The Wound That Will Never Heal:
An Allegorical Interpretation of Richard Wagner's *The Ring of the Nibelung*

Paul Brian Heise

The Wound That Will Never Heal:
An Allegorical Interpretation of Richard Wagner's
The Ring of the Nibelung

Paul Brian Heise

Academica Press
Washington~London

Library of Congress Cataloging-in-Publication Data

Names: Heise, Paul Brian (author)
Title: The wound that will never heal : an allegorical interpretation of richard wagner's the ring of the nibelung | Heise, Paul Brian
Description: Washington : Academica Press, 2021. | Includes references.
Identifiers: LCCN 2021945675 | ISBN 9781680538120 (hardcover) | 9781680538137 (paperback) | 9781680538144 (e-book)

Copyright 2021 Paul Brian Heise

Contents

Acknowledgments ix

Abbreviations xv

Key References xvii
Ludwig Feuerbach xvii
Richard Wagner xvii
Ring Subdivisions xviii

Introduction by Roger Scruton 1
Paul Heise's Interpretation of Wagner's *Ring* Cycle 1

Prologue 5
Do We Really Understand Wagner's *Ring*? 5
The Importance of Wagner's *Ring* 6
The Problem 6
The Solution 7
A Brief History of My Book: *The Wound That Will Never Heal* 9
The Twelve Pillars 12

The Rhinegold 29
THE RHINEGOLD ≠ SCENE ONE 29
THE RHINEGOLD ≠ SCENE TWO 39
THE RHINEGOLD ≠ SCENE THREE 70
THE RHINEGOLD ≠ SCENE FOUR 89

The Valkyrie 121
THE VALKYRIE ≠ ACT ONE, SCENE ONE 121
THE VALKYRIE ≠ ACT ONE, SCENE TWO 124

THE VALKYRIE ⚡ ACT ONE, SCENE THREE 129
THE VALKYRIE ⚡ ACT TWO, SCENE ONE 135
THE VALKYRIE ⚡ ACT TWO, SCENE TWO 144
THE VALKYRIE ⚡ ACT TWO, SCENE THREE... 175
THE VALKYRIE ⚡ ACT TWO, SCENE FOUR.. 177
THE VALKYRIE ⚡ ACT TWO, SCENE FIVE 182
THE VALKYRIE ⚡ ACT THREE, SCENE ONE 184
THE VALKYRIE ⚡ ACT THREE, SCENE TWO... 190
THE VALKYRIE ⚡ ACT THREE, SCENE THREE.. 195

Siegfried... 209
SIEGFRIED ⚡ ACT ONE, SCENE ONE... 209
SIEGFRIED ⚡ ACT ONE, SCENE TWO... 223
SIEGFRIED ⚡ ACT ONE, SCENE THREE 233
SIEGFRIED ⚡ ACT TWO, SCENE ONE... 247
SIEGFRIED ⚡ ACT TWO, SCENE TWO 259
SIEGFRIED ⚡ ACT TWO, SCENE THREE 274
SIEGFRIED ⚡ ACT THREE, SCENE ONE 286
SIEGFRIED ⚡ ACT THREE, SCENE TWO 306
SIEGFRIED ⚡ ACT THREE, SCENE THREE 317

Twilight of the Gods 355
TWILIGHT OF THE GODS ⚡ PROLOGUE, PART A....................................... 355
TWILIGHT OF THE GODS ⚡ PROLOGUE, PART B...................................... 366
TWILIGHT OF THE GODS ⚡ ACT ONE, SCENE ONE 378
TWILIGHT OF THE GODS ⚡ ACT ONE, SCENE TWO 387
TWILIGHT OF THE GODS ⚡ ACT ONE, SCENE THREE, PART A 406
TWILIGHT OF THE GODS ⚡ ACT ONE, SCENE THREE, PART B............ 419
TWILIGHT OF THE GODS ⚡ ACT TWO, SCENE ONE 427
TWILIGHT OF THE GODS ⚡ ACT TWO, SCENE TWO 437
TWILIGHT OF THE GODS ⚡ ACT TWO, SCENE THREE............................ 440
TWILIGHT OF THE GODS ⚡ ACT TWO, SCENE FOUR............................... 444

TWILIGHT OF THE GODS ≠ ACT TWO, SCENE FIVE.............................. 458
TWILIGHT OF THE GODS ≠ ACT THREE, SCENE ONE 469
TWILIGHT OF THE GODS ≠ ACT THREE, SCENE TWO.......................... 480
TWILIGHT OF THE GODS ≠ ACT THREE, SCENE THREE...................... 502

Allen Dunning's Numbered List of
The *Ring*'s Musical Motifs, with 23 Motifs added by Paul Heise 531
Musical notation by Allen Dunning and commentary by Paul Heise 531
Symbols Employed to Characterize Musical Motifs 535

Guide to Motifs in Richard Wagner's *The Ring of The Nibelung*.............. 539
The Rhinegold 539
The Valkyrie 551
Siegfried... 561
Twilight of the Gods.. 573

References.. 583

Index 589

Acknowledgments

I wish to thank Dr. Paul du Quenoy, President and Publisher of Academica Press, for offering me my first opportunity to publish a book-length version of my allegorical interpretation of Wagner's *Ring*.

It is an honor for me to acknowledge the keen understanding of—and sympathetic encouragement granted to—my original research into the philosophical implications of Wagner's *Ring*, offered by the late Sir Roger Scruton. Roger Scruton's primary contribution to our knowledge of Wagner, aside from various lectures and articles, is four books: *Death-Devoted Heart: Sex and the Sacred in Wagner's 'Tristan and Isolde'* (2004), *Understanding Music* (2009), and *The Ring of Truth—The Wisdom of Wagner's 'Ring of the Nibelung'* (2016), and *Wagner's 'Parsifal'—The Music of Redemption* (2020). Having completed my first revised edition of *The Wound That Will Never Heal* in the summer of 2009, I emailed an announcement of its completion, along with attachments of my Introduction and book proposal, to over 300 Wagner scholars, officers of many Wagner Societies, and others with significant direct or indirect links to the Wagner world. Of the responses I received, by far the most substantial was from Scruton, who made the creation of www.wagnerheim.com possible, and who also provided financing for my project. Through his aid I was able to obtain the help of "webmeister" Justin Jeffrey of Mindvision, who built www.wagnerheim.com taking my specific needs into account, and who, despite my wholesale ignorance, never gave up on me. Scruton is the first to have read the entirety of my text. His critical responses can be found in the Introduction he wrote for www.wagnerheim.com, his article *The Ring of Truth* published in *The American Spectator* (May 27, 2011) and in a variety of citations of my online *Ring* study in his book *The Ring of Truth*. I thank Roger's widow, Lady Sophie Scruton, for having granted me permission to include his Introduction in my book. Sir Roger not only read my entire text, and understood it in considerable detail, but he grasped some of its widest implications, despite expressing doubts about my allegorical approach in his recently published book on the *Ring*. I thank him for his critique because it bore fruit in my fourth and final revision of this book, which I partly rewrote to accommodate it.

At the risk of oversimplification, that while Scruton and I agree that Wagner's *Ring* represents his quest to restore religious sanctity and feeling to an increasingly secular and scientific world, unlike Scruton I maintain that Wagner's *Ring* is a dramatization of this, that its plot is an allegory whose subject is the quest of revolutionaries with a social conscience (Siegmund) and inspired secular artists (Siegfried) to preserve and perpetuate religious feeling in an age in which religious faith (Wotan and the Valhallan gods) is dying out in the face of the advancement of scientific knowledge. It is also an oversimplification to add that a crucial distinction between our views is that Scruton in his book *The Ring of Truth* has presented a thoughtful approximation of what Wagner wished ideally for his *Ring* to mean (which of course is a significant part of its authentic meaning), whereas I presented what the *Ring* actually does mean, in the sense that my interpretation not only encompasses, like Scruton's, the ideal towards which Wagner was reaching, but also Wagner's grave doubts about what he wished for his *Ring* to mean. My study has shown that Wagner's doubts constitute a significant portion of what the *Ring*, taken as a whole, does mean. My reading's cogency is enhanced by the fact I can demonstrate its coherency with Wagner's other canonical operas and music-dramas, from *The Flying Dutchman* through *Parsifal*, as well as his writings and recorded remarks, and those of Ludwig Feuerbach, which influenced him. However, despite Scruton's reservations about my allegorical approach, which he feels (I think incorrectly) loses touch with the actual drama, he did state in his *The Ring of Truth* that he finds my allegorical interpretation of the *Ring* more plausible than that of George Bernard Shaw (Scruton, p. 191), which is saying a lot, since Shaw's interpretation is by far the most popular and influential. So let me say again that were it not for his astute assessment of the value of my research project not only for Wagnerians, but for all thinking people, it would not have been possible to present the original version of my book and its scholarly apparatus online at www.wagnerheim.com, nor would my now published version of this online book have reached the light of day, at least in its present form.

With respect to other responses to my 2009 announcement, special thanks are also due to the eminent Wagner scholar Dr. Thomas Grey, Professor of Music at Stanford University, who wrote a detailed response to my Introduction, and engaged in significant correspondence with me regarding the claims I make in my book.

I thank the distinguished Wagner scholar Barry Millington for agreeing during the summer of 2016 to read significant portions of *The Wound That Will Never Heal*. He offered his initial critical response in an e-mail in the winter of 2017, stating that though he could not entirely endorse my allegorical interpretation of Wagner's *Ring*, nonetheless he could not imagine a more thorough exegesis of it, feeling that I had to a large degree sustained my claim to have offered a coherent conceptual account of the *Ring* in its entirety, and noted that my study has gone much further than prior studies in exploring the influence of atheist philosopher Ludwig Feuerbach on Wagner's *Ring*. The reader can find his brief critical review in the archive of the discussion forum at www.-wagnerheim.com, on page 3 under the title "Barry Millington's first thoughts on my online *Ring* book" (posted 1/25/2017). Special thanks are also due renowned Wagner scholar John Deathridge, who answered a variety of questions I had about Stewart Spencer's translation of specific passages from the *Ring* libretto.

I wish to thank my late father and mother, Richard Edward Heise Jr. and Marjorie Lois Heise (née Cox), for their life-long moral encouragement, and long-term practical aid in financing my work with loans so that I could devote myself full-time to this project for several years without interruption. Much needed financial aid was also provided through a loan donated by fellow Annapolitans Dorothy and Bruno Szymanski, who made it possible for me to devote a whole year exclusively to this project. Since Bruno's passing, Mrs. Szymanski has also provided aid whose value to me cannot possibly be overestimated, not the least being a safe and quiet space where I was able to complete my project without distraction. Andrew Gray (translator of Wagner's autobiography *My Life* for Cambridge University Press: 1983) financed my first and only trip to the Bayreuth Festival in 2001 and has provided invaluable practical aid over the years (such as his fluency in German), including putting me in touch with some key Wagner pundits and major university presses in my quest to seek critical reviews and potential publishers, and providing me an excellent forum to test my ideas. Dr. Denis Donovan, and Tom and Nancy Marks, bought me a new computer when I was down and out, making it possible to complete the text currently in your hand. Furthermore, Dr. Donovan, a worldly child psychiatrist with a great breadth of knowledge and experience, who has posed searching questions about the nature of music, language, and meaning, as well as making signal contributions to our knowledge of child-rearing and adoptions, has provided me a unique opportunity to discuss my ideas as they evolved, providing extraordinarily helpful criticism and practical advice, including employing his expertise to help me organize PowerPoint lectures on my interpretations of Wagner operas and music-dramas. He continues to work with me to seek paths for the wide dissemination of my work. My wonderful friend and intellectual comrade of recent years, Alexander Balko, has provided me a sounding board and critical advice, as well as many helpful editorial suggestions, as I have brought my project to its conclusion. I also wish to thank Stephen Klemawesch, MD (allergist), and Louis Apter, MD (ophthalmologist), for medical services granted to me pro bono in order to aid me in the completion of my book.

There is a long list of friends who willingly listened as I developed my hypotheses about Wagner, some of whom I have known since I began this project back in 1971 (and even earlier). My oldest friend, Mary Conrad (Bird) Rubino, and my cousin Susan Dapkunas (née Taylor—an older friend yet, since we virtually grew up together) lent their sympathetic ear to my ever more involved hypotheses and provided life-long moral encouragement. More recent friends with whom I have had lengthy and very useful discussions about my life's work are my loving companion Dotti Szymanski (neé Englert), Thomas Stanley, Jeff Smith, Steven Alm, Jay Moroughan, Chad Taylor, John Jarvis, Bill Weiss, Joan Bishop, James Weaver, Marita (former President of the Richard Wagner Society of Florida) and Richard Rotella, Rick Baker, and Trevor Clarke (former president of the Richard Wagner Society, Victoria, Australia). Trevor offered me a valuable sounding board as I brought my final revision of my book to its conclusion, and has helped me solve some key editorial problems, and suggested important improvements to www.wagnerheim.com which webmeister Justin Jeffrey put into action. His help has been invaluable in preparing my manuscript for publication by Academica Press. He also discovered in the Art Gallery of Western Australia the "Ride of the Valkyries" by John Charles Dollman (1909) and obtained permission for its use on the cover of my book. Needless to say, my various friends' discussions do not imply any adherence on their part to the views expressed in this book. In fact, quite often, their disagreements have been of inestimable value.

I would like to make special mention of two very astute students of Wagner who worked closely with me for several years as I developed my interpretation of Wagner's artworks. Dr. Allen Dunning has collaborated with me in developing this project by acting as my music consultant. Without Dr. Dunning's endeavor to identify all the motifs and motif variants in the *Ring*, and to locate each occurrence in the score, so that I could indicate each in Wagner's libretto, I could never have completed my project. Dr. Dunning worked with me virtually weekly by e-mail, from 2001 until 2005, answering numerous questions about Wagner's employment of musical motifs in the *Ring*. My current guide to the *Ring* motifs is based squarely on Dr. Dunning's revision of Deryck Cooke's list. Our mutual friend Derrick Everett, a first-class expert on Wagner in general and Wagner's *Parsifal* in particular, offered enormously helpful critical editorial advice, in remarkable detail, as I wrote my chapters on *The Flying Dutchman*, *Tannhäuser*, and *Lohengrin*, as well as the *Ring*. His stunning website www.monsalvat.com is entirely devoted to Wagner's final mystical music-drama *Parsifal* and has no peer as a source of knowledge of Wagner's final essay in music-drama.

There's a long list of august Wagnerians, including academics, publishers, and officers of Wagner societies, who over the years have taken the time to provide critical reviews of my work, and on occasion have provided other encouragement for my never-ending project. These include Philip Winters, Dr. William Webster of Stanford University, Jim Holman, Dieter Borchmeyer, Nike Wagner, Paul Lawrence Rose, Elliott Zuckerman, Hans Rudolf Vaget, Bryan Magee, Monte Stone, Michael Tanner, Harry and Nathalie Wagner, Laurence Lueck, Robert Donington, Walter Lippincott (former Director of Princeton University Press), Speight Jenkins, and John Cerullo (Director of Amadeus Press)

I especially thank Stewart Spencer for providing me my first opportunity for publication. As Editor of *Wagner*, the scholarly publication of The Wagner Society (London, UK), he provided editorial advice, forwarded the critical responses of three anonymous reviewers, and published my seminal essay "How Elsa Showed Wagner the Way to Siegfried" in the May 1995 edition. With respect to this, my first published article, I am indebted to my editor Chad Taylor for exhibiting such heroic patience in working with me until we were finally able to submit an ultimately publishable version to Stewart Spencer.

I am especially indebted to Stewart Spencer and Thames & Hudson for granting me permission to quote extensively from Spencer's English translation of Wagner's *Ring* (Thames & Hudson: 1993) and thank Nancy Elder for securing their permission. Without this foundation, my book would never have gotten off the ground.

Having mentioned the Wagner Society (London, UK), I have to thank its President, Alan Ridgewell, for publishing the transcript of my lecture "The 'Ring' as a Whole" (which I presented to The Wagner Society of Washington, DC, on 4/27/2000, at the invitation of its Chairman Jim Holman) in the March 2021 issue of *Wagner News*.

For the inestimable opportunity of seeing my work published in translation, I have to thank Ilkka Pajaanen and Markus Ilmonen, President and Vice President, respectively, of the Richard Wagner Society of Helsinki, Finland, for publishing my essay "The 'Ring' as a Whole" (translated into both Finnish and German) in the 11/04 and 4/05 issues of their scholarly journal devoted to Wagner, "Grane." Furthermore, Dalia Geffen, Founder and President of the Boston Wagner Society, has published all or part of several of my papers in the newsletter of the Boston Wagner Society, "Wagneriana." The Boston Wagner Society has posted several of my essays and my complete critical chronological anthology of Wagner's writings and recorded remarks on their website: www.bostonwagnersociety.org.

I wish also to pay tribute to various academics, and Wagner Society presidents and officers, who made it possible to present various aspects of my Wagner project in a series of lectures around the USA. Dr. John Weinstock (Germanic Studies Department) and Dr. Tom Seung (Jesse H. Jones Regents Professor in Liberal Arts, Department of Philosophy), both of the University of Texas in Austin, graciously invited me in 2005 to present two lectures on my *Ring* interpretation to the faculty and students of the Germanic Studies, Philosophy, and Music Departments. I had the opportunity to teach one of Dr. Weinstock's classes. Dr. Seung also did me the honor of critiquing my unpublished work on the *Ring* in the final pages of his book *Goethe, Nietzsche, and Wagner: Their Spinozan Epics of Love and Power* (2006). You'll find my review of his book on www.amazon.com. Dr. Weinstock has also posted several of my essays and my critical chronological anthology of Richard Wagner's writings and recorded remarks on his website devoted to Wagner's *The Ring of the Nibelung*, "The Wagner Experience," at https://www.laits.utexas.edu/wagner/home.html.

With respect to the various Wagner Societies, I owe a great debt of gratitude to Nathalie Wagner, President of the Wagner Society of New York, and the late Harry Wagner, editor of its newsletter *Wagner Notes*, for providing me my first lecture opportunity in the early 90's. Since then I presented a lecture at Southern Methodist University to the Wagner Society of Dallas in response to my invite by the founder, Virginia Abdo; multiple lectures for the Richard Wagner Society of Florida, hosted by the President Marita Rotella and her husband Dr. Richard Rotella; two lectures for the Boston Wagner Society (the latter of which was recorded for posterity on DVD by a cable TV station in Wellesley, MA) in response to the invitation of President and Founder Dalia Geffen; a lecture at George Washington University in Washington, DC, to the Wagner Society of Washington, DC, at the request of its Chairman, Jim Holman, and President, Aurelius Fernandez; and finally, two lectures for the Washington National Wagner Society at the instance of the Founder and President, Janice Rosen, and her good friend—and stalwart Wagnerian—Justin Swain. I also wish to thank Bill

Smith, President of the Wagner Society of America in Chicago, for bringing me up to Chicago some years ago to meet with various members of his Wagner club to discuss my work.

I wish to especially thank the co-founders of our Richard Wagner Society of Florida, Marie Jo Bell and Carmen Wagner. By creating this educational institution these two ladies provided me with an immeasurably valuable forum to disseminate my ideas. Furthermore, former president Marita Rotella, and her husband Dr. Richard Rotella, who graciously hosted most of our meetings since the society's inception in 4/01, kept our society thriving for years through considerable personal expenditure in time, labor, and financing, without which our society could not have survived.

I wish to mention several students of Wagner I have met at Wagner functions or online, whose discussions with me regarding my hypotheses have been helpful in my effort to sharpen my arguments. These include John Jarvis, Wolram, Robert Pelletier, Timothy Fisher, Dr. Kevin Hill, Albert Reiner, Laon (New Zealand), Cruz Tijerina, Jerry Hashimoto, Glen Wolfson, Kimberly Cornish, Peter Cresswell, Michael Mountain, A.C. Douglas, Anselm, Chenlei (Shanghai, China), Dave Shifrin, Christine Rothauser, Steven Liening, Henry Fogel, Father James O'Leary, Robin Hobbes, Patrick Swinkels, Jon Szostak Sr., Richard Loeb, Richard Smith, Dick, William, John, Pavel, and Leonardo. Your interest in my work and intelligent commentary has kept my project alive in dark times.

Finally, I wish to thank the donors (and contributors of discussion) to www.-wagnerheim.com and to my cause, for helping to keep my research project alive.

Abbreviations

All the extracts from the following key sources used in this book are from a chronological anthology of 1,151 numbered passages (see Appendix II at www.-wagnerheim.com, pages 1047–1346) which I selected from the writings of Ludwig Feuerbach (whose published works had an incalculable impact on Wagner as he wrote the *Ring* libretto and music), and from the writings and recorded remarks of Richard Wagner. All these extracts are from translations of the original German into English. My choices were based on the value of these passages for grasping the allegorical meaning of Wagner's ten repertory operas and music-dramas, from *The Flying Dutchman* through *Parsifal*. Because the main body of Feuerbach's writings preceded most of Wagner's important writings and recorded observations, the chronological anthology begins with Feuerbach. Therefore, the numbered passages from 1F through 352F are drawn from Feuerbach's writings in chronological order (dictated by date of publication of his four books on which I drew for this anthology, and within each book by following the order in which the passages are presented). The remaining numbered passages, from 353W through 1,151W, are selections from Wagner's writings and recorded remarks (as found in Wagner's published writings, personal diary entries, letters, autobiography, and remarks attributed to him on certain dates by his second wife Cosima in her diaries, and by others), and are numbered in correspondence with the relative date of origin of each extract.

In the body of my text, after each quotation from Feuerbach or Wagner drawn from this anthology, I've placed in brackets the following reference information, reading from left to right: the number identifying the quotation; "F" for a passage from Feuerbach, "W" for a passage from Wagner; the date of the passage if it's from Wagner's writings or recorded remarks (in some instances having this date is very important to interpretation); the title (solely in abbreviated form if it's from one of Feuerbach's four books, such as TDI—see list below); the volume number if relevant, and finally the page number where this quotation can be found in the source.

Key References

Ludwig Feuerbach

TDI   *Thoughts on Death and Immortality.* Translated from German by James A. Massey. Originally published in 1830.

EOC   *The Essence of Christianity.* Translated from German by George Eliot (the British novelist). Originally published in 1841.

PPF   *The Principles of the Philosophy of the Future.* Translated from German by Manfred Vogel. Originally published in 1843.

LER   *Lectures on the Essence of Religion.* Translated from German by Ralph Manheim. Based on a book published in 1845 entitled *The Essence of Religion*, which was intended to fill in some gaps left by *The Essence of Christianity*.

Richard Wagner

BB   *The Diary of Richard Wagner: The Brown Book*—1863–1882: Presented and annotated by Joachim Bergfeld, and translated by G. Bird

CD   *Cosima Wagner's Diaries*: two volumes ed. By Martin Gregor-Dellin and Dietrich Mack, and translated by Geoffrey Skelton

CWL   *Correspondence of Wagner and Liszt.* Trans. by Francis Hueffer. Originally published by Charles Scribner's Sons in 1897.

ML   Wagner's autobiography *My Life*: Edited by Mary Whittall and translated by Andrew Gray

PW   *Richard Wagner's Prose Works*: eight volumes translated by Ashton Ellis

RWMW   *Richard Wagner's Letters to Mathilde Wesendonck*: translated by Ashton Ellis

SLRW   *Selected Letters of Richard Wagner*: a chronological anthology of Wagner's letters translated and edited by Stewart Spencer and Barry Millington

WCR   *Richard Wagner's Letters to August Röckel*: translated by Eleanor C. Sellar

WRR   *Wagner Rehearsing the 'Ring:'* Heinrich Porges' record of Wagner's comments during the rehearsals for the 1876 premier of *The Ring of the Nibelung* at Bayreuth.

WR   *Wagner Remembered*: translated and edited by Stewart Spencer. An anthology of reminiscences of Wagner by those who knew him.

Due to Wagner's subdivision of the *Ring* into four music-dramas and numerous scenes (36), and my need to further divide two of Wagner's scenes into two separate parts for purposes of discussion, and so readers can quickly look up specific moments from the drama, I've employed the following abbreviations to identify specific parts of Wagner's libretto according to both Wagner's arrangement and two of my own more refined subdivisions.

Ring Subdivisions

R.   *The Rhinegold*
V.   *The Valkyrie*
S.   *Siegfried*
T.   *Twilight of the Gods*

R.1   *The Rhinegold,* Scene One (and so on through the four scenes of *Rhinegold*, which has no acts but is divided only into scenes)

V.1.1   *The Valkyrie,* Act One, Scene One (and so on through the three acts composed of three, five, and three scenes, respectively, of *Valkyrie*)

S.1.1   *Siegfried,* Act One, Scene One (and so on through the three acts composed of three, three, and three scenes, respectively, of *Siegfried*)

Twilight of the Gods is a special case, because, though otherwise organized into acts and scenes, it begins with a Prologue, which I designate "T.P,"—"T" representing *Twilight of the Gods,* and "P" the *Prologue.* Furthermore, though both the Prologue, and Act One Scene Three, seem naturally to break down dramatically into two separate scenes, nonetheless Wagner didn't make such a division, but I have. I distinguish the two parts of the Prologue into Prologue Part A, designated by T.P.A (the Norns' Scene), and Prologue Part B, designated by T.P.B (Siegfried's and Brünnhilde's second love-duet), using capital letters to designate such large divisions of a scene. Similarly, I divided *Twilight of the* Gods Act One Scene Three into two parts, designated T.1.3.A (Waltraute's confrontation with Brünnhilde), and T.1.3.B (Siegfried's confrontation—disguised as Gunther—with Brünnhilde), respectively. Here are some examples:

T.P.A   *Twilight of the Gods*—Prologue, Part A (and so on through part B)

T.1.1   *Twilight of the Gods,* Act One, Scene One (and so on through the three acts composed of three scenes, five scenes, and three scenes, respectively, of *Twilight of the Gods.* Keep in mind that I've divided T.1.3 into two parts—see below)

T.1.3.A *Twilight of the Gods,* Act One, Scene Three, Part A (and so on through part B)

Aside from my use of brackets "[ ]" to enclose my abbreviations of passages from the *Ring*, or the reference information for a quotation, all other brackets enclose my own editorial remarks. For instance, within the context of specific passages of text from the *Ring* or of quotations from Feuerbach and Wagner, when I enclose anything in brackets "[ ]," this represents either my summation in my own words of a passage from the libretto of the *Ring* which I didn't deem necessary to quote in full, or my editorial commentary on the libretto text or on some extract from Wagner or Feuerbach.

There are numerous extracts from Wagner and Feuerbach in which it's extremely helpful to draw attention to links between them and their allegorical equivalent in the *Ring* drama, right within the context of the extract, *so that the reader can see what the author of this study has seen,* directly.

Introduction by Roger Scruton

The late Roger Scruton sponsored and financed the creation of my website www.wagnerheim.com as an online venue to present the entire body of my research into the allegorical, conceptual unity of Richard Wagner's *The Ring of the Nibelung,* as a free resource for students and admirers of Wagner's art, as well as dedicated Wagner scholars. www.wagnerheim.com went online in the spring of 2011, at which time he wrote an introduction to it which is reproduced below:

Paul Heise's Interpretation of Wagner's *Ring* Cycle
Roger Scruton

No composer has ever been more of a philosopher than Richard Wagner, and in none of his works is Wagner more philosophical than in *The Ring of the Nibelung*. In this work—surely the greatest drama composed in modern times—Wagner attempts to convey a picture of the human condition that will identify the origins of good and evil, the place of man in the *cosmos*, and the secret source of human freedom. When he wrote the poem, Wagner was under the influence of Ludwig Feuerbach, the philosopher whose materialist re-working of Hegel's social and political philosophy inspired the early thoughts of Karl Marx. And many commentators (not least George Bernard Shaw) have seen strong parallels between the vision of the *Ring* and the Marxist critique of capitalism. Heise shows that the influence of Feuerbach is indeed all-pervasive in Wagner's music-drama. But he also shows that the *Ring* is concerned with far deeper and more lasting questions than those raised by the discussion of property and revolution. The drama touches on aspects of the human psyche that are hardly acknowledged in the writings of 19th century socialists. Briefly put, *The Ring*, on Heise's interpretation, is an exploration of man's religious sense, of the human need for the transcendental, and of the hope for redemption that endures even in our time of cynicism and materialist frivolity, and which can be satisfied, now, only through the truthful enchantment conveyed to us by art.

In developing that theme Heise has made, it seems to me, one of the most important contributions to Wagnerian scholarship that we have seen. As yet his work takes the form of a scene-by-scene analysis of the whole drama, in which the symbolism of the motives and the allegorical meaning of the action is minutely dissected. In making it available in this form, Heise has opened his ideas to public discussion, and made it possible for fellow Wagnerians to question them, to amplify them and to contribute to the kind of debate that is surely needed, if this great work is to take its proper place at the center of modern philosophy and at the center, too, of modern life.

The text of the *Ring* is derived, with imaginative flair and brilliant strokes of synthesis, from old German myths that were once the theological heritage of the German people. The seamless plot of the tetralogy can be read as a retelling of the myths of a dead religion. And yet this is also the *meaning* of the drama, on Heise's reading: *The Ring* is about the death of religion—not the old Germanic religion only, which, in the Icelandic sagas, foresaw its own demise—but all religion. The religious need is the original need—the *Urnoth*—of humanity itself, which arises with our conscious separation from the cosmic order. Consciousness is the human lot, and the root of freedom; but it is also the cause of our fall—and Wagner's telling of the "Fall" is surely a poetic achievement to match those that we know from the Book of Genesis, and from *Paradise Lost*.

On Wagner's understanding, consciousness is the origin, not only of the distinction between good and evil, but of the "hoard" of scientific knowledge, which alienates us from our roots in species life. We long to regain the innocent oneness with the world that is the lot of animals and which was the lot of our pre-conscious ancestors. And we project that longing into the heavens, imagining there a blessed resting place where the wound of consciousness will be healed, and we will regain the serenity that we lost in our first attempts at self-understanding.

That is the theme of Wagner's drama as Heise understands it. And in his subtle exposition he shows, one by one, how each scene of the work spells out some necessary feature of the allegory. Wagner's work is a meditation on our condition, as spiritually needful beings, whose sparse allocation of happiness has created a lasting need for the transcendental. We seek for the transcendental in love, in power, in the accumulation of knowledge. But always it eludes us. What then is the redemption? Alberich renounces love, for the sake of the Ring, which is (on Heise's interpretation) the spell-making and spell-deciphering power of science. And Alberich's sin is both a sin against religion and the sin required by religion. For without science, in its elemental aspect, the illusory kingdom of the gods cannot be built or maintained. The intricate thought here, which is so difficult to grasp in plain prose, is wonderfully presented in the music and the drama of *Das Rheingold*, and lucidly explained by Heise in his commentary.

If we cannot redeem ourselves by renouncing love, then from whence does redemption come? Two ideas animate the subsequent dramas. The first is that we are redeemed not by renouncing love, but by renouncing life for the *sake* of love. The second is that we are redeemed through art, and through the artist-hero (Siegfried) who takes on the task that religion failed to accomplish. The artist-hero presents a new kind of redemption, which is the redemption of "wonder." Instead of looking for vindication in the transcendental world, art shows that we are vindicated here and now, by our own capacity to recognize the beauty of the world, and to weave love and allusion into the sensory order. Which of these two forms of wisdom does Wagner recommend? Heise suggests that the two philosophies coincide: redemption through loving renunciation, and redemption through art involve the same sacrificial stance. Consciousness needed the gods, as a mirror in which to smile. Science smashed the mirror. And art replaced the mirror with a refracting window on the world, in which all the colors of our joy and suffering are harmonized. In the place of the certainties of religion and the doubts of science, art gives us wonder. Through wonder we accept the world, and this wonder is exemplified by the *Ring* itself. Wagner's music shines a light of allusion and suggestion that reaches to the ends of the universe, and by *showing* what art can achieve, Wagner also justifies his view that art is the way in which we can live with the unhealing wound of consciousness.

Heise's book is not an easy book. But it is a deep book. All Wagnerians know that *The Ring* is full of enigmas. But the enigmas are resolved by Heise in a most pleasing, intense and persuasive way. The Wanderer, Wotan's missing eye, the Norns and their rope, the head of Mime, the many drinks brewed and refused or stored and consumed, the Ring, the Tarnhelm, the sword Nothung, the spear, the wood-bird—so many obscure seeming symbols, which become bright and transparent in Heise's reading. I don't agree with all that he says. But he awakens interest, argument, dissent and wonder at every point, linking the text minutely to the musical realization, and bringing this great work to life in a way that I hope you will appreciate as much as I have.

Prologue

Do We Really Understand Wagner's *Ring*?

I once attended a Wagner Society luncheon at which I was introduced as the author of a new book on Wagner's *Ring* to a gentleman who made me the following proposition: he said anyone trying to write a new book on Wagner's *Ring* in our time was on a fool's errand. I asked him why. He answered that everything worth saying about the *Ring* was said long ago. But I have a counterproposition: what if I suggest that we have only just begun to grasp the depths of meaning hidden in Wagner's *Ring*, that our received wisdom on the subject of not only his *Ring*, but his other canonical operas and music-dramas, is a mere fragment of the meaning comprehended within his life's work, and that our heritage of scholarship on the subject often as not throws us off the scent of true understanding! There is so much that occurs musico-dramatically in his *Ring*, and that he said about it, that remains mysterious for us, so many questions raised in it that most just let pass without pursuing them further, because they seem to resist comprehension.

Why, for instance, did Wagner say in his essay "A Communication to My Friends" that Elsa [from *Lohengrin*] taught him to unearth his Siegfried? Why did Wagner write to King Ludwig II that Wotan is reborn in Siegfried as the artist's intent is reborn in his work of art, but forgotten in it? What is the significance of the fact that Alberich's Ring Motif H17ab transforms into the first two segments of Wotan's Valhalla Motif H18ab during the transition from Scene One to Scene Two of *The Rhinegold*? Why did Wagner say that the most important scene in the *Ring* is Scene Two, in Act Two, of *The Valkyrie,* Wotan's confession to Brünnhilde? Why does Siegfried forget what the Woodbird had just told him of the use he could make of the Tarnhelm and Ring it instructed him to retrieve from the dragon Fafner's lair as soon as he emerges from it? Why does Siegfried fear to wake Brünnhilde, and Brünnhilde initially suffer panic at the thought of consummating a loving union with him? Why do we hear the Dragon/Serpent Motif H47 at the height of Siegfried's and Brünnhilde's ecstatic love duet in *Siegfried* Act Three, Scene Three? Why did Wagner state in his *Epilogue to the 'Nibelung's Ring*' that the plots of *Twilight of the Gods* and *Tristan and Isolde* are identical, and what consequences follow from this? These are a few of the hundreds of questions and conundrums in Wagner scholarship which remain unresolved or unexplored. What would you think if I told you that not only can each of these questions and dozens of others be solved, but solved within a coherent interpretation of Wagner's *Ring* which demonstrates its musico-dramatic and philosophic unity, and that this interpretation also reveals an allegorical logic which can be applied to unlocking many of the remaining unresolved questions about Wagner's other canonical operas and music-dramas from *The Flying Dutchman* to *Parsifal*?

Here's my opening gambit: I propose that Wagner's *Ring* is, figuratively, '*radioactive* with potential force and meaning' which, once grasped, penetrates like a virtual X-ray inside many things that previously defied understanding, and reveals previously undisclosed wonders, perhaps the innermost secrets of Wagner's creative inspiration. Wagner once declared that through his musical motifs he could make you, his audience, fellow-sharers in the profoundest secret of his artistic aim, an aim which he confessed was as mysterious to him as to his audience. We all who love Wagner feel that there is much more at stake in his *Ring* than we can ever consciously comprehend; that there is a latent power in it which always seems just beyond our reach. Feeling this since I first discovered his *Ring* at age eighteen, for fifty years I've been impelled to grasp the *Ring*'s secrets in a way which recalls, to me, how Marie and Pierre Curie were prompted to devote their lives to the quest for the hidden source of the radioactivity in a conglomerate of three known elements which was more than the amount that should have been generated chemically from them. It was only after years of ever more refined chemical analysis that they finally distilled that almost negligible powder of the radioactive element radium that gave birth to the explosive nuclear age.

Why, then, did I undertake this lifelong task?

The Importance of Wagner's *Ring*

Richard Wagner's four-part music-drama, *The Ring of the Nibelung*, can justifiably be called the Holy Grail of art criticism. It is not only the most extensive in scope of all the canonical stage-works in the Western theatrical and operatic traditions, but is arguably the most comprehensive vision of the human experience presented on any stage since its premier in 1876. It remains the single work of art which most fully expresses that angst which is the hallmark of the modern world. Its great magnitude is a tribute to Wagner's belief that in it he was unveiling a world-myth (i.e., disclosing the essence of universal human nature, which he described as the "purely-human") beneath the façade of diversity in the world's distinct races, languages, cultures, mythologies, religions, traditions, customs, and modes of government. What it means, and how its music in general and musical motifs in particular convey this meaning, is still to be determined after more than 140 years' effort. A key purpose of the present study is to demonstrate how completely absurd it is to treat it as just another opera, and that it can best be understood as a music-drama which expresses a unified philosophy or world-view through allegory.

The Problem

The *Ring* remains a mystery to this day, and is what Deryck Cooke called a "problematic" work (like *Hamlet* or Goethe's *Faust*). [Cooke, pp. 12–13] Given its world-historical importance, it's astonishing that no study has yet been produced which comprehends the entirety of the drama and its music. George Bernard Shaw's socialist, and Robert Donington's Jungian interpretations are universally regarded as one-sided and incomplete today, and the most serious effort to encompass the entire work in a single study, by Deryck Cooke, was left incomplete by his premature death. For the most part students and admirers of the *Ring* now remain content to enjoy it in the theater without troubling themselves further about any deeper meaning. It is generally assumed that it is too densely packed with a variety of sometimes contradictory meanings, on multiple levels, which are in any case largely subliminal (thanks at least partly to its music) and therefore inaccessible to reasoned discussion, to be grasped as a whole.

Warren Darcy, in his *Wagner's 'Das Rheingold'* (1993), noting that Deryck Cooke "proposed to follow Wagner's own suggestion ... that the transformation of each [musical] motif should be pursued carefully 'through all the changing passions of the four-part drama,'" observed that "unfortunately, Cooke died before he could carry out this task, and no one else has attempted it." [Darcy, p. 50] Cooke himself, speaking—in his *I Saw the World End* (1976)—of a particular example of the confusion Wagner caused by associating a single musical motif with two passages of text from the *Ring* poem which seem conceptually inconsistent, stated that "there are many others in the *Ring*, all of which lead away from their immediate dramatic contexts to the whole involved story, and to its complex tangle of symbols, which seem intended to bring some great revelation but has always eluded our understanding." [Cooke, p. 10] It appears, then, that much of the *Ring*'s meaning remains unconscious for its audience, something "felt" but not "thought." On this subject, Michael Tanner, in his *Wagner* (1996), quotes Hans Keller: "'Wagner's music, like none other before or after him, let what Freud called the dynamic unconscious, normally inaccessible, erupt with a clarity and indeed seductiveness which will always be likely to arouse as much resistance (to the listener's own unconscious) as its sheer power creates enthusiasm.'" To this Tanner retorts: "The trouble with that highly plausible-sounding suggestion is that no one has succeeded in developing it any further, no doubt because to do so would involve independent research of a kind that musicologists are unwilling or unable to undertake." [Tanner, pp. 4–5]

The Solution

The Wound that Will Never Heal, Volume One, picks up the threads of debate where the major studies of the past dropped them, from an entirely new perspective. It is the first attempt since Deryck Cooke's passing to provide a comprehensive conceptual interpretation of Wagner's *Ring* which includes a complete assessment of its dramatic poem and musical motifs' enhancement of the drama in unprecedented detail. It explores Wagner's musico-dramatic meaning in a way intended to illustrate his remark to Mathilde Wesendonck that "there never was another man who was poet and musician at once in my sense, and therefore to whom an insight into inner processes has become possible such as could be expected of no other." [665W—{12/8/58}] RWMW, P.78] Wagner seems to have recognized that his unique artistic insight into unconscious processes might have unforeseen, troubling consequences. As Cosima Wagner recorded in her diary, "[Wagner] says that he sometimes has the feeling that art is downright dangerous—it is as if in this great enjoyment of observing he is perhaps failing to recognize the presence of some hidden sorrow." [753W—{7/27/69} CD Vol. I, p 130] How could he fail to recognize some sorrow hidden within his own work of art? This is possible because, he said, his artistic creations were to a large degree the product of involuntary, unconscious inspiration: "how can an artist hope to find his own intuitions perfectly reproduced in those of another person, since he himself stands before his own work of art—if it really is a work of art—as though before some puzzle, which is just as capable of misleading him as it can mislead the other person." [641W—{8/23/56} Letter to August Röckel, SLRW, p. 357] In other words, Wagner's *Ring* means much more than he could consciously grasp, in much the same way that our dreams are ours, yet come to us involuntarily, seemingly from a mysterious elsewhere. Wagner is warning us that his art contains an allegorical subtext which might be its primary level of meaning, to which his music, the language of our unconscious, points.

This study will examine this question in depth to demonstrate that Wagner's notion that he was uniquely capable of accessing heretofore unconscious (and potentially dangerous) knowledge, knowledge of which he was only subliminally aware and therefore at risk of unwittingly revealing it to his audience (and perhaps even to himself), may provide the key to a coherent, unified understanding of the entire *Ring*, and even several of Wagner's other canonical artworks.

Most Wagner scholars of both the past and present, including George Bernard Shaw [Shaw, pp. 76–78], Cooke [Cooke, p. 247], Tanner [Tanner, p. 182], and Jean-Jacques Nattiez [Nattiez, p. 275; p. 286; pp. 299–300], have assumed that the *Ring* has no global meaning which will allow us to grasp it as a whole on one level of interpretation. A primary task of this study is to demonstrate that though such writers have made important contributions to our knowledge of this subject, some of which have been incorporated into this study, it is possible to propose an alternative interpretation which may grant us a depth of insight into the *Ring*'s conceptual unity, and into its status as the conceptual framework for Wagner's other repertory operas and music-dramas, which was previously largely unsuspected. In a private email forwarded to me by the eminent Wagner scholar Barry Millington on January 23, 2017, in critical response to his first attempted reading of my online book on Wagner's *Ring* posted since 2011 at www.-wagnerheim.com, he stated that though he was initially skeptical of my claim to have posited a global, unified allegorical reading of Wagner's *Ring*, he was pleasantly surprised to see that my claim was not as preposterous as he had feared. You can find his brief critical response to the online version of my book in the www.wagnerheim.com discussion forum archive on page 3, posted on January 25, 2017.

To initiate you into my novel reading of the *Ring*, I offer a brief history of my development of this research project, from its inception in the summer of 1971 to its final incarnation as a full-fledged interpretation, posted under the title *The Wound That Will Never Heal*, Volume One, at www.wagnerheim.com in 2011, and now in the much briefer, user-friendly revision which you're reading (please consult the considerably longer version at www.wagnerheim.com for more extensive consideration of the documentary evidence). My purpose is to show what distinguishes my *Ring* interpretation from all others.

A Brief History of My Book: *The Wound That Will Never Heal*

By age eighteen, in 1971, the only thing I knew about Richard Wagner was what everybody else knows: the wedding march ("Here Comes the bride") from *Lohengrin*, and "The Ride of the Valkyries," the most famous excerpt from Wagner's *Ring*. I knew nothing of *Lohengrin* and the *Ring* as works for the theater. One hot summer Friday evening, my parents were out of town (Annapolis, Maryland), and one of our two Washington, DC, classical radio stations, WETA, was broadcasting what was the most curious, searching, and novel piece of classical music I had ever heard. It consisted of a series of orchestral vibrations and oscillations, rising and falling, interspersed with what sounded like birdsongs. I became acutely alert and lucid (clairvoyant), as if I had woken up for the first time. At its conclusion, I ran for paper and pencil to record the host's naming of the piece's composer, Richard Wagner, and the piece's name, "Siegfried's Forest Murmurs," from Wagner's *Ring*. Afterwards, the host advertised a sale of Angel Records at a book and record store on Connecticut Avenue, near Dupont Circle, for Saturday. I intended to drive to Washington, DC, in the morning to buy an anthology of Wagner's orchestral highlights which would include my chosen piece. I felt this music was striving to give birth to words.

I arrived at the store next morning and told the manager my request. He noted I must have been very moved by this musical excerpt to drive all the way over to Washington just to obtain it and asked me what I knew about Wagner. Little or nothing, I said. He filled me in. "Siegfried's Forest Murmurs," he said, is an eight-minute-long orchestral excerpt from *The Ring of the Nibelung*. This four-part music-drama, requiring some fifteen hours to perform, was the most ambitious work in the entire history of musical theater. Wagner had taken approximately five years, from 1848 to 1853, to write the libretto, and took from 1853 through 1874 to compose all the music, a total of 26 years from gestation to completion (later I learned that Wagner took a break from his *Ring* to author and compose *Tristan and Isolde* and *The Mastersingers of Nuremberg* from 1857 to 1869). Among opera composers, in writing his own libretto he was almost unique, and the librettos of his mature music-dramas were surely the best, considered as dramas, ever penned. In order to perform this grand work, Wagner designed a special theater unlike any other in Europe (though it was patterned roughly after the amphitheaters in which ancient Greek tragedy and comedy had been performed). I was mightily intrigued. By the way, I cannot guarantee that a single thing I recorded above of the store manager's conversation with me is precisely accurate, so much have I mythologized this foundational event in my life. But I can guarantee what follows.

He made an astounding offer: he asked me how much money I had in my pocket. I told him I had $30.00 (which in those days could buy perhaps 5 or 6 Angel records). He suggested I climb up a ladder and retrieve a big, burgundy-colored, box-set of LP records from the topmost shelf, which had evidently been gathering dust for months. It was the Seraphim (a subsidiary of Angel Records, for old classic recordings, available at a lower price) 1951 mono recording of the entire *Ring*, including English/German libretto, with Wilhelm Furtwängler conducting the Italian Radio Orchestra. It contained some 19 albums. He offered it to me for my $30.00, saying it would normally retail for about $120.00 or so, but since it had sat for so long without attracting a buyer he would more or less give it away to me in honor of my profound initiation into Wagner's world.

Taking it home, I immediately fell into the bad habit of listening to a short, never-changing list of favorite orchestral passages. After some months of my wallowing in these few selections from the whole, mostly orchestral preludes to acts and interludes between scenes, my parents went away again for a weekend. So, having the house to myself, I did the experiment for the first time and sat down, libretto in hand, to follow along in English to at least a part of *The Rhinegold*, the first of the four *Ring* dramas. I had no intention of sitting for more than an hour, but hadn't anticipated the life-altering adventure on which I was about to embark. From the opening E flat major chord, I first recognized who I truly am. Oblivious to everything else, I experienced the *Ring*, libretto in hand, following the entire narrative, words and music, from beginning to end, with a few bathroom and sandwich and iced tea breaks along the way. I must have sat, including breaks, for twenty-four hours. It was the signal event of my life, the most fully alive I've ever been, one of those privileged moments when one floats and loses touch with the ground in a complete loss of self in another's dreamwork. I felt as though I had acquired a sixth sense, a sort of clairvoyance, experiencing felicity of this magnitude. This was the closest approximation to a numinous experience I've ever had, a secular version of what can otherwise only be described as a divine revelation. From that day to the present, I've tried to grasp the meaning of this experience for me, and hopefully for others. The book you're reading is the culmination of half a century of unremitting labor to get "inside" Wagner's creations in such a way that I can make sense of them both subjectively and objectively, as something both felt and thought. The following is my account of the high points of my quest for (self-)knowledge.

My initial impression of the *Ring* was that it had the most remarkable, powerful dramatic coherence, from beginning to end. Was this due, as Michael Tanner suggested [Tanner, p. 182], solely to the *Ring*'s well known musical unity, merely a product of Wagner's continual development of a small number of identifiable musical motifs (most being members of specific motif families) throughout the entire drama? Or was the *Ring*, as I experienced it, just as dramatically and conceptually coherent as it was musically coherent, capable of being grasped as a whole? I felt the musical coherence was the product, not the cause, of the dramatic and philosophic coherence. So I undertook a deep, systematic reading of the *Ring* libretto, to determine to what extent a global interpretation could be applied to the *Ring*'s entire text in fine detail. I wrote out and strove to solve all the philosophical problems raised by the libretto and its associated music at each point. I had the repeated good fortune to discern that Wagner regularly solves all the problems he raises in the *Ring*, once one properly construes his allegorical language.

From the beginning, however, the fact that Wagner's *Ring* is so heavily indebted to Norse and German mythology and legend as the primary source for its dramatic situations and characters (including their names) seemed an insurmountable objection to my attempt to apply an allegorical reading based on a modern mindset. I long feared this might be the case until I read Cooke's *I Saw the World End* in the late 1970s. He taught me how remarkably creative Wagner was not only in selecting only those things in his sources which he could manipulate for his own purposes, but furthermore how artfully he repurposed this material until it had become entirely his own. Cooke added that whenever Wagner needed to say something not found in his sources, he merely invented it, and he did this so skillfully that it would be difficult to distinguish—without prior knowledge of the sources—the dramatic incidents Wagner invented, from those he found in his source material. [Cooke, pp. 74–131] Furthermore, I learned that though most of the *Ring*'s dramatic situations and characters Wagner derived from Teutonic or Norse sources, a significant number were based on situations and characters drawn from Greek mythology and tragedy and from the Bible. Wagner found such a rich treasury of material in his diverse mythological sources that he manipulated it to carry any allegorical significance he desired. He believed that through his intuitive rearrangement of his source material he was disclosing its primal, purely-human, universal significance, cutting away the chaff of history to unearth the timeless, self-generating seed that gave birth to the original, pristine myths. Wagner's *Ring* could be construed as the universal master myth, a template or blueprint which embraces all possible myths, since he believed he had through a deep study of a plethora of mythological material disclosed its essence, the very nature of naked man, in his *Ring*.

In this way, I soon established the twelve "pillars" of my interpretation, which in most instances set my interpretation apart from all others. These pillars support what I've long believed is the true subject of the *Ring* allegory, that it's Wagner's account of human history from its beginning to its end, and that its conflict between power and love is Wagner's metaphor for man's existential dilemma, that we humans are torn between our quest for worldly power, attained through acquisition of objective knowledge of man and nature, as expressed in science, technology, and politics, and our counter-impulse to assert our transcendent human value, as expressed in religion, altruistic morality, and art. In this scheme, truth (the ultimate source of power), or "is," is incommensurable with the good (love) and the beautiful (love), or "ought." This is man's tragedy, his 'existential dilemma,' our un-healing wound.

The Twelve Pillars

(1) Nature and its laws (Fate, represented by Erda and her daughters, the Norns, and our egoistic animal instincts, the Giants) are the foundation of all events and characters in the *Ring*, including the so-called gods of Valhalla and their proxies the Wälsungs and Brünnhilde.

(2) The Ring of power Alberich forges is Wagner's metaphor for the power of the human mind. The Tarnhelm represents imagination (Wagner's "Wonder"), and the Nibelung Hoard represents objective knowledge (its accumulation increasing the power knowledge gives us).

(3) Alberich's accumulation of a Hoard of Treasure in the bowels of the earth (Erda) and Wotan's (Light-Alberich's) accumulation of a hoard of knowledge of the earth (Erda) during his world-wandering, are Wagner's metaphors for man's gradual acquisition of objective knowledge of man and Nature.

(4) When Alberich warns Wotan that he'll be sinning against all that was, is, and will be if he steals Alberich's Ring and co-opts its power for the sake of the gods (the self-deception necessary for religious faith), this is Wagner's metaphor for religious man's sin of world-denial, or pessimism.

(5) Alberich's motive in placing a Curse on his Ring is to punish Wotan and his proxies (the Wälsungs and Brünnhilde) for committing the religio-artistic sin of world-denial-and-renunciation.

(6) Siegmund is Wagner's metaphor for his Feuerbach-inspired secular social revolutionary. Having acknowledged the futility of hoping a social revolution could establish justice and truth in the world, Wagner dramatized his loss of faith in Wotan condemning his beloved son Siegmund.

(7) Since Wotan represents collective man during the religious phase of history, his confession to Brünnhilde of knowledge he can't bear to speak aloud is Wagner's metaphor for religious man's repression of unbearable knowledge into man's collective unconscious. Wotan's confession to Brünnhilde is Wagner's dramatization of his own turn inward towards his art, his creative unconscious (Brünnhilde), after giving up hope for redemption through politics.

(8) Siegfried is Wagner's metaphor for man's second post-religious bid for redemption in the inspired artist-hero, creator of the artwork of the future. Siegfried's loving union with Brünnhilde is Wagner's dramatization of unconscious artistic inspiration of Wotan's (dying religious faith's) heir, the music-dramatist Siegfried, by his muse, his unconscious mind, Brünnhilde.

(9) When Wotan tells Erda he no longer fears the twilight of the gods she foresaw but gladly embraces it because his heirs Siegfried and Brünnhilde will redeem the world from Alberich's Ring Curse, this is Wagner's metaphor for his notion that when religious faith (the gods) could no longer be sustained in the face of science's advancement in knowledge (Erda's knowledge), religious faith could live on, reborn as feeling, in secular art, particularly in the non-conceptual art of music.

(10) Siegfried's betrayal of his lover, muse, and unconscious mind Brünnhilde, under Alberich's son Hagen's influence, by unwittingly and involuntarily giving her away to his blood-brother Gunther, is Wagner's metaphor for the fact that in his *Ring* he's betrayed the hitherto secret process underlying religious revelation and unconscious artistic inspiration to his audience, through his musical motifs, represented by the Woodbird's songs Siegfried interprets for his audience.

(11) Wagner's creative advance from author and composer of romantic operas (*The Flying Dutchman, Tannhäuser,* and *Lohengrin*), in which his music had what he described as only a mechanical relationship to the development of the plot, to the revolutionary music-dramas (the *Ring, Tristan and Isolde, The Mastersingers of Nuremberg,* and *Parsifal*), in which Wagner's music, and his musical motifs, develop in an organic association with the drama, is allegorically dramatized in a crucial distinction between the plot of *Lohengrin*, the last of his romantic operas, and the *Ring*, the first of his music-dramas. This distinction is the following: where Lohengrin refuses Elsa's request that he share with her the secret of his true identity and origin, so she can help preserve his secret to protect him from the "Noth" (anguish) she supposes he would suffer if his secret was revealed, Wotan acquiesces to Brünnhilde's plea that he confess to her what ails him, the unspoken secret of his divine "Noth" ("Götternoth"). Wotan's confesses the truth he learned from Erda, that the gods (i.e., man's religious beliefs) are predestined to destruction by man's gradual accumulation of a hoard of objective knowledge. In the *Ring*, drama (Wotan's confession of the unthinkable guilt in man's history) and redemptive musical motifs of foreboding and reminiscence (Wagner's artistic "Wonder" distilled from Wotan's confession by Brünnhilde's magic) attain complete organic union, redeeming man's terrible history by transforming it into timeless myth.

(12) Wagner's three canonical romantic operas and his four mature music-dramas can best be construed as a single work of art in continuous development, the *Ring* being the overall allegorical frame of reference for Wagner's other canonical artworks, their master-myth.

A key purpose of *The Wound That Will Never Heal* is not merely to demonstrate the *Ring* can best be grasped as a unified whole if we approach it as an allegory along the lines of interpretation outlined in my list of "pillars," but also to show how our new allegorical understanding will establish the *Ring* as the basic frame of reference within which we can understand all of Wagner's other canonical romantic operas and music-dramas (which could be the subject of a second volume). For they're each systematically linked conceptually with all or part of the *Ring*, which can be construed as their master myth or archetypal model. *The Flying Dutchman*, for instance, is a cryptic version of what would become the *Ring*. *Tannhäuser* is a seedbed for the plots of *Siegfried, Twilight of the Gods, Tristan and Isolde, The Mastersingers of Nuremberg,* and *Parsifal*. *Lohengrin* isn't only the seminal point of departure for the revolutionary music-dramas which followed, but is specifically the basis for two key plot elements of the *Ring*: (a) Wotan's confession to Brünnhilde, and (b) Wotan's punishment of Brünnhilde with banishment, loss of divine virginity, and deprivation of godhead in order that his heir Siegfried, the mortal, secular artist-hero, can win her and take aesthetic possession of the hoard of fearful knowledge Wotan imparted to her, thus redeeming him from Alberich's Ring Curse. Please see my two studies of *Lohengrin* in the discussion forum archive at www.wagnerheim.com: My article "How Elsa Showed Wagner the Way to Siegfried" is in the archive on page 14, posted in three parts (corresponding with its three acts) on 10/2–3/2011. My elaboration of this paper, titled "Feuerbach's Influence on *Lohengrin*," can be found in the archive on page 7 posted in four numbered parts on 6/16–17/2015. The plots of *Tristan and Isolde* and *Twilight of the Gods* are, as Wagner said himself, essentially identical. *The Mastersingers of Nuremberg* is a variation on the plots of *The Valkyrie* and *Siegfried*, while at the same time being the satyr-play to *Tannhäuser*, and the anti-thesis to *Tristan and Isolde*. And *Parsifal*, as has long been suspected, is virtually the fifth and final part of the four-part *Ring*, in which many of its unresolved issues are resolved, but it's also the music-drama in which all of Wagner's prior canonical artworks culminate, for all of their primary protagonists are, so to speak, reborn in those of *Parsifal*, their final incarnation. My study "Feuerbach's Influence on *Parsifal*" can be found in the archive on page 7 posted in seven numbered parts on 6/17/2015.

Dozens of hitherto incomprehensible conundrums and seemingly irresolvable contradictions in Wagner's drama, music, and their relationship, in the *Ring* and his other canonical artworks, can be construed with clarity or resolved thanks to this allegorical approach. Its success suggests that those exegetes who described the *Ring* as unsusceptible to dramatic or conceptual analysis within one frame of reference hadn't asked the right questions, and/or hadn't proposed a sufficiently all-embracing thread of narrative logic, to grasp the *Ring*'s allegorical grandeur and dramatic unity. This I believe explains why, during the early years in which I developed my unique reading of the *Ring*, when I read everything available on Wagner by other authors, I discovered, often to my surprise, that though a number of talented writers on Wagner's artistic legacy had made discoveries of great explanatory value, which I was able to incorporate into my own work, many of these same authors often failed to follow up the implications which logically followed from their seminal insights. And in many instances the very insights that gave them an authentic purchase on Wagner's creative work became a stumbling block to further exploration. A few examples will suffice.

Nietzsche, Wagner's erstwhile champion and latter-day critic, had more access to Wagner and his works than anyone, and should have known, as no one else could, just how extraordinarily prescient the plot of Wagner's *Ring* was—especially considering its colossal debt to Ludwig Feuerbach's critique of religion—with respect to Nietzsche's own mature philosophy. Yet, when one surveys the entire body of Nietzsche's critique of Wagner, the *Ring* libretto is rarely discussed at all, and if so, generally only with biting condescension. In one notorious example, Nietzsche argued that the sole reason Wotan, in his role as the Wanderer, wakes Erda in *Siegfried* Act Three Scene One, is that we haven't heard a soprano voice in a long while, so Wagner needed a pretext to produce one at this point. [*The Case of Wagner*, p. 175] Nietzsche's critique is preposterous in view of the fact that this is one of the crucial moments in the *Ring*, when Wotan wills the end of the gods (religious faith), which Erda foretold, only because he's persuaded that his ideals will live on in the love of his heirs (metaphor for secular art), the hero Siegfried and heroine Brünnhilde. S.3.1 is a dramatic turning point in the *Ring*, for Wotan passes the torch, the responsibility for preserving our human illusion of our transcendent value, from traditional religious belief to inspired secular art, by leaving his daughter Brünnhilde, who holds the key to the secret of the religious mysteries (Wotan's confession), for the music-dramatist Siegfried to wake. Virtually every sentence in Wotan's contentious dialogue with Erda is deeply meaningful (and steeped in Wagner's musical motifs, which hugely amplify both the emotional and the conceptual resonance of the words they accompany), linking this passage musico-dramatically not only with the entirety of the *Ring* plot but also with Wagner's other repertory operas and music-dramas.

George Bernard Shaw famously described the *Ring* as a thinking man's allegory whose subject was the coming political and social revolution in Europe, a revolution incited by the evil effects of rampant capitalism and greed for money and power. Shaw's reading is, of course, to some extent accurate, but he admitted it could only be applied to the first two thirds of the *Ring*. [Shaw, pp. 76–78] In truth, Shaw based most of his interpretation on a metaphorical reading of approximately one thirtieth of the *Ring*, Scene Three of *The Rhinegold* (in which Wotan and Loge visit Alberich and his fellow Nibelungs in Nibelheim), and general knowledge about Wagner's revolutionary activities in 1849. That this reading has become a stumbling block to understanding was illustrated by one of the participants in a seminar on Wagner I attended in Chicago many years ago, who informed me after a provocative lecture that it was too bad Wagner couldn't have engaged Shaw to write the *Ring* libretto for him, since in that case Shaw would have gotten it right and made the last third of the *Ring* consistent with the first two thirds. Consistent with Shaw, at least!

Shaw argued that Wagner's alleged inconsistency was due to the fact that the libretto of *Twilight of the Gods*, the last part of the four-part *Ring* drama, was the first part of the *Ring* to be completed, and that it therefore still contained elements drawn from conventional romantic opera which Wagner finally emancipated himself from by the time he wrote the libretto of *The Rhinegold*, the last part of the four-part *Ring* libretto to be completed. This might seem convincing until we recall that Wagner acknowledged [See 811W-{12/71} 'Epilogue to *The Nibelung's Ring*,' PW Vol. III, pp. 268–269] that the plot of Tris*tan and Isolde*, a full-fledged revolutionary music-drama created after Wagner had completed the entire libretto of the *Ring* and two thirds of its music, is virtually identical to the plot of *Twilight of the Gods*. In both instances the hero, as if under a spell, gives his own true love away in marriage to another man, and thereby dooms himself. Though we can all agree that there are holdovers from his romantic opera days in *Twilight of the Gods* which Wagner would omit from his subsequent music-dramas, evidently this plot which the *Ring* and *Tristan and Isolde* share was central to Wagner's concept of the revolutionary music-drama, something which distinguished it from romantic opera. In his too-strict adherence to a topical reading of the *Ring* as an allegory of 19th Century social, political, and economic revolution, Shaw blinded himself to this fundamental aspect of Wagner's whole conception of music-drama. But Shaw's virtue was that he understood the *Ring* is allegorical.

The Jungian Robert Donington had several signal insights into the *Ring*'s allegorical logic which will be detailed in the course of this study. The first of these will serve for illustration. Donington surmised that Alberich's rejection by the Rhinedaughters, his renunciation of love, and forging of the Ring of power represents an important stage in the evolution of human consciousness. [Donington, p. 60] His insight led me to consider the possibility that Alberich's Ring represents the human mind itself. Donington described Alberich's Ring as Wagner's metaphor for the "Self" in its Jungian sense, i.e. the entire human being, both good and bad, conscious and unconscious. [Donington, pp. 227–228] However, Donington failed to follow up this insight. The remainder of his book, after the first provocative chapter on *The Rhinegold*, and occasional world-class insights in subsequent chapters, becomes ever more arbitrary and divorced from the actual dynamics of the plot, as he tries to force Jungian categories on everything in the *Ring*, until by the end of his book this has reached the point of absurdity. Donington's fatal mistake, it seems, was his failure to grasp that the *Ring* is an allegory of human history. He instead construed the *Ring* as an allegory of the maturation of the "self" from a psychological standpoint only. This gave him insight into some of the *Ring*'s secrets—such as the fact that Wotan, as a symbol for man per se, the "self" which is maturing in the course of the drama [Donington, p. 67], subsumes all the other protagonists of the *Ring*—but blinded him to many others.

However, since Donington provided the initial spark of inspiration for my lifetime of labor to grasp Wagner's *Ring* and his other artworks, I must pay him due credit. First, he gave me the idea for the title of my book, *The Wound That Will Never Heal*. Donington's seminal idea, that so influenced my own work, was that the Nibelung dwarf Alberich must become creative to compensate himself for his inherent incapacity to find normal contentment, what Donington calls "the wound in the psyche," the price man pays for his acquisition of the gift of consciousness (Alberich's forging of his Ring). [Donington, p. 82] This was the seed which gave birth to my central idea, that Alberich's Ring Curse represents the price we humans pay for our gift of reflective consciousness, that we're inherently incapable of accepting the world as it is, which inspires us to compensate ourselves for its deficiencies psychologically through religious faith, morality, and art, and practically through science, technology, and politics. An obvious source for this concept are the un-healing wounds from which Tristan and Amfortas suffer. It's worth adding that another influence on my title of equal importance was the un-healing wound that Prometheus, exposed (like Brünnhilde) to the elements on a mountaintop, suffers as the god Zeus's punishment for having (like Brünnhilde) aided mortal man against Zeus's will by granting man god's divine gifts (not only fire, but specifically the gift of "foresight," for Prometheus in Greek means foresight). This comes to the same thing as Donington's "wound in the psyche," for foresight is a key property of man's uniquely reflective consciousness, one which though it grants us the greatest power of all animal species, also exacts the greatest price, man's foresight of inevitable death.

A brief reckoning of some of Donington's other contributions will illustrate my debt to him. I've mentioned Donington's crucial insight that Wotan, a symbol for humanity, subsumes all the other characters in the *Ring*. This led Donington to suggest that Brünnhilde represents specifically Wotan's unconscious desire [Donington, p. 164], that Mime represents Siegfried's fear [Donington, pp. 176–177], that Wotan's contest of knowledge with Mime can only be understood if we recognize them as the same character [Donington, p. 180], and that Dark-Alberich is Wotan's (Light-Alberich's) Jungian shadow [Donington, p. 63]. Each of these enlightening ideas have been my springboards to further discoveries. Especially helpful with respect to my endeavor to grasp Wotan's character and fate was Donington's remark that our "fate" is actually one with our true character, [Donington, p. 235] an idea I subsequently discovered was expressed by Wagner's mentor Ludwig Feuerbach.

On the subject of religion and art as an evasion of truth, Donington provided four insights which have been very helpful to me in my quest to plumb the *Ring*'s depths. He noted, for instance, that a great artist half reveals and half conceals the truth, concealing it because the full light of the truth would be insupportable. [Donington, p. 15] Yet he went on to say that if illusion is the disease, the truth, no matter how bitter, heals. [Donington, p. 262] These insights were immensely helpful to me in my effort to understand Wotan, though Donington didn't specifically apply them to Wotan. Equally helpful were his observations that both religion and art reflect human infantilism, our longing to return to the womb, and that art allows us to play with reality and enjoy its benefits symbolically without suffering the consequences which would follow if we engaged in actual life [Donington, p. 247]. These astute observations were helpful when I began to see Siegfried as an artist-hero in whom Wotan (man's religious impulse) sought redemption from truth, though Donington never construed Wotan or the gods specifically as a symbol for man's religious impulse, nor did he ever describe Siegfried as Wagner's metaphor for an artist.

However, in spite of the fact that my engagement with the *Ring* as an allegory began with a close reading of Donington's Jungian study, which gave me many fruitful ideas for further development, my book isn't a Jungian interpretation. Rather, I've drawn insight from Donington's Jungian interpretation, among many other sources equally important, such as the work of the French anthropologist Claude Lévi-Strauss, and others too numerous to name.

My debt to Claude Lévi-Strauss, whose writings I studied as an undergraduate and graduate student in anthropology, is also considerable. His books introduced me to several key concepts which have greatly influenced my understanding of Wagner. One of the most beneficial was his constant emphasis on the foundational trauma represented by man's evolutionary transition from the state of Nature (preconscious animal instinct) to Culture (communication through symbols, language), which produced a series of perhaps irresolvable contradictions. It's the underlying purpose of myth to resolve these. Another seminal Lévi-Straussian observation was that Wagner was the founder of Lévi-Strauss's enterprise, the structural analysis of myths, and that the conceptual structures of myths are reproduced in music. [Lévi-Strauss—*The Raw and the Cooked*, p. 15] A close reading of my book will leave you in no doubt how deeply Lévi-Strauss's following tribute to Wagner has influenced my own outlook: "Before taking the place of religion, the fine arts were in religion, as the forms of contemporary music were already in the myths before contemporary music came into being. It was doubtless with Wagner that music first became conscious of the evolutionary process causing it to take over the structures of myth ... ." [Lévi-Strauss—*The Naked Man,* pp. 653–654] Finally, Lévi-Strauss's elaboration of Vladimir Propp's idea that there's a sort of archetypal folktale (or myth) which lies behind the actual folktales (or myths) recorded in the field, in reference to which one can grasp details in specific folktales (or myths) which otherwise would be incomprehensible, was partly what prompted my decision to treat Wagner's four mature music-dramas as if they're one, single, unified work of art.

The musicologist Deryck Cooke made the most ambitious effort yet to comprehend the entire *Ring*, libretto and music, within one interpretation. He passed away prematurely while still completing the second of four projected parts, on *The Valkyrie*. One of his greatest contributions to Wagner scholarship is his unprecedented analysis of the evolution of, and family relationships among, the *Ring*'s musical motifs, in *An Introduction to Der Ring Des Nibelungen,* surely the greatest lecture on the *Ring*'s musical motifs ever recorded. Cooke demonstrated that Wagner's *Ring* has a musical/motival coherence on a mass scale which is unique in the history of Western music (and of course entirely unique in drama, since Wagner was the only great dramatist who was also a great composer). Dr. Allen Dunning's list of 177 of the *Ring*'s musical motifs was based on Cooke's lecture, though Dr. Dunning corrected some of Cooke's errors and added his own discoveries. My new list of 193–194 motifs incorporates most of Dr. Dunning's list (minus a few I've eliminated), and includes his musical notation for motifs not included in his numbered list which I've added.

Cooke began well but was unable to follow up many of his fine insights into the genealogical relationships among the motifs, when in his *I Saw the World End* (1976) he attempted to describe their dramatic significance, because the frame of reference within which he tried to describe the *Ring* libretto and tease out its allegorical elements was too narrow and inflexible. Aside from a few helpful observations, he simply could not discern and describe the more far-reaching allegorical significance of his great insights into the evolution of, and mutual relations among, the musical motifs, and thus he missed dozens of clues to Wagner's allegorical logic in the libretto.

He made one fundamental error in interpretation which was bound to have a dire effect on his entire enterprise. He stated categorically that in the *Ring* meaning lies ultimately in the music, not the dramatic text or action: "All that really matters is that the ultimate meaning of a Wagner 'drama' is achieved through the music, as Wagner himself was perfectly well aware." [Cooke, p. 65] The example he chose to illustrate this illustrates just the opposite. In *The Valkyrie* Act Two, Scene Two, Wotan has just been convinced, against his will, that he must follow his wife Fricka's advice that he support her protege Hunding's intent to kill Wotan's beloved son Siegmund for breaking the divine prohibition of adultery and incest, to ensure that the gods' rule will be respected. When his daughter Brünnhilde asks him what ails him, he explodes in a semi-coherent tirade (which I reproduce here in Cooke's version, plus musical motifs numbered according to my newly revised version of Allen Dunning's original list, which he based on Cooke's list):

"(H81; H50) Oh divinity's disgrace!
(H81; H50) Oh shameful wrong!
(H78) God's distress ["Götternoth"]!
(H78) God's distress!
(H39) Unending wrath!
(H39) Eternal grief!
(H35) I am the unhappiest of all beings!"

Cooke notes Wotan's verbiage is purely emotional and expresses no concepts:

... even Wagner's original [German text] is no more than a generalized indication of thought and feeling, conveying nothing in itself as to the essential nature of Wotan's self-disgust, rage, and despair, or the wider implications of them. If this passage of the text were offered at such a crucial moment in a poetic drama, we should rightly regard it as so much empty mouthing; we should expect a more masterly use of language, peculiar to the character concerned, expressing his state of mind and feeling in a much more complex way, and setting up all kinds of resonances backwards and forwards throughout the drama. / In fact, we are offered just such an experience by this brief passage, which is one of the most supreme moments in *The Valkyrie*, but the language used to provide it is the language of music. ... the resonances backwards and forwards are set up by the development and transformation of previous musical ideas, in the orchestra and in the voice. [Cooke, pp. 66–67]

Cooke then describes the origins and dramatic associations, within the context of the *Ring* drama, of the five motifs in play during Wotan's explosion of despair. But he's gotten this entirely wrong. The reason these five motifs have so much dramatic resonance, aside from their purely musical expressive power, is their former association with passages of libretto text and dramatic incidents, which demonstrates that poetic drama is clearly the source of the motifs' accumulated resonances. Wagner's motifs are messengers of Wagner's thoughts as expressed by his characters and their dramatic situations. The ultimate source of "meaning" remains the poetic text of the drama, even when that meaning is carried by identifiable musical motifs with which it's been associated in the course of the drama.

Another example of an opportunity Cooke missed will illustrate how I've been able to employ partial insights from prior pioneers in Wagner studies while leaving the burden of their interpretation behind as unusable. In a chapter covering the various allegorical subjects embraced by Wagner in his *Ring*, Cooke quotes Wagner [Cooke, pp. 250–254] on the subject of the evolution of human consciousness, and the development of religio-artistic thought, and scientific thought, which is where my interpretation begins and ends. Cooke has within his grasp in these few passages, and in his astute commentary on them, the means to construe the entire *Ring* allegory, but misses the opportunity completely. A brief extract from his book will suffice to illustrate:

"At first [i.e., after natural evolution had produced the human species], humanity followed its natural instincts, which were as follows: (a) a need to wrest from nature the means of existence; (b) a need for communication, which led to the evolution of language; (c) a need for mutual love and fellowship, which led to the establishing of the family and eventually, of society; and (d) a need to explain to itself its relationship to nature, which led to the creation of myths, and thus to religion and art. / It is the third of these four instincts which mainly concerns us here—the Need for mutual love and fellowship that led to the establishment of society." [Cooke, p. 253]

By skipping over instinct (a), the acquisition of knowledge which leads to science and technology, and instinct (d), the creation of myths, of religion and art, and never invoking these again for the remainder of his study, Cooke misses two of the main allegorical strands of meaning in the *Ring*. He then discusses the influence of the atheist philosopher Ludwig Feuerbach on Wagner, whose critique of religion and celebration of science and secular art is an influence which I find throughout the *Ring*, but which Cooke quickly passes over without bringing it up again. An equally fateful omission occurs two pages later, in which he discusses an extract in which Wagner paraphrases Feuerbach's critique of religion:

"This 'error' on the part of primitive peoples—the creation of gods and of religion was, Wagner maintained, a magnificent one, since it arose from that natural instinctive need of humanity to explain to itself its relationship to nature, and it led to the creation of the great myths, which were marvelous projections of humanity's own highest ideals and aspirations. And the factual error itself was eventually corrected by science, which discovered the causes of nature's effects inside nature." [Cooke, p. 254]

After a few pages Cooke leaves this profound subject behind, never to bring it up again for the remainder of his study. But it's the whole affair! The entire *Ring* plot is contained in brief in these few remarks. Nonetheless, Cooke was the first to draw attention to this subject, and ultimately inspired me to undertake a comprehensive survey of the entire body of Wagner's writings and recorded remarks, and compare them with the libretto texts of his operas and music-dramas (and their music). Had he lived to complete his study of the *Ring*, would Cooke eventually have incorporated these insights? Perhaps. But if one peruses the final chapters he completed in his study of *The Valkyrie* one finds increasingly strained efforts to construe the complexities of the plot according to his assumptions.

The last author I'll consider in detail is Jean-Jacques Nattiez, whose *Wagner Androgyne* (1990) is one of the most insightful studies of the *Ring* in the literature, but which only influenced my own interpretation after-the-fact, since I'd already developed its essentials (such as my twelve "pillars"), and particularly those insights in which our work overlaps, before I first became familiar with Nattiez's work in 1983. One of Nattiez's primary insights (which we have in common) is that in Wagner's mature music-dramas, the hero and heroine, particularly Siegfried and Brünnhilde, are metaphors for the poet-dramatist, and music, respectively. Therefore, their loving union is Wagner's metaphor for his revolutionary music-drama, in which the poetic drama and music serve each other in an organic (i.e., loving) way unknown, according to Wagner, to traditional opera, in which vocal music is usually the main affair and the staged drama and libretto merely provide a pretext for beautiful song. In my original and independently developed take on this reading, I concurred with Nattiez in construing Siegfried as a metaphor for the music-dramatist, but I differed from him in seeing Brünnhilde as Siegfried's unconscious mind, and therefore as his muse of unconscious artistic inspiration. Nattiez noticed that this metaphor—the loving union of hero and heroine as Wagner's image of the relationship of drama to music—was explicit in Wagner's theoretical writings, and implicit in the opera prose scenarios Wagner wrote between 1848 and 1853, while he was also writing the *Ring* libretto. But he also noted that it is made quite explicit by Cosima Wagner, Wagner's second (and last) wife, in a passage from her diaries: "We speak also about my last conversation with Herr Levi. He does not seem to fully understand 'Parsifal,' and I tell him that R's [Wagner's] article theoretically bears almost the same relationship to the poem as his words on music (the loving woman) and on drama (the man) in 'Opera and Drama' bear to Brünnhilde and Siegfried." [933W-{8/2/78} CD Vol. II, p. 128]

In this one subject in which our hypotheses overlap, however, my interpretation differed from Nattiez's in one crucial respect. Nattiez read Siegfried's betrayal of Brünnhilde in *Twilight of the Gods*, his courtship of the false muse, the coquette Gutrune, and subjection to the will of Hagen (in Nattiez's reading a half-Jewish impresario of sorts, who lures Siegfried into betraying his true art for a false one), as the music-dramatist's betrayal of his true genius (expressed solely in revolutionary Wagnerian music-drama) for the sake of a retro art-form, Parisian grand opera, as instanced in Siegfried's performance of a song narrating the story of his life, at Hagen's behest, in T.3.2. [Nattiez, pp. 87–88]. But Nattiez failed to see that the whole purpose of Siegfried's song is to narrate the authentic story of his heroic life as the music-dramatist, and in particular to explain how he came to understand the meaning of birdsong, which is Wagner's metaphor for his concept that as both author and composer of his music-dramas he had insight into the creative unconscious (i.e., Brünnhilde) that was unique. Siegfried's sung narrative of the story of his heroic life, which culminates in his death, is Wagner's play-within-the-play, a miniaturization of, and a metaphor for, a performance of the *Ring* itself. What Siegfried betrays in his performance of his greatest artwork (this betrayal the consequence of his having given his muse Brünnhilde away to Gunther, Wagner's metaphor for his audience) is the secret of his unconscious artistic inspiration, by sharing it with his audience, through his musical motifs.

I didn't read Sandra Corse's *Wagner and the New Consciousness* (1990) until long after I'd fully developed my allegorical reading of the *Ring*, but was interested to learn she anticipated my employment of the term "artist-hero" [Corse, p. 23], and that, like my reading, she conceives the *Ring* as an allegory of the evolution of consciousness, but unlike my reading construes this advancement as one of love alone, not reason (advancement of knowledge). [Corse, p. 30, 37] Similarly, I only read Mary Cicora's *Mythology as Metaphor—Romantic Irony, Critical Theory, and Wagner's 'Ring'* (published in 1998) long after I'd developed my interpretation. The primary overlap between our two books is that she construes Wotan's confession as his (i.e., Wagner's) deconstruction of the *Ring* as myth, which in a general way approximates my emphasis on the importance of his confession as containing his admission that he lives by self-deception.

I would be remiss if I didn't explain my reason for not reviewing the contribution of Dr. Mark Berry in his fairly recent book on Wagner's *Ring*, *Treacherous Bonds and Laughing Fire: Politics and Religion in Wagner's 'Ring'* (Ashgate, 2006; based on a dissertation from 2004), in any detail. Some years ago, my music consultant Dr. Dunning suggested I read Berry's book because he detected some significant overlap between Berry's reading of the *Ring* and my interpretation of it, which I'd been posting online for several years, and presented in lectures, prior to publication of Berry's book in 2006. One such lecture was "The *Ring* as a Whole," which I presented (having been invited to speak to the Wagner Society of Washington, DC by its Chairman Jim Holman) at George Washington University on April 27, 2000. The WSWDC posted a transcript of my lecture in their archive of past lectures on their website wagner-dc.org on 5/20/2000, and it remained there for years until their entire archive of past lectures was deleted. For this reason I re-posted it in the discussion forum at my website www.wagnerheim.com. It can be found on page 13 of the discussion forum archive, posted on 10/5/2011. The significance of this lecture is that in it I anticipated a number of Berry's observations, no doubt because Berry delineated the influence of Ludwig Feuerbach on Wagner's *Ring*, and though in 2000 I hadn't yet read Feuerbach's books, my evolving interpretation of Wagner's *Ring* had analyzed in detail the elements in Wagner's allegory which I later discovered stemmed from Feuerbach's influence. In my critique of Berry's *Treacherous Bonds and Laughing Fire*, posted in the discussion forum archive at www.-wagnerheim.com in eight numbered parts (on pages 11 and 12) between 5/4/2012 and 6/19/2012, I detailed the many threads of argument our two studies have in common. I found almost nothing in Berry's book which details Feuerbach's critique of religion as an influence on Wagner's *Ring* that wasn't already discussed by me in my prior copyrighted work. This isn't to denigrate Berry's contribution, however, because he helped to pave the way for acceptance of a Feuerbachian reading of Wagner's *Ring*.

There are two more recent books on Wagner's *Ring* which present earnest, detailed, thoughtful and original interpretations, which I'd thought initially I should critique in my introduction, namely, Dr. Philip Kitcher's and Dr. Richard

Schacht's *Finding an Ending—Reflections on Wagner's 'Ring'* (Oxford Univ. Press, 2004) and Roger Scruton's *The Ring of Truth—The Wisdom of Wagner's 'Ring of the Nibelung'* (Allen Lane, an Imprint of Penguin Books, 2016). However, I've saved them instead for an Epilogue (which I hope to post at www.wagnerheim.com some time this year, 2021) for the following reasons: (1) they were published long after I'd completed my *Ring* interpretation, and therefore had no influence on my online *Ring* book; (2) I needed to critique them in somewhat greater detail than I have the books dealt with so far in my Prologue, since they proffer interpretations which are in some key respects antithetical to my own; and (3) Kitcher and Scruton have written critiques of the online version of my *Ring* interpretation to which I must respond in greater detail than could reasonably be accommodated in this Prologue. The main theme of my critique of all three authors is that in their two books they're unable to make any sense of Siegfried because they fail to grasp his status as an allegorical being.

And last, there's a recently published book *The Consolations of History: Themes of Progress and Potential in Richard Wagner's 'Götterdämmerung'* (Routledge, 2019) which has special relevance because my online *Ring* interpretation at www.wagnerheim.com (posted since 2011) anticipated dozens of author Alexander H. Shapiro's insights and arguments, and in many cases employed identical quotations of passages from both Feuerbach and Wagner to make somewhat similar points. Mr. Shapiro's sole citation of my prior study is footnote #10 to a remark he made about Mark Berry's *Ring* interpretation, in Chapter One 'Siegfried as historical anomaly.' In order to prove the priority of my claim to these insights and arguments, I wrote a critique of Shapiro's book in which I methodically compared passages from my older online *Ring* study at www.wagnerheim.com with corresponding passages from Shapiro's newer book, and posted it on October 7, 2020, in 21 numbered parts in the archive of my discussion forum at www.wagnerheim.com, on pages 1 and 2. On page 1 you'll find my reader's guide to this critique. Though Shapiro bases much of his argument on a concept he has in common with my interpretation, that Brünnhilde is the bearer of a hoard of knowledge which is instrumental in advancing humanity's potential and progress, his argument departs from mine in construing this knowledge only in a positive light, whereas I proved in detail that Wagner identified man's gradual accumulation of a hoard of scientific knowledge as antithetical to man's religious impulse as found not only in traditional faith but in altruistic ethics and secular art. Aside from that key distinction between our interpretations, readers can easily discern their underlying similarity by performing a simple substitution: wherever Shapiro invokes Nature, substitute my concept of unconscious artistic inspiration.

As with most of the authors aforementioned from whom I drew occasional benefit but much of whose work I had to discard, I had a similar experience with the writings of perhaps a dozen other Wagner scholars, i.e., discovering in them the occasional earth-shaking insight, but frequently a failure to follow up the implications of that insight. Believing that my independent research could complement their own, I began to forward portions of my unpublished manuscripts to the published Wagner scholars for their review, and occasionally received promising reviews, but more often than not I was told, in so many words, that Wagner couldn't possibly have conceived his artworks in the way that I'd described. This was one among other reasons that I made a methodical study of a huge and representative body of Wagner's writings and recorded remarks, and of Feuerbach's writings which demonstrably influenced Wagner, which culminated in my creation of a comprehensive chronological anthology of 1,151 numbered passages from this material as evidence for (and sometimes against) my interpretation. You'll find this anthology in Appendix II at www.wagnerheim.com.

One area where my competence was lacking, and I needed a consultant, was the music. Having no musical training and being unable to read music, I've not attempted to enhance my allegorical reading of Wagner's *Ring* with musicological analysis of its tonal and harmonic structure. My treatment of Wagner's music is limited to a close analysis of the far-reaching cross-references engendered by Wagner's 193 or so identifiable musical motifs, heard in intimate association with passages from the libretto, which point to meanings within the drama, such as my allegorical reading, which might otherwise have remained undetected. In 2001 Dr. Allen Dunning, who'd made his own study (based on that of Deryck Cooke) of the *Ring* motifs, and who described and assembled by far the most comprehensive numbered list of motifs (177) to date, offered to be my music consultant and let me use his motif list in my book. He worked with me to embed the *Ring* libretto (both in the German original and Stewart Spencer's English translation) with numbers representing each numbered motif's occurrence where it can be located in the orchestral score, at those points in the drama which correspond with the score. I've revised Dunning's list of 177 motifs, eliminating several which I feel don't deserve status as numbered motifs, and adding some others which Dunning omitted, some of which Roger Scruton included in his *The Ring of Truth—The Wisdom of Wagner's 'Ring of the Nibelung.'* In order for readers to instantly compare Dunning's original list of 177 motifs, my newly revised list of 193 (perhaps 194) motifs, and Roger Scruton's list of 186 motifs, in my motif guide I've designated Dunning's motifs with a hashtag # followed by their number, while my revised list's motifs are designated by "H," for Heise, and Scruton's by "S." Needless to say, my *Ring* study could benefit from expert musicological analysis.

The last major untapped area of research was Ludwig Feuerbach's writings, with which I was familiar only through occasional references in some of the books on Wagner I'd acquired over the years. I'd already read and vetted virtually everything Arthur Schopenhauer and Friedrich Nietzsche had written, and grasped in some detail Schopenhauer's influence on Wagner, and Wagner's influence on Nietzsche. But I felt I couldn't propose a comprehensive interpretation of Wagner's *Ring* until I'd thoroughly ascertained the degree and quality of influence of Feuerbach's writings on Wagner's operas, music-dramas, writings, and recorded remarks. I was encouraged in this endeavor by fellow Wagnerian Derrick Everett, creator of the superb website devoted to Wagner's

Parsifal, www.monsalvat.com. I vetted the four books by Feuerbach which Wagner admitted having read, or having been familiar with. As I'd done with Wagner's writings and recorded remarks, I produced a comprehensive chronological anthology of key passages from all four of Feuerbach's books which demonstrably influenced Wagner. This enabled me to make a point-by-point comparison, matching Feuerbach's original ideas with what appeared to be Wagner's paraphrases of them. My book regularly draws on such matched passages from Feuerbach and Wagner to enhance our allegorical reading. At www.wagnerheim.com you'll find Appendix II, which contains my entire chronological anthology of Ludwig Feuerbach's writings, followed by Richard Wagner's writings and recorded remarks.

As my exhaustive study of Feuerbach's profound and broad influence on Wagner made clear, Wagner, prior to his first known acquaintance with Schopenhauer in the summer of 1854 (who according to Wagner supplanted Feuerbach in his esteem), had already built his critique of Feuerbach's materialistic philosophy into the plot of the *Ring*. Wotan and his proxies Siegmund and Sieglinde, Siegfried and Brünnhilde, though operating within a world Wagner pre-supposed was built according to Feuerbach's natural, materialistic principles, strive with all their being to transcend the limits of this Feuerbachian foundation. Nonetheless, to an extraordinary extent the musico-dramatic and conceptual content of the *Ring* expresses Wagner's Feuerbach-inspired doubts about the ideals and longing for transcendent value to which Wotan, his daughter Brünnhilde, and the Wälsungs Siegmund, Sieglinde, and Siegfried dedicate their lives. Feuerbach's materialistic realism and doubt lie behind, and eventually undermine, all of their heroic strivings. This is a primary premise of the *Ring*'s plot. For this reason alone, my *Ring* interpretation shouldn't be misconstrued as a purely Feuerbachian interpretation: Wagner's *Ring*, as I understand it, is Wagner's attempt (perhaps futile) to redeem himself and the world from the natural limitations of Feuerbach's worldview.

Three things became apparent through my detailed comparison of Feuerbach's work with Wagner's. (1) Feuerbach must have had a crucial influence on at least the last two of Wagner's three canonical romantic operas, *Tannhäuser* [first version completed in 1845] and *Lohengrin* [completed in 1848]. (2) Feuerbach continued to be a major influence on Wagner's writings, recorded remarks, and most importantly, the librettos (and therefore the music) of his music-dramas, long after 1854 when he said he renounced Feuerbach for the sake of Schopenhauer. (3) I could see in remarkable detail that Feuerbach had a pervasive influence on virtually every scene of the *Ring*. But what's particularly interesting is that the content of a study I completed at break-neck speed in 1983 (because I wanted to disseminate it to the Wagner scholars engaged to speak at the "Wagner in Retrospect—A Centennial Reappraisal" symposium at the University of Illinois, Chicago Circle, and had little time to prepare it), entitled *The Doctrine of the Ring*, which was my first detailed effort to disclose the philosophic unity underlying Wagner's mature music-dramas, corresponded in extraordinary detail with numerous passages from Feuerbach which Wagner paraphrased in his own writings and recorded remarks. What made this startling is that my 1983 study was based solely on my knowledge of Wagner's operas and music-dramas. It was written before I'd studied his own writings and recorded remarks in any detail, and long before I'd read more than a few passages from Feuerbach. I had, in other words, reconstructed the essential points, and many of the specific details, of Feuerbach's world-view from my study of Wagner's *Ring*. This has been the capstone of my life's work, and convinces me I've genuinely discerned several key aspects of the subject of Wagner's *Ring* allegory which previously had remained largely obscure.

Having received a private communication by email from the eminent Wagner scholar Barry Millington containing his initial critical response to his first attempted reading of the earlier, online version of my book on Wagner's *Ring* (posted at www.wagnerheim.com), on January 23, 2017, I'm grateful for his acknowledgment of my achievement in having carried further than prior scholars research into the pervasive influence of Feuerbach on Wagner, even after his conversion to Schopenhauerian pessimism after 1854. You can read his thoughts on p. 3 of the discussion forum archive at www.wagnerheim.com.

I close this Prologue with the following observations. It should be obvious that my allegorical reading of Wagner's *Ring* and my twelve pillars of interpretation aren't self-evident from your experience of the *Ring* at the theater or a private study of it. Had it been self-evident someone else would have stolen a march on the insights I present here in *The Wound That Will Never Heal* long ago. What I wish to argue is that a good deal of the "meaning" of Wagner's *Ring*, including the meaning of much of the libretto, is unconscious for us, something felt but rarely if ever thought, and probably was so to an extent for Wagner (who said that for the authentic artist, his art remains a mystery to him). But because Wagner unites music, which is inherently non-conceptual (felt, not thought), with words and the drama founded on them, which are conceptual, but like the myths on which Wagner modeled his *Ring* are often mysterious and not easily grasped, it's possible to unearth some of this unconscious content for conscious contemplation through a very close-reading of the libretto (which the average opera-goer, even the average dedicated Wagnerian, is unlikely to undertake) in its relation to the most far-reaching cross-references contained in Wagner's employment of his musical motifs in conjunction with the drama. This unconscious or subliminal component of the libretto, to which Wagner's musical motifs hold the key (just as Siegfried was able to translate the Woodbird's music into words for himself after sucking dead Fafner's blood, and later for the Gibichungs at Hagen's request, under the influence of Hagen's antidote to his potion of love-and-forgetting), constitutes a large component of the *Ring*'s plot which, among other things, is the tale of how the music-dramatist Wagner unwittingly and involuntarily betrayed the heretofore unconscious religious mysteries and secrets of his artistic inspiration up to the light of conscious day, in his *Ring*, through his musical motifs. As I'll show later in extraordinary detail, there's much in the *Ring*'s music and libretto which would remain mysterious and incomprehensible unless one consults my allegorical (though previously subliminal) interpretation. Roger Scruton posed the question whether this allegorical level of meaning had only private significance for Wagner and therefore doesn't become part of his audience's emotional response to the *Ring*, or whether it's an integral part of what the audience responds to in performance. You'll find my response to his critique in the Epilogue at www.wagnerheim.com.

In completing my study I have depended exclusively on Stewart Spencer's English translation of Richard Wagner's German libretto for the *Ring* 'From Wagner's *Ring of the Nibelung: A Companion*, © 1993 Stewart Spencer, Barry Millington, Roger Hollinrake, Elizabeth Magee and Warren Darcy. Published by Thames & Hudson Ltd., London and Thames & Hudson Inc., New York. Reprinted by kind permission of Thames & Hudson Ltd., London.' I've quoted from Spencer's translation extensively, since my study is the first to undertake analysis of all of its monologues and conversations, in all 36 scenes.

* * *

Readers may contact me by email at alberichnibelung276@gmail.com or paul@wagnerheim.com. I hope to update my website www.wagnerheim.com by replacing Dunning's list of 178 numbered motifs (identified with a hashtag #) with my new list of 193 numbered motifs (identified by "H" for Heise) introduced here in *The Wound That Will Never Heal*. The motifs' numbers in my published book don't correspond with Dunning's list used at www.wagnerheim.com. Furthermore, in my published book I've corrected many errors re indications of motif occurrences in context within the passages of libretto I quoted at www.wagnerheim.com. Also, I'm seeking someone with the skill to convert the musical notation of the 23 motifs I added to Dunning's list into sound files based on Wagner's score, like those Dunning created, as found at www.wagnerheim.com. And last, please register to join our discussion forum at www.wagnerheim.com.

The Rhinegold

THE RHINEGOLD ≠ SCENE ONE
(IN THE RHINE RIVER)
ALBERICH AND THE RHINEDAUGHTERS

Wagner's orchestral prelude to *The Rhinegold* is his metaphor for the "creation" in this sense, that we gradually become aware of the ageless, endless, uncreated world, and witness the evolution of life from animal to man. Wagner and Feuerbach agreed that the idea that a god created the world was absurd. Feuerbach suggested that the pre-existence of a perfect god makes an imperfect creation, supposedly emanating from him, superfluous: "It has often been said that the world is inexplicable without a God; but the exact opposite is true; if there is a God, the existence of a world becomes inexplicable; for then the world is utterly superfluous." [238F-LER, p. 143] And here's Wagner's paraphrase: "If Mind has manufactured Nature, if Thought has made the Actual, ... then Nature, Actuality and Man are no more necessary, and their existence is not only superfluous but even harmful; for the greatest superfluity of all is the lagging of the Incomplete *when once the Complete has come to being.*" [428W—{9-12/49} 'The Artwork of the Future,' PW Vol. I, p. 83] Furthermore, Wagner expressed his doubt about our religious assumption of pre-fallen innocence: "R. [Wagner] ... sees a lizard catching a glowworm, but the children rescue it. 'If it were not for the assumption that the world was made by a good God, one would find it all easy to understand. But none ... can free himself of the idea that once all was Paradise ... .'" [1017W-{6/25/80} CD Vol. II, p. 496]

Feuerbach and Wagner also agreed that man is a product of the natural evolution of animal life which culminated, in one evolutionary lineage, in human consciousness. Feuerbach said, for instance, that: "Man ... owes his existence and origin to the interrelation of all nature. (...) The earth is what it is only because of the place it occupies in the solar system, and it was not so placed in order that man and animals might be able to live on it, but the other way around." [231F-LER, p. 128; see also 232F-LER, p. 129] Wagner's version of Feuerbach's pre-Darwinian theory of evolution is the following: "Just as we know that there are heavenly bodies which have not as yet, or never will have, attained the birth of those conditions fundamentally necessary to the existence of human beings: so do we know that at one time our own Earth, also, had not as yet evolved such attributes. (...) Only where this 'Climate' resolves ... its influence into a pliant chain of broken contrasts, do we see arise that infinitely manifold series of organic creations whose highest grade is conscience-gifted Man." [446W-{2/50} 'Art and

Climate,' PW Vol. I, pp. 251–252] In this light we may consider the Prelude to *The Ring of the Nibelung*.

The three related motifs introduced in the prelude, H1, H2, and H3, are, taken in conjunction with the first words of the *Ring* sung by the Rhinedaughter Woglinde, Wagner's musical metaphor for the natural evolution of human life from simpler forms of animal life, expressing what both Feuerbach and Wagner called natural necessity:

> **[p. 57]** (Prelude: the orchestra begins while the curtain is closed: [[H1 orch:]]; [[H2 orch:]] [= H1 vari]; [[H3 orch:]] [= H2 vari] … . The top of the stage is filled with billowing waters that flow unceasingly from left to right. …)

The audience, enveloped in darkness, is supposed to become slowly aware of a pre-existing, eternal motion of the cosmos, as the sound of the orchestra gradually becomes audible. Motif H1, described by Cooke as the Primal Nature Motif, is a diatonic arpeggiated figure, which for Wagner apparently represented the fundamental component of music from which all musical development arises, just as it's a musical metaphor for our rising consciousness of the pre-existing, timeless world. [Darcy, pp. 77–78] This ur-motion becomes incarnate in the flowing Rhine River, represented by the final development of motif H1 into H3. Feuerbach's following two observations about water, the first as a metaphor for a timeless, unending, yet ever changing cosmos, and the second describing water as our link with our preconscious animal ancestors, seem to find voice in Wagner's Prelude, an image of a preconscious golden age when instinctive impulse alone impelled life forms: "The universe is the water, time is the motion of the water … . (…) Is it not just as absurd to conceive of a point in time as the beginning of the world as to conceive of the flow of water as the origin of water?" [225F-LER, p. 114] "Water as a universal element of life, reminds us of our origin from Nature, an origin which we have in common with plants and animals. … water is the element of natural equality and freedom, the mirror of the golden age." [142F-EOC, p. 276]

Heinrich Porges, Wagner's secretary who recorded Wagner's observations about the proper performance and understanding of the *Ring* during the rehearsals for its premier at Bayreuth in 1876, made the following remarks about the prelude which presumably echo Wagner's opinion: "Regarding the orchestral prelude [to *The Rhinegold*] as a whole, built on a single E flat major triad, Wagner insisted that its huge crescendo should throughout create the impression of a phenomenon of nature developing … of its own accord … . (…) It will be as though …, no longer conscious of the music, we had become immersed in the primal feelings of all living things and were peering directly into the inner workings of natural forces." [862W-{6–8/76} WRR, pp. 7–8; see also 353W-{11/40} 'A Pilgrimage to Beethoven,' PW Vol. VII, pp. 41–42]

Suddenly, as the orchestral prelude reaches its climax, the Rhinedaughter Woglinde introduces speech into the *Ring* out of newly introduced motif H4:

[p. 57] **Woglinde:** [[H4 voc:]] Weia! Waga! Welter, you wave, swirl round the cradle! [Wellgunde, Flosshilde and Woglinde converse: (…)]

Flosshilde: The sleeping gold you guard badly; pay better heed to the slumberer's bed (H3:) or you'll both atone for your sport (:H3).

Here, in Woglinde's lullaby H4, the first words of the *Ring*, in which onomatopoeic syllables develop into meaningful words, we find Wagner's metaphor for the origin of human language, which originated in instinct. Wagner identified ur-melody (mother-melody) with instinctive feeling. Out of this primal feeling evolved language, and therefore ultimately human history and drama: "Starting with an infinitely confluent fund of Feeling, man's sensations gradually concentrated themselves to a more and more definite Content; … their expression in that Ur-melody advanced at last, by Nature's necessary steps, to the formation of Absolute Word-speech." [535W-{50–1/51} *Opera and Drama*: PW Vol. II, p. 281; see also 512W-{50–1/51} *Opera and Drama*, PW Vol. II, pp. 200–201] By singing her lullaby H4, it's as if Woglinde wishes to keep the world from waking. But her effort is futile, because the Nibelung dwarf Alberich scrambles up to observe the three Rhinedaughters in play, spellbound by their beauty. The Rhinedaughters cruelly decide to teach him a lesson, so that, in spite of appearances, he'll learn he can never obtain love from them. Their mockery of his desire for love expresses the fact that, at least for him, there's no love in Nature:

[pp. 58–9] **Woglinde and Wellgunde:** (H8 embryo:) Ugh! The foul creature! (…)

Flosshilde: Look to the gold! Father warned against such a foe! (…) [Alberich and the Rhinedaughters converse: (…)]

Alberich: (…) How I long to embrace just one of those slender creatures, if only she'd deign to slip down here! [**Flosshilde:** (…)]

Wellgunde: The lecherous rogue!

Woglinde: Let's teach him a lesson!

Wagner initially felt sympathy for Alberich's plight: " … R. tells me that he once felt every sympathy for Alberich, who represents the ugly person's longing for beauty. In Alberich the naiveté of the non-Christian world … !" [907W-{3/2/78} CD Vol. II, p. 33] Now Alberich introduces the second of Wagner's many metaphors for the birth of human consciousness, expressing the idea that higher consciousness is a stumbling block to the ease with which man's animal ancestors spontaneously, instinctively negotiated their way through life:

[pp. 59–60] **Alberich:** ([[H5 orch:]] [[H6 orch:]] His progress repeatedly obstructed, Alberich clambers up to the top of the ledge with goblin-like agility.) (…) With my hands and my feet I can't capture or hold those delightfully slippery creatures. [Woglinde and Alberich converse (…)] What you scaled with such ease was much harder for me.

It was Wagner's viewpoint that human consciousness interferes with spontaneous, instinctive freedom of action: " ... this will to live, ... the actual metaphysical basis of all existence, demands solely to ... eat and reproduce itself perpetually, and this tendency is ... the same whether it be found in the dull rock, in the more delicate plant, or, finally, in the human animal; the only difference lies in the organs which man ... must use in order to satisfy more complicated needs which, for that reason, are increasingly contested and harder to meet." [634W-{6/7/55} Letter to Franz Liszt, SLRW, p. 345]

The new motif H5 is introduced as one of several motival incarnations of this notion that human consciousness is brutal and ugly, i.e., unnatural. H6, a slithering motif of six descending chromatic notes, Cooke called Alberich's Motif because, he claimed, it's the only motif associated exclusively with Alberich's character. I call it "Alberich's Futile Wooing Motif." It represents the incommensurability of reflective human thought, which is arduous, with instinctive feeling. This Wagner dramatized in the futility of Alberich's attempt to capture the Rhinedaughters.

After Wellgunde gives voice to new motif H7 in mockery of Alberich's bid for love, Alberich introduces a third metaphor for human consciousness, Wagner's notion that it's inherently egoistic and coercive, constituting a figurative rape of Nature (though being, nonetheless, a product of natural necessity, or evolution):

> **[pp. 61–2] Wellgunde: [[H7 voc:]]** Hey, my sweetheart (:H7 voc)! Can you not hear me? [Alberich and Wellgunde converse: (...)] If you're in love and lusting for love's delights let's see, my beauty, just what you are like!—(H38 embryo:) Ugh! You hairy, hunchbacked fool! Brimstone-black and blistered dwarf (:H38 embryo)! Look for a lover who looks like yourself! (...)
>
> **Alberich:** Although you don't like me, I still hold you tight. (...) (H2 end frag)

Feuerbach tells us that man must force Nature to satisfy his needs: " ... nature gives me nothing, I myself must take everything ...—and moreover I must take it by extreme violence. (...) To whom then does it really belong? To the one who takes it." [336F-LER, pp. 316–317]

The Rhinedaughters Woglinde and Wellgunde, having decided to befool Alberich into believing they really might satisfy his longing for love (while holding him in contempt), have flattered him with the sadistic intent to set him up for a brutal failure. Then Flosshilde chimes in:

> **[pp. 62–4] Alberich:** What lovely singing wafts this way.—How good there's not just one of you: with many, one might like me, with one, none would choose me! (...) [Alberich and Flosshilde converse: (...)]
>
> **Flosshilde:** (H23 embryo:) How your charm cheers my eye ... (:H23 embryo)! [Alberich and Flosshilde converse: (...)] (H112 embryo:) Your piercing eyes, your bristling beard, might I always see and hold them! (...) Your toad-like build, the croak of your voice ... (:H112 embryo).
>
> **Woglinde and Wellgunde:** Hahahahahaha!

In the course of Flosshilde's mocking praise of Alberich's toad-like charm, Wagner introduces the Embryo for Motif H23 which is the basis for what Cooke rightly described as the primary Love Motif of the *Ring*. But at H23's inception as an embryo we associate it with love as an expression of brutality and sadism, the triumph of the beautiful over the ugly in the competition for mates. Alberich's longing for love being thwarted, he'll conclude that love is an illusion, and will act accordingly, with nothing to lose. His cynicism has already reached the point that he acknowledges that the quest for a love-mate is based on statistical probability. But having failed to seduce any of the three Rhinedaughters, Alberich concludes that no matter how often he might make the experiment, he'd fail to find love for himself in the world. He expresses his existential angst in the following despairing cry:

> **[p. 64] Alberich:** (In a screeching tone of voice: **[[H8a voc:]]** Woe! **[[H8b voc:]]** Woe is me (:H8ab)! (H37 embryo voc:) Has the third one, so true, betrayed me as well (:H37 embryo voc)?

Alberich's cry "Wehe! Ach, Wehe!" introduces the definitive motif H8ab, which will be heard in association with woe throughout the *Ring*, and generates motifs H43ab and H173ab. Alberich is establishing himself as a metaphor for objective thought, not in the sense that it's passionless, but in the sense that its passion is the objective truth, the sole benefit to be derived from disillusionment of one's longing for illusory consolations. Alberich is acquiring the fortitude to face the bitter truth of the world, its indifference and lovelessness, without hope. But there's compensation: an unending quest for the earthly power to be won solely through arduous acquisition of knowledge of the world as it really is. He now grasps the distinction between the world as it really is, and the world as men—in their fear and longing—feel it ought to be. However, Porges described Alberich's expression of woe as representing merely uncontrollable greed: "The passage indicating most clearly how Alberich should be characterized is his lament after Flosshilde has deceived him so humiliatingly: 'Wehe! Ach wehe! O Schmerz! O Schmerz! Die dritte so traut, betrog sie mich auch!' ... the revelation should be that of an uncontrollable yet base and common greed. This is the fundamental trait of this child of the night ... ." [863W-{6–8/76} WRR, pp. 9–10] But we'll eventually learn that this primal, insatiable greed develops in the course of the *Ring* into a phenomenon of greater scope, man's insatiable impulse to control his environment, and his fellow men, through knowledge and the power which this brings.

Alberich's woe introduces another of the key themes of the *Ring*, that the gift of human consciousness is also, as Donington suggested [Donington: p. 38]), the source of man's existential woe, because man alone among animals is sufficiently self-conscious to conceive the conflict between the ideal and real. Man alone, with his ability to summarize experience in symbols, can construct an ideal which experience of reality often contradicts. As Wagner put it: "... a review of all the races makes it impossible to deny the oneness of the human *species*; ... that common factor may be defined, in its noblest sense, as the capacity for conscious suffering ... ." [1087W-{6–8/81} 'Herodom and Christendom,' 3rd Supplement to 'Religion and Art,' PW Vol. VI, pp. 276–277]

The Rhinedaughters at this early stage represent spontaneous animal instinct, which Wagner regards as unreflective joy in existence for its own sake, the basis for artistic expression. Such instinctive feeling for life Wagner identifies with "love," while Alberich's practical interests which exclude love are the basis for that quest for objective knowledge which grants us actual power. Having lost his chance at love through natural affection, Alberich desperately tries to coerce love (an oxymoron) from the Rhinedaughters and fails miserably:

> [p. 65] **Alberich:** Though you may laugh and lie, lusting, I languish after you and one of you must yield to me! (...) Might this fist catch only one! (He remains where he is, speechless with rage, his gaze directed upwards where it is suddenly attracted and held by the following spectacle. [[H9ab orch:]] An increasingly bright glow penetrates the floodwaters from above, flaring up as it strikes a point high up on the central rock and gradually becoming a blinding and brightly beaming gleam of gold; a magical golden light streams through the water from this point: [[H10 orch:]])
>
> **Woglinde:** Look, sisters! The wakening sun smiles into the deep. (H9ab)

Alberich's abject failure, and consciousness of its irrevocability, seems, of itself, to have appeared as a ray of the sun (consciousness) which lights up the previously invisible Rhinegold sitting on top of a massive crag under water. This produces two new motifs, H10, a shimmering motif which Cooke noted is often heard as a premonition of magical moments, and H9ab, the Rhinegold Motif, which is in the same family of diatonic arpeggiated figures as the Primal Nature Motif H1. The Rhinedaughters, in ecstasy, celebrate its beauty with song (i.e., poetry and music), dance and play:

> [p. 66] **The Rhinedaughters:** [[H11 voc:]] [= H8b vari] Heiajaheia! Heiajaheia (:H11 voc)! Wallalalalala leiajahei! [[H12 voc:]] [= H8a vari] Rhinegold! Rhinegold! (:H12 voc)! [[H13 voc:]] Light-bringing joy, how bright and sublime your laughter! (...) Gladdening games we'll play for you now: when the river glows and the flood is aflame, your bed we encircle, diving and dancing and singing, in blithely blissful abandon (:H13 voc)! (...)
>
> [[[H14 orch:]] is introduced as they swim around the gold in delight. Alberich asks about the gold.]

The Rhinedaughters' song in celebration of the Rhinegold introduces four new motifs, two of which are important in the development of the plot and the evolution of motifs associated with it, namely, H11 and H12, both of which derive ironically from Alberich's cry of woe at his inability to find love in Nature, H8ab ("Wehe! Ach, Wehe!"). H11 is their cry "Heiajaheia! Heiajaheia!" and H12 their cry "Rhinegold! Rhinegold!" As if that weren't irony enough, H11, at its inception here associated with joy, will—Cooke noted—give birth to the Nibelungs' Forging (or Labor) Motif H38, symbol of Alberich's enslavement of his fellow Nibelungs. Of the other two new motifs H14 is merely descriptive of the

Rhinedaughters' joyously swimming in the Rhine, one of Cooke's Motions of Nature. H13 is the beautiful song of the Rhinedaughters celebrating the Rhinegold's aesthetic splendor, evoking the arts. Nattiez, in *Wagner Androgyne*, referenced Tibor Kneif as the source of a fascinating insight into Wagner's allegorical intentions apropos the Rhinedaughters. The three Rhinedaughters represent the three muses of drama and poetry (Flosshilde), song (Woglinde), and dance (Wellgunde). [Nattiez, pp. 55–56] As noted by Kneif, Wagner provided our clue to this metaphorical reading: "The arts of Dance, Tone, and Poetry ... call themselves the three primeval sisters whom we see at once entwine their measures wherever the conditions necessary for artistic manifestment have arisen. ... this dance ... is the very cadence of Art itself ... ." [433W-{9–12/49} 'The Artwork of the Future,' PW Vol. I, pp. 95–96] Wagner thus links what for him were the three key arts of the theater with spontaneous animal instinct, or feeling. But there's more. The Rhinedaughters are engaged in a seemingly childish game, and art for Wagner is a profound form of play, which, like love, seems antithetical to the quest for power. The splendor of the Rhinegold is enjoyed for its own sake: " ... it is permissible for art to use these [the church's] symbols, but in a free spirit and not in the rigid forms imposed by the church; since art is a profound form of play, it frees these symbols of all the accretions the human craving for power has attached to them." [1012W-{4/27/80} CD Vol. II, p. 470] Alberich, clear-sighted about the world's true, earnest nature now that he knows he'll never find love in it, makes this distinction himself, disdaining the Rhinegold if it only serves for the Rhinedaughters' games, since in that case it's little use to him:

> **[p. 67] Alberich:** Is the gold only good for your diving games? Then it would serve me little!
>
> **Woglinde:** ([H?—a transformation of joyous Rhinedaughter music into the "World Mastery Motif" H15ab, which remains essentially Rhinedaughter music but is also an embryo for the "Ring Motif" H17ab:]) The golden jewel he'd not despise if only he knew all its wonders.
>
> **Wellgunde:** [[H15ab voc:]] The world's wealth would be won by him who forged from the Rhinegold the ring that would grant him limitless power (:H15ab voc).

Alberich has made one of the *Ring*'s crucial distinctions between human thought under the sway of feeling and play, which produces religious mythology and art, and objective human thought, through which we obtain the knowledge to draw power from our world. This latter is the practical utility which Alberich values, now that he knows the real world contains no subjective consolation. But Woglinde retorts that Alberich wouldn't despise the Rhinegold if he knew its latent power. The limitless power of the world's wealth she says can be obtained if one forges the Rhinegold into a Ring. In this musical dramatization of the transformation of the Rhinegold, which gave the Rhinedaughters aesthetic bliss, into the Ring of worldly power, Woglinde's music celebrating the Rhinegold subtly transforms to become H15ab, the "World Mastery Motif," which will in turn transform into the Ring Motif H17ab. Evidently what begins as love, or feeling, naturally evolves into a conscious motivation to gain power. Wagner drew a similar distinction between the Rhinedaughters' aesthetics and Alberich's insistence on seeking only practical "use," in his contrast between what he calls "German," i.e., enjoyment for its own sake (art for art's sake), and ulterior, utilitarian motives, which he describes as un-German (and which he tended to identify with Judaism). [See 732W-{9–12/67} 'German Art and German Policy,' PW Vol. IV, pp. 107–108] Wagner prized the aesthetic value of religious mythology, altruistic ethics, and art above the practical realm of knowledge in science, technology, and politics, which he regarded merely as expressing vulgar physical need. It's the psychological or spiritual need which religion and art satisfy which Wagner says "makes life worth living."

But Woglinde delivers the sticking point: to forge a Ring of power from the Rhinegold one must forsake love, i.e., forsake the psychological consolations of belief in love, which embrace religious mythology, morality, and art. She thus introduces one of the most famous *Ring* motifs, H16, the so-called "Renunciation of Love Motif":

> **[p. 68] Woglinde: [[H16 voc:]]** Only the man who forswears love's sway, only he who disdains love's delights (:H16 voc) can master the magic spell (H15ab:) that rounds a ring from the gold (:H15ab)
>
> **Wellgunde:** We're safe enough, and free from care since all that lives must love; no one wants to abjure its delights.
>
> **Woglinde:** Least of all he, the lecherous elf: he's almost dying of lustful desire ["Liebesgier"]!

Wagner's philosophic mentor Ludwig Feuerbach felt that only objective thought, freed from the bias of subjective feeling which taints religious faith's relationship with the truth, could get at Nature's truths to obtain that knowledge which grants man power over his environment: "It is only by the understanding that man reduces the things around and beneath him to a mere means to his own existence." [53F-EOC, p. 39] But, according to Feuerbach, those whose religious faith promises only supernatural consolation, who abjure reason and earthly labor, will never experience that feeling of lack (such as Alberich experienced after his bid for love was rejected, i.e., when Nature failed to satisfy him) necessary to the evolution of culture and mastery of the real world: "But how can he who has all in God, who already enjoys heavenly bliss in the imagination experience that want, that sense of poverty, which is the impulse to all culture?" [126F-EOC, p. 217] One must renounce subjective emotional consolations, which engender self-deception, to win the power granted only by effortful acquisition of knowledge of the real world. Alberich, in other words, is the first conscious being, because he's the first—thanks to his experience of need, "Noth"—in whom our mind's divorce between object ("is") and subject ("ought") becomes thought's object. As Feuerbach put it: "Conscious Spirit has arisen, this universal, self-beholding light has broken forth out of the break and division in nature's simple unity with itself." [14F-TDI, p. 112] And Wagner's more elaborate paraphrase of Feuerbach was: "To the Feeling the at-one-with-itself alone is understandable; whatsoever is at variance with itself ... confounds the Feeling and drives it into thinking ... ." [511W-{50-1/51} *Opera and Drama*, PW Vol. II, p. 198]

Alberich has been driven to thinking because he can't satisfy his fundamental instinct to enjoy the bliss of sexual reproduction, and so contemplates his formerly preconscious animal drives as an object of bitter reflection, a philosophic problem. Presumably the evolution of species gave birth to our conscious mind when formerly preconscious instinct was no longer adequate, in our human lineage, to satisfy all of our life needs and desires, and when the gift of generalization gave us humans an advantage in survival and propagation over other animals. The Rhinedaughters' rejection of Alberich's need for love, and their offer of a substitute, power, is Wagner's metaphor for that epoch in the evolution of life when Mother Nature no longer satisfied our human need through the gift of natural instinct, so we were forced to satisfy our need by compelling Nature to provide it, through conscious learning and hard labor. Here, in a passage introduced to me by Cooke's *I Saw the World End*, is how Wagner described this evolutionary process which culminated in human consciousness: " ... where Climatic Nature draws Man beneath the all-sheltering influence ... , and rocks him in her bosom as a mother rocks her child [Woglinde's lullaby H4], — where we must therefore place the cradle of newborn mankind: — there has Man remained a child forever ... . (...) Only through the force of such a Need as surrounding Nature did not ... still at once ... , but for whose appeasement he must himself provide, did he gain consciousness not only of that need but also of his *power*. This consciousness he reached through learning *the distinction between himself and Nature*; and thus it was that she, who no more *offered* him the stilling of his need, but from whom he now must *wrest* it, became the object of his observation, inquiry, and dominion. / The progress of the human race in the development of its innate capabilities of winning from Nature the contentment of those needs that waxed with its ever-waxing powers, is the *history of Culture*." [447W-{2/50} 'Art and Climate,' PW Vol. I, p. 252]

This extract seems to be the conceptual basis for the Rhinedaughters' rejection of Alberich's love, and his desperate decision to renounce love for the sake of power over the world which forging a Ring from the Rhinegold alone confers. For Wagner world-history is man's quest to satisfy his need by observing Mother Nature (obtaining objective knowledge) and dominating her. Why would Alberich reject love for power's sake? Reason, Feuerbach says, requires that we constrain our heart's feeling for the sake of clear sightedness and objectivity: "... reason ... is not satisfied by the heart; I think only in the interest of reason, from pure desire of knowledge." [156F-EOC, p. 296] Wagner, in an essay of his later years entitled 'Beethoven,' gave Schopenhauer credit for an idea he'd found first in Feuerbach, that objective thought (scientific inquiry) requires that we suppress our subjective feeling to get at the truth. Wagner identifies Schopenhauer's concept of the "Will" with subjective inner feeling (i.e., love), which Wagner says must be suppressed (love renounced) for the sake of the purity of the outward facing (objective, scientific) consciousness: "... our consciousness has two sides: in part it is a consciousness of *one's own self*, which is the will; in part a consciousness of *other things*, ... a *visual* knowledge of the outer world, the apprehension of objects. (...) / (...) If this consciousness ... is the consciousness of one's own self, i.e. of the Will, we must take it that its repression is indispensable ... for purity of the outward-facing consciousness ... ." [766W-{9–12/70} 'Beethoven,' PW Vol. V, pp. 66–67] It was Donington who first brought the association of man's evolutionary acquisition of reflective consciousness with the world-wide myth of the "Fall" to my attention, construing man's consciousness as the gods' punishment of a transgression. [Donington, pp. 37–39]

Alberich, having no prospect of love and nothing to lose, now will compensate himself for the lovelessness to which he's doomed, by seeking power through the Ring, power through knowledge:

> [p. 68] **Alberich: [[H17ab: voc]]** [= H15ab vari; almost definitive] The world's wealth might I win through you? Though love can't be gained by force, through cunning might I enforce its delights (:H17ab voc)? (H16)

Alberich has introduced the Ring Motif H17ab in almost definitive form. There's a mystery in his remark which can only be solved once we consider, in advance of the event, that the Ring Motif H17ab will—during the transition from R.1 to R.2—transform subtly into the first two segments of the Valhalla Motif H18ab, symbol of the gods's heavenly abode, a metaphor for man's religious impulse. To grasp Alberich's otherwise perhaps inexplicable remark that if love can't be gained by force, through cunning he might win its delight (it doesn't mean merely that Alberich intends to get through rape what he couldn't through love), we must grasp that his acquisition of the power of the conscious human mind, by forging the Ring, is the precondition for the development of religious thought, our earliest form of thought. It's by virtue of religious belief that man can, through artistic cunning, restore the delights of love (subjective feeling) which had to be renounced in order to gain the power of the Ring (our mind). Through religious belief and art, products of our mind (Alberich's Ring), we restore in some measure the animal instinct, the feeling of oneness with Nature, lost to us through our acquisition of consciousness, though this grants only an artificial restoration of lost innocence. For our reflective consciousness can be devoted both to the acquisition of objective knowledge of the world (Alberich's quest for power), and to subjective modes of thought under the influence of feeling, such as religious belief and art. Alberich's conscious wakefulness, representing our quest to force Nature to satisfy our needs, our ambition to grasp the whole, is the hallmark of our alienation from our primal feeling of oneness with Nature. Unconsciousness, the bliss of dreaming, by contrast, can be identified with our artificial attempts to restore this feeling of oneness in religion and art.

Another intriguing insight into Alberich's acquisition of power by renouncing love we find in Wagner's oft-stated view that his artistic creativity was compensation for his inability to find love in the real world: " ... art for me is a substitute for a life of unsatisfied desire ... ! I pour out into my art the violent need I feel for love, a need which life cannot satisfy ... ." [593W-{11/11/52} Letter to Luise Brockhaus: SLRW, p. 274; See also 592W-{10/28/52} Letter to Robert Franz, SLRW, p. 271; and 975W-{8/16/79} CD Vol. II, p. 355] Donington noted how similar this makes Wagner to Alberich [Donington: pp. 56–57], who's able to forge his Ring of power only after being thrice rejected in his quest for love. One suspects that Wagner saw himself in Alberich's plight, that Alberich figuratively gives birth to the *Ring* tetralogy through his artificial attempt to compensate, with the Ring's power, for his irrevocable loss of love. Alberich therefore now makes his desperate bid for world-power by renouncing and cursing love:

> **[p. 69] Alberich:** (H9) Your light I'll put out, (H9) wrench the gold from the rock (H9) and forge the avenging ring: (H17ab orch) ... (H16:) thus I lay a curse on love (:H16)! (He tears the gold away and plunges into the depths. H9. Impenetrable darkness suddenly descends on all sides.) (...) (H16: Gradually the waves turn into clouds, which resolve into a fine mist as an increasingly bright light emerges behind them. **[[H17ab definitive orch:]]>[[H18ab orch:]** [= H17ab vari] ... an open space on a mountain summit becomes visible in the dawning light. At one side, on a flowery bank, lies Wotan with Fricka at his side. Both are asleep)

Alberich's quest to obtain worldly power through objective knowledge of the earth (Erda) seems a sort of vengeance of the conscious mind against Mother Nature (which gave birth to human consciousness) to obtain compensation from Nature for the angst, the existential "Noth" which man inherits as the natural price of consciousness. This vengeance, expressing man's resistance to accepting nature as she is, will first produce religious belief, the positing of a divine realm (Valhalla) as the human imagination's alternative to the real world. Though religious faith promises supernatural assuagement of man's ills, the fact that its promises are illusory means that the satisfaction it offers is psychological, not actual. Religion posits a transcendent realm as a consoling alternative to Mother Earth's harsh truths, and thus sins against Mother Nature's truth. In this way Alberich's forging of his Ring of consciousness launches the war between science (objective man) and religion (subjective man). The light of the Rhinegold which Alberich puts out will be artificially re-lit in the splendors of Valhalla, as Loge puts it in the finale to *Rhinegold*.

THE RHINEGOLD ≠ SCENE TWO

(ON A MEADOW OUTSIDE VALHALLA)
WOTAN, FRICKA, FREIA, FROH, DONNER, FASOLT, FAFNER, AND LOGE

During the orchestral transition from R.1 to R.2, one of the most momentous musico-dramatic events has transpired, the gradual transformation of the Ring Motif H17ab into the first two segments of the new Valhalla Motif H18ab: The gods Wotan and Fricka have it seems slept in a meadow beneath the mountain on which the Giants have been building Valhalla during the entire course of its construction:

> [pp. 70–71] ([[H18abcd orch:]] In the growing light of the dawning day a castle with glittering battlements can be seen standing on a rocky summit in the background .... Wotan and Fricka asleep. (...))
>
> **Fricka:** (alarmed) Wotan, husband! Awake!
>
> **Wotan:** (still dreaming) (H17:) The happy hall of delight ... (:H17). (H18b:) Manhood's honor (:H18b), (H18c:) boundless might redound to endless renown (:H18c)!
>
> **Fricka:** (shaking him) Awake from the blissful deception of dreams! (H19 embryo:) Husband, wake up and reflect (:H19 embryo)!
>
> **Wotan:** (Waking ...) [[H18a orch:]] The everlasting work is ended (:H18a)! (...) On mountain peak the gods' abode; resplendent shines the proud-standing hall! As in my dream I conceived it, just as my will decreed it, [[H18b orch:]] sturdy and fair (:H18b) [[H18c orch:]] it stands on show (:H18c), [[H18d orch:]] august and glorious building (:H18d)!
>
> **Fricka:** You feel only joy at what fills me with dread? (...) (H19 embryo:) The fortress is finished, the forfeit is due (:H19 embryo): (H25a embryo:) have you forgot what you gave away (:H25a embryo)?
>
> **Wotan:** Well I remember what they demanded who built the stronghold for me there; [[H19 orch:]] through a contract I tamed their forward breed (:H19 orch), bidding them build the lordly hall. [[H19 orch:]] It stands there—thanks to the giants (:H19 orch)—as for the payment, give it no thought.

Cooke noted that the Valhalla Motif has five distinct segments, H18abcde, but the fact that Alberich's Ring of power H17ab gives musical birth to Valhalla by transforming into H18's first two segments H18ab has far-reaching implications. If we grant that Alberich's forging of his Ring represents man's acquisition of symbolic consciousness, it's important to recall that the first form of human speculation on the origin, nature, meaning, and destiny of human life, was religious mythology. That is, Alberich's Ring, the human mind, gives birth to the heavenly realm of the gods, Valhalla, and therefore to the gods themselves. Our imagination, our gift for creating symbols for things which aren't identical with the things they represent, and which seem autonomous from our experiences, gives birth to our belief in religious mythology. How did newly evolved man come to posit a supernatural realm which transcended the natural limitations of physical existence? Feuerbach finds this propensity in our mind's ability to extrapolate from limited experience to posit limitless possibilities. He described how our mind's tendency to perfect what Nature presents as imperfect, to round the circle, gave birth to belief in a transcendent realm peopled by beings like ourselves who are, however, not subject to our physical limitations: " ... from man's ... infinite thirst for knowledge, which is not and cannot be satisfied here below, from man's infinite striving for happiness, which no earthly possession or good fortune can satisfy, from his yearning for perfect morality, sullied by no sensuous drives, don't Christians ... infer the ... reality of an infinite life and existence for man, ... unfettered by the body or by death? (...) / But what does this infinity of the divine attributes reveal? Nothing but the infinity or unlimitedness of human desires, of the human imagination and faculty of abstraction ... ." [300F-LER, pp. 262–263; See also 215F-LER, p. 97] Wagner paraphrased Feuerbach, suggesting that our mind's inherent incapacity to find absolute satisfaction of desires or freedom from fear in the imperfect world impels it to posit a perfect realm where absolute satisfaction is possible: "To the religious eye ... the truth grows plain that there must be another world than this, because the inextinguishable bent-to-happiness cannot be stilled within this world, and hence requires another world for its redemption." [701W-{64–2/65} 'On State and Religion,' PW Vol. IV, p. 24]

Alberich's "Noth," his need to compensate himself for what Nature didn't provide by seeking absolute power, gives birth to the gods who men imagine have absolute power. Man imagined beings in whom his unique properties of mind are freed from our natural limits, limits which, however, were the foundation for the evolution of our mind in the first place. Over time early man reified the nature of his symbolic mind and called it god. One step more, and religious man could posit this image of his own mind as a god who created the physical realm of our experience. Feuerbach explained how early man would naturally construe his symbolic capacity for abstraction and generalization as proof of the gods' autonomy from Nature's laws, and in some instances (the God of monotheistic religions) as the creator of the world, the thought giving birth to the thing: " ... since the universal, that is, the abstract, has ... become the foundation of the real, man comes to regard the being who is nothing but a bundle of universal concepts, the ... spiritual being, as the first being, as the being who precedes all other beings not only in rank but also in time, who is ... the ... cause of all being and the Creator of all beings." [228F-LER, p. 119; see also 187F-PPF, p. 69; 345F-LER, p. 334; 258F-LER, pp. 174–175; 264F-LER, p. 184; and 545W-{50–1/51} *Opera and Drama*, PW Vol. II, pp. 338–339]

This is what Wagner has done in musically invoking Alberich's forging of his Ring of power as the foundation for the heavenly abode of the gods, Valhalla, and of the gods themselves. Our unique gift of abstract, symbolic thought, gave us humans a power over our environment and other life forms which was unique. As Feuerbach said, knowledge is power: "In divine omnipotence, man merely fulfills his desire to be able to do everything, a desire that is related to, or a consequence of, the desire to know everything; for ... knowledge is power ... ." [308F-LER, p. 274] Thus the Rhinedaughters told Alberich that if he can forge a Ring from the Rhinegold he'll control the world. Significantly, Feuerbach added that power is God's [i.e., Wotan's] first predicate: "Power is the first predicate of the Godhead or rather, it is the first god. (...) But what is this power distinguished from will and reason if not the power of nature?" [220F-LER, pp. 104–105] In sum, Nature gives birth to man, who—thanks to his imagination, itself a product of evolution—invents the supernatural, thereby cheating his Mother Nature of her natural rights and our debt to her.

Cooke's *I Saw the World End* drew my attention to Wagner's Feuerbachian disquisition on the evolution of human consciousness from animal forebears, and how man's first form of thought, the error in religious mythology, grew out of his newfound gift of abstract, symbolic thought: "From the moment when Man perceived the difference between himself and Nature ... by breaking loose from the unconsciousness of natural animal life and passing over into conscious life, — when he ... evolved the faculty of Thought, — from that moment did Error begin, as the earliest utterance of consciousness. But Error is the mother of Knowledge; and the history of the birth of Knowledge out of Error is the history of the human race, from the myths of primal ages down to the present day. / Man erred, from the time when he set the cause of Nature's workings outside the bounds of Nature's self, and for the physical phenomena subsumed a superphysical, anthropomorphic ... cause ... . Knowledge consists in the laying [correcting] of this error ... . / Through this knowledge does Nature grow conscious of herself ... by Man himself, who only through discriminating between himself and Nature has attained that point where he can apprehend her, by making her his 'object.' But this distinction is merged once more, when Man recognizes the essence of Nature as his very own ... ." [414W-{9–12/49} 'The Artwork of the Future,' PW Vol. I, pp. 70–71] Our first form of thought, arising long before we'd acquired sufficient knowledge of Nature to grasp it objectively, was religious mythology, in which we were in error about the world and our true place in it. Wagner describes history as the process through which we, originally religious, gradually corrected our false view that the cause of Nature (the true creator) is outside of Nature, i.e., that Nature was created by a supernatural god. We corrected our error through advancement in knowledge. In the *Ring*, not only is the creation depicted as an impersonal natural process devoid of supernatural influence, but the gods of Valhalla are presented as subject to Erda (Mother Nature): Wotan isn't a creator god, but lives in, and is subject to, Erda's world, which predated the gods.

Wagner employs the term "knowledge" in two distinct ways. The first kind of knowledge is objective knowledge of the natural world, including objective knowledge of man's origin and nature. This we obtain by making Nature our object of knowledge. The second kind of knowledge is aesthetic intuition, knowledge through feeling. Wagner describes this when he says that the distinction between the self (the subject) and Nature (the object) is merged, when man recognizes the essence of Nature as his own. Though he doesn't say so, he's speaking of music, which he describes elsewhere as disclosing the inner necessity of all things outside of us, and our unity with them. Grasping this distinction is a clue to understanding the two distinct kinds of knowledge Wotan will later seek to acquire from Erda, Mother Nature, in his wanderings.

A potential cause of confusion is the relative chronology of Alberich's implication in the "Fall" through his renunciation of love to obtain the Ring of world-power, and Wotan's implication in the "Fall" (which we'll learn about in

S.1.2) by breaking off the most sacred branch of the World-Ash Tree to make his Spear of divine authority and law. This seminal act killed the World-Ash and dried up the spring of wisdom which seeped from its roots. Cooke highlighted the underlying equivalence of these two foundational events. [Cooke, pp. 146–149] Here's my solution: When we first see the gods Wotan and Fricka they're asleep, but evidently Wotan has previously been involved in negotiations with the Giants to get them to agree to a contract to build Valhalla, so it seems Wotan's original sin predated Alberich's. The subject of the gods' origin is never broached in the *Ring*, but they're presented as only contingently immortal, and there's no definitive evidence that the gods existed prior to Alberich's theft of the Rhinegold. There are many reasons for taking Alberich's theft of the Rhinegold and forging of his Ring as the seminal act which set in motion all the other actions described in the *Ring*, including Wotan's making his contract with the giants to build Valhalla, and even his breaking a branch off of the World-Ash to make his Spear of divine authority. Warren Darcy distinguished R.1, during which Alberich steals the Rhinegold, from all the *Ring*'s other scenes, as standing outside the time-frame of the rest of the drama. [Darcy, p. 87] Furthermore, not only does Alberich's Ring (H17ab) give musical birth to Wotan's heavenly abode Valhalla (H18ab), but Wotan in S.1.2 describes himself to Mime as "Light-Alberich." Since Alberich is also described in S.1.2 as Dark-Alberich, it might seem Alberich and Wotan are two aspects, dark and light, of the same personality. Some scholars argue that this distinction reflects Wagner's reference to Teutonic and Norse myth, in which Alberich is Lord of the dark elves (Nibelungs), and Wotan Lord of the light elves (gods). On this view, the name "Alberich" is construed as "Elf-Lord," Albe being "elf," and "reich," the German word for kingdom, implying that this elf rules a kingdom of elves. But a key problem with this reading is that Alberich alone possesses the generic name "Alberich." Alberich is never called "Dark-Wotan," but Wotan calls himself "Light-Alberich." The fact that Alberich alone possesses the name for Elf-Lord in general suggests he's Lord of all elves, both dark and light. But the best way to see this is that he's (his Ring is) the precondition necessary for the creation of the gods (Valhalla).

Both Feuerbach and Wagner provide impressive evidence for our reading. Feuerbach describes the oldest god as physical need (which we can construe as Alberich in his quest for worldly power), which he says is both before and behind the ethical and spiritual god [See 322F-LER, pp. 294–295], who in the *Ring* is represented by Wotan. Wagner paraphrases Feuerbach: "The quintessence of this constant motion, thus of Life, at last in '*Wuotan*' [Wotan] (Zeus) found expression as the chiefest God ... . Though his nature marked him as the highest god, ... father to the other deities, yet was he nowise an historically older god, but sprang into existence from man's later, higher consciousness of self; consequently he is more abstract than the older Nature-god, whilst the latter is more corporeal and ... more personally inborn in man." [368W-{6–8/48} 'The Wibelungen'—Revised summer of 1849, PW Vol. VII, p. 275] We can construe Wagner's "Nature-god," who is more inborn in man, as Alberich, and Wagner's later god, higher and more abstract than the Nature god, as Wotan, who's higher and more abstract than

Alberich because Wotan represents what our imagination conceives as a supernatural being, created by us as an alternative to actual beings.

Wagner's meditation on the origin of the Holy Grail legend, so important to his two great works *Lohengrin* (whose creation just preceded that of the *Ring*) and *Parsifal* (created immediately after Wagner finished the *Ring*), provides striking evidence for our thesis. For Wagner said that through a process of sublimation the Nibelung Hoard eventually lost its bond with the material world and was transformed into the spiritual Grail: "... the legend of the Holy Grail ... makes its entry on the world at the very time when the Kaiserhood attained its more ideal direction, and the Nibelung's Hoard accordingly was losing more and more in material worth, to yield to a higher spiritual content. The spiritual ascension of the Hoard into the Grail was accomplished in the German conscience .... (...) / The quest of the Grail henceforth replaces the struggle for the Nibelungen-Hoard ... ." [373W-{6–8/48} 'The Wibelungen'—Revised summer of 1849, PW Vol. VII, pp. 293–294] But note, the Nibelung Hoard (for our purpose Alberich with his Ring) came first, and only later did the Holy Grail (the gods in their heavenly abode Valhalla) evolve from it. This corresponds with the evolution of the Ring Motif H17ab (the Nibelung Hoard accumulated under the Ring's power) into the first two segments of the Valhalla Motif H18ab.

Wagner seems to have based his distinction of Alberich from Wotan (Light-Alberich) as much on Feuerbach's analysis of the origin of the concept of Godhead as he did on Norse and/or Teutonic mythology. Feuerbach explained that to describe how a perfect god could produce an imperfect creation called Nature, to be consistent the inventors of god had to posit in god both light and dark principles, the light principle identified with the realm of spirit, and the dark principle with the material world, out of which, however, the realm of spirit was born, since the material world is its precondition. [See 78F-EOC, p. 87; 244F-LER, p. 156] On this reading evil is identified with the material world, and good, the ideal, with the supernatural. Thus we have our villain Alberich, identified with worldly power, and the god Wotan identified with divine power and man's quest for an ethical order grounded in divine law. Wagner was deeply impressed with Feuerbach's analysis of God into light and dark, good and evil, spiritual and earthly principles, in order to bridge the gap between an immaterial, good god and an imperfect material creation, Nature, incorporating evil. Wagner drew a moral conclusion from this, that Spirit and Nature are only antitheses for the religious imagination, and that the primal being is neither good nor evil, and is therefore amoral: "'But, alas, how is culture possible when religion has such defective roots, and even terminology is so little defined that one can talk of spirit and Nature as if they were antitheses?'" [828W-{6/29/72} CD Vol. I, p. 505] "R. spoke recently of the heresy of the Marcionites, which consisted in recognizing a primal being who was neither completely good nor completely evil; admiration for this sensible form of cognition." [854W-{7/1/74} CD Vol. I, p. 770]

In fairness, we do occasionally find indirect evidence that Wagner didn't think Alberich's theft of the Rhinegold and forging of the Ring preceded Wotan's manufacture of his spear. On one occasion he said Alberich couldn't have harmed the gods unless they were already susceptible, and that the germ of evil in the *Ring* wasn't the Rhinedaughters' rejection of Alberich's bid for love, but was Wotan's artificial attempt to sustain his love for his wife Fricka long after it had ceased to have heartfelt conviction. [614W-{1/25–26/54} Letter to August Röckel, SLRW, p. 307]. Furthermore, Wagner once considered depicting Wotan bathing in the Rhine as a witness to the events of R.1, the opening scene of the *Ring* during which Alberich steals the Rhinegold from the Rhinedaughters. [Darcy, pp. 39–40] We can resolve this apparent contradiction if we grasp Alberich and Wotan as the objective and the subjective aspects of the human mind, and that Alberich's contribution to the Fall by forging consciousness (the Ring) isn't so much prior chronologically to Wotan's creation of the Spear, the social contract founded on religious belief, as prior logically, since the human mind is the precondition for the imagination's creation of the gods.

This raises the question of Wagner's anti-Semitism and whether it influenced him in writing the *Ring*'s libretto and music. The distinctions delineated above between Alberich and Wotan are similar in many respects to Wagner's distinction between Judaism and Christianity. Much of this Wagner derives, again, from Feuerbach. Though Wagner was anti-Semitic in his private life, the distinctions he draws between sympathetic and unsympathetic characters in the *Ring* are universalized in such a way that racism is left far behind. For instance, Franz Liszt once noted (in a remark whose source I've forgotten) that what Wagner meant when he said "Jew" is actually a cultural philistine. Obviously Wagner isn't absolved of the sin of racism in using the word Jew to describe a person of any race who he thinks is a philistine, but we can best grasp the universal meaning of the *Ring* if we stick to the concept philistine in its generic sense whenever we're inclined to read a Jewish stereotype into one of its characters or incidents. We aren't going to be able to grasp the breadth of vision of the *Ring* if we insist on looking for topical meanings when a universal, generic meaning is far more explanatory.

Under Feuerbach's sway, Wagner identified Judaism as a worldly religion, which for him was motivated by egoism. Insofar as Christianity owed anything to its Jewish roots, it was, according to Wagner, tainted by this debt. This is partly a basis for Wotan's dependence on Alberich's actions (his forging of the Ring and accumulation of a Hoard of treasure) to pay off Wotan's debt to the Giants, so Wotan can establish Valhalla as the gods' refuge. It's also the cause of Wotan's desperation to escape his dependence on Alberich which was implicit in the founding of Valhalla on the basis of Alberich's Ring-power (i.e., H17ab>H18ab). Feuerbach gave Wagner his cue: "Judaism is worldly Christianity; Christianity, spiritual Judaism." [88F-EOC, p. 120] Wagner broached the implications of Feuerbach's remark in his observation that, given all that Christianity owes to its Jewish roots, it was through this influence that the Jews could one day dominate the world, fulfilling their god's promise of world-rule: "The tribal God of a petty nation had promised his people eventual rulership of the whole world and all that lives and moves therein, if only they adhered to laws whose strictest following would keep them barred against all other nations of the earth. (...) But the Jews

... could fling away all share in this world-rulership of their Jehova, for they had won a share in a development of the Christian religion well fitted to deliver it itself into their hands in time ... ." [1031W-{6–8/80} 'Religion and Art,' PW Vol. VI, pp. 232–233] We're reminded of the Rhinedaughters' promise to Alberich that if he renounced love he could forge a Ring from the Rhinegold and with it rule the world.

But Wagner goes further and traces not only the Christian religion back to Judaism, but also the world-economy and the State, offering us a conventional interpretation of Alberich's amassing his hoard of treasure and quest for power: " ... the astounding success of our ... Jews in the ... amassing of huge stores of money has always filled our Military State authorities with nothing but respect and ... admiration ... . (...) / If the application of 'Know Thyself' to our Church's religious descent would turn out poorly for our case against the Jews, the result will be no less unfavourable if we investigate the nature of the only thing our State systems understand by possession, before endeavouring to secure it from the Jews' encroachments." [1065W-{1–2/81} 'Know Thyself'—2nd Supplement to 'Religion and Art,' PW Vol. VI, p. 267] What's at stake here isn't, however, the presumed influence of any given human stock, Jewish or otherwise, on modern society, but Wagner's profounder suspicion that all human society is ultimately predicated on egoism. He's confessing that if his fellow Europeans truly knew themselves, they'd acknowledge the egoism at the root of their own nature before seeking to blame their problems on the Jews, a point Wagner sadly often forgot himself. However, this more universal Feuerbachian point, that egoism is the root of all, he dramatized in *The Rhinegold*, an allegory about the origin of human society per se, not some particular phase of subsequent human history or narrative about a particular society.

There's another intriguing aspect of this transition from R.1 to R.2, a plausible explanation of the beginning of R.2 where we find the gods sleeping as the dawn lights up their newly built fortress (Valhalla), completed by the Giants while the gods slept. Feuerbach taught Wagner that we're the involuntary creators of our gods, that we humans must have collectively, unconsciously dreamed the gods into existence in the earliest days after the evolutionary onset of our human consciousness. We must have dreamed them into existence unconsciously and involuntarily because, had we been conscious of inventing them, we could never have believed in them or have faith in their power to help or hinder us. Since neither Feuerbach nor Wagner believed in gods, the Valhallan gods in the *Ring* may be construed as representing man's religious impulse, religious mythology, which has been the primary source of all value, and all explanations of the world, for most history from our earliest times up to the present. We, who invented the gods, are the gods in whom, as Feuerbach put it, we merely project our own idealized nature. But religious folk remain unconscious of this fact. Wotan is Wagner's poetic metaphor for Feuerbach's concept that collective, historical man, is the foundation of our concept of God, that allegedly divine knowledge is the collective wisdom of all men, accumulated over time. Thus, when Wotan— collective man, the unwitting and involuntary product of evolution—sleeps during the Giants' construction of Valhalla, Wotan is dreaming the gods and their abode into existence. This is why Wotan says, on waking and observing the newly built Valhalla, that it appears as he dreamed it.

Feuerbach was Wagner's guide in describing religion as the product of man's collective dreaming: "It is the same ego, the same being in dreaming as in waking; the only distinction is that in waking, the ego acts on itself; whereas in dreaming it is acted on by itself as by another being. (…) Feeling is a dream with the eyes open; religion the dream of waking consciousness: dreaming is the key to the mysteries of religion." [102F-EOC, pp. 140–141; See also 268F] What's called divine revelation Feuerbach would describe as a message from within ourselves, from our unconscious mind. The same can be said of what Wagner described as unconscious artistic inspiration. It seems as if it came from another world because it comes involuntarily, though its hidden source is us. But Wotan's wife Fricka has equated waking with sober reflection and objective knowledge, and equated Wotan's dreaming, and his dream-inspired fortress, with self-deception, for she asks him to wake from the self-deception of dreams and reflect. Fricka is indirectly suggesting that Alberich has a monopoly on objective, waking consciousness of the bitter truth, which will be a stumbling block to Wotan's ideal plans, while Wotan seeks contentment in the self-deception of dreams.

Wagner described religious belief as the product not so much of a single artist, who presumably would be largely conscious of the part his own imagination plays in creating a fictional or musical world (even if he isn't conscious of the creative process within him), but of collective man, the Folk, the artist in the aggregate, who unwittingly and involuntarily created imaginary supernatural beings believed to be more real than reality. The gods, Wagner says, are the Folk's condensation of the inexhaustible phenomena of Nature and of human life into idealized human forms, an involuntary act of the imagination which lends such beings a supernatural aura: "Just as the human form is to him [man] the most comprehensible, so also will the essence of natural phenomena—which he does not yet know in their reality—become comprehensible only through condensation to a human form. (…) [This "faculty"] … appears superhuman and supernatural by the very fact that it is ascribed to one imagined individual … in the shape of Man. By its faculty of thus using its force of imagination to bring before itself every thinkable reality and actuality, in widest reach but … succinct … shaping, the Folk … becomes in Mythos the creator of Art … ." [489W-{50–1/51} *Opera and Drama*, PW Vol. II, pp. 154–155] This process by which the variety of human experience is condensed by our imagination into the form of a god is identical to Wagner's concept of the "Wonder" through which he could capture the pillars of a drama, its most essential events, characters, and ideas, in distinctive, memorable musical motifs, which carry the power of all those elements of the drama, thematically akin, with which they've been associated in the course of the drama. Feuerbach's description of the "Wonder" is the basis of Wagner's description of the process whereby the folk created their "Mythos": "… an object considered as subject, the essence of nature differentiated from nature and seen as a human being, the essence of man differentiated from man and seen as a not-human being—this is the essence of divinity and religion, the secret of mysticism ... , ... the great thauma, the wonder of all wonders, which fills men with the profoundest amazement and rapture." [338F-LER, pp. 320–321]

In the modern world, in which man is far more self-conscious than early man was, the individual artistic-genius, Wagner says, inherits what once was the collective mythic creativity of the Folk who invented the gods, and becomes the Folk's voice. What links the modern, individual artistic genius to the primal Folk who collectively dreamed the various religions into existence is the involuntary, unconscious nature of inspiration, which Wagner describes as a "force" or "faculty": "[Speaking of] ... so-called prehistoric times, the times when Speech, and Myth, and Art were ... born ... [Wagner says that] the thing we call Genius was unknown: no one man was a Genius, since all men were it. Only in times like ours, does one ... name these 'Geniuses;' the sole name that we can find for those artistic forces which ... open out new pathways ... ... these new openings are ... [not] arbitrary and private paths, but continuations of a long-since-hewn main causeway ... ." [559W-{6–8/51} 'A Communication To My Friends,' PW Vol. I, pp. 288–289]

One way of understanding Wotan's (the Folk as artist's) creative dream of inspiration which gives birth to Valhalla (a religious society) is that Alberich's renunciation of love, theft of the Rhinegold, and forging it into the Ring of conscious mind, is Wotan's dream of inspiration which gave birth to Valhalla. But Wotan on waking has forgotten the true source of his inspiration, which remains unconscious, and instead credits himself with this inspiration, just as religious man, the product of unconscious processes of Nature, credits figures of his own imagination, his gods, with his creation. Here we have Wagner's description of the process of unconscious artistic inspiration (which we can surmise took place in Wotan while he slept and dreamed of Valhalla): "... the prodigious force ...framing appearances from within outwards, against the ordinary laws of Nature, must be engendered by the deepest Want (Noth). (...) What we here experience is a ... vast compulsion to unload without, only to be compared with the stress to waken from an agonising dream; and the important issue for the Art-genius of mankind, is that this special stress called forth an artistic deed ... ." [786W-{9–12/70} 'Beethoven,' PW Vol. V, pp. 111–112] If we compare this passage with the events in R.1 and R.2 we've witnessed (and events which transpired between these two scenes which we'll learn about later), then Alberich's "Noth," his anguish which inspires in him the wish to avenge himself on Nature for not satisfying his desires, and to attain world-power, involuntarily gives birth to God, Wotan (Light-Alberich), and the heavenly abode of the gods, Valhalla, through what may be described as Wotan's (the Folk's) dream. Wotan remains unconscious of the part his dark, unconscious half, Alberich, played in creating Valhalla. Alberich's love-curse, theft, and forging of the Ring in Nibelheim, with all its attendant horror (see R.3), becomes for Wotan his obsessive vision of profoundest sleep, the nightmare he forgets on waking but which gave birth to his waking dream Valhalla. Valhalla can be construed as a waking allegory which is the sublimation of Nibelheim. But Nibelheim remains in the dark, repressed and unconscious. As Wagner said: "In this sacred allegory an attempt is made to transmit to worldly minds ... the mystery of divine revelation: but the only relation it can bear to what the Religious had immediately beheld, is the relation of the day-told dream [Wotan's waking dream of Valhalla] to the actual dream of night [Alberich's forging of this Ring in his realm of mist and night, Nibelheim]. / ... the record left upon our own mind by a deeply moving dream is strictly nothing but an allegorical paraphrase [Valhalla], whose intrinsic disagreement with the original [Alberich's Nibelheim] remains a trouble to our waking consciousness ... ." [704W-{64–2/65} 'On State and Religion,' PW Vol. IV, pp. 27–28; See also 767W]

Fricka gives Wotan's dreamy nature a jolt, waking him to remind him bluntly that a forfeit is due the Giants for building Valhalla, accompanied by an embryonic form of the Spear Motif H19. H19 is one of the most important *Ring* motifs, proved by its power of generation, for, Cooke noted, it generates many other significant motifs. The Giants Fafner and Fasolt, soon to appear, represent, respectively, our two fundamental animal instincts, namely, the self-preservation instinct (Fafner), which we experience as fear of pain and death, and the instinct for sexual reproduction (Fasolt), both of which, through natural evolution of species, gave birth to human civilization during that transitional period when evolving man hadn't yet attained fully human status. Man had in a sense been sleeping, impelled by preconscious instinct, but on becoming fully conscious found himself already in possession of language and religion, as if he'd always possessed them, just as Wotan and Fricka, having slept while the Giants built Valhalla, wake to find it (and themselves) an established fact. But now a forfeit is due our instincts of self-preservation (fear—Fafner) and sexual reproduction (love—Fasolt) for building our civilization modeled on the gods' ideal realm, whose divine law guides earthly men. Religious faith in the promises the gods make (Wotan's contract with the Giants) satisfies instincts which aren't divine, namely, fear of death, which is selfish, and longing for endless bliss (love) which, though founded on selfish lust, through a process of abstraction bonds family members with each other and with outsiders, i.e., friends and associates, creating a society under moral authority.

Wotan's retort to Fricka is that she begged him to make his contract with the Giants to build a home for the gods, but Fricka asserts she did so for the sole purpose of ensuring Wotan's fidelity:

[pp. 71–2] **Fricka:** Had I known about your contract, I'd have hindered such deceit .... (...) What is still sacred and precious to hard hearts such as yours when you menfolk lust after power? (H17ab)

Wotan: Was such lust unknown to Fricka (H17ab>H18ab orch) when she begged me for the building?

Fricka: [[H20 voc:]] Heedful of my husband's fidelity, I'm bound in my sadness to brood on ways of binding him fast whenever he feels drawn away (:H20 voc): [[H21 voc:]] A glorious dwelling, domestic bliss were meant to entice you to tarry and rest (:H21 voc). But ... it is meant to enhance your dominion and power ... .

Wotan: [[H21 voc:]] If your aim, as my wife, was to hold me fast in the fortress, you must grant that I, as a god (:H21 voc), while confined to the stronghold, might win (H18a:) for myself the world outside (:H18a). (H18c:) All who live love renewal and change (:H18c): (H18d:) that pleasure I cannot forego (:H18d)!

Fricka's defensive response to Wotan introduces two new motifs, H20 and H21. At its inception H20 is associated with marital fidelity. H21 at the outset is linked with Valhalla as the source of that domestic tranquility which Fricka hopes will inspire Wotan's loyalty. But Fricka is the goddess of marriage, the domesticity of hearth and home, the family, the basic unit of a society founded on belief in gods. So she hopes Wotan will maintain his fidelity to the values validated by the Valhallan gods, the religious basis for ordered society. A possible conceptual basis for H21 is Feuerbach's statement that "Feeling, the heart, is the domestic life ... ." [147F-EOC, p. 285] But religious man (Wotan) is also historical man. Wotan isn't only an exponent of the consolations of religious faith, but also an agent of cultural evolution through which, as he tells Fricka, he must seek to conquer the world, acquiring earthly power outside the safe walls of religious faith and tradition. It's inevitable that man's historical experience of the earth (Erda), his gradual acquisition of world-and-self-knowledge, will contradict our fidelity to religious belief and its values. Wotan the Wanderer will later wander the earth (Erda) seeking knowledge from experience.

Fricka accuses Wotan of a cynical (Alberich-like) eagerness to gamble away love and woman's worth for the sake of power as we hear H16 (so-called Renunciation of Love):

[p. 72] **Fricka:** Loveless husband ... ! For the barren bauble of might and dominion you'd gamble away, with ungodly contempt, (H16:) love and womanhood's worth (:H16)?

Wotan: (H19:) In order to win you as wife, my one remaining eye I staked that I might woo you (:H19) ... . (...) Freia the good I'll never give up: it never seriously entered my thoughts.

Fricka identifies love (feeling) with woman, and power (the Ring power of thought) with man, as Feuerbach did when he proclaimed that "Love is ... essentially feminine ... ." [71F-EOC, p. 72]. The conflict between Fricka and Wotan over the price they must pay the Giants to build Valhalla, Freia, the goddess of divine love and sorrow-less youth eternal (immortality), reveals a contradiction at the heart of Wotan's dream of securing a safe refuge for religious faith in Valhalla. Even though Valhalla is the domestic refuge of divine love and transcendence (Freia), it can only be built with the aid of the egoistic, corporeal animal drives fear and desire (Fafner and Fasolt), by promising those drives satisfaction. Though Wotan has to satisfy our egoistic animal instincts to build his allegedly supernatural heaven, he can't acknowledge this contradiction because this would expose Valhalla as nothing more than a sublimation of physical nature and mortal man's mundane animal impulses. As Feuerbach said, " ... the ... true Christian ... is bound to deny Nature, while he satisfies it ... . he publicly disavows what he privately does." [165F-EOC, p. 314] To resolve this Wotan had to fool the Giants into thinking he'll pay them the goddess Freia, yet persuade them to forego their pay and accept a substitute Wotan can afford, in a classic 'bait and switch.'

And now Freia, the price Wotan agreed to pay the Giants for building Valhalla, makes her dramatic entrance running from them in desperation, begging Wotan and her brothers to protect her:

> [p. 72] **Fricka:** Then shield her [Freia] now: in defenseless fear she comes running hither for help! (**[[H22 orch]]**; **[[H23 orch]]** [Freia] entering, as if in headlong flight)

With Freia's entrance we hear fast, urgent versions of two new motifs which Cooke says can be regarded initially as Freia's motifs, H22, which quickly ascends, and H23, which more slowly descends. H63, which stems from H23, is what Cooke described as the definitive Love Motif. It's significant that as this basic love motif is introduced, love (Freia) is running from the natural claim that our base animal instincts (the Giants) make on it. Our human impulse to love, which produces altruistic self-sacrifice and compassion, seeks to transcend its roots in our base animal drives. But Wotan looks to the fire (liar) god Loge, the Trickster, to redeem Freia—as Loge promised—from the Giants' rightful claim to her. Loge incarnates our artistic imagination, which has the power to delude us since it's solely through self-deception that Wotan can deny the Giants' claim to Freia. However, Fricka bitterly observes that though Loge has caused the gods much ill, nonetheless he always ensnares Wotan again:

> [p. 73] **Wotan:** Did you see Loge?
>
> **Fricka:** So you still prefer to trust in that cunning trickster? Much ill he has caused us already, yet ever again he ensnares you.
>
> **Wotan:** Where freedom of mind is called for, I ask for help from no man; **[[H24 orch/voc:]]** but to turn to advantage an enemy's grudge ["Neid"] is a lesson that only cunning ... can teach of the kind that Loge slyly employs (:H24 orch/voc). He who counseled me on the contract promised to ransom Freia: on him I now rely.

H24, introduced in association with the concept that Loge's cunning can transform the enemy's threat into an advantage, is the first of four motifs which will characterize Loge. H24 is the basis for H26, linked later in R.2 with Wotan's intent (based on Loge's promise to redeem Wotan from having to honor his agreement to pay the Giants Freia) to break the contract, engraved on his spear, that he made with the Giants. To grasp Loge's nature and his relationship with Wotan, consider Wagner's remark that the Folk involuntarily, unconsciously created their gods by condensing human and natural phenomena into idealized human forms, creating the religious myths through which the Folk unwittingly deluded themselves. Loge transforms mundane experience into Wonder. He embodies man's artistic capacity for self-deception motivated by desire and fear (the Giants). In T.P.B, the Norns—in their recitation of world history—will describe how Loge strove to win his freedom from service to Wotan, just as Feuerbach described how the individual artist of modern times won his freedom from former servitude to religious belief. [See 263F-LER, p. 183] Wagner believed that the Folk's (Wotan's) artistic creativity, which involuntarily invented the gods, lives on in the modern, individual artist as unconscious inspiration. Wagner's description of his artistic nature is a basis for Fricka's accusation that Loge repeatedly ensnares Wotan. He said that his artistic nature ensnares him with self-delusion ever and again, hiding from him the bitter truth of the world which, if contemplated without this protective screen (the veil of Maya, self-deception), would be unbearable: [630W-{5/12/55}Letter to Jacob Sulzer, SLRW, pp. 338–339]

Wotan tries to reassure Fricka by telling her that Loge was able to persuade Wotan to make what seemed to her a cynical contract with the Giants, in which Wotan would pay them Freia in exchange for building Valhalla, only because Loge promised to redeem Freia from them. Loge in other words offered to redeem the gods' dependence on self-deception (our illusory religious belief in transcendent love and immortality) from truth's threat to self-deception (the Giants' claim on Freia). It's only through our artistic imagination that we could (seemingly) free heaven (Valhalla) from its basis in the earth (Alberich's Ring and the Giants). But with Loge's tardiness weighing on Wotan, the Giants, having built Valhalla while the gods slept, now stake their claim on Freia:

[pp. 73–4] ([[H25a orch:]] Enter Fasolt and Fafner, both of gigantic stature and armed with stout staves)

Fasolt: (H19:) Gentle slumber sealed your eyes (:H19): we both, unsleeping, built the stronghold. [[H25b voc:]] Never tiring of mighty toil, we stowed the heavy stones away ... (:H25b voc). (pointing to the castle: H18a modulation) There it stands, what we hewed (H18a modulation); shimmering brightly the day shines upon it (H18a modulation): move in now, to pay us our due. (H25a orch)

The orchestra introduces the Giants' pounding motif H25a. Fasolt, backed up by H19 (Wotan's Spear), affirms that while the gods slept the Giants, unsleeping, built their fortress. H19 is a subtle reminder that whatever Wotan or others later say about his motives in making his Spear from a branch of the World Ash, and his negotiation of a contract with the Giants to build Valhalla (engraved on his spear), these events occurred while Wotan slept, during man's preconscious dreamtime in the evolution from instinctive animal life to conscious humanity. This is an astounding example of Wagner's talent for translating the most arcane aspects of Feuerbach's critique of religion into fairy-tale metaphors by employing his musical motifs in the most subtle ways. It was in that transitional period of collective dreaming (involuntary myth-making), during which our animal drives (the Giants), enhanced by the growing power of conscious human thought

(Alberich's Ring), gave birth to the first human societies and the religions (Valhallas) which laid their foundation. So, as the gods (early man) slept, the Giants built Valhalla. In Wagner's sophisticated yet naively expressed *Ring* libretto, seemingly negligible remarks such as this, when transfigured by his infinitely suggestive motifs of foreboding and reminiscence, carry portentous allegorical significance.

I noted that Wotan, in his desire to deny the Giants their due payment for building Valhalla, is denying that egoism is the root motivation for human feeling, thought, and action, even the root of our more abstract impulse to posit transcendent ideals. According to Feuerbach: " ... in reality states, even Christian states, are built not on the power of religion, ... but on the power of bayonets and other instruments of torture. In reality men act out of entirely different motives than their religious imagination leads them to *suppose*." [325F-LER, p. 302; See also 245F-LER, p. 156; 212F-LER, p. 87; and 96W-{1–2/49} *Jesus of Nazareth*: PW Vol. VIII. p. 339] If we analyze each Giant's individual claim to Freia, the characteristics which distinguish Fafner from Fasolt also distinguish Freia's two aspects, as goddess of love and immortality. Fasolt represents the animal instinct of sexual desire and the more general desire for love and family, the social desire to belong, whereas Fafner, to whom Siegfried will later look to teach him fear, represents the animal instinct of fear of death, the lonely self-preservation instinct. Fear is lonely because under its sway an individual will often (perhaps always) sacrifice love, heartfelt relations with others, to preserve himself. The self-preservation instinct is the basis of man's loveless lust for self-aggrandizement and worldly power. When evolution produced man's reflective consciousness (Alberich's Ring), our newfound capacity for symbolic abstraction expanded the imaginative reach of the basic animal impulses to infinity. Our fear of death could seek assuagement in the religious belief that a god can grant us the divine gift of immortality. And the otherwise egoistic impulse of sexual desire, the foundation of the family and social sentiments like love and compassion, can be sublimated into belief in a love which is infinite, sorrow-less never-ending bliss. So the Giants (animal impulses which seek satisfaction), when multiplied to infinity by the Ring's power (the unlimited power of our imagination), produce Freia, goddess of divine love and immortality. This is the basis of their rightful claim to Freia. It's this troubling claim of the mundane on the sublime which the archetypal artist-hero Loge promises to help Wotan deny, by employing his artistic cunning to redeem Freia from the Giants' rightful claim.

So Wotan attempts to weasel his way out of granting the Giants the agreed-on payment Freia, to buy time until Loge saves the day. But Fasolt brusquely declares that the gods only rule because they keep faith with their allegedly divine social contract:

[pp. 74–5] **Fasolt:** (H19:) We already asked for what seems to us fitting (:H19) ... . (H22:) Freia the fair, Holda the free—it's already agreed: we carry her home.

Wotan: (...) Freia isn't for sale.

Fasolt: (...) (H19 vari) You're plotting betrayal? (...) (H19: [plus pulsations]) The runes of well-considered contract, safeguarded by your spear, are they no more than sport to you (:H19 plus pulsations)?

Fafner: (H32B embryo:) Most trusty brother, you see their deception now, you fool (:H32B embryo)?

Fasolt: Son of light, lightly swayed, [[H26 voc:]] [= H24 vari] listen and beware: keep your faith with your contracts (:H26 voc)! (H19 [in a new vari plus pulses] (H123 embryo:) What you are you are through contracts alone: your power ... is bound by sworn agreements (:H123 embryo). Though you are wiser than we ... , you bound us freemen to keep the peace: I'll curse all your wisdom, fly away from your close [[H27 voc:]] [= H19 vari] if, openly, fairly and freely, you cannot keep faith with your contracts (:H27 voc)! (...)

Wotan: How cunning to take in earnest what was decided in jest! (...)

Fasolt: (...) (H22:) You who rule through beauty, you augustly glittering race (:H22), how foolish to strive (H18a modulation:) after towers of stone (:H18a modulation), (H16:) placing woman's delights in pawn (:H16) ... ! (H22, H23)

Fasolt introduces the second in a fascinating family of motifs described by Cooke, H26, which is based on Loge's first motif, H24, and includes the two motifs associated with Mime's Scheming, H42 and H106, and H124, associated later with Wotan's contracts he engraved on his spear. H26 bespeaks Fasolt's intuition that through Loge's cunning Wotan intends to break their contract. He reminds the gods that they're only gods by virtue of having made their contracts and honoring them, noting that the gods bound freemen such as the Giants to keep the peace among themselves with contracts. As Fasolt observes that the Giants will flee the gods' rule if they can't keep faith, we hear another new motif H27, "Treaty," a variant of H19 (Wotan's Spear), which represents the honoring of contracts which restrain our egoistic impulses (the Giants), guaranteed by divine law. Wotan's Spear, made by him from the World-Ash's "holiest bough," and engraved with the runes spelling out the dubious contract Wotan (under Loge's influence) made with the Giants to build Valhalla in exchange for Freia, is Wagner's metaphor for the Social Contract. Wotan's contract with the Giants, i.e., with man's egoistic tendency toward selfishness rather than social cooperation, is the archetype for all contracts and laws which govern society. Feuerbach said (figuratively) that the state, human history, and language originated by contract [10F-TDI, p. 79].

Feuerbach also noted that egoism (the Giants) is the underlying motive which guarantees all contracts, all reckoning of good and evil (morality), even in the absence of divine sanction: " ... nothing is more groundless than the fear that the distinction between right and wrong, good and evil, must vanish with the gods. The distinction exists and will continue to exist as long as there is a difference between me and thee, for this is the source of ethics and law. My egoism may permit me to steal, but my fellow man's egoism will sternly forbid me; left to myself I may know nothing of unselfishness, but the selfishness of others will teach me the virtue of unselfishness." [327F-LER, p. 303] In the social contract we all agree to restrain the satisfaction of our egoistic impulses (the Giants make peace) for the sake of the satisfaction of our egoism on a tolerable scale which isn't disruptive and tends towards social order, as Wagner put it in his paraphrase of Feuerbach: "To the fear of violence from ... [" ... the violent, ... passionate individual ... "], as also to ... knowledge thus acquired of basic human nature, we owe the State. It is a contract whereby the units seek to save themselves from mutual violence, through a little mutual practice of restraint. ... in the State the unit offered up just so much of his egoism as appeared necessary to ensure for himself the contentment of its major bulk." [695W-{64–2/65} 'On State and Religion,' PW Vol. IV, p. 11] The essence of society, according to Wagner, is stasis, security, quiet based on wont, custom, care, fear of the new and dislike of innovation, that is, peace at the cost of individual freedom of expression [See 504W-{50–1/51} *Opera and Drama*, PW Vol. II, p. 186; See also 1126W].

Fasolt provides further insight into the gods' nature. He not only tells Wotan that the gods can sustain their rule only by honoring the laws they themselves make, but adds that the gods rule through beauty. Fasolt reminds us that though religious thought partakes of the power of objective thought (Alberich's Ring), nonetheless religious thought is tempered by subjective value, feeling, not by objective truth. The gods rule by laws indeed, but laws guided by feeling (good, and beauty).

We can now grasp why the Giants contracted with the gods to build their heavenly home Valhalla. It's because the religious illusions of transcendent love (Freia's aspect which appeals to the amorous Fasolt) and sorrow-less youth eternal, i.e., immortality (which appeals to Fafner as the promise of immortality assuages our fear of death), offer to satisfy our egoistic instincts in a manner with which natural human life can't compete. Religious faith achieves this by deluding our animal instincts into supposing they can obtain infinite satisfaction, just as the Rhinedaughters told Alberich that through the Ring he would obtain limitless power. Wagner explained this in the following way. We invented the gods, making a contract with them to ensure they'll grant us a heavenly reward for the world's ills and imperfections. As Wagner put it: "The really perplexing problem ... is always how, in this terrible world of ours, beyond which there is only nothingness, it might be possible to infer the existence of a God who would make life's immense sufferings merely something apparent, while the redemption we long for is seen as something ... real that may be consciously enjoyed. This may not be a problem for philistines ... : the reason they get on so splendidly with their God is because they enter into a contract with Him, according to whose terms they have to fulfil ... contractual points, so that, ..., as a reward for various shortcomings in this world, they may enjoy eternal bliss in the world to come. But what do we have in common with such vulgar ideas?" [633W-{6/7/55}Letter to Franz Liszt, SLRW, p. 344]

Fafner tells Fasolt he knows where the gods are vulnerable, because Fafner, our fear of death, the basis of our religious beliefs, is also religious faith's Achilles heel. Wagner dramatizes this in Fafner's threat to take Freia away from the gods, exposing them as merely mortal, finite beings:

> **[pp. 75–6] Fafner:** ... holding Freia helps us little; much, however, will be gained if we wrest her away from the gods. **[[H28 voc/orch:]]** softly:) Golden apples grow in her garden; she alone knows how to tend them; the taste of the fruit confers on her kinsfolk endlessly never ageing youth (:H28 voc/orch); **[[H29a voc/orch:]]** but, sick and wan, their bloom will wither (:H29a voc/orch), **[[H29b voc/orch:]]** old and weak they'll waste away, if Freia they have to forego (:H29b voc/orch): (roughly) so let her be plucked from their midst! (H28; H25a)
>
> **Wotan:** Loge delays too long!

H28 is introduced as the Motif of Freia's Golden Apples of Sorrow-less Youth Eternal. H28 is the basis for the motif belonging to her optimistic brother Froh, H30. Since fear of death is assuaged by religion's promise of immortality, H28 is always heard associated with Fafner, whereas Freia's motifs H22 and H23, which represent her as the love goddess, are always heard in association with Fasolt, smitten with love. But Fafner seems more interested in obtaining Freia in payment solely in order to deprive the gods of that which makes them gods, their immortality, than in enjoying the immortality which Freia would presumably grant the giants if they acquired her as payment for building Valhalla. This seeming contradiction is resolved by grasping that if the gods actually accepted the egoistic Giants' valid claim to Freia, the gods' ideal of transcendent love and immortality would be exposed as having an earthly rather than supernatural origin. So fear of death (Fafner), the foundation of religious faith, is also its greatest threat. Accordingly, Fafner introduces another motif which has two distinct segments, H29ab, Dunning's "Godhead Lost," as Fafner describes to Fasolt how the gods would wither away and die if they could no longer taste Freia's golden apples. Dunning noted that H29b is the basis for H101 (which also contains harmony based on the Ring Motif H17ab), "Brünnhilde's Magic Sleep," introduced in V.3.2 to dramatize Wotan's threat to punish his daughter Brünnhilde by taking away her divinity (and by putting her to sleep so she'll be vulnerable to any mortal man to wake and win her). Fafner is a greater threat than Fasolt because Fafner, fear of death, is inimical to our social instincts, and love. What irony that the Ring and its product fear are the mainsprings of religious faith!

Fafner (fear) stands for a key concept in the *Ring*, and his importance lies in two special facts about him. One is that, unlike Fasolt, he'll employ Alberich's wondrous cap the Tarnhelm to transform himself into a serpent (emulating Alberich, who'll employ the Tarnhelm for this same purpose in R.3). Wagner highlights Fafner's kinship with Alberich by employing Motif H47 (Serpent/Dragon) to represent the serpent into which both Alberich and Fafner transform themselves. Fafner's antisocial egoism is directly linked with Alberich's quest to obtain loveless power over the world and his fellow men through his Ring. Two, Fafner lives on after persuading his brother Fasolt to renounce love for the sake of power, and then killing Fasolt. Fafner is more important, and therefore absorbs Fasolt. This fear which gives birth to the gods ultimately expands beyond the fear of death, through the unlimited scope of the imagination, to embrace what Feuerbach describes as abstract fear in general, existential fear: "When we explain religion by fear, we must ... take into account not only the lowest form of fear, fear of one natural phenomenon or another, ... but also the fear that is limited to no particular object, the perpetual, ever present fear which embraces every conceivable misfortune, ... the *infinite* fear of the human soul." [319F-LER, p. 287; See also 269F-LER, p. 196; and 196F-LER, p. 25] Wagner, echoing Feuerbach's remark below, tells us that the gods' hold over man's imagination is rooted in their power to save, especially to grant man the divine gift of immortality: "A God is essentially a being who fulfills man's desires. And the most heartfelt desire ... is the desire not to die, to live forever ... ." [305F-LER, p. 269] "He [Wagner] ... says how much to be preferred are the ideas of the ancient world to those of the church today, whose power is rooted in the fear of death, or, rather, the life after death." [944W-{10/10/78} CD Vol. II, p. 168]

But fear must remain an unconscious source of inspiration for our belief in immortality and the gods. If the truth was consciously acknowledged that our corporeal life-instincts are the basis for our involuntary invention of gods and redemption in heaven, we'd be forced to confess our allegedly transcendent heaven is merely our own body and earth, sublimated into an ersatz spiritual realm freed by our imagination from natural limits. As Wagner put it: "... the naïve saints of Christianity ... were able to deceive their confused imagination by seeing that longed-for state [i.e., our supernatural redemption from subjection to egoistic impulse, and our mortal body, in heaven] as a perpetual continuation of a new state of life freed from nature ... ." [636W-{6/7/55} Letter to Franz Liszt, SLRW, pp. 345–346] Freia, goddess of divine love and immortality, represents our futile (because unassuageable) desire for endless life freed from those natural conditions which alone make life possible. As Wagner implied, when we posit the possibility of our redemption from our earthly coils in heaven, we do so by imaginatively smuggling into heaven the earthly things for which we long, minus all those natural limitations which make it impossible to satisfy our desires and assuage our fears in actual life. So Wotan's task (which will be accomplished for him by Loge, our—Wotan's—artistic capacity for self-deception) is to seemingly satisfy the Giants' demand for what Freia represents, without consciously acknowledging their true claim on her. Only in this way can religious man mistake illusion (Freia's gifts) for truth and get away with it.

Wotan, in a panic at the possibility that Fafner's threat fulfilled might overthrow the illusions which sustain the gods' rule, cries out that Loge (through whose artistic cunning alone the gods can deceive themselves) delays too long. At this desperate moment Freia's brothers Froh and Donner, responding to her cry for help, enter to save her from the Giants' threat, Donner in particular threatening to use force, an affront to the contract Wotan made with the Giants:

[pp. 76–77] **Froh:** ([[H30 orch:]] [= H28 vari]: taking Freia in his arms) (...) Get back from her, you bully! Froh protects fair Freia (:H30 orch).

Donner: (... [[H31ab orch:]]) Fasolt and Fafner, you've felt my hammer's blow before (:H31ab orch)? [Fafner, Fasolt, and Donner debate: (...); Donner threatens to strike with his hammer]

Wotan: (stretching out his spear between the disputants: [[H19 Definitive orch:]] Stop, you firebrand! Nothing by force (:H19 Definitive orch)! (H26:) My spearshaft safeguards contracts (:H26): spare your hammer's haft.

The eternal optimist Froh's arrival is heralded by his own, new motif in the orchestra, H30, which is closely related to the Motif of Freia's Golden Apples of Sorrow-less Youth Eternal H28. Donner the Thunder God's motif H31ab expresses his nature as the god of storm and thunder with two segments, a choppy descending segment followed by a rising and falling segment representing rolling thunder, which as Cooke noted is a basis for the Storm Motif H59 with which the following music-drama *The Valkyrie* opens. H31b is based on the embryo for H19, the Spear Motif. Donner is the terrifying enforcer of the gods' divine law and authority. Wagner's characterization of Donner may owe something to Feuerbach who suggested that our fear of thunder was God's womb: "Certain peoples ... have no other word for God than thunder ... . (...) Considering that it was thunder which pounded religion into man, we may ... term the eardrum the sounding board of the religious sense and the ear the womb of the gods." [197F-LER, p. 27]

As Freia's brothers imprudently try to intervene in her behalf, disregarding the Giants' rights, Wotan wields the power of his spear to protect them from Donner's threatened hammer blow, crying out "(H19) Nothing by force! (H26) My spear guards contracts," as we hear the Definitive Spear Motif H19. Wotan's attempt to invoke the law by force, in order to pre-empt Donner's use of force outside the law, bespeaks a contradiction at the root of the concept of law itself. Feuerbach captured the essence of this in his observation that the state isn't based on religious belief, but on force. [See 325F-LER, p. 302] Wagner concurred, noting the irony in man's hope that through law violence can be restrained by the prudent use of violence, which Wagner describes as loveless [1030W-{6–8/80} "Religion and Art": PW Vol. VI, pp. 230–231; see also [394W-{1–2/49} *Jesus of Nazareth*, PW Vol. VIII. p. 321]. Wagner summed up the hypocrisy in our use of law to enforce morality in this way: "Misunderstanding his own impulses, to himself Man seemed outside God, i.e., wicked: over against themselves men set the Law, as come from God, to force themselves to good." [391W-{1–2/49} *Jesus of Nazareth*, PW Vol. VIII. pp. 310–311]

As Loge arrives Wotan chastises him for making what Wotan describes as Loge's bad bargain with the Giants, but Loge demurs:

[pp. 77–8] **Wotan:** ([[H32A orch:]]) Loge at last! [[H33 orch:]]; [[H34 orch:]] Have you come in such haste to resolve the bad bargain you struck (:H33 orch; :H34 orch)?

(Loge has climbed up through the valley at the back: [[**H32B**]])

Loge: (H34:) (...) Which bargain is that that I'm said to have struck? (H33:) The one you discussed with the giants in council (:H33)?—(H18a:; H32B:) To hollow and height my hankering drives me; house and hearth (:H18a; :H32B) delight me not: Donner and Froh think only of house and home; if they'd go awooing, a home must make them happy: a stately hall, a sturdy keep, such was Wotan's wish. (H18a:) House and court, hall and keep, your blissful abode now stands there, solidly built; the proud-standing walls (:H18a) (H18b:) I tested myself ... .

All but one of the four motifs which characterize the Fire God Loge (the exception being H24) are introduced with his arrival. These are H32ab, which ascends and descends, H34, which represents fire per se, and H33. H33 (Dunning's "Loge's Transformations") generates the two Tarnhelm motifs H40A and H40B, Wotan's (& Brünnhilde's) Magic Fire Music H105, and ultimately Hagen's Potion Motif H165. Dunning also included in this list of related motifs the first of Wotan's Wanderer Motifs H119. Since this set of Loge motifs is first heard as Wotan debates with him which of them is responsible for having made the bad bargain with the Giants, Loge's motifs express his shifty relationship with the truth. But he incarnates the gods' own self-deception. Loge has much in common with the Christian notion of the Serpent in paradise, who lures Eve with the false promise that mortal humans can partake of both divine knowledge and immortality (fruit of the Trees of Knowledge and Life, respectively) without paying the price of death which God has threatened. The Serpent lures Eve/Adam (man) into bringing about man's irrevocable Fall through hubris, which exiles us from paradise and deprives us of immortality (i.e., deprives us of our former unconsciousness of our mortality). Similarly, Loge lures Wotan into making the bargain with the Giants to build Valhalla on the false promise that through Loge's cunning he can redeem the gods from paying the price the Giants require, Freia, who grants the gods immortality. Loge's cunning persuades the Giants to believe the gods' debt to them has been satisfied, when it hasn't. And in Wotan's futile attempt to blame Loge for Wotan's self-deception we find the Christian's attempt to project his need for self-deception, and its guilt, on to the Serpent, or Satan.

Loge's self-description as one who's driven to hollow and height by his longing, for whom home and hearth hold no delight, aligns him with the natural necessity for change to which Wotan pledged allegiance when he warned Fricka that though he'd make the domestic tranquility of Valhalla his base of operations, he's driven nonetheless to step outside the bounds of Valhalla to conquer the exterior world, for as he says, all who live love renewal and change. Loge glibly yet implausibly affirms that the gods' new fortress is solidly built, knowing perfectly well that, thanks to the role his cunning played in securing this fortress through false promises, its walls are porous. Loge, redeemer from truth, as an agent of creative change is also dangerous for religious faith.

Wotan confronts Loge, reminding him that Wotan only agreed to pay the Giants Freia because Loge promised to redeem her. But Loge begs to differ: what he did was merely promise to seek a way to redeem her. After all, how could he promise the impossible?:

[pp. 78–9] **Wotan:** ... (H32B:) take care ... that you don't deceive me (:H32B). Of all the gods your only friend, I took you into the ill-trusting tribe. (...) (H19) When the citadel's builders demanded Freia by way of thanks, (H32B) you know that I only acquiesced because you promised on oath to redeem the noble pledge. (H32A)

Loge: With utmost care to ponder on ways by which to redeem it—that I did indeed promise. (H32A:; H34:; H33:) but that I would find what never befell and what's bound to fail (:H32a; :H34; :H33), how could such a promise be made? [Fricka and Froh insult Loge: (...)] (H33: [as embryo for H105]) To hide their shame the fools defame me (:H33). (...)

Wotan: (...) You don't know Loge's art ["Kunst"]: (H24:) greater the value of his advice (:H24) when he pays it out delayingly.

The gods need Loge, but, just as with their debt to the Giants and Alberich, they also need to disavow him. They can't acknowledge that their allegedly divine world is founded on self-deception as a mask for earthly egoism. Feuerbach decried religion's confusion of illusion with truth: "... unless religion enters in, an artist merely expects his images to be faithful and beautiful; he does not claim that a semblance of reality is reality itself. Religion, on the other hand, deceives people, or rather people deceive themselves in religion; for it does claim that the semblance of reality is reality, that an image is a living being. But this being lives only in the imagination ... ." [262F-LER, p. 183] According to Porges Wagner described Loge as the gods' (i.e., religion's) bad conscience: "... it is he [Loge] who embodies the bad conscience of the world of the gods presented to us in all its glitter and glory." [864W-{6–8/76} WRR, p. 21] Wotan tries to reconcile the gods to his friendship with, and dependence on, Loge, noting—accompanied by the first Loge Motif H24—that Loge's advice's value increases the more he delays giving it. Dunning coined H24 "Loge's Deceptions." Loge's greatest deception has been persuading Wotan that Loge can find a substitute payment the giants will accept in lieu of the originally agreed on price for building Valhalla, Freia. In other words, Loge offers to redeem Wotan's self-deception from the truth. H24 conveys the embarrassing fact that the gods depend on Loge to help them deceive themselves. The logic behind the link of the family of motifs generated from H24 with Mime's scheming will become clear later when we recognize in Mime the loathsome egoism which Wotan is horrified to discover at the root of his own allegedly noble motives. This is the source of all of Wotan's self-deceptions.

Loge, in a narrative of extraordinary musico-dramatic beauty, describes how in his quest to find a substitute for Freia the Giants would accept as payment, he found that none among the living will forsake love and woman's worth, a statement he knows to be untrue:

[pp. 79–82] **Loge:** I looked all around me, stormily scouring the ends of the earth seeking a ransom for Freia that the giants might approve. I sought in vain and see full well: in the whole wide world there's naught so rare as to strike mankind as a worthy ransom [[**H35 voc:**]] [= H16 vari] for woman's delights and worth (:H35 voc). (...) ([[**H36 orch**]]; H22) (...) Wherever there's life and breath, my inquisitive skill was laughed to scorn: in water, earth and air none will relinquish love and woman.—(...) (H22) Only one man I saw who forswore love's delights (H9): for the sake of red gold he forwent women's favours. (H8:) The Rhine's fair children (H13:) complained to me of their plight ["Noth"] (:H13): the Nibelung, Night-Alberich, (H4:) wooed in vain for the nixies' favours (:H4); the thief robbed the Rhinegold then in revenge (H9): (H17:) it seems to him now the rarest jewel (:H17) ... . (H12 orch:) For the glittering toy that was torn from the deep the daughters' lament rang out (:H12 orch): to you, Wotan, they now appeal to call the thief to account (... H9:) and give back the gold to the waters, to remain their own (H9) forever.—(...) [Wotan, Fasolt, and Fafner converse: (...)]

Fafner: ... what is the gold's great virtue that it satisfies the Nibelung?

Loge: (H12:; H11:) A toy it is in the watery deep, delighting laughing children (:H12; :H11): (H15>H17:) but once it is forged to a rounded hoop, it helps to confer unending power and wins the world for its master (:H15>H17). (H17)

Wotan: (... H17:) Of the gold in the Rhine I've heard it whispered (:H17) (H18ab:) that booty-runes (H17:) lie hid in its fiery glow (:H18ab); power and riches beyond all measure may be gained through a ring (:H17)

Fricka: Might the golden trinket's glittering gem ... serve as fair adornment?

Loge: (H21:) A wife might ensure that her husband was true if she lovingly wore the bright-shining jewel which ... dwarves have (H11>H38 Embryo:) forged, bestirred by the spell on the ring.

In his statement that he found nothing in the world which is a worthy ransom for woman's delights and worth, Loge introduced two new motifs. The first, H35, Dunning calls the "Loveless Motif" because it's derived, Cooke observed, from the second segment of H16, which Wellgunde sung as she told Alberich he could only forge a Ring from the Rhinegold granting him limitless power if he renounced love. H35, an oft-heard motif, can be regarded as an abbreviated version of H16, though its range of reference (it's dramatic profile) is far greater than that of H16 per se, which is only heard complete a few times in the entire *Ring*. The second motif, H36, is what Cooke describes as a Motion of Nature. It's related to H2, the first variant of the Original Nature Motif H1 in which we hear the motion of the Rhine River, and to H14, the Rhinedaughters' jubilant dance-like swimming in celebration of the shining Rhinegold. H36 will be heard as the herald of Siegfried's Forest Murmurs in S.2.2, and only a few other times in an abbreviated variant (when Wotan wakes Erda to ask her for knowledge in S.3.1, for instance). Woman's delight and worth (a figure for love), as Loge describes it here, isn't merely a description of woman's sexual delights, or romantic love, or even sympathy of one living being for another, but conveys a feminine essence which for Wagner embraces feeling, animal instinct, preconscious animal life, human love of all kinds, and even music. It represents the life of feeling, animal life's innocence before the birth of human consciousness and its power (which Wagner identifies with language, masculinity, and ultimately with the Fall, with which H35 can be identified).

Loge immediately contradicts what he just said (that no living being will renounce love) when he adds that he found only one man who forswore love for gold's sake, Alberich. The Giants will also forswear love for gold's sake when they agree to accept Alberich's Hoard of treasure in lieu of Freia. The Rhinedaughters complained to Loge of their "Noth," the existential angst which is the Fall's hallmark, calling on Wotan to restore lost innocence. Since, in many origin myths, we humans had to steal divine power to obtain it, and the Fall is our punishment by the gods for our theft of the divine prerogative of consciousness (our original sin), the Rhinedaughters' plea that Wotan restore what's been lost through Alberich's forging of the Ring expresses man's longing that religious faith redeem us from our intolerable punishment, consciousness. This explains the Prometheus Myth. Prometheus was punished by Zeus with an un-healing wound for giving mortal man the divine privilege of fire (Loge), and, significantly, foreknowledge (Prometheus means "foresight") of death. In Wagner's world, initially religious faith, and later, secular ethics and art (music), are man's artificial attempts to restore the life of feeling which has been lost to thinking.

Wotan's curiosity gets the better of him, and he asks Loge how one might make such a Ring:

> **[p. 82] Wotan:** (... H9:; H17:) To wield the ring seems wise to me (:H9; :H17).—but, Loge, how might I learn the art? How could I make the jewel?
>
> **Loge:** (H17:) A rune-spell makes a ring from the gold (:H17): no one knows what it is, (H16:) yet the spell is easily cast by him who forswears love's delights (:H16). (Wotan turns away in displeasure.) You'd rather not; you'd be too late in any case: Alberich did not hesitate; (H17:) fearless, he gained the magic power (harshly: H35:) and managed to make the ring (:H35).

As Loge answers (accompanied by H16) with brutal abruptness that this spell to forge the Ring of power is cast easily by him who forswears love, Wotan turns away, repulsed. Loge, quick to note Wotan's inaptitude for taking the drastic step which alone would make him worthy to use the Ring's power, with a touch of sadistic pleasure tells him that Alberich didn't hesitate to make the sacrifice Wotan finds so repugnant, and fearlessly obtained the power he needed to make the Ring (as we hear H35—Loveless) by, Loge implies, renouncing love. Loge's point is that while Wotan's thinking (religious thought) is guided by feeling (love), Alberich, our impulse to obtain real power through objective knowledge unimpaired by feeling (love), is alone able to forge the Ring to employ thought's power to the fullest degree. Feuerbach expressed Wotan's quandary in the following extracts which distinguish theological thought from objective thought:

" ... although in theory the theists place truth above good cheer, in practice the power to provide consolation is their sole criterion of truth or untruth ... ." [273F-LER, p. 204] Feuerbach identifies what he calls the heathen God with the understanding and with pantheism (the natural world understood objectively), and identifies the Christian God with the human heart: *"The distinction between the "heathen," or philosophic, and the Christian God—the non-human, or pantheistic, and the human, personal God—reduces itself only to the distinction between the understanding or reason and the heart or feelings."* [146F-EOC, p. 285; See also 148F-EOC, p. 285] We see Alberich, who eagerly renounces love for the Ring's worldly power, in Feuerbach's heathen God of the heartless understanding, a partisan of Nature by grasping it objectively through reason. Wotan we see in Feuerbach's Christian God of the heart, who, being social, needs love, and who acknowledges Nature only insofar as it doesn't contradict his consoling illusions.

Donner states the obvious, that Alberich with his Ring power threatens the gods, who therefore ought to wrest the Ring from him. Wotan concurs:

[pp. 82–3] **Donner:** (to Wotan) The dwarf would enslave us all were the ring not wrested from him.

Wotan: I must have the ring!

Froh: (H35:) It's easily won now, without cursing love (:H35).

Loge: ... it's child's play indeed! [**Wotan:** (...)] By theft! (...) (H32B) But with cunning defense is Alberich armed; (H15:) shrewd and subtle must be your approach when you call the thief to account (:H15) (H12:; H11:) and make him give back ... the gold ... to the daughters of the Rhine (:H12; :H11): (H9) ... .

Wotan: (H12:) The daughters of the Rhine (:H12)? What use is such advice to me?

Loge suggests the gods take advantage of Alberich's sacrifice of love by relieving him of his Ring through theft. As Wotan noted, Loge's cunning draws advantage from the enemy's envy. Loge is scheming that religious man (Wotan), aided by Loge's artistic cunning (self-deception), take our mind (Alberich and his Ring) prisoner, to draw advantage from the power Alberich alone possessed the ruthlessness to win. They'll capture Alberich and his Ring to convert its power to subjective employment, i.e., to sustain the gods' rule through artistic self-deception in Valhalla. Religious belief (Valhalla—H18ab) is, after all, an expression of the Ring's (H17ab's) power, the power of our mind tempered by feeling (love).

But Loge adds—supported by the Ring Motif's Rhinedaughter-flavored embryo H15ab—that the gods must be shrewd and subtle if they hope to make the thief Alberich give his Ring back to the Rhinedaughters. Wotan asks the first of his great questions when he asks Loge what "use" giving the Ring back to the Rhinedaughters would be. Wotan's question recalls Alberich, who couldn't for a moment grasp what "use" the Rhinedaughters' song, dance, and play in aesthetic celebration of the Rhinegold could be. Ultimately we'll learn that the use of giving the Ring back to the Rhinedaughters is to redeem the world from the curse Alberich will place on his Ring. But this seemingly innocent remark foreshadows the subtle method Wotan's free hero (and grandson) Siegfried and Wotan's daughter Brünnhilde, Siegfried's lover and muse, will use to redeem the gods (man's religious impulse) temporarily from Alberich's Ring Curse. This alternative to returning the Ring to the Rhinedaughters is the shrewd and subtle method to which Loge, who plays the long-game, alludes. Though we'll only grasp its significance much later in the drama, we're offered a clue to it by Loge's response to Fricka's hope to use Alberich's Ring, or jewels forged under its spell, for adornment, for he says, accompanied by H21, that with such jewels a woman could preserve her husband's fidelity. This foreshadows Siegfried's and Brünnhilde's taking Alberich's Ring as the symbol of their wedded troth, troth they'll betray.

Fafner the cynic now whispers to his brother Fasolt that the gold is worth more than Freia, since eternal youth could also be obtained through the Ring's spell:

> **[pp. 83–4] Fafner:** [addressing Fasolt] (H22 vari:) ... the glittering gold is worth far more than Freia: eternal youth may also be gained by him (:H22 vari) (H28; H9) who obtains it by force through the gold's magic spell. (Fasolt's reaction indicates he has been persuaded against his will. ... (H25a)) (...) Freia may live in peace with you; an easier payment I've found as ransom: (H26:; H25a:) we uncouth giants will be content (:H26; :H25a) with the Nibelung's bright red gold. [Wotan and Fafner converse: (...)]
>
> **Wotan:** (...) For you should I capture your foe? Unabashed and over-demanding my debt has made you, you fools.

Given his strong desire for Freia, Fasolt is surprisingly acquiescent in his brother's cynical plan to renounce Freia (goddess of love and immortality) in favor of the power Alberich's gold can win them. The fact that Fafner's appeal to egoism persuades Fasolt (however reluctantly he concurs with Fafner) proves Fasolt's love is weaker than Fafner's lust for self-aggrandizement and immortality. In a loveless, material world lacking supernatural influence, the self-preservation instinct would always trump higher ideals such as compassionate love for others.

Fafner has made the astonishing assertion that one of the powers won by the Rhinegold's owner will be the immortality which heretofore we'd believed could be granted by Freia's golden apples alone. True, the Ring confers theoretically limitless practical power over the world, but this doesn't embrace a supernatural power to confer unending life. There must be something more at stake here unless Fafner is lying to convince his brother to renegotiate their contract. Fafner prefers whatever reality can give him, enhanced by the power over our world granted us by our mind (Ring), over the psychological pleasure which the consolations of illusion can provide. He'd rather obtain a fuller and longer life through objective knowledge and the power it wins, than enjoy belief in eternal youth predicated on illusion. This is the danger his cynicism (instinct for truth) presents to the gods, that it's skeptical of the consolation of faith which it suspects is predicated on illusion, not substantial, physical satisfaction. Fafner is a realist like Alberich, for both seek an earthly utopia which will sate their egoistic desires and assuage their fears within the practical limits of reality. Fafner is a good student of Feuerbach: "Culture has no other object than to realize an earthly heaven ... ." [127F-EOC, p. 217] Wagner identified this acknowledgment of the earthly origin of our purportedly spiritual aspirations, and Judaism's alleged rejection of the notion of supernatural immortality for more abundant life on earth, with Christianity's debt to Judaism, a notion he borrowed, again, from Feuerbach, who described Jewish morality as love of the temporal and earthly life: "The only difference between Judaism and Christianity is that in Judaism morality is based on the love of temporal, earthly life, and in Christianity on the love of eternal, heavenly life. ... egoism alone is the secret of faith as distinct from love ... ." [324F-LER, p. 300]

In our extract below which echoes the passage from Feuerbach which precedes it, Wagner provides the conceptual basis for Fafner's willingness to forego the illusory immortality offered by religious faith, for more abundant life provided by earthly power: "Christianity has ... changed the desire for earthly happiness [Alberich's worldly Ring power], the goal of the Israelitish religion, into the longing for heavenly bliss [the sorrow-less youth eternal conferred on the gods by Freia], which is the goal of Christianity." [91F-EOC, p. 121; See also 304F-LER, p. 268] "... he [the Jew] has no religion at all—merely the belief in ... promises of his god which [don't] ... extend to a life beyond this temporal life of his, as in every true religion, but simply to this present life on earth, whereon his race is certainly ensured dominion over all that lives and lives not. ... ." [1068W-{1–2/81} 'Know Thyself'—2nd Supplement to 'Religion and Art,' PW Vol. VI, p. 271] In Wagner's remark that Jews don't believe in eternal life but only in the promise of their god (egoism, according to Wagner) that they'll have power to dominate life here on earth, we find the basis for Fafner's choice of the gold over Freia. But Fafner's alleged Judaism is merely the egoism which underlies all human behavior, whether of Gentile or Jew.

Having convinced Fasolt of the advantage to be gained by exchanging Freia for the Rhinegold, Fafner, accompanied by H26, tells Wotan they'll be content with the Nibelung's gold instead. Fafner's willingness to accept this substitute represents the fact that our instincts can only be satisfied by an illusory promise if convinced this satisfaction is more substantial than actual satisfaction here on earth. The result is that Fafner believes his concrete, base desires are satisfied while Wotan and the gods get to keep their illusions. Wotan is shocked that as an alleged god, if he aids the lowly, despised Fafner in this scheme he'll be troubling himself for the sake of an ignoble motive which Wotan doesn't wish to own. He's embarrassed that loathsome egoism and fear are behind his intent to win the Ring from Alberich. The Giants are the gods' (our) motivating animal impulses, a constant reminder that the gods aren't gods, but merely mortal humans. Both Feuerbach and Wagner explain Wotan's disdain for acknowledging his base motives. Feuerbach says that for those who believe in a transcendent realm of being, the body and the natural processes are repugnant: "The more man alienates himself from Nature, the more subjective, ... antinatural, is his view of things, the greater the horror he has of Nature." [99F-EOC, pp. 136–137] This inspired Wagner's insight that if we (religious men) disown our true relationship with the beasts (don't acknowledge that we evolved from animal ancestors, but believe instead that have a divine origin), we see the real world, including our bodies and physical impulses, as abhorrent and evil: "... with the disowning of our true relation to the beasts, we see an animalised—in the worst sense—and more than an animalised, a devilised world before us." [986W-{10/79} Letter to E. von Weber 'Against Vivisection,' PW Vol. VI, p. 204] But Alberich, unlike Wotan, has the courage of his convictions and openly proclaims himself egoistic without guilt, since he accepts his status as a mortal in a world circumscribed by natural limits.

Feuerbach noted how ironic it is that the human mind (which is after all the product of a natural evolution of species) invented the gods, in whom religious man disavows his true origin in, and dependence on, Mother Nature, and his subjection to the needs of his body: "The mind ... is the highest part of man; it is man's badge of nobility, which distinguishes him from the animals; but first in man is not first in nature. On the contrary, what is highest and most perfect is the last and latest. ... to make mind or spirit into the beginning, the origin, is to reverse the order of nature." [243F-LER, p. 155] Wagner emulated Feuerbach's opinion obliquely in his observation that, because our "... most conditioned faculty, the mind ...," hubristically exalts itself, in its arrogance it thinks it can employ its preconditions as "the handmaids of its own caprice." [432W-{9–12/49} 'The Artwork of the Future,' PW Vol. I, p. 94] This offers us a novel perspective on the question whether Alberich's original sin preceded Wotan's. Wotan and the gods can't escape their debt either to the Giants, their underlying animal motives for all they feel, think, do, and say, or their debt to Alberich's forging of the Ring of consciousness, which made our involuntary, unconscious invention of the gods (the building of Valhalla) possible.

The essence of religion's consoling illusions is that we must believe they're true. This is only possible if religious man consigns any knowledge of the truth which would undermine our beliefs, to oblivion, or to the status of an illusion. Religious man can't afford to admit that the redemption we seek in paradise satisfies our animal instincts (the Giants), since we would intuit that our bodily needs gave birth, when magnified by our heightened imaginative powers, to the belief we can find redemption from all that troubles us in the natural world, in a supernatural paradise. So Wotan had to lure the Giants into creating Valhalla (the illusion of heavenly paradise, and a society founded on this self-deception) on the promise of a satisfaction even greater than real life can offer, embodied in the goddess Freia. But Wotan at the same time must deny the Giants' rightful claim to Freia, by buying them off. So the Giants can only obtain satisfaction from the illusion Freia represents, if they stake their claim to her subliminally. Though our ideal is a product of the real, Wotan is striving to ensure that the real can't stake a claim on our ideal, yet pay off our debt to it secretly. These subtle machinations are the foundation of religious man's (specifically, Christians') unconscious hypocrisy. Feuerbach noted that the Christian is bound to deny Nature (Wotan denies the Giants their due for building Valhalla), yet satisfy Nature secretly (he persuades them to accept the Rhinegold in lieu of Freia). [See 165F-EOC, p. 314] The basis of religious morality, says Feuerbach, is the renunciation of the ego here on earth for its fuller satisfaction in heaven: "Why does man deny himself in religion? In order to gain the favor of his gods who grant him everything he desires." [206F-LER, p. 67] This suggests that we unconsciously smuggle into our idea of heaven only those earthly things which can be adapted by our imagination to our illusion of divinity, while denying the physical origin of the impulses which inspired us to involuntarily invent heaven in the first place. As Feuerbach said: "Even if that which pleases him cannot exist without being associated with that which displeases him, the subjective man is not guided by the wearisome laws of logic and physics, but by the self-will of the imagination; hence he drops what is disagreeable in a fact, and holds fast alone what is agreeable." [100F-EOC, p. 137]

Wotan, with Loge's help, has through "Wahn," self-deception, persuaded our instincts (Giants) to renounce immediate physical satisfaction for the sake of distant symbolic satisfaction, but only by assuring them that their egoistic fears and desires will have even more substantial assuagement through this religious illusion than the actual world could ever provide. As Wagner said: "The individual's egoism is ... assumed ... to be so invincible that arrangements beneficiary ... to the species ... at cost of the transient individual, would never be consummated by that individual with ... self-sacrifice, were it not guided by the fancy (Wahn) that it is thereby serving an end of its own ... . without its [Wahn's] intervention the individual in narrow egoistic care for self, would gladly sacrifice the species on the altar of its personal continuance." [698W-{64–2/65} 'On State and Religion,' PW Vol. IV, pp. 14–15]

The Giants, deciding that Wotan can fulfill their contract by granting them Alberich's Hoard of Treasure instead of the originally agreed on payment, Freia, now hold her in pawn until the gods can redeem her. As they haul her away the gods suffer the ill-effect of the loss of her golden apples of sorrow-less youth eternal, and are exposed as mere mortals:

> [p. 86] **Loge:** (H28: [sad vari, in minor]) (...) Hear what you lack (:H28 sad vari)! (H28) Of Freia's fruit you've not yet tasted today: (H28:) the golden apples in her garden kept you hale and young when you ate them every day (:H28). (H29a:) She who tends the garden has now been placed in pawn (:#29a); (H29b:) on the branches the fruit dries out and withers (:H29b): soon it will rot and fall. (H32B)—It troubles me less: in her niggardly fashion Freia always begrudged me the luscious fruit: (H32A) (H29b:) for I'm only half as godlike (:H29b) as you, you immortals! (... H34) But you staked all on the youth-giving fruit, as the giants knew full well; your very lives they've threatened ... . (H28:) Without the apples (:H28) , ... (H29a:) withered and scorned by the whole of the world (:H29a), (H2 chords:) the race of gods will perish (:H2 chords).

As the gods age we initially hear Freia's love motifs H22 and H23, but H28 (Freia's golden apples) is in play as Loge explains that they're aging because they haven't tasted her golden apples today. We hear H29ab, Dunning's "Godhead Lost," as Loge adds that the gardener has been placed in pawn. Feuerbach observed that belief in God is motivated by our longing for immortality, i.e., by fear of death, our irrevocable end in a natural world sans gods: "... in *doctrine*, *immortality* is merely a consequence of the belief in God; but in *practice*, in reality, the *belief in immortality* is the *motive* for the belief in God. (...) ... the divinity and eternity of a nature god ... do not imply human immortality: nature is heartless, impervious to man's wishes, without concern for man." [303F-LER, p. 267; See also 302F-LER, p. 266] That the gods will perish if they can't eat Freia's golden apples of sorrow-less youth eternal means that our belief in the gods will perish: since the gods are our invention, if we cease to believe in them, they cease to exist. Loge sees through the gods' pretensions, knowing they depend on the illusions he creates. It's no wonder he says he's only half as godlike as the gods, and that unlike them he doesn't depend on Freia's golden apples. Unlike the gods, he hasn't staked the meaning of life itself, and happiness, on the illusion of transcendence provided by her youth-giving fruit. But Loge points out that the Giants (the truth behind the gods' self-deception) knew the gods depend on the illusions represented by Freia, and that the Giants' stake in the truth is a mortal threat to the gods' survival. Loge's self-proclaimed autonomy from the gods he serves anticipates the emancipation of the Wälsung heroes Siegmund and Siegfried from subjection to the gods' (religious faith's) rule.

But for now, the Giants have placed the gods' rule (our belief in them) at risk, by temporarily staking their rightful claim to Freia. So Wotan, with Loge's aid, must restore the faith which has been temporarily lost, by stealing Alberich's gold, so he can redeem Freia from the Giants with it:

[p. 87] Wotan: (H17) Get up, Loge! (...) To Nibelheim let's descend: the gold I mean to win. (H12; H11)

Loge: The Rhinedaughters cried out for your help: so may they hope to be heard?

Wotan: (...) Silence, you babbler! ... Freia must be redeemed. [Loge and Wotan converse (...)] (H17:) I go in search of redeeming gold to ransom (:H17) (H8:) our lost youth (:H8)!

Wotan is prompted to redeem Freia from the Giants by fear of perishing, not because he regrets loss of love. Furthermore, since it's only through Alberich's sacrifice of love that he was able to forge the Ring, make the Tarnhelm, and amass that Hoard of treasure with which Wotan will redeem Freia, Wotan must confess not only that he depended on the Giants to build Valhalla, but that he can only take possession of it and keep Freia (the soul of religious belief) safe by virtue of Alberich's Ring power. It was the forging of our conscious mind by evolution which made our involuntary invention of the gods possible (H17ab>H18ab). So it's solely thanks to Alberich's Ring, which produced our human imagination

(Tarnhelm), that Wotan can redeem heavenly Valhalla and its soul, Freia, from the natural world's claim on them. Even the artistic imagination represented by Loge is a byproduct of the human mind's gift of symbolic abstraction. This brings us to the musical transition from R.2 (the meadow before Valhalla) to R.3 (Alberich's cavernous hell Nibelheim), which introduces three new motifs, H37, H39, and H38:

> [p. 88] (**Interlude:** … a solid, rocky chasm … continues moving upwards, … giving the impression that the stage is sinking deeper and deeper into the earth. H35; H8; [[**H37 orch**]] [= H23 vari]; H9; H17; [[**H38 orch**]] [= H11 vari]; [[**H39 orch**]] [= H37 vari]; a dark red light begins to glow at various points in the distance: a noise as though of people forging can be heard on all sides. The ringing of the anvils dies away. A subterranean cavern, stretching away endlessly into the distance … .)

Cooke offered an insightful analysis of this musical transition. H37, he notes, is a variant of Freia's Motif H23, embryo for the definitive Love Motif H63. Cooke discovered that H37, heard here in conjunction with H8, harks back to a pre-H23 embryo of the love motif, and the introduction of H8, sung by Alberich in despair at his rejection by the three Rhinedaughters: "(H8a:) Wehe! (H8b:) Ach, Wehe! (…) (H23 Embryo or H37 Embryo:) Has the third one, so true, betrayed me as well?" As Cooke said, the conjunction in this interlude of H8 and H37 recalls Alberich's cry of woe at his irrevocable loss of love. Cooke also observed that H37 here slows down and transforms into a tragic, dark variant of the essential Love Motif, H39, which he described as a symbol for love lost from the world thanks to Alberich's love-curse. Though H39 is a love motif Cooke said it incorporates the Ring Motif's (H17's) harmony. One of Cooke's stellar insights is that this musical prelude to R.3—which dramatizes the consequences of the Rhinedaughters' rejection of Alberich's bid for love—provides a psychological portrait of Alberich as he converts what had been his hope of finding love into a vengeful desire to destroy it (by exposing it as an illusion). As Cooke explained, the Rhinedaughters' joyous cry of "(H11:) Heiajaheia!" in celebration of the Rhinegold's aesthetic splendor, is transformed in this prelude into the harsh, rhythmic motif of the Nibelungs' slave labor, their Forging Motif H38 which conveys their arduous forging of Alberich's Hoard of treasure in Nibelheim's mines under his loveless coercion.

Alberich's renunciation of love (emancipation from dependence on animal instinct) for power's sake (the power of the human mind) was the precondition for our invention of the gods, who embody our artificial, futile attempt to restore lost innocence. As Wagner said: "(The state of Innocence could not come to men's consciousness until they had lost it. This … struggle for its re-attainment … is the soul of the whole movement of civilisation … . It is the impulse to depart from a generality that seems hostile to us, to arrive at egoistic satisfaction in ourselves … .)." [393W-{1–2/49} *Jesus of Nazareth*, PW Vol. VIII. p. 320]

THE RHINEGOLD ≈ SCENE THREE
(NIBELHEIM)
WOTAN, LOGE, MIME, ALBERICH, THE NIBELUNGS,
AND ALBERICH TRANSFORMED INTO A SERPENT/DRAGON
AND TOAD

Having followed Wotan and Loge into Alberich's underworld hell, Nibelheim's mines, we've entered what Mime will describe in S.1.2 as the earth's (Erda's) navel-nest ("umbilical nest"). After starting to familiarize himself with Schopenhauer's philosophy in 1854, Wagner was influenced by Schopenhauer's thought in all his future endeavors, but also in his reassessment of his completed artworks. But Feuerbach's influence on the *Ring* was so pervasive that Wagner found ways to incorporate Schopenhauer's philosophy mostly where he found parallels to it either in Feuerbach's philosophy, or Wagner's own pre-Schopenhauerian conception of the *Ring*. An excellent introduction to R.3 is Wagner's Schopenhauerian comparison between the unconscious inspiration which he presumed generated Beethoven's music, and the (Schopenhauer's) Will's workshop, where (evoking Nibelheim) all moves and stirs as in the earth's (i.e., Erda's) bowels: " ... Rub. plays us the first part of the (Opus) 106 Sonata [Beethoven], and our delight is boundless! ... R: 'It is like being taken into the workshop of the Will, one sees everything moving and stirring as if in the bowels of the earth.'—'Anyone who could translate this into words would have the key to the enigma of the world.'" [1055W-{1/17/81} CD Vol. II, p. 600] Wagner's observation that by translating this inspired music into words (as Siegfried will grasp the conceptual meaning of the Woodbird's songs H137ab and H138ab) we'd find the key to the world's enigma is also a key to the *Ring*. We'll be less ambitious and merely suggest that Alberich's nefarious doings in Nibelheim might provide a key to the enigma of human nature.

The action begins with Alberich's demand that his brother Mime hand over a magic helmet, the Tarnhelm, which Alberich designed, but Mime manufactured:

> **[pp. 89–90] Alberich:** Give me the trinket! (...) ([[H40A orch]] [= H33 vari]) (...) Everything forged and fitted together just as I asked! So the simpleton slyly wanted to trick me, keep for himself the costly jewel that my cunning alone taught him to craft? (...) (H40A: he places the metalwork on his head as a 'Tarnhelm.') (...) [[H40B orch:]] [= H40A continuation] 'Night and mist, like to none (:H40B orch)!'—(He disappears and in his place can be seen a column of mist.) [Alberich and Mime converse: (...)] [Alberich, invisible, whips Mime] (...) Nibelungs all, bow down to Alberich! [modulating chromatically and featuring a falling diminished fifth, a key ingredient of H17:] Everywhere now he lies in wait in order to keep you under guard; rest and repose have melted away; for him you must toil where you cannot see him; where you don't expect him, there you shall find him: you're subject to him for ever!

As Alberich speaks to Mime of the Tarnhelm, and demonstrates its power of transformation, we hear two distinct parts of the Tarnhelm Motif, H40AB. For Dunning the first version H40A is the Tarnhelm Motif per se, and H40B, a continuation of H40A, the "Tarnhelm's Transformations." Since Loge represents man's capacity for artistic self-deception, the Tarnhelm motifs' derivation from Loge's H33 suggests that the Tarnhelm's power to transform is the imagination. Initially, Alberich employs it to make himself invisible, but we'll later learn it can be used to alter one's form, or to travel instantly to another place. It represents imagination's mobility, a faculty of the human mind (Ring). Through imagination we can either organize aspects of our objective experience for analysis, or reconstruct experience according to our subjective feelings. We can travel in time through memory of the past and imaginative anticipation of the future, or travel in space in an instant by imagining things which aren't present. Alberich through the Tarnhelm has made himself the invisible spur compelling his fellow Nibelungs into slavery to obtain a hoard of treasure from earth's bowels. But Wagner means by this something more serious than mining. After making himself invisible, Alberich whips Mime in triumph, boasting that now Alberich keeps him under guard, and rest and repose are gone. Mime and the other Nibelungs must toil for Alberich where they can't see him, and, most importantly, they'll find him where they least expect him. Thus the Nibelungs are subject to him forever. He's stating that his egoism is the hidden influence of the mind's power upon all men. He's saying also that our restless striving, which I've previously described as the product of our inherent inability to accept things as they are, but to always strive to surpass our limitations, is human nature. The enslaved Nibelung dwarfs are Wagner's prosaic vision of human nature, what humans are in reality rather than ideally.

With respect to Alberich's ego's invisible yet all-powerful, omnipresent influence, Feuerbach noted that because our mind's operations were invisible to early men, who were ignorant of the physical process behind thought and feeling, man mistook thinking for something transcendent and spiritual: "... because the activity of the brain is the most hidden, withdrawn, soundless, and imperceptible activity, man has come to look upon this activity as an absolutely *disembodied*, ... abstract being, to which he has given the name of spirit. But since this being owes its existence solely to man's ignorance of the organic conditions of thought and to the imagination with which he compensates for his ignorance ... , all the difficulties it involved are dispelled." [242F-LER, pp. 154–155] Alberich's warning to his fellow Nibelungs that he can be found where least expected suggests that his egoism is the foundation even of the gods, and of our human ideals, where we'd least expect to find this mundane, vulgar influence. As Feuerbach put it, egoism is the hidden motive behind all our actions, even our longing to transcend our bodily and natural limitations and liberate ourselves from subjection to our egoistic drives: "... *he* [man] *cannot break with his nature; even the wish fantasies which depart from it are determined by it; they may seem to go far afield, yet they always fall back on it, just as a stone thrown into the air falls back on the ground.*" [250F-LER, p. 164; See also 343F-LER, p. 324; and 218F-

LER, p. 101] Alberich's remark that the Nibelungs are subject to him forever tells us we can never transcend our nature, can't escape subjection to egoism or the bonds of natural law. In the *Ring*, these natural bonds are Fate: everything is inevitable, is as it must be. As Wotan the Wanderer will confess to Alberich in S.2.1, everything goes its own way, and one can alter nothing.

Loge, finding Mime in despair wondering how he might free himself from Alberich's steel grip, offers to help him, while the orchestra introduces a new motif H41 ("Servitude"), a variant of H8, which is initially associated with Mime's servitude to Alberich, but later expands its meaning. Introducing another new motif H42, Mime asks who'd ever help him, since he must obey Alberich:

> [p. 91] Loge: Hey, Mime! (...) What plagues and pinches you so? [[H41 orch]] [= H8a vari] [Mime and Loge converse: (...)] ... I want to help you, Mime! (...)
>
> Mime: [[H42 voc/orch:]] [= H24 vari] Who'd ever help me? I'm bound to obey my own bloodbrother (:H42 voc/orch) (H42 orch), (H17:) who's bound me in fetters fast (:H17).

H42, "Mime's Scheming," is based on H24 (a Loge Motif), related to H26, and is the basis for H106 (associated with Mime's Scheming to exploit Siegfried) and H124 (the Norns' unwittingly ironic comment that Wotan engraved honorable treaties on his spear, when we know they weren't made in good faith). H26 was associated at its inception with Wotan's propensity—inspired by Loge—to break the contracts Wotan has made, and H24 represents the advantages to be drawn from one's enemy's envy by Loge's cunning. Since the Nibelungs represent us men as the objective, cynical Alberich sees us, i.e., as a craven animal without inherent value, an object, rather than as man the idealist views us, as a subject (even as a god or hero), Loge's offer to help Mime escape his subjection to Alberich's Ring power is an expression of the religious imagination's capacity to lift us above the level of a moral dwarf, by granting us the illusion we have divine status and transcendent value. It's only through the gods and their agent of self-deception Loge that lowly man can free himself from his prosaic existence, at least in imagination.

Loge inquires of Mime how he found himself in this pickle. Mime recounts the pre-*Ring* mythological history of the Nibelungs, an imaginary paradisal period during which Nibelung craftsmen labored with love to produce jewels for ornament and play. But, Mime complains, Alberich has now employed his Ring-power to make them amass a golden hoard for him by mining it under his whip's coercion in the earth's bowels:

> [pp. 91–2] Mime: (H42:) With cunning artifice Alberich crafted a yellow ring of gold from the Rhine: at its powerful spell (H17:) we tremble in awe (:H42) for with it he bends us all to his will (:H17), the Nibelungs' army of night. (H38:; H112 embryo voc:) Carefree smiths, we used to fashion trinkets for our womenfolk, delightful gems and delicate Nibelung toys: we cheerfully laughed at our pains (:H112 embryo voc). (H38:; H8:) Now the criminal makes us crawl into crevices (:H8), ever toiling for him alone.

Through the gold of the ring his greed can divine where more gleaming veins lie buried in shafts: there we must seek and search and dig, (H17:) smelting the spoils and working the cast without rest or repose (:H17), to heap up the hoard for our lord (:H8; :H38). (H38)

Mime's account of a pre-fallen carefree humanity which once produced goods for the enjoyment of all, in love and beauty, is Wagner's pre-Marxist romantic metaphor for a fantasy golden age of handicraft when the worker took pleasure in the process of production, rather than seeking only profit or slaving under the sting of coercion enforced by those who controlled the means of production and property. Mime is distinguishing what's produced for ulterior motives, for "use," within Alberich's world, from art produced for its own sake, from sheer love of it. Feuerbach gave Wagner the cue for Mime's mytho-historical narrative in his remark that true works of genius don't merit praise because the genius produces out of his own nature, reaping joy instead of suffering drudgery: "... the poet *must* bring forth poetry, the philosopher *must* philosophise. They have the highest satisfaction in the activity of creation, apart from any collateral or ulterior purpose." [169F-EOC, p. 321] And here's Wagner's take on Feuerbach's distinction of labor under outside coercion from the labor of love, whose value lies in the act of creation itself: "The true artist finds delight not only in the aim of his creation, but also in the very process of creation .... (...) The journeyman reckons only ... the profit which his toil shall bring him; the energy which he expends, gives him no pleasure; ... his toil is but a fettering chain. (...) [This] ... is the lot of the Slave of Industry; and our modern factories afford us the sad picture of the deepest degradation of man,—constant labour, killing both body and soul, without joy or love, often almost without aim." [406W-{6–8/49} 'Art and Revolution,' PW Vol. I, pp. 48–49; See also 399W-{4/49} 'The Revolution,' PW Vol. VIII, p. 236]

If, as Feuerbach asserts, egoism is the primary motive behind all human action (behind both the Nibelungs' fearful obedience, and Alberich's tyrannical command), then to avoid becoming a slave one must make all others one's slaves. In such a world there could be no motive to sacrifice one's own interests for others, no compassion, no love. But there's more going on here than G.B. Shaw supposed when, in his *The Perfect Wagnerite*, he concluded that the Nibelungs' enslavement in Nibelheim is Wagner's indictment of the ill-effects of rampant capitalism and the exploitation of labor in the industrialization of Europe. Though Wagner surely had the wage-slaves of capitalistic industrialization in mind when he first conceived this scene, his *Ring* grew to embrace a far more timeless, universal understanding of human nature, of which the terrible condition of 19th century Europe's working class was just one instance. The Nibelungs' forced labor represents the Biblical notion that fallen man, having lost his preconscious paradise of animal instinct, must laboriously learn and work to satisfy his needs. Their endless labor is Wagner's metaphor for human nature.

Now Mime explains why his interests might correspond with those of Wotan and Loge, for he sought to keep the Tarnhelm he'd made, at Alberich's behest, to free himself from enslavement (as they are), hoping instead to force Alberich to serve Mime's needs:

> [p. 92] **Mime:** On me, the most wretched of all, he forced the worst of all tasks: (H40A:; H38:) a metal helm he bade me weld; he told me exactly how to craft it (:H38). (...) (:H40A) (H17 varis:) ... I wanted to keep the helm for myself, by means of its magic free me from Alberich's sway—... perhaps outwit my tormenter and, placing him in my power, (H17 vari:) wrest the ring away from his grasp, so that, just as I'm now a slave to that bully, (H17 in jaunty vari with triangle: harshly) he'd serve me, a free man, in turn (:H17 vari)! (H8; H15)
>
> **Loge:** ... why did you fail?
>
> **Mime:** Alas, I who wrought the work (H40A:) failed to guess the spell aright ... (:H40A)!

In this respect Mime is like Wotan, wishing to free himself from Alberich's threat by co-opting Alberich's Ring-power and using it to serve Mime's needs and desires, compelling Alberich to serve Mime instead. This suggests an underlying kinship between Wotan and Alberich's brother Mime, a kinship implicit both in Wotan's description of himself in S.1.2 as "Light-Alberich," and in Alberich's Ring (H17ab) giving motival birth to the gods' heaven Valhalla (H18ab). The clue to their underlying identity is Feuerbach's remark that religious belief satisfies our practical motives: " ... the religious imagination [the Tarnhelm in Wotan's hands] is not the free imagination of the artist, but has a practical egoistic purpose ... ." [269F-LER, p. 196; See also 271F-LER, p. 200]

This culminates in Loge's offer to free the Nibelungs from their "Noth," their anguish at being the victims of Alberich's will-to-power, embodied by their Labor (Forging) Motif H38:

> [p. 93] **Wotan:** (H32B:) ... our foe will fall with the help of your [Loge's] cunning (:H32B). (...)
>
> **Mime:** Who are you strangers ... ?
>
> **Loge:** Friends of yours; from their plight ["Noth"] we shall free the Nibelung folk. (H38)

If the gods, with the help of their artist-savior Loge, are able to co-opt the objective power of our human mind (Alberich's Ring), especially the imagination (the Tarnhelm), to serve their subjective desire for illusory consolations, Mime and the other Nibelungs might be exalted to a near-divine dignity and seeming freedom from subjection to their egoistic drives which are the basis of their enslavement by Alberich. Believing in immortal gods as founders and lawgivers, or even as ancestors, men can exalt themselves above their otherwise animal existence, giving life transcendent meaning and value. If Wotan and Loge can take possession of Alberich's Ring, Tarnhelm, and Hoard, thus taking our mind (Alberich's Ring) prisoner, Wotan and Loge can transform Mime's prosaic needs, desires, and fears into the illusion we possess transcendent value.

Alberich reappears, demonstrating the power he wields with his Ring. He holds his fellow Nibelungs in contempt, as a downtrodden, craven herd:

> [pp. 93–4] **Alberich:** (H8:; H38:) You idle herd, there in a heap pile up the hoard (:H8; :H38)! (...) Contemptible creatures ... ! (...) (He suddenly becomes aware of Wotan and Loge.) (H49 embryo:) Hey! (...) Who's broken in here (:H49 embryo)? (...) [Alberich forces Mime to join the Nibelungs in smelting and smithing] (...) You'll taste my whip if you don't dig quickly! That none shall be idle Mime shall answer ... : that I'm lying in wait where no one expects me—he knows ... well enough. (...) (He draws the ring from his finger, kisses it and holds it out threateningly: H17) **[[H43a orch:]]** [= H8a vari with H17 harmony] Tremble and quail, downtrodden herd (:H43a orch): **[[H43b orch:)]** [= H8b vari with H17 harmony] be quick, and obey the lord of the ring (:H43b orch)! (amidst howling and shrieking the Nibelungs—Mime among them—scatter and slip away into the shafts all around them.)

Alberich's suspicion of his two new visitors, Wotan and Loge, and his exercise of Ring-power over his fellow Nibelungs, has introduced two new motifs to the *Ring*, respectively. We hear a H49 embryo (Resentment/Greed/Envy—"Neid") as Alberich, in his resentment of potential rivals for his Ring-power, inquires who his new visitors are, presuming they envy his treasure and are a threat. Cooke notes it's a syncopation of the Ring Motif's (H17's) harmony. H43, Cooke's "Power of the Ring Motif," stems, he says, from Alberich's cry of woe "(H8a) Wehe! (H8b) Ach, wehe!," and incorporates harmony drawn from the Ring Motif H17. Alberich concluded that love is an illusion and will swear to make all others renounce love as he had. His cry expresses our anguish at irrevocably lost innocence. Cooke noted that H43ab later produces a variant H173ab, Hagen's Watch Motif.

Alberich's assessment of Nibelung (human) nature as contemptible, according to Wagner's later writings, is the view of ourselves modern science would compel us to accept, that we're merely physical animals, a product of the evolution of species with a uniquely symbolic consciousness, who have no free will, no transcendent spirit (no basis of hope for immortal life), no divine origin, and no capacity for love and compassion which can't be trumped by fear and pain (regard for self). For Wagner, this modern understanding of man was intolerable to contemplate. He found a basis for it in Feuerbach. For Feuerbach, where the objective, scientific man (described as "heathens" who make no effort to set themselves or their gods outside Nature) knows man as animal and common, the religious (Christian) man exalts himself with the pride stemming from his illusion he has a divine origin and immortal soul: "If the Christian severed man from all community with nature, ... which stigmatised the remotest comparison of man with the brutes as an impious violation of human dignity, the heathens ... fell into the opposite extreme, into that spirit of depreciation which abolishes the distinction between man and the brute... ." [104F-EOC, p. 151; See also 162F-EOC, p. 309]

Wagner was greatly troubled by a problem in Feuerbach's thinking which seems not to have troubled Feuerbach, who seems never to have reconciled his optimistic appraisal of modern secular, scientific life with the consequence for man which must follow logically from it, that egoism underlies all human feelings, thoughts, and actions in such a prosaic, spiritless world. Wagner feared such an objective understanding of man would encourage expression of our inherent and universal egoism at the expense of benign impulses. He saw acceptance of egoism's primacy behind what he regarded as the inexorable decline of civilization, a fate he described as inimical to all spiritual aspiration: "The crime and the curse of our social intercourse have lain in this: that the mere physical maintenance of life has been till now the one object of our care, — a real care that has devoured our souls and bodies and well nigh lamed each spiritual impulse." [411W-{6–8/49} 'Art and Revolution,' PW Vol. I, p. 57] Alberich's sadism toward his own kind is Wagner's dramatization of his reluctant insight that accepting our status as mere animals, with all that follows from this cynical admission, requires us to renounce transcendent love and compassion as unnatural: "'A human being should not feel pity,' R. says. 'Nature doesn't want it; he should be as cruel as the animals; pity has no place in the world.'" [812W-{2/8/72} CD Vol. I, p. 456] And he recorded a striking instance of his terrible insight into the sadism and cynicism of the powerful, inspired by a story about the Zulu King Chaka's cruel imagination: "R. relates to me the biography of the Zulu King ... ; 'No animal is as cruel as a human being, it is only the human being who takes pleasure in tormenting; the cat playing with a mouse does not know what this means to the mouse, but a human being does know.'" [961W-{3/23/79} CD Vol. II, p. 281]

It's possible that Wagner's anti-Semitism was his unconscious projection of his suspicion that all humans are by nature craven, unspiritual beings, on to the Jews, as a means to purge his favored Aryans or Germans of what's after all just human nature. In this reading Mime, considered by some to be Wagner's stereotype for the Jews, represents Wotan's egoistic nature which he must disavow, Wotan's true, prosaic motive in wishing to (like Mime) dispossess Alberich of his Ring. It was Feuerbach who described the Jews' God as the embodiment of egoism and practical need: "Their [the Jews'] principle, their God, is the most practical principle in the world,—namely, egoism; and moreover egoism in the form of religion." [84F-EOC, p. 114] But why, if Alberich like Mime is construed as Wagner's stereotypical representation of Jews, is he heartless towards his own kind, the Nibelungs? One would have thought, given anti-Semites' assumption that the Jews as a cultural entity have evil designs on the Gentiles among whom they live, that Alberich wouldn't have enslaved the Nibelungs but instead led them as a free people to enslave the gods and Giants. Though (we'll soon learn) Alberich does intend to storm Valhalla with his host of night (the Nibelungs), this is a metaphor for Alberich's intent to confront our illusory ideals with the bitter truth about human nature. The Nibelungs remain Alberich's slaves under all circumstances. The Nibelungs' forced labor, aside from being Wagner's metaphor for the Biblical concept of man's "Fall" (the price we pay for our acquisition of symbolic consciousness), is also his metaphor for Feuerbach's notion that men objectively attuned to the bitter realities and limits of Nature (as Alberich is), instead of the consolations of religious and artistic illusion, work, rather than pray: "The man who does not exclude from his mind the idea of the world, ... that every effect has its natural cause, ...—such a man does not pray: he only works; he transforms his attainable wishes into objects of real activity ... ... he limits ... his being by the world, as a member of which he conceives himself ... ." [94F-EOC, p. 123] Alberich's enslavement of the Nibelungs expresses the price of anguish ("Noth") we pay for our gift of conscious mind, which compels us to gain knowledge of Nature by force, to satisfy our need through laborious effort.

Loge, describing himself as Alberich's kinsman and friend, expresses outrage that Alberich has denied this bond and regards himself as Loge's enemy. However, as Alberich points out, in that case it's Loge who, in allying himself with the gods, has betrayed Alberich:

[pp. 94–5] Alberich: (H32B:) Envy ["Neid"] brings you to Nibelheim: such dauntless guests, believe me, I know well (:H32B).

Loge: You know me well, you childish elf? Then say who I am that you yelp like that. In a frozen hole where you coweringly lay, who'd have given you light and warming fire if Loge hadn't smiled upon you? What use would your forge-work have been (H33:) if I hadn't heated your forge? I am your kinsman and once was your friend ... (:H33)! (H33)

Alberich: (H33:) So Loge now smiles on the light-elves, cunning rogue that he is? If, false traitor, you're now their friend, as you once were a friend to me, haha!—I'm glad—from them I've nothing to fear (:H33). (...) (H47 embryo?:) I trust your dishonesty, not your honesty! (adopting a defiant attitude :H47 embryo?) I can safely defy you all! [[H44a orch]]

Alberich, observing that Loge betrayed his kinship and friendship with Alberich by working now on behalf of the gods, introduces a new motif H44 as he explains that, thanks to this betrayal, he trusts Loge's dishonesty, not his honesty, and that for this reason he can now safely defy the gods. H44, Dunning's "Alberich's Revolt," in effect inverts Wotan's Spear Motif H19. H44 is also an embryo of a very important motif H81 ("Wotan's Revolt"), which will be introduced in V.2.2 when Wotan explodes in inchoate despair, just prior to granting Brünnhilde's wish that he confess what troubles him to her, his acknowledgment of the inevitability of Alberich's victory over the gods. H44 at its inception here and in several subsequent instances in R.3 expresses Alberich's intent to overthrow the gods' rule. Alberich's confidence is founded on the fact the gods depend on Loge's cunning, our artistic self-deceit, whereas Alberich's Ring power is founded on truth. The gods' dependence on the liar god Loge is predestined to failure because Alberich's objective truth will overthrow the illusions which sustain the gods. In this sense Loge, posing as the gods' redeemer, will in the end betray them. Alberich has foreseen that the means Wotan employs to redeem the gods from Alberich's Ring Curse will fulfill it.

Loge's claim of blood-kinship with Alberich Wagner probably based on the Greek myth of Prometheus, who provided Wagner a model for both Loge and Brünnhilde. Prometheus was originally a pre-Olympian Titan who formerly supported his kin, but he betrayed them for the sake of the upstart gods of Olympus, employing his cunning to help them overthrow their forefathers, the Titans. Through Prometheus's treacherous cunning the Olympian gods co-opted the Titans' power and consigned them to oblivion, much as Wotan employs Alberich's relative Loge both to consign the Giants and the gods' debt to them to oblivion, and to overthrow Alberich's foundational power and co-opt it to secure the newfound power of the upstart gods in Valhalla. But Prometheus, having helped establish the Olympian gods by betraying his fellow Titans, betrayed the gods in turn by supporting mortal man's bid to share in the gods' power, stealing the gods' prerogative fire for mortal man's sake, and giving mortal man the divine gift of foresight, which granted men divine wisdom minus the virtue—immortality—which made that wisdom tolerable. For mortal man could now foresee his inevitable death, just as Erda's prophecy of the gods' inevitable end in R.4 will plunge Wotan into irredeemable despair. This foresight of death is the cause of Prometheus's un-healing wound, which in the myth is Zeus's punishment for Prometheus' betrayal of the gods, a Greek version of the "Fall." Prometheus's betrayal of the gods for mortal man's sake is the basis for Brünnhilde's betrayal of Wotan for the mortal Wälsungs' sake. Similarly, Wotan's punishment of Brünnhilde for supporting his mortal spawn the Wälsungs in defiance of the gods' law, by exposing her, asleep, on a mountaintop, to be subjected sexually to any man who wakes her, is modeled on Zeus's punishment of Prometheus by exposing him on a mountaintop, where he suffers from an un-healing wound perpetually picked at by vultures. This is part of the received wisdom of Wagner scholarship, but its implications seem never to have been adequately explored.

Loge—embodying man's artistic imagination, and thus linked not only musically but conceptually with Alberich's Tarnhelm whose motif H40AB Loge's H33 produces—once served Alberich's quest for the power which only the human mind with its imagination can acquire, but as servant of the gods (of our religious illusions) Loge has become the archetypal artist-hero who helps us redeem ourselves from the truth by deceiving ourselves unwittingly, substituting consoling illusion for unbearable knowledge which is consigned to oblivion. In other words, our artistic imagination Loge is about to trick Alberich into giving up the truth (the Ring) for the sake of a consoling illusion, that the gods rule our lives and give them transcendent meaning. This is what's behind Loge's conspiracy with Wotan to co-opt Alberich's Ring power, Tarnhelm, and Hoard of Treasure. In this way Alberich's power of thought (imagination) will serve feeling (the Giants, and gods) instead of Alberich's quest for objective knowledge, allowing Wotan to enjoy the benefits of the mind's (Ring's) power without having to sacrifice love.

In order to intimidate Wotan and the Valhallan gods Alberich draws Wotan's attention to the means through which he'll overthrow their rule, his accumulation of his Hoard of Treasure, whose motif H45, introduced here, Cooke says is derived from H17b, the Ring Motif's second segment:

[pp. 95–6] (H44a orch)

Alberich: Do you see the hoard that my army has heaped up for me there? [**Loge:** (…)] [[**H45 orch:**]] [= H17b vari] That's just for today, a pitiful pile: daunting and great it shall grow hereafter (:H45 orch).

Wotan: But what good is the hoard since Nibelheim's joyless and naught can be bought here with wealth?

Alberich: To create yet more wealth and to hide away wealth Nibelheim's night serves me well; (H45:) and yet with the hoard, heaped up in the cave (:H45), I shall … work wonders: The whole of the world I'll win with it as my own. (H17)

Wotan's question to Alberich, what possible use his Hoard could be to him, since nothing can be bought with it in Nibelheim, is the only instance in the *Ring* in which Alberich's hoard is spoken of as wealth which can be used to acquire other things of use and value. After this, and especially when Wotan gathers what's described as a hoard ("Hort") of knowledge from Erda by consorting with her in the bowels of the earth, or what's the same thing, gathers a hoard of knowledge or runes during his wanderings over the earth, the hoard becomes a metaphor for man's historical experience of the world (the earth, Erda), man's gradual acquisition of objective knowledge. This embraces both man's self-knowledge, and knowledge of Nature (Erda), which gave birth to man. Alberich's and Wotan's gradual enlargement of this treasury of knowledge, a natural outgrowth of our power of thought (the Ring), is what grants us actual power. This is one of the most important metaphors in the *Ring*, and many subsequent plot developments depend on grasping this.

Feuerbach's and Wagner's writings (and Wagner's recorded remarks) are an especially rich source for our metaphorical reading. A basis for Alberich's insatiable need to accumulate an ever larger hoard can be found in Feuerbach's remark: "The desire of knowledge is infinite; reason then is infinite." [153F-EOC, p. 287] Having read—following Feuerbach's lead—Alberich and Wotan (Light-Alberich) as metaphors for collective, historical man instead of individual characters, we can see how Alberich's and Wotan's slow accumulation of their respective hoards of treasure and knowledge finds its basis in Feuerbach's observation that though each individual man's knowledge and power is limited, collective human knowledge and power is unlimited and infinite, since many contribute and new knowledge incorporates prior knowledge: "The knowledge of a single man is limited, but reason, science, is unlimited, for it is a common act of mankind, … not only because innumerable men co-operate in the construction of science, but also in the … profound sense … that the scientific genius of a particular age comprehends in itself the thinking powers of the preceding age … ." [77F-EOC, p. 83] We recall that the Rhinedaughters told Alberich that through the Ring (the human mind) he could obtain limitless power. Alberich's Ring doesn't grant him immediate world-power. Rather, thanks to the Ring's power Alberich compels all men to contribute, over time, to the gradual accumulation of his hoard of knowledge which will eventually grant him (man) world dominion. This, according to Feuerbach, highlights the distinction between what religion (Wotan) promises, allegedly infinite satisfaction of all desires and alleviation of all fears, and what natural man (scientific and technological man) can reasonably gain for himself from Nature by virtue of his labor: " … unlike … religious imagination, civilization is not all-powerful. No more than nature can make gold out of leather after the manner of God, can civilization, which masters nature … by natural means, perform miracles." [276F-LER, p. 208]

After Wotan co-opts Alberich's Ring-power, the Tarnhelm's (imagination's) Wonder, and Alberich's ever growing Hoard, Wotan will carry on Alberich's acquisition of power by obtaining knowledge from Mother Nature (Erda) in the course of his historical experience, as the Wanderer. But Wotan's knowledge will temporarily be subject to censorship by religious man's fear of the truth, which will be embodied by Fafner, transformed by the Tarnhelm (like Alberich) into a serpent or dragon. Once they come into his possession in R.4, Fafner, guarding Alberich's Hoard, Tarnhelm, and Ring, will deny man access to that (scientific) knowledge which will overthrow our belief in gods, a virtual incarnation of religious faith's fear of intellectual inquiry. Feuerbach lends support to this through his identification of god with the collective experience of historical man, particularly in his acquisition of that knowledge which eventually reaches critical mass in the Western World by producing self-consciously objective scientific inquiry: "My knowledge, my will, is limited; but my limit is not the limit of another man, to say nothing of mankind; what is difficult to me is easy to another; what is impossible, inconceivable, to one age, is to the coming age conceivable and possible. … the future always unveils the fact that the alleged limits of the species were only limits of individuals. The most striking proofs of this are presented by the history of philosophy and of physical science." [105F-EOC, pp. 152–153] God (Wotan) can be construed as the totality of perfections belonging to the human species, attributes dispersed in bits and pieces among real men, this perfection realizing itself in the course of world history: "… God as the total of all realities or perfections is nothing other than the total of the attributes of the species—dispersed among men and realizing themselves in the course of world history … . (…) … what the individual man does not know and cannot do all of mankind together knows and can do. … the divine knowledge that knows simultaneously every particular has its reality in the knowledge of the species." [177F-PPF, p. 17] This power we obtain by virtue of our gift of conscious thought (the Ring), through acquisition of knowledge of the world, is the world-power which the Rhinedaughters promised Alberich he could obtain by forging a Ring from the Rhinegold.

It's noteworthy that Feuerbach construed this gradual accumulation of worldly power through the advancement in human knowledge as secular man's substitute for the gods' offer of immortality in the hereafter, a future of ever greater power and wisdom for collective (but not the individual) man: "Those human desires that are not imaginary and fantastic are fulfilled in the course of history ... . innumerable things that today we do not know but would like to know, will be known to our descendents. We must therefore modify our goals and exchange divinity, in which only man's groundless and gratuitous desires are fulfilled, for the human race ... , religion for education, the hereafter in heaven for the hereafter on earth, ... the ... future of mankind." [316F-LER, p. 281] Wagner paraphrased Feuerbach's thesis that man's true "hereafter" lies in collective, historical man's future, not in a supernatural heaven of redemption, but from the uniquely Wagnerian perspective that this hereafter can be found in his own art. [See 598W-{4/13/53} Letter to Franz Liszt, SLRW, p. 284] Feuerbach's thesis explains why Fafner told Fasolt that the immortality the Giants could obtain from the goddess Freia's golden apples, could also be obtained by possessing Alberich's Hoard of Treasure. Feuerbach's observations on man's historical advancement in knowledge recall the passage from Wagner's "Art and Climate" I cited previously [See 447W-{2/50} 'Art and Climate,' PW Vol. I, p. 252], in which he described how Nature eventually left man to fend for himself, and that his growing consciousness of his need made him aware also of his power. Nature thus "... became the object of his observation, inquiry, and dominion." And Wagner added that the process whereby man forced Nature to satisfy "... those needs that waxed with his ever-waxing powers, is the history of Culture." It's Alberich, not Wotan, who became conscious of his "Noth" and power by making Nature his object of observation, inquiry, and dominion, after the Rhinedaughters (Voices of Nature) forced him to satisfy himself when they wouldn't.

But there's also ample evidence in Wagner's writings that he construed the Nibelung Hoard as a metaphor for money, capital accumulation, property, a reading suggested by Wotan when he wondered why Alberich would bother amassing his hoard in joyless Nibelheim where nothing can be bought. In the following passage Wagner interpreted Alberich's Ring Curse as expressing what Wagner describes as the curse of money: "Clever though be the many thoughts expressed ... about the invention of money and its enormous value as a civiliser, against such praises should be set the curse to which it has always been doomed in song and legend. ... gold here figures as the demon strangling manhood's innocence ... . The Nibelung's fateful ring become a pocket-book, might well complete the eerie picture of the spectral world-controller." [1066W-{1–2/81} 'Know Thyself'—2nd Supplement to 'Religion and Art,' PW Vol. VI, p. 268] Who can fail to see in Wagner's description of the Ring transformed into a pocket book which becomes the "spectral world-controller," Alberich, made invisible by the Tarnhelm, enslaving the Nibelungs to serve him forever even where they can't see or least suspect him, or fail to identify Alberich's Ring Curse with the curse of money? Such evidence was the basis for G. B. Shaw's hugely influential *Ring* interpretation. Wagner couldn't have provided a more definitive declaration of this particular allegorical intent than the following comment recorded by Cosima in 1881: "Recently R. expressed his pleasure at having provided in 'Der Ring des Nibelungen' a complete picture of the curse of greed for money, and the disaster it brings about." [1074W-{2/15/81} CD Vol. II, p. 624] Our main problem in accepting this evidence from Wagner himself is that it only makes sense of a few of the *Ring*'s details seen in isolation, whereas the other evidence we find in such profusion not only in the *Ring* libretto and music, but in Feuerbach's and Wagner's writings (and Wagner's recorded remarks), and in Wagner's other repertory operas and music dramas, for our broader reading, makes sense of virtually the whole *Ring*, even those portions oft invoked to support the notion that it's an allegory about the curse of money. Though Wagner's conception of his *Ring* drama in its earliest phase may have been an allegory of the cultural damage which was the price for industrialization and capitalism, an emphasis on profit at the expense of our humanity, in the course of writing it he broadened and deepened his vision, realizing that greed for money or property or political power are just a few expressions among many of an inherent egoism which Wagner acknowledged had poisoned human history, and might end in our self-destruction.

Alberich now describes what will happen when he fully asserts his Ring's and Hoard's power to threaten the gods' rule (religious faith):

> **[p. 96] Alberich:** You who live, laugh, and love up there in the breath of gentle breezes (H22 vari violin): in my golden grasp I'll capture all you gods! (H44a[[b]]; H17) (H16:) As love has been forsworn by me, so all that lives shall also forswear it (:H16); (H22 vari violin:) lured by gold, you'll lust after gold alone (:H22 vari violin). (H44ab; H17)

We hear H44 again as Alberich threatens that someday he'll capture in his golden grasp the gods who up until then have lived, laughed, and loved on the heights above Nibelheim, this time including segment H44b (only heard thrice), an agitated descending figure which expresses anxiety. H16 accompanies Alberich as he explains what he means by this: just as he renounced love, all that lives will renounce it. Lured by gold, the gods will lust after it alone. Given the premises of our allegorical reading, Alberich means that in the long run we (Wotan) will forsake our religious mythology, which grants us only psychological and emotional satisfaction, in favor of that knowledge which can bring us concrete, worldly power. Man, Alberich suggests, will eventually turn secular and scientific. Light-Alberich (Wotan) will become (or be indistinguishable from) Alberich himself (Dark-Alberich). Since I've interpreted Alberich's hoard of treasure as a metaphor for objective knowledge of Nature, the notion that we humans will be lured by gold alone doesn't merely allude to the power we accrue through money and property, but also the power we accrue over our environment and fellow men through scientific knowledge and technology, and perhaps even political power. It was this power, granted by scientific and secular man's self-emancipation from rule by gods, his freedom of inquiry unencumbered by religious faith's censorship of knowledge, which has allowed us to obtain that objective knowledge of Nature which, according to Feuerbach, has given the Western World its modern hegemony (now fast eroding) in political, military, economic, and cultural power: "Let us not ... find fault with Western man for ... ignoring the implications of his ["religious"] faith and .. in practice ... abjuring it; for it is solely to ... this practical unbelief, this instinctive atheism and egoism that we owe all progress, all the inventions which distinguish Christians from Mohammedans, and Occidentals in general from Orientals." [253F-LER, p. 167]

This grants us further insight into the meaning of the Nibelungs' slave labor, dedicated to accumulating a hoard of treasure in Mother Earth's (Erda's) bowels. For Feuerbach said that the illusion of Godhead (Wotan) has two parts, imagination (say, Loge) and Nature (Erda): " ... *Godhead consists ... of two components, one originating in man's imagination, the other in nature. 'You must pray,' says the one component, the god differentiated from nature* [Wotan]. *'You must work,' says the other, the god who is not differentiated from nature and merely expresses the essence of nature* [Alberich]. *For nature is a worker bee, while the gods are drones.*" [337F-LER, p. 317]

So let's ask one of the most important questions posed by Wagner's *Ring*. Is Alberich's threat to demonstrate that all human beings will forsake love for gold and the power it can bring, that everyone has their price, founded in truth? Is it true that all our other motives, especially those of compassion and self-sacrifice for the sake of others, will always be trumped by egoism when put to a drastic test? Wagner's *Ring* is dedicated to answering this question. This is what's at stake as Alberich enlarges on his threat, foreseeing the day when even Wotan's heroes will yield to Alberich's power, and Alberich will force himself, without love, on the gods' women (it's not clear whether Alberich means the Valhallan goddesses, or other women, perhaps even the Valkyries):

[pp. 96–7] Alberich: (H18a modulation: Rocked in (:H18a modulation) (H18c:) blissful abandon on radiant heights (:H18c), (H18a:) you eternal free-livers (:H18a) (H17:) scorn the black elf (:H17):—Beware! Beware! For when your menfolk yield to my power, (H37 voc:) your pretty women, who spurned my wooing (:H37 voc), shall forcibly sate the lust of the dwarf, though love may no longer smile upon him. (H44ab)

Wagner's juxtaposition of the Valhalla Motif H18 with Alberich's Ring Motif H17 as Alberich complains that the free-living gods scorn the black elf reminds us subliminally that Valhalla, the gods' allegedly spiritual realm, a supposed refuge from the truth, is a product of Alberich's Ring-power, and that the gods are free-living and blissful only thanks to Alberich, whom they scorn. Alberich has contempt for the gods' heedless luxuriating in their false feeling of freedom from the constraints of that real world within whose limits Alberich is content to pursue his quest for real power, because the gods owe all they are to him. It's his (and his fellow Nibelungs') labor in Nibelheim which has made the gods' life of luxury and magical thinking possible, a point to which Karl Marx devoted a rather large proportion of his *Das Kapital*.

Alberich's prediction that he'll ultimately control Wotan's heroes and force his lust on the gods' women foreshadows Alberich's son Hagen's influence over Wotan's allegedly free hero Siegfried, who, through Hagen's machinations, will be compelled to force himself on Siegfried's own true love and muse, Brünnhilde, Wotan's daughter, and rip Alberich's Ring (which Siegfried previously presented to her as a wedding ring) off her finger. Siegfried will figuratively rape and forcibly abduct her to present her as prize in a loveless marriage to his blood-brother Gunther, echoing what Wagner described as Alberich's rape of the Rhinegold. Accordingly, Alberich's threat against the gods culminates with his warning to Wotan to beware Alberich's army of night, when Alberich's Nibelung Hoard rises from the silent depths to the light of day:

> [p. 97] **Alberich:** (H45:) Beware of my army of night (:H45), (H8) (H44a:) when the Nibelung's hoard (H8) arises (:H44a) (H43/H9:) from silent depths to the light of day (:H43/H9)!

Alberich's Revolt Motif H44 (including either both its segments H44ab, or its first segment alone H44a) has now been heard in R.3 in association with Alberich's threat to exploit the fact that the gods depend on Loge's (artistic cunning's) dishonesty to overthrow the gods, to do this by employing Alberich's ever larger Hoard of knowledge as a weapon his Nibelung army of night can use to storm Valhalla, to make all the living renounce love as Alberich did to obtain his Ring, to turn Wotan's own heroes against him, and to force Alberich's lust on the gods' women lovelessly. It's extremely important to consider that H44a is a basis for the motif Dunning coined "Wotan's Revolt" H81, introduced just prior to Wotan's confession to Brünnhilde in V.2.2. Alberich's prophesy will come true in the following sense. When Siegfried, under the influence of Hagen's Potion (H165), having forgotten his true relationship with Brünnhilde, forces Alberich's Ring off her finger, and abducts Brünnhilde to present her as a wife to his blood-brother Gunther, Siegfried will have become, in effect, Alberich's host of night, and in so doing reveal his true nature as a Nibelung, reminding us that Wotan, Siegfried's grandfather, describes himself to Mime in S.1.2 as "Light-Alberich." Brünnhilde, not recognizing Siegfried disguised as Gunther, will ask him whether he's from "Hella's night-dwelling host," i.e., from Nibelheim's army of night. By this point in the tale Alberich's Ring will have become a stand-in for the Nibelung Hoard. When Siegfried forces it out of Brünnhilde's protective hands and exposes it to the public, he'll have fulfilled Alberich's threat that his Nibelung Hoard of knowledge will rise from the silent depths to the light of day, culminating in the twilight of the gods.

Wagner acknowledged that scientific inquiry will eventually overthrow religious mythology, that what was once unknown will inevitably become known, rising from the silent depths of man's unconscious mind (Alberich's realm of night) to the daylight of full consciousness. Feuerbach's remark that what was once explained supernaturally will eventually be construed objectively as natural phenomena, through advancement in scientific understanding, comes to mind: "... though there are numerous phenomena in nature whose physical, natural ground we have not yet discovered, it is absurd to resort to theology for that reason. What we do not know, posterity will find out. How many things that our ancestors could explain only through God and His purposes we have derived from the workings of nature!" [234F-LER, p. 134] Wagner similarly observed that an arbitrary (and false) view of Nature which we'd involuntarily formed through the influence of religious mythology, would eventually be the subject of our scientific scrutiny, liberating us from error, fancy, and religious belief, so that we can embrace knowledge, reality, and Nature: "Whilst Man involuntarily moulds his Life according to the notions he has gathered from his arbitrary views of Nature, and embalms their intuitive expression in Religion: these notions become for him in Science the subject of conscious, intentional review and scrutiny. The path of Science lies from error to knowledge, from fancy ... to reality, from Religion to Nature." [417W-{9–12/49} 'The Artwork of the Future,' PW Vol. I, p. 72]

Since Wagner resigned himself to the fact that there was no point in trying to increase human happiness and social equality and fairness through political reforms and laws, because we're intrinsically and irrevocably subject to egoism, he was forced to conclude that the Jews, on whom he'd falsely but exclusively projected his cynical realization of the egoistic foundation of human nature, would inevitably compel the world to endorse what he construed as their materialist philosophy. That is, we'll all eventually renounce love for the power of gold. According to Feuerbach this materialist philosophy was the basis of what he described as a faux Christian spirituality masquerading as autonomous from its roots in Judaism. The ever increasing influence of a science-based secularism and materialism, with which Wagner identified Judaism, would, he believed, spell the death not only of religious belief but of all that stems from it, such as the high value placed on compassion and love, moral idealism, and art for art's sake. Within a scientific secular world dominated by the allegedly exclusively Jewish notion that everything must have a "use," a material profit, there could be no basis for higher spiritual aspiration. The irresolvable existential dilemma for Wagner was that, while his intellectual conscience forced him to recognize the bitter truth of the objective scientific understanding of man and Nature, his heart couldn't abide this unbearable thought: that the good and the beautiful are as incommensurable with the truth as love in the *Ring* is incommensurable with the Ring's power.

Nonetheless Wagner believed that in the context of this scientific secular age in which he was born, his revolutionary music-drama was the last refuge of our inherent metaphysical impulse, our age-old longing for transcendent value, in the face of what he described to King Ludwig II of Bavaria as a Judaism which had grown all-powerful because, after all, it represents the tendency of the modern age, a philosophy gaining universal acceptance: "If I have friendly and sympathetic dealings with many of these people, it is only because I consider the Jewish race the born enemy of pure humanity and all that is noble in man: there is no doubt that we Germans especially will be destroyed by them, and I may well be the last remaining German who, as an artist, has known how to hold his ground in the face of a Judaism which is now all-powerful." [1107W-{11/22/81} Letter to King Ludwig II of Bavaria, SLRW, p. 918] Wagner also described the Jews as being destined to rule the world due to the promises of their god (by which Wagner meant egoism) which extend only to earthly, not spiritual wellbeing. He added that this grants them the status of being: "A wonderful, unparalleled phenomenon: the plastic daemon of man's downfall in triumphant surety ... ."

[1068W—{1–2/81} 'Know Thyself'—2nd Supplement to 'Religion and Art,' PW Vol. VI, pp. 271-272]

Wotan and Loge must launch a pre-emptive strike to ensure that Alberich doesn't act on his threat. But no matter how they manage to bring this off, their victory will only be temporary. Toward this end, Loge cunningly tricks Alberich into relinquishing his power to the gods, employing a classic ruse which Wagner (as is well known) based on the folktale "Puss & Boots." Loge flatters Alberich by describing him as virtually unstoppable, destined to be lord of the universe, but then slyly suggests that since Alberich has made enemies of all men, he can't sleep securely:

> **[p. 97] Loge:** (H32B vari:) If your marvelous guile can achieve what you claim with the hoard, as the mightiest of men I must hail you (:H32B vari): **[[H46 orch:]]** [= H18ab/H33 vari] for the moon and the stars and the beaming sun, they too have no choice but to serve you (:H46 orch). (H38) Yet I think it important above all else that those who heap up the hoard, the Nibelung army, should bow before you ungrudgingly. A ring you boldly flourished (H17); trembling, your people shrank before it: (H38) (H17 varis; H40A varis:) but what if a thief crept upon you, asleep, and slyly snatched it away—how would you ward yourself then in your wisdom (:H17 varis; H40A varis)?

As Loge mockingly celebrates the invincibility of Alberich's power we hear a new compound motif H46 ("Arrogance of Power") comprised of H18b (the Valhalla Motif's second segment) and H33 (Loge's Transformations). Loge notes that Alberich's quest for power, having left so many of his fellow Nibelungs oppressed and resentful, leaves him vulnerable to theft during sleep, as we hear the Tarnhelm Motif H40A. Perhaps the Nibelungs' oppression stems more from the objective, ugly view of their nature which Alberich compels them to acknowledge, than from any literal physical suffering he inflicts, an abhorrent self-image which Wotan, aided by Loge's artistic cunning, could amend if we grant religion power over our mind, and abjure objective reason. As so often in the *Ring*, this passage has both a conventional meaning and an allegorical import of greater scope. We must consider not only that Wotan is Light-Alberich, i.e., in some sense identical with Alberich, but recall that, while Wotan and the other gods slept, Alberich's Ring (H17ab) of earthly power gave birth musically to the gods' heavenly abode Valhalla (H18ab). The point is that Wotan dreamed Valhalla into existence while the Giants (our instincts), newly empowered by Alberich's Ring (human consciousness), built Valhalla. So we might say that when Alberich (Wotan as Light-Alberich) sleeps, his involuntary and unconscious mind, subject to feeling (i.e., imagination freed from the constraint of natural necessity), takes over in spite of his conscious intent. Thus, if Alberich sleeps, he dreams, and his involuntary dreaming may well place his Ring of power, the human mind, in Wotan's hands, precisely because his waking knowledge of man's craven nature is so oppressive and needs relief in dreaming, so that feeling (love) will trump thinking (power). What's already happened musically in the transition from R.1 to R.2 is being dramatized now. Alberich's doings in Nibelheim are Wotan's unremembered nightmare, which on waking he's forgotten, but which are sublimated into a waking dream of consolation.

Alberich, amused at Loge's apparent naiveté, boasts that he's made provision for this danger, by inventing a masking helmet, the Tarnhelm, which he compelled Mime to forge for him (bespeaking the prosaic origin of the "Wonder" of our human imagination, which gave our human species an advantage in the competition for life). Through this Tarnhelm Alberich can change his form or even become invisible, so the envious Nibelungs couldn't find him and steal his Ring. To clarify he repeats his prior point that his Ring power is what invisibly prompts all Nibelungs to action, and that because this power is behind everything and is found where least expected, he can never truly be deprived of his Ring. But then Loge springs his trap:

> **[pp. 98–100] Alberich:** (H40A:) The masking helmet I thought up myself; but Mime—most heedful of smiths—had to forge it for me (:H40A): (H40B:) to transform me swiftly and change my shape to whatever I want the helmet serves; no one sees me, though he may seek me; yet I am everywhere, hidden from sight (:H40B). And so, free from care, I'm safe from you ... ! (H46; H33)
>
> **Loge:** ... strange things I have found, but such a wonder ["Wunder"] I've never beheld. [Loge and Alberich converse: (...)] [Loge suggests Alberich choose the form he wishes to take]
>
> **Alberich:** (putting on the helmet: H40B:) 'Giant dragon, wind in coils (:H40B)!' (**[[H47 orch:]]** He immediately disappears and in his place an enormous giant serpent writhes on the ground ...)
>
> [Loge, Wotan, and Alberich converse about his amazing transformation: (...) Alberich reappears in his own shape. Loge and Alberich converse: (...) Loge suggests Alberich transform himself into something small, and they discuss it: (...)]
>
> **Alberich:** (H40A:) ... (:H40A)! (He puts on the helmet.) (H40B:) 'Crook-legged and grey, creep, you toad (:H40B)!' (He disappears: the gods become aware of a toad ... : **[[H48ab orch]]** [H48a = H47 vari]) (...) (H44a: Wotan places his foot on the toad: Loge seizes it by the head and takes the Tarnhelm in his hand.) (H8a orch)
>
> **Loge:** Hold him fast until I've bound him. (H44a: Loge binds his hands and feet with a length of rope: H8). Quickly up now! There he'll be ours! (H46 orch) (Both of them seize their prisoner ... and drag him with them ... . H17 varis. (...) (H35) (...) (Once again the change of scene leads past the forges. H38; H8; H39; H25a; H18ab modulation or H18b vari?. Continuous upward movement. H8; H25a; H18ab modulation or H18b vari?; H8; H32B; H8 vari; H32B:; H34: Wotan and Loge emerge from a cleft, leading the bound figure of Alberich.) (H8)

When Loge asks Alberich to choose the form he'll take to demonstrate the Tarnhelm's "Wonder," Alberich transforms himself into a Serpent (Dragon). The new new Dragon Motif H47 represents not only fear of death, but fear of truth (which would overthrow our religious beliefs, including faith in the promise of immortal life which assuages fear of death), the basis of religious faith's prohibition on freedom of inquiry. It's this fact, that Alberich alone has the courage to face the truth, to pay the price for owning the Ring and wielding its power, which ensures it ultimately can't be stolen from him. No matter what form the Tarnhelm (imagination) transforms our image of ourselves into, Alberich's egoism is the driving force behind it. Just as Loge's cunning exploited Alberich's Tarnhelm so the gods could co-opt his Ring power, perhaps someday the Tarnhelm will play a role in restoring the Ring's power back to Alberich. But he hadn't anticipated the wonders which our gift for self-deceit (another Ring power) could perform. He hadn't foreseen that through the imagination (Tarnhelm), product of our gift for abstraction, generalization, abbreviation, symbolism, and language in general, we can delude ourselves (at least temporarily) by transforming illusion into truth, and consigning truth to oblivion. We're predisposed to take our symbols for things for the things themselves, and to believe, wrongly, that the operations of our imagination on symbols which represent actual experience, are actual and real, when instead, through our imagination (under the sway of feeling) we move further away from actuality. This is the "Wonder" of which Loge speaks, that through imagination we can will the miraculous, even if in reality the miraculous is an impossibility. As Feuerbach put it: "Christians designate the theoretical religious faculty by the word faith or belief. (...) But on closer scrutiny the words mean nothing other than imagination." [259F-LER, pp. 177–178; See also 258F-LER, p. 175]

But Alberich's second transformation into a toad (at Loge's suggestion) places him and his Ring in Wotan's and Loge's hands. The new Toad Motif H48ab, whose first segment H48a is derived from the Dragon Motif H47, is merely descriptive, and isn't heard after its inception here. As an amphibian, however, it can be construed as a symbol for a transition from one world to another.

Though Wagner had several sources in Norse and Teutonic myth and legend for Wotan's and Loge's capturing Alberich and forcing him to ransom himself with his Ring, Tarnhelm, and Hoard, his primary conceptual source was probably Feuerbach, who said that Christianity (considering that many aspects of the *Ring*'s purportedly pagan gods are drawn from Christian theology) overpowers human reason, taking the mind prisoner (as Wotan and Loge take Alberich prisoner), by making the articles of religious faith undoubted facts: [Footnote:] "The denial of a fact is not a matter of indifference; it is something morally evil ... . Christianity made its articles of faith objective, i.e., undeniable, unassailable facts, thus overpowering the reason, and taking the mind prisoner by the force of external reality ... ." [120F-EOC, p. 205] Wotan and Loge co-opt Alberich's mind by taking him prisoner along with his Ring to ensure the gods' survival, i.e., to sustain man's faith in them. Wagner echoed Feuerbach, stating like him that Judeo-

Christian miracle ("Wonder") is predicated on faith which denies understanding and nature's laws: "The Judaeo-Christian Wonder tore the connexion of natural phenomena asunder, to allow the Divine Will to appear as standing over Nature. (...)... the characteristic of the Dogmatic Wonder consists ... in this, that, through the obvious impossibility of explaining it, it tyrannously subjugates the Understanding despite the latter's instinctive search for explanation ... ." [522W-{50–1/51} *Opera and Drama*, PW Vol. II, pp. 213–214] And it's the Tarnhelm (H40AB derived from Loge's Motif of Transformation H33), as manipulated by Loge's artistic cunning, that's the source of this "Wonder."

Having bound Alberich, Wotan and Loge now retrace their steps up from the depths of hellish Nibelheim (Erda's Umbilical Nest) to the meadow before Valhalla where they left Froh, Donner, and Fricka anxiously waiting. Their progress is depicted in another of Wagner's remarkable orchestral interludes between scenes.

THE RHINEGOLD ≠ SCENE FOUR

(ON A MEADOW OUTSIDE VALHALLA)
WOTAN, LOGE, ALBERICH, FRICKA, FROH, DONNER, FREIA, FAFNER, FASOLT, ERDA, AND THE RHINEDAUGHTERS

Having brought Alberich, bound, from Nibelheim to the meadow opposite Valhalla, Wotan tells Alberich he'll be freed if he ransoms himself with his Hoard of Treasure. Alberich, reluctant to lose the source of his power to the gods, consoles himself thinking that if he can retain his Ring he can command the Nibelungs to mine another treasure for him. Likewise, when Loge insists Alberich's Tarnhelm must also be included in his ransom, he's confident that if he can keep his Ring, through its power he'll compel Mime to forge another:

[pp. 101–4] **Wotan:** You're captured and firmly fettered, just as you thought that the world and all that lives and moves in it was already in your power. ... to set you free a ransom is needed.

Alberich: O dunce that I am! A dreamy-eyed fool ["träumender Thor"]! (...) Fearful revenge shall atone for my failing!

Loge: (...) If you're plotting revenge, ... think first of the ransom! (H46 ...)

Alberich: Then say what you desire!

Wotan: The hoard and your bright-shining gold.

Alberich: (H17:) (...) (aside) But if I can keep the ring for myself (:H17), I can easily manage without the hoard ... . [Alberich notes, accompanied by H24, that he can replenish his hoard with his Ring, and that this will teach him a valuable lesson: (...)]. [**Wotan:** (...)] Untie my hand and I'll call it here. (Loge unties the rope ... .) (H19 frag: Alberich raises the ring to his lips and secretly murmurs a command: H17; H43; H38) Well then, I've called the Nibelungs here: (H45:) obeying their lord, I hear them bringing the hoard from the depths to daylight (:H45). (...) [**Wotan:** (...)] (H38; H8;

H45 ... Throughout the following, the Nibelungs pile up the hoard.) (...) (H40A) And the metal helm that Loge's holding, kindly give it me back!

Loge: (tossing the Tarnhelm on to the hoard) The booty is part of the ransom.

Alberich: (...) (H17 vari:) He who made the old one will make me another: I still wield the power that Mime obeys (:H17 vari). (H24:) It's hard ... to abandon this cunning defense to my craftily scheming foe (:H24)! (...) [**Loge:** (...)]

Wotan: A golden ring stands proud on your finger ... . It too is part of the hoard, I think. [Alberich and Wotan converse: (...)]

Alberich: (...) My life, but not the ring! [**Wotan:** (...)] If I ransom life and limb, I must also ransom the ring; (H8 loose vari:) hand and head, eye and ear are no more my own than this bright red ring (:H8 loose vari)?

Wotan: (H57ab embryo?:) You call the ring your own (:H57ab embryo?)? (H8) (...) (H12:) Consult with the Rhine's fair daughters and ask if they gave you the gold as your own (:H12) which you stole to make a ring.

Through his Ring-power Alberich compels his Nibelung slaves to carry his hoard of treasure from Nibelheim's silent depths to the light of day so he can ransom his life. This isn't, however, the fulfillment of Alberich's threat in R.3 that he'll overthrow the gods once his hoard has risen from the silent depths to daylight, because Alberich's powers, deriving from the Ring, have been co-opted by Wotan and Loge, and are emerging into the light of day under their control. Thanks to Loge's cunning the gods can draw advantage from Alberich's envy (H24). This transfer of Alberich's Ring power from Alberich to Wotan (and the Tarnhelm's power to Loge) dramatizes what was already implicit in the musical transformation of Alberich's Ring H17ab into the first two segments of Wotan's Valhalla H18ab during the transition R.1–2. Alberich has lost his Ring power, at least temporarily, to the gods. However, a secret hidden deep within this apparent transfer of power from Alberich to Wotan is that Wotan is Light-Alberich. Wotan and his future proxies will, according to Alberich's prophecy in R.3, eventually serve Alberich, so in the most far-reaching sense Alberich doesn't lose his Ring's power to Wotan after all.

Nonetheless, when Wotan demands even Alberich's Ring as ransom, Alberich protests that the Ring is his very essence, his identity. The original sin which brought about our fall from grace with our preconscious animal existence was the natural evolution of human consciousness (Alberich's Ring). It was this that made us who we are. Alberich is saying that if Wotan steals Alberich's Ring, whose price Wotan would never willingly pay, Wotan will be committing the sin of self-deception. Alberich is on to the hypocrisy in Wotan's grandstanding in defense of the Rhinedaughters' alleged right to claim Alberich's Ring. He notes bitterly that Wotan, intending to co-opt Alberich's Ring power, not only has motives as ignoble as those which impelled Alberich to steal the Rhinegold and forge the Ring, but what's worse, Wotan has drawn advantage from Alberich's sacrifice of love for power (his "Noth") so Wotan can employ Alberich's Ring power without paying its price:

> **[p. 104] Alberich:** You upbraid me, you crook, for the wrong you so fondly desired? (...) How lucky for you ... that I ... from shameful necessity ["Noth"], slave to my anger, mastered the fearful magic whose work now smiles so gaily upon you. (...) (H17 vari:) Shall my curse redound to your joy (:H17 vari)?—(H17)

Feuerbach's following diatribe against Christian hypocrisy is echoed in Alberich's accusation that Wotan's motive in stealing the Ring from Alberich is no nobler than the motive which impelled Alberich to sacrifice love for the sake of the Ring's power: "The Christians blamed the Jews for this arrogance [the notion that God exists to serve our, or exclusively the Jews,' needs], but only because the kingdom of God was taken from them and transferred to the Christians. Accordingly, we find the same thoughts and sentiments in the Christians as in the Israelites." [159F-EOC, p. 299; See also 91F-EOC, p. 121] Alberich hopes to ensure that the gods can't draw advantage (through Loge's cunning) from his "Noth" to benefit from the Ring's power, which cost Alberich so much, without paying his price. The price he'll exact is that, in the end, those who co-opt his Ring power to sustain their happiness through self-deceit, will have to confront the bitter truth which is predestined to overthrow their illusions. At an early phase in his development of the *Ring* plot (1848) Wagner described Alberich as the gods' conscience, i.e., consciousness of their guilt which lies in Wotan and Loge co-opting Alberich's Ring power for no higher end than Alberich had in forging his Ring. For this reason Alberich's complaint against the gods is just: "From the depths of Nibelheim the conscience of their guilt cries up to them [the gods]: for the bondage of the Nibelungen is not broken; merely the lordship has been reft from Alberich, and not for any higher end ... : Alberich thus has justice in his plaints against the Gods." [376W-{6–8/48} 'The Nibelungen Myth,' PW Vol. VII, p. 302]

Some might say my reading of Alberich's Ring power as a metaphor for exercise of reason's power is off the mark, because Alberich is too passionately self-involved to be capable of objective thought. But Wagner felt scientific inquiry isn't emotionless or without ulterior motive. He believed scientific endeavor is an aspect of our will to control our world, similar in this respect to religious belief, but, unlike religious faith, not subject to fantasy. It's not that Alberich is spurred by pure reason, but rather, that his greed for power can only be assuaged by acquiring objective knowledge of Nature and man, unimpaired by religiously inspired illusion. For Feuerbach, to grasp the true nature of his object of contemplation the scientific inquirer doesn't let imagination or feeling impose a subjective bias, even though, like any other human, he or she is subject to passion: "Even to a believer in natural process ... nature is an object of the striving for happiness ... . Even to a scientific thinker it is an object of imagination and of feeling, ... but only on the basis of its real, objective character; he is not so hoodwinked by his feeling or so overwhelmed by his imagination as to take a subjective view of nature ... ." [286F-LER, p. 229]

Now Alberich levels an extraordinary accusation against Wotan, an imputation of metaphysical guilt, which seems to have been misunderstood by the other published Wagner scholars who've discussed it, but which is a key to grasping the *Ring* as a coherent allegory. Alberich confronts Wotan with the drastic observation that if Alberich sinned in renouncing love for the sake of the Ring's power, Alberich sinned only against himself, but if Wotan co-opts Alberich's Ring power for the gods' sake, he'll be sinning against all that was, is, or shall be:

> [pp. 104–5] **Alberich:** (H17 vari:) Be on your guard, you haughty god (:H17 vari)! If ever I sinned, I sinned freely against myself: but you, you immortal, will sin against all that was, is and shall be—if you brazenly wrest the ring from me now!
>
> **Wotan:** Give the ring here! (H19) (...) (He seizes Alberich and tears the ring from his finger with terrible force: H44a; H9ab minor)
>
> **Alberich:** (with a hideous scream) Ha! Ruined! Crushed! (H35:) The saddest of all sad slaves (:H35)!
>
> **Wotan:** (contemplating the ring: H18b vari?:) Now I hold that which exalts me, the mightiest lord of the mighty (:H18b vari?)! (H17: He puts on the ring.)

The significance of Alberich's accusation can only be grasped by anticipating Erda's (Mother Nature's) appearance after Alberich's exit. When Wotan, having stolen Alberich's Ring and placing it on his finger, refuses to give it to the Giants to redeem Freia, Erda will rise from the earth (as if, by taking possession of Alberich's Ring, the world's essence or soul rises to consciousness in Wotan) to tell him that she possesses knowledge of all that was, is, or shall be. Erda (Nature) possesses knowledge of the real world which exhibits itself to us in time, space, matter, and energy, under the laws of causation (or other laws expressing Nature's coherence not yet fully understood by science), which in the *Ring* can be construed as the scientific equivalent of Fate. Alberich is telling Wotan that Alberich, by possessing the Ring, doesn't sin against the real world (but only against himself), while if Wotan co-opts Alberich's Ring he'll be sinning against the actual world. This is Wagner's metaphor for the distinction between Alberich's relationship with the truth, and Wotan's relationship with it. Where Alberich has the courage to accept Nature's truth, because only objective knowledge of the world grants us the means to acquire concrete power, Wotan, man's religious impulse, has a false relationship to reality, having invented an "other world" of the imagination conceived as antithetical to the real world. Alberich is an optimist in the sense that he affirms the world, no matter how abhorrent this might be to his self-esteem, while Wotan is what Nietzsche would regard as a romantic pessimist and religious nihilist because he denies the real world, finding it loathsome and frightening, and substitutes for it a consoling, imaginary reality. Wotan's denial of Nature's truth is a sort of matricide: Wotan, embodiment of our illusion that gods exist, figuratively kills our mother, Nature, by repudiating the real world which is ephemeral, existing in the past, present, and future, and positing a false, allegedly spiritual (eternal) substitute. It's in this sense that Wotan sins against all that was, is, and will be.

In what sense does Alberich sin against himself? Wotan affirms natural feeling but renounces objective knowledge of Nature. As Feuerbach put it: "The divine being is the pure subjectivity of man, freed from all else, from everything objective ...—... his inmost self." [79F-EOC, p. 98; See also 67F] It's this subjective, inner self of feeling (aesthetic intuition) which Alberich sins against but Wotan affirms. Wotan's religious sin against truth, Erda's knowledge of all that was, is, and will be, is that he, the most conditioned product of Nature, acquires a pride which deludes him into seeing himself as a first cause, and therefore as free and autonomous from Nature, as Feuerbach suggested: [See 193F-LER, p. 21; See also 228F, 243F-LER, p. 155, 51F-EOC, p. 37, and 427W-{9–12/49} 'The Artwork of the Future,' PW Vol. I, p. 83] Here's how Wagner, paraphrasing Feuerbach, described hubris of the kind of which Wotan is guilty, and suggests how his sin will be punished: "... Thought, the highest and most conditioned faculty of artistic man, had cut itself adrift from fair warm Life, whose yearning had begotten and sustained it, as from a ... fettering bond that clogged its own unbounded freedom: — so deemed the Christian yearning, and believed that it must break away from physical man, to spread in heaven's boundless aether to freest waywardness. But this very severance was to teach that thought and this desire how inseparable they were from human nature's being ... ... they could not take the carcass with them, bound as it was by laws of gravitation ... ." [439W-{9–12/49} 'The Artwork of the Future,' PW Vol. I, pp. 138–139] Wotan's hubristic, religious quest to transcend the limits of our only world and human nature, is the essence of Wotan's sin against Erda's knowledge of all that was, is, and will be. This pessimistic world-denial, Wagner says, is the very essence of religion: "Religion ... is radically divergent from the State. (...) Its basis is a feeling of the unblessedness of human being ..... Its inmost kernel is denial of the world—... and struggle for redemption from it, prepared-for by renunciation, attained by Faith." [701W-{64–2/65} 'On State and Religion,' PW Vol. IV, pp. 23–24]

Some might protest against identifying Alberich with Mother Nature, Erda, on the basis that Alberich's greed seems unnatural and excessive, while Erda's natural wisdom is conceived as unchanging and dispassionate. But Wagner came to see Nature (Erda) as heartless and devoid of feeling like Alberich: "... I can't stand hearing anyone appeal to Nature: ... for Nature is heartless and devoid of feeling, and every egoist, ay, every monster, can appeal to her example with more cause and warranty than the man of feeling." [658W-{9/30/58} Letter to Mathilde Wesendonck, RWLMW, p. 46] It's also worth adding that Wagner associated Judaism with Alberich's cold, scientific, objective way of affirming Mother Nature (Erda), i.e., with Alberich's sin against himself, our innermost self of feeling, or love. Wagner said the Jews' very nature condemns them to the world's reality, so they're irredeemable: "Whether the Jews can ever be redeemed is the question which ... occupies our thoughts—their nature condemns them to the world's reality." [1071W-{2/10/81} CD Vol. II, p. 618] It may help to persuade those inclined to insist on Erda's dissimilarity to her alleged advocate Alberich, that we find decisive evidence of his identification with her not only in the fact that her most profound observation in the *Ring* is her prophecy of the inevitable victory of Alberich (and his son Hagen) over the gods, but also in the fact that in S.3.1, during Wotan's last conference with Erda, he'll equate her as "Primeval mothers' fear!" with his fear of the end she prophesied Alberich's Ring Curse would bring to pass, and consign her, with her knowledge of all that was, is, and will be, to oblivion.

But with respect to Wotan's greater sin, Feuerbach regarded natural human egoism as essential, inevitable, and necessary, but religious man's sin in reaching for the impossible to satisfy infinite desires and suppress infinite fear he regarded as unnatural, a sin which greatly exceeded that of normal egoistic striving: "... religion has wishes that can be fulfilled only in the imagination, in faith, whereas ... the man who replaces religion with culture, reason, science and replaces heaven by earth, has desires that do not exceed the limits of nature and reason and whose realization lies within the realm of natural possibility." [296F-LER, p. 249; See also 204F-LER, p. 62] The practically limitless power Alberich can attain over time through his Ring power, through the labor of those men compelled to serve it, is within the limits of natural possibility. It's limitless in the sense that our knowledge and the power it generates can always advance, but, unlike the power of the gods, it isn't omnipotent and absolute.

We find a basis for Alberich's accusation that Wotan sins against Mother Nature (Erda) if he co-opts Alberich's Ring (to preserve religious illusion from the truth) in Feuerbach's suggestion that by positing the existence of the supernatural, a ground for Nature outside Nature's self, we kill life, betray, sin against, and therefore figuratively murder our Mother, Nature: "... if you imagine that natural life ... has its ground outside of itself, ... you strike life dead." [11F-TDI, p. 86] "How untrue we Germans have become to our source, our mother, and how unlike her, thanks to Christianity which taught us that heaven is our home." [211F-LER, p. 85] "Nature has terminated and ended, and with its death, there arises over it a new world, the spirit." [8F-TDI, p. 73; See also 336F] Wagner paraphrased Feuerbach, suggesting the day will come when we'll free ourselves from the heresy through which we denied Nature by seeing ourselves as the means to a supernatural end (God) which lay outside us: "Let us glance ... for a moment at this future state of Man, when he shall have freed himself from his last heresy, the denial of Nature, — that heresy which has taught him hitherto to look upon himself as a mere instrument to an end which lay outside himself. When Mankind knows, at last, that itself is the one and only object of its existence ... , (...) This Heavenly Father [Wotan] will then be no other than the social wisdom of mankind ... ." [410W-{6–8/49} 'Art and Revolution,' PW Vol. I, p. 57] Wagner echoed Feuerbach in describing the heavenly father (Wotan) as collective man's social wisdom. Wagner is saying that Wotan (we) will be redeemed from his (our) sin against Mother Nature only after we've acknowledged Nature as our Mother, and have recognized that we (collective humanity), having invented God, are god.

The radical importance of this metaphor—that by positing the existence of the supernatural we not only sin against our true mother, Nature, but figuratively kill her—lies not only in the fact that it's the basis for Alberich's accusation against Wotan, but that it's perhaps the basis for a striking likeness among three of the four heroes of Wagner's mature music-dramas. Not only will Wotan's heir (heir both to Wotan's desire for redemption and to Wotan's sin) Siegfried meditate on the philosophical problem that his mother (literally his blood-mother Sieglinde—but figuratively Erda) died giving him birth, but Tristan's mother also died giving him birth, a tragedy he meditates on at length in Act Three of *Tristan and Isolde*. And Parsifal (in *Parsifal*) holds himself responsible for his mother's death because, after he neglected her and never returned home to her, she died of a broken heart. The artist-hero Walther von Stolzing from *Mastersingers* is an exception among Wagner's mature music-drama heroes for reasons wholly consistent with the allegorical logic I've detailed here, which will be explained in Volume Two devoted to these other music-dramas.

Feuerbach gave Wagner more impetus for Alberich's description of Wotan as a sinner, an immoral man, when he said religion contradicts morality by dishonoring the truth and understanding: "... *wherever religion places itself in contradiction with reason, it places itself also in contradiction with the moral sense. Only with the sense of truth coexists the sense of the right and good. Depravity of understanding is always depravity of heart.*" [133F-EOC, p. 246] Feuerbach summed up this indictment in his drastic assertion that: " ... I would rather be a devil in alliance with truth [Alberich], than an angel in alliance with falsehood [the gods of Valhalla]." [117F-EOC, p. 188]

Having co-opted Alberich's Ring power by taking possession of his Ring, Tarnhelm, and Hoard of Treasure (knowledge), Wotan instructs Loge to free Alberich from his bonds. But Alberich knows that so long as Wotan holds Alberich's Ring, i.e., so long as our age-old religious mythology sways our thinking, Alberich (our objective human mind) can never truly be free:

[p. 105] **Wotan:** Set him free! (H6 orch?: Loge frees Alberich from his bonds) [**Loge:** (...)]

Alberich: (... [[H49 orch]] [= H17 harmony syncopated]) Am I free now? (laughing wildly: [[H49 orch]]) Really free?—[[H49 orch:]] Then let my freedom's first greeting salute you (:H49 orch)!—[[H50 voc:]] [= H17a inversion] Just as it came to me through a curse so shall this ring be accursed in turn; just as its gold once endowed me with might beyond measure, so shall its spell now deal death to whoever shall wear it (:H50 voc)!"

Alberich introduces the definitive version of H49 (Greed/Grudge/Resentment/ Envy—"Neid") as he asks rhetorically whether he's really free. Cooke noted H49 is basically H17's (the Ring's) harmony syncopated. H49 is emblematic of Alberich's resentment toward anyone claiming title to the Ring who hasn't paid his price of lovelessness to obtain it. In V.2.2, when Wotan confesses to Brünnhilde the knowledge her mother (his lover) Erda imparted to him, he's accompanied by H49 as he speaks of Alberich's as yet unborn son (Hagen), telling Brünnhilde that Alberich's force of Envy (Hagen) stirs in a mortal woman's womb. Hagen will fulfill Alberich's Ring Curse, carrying out Erda's prophecy that the twilight of the gods will have dawned not long after Alberich's child is born. Hagen embodies the Ring Curse. Alberich introduces the famous Curse Motif H50 as he sings that as the Ring came to him through a curse (his curse on love), his Ring shall now be cursed. H50, Cooke observed, is the inversion of H17a, the first segment of the Ring Motif H17.

Then Alberich states the conditions of his curse. He declares that just as the Ring gave him measureless power, its spell will now doom to death whoever wears it. This is the old conundrum in the gift of human consciousness, that our mind's property which grants us seemingly limitless power to shape our world, the foresight and symbolic consciousness which allows us to plan ahead and accumulate knowledge, also grants us the troubling ability to foresee our inevitable death, and is therefore the basis for our existential fear. This fear of death, the fact of death as a problem, Socrates said was the basis for philosophy, and Feuerbach described as the ultimate inspiration for religious belief. Our unique gift of foresight is the Fall. We'll soon learn that Wotan's foresight of the inevitable end of the allegedly immortal gods (the inevitable victory of science over religious faith), granted him courtesy of Erda's prophecy of the gods' fated doom, will paralyze him into inaction with existential fear. This is Alberich's punishment of us humans for our hubris in drawing benefit from the allegedly divine gift of foreknowledge, of full, abstract, reflective consciousness.

Alberich's threat to doom anyone to death who wears his Ring doesn't mean literally that the Ring's owner will die the moment he takes possession of it. It means he'll be troubled by the thought of the inevitability of his eventual death, and/or by the thought of the inevitability of the destruction of those ideals, values, and beliefs which are predicated on the illusion that we have transcendent value, or a special relationship with supernatural beings. Wagner borrowed this concept from the Bible. In the *Book of Genesis*, Adam and Eve have been told that if they eat the fruit of the Tree of Knowledge, they'll surely die. They do eat it, but God doesn't strike them dead. Instead, God punishes them with exile from paradise, which means they'll no longer be able to eat the fruit of the Tree of Life which presumably grants them eternal youth. Exiled from paradise, they'll foresee their inevitable death (the price of their Fall and breach of faith) and have to work. Alberich spells out the other punishments which the Ring's owner will suffer through its Curse:

> **[pp. 105–6] Alberich:** (H17 vari:) No joyful man shall ever have joy of it; on no happy man shall its bright gleam smile (:H17 vari); (H49:) may he who owns it be wracked by care, and he who does not be ravaged by greed ["Neid"]! Each man shall covet its acquisition, but none shall enjoy it to lasting gain (:H49); (H17:) its lord shall guard it without profit and yet it shall draw down his bane upon him (:H17). [[**H51 voc:**]] Doomed to die,

may the coward be fettered by fear; as long as he lives, let him pine away, languishing (:H51 voc), (H43:) lord of the ring, as slave of the ring (:H43): till the circlet I hold in my hand once again!—And so in highest need ["höchster Noth"] the Nibelung blesses his ring. (...) Keep it now (laughing) and guard it well: (... [Hint of H35:]) you'll not escape from my curse (:H35 Hint)! (H43 vari orch: He disappears quickly into the crevice. H8. The thick mists in the foreground slowly clear: H6)

The whole purpose of Alberich's Ring Curse is to punish those whose happiness depends on the self-deceptions of religion, altruistic morality, and art, i.e., those (like Wotan) who can't bear to sacrifice love (feeling) for power. As Alberich says, the Ring's (objective consciousness's) owner will be wracked by care. This existential angst isn't only the price we humans pay for our gift of self-consciousness in being able to foresee our death, a price religious faith, ethics, and art are meant to ameliorate. It's also the price those pay who're dedicated to affirming our transcendent value, who, having over-reached the bounds of the possible, are fated to be humiliated by truth.

When Alberich adds that whoever doesn't own the Ring will be ravaged by greed to possess it, some may read this conventionally as Wagner's warning that those possessed by greed for money or property or the political power which naturally entails increase of money, property, and sway, will never be content with what they have. While that is true, Wagner is invoking something of greater scope. He's saying it's the very nature of our mind, especially highly developed minds such as geniuses, to be incapable of finding contentment in things as they are. Alberich's Ring Curse follows naturally from the nature of our reflective consciousness. Our inherent inability to find satisfaction is both a source of anguish, or "Noth" (want, need, care), and a source of creativity, for it inspires us to seek new ways to satisfy our needs and desires and to assuage our fears when we're thwarted in our quest to address them. And since possessing the Ring means being fully conscious, the insatiable greed of those who don't possess it to possess it is a poetical description of historical, collective man's (Wotan's) quest for knowledge and the power which flows from it.

A new motif H51, rarely heard and evidently unrelated musically to other motifs, is heard as Alberich tells Wotan that the Ring's owner, doomed to die, will be fettered by fear. This isn't only everyman's fear of inevitable death, but specifically Alberich's premonition that Erda will forewarn Wotan of the gods' fated doom, leaving him to meditate on the gods' (religion's) end in care and fear. Wotan will be paralyzed into inaction by this foreknowledge, and will have to depend on his proxies the Wälsung heroes and his daughter Brünnhilde, who, unlike Wotan, won't be aware of the full implications of Alberich's Ring Curse.

Our insatiable quest for power, the essence of Alberich's Ring Curse, expresses Feuerbach's notion that it's man's nature to seek the truth, to perfect what experience presents to him as imperfect. By our nature we're bound to do this, yet the truth, if ever we could learn it, we might well find unbearable, a point Donington made in the introduction to his seminal *Wagner's 'Ring' and its Symbols*. [Donington: p. 15]. This is Wagner's poetical metaphor for historical man's Promethean quest for that knowledge which, once found, will retrospectively nullify the value of the quest for it. Wagner once wrote, with unblinking honesty, that it's our inmost nature, our natural necessity, to seek the fateful Nibelung Hoard, which contains the secret of earthly might: "Though doomed to death by acquisition of the Hoard, each sequent generation strives to seize it: its inmost necessity drives it on, as with necessity of Nature .... . For in the Hoard there lies ... the secret of all earthly might: it is the Earth itself with all its splendour ... ." [370W-{6–8/48} 'The Wibelungen'—Revised summer of 1849: PW Vol. VII, p. 276] This cognitive drive is the basis for all human creativity in both the objective realm of science (which values only the physically real, the possible), and in religious belief and art (which tap our imagination to satisfy our desires and assuage our fears where objective experience of Nature can't).

It's our mind's insatiable nature, its need to complete what Nature presents to it as incomplete, in reality if possible, and symbolically and mythologically if impossible, which according to Feuerbach gives birth to our religious illusion that there must be another, transcendent realm, where our desires, that are thwarted here in the real world, are satisfied: " ... they ["the Christians"] ... conclude that ... because in this life man cannot fulfill all his desires and potentialities—there must be an eternal, infinite life to come; they conclude that because man wants to know everything, because his thirst for knowledge is unlimited, he will inevitably know everything some day; that because man has ... an infinite drive toward perfection and happiness, which can never be fulfilled on this small earth, in this brief life span, ... therefore man ... must some day become perfectly ethical and happy .... " [301F-LER, p. 265] Wagner paraphrased Feuerbach's suggestion that because our mind has a seemingly limitless desire for satisfaction which can't be fulfilled in this world, it necessarily posits a supernatural realm in which infinite desire can be sated, such as the gods' promise that men, mortal on earth, can enjoy immortality in heaven. We'll learn in *The Valkyrie* that Wotan offers immortal life in Valhalla, granted by Freia, to heroes inspired by his Valkyrie daughters to martyrdom on the field of battle. But Wagner, unlike Feuerbach, locates the value of life solely in this metaphysical quest to affirm our transcendent value. In a previously cited passage Wagner stated that since our world can't satisfy us we need another world for our redemption. [701W-{64–2/65} 'On State and Religion,' PW Vol. IV, pp. 23–24; See also 1021W-{6–8/80} 'Religion and Art,' PW Vol. VI, p. 215]

We can now see how Wotan's co-opting of Alberich's Ring power, i.e., religion's manipulation of the human mind through imagination in service to subjective fear and desire (multiplied to infinity by the limitless scope of conscious thought), is the fulfillment of Alberich's Ring Curse, and is its own punishment. The essence of religion is that under its spell we seek transcendent value and being, a quest which because it's predicated on ignorance and self-deception is inherently unfulfillable, irredeemable, futile, and therefore insatiable. Alberich's curse on his Ring to punish Wotan and the gods for co-opting his Ring-power is the punishment which inheres in our futile quest to transcend natural law and the limits of our mortal body, to figuratively kill our Mother, Nature, by denying her truth and positing an untruth as substitute. Thus, according to Alberich's Ring Curse, religious man is historically fated to seek that power through knowledge which will eventually overthrow his religious self-deception and replace it with the bitter truth, thus effectively placing the Ring back in Alberich's hands and bringing to pass the twilight of the gods.

Another component of his Ring Curse is that the coward, doomed to die by virtue of it, will be fettered by fear and pine away as long as he lives. The religious man of faith pines away because he can't accept the fact of death and finitude, but is impelled to seek transcendent meaning where there is none. His inability to reconcile himself with his true, mortal nature, is the source not only of his existential fear, which religious faith is meant to assuage, but also of his fear of any knowledge of the truth which might undermine his faith in the gods. Wagner found in Feuerbach the basis for his emphasis in the *Ring* on the overwhelming import and scope of existential fear, which transcends even the fear of death, its original source. This fear which gave birth to religion isn't a specific fear of any particular object, but the generalized fear which is the inevitable product of the universal, limitless power of the human mind and imagination (Ring and Tarnhelm). [See 196F-LER, p. 25, 319F-LER, p. 287, and 269F-LER, p. 196] Wagner said that the whole purpose of his *Ring* was to show how existential fear came into being, and came to rule the affairs of men: " … fear of the end is the source of all lovelessness, and this fear is generated only when love itself is beginning to wane. How did it come about that a feeling which imparts the highest bliss to all living things was so far lost sight of by the human race that everything that the latter did, ordered and established was finally conceived only out of a fear of the end? My poem [the *Ring*] shows the reason why." [613W-{1/25–26/54} Letter to August Röckel, SLRW, pp. 306–307] Wotan's waking dream, the gods' heavenly abode Valhalla, with its soul, the goddess of divine love and immortality, Freia, has been established by Wotan (thanks to Alberich's Ring-power, the Giants' labor, and Loge's artistry) as our illusory refuge from this existential care and fear, a point Wotan will make in the finale of *The Rhinegold* when he describes Valhalla, with Freia now safely restored to the gods, as a fortress safe from "dread and dismay," accompanied by H57b. In a moment of rare candor, Wagner described the power of our human mind (Alberich's Ring) as the source of paralyzing fear and the reason for the primacy of the self-preservation instinct (Fafner) as a motive for human thought and action: "At lunch R. told the story of a woman who threw her children to the wolves; I observed that a mother dog would have sacrificed herself first, and R. says, 'Yes, because she has no reasoning power.'" [1142W-{12/17/82} CD Vol. II, p. 975]

During his confession to Brünnhilde in V.2.2 Wotan will echo the conclusion of Alberich's Ring Curse when he tells her that "(H19) I, lord of treaties [engraved on his Spear], am now a slave to those treaties." This highlights another aspect of the existential trap Nature set for us when it gifted us with symbolic consciousness, that the very universality of our human mind and imagination, which grant us such wide sway over our world and scope for action, also compels us to acknowledge ever more irrevocably our unfreedom, the more we learn about ourselves and how all things in our world are necessary. As Feuerbach opined, as our worldly knowledge and self-knowledge grows we seem more and more a mere product of Nature rather than an active creator with a free will: [Footnote:] " ... a man can go so far as to disclaim all credit; for ultimately my feeling, my consciousness, my very being result from premises which are situated outside the I, which are the work of nature or of God. Indeed, the deeper man looks within, the more the distinction between nature and man or I vanishes, the plainer it becomes to him that he is only *consciously unconscious*, a *not-I that is an I*. That is why man is the deepest and most complex of all beings. But man cannot understand or endure his own depth, and for that reason he splits his being into an I without a not-I, which he calls God [say Wotan, a god who renounces Nature] and a not-I without an I, which he calls nature [Erda]." [334F-LER, p. 313]

Having delivered this drastic warning, Alberich now scuttles off to plot his eventual return to power by destroying (discrediting) the usurpers, the so-called gods. Fricka, Donner, and Froh welcome Wotan and Loge back, while the Giants appear in the distance returning with Freia to see whether the gods will redeem her with Alberich's gold. Froh, the eternal optimist, speaks for all when he sings an apostrophe to Freia, saying how great a loss it would be were the gods forever deprived of the jubilant bliss of sorrow-less youth everlasting which Freia's golden apples provide them:

> [p. 107] Froh: (H28 fragments:) What sweet-scented air wafts around us again as blissful emotion steals over our senses (:H28 fragments)! Sad it would be for us all (H35 vari?:) to be severed for ever from her (:H35 vari?) who grants us the jubilant bliss of sorrowless youth everlasting. (the front of the stage is now brightly lit again; the light restores the gods' former youthful appearance ... . Fasolt and Fafner enter, leading Freia between them.)

Froh's characteristic emotion of gratitude, in distinction from Donner's dependence on threats to instill fear as the gods' enforcer, calls to mind what Feuerbach described as the two aspects of our feeling of dependence on Mother Nature (Erda) which gave birth to belief in gods: "... the true reason why fear does not offer a complete explanation of religion is that, once the danger is past, fear gives way to an opposite emotion ... . This is the feeling of release from danger, from fear and anxiety, a feeling of delight, joy, love, and gratitude." [198F-LER, pp. 29–30] But now that the Giants have returned with Freia, and Wotan seems prepared to honor the agreed-on change in his original contract with them, that they'll accept the Nibelung Hoard instead of Freia as payment for building Valhalla, Fasolt expresses qualms which will result in Wotan redeeming Freia not merely with the agreed-on Hoard per se, but also with those portions of it of greatest value, Alberich's Tarnhelm and even his Ring:

> [pp. 108–11] Fasolt: To lose the woman ... grieves me deeply: (H22:) if she's to fade from my thoughts, then heap up the hoard of trinkets so that it hides (:H22) (H35:) the radiant child from my sight (:H35)!

Wotan: Then set the measure to Freia's form ["Gestalt"]. (...)

Fafner: (H25a; H27:) Our staves have been set to the pledge's size (:H25a; :H27): let the hoard, when heaped high, fill the space! [Wotan, Loge, and Froh comment on the shameful situation: (...)] (Loge and Froh hurriedly pile up the trinkets between the staves: H27; H38; H25a) [Fafner and Loge debate how best to pile up the hoard: (...)]

Wotan: (...) Deep in my breast (H38:; H23:) the shame of it sears me. (...)

Fafner: (H45: H38: casting a careful eye over the hoard, looking for chinks: H28:) Holda's hair still glints through the gold (:H28): that trinket yonder add to the hoard! [Fricka, Fafner, Donner, and Loge discuss the situation, and Fafner demands the Tarnhelm to block sight of Freia's hair: (...)]

Wotan: All right, let it go! [Loge tosses the Tarnhelm on the hoard, and asks if the Giants are content: (...)]

Fasolt: (...) (H45; H38) (He moves closer and peers through the hoard: H22:; H23:) Alas! Her ... starry eye still shines upon me ... ! (...)—While I still see this lovely eye (:H22; H23), (H35:) I'll not give up the woman (:H35). [Fafner and Loge debate: (...)]

Fafner: (...) On Wotan's finger a ring of gold still glints: give that to fill the cranny! [**Wotan:**(...)]

Loge: (H12:) (...) This gold belongs to the Rhine's fair daughters: Wotan is giving it back to them (:H12).

Wotan: What nonsense is that? What was hard for me to capture I'll fearlessly keep for myself. (H9) [Wotan and Loge debate: (...); **Fafner:** (...)] ... ask for whatever you want ... ; but not for the world shall I give up the ring!

Fasolt: (angrily pulling Freia out from behind the hoard) (...) Freia will follow us now for ever.

[Freia, Fricka, Froh, and Donner beg Wotan to give the Ring to the Giants to redeem Freia: (...)]

Wotan: Leave me in peace: the ring I'll not give up.

The vulgarity with which the Giants transform sacred Freia into a commodity to be weighed in value against a golden treasure plunges Wotan into an apoplexy of shame. This dramatizes how entirely dependent our ideal is on the real. Fafner having claimed the Ring Wotan is wearing in order to block Fasolt's view and wipe out love forever from his heart, Wotan shows his true colors and refuses to yield the Ring to the Giants, even if this means he must forfeit Freia and the world (his ideal world). Though Freia represents our hope for transcendent value and eternal life, the imaginary things promised by religious faith, our longing for these ideals has a physical basis. Wotan therefore grasps at reality when he has the opportunity, disavowing for the moment his emotional attachment to the illusion of infinite enjoyment which religion's promises provide. But Wotan's insistence on trading the illusion of transcendent value and immortal life for concrete power in the real world calls up from the depths the World Soul, Erda, Mother Nature. Nature fully wakes in Wotan, becomes conscious of herself in him. Her rising is heralded by an orchestral explosion of a H17/H18a hybrid or variant which motivally highlights the underlying identity of Wotan's quest for divine power in Valhalla, and Alberich's quest for actual power on earth:

> **[p. 112]** ([[H?51.5 orch:]] [[H17ab/H18ab orch or a H17ab vari?]]: [[possibly a distinct, compound motif which ought to be numbered]]) (...) All stand dismayed. Wotan turns away in anger. The stage has grown dark again: **[[H52 orch:]]** [= H2 vari] ... Erda suddenly appears ... .)
>
> **Erda:** ([[H52 orch:]] ...) Yield, Wotan! Yield! Flee the curse on the ring! To irredeemably dark destruction its gain will ever ordain you. [**Wotan:** (...)] **[[H52 orch:]]** How all things were—I know; (H52:) how all things are, (H52 modulating:) how all things will be, I see as well (:H52 modulating): (H52:) the endless earth's (:H52) primeval Wala, Erda, bids you beware. (H52:) Ere the world was, my womb brought forth three daughters: what I see the Norns unfold each night (:H52).

Alberich's Ring speaks its truth through Erda. Having attained full objective consciousness in us, Mother Nature becomes self-conscious and wakes in Wotan as she did in Alberich. Wagner found a basis for this concept in Feuerbach: " ... the reason is the most indispensable being—the profoundest and most essential necessity. In the reason first lies the self-consciousness of existence ... ; in the reason is first revealed the end, the meaning of existence." [55F-EOC, p. 43; See also 193F-LER, p. 21] In one of Wagner's paraphrases of Feuerbach previously cited, he observed that though at its inception man's newborn consciousness—thanks to our limited knowledge of the world—begins in error (religious belief), the history of the birth of knowledge from error is the history of our scientific correction of our prior religious view that the cause of Nature is outside of Nature in supernatural beings. [See [414W-{9–12/49} 'The Artwork of the Future,' PW Vol. I, pp. 70–71] And Wagner explained that: "Through this knowledge does Nature grow conscious of herself, ... by Man himself, who only through discriminating between himself and Nature has attained that point where he can apprehend her, by making her his 'object.'"

Now that Wotan has taken possession of Alberich's Ring and is preparing to exploit its full power, Erda, Mother Nature as known to man objectively, has woken to offer Wotan a vision of the bitter truth which he can't face, but Alberich can. Erda's waking for Wotan is automatically tantamount to the twilight of the gods she'll soon foretell. Erda will tell Wotan the price he must pay if he insists on staking his claim to the power of truth by retaining possession of Alberich's Ring of consciousness. Consciousness of truth means the end of the gods, i.e., the end of our belief in them. As Erda delivers her initial warning that Wotan should flee the Ring Curse, presumably by yielding it to the Giants (she never suggests he return it to the Rhinedaughters), and proclaims that its gain will ordain him irredeemable dark destruction, H52 ("Erda's Motif") is introduced. It's a slower, heavier, darker, harmonized variant of H1 via H2, the Primal Nature Motif and its first variant which included the Rhine River's Motion, with which the *Ring* began. H52 is associated here with Erda's description of her (Nature's) self-knowledge, that it embraces all that was, is, and will be (the cosmos composed of time=space, matter=energy, abiding by the ur-laws of Nature's coherence including causation, the scientific equivalent of Fate). H52, stemming from the Primal Nature Motif H1 out of which the music (and thus the words and drama) of the entire *Ring* develops, can be understood as the motival incarnation of the natural necessity of change, the ephemeral world. It's natural necessity, fate in its scientific sense, Erda's knowledge, which Erda's daughters the Norns spin into their rope of fate. This includes the necessity of death. This confirms that the sin against all that was, is, and will be, which Alberich said Wotan would commit if he stole Alberich's Ring and co-opted its power, is religious man's sin of world denial, the symbolical murder of Mother Nature. However, since Alberich's Ring Motif H17ab evolved into the first two segments of Wotan's Valhalla Motif H18ab (where Wotan intends to live), Wotan has already co-opted Alberich's Ring power: what's being enacted now merely dramatizes this. Wotan couldn't really give away Alberich's Ring if he wanted to. Erda must mean something else by her plea.

It's noteworthy that Erda, who incarnates and speaks Nature's wisdom (in the *Ring* Nature is the creator and embraces even the gods), doesn't suggest Wotan restore the Ring to the Rhinedaughters, but insists that he yield it to the Giants. When Erda warns Wotan that he ought to flee the Ring Curse by yielding it to the Giants, she's figuratively telling him he should escape the curse of consciousness by placing the Ring under the control of his emotions of fear (Fafner) and desire (Fasolt). Yielding the Ring to the Giants (feeling under the influence of thought) is a sort of ersatz, artificial restoration of it to the Rhinedaughters, preconscious feeling. Erda can either be known objectively as Alberich does, in which case he who possesses full Ring consciousness can't console himself with illusions inspired by heartfelt feeling, or she can be known subjectively, sympathetically, through feeling, i.e., through restoration of that feeling of oneness with Nature which presumably preceded consciousness's split into subject and object, such as the Rhinedaughters enjoyed. Since we can no longer restore the innocence lost to us through consciousness, we must resort to artificial means, a surrogate, our unconscious mind.

Though Feuerbach had high praise for conscious scientific endeavor, he believed our most authentic contact with the reality of the ephemeral world is through the unique particularity of feeling, because feeling can capture Nature's essence as change. Feuerbach's ruminations on this subject had a huge influence on Wagner's concept of music as feeling which offers us redemption from the burdens of thought. These include the following: "Transitoriness [Erda's "All things that are, end!"] is the essence of all feeling." [2F-TDI, p. 51; See also 28F-TDI, p. 200, and 349F-LER, p. 351] " ... only the sensuous is clear as daylight; all doubt and dispute cease only where sensation begins." [183F-PPF, p. 55; See also 342F-LER, pp. 322–323, 179F-PPF, pp. 43–44, and 346F-LER, p. 335] "... life is music. Every moment is a melody or a fulfilled, soulful, inspired tone. (...)

Transitoriness disappears as a meaningless reality without significance in comparison to this inner ... soul of the musical tone." [24F-TDI, p. 171]

Wagner saw our scientific impulse to accumulate an ever greater and increasingly truthful hoard of objective knowledge of the world as our futile quest to grasp the world as a whole, to continually forge Alberich's Ring. He called on us to redeem ourselves through subjective feeling (music), as Erda calls on Wotan to do in yielding the Ring of consciousness to the Giants to flee Alberich's Ring Curse of consciousness: "... reality ... can be grasped ... only if we recognize that the essence of reality lies in its endless multiplicity. This ... can be apprehended, however, by feeling [music] ... : this sense of change [Erda's "All things that are, end!"] is the essence of reality, whereas only what is imagined is changelessly unending [the Valhallan gods' alleged immortality]. Only what changes is real: to be real, to live—... is to be created, to grow, to bloom, to wither and to die; without the necessity of death, there is no possibility of life ... . (...) But in order to make such a consummation possible, we must abandon completely our search for the 'whole' ... . How is this marvellous process most fully achieved? Ask Nature [Erda]! Only through love [feeling, or music]!" [607W-{1/25–26/54} Letter to August Röckel, SLRW, pp. 302–303; See also 606W-{1/25–26/54} Letter to August Röckel, SLRW, p. 302; 1059W, and 1115W] This quest for the whole—which according to both Feuerbach and Wagner is the basis for human history (the basis of human consciousness per se)—is the foundation both of scientific, technological man's quest to transform the real world into his personal property, and to know all things, such as the unchanging laws of Nature, and of religious man's quest for union with what he regards as the eternal, immutable, supernatural basis of the ephemeral world. Erda seems to be warning Wotan that if he co-opts Alberich's Ring power, Wotan's hope to sustain the illusory realm of the gods will be predestined to destruction.

But we'll soon learn that the gods' doom Erda foretold can't be preempted by Wotan's decision to take her advice and yield the Ring to the giants. Wotan, exponent of our belief in the supernatural, seeks the whole which can never be found because his object is illusory. This is the basis for religious man's existential dilemma, which I, following Wagner's lead in *Parsifal*, have called the wound that will never heal. This is why Erda now foretells the inevitable doom of the gods:

> **[p. 112] Erda:** (H49:) But gravest danger brings me myself to you today (:H49): (H8:) Hearken! Hearken! Hearken (:H8)! (H52:) All things that are—(H52 modulating [with octave drop:]) end (:H52). **[[H53 orch:]]** [= approximately H52 inversion] A day of darkness dawns for the gods (:H53 orch): (H17:) I counsel you: shun the ring (:H17)!

In her proclamation that all things that are, end, Erda proclaims Mother Nature's self-knowledge: transience and change are the essence of Mother Nature's phenomena. This puts Erda, spokeswoman for the truth, at odds with the gods, who proclaim their immortality and the divine inalterability of their mandate and laws. Feuerbach's meditations on Nature's transience gave Wagner the cue for both Erda's expression of her nature as change, and for her prophecy of the twilight of the gods: "Nature brings death, God alone confers immortality." [302F-LER, p. 266] " … in nature it is impossible to tell who is the lord and who the vassal, because all things are … equally essential … . And this very fact that the organism … owes its existence to cooperation among equal beings, is the source of material evil, of struggle, illness, and death; but the cause of death is also the cause of life, the cause of evil is also the cause of good. A God, on the other hand, is … an absolute, unrestrained monarch who does what he pleases, who is 'above the law' … ." [237F-LER, p. 137; See also 303F-LER, p. 267] But according to Erda even the gods, like all other natural phenomena, are subject to change, to mortality. Their fated doom is a logical consequence of Erda's essential law that all things which are, end. Since our *Ring* allegory is predicated on the idea that mortal humans involuntarily and unconsciously invented the gods, who're therefore illusions of our own making, it goes without saying they're predestined to destruction by us, their unwitting makers, once we mature in knowledge of the truth.

A crucial omission in Erda's prophecy is that she doesn't tell Wotan the gods can escape the fated doom she foretold, but rather, offers them a suggestion of how they can temporarily avoid foreseeing it, how they can redeem themselves from consciousness of it and fear of it (the end), by submerging thinking (the Ring) in feeling (yielding it to our animal instincts, the Giants). This they can do by resorting to the refuge of consoling illusions founded in subjective feeling (Valhalla), called religious faith in earlier times, and art, particularly the art of music (feeling sans thought), in secular times. Initially, Wagner planned to have Erda say a gloomy day was dawning for the gods if they don't yield the Ring (to the Giants), but he altered this passage. In the version we experience in performance Erda drops this condition, stating flatly that a day of darkness dawns for the gods: "For me my poem [*The Ring of the Nibelung*] has only the following meaning: … Instead of the words: 'a gloomy day dawns on the gods: in shame shall end your noble race, if you do not give up the ring!' I now make Erda say merely: 'All that is—ends: a gloomy day dawns on the gods: I counsel you, shun the ring!'—We must learn to die … in the fullest sense of the word: fear of the end is the source of all lovelessness … ." [613W-{1/25–26/54} Letter to August Röckel, SLRW, pp. 306–307] We'll only learn much later what Wagner means by his alteration to Erda's prophecy, when he adds that we must learn to die, and that fear of the end is the source of all lovelessness. Wagner enlarged on this in his commentary on Wotan's fateful decision to will the necessary, the destruction of the gods, in S.3.1: " … the remainder of the poem [the *Ring*] is concerned to show how necessary it is to acknowledge change, variety, multiplicity and the eternal newness of reality and of life, and to yield to that necessity. Wodan rises to the tragic heights of willing his own destruction. This is all that we need to learn from the history of mankind: to will what is necessary and to bring it about ourselves." [615W-{1/25–26/54} Letter to August Röckel, SLRW, p. 307] As we'll see, Wagner is referring to a post-religious path to redemption.

Erda's prophecy of the twilight of the gods has foreseen the following: the day will come when we'll recognize ourselves as the formerly unwitting authors of the imaginary ideal we call divinity, and take responsibility for ourselves by casting off our belief in the gods' protection, and renouncing our age-old hope that redemption from our earthly coils can be found in the gods' heavenly abode. This will come to pass as the natural, inevitable consequence of man's gradual advancement in objective knowledge, i.e., Wotan's wandering into and over the earth (Erda) in quest of a hoard of knowledge, in his role as the Wanderer. Erda counsels Wotan to shun the Ring but not with any prospect that he can thereby redeem the gods from Alberich's Ring Curse. Belief in the gods is predestined to destruction. Since, along with faith in the divine, man will also lose his dependence on religion's illusory promise of immortality, Wagner added that we must learn to die. But that ultimate loss of faith is a long way off. In the meantime Erda's warning has granted the gods a temporary lease on life. Wotan can for a time redeem himself from having to foresee the inevitable end of the gods so long as he doesn't possess the Ring of consciousness. He can replace truth with an illusion held to be the truth, and prohibit freedom of inquiry which can contradict this false belief, by establishing unquestioning religious faith, sanctioned (at least subliminally) by fear. Faith's fear of truth will later be represented by Fafner.

Wotan, paralyzed now by that existential fear which Alberich's objective consciousness (the Ring's power, expressed by Erda) has instilled in him, seeks to know everything, to understand why he must live his entire life under the burden of this inescapable dread:

[pp. 112–13] **Wotan:** [to Erda] ... tarry, till I know more! (...)

Erda: (sinking: H52:) I've warned you—(H52:) you know enough: (H52—fading:) brood in care and fear! (She disappears completely ...) (...)

Wotan: If care and fear must consume me then I must seize you and find out everything!

Wotan's attitude is that of the jealous lover who, though knowing the full truth might forever disillusion him, can't rest until he learns whether his lover has been betraying him behind his back. Or like the sick man who, believing his doctor is hiding the worst from him, insists on learning the bitter truth, no matter the cost to his peace of mind, since uncertainty is worse even than the bitterest truth. Wotan intends to find out all that Mother Nature can teach him objectively, to know Nature as cold science (Alberich's quest for objective power) knows it, to grasp the full price he must pay for possessing Alberich's Ring of consciousness. But Wotan will abruptly change his mind after he witnesses a dramatic incident which demonstrates the cost to him of acknowledging the truth. Erda has implanted in him that existential fear, doubt, with no specific (i.e., conscious) cause of which Feuerbach spoke, and which Alberich described as the essence of his Ring Curse of consciousness. Erda has prepared for the gods a day of judgment on their pretension to divinity, i.e., their alleged immortality, in a formulation straight out of Feuerbach: " ... love [say, the Rhinedaughters' joy in the Rhinegold which Alberich renounced] goes back to the beginning of the world, but fear extends to the end of the world; love made the First Day, but fear made the Day of Judgment." [320F-LER, p. 290]

Thanks to Erda's warning about the price Wotan must pay to possess Alberich's Ring power, i.e., consciousness of the objective truth, he decides he prefers the consolation of self-deception, and agrees after all to yield the Ring of consciousness to the Giants, so his conscious mind can be controlled by his subjective feelings:

> [p. 113] (All stare expectantly at Wotan; H52: the latter rouses himself from his thoughts, seizes his spear and brandishes it, as though to indicate a courageous decision: H19)
>
> **Wotan:** To me, Freia! You are freed: now it's brought back, (H35:) may our youth return (:H35)! You giants, take your ring! (He throws the ring on to the hoard. The giants release Freia ... .)

Thanks to Wotan's choosing illusion over truth, the Giants grant him his illusion of transcendent love and immortality by restoring Freia to him, which can only freely be enjoyed by the gods if the Giants (mortal man's egoism) don't openly stake their rightful and natural claim to her. But by covertly satisfying the Giants' demand for the sole true source of satisfaction in life, the Ring's worldly power, Wotan subliminally acknowledges that our egoistic animal instincts own the truth. The first fruit of Wotan's decision to place the Giants in control of Alberich's keys to worldly power is that they fight over the spoils until Fafner kills his brother Fasolt in a manner so brutal and cynical that it shocks the gods into speechlessness:

> [p. 114] **Fasolt:** (to Fafner: H25a:; H38:) Don't be so greedy. Grant me some, too! Equal shares befit us both (:H25a; :H38).
>
> **Fafner:** (H25a:; H38:) You set greater store by the maid than you did by the gold, you lovesick loon! (... (:H25a; :H38). (H24:) You wouldn't have shared her if you'd wooed Freia (:H24); if I now share the hoard, it's fair that I keep the biggest half for myself.
>
> **Fasolt:** (...) (to the gods) I call on you as judges: justly and fairly divide the hoard! (Wotan turns contemptuously away.) [**Loge and Fasolt:** (...); Fasolt and Fafner struggle over the Ring]
>
> **Fafner:** (H17:) Take your hands off! The ring is mine (:H17). (Fasolt tears the ring from Fafner's hand) [**Fasolt:** (...)] (preparing to strike him with his stave) Hold it fast or else it may fall! (He fells Fasolt with a single blow, drumbeat repeated: then wrenches the ring from his dying brother.) (H17:) Now gaze your fill on Freia's glance: never again will you touch the ring (:H17)! (H50: He puts the ring in the sack, then calmly finishes packing away the rest of the hoard. All the gods look on in horror: solemn silence.)

We could call this fratricide the first fruits of the Fall, of Alberich's forging the Ring and laying his Curse on it. We're reminded of Cain's slaying of Abel in the

Bible's *Book of Genesis*. This isn't only an expression of our Fall (from grace with Nature) through acquisition of consciousness, but also suggests our self-preservation instinct is stronger than our social instinct of love, since we see Fafner, the incarnation of self-preservation, kill his brother, the amorous Fasolt. Fafner has now absorbed his brother, as both are motivated by the same thing, egoism. In Fafner's assumption that his brother Fasolt didn't bargain in good faith in seeking possession of Freia, because Fasolt wouldn't willingly have shared her love if the Giants had won her in payment (accompanied, significantly, by Loge's Motif H24), Fafner cynically points out the egoism hidden within the alleged virtuousness of monogamy, love's fidelity. The egoistic underside of romantic love is that it's another form of competition in the quest for exclusive power, our quest to stake our claim to personal property at the expense of others. The inextricable link of jealousy with romantic love strongly suggests egoism is the root of romantic love's exclusivism. Wagner's beloved Schopenhauer often exercised his caustic wit at the expense of lovers on the basis of this argument, that romantic love is just a gloss for the selfish drive to sexual reproduction, the Will.

Having witnessed this terrible event, the initial impact of Alberich's Ring Curse among men, Wotan decides after all he doesn't wish to learn from Erda the full truth:

> [pp. 114–15] **Wotan:** (shaken) Fearful now I find the curse's power! (H50)
> [**Loge:** (...)] (H50:) ... how a sense of unease binds me fast (:H50)! (H52:) Care and fear fetter my thoughts—how I may end them (:H52) (H53:) Erda shall teach me: to her I must descend (:H53)!

In Fafner's murder of his brother Fasolt for the sake of the Ring's power Wotan recognizes the essence of the Ring Curse, that we're destined to acknowledge self-preservation and self-aggrandizement (all will lust for gold and renounce love) as the fundamental motives underlying all human feeling, thought, and action, including those seemingly exceptional cases in which we strive to escape our subjection to egoism and natural law. After witnessing this effect of the Ring Curse, Wotan has found the implications of it unbearable, so he's changed his mind. He no longer wishes to learn from Erda the full truth about why he must live in care and fear, since he's just obtained his answer in Fafner's victory over Fasolt. He now desires instead to follow Erda's original suggestion that he flee Alberich's Ring Curse of consciousness. He's already followed her advice to yield Alberich's Ring to the Giants, but that isn't enough. He no longer expresses hope he can alter those things which engender care and fear, but wishes now to learn from Erda how he can cease to feel care and fear, i.e., how he can become unconscious of it. Wotan wishes, in other words, to substitute consolation for truth, illusory bliss (Wahn) for woe ("Noth"), blindness for sight. Through this unconscious process of repression and sublimation, Wotan will draw inspiration (Loge's advantage) from the fear engendered by Erda's prophecy of the gods' end, to create a veil of self-deception (Wahn, or Maya) as a means to forget the fear she taught. We must in some sense know the truth to be inspired to (have any motive to) deceive ourself about it, but we can only deceive ourself about something we know if we only know it unconsciously. Just as Wotan drew unconscious inspiration from the nightmare of Alberich's forging of his Ring in Erda's Navelnest Nibelheim in order to involuntarily dream Valhalla into existence (H17ab>H18ab), so he must descend to Erda to draw unconscious artistic inspiration from what he can't bear to think.

Though Wotan can't afford to possess the Ring himself, because to do so would make him conscious of this fatal truth, he must find some way of keeping Alberich from regaining it which doesn't place the Ring's guardian at risk of exposing its truth to the light of day. Wotan and Alberich are essentially one being, in whom the light-side, Wotan, now takes precedence and suppresses the dark side, hiding it in his unconscious mind, where it will sit lurking, waiting for its chance to rise from the silent depths to daylight. How to keep this from happening will be Wotan's obsession.

In a passage previously cited [See 704W-{64–2/65} 'On State and Religion,' PW Vol. IV, pp. 27–28; See also 767W] Wagner developed a theory of unconscious artistic inspiration which presumably was based both on his personal experience of it, and received tradition. According to his thesis the authentically unconsciously inspired work of art is a waking dream, an allegory for the true, unconscious source of inspiration which remains hidden even from the artist himself. While on some deep level of consciousness the artist must confront this true source, upon waking from what Wagner described as a nightmare, the artist forgets the original dream of inspiration and produces for himself and his audience a waking dream which is a mere allegory for the original, which is "unspeakable." He applied this thesis equally to both religious revelation and unconscious artistic inspiration. The portion of this extract of greatest import is the following: " ... the record left upon our own mind by a deeply moving dream is strictly nothing but an allegorical paraphrase, whose intrinsic disagreement with the original remains a trouble to our waking consciousness ... ." Wotan's unease is a metaphor for what Feuerbach suggested is the unease the religiously faithful feel in staking their happiness on what their unconscious mind knows to be their own self-deception. Wotan knows deep down that he's cheating (i.e., depending on the Liar God Loge), that he's dishonoring the truth. He's at risk of becoming too conscious of the egoism underlying our belief in the gods. It's his fear that the beliefs and ideals on which the gods (i.e., mortal men) staked all their happiness might have an insecure foundation which troubles him so much he feels he must descend to Erda, Mother Nature, to confront this seemingly irresolvable existential dilemma, the source of his self-doubt, to find the means to allay it.

Wotan seeks Erda to obtain two types of knowledge, (1) objective knowledge of the bitter truth he fears, and (2) subjective, aesthetic intuition through which he can sublimate her terrible knowledge into a safe form as religious mythology, and later, secular art (especially music), and thereby forget the fear engendered by objective truth. The first kind of knowledge (1) is comparable to the fatal knowledge Eve obtained from the fruit of the Tree of Knowledge in paradise and imparted to Adam, thereby prompting God to exile them from paradise in punishment, and to make them subject to shame and fearful death, and the need to labor in order to sustain life. The second kind of knowledge acquisition (2) is an attempt to restore the paradise which has been lost due to obtaining the first kind of knowledge, just as Eve's crime, which banished us from paradise, is the inspiration for Christ's offer of redemption, the restoration of paradise. Eve is for Wagner the archetypal muse for secular art which he dramatized in *The Mastersingers of Nuremberg*, in which Eva is the muse who unconsciously inspires the composer and poet Walther von Stolzing, in a dream, to create his Mastersong, in which the Tree of Knowledge (Erda's objective knowledge, the cause of the Fall, our exile from paradise) and the Tree of Life (aesthetic intuition, i.e., Erda known sympathetically through love rather than through objective understanding, the promise of paradise regained) become one. As Hans Sachs tells Eva during his cobbling song confession in Act Two of *Mastersingers*, since Eva in paradise was responsible for committing that original sin which made God punish both Adam and her with exile from paradise, Eva must compensate for her crime by serving as muse of unconscious inspiration for Walther von Stolzing's redemptive work of art, the Mastersong, which is our substitute for the sacred in a secular age. The significance of this for Wotan's relationship with Erda is that she both delivers the wound and heals it. In Volume Two I'll show how this key trope underlies and illuminates much that has previously been obscure in Wagner's canonical operas and music-dramas from *The Flying Dutchman* through *Parsifal*.

While Wotan is tremulous with unease contemplating the compromising machinations, subterfuge and self-deception in which he's had to engage to enter the gods' abode Valhalla with religion's essential beliefs (Freia as goddess of transcendent love and immortality) intact, Fricka, wholly oblivious to these subterranean contradictions which burden Wotan, suggests he allay all doubt and enjoy the welcoming shelter of the as-yet-to-be-named fortress, accompanied by H21. But Wotan's doubts aren't allayed, for he notes he paid for Valhalla with evil wage, as we hear H17ab, reminding us again that H17ab (Alberich's Ring) gave birth to H18ab (Valhalla):

> **[p. 115] Fricka:** (... H21:) Your thoughts are elsewhere. Does the noble stronghold not beckon you gladly (:H21), (H18ab:) awaiting its lord with its welcoming shelter? (H18ab [seems to transform into H17])
>
> **Wotan:** (sombrely: H17:) With evil wage I paid for the building (:H17)! (H50 frag)

Loge of course was lying when he declared Valhalla's walls solidly built. It was egoism, our selfish animal instincts, which built these walls of religious self-deception on which we depend for our sense of transcendent self-worth. Through Wotan's self-doubt Wagner is suggesting that we, the historical Folk, who involuntarily and unconsciously invented our religions and our gods, are subliminally aware we're lying to ourselves, i.e., that we're dependent on the liar-god Loge.

Porges, evidently referencing Erda's last confrontation with Wotan in S.3.1, recorded Wagner's view that Erda, Mother Nature, is Wotan's superior, the "inexorable voice of his conscience," i.e., his objective, intellectual conscience: "Although he [Wotan] compels her [Erda] with his magic ('she can only withdraw when he allows her to,' Wagner said) she is his superior in that it is from her lips that he hears the inexorable voice of his conscience which nothing can silence." [877W-{6–8/76} WRR, p. 103] It's noteworthy that in a passage previously cited Wagner observed that Alberich's accusations that Wotan is a hypocrite, that he's motivated by the same egoism that motivates Alberich, and that Wotan is a sinner, are accurate and just: "From the depths of Nibelheim the conscience of their [the gods'] guilt cries up to them ... ." [See 376W-{6–8/48} 'The Nibelungen Myth,' PW Vol. VII, p. 302] Alberich, like Erda, is the gods' conscience. Alberich affirms Erda's objective knowledge, while Wotan sins against it by denying it. Since Wotan in S.3.1 will consign Erda and her wisdom to the oblivion of sleep, describing her as the embodiment of "mothers' fear," Porges' remembrance of Wagner's observation that Erda is Wotan's conscience has special resonance. Similarly, since Wagner so often equated Judaism with the stance of modern, secular, scientific thought, and described the Jews as condemned to the reality of this world (i.e., condemned to egoism, and subjection to natural law), it's not surprising to find him stating that " ... Judaism is the evil conscience of our modern Civilisation," [460W-{8/50} 'Judaism in Music,' PW Vol. III, p. 100] thus equating Judaism with both Alberich and Erda.

Alberich will for aeons sit outside Fafner's lair waiting for his chance to regain possession of the Ring power (control over man's conscious mind) which has now been co-opted temporarily by our first form of thought, religious mythology. At Fafner's Envy-Cave, transformed into the serpent or dragon whose form Alberich also took, Fafner (in whom man's fear of death is transmuted into religious faith's fear of the truth) will guard access to the truth (Alberich's hoard of knowledge), to keep the faithful from seeking it. Alberich will wait for man in the course of history to breach his faith so Alberich can restore his lost Ring power and reaffirm Mother Nature's objective truth. Wotan, deep down, knows this, and he's troubled because he must find some means to pre-empt Alberich's intent, without disturbing the religiously faithful (exemplified by Wotan's wife Fricka, who doesn't share Wotan's self-doubt). Alberich's sole concern henceforth will be to discredit religious mythology (the gods), so he can replace it with that knowledge which grants us earthly power. Feuerbach described the kind of doubt (Wotan's unease) which must inevitably beset religious man over time, suggesting that in the course of history our experience of the world will eventually engender doubt in religion's articles of faith: "But whence comes this weakness of faith? From the fact that the power of belief is nothing other than the power of imagination, and that reality is an infinitely greater power, directly opposed to the imagination. (...) ... as even the greatest heroes of faith have confessed, it flies in the face of sensory evidence, natural feeling, and man's innate tendency to disbelief. How, indeed, can anything built on constraint, on the forcible repression of a sound inclination, anything exposed at every moment to the mind's doubts and the contradictions of experience, provide a firm and secure foundation?" [326F-LER, pp. 302–303]

Valhalla at its founding having been tainted by its disreputable origin, Donner now strives to clear the air of all doubt through a miraculous, sensational proof of divine power over Nature, which will hopefully clear the way for the gods to enter their new, heavenly abode without fear of Alberich's host of night (i.e., without dread of the truth):

> [pp. 115–16] **Donner:** A sultry haze hangs in the air; its lowering weight lies heavy upon me. The leaden clouds (H10:) I'll gather into a raging storm; it will sweep the heavens clear. (…) **[[H54 voc:]]** Heda! Heda, hedo (:H54 voc)! To me, you haze! You mists, to me! Donner your lord, musters his hordes. (He swings his hammer.) At the swing of my hammer sweep to me here! [etc. … .] (H54 voc:) Heda! Heda! Hedo! (:H54 voc)! (H54:;; H10: (…) (The blow of his hammer is heard striking the rock. A brilliant flash of lightning issues from the cloud, followed by a violent clap of thunder. (…)) (invisible): Brother, this way! Mark out the way for the bridge! (The cloud suddenly lifts, revealing Donner and Froh. **[[H55 orch:]]** From their feet a rainbow bridge of blinding radiance stretches out across the valley to the castle, which now glints in the glow of the evening sun.)
>
> **Froh:** (…) The bridge leads to the stronghold, light yet firm to the foot. Tread undaunted its terrorless path!

Donner's new motif H54, sung to his "Heda! Heda! Hedo!," is in the Nature Motif Family stemming from H1, the Primal Nature Arpeggio. H54 is in turn the basis for H60, which depicts lightning during the storm (produced by Wotan) which drives Wotan's mortal son Siegmund in desperation to seek shelter in Hunding's hut in the opening scene of *The Valkyrie*. Dunning suggests H60 may influence H83 and H85, motifs which will be associated with Wotan's anger against his mortal family the Wälsungs, and anger at his daughter Brünnhilde for defying the gods' law to support the Wälsungs.

As Donner's storm clears to make way for the stunning appearance of the Rainbow Bridge leading from the meadow to Valhalla, we're introduced to its "Rainbow Bridge Motif" H55, the only instance in which it's heard in the entire *Ring* (though Wagner grants it an impressively broad sweep in this, its one dramatic occurrence, in the finale of *Rhinegold*). H55 is also in the Nature Motif Family. It's the bridge of transition between our evolutionary status as preconscious animals, and new status as reflectively conscious humans, since only with the finale of *Rhinegold* are the foundations of human civilization laid. All the gods and other beings of *The Rhinegold* represent aspects of humanity, of the human psyche and heart, rather than specific beings, or represent collective, historical man. The essence of this transition, this collective dreaming which gave birth to civilization founded on religious faith in the rule of supernatural gods, is that all trace of our true, natural origin in evolution is wiped out and replaced by a false mythological past which we recount as our own, though it's our involuntary, unwitting invention. All memory of our debt to Nature (Erda), to our animal instincts (first the Rhinedaughters, and then, with the split of instinct into desire and fear, good and evil, the Giants), and to the power of our conscious human mind (Alberich's Ring and Tarnhelm), is forgotten, or rather, never rose to consciousness. As Feuerbach put it, all trace of our Christian God's origin in Nature is effaced by our religious mythology, and all intellectual inquiry and curiosity which might reveal this origin is instinctively censored so the physical origin of what we call the supernatural can never be known. We can't help thinking of Lohengrin's taboo against revealing his true origin and identity: "... the God of Christian monotheism is a withered, dried-out God in whom all traces of His origin in nature is effaced; there He stands like a creation out of nothing; on pain of the rod He even forbids the inevitable question: ... 'What was He before nature?' In other words, He makes a secret of His physical origin, hiding it behind a metaphysical abstraction." [341F-LER, pp. 321–322]

Wotan now invokes the weighty burden of the epic labor we humans, in the earliest epoch of our history, undertook to win for ourselves this strange compromise between truth and self-deception in a civilization predicated on both practical knowledge of the means to survival, and the illusion that we mortals have one foot in a spiritual, transcendent realm:

> [pp. 116–17] **Wotan:** (H18a:) In the evening light the sun's eye gleams; in its glittering glow the stronghold shines resplendent: (H18b:) glinting bravely in the morning light, (H18c:) it still lay lordless and (H18d:) nobly alluring before me (:H18d). (H17:) From morn until evening in toil and anguish ["Angst"] it wasn't happily won (:H17)! Night draws on: from its envious ["Neid"] sway may it offer shelter now. (**[[H56ab orch:]]** [H56a = Octave drop on Erda's "Endet;" H56b = H1 vari] very resolutely, as though seized by a grandiose idea:) **[[H57a voc:]]** Thus I salute the stronghold (:H57a), **[[H57b voc:]]** Safe from dread and dismay (:H57b). (H56ab) (... : H18d) Follow me, wife: in Valhalla dwell with me!
>
> **Fricka:** (H18ab:) What meaning lies in the name? Never, I think, have I heard it before (:H18ab).
>
> **Wotan:** (H18ab:) What, mastering fear, my mind conceived, shall reveal its sense if it lives victorious (:H18ab)! (He takes Fricka by the hand and moves slowly with her towards the bridge; Froh, Freia, and Donner follow)

Wotan proclaims the essence of the gods' newly won abode he's named Valhalla. It's our refuge from night's (Alberich's) envious sway, religious man's refuge from the truth which Alberich wishes to raise up from the silent depths of Nibelheim's night to the light of day. Wotan proclaims his grand idea, his revelation that he'll find a way to redeem the Valhallan gods from the dread and dismay engendered by Wotan's own skepticism about its dismal origins. We hear a loud proclamation on the trumpet of the new and supremely important Motif H56ab, the Sword Motif (the sword Nothung Wotan makes so his Wälsung heroes can wield it in their unwitting quest to redeem the gods from Alberich's Ring Curse). It's also called the "Motif of Wotan's Grand Idea": he'll create a race of mortal heroes, the Wälsungs, who can (all unwitting) free themselves from the gods' laws and religious faith, in order to retrieve Alberich's Ring from Fafner (something Wotan is bound on oath, through his social contract, not to do) to preempt Alberich's plot to regain its power. Wotan will live in the hope that the Wälsungs can somehow redeem the gods from the fate Erda foretold, the gods' fated doom which (as he'll tell Brünnhilde in V.2.2) necessarily follows on the birth of Alberich's son Hagen. This twilight of the gods is a metaphor for the inevitability that we'll eventually outgrow our belief in gods as we, in the long course of world-history, gradually substitute objective knowledge of natural causes for phenomena previously attributed to the gods.

H56ab is a classic example of Wagner's concept of a musical motif of premonition, since it's not clear that Wotan is conscious yet of his long-term plan to redeem the gods from Alberich's Ring Curse. We don't see the sword, whose motif sounds without its proper object, until scene three of the first act of *The Valkyrie*. We can grasp the Sword's (Wotan's grand idea for redemption's) significance in its motival components, for it's composed of two distinct segments, the first, H56a, being composed of the octave drop on "Endet" as Erda sang, "All things that are, end!" This segment implies the transitory nature of the world's phenomena, and the necessity of death. Segment H56b is composed of the Primal Nature Motif H1, the music with which the *Ring* began, which gave birth to it. It represents the time prior to our Fall from grace with our preconscious animal nature caused by the evolution of human consciousness. The Wälsung heroes, who unwittingly wield this sword in behalf of Wotan's quest to redeem the gods from Alberich's Ring Curse of consciousness, will unknowingly strive to restore the innocence and love (the life of feeling) lost with the onset of human thinking (the Ring).

Wotan's visit to Mother Nature, Erda, is an unconscious process, very similar to that collective dreaming through which Alberich's forging of the Ring gave birth to Valhalla while the gods slept. Wotan's daughter Brünnhilde (and her Valkyrie sisters) will be the spawn of his union with her mother Erda. The implications of this for our allegory are momentous, since Brünnhilde will be born of Wotan's two distinct motives in seeking out Erda. First, Wotan wished to learn from Erda the full truth about why he must live his life in care and fear, and presumably to learn whether he can somehow escape the gods' fated doom she foresaw. But what Erda foresees is the objective truth, the nature of the world. Since she is the world, her knowledge is self-knowledge, knowledge of necessity, of what is, what must be. Wotan therefore can't escape his fate. And he can't escape the bitter truth: having witnessed Fafner kill his brother Fasolt for the sake of Alberich's Ring, Wotan has amended his original desire of Erda, and now no longer wishes to confront the truth. So his second, amended desire of Erda is to learn from her how he can free himself from the dread and dismay, the existential fear of the end, which her prophecy has engendered. Since the gods' rule depends on our fear of the truth, and this is a liability which makes faith in the gods vulnerable, perhaps the ultimate redemption Wotan seeks will be a mode of expression of religious man's longing for transcendent value and immortality which needn't fear truth. Brünnhilde, in any case, will have to satisfy both

Wotan's desire to learn the meaning of the fear Erda's prophecy of the gods' doom implanted in his heart, and his antithetical desire to forget this fear.

Alongside H56ab (Sword), Wagner also introduces another new motif, H57ab, as Wotan salutes the newly built abode of the gods, Valhalla: "(H57a) Thus I salute the fortress, (H57b) safe from dread and dismay!" Cooke observed that H57b breaks off from H57ab to highlight the dramatic moment in V.1.3 when Wotan's son Siegmund, the first of the Wälsung heroes through whose freest act Wotan hopes to redeem the gods from the fate Erda foretold, i.e., from the "dread and dismay" caused by Alberich's Ring Curse, sings it while saluting the sword Nothung which Wotan, in disguise, has left for him in Hunding's Ash-tree house pillar. H56b, Cooke noted, gives rise to H79, which in V.2.1 will express Fricka's fear that the Wälsungs threaten the gods' rule.

I've already cited Wagner's remark that world history is the account of how we humans, having risen to consciousness, became aware of our "power" and, having made Nature (Erda) our object of knowledge, set out to force Nature to satisfy our needs through acquisition of knowledge. Here Wagner describes our acquisition of a second kind of knowledge, aesthetic intuition, loving knowledge of the earth (Erda), as the task of world history: "I have succeeded in viewing natural and historical phenomena with love and with total impartiality ... , and I have noticed nothing amiss except for—lovelessness.—But even this lovelessness I was able to explain as an aberration ... which must inevitably lead us away from our state of natural unawareness towards a knowledge of the uniquely beautiful necessity of love; to acquire this knowledge by active striving is the task of world history; but the stage on which this knowledge will one day act out its role is none other than the earth and nature herself [Erda], which is the seed-bed of all that will lead us to this blissful knowledge." [597W-{4/13/53}Letter to Franz Liszt, SLRW, p. 284] This contradiction in our human nature has developed into the war between science and religion (including, according to Wagner, those secular forms of expression, social revolution in the name of social justice and compassion, and inspired art, in which religious man's longing for transcendent value lives on). Wotan's desperate quest to seek redemption from the hoard of knowledge of the truth which he inevitably amasses throughout his historical experience of the world, is represented by H56, his grand idea of how the gods can redeem themselves from the objective truth by restoring lost innocence, retreating from thought into feeling, from power into love, in religious faith, ethics, and art. As Wagner said, world history is the record of our attempt to restore the innocence we lost. [393W-{1–2/49} *Jesus of Nazareth*, PW Vol. VIII, p. 320]

This may be what's behind the peculiar explanation Wotan gives his wife Fricka when she asks him the meaning of the name he's given the newly built fortress, Valhalla, which she's never heard before. Wotan's answer, a bit tortured, nonetheless captures the essence of his hope for redemption. He tells her that what, mastering fear, his mind conceived, shall reveal its sense if it lives on in victory ("wenn <u>sieg</u>end es lebt"). Significantly, all three Wälsungs in whom Wotan hopes to secure Valhalla (the gods' rule in men's hearts) from Alberich's threat, will have names whose root is "Sieg," i.e., victory. They're the sibling twins Siegmund and Sieglinde, and their son Siegfried.

Loge, who—as author of the gods' dependence on self-deceit to make life meaningful—sees through the gods' pretensions to divinity and immortality, finds all this very amusing, and sums up the ironies of the gods' current position astutely, accompanied by that same "Arrogance of Power" motif H46 which sounded as Loge mocked Alberich's ambition for world-power:

> **[p. 117] Loge:** (H32b: remaining at the front of the stage and looking back at the gods) (H46:) They're hurrying on towards their end, though they think they will last for ever (:H46). (H34:; H17 frag:) I'm almost ashamed to share in their dealings ... . To burn them up who formerly tamed me, instead of feebly fading away with the blind—and were they the godliest gods—that seems to me not so foolish (:H34; :H17 frag)! I'll think it over: who knows what I'll do! (He goes nonchalantly to join the gods. H18bc)

Loge symbolizes our (the gods') dependence on artistic self-deceit to make our mortal lives meaningful, and is the archetype for Wotan's race of Wälsung heroes (particularly Siegfried), who can only redeem the gods by breaking their law, as Loge did in persuading Wotan to break his original contract with the Giants. He's the model for the friendly foe and redeemer Wotan will tell Brünnhilde he's seeking in his confession to her in V.2.2. Only a mortal hero, freed from the gods' law (the stranglehold of religious faith, Fafner), can redeem the gods (our religious illusions) from destruction at the hands of truth (Alberich's Ring Curse). Just as Loge has redeemed the gods temporarily from both Alberich's and the Giants' threat by employing his cunning to steal Alberich's Ring, Tarnhelm, and Hoard, so that the gods can redeem Freia from the Giants' claim, so Siegfried, the last of Wotan's Wälsung heroes, will keep Alberich from regaining his lost Ring power by taking possession of his Ring after killing its guardian Fafner. The underlying equivalence of these two incidents is implicit in the fact that both Alberich and Fafner transform themselves into a serpent (dragon), accompanied by the Serpent/Dragon Motif H47, prior to the two distinct thefts of the Ring by Wotan and Loge, and Siegfried, respectively. Loge's expression of ironical amusement at the gods' expense—noting that though they think themselves immortal they're hurrying toward their end, and that therefore he's almost ashamed to share in their doings—describes what's at stake behind the unwitting involvement of the Wälsung heroes Siegmund and Siegfried in the gods' fate. Though the Wälsung heroes will act instinctively and spontaneously, unconscious of the role they're playing in preserving Valhalla from Alberich's threat, Loge is the heroes' hidden conscience and archetype.

Just when Wotan and the gods think they've put all their problems behind them and can freely enter their refuge from dread and dismay Valhalla, the Rhinedaughters cry up from the Rhine to check the gods' hubris with their haunting lament for the lost Rhinegold and indictment of the gods, which introduces the last of the musical motifs presented in *The Rhinegold*: H58abcd:

[pp. 117–18] **Rhinedaughters:** (from the depths of the valley, invisible: **[[H58a voc:]]**) Rhinegold! Rhinegold! Guileless gold (:H58a voc)! (...) **[[H58b voc:]]** For you, bright toy, we now lament (:H58b)! **[[H58c voc:]]** Give us the gold (:H58c voc), **[[H58d voc:]]** O give us the guileless gold back again (:H58d voc)! (H3 harps; H4 horns:)

Wotan: (on the point of setting foot on the bridge, stops and turns round: H9) What sounds of wailing waft this way?

Loge: (...) The river Rhine's children bewail the rape of the gold.

Wotan: (...) Put an end to their teasing!

Loge: (calling down into the valley: H18a modulation:) (...) Hear what Wotan wishes of you: if the gold no longer gleams on you maidens, blissfully bask henceforth in the gods' new-found splendour (:H18a modulation)! (H46 vari: The gods laugh and, during the following, stride across the bridge)

The Rhinedaughters describe their stolen Rhinegold, which they once celebrated in song, dance, and verse, as guileless. Before Alberich took it, it represented the preconscious innocence of the golden age before evolution produced human consciousness with its inherent contradictions and associated ills. According to Loge the Rhinedaughters had begged of Wotan that he restore the lost gold to them, specifically the Ring, and Wotan refused because we humans are conscious beings who by our very nature can never return to a prior stage of the evolution of consciousness now long past. However, as Wagner oft said, in music, which for him was the distillation of our aesthetic intuition of the world, we possess an artificial means of restoring our lost innocence. Wagner seems to have encapsulated this concept, that through music we can redeem ourselves from Mother Nature's terrible Truth, in his following observation about the meaning of one of his favorite operas, Weber's *Der Freischütz*: [Speaking of " ... the legend of the '*Freischütz*,'" Wagner said:] "It seems to be the poem of those Bohemian woods themselves, whose sombre aspect lets us grasp at once how the lonesome forester would believe himself, if not the prey of a daemonic nature-power, at least irrevocably subject to it. (...) Albeit terrible, this notion does not here become downright remorseless: a gentle sadness shimmers through its awe, and the lament over Nature's lost Paradise knows how to soften the forsaken mother's vengeance. And that is just the German type." [354W-{5/41} *Der Freischütz*: PW Vol. VII, pp. 174–175] Here in one brief passage we find the two kinds of knowledge Wotan seeks to obtain from Erda (Mother Nature), both the objective knowledge which engenders fear of the truth (i.e., that we're "irrevocably subject" to a "daemonic nature power," the fate incarnate in Erda's knowledge), and aesthetic intuition (i.e., "the lament over Nature's lost Paradise," the Rhinedaughters' lament for the lost Rhinegold). It's through aesthetic intuition, music (which for Wagner is the foundation of our aesthetic sense in general), that Wotan can sublimate the terrible world (Erda's fearful prophecy of the gods' doom) aesthetically into a sympathetic being (Erda's daughter, the muse Brünnhilde and her music, who softens Mother Nature's—Erda's—vengeance.). In Alberich's intent to punish the gods with his Ring Curse for their sin against all that was, is, and will be, Erda's knowledge, he (through his son Hagen) becomes the instrument of Mother Nature's (Erda's) vengeance against the gods for denying her. But Brünnhilde will offer the gods (dying religious faith) redemption by temporarily neutralizing Alberich's Ring Curse. The remainder of the *Ring* drama tells how.

Wotan, much annoyed because the Rhinedaughters, speaking truth to power, are telling him what he already knows but can't afford to admit, that by refusing them the guileless gold the gods are establishing themselves as the very incarnation of guile, ironically asks Loge, the lord of guile, to shut them up. Loge's retort to the Rhinedaughters is that if their gold no longer gleams on them, they should bask henceforth in the gods' newfound splendor. The gods' newfound splendor, in Valhalla, is the foundation of civilization under the sway of belief in supernatural beings. The Valhallan gods are the product of the power of thought (Alberich's Ring) tempered by feeling, or love, the very thing Alberich had to renounce to obtain the power of objective thought. And it's love, preconscious feeling, which the Rhinedaughters embody, which is artificially restored in the splendor of the gods. So in this sense Loge is right: the light that went out when Alberich stole the Rhinegold is artificially restored by the gods' splendor. It's noteworthy that just before he stole the Rhinegold to forge his Ring (which gave birth to Valhalla), Alberich stated that if he couldn't obtain love by force, perhaps he could gain it by cunning. That was Loge's cunning.

The Rhinedaughters' lament H58abcd is the lament for lost paradise, the motival expression of our longing to restore lost innocence, which according to Wagner is the primary drive impelling historical man after he's satisfied his first, fundamental drive, physical need. For Wagner, this is the essence of music itself. Witness his following poetical description of the Fall: "From the earth gushes sweet juice; with this, longing refreshes itself until it has imbibed fresh love of life: then the juice runs dry; rice sprouts forth unsown, satiety to abundance; then it comes to an end. Now one has to do one's own planting, ploughing and sowing. Life's torment begins: Paradise is lost. The music of the brahman world recalls it to the memory: it leads to truth. Who understands it? The milk that has flowed from no cow?" [738W-{5/68} BB, p. 148] Now the Rhinedaughters sing the last lines of *The Rhinegold*, their indictment of the gods' artificial restoration of lost paradise in Valhalla's newfound splendor, based as it is on self-deception and therefore fated to destruction:

> [p. 118] **Rhinedaughters:** (H12 harmonic vari or H58a modulation?:) Rhinegold! Rhinegold! Guileless gold (:H12 harmonic vari or H58a modulation?)! (H58b modulation?:) Would that your glittering toy still shone in the depths (:H58b modulation?)! (H9) Trusty and true it is here in the depths alone: false and fated is all that rejoices above!
>
> (H18ab modulation; H56ab: As the gods pass over the bridge on the way to the castle, the curtain falls.)

The Rhinedaughters sing that it's trusty and true only in the depths of the Rhine because there's no self-deception in preconscious animal instinct, no concern with truth in the abstract. No doubt the world-historical conflict, which will drive Wotan to despair in the course of the *Ring*, between our scientific quest to advance knowledge for the sake of power over ourselves and our world, and religious man's counter-impulse to deny this prosaic world and seek redemption from it in an imaginary world, is no concern of feeling as such, but only of thinking. Reason, which judges the conflict between falsehood and truth, is no concern of music, that most recently developed of the arts, that distilled nectar of the aesthetic sense which seems to restore our pre-lingual innocence. The beauty of music, according to Wagner, is that it satisfies our religious longing for transcendence through feeling alone, within our subjective depths, without staking a claim to the objective world's truth (and to the power which can only be sought there): "As Christianity stepped forth amid the Roman civilisation of the universe, so Music breaks forth from the chaos of modern civilisation. Both say aloud: 'our kingdom is not of this world.' And that means: we come from within, ye from without; we spring from the Essence of things, ye from their Show." [790W-{9–12/70} 'Beethoven,' PW Vol. V, p. 120; See also 776W-{9–12/70} 'Beethoven,' PW Vol. V, pp. 86–87; and 430W-{9–12/49} 'The Artwork of the Future,' PW Vol. I, p. 91] "He is a fool who would seek to win the world and a feeling of peace from outside himself! (...) Only ... within us, deep down does salvation dwell!" [655W-{4/7/58} Letter to Mathilde Wesendonck, SLRW, p. 383]

As Wagner said, music makes us feel as if it's the ultimate truth, the essence of the world, without any debate over good and evil, truth or falsehood, or any claim to factuality: "Hear my creed: Music can never and in no possible alliance cease to be the highest, the redeeming art. ... what all the other arts but hint at, through her and in her becomes the most undoubtable of certainties, the most direct and definite of truths. ... she transfigures everything she touches." [650W-{2/57} 'On Liszt's Symphonic Poems,' PW Vol. III, pp. 246–247] It's in music, he says, that we can consign our reasoning power and its problems to oblivion, as if by supernatural grace, though music comes not from a transcendent heaven, but from those depths (of the self) which the Rhinedaughters say are alone trusty and true: "In this Symphony [Beethoven's] ... the purely-musical Expression enchains the hearer ... ; rouses his inmost being, to a degree unreachable by any other art; and ... reveals an ordering principle so free and bold, ... [that] the reasoning march of Thought, with its track of causes and effects, here finds no ... foothold. ... this Symphony must ... appear to us a revelation from another world; ... whereof one foremost thing is undeniable: — that it thrusts home with the most over-whelming conviction, and guides our Feeling with such a sureness that the logic-mongering Reason is completely routed and disarmed thereby." [681W-{9/60} 'Music of the Future,' PW Vol. III, pp. 317–318]

The Rhinedaughters' final salvo is that those (the gods) who rejoice above are false (dependent on self-deception) and fated (doomed to destruction). It's because the gods' rule depends on illusion that it's false and also doomed by

Alberich, who alone has the courage for the truth and no illusions to lose. But if the gods can return to the refuge of music, which stakes no claim to the truth (the Ring's power), the gods can perhaps free themselves from fear of it.

We've come to the end of the first of the four *Ring* dramas, *The Rhinegold*, which Wagner regarded as an introductory prologue, a fore-evening, for the *Ring* trilogy. Being the last of the libretto texts of the *Ring* dramas which Wagner completed, having worked his way back to the beginning of human history to explain why Siegfried had to die, we've found *The Rhinegold* to be one of the most densely philosophical works in world-literature, an inexhaustible allegory of breathtaking scope, depth, and resonance. This is all the more surprising since Wagner maintains throughout an extraordinary naiveté of verbal expression, though made "Deep" by its musical component. It will always have a freshness unknown to even the greatest of Wagner's other, later music-dramas, because it was here that he introduced the world to his new art-form, one of the most original creations of the human spirit, the revolutionary music-drama. It would set the example for the others he had yet to complete, the three following *Ring* dramas *The Valkyrie*, *Siegfried*, and *Twilight of the Gods*, and *Tristan and Isolde*, *The Mastersingers of Nuremberg*, and *Parsifal*.

We've also experienced for the first time in Wagner's output the full potency of his musical motifs as a means of expression for the drama, which will develop, grow, alter, transform, break apart and recombine themselves in new forms in direct relationship with the evolving characters and ever more complex ramifications of the drama. The *Ring*'s music enhanced Wagner's drama with a numinous, infinitely suggestive meaningfulness which linked words and actions inextricably with what was normally inexpressible in language or images, a sort of magical aid to Wagner in carrying out his poetic intent, to make what's unconscious conscious, to bring what's hidden in the silent depths up to the daylight for aesthetic contemplation, the portal to a previously undiscovered interior world. As he said: "The completion of the Rhinegold …has restored my sense of self-assurance … . I have once again realized how much of my work's meaning (given the nature of my poetic intent) is only made clear by the music: I can now no longer bear to look at the poem without the music." [623W-{1/25–26/54} Letter to August Röckel, SLRW, p. 310]

Before we proceed to our next drama, *The Valkyrie*, it's worth contemplating Wagner's thoughts on the Rhinedaughters' lament for the lost gold, as these aren't only the last words of *The Rhinegold*, but inspired Wagner's last thoughts, recorded—just hours before he passed away—by Cosima: "When I am already lying in bed, I hear him talking volubly and loudly; I get up and go into his room. 'I was talking to you,' he says, and embraces me tenderly and long. (…) 'I was talking about Undine, the being who longed for a soul.' He goes to the piano, plays the mournful theme 'Rheingold, Rheingold,' continues with 'False and base all those who dwell up above.' 'Extraordinary that I saw all this so clearly at that time!'—And as he is lying in bed, he says, 'I feel loving toward them, these subservient creatures of the deep, with all their yearning.'" [1151W-{2/12/83} CD Vol. II, p. 1009–1010]

The Valkyrie

THE VALKYRIE ≠ ACT ONE, SCENE ONE

(HUNDING'S HUT)
SIEGMUND AND SIEGLINDE

The Valkyrie begins with an orchestral prelude which depicts Wotan's storm driving his mortal son Siegmund through the forest. He'd striven futilely to save a woman, a stranger, from being forced by her relatives into a loveless, arranged marriage, and in killing her brothers brought down the storm of their clan on himself, from whose wrath he seeks to escape. He takes shelter, ironically, not only in his enemy's home, but specifically his long-lost twin-sister Sieglinde's home:

[pp. 122–123] (**Prelude—storm:** The curtain rises. The interior of a dwelling. The room is built around the trunk of a mighty ash-tree … . (…) [[H59 orch]] [= H19 vari]; [[H60 orch]] [= H54 vari] Siegmund opens the main door from outside and enters. H59 orch>[[H61 orch]] [= H19 Embryo vari] … it is evident from his clothing and appearance that he is on the run. (…) (H8a vari:) … with the extreme effort of someone half-dead with exhaustion, [he] moves towards the hearth, where he throws himself down on a bear-skin rug.) (…)

[Sieglinde is surprised to see that a stranger, not her husband Hunding, has come in (…)]

Sieglinde: An unknown man! I must ask who he is. (…) (H61) Weary he lies from the toils of his way here: (H61) … . Could he be ill?—(She bends over him and listens: H61; [[H62 orch]]) (…) … stout-hearted the man seems to me, though he sank wearily down. (H61) (…)

Siegmund: A drink! A drink!

Sieglinde: I'll fetch some refreshment. … H61; H62) Comfort I offer to lips that are parched: water, just as you wanted! (H61: Siegmund drinks and hands back the drinking-horn. [[H63 orch:]] [H63a = H22 vari; H63b = H39 vari] As he signals his thanks with a movement of his head, his gaze fixes on her features with growing interest.)

Several motifs are introduced in this prelude. Cooke provided their genealogy: H59 (Wotan's Storm) is a compound motif comprised of the embryonic form of H19 (Wotan's Spear) and H31b (Donner's thunder); H60 (Wotan's Storm's lightning) is based on H54 (Donner's "Heda! Heda, hedo!"), and is possibly a partial basis for H83 (first motif of Wotan's Anger) and H85 (second motif of

Wotan's anger); H61, Siegmund's motif, is a slowed down variant of the embryonic form of H19 (Wotan's Spear) and H59 (Wotan's Storm); H62 (Sieglinde's sympathetic Motif); and H63, the Definitive Love Motif. H63a may be based on H20, but H63 as a whole is based on H23, H37, and H39, and is the basis for H79b, H142, and H150.

H59 (Storm) signifies that Wotan, the Wild Huntsman, is hunting down his son Siegmund for defying society's rules, which is ironic since we'll soon learn that Wotan, disguised as a mortal, has deliberately brought Siegmund up to defy divine law. This suggests that Wotan's storm H59 is driving the lawless Siegmund deliberately to the home of his twin-sister Sieglinde. Wotan's divine authority (H19), and authoritarian persona, are embodied on earth by the conservative social establishment under divine law which cares more for social quiet and security than for the expression of individual character and conscience. Sieglinde's husband Hunding and his clan represent this "establishment" dedicated to family-and-clan honor, which instinctively feels danger in the presence of any man who, following his private conscience, exhibits freedom of thought and feeling. H60 is a descriptive motif which depicts Donner's lightning, symbolizing the importance of fear to social order and belief in divine beings. [See 197F-LER, p. 27] H59 (based on Wotan's Spear H19) slows down to transform into Siegmund's Motif H61. H61's derivation from H19 expresses the irony that though Siegmund is the social revolutionary Wotan desired, whose individualistic conscience disdains the need to compromise for the sake of social acceptance, nonetheless Siegmund's alleged freedom is a product of Wotan's (i.e., religious belief's) influence. This will catch up with Wotan in V.2.1 when his wife Fricka, religious faith's conscience, compels him to acknowledge that Siegmund is merely Wotan's product, not the free hero he'd longed for. Siegmund's seemingly independent conscience, expressed by his compassion, is a residuum of religious faith's emphasis on the human spirit's transcendence, an ideal which in secular society survives the decline of religious belief.

H62 (Siegmund's twin-sister Sieglinde's motif) expresses her nature as a woman who suffers the burden of a forced, loveless marriage, but who's sympathetic to the plight ("Noth") of her social revolutionary twin-brother Siegmund, who suffers unwittingly for the gods' sake the anguish of Alberich's Ring Curse. As they stare into each others' eyes we hear H63ab, which Cooke called the Definitive Love Motif. Cooke demonstrated that H63b stems ultimately from Freia's Love Motif H23 (via H39 and H37), which at its inception identified her as goddess of love in flight from the Giants' (egoism's) claim to her, a situation akin to that under which Sieglinde suffers now. Siegmund expresses his gratitude for the refreshment Sieglinde has provided, both physical and spiritual, but she warns that she'll have to explain his presence to her rough husband Hunding:

[pp. 123–25] **Siegmund:** Cooling comfort (H62) came from the spring, (H62) the weary man's burden it helped to make light; my courage revives, my eye is rejoiced by the blissful delight of seeing:—(H62) who is it who comforts me so?

Sieglinde: This house and this wife are Hunding's own; as host he may grant you rest: tarry until he comes home. (H61)

Siegmund: Weaponless am I: a wounded guest won't be turned away by your husband.

Sieglinde: (with anxious haste) Quickly, show me your wounds! (...)

Siegmund: But slight they are, not worthy of mention ... . (...) (H59) the enemy horde hounded me till I was weary; a raging tempest battered my body; but, fast as I fled the hounds, (H62) my faintness has fled yet faster: (H61) though night had closed on my eyelids, (H61) the sun smiles upon me anew. (...)

Sieglinde: A sweetened draught (H62:) of honeyed mead you'll not, I hope, disdain (:H62). (H62)

Siegmund: Will you not taste it first?

(Sieglinde sips from the horn and hands it back to him. H62 on clarinet & horns:; H63: Siegmund takes a long draught, while fixing his eyes on her with growing warmth. He takes the horn from his lips and slowly lets it sink, while the expression on his face turns to one of powerful emotion. H39: He sighs deeply, and gloomily casts his eyes to the ground: H61)

Siegmund: (...) You've tended an ill-fated man:—(H62:) may Wunsch [wish/Wotan] avert ill-fortune from you (:H62)! (H62) I've rested now and sweet was my ease: (H62) now shall I wend my way further. (...)

Sieglinde: (...) Who's hunting you down, that you flee so soon?

Siegmund: (stopping: [[H64 voc:]]) Ill-fortune follows wherever I flee; ill-fortune draws near me wherever I turn (:H64 voc): (H63) from you, woman, may it stay far away! I'll turn my steps and eyes from here. (...)

Sieglinde: (...) Then tarry here! (... H39 voc:) Ill-luck you cannot bring ... to a house where ill-luck lives (:H39 voc)! ([[H65 orch:]]; H61:; [[H65 orch:]] Deeply shaken, Siegmund remains where he is; he gazes searchingly at Sieglinde, who lowers her eyes, ashamed and sad. H61) (...)

Siegmund: (...) Woeful ["Wehwalt"] I have called myself. Hunding I'll await. (H65:; H62:; H65:; H62:... his gaze is fixed on Sieglinde in calm and resolute sympathy: the latter slowly raises her eyes to his. H63: A deep silence ensues, during which they both gaze into each others' eyes with an expression of great emotion.)

H64 expresses the plight or ill-fortune ("Noth") the individualistic social revolutionary Siegmund has inherited as a man with a personal conscience in a society which caters to political and social expedience, as established under Wotan's "Social Contract," to which love and goodness must often be sacrificed. The name Siegmund calls himself, Woeful, expresses his low status, his fate in a society concerned only for the status quo, quiet at all costs (including religious faith, which embodies our desire to be relieved of the burden of thinking or feeling for ourselves). H65, much more important than H64, is introduced as Sieglinde suggests Siegmund needn't worry that he's bringing his ill-fortune to her, since she suffers it already. H65 like H64 expresses the Wälsungs' fated plight ("Noth") and, as Cooke says, incarnates their sympathy for each other's anguish. They're destined to tragedy because Wotan has foredoomed them to pay the price of Alberich's Ring Curse to redeem the gods from Alberich's threat. H65 will later take on a special role as a reminder specifically of Sieglinde's compassion, and of the fact that she died, suffering the greatest "Noth," giving Siegfried birth.

THE VALKYRIE ≠ ACT ONE, SCENE TWO

(HUNDING'S HUT)
SIEGMUND, SIEGLINDE, AND HUNDING

Sieglinde's gruff, authoritarian husband Hunding enters, instinctively suspicious of Siegmund:

[pp. 125–28] ([[H66 orch:]] Hunding, armed with shield and spear, enters and stops in the doorway on noticing Siegmund. Hunding turns to Sieglinde with an expression of stern inquiry.)

Sieglinde: (…) Faint by the hearth I found this man: need ["Noth"] has brought him to our house. (H61)

Hunding: You tended him?

Sieglinde: (calmly) His lips I moistened, I cared for him as any host would. [**Siegmund:** (…)]

Hunding: [[H67 voc:]] [= H17a vari] Sacred is my hearth:—may my house be sacred to you (:H67 voc)! [Hunding orders Sieglinde to prepare a meal, which she does.] (…) (Involuntarily she stares at Siegmund … . (H25a) Hunding examines Siegmund's features closely and with surprise, comparing them with those of his wife. (H62; H63)) (aside) How like the woman he looks! The selfsame glittering serpent is glinting in his eye, too. (H19 vari on bass clarinet: He conceals his dismay and turns to Siegmund as though quite naturally.) (H66) Far indeed have you fared on your way; … what impassable pathways caused you pain? (H59)

Siegmund: … storm and great need ["Noth"] have driven me here: I know not the way that I came. whither I've wandered I know still less … .

Hunding: (at the table, offering Siegmund a seat) He whose roof is your shelter, whose house is your haven, Hunding's ["Hounding"] the name of your host (H66); if you turn your steps to the west of here, in wealthy homesteads kinsmen dwell who safeguard Hunding's honour (H66). My guest would do me honour by telling me his name. (…) [**Sieglinde:** (…)]

Siegmund: (H65: looks up, gazes into her eyes … .) Friedmund [Peaceful?] I may not call myself; Frohwalt [Joyful] fain would I be: but Wehwalt

[Woeful] I must name myself. (H65) Wolfe was my father; as one of twain I came into the world, a twin-born sister and I. (...) Stout-hearted and strong was Wolfe; many foes he made. With the boy the old man used to go hunting; from chase and encounter they came home one day: ... burned to ashes the splendent hall ... ; murdered lay my valiant mother, all trace of my sister lost in the embers:—the Neidings' hard-hearted host had wrought us this bitter distress ["Noth"]. (H66) Outlawed, the old man fled with me; deep in the wildwood the youngster lived with Wolfe for many a year: many's the time they were hunted down; but wolf and whelp would put up a stout defence. (turning to Hunding: (H69 embryo:) A Wölfing tells you this, whom as Wölfing many know well (:H69 embryo). (H66) [**Hunding:** (...)]

Sieglinde: ... where is your father now?

Siegmund: The Neidings launched a fierce onslaught against us: full many a huntsman fell to the wolves .... But I from my father was parted; the longer I searched, the more I lost his trail; a wolfskin was all that I found in the forest: empty it lay there before me, my father I could not find (H18ab [with great emphasis]).

This passage introduces Hunding and his impressively intimidating motif H66. We also hear H67, "Hunding's Rights Motif," associated with Hunding's warning to Siegmund to honor the sacredness of Hunding's hearth and home, i.e., his wife Sieglinde. Cooke demonstrated that H67 is based on H17's chord. H67 expresses "power" and "possession" as found in the honor of name, status, family, clan, unthinking obedience to the gods's laws, etc. Cooke showed how it will later (in *Twilight of the Gods*) transform into H172, the "Oath of Atonement Motif," part of an oath Siegfried (Siegmund's son) and his new blood-brother Gunther swear, that they'll exact vengeance on anyone who dishonors the blood-brothers' bond.

Wagner's irony comes into play: Siegmund has narrated the tale of how he lost his mother and sister to the predations of the Neidings (the envious ones) who, as we'll learn later, abducted Siegmund's twin sister Sieglinde and gifted her in forced marriage to Hunding, indicated here by the sounding of Hunding's Motif H66 as we hear Siegmund's description of the death of his mother and presumed death of his twin-sister Sieglinde. So it's Siegmund and Sieglinde who're the honorable ones, Hunding and his minions slaves to the system who've learned to "play the game" to get along. Wagner offers a vivid portrait of a personality which seems an apt portrait of Hunding's mindset in his comparison between established society and the individual who nobly strives for freedom from society's arbitrary restrictions: "... the 'view' of Society, so long as it does not fully comprehend the essence of the Individual and its own genesis therefrom, is a hindering and shackling one; and it becomes ever more tyrannical, in exact degree as the quickening and innovating essence of the Individual brings its instinctive thrust to battle against habit. (...) ... Society appears as the conscious, the capricious (Willkürliche), the true thing to be explained and exculpated." [500W-{50-1/51} *Opera and Drama*, PW Vol. II, pp. 179–180]

We hear a variant of H19 (Spear) as Hunding notes the twins' resemblance, informing us that Wotan the lawgiver (founder of that corrupt society of which Hunding is the exemplar) is their father, just prior to the more dramatic sounding of the Valhalla Motif's first two segments H18ab. One of the most moving examples of Wagner's motifs of reminiscence is the sounding of H18ab (Valhalla) in the orchestra after Siegmund tells how he lost track of his father Wolfe in the forest after a battle with the Neidings. Wolfe is Wotan disguised as a mortal man. It was while visiting the earth's surface that Wotan fathered the twins Siegmund and Sieglinde on a mortal woman whom Wagner never identifies. The pathos of the Valhalla Motif H18 sounding as a distant reminder to us (but not to Siegmund) that Wotan is his father, arises partly from the fact that neither Siegmund nor Sieglinde will ever learn their father's true identity as Lord of the Valhallan gods, and partly also from the derivation of H18ab from Alberich's Ring Motif H17ab. Siegmund's hidden back-story, his virtual raison d'être, is Wotan's futile desire to redeem the gods from Alberich's Ring Curse, futile because the gods' rule is founded on Alberich's Ring power.

Siegmund now continues the narrative of his troubled life, inadvertently exposing himself to Hunding as the enemy of Hunding's clan, who they've literally chased into Hunding's own home:

[pp. 128–130] **Siegmund:** I longed to leave the wildwood and felt drawn to men and women:—(H22; H63 Clarinet) However many I met, wherever I might find them, though I sued for a friend or for women,—ever was I treated as an outcast. (…) Whatever I held to be right others thought was wrong … . (…) … though I craved for bliss, I caused only woe. (H8)—And so I must call myself Wehwalt ["Woeful"], for woe is all I have known. (He looks up at Sieglinde and notices her sympathetic glance. H66; H62; H63; H8) [**Hunding:** (…)]

Sieglinde: (…) (H62) Tell us, guest, how at last you lost your weapon in the fray. (H65)

Siegmund: A sorrowing maid had called me to arms: her kinsmen's clan was wanting to marry the maid, unloved, to a man. … I flew to her aid; the horde of oppressors I faced in battle: the enemy fell to the victor. Her brothers lay there slain: the maid enclasped their corpses; grief drove out her anger. (H8:; [[**H68 orch:**]]) In floods of unstaunchable tears she bathed the slain with her weeping: the murder of her brothers the hapless maid bewailed (:H8; :H68 orch). (…) (H8:; [[**H68 orch:**]]) … the maid would not stir from the slain; with shield and spear I long gave her shelter till shield and spear (:H8; :H68 orch) were hewn from my hand in the fray. (H61) Wounded and weaponless, there I stood (H61)—and saw the maiden die: (H59:) I was harried by the wild hunt (:H59)—on the lifeless bodies she lay dead. (H65: Turning to Sieglinde with a look of sorrowful fervour: [[**H69 voc:**]] Now you know, you questioning woman, why Friedmund is not my name (:H69 voc)! ([[**H70 orch:**]] [H70 rises out of last three notes of H52] He stands up and walks over to the hearth: Sieglinde turns pale and stares, deeply shaken, at the ground.)

Hunding: (...) I know an unruly race: what others hold dear they deem unholy: (...) they're hated by all—and by me. (H66) I was called to vengeance, (H66) to seek requital for kinsmen's blood: I came too late and now come home to find the fleeing traitor's trace here inside my own house.—(...) My house, Wölfing, protects you today; ... : (... H66:) but with sturdy weapons defend yourself in the morning; ... you'll pay me tribute for all who died. (...) [Hunding orders Sieglinde out and to make his night drink: (...)]

(...) (H69:; H63: With quiet resolve she opens the cupboard, fills a drinking-horn and shakes some spices into it from a container. (...) On the steps she turns round ... , gazes yearningly at Siegmund and indicates with her eyes ... with eloquent explicitness ... a particular spot in the ash-tree's trunk. H56ab. (...) With a final glance at Siegmund (H56ab) ... she goes into the bedchamber ... .)

Hunding: (...) (... H66 varis:) Tomorrow, Wölfing, we shall meet ... (:H66 varis) ... ! (He goes into the bedchamber and can be heard closing the bolt from within. H62)

This passage introduces motif H68, which evokes the tears of the anonymous woman for her brothers whom Siegmund had to kill in order to defend himself and her from the revenge of her family. They were forcing her into an unloving arranged marriage, and Siegmund, responding to her appeal for help, attempted to free her. H68 carries the bittersweet quality which can tear at our loyalties in contradictory ways. H68 is the basis for H79a. H79ab will first be heard in V.2.1 in the context of Wotan's wife Fricka's complaint to him that thanks to his infidelities to her, he's given a poor example to these illicit Wälsung twins who thumb their noses at the gods' divine laws and the society founded on them.

This passage also introduces the famous motifs H69 and H70, both of which are associated, Cooke notes, with the heroic yet tragic destiny of the Wälsungs. H69's inception calls to mind Wotan's intent to bring up his Wälsung heroes independent of society and its mores, destining them to lives as social outcasts and martyrs. Cooke concluded that H70 rises out of the last three notes of Erda's H52, which recalls her proclamation of the ephemeral nature of all things, including the gods' inevitable doom. The Wälsungs' tragic destiny is to unwittingly strive to forestall this doom, to redeem the gods (religion) from it, but they can only do this by breaking divine law and breaching faith in the gods. This trope lends unity to almost the entire family of heroic motifs which Cooke noted stem from the last three notes of H52. This family includes H76 (the Valkyries, illicit spawn of Wotan and Erda, to whom Wotan looks to inspire heroes to martyrdom who'll aid the gods to defend Valhalla in the final battle against Alberich's host of night); H88 ("Brünnhilde's Annunciation of Death to Siegmund"); and H92 (the fearless hero Siegfried, Wotan's last hope of redemption).

By risking his life to aid this anonymous but needy woman, because she's suffering injustice, Siegmund the social revolutionary demonstrates his bent to redeem that society which considers any individual who threatens the status quo, even if it's unjust, its enemy. Hunding's self-righteous indignation is due to the fact that Siegmund helped a maiden to avoid a loveless marriage with a member of Hunding's clan, echoing the situation Siegmund finds his twin sister Sieglinde suffering under Hunding's coercion. Siegmund will try to save his sister Sieglinde from her loveless marriage to Hunding by offering himself to her in marriage. The god Wotan, disguised, bringing up Siegmund in the wilderness to fight for what's ethically right in the face of society's craven dependence on thoughtless tradition, is Wagner's metaphor for the moral legacy which modern secular man inherits from our religious ancestors' belief in our divine origin, immortal soul, and transcendent value, which ground our ethic of self-sacrifice and compassion for others in an allegedly spiritual foundation freed from earthly egoism. These religious beliefs influenced us to establish moral values which survive the decline of those religious beliefs which prompted their creation in the first place. Siegmund is heir to religious man's (Wotan's) longing for redemption from corrupt society—a society predicated on fear of the new, on habit, on lust for possessions and property, ersatz (unearned) honor, etc.—through personal conscience, the basis for sympathy for other mens' plight which is the essence of moral heroism. This religious influence, or at any rate, the influence of that longing for noble, selfless motivation which inspired us to look to gods as the secure ground of the value we place on actions done for the sheer moral beauty of them, without thought of material profit to the doer, we'd prefer to trace to a spontaneous impulse of the soul rather than see it as a product of consciously calculated egoistic advantage and learned behavior.

Feuerbach, though tending to emphasize egoism as the basic motive behind all human behavior, including our invention of the gods, nonetheless proclaimed our morality of self-sacrifice to be not only the essence of Christianity (once one purifies Christianity of its egoistic obsession with our longing for immortality), but as our spontaneous instinct which expresses what's truest and best in Christian faith: "... out of the heart, ... the inward impulse to do good, to live and die for man, ... out of the human nature, therefore, as it reveals itself through the heart, has sprung what is best, what is true in Christianity—its essence purified from theological dogmas and contradictions." [64F-EOC, p. 60] Wagner's explanation of "purely human" sentiment and its distinction from the morality of established society ("Public Opinion") in our extract below echoes Feuerbach: "... the Purely-human, which inspired it, came into conflict with the strongest social interest, that of absolute Wont, i.e. of joint self-seeking [the social contract Wotan engraved on his Spear]. Wherever this ethical conscience fell into conflict with the practice of society, it severed from the latter and established itself apart, as Religion; whereas practical society shaped itself into the State." [504W-{50–1/51} *Opera and Drama*, PW Vol. II, p. 186]

According to both Feuerbach and Wagner, love is an expression of natural necessity, an animal instinct which is the basis for the mutual affection of (and mutual loyalty among) lovers, family, friends. But Feuerbach also declared that when put to the test by overwhelming physical need or duress, such sympathetic other-directed sentiments fall by the wayside as the all-powerful selfish ego takes over: "Hunger and thirst destroy not only the physical, but also the mental and moral powers of man; they rob him of his humanity … ." [143F-EOC, pp. 277–278] This is the point of Alberich's assertion in R.3 that by virtue of his gradual accumulation of his hoard (of objective knowledge), all will renounce love for power's sake as he has. This is the basis of one of the key indictments of atheism proffered by religious men, that without the supernatural, the immortal, loving soul (or at least, without belief in supernatural influence over human affairs), we'd act solely in self-interest. Both Feuerbach and Wagner looked to "Nature" as the origin of the only love worth considering, in spite of the war of all against all that seems to characterize natural life, including human life.

Since Hunding adheres to the social norm that one must extend courtesy to a guest, he's granted Siegmund a single night of rest in his home prior to the duel of honor. What follows is the famous pantomime sequence during which Sieglinde prepares Hunding's night-drink, putting a sleeping potion in it, and, accompanied by H56ab (Wotan's Grand Idea for redeeming Valhalla from Alberich's Ring Curse, embodied by the sword Nothung) indicating with her eyes the hilt of the sword Wotan (in disguise) thrust into Hunding's house-ash-pillar the day she was wed, against her will, to Hunding. H56b expresses Wotan's hope his Wälsungs will restore lost innocence.

THE VALKYRIE ⁎ ACT ONE, SCENE THREE
(HUNDING'S HUT)
SIEGMUND AND SIEGLINDE

Siegmund, left alone, mulls his desperate moment of truth. His destiny (Wotan's influence) has brought him to Hunding's hut and his twin-sister Sieglinde, though Siegmund will never become conscious of the role which Wotan's (man's religious longing for transcendent value) influence has had on his personal history. Siegmund—in a rapturous meditation of lyrical profundity—contemplates the meaning of the events which have brought him to this moment of decision about newfound love and the price he must pay for it, and invokes the promise made by his father Wälse (Wotan in disguise as known to his Wälsung children Siegmund and Sieglinde; "Wolfe" is how Wotan is known to others) to grant him a sword in his time of direst need ("höchster Noth"):

[pp. 131–4] **Siegmund:** (H57a:) My father promised me a sword (:H57a): (H19 frag) (H57b:) I'd find it in direst need ["höchster Noth"] (:H57b)! (H66) (…) (H63:) I saw a woman, winsome and fair; exquisite terror consumes my heart (:H63):—(H66:) she to whom yearning draws me now and who wounds me with sweet enchantment is held in thrall by the man who mocks me, weaponless as I am (:H66).—(H56a:) Wälse! Wälse! (:H56a)! Where is your sword? The mighty sword that I'd wield in the fray (H8 varis:) when forth from my breast breaks the furious rage yet harboured within my heart (:H8 varis)? (The fire collapses, causing a fierce glow to flare up and strike the spot on the ash-tree's trunk indicated by Sieglinde's eyes, where the hilt of a buried sword can be clearly seen. H56ab) What glints there so bright in the glimmering light? (...) (H56ab) Is it the glorious woman's glance, which she left behind her ... when she passed out of the hall? (H56ab: From this point on, the fire in the hearth gradually dies out.) Nighttime's shadows shielded my eyes; the flash of her glaze then glanced upon me, bringing me warmth and light. (H56ab) (...) ... (H56ab) now the blossom fades, the light dies out; nighttime's shadows shielded my eyes: deep in my sheltering breast a flameless fire still smoulders. (The fire has gone out completely: total darkness. (...) Sieglinde enters in a white nightdress and moves softly but quickly over to the hearth. H69; H62) [Sieglinde tells Siegmund she's drugged Hunding and Siegmund should make his escape, but Siegmund won't abandon her: (...)]

Sieglinde: Let me show you a weapon: if only you could win it! As the noblest of heroes might I hail you ... . [[H71 orch]] [= H56b/H18a] Heed well what I have to tell you. The men from his clan sat there in the hall, as guests at Hunding's wedding: he was wooing a woman whom villains, unasked, had given him as his wife. Sadly I sat there while they were drinking: a stranger then came in—(H18ab) an old man dressed in grey; (H18ab) his hat hung so low that one of his eyes was hidden, (H18ab:) but the flash of its fellow struck fear all around ... (:H18ab): (H8: [repeated in descending pattern]) in me alone his eye awakened sweetly yearning sorrow, mingled with tears and solace (:H8 descending pattern). (H56ab) ... he brandished a sword in his hands; (H56ab) he then drove it deep in the ash-tree's trunk ... (H56ab) up to the hilt: (H56ab)—(H18a frag:) The steel would rightly belong to him who could draw it forth from the trunk (:H18a frag). Of all the menfolk, much as they struggled, none could win the weapon. (...) (H18ab:) I knew then who greeted me in my grief (:H18ab): I also knew for whom alone (H56ab) he destined the sword in the tree. [[H71 orch]] Might I find him here today, that friend; ... however I smarted from shame and disgrace, [[H71 orch]]—sweetest revenge would atone for it all! I'd then have recaptured whatever I'd lost, whatever I'd wept for would then be won back, [[H71 orch]] were I only to find that hallowed friend ... .

Siegmund: (... H70) That friend now holds you, (H56ab) thrice-blessed woman, to whom both weapon and wife were destined! [[H71 orch]] (...) Whatever I longed for I saw in you; in you I found whatever I lacked! Though you suffered shame and though sorrow pained me; though I was an outlaw and you were dishonoured, [[H71 orch:]] joyful revenge now bids us rejoice (:H71).

The sword (H56ab) which Wotan thrust into Hunding's House-Ash represents Wotan's need of love in a loveless, corrupt world, Hunding's world, to be regained by restoring lost innocence. Siegmund's "höchster Noth" (direst need of lost love) is the suffering caused by the lovelessness of the world Alberich's Ring-power has created. Loveless marriage between the sexes based on profit and/or coercion is the source of Sieglinde's lifelong woe, from which her twin brother Siegmund will save her. This is a key Wagnerian example of the hatefulness of

Alberich's world, based on power instead of love: " ... it is our task to recognize as infallibly certain that marriage without mutual affection for the human race has been more pernicious than anything else." [1125W-{3/21/82—4/9/82} BB, p. 204] Motif H71, introduced here in association with the notion that the Wälsung siblings' loving union (sibling incest and adultery) will avenge all the suffering ("Noth") which society has foisted on them, Dunning suggests is a compound motif comprised of the Sword Motif (Wotan's Grand Idea For Redemption) H56ab, and the Valhalla Motif's (H18ab) first two segments. H71 represents the temporary triumph of Wotan's hope to find redemption in his Wälsung hero Siegmund, and Sieglinde.

What follows is the famous lyrical interlude in which Siegmund and Sieglinde sing a love duet extolling the union of spring with love, brother with sister (though not yet conscious of their true blood relation to each other, a fact which notoriously often causes confusion):

[pp. 134–6] (The main door flies open.) [**Sieglinde:** (...)] (... a glorious spring night outside; the full moon shines in and throws its bright light on the pair, so that they can suddenly see each other in total clarity.)

Siegmund: ... see how spring smiles into the hall! (H36/H10: He draws Sieglinde to him ... .) **[[H72 voc:]]** Winter storms have waned at May's awakening; spring is aglow with gentle light; on balmy breezes, light and lovely, working wonders he wafts his way ... . **[[H72 voc:]]** In blissful birdsong sweetly he sounds and fragrant perfumes scent his breath; from his warming blood bloom wondrous flowers ... . (...) (:H72 voc) (H63:) To find his sister he flew this way (:H63); (...) (H72 voc:) love has lured spring here (:H72 voc). (...) The sister-bride was freed by her brother ... ... : **[[H73 voc:]]** united are love and spring (:H73 voc)!

Sieglinde: (H39 voc:) You are the spring for which I longed in frosty wintertime (:H39 voc) ... .—All I'd ever seen seemed strange, (H63) friendless was all that was near me ... . (H63:) But you I recognized ... clearly ... (:H63): (H22?:) ... . what I am, it came to me as bright as day (:H22?); (H63) like an echoing sound it struck my ear, when in frostily foreign wasteland I first beheld my friend. (H22: She throws her arms round his neck in her ecstasy and looks closely into his face.)

Siegmund: (... **[[H74A voc:]]** O sweetest delight, most blessed of women (:H74A voc)

H36 and H10, last heard in R.2 as an orchestral prelude to Loge's narration of his tale about the futility of seeking to find anything for which one would willingly renounce love and woman's delight, are heard now as Siegmund heroically embraces Sieglinde in love in the face of society's hostility. Siegmund sings the famous aria H72, "Winterstorms," in which spring and love, brother and sister, escape the bonds of winter and are united in adulterous and incestuous love. H73 is first heard in the context of Siegmund's aria in association with the notion that spring and love, brother and sister, are united. These love motifs are in striking contrast with Sieglinde's description of Hunding's conventional, hide-bound world as a trap, a strange, friendless, foreign wasteland, to which she was condemned until she found herself again, found herself at home, in her twin-brother Siegmund's embrace. Motif H74, first heard in Siegmund's response to Sieglinde's ecstatic and equally beautiful aria answering to Siegmund's "Winterstorms" aria, and related to H7 and H20, is a purely expressive motif which sings of longing for love, first heard as Siegmund, enraptured, sings "O sweetest delight, most blessed of women." It's sometimes called the "Bliss" or "Rapture" Motif.

Now they embark on a journey of reminiscence as they gradually recognize the physical features which link them with each other and with the old one-eyed man who long ago thrust the sword up to the hilt into Hunding's house-ash on the occasion of Sieglinde's dreary wedding to Hunding, and finally acknowledge each other as long-lost twin brother and sister:

[pp. 136–8] **Sieglinde:** [[H74B:]] [she notices the veins of his brow] [[H74B:]] I tremble to tell of the bliss that transports me (:H74B)—(H18ab:) a wonder seeks to forewarn me: you whom I first beheld today my eyes have seen before (:H18ab)!

Siegmund: (H22:) A dream of love forewarns me, too (:H22): [[H75 orch:]] in fervent longing I've seen you before!

Sieglinde: (H74:) My own likeness ["Bild"] I glimpsed in the brook—and now I see it again: as once it rose from the pool, to me now you show that likeness (:H75 orch; :H74)!

Siegmund: (H63 voc:) You are the likeness I hid within me (:H63 voc).

Sieglinde: (…) O hush! (H63:) Let me hark to your voice: I think that I heard its sound as a child—but no! I heard it of late when the ring of my voice re-echoed throughout the wood (:H63). (…) (… H70; H56ab:) Your eye's smouldering glance glinted upon me ere now:—(H18ab:) so the greybeard looked as he greeted me once and brought comfort to me in my sadness. By his glance his child knew who he was (:H18ab)—I wanted to call out his name—is Woeful really what you are called? [**Siegmund:** (…); **Sieglinde:** (…)]

Siegmund: Name me yourself as you'd like me called: (H73 voc:) I'll take my name from you (:H73 voc).

Sieglinde: But Wolfe, you said, was your father?

Siegmund: A wolf to fearful foxes! (H18ab) But he whose eye once flashed as proudly as yours, fair woman, flashes now (:H18ab)—Wälse was his name.

Sieglinde: (…) If Wälse's your father and if you're a Wälsung; if he thrust the sword in the tree for you—then let me name you as I love you: Siegmund—thus do I call you!

As Sieglinde's remembrance of her past life with Siegmund gradually wakens, the exquisite and mysterious new motif H75, capturing the pathos of remembrance of things past, comes into play, in relation to the metaphor of seeing her likeness reflected in a brook, as now she sees her image reflected in Siegmund. Sieglinde experienced this also when, having heard her voice echo in the woods, she now hears it echoing again in Siegmund's voice. It's well known that one of Wagner's key sources for this scene was the similar scene in the second drama (*The Libation Bearers*) of one of his favorite Greek tragedies, Aeschylus's trilogy the *Oresteia*, in which Orestes returns to his homeland, disguised, in order to exact vengeance on his mother Clytemnestra for murdering his father Agamemnon. For when they meet his sister Electra doesn't at first recognize her long-lost brother Orestes. By comparing reminiscences Siegmund and Sieglinde eventually realize they're twin brother and sister, long separated, Wälse's children, and thus Wälsungs. However, neither of them will ever learn that their father Wälse was Wotan disguised as a mortal man.

Siegmund accepts his destiny, to live for love and, if necessary, to die for it, as he manfully extracts Wälse's sword, which he names Nothung ("Needful"), from Hunding's house-ash, and declares himself husband to his twin-sister Sieglinde, so the blood of the Wälsungs may flourish:

> [pp. 138–9] **Siegmund:** (... H70) Siegmund I'm called (H56ab) and Siegmund I am: (H57b frag:) be witness this sword ... ! Wälse promised that I'd find it one day in my time of greatest need ["höchster Noth"] (:H57b frag): I seize it now! (H16:) Highest need ["höchste Noth"] of holiest love, consuming need ["Noth"] of yearning desire (:H16) burns brightly within my breast, urging me on to deed and death! (H56a:) Nothung ["Needful"]! Nothung (:H56a)! So I name you, sword! (...) (H57b:) Show me your swordblade's sharp-cutting edge (:H57b): come forth from the scabbard to me! (With a violent effort he draws the sword from the tree and shows it to Sieglinde, who is seized by astonishment and ecstasy. H56ab) Siegmund the Wälsung you see here, wife! (H70) As bridal gift he brings this sword: (H70) for so he woos the most blessed of women; (H71) from his enemy's house he thus carries you off (H71). (H72:) Far from here follow me now, (H56ab) away to springtime's smiling home (:H72): there Nothung the sword shall shield you, (H63) when Siegmund succumbs to your love.

Siegmund's highest need ("Noth") is the need of love in a loveless world. This is represented musically on the one hand by the recurrence of H57b, to which Wotan had sung: "(H57a) Thus I salute the fortress [Valhalla], **(H57b) safe from dread and dismay!**" in R.4, expressing his grand idea of producing a race of mortal heroes who could redeem Valhalla's gods from their dread and dismay in the face of loveless Alberich's threat to destroy them and the human ideals which spring from them, by restoring lost innocence and love. This restoration is represented by H56ab, first heard in conjunction with H57ab's first occurrence. But on the other hand, most importantly, this concept is conveyed by the otherwise surprising recurrence here of H16, first heard in association with Woglinde's warning that Alberich must renounce love to forge a Ring of power. This isn't a contradiction: it's because of Alberich's renunciation of love that Siegmund and Sieglinde have the highest need (Noth) of love, love that's been lost. As Wagner said, we weren't aware of our innocence, and didn't long to restore it, until we'd lost it, and the history of this longing is the history of man. [see 393W-{1–2 [/49} *Jesus of Nazareth*, PW Vol. VIII. p. 320] This is one solution to a famous problem in Wagner exegesis, the question why Wagner employed H16 both to dramatize Alberich's renunciation of love for power, and Siegmund's renunciation of power for the sake of love. In a passage previously cited, Wagner provided conceptual justification for this reading. Wotan's Wälsung heroes are in the greatest need of love not only in the loveless world produced by Alberich's renunciation of love to forge his Ring, but also in the loveless world perpetuated in a different way by Wotan's divine authority embodied by his Spear's social contract. Wagner wrote to Liszt that he found "nothing amiss [with the world] except for lovelessness," which he stated would lead us "towards knowledge of the uniquely beautiful necessity of love: to acquire this knowledge ... is the task of world history." [597W-{4/13/53}Letter to Franz Liszt, SLRW, p. 284]

Siegmund has forcibly removed his birthright from Hunding's house-ash, the sword Wotan left for him, thereby severing the Wälsung race symbolically from dependence on Wotan's divine authority inscribed on his Spear, which is perhaps symbolized by the house-ash which sustains Hunding's habitation and life, given that Wotan made his Spear from a branch of the World-Ash. Sieglinde's ecstatic response as Siegmund pulls Nothung from Hunding's House-Ash can be given a phallic reading. This isn't strained: Wagner will later, both in explicit sexual imagery during Siegfried's smelting and re-forging of Nothung in S.1.3, and in Brünnhilde's chastisement of Siegfried in T.2.4 for denying his prior sexual involvement with her (by invoking his sword, i.e., Siegfried's phallus, and its sheath, i.e., Brünnhilde's vagina), link Nothung (natural necessity, Nature's fertility) with the penis. This is why Nothung, the sword Wotan offers as a legacy for his Wälsung heroes, is embodied musically by Motif H56, whose second segment, H56b, replicates the Primal Nature Motif H1, which represents preconscious life, unconscious natural necessity. Wagner subtly hints at the natural necessity which underlies both Alberich's renunciation of love, and Siegmund's need of love and heroic embrace of it, not only by associating H16 with both Alberich and Siegmund at their moments of decision, but also through a verbal motif which they both utter, "höchster Noth." In R.4, Alberich blessed his Ring with "höchster Noth" while laying his curse on it so Wotan, having stolen it from Alberich, couldn't draw bliss from it without paying the Ring's price, renunciation of love.

Thanks to this consideration of the symbolism of Siegmund's sword Nothung as the embodiment of both Feuerbach's natural necessity and Wotan's grand idea for the restoration of lost innocence, we can grasp Siegmund's special function in the *Ring* as one of the two Wälsung heroes (his son Siegfried being the other) who wield Wotan's sword Nothung. Siegmund represents Wotan's hope (ultimately futile) to restore pre-fallen innocence through nobility of action, as Wotan's allegedly free moral hero and social revolutionary, and Siegfried, after Siegmund's death falling heir to Nothung, will represent Wotan's hope for redemption through the secular artist-hero. Both equally represent what Feuerbach described as natural necessity. Wagner acknowledged his debt to

Feuerbach on this score in his following tribute from Wagner's autobiography: [Speaking of Feuerbach's book *Thoughts on Death and Immortality* (1830), Wagner stated that:] "I found it elevating and consoling to be assured that the sole authentic immortality [thus disqualifying the allegedly divine, but illusory, immortality granted by Freia in Valhalla] adheres only to sublime deeds [such as Siegmund's compassionate interventions in the lives of two suffering women, including his own sister Sieglinde] and inspired works of art [the muse Brünnhilde's inspiration of the artist-hero Siegfried to undertake heroic deeds of art]. (...) ... Feuerbach became for me the proponent of the ruthlessly radical liberation of the individual from the bondage of conceptions associated with the belief in traditional authority ... ." [387W-{?/49 ML, p. 430]

Having finally recognized each other, Siegmund acknowledges himself as Sieglinde's twin-brother and joyfully proclaims their newfound status as incestuous and adulterous husband and wife, as he prepares to wed her with his newly named sword Nothung ("Needful"), so the Wälsung blood can flourish without taint by the blood of such unheroic, uninspired men as Hunding.

> [p. 139] **Sieglinde:** If you are Siegmund whom I see here—Sieglinde am I, who has longed for you: your own true sister you've won for yourself with the sword! (...)
>
> **Siegmund:** (H63:) Bride and sister you are to your brother—so let the blood of the Wälsungs blossom (:H63)! (He draws her towards him with furious passion: H56ab, H63, H75 vari: the curtain falls quickly.)

Siegmund introduces the concept of sibling incest in conjunction with the transmission—safe from taint of ignoble blood—of noble blood within the Wälsung clan. Wagner discussed the symbolic significance of Oedipus's unwitting incest with his mother Jocasta in light of the concept that this involved him in an unconscious crime against established society, a crime however which expressed the emancipation of the ever new individual, exemplar of natural necessity, from the strictures of an age-old, conservative world. However, once Oedipus and his mother became conscious of their true relationship, they were covered in shame thanks to societal judgment, their social conscience, though their loving relationship had seemed quite natural before they became aware of Oedipus's true identity. [See 501W; and 502W-{50-1/51} *Opera and Drama*, PW Vol. II, pp. 182-183] But here, unlike Oedipus and Jocasta, who, once conscious of their formerly unconscious crime, allowed their collective social conscience to make them ashamed of it, Siegmund and Sieglinde openly celebrate their sibling incest and adultery because they've transcended the limitations of society and its mores.

THE VALKYRIE ⁎ ACT TWO, SCENE ONE

(A MOUNTAIN PASS)
WOTAN, BRÜNNHILDE, AND FRICKA

We'll now be reintroduced to Wotan and his wife Fricka, and meet for the first time Wotan's favorite daughter via his sexual union with Erda (Mother Nature),

Brünnhilde, of supreme importance to the *Ring* drama, as Wotan encourages her to protect Siegmund in his coming duel of honor with Hunding:

> **[pp. 140–1]** (**Prelude:** H56ab:; H39:; **[[H76 orch:]]** [H76 rises out of last three notes of H52] A wild and rocky mountain landscape. (...) Wotan, armed for battle, with his spear; before him Brünnhilde, as a Valkyrie, likewise fully armed)
>
> **Wotan:** (...) A furious fight will soon flare up: let Brünnhilde fly to the fray; (H19) for the Wälsung let her choose victory! (H19) Hunding may choose to whom he belongs: he's no use to me in Valhalla. (H19) (...)
>
> **Brünnhilde:** (...) **[[H77 voc:]]** Hoyotoho! Hoyotoho! Heiaha! Heiaha! Hahei! Hahei! Heiaho (:H77 voc)! (...) I warn you, father ... : Fricka, your wife, draws near in a chariot drawn by a team of rams. (H8 orch:) Ha! How she whirls the golden whip; the pitiful beasts are bleating with fear (:H8 orch) ... . (...) [Brünnhilde leaves, singing H77: (...)] (H8 vari: Fricka arrives on the mountain ridge from the gorge in a chariot drawn by two rams ... .)
>
> **Wotan:** **[[H78 voc:]]** [= H57b vari] The same old storm, the same old strife (:H78 voc)! But here I must make a stand. (H52 in a free vari or translation?: [H78 possibly mixed with H52?]) the closer she comes, the more she moderates her pace and at last places herself with dignity before Wotan)

The exciting prelude to V.2.1 introduces the most popular and famous of the *Ring* motifs, the "Valkyrie Motif" H76, heard later as a major component of the "Ride of the Valkyries," the prelude to V.3.1. According to Cooke, it's one of a family of heroic motifs stemming from Erda's Motif H52's last three notes. H76, which represents Brünnhilde and her eight Valkyrie-sisters, is based on H52 presumably because the nine Valkyries are the warrior-daughters born to Erda through Wotan, whose sole purpose as angel-like muses of death is to inspire mortal warriors to martyrdom so the Valkyries can gather them in Valhalla, restored to life, to help Wotan forestall Alberich's threat to storm Valhalla and overthrow the gods' rule. Other motifs of this heroic family include H70, the Wälsung race's tragic fate, H88, the fated doom of the heroes the Valkyries inspire to martyrdom, and H92, belonging to Siegfried. Most motifs in this family express Wotan's hope for a restoration of the innocence both he and Alberich have lost, won through his proxies the Valkyries and Wälsungs. We also hear for the first time the Valkyrie war-cry, H77, sung by Brünnhilde. H77 will also feature prominently in the famous prelude to V.3.1. Unlike H76, which is integrated musico-dramatically into the *Ring* and accrues a storehouse of meaning, H77 is primarily evocative of the Valkyries as warrior-maidens and rarely heard.

Wotan tells Brünnhilde to give the Wälsung hero Siegmund, his son, victory, rather than death. In the past, as we'll learn from Wotan in his confession to Brünnhilde in V.2.2, Wotan's heroes chosen for service in Valhalla to fight for good (heavenly Valhalla) against evil (Alberich's hell Nibelheim), at the end of times, were inspired by his nine Valkyrie daughters to martyr themselves in battle, but Wotan's Wälsung heroes are distinguished from his resurrected martyrs by serving him while living. The resurrected heroes Wotan assembles in Valhalla to preserve the gods' rule, whereas he intends his Wälsungs to fight for his ideals while living in a post-religious world. These martyred heroes we may take for religious martyrs and other culture-heroes who, deluded by the promises of religious self-deception, produced a cultural legacy which had its greatest effect only after their death. But now, ethics and art and science are liberating themselves from religious belief, the protection of the gods, and Siegmund, Wotan's secular social revolutionary with a conscience inspired by love, is to bring about the revolution in his lifetime. The reason for this is that during the mytho-poetic phase of human history, when religious self-deception was the primary source of value and knowledge, faith couldn't be openly questioned. When religious practice was questioned by reformers (who often wished merely to return society to purer, holier times) they were often repelled and sometimes martyred as threats to the establishment. But as the *Ring* allegory proceeds we're entering that phase of history during which individual men and women of genius gradually emancipated themselves from what had been regarded as divine authority, and with the eventual acceptance of individualism and personal originality as values, a culture-hero could make a signal contribution to civilization and be honored for it in his or her lifetime.

Some of the music portraying Fricka's progress in her chariot is reminiscent of music heard in association with Alberich earlier, such as H8 and a H38 Variant, and we're reminded that he whipped his fellow Nibelungs as she whips her rams. Like Alberich, Fricka, symbol for religious conservatism, is now aligned with the forces which are inimical to free self-expression, creativity, loving kindness and affection, and individual conscience. Wotan, who favors the Wälsungs and brought Siegmund up expressly to challenge the gods' rule, complains—accompanied by a new motif H78—that the same old storm and strife approaches. H78 is based on H57b, introduced in R.4 as Wotan saluted the fortress Valhalla, saying it will protect the gods from dread and dismay. It was to this motif that Siegmund sang how desperate he was to obtain the sword his father Wälse had promised him in his time of need. H57b, in its new incarnation as H78, expresses the ambiguity that though both Fricka and Wotan seek to preserve Valhalla, Fricka's insistence on the immutability of the gods' laws will, as Wotan alone knows, ensure Valhalla's destruction. The only way for the gods' ideal realm to survive the inevitable end of religious belief is to break divine law and breach faith by acknowledging mortal man as the author of the gods' divinity and of his own redemption. But Fricka can't afford to admit this. So he insists he must make a stand against her blind conservatism, followed by the sounding of what Dunning describes as a loose variant of H52, the motif to which Erda informed Wotan that all things come to an end.

Fricka, wedlock's guardian, has promised Hunding she'll avenge his shame—that he's been cuckolded by Siegmund and Sieglinde, guilty of adultery and incest—on the Wälsung twins. With dignified, self-righteous bearing, she now confronts Wotan with her complaints, expressing her fear that through his encouragement the illicit twin-pair's irreverence towards the gods' laws will engender social instability:

> **[pp. 141–2]** (H66) **Fricka:** (H50 voc:) Hunding's distress ["Noth"] I heard; he called on me (:H50 voc) (H67:) for vengeance: wedlock's guardian gave him ear and promised to punish severely the deed of that brazenly impious pair (:H67) that dared to wrong a husband.
>
> **Wotan:** What was so wrong that was done by the couple that spring united in love? (H63:) ... who'll make me amends for the power of love (:H63)?
>
> **Fricka:** ... (H67:) ... I grieve for wedlock's holy vow, a vow most harshly broken (:H67)!
>
> **Wotan:** Unholy I deem the vow that binds unloving hearts; ... (H19) wherever forces are boldly stirring, I openly counsel war. (H78 frag)

Fricka regards the vow of fidelity in wedlock as more important than whether authentic love sustains it. For her the stability of society is more important than self-expression, which she regards as egoistic and an affront to divine rule. This insistence on stability at the expense of individual freedom of expression is expressed in H67 (Hunding's Rights). This conflict between conservatism and the revolutionary impulse toward more freedom is the central conflict of our time.

The basis for Wotan's retort to Fricka can be found in Feuerbach: " ... marriage as the free bond of love—is sacred ... . (...) [Footnote:] ... a marriage the bond of which is merely an external restriction, not the voluntary, contented self-restriction of love, ... a marriage which is not spontaneously concluded, ... is not a true marriage, and therefore not a ... moral marriage." [140F-EOC, p. 271] Wagner argued marriage without love is a sin, because it makes woman man's property, and converts her natural, healthy quest for true love into an artificial sin: " ... the idea of Marriage, its sacredness, its right ... became embodied in the Law. (...) If a woman was wed by a man for whom she had no love, and he fulfilled the letter of the marriage-law to her, through that law she became his property: the woman's struggle for freedom through love thereby became a sin, actual contentment of her love she could only attain by adultery." [390W-{1–2/49} *Jesus of Nazareth*, PW Vol. VIII. p. 302]

Fricka wonders aloud that even if the twins' adultery doesn't horrify Wotan, how can he fail to find their sibling incest abhorrent! Significantly, her main reason for saying this is that sibling incest is without precedent. Wotan, who'd formerly (in R.2) extolled variety and change, takes the spontaneity of the twins' love as a sure sign of its virtue:

> **[p. 142] Fricka:** If you think breach of wedlock worthy of praise, then ... deem it holy that incest springs from the bond of a twin-born pair! My heart is quaking, my brain is reeling ... ! When was it witnessed that natural siblings loved one another?
>
> **Wotan:** (H72 orch:) Today you have witnessed it happen: learn thus that a thing might befall of itself though it never happened before (:H72 orch).

Unlike Oedipus and Jocasta (Oedipus's mother), who freely commit incest only so long as they're unconscious of their crime, but on learning their true relation to each other condemn themselves (as Wagner explains in the following extract), the Wälsung twins self-consciously glory in their sibling incest: "The hapless pair [Queen Jocasta of Thebes and her son, Oedipus], whose Conscience ... stood within the pale of human Society, passed judgment on themselves when they became conscious of their unconscious crime: ... ... Oedipus had solved the riddle of the Sphinx! ... he called the kernel of this riddle Man. (...) It is we who have to solve that riddle ... by vindicating the instinct of the Individual from out Society itself; whose highest, still renewing and re-quickening wealth, that Instinct is." [502W-{50–1/51} *Opera and Drama*, PW Vol. II, pp. 182–183] Siegmund and Sieglinde glory in their incestuous love and adultery because through this means alone can they preserve in purity the blood of the Wälsung race which Wotan introduced into the world for its redemption (blood which will eventually produce the greatest Wälsung hero Siegfried). Their conscious breach of one of the oldest and most universal (with rare, special exceptions) social prohibitions, the taboo against incest, exhibits their almost animal-like innocence, their insistence on living for feeling rather than subscribing to learned social norms. The genius, in his or her inherent originality, similarly maintains a child's plasticity and adventurousness and freedom from learned prejudice long after average adults' minds have ossified with little likelihood of future self-development.

Fricka exclaims that the Wälsungs' lawlessness, if unpunished, will bring about the twilight of the gods because they'll lose man's respect if divine law isn't strictly enforced. Laws of divine origin are by definition infallible and immutable, so to permit innovation and breaking of tradition calls the gods into question. H78, heard as Fricka warns Wotan that the gods' rule is threatened by Wotan's tolerance of disobedience by his favorites, is ironic, since Wotan, unlike Fricka, knows they can't hope to be redeemed from Alberich's Ring Curse without the Wälsungs' lawlessness:

> [pp. 142–3] Fricka: (... [[H78:]]) So this is the end of the blessed immortals, since you begot (:H78) those dissolute Wälsungs? (...) ... (H6 staccato vari?) you ... laughingly loosen heaven's hold (H56) that this impious twin-born pair, your falsehood's wanton fruit, might obey the dictates of pleasure and whim! [[H79ab voc:]]) [= H68/H23 vari] Oh why do I wail over wedlock and vow, (H78) when you were the first to infringe them! (...) (:H79ab). Where was the hollow, where the height where your lustful look didn't pry in seeking out ways of indulging your fondness for change ... !

Fricka accuses Wotan of encouraging such illicit love by engaging in affairs himself, accompanied by a new compound motif H79ab whose first segment H79a is based on H68 (the weeping of the maid whom Siegmund futilely tried to rescue from a loveless marriage), and whose second segment H79b is based on H63b, the definitive love motif. Wotan has had two illicit sexual liaisons which produced children, his first with Erda, which produced their daughters, the nine Valkyries (including Brünnhilde), and the second with the anonymous mortal woman who gave birth to Siegmund and Sieglinde. His hope to redeem the gods is served by both of his sexual affairs. He must break his own law to preserve it. We find a parallel in the Christian distinction between the Old and New Testaments: Christ the savior makes a new contract with man, distilling the 10 commandments, the "thou shalt nots" predicated on fear of the Lord, into the new law of love. Christians hold that Christ's new law superseded the old, but Christ was martyred by adherents of the old law as a blasphemer and threat to the faithful.

Fricka accuses Wotan of seeking to indulge his fondness for change through these affairs, and we're reminded that in R.2 he told her that though she wished to entice him with domestic tranquility to remain content within the secure walls of Valhalla, he had an impulse for change which would lure him outside Valhalla's safe confines to seek dominion over the outer world. But his trips outside Valhalla (outside religious faith) are inspired by his hope to save Valhalla's soul from destruction by Alberich's envious revenge. Fricka, the incarnation of unexamined religious faith, can't afford to acknowledge the truth. But she at least acknowledges that the Valkyries, Wotan's illicit daughters, serve the gods, though she complains that now that Wotan has resorted to taking on new identities and disguises in order to produce a mortal race of heroes, he may as well finish the gods off:

> [p. 143] **Fricka:** (H78 varis & frags:; H79 varis & frags:) In sadness of spirit I had to stand by, while you fared to the fray with those ill-mannered girls, who were born of the bond of a dissolute love; for you still held your wife in sufficient awe that the Valkyrie band, and Brünnhilde herself, the bride of your wishes, you gave to me to obey as their mistress. (H86 embryo bass clarinet:) But now new names have taken your fancy, wolf-like you roam through the forest as Wälse (:H86 embryo bass clarinet); now that you've fallen to fathomless shame and fathered a couple of common mortals, would you ... fling your wife at the feet of the she-wolf's litter?

The mere fact that Wotan, ruler of gods and man, should seek redemption for the gods through a race of mortal men, foreshadows the twilight of the gods which Alberich threatens. This irony stems from the Feuerbachian idea that through the Christian belief that God had to take human form in order to redeem man, the Christians unwittingly admitted that God is, after all, merely the human species as such: " ... the true reason why at the end of religion ... eschatological doctrine represents man as a divine being, ... is that God, at least the Christian God, is nothing other than the essence of man." [306F-LER, p. 270]

Wotan tries to persuade Fricka that depending on the alleged infallibility of particular laws, customs, traditions, and beliefs, will leave one vulnerable to tide and time if one doesn't acknowledge necessary change. He confesses that the gods need a hero, independent of them, who can do what they, bound by faith, can't do, breach faith and break divine law to preserve what's truly valuable in Valhalla's legacy from the inevitable twilight of the gods:

[pp. 144–5] Wotan: Age-old custom is all you can grasp: but my thoughts seek to encompass what's never yet come to pass. (H56ab) (…) A hero is needed ["Noth thut ein Held"] who, lacking godly protection, breaks loose from the law of the gods: (H19) thus alone is he fit to perform that feat (H17:) which, needful though it is to the gods ["wie noth sie den Göttern"], the god is forbidden to do (:H17). (H27)

Fricka: (…) What lofty feat could heroes perform that their gods were prevented from doing, whose grace informs their actions alone?

Wotan: You have no heed of their own independence?

Fricka: (…) Sheltered by you they seem to be strong; spurred on by you, they strive for the light: you alone urge them on whom you thus praise to me, the immortal goddess. (H78 frag orch) … and yet you'll not win this Wälsung yourself: in him I find only you, for through you alone he defies us.

Wotan: (H64 harmony on horns:; H64 voc:) In grievous distress … he grew up by himself (:H64 orch & voc). (H19:) My shelter (:H19) never shielded him.

Fricka: Don't shelter him today then; take away the sword you bestowed upon him. (H56ab) [**Wotan:** (…); **Fricka:** (…)]

Wotan: … Siegmund won it himself … in his need ["Noth"]. (from this point onwards, Wotan's whole demeanor expresses increasing gloom and dejection: [[H80 orch]] [= H19 vari])

Fricka: … [[H80 orch:]] You fostered that need ["Noth"] no less than you fashioned the fearsome sword (:H80 orch) … . [[H80 orch]] For him you thrust the sword in the tree trunk; [[H80 orch]] you promised him the noble weapon: [[H80 orch]] will you deny that your cunning alone lured him to where he might find it?

Wotan needs a hero who can obtain Alberich's Ring from Fafner before Alberich wins it back to bring about the gods' doom (end of belief in gods). He fears Alberich's scientific consciousness based on the power of objective knowledge will become the guiding force in society, and supplant religious belief and the ideal of selfless love it engendered. He can't get involved because, to admit that faith might be under threat from the truth is to lose the battle before it's started. Wotan's fear of self-knowledge, Fafner transformed by the Tarnhelm into a Serpent embodying religious faith's fear of truth, now guards access to Alberich's Hoard of knowledge, the wondrous Tarnhelm (imagination), and the Ring (symbolic consciousness), to ensure that knowledge sleeps and is never woken by free intellectual inquiry. But Wotan, knowing Fafner's vulnerability to Alberich, hopes his free hero can win Alberich's Ring from Fafner in a manner that will void its curse.

Feuerbach assessed the manner in which unexamined customs, laws, institutions, and religious beliefs, established in the earliest period of human culture, stifled change and innovation for millennia. His following remark may be a basis for Fricka's fear of the new, Fafner's prohibiting man's access to Alberich's hoard of knowledge, and for Wotan's praise of innovation: "... precisely because man made sacraments ... of the first elements of human civilization and well-being, religion always became, in the course of development, the antithesis of true civilization, an obstacle to progress; for it opposed every innovation, every change in the old traditional ways." [279F-LER, pp. 211–212; See also 85F-EOC, p. 117] And Wagner could scarcely have penned a better description of Fricka's conservatism and fear of the new than the following: "... the State, which had imperceptibly waxed from out ... Society, had fed itself on the latter's habit ... , and had so far become the attorney ... of this habit, that now it represented abstract Wont alone, whose core is fear and abhorrence of the thing unwonted." [503W-{50–1/51} *Opera and Drama*, PW Vol. II, p. 184]

Fricka's contempt for Wotan's assertion that his mortal hero has acted spontaneously from his own need (Noth) finds justification in Feuerbach's observation that cultures which assign gods, imaginary beings, the role of creator, or just the role of ruler and adjudicator of man, deprive man and Nature, the true creators, of this honor, and give all credit to the gods: " ... if you look on God as ... the cause of the good—... then do not deny that God is also the cause of the evil that is done men by other men ... . (...) ... if you refuse to honor man as a benefactor, you must also refuse to condemn him as an evildoer ... . How absurd ... to dispose of the good a man does as the grace of God, but to hold man guilty of the evil he does." [248F-LER, p. 162; See also 247F-LER, p. 161] Wagner reiterated Feuerbach's sentiment in his observation (cited previously) that the good, or "the Helpful," man identifies with God, but evil, or harm, man attributes to man. [See 391W-{1–2/49} *Jesus of Nazareth*, PW Vol. VIII. pp. 310–311]

But Wagner offered a deeper analysis of the question Fricka raised, whether mortal man can have free will. He notes that if we only act because of outside coercion, only because, let's say, we fear God, our good is deprived of merit: "... so long as a virtue is demanded, it will never ... be exercised. Either the exercise of this virtue was an act despotically imposed—and thus without that merit of virtue imagined for it; or it was a necessary, an unreflective act of free-will, and then its enabling force was not the self-restricting Will, — but Love." [551W-{50–1/51} *Opera and Drama*, PW Vol. II, p. 352] But anything we do of our own volition isn't free either, because it's the direct product of our true character, which we inherit by virtue of our genes and the environment in which we develop, or by virtue of our allegedly immortal soul, none of which can be altered: "... he [Wagner] talked to me about character and said it was foolish to praise it, for either it was meaningless, or a person could not act otherwise than he had done. (...) I ask him whether he does not admit struggles inside a noble person. 'Yes, but the decision is preordained.'" [1139W-{11/15/82} CD Vol. II, pp. 952–953] We find a basis for Wagner's reflections in Feuerbach: [Footnote:] "Can an individual really outdo himself? Isn't that which enables me to outdo myself simply my own individual energy and predisposition, which has been released and developed on this particular occasion? But most people mistake phrases for reality." [348F-LER, p. 348] In other words, there's no free will. The real question is whether the ultimate ground of our impulses and/or conscious motives is divine or natural, and if solely natural, whether the cause is inherent nature, or nurture, or both. The problem for Wotan is that the inevitability of Alberich's victory has forced him to acknowledge that the gods' alleged freedom of will is illusory. If this is true, how much less free are mortal men, contingent products of Nature and bound by its laws!

A new and extremely important motif, H80, "Wotan's Frustration," is introduced here as the hallmark of Fricka's critique of mortal man's freedom of will, and is heard repeatedly as her accusation that Wotan alone is behind all of Siegmund's allegedly free and heroic acts starts to have its depressing effect on his morale. He's gradually forced to acknowledge what his religious conscience Fricka has proclaimed, that Siegmund's love and heroism are due to Wotan's influence, since Wotan brought him up to exercise his individual judgment and conscience. H80 is according to Cooke derived from the Spear Motif H19 embryo, that spear whose laws Wotan desires his Wälsung heroes will break to redeem the gods from Alberich's threat. All future occurrences of H80 (and its derivatives H147 and H176) will recall both Wotan's need for a free hero and his recognition of the futility of seeking him, because Wotan has been forced to concede that all such heroes are products of Wotan's fearful, loathsome egoism.

Fricka, cashing in on the categorical triumph of her invincible argument, forces Wotan to abandon Siegmund because he's a threat to the gods' rule, even though Wotan knows what Fricka can't, that without a hero freed from the gods' authority the gods are predestined to destruction anyway:

[pp. 146–7] **Fricka:** ... Siegmund was destined to be my slave. (...) (H78 vari; H19 frag) Should he who, as bondsman and vassal, obeys you, his lord, bend your own eternal wife to his will? (...) My husband cannot want such a thing, he'd not profane the goddess so. (H80) [**Wotan:** (...)] Abandon the Wälsung! (H80) (...)

[Contradicting Wotan's attempts to give Siegmund a fighting chance, Fricka insists neither Wotan nor Brünnhilde protect him: (...)]

Wotan: (... H80:) I cannot kill him: he found my sword (:H80)! (H56ab)

Fricka: (H97 embryo voc?:) Withdraw its magic, let it break in his servile hands (:H97 embryo voc?): let his enemy find him defenceless! (...) [**Brünnhilde:** (...)] Here comes your valiant maid ... ! [**Brünnhilde:** (...); **Wotan:** (...)] Your eternal spouse's sacred honour her shield must defend today: derided of men, deprived of our might, we gods would go to our ruin were my rights not avenged ... by your mettlesome maid today.—The Wälsung falls for my honour's sake: (H19 [with finality]) will Wotan give me his oath?

Wotan: (H80: ...) (H19: [broken up]) Take my oath (:H19 [broken up])!

([Alex Ross's "Microlude":] Fricka strides towards the back of the stage: there she meets Brünnhilde and pauses for a moment before her.)

Fricka: The lord of battles awaits you: let him explain the fate he has chosen! (she drives quickly away: H50; H80: ... Brünnhilde moves towards Wotan, who, leaning on the rocky seat, is sunk in gloomy brooding)

Feuerbach denigrated Fricka's belief that all honor and freedom is accorded to God alone: "... is a God who accords no merit to man, who claims all exclusively for himself, who watches jealously over his honour—is a self-interested, egoistic God like this a God of love?" [173F-EOC, p. 327] We see in the conjunction here of H50 (Alberich's Ring Curse) and H80 (Wotan's Frustration, which informs us that he's bound by his own law to destroy the sole possible means of redemption from its constraints and contradictions, namely, individual freedom and love) that Fricka—though wishing to preserve our ideal of transcendent love, Freia, and divine law—isn't sufficiently flexible to accept the changes necessary to give our religious longing for transcendent meaning a fighting chance to live on in the face of Alberich's threat, to which she's oblivious.

In describing the tragic responsibilities of a king Wagner captured Wotan's despair in having to destroy Siegmund for what seems to be social good, but what in fact is just collective egoism: "[Describing "Public Opinion" as a reflection of "the vulgar egoism of the mass," Wagner says that:] ... the necessitation to yield to its requirements ... becomes the earliest source of that higher form of suffering which the King alone can personally experience ... . If we add ... the personal sacrifice of private freedom which the monarch has to bring to 'reasons of State,' and if we reflect how he alone is in a position to make purely-human considerations ... his personal concern, and yet is forced to immolate them upon the altar of the State: then we shall understand why the legends and the poetry of every age have brought the tragedy of human life the plainest ... to show in ... the destiny of Kings. (...) True justice and humanity are ideals irrealisable: to be bound to strive for them, nay, to recognise an unsilenceable summons to their carrying out, is to be condemned to misery." [700W-{64–2/65} 'On State and Religion,' PW Vol. IV, pp. 21–22] However, as we'll learn in Wotan's confession to Brünnhilde, he's troubled by something more insidious than the impracticality of hoping for social revolution's success in the face of society's immobility.

THE VALKYRIE ≠ ACT TWO, SCENE TWO

(A MOUNTAIN PASS)
WOTAN AND BRÜNNHILDE

For Wagner, Wotan's confession to Brünnhilde was the most important scene in the *Ring*: "In disconsolate ... hours what I was most afraid of was Wodan's great scene, and especially the revelation of his fate to Brünnhilde ... . (...) This is the most important scene for the development of the whole of the great four-part drama ... ." [639W-{10/3/55} Letter to Franz Liszt, SLRW, pp. 351–352] Brünnhilde's sympathy for his divine "Noth," reflecting both his desperate need for a hero freed from the gods' laws who can redeem them from Alberich's Ring Curse, and his concession that such a hero is an impossibility, is what prompts him to confess his futile hope and most terrible fears to her. She longs to have him confide to her what troubles him:

> [pp. 148–9] **Brünnhilde:** (H80) What is it, father, your child must learn? (H80) Sad you seem and downhearted. (H80)
>
> **Wotan:** (...) (H80:) In my own fetters I find myself caught:—I, least free of all things living (:H80)!
>
> **Brünnhilde:** Never have I seen you so! What is it that gnaws at your heart? (...)
>
> **Wotan:** ([[H81 orch:]] [= H19 inversion = H44 vari?]; H50 orch:) O righteous disgrace! O shameful sorrow (:H81 orch; :H50 orch)! (H78:) Gods' direst need ["Götter<u>noth</u>"]! Gods' direst distress ["Götter<u>noth</u>"] (:H78)! (H39:) Infinite fury! Grief neverending (:H39)! (H35:) The saddest am I of all living things (:H35)!
>
> **Brünnhilde:** (...) Father! Father! Tell me, what ails you? (...) Confide in me: I'm true to you; see, (H39 voc:) Brünnhilde begs you (:H39 voc) (H39; H63: Lovingly and anxiously she rests her head and hands on his knees and lap.)
>
> **Wotan:** (...) If I let it be spoken aloud, shall I not loosen my will's restraining hold?
>
> **Brünnhilde:** (... H23 voc major frag:) To Wotan's will you speak when you tell me what you will (:H23 voc major frag): (H?—Possible Embryo for H177: [some chord changes suggest H58a or H12 as heard with H18c in T.3.3 when Brünnhilde sings "Ruhe! Ruhe!":]) who am I if not your will (:H?—possible hint of H58a or H12?)?
>
> **Wotan:** (...) What in words I reveal to no one, let it stay unspoken for ever: with myself I commune when I speak with you.

Cooke examined this passage in which Wotan explodes, expressing the depths of his despair, in detail from a motival standpoint, and said, strangely enough, that it illustrates just how little the meaning of the *Ring* owes to the words, or drama, since most of the meaning of this passage is carried by the resonances of the five motifs in play. [Cooke: pp. 65–72] It's odd that Cooke said this, because though it's true that, as he said, the words which here are accompanied by these five motifs convey little conceptual meaning, he knew perfectly well that a large part of the resonance of these motifs at Wotan's moment of decision stems from their prior association with remarks and events located squarely in the language and drama of the *Ring* elsewhere.

A new, compound motif, heard only a few times in the *Ring*, but of profound significance, is introduced here prior to Wotan's confession, H81. H81 can be regarded as the hallmark of Wotan's confession. Dunning observed that H81 is a compound of H80's four-note (grace-note) flourish, Alberich's Revolt H44 (which is itself an inversion of Wotan's Spear Motif H19), and the last three notes of the motif associated with Erda's knowledge of all that was, is, and will be, H52.

H80 represents the futility of Wotan's hope for a free hero who'll redeem the gods from Alberich's Ring Curse. Alberich's H44 calls to mind his resistance to the gods' rule and intent to overthrow it. The last three notes of H52, which brings up the rear of this compound motif, remind us of Erda's knowledge that all things end, and that the gods themselves are doomed. The sum of H81's meaning would be that Wotan grasps the inevitability of the victory of bitter truth over illusion. As Cooke pointed out, the other motifs at play in this intense, compact passage, include H50, Alberich's Ring Curse, his intent to make the gods pay for co-opting his Ring. There's the tragic version of the love motif, H39, which Cooke said conveys love lost from the world. As Wotan exclaims "Gods' Noth," we hear H78, linked in V.2.1 with Fricka's accusation that the Wälsungs' lawlessness Wotan has encouraged will doom the gods. And last, we hear H35 (Loveless) as Wotan says he's the saddest of all living things. H35 is the sign of The Fall.

Consider Wotan's conundrum: he tells Brünnhilde that he, the (alleged) God, is the un-freest of men, caught in the fetters of his own law which compels him to disavow, punish, and destroy those free individuals to whom he'd looked for redemption. It's self-evident that Wotan's trap entails at least partly what both Feuerbach and Wagner complained of, that through man's earliest laws and institutions, regarded as sacred and therefore immutable, man condemned himself to stick with a guide to life which was once beneficial but was unadaptable to change. But to fully grasp the irony of Wotan's position, note Feuerbach's observation that the very definition of a God is someone who can make, and unmake, his own laws: " ... a God can only prove His divinity by His power to abolish laws .... The only proof that He has made the laws is that He also *unmakes* them. And such proof is provided by miracles." [292F-LER, p. 241] Wotan, though a self-proclaimed god, has lost faith in the miraculous, in his very identity as an allegedly supernatural being. But his problem lies deeper than this. The power we humans grant our gods is that all value and truth stem from them. Since we invented the gods, and they therefore didn't create us, this means those among us who're believers have predicated life's meaning on self-deception. Recall Loge's remark in R.2 that the gods staked everything on Freia's golden apples of sorrow-less youth eternal, i.e., on the illusory belief in immortality. This is the trap Wotan set for himself, that we set for ourselves, by inventing illusory gods as the primary source of all value and knowledge. Wotan has begun to grasp that his dilemma, self-made, is irresolvable. This thought is so unbearable that he's virtually telling his daughter Brünnhilde that he daren't think it aloud, i.e., consciously, lest he lose his mind.

Schopenhauer, whose books Wagner evidently hadn't yet read when he penned this portion of the *Ring* libretto, said the cause of madness is the inability of our human mind to consciously confront thoughts which are so destructive of all those assumptions by which we sustain our happiness and self-image, that they must be repressed and replaced by fantastical thoughts no longer in touch with reality. This extraordinary passage describes religious belief as Feuerbach conceived it, a sort of collective dream or madness (Wahn) in which the objective truth about themselves which men can't stomach is repressed, and a consoling illusion which sustains our preferred assumption of our transcendent value, considered now to be the truth, is substituted for the truth: "In this resistance on the part of the will to allow what is contrary to it to come under the examination of the intellect, is to be found the place where madness can break in on the mind. (...) ... if certain events or circumstances are wholly suppressed for the intellect, because the will cannot bear the sight of them; and then, if the resultant gaps are arbitrarily filled up for the sake of the necessary connexion; we then have madness. For the intellect has given up its nature to please the will; the person then imagines what does not exist. But the resultant madness then becomes the Lethe [a stream of forgetting in Hades, a trope of Greek mythology] of unbearable sufferings; it was the last resource of worried and tormented nature, i.e., of the will." [Schopenhauer: pp. 400–401] What Schopenhauer has described is repression of unbearable knowledge into the unconscious, a repository where it can be securely stored without troubling the conscious mind, and its sublimation into consoling illusions, influenced by feeling, which can safely reach consciousness. This is what Wotan is doing in confessing his unspoken secret to Brünnhilde, whom he describes as part of his own self, effectively his unconscious mind. The thoughts so terrible he daren't speak them aloud, the hoard of forbidden knowledge he imparts to her, which he tells no one in words, leaving it forever unspoken, presumably remains unconscious for him.

Wotan, as not only a figure for "Godhead," but also as a metaphor for Feuerbach's interpretation of god as the collective spirit of historical man, has a more all-embracing consciousness than is given to any one man. He's the all-embracing human spirit who can see, and feel, what individual men can't. He's had a revelation of the full tragic significance of our human existence. Wagner spoke of the universal, tragic consciousness of the human species in his description of the Dutchman in his early romantic opera *The Flying Dutchman*. The Dutchman's "unmeasured sorrows of the damned," his unbearable consciousness of the futility of his quest for redemption from Satan's curse [See 600W-{5/53} 'Explanatory Program: *The Flying Hollander* Overture,' PW Vol. III, p. 229], is comparable to Wotan's existential paralysis conceding the futility of seeking redemption from Alberich's Ring Curse. Wagner's following description of the unique suffering of the "truly noble spirit" corresponds with Wotan's "Noth": "... the great, ... truly noble spirit is distinguished from the ... [common man] by this; to it every ... incident of ... world-intercourse is capable of swiftly displaying its widest correlation with the essential root-phenomena of all existence, thus of showing Life and the World ... in ... their terribly earnest meaning. The naïve, ordinary man—accustomed merely to seize the outmost side of such events, ... of practical service for the moment's need—when once this awful earnestness ... reveals itself to him through an unaccustomed juncture, falls into such consternation that self-murder is very frequently the consequence." [707W-{64–2/65} 'On State and Religion,' PW Vol. IV, p. 32] This explains why Wotan, whom brief possession of Alberich's Ring of consciousness has endowed temporarily with this shocking vision of the terrible sin in our human existence, represses this unbearable knowledge of his true identity, and corrupt history which follows from it, into Brünnhilde, his unconscious mind, the womb of our involuntary dreaming. As Feuerbach put it in a passage previously cited: "... in waking, the ego acts on itself; whereas in dreaming it is acted on by itself as by another being. (...) ... dreaming is the key to the mysteries of religion." [102F-EOC, pp. 140–141]

A basis for the idea that Brünnhilde is Wotan's unconscious mind is Wagner's discussion of the meaning of Elsa's relationship with Lohengrin in 'A Communication To My Friends': "In 'Elsa' I saw ... my desired antithesis to Lohengrin, ... the other half of his being ... . Elsa is the unconscious, the undeliberate (Unwillkürliche), into which Lohengrin's conscious, deliberate (willkürliche) being yearns to be redeemed ... . (...) I grew to find her so justified in the final outburst of her jealousy [i.e., Elsa's insistence that Lohengrin share with her, his wife, the secret of his true identity and origin, so she could help him keep the secret which she supposes might, if exposed, bring him great suffering (Noth), akin to Brünnhilde's sympathetic desire to hear Wotan confess his "divine Noth" which he daren't speak aloud], that from this very outburst I learnt first to thoroughly understand the purely-human element of love ... . this woman, ... who, by the very outburst of her jealousy, wakes first from out the thrill of worship [religious faith] into the full reality of love, ... I had found her now: ... my ... Lohengrin ... I must give up as lost [Lohengrin and Wotan sever themselves from Elsa and Brünnhilde, respectively, and withdraw from active involvement with the world]; to track ... the footsteps of that true Woman-hood, which should one day bring to me and all the world redemption, after Man-Hood's egoism, even in its noblest form [religious faith], had shivered into ... dust before her. Elsa ... made me a Revolutionary at one blow. She was the Spirit of the Folk, for whose redeeming hand I ... , as artist-man, was longing." [573W-{6–8/51} 'A Communication To My Friends,' PW Vol. I, pp. 346–348]

Elsa's request that Lohengrin share with her the secret of his true identity and origin, a secret which, if divulged, she believes would bring him great suffering (Noth), and her offer to help Lohengrin keep this secret to protect him from this Noth, is the basis for Brünnhilde's request that Wotan share with her the secret of his divine Noth, which he daren't speak aloud in words. Lohengrin's prohibition against revealing the secret of his true identity and origin has the same cause as Wotan's inability to speak aloud (consciously) the origin of his divine Noth. It's that religious faith is predicated on an illusion inspired by man's fear of truth. Lohengrin refuses Elsa's request until her insistence compels him to answer her question, but Wotan acquiesces voluntarily to Brünnhilde's request that he tell her what gnaws at his heart, sharing with her the unspoken secret of his divine Noth. Lohengrin's coerced, public confession that he was sent to earth from the divine Grail realm is self-deception akin to Wotan's insistence on outwardly supporting the demands made by Fricka's faith in the face of his unconscious knowledge of its futility, which he'll confess to Brünnhilde. Elsa is the revolutionary whose breach of religious faith emancipated Wagner from the limitations of his traditional romantic operas to create his revolutionary music-dramas. The distinction between Lohengrin's refusal to share with Elsa forbidden knowledge, and Wotan's acquiescence to Brünnhilde's plea that he confide his divine Noth to her, is the key.

Wagner described Elsa not only as Lohengrin's unconscious mind, in whom Lohengrin's conscious mind sought redemption, but also suggested that had Lohengrin shared the unspoken secret of his true identity and origin with her, she'd have become the agent of universal redemption. Considering that I've described Wotan not only as god but as a metaphor for Feuerbach's identification of god as collective, historical man, i.e., the Folk who involuntarily and unconsciously invented the gods, it's striking that Wagner describes Elsa (embryonic Brünnhilde) as the "Spirit of the Folk." Brünnhilde isn't just a single man's unconscious mind, but man's (Wotan's) collective unconscious. The fact that Alberich's nightmarish forging of his Ring (H17ab) is the unconscious source of inspiration for Wotan's waking dream Valhalla (H18ab), and that Brünnhilde affirms her status as Wotan's unconscious mind prior to his confession, suggests she (like her mother Erda) will play a key role in redeeming Wotan from Alberich's Ring Curse of consciousness. This she'll do not by saving the gods from their fated demise (the death of religious faith), but rather, in redeeming them (redeeming those who believe in gods) from consciousness of the fatal truth. Wotan tells Brünnhilde as he prepares to confess his secret: "What in words I reveal to no one, let it stay unspoken forever ... ." The forbidden, dangerous secret Wotan confesses to her may remain unspoken in words, but it can be spoken in the language of the unconscious, Wagner's musical motifs of reminiscence and foreboding.

Wagner links the plots of *Lohengrin* and the *Ring* in his following comparison between the two works, in which he says that the *Ring* (in which Wotan acquiesced to Brünnhilde's plea that he share with her his unspoken secret, the Noth which ails him) resolves the difficulty presented in *Lohengrin* by Lohengrin's refusal to lovingly share the secret of his true identity and origin with Elsa. Thanks to his acquiescence, Wotan obtains through Brünnhilde healing from the wounds of consciousness, which Lohengrin doesn't: "... I remain convinced that my Lohengrin ... symbolizes the most profoundly tragic situation of the present day, namely man's desire to descend from the most intellectual heights [Wotan's desire to repress his hoard of unbearable knowledge] to the depths of love [into his unconscious mind, Brünnhilde], the longing to be understood instinctively [to let feeling (music) replace reflective thought as expressed by dying religious faith], a longing which modern reality cannot yet satisfy. (...) This is where my art must come to the rescue: and the work of art that I had no choice but to conceive in this sense is none other than my Nibelung poem." [612W-{1/25-26/54} Letter to August Röckel, SLRW, p. 306; See also 686W] The essential distinction between Lohengrin and Wotan is that Lohengrin's refusal to share his secret Noth with Elsa symbolizes the fact that in Wagner's romantic operas drama (the word) and music only had what Wagner described as a mechanical (unloving) relationship to each other, whereas Wotan's acquiescence to Brünnhilde's loving plea symbolizes the organic, loving union of drama (Wotan's confession of world-history, the story of man's inherent guilt) with music, in which the drama's guilt is redeemed through its sublimation into Wagner's musical motifs, born of Wotan's unconscious mind Brünnhilde. [See 557W-{5/31/51} Letter to Adolf Stahr: SLRW, p. 225] It's as if historical man (Wotan) had been transformed back into timeless, mythical man, whom we'll later recognize as Siegfried.

Wotan, symbol for collective man's dying religious faith, having lost hope that man's religious impulse could be redeemed by social revolution, turns inward (emulating Wagner) to seek redemption instead in inspired secular art, particularly music. As Brünnhilde will tell Siegmund's son Siegfried in S.3.3, what Wotan thought (his confession), she felt (sublimated into music), and what she felt was her love for Siegfried. Music, the language of the unconscious, will keep Wotan's unutterable secret which, as he told Brünnhilde, will remain forever unspoken in words, but will be spoken aloud only in music. As Wagner said: "It is terrifying, and makes one dizzy, to gaze into the awful caverns of the human heart. For the poet it is impossible to render in words all that passes at the bottom of this stanchless fount ... . It is reserved for Music alone, to reveal the primal elements of this marvellous nature; in her mysterious charm our soul is shown this great, unutterable secret." [356W-{2–4/42} 'Halevy and *La Reine De Chypre*,' PW Vol. VIII, p. 179] In other words, it's Wagner's musical motifs, engendered by the womb of Wotan's wishes Brünnhilde, in whom he represses and sublimates the horror of his unbearable confession, which will keep Wotan's unspoken secret: "The poet [Wotan] can only hope to realise his Aim, from the instant when he hushes it and keeps it secret to himself: ... when, in the language wherein alone it could be imparted as a naked intellectual-aim [words], he no longer speaks it out at all. (...) ... Tone-speech ... is therefore the organ of expression proper for the poet who would make himself intelligible by turning from the Understanding [Wotan's Hoard of knowledge] to the Feeling [his sympathetic daughter Brünnhilde] ... ." [529W-{50–1/51} *Opera and Drama*, PW Vol. II, pp. 233–234]

Wagner further suggests how the Poet (Wotan) can redeem his aim (escape Alberich's Ring Curse of consciousness) by submerging his hoard of knowledge of the terrible world and its history in music (confessing it to Brünnhilde): "The Understanding is ... driven by necessity to wed itself with an element [music] which shall be able to take-up into it the poet's Aim [Wotan's confession] as a fertilising seed, ... that it may bring it forth as a ... redeeming utterance of Feeling. This ... is that same mother-element, the womanly, from whose womb—the ur-melodic expressional-faculty, — there issued ... Word-speech [Woglinde's Lullaby H4, music which evolved into meaningful words, but which also evolves into a variant motif, the second of the Woodbird's Songs H138ab] ... ." [530W-{50–1/51} *Opera and Drama*, PW Vol. II, p. 235; see also 512W]

And Wagner equated music not only with Wotan's unspoken secret, described here as the "unspeakable," but also with the religious mysteries, which he confesses to Brünnhilde: "That this Unspeakable is not a thing unutterable per se, but merely unutterable through the organ of our Understanding; ... is shown plainly ... by the Instruments of the orchestra ... . This ... explanation of the

'Unspeakable,' one might extend ... to the whole matter of Religious Philosophy ... ." [539W-{50–1/51} *Opera and Drama*, PW Vol. II, pp. 316–317] Wotan's seed, his confession of his unbearable hoard of knowledge to Brünnhilde, will be converted by her into redemptive musical motifs, the subliminal messengers of Wotan's thoughts: "This faculty ["... of uttering the unspeakable ..."] the ear acquires through the language of the Orchestra, which is able to attach itself just as intimately to the verse-melody as earlier to the gesture, and thus to develop into a messenger of the very Thought itself, transmitting it to Feeling ... ." [540W-{50–1/51} *Opera and Drama*, PW Vol. II, p. 324] Brünnhilde's status as both the repository of Wotan's confession of his unsettling, secret hoard of forbidden knowledge (which embraces the essential elements of Wagner's *Ring* drama), and as the musical messenger of these thoughts, will have the most extraordinary bearing on our understanding of her future, loving relationship with Wotan's last bid for redemption through a Wälsung hero, Siegfried.

What follows is Wotan's confession to Brünnhilde, whose importance can't be overestimated:

> **[p. 149]** (H80) **Wotan:** (starkly unmusical recitative:) When youthful love's delights had faded, I longed in my heart for power: ... I won for myself the world.

What Wotan describes as his "youthful love's delights" is Wagner's metaphor for the pre-cultural time when our ancestors were only impelled by animal instinct or feeling (the Rhinedaughters), not reflective thought involving complex language. This youthful love faded during the evolutionary transition from instinctive feeling to reasoned thought (Alberich forged his Ring; Wotan made his Spear of Divine Authority), as we obtained power over our world through knowledge. Wotan then tells how, aided by our artistic cunning Loge, he unwittingly, unconsciously deluded himself, through religion's illusions, into believing he could restore lost innocence (love) in the face of man's acquisition of that knowledge which grants us power:

> **[p. 149] Wotan:** Unwittingly false I acted unfairly, binding by treaties what boded ill: cunningly Loge lured me on but vanished while roaming the world.—(H80) Yet I did not like to give up love; (H80 frag) in the midst of power I longed for love's pleasures ... .

Wotan's troubles (represented by H80, Wotan's Frustration) began when he thought he could safely follow Froh's suggestion and enjoy the Ring's—consciousness's—power, without sacrificing love. He unconsciously deceived himself (and therefore deceived all men, since all are subsumed under Wotan). H80 embodies his existential dilemma, that he desires to possess both love and power even though they're incommensurable. But in spite of the fact that Wotan starts his account of world-history with his own primal crime, Wotan's and Alberich's primal crimes represent the Fall seen from two different viewpoints, one subjective (Wotan's), the other objective (Alberich's).

Wotan now introduces his nemesis and dark-side Alberich, but without comparative information which allows us to locate Alberich's primal crime in the *Ring*'s chronology of events:

> **[p. 149] Wotan:** ... born of the night, the fearful Nibelung, Alberich, severed its bonds; he laid a curse upon love and, by that curse, won the glittering gold of the Rhine and, with it, measureless might. (H17ab) The ring that he forged I cunningly wrenched away from him: not to the Rhine though did I return it. With it I paid for Valhalla's battlements, (H18ab:) ... (:H18ab), (H18d:) from which I now ruled the world (:H18d).

In view of Wotan's self-serving manipulation of world-history to give the gods precedence over Alberich not only in dignity but in chronology, Feuerbach's observation that though the creation of the human mind (Alberich's forging of the Ring) is the last event in natural evolution, our vain assumption that we have a divine origin inspires us to grant what's first in dignity, but not in time, our human mind (i.e., the gods it invented), precedence in time also [See 243F-LER, p. 155], is very helpful in grasping Wotan's self-delusion.

Wotan then describes how, after hearing Erda's prophecy of the twilight of the gods, he sought her to obtain more complete knowledge of the bitter end she foresaw (presumably also to learn whether the gods' fate could be altered, or, if not, how their fate could be borne). So he entered—and planted the seed of his fear and hope for redemption in—"the womb of the world," Erda, who gave birth to their daughter Brünnhilde:

> **[pp. 149–50] Wotan:** (H52:) She who knows all that ever was, Erda, the awesomely all-wise Wala, told me to give up the ring and warned of an end everlasting (:H52). ... Of that end I wanted to know yet more ... ... (H80:) Then I lost all lightness of heart; the god desired knowledge (:H80): into the womb of the world I descended, (H97 hint?:) mastered the Wala with love's magic spell (:H97 hint?) ... . Knowledge I gained from her; from me though she gained a pledge: (H88 Embryo:) the world's wisest woman (:H88 foreshadowed) bore to me, Brünnhilde, you.

Brünnhilde was born of the seed produced by Wotan's self-doubt, fear, and hope, and his two distinct intentions towards Erda. Wotan descended to Mother-Earth (Nature) to learn both the full truth about why Erda says he must live in fear, and, through loving union with her, how to end his fear. These two motives constitute Wagner's metaphor for our ability to know Nature (Erda) either conceptually through objective understanding, as the scientist does, or to know the world (Erda—Nature) sympathetically through feeling, as in religious belief (which creates an alternative world of the imagination, held to be more substantial than our objective world) and art (which transfigures our objective world by taking possession of it aesthetically).

Brünnhilde is Erda's daughter because that part of us, "man's inner nature," which acts unconsciously by instinct, is, according to Feuerbach, Nature itself, as much as the outer world in which we live. Wotan's unconscious mind, his "Will" Brünnhilde, is our inner nature, the involuntariness and spontaneity of unconscious human thought, our collective dreaming, the ultimate religious mystery: "The object of religion is nature [Erda], which operates independently of man and which he distinguishes from himself. But this nature is more than the phenomena of the outside world; it also includes man's inner nature [Brünnhilde], which operates independently of his knowledge and his [conscious] will. (...) The ultimate secret of religion [Wotan's unspoken secret, which Erda imparted to him, and he imparts in turn to Brünnhilde] is the *relationship* between the *conscious* and *unconscious*, the *voluntary* and *involuntary in one and the same individual.*" [331F-LER, pp. 310–311; See also 213F] Again, why is Brünnhilde Erda's—i.e., Mother Nature's—daughter? Wagner distinguished Nature—Erda—as known to us objectively through our understanding (Alberich's Ring power), from Nature as known to us sympathetically through subjective feeling, or music, which we can identify with Brünnhilde: "Nature in her ... reality is only seen by the Understanding, which de-composes her into her separatest of parts; if it wants to display to itself these parts in their living organic connexion, then the quiet of the Understanding's meditation is involuntarily displaced by a more and more ... agitated mood ... of Feeling. (...) In Feeling's highest agitation, Man sees in Nature [Erda] a sympathising being [Brünnhilde] ... ." [526W-{50–1/51} *Opera and Drama*, PW Vol. II, p. 218; See also 1126W-{3/21/82—4/9/82} BB, p. 204]

The cause of our un-healing wound, our natural evolution into reflectively conscious beings, is also our sole source of consolation and healing. For Erda, who delivers Wotan's wound of unbearable foresight of the gods' inevitable doom, knowledge he so feared he couldn't contemplate it consciously, gives birth to Brünnhilde, through whom Wotan can redeem himself from consciousness of Erda's knowledge and forget his fear. Wotan's heir, the artist-hero Siegfried, will both learn the meaning of Wotan's fear from Brünnhilde (to whom Wotan has imparted the hoard of fearful knowledge he obtained from her mother Erda), and forget his fear through the consummation of their loving union, i.e., through her unconscious inspiration of his redemptive art.

Wagner wrote of what I've described as man's un-healing wound, the price of our natural gift of consciousness, as the special characteristic of humanity, "its aptitude for Conscious Suffering," and described Nature [Erda], which he identified with Schopenhauer's concept of the "Will," as possessing a mysterious capacity for "willing of Redemption": "... the human species' bond of union ... [is] its aptitude for Conscious Suffering. This faculty we can ... regard as the last step reached by Nature in the ascending series of her fashionings; ... in it she ... attains her unique freedom, the annulling of the internecine warfare of the Will. The hidden background of this Will, inscrutable in Time and Space, is nowhere manifest to us but in that abrogation; and there it shows itself divine, the willing of Redemption." [1090W-{6–8/81} 'Herodom and Christendom'—3rd Supplement to 'Religion and Art,' PW Vol. VI, pp. 280–281] In other words, the bitter truth we daren't contemplate consciously, unconsciously inspires us to create that Wahn, a veil of illusion as found in both religion and secular art, which redeems us from it. This is a gift from Mother Nature. Wotan's unconscious mind, Brünnhilde, and its language music, remains Wotan's link with Erda (Nature).

Wotan is repressing knowledge in Brünnhilde which hasn't yet attained consciousness (but which threatens to wake in him and become conscious, as Alberich threatened that his hoard of knowledge would rise from silent depths to the light of day to overthrow the gods' illusions) by restoring it to his unconscious, his secure repository, through his confession to Brünnhilde.

Wotan now informs us what role his daughters by Erda—Brünnhilde and her Valkyrie sisters—have played as muses of inspiration for the martyred heroes on whose legacy he's up until now been able to depend to keep Alberich's inevitable assault on Valhalla and its values at bay. The Valkyrie muses have inspired Wotan's chosen heroes with the same subliminal fear of truth (Erda's prophecy of doom) and longing for redemption from it, which prompted Wotan to seek consolation through Erda, the Valkyries' mother, in the first place:

> [p. 150] **Wotan:** With eight sisters I brought you up: through you Valkyries I hoped to avert the fate ... the Vala had made me fear—a shameful end of the gods everlasting. (H76:) That our foe might find us stalwart in strife I bade you bring me heroes (:H76): those men whom ... we tamed by our laws, ... whose mettle we held in check by binding them to us in blind allegiance through troubled treaties' treacherous bonds. (H76:) You'd [?] to spur them on ... to onslaught and strife ... (:H76), so that hosts of valiant warriors I'd gather in Valhalla's hall.

The Valkyries are muses through whom culture-heroes—chosen by virtue of their own genius to help save Valhalla from Alberich's threat to overthrow the gods (religious belief)—are inspired to martyrdom and enter Valhalla as a realm of memory and tradition, who sustain a civilization predicated on the self-deception of religion and art. They (creators and sustainers of the veil of Wahn which protects Valhalla, religious belief, from contradiction by the objective truth) are legatees of the archetypal artist and trickster Loge. Wotan notes that his heroes were bound to the gods, to religious belief and its social contract, by blind allegiance to troubled, treacherous treaties (self-deceit). Since the Valkyries have served Wotan well in this respect, gathering for him in Valhalla a great hero-host against the judgment day when Alberich and his host of night will launch their final assault on Valhalla, Brünnhilde wonders why Wotan is troubled. It's because his deluded, blindly faithful band of resurrected heroes can only protect Valhalla until Alberich regains his Ring:

> [p. 151] **Brünnhilde:** What is it you fear since we've never yet failed?
>
> **Wotan:** (H52: ...) (H19 bass:) There's something else (:H19 bass) (H17) ... of which the wala warned me. (H17:) Through Alberich's host our end now threatens (:H17): (H45:) burning with envious ["neidischem"] rage, the Nibelung bears me ill-will; ... but I'm not now afraid of his forces of night— my heroes would defeat him (:H45). (... H17:) Only were he to win back the ring ... would Valhalla then be lost (:H17): he who laid a curse on love, he alone in his envy ["Neidisch"] would use the runes of the ring to the noble gods' unending shame; my heroes' hearts ... he'd turn against me, ... to ... wage war against me.

Wotan isn't yet afraid Alberich's accumulation of a hoard of knowledge (represented by the Hoard Motif H45) will overthrow the gods, because society is still predicated on the beliefs and values invented and imparted to it by the culture-heroes whom the Valkyries unconsciously inspire with Wotan's fear of the truth, to produce those works which sustain a culture dependent on religious illusion, Valhalla. But if Alberich ever regained the ring, if objective thought ever gained control over our consciousness (if science supplants religion as an explanation of the world), Alberich would employ this knowledge to discredit faith by exposing religious man's hypocrisy and self-deceit, and reveal Nature's bitter truths which religious man had ignored or censored. What's more, Wotan's own heroes (whose archetype is the treacherous Loge) Alberich would turn against him. These heroes aren't only Wotan's heroes of religion, social revolution, and art dedicated to restoring lost innocence, but also Alberich's host of night who labor in the shadow of the dominant religious society to reveal the secrets of Nature. But both sets of heroes will eventually fight for individual freedom of thought from religious man's dogmatic faith as they gradually emancipate themselves from fear of breaching it, in order to access life's unexplored dimensions on which religious faith's fear of the new (Fafner) had sat for millennia like a dragon guarding its hoard of treasure. So even Wotan's chosen heroes will play a role in storming Valhalla. Wotan's prophecy that Alberich will eventually make Wotan's own heroes betray him echoes Alberich's prophecies (in R.3) of Loge's role in betraying the gods, and of Alberich's use of Wotan's heroes to fight against him, and it looks forward to Alberich's son Hagen's manipulation of Siegfried to betray Brünnhilde's love and restore the ring to Alberich.

There's a rational explanation for this betrayal. Though in earlier times the gods were presumed to control all things, as human societies matured many who were once committed to the old faith found themselves in a position to obtain objective knowledge which wasn't initially regarded as a threat to received opinion and religious faith, but whose ultimate implications eventually threatened social stability predicated on the illusion of man's transcendent origin and/or value. Feuerbach, referencing the learned, elite keepers of the faith such as priests who eventually came into possession of the very knowledge which will ultimately undermine their faith, said that: "The original elements of the ancient religions are merely ... the impressions which physical and astronomical phenomena arouse in man so long as he does not see them as objects of science. Later, ... even among ancient peoples, notably in the priestly caste who alone had access to science and learning, observations—the rudiments of science—took their place side by side with the religious view of nature ... ." [200F-LER, p. 36] "Everything which later became a field of independent human activity, of culture, was originally an aspect of religion: all the arts, all the sciences ...—for as soon as an art or science achieves a high state of development, it ceases to be religion—were originally the concern of religion and its representatives, the priests." [278F-LER, pp. 209–210; See also 170F-EOC, p. 323] Eventually, even reformers of religion, in winning their right to express their views and cause change from within, won for all thinkers the right to individual freedom of inquiry, freeing those formerly specializing in theologically authorized science and art to venture into new territory which threatens faith itself: *"... it is to doubt of Christian faith, to the victory of religious scepticism, to free-thinkers, to heretics, that we owe tolerance, freedom of opinion."* [171F-EOC, p. 323]

Having reached the nub of his existential dilemma, Wotan now explains both why the gods can only find redemption from Alberich's Ring Curse in the allegedly spontaneous actions of a hero freed from the gods' authority and influence, and why Wotan has become convinced that such a hero is a mere figment of his imagination:

> [pp. 151–2] **Wotan:** (... H17:) Troubled, I brooded ... how to wrest the ring from my foe (:H17): ... (H25a) Fafner broods on the hoard for which he killed his brother. (H17 harmony:) From him I must wrest the ring (:H17 harmony), which I paid him once as tribute: (H27:) having treated with him, I cannot meet him; fatally weakened, my courage would fail me (:H27). (H19) ... (H19:) I, lord of treaties, am now a slave to those treaties (:H19). **[[H82ab orch]]** [= H52/H52's inversion—almost H53/H80 frag]; H56ab) One man alone could do what I myself may not: **[[H82ab orch:]]** a hero I never stooped to help; who, unknown to the god and free of his favours, all unwitting, without his bidding, by his own need ["Noth"] alone and with his own weapon (:H82ab orch) might do the deed which I must shun and which my urging urged not on him, though it were wished by my wish alone.

This passage introduces a new compound motif H82ab, the "Need of the Gods." It's composed of H52 followed by its inversion (Dunning says not by H53, as is so often supposed), overlaying H80. For our purposes, though, we may construe H52's inversion in H82 as tantamount to H53, as the sequence of H52 and H53 represents the entirety of Erda's proclamation of her knowledge that all things must end, and that the gods' doom is inevitable. It's this fate from which Wotan hopes his hero will redeem the gods. H82 embodies Wotan's need for a hero who can emancipate himself from the trap set for Wotan by his own actions, that Wotan, lord of treaties, is slave to them (just as Alberich said that the lord of his Ring will be enslaved by it). Wotan needs a hero who can unwittingly resolve the dilemma represented by H80, who's freed from the egoistic motives which underly the social contract engraved on his Spear, but who, crucially, will breach it only symbolically, unconsciously, rather than in conscious actuality, to redeem the gods.

Wagner described this redemption as the state's "going-under": "... the Going-under of the State can mean nothing else but the self-realisation of Society's religious conviction ... of its purely-human essence. ... this conviction can be no Dogma stamped upon us from without, i.e. it cannot rest on historical traditions, nor be drilled into us by the State. ... when we act from the dictates of religious conscience we act from out ourselves, ... as we cannot act otherwise. But Religious Conscience means a universal conscience ... ; and conscience cannot be universal, until it knows the Unconscious, the Instinctive, the Purely-human, as the only true and necessary thing ... ." [513W-{50–1/51} *Opera and*

Drama, PW Vol. II, p. 201] Wotan, by virtue of confessing the knowledge of his historical trap to Brünnhilde, his unconscious mind, and thus repressing it, is in the process of accomplishing "the Going-under of the State" and its foundation on religious faith, in favor of a new dispensation as yet undefined. Wotan fears that in the course of world history Alberich (i.e., his host of night, including Wotan's heroes) will eventually break religious faith's prohibition on freedom of thought and liberate the Ring, Tarnhelm, and Hoard of knowledge, the sources of Alberich's power, to serve Alberich's intent to overthrow the gods, unless Wotan's free hero launches a pre-emptive strike and removes Alberich's Ring from Fafner's (religious faith's, fear of truth's) hands. If Wotan hopes to salvage any of the poetry and beauty of our old religion, he must find a hero who can, as religious faith once did, take the mind (the Ring) prisoner, but unlike religious faith, without staking a claim to truth's power which would force him into an unwinnable conflict with Alberich, who alone can claim the terrible power of objective truth. Wotan needs a hero who, of his own nature, without ulterior (conscious) motive, will take aesthetic possession of Alberich's Ring, Tarnhelm, and Hoard.

Wotan is paralyzed into inaction because he's hamstrung by rising consciousness of an irresolvable contradiction between illusory religious belief and reality, a contradiction which could be suppressed so long as we remained secure within the mytho-poetic phase of human history, but which will rise to consciousness if Alberich regains control of his Ring. Wagner may have based his conception of Wotan as paralyzed into inaction by virtue of his too great consciousness of the existential dilemma which lies at the root of human existence, on Shakespeare's Hamlet: "… 'Hamlet.' R. … says that everything in this is … dawning madness, Hamlet the modern man, disintegrated and incapable of action, seeing the world for what it is." [1062W-{1/31/81} CD Vol. II, p. 612; See also 1100W] And not only Hamlet, but another of Shakespeare's tragic heroes, Othello, granted Wagner an insight into the paralyzing effect caused by too great consciousness of the egoism which is presumably at the root of all human behavior, even (counter-intuitively) at the root of self-sacrificial action which is presumed to be the antithesis of egoism: "… I remind him [Wagner] of the remark he once made to me—that O. [Othello] killed Desdemona because he knew she must one day be unfaithful to him. He continues by saying that natural tendencies hold sway over acts of enthusiasm [idealism], and once the image had arisen in his mind, even if put there by such a despicable rogue [Alberich, in lieu of Iago], life became impossible, everything was finished … ." [978W-{10/1/79} CD Vol. II, p. 373]

By confessing his horrific history of unwitting corruption and self-deception, and his true but loathsome identity, to his unconscious mind Brünnhilde, and thus distilling the essential elements of the *Ring* drama into redemptive musical motifs, Wotan can purge his mind of the guilt-ridden burden of conscious thought in order to restore the involuntary unconsciousness which he's lost, but which lives in Brünnhilde. By imparting his unbearable thoughts to feeling, and thus to forgetting, it's as if Alberich's Ring Curse of consciousness can be obviated, as if

Wotan can regain pristine, childlike innocence. Perhaps in this way Wotan can purge himself of his self-knowledge of paralyzing guilt in order to be reborn in the hero-redeemer for whom he longs, who must do what Wotan needs for him to do, but without conscious awareness that Wotan's fears and hopes motivate him. In this way Wotan's seed, his confession (god's "word"), can figuratively give birth, through insemination of the womb of his wishes Brünnhilde, to his ideal hero who's freed from Wotan's intolerable awareness of his egoism and fear, and from the residue left to us by our tainted religious heritage, who acts seemingly only on the prompting of spontaneous instinct, Siegfried. By making Brünnhilde the unconscious repository for his unspoken secret Wotan is planting the seed of his longing for redemption in the hero Siegfried's unconscious mind. For Wotan will leave Brünnhilde for Siegfried as his inheritance. Brünnhilde will be for Siegfried what she is for Wotan, a secret repository of dangerous knowledge, and his muse of unconscious inspiration. As Wagner put it: "… only a free Will, independent of the Gods themselves, and able to assume and expiate … the burden of all guilt [Wotan's sin against all that was, is, and will be, his denial of the truth], can loose the spell; and in Man the Gods perceive the faculty of such free-will. In Man they therefore seek to plant their own divinity [through his muse, his unconscious mind Brünnhilde, Siegfried will draw subliminal inspiration from Wotan's confession, his hoard of knowledge of the religious mysteries], to raise his strength so high that, … he may rid him of the Gods' protection, to do of his free will what his own mind inspires. So the Gods bring up Man [first Siegmund, and then Siegfried] for this high destiny, … and their aim would be attained even if in this human creation they should perforce annul themselves [the "going-under" of State and Religion] … ." [377W-{6–8/48} 'The Nibelungen Myth,' PW Vol. VII, pp. 302–303] [See also 440W, and 280F-LER, pp. 212–213; and 263F-LER, p. 183]

The creative genius Wagner once identified with the collective, historical Folk, i.e., with Feuerbach's definition of God (Wotan), will now be inherited by the individual revolutionary genius of art, Siegfried. Only the single secular artist, freed to breach religious faith, can preserve religion's essence which is the feeling of transcendence, the sublime, when religious thought, its dogmatic beliefs, trapped in contradictions which have become too conscious, can no longer be sustained in the face of the advancement of objective knowledge. Staking no indefensible claim to the power of truth (Ring), the artist-hero should be invulnerable to collective man's accumulation of a hoard of objective knowledge, since his province is feeling, not dispute about facts.

Now that Wotan has introduced his longing for an heir into his confession, we can better understand the *Ring*'s conceptual structure. While it's well known that Wagner based his four-part tetralogy on the plan for Greek tragedies, i.e., a trilogy and satyr-play (though in the *Ring* the order is reversed, *The Rhinegold*, the first of the *Ring* dramas, standing in for the satyr-play before rather than after the tragic trilogy), the fundamental structure of the *Ring* is a division into two halves. The first—embracing *The Rhinegold* and *The Valkyrie*—is Wotan's half, the history of God-the-Father and his involvement with man, as in the Christian

Old Testament. The second half, Siegfried's half, covering *Siegfried* and *Twilight of the Gods*, presents the history of the savior (god as mortal man) as in the Christian New Testament, but with a difference. The first half, Wotan's story, concerns the history of religious belief, while the second half, Siegfried's (and Hagen's) half, details the history of Wotan's (Dark-Alberich's and Light-Alberich's) heirs, Hagen and Siegfried. Dark-Alberich's son Hagen will be Wagner's metaphor for the scientific, secular world-view which brings its cynical critique to the demythologization of society, and the acquisition of earthly power. Wotan's grandson Siegfried will present as the secular artist who falls heir to religious man's longing for transcendent value, which will be expressed in the subjective feeling of art rather than through objective thought. In this scheme, God-the-Father, The Old Testament and its laws of fear and prohibition, stands toward Christ the Savior and his New Testament law of love, as Wotan, identified here with religious belief (the Valhallan gods), stands toward the secular artist Siegfried, to whom Wotan looks as savior. This explains, by the way, why Walther von Stolzing, the artist-hero and unconsciously inspired poet-composer in Wagner's only mature comedy *Mastersingers*, is equated with Christ the Savior throughout the entirety of that music-drama. In the following extract Wagner justifies his identification of Wotan with Christianity's God-the-Father, and of Siegfried with Jesus: "The abstract Highest God of the Germans, Wuotan, did not really need to yield place to the God of the Christians; rather could he be completely identified with him: merely the physical trappings with which the various stems had clothed him ... were to be stripped off; the universal attributes ascribed to him ... completely answered those allotted to the Christian's God. (...) In the German Folk survives the oldest lawful race of Kings in all the world: it issues from a son of God, called by his nearest kinsmen Siegfried, but Christ by the remaining nations of the earth ... ." [372W-{6–8/48} 'The Wibelungen'— Revised summer of 1849, PW Vol. VII, p. 287; p. 289]

Wotan now describes the hero-redeemer of his dreams as a friendly foe who, in breaching faith with the gods, will unwittingly serve their need for redemption from Alberich's Ring Curse. But Wotan despairs of ever finding such a hero because he'll always find only his own craven, egoistic, fearful self behind his longing for this hero, and therefore in the hero himself:

> [p. 152] **Wotan:** (H82:) He who, against the god, would fight for me, O how might I find that friendly foe? (...) How can I make that other man who's no longer me and who, of himself, achieves what I alone desire (:H82)?—(H82a orch: [based on H52]; [[**H83 orch:**]]) [Possible H54 influence] O godly distress ["göttliche Noth"]! O hideous shame (:H82a orch; :H83 orch)! [[**H83 harmony orch:**]] To my loathing ["Ekel"] I find only ever myself in all that I encompass (:H83 harmony orch)! (H82a:) That other self ... I never see; for the free man has to fashion himself (:H82a)—Serfs are all I can shape! (H83 harmony orch; H78)

The most difficult concept in our *Ring* allegory is probably the following: by virtue of repressing unbearable foreknowledge of religious faith's fated doom into his unconscious mind Brünnhilde, Wotan plants a seed in his wish-womb with this knowledge. It's this seed, Wotan's confession of his need for a hero freed from the gods' (religion's) corrupting influence, and his despair that this need can ever be met, which figuratively gives birth to his longed-for hero Siegfried. Through Brünnhilde's sympathetic absorption of his confession of his guilt and longing for redemption, Wotan is, effectively, reborn in Siegfried, in innocence, minus consciousness of his true origin and identity and guilt, which Brünnhilde knows for him. For the essence of Siegfried's heroic fearlessness will be that he doesn't know who he is, whereas Wotan's confession to Brünnhilde is the despairing cry of a man so much aware of who he is (an egoist no better than Alberich) that he loathes and can't bear to know himself. Wagner in Wotan has flatly contradicted that old Greek saw: "Know Thyself."

We find a basis for this transmutation of Wotan into Siegfried in both Feuerbach and Wagner. Feuerbach noted that: "Only when history is nothing, only when the naked individual ... who is stripped of all historical elements, of all destiny, determination, purpose, measure, and goal, only when the vain, abstract, meaningless, empty individual is something, and therefore only when nothing is something ... [could one posit immortality of the human soul]. Thus those peculiar beings ... who think that they live only after life do not reflect that they attain ... nothing ... with their afterlife, that as they posit a future life, they negate the actual life." [20F-TDI, p. 133] Wotan's futile desire to purge his imaginary, free hero of his origin in Wotan's fear of truth echoes Feuerbach's thesis. Wagner described how, through a similar process of purgation of all our links to our history (our debt), a purgation of all things which make us human—it's possible to posit a mythical, purely-human being freed from all implication in the world's corruption, a timeless, pristine, innocent man, such as Wotan hopes Siegfried will be. It's noteworthy that in our first extract Wagner echoes Feuerbach by describing Siegfried as the "real naked man," just as Feuerbach critiques the history-less immortal man—which religious belief has conjured from the imagination—as the "naked individual": "In the struggle to give the wishes of my heart artistic shape, ... I drove step by step into the deeper regions of antiquity, where at last to my delight, and truly in the utmost reaches of old time, I was to light upon the fair young form of Man ... . My studies ... bore me, through the legends of the Middle Ages, right down to their foundation in the old-Germanic Mythos ... . What here I saw, was no longer the Figure of conventional history [Wotan], whose garment claims our interest more than does the actual shape inside; but the real naked Man [Siegfried] ... . I had sought this human being in History too. ... the human being I could only see in so far as ... relations ordered him: and not as he had power to order them [Wotan, Lord of treaties, trapped by his treaties]. (...) ... Mythos led me to this Man ... as to the involuntary creator of those relations [Wotan], which ... , as the excrescences of History ... , as traditional fictions and established rights, have ...usurped dominion over Man and ground to dust his freedom." [574W-{6–8/51} 'A Communication To My Friends,' PW Vol. I, pp. 357–358] "With the conception of 'Siegfried,' I had pressed forward to where I saw ... the Human Being in the most natural and blithest fulness of his physical life. No historic garment more [Wotan's confession], confined his limbs ... . It was 'Elsa' who had taught me to unearth this man: to me, he was the male-embodied spirit of perennial and ... creative instinct (Unwillkür) [an unconsciously inspired artist-hero], of the doer of true Deeds ... ." [579W-{6–8/51} 'A Communication To My Friends,' PW Vol. I, p. 375; See also 498W]

Wagner seems to have found his model for the free, fearless, purely-human hero, miraculously disconnected from Wotan's historical time, context, collective guilt, and fate (Erda's knowledge), in Feuerbach's critique of immortality. But Wagner added the most striking point of all, that it was his heroine Elsa, from *Lohengrin*, who taught him to unearth his de-contextualized Siegfried, a man freed from all natural preconditions and debts. Presumably what Wagner meant was that it was Elsa's breach of Lohengrin's demand of unquestioning faith, her insistence that he share with her his prohibited knowledge of his true origin and identity so she could help protect him from the anguish (Noth) she believed he'd suffer if his secret was revealed, that somehow gave birth to Siegfried, the hero whose virtue is that he's fearless because he doesn't know who he is.

Our backstory for this mystery can be found in a comparison between the following extract from Feuerbach and Wagner's paraphrase of it. In our first, cryptic passage, Feuerbach implies that illusion (Maya, or Wahn) protected the world-creator Brahma from foreseeing the terrible nature of the world he was about to create so well, that instead of being paralyzed into inaction by depressing foreknowledge of his prospective creation, he joyously gave birth to the world: "Maya once drove away the melancholy of the ancient Brahma So that a depressed person was changed into a creator of the world." [38F-TDI, p. 250] We're reminded of the relationship between the sorrowful Wotan (who confesses his self-loathing and abhorrence of the world he's created, and inability to act in his own behalf to redeem himself, to his daughter Brünnhilde) and Siegfried, who, thanks to Brünnhilde's protection, will be unconscious of the knowledge which paralyzed Wotan into inaction, so Siegfried can spontaneously, fearlessly create redemptive secular art. To grasp Wagner's paraphrase of Feuerbach consider that "Prometheus" means foreknowledge in Greek: "... R. says to me, 'Prometheus's words "I took knowledge away from Man" ... gave me a profound insight; knowledge, seeing ahead is ... a divine attribute, and Man with this divine attribute is a piteous object, he is like Brahma before the Maya spread before him the veil of ignorance, of deception; the divine privilege is the saddest thing of all.'" [809W-{11/29/71} CD Vol. I, pp. 435–436] The implication for Wagner's reading of the Prometheus myth is that when Prometheus stole fire from the Olympian gods for mortal man's sake, he also bestowed foresight (divine knowledge) on mortal man. Foresight not only granted us conceptual power through which we surpassed all other animals, but through it we can contemplate the inevitability of our death, and perhaps assuage our fear of it through religion. This evidently is what Wagner meant when he said Prometheus, who granted mortal man forbidden, divine knowledge (like Eve), took knowledge away from man, thus protecting us from paying the price for conscious knowledge. In other words, he who delivered the wound of consciousness alone can heal it. The following striking passage from *Prometheus Bound* was likely a key influence on Wagner's reading of this myth recorded by Cosima:

> "**Prometheus**: Through me mankind ceased to foresee death.
> **Leader [of Chorus]**: What remedy could heal that sad disease?
> **Prometheus**: Blind hopes I made to dwell in them.
> **Leader**: O merciful boon for mortals.
> **Prometheus**: And more than all I gave them fire.
> **Leader**: And so in their brief life they are lords of flaming fire?
> **Prometheus**: Through it they will learn many arts.
> **Leader**: And was it for crimes like this Zeus —
> **Prometheus**: Tortures me, and ceases not nor relents."
>
> [*The Complete Greek Drama*, Volume One, translator Paul Elmer More, pp. 134–5]

The punishment Zeus metes out to Prometheus for granting mortal man these divine gifts is to be bound to the top of a mountain (Wotan's punishment of Brünnhilde in V.3.2–3) where a vulture perpetually eats his liver, inflicting a wound that will never heal, the very wound which seems to be the basis for the wounds (literal and figurative) which belabor so many of Wagner's protagonists. It's our inherent gift of foresight, man's hallmark, which is the initial cause of our un-healing wound. Prometheus, who delivered the gift and wound of foresight to mortals, is also the inspirer of that Wahn through which we no longer foresee our end, and can assuage our existential fear. It's no accident that Wotan echoes the last line from this passage in Cosima's Diaries, that he's the saddest of all the living, for Erda granted him foresight of the gods' fated end. In saying this, Wotan is merely saying that we humans are the saddest of all living creatures. Like Prometheus, just as Erda delivers the wound of fatal knowledge, her daughter Brünnhilde offers temporary healing by taking knowledge away from Wotan. So Brünnhilde, having taken Wotan's self-knowledge away, grants him rebirth as Siegfried, who is Wotan himself, minus conscious self-knowledge. This is why Brünnhilde in S.3.3 tells Siegfried that what he doesn't know she knows for him (Siegfried having previously told the dying Fafner "I still don't know who I am!"). The fact that the Fate Motif H87 sounds at the instant Brünnhilde tells Siegfried this clinches the matter. And this also explains why Wagner stated that Elsa taught him to unearth Siegfried. While Elsa only begged Lohengrin to share his forbidden self-knowledge with her, Brünnhilde, by hearing Wotan's confession of his unspoken secret, allows him to be reborn as Siegfried, minus consciousness of this secret which she keeps for Siegfried, protecting him from Wotan's divine Noth.

What is it Wotan finds so abhorrent in his own nature that he longs for a hero wholly purged of it, or better, longs to be reborn purified of it? Wagner provided a vivid description of our religious impulse to seek freedom from our bondage to our egoistic Will, an impulse which Wotan in his confession to Brünnhilde recognized is inherently insusceptible to satisfaction: "Whoever rightly weighs these aptitudes of the human race ... must come to the conclusion that the giant force which shaped the world [Erda's ur-law] ... had reached its goal in bringing forth this Man; for in him it became conscious of itself as Will [Erda wakes for both Alberich and Wotan when they possess the Ring], and, with that knowledge, could henceforth rule its destiny [they win the Ring's limitless power]. To feel that horror at himself [Wotan's self-loathing] so needful for his last redemption, this Man was qualified by ... that knowledge, ... the recognition of himself in every manifestation of the one great Will [Wotan finds egoism in all he does, just as Alberich tells his fellow Nibelungs in R.2 that his Ring power is everywhere, even where least expected]; and the guide to evolution of this faculty was given him by Suffering [Wotan (man) is the saddest of all living things], since he alone can feel it in the requisite degree." [1034W-{6–8/80} Religion and Art: PW Vol. VI, p. 244; See also 636W-{6/7/55}Letter to Franz Liszt, SLRW, pp. 345–346; and 635W]

For those who're convinced that Wagner depended exclusively on Schopenhauer's writings (with which—it's generally agreed—he first became familiar in the second half of 1854) to find the inspiration for a pessimistic outlook on human nature such as he gives voice to in our extract above (and in Wotan's confession), Feuerbach in 1830 distilled Schopenhauer's pessimism into a few brief sentences in a book well known to Wagner: "The birth of one being is another's death. The drive of self-preservation in nature is also a drive to destruction. ... how unfortunate existence and life are for a single being, which cannot exist without opposing and contradicting another being ... ... it therefore seems as if it might be ... a misfortune to live, to be a living, single being, an individual." [9F—TDI, p. 78] Feuerbach might have been familiar with the first volume of Schopenhauer's *The World as Will and Representation*, which Schopenhauer had published prior to 1830, when he wrote what appears to be a cryptic reference to Schopenhauer above. But Wagner was capable of conceiving Wotan's pessimistic outlook and Siegfried's death without help from either Feuerbach or Schopenhauer: in the very process of tracing the cause of Siegfried's death back to man's origin he asked the deepest questions about what it means to be human.

Wotan's self-loathing opens a portal into the inner motive of Wagner's idiosyncratic anti-Semitism. He, like Wotan, couldn't tolerate the idea that all men (especially in Wagner's case the Germans or semi-mythical Aryans) are ultimately motivated only by egoism (even in their striving to transcend it). This thought evidently became so intolerable that it seems Wagner, perhaps subliminally, tried to project this universal egoism on to the Jews to purge his ideal German (Aryan) of all taint. This is what Wotan tries to do by seeking a hero, Siegfried, whose heroism can't be traced back to Wotan's self-confessed egoism, who presumably will be freed from Wotan's debts to Alberich and his Ring, Erda, the Giants, and even Loge. But this self-purgation is impossible because what Wagner described as the Jews' inherent egoism is the basis for all feelings, thoughts, and actions of man per se. Wagner's anti-Semitism was a cover for man's religious longing to redeem himself from his inherent egoism. Wotan's longing to transcend his true nature in a hero freed from all that Wotan loathes in himself (Siegfried) is Wagner's metaphor for this universal yet futile religious ideal. Wagner linked what he described as the German's involuntary repugnance for Jewish nature with that loathing of egoism which is the fount of all traditional conceptions of morality, all notions of human nobility of character which are predicated on religious belief: "... with all our speaking and writing in favour of the Jews' emancipation, we always felt instinctively repelled by any actual ... contact with them. ... we have to explain to ourselves the involuntary repellence possessed for us by the nature and personality of the Jews, so as to vindicate that instinctive dislike ... ." [456W-{8/50} 'Judaism in Music,' PW Vol. III, pp. 80–81] We can see in the following extract how, through Wotan's confession to Brünnhilde, his figurative Jewishness or Nibelung-nature (i.e., the egoism he loathes in himself) goes under, so Wotan can be reborn as Siegfried minus consciousness of his true, craven identity and corrupt history. And note, Wagner invites the Jews to join the Germans in this alleged regeneration: "[Addressing the Jews, Wagner states:] To become Man at once with us, ... means firstly for the Jew [Wotan] ... ceasing to be Jew [Wotan reborn minus consciousness of his true identity, as Siegfried]. (...) ... take ... your part in this regenerative work of deliverance through self-annulment (*Selbstvernichtung*); then are we one and Un-dissevered! But ... only one thing can redeem you from the burden of your curse [Wagner alludes here unwittingly to the curse in man's irrevocable subjection to egoism, which ultimately makes a truly supernatural redemption impossible]: the redemption of Ahasuerus—Going under!" [461W-{8/50} 'Judaism in Music,' PW Vol. III, p. 100]

But it's Brünnhilde, not Wotan, who'll be the advocate for this new lease on life for man's religious longing for redemption in an artist-hero, a prospect she doesn't yet recognize in her loyalty to Wotan's original longing for redemption through the social revolutionary Siegmund. Brünnhilde, the exponent of Wotan's feeling rather than his thought, can't grasp Wotan's tragic insight into Siegmund's hidden motives (historical preconditions of, and religious influences on, the high value man ascribes to compassionate self-sacrifice), can't understand why Wotan would conclude that Siegmund can't be the free hero he's longed for, so she impulsively rushes to Siegmund's defense:

[pp. 152–3] Brünnhilde: But the Wälsung, Siegmund? (H23 voc vari?:; H61:) Does he not act of himself (:H23 voc vari?; :H61)?

Wotan: ... (H61) against the gods' advice, I boldly urged him on—against the gods' revenge, he's shielded now by that sword (H56 frag) ... which the grace of a god bestowed upon him. (H80 vari)—How slyly I sought to deceive myself! (H80 vari) How easily Fricka uncovered the fraud! (H24 voc:) To my deepest shame she saw straight through me (:H24 voc): now I must yield to her will!

Brünnhilde: (H81:) And so you'll not let Siegmund win (:H81)?

Wotan: (H17:) I once held Alberich's ring, greedily grasped the gold (:H17)! (H39:) The curse that I fled won't flee from me now (:H39): (H39 vari:) what I love I must relinquish, murder him whom I cherish (:H39 vari) (H35 voc:) and foully betray him who trusts me (:H35 voc)! (H50)

Wotan, tracing the motivation for Siegmund's heroic self-sacrifice and compassionate love back to Wotan's own ulterior influence in bringing him up, is forced to recognize Wotan's fear of the gods' fated doom (expressed here by H81, H39, H35 and H50, motifs which conveyed Wotan's explosion of despair that prompted Brünnhilde to beg him to confide in her the cause of his divine Noth) behind Siegmund's seemingly spontaneous actions. He confesses to Brünnhilde what Fricka forced him to concede, that Siegmund isn't free, but is the legatee of our religion-inspired moral heritage based on self-deceit and our inherent human egoism. H80 recalls that Fricka, Wotan's religious conscience, forced him to admit that only a god, a supernatural being, could be free, and that the mortal Siegmund is unfree. Yet Wotan has called himself, the alleged god, the un-freest of men. If he's the un-freest of men, any man who would do Wotan's bidding, including breaking the gods' law to win the ring back from Fafner, is even more unfree. H24, heard as Wotan admits he was deceiving himself and that his religious conscience, Fricka, has found him out, recalls Loge's influence on Wotan's unacknowledged intent to deceive himself and others, and its futility. As the embodiment of unexamined faith Fricka couldn't afford to admit that deceit might be necessary to preserve that faith, that the gods might in any way be threatened by the truth, but Wotan has confessed this terrible secret to his unconscious mind Brünnhilde. He's imparted to her subliminally that egoism trumps love in the real world, and therefore Wotan must betray his longed-for hero, love, and hope for redemption, to preserve a corrupt society whose stability is founded on fear and self-deception, which for these reasons is predestined to self-destruct. Wagner captured Wotan's profound feeling of impotence in his following melancholy reflection: " ... by the nature of things, ... superlative friendship can be nothing but an ideal; whereas Nature, that hoary old sinner and egoist, ... can do no else than deem herself the whole exclusive world in every individual, and merely acknowledge the other individual so far as it flatters this illusion of Self. (...) God, what a worth it must have, the thing for whose sake one holds on, with such a knowledge!" [661W-{10/3/58} Letter to Mathilde Wesendonck, RWLMW, pp. 52–53]

Wotan, having acknowledged that he's founded his life and most sublime ideals on self-deceit, in an access of self-loathing and bottomless depression expresses his desire to end his life and the ideal world he's created, including his hope of redemption:

[pp. 153–4] (H56ab: Wotan's demeanor passes from an expression of the most terrible anguish to one of desperation)

Wotan: Farewell, then, imperious pomp! Godly show's resplendent shame! Let all I raised now fall in ruins! My work I abandon; one thing alone do I want: (H56a: [i.e., Erda's octave drop on "endet!"]) The end! The end

(:H56a)! (H52: ...) And Alberich will see to that end! (H52)—Only now do I fathom the silent sense of the vala's mysterious words:—(H49:) "When love's dark foe begets a son in his fury, the end of the gods won't be long delayed (:H49)!" **[[H84 orch]]** [= H18ab vari/H9b vari] Of the Nibelung I lately heard it told that the dwarf had had his way with a woman, whose favours gold had gained him. (H51 harmonic hint?:; H49:) A woman harbours the seed of hate (:H51 harmonic hint?); The force of envy ["Neides"] stirs in her womb (:H49): (H35 loose vari:) this wonder befell the loveless dwarf (:H35 loose var); yet I who wooed in love cannot father one who is free!—(... **[[H84 orch:]]**) So take my blessing, Nibelung son! What I loathe most deeply I leave as your legacy (:H84 orch): godhood's empty glitter. May your envy ["Neid"] greedily gnaw it away!

Wotan is now resigned to the fact that Erda's prophecy of the gods' doom is true and unalterable, and that Alberich's son will bring it about. Wotan's prophetic vision of this inevitable doom of the gods, and that Alberich's son will be the heir to all Wotan hoped to achieve with his preferred heir, his free hero whom he now believes discredited, is captured by a new, compound motif H84, comprised of a variant of the first two segments of the Valhalla Motif H18ab, and the second segment of the Rhinegold Motif H9b. Erda (Mother Nature) has told Wotan that all his illusions about the world, including his assumption of godhead, are destined to destruction by those who affirm her objective knowledge, Alberich and his yet-to-be-born son (Hagen). Hagen we'll recognize later as Wagner's metaphor for the modern, secular, scientific spirit of skepsis, destined to overthrow religious faith and the transcendent ideals it entails. Science will replace the gods with Mother Nature (Erda known objectively), thereby punishing Wotan (man) for the religious sin of world-denial, matricide in its Feuerbachian sense.

Wotan's self-destructive craving for world-end, in despair at his inability to transcend his own nature and the world, because he's the victim of that religious self-deceit (Loge's false promises) which inspired his unnatural longing for what can't be fulfilled in real life, is the essence of what Nietzsche described as Nihilism. According to Nietzsche the ultimate consequence of Christian theology, which despises the real world in favor of an illusory one, once modern man confronts the fact that religion's claims and promises are an illusion, and that there's no alternative but the scientific world-view which provides no sanctuary for Christian ideals, is self-destruction and longing for world-annihilation. Those whose values, even subliminally, are founded on the old religious longing for an "other world" of redemption from this one, face the following irresolvable dilemma: on the one hand, thanks to man's advancement in knowledge, the consoling illusions of our transcendent value which once made life meaningful can no longer be sustained, while on the other hand, the only world left to us, the real world presented to us by science, is held to be intolerable: "This antagonism—not to esteem what we know, and not to be *allowed* any longer to esteem the lies we should like to tell ourselves—results in a process of dissolution." [Nietzsche: note from 6/10/87 collected in *The Will to Power*: p. 10] Nietzsche located this self-destructive nihilism squarely in Wagner's *Ring*: "Art and the preparation of nihilism: romanticism (the conclusion of Wagner's *Nibelungen*)." [Nietzsche: note from 1885–1886 collected in *The Will to Power*: p. 8] Feuerbach described this nihilistic longing for world-end as the "inmost essence of Christianity," the consequence of its renunciation of Nature's truth: "Faith does not limit itself by the idea of a world, a universe, a necessity. (...) Faith in the real annihilation of the world ... is therefore a phenomenon belonging to the inmost essence of Christianity ... ." [96F-EOC, p. 128] And here's Wagner's take on our religious impulse to seek world-end because the real world, what "is," won't support religious man's notion of what "ought" to be: "[Speaking of the existential dilemmas which beset modern man, Wagner described their source as:] The restless inner discord of this Man, who between 'will' [the ideal] and 'can' [the real] had created for himself a chaos of tormenting notions, driving him to war against himself, to self-laceration and bodiless abandonment to the Christian death ... ." [497W-{50–1/51} *Opera and Drama*, PW Vol. II, p. 169]

Wotan expresses this sentiment by seeking the end of all things because he can't reconcile his ideal with the real. Wotan's nihilistic self-loathing, and his bid to rid himself of his false, futile hopes and dreams rather than try any longer to perpetuate them in the face of the world's horrific nature, is summed up in Wagner's reflection on the possibility that human existence is meaningless: "At supper he again became absorbed in reflections as to whether the sum of existence ... might not in fact have an ethical purpose, as has indeed been finely surmised. 'Or are we really just here to eat grass? It's possible.'" [1110W-{12/12/81} CD Vol. II, p. 768]

The ironic soul of Wotan's catastrophic nihilist urge to self-destruction is his final conclusion that, while he, though loving, couldn't create a free hero of redemption, Alberich, though loveless, has evidently produced a free hero in his son (Hagen), who'll destroy any hope of redemption. Alberich's son Hagen will be free in a way that Wotan's Wälsung heroes aren't because Alberich, unlike Wotan and his progeny, isn't dependent on self-deception, but accepts the real world as he finds it, and acquires power through means the world presents to him. He'll be free in a limited sense, free from illusion. Alberich has nothing to lose in admitting the truth about the world, so his consciousness is coherent, unified, single and not divided against itself, whereas Wotan, though living in the real world, and a product of it, is dissatisfied with the nature of things, so he's invented an "other world" of redemption from this one, Valhalla. This single-minded adherence to one, coherent truth, based on an honorable effort to grasp Nature objectively, will be a signal characteristic of the coming secular, scientific world order, which Hagen will exemplify. Wotan, on the contrary, representing the dying mytho-poetic world-view which depends on consoling illusions, is two-faced and hypocritical in comparison to Alberich, a fact Wotan has now admitted.

While Alberich and Hagen have no need to lie because they accept the one world we have, Wotan's hero Siegfried will be free only by default: he'll have no reason to consciously lie because his self-deception (his perpetuation of Wotan's sin against Mother Nature's truth) will be unconscious. He'll not be conscious of lying to himself any more than religious man is until an objective mind like

Alberich/Hagen points it out to him. Wotan's division against himself is the basis of his relationship with his daughter Brünnhilde: Wotan stands to Brünnhilde as his conscious stands to his unconscious, as thought does to feeling, as power does to love. By contrast, Alberich and Hagen affirm the world, which Wagner said (emulating Wotan's despair) belongs to Alberich: "... let us treat the world only with contempt ... : ... let no hopes be placed in it, that our hearts be not deluded! It is evil, evil, fundamentally evil ... . (...) It belongs to Alberich: no one else!! Away with it! (...) I hate all appearances with lethal fury: I'll have no truck with hope, since it is a form of self-lying." [627W-{10/7/54}Letter to Franz Liszt, SLRW, p. 319] In much the same way Christians say the physical, fallen creation belongs to Satan, though they only grant the physical world to Satan because they presuppose a more substantial spiritual world of redemption from this one. But what if there be no "other world"!

Because secular materialists like Alberich and Hagen adhere to the natural laws of this world, Wagner predicts the inevitable victory of their objective worldview over that of idealism, which follows from Feuerbach's estimation of the fate of Christianity in its conflict with science. This is the scientific basis for Erda's prophecy of the twilight of the gods at Alberich's hands. Wagner similarly accords the Jews eventual, inevitable rule over the world, just as Wotan acknowledges that Alberich's son Hagen will inherit the world, and destroy the gods, because according to Wagner the Jews, like Alberich, adhere to the laws of this world, the laws which alone have power, while religion and art, which express longing for our transcendent value, are powerless. [See 1068W-{1–2/81} 'Know Thyself'— 2nd Supplement to 'Religion and Art,' PW Vol. VI, pp. 271–272; See also 1107W-{11/22/81} Letter to King Ludwig II of Bavaria, SLRW, p. 918]

In his nihilistic desire to end the world and all the ideals and beliefs he's striven for within it, Wotan was prompted by his conviction of the futility of fighting against Alberich, who has the truth on his side. However, there's still a way out, a temporary form of redemption, that Wotan has only dimly foreseen. If he accepts the end of the gods as an idea, as belief or faith, and no longer stakes religious faith's falsifiable claim on the power of truth (the Ring), religious feeling, man's longing for transcendent value, can live on in art, minus refutable claims to truth. The free, fearless hero Wotan seeks (to become) is the Feuerbachian hero of art, who, according to Feuerbach and Wagner, has the advantage of freedom of expression not bound to any practical claim, such as Christianity's false promise of immortality which assuages fear of death and satisfies our unnaturally excessive desire for eternal bliss. The secular artist enjoys this privilege because, unlike the religiously faithful who claim their illusory beliefs are the truth, the artist stakes no claim to it (Siegfried, unlike Wotan, will not seek the Ring's power). For these reasons Feuerbach says that while religion's basis is existential fear, the artist is freed from it. We again find in Feuerbach the origin of Wotan's free, fearless hero Siegfried: " ... a God is an imaginary being, a product of fantasy; and because fantasy is the essential form or organ of poetry, it may also be said that religion is poetry, that a God is a poetic being. If religion is taken as poetry, may it not be inferred that to abolish religion ... is to do away with poetry and all art? (...) My adversaries throw up their hands in horror at the hideous desolation to which my doctrine would reduce human life .... (...) Far from annulling art, poetry, imagination, I deny religion only insofar as it is not poetry [not Wotan's ideal self, Siegfried], but common prose [Wotan's prosaic, practical self, which he loathes, represented by Siegfried's antithesis Mime]. (...) In a sense it is poetry, but with one important difference: poetry and art ... do not represent their creations as anything but what they are, ... products of art, whereas religion represents its imaginary beings as real beings." [261F-LER, pp. 180-181; See also 262F-LER, p. 183] " ... the religious imagination is not the free imagination of the artist, but has a practical egoistic purpose .... (...) This feeling of anxiety, of uncertainty, this fear of harm that always accompanies man, is the root of the religious imagination ... ." [269F-LER, p. 196] "The object of religion ... is not the thauma, the wonder [which we experience in inspired secular art], but the oneiar, the blessing, i.e., the god as an object not of astonishment, but of fear and hope; he is worshiped ... not because of those attributes that arouse astonishment and admiration, but because of those that establish and preserve human existence [Fafner, man's invulnerable instinct of self-preservation] ... ." [202F-LER, p. 47]

Wagner paraphrased Feuerbach's argument point by point, and it's remarkable that he did so in an essay written for King Ludwig II many years after Wagner proclaimed himself freed by Schopenhauer (in 1854) from adherence to Feuerbach's materialist philosophy: "... an irrecusable yearning to turn his ["... the great, the truly noble man ..."] back completely on this world must necessarily surge up within his breast were there not for him—as for the common man who lives away a life of constant care [i.e., fear]—... a periodical turning-aside from that world's earnestness [existential fear] which else is ever present to his thoughts. What for the common man is entertainment and amusement, must be forthcoming for him as well, but in the noble form befitting him; and that which renders possible ... this noble illusion, must ... be a work of that man-redeeming Wahn [self-deception] which spreads its wonders wherever the individual's normal mode of view can help itself no farther. But in this instance the Wahn must ... confess itself in advance for an illusion ... . The fancy-picture ... must never afford a loophole for re-summoning the earnestness of Life through any possible dispute about its actuality and provable foundation upon fact, as religious Dogma does ... . This office is fulfilled by Art; ... I therefore point my highly-loved young friend [King Ludwig II] to Art, as the kindly Life-saviour who does not really ... lead us out beyond this life [i.e., unlike religion, art doesn't promise man immortality or supernatural transcendence], but, within it, lifts us up above it and shows it as ... a game of play; a game that, take it ne'er so terrible and earnest an appearance [as in Wotan's confession to Brünnhilde of all that he abhors in himself and fears], yet ... is shown us as a mere Wahn-picture, ... which ... comforts us and wafts us from the common truth of our distress (Noth). ... in his most rapt beholding of this wondrous Wahn-play (Wahnspiel) there will return to him the ... dream-picture of the holiest revelation [inspired secular art is a new religion unencumbered by religious faith's fatal flaws], ... that same divine dream-picture which the disputes of sects and churches had made ever more incognisable to him ... . The nothingness of the world, here it is harmless, ... avowed as though in smiling ... ; for our willing purpose to deceive ourselves [which Wotan admitted to Brünnhilde in his confession] has led us ... to recognise the world's real state without a shadow of illusion [Wotan's confession of the intolerable truth]." [708W-{64–2/65} 'On State and Religion,' PW Vol. IV, pp. 33–34]

In the following extract Wagner offers a succinct version of his Feuerbachian meditation on the redemptive potentiality of secular art as heir to dying religious faith, but adds that religion has sought art's aid, a notion echoed in Wotan's longing for a free hero who can redeem the gods: "One might say that where Religion becomes artificial, it is reserved for Art to save the spirit of religion by recognising the figurative value of the mythic symbols which the former would have us believe in their literal sense, and revealing their deep and hidden truth through an ideal presentation. Whilst the priest stakes everything on the religious allegories being accepted as matters of fact, the artist has no concern at all with such a thing, since he freely and openly gives out his work as his own invention. (...) Feeling this, she [religion] has always sought the aid of Art ... ." [1019W-{6–8/80} 'Religion and Art,' PW Vol. VI, p. 213] For it was only after Wotan confessed to Brünnhilde (unconsciously) that he'd been deceiving himself and others, and abhorred his own motives, that the possibility of redemption through the free hero Siegfried was attained. As Wagner put it in a passage previously cited in part: " ... there are certain things human beings have been able to express only in symbols, and the church has committed the crime of consolidating these and forcing them on us as realities through persecution; it is permissible for art to use these symbols, but in a free spirit and not in the rigid forms imposed by the church; since art is a profound form of play, it frees these symbols of all the accretions the human craving for power [H17ab>H18ab] has attached to them." [1012W-{4/27/80}CD Vol. II, p. 470; See also 1048W]

And here Wagner further develops this notion of secular art, particularly music, as an alternative to the self-destructive nihilism inspired by religious man's despair at the failure of faith in the face of the modern world's scientific, secular skepticism: "... I had ... finally completed, the poem of my 'Ring des Nibelungen.' With this conception I had unconsciously admitted to myself the truth about things human. Here everything is tragic through and through, and the Will, that fain would shape a world according to its wish, at last can reach no greater satisfaction than the breaking of itself in dignified annulment. It was the time when I returned ... exclusively to my artistic plans, and ... acknowledging Life's earnestness with all my heart, withdrew to where alone can 'gladsomeness' abide." [694W-{64–2/65} 'On State and Religion,' PW Vol. IV, pp. 8–9]

Wotan the Wanderer's similarity to the Dutchman wasn't lost on Wagner: "I read 'The Nibelung Myth' and 'Siegfried's Tod' and talk to R. about them. Later he tells me that he originally designed this more in the mode of antiquity; then, during his secluded life in Zurich, he became interested in Wotan's downfall; in this work he was more a kind of Flying Dutchman." [957W-{1/23/79} CD Vol.

II, p 258] We find this concept of art as dying religious faith's savior first broached in cryptic form in Wagner's meditations on the meaning of his first important opera, *The Flying Dutchman*, whose hero, resembling the Wanderer Wotan, is cursed to roam the world's oceans without finding redemption, and therefore seeks world-end, though an alternative form of redemption is in store for him if he can find a sympathetic woman, on earth, who'll lovingly sacrifice herself for him, or at least be willing to do so. The curse of irredeemable world-wandering the Dutchman (or Wandering Jew) suffers from was, like Alberich's Ring Curse directed against Wotan, the consequence of the religious sin of world-denial: when the Dutchman was unable to round the Cape of Good Hope because of physical conditions which made it impossible, he swore he'd never stop trying until he rounded it. Satan (a cryptic synthesis of Alberich and Loge) took him at his word, cursing him to strive futilely to transcend the laws of Nature throughout world-history, and to forever lose hope in promises of redemption which seduce him (as Loge does Wotan) from time to time. Satan's curse is a model for Alberich's Ring Curse, and both are metaphors for man's un-healing wound, our inherent inability to accept the world as it is, which produces our futile longing for redemption from the real world in an "other world" which is the product of imagination. Like Wotan, the Dutchman, though forever seeking but unable to find earthly or heavenly redemption, reluctantly gathers a hoard of treasure from other ships (a metaphor for man's historical experience of the real world through his advancement in knowledge) during his endless voyage without rest, a hoard which is useless to him and pushes redemption ever further away from realization. We find in Wagner's notion of woman's (Senta's) love unto death as an alternative to the Dutchman's Nihilist longing for world-end (paralleled by Wotan's longing for world-end) Wagner's anticipation of his concept that art (the redemptive woman, Senta, the muse for art, particularly music) can offer our religious impulse a means of expression even in the face of the futility of seeking an actual religious redemption from the real world. [See 562W-{6–8/51} 'A Communication To My Friends,' PW Vol. I, pp. 307–308]

In other words, Wagner withdrew to the subjective consolation of innermost feeling, the refuge of his unconscious mind, in music, which knows nothing of our existential dilemma, the irresolvability of the conflict between truth and the illusion that we have transcendent value, and dramatized this in Wotan's confession to Brünnhilde.

In the following striking extract he offers us his cryptic blue-print for the *Ring*'s plot, which is that god (religious belief) is sacrificed to science (Wotan and the Valhallan gods sacrificed to Alberich's Ring Curse) in order to free Jesus (the artist-hero, Siegfried) to express religious feeling (the love Siegfried and Brünnhilde share), when religious belief, as thought, can no longer be sustained in the face of man's increase in knowledge: "Is it so utterly impossible to Theology, to take the great step that would grant to Science its irrefutable truths through surrender of Jehova, and to the Christian world its pure God revealed in Jesus the only?" [928W-{3–7/78} 'Public and Popularity,' PW Vol. VI, p. 79; See also 1023W] And in the following passage he affirms that Wotan's self-destruction gives birth, through his "Will" Brünnhilde, to the redeemer Siegfried: "Wodan rises to the tragic heights of willing his own destruction. (...) The final creative product of this supreme, self-destructive will is a fearless human being, one who never ceases to love: Siegfried." [615W-{1/25–26/54} Letter to August Röckel, SLRW, p. 307]

However, by seeking escape from the conflict between science (truth) and religion (error) in art, which stakes no claim to the truth (the Ring's power) and therefore seems free from refutation by science, Wotan doesn't secure redemption, but merely a new opportunity for the unconscious to hide from us, temporarily, the world's bitter truth, which will eventually rise to consciousness as man (Wotan) accumulates that hoard of knowledge which will expose secular art as covert religion. Wagner freely admitted that his art merely served to hide from him the earnest, horrific nature of the real world, in an elaborate complaint in which he confessed he could scarcely go on living after gaining insight into the terrible nature of the world, except that his artistic nature kept offering him a veil of Maya, of self-deception, which obscured this horror by creating an illusory substitute for it. [See 630W-{5/12/55}Letter to Jacob Sulzer, SLRW, pp. 338–339] So Wotan's suicidal despair has a potential outlet in secular art, which the artist-hero Siegfried's loving union with his muse Brünnhilde will create. But this desperate expedient will set both Wotan and Siegfried up for an even greater Fall, since even the redemptive art in which Wotan (man) can lose himself and forget his fear is predestined to betray its secrets. But having resigned himself unconsciously to his fate, which will come to fruition in the distant future, Wotan goes through the motions of ordering Brünnhilde to sustain Fricka's honor by fighting against Siegmund for Hunding's sake, because Wotan's conscious mind must still sustain man's sole source of transcendent value, the belief in the gods, for as long as this is possible. He therefore ostensibly disavows any interest in pursuing another path to redemption which he's confessed to his unconscious mind he believes to be futile, but which his unconscious "Will" Brünnhilde will now take to heart as her sole purpose in life:

> [p. 154] (H82 [agitated]) **Brünnhilde:** ... o tell me, what must your child do now? (H83 hint)
>
> **Wotan:** (embittered) Fight bravely for Fricka, (H67 voc:) for her, guard both wedlock and vows (:H67 voc)! ... What use would my own will be to me? I cannot will a free man—for Fricka's slaves now fight!

Just before Brünnhilde asks Wotan what she must now do, we hear H82 (the gods' need of redemption) in an agitated variant, which contradicts what Wotan is about to say in answer to her: deep down he wants her to do whatever is necessary to secure the gods' redemption. To clinch our argument, Wotan asks what use his "Will" (Brünnhilde) could be to him, since he can't will a free man. But that's the point. By virtue of Wotan having confessed his seemingly futile longing for a free hero of redemption to Brünnhilde (who described herself as Wotan's "Will") and thereby repressing it in his unconscious, she'll metaphysically give birth to his free hero Siegfried. As his muse, she'll allow Siegfried to draw unconscious and therefore safe artistic inspiration from Wotan's unspoken secret, his forbidden hoard of fearful knowledge, to perpetuate Loge's veil of illusion (Maya; Wahn) in a new form of religion, secular art. But Wotan seems to be contradicting himself. If, as he told Brünnhilde, he now wills the "end," why does he care whether Brünnhilde fights for Fricka, or for Siegmund, or nothing? It's because Wotan both wills the gods' doom, and doesn't. He consciously sustains the gods' rule (religious faith) by ostensibly supporting Fricka, yet unconsciously acknowledges to Brünnhilde that if he supports Fricka the gods' rule is predestined to end. He's not involved in a contradiction once one understands that though he wills the end of religious belief as an affirmation of fact, Brünnhilde has secretly offered him an alternative to religion's self-destruction, the hope man's religious impulse will live on in secular art.

Siegfried's and Brünnhilde's unconsciously inspired art will redeem man from the unbearable truth by taking possession of it aesthetically, transmuting the world's horrific history (Wotan's confession of the *Ring*'s plot) into redemptive art, transfiguring it through music's Wonder. Wotan's hoard of intolerable knowledge of himself and the world and his longing for redemption from it is the seed, the poetic intent, which he plants in his wish-womb Brünnhilde to give birth to Siegfried, the artist who'll void Wotan's existential fear through the creation of redemptive works of art inspired by his muse Brünnhilde. [See 418W-{9–12/49} 'The Artwork of the Future,' PW Vol. I, pp. 72–73; and 439W-{9–12/49} 'The Artwork of the Future,' PW Vol. I, p. 139] The distillate of Wotan's horrific history is sublimated by Brünnhilde's sympathy into redemptive musical motifs which erase our terror, allowing us to forget our fear, as Wagner suggested: "... seeing how fond people are of ascribing to Music, particularly of the passionate and stirring type, a simply pathologic character, it may surprise them to discover ... how delicate and purely ideal is her actual sphere, since the material terror of reality [Wotan's confession to Brünnhilde of thoughts so abhorrent he can't bear to be conscious of them] can find no place therein, albeit the soul of all things real in it alone finds pure expression." [800W-{3–6/71} 'The Destiny of Opera,' PW Vol. V, pp. 152–153]

Brünnhilde's compassion for Siegmund, product of Wotan's original grand idea to redeem the gods, has been woken by her sympathy for Wotan's Noth. She incarnates his inability to bear having to give up his ideal of a free hero by turning against Siegmund, though Wotan has clearly expressed in words this intent. However, reacting against Brünnhilde's sympathy for his highest ideal (against the division within him), he explodes in anger expressed by motifs H83 and H85. Both motifs, H85 introduced now, and H83 (occurring in embryo briefly when Wotan was overwhelmed by self-loathing—"Ekel"—during his confession), seem to express his anger at Brünnhilde's rebellion against his conscious will:

[pp. 154–6] **Brünnhilde:** In pity's name take back your word! You love Siegmund: out of love for you—I know—I'll shield the Wälsung.

Wotan: (H82a:) Siegmund you must kill and master the field for Hunding (:H82a)! (...)

Brünnhilde: (H82ab:) Him whom you always taught me to love, whose lofty valour is dear to your heart (:H82ab)—never will your two-faced words force me to turn against him.

Wotan: Ha, insolent child! (...) What are you if not the blindly elective tool of my will? (H19)—(H59 chromatic vari?:) In conferring with you, have I sunk so low that I'm scorned by creatures of my own making (:H59 chromatic vari?)? (...) Within my breast I harbour the rage that can plunge into dread and confusion a world which once smiled upon me in joy: woe unto him whom it strikes! (H19 frag) His defiance would bring him grief! (H59 chromatic vari?:) ... Siegmund shall fall!—Let this be the Valkyrie's task (:H59 chromatic vari?). (H82ab orch:; H83 orch:; **[[H85 orch:]]** [Possible H54 influence]; H35: He storms away ... .)

Brünnhilde: (H80: remaining where she is, shocked and stunned) (...) (H65; H63 vari on oboe; H65) (H63 vari on oboe: ...) Alas, my Wälsung (:H63 vari on oboe)! (H80) In deepest grief a faithful woman must faithlessly forsake you! (... H82ab develops)

Since H83 was introduced as Wotan complained to Brünnhilde in his confession that he found with loathing ("Ekel") always only himself in all he endeavored to do (in all his efforts to redeem the gods from Alberich's Ring Curse), Wotan's anger at Brünnhilde really expresses his anger at his own folly in having staked the meaning of his life on an illusion, an illusion to which she—who freely expresses feeling without having to confront ideas and their contradictions—now gives voice after Wotan has already acknowledged he'd been deceiving himself, and that his hope for redemption is futile. But as Wotan proclaims decisively that Siegmund shall fall we again hear H82 telling us of Wotan's need for a hero freed from the gods' laws who can redeem them. This immensely powerful scene ends with an extraordinarily poignant, drawn out variation of H63 (juxtaposed with H65, the Wälsungs' Noth, hallmark of their unwitting implication in Wotan's guilt), the main love motif, on oboe, as Brünnhilde contemplates the shocking necessity of betraying Siegmund, conveyed here by H80 (Wotan's Frustration).

Since Wotan has rejected his first Wälsung hero, the social revolutionary Siegmund, this is the place to examine a source of immense confusion in standard *Ring* exegesis. It's received wisdom in contemporary Wagner scholarship that Wagner intended Siegmund's son Siegfried to be the social revolutionary who'd redeem the gods, but that Wagner, influenced both by Schopenhauer's pessimism and by the failure of European social revolutions (in which Wagner participated) in the face of all-powerful conservative institutions, renounced his original Feuerbachian program of social revolution and turned inward away from outward revolution towards his own art for consolation, eventually losing interest in Siegfried as a social revolutionary, and focusing all interest instead on Wotan, and especially Brünnhilde, whom Wagner anointed the true redeemer. According to this thesis Wagner abandoned Siegfried, for whom he conceived the *Ring* in the first place. This tired and utterly false thesis is based on the incorrect assumption that Siegfried was Wagner's Feuerbachian social revolutionary, when in truth

Wagner's social revolutionary was Siegfried's father Siegmund. Wagner dramatized his loss of faith in social revolution as the path to redemption in Wotan's loss of faith in, and rejection of, his beloved son Siegmund. Wagner had concluded that the social revolutionaries with whom he'd collaborated in 1849 were ultimately driven by the same egoistic motives as their nemeses, political reactionaries and adherents of traditional authority. Who then is Siegfried? Wagner dramatized his renunciation of outward social revolution as a means to redemption, and turning inward to his own art as the sole means of redemption, in Wotan's confessing his sense of futility which led him to betray his hope for Siegmund, and desperate wish for a hero who'd be freed from Siegmund's vulnerabilities, to Brünnhilde. The unconsciously inspired artist-hero Siegfried is the product of Wotan's confession of god's word to his wish-womb Brünnhilde, who'll be Siegfried's metaphysical (not literal) mother. Siegfried is a purely allegorical being. This solves a plethora of problems in Wagner scholarship, and also establishes numerous allegorical links between Siegfried and Wagner's other heroes from at least Tannhäuser onward.

THE VALKYRIE ⁊ ACT TWO, SCENE THREE

(A MOUNTAIN PASS)
SIEGMUND AND SIEGLINDE

Siegmund and Sieglinde, pursued by Hunding and his minions, are accompanied as they escape by H37 and/or H39, the older versions of the basic Love Motif H63 which Cooke noted are introduced in the transition from R.2 to R.3, when Wotan and Loge descend to Nibelheim, where Alberich has won the first fruits of his quest for the power he can obtain only by renouncing love. H37 and H39, though love motifs, are saturated with Alberich's curse on love: in his world love is on the run and at risk, as it was when Freia's Love Motif H23 was introduced as she fled the Giants:

> [pp. 156–7] (H37 and/or H39?: [repeated obsessively] ... Brünnhilde gazes down into the gorge and sees Siegmund and Sieglinde ... . (...) Sieglinde is hurrying on ahead; Siegmund tries to restrain her.) [**Siegmund:** (...); **Sieglinde:** (...)]
>
> **Siegmund:** ... No further now! (He clasps her firmly to him.) (H37 &/or H39 frags?:) (...) From the transports of bliss you started up and rushed away in headlong haste: I could scarcely follow your breakneck flight: through forest and field, over crag and rock, speechless, silent, onward you sprang; no call would bring you to rest. (...) (H37:) End this speechless fear (:H37)! (H63:) ... (:H63): (H73:) ... (:H73) (H8 repeated in series)
>
> **Sieglinde:** (H23 ...) (...) Flee one who's defiled! Unhallowed her arm enfolds you; dishonoured, disgraced, this body is dead: flee from the corpse and let it go! May the wind waft her away who, honourless, gave herself up to the hero!—(H39) ... (H22 minor vari:; H23 minor vari with H39 hint:) what horror and dread at most horrible shame were bound to inspire with terror the whore who had ever obeyed a man who held her without any

feelings of love (:H22 minor vari; :H23 minor vari with H39 hint)! Forsake the accursed creature, (H63:) let her flee far away! Depraved am I and devoid of all worth! You purest of men, from you I must run (:H63) ... ! (H70)

Siegmund: (H70:) Whatever shame has done to you the villain's blood shall now blot out (:H70)! (... (H56))

Sieglinde, in hysterics, is harassed by contradictory emotions. On the one hand she's in a panic at the prospect of facing the consequences of having broken society's code, making her and her lover pariahs, destined for punishment, even death. On the other hand, an even stronger impulse is her personal conscience, which tells her that having succumbed to the humiliation of letting Hunding force her into sexual intimacy without love, she's become a whore and dishonors the heroic Siegmund (his heroism represented here by H70) by her presence. Siegmund tries futilely to console her by his promise to wreak vengeance on Hunding, the vengeance his sword Nothung (instrument for restoring man's lost innocence) will wreak on Fallen, corrupt society for dishonoring Sieglinde, the soul of sympathetic fellow-feeling.

But she's inconsolable. She vividly imagines Hunding, wakened, gathering his clan and hounds to pursue the illicit couple, and wreaking terrible vengeance on Siegmund. This frightful image is accompanied by a H59 (Storm) variant, based (like Siegmund's Motif H61) on Wotan's Spear H19. H59 was first heard at the beginning of V.1.1 when Siegmund was being pursued for precisely the same crime he and Sieglinde have now committed, breaking the official marriage bond. Sieglinde, wholly overcome with the magnitude of the crime they're committing against divinely established society, faints after envisioning Siegmund torn to shreds by the hounds (Hunding means "Hounding"), and prophetically foreseeing not only Siegmund's sword broken by the force of vengeance (as it will be by Wotan using his Spear), but even the death of the World-Ash tree. Sieglinde's hysterical fear of Hunding's revenge is accentuated by a new motif H86 which Dunning christened "Hunding's Pursuit." H86, Dunning showed, is a slower, heavier variant of Alberich's slippery Motif of Futile Wooing, H6, which in R.1 expressed Alberich's ineptitude in striving to coerce love from the Rhinedaughters. The World-Ash, we'll learn from Erda's daughters the Norns in T.P.A, died after Wotan broke off its most sacred branch to make his Spear of divine law (the law which according to Wagner stifles the free movement of life) and authority:

> **[pp. 158–9] Sieglinde:** ... Hark! The horns—do you hear their call? (...) Hunding has woken from heavy sleep; (H59 chromatic vari:) kinsmen and hounds he calls together; soundly harried, the pack is howling and baying wildly heavenwards at wedlock's broken vow (:H59 chromatic vari)! (...) **[[H86 orch:]]** [= H6 vari] His pack is approaching, mightily armed! No sword can resist the hounds' seething horde: cast it off, Siegmund! (...) (:H86 orch) **[[H86 inverted staccato orch:]]** (...) I can see you—terrible sight! Scenting flesh, the dogs bare their fangs .... Their firm-gripping teeth tear at your feet—you fall—the sword is shivered in shards: (H56ab) the ash-

tree topples—the trunk is riven (:H86 inverted orch)! (...) (She sinks senseless into Siegmund's arms.)

[**Siegmund:** (...)] (H23 or H39 alternating with H63 on bass clarinet: (...) ... Siegmund bends over Sieglinde with tender care and presses a long kiss upon her brow.)

THE VALKYRIE ⁂ ACT TWO, SCENE FOUR

(A MOUNTAIN PASS)
SIEGMUND, SIEGLINDE, AND BRÜNNHILDE

Brünnhilde, preparing to inform Siegmund of his fated doom, of Wotan's requirement that he must be martyred on earth to serve the gods in an afterlife in heavenly Valhalla, now appears before Siegmund, having just witnessed his despairing love for his sister Sieglinde. She sublimely approaches with dignity, reserve, and with respect for her appointed victim. The brief instrumental prelude to V.2.4 which expresses her quiet approach to Siegmund opens the scene known as Brünnhilde's annunciation of death to Siegmund. This "Todesverkündigung" introduces two new motifs, H87, the "Fate Motif," and H88, the "Annunciation of Death" or "Doom" motif. This awe-inspiring moment carries the conviction of a sacred revelation:

[**pp. 159–61**] (Prelude: [[**H87 orch:**]]; H87 orch:; [[**H88 orch:**]] [Rises out of last three notes of H52]: Leading her horse by the bridle, Brünnhilde emerges from the cave and advances slowly and solemnly to the front of the stage. She pauses and observes Siegmund from a distance. H87:; H87:; H88: Again she advances slowly. She stops, somewhat closer to him. (...)) (H18 harmonic invocation of Valhalla) [**Brünnhilde:** (...); **Siegmund:** (...)]

Brünnhilde: (H87:) The death-doomed alone are destined to look on me: he who beholds me goes hence from life's light (:H87). (H18b:) In battle alone I appear before heroes (:H18b): (H18c:) him who perceives me (:H18c) (H18d:) I've chosen as one of the slain (:H18d). (...)

Siegmund: (...) (H88 voc:) The hero who follows you—where will you lead him (:H88 voc)?

Brünnhilde: (H18b:) the Lord of the Slain has chosen you—to him do I lead you now (:H18b): (H18a:) you'll follow me to Valhalla (:H18a).

Siegmund: (H88:) In Valhalla's hall shall I find the Lord of the Slain alone (:H88)?

Brünnhilde: (H18a harmony?:) The noble host of fallen heroes welcomes you fondly with greeting most holy (:H18a harmony?). (H76)

Siegmund: (H88:) Might I find my own father, Wälse, in Valhalla (:H88)?

Brünnhilde: (H18ab:) The Wälsung will find his own father there (:H18ab).

Siegmund: (H88 voc:) Will a woman greet me gladly in Valhalla (:H88 voc)?

> **Brünnhilde:** (H22:; H76:) There wish-maidens hold sublime sway: Wotan's daughter will lovingly hand you your drink (:H22; :H76).
>
> **Siegmund:** Awesome you are, and Wotan's child I behold with holy wonder: but tell me one thing, immortal! (H88 voc:) Will the sister-bride go with her brother? Will Siegmund embrace Sieglinde there (:H88 voc)?
>
> **Brünnhilde:** Earthly air she must breathe awhile: Siegmund will not see Sieglinde there!
>
> **Siegmund:** (... H63; H39) Then greet for me Valhalla (H18b), greet for me Wotan (H18b), greet for me Wälse, and all the heroes (H18b)—greet, too, Wotan's (H22) gracious daughters: (... H87:) to them I follow you not (:H87). ([[**H89**]]; H87; [[**H89**]])

Fate (H87) is Nature's ur-law which Erda's daughters the Norns spin into their rope of fate recording Erda's knowledge, which represents the coherence of Nature, the natural course of events which includes human history. While Cooke didn't identify musical links between H87 and other motifs, he affirmed that H88 (Annunciation of Death) is in that family of heroic motifs stemming from the last three notes of H52 (Erda), which represents all that Wotan sets in motion to redeem the gods from the fated doom which Erda (who introduced H52) foresaw, including assembling dead heroes to protect Valhalla.

This is one of the most sublime and memorable scenes in the *Ring*, in which Siegmund's exalted moral nature, his instinctively compassionate, personal conscience, bravely confronts death and even renounces Wotan's promise of immortal bliss in Valhalla, to remain with his beloved Sieglinde as her helpmate on earth. Siegmund will live a life of weal and woe, for earthly love's sake, rather than seek eternal glory with the gods, bespeaking Wagner's Feuerbachian preoccupation with affirmation of our earthly and mortal but real life over the imaginary heavenly life. Siegmund's heroic resistance to the fate Brünnhilde has announced is embodied in the expressionistic new motif H89, which in variant forms will (in V.3.3) convey an almost unbearably sublime poignancy to Brünnhilde's immortal defense of her choice to defy Wotan by supporting the Wälsungs. Now Siegmund's Noth, the tragic mesh of circumstance in which Wotan's manipulation of events has trapped Siegmund and Sieglinde, gradually awakens Brünnhilde's active sympathy:

> **[pp. 161–2] Siegmund:** (H63 voc:) Where Sieglinde lives in delight and sorrow, there, too, shall Siegmund tarry (:H63 voc): (H87 voc:) your gaze has yet to make me blench: it will never force me from staying (:H87 voc)! (H87; H89)
>
> **Brünnhilde:** ... (H88 voc:) ... death, you fool, will force you (:H88 voc):— (H89) ... .
>
> **Siegmund:** (H89:) Where might the hero be found to whom I'd fall today (:H89)? (H89)
>
> **Brünnhilde:** (H87:) Hunding will slay you in single combat (:H87).

Siegmund: Threaten things stronger than Hunding's blows! (H87 vari >>:) If you're lurking here, lusting for slaughter, choose Hunding as your booty: I mean to slay him in battle (:H87 vari).

Brünnhilde: (... H87) For you, Wälsung, (H89; H87) ... (H89:) ... the lot was cast (:H89).

Siegmund: Do you know this sword? (H56ab:) He who sent it decreed I should win: with it I'll defy your threats (:H56ab)!

Brünnhilde: (... H56 hint:) He who sent it has now decreed your death: its virtue he takes from the sword (:H56 hint)!

Siegmund: (...) (H39 inversion:) Woe! Ah woe! O sweetest of wives! You saddest of all who are true (:H39 inversion)! (H23/H39:) Against you the world has taken up arms: and I, whom you trusted alone, and for whom you defied the world alone (:H23/H39), ... must I betray my brave sister in battle? Ha, shame upon him who sent me the sword if he now decrees not conquest but shame! (H39/H23 heavy brass) If I must fall, I'll not go to Valhalla—hell shall hold me fast! (H39 heavy brass: ...)

According to Wotan's Fricka-inspired dispensation, Siegmund was to have joined the other great martyrs of cultural history in death, thereby contributing to that grand tradition of heroic memory which sustains Valhalla and its ideals throughout history, the traditional pattern through which those reformers and revolutionaries who in life were regarded as threats by established society, became the pillars of that society as it gradually transformed into something new after their death, when their life's meaning became mythologized. But Siegmund, defying the fate assigned him by Wotan, says he'd seek Hell (i.e., Alberich's Nibelheim) rather than Wotan's Valhalla, if the price of embracing Valhalla's heavenly life is renunciation of his earthly love for his sister Sieglinde. Siegmund's defiance recalls Wotan's risky longing for a friendly foe who in challenging the gods will unwittingly save them from Alberich's Ring Curse.

Brünnhilde futilely tries to tempt Siegmund to renounce his love for his sister Sieglinde for the sake of privileged existence in Valhalla, whose denizens enjoy sorrow-less youth eternal thanks to Freia's golden apples. This, by the way, proves that Wagner regarded the immortality granted by Freia's golden apples as distinct from Freia's virtue as goddess of love, for Siegmund, in the name of authentic love, disparages the endless bliss the gods and martyred heroes enjoy in Valhalla by virtue of her golden apples, just as his father Wotan will in the end when (as described by Waltraute in T.1.3.B) he refuses to partake of Freia's golden apples any longer:

[pp. 162–3] **Brünnhilde:** (shaken) (H87 vari:) You're so little heedful of bliss everlasting (:H87 vari)? ... Is she all to you, this pitiful woman who, tired and sorrowful, lies there, faint, in your lap? (H89) Is there nothing else you hold dear?

Siegmund: (... H39 vari) (H88 vari: [a flowing, urgent vari]) Young and fair though you shimmer before me (:H88 vari): (H63 hint:) cold and hard my heart now knows you to be (:H63 hint)! (H22:; H39 vari:) (...) (:H22; :H39 vari)! (H88 vari:) ... if you must gloat at this grief of mine, (H63:) ... (:H88 vari; :H63); may my plight ["Noth"] regale your spiteful ["neidvolles"] heart:—(H90 frag hint?:) but of Valhalla's cold delights speak not, in truth, to me (:H90 frag hint?)! (H22; H23; H39)

Siegmund has renounced Freia as goddess of transcendent love, and immortality. He's expressed Feuerbach's conclusion that what we look for in heaven is only an imaginary, idealized projection of what can only be found imperfectly on earth during our mortal life, and that we hide this contradiction from our conscious mind by unconsciously smuggling the earthly into our conception of heaven to give it substance: "But into the idea of the personal God, the positive idea of whom is liberated, disembodied personality, released from the limiting force of Nature, to smuggle again this very Nature, is as perverse as if I were to mix Brunswick mum with the nectar of the gods, in order to give the ethereal beverage a solid foundation." [80F-EOC, p. 100] Siegmund seems to know instinctively what Feuerbach knew, that what heaven promises is illusory, and that all value is found in our physical life on earth: " ... all wishes of the heart, even the wish for a personal God and for heavenly felicity, are sensuous wishes;—the heart is essentially materialistic, it contents itself only with an object which is seen and felt." [155F-EOC: p. 295] Also, Siegmund's moral repugnance at the idea of renouncing earthly love for heaven's eternal bliss finds a basis in Feuerbach: "... your morality is the most immoral, the most pitiable, the most vain, and the most futile morality in the world if it derives from the belief in immortality ... ." [18F-TDI, p. 126] Wagner similarly took offense at the idea that great men of good will, like the saints, perform their good deeds solely in hope of winning eternal bliss in heaven: "... our conversation turns to the saints, and R. gets heated about the idea, so common nowadays, that they are virtuous in the hope ... of future profit." [1084W-{6/18/81} CD Vol. II, p. 678]

Wagner emulated Feuerbach, insisting that love isn't transcendent, coming to us from above, but that it comes from below, our concrete, physical existence: "... the redeemer without whom Power remains but violence ... is ... Love; yet not that revelation from above, imposed on us by precept and command, — and therefore never realised, — like the Christian's: but that Love which issues from the Power of true and undistorted human nature; ... that proclaims itself in pure delight of physical existence and, starting from marital love, strides forward through the love for children, friends and brothers, right on to love for Universal Man./This Love is thus the wellspring of all true Art .... ." [452W-{2/50} 'Art and Climate,' PW Vol. I, p. 263; See also [565W-{6–8/51} 'A Communication To My Friends,' PW Vol. I, pp. 334–335; 580W; and 22F-TDI, pp. 145–146]

Brünnhilde's growing sympathy for Siegmund's Noth now rises to its greatest pitch, inspiring her to break faith with Wotan to support the mortal Siegmund against the gods' will. Brünnhilde's change of heart in Siegmund's favor can be heard in the new motif H90, a change inspired by sheer compassion for Siegmund's brave defiance of the gods for love's sake, but perhaps more by her intuition that the greatest of heroes, Siegmund's as yet unborn and unnamed son Siegfried, will be born of Sieglinde. So Brünnhilde attempts to persuade Siegmund to leave Sieglinde in Brünnhilde's care, so Siegmund's as yet unborn son can be brought to birth. Her decision in Siegmund's favor preempts his threatened murder-suicide involving himself, his wife, and his unborn child:

> **[pp. 163-4] Brünnhilde:** (H88 voc:) I can see the need ["Noth"] that gnaws at your heart (:H88 voc); (H63:) I can feel the hero's holy sorrow (:H63). (H90A hint:) Siegmund, commend your wife to me: (H39:; H63 hint:; H88:) let my shelter shield her securely (:H39; :H63 hint; :H88; :H90A hint)!
>
> **Siegmund:** (H22:; H23 or H39:) ... if I'm fated to die, I shall kill her first as she lies here ... (:H22; :H23 or H39).
>
> **Brünnhilde:** (...) (H63:) ... commend me your wife (:H63) (H39:; H63:; H93c hint voc?:) for the sake of the pledge she received from you in her bliss (:H39; :H63; :H93c hint voc?).
>
> **Siegmund:** (drawing his sword) This sword—which a traitor gave to one who is true ... : if it cannot avail against that foe, then let it avail against a friend! (H56ab: He aims the sword at Sieglinde.) (H8 varis:) Two lives smile upon you here:—take them, Nothung, envious steel! Take them at a stroke (:H8 varis)!
>
> **Brünnhilde:** (in the most passionate and tempestuous show of sympathy H87:; H88 vari:; H8:; **[[H90A orch:]]**) Stay your hand, Wälsung (:H87)! (...) Sieglinde shall live and Siegmund with her! My mind is made up; I'll change the course of the battle: Siegmund, on you both blessing and victory I bestow (:H8; :H88; :H90A orch). (...) Fare you well, Siegmund, most blessed of heroes! I'll see you again on the battlefield.

Brünnhilde, like Antigone, is spontaneously moved to a self-sacrificial act of compassion against the power of the state and divine law, in order to save the as-yet-unborn Wälsung, the future artist-hero Siegfried, from destruction. As Wagner said: "In this State [Thebes under the Machiavellian King Creon] there was but one sorrowing heart, in which the feeling of Humanity had sought a shelter: — it was the heart of a sweet maiden, from whose soul there sprang ... the flower of Love. Antigone knew nothing of Politics: — she loved." [506W-{50–1/51} *Opera and Drama*, PW Vol. II, pp. 188–189] Siegfried will someday wake, woo and wed Brünnhilde, the muse whose compassionate intervention has paved the way for his birth, and their union will produce that art in which Wotan hopes to find the ideal soul of Valhalla redeemed. What has ultimately moved her to take decisive action in Siegmund's and Sieglinde's behalf was Wotan's confession of his need for a free hero, the seed which Wotan planted in his unconscious mind Brünnhilde. It's her womb which will figuratively (while Sieglinde will literally) give birth to Wotan's reincarnation as Siegfried, Wotan's hoped-for redeemer of religious feeling from objective consciousness in art.

THE VALKYRIE = ACT TWO, SCENE FIVE

(A MOUNTAIN PASS)
SIEGMUND, SIEGLINDE, BRÜNNHILDE, HUNDING, AND WOTAN

Siegmund notices that Sieglinde—having fainted—seems to be dreaming a happy dream, perhaps inspired by Brünnhilde's consoling presence, and runs off to fight Hunding. Sieglinde's happy dream now turns, ironically, into a vivid nightmarish remembrance of the terrible day her mother was murdered, and Sieglinde was abducted by the Neidings who gave her to Hunding, separating her from Siegmund and their father Wälse (Wotan). Her nightmare from the past culminates in her waking in the present to witness Siegmund being killed by Hunding, i.e, martyred by society:

> [pp. 164–6] **Siegmund:** ... slumber soothes my sweetheart's pain and sorrow:—(H63:) when the Valkyrie came to my side, did she bring her this blissful solace (:H63)? (H87) Should so fell a choice not affright a sorrowing woman? Lifeless she seems who is yet alive: a smiling dream now speaks to her in her sadness. (H72)—(H59 chromatic vari) (...)
>
> [Siegmund declares he'll pay Hunding what he deserves, draws Nothung, and disappears at the back of the stage into stormclouds flashing lightning, as we hear H56ab repeated (...)]
>
> **Sieglinde:** (H86:; H59 chromatic vari:; H60: beginning to stir more restlessly in her dreams: [[H91 orch]] [Independent musical theme for Faust, from the first—"Faust"—movement of Liszt's Faust Symphony on cellos]; H59 orch:) Would that our father were home! With the lad he yet lingers far away in the wildwood. (H66) Mother! Mother! (H86:) My spirit fails me:—the strangers seem neither friendly nor peaceful (:H86)!
>
> [Sieglinde describes how the fire the Neidings set burned her home after they killed her mother and abducted her, and calls out to Siegmund for help. Siegmund shouts for Hunding to stand where he can find him, while Sieglinde anxiously looks for them in clouds: (...)]
>
> **Hunding:** This way, you wicked wooer: let Fricka fell you here!
>
> **Siegmund:** (...) From your house's (H56ab) home-built trunk I fearlessly drew forth the sword; its edge you now shall taste! (H56)
>
> [**Sieglinde:** (...)] ((...) Brünnhilde appears in the blaze of light, hovering over Siegmund and protecting him with her shield: H66) [**Brünnhilde:** (...)] (Siegmund is on the point of dealing Hunding a fatal blow when a bright red glow breaks through the clouds on the right; in it can be seen Wotan, standing over Hunding and holding his spear diagonally at Siegmund: H76; H56ab)
>
> **Wotan:** Get back from the spear! In splinters the sword! (Still holding her shield, Brünnhilde recoils in terror before Wotan: H19. Siegmund's sword shatters on the outstretched spear. H56ab. Hunding plunges his spear into the defenceless Siegmund's breast. Siegmund falls to the ground dead: H70)

As Sieglinde's initially happy dream turns into a nightmare, we hear motifs H59 and H60, associated at the beginning of *The Valkyrie* with Siegmund's escape through the forest from Hunding and his men, themes which invoke Wotan's Spear and Donner's hammer, the gods' rule over a coercive society which flattens individuals who stand for compassion and creativity instead of power and stability. Also heard here is H86 (Hunding's Pursuit). It reminds us that Alberich's vengeful desire to rape the Rhinedaughters is an archetype for Hunding's inability to win Sieglinde except by coercion. During Sieglinde's nightmare Wagner introduces, curiously, the "Faust" Theme from the first ("Faust") movement of Franz Liszt's *Faust Symphony*, which I've designated H91 because Wagner rated his friend Liszt and his *Faust Symphony* so highly. H91 may be the most significant quotation from another composer's music among the *Ring*'s motifs. H91 conveys the portentousness of Sieglinde's nightmare, which links the tragic present with her troubled past. I don't believe it's heard again in the *Ring*.

Wotan, in one of the *Ring*'s most "Homeric" moments, intervenes as Brünnhilde strives to save Siegmund from Hunding's spear-thrust, breaking Siegmund's sword Nothung. Siegmund is speared by Hunding and dies. As in the *Iliad*, two rival divinities have stood behind their respective hero, except that in this case Wotan's innermost desire is that Brünnhilde intervene to save Siegmund, though Wotan's conscious mind must preserve Fricka's honor by helping Hunding. Wagner's inspiration for Wotan's virtual murder of his own son to sustain the gods' rule is Laius's attempt to cast his son Oedipus's life away because of a prophecy that Oedipus would one day murder his father Laius, as found in Sophocles' *Oedipus the King*: "Quiet and order, even at the cost of the most despicable outrage on human nature ..., — at the cost of a conscious, deliberate murder of a child [Oedipus] by its own father [Laius], ... — this Quiet and Order were ... more worth considering than the most natural of human sentiments, which bids a father sacrifice himself to his children, not them to him. What ... had this Society become, whose natural moral-sense had been its very basis? The diametrical opposite of ... its own foundation: the representative of immorality and hypocrisy. (...) The passion for use-and-wont, for unconditional quiet, betrayed it into stamping down the fount from which it might have ever kept itself in health and freshness; and this fount was the free, the self-determining Individual." [505W-{50-1/51} *Opera and Drama*, PW Vol. II, pp. 187–188] Not Siegmund, but his son (Wotan's grandson) Siegfried, will one day destroy Wotan's power by cutting his spear in two with Siegmund's (Wotan's) sword Nothung, which Siegfried has re-forged, the cycle of revenge complete. Siegmund's martyrdom by established society as punishment for his social revolution is the sacrifice required of all past revolutionaries to free society in order to allow an original artist-hero such as Siegfried to flourish.

Brünnhilde, appraising the situation, takes advantage of Wotan's paralysis in the face of the terrible shock to his soul of his involvement in his son's death, to both save Sieglinde and preserve the two halves of Siegmund's Sword Nothung for Sieglinde which Wotan's Spear cut in twain:

[pp. 166–7] Brünnhilde: [to Sieglinde] To horse, that I may save you!

(She lifts Sieglinde quickly on to her horse, ... and immediately disappears with her. H76. The clouds ... part in the middle, revealing Hunding in the act of drawing his spear from the fallen Siegmund's breast. H87. ... Wotan can be seen standing on a rock behind him, leaning on his spear and gazing in anguish at Siegmund's body. H61 hint?)

Wotan: (to Hunding) Be gone, slave! Kneel before Fricka: (H67 voc:) tell her that Wotan's spear has avenged what brought her disgrace (:H67)! (H19) Go! Go! (At a contemptuous wave of his hand, Hunding falls to the ground, dead.) (suddenly erupting in terrible anger: H80:; H76:; H83:; H85:) But Brünnhilde—woe betide the betrayer! The shameless child shall be fearfully punished once my horse overtakes her flight (:H80; :H82; :H83; :H85?)!

Wotan is stricken with despair and crippling self-reproach at the role he felt compelled to play in punishing Siegmund for breaking the gods' law, an act which, after all, he brought Siegmund up to perform. [See 700W-{64–2/65} 'On State and Religion,' PW Vol. IV, p. 22] The presence at the end of V.2 of the anger motifs H83 and H85, as well as H80 (Wotan's Frustration), convey Wotan's disturbing mix of emotions. Both H80 and H83 recall his recognition that he could never find a hero truly freed from all that Wotan loathes in himself. It's his self-loathing which is the root of his anger at Brünnhilde for supporting an ideal which Wotan has unconsciously begun to acknowledge is illusory and futile. But it's only through Brünnhilde's rebellion against Wotan's conscious will that the free hero he longs for can win the gods a temporary lease on life, through dying religious faith's sublimation into feeling in unconsciously inspired secular art.

THE VALKYRIE ≠ ACT THREE, SCENE ONE
(BRÜNNHILDE'S ROCKY PEAK)
THE VALKYRIES, BRÜNNHILDE, AND SIEGLINDE

V.3.1 begins with the prelude known as "The Ride of the Valkyries," the most famous part of the *Ring* in the popular imagination. Of all Wagner's music the general public, even those who resist classical music or opera, are always familiar with the music of this prelude, and the wedding music from *Lohengrin* Act Three. In its dramatic context this prelude is a highly picturesque musical representation of Brünnhilde's Valkyrie sisters gathering a horde of valiant warriors they've inspired to martyrdom in battle to bring them to Valhalla and enlist them, resurrected, for Wotan's final battle against Alberich's host of night. This prelude reintroduces, in definitive orchestral form, the older motifs H76 and H77, and now introduces a new one, H92, descriptive of Valkyries riding which is associated exclusively with the Valkyries' role as angels of death. Late in the prelude, as Brünnhilde approaches, H90B is introduced, the second version of the motif which conveys her change of heart in Siegmund's behalf, as she desperately begs her sisters to shield and help her in her greatest need ("höchster Noth") to protect Sieglinde and herself from Wotan's wrath:

[pp. 167-75] (**Prelude: [[H92 orch:]]** On the summit of a rocky mountain. (...) Isolated cloudbanks scud past the edge of the cliff, as though driven by a storm. Gerhilde, Ortlinde, Waltraute, and Schwertlinde have taken up their positions on the peak ... ; they are fully armed.) (H76>>; H92>>; [a vivid portrayal of Brünnhilde's eight Valkyrie-sisters gathering slain heroes for Valhalla, including numerous repetitions of H77: Several Valkyries exchange humorous banter about how their mares' fighting is inspired by their martyred heroes' rivalries. (...)]

Rossweise: If we're all assembled, delay no longer: (H18ab:) to Valhalla let's set out and bring the slain to Wotan (:H18ab). **[Helmwige:** (...); **Gerhilde:** (...); **Waltraute:** (...)]

Siegrune: (...) (H77:; H76:) At a furious pace Brünnhilde flies this way. (...) (**[[H90B orch]]**; H63) [Several Valkyries describe Brünnhilde's desperate flight towards them: (...)] She's bringing a woman. (...) (**[[H90B orch]]** All eight Valkyries return to the stage; with them comes Brünnhilde, supporting and leading Sieglinde.)

Brünnhilde: (breathlessly) Shield me and help me in direst need ["höchster Noth"]! [**The Eight Valkyries:** (...)] For the first time I flee and am being pursued! Father of battles is hunting me down!

The Eight Valkyries: ... Have you lost your senses? (...) (H82) [**Brünnhilde:** (...)]

Ortlinde: (H82:) A thunder-storm's blowing from the north! [**Waltraute:** (...); **The Other Six Valkyries:** (...)]

Brünnhilde: The Wild Huntsman, who hunts me down in his fury, ... draws near from the north (:H82). Shield me, sisters! Save this woman! [**Six Valkyries:** (...)] [Brünnhilde briefly recounts how she came to this pass: (...)] ... I fled away with the woman: to save her I hurried to you, that ... you might hide me away from his [Wotan's] punishing blow.

Six Valkyries: ... O foolish sister! (...) Has Brünnhilde willfully broken the battle-lord's holy behest? [Various Valkyries express their fear of Wotan's approach: (...)]

Brünnhilde: Woe betide the wretched woman if Wotan finds her here: he threatens the ruin of all the Wälsungs!—Which of you'll lend me the fleetest of steeds that will swiftly spirit the woman away? [One after another Brünnhilde's sisters refuse to help her (...)] Grimgerde! Gerhilde! Grant me your horses! Schwertleite! Siegrune! See, I'm afraid! Dear to you as I was, be true to me now and save this sorrowing woman.

Brünnhilde has arrived with Sieglinde desperately seeking her Valkyrie sisters' help to protect the Wälsung Sieglinde from Wotan's wrath, but Brünnhilde's sisters mechanically affirm their obedience to Wotan, castigating Brünnhilde as mad for having defied him. Many wonder why Wotan is in such a rage with Brünnhilde for doing what, in his heart of hearts, he wanted to do himself. The reason is that she's his unconscious mind: he's not angry with her for the sympathy she expressed for his unconscious desires, but rather, for openly, consciously standing up for what should remain unconscious, an unspoken secret which can be safely expressed now only in art, not through open competition with Alberich. Valentina Serova's reminiscence of Wagner's interpretation of Wotan's anger at her confirms that it expresses his anger at himself: "Someone made so bold as to ask why Wotan could rejoice in Siegfried's protest, yet punish his daughter so cruelly for her disobedience. Wagner glanced fiercely at the questioner. 'Because,' he replied, 'Brünnhilde herself is no more than Wotan's desire (his "Wunschkind"). When his desires begin to contradict his own will, ... the violence of his anger is directed not against Brünnhilde but against himself. Brünnhilde may be the outward manifestation but its essence lies in Wotan's inner discord.'" [752W-{7/8/69} Valentina Serova's reminiscence of a visit to Tribschen on 7/8/69, WR, p. 203]

At the moment when Brünnhilde, begging her sisters for aid in her time of need, introduces H90B, she says: "(H90B) Shield me and help me in direst need ("höchster Noth")." Her invocation of this trope is the third time in the *Ring* that this verbal motif has occurred since Alberich blessed his Ring Curse in "direst need" ("höchster Noth"). Siegmund's invocation of "höchster Noth" occurred in V.1.3 when he spoke of his father Wälse's (Wotan's) promise to give Siegmund a sword in Siegmund's moment of highest need. The allegorical logic behind Wagner's use of a verbal motif to link these three incidents, the latter two of which, involving Siegmund and Brünnhilde, seem to contradict the first involving Alberich, is likely identical to that which explains Siegmund's singing the motif previously associated with Alberich's renunciation of love for power (H16) when he embraced love and death for the sake of his twin-sister Sieglinde. Alberich's renunciation of love for power has engendered a desperate need for love that's been lost.

Sieglinde, suicidally depressed by her loss of Siegmund, appeals to Brünnhilde not to intervene in her behalf but to let her join Siegmund in death, until Brünnhilde puts the spark of life back in her by announcing (how would Brünnhilde know?) that Sieglinde is carrying Siegmund's as yet unborn child, whom Brünnhilde will name (how presumptuous!) Siegfried:

> [pp. 175–7] **Sieglinde:** Who bade you, maid, bear me hence from the fray? In the onslaught there I'd have been struck down by the selfsame spear to which Siegmund fell: I'd have met my end united with him! Far from Siegmund—Siegmund, from you! Let death enfold me lest I think of it! Ere I curse you, maid, for fleeing with me, (H95 hint or embryo orch?:) hear my holy entreaty and drive your sword into my heart (:H95 hint or embryo orch?)!
>
> **Brünnhilde:** O woman, live for the sake of love! Save the pledge you received from him: ... a Wälsung stirs in your womb! (...)
>
> **Sieglinde:** Save me, brave woman! Rescue my child! Shield me, you maidens, with mightiest shelter! (...) [**Waltraute:** (...); **Ortlinde:** (...)]

The Six Other Valkyries: Away with the woman, if danger besets her: let none of the Valkyries dare to protect her!

Sieglinde: (kneeling before Brünnhilde) Save me, o maiden! Rescue a mother!

Brünnhilde: (...) Flee then in haste—and flee alone! I'll stay here and face Wotan's vengeance: here I'll forestall the furious god, while you escape from his frenzy.

Sieglinde: (H82:) Whither then should I turn?

Brünnhilde: Which of you sisters (:H82) has roamed to the east?

Siegrune: (H17 chromatic vari on winds:) Away to the east a forest stretches: there Fafner has taken the Nibelung hoard (:H17 chromatic vari on winds).

Schwertleite: (H17:) The savage assumed the shape of a dragon and in a cave he guards Alberich's ring (:H17).

Grimgerde: (H47:) No place it is for a helpless woman.

Brünnhilde: And yet the forest will surely shield her from Wotan's wrath: the mighty god shuns it and shies from the spot (:H47).

Sieglinde, suicidal at first like Siegmund, has had an entire change of heart after Brünnhilde informs her, with what seems supernatural prescience, that the Wälsung seed, Siegmund's and Sieglinde's as yet unborn child, stirs in her womb. Brünnhilde knows what Siegfried's blood-mother Sieglinde doesn't know, for Brünnhilde is Siegfried's metaphysical mother, just as Brünnhilde's mother Erda (Nature) is man's metaphysical mother. Brünnhilde figuratively gives birth to Siegfried and is in this sense co-mother with Sieglinde, Siegfried's literal blood-mother.

After Brünnhilde promises that if Sieglinde will escape, she'll stay behind and confront Wotan, she suggests Sieglinde seek shelter "in the east" where Fafner, now transformed into a serpent (dragon) by virtue of the Tarnhelm, guards Alberich's Ring and Hoard. She suggests this because Wotan shuns Fafner's cave. But why? Because Fafner embodies religious man's fear of inquiry, his dependence on unquestioned faith, which makes consciously accumulating Alberich's hoard of objective knowledge of man and Nature a psychological impossibility. Fafner sitting on the inert hoard, without using it to increase power, embodies the stranglehold of religious faith—and of the age-old traditions created by man yet regarded as divinely instituted—on progress, which depends on freedom of thought and uncensored acquisition of objective knowledge. Fafner's lair is therefore taboo for Wotan and for all those under the sway of religious faith. Brünnhilde instructs Sieglinde to take refuge near Fafner's lair so she can—as reward for unprecedented suffering (Noth)—give birth to the greatest of heroes Siegfried, whom Brünnhilde names without asking Sieglinde's leave. She takes this liberty because they know intuitively that Siegfried and Brünnhilde will someday join in loving union. Siegfried is to be born near Fafner's lair because

Wotan never goes there: Siegfried, in other words, will be safe from Wotan's wrath against Brünnhilde and the Wälsungs (Wotan's self-deception) in the tabooed realm of Wotan's repressed hoard of self-knowledge:

> [pp. 177–8] **Brünnhilde:** Then hurry away and head for the east! In brave defiance bear all burdens—hunger and thirst, thorns and stones: laugh if need ["Noth"] or suffering plague you! Know this alone and ward it always: (**[[H93a voc:]]** [Rises out of last three notes of H52] the world's noblest hero, O woman (:H93a voc), **[[H93b voc:]]** you harbour within your sheltering womb (:H93b voc)! (**[[H93a orch; H93c orch]]** [= H58d vari?])—(H56ab: She takes the fragments of Siegmund's sword from beneath her coat of mail and hands them to Sieglinde.) For him keep safe the sword's stout fragments; from his father's field I haply took them: **[[H93ab voc:]]** let him who'll wield the newly forged sword receive his name from me (:H93ab)—may (H56a:) 'Siegfried' (:H56a) joy in victory! (H56ab)
>
> **Sieglinde:** (deeply stirred: **[[H94 voc:]]**) Sublimest wonder! Glorious maid (:H94 voc)! You true-hearted woman, I thank you for sacred solace! (H93a voc:) For him whom we loved I'll save what's most dear (:H93a voc): may my gratitude's guerdon smile upon you one day! Fare you well! Let Sieglinde's woe be your blessing! (She hurries away downstage left.)

Brünnhilde, naming him, introduces Siegfried—Sieglinde's and Siegmund's son to be—as the greatest of heroes. The fact that Brünnhilde conceives and gives Siegfried his name, without taking Sieglinde's wishes into account, suggests Brünnhilde has a claim on Siegfried which his natural mother Sieglinde doesn't. This Sieglinde feels and accepts without comment. In Siegfried Wotan's hope for redemption of the Valhallan gods from Alberich's Ring Curse will be realized, but not in the way Wotan at first imagined. H92abc (Siegfried as a fearless hero, introduced as Brünnhilde heralds him as the world's noblest hero, and names him), like H70, H76, H88, and H98, stems initially, according to Cooke, from the last 3 notes of H52, which means that Siegfried, like his father Siegmund (represented in this list by H70), like the Valkyries, is an agent to whom Wotan looks to redeem the allegedly immortal gods from Erda's fearful truth. Siegfried will be motivated subliminally by Wotan's fear to undertake Siegfried's adventures, except that for Siegfried this impulse won't be experienced as fear, but rather, as love's inspiration.

Brünnhilde, like her mother Erda a prophetess, foretells that Siegfried will re-forge his father Siegmund's sword Nothung, whose pieces she salvaged from the battlefield. Sieglinde, inspired by Brünnhilde's gift of prophecy, anticipates that Siegfried will smile on Brünnhilde someday. Sieglinde, Brünnhilde also foresees, will suffer the special misery (Noth) to which the Wälsung race are doomed by having to take on the burden of Alberich's Ring Curse to free the gods from it. She'll suffer this Noth to bring the greatest Wälsung hero to birth. Sieglinde suggests her woe may be Brünnhilde's blessing. This concept that the Wälsungs' Noth is the basis for Siegfried's and Brünnhilde's marital bliss will be echoed when the Woodbird (Wagner on several occasions said the Woodbird is the spirit of dead Sieglinde) in S.2.3 tells Siegfried the lovers' secret, that bliss is made from woe. This is a variant of Wagner's metaphor for redemption through unconscious artistic inspiration: through the artist's muse (Siegfried's lover Brünnhilde) the artist-hero, like Loge, draws advantage—i.e., inspiration—from the most terrible things, to transform them into the sublime. This is the "sublimest Wonder" of inspired art.

The new, transcendently beautiful motif Sieglinde introduces while singing her hymn of praise to Brünnhilde, in which she extols the "sublimest wonder" or miracle of Brünnhilde's intervention to save Sieglinde's child Siegfried, is H94. H94, the primary motif which will be heard in the finale of the *Ring* (T.3.3), is called the "Motif of Redemption by Love." Porges provided the following evidence for this reading, which probably corresponds with Wagner's own remarks at the time: "Into her ecstatic outcry: 'O hehrstes Wunder!' Sieglinde must put all the intensity of which she is capable, she must release a great flood of emotion, enraptured and enrapturing." [* Porges' Footnote: "It is well known that this supremely lovely melody, banishing the terror of death, is employed at the close of Götterdämmerung as the song of redemption that overcomes the power of fate."] [872W-{6–8/76} WRR, p. 69] Porges' interpretation presumably had Wagner's imprimatur, but Wagner never, so far as I know, described H94 as a redemption motif in writing. He said, rather: "I am glad that I kept back Sieglinde's theme of praise for Brünnhilde, to become as it were a hymn to heroes.'" [832W-{7/23/72}CD Vol. I, p. 515] Wagner also described H94 as "The Glorification of Brünnhilde." But we mustn't let our enthusiasm for the sublimity of the *Ring*'s finale, and the passionate hopes we invest in the *Ring*'s sympathetic heroes and heroines, delude us into canonizing H94 as a motif representing "Redemption by Love" for many reasons, not least of which is that both Siegfried and Brünnhilde will betray their love before we reach the drama's denouement. And there are many other reasons as well. We mustn't forget the historical context in which the heroes and heroines of the *Ring* live and lose their lives, and Wotan's opinion that all these heroic characters are mere products of his craven needs and fears.

Cooke assigned H94 to the motif family which includes H7, H21, and H160, a family which he described as representing woman's inspiration. H7 conveyed the Rhinedaughters' mocking pretense of love toward Alberich in R.1. H21 captures the domestic tranquility of life in Valhalla, in both its initial form as the gods' refuge from dread of truth, and in its subsequent incarnation anticipating the love Siegfried and Brünnhilde will share (H21 will be heard as Siegfried in S.3.3 surveys in wonder the scene at the summit of the mountain on which Wotan has left Brünnhilde asleep), in which Wotan's hope to preserve Valhalla's spirit from Alberich's threat is embodied. Wotan's resistance to Fricka's hope that Valhalla will content him, both when H21 is introduced early in R.2 (he protests that he must leave Valhalla to conquer the outside world and express his need for change), and later in R.4 when Fricka suggests they enter Valhalla together (he protests it's been won with evil wage), shows Fricka's inspiration to be ineffective, just as the Rhinedaughters' flattery of Alberich's romantic inclinations was false. But Cooke's identification of this motif family with woman's inspiration is true of its ultimate incarnation H160 (in T.P.B when Brünnhilde defines her love as inspiring Siegfried to undertake new adventures), since we'll recognize Brünnhilde's love as Wagner's metaphor for her unconscious inspiration of the artist-hero Siegfried! In this final instance, Brünnhilde, unlike Fricka, doesn't attempt to inspire Siegfried to stay at home, but instead inspires Siegfried with her love to send him into the world outside their enchanted realm of love (protected by Loge's, self-deception's, ring of fire). The grand result of this last adventure inspired by his muse Brünnhilde is that Siegfried will betray his love for her, and she'll betray him. There's therefore something suspect in conceiving H94 as the Motif of "Redemption by Love."

However, a grand motif which will be introduced in S.3.1 during Wotan the Wanderer's final confrontation with Erda, H143 (World-Inheritance, or Wotan's Second Bequest—Scruton), Wagner did describe as "the redemption theme," according to Porges. He said that Wagner felt it should sound, at first hearing, as if it's the declaration of "... the proclamation of a new religion." [878W-{6–8/76} WRR, p. 103] This new religion will be secular art (revolutionary Wagnerian music-drama), the redemptive art which Siegfried's muse Brünnhilde will inspire him to create and present to audiences in the outside world. Accordingly, H143 is introduced in S.3.1 as Wotan embraces his destruction (religious faith's decline) because he knows his heirs Siegfried and Brünnhilde (inspired secular art) will redeem the world from Alberich's Ring Curse.

THE VALKYRIE = ACT THREE, SCENE TWO
(BRÜNNHILDE'S ROCKY PEAK)
THE VALKYRIES, BRÜNNHILDE, AND WOTAN

Wotan arrives in a tempestuous rage over Brünnhilde's disobedience, preparing to administer severe punishment once he has her in hand:

> [pp. 179–80] (H83 orch:; H85 orch: Wotan emerges from the pinewood in an access of fury ... .) [**Wotan:** (...); **The Eight Valkyries:** (...)]

> **Wotan:** I know that you're hiding Brünnhilde from me. From her, the eternal outcast, turn aside, as she herself has cast aside her worth! (H80 frag) [**Rossweise:** (...)]

> **The Eight Valkyries:** (...) For our faint-hearted sister we beg ... that you curb your initial anger. [**Helmwige, Gerhilde:** (...)]

> **Wotan:** (...) (H80 free vari) Know then, you whimperers, what she did wrong, for whom you fainthearts shed a hot tear. No one, as she did, knew my innermost thinking; (H80 free vari) no one, as she did, watched at the well-spring of my will; (H80 free vari) she herself was my wish's life-giving womb: (H80 vari)—and now she has broken the holy bond by faithlessly flouting my will and openly spurning my sovereign command, turning against me the very weapon my will ["Wunsch," i.e. wish] alone had created for her! (H81 vari) Do you hear me, Brünnhilde? You on whom brinie,

helmet and weapon, bliss and favour, name and life I bestowed? (H95 frag hint:) Do you hear me make complaint (:H95 frag hint) and hide in fear from the plaintiff in the faint-hearted hope of avoiding chastisement?

In Wotan's description of the crime Brünnhilde committed against him he leaves little doubt that our assumption that Brünnhilde is his unconscious mind is correct. He says, for instance, that no one as she did knew his innermost thinking, no one else watched at the well-spring of his will: she was his wishes' life-giving womb. Since Wotan is collective, historical man, she's man's creative unconscious. The weapon his wish alone created for her, which he accuses her of turning against him, is his unconscious confession, which should have remained a hidden motive and not inspired any outward, conscious act in defiance of Wotan. We hear an H81 variant several times as Wotan storms up in anger, and then after Wotan's complaint that she flouted his will by "openly" breaking faith with his intent, i.e., by consciously, actively doing so. H81 (Wotan's Revolt) in V.2.2 heralded his repression of his unbearable hoard of knowledge into his unconscious mind Brünnhilde, in his confession. She can only help him by keeping his unspoken secret unconscious so it remains a feeling and doesn't consciously motivate action in the outer world. Brünnhilde is to accomplish subliminally, through inspiration of Siegfried's art, what Siegmund attempted to accomplish outwardly by staking morally conscientious claims on his unreflective society, as a social revolutionary. Morality demands one take action in the real world, but art—what Wagner called a profound form of play—accomplishes this symbolically.

As Wotan demands to know whether Brünnhilde will acknowledge his complaint's justification and own her need to accept punishment, and she accedes to this, we hear a new motif H95 which, though it's preceded by H80's initial grace-note twist, is a distinct motif (Dunning, however, incorporated it into the second half of his musical notation of H80, as if it's H80B) which expresses Wotan's intent to punish Brünnhilde for her disobedience. She now steps forward to take what's coming to her at Wotan's hands:

[pp. 180–82] Brünnhilde: Here I am, father, dictate my punishment! (**[[H95 orch]]** [low, heavy brass & strings])

Wotan: It is not for me to punish you: your punishment you yourself ordained. (Free varis and combinations of frags from H59:; H80; H95:; H82:; & H87 in orch:) **[[H96 voc:]]** Through my will alone you existed: but against me you have willed; ... wish-maid you were to me: (H19 or H80? orch) but against me you have wished; (H19 or H80? orch) ... (H19 or H80? orch) chooser of lots you were to me: but against me you have chosen lots; inciter of heroes you were to me: (H19:; H59: [as heard during Siegmund's desperate run through the storm in the prelude to V.1.1]) but against me you have incited heroes (:H96 voc). (H95 orch, in an extended, loose vari on heavy brass [ending with a segment of H19 and a hint of H87]) (H17 bass line on trombones: [in the form of an interval falling from diminished 5th, to an augmented 4th, the "diabolus musica"]) What you once were Wotan has said to you: what you are now say to yourself (:H17 bass line on trombones)! (...)

Brünnhilde: ... You're casting me out? (...)

Wotan: No more shall I send you forth from Valhalla, (H88 urgent vari: [as heard when Siegmund challenged the fate Brünnhilde said was chosen for him]) no more show you heroes to add to the slain (:H88 urgent vari); (H88 definitive:) no victors you'll guide again to my hall (:H88 definitive): ... (H88:) .... From the gods' own host you're now cut off (:H88), cast out from the kin of immortals; our bond is broken: (H19:) you're banished from my sight (:H19)!

Brünnhilde has ordained her own punishment by taking on herself the Wälsungs' Noth, i.e., by supporting the revolutionary individualism of the Wälsungs on whom Wotan depends to salvage Valhalla's soul from Alberich's threat to destroy it. Wotan's complaint that her defiance of the fate Wotan had condemned Siegmund to suffer has put her at odds with Wotan is merely rhetorical, since she's paved the way for the friendly foe whom Wotan confessed to her he desired. Because she—Wotan's unconscious mind—has chosen this path, she must be prepared to suffer the Wälsungs' tragic fate. But Wotan had confessed to her that the values Wotan and his Wälsungs are fighting for are predicated on self-deception, on fear of the truth. There will always be a risk that what he repressed in her will rise to consciousness, fulfilling Alberich's threat that someday he'd bring his hoard from the silent depths up to the light of day and overthrow the Valhallan gods. Wotan reminds us how he confessed to her his need for a free hero who'll create himself, when he says that though he's told her what she once was, she must now say what she is. Wotan is banishing her from Valhalla, but Wotan requires of his hero-redeemer that he be free from the gods' protection anyway. What appears as Wotan's intent to punish Brünnhilde is actually the precondition for the hero's freedom to do, spontaneously, what will ultimately serve the gods' need for redemption.

Wotan introduces in the vocal line of his multi-part indictment of her another new motif, H96, which Scruton christened "Wotan's Reproach," in which he condemns her for having undertaken all those tasks in Siegmund's favor which he'd formerly appointed her to accomplish but which Fricka persuaded him to rescind. He now spells out her punishment. He'll put her to sleep on the mountaintop, leaving her vulnerable so any man, even a loveless or unheroic one, can wake and win her as wife. Wotan's dread sentence, that a Valkyrie (his favorite daughter) must sacrifice her holy virginity to any mortal man who discovers her asleep, elicits a spirited defense of her from her erstwhile cowardly and disloyal sisters:

[pp. 182–3] **Brünnhilde:** Will you take away all that you ever gave me?

Wotan: He who subdues you will take it away! (H41 "Servitude" vari:—[as heard in S.3.2 when Wotan warns Siegfried away from Brünnhilde's rock, saying his ravens have scared Siegfried's Woodbird guide away]) (H99A embryo voc:) Here on the mountain I'll lay you under a spell (:H99A embryo voc); **[[H97 voc:]]** in shelterless sleep I'll shut you fast (:H97 voc); (H19 vari in triplets) the maiden shall fall to the man (H19) who stumbles upon her and wakes her.

The Eight Valkyries: (... **[[H98 voc/orch:]]** [= H88/H93] Stop, o father, stay the curse! Is the maiden to fade and grow wan with a man? Hear our entreaty! (...) (:H98 voc/orch)!

Wotan: (...) (H19) From your host shall your faithless sister be sundered (H19) ... ; (H19) (H87 drum rhythm—"Crisis":; H99A embryo voc with H97's harmony orch:) the maid's maidenly flower will fade; a husband will win her woman's favours (:H87 drum rhythm; :H99A embryo voc with H97's harmony orch); (H97 voc:) henceforth she'll obey the high-handed man (:H97 voc); (H19) she'll sit by the hearth and spin, (H19 vari in minor) the butt and plaything of all who despise her. (...) Does her fate affright you? (...) If anyone dares to tarry here with her, if any defies me and helps the sad child—that fool shall surely share her fate ... ! (H80 vari; H87) Now get you all gone! (...)

[The Valkyries scatter on horseback in storm and lightning accompanied by H76 and H92]

The Valkyries pride themselves on their divine virginity. Though they're the heroes' muses they presumably only inspire heroes worthy of resurrection in Valhalla through action at a distance, like divine inspiration, because it's clear (or is it?) they don't become the heroes' lovers. Valhalla's host of heroes are dedicated to preserving the gods' rule (religious faith). But Wotan's punishment of Brünnhilde, compelling her to accept marriage with any mortal man who wakes her, is Wagner's metaphor for the fact that secular art, unlike man's religious longing for transcendence from which it sprang, doesn't renounce the physical world and the body for the sake of immortality, but replaces belief in transcendence with the feeling of transcendence, produced through natural means. The artist's muse must join him in sexual union to inspire him, just as the secular artist embraces the earth (Erda) rather than renouncing her. Wagner captured the contradiction at the root of religious man's propensity to deny sexuality for the sake of an allegedly sexless life in heaven, in his critique of Christianity's emphasis on chastity as a means to renounce this world in order to make oneself worthy of entry into the spirit realm: "... we [Richard and Cosima] decide that the excesses to which the insistence on chastity led constituted a terrible feature; they were due to the impossibility of realizing something felt to lie deep within the human character, the desire to set oneself outside nature and yet to go on living." [948W-{11/3/78}CD Vol. II, p. 188] By sacrificing his once virgin Valkyrie daughter Brünnhilde to become the artist-hero's wife, and taking away her divinity so that as a mortal woman she can love Siegfried, Wotan imparts his divinity as feeling, not as dogmatic belief, to his artist-hero heir Siegfried.

But there's more. When Brünnhilde asks Wotan if he'll take away from her all he gave her, and he responds that the hero who wakes and wins her will take it, he's speaking not only of the "… brinie, helmet and weapon, bliss and favour, name and life …" he bestowed on her, but of his unspoken secret which she, his unconscious mind, guards, the hoard of forbidden knowledge he confessed to her. Siegfried, on waking her, won't only inherit religious faith's essence, its feeling of transcendent bliss, but also the hoard of fatal knowledge which the faithful have suppressed in order to believe in the gods. But as an inspired artist he'll take aesthetic, not objective, possession of this hoard, thereby redeeming it from its terrors, and never using its power. By leaving the repository of his unspoken secret, Brünnhilde, vulnerable to be won by any man who finds her, Wotan leaves his hoard of forbidden knowledge vulnerable to exposure to the light of day. This is why only an artist-hero inspired subliminally both by Wotan's fear of the truth, and longing for redemption from it, can be allowed access to Brünnhilde. She, intuiting this, will persuade Wotan to protect her vulnerable sleep from all but a free and worthy artist-hero.

Two new motifs are introduced here. H97 conveys Wotan's intent to punish her for her disobedience by putting her to sleep, shelterless, on this mountaintop, to be won by any man who chances upon her. H98, which Dunning suggests is a combination of H88 (the Valkyries' inspiration of heroes to martyrdom) and H92, Siegfried's motif, expresses the Valkyries' and Brünnhilde's horror at the thought that the once divinely virgin, chaste maid will become the object of a mortal man's desire. A third new motif H99A is introduced only in embryo as Wotan threatens to put her to sleep so she'll belong to any man who finds her. H99A is the basis for one of the most exalted motifs of the *Ring*, first heard in more developed form (H99B) in V.3.3 when Brünnhilde strives to persuade Wotan either to relent and not leave her vulnerable, or, if that must be, to ensure that only a worthy hero wins her as wife.

Wotan closes this scene by warning Brünnhilde's eight Valkyrie sisters to avoid this crag and never to help her, lest they share her fate. I noted previously that Wotan's punishment of Brünnhilde is reminiscent of Zeus's punishment of Prometheus (foreknowledge) for stealing the Olympian Gods' divine gift of fire and privilege of foresight, and granting them to mortal man. Hermes (Zeus's messenger), like Wotan, warns that anyone who tries to intervene and help Prometheus will share his fate. But Prometheus possesses fateful foreknowledge—granted to him by his mother, the Titan Themis—of the Olympian Gods' predestined doom, and how to avert that doom. The Olympian gods' predestined doom is the fate engendered by the Titan Cronos's curse (time, Erda's knowledge of all that was, is, and will be, that all things that are, will end, and that a day of darkness dawns for the gods) he placed on the Olympian gods who overthrew the Titans, usurping their power. [*Prometheus Bound*—from 'The Complete Greek Drama,' pp. 152–156] This is a model for Alberich's cursing his Ring in vengeance against the Valhallan gods for usurping his rightful power, and for Erda's prophecy of the gods' fated doom. Prometheus is a model for Brünnhilde, who possesses knowledge inherited from her mother Erda (repressed into Brünnhilde by Wotan during his confession to her) of the gods' predestined end which Erda foretold and which Alberich's Ring Curse will bring to pass, and who also, again like Prometheus, knows how the gods can allay their fear of this doom.

Having broached the remarkable influence of the Greek tragedy *Prometheus Bound* (attributed to Aeschylus) on Wagner's *Ring*, it will be helpful before proceeding to *The Valkyrie*'s final scene to cite some other striking similarities between these two great artworks, which provide further evidence for our overarching thesis that the *Ring* can best be construed as one single, coherent narrative, of immense dramatic force and unity. It's clear that just as Wotan is to some extent modeled on Zeus, Fricka on Zeus's wife Hera, and Brünnhilde on both Prometheus and Athena (the latter referencing the influence of Aeschylus's *Oresteia*), Siegfried is partly modeled on Herakles. According to Prometheus, Herakles, Zeus's mortal son, will some day liberate Prometheus and overthrow those Olympian gods who brought Herakles into the world in the first place to serve them. Speaking of Zeus, Prometheus tells Zeus's lackey Hermes: "A mighty wrestler he is preparing against himself, an irresistible champion, ... who shall break in pieces that sea-scourge and shaker of the earth, the trident-spear of Poseidon. And Zeus, broken on this rock, shall learn how far apart it is to rule and be a slave." [*Prometheus Bound*—from 'The Complete Greek Drama,' p. 153] Prometheus' description of Herakles is echoed in Wotan's description of that hero who alone can free the gods from Alberich's Ring Curse, as Wotan's friendly foe, and Herakles breaking the god Poseidon's Trident to express his emancipation from the gods' rule, is undoubtedly a basis for Siegfried's breaking of Wotan's spear in S.3.2.

THE VALKYRIE ≠ ACT THREE, SCENE THREE
(BRÜNNHILDE'S ROCKY PEAK)
BRÜNNHILDE AND WOTAN

Brünnhilde now, in one of the most eloquent passages in the *Ring*, or for that matter in the entire history of the theater (drama or opera), appeals to Wotan to relent: this passage—and that which immediately follows, during which her plea conquers Wotan's resistance—is of such surpassing sublimity that it's almost unbearable when performed with conviction. It's blinding.

[pp. 183–4] **Brünnhilde:** (... [[H99A orch:]]; H80:; [[H99A orch:]]; H80: ... [[H99A voc:]]) Was it so shameful what I did wrong that you punish that wrong in so shameful a way? (...) (H89 orch: [repeated 5 or 6 times in following passage]) Was what I did so lacking in honour my lapse must deprive me of honour (:H99A voc; :H89)? (H80 oboe: ...) (H80 vari >>:; [[H99A orch:]]; H87 hint?:) O tell me, father! ... curb your wrath and explain to me clearly what hidden guilt forces you now, in stubborn defiance, your dearest child to disown (:H80 vari; :H99A)! (H80; H87 hint?) [**Wotan:** (...); **Brünnhilde:** (...)]

Wotan: Did I order you (H87) to fight for the Wälsung?

Brünnhilde: (H19 vari orch) So you bade me act (H19 vari orch) as Lord of the Slain. (H19)

Wotan: But I took my instruction back again.

Brünnhilde: (… H78's rhythmic pick-up note and first chord in Orch:; H89 vari?:) When Fricka had turned your own mind against you: in conforming with her thinking, you became an enemy unto yourself (:H78 frag & first chord; :H89 vari?). (H80)

Wotan: (…) I believed you had understood me and punished your knowing defiance ["wissenden Trotz"] … !

Brünnhilde now, in one of the musico-dramatic highlights of Wagner's entire career, introduces the embryonic form (H99A) of one of the most poignant and meaningful motifs in the *Ring*, H99. Its' definitive form is H99B. Cooke demonstrated it's based on H80 and therefore indirectly on H19's (Spear's) embryonic form. She introduces it in the context of her argument that in breaking the letter of Wotan's law she was actually doing Wotan's truest bidding. Therefore, as Cooke pointed out, H19's lineaments are softened and rounded in a baroque manner, and octave leaps upward seem to challenge the formerly remorseless downward thrust of H19, to suggest the softening of Wotan's authoritarian stance in the face of her overwhelming conviction of love's power. We also hear H89, expressing Siegmund's defiance of the fate Wotan—under Fricka's influence—had chosen for him, as Brünnhilde's appeal proceeds. H89 in this context, mixed with so many other poignant motifs, acquires a new resonance surging with tragic meaning, for Siegmund's heroic example has imparted to Brünnhilde a new ideal, a mortal paragon of altruistic virtue whose willingness to forego eternal bliss in heaven for the sake of earthly love has made all her past life seem meaningless by comparison.

We hear H80 as Brünnhilde asks her father what hidden guilt forces him now to disown his child, and are reminded that Fricka convinced him that no mortal hero could be free from the gods' will, since she found only Wotan behind Siegmund's alleged virtues. H80 represents Wotan's recognition that he can ever find only his egoistic self, with loathing, in all that he does to transcend himself, and that all of his proxies, including Brünnhilde and the Wälsungs who're oblivious to this limitation, are equally subject to this law of gravity. Brünnhilde complains that when Wotan rescinded his original order to protect Siegmund, Wotan wasn't acting according to his true convictions, but under Fricka's coercion. But Brünnhilde doesn't grasp that Fricka's coercion is Wotan's own recognition that he's in contradiction with his beliefs in seeking redemption through mortal heroes who're by definition unfree. Wotan retorts that he believed Brünnhilde had understood him (i.e., how he wished to be redeemed) and punished her "knowing defiance." That is, she should have grasped from Wotan's confession that the real world now belongs to Alberich, that egoism is the basis for society and human history, so that his longing for restoration of lost innocence can now only be expressed subliminally in art, not in open challenge to the bitter truth, a fight Alberich will inevitably win. It's not that she defied Wotan that angered him, but rather, the fact that her defiance was "knowing," i.e., conscious. Wotan is seeking a hero whose defiance of Wotan's law will be subliminal, an expression solely of feeling, not open, public, conscious, active. He's seeking an artist-hero in whose art, a profound form of play, the terrible world can be redeemed aesthetically without actively asserting power in the real world.

Brünnhilde now attempts to impart to Wotan the depth of compassion Siegmund's stellar example sparked in her. This is the essence of her sympathetic nature, and it tears our heart out experiencing it in the theater when the performance rises to the level of its material, a rare event:

> [pp. 185–6] **Brünnhilde:** (H99A:) Not wise am I, but one thing I knew (:H99A)—(H80) ... that you loved the Wälsung: (... H88:) (...) (:H88). (H65? >>:; H80: [the version heard when Wotan realized Fricka's argument had trapped him in V.2.1]) Yet something else you had to see, the sight of which so sorely pained your heart (:H65?; :H80) you withheld your protection from Siegmund.
>
> **Wotan:** You knew it was so and yet you dared to protect him?
>
> **Brünnhilde:** (... **[[H100 on strings:]]** [= H80/H89]) Since, for you, I kept sight of that one thing alone on which, painfully torn by the other's constraint, you helplessly turned your back (:H100 on strings)! (**[[H100 vari on strings?:]]** [i.e., H100 in a different key, &/or H80 vari?: a downward syncopated vari of great nobility]) She who, in battle, guards Wotan's back, she saw only (H87) what you did not see:—(H87) Siegmund I had to see. (H88) (H88:) Heralding death ... (H88) **[[H100 orch:]]** ... (H87) I noted the hero's hallowed need ["heilige Noth"]; ... (:H100 orch)—the fearful pain of freest love, the mightiest scorn (H39 or H63?:) of the saddest of hearts (:H39 or H63?) ... (H87) ... (H87) and my eye beheld what ... caused my heart to tremble in holy awe. **[[H100 orch]]** ... **[[H100 orch]]** all I could think of was how to serve him: (... H97 voc:) victory or death to share with Siegmund (:H97 voc)—(H35 voc?:) this I now knew (H89 vari:) was the fate I must choose (:H35 voc?; :H89 vari)! (H80 vari) (... **[[H99B voc/orch:]]** [= H19 vari]) Inwardly true to the will which inspired this love in my heart and which bound me to the Wälsung (:H99B voc/orch)—**[[H99B orch]]** ... I flouted your command!

In one of the most terribly moving monologues of the entire *Ring* (or Wagner's entire output), Brünnhilde describes in detail the overwhelmingly sympathetic impression made on her by Siegmund's plight (Noth), the dire threats the world holds for his attempt to preserve the love he shares with Sieglinde. Siegmund's Noth has revealed to her the full tragic implications of his unwitting involvement in Wotan's plan for redeeming the gods, which employs man's noblest impulses in a revolutionary fight against the dead weight of the social establishment with its prejudices, traditions, and beliefs, which after all can be reformed or changed over time. But what Wotan repressed and she doesn't see is that she's devoted now to a futile fight against the prosaic truths inevitably revealed over time by science about human nature, which aren't subject to reform or redemption. She declares that her passionate change of mind to support Siegmund, and die for him if needs must, wasn't a matter of intellect ("Not wise am I"), but of the heart. Unlike Wotan, who's labored under his ever more conscious awareness of the irresolvable contradictions which beset his futile quest to preserve man's belief in the gods, Brünnhilde has acted solely on feeling, which is freed from conceptual contradiction. In Wotan's confession to her he's foreseen the inevitable end of all human self-deceptions where no one else sees them, so he can't find hope where she does, in mere feeling. This is that "something else" which, according to her, Wotan had to see, which so sorely pained his heart he renounced hope of redemption through Siegmund. If Siegmund, surely the most sympathetic—with the exception of Brünnhilde and Sieglinde—and genuinely loving and courageous of the *Ring*'s characters, is ultimately only natural law's puppet and merely a product of Wotan's idiosyncratic program of training for the role of social revolutionary, then what hope is there? Wotan is convinced that Alberich's threat to make all the living renounce love as he has is more substantial than all that Brünnhilde can convey to him of Siegmund's stand-alone heroism and compassion. He's convinced of this because he knows it's true of himself: Wotan (religious man) invented the ideal represented by Siegmund in the first place. Wotan's conviction is that Alberich's vulgar materialism and selfishness more closely reflect the truth, the world (Erda), than all of Wotan's fantasies of transcendent meaning.

Aside from H99AB, the most characteristic motival expression of Brünnhilde's moving defense of her rejection of Wotan's divine injunction is a new compound motif H100: it partakes both of Wotan's conviction, represented by H80, that Siegmund's heroism, love, and compassion are merely the product of Wotan's fear of the truth, self-deception, and loathsome egoism (since Wotan brought Siegmund up to be a free hero), and H89's expression of Siegmund's instinctive resistance to his fate, his spontaneous assertion of freedom of will in love's behalf. H100 expresses the irresolvable contradiction at the heart of Wotan's moral paralysis, his nihilistic resignation to Alberich's inevitable victory over man's transcendent ideals, confronted nonetheless by his love for his ideal, Siegmund, voiced by Brünnhilde.

Brünnhilde notes that in battle she guards Wotan's back. This references the fact that Wotan, fearful of Erda's knowledge of the truth, turns his back on it, trying to leave it behind him, as he did in his confession to Brünnhilde by storing Erda's fateful knowledge out of sight and mind, putting it behind him in the realm of forgetting. Brünnhilde sees what he can't see (but only as feeling), not only the abhorrent knowledge of his impotence which he repressed into her, but also the means through which his seemingly futile bid for redemption through a free hero might be salvaged, which he can't consciously acknowledge either. By acquiescing in her plea to share with her his unspoken secret of his divine Noth, his foreknowledge of the fated end Erda foretold, he's ensured his hoped-for hero Siegfried will be protected from foreknowledge and fear of the gods' doom. We'll learn only late in the *Ring* (T.2.5) that Brünnhilde's magic, unbeknownst to

Siegfried, protected him from wounds (inflicted by Alberich's Ring Curse of consciousness) only at the front (from Wotan's foreknowledge), since no fearless man ever turns his back on his foe.

Brünnhilde acknowledges that her overwhelming compassion for Siegmund's Noth compelled her to offer herself in his service and to suffer the Wälsungs' fate. It's in this sense that, as Wotan says, she's already chosen her punishment for disobedience. Singing the astoundingly beautiful definitive form of H99, H99B, she declares that in her apparent defiance of Wotan's outwardly expressed wishes she remained true to his innermost (authentic) self. Given Wotan's knowledge of the overall historical context in which the Wälsungs and Brünnhilde are fighting to preserve a hope of redemption, a hope he's already relinquished (unconsciously) in favor of the sheer pride of intellectual honesty toward the truth, Wotan observes bitterly that it's easy for her—who inhabits solely the world of feeling, which isn't troubled about conceptual contradictions which beset the conscious mind—to live for love, which Wotan not only presumes is lost forever, but which he believes never existed nor can exist. In so doing he, ironically, paraphrases the complaint Alberich once made to him in R.4, that thanks to Alberich's having already paid the price of Noth to possess the Ring's power, Wotan, if he and the other gods co-opt it, can draw advantage from Alberich's sacrifice without paying the price he did:

> [pp. 186–7] **Wotan:** So lightly you thought that heartfelt delight might be won, (H100:) when burning pain broke into my heart (:H100) and hideous need ["Noth"] aroused my wrath, so that, (H87 hint?:) out of my love for the world (:H87 hint?), I was forced to staunch the well-spring of love in this harrowed heart of mine? (H100:) When I turned on myself in consuming torment, ... furious longing's fervent desire inspired the terrible wish (H85:) to end my eternal grief (:H85) (H35 voc:) in the ruins of my own world (:H35 voc): (H50) ... (H63:) then blissful abandon solaced you sweetly; rapt emotion's heady delights you drank from love's cup with lips parted in laughter (:H63)—(H87:) while my drink was mixed with the griping gall of godly distress ["göttlicher Noth"] (:H87:)? ... (H19 vari [broken up]) Be guided now by your own light thoughts: from me you have cast yourself free. (H99B) Now I must shun you and nevermore share any whispered counsels with you; (H100) divided, we may not act in close concert; (H83 & H85 hint:) ... the god may no longer meet you (:H83 & H85 hint)! (H19 vari [broken up]; H80)

When Wotan says that, thanks to the exigencies of the Noth he was forced to acknowledge, he had to staunch the well-spring of love in his heart for the sake of his love for the world, this is an oblique way of saying two things: (1) that for the sake of social order he had to suppress individual freedom, personal conscience, and creativity, and (2) that his motives, like those underlying the social order he created, were based on self-interest and fear rather than love or any divine sentiments. Wagner stated on many occasions that the true fount of all good in society is the new things which independent individuals bring to it, a fresh source of vitality which established society generally tries to suppress. [See 505W—{50-

/51} *Opera and Drama*, PW Vol. II, pp. 187–188; See also 500W-{50–1/51} *Opera and Drama*, PW Vol. II, pp. 179–180; and 502W-{50–1/51} *Opera and Drama*, PW Vol. II, pp. 182–183]

    Wotan chastises Brünnhilde for the lightness of heart with which he assumes she's taken sides with his ideal of love in the face of facts which contradict it. Cooke felt that Wotan's critique of her was unfair because, in her compassionate desire to sacrifice all, even risk her life, for the sake of the Wälsungs and Wotan's ideal, she can hardly be described as enjoying the bliss of love while ignoring the world's anguish. [Cooke, pp. 350–351] However, Wotan is getting at something else. He's suggesting that even the compassionate, self-sacrificial love for which she now says she lives, the love which Siegmund and Sieglinde share, is itself self-delusion which ignores the egoistic basis underlying all human motivation, a bitter truth which Wotan's inability to defeat Alberich has forced him to own. Brünnhilde's and Siegmund's apparent selflessness is either an inevitable product of natural law, including animal instinct (magnified by the influence of human consciousness), which also inevitably produces all the supposed evil in the world, or, if the product of learning, of training (as in Wotan's bringing up Siegmund to be a social revolutionary), remains nonetheless a product of natural law and animal instinct, and therefore not only isn't transcendent, but is subject to being changed into its direct opposite under certain circumstances. But Wotan's growing sympathy for her appeal manifests his abhorrence of the only alternative left to him, to live in a world guided by Alberich's cynical, objective understanding. Wotan would rather die than live in such a world, but Brünnhilde's decision to stand up for an ideal that Wotan knows is a false one, but which can give his dreams a temporary lease on life, is the path Wotan will eventually take.

    Brünnhilde can only freely live for love because she's—as she tells Wotan—not wise, i.e., not objectively conscious, but only feels. This is the point Wotan is trying to drive home to her. Were she forced to confront the truth, as he's been, she couldn't live for love. The recurrence here of H87 reminds us that Wotan can't help fearing the fated end of the gods which Brünnhilde's mother Erda foretold. But he draws an unexpected advantage from his intent to punish Brünnhilde with exile from Valhalla: by casting her free from the gods, religious faith, and divine laws (and vulnerability to truth), he frees the newly mortal Brünnhilde to live for love of the Wälsung hero she's chosen, her future lover, the secular artist-hero Siegfried, and to suffer his fate as well.

    Since he declares he'll no longer share whispered counsel with her, i.e., no longer repress his intolerable knowledge into her through confession, he's saying that she'll now transfer her role as man's collective unconscious to Siegfried, the individual artist-hero, for whom she can perform her new role as his muse of unconscious artistic inspiration. As Wotan said, what he once gave to her, his hoard of forbidden knowledge, will now be taken away from her by her new lover (who'll draw inspiration from it). Wotan's seed, planted by him in the womb of his wishes Brünnhilde through his confession, can now figuratively give birth to Siegfried, the individual artist-hero in whom the artistic cunning (Loge) of the primal Folk (Wotan) will now live on. Wotan asked what "use" his "Will" could be to him, because he can only will the creation of heroes who're as unfree (lacking in objective power) as the contingent imagination which dreamed them into existence. Her (his will's) use to him is that she'll give birth to his hero Siegfried, who is Wotan himself, minus consciousness of his true identity, history, and purpose.

Brünnhilde now reminds Wotan that since she's his other half, his unconscious repository for his dangerous hoard of knowledge, the unspoken secret he expected her to keep, he'd be exposing himself to shame if he let just any passing man, rather than an authentically inspired hero, win her and fall heir to the forbidden knowledge which is the cause of Wotan's shame and fear:

> **[pp. 187–9] Brünnhilde:** ... Little use, I fear, was the foolish maid, who, stunned by your counsel, understood nothing, for my private counsel counseled but one thing—to love whatever you loved. (H99B:) ... if you must sunder what once was whole, and hold far off one half of yourself—O god, don't forget that it once belonged to you wholly (:H99B)! (H80:; H82 hint:) You cannot want to dishonour that part of you which is ageless nor suffer a shame that brings you disgrace (:H80; :H82 hint) ... ! **[Wotan:** (...)**]** If I must leave Valhalla, no more to work beside you, (H44a free vari orch:; H97 voc:) henceforth obeying a high-handed husband (:H44a free vari orch; :H97 voc)—don't give me as prey to some craven braggart: let him who wins me not be worthless. **[Wotan:** (...)**]** (H70: ...) You fathered a noble race; (H70) (H93b:) no coward can spring from its stock (:H93b). (H93a voc:) The holiest hero—I know—will arise from the race of the Wälsungs (:H93a voc)!
>
> **Wotan:** (H100?:) (...) Parted from you, I have parted from them: spite ["Neid"] was bound to destroy them (:H100?).
>
> **Brünnhilde:** (H100:) She who tore herself from you (:H100) has saved them: ... (H93a voc:) Sieglinde nurtures the holiest seed (:H93a voc); (H39:) in pain and grief such as no woman suffered she'll one day bring forth what she hides in her fear (:H39). **[Wotan:** (...)**]** (... H56ab:) She safeguards the sword you made for Siegmund (:H56ab) —
>
> **Wotan:** ... And which I struck in splinters!—(H87; H87) (...) Await your fate ... , I cannot choose it for you! (H87) —but now I must leave you and fare far from here ... . I may not know what she ["the Turncoat"] wants: the sentence alone I must see carried out.

When Brünnhilde tells Wotan she's one half of himself, his ageless part, to remind him that in subjecting her to a shameful punishment he'd be shaming himself, she's describing herself as his unconscious mind. As I noted in my discussion of a prior citation, Wagner spoke in precisely this sense of Elsa's relationship to her husband Lohengrin: "In 'Elsa' I saw ... my desired antithesis to Lohengrin, ... the other half of his being ... . Elsa is the unconscious, the undeliberate ..., into which Lohengrin's conscious, deliberate ... being yearns to be redeemed." [573W-{6–8/51} 'A Communication To My Friends,' PW Vol. I, p. 346] When Brünnhilde describes herself as Wotan's ageless part, she's referencing Wagner's notion that while political establishments change over time, and religions die, the great, immortal artworks live on forever, fresh and new: "… the wisest-constituted States fall through, ay, the sublimest Religions outlive themselves and yield to superstition or unbelief, whilst Art eternally shoots up, renewed and young, from out the ruins of existence." [729W-{9–12/67} 'German Art and German Policy,' PW Vol. IV, p. 80] I previously cited Wagner's praise of Feuerbach's idea that the only true immortality is that of heroic deeds (such as Siegmund's) and divine works of art (such as those which Brünnhilde will inspire the artist-hero Siegfried to create), and that what we've traditionally called "spirit" (i.e., Valhalla) is actually the product of our "aesthetic perceptions of the tangible world" (i.e., art). [387W-{?/49} ML, pp. 430–431]

Wagner's praise of Elsa for doing what's normally regarded as an irredeemable crime, breaching faith, and thus renouncing worship of God (or the gods) for the sake of love (feeling), tallies perfectly with his notion, borrowed from Feuerbach, that religious faith as a set of beliefs had to end in order to free the artist (who formerly served religion) from staking a claim on the truth which is indefensible, since the artist offers us the feeling of having transcended the world, without staking a factual claim that the world has actually been transcended. Only in this way could the secular artist emancipate himself from the contradictions which undermine religious faith, and only in this way can Brünnhilde redeem Wotan (religious faith) by freeing his chosen hero Siegfried from Wotan's overt influence. Both Elsa's breach of Lohengrin's demand for unquestioning faith, and Brünnhilde's breach of Wotan's demand that she keep his unspoken secret without acting on it in the objective world, are steps towards religious faith's only means of redemption in the face of science's advancement in knowledge, in unconsciously inspired art. Just as Lohengrin separates himself from Elsa forever, so she can offer her restored brother (and Lohengrin's heir) Godfrey inspiration by giving him Lohengrin's horn, sword, and ring (models for Siegfried's horn, sword, and ring, as John Deathridge noted in an essay published in a program not available to me), so Wotan severs all contact between himself—the divine world—and the newly mortal Brünnhilde, so she can freely offer her services as muse to the artist-hero Siegfried. Wagner expressed this need for art, especially music, to sever itself from the church, in the following passage: "Only her [music's] final severance from the decaying Church could enable the art of Tone to save the noblest heritage of the Christian idea in its purity … ." [1026W-{6–8/80} 'Religion and Art,' PW Vol. VI, pp. 223–224] However, in disavowing any further concern with his daughter Brünnhilde and his beloved Wälsung race she's championed, his only hope of redemption, Wotan has foretold what will become of Siegfried, for he tells Brünnhilde that spite ("Neid") was bound to destroy the Wälsungs. Alberich's son Hagen, who embodies "Neid," will destroy Siegfried.

Brünnhilde now asks Wotan to describe the punishment he's planned for her. When he confirms what he'd already threatened, that he'll seal her in soundest sleep so she'll remain vulnerable to any man who wishes to wake and win her (introducing one of the most memorable *Ring* motifs H101, "Brünnhilde's Magic Sleep") she's thrown into a panic. She begs that Wotan preserve their honor by ensuring that only a great hero (only an artist-hero capable of unconscious inspiration, and thus worthy to woo art's muse Brünnhilde), not an unworthy man, take her as wife. Siegfried, she suggests, greatest scion of Wotan's beloved Wälsung race, would be the perfect choice. Though Wotan disingenuously disavows all interest in her plans, his spirit is involved every step of the way:

> **[pp. 189–90] Wotan: [[H101 orch:]]** [= H29b vari with H17ab harmony] I'll seal you in soundest sleep (:H101 orch)—(H18c:) he who wakes the defenceless woman (:H18c) **[[H101 orch:]]** shall take her, awakened, as wife (:H101 orch).
>
> **Brünnhilde:** If fettering sleep is to bind me fast, as easy prey to the basest of cowards, **[[H102:]]** this one thing alone you must grant me that holy fear entreats of you (:H102). **[[H102 modulating:]]** Shield the sleeper with hideous terrors (:H102 modulating) (... H93a voc:) that only a fearlessly free-born hero shall find me here on the fell (:H93a voc)! **[Wotan:(...)]** (H19) ... pitiless god, don't give her up to the shamefullest of fates! (... H76:) At your behest let a fire flare up (:H76); (H33:) let its flames encircle the fell (:H33); (H32B:) ... its tooth consume the coward who dares to draw near to the fearsome rock in his rashness (:H32B). (H76 vari; H89 vari?; H76 vari; H89 vari?)
>
> **Wotan:** (overcome and deeply stirred ... H76) Fare well ["Leb' wohl"], you valiant, glorious child! (...) Fare well! Fare well! (... [H: An independent aria based partly on H102:]) If I must shun you ... ; if I must lose you whom I loved, ... : (H101/H34:) a bridal fire shall burn for you such as never blazed for a bride (:H101/H34)! (H33:) Fiery flames shall encircle the fell (:H33); (H101:) ... (:H101); (H76:) the coward shall flee from Brünnhilde's fell (:H76):—(H93a voc:) for one man alone shall woo the bride, one freer than I, the god (:H93a voc)!

The only means for Wotan to find a free, fearless hero who'll do, of himself, involuntarily yet spontaneously, what Wotan desires him to do, without becoming aware that it's Wotan's fear of the end which motivates him, had been for Brünnhilde to receive Wotan's confession and impart it, through unconscious inspiration, to his heir, the artist-hero Siegfried. In works of art which his muse Brünnhilde inspires Siegfried to create, Valhalla can live on again, figuratively reborn, as a New Valhalla (religion of art) freed from vulnerability to Alberich's Ring Curse of consciousness. This may explain what otherwise seems inexplicable, the fact that H18c, the third segment of the Valhalla Motif H18, is heard as Wotan tells Brünnhilde that he who wakes her will take her, awakened, as wife. Siegfried, on waking her, will fall heir to Valhalla's legacy, including Wotan's hoard of forbidden knowledge, the religious mysteries which he confessed to her. H18ab, the Valhalla Motif's first two segments, are derived from Alberich's Ring Motif H17ab, but segments H18cd aren't. Though Siegfried, by winning Brünnhilde, Wotan's collective unconscious, will also fall heir to Wotan's unpaid debt to Alberich (Wotan's sin against all that was, is, and will be), he'll redeem man from the danger inhering in it by taking possession of it aesthetically. H18c will also, alongside H58a in compound Motif H177, play an important role in Brünnhilde's summation of the drama and judgment of Wotan in the *Ring*'s finale in T.3.3, when she tells her father to "Rest! Rest!" from his endless, futile wanderings in quest of redemption.

   The motif which expresses Wotan's intent to put her to sleep is H101 (Brünnhilde Magic Sleep). According to Dunning H101 is based directly on H29b (Godhead Lost), introduced in R.2 when Fafner noted that the gods, deprived of Freia's golden apples of sorrow-less youth eternal, would wither away and die. Wotan will take away her divinity (godhead) just before putting her to sleep. Dunning noted that the Ring Motif H17's harmony rises upward in thirds simultaneously with H101's downward descent. Brünnhilde possesses foreknowledge of the gods' fated doom. By putting her to sleep he's putting his forbidden knowledge to sleep, so it may waken only for the authentic artist-hero gifted with that unconscious artistic inspiration through which he may draw subliminal inspiration from this knowledge without suffering the paralyzing effect it would have were it conscious. In this way Alberich's Ring Curse can be made dormant, tamed aesthetically, by virtue of its transmutation into that profound form of play Wagner calls inspired art.

   Since only an authentically unconsciously inspired artist-hero can safely access Alberich's and Wotan's hoard, Brünnhilde forcefully argues that Wotan must protect her defenseless sleep with a protective ring of fire (represented initially by Loge's motifs H33, H34, and H32B), Loge's gift of artistic self-deception, the veil of Maya which religion and art have constructed over millennia to hide the truth from humanity and replace it with a consoling illusion. The fear of penetrating it stems from intuition of the fearful truth hidden within it. Our reluctance to inquire deeply into the source of the felicitous magic of art and love stems from the same cause as religious man's fear of bringing his faith into question (Fafner). Wagner identified Brünnhilde with music. Accordingly, he said: " ... if I wish to demonstrate that music (as a woman) must necessarily be impregnated by a poet (as a man), then I must ensure that this glorious woman is not abandoned to the first passing libertine, but that she is made pregnant only by the man who yearns for womankind with true, irresistible love." [464W-{11/25/50}Letter to Franz Liszt, SLRW, pp. 220–221] Our fear of examining the basis of our religious faith and art's (music's) and love's magic will keep all humans except the inspired artist-hero from accessing the tabooed secret of religious revelation and artistic inspiration. But this hero, Siegfried, will be involuntarily impelled by the same inner doubt (transformed in his case into love's longing) which led Wotan to seek out Erda for knowledge both of what caused him fear, and of how he might end his fear, to seek out Siegfried's muse of inspiration and healing, Brünnhilde, Wotan's and Erda's daughter. That fear which repels others but lures Siegfried is expressed by the new motif H102 which Brünnhilde introduces in the context of her plea that Wotan protect her defenseless sleep with terrors from all but a fearless hero. H102 is, Cooke notes, a pentatonic melody of five notes in the same family as the other pentatonic motifs such as H4 (Woglinde's Lullaby from R.1), H137ab and H138ab (the Woodbird's songs introduced in S.2.2–3, H138ab being a variant of H4), and H184abc (the Rhinedaughters' final lament for their lost gold from T.3.1, a portion of which, according to Dunning, is a loose inversion of Woglinde's Lullaby H4). These pentatonic tunes are unified by the concept that in answer to the Fall music restores lost innocence. By inseminating the womb of music with the knowledge Wotan fears, he's repressed it and sublimated it into musical motifs. Pentatonic music is music's most primal form, what Wagner called "Mother-melody." In this way Wotan's unspoken secret is safely transmuted into primal motifs which keep his secret unspoken, speaking it aloud only in tone but not words.

Brünnhilde's plea finally breaks Wotan's resolve to punish her remorselessly without hope of redemption from a loveless marriage, when, inspired, she begs him to call on Loge to protect her sleep with his fire to ensure only a worthy hero win her. Overcome with love for his favorite daughter and overwhelmed with nostalgic remembrance of past days of joy shared with her, he now launches into another of the most poignant passages of the *Ring*, singing his final farewell to her in three iconic melodies achingly expressing all that he loses forever in losing her, the first of these an independent melody which Dunning says is a loose variant of H102. This first part of his song of farewell culminates in his proclamation that he'll acquiesce to her final wish by making a bridal fire to protect her sleep such as the world's never seen, and his declaration that one man alone will now woo the bride, one freer than Wotan the god. As they embrace, looking deep into each others' eyes, we hear the most sweeping, climactic variant of H99B, which expresses both her rebellion and longing for reconciliation with Wotan. What will make Wotan's hero Siegfried freer than the god Wotan is what makes Wagner's secular art freer than religious faith. As Wagner said in a passage previously cited, secular art, which openly proclaims itself illusory, a game of play, is free from religion's false claim to truth and its power. [See 1012W-{4/27/80} CD Vol. II, p. 470] The secular art, successor to dying religious faith, which his muse Brünnhilde will inspire Siegfried to create, will (at least ostensibly) be freed from the "accretions" which man's craving for power has attached to religious symbols, will in a sense free Valhalla from its origin in Alberich's forging of his Ring of consciousness. Religious faith, unlike art, is unfree, because its insistence that its mythic beings are real beings who can miraculously intervene in our behalf proves it to be motivated by egoism, a craving for the power that only truth, actuality, can bring. Siegfried's freedom will instead express Rhinedaughter-like playfulness and innocence.

In the second portion of Wotan's farewell to Brünnhilde he sings a more extensive aria of unforgettable beauty, in two distinct parts. The first, associated with his remembrance of her radiant eyes, is H103. It won't re-occur later, but is of such iconic status that it warrants designation as H103. The other new motif H104 (key theme of the second part of this aria), when sung by Wotan, invokes his last joyful glance into her eyes as he delivers "… valediction's final kiss" to his beloved daughter whose eyes' stars will shine on a happier man, kissing her godhead away. H104 will be reintroduced much later in T.1.2.A as a moving reminiscence of Wotan's last moments with her during her confrontation with her sister Waltraute. He ends his song of farewell by delivering his parting kiss and taking away her godhead as he puts her to sleep:

> **[pp. 190–1]** (Moved and inspired, Brünnhilde sinks down on Wotan's breast; he holds her in a long embrace. she ... gazes with solemn emotion into Wotan's eyes. H76 vari; H99B; H89 vari?; H102 [repeated numerous times])
>
> **Wotan:** (**[[H103 voc:]]**/H102 vari orch:) That radiant pair of eyes which I often caressed with a smile ...:—(H102) ... (:H103 voc): (H102) **[[H104 voc:]]** for one last time let them joy me today (H102) with this valediction's final kiss (:H104 voc)! (H102) On a happier man (H102) their stars shall shine: (H102) on the hapless immortal they must close in parting! (H87: He takes her head in both hands.) (H16 Definitive:) And so –the god turns away from you (:H16 Definitive): (H35:) so he kisses your godhead away (:H35). (H103 orch [etc.].:; H102 orch: ... . H101 orch: She sinks back ... as consciousness gently slips away. ... Slowly he turns away, before turning round again with a sorrowful expression. (H18c; H102; H87)

Cooke observed that H104, in which Wotan expresses his anguish knowing he's looking into her eyes for the last time, but must now relinquish her to the happier man on whom they'll shine someday, is in the same family as H20 (Fricka's hope to preserve Wotan's fidelity to her by offering him Valhalla's consolations), H74 (the bliss of Siegmund's and Sieglinde's love), and H113 (which when introduced in S.1.1 will embody Siegfried's longing for parental love—particularly his mother's). We hear H87 (Fate) as Wotan takes her head in his hands to give her his final kiss (she's his repository for knowledge of the gods' fate), and then H16 (Renunciation and Need of Love) in its original form, as he says he now turns away from her. As he tells her he's kissing her godhead away, we hear H35 (Loveless), that segment of H16 which conveys the unfathomable sorrow of the Fall, our loss of innocence. The Fall brought about by Alberich was the first Fall, which gave birth to religion as an antidote. The dying of religious faith is the second Fall, which calls forth its replacement by inspired secular art's "Wonder," which Wagner identifies with romantic love between the sexes. We hear H18c again as Wotan walks her to the mossy bank to leave her, asleep in her armor, for the fearless hero Siegfried to wake, reminding us that Valhalla is figuratively reborn and lives on in the inspired art which Siegfried and his muse will create, just as Wotan (godhead) is reborn, minus consciousness of his true identity and history, in Siegfried.

Wotan now calls up Loge—the archetypal artist-hero redeemer—to surround sleeping Brünnhilde (the secret repository of Wotan's religious mysteries) with his protective ring of fire to keep all men away except the greatest Wälsung hero Siegfried, introducing the last new motif generated by *The Valkyrie*, H105, the "Magic Fire Music":

> **[p. 191] Wotan:** Loge, listen! (H34 vari:) ... (:H34 vari), just as I bound you, (H19) I tame you today! (H33; H32B) Arise, you flickering flame, enfold the fell with fire! (During the following, he strikes the stone three

times with his spear.) Loge! Loge! Come hither! ([[**H105:**]] [= H33 vari] A stream of fire springs from the rock, gradually increasing in intensity until it becomes a brilliant fiery glow. (...) With his spear, he directs the sea of fire to encircle the edge of the rock ... . H102; H101) (H93a voc; H102 orch:) He who fears my spear-point shall never pass through the fire (:H93a voc)! (H93a orch: He stretches out his spear as though casting a spell. He ... gazes sorrowfully back at Brünnhilde, turns slowly to leave and looks back once again before disappearing through the flames. H104; H105; H93a; H102; H87; H34)

The Magic Fire Music H105 (variant of Loge's motif H33) is from the family which includes the two Tarnhelm Motifs H40A and H40B, possibly the Serpent (Dragon) Motif H47, and Hagen's Potion Motif H165. This thematically unified motif family expresses Wagnerian "Wonder," secular art's antidote to man's existential fear which previously religious faith's wonder alone provided. Wagner's artistic Wonder is his substitute for the Folk's collective dreaming which gave birth to the gods. Loge, the Folk's (Wotan's) artistic cunning, gave birth to this "Wonder," and Siegfried is heir to Loge's cunning.

By leaving Brünnhilde asleep on a mountaintop protected by Loge's veil of self-deception, Wotan has left as a legacy for Siegfried what Feuerbach described as religion's essence, its feeling, or music, when God (Wotan) as a concept has had to pass away in the face of the rise of secularism and scientific knowledge. This is the ever increasing hoard of knowledge which Wotan as Wanderer (Wagner's metaphor for historical man's collective experience of the earth—Erda) accumulates. Feuerbach expressed this in the following passages: "The last refuge of theology ... is feeling. God is renounced by the understanding; he has no longer the dignity of a ... reality which imposes itself on the understanding; hence he is transferred to feeling; in feeling his existence is thought to be secure. And doubtless this is the safest refuge ... . as certainly as I exist, so ... does my feeling exist; and as certainly as my feeling exists, so ... does my God exist." [145F-EOC, p. 283] " ...is there a God or not?—questions and doubts which vanish, ... are impossible, where feeling is defined as the essence of religion." [43F-EOC, pp. 10–11]. "This timid crowd [the religious community of faith] can no longer erect temples or cathedrals, So now the only temple left for God is a chamber of the heart." [26F-TDI, p. 192] "What would man be without feeling? It is the musical power in man. (...) Just as man has a musical faculty and feels an inward necessity to breathe out his feelings in song; so ... he in religious sighs and tears streams forth the nature of feeling as an objective, divine nature." [65F-EOC, p. 63; See also 41F]

And Wagner, as always, has paraphrased Feuerbach: "Men of science persuade us that Copernicus reduced the ancient Church-belief to ruins with his planetary system, since it robbed God Almighty of his heavenly seat. (...) Yet this approachless god of ours had begotten much within us, and when at last he [Wotan] had to vanish, he left us—in eternal memory of him—Music [Brünnhilde]." [999W-{12/25/79} 'Introduction to the Year 1880,' PW Vol. VI, p. 34] "[Speaking of science rejecting religious dogma in favor of reason, Wagner says:] But does this mean that Religion itself has ceased? –/No, no! It lives, but only at its primal source and sole true dwelling-place, within the deepest, holiest inner chamber of the Individual; there whither never yet has surged a conflict of the rationalist [Alberich] and supranaturalist [the alleged god Wotan] …. (…) Profoundest knowledge teaches us that only in the inner chamber of our heart, in nowise from the world presented to us without, can true assuagement come to us." [705W-{64–2/65} 'On State and Religion,' PW Vol. IV, pp. 28–30] Wagner also explained why Wotan has left music, Brünnhilde, within the protective ring of Loge's fire, the veil of Maya (Wahn) which is our artistic imagination's cunning, to be woken solely by the music-dramatist Siegfried, in whom Wotan has found rebirth. It's Siegfried who in his unconsciously inspired music-drama will confer on us our "last religion": "Our Music … is the living god within our bosom. Let us guard it therefore, and ward off all profaning hands. (…)/(…) … it wakes in us no little pain, to see the downfall of our musical affairs so utterly unheeded; for so our last religion melts away in jugglery. (…) [We] … put out thereby the last light [Brünnhilde] the German God [Wotan] had left in us to find our way back to him!" [1000W-{12/25/79} 'Introduction to the Year 1880,' PW Vol. VI, pp. 34–35]

Siegfried

SIEGFRIED ⸗ ACT ONE, SCENE ONE

(MIME'S FORGE)
MIME AND SIEGFRIED

Siegfried begins with a prelude of foreboding initiated by a new motif H106, a variant of Mime's Scheming Motif H42, which, according to Cooke, is basically Loge's H24 with H17's (the Ring Motif's) harmony. It's also related to H26 and H124. The curious thing about this motif family is that H26 and H124 convey the subterfuge, dishonesty, and self-deception at the root of Wotan's rule through his Spear of divine authority, rule sustained only by Loge's cunning. The prelude is composed also of H8, which expressed that anguish ("Wehe!") at being rejected by the Rhinedaughters which led Alberich to renounce love to forge his Ring of power; H38, Nibelung (Forging) Labor as symbol of the Fall; H43 (Power of the Ring); H45 (Nibelung Hoard), variations of the Ring Motif H17, and H56 (Sword), Wotan's Grand Plan for redemption. We find Mime forging a sword:

> [p. 195] (Prelude: ... a cave in the forest; inside it is a natural forge, with a large set of bellows. At the anvil in front of it sits Mime, busily hammering at a sword. [[H106 orch]] [= H42 vari]; H45; H38; H8a over H38; H45 over H8/H38; H45; H45/H38; H8b/H38; H43/H38; H17 varis; H56, H38 over H8b/H45/H8a)

After this gloomy prelude, which conveys Mime's brooding over how he'll win his brother Alberich's Hoard and Ring, and describes the spooky forest which lies near to Neidhöhle (Envy-Cave), where Fafner has—using the Tarnhelm—transformed himself into a serpent to guard Alberich's Hoard, Tarnhelm, and Ring, Mime complains he's been futilely laboring to produce a sword which his foster-son Siegfried could wield, but that Siegfried snaps them all in two. Mime tells us Nothung alone (which Mime either received, or stole, from Siegfried's dying mother Sieglinde) would do, though Mime's art (Kunst) is unable to re-forge its pieces into a new sword:

> [p. 195] **Mime:** (pausing) Punishing torment! Toil without purpose! (H38>>:) The finest sword that ever I forged would have held quite firm in giants' hands: but the rascally lad for whom I wrought it bends and snaps it in two as though I'd made some childish trinket (:H38)! (...) [[H106 orch]]; H56 frag) One sword there is which he'd never shatter: (H56) Nothung's fragments he'd not defy, (H38) could I but weld the mighty shards which no art ["Kunst"] of mine can piece together. (H56)

It's often said that Mime is one of Wagner's stereotypes for Jews. To my knowledge, on one occasion only did Wagner describe Mime as a Jew: "First act 'Siegfried.' Mime 'a Jewish dwarf,' R. says, but excellent ... ." [1082W-{5/3/81} CD Vol. II, p. 662] Wagner was speaking of a particular singer who sang the role, and we'd need to learn whether that singer was Jewish to speculate whether he was speaking of the character Mime per se, or merely of the ethnic origin of the particular singer who performed the role. Of course, Wagner may have been offering his own impression of a singer who wasn't Jewish. This is an important question, because Wagner, taking his cue from Feuerbach, regarded the Jews (whether descriptive of their culture alone, or of an allegedly inherited racial characteristic, is never quite clear from Wagner's writings) as being bound by utilitarian, egoistic, earthly motives which preclude all longing for the ideal, the realm of spirit, and which disavow altruistic values like compassionate, self-sacrificing love. Mime fits this description. It's also true that Wagner described the newly emancipated Jews of Germany as mere imitators, while, according to him, authentic German geniuses alone produced what was truly new and original. Mime's status as a mere imitator is verified by his name (the mime), and by the fact that Mime's only creative act, manufacture of the Tarnhelm, was done under Alberich's direction, according to Alberich's design. However, though Mime and Alberich are siblings, Alberich, unlike his brother, is capable of introducing the new, though only within the practical world, not the world of utmost importance to Wagner, the religio-artistic imagination. Assuming that Wagner inscribed his anti-Semitism in his depiction of certain *Ring* characters, perhaps he distributed what he regarded as distinctly Jewish traits over several characters, like Alberich, Mime, and Hagen. However, the key to grasping the *Ring* is that these are universal human traits, a fact of which Wagner was well aware, and any interpretation based on the assumption that the *Ring*'s meaning depends on ascribing Jewish stereotypes to its less sympathetic characters misses the essence of this all-embracing artwork. It's an indictment of human nature per se. Mime now explains how he'll exploit Siegfried to win Hoard and Ring from Fafner:

> [pp. 195–6] **Mime:** Fafner, the grim-hearted dragon, (H47) ... (H50 hint voc:) watches over the Nibelung hoard ... (:H50 hint voc). (H47; H106; H56 frag) To Siegfried's childlike strength (H47) Fafner would no doubt fall. (H47) (H17:) The Nibelung's ring he'd win for me (:H17). One sword alone befits the deed (H56) and only Nothung serves my grudge ["Neid"] ... : (H46 frag orch)—[[**H107 voc:**]] yet I cannot forge it, Nothung, the sword (:H107 voc)! (...) (H8/H38) The finest sword that ever I forged will never serve for that single deed! (H38:) I fumble and hammer away because the boy demands it ... !

Mime asserts that Nothung alone—which he can't re-forge—could serve Siegfried to kill Fafner, so Mime can exploit Siegfried's heroism to gain the Nibelung's Ring. The new motif H107, heard as Mime complains he can't forge Nothung, stands for his lack of the unconscious inspiration necessary to produce the truly new in man's age-old quest for transcendent value and redemption from prosaic existence. His forge-work is motivated solely by conscious, practical need and profit. For this reason Mime is unable to re-forge that sword which is the soul of the Wälsung heroes' predestined attempt to restore lost innocence. Dunning suggests H107 is influenced by H35, the Loveless Motif. H107 is virtually identical in melodic outline to the first seven-note segment of Motif H170, which in T.1.2 will be part of the blood-brotherhood oath which Siegfried and Gunther swear. The link between these motifs suggests a link between Gunther's and Mime's craven character: Gunther will exploit Siegfried through deceit and resort to Hagen's potion to get Siegfried to win Brünnhilde for him, because Gunther's pedestrian, unheroic nature isn't up to the task, just as Mime employs deceit to exploit Siegfried's heroism to win for him Alberich's Ring, and will later try to employ a potion to bring this to pass. Mime typifies what Wagner considered the vulgar masses, irredeemably fallen, who're often hostile to more intellectually and emotionally developed human beings. This tells us much about Mime's fraught relationship with his foster-son Siegfried. But as Mime says, it's Siegfried's childlike strength (his pre-fallen innocence) which alone will kill the Serpent Fafner. Fafner embodies the Fall, the malign consequence of the birth of reflective consciousness (Alberich's Ring). Mime's true nature is well described by Wagner's critique, previously cited, of established society's primary concern, the self-preservation instinct, which according to Wagner lames all spiritual impulse in favor of egoistic pursuits. [See 411W-{6–8/49} 'Art and Revolution,' PW Vol. I, p. 57]

Siegfried now bursts into the cave, introducing Siegfried's Youthful Horncall Motif H108 as he blows his horn and, to amuse himself at Mime's expense, drives a bear (representing "Nature" in opposition to Mime's unnatural, artificial mind) before him to set it on Mime:

[pp. 196–8] ([[H108 orch:]] Siegfried, in wild forest clothing, with a silver horn on a chain, bursts in from the forest with sudden impetuousness, driving a large bear ... which he ... sets on Mime ...) [**Siegfried:** (...); **Mime:** (...)]

Siegfried: (H108>>:) I came as a pair, the better to plague you: ask him, bruin, about the sword!

Mime: (H108>>:) (...) There lies the weapon: I finished furbishing it today. (...) [Siegfried sends the bear packing: (...)] (H108 inverted: The bear runs back into the forest ... .) [**Mime:** (...)]

Siegfried: ... I was seeking a better companion than the one sitting here at home; deep in the forest I wound my horn till it echoed far and wide: would some good-hearted friend be glad to join me, I asked by means of that sound. (H108) From the bushes came a bear ... ; I liked him better than you ... . (...)

Mime: (H108 frags >>>:) I've made the weapon sharp, you'll be pleased with its keen-edged blade. (...)

Siegfried: (...) (testing the sword H93a) (...) (H93a) This puny pin you call a sword? (He smashes it on the anvil, so that the splinters fly off in all directions ... .) [[H109 orch >>>:]] There, take the pieces, you shameful bungler: (H109 scale varis) ... . [[H109 orch >>>:]] ... he makes me weapons and fashions swords; he vaunts his art ["Kunst"] as though he could do aught aright: when I take in my hand whatever he's hammered, I can crush the trash in a single grip (:H109)! (H109 scale varis:) Were the knave not simply too scurvy, I'd smash him to pieces with all his smith-work, the old and addle-headed elf (:H109 scale varis)! (...) (H109>>>: In his anger Siegfried throws himself down on a stone bench. .... H109 [sounding like a big laugh])

Siegfried's Youthful Horncall Motif H108 is, Cooke notes, a member of the family of Nature motifs, arpeggiated figures in Major Key, akin to the Primal Nature Motif H1, the Rhinegold Motif H9, and the Rainbow Bridge Motif H55. It later evolves into the harmonically richer Mature Siegfried Horncall Motif H159. At its inception it represents two things: (1) Siegfried's tempestuous, youthful, spontaneous and independent spirit (his will to self-expression), and (2) his seeking for a natural companion superior to the calculating, scheming Mime. It will take on richer meaning as the *Ring* drama proceeds, including an incarnation in fragmentary form in S.1.3 as the embodiment of Siegfried's vital creative force, H127, Siegfried's labor of love in re-forging his father Siegmund's sword Nothung.

As Siegfried tests Mime's new sword, knowing in advance it will shatter on Mime's anvil, we hear Siegfried's motif H93, which reminds us that he, unlike Mime, is the fearless hero Wotan longed for, who must create himself, forge his independence free from Wotan's influence. It's implicit that Siegfried alone, not Mime, will be able to re-forge his father Siegmund's sword Nothung. Nothung is Wotan's Grand Idea, that through inspired acts of compassionate heroism (exemplified by Siegmund, Sieglinde, and Brünnhilde), or deeds of art (created by Siegfried, inspired by his muse Brünnhilde), the innocence which is lost as religious belief begins to wane, will be restored. Siegfried as an inspired artist-hero, fount of creativity, is an exponent of what Feuerbach described as "natural necessity," for he expresses the new and ever-changing, the natural, which Wotan once extolled. However, as a self-proclaimed God whose authority allegedly establishes infallible law, immutable values, and eternal bliss, Wotan has found his impulse for change in constant contradiction with his desire for security and quiet (his socio-religious conscience, Fricka). Mime's vulgar opportunism in striving to draw profit from the original creations of his superiors (Alberich and Siegfried) to enjoy a complaisant existence, represents the covert egoism which underlies the gods' quest for quiet and security in established society, and hostility towards authenticity.

After Siegfried smashes Mime's newest sword, he vents his contempt for Mime in a diatribe set to the new Motif H109, which expresses Siegfried's instinctive loathing for Mime. Mime, Siegfried's polar opposite, represents all those things in Wotan's character which Wotan said he loathed (Ekel). Since Siegfried is Wotan reborn, minus consciousness of his true identity and origin, Siegfried's contempt for Mime expresses Wotan's self-loathing. Wotan, Light-

Alberich, is a covert Nibelung (as instanced in his confession to Brünnhilde that he finds with loathing always only himself in all that he undertakes), by virtue of the transformation of Alberich's Ring (H17ab) into Valhalla (H18ab). It's this "going-under" of our inherent egoism, of what Wagner might have disgracefully described as the Judaism in ourselves, which Wotan accomplished by submerging his consciousness of his loathsome nature and corrupt history (both now embodied by Mime) in his unconscious mind Brünnhilde. Wotan's two-fold nature as both a realist (Nibelung) and idealist (first God, then a mortal Wälsung) is embodied in two distinct characters, Mime shamelessly exemplifying Wotan's utilitarian, prosaic, egoistic impulse, and Siegfried inheriting Wotan's idealistic, poetical, metaphysical impulse. These two impulses being inimical to each other, Siegfried and Mime naturally despise each other.

Mime now chastises Siegfried for his ingratitude almost as if Mime was his mother, reminding Siegfried of how much Siegfried owes to Mime, who brought him up. But Siegfried retorts that though Mime taught him much, he'd rather remain ignorant of anything Mime can teach:

[pp. 198–200] **Mime:** (H109 orch:—[sounding like laughing]) ... your ingratitude's gross indeed (:H109). If I don't do everything right for the wicked boy straightaway, **[[H110 orch>>:]]** [= H38 duple vari] he all too soon forgets whatever good I've done him (:H110 orch)! (H109 orch>>:; **[[H111A orch:]]**) Will you never recall what I said about being grateful? (...) (:H109 orch: :H111A orch). (...) (**[[H110 orch >>>:]]**; H? voc: [Possible embryo for Gibichung motifs in *Twilight of the Gods* such as H167, H168ab, and H183?]) No doubt you'd like some food. I'll fetch the roast from the spit: or would you like to try the broth? I boiled it thoroughly for you (:H110 orch; :H? voc—Possible embryo for Gibichung motifs?) (... Siegfried ... knocks the pot and roast meat out of Mime's hands. H109) [**Siegfried:** (...)] **[[H112 voc >>:]]** From a suckling babe I brought you up, warmed the little mite with clothes: food and drink I brought to you and tended you like a second self ["eig'ne Haut"] (:H107 hint). (...) I forged you toys and a winding horn; (H110>>:) ... : with clever counsel I counseled you cleverly, with lucid lore I taught you wit. ... : (H110 >>:; H8 hint >>:) ... for you alone I suffer affliction and wear myself out ... (:H112 voc)! And that's my reward for the burdens I've borne, that the quick-tempered boy torments (sobbing) and abhors me! (...)

Siegfried: (H109 vari orch>>>:; H111A orch:) Much, Mime, have you taught me and much from you have I learned; but what you most wanted to teach me, I never managed to learn (:H111A orch): how I could ever abide you. (H109:; H112 vari over H110:) Although you may bring me food and drink (H109), I'm fed by my loathing ["Ekel"] alone; ... ; (H110:) although you would teach me to use my wits, (H109:) I'd still rather stay dull and stupid. (H109:; H110:; H111A hint orch:) I only need set eyes upon you to recognize evil in all that you do (:H111A hint orch:): (H110 orch:; H? voc: [Siegfried imitates Mime's vocal line from "No doubt you'd like some food. I'll fetch some roast from the spit."]) when I see you standing, shuffling and shambling, week-kneed and nodding, blinking your eyes (:H? [Mime's vocal line]): (H109 >>>:) I long to seize the dodderer's neck and finish off the filthy twitching creature! (...) (H109)

Several new motifs are introduced in this passage. H110 is a syncopated four-note motif which Dunning describes as a duple variation of the Nibelung Forging Motif H38. It conveys something of Mime's quirky locomotion and also his character (or lack thereof), and is heard frequently in association with Mime in S.1–2. H111A is the first of two musically unrelated but conceptually linked motifs (the other being H111B: both are introduced in S.1.1) which express Siegfried's longing for relief from the obsequious, artificial, and fake Mime by seeking refreshment in Nature. They are both, in a sense, conceptual (but not motival) premonitions of Siegfried's Forest Murmurs H136, which will be introduced in S.2.2. H112, called "Mime's Starling Song" (because Siegfried, exasperated with Mime's incessant grubbing for gratitude, demands that he stop this everlasting "Starling Song") is introduced as Mime describes all the sacrifices he's made to bring Siegfried up, and all that Siegfried owes to Mime. The implication is that all that Siegfried is he owes to Mime, and ultimately to Alberich, whose renunciation of love (of animal instinct) for the sake of the Ring's power (consciousness) gave birth not only to the human mind, but to its impulse to transcend its very preconditions, its origin and nature, in godhead (Wotan), and in man's idealistic, metaphysical impulses. H112 introduces a small family of motifs which includes two variants of H112 which will be introduced in S.1.1 and S.2.1 respectively, the first being H118, "Siegfried's Mission," which expresses Siegfried's joyful feeling of emancipation from Mime, the last being H135, to which Wotan (Wanderer) will tell Alberich Wotan expects Siegfried to stand on his own.

I've suggested that Siegfried's loathing ("Ekel") for Mime is Wotan's self-loathing, Wotan's abhorrence of his true nature and origin as a Nibelung, a natural man whose primary instincts are self-preservation and self-aggrandizement. Where Wagner speaks of the Germans' allegedly instinctive abhorrence of Jews, he's really speaking of the higher man's universal abhorrence for all that is low, craven, or egoistic in his own nature, for which he feels guilt. That Wagner in his innermost self acknowledged this truth is proved by his having dramatized it in Wotan's self-loathing, for Wotan, as Wagner's Feuerbachian metaphor for collective, historical man, is really the *Ring*'s main protagonist and subsumes all the other characters, both those who're unsympathetic like Alberich and Mime, and those who're sympathetic like Brünnhilde and the Wälsungs. An approximation of this contrast of the two types of human being represented, respectively, by Mime and Siegfried, Wagner finds in a lesson from the story of Wieland the Smith: "... 'the ne'er contented mind, that ever broods the New,' the youngest Norn holds out to all of us when we are born, and through it alone might we each one day, become a 'Genius:' but now, in our craze for education [i.e., Mime's futile attempt to instruct Siegfried in the mundane ways of the conventional world], 'tis Chance alone that brings this gift within our grasp, —

the accident of not becoming educated ... ... perchance the Norn ... bestowed on me her gift; which never left poor untrained me, and made Life and Art and mine own self my only, quite anarchic, educators ... .." [560W-{6–8/51} 'A Communication To My Friends,' PW Vol. I, p. 290] Wagner saw himself in Siegfried, who instinctively prefers to educate himself rather than be tainted by an upbringing designed for the vulgar masses' needs. We can see in Wagner's remark that nowadays education destroys genius an echo of Siegfried's complaint that though Mime wishes to teach him Siegfried wishes to remain ignorant of his lessons. Mime represents what Wagner described as the hostile philistine element among whom the truly creative genius must make his way, to whose needs and desires he must often cater to survive, yet whose lessons the man or woman of genius would rather never learn.

In several remarkable passages from his writings Wagner compared the truly original artist with the imitative mime, suggesting that all great artists begin as mimes but eventually develop into original re-interpreters of the world, who transmute the real into the ideal. [See 730W-{9–12/67} 'German Art and German Policy,' PW Vol. IV, pp. 80–82] This may explain Mime's insistence that Siegfried acknowledge a debt of gratitude to him for bringing Siegfried up. Siegfried, while acknowledging he owes Mime much, desires to disavow all debt to him. Such an idealistic artist comes to feel contempt for the merely imitative, realistic mime, his immature self, just as, according to Wagner, the fully evolved human being feels repugnance toward (his ancestor) the imitative ape. Wagner described the imitative mime as representing a transitional phase in evolution between animal and man, for in his view the genius stands to the average man as the average man stands to his immediate animal ancestors, the apes, adding that this could explain why states and religions decline "... whilst art eternally shoots up, renewed and young from out the ruins of existence." [See 729W-{9–12/67} 'German Art and German Policy,' PW Vol. IV, pp. 79–80] Mime (miming, imitation), with his practical intelligence, represents the precondition for Siegfried's ability to posit an ideal realm which transcends reality, just as Alberich's forging of his Ring of consciousness was the precondition for man's involuntary (dreaming) invention of the gods and their heavenly abode, Valhalla. While Mime can be identified with both State and Religion, i.e., with Wotan's establishment in its practical aspect, Siegfried represents the artist whose originality transcends the conservative limits of a religion-based society. This surely also explains why Mime made the Wondrous Tarnhelm to Alberich's design. Wagner summarized this distinction between authentic genius (Siegfried) and the vulgar masses (Mime) in imagery that recalls his comparison of the interpretive artist with the imitative mime: "He [Schopenhauer] regards it as an ineptitude of Nature not to have created yet another species, since between gifted and ungifted human beings there is ... a gap wider than between human beings and animals. (...) One has only to watch a theater audience, in which one person is utterly absorbed and concentrating, the other inattentive, fidgety, vapid. Between these two persons no understanding is possible, and therein lies the mystery of the gifted person in a world in which he must regard as identical with himself a creature who no more resembles him than an ape does." [760W-{9/18/70} CD Vol. I, p. 272]

Siegfried poses the following question to the "wise" Mime: why is it that though Siegfried prefers the instinctual beasts of the forest to the ulterior, calculating Mime, whom he abhors, he always returns to Mime? Mime answers that this is because Siegfried feels natural love for his parent, Mime. Mime has been hiding Siegfried's true parentage in order to pose as his sole parent:

> [pp. 200–1] **Siegfried:** If you're so wise, then help me to know what I've thought about in vain:—(H109 orch:; H111A orch:) though I run off into the forest to leave you, how is it that I come back: (:H109; :H111A orch)? (H109 varis:; H111A orch develops [possible hint of H102?:]) All the beasts of the forest are dearer to me than you: every tree and bird, the fish in the brook I can far more abide than you—how is it, then, that I always come back (:H109 varis; :H111A orch [:possible hint of H102?])? (…)
>
> **Mime:** (… **[[H113 orch:]]** [Possible influence of H104?]) My child, that makes you understand how dear to your heart I must be (:H113 orch). [**Siegfried:** (…)] **[[H114 voc:]]** Whimpering, young things long for their parents' nest: love is the name of that longing: (H113 orch:; **[[H114 vari orch:]]**) so you, too, pined for me, so you, too, love your Mime—so you have to love him (:H114 voc/orch)!

Though Siegfried instinctively abhors Mime and denies him credit for having contributed in any way to making Siegfried what he's become (recalling Wotan's hope that his chosen hero would do what Wotan desires spontaneously, wholly free from Wotan's influence, which Wotan now loathes), nonetheless Siegfried can't escape his roots, his true identity and origin, any more than Wotan and the gods (or their proxies) can. Siegfried is the product of Wotan's artificial endeavor to purge himself of all that's craven, fearful, egoistic, narrow, stilted, mundane, etc. Siegfried's origin and identity lie ultimately in Wotan's futile quest for redemption from the truth.

Mime introduces two new motifs. As he suggests that Siegfried has always returned to him because Mime is dear to his heart, we hear H113, part of the motif family which includes H20, H74, and H104. H20 was first heard in R.2 when Fricka asked herself how she could preserve Wotan's fidelity to her, hoping that the domestic tranquility of Valhalla (H21) would serve; H74 expressed the tenderness of Siegmund's growing love for Sieglinde; and H104 was that extraordinarily poignant theme in which Wotan's farewell to Brünnhilde culminated, as he sung his nostalgic reminiscence of all the love he's shared with her, which he must now relinquish forever. Mime is engaging in a subtle manipulation of Siegfried's instinctive longing for parents and trying to thwart his longing for a heritage more exalted than that which Siegfried could ever hope to obtain by being Mime's son. H114 is introduced as Mime describes how young children long for their parents' nest. Mime describes this longing as "love." But Mime isn't Siegfried's blood-parent but only his foster-parent by default. He's been posing as Siegfried's father and mother, offering his lowly self as a poor substitute for Siegfried's heroic parents Siegmund and Sieglinde. Siegfried is striving to emancipate himself from the society of philistines (represented by Mime) to discover his place among the culture heroes who tried to restore lost innocence in religion, morality, and art.

Siegfried pursues his suspicion that something is amiss in Mime's claim to be his parent, for Siegfried has noted that in the natural world children have both father and mother, and what's more, children in the natural world resemble their fathers and mothers:

> [pp. 201–3] **Siegfried:** Hey, Mime, if you're so clever, tell me one thing more! (H113 >>:) In spring the birds would sing so blithely, ... the one would entice the other (:H113): you said ... (H113 >>:) that these were fathers ... and mothers (:H113). **[[H115 orch:]]** They dallied so fondly, not leaving each other but building a nest and brooding inside it (:H115 orch): (H?—Orchestral birdcalls:) young fledglings then would flutter out and both of them tended their brood. (:H?—Orch birdcalls)—(H113, H23) Deer, too, would rest in pairs in the bushes with even wild foxes and wolves: (H113 varis >>>:) the father brought food to the lair, the mother suckled the whelps. There I learned the meaning of love: (H113:; H23 [emphatic!]) (**[[H115 orch>>:]]**) Where, Mime, is your loving wife, that I may call her mother (:H115 orch)? [**Mime:** (...)] **[[H111B orch:]]** That the young look like their parents I've luckily seen for myself. When I came to the limpid brook, I glimpsed trees and beasts in its glassy surface ... . (:H111B orch). (H93b voc:) And then I saw my own likeness too (:H93b voc), (H70) quite different from you I thought myself then: (H38/H8 vari:) as like to a toad were a glittering fish, though no fish ever crept from a toad.

Siegfried isn't interested in what the child owes its parent but rather in the loving care which the parent provides for the child. This is a direct—yet unwitting—slap at Wotan, who, under Fricka's influence, put egoistic concern for his power and her honor, the gods' rule, ahead of his love for his children Siegmund and Sieglinde. H115 is introduced as Siegfried describes how such fathers and mother's bond with each other to build a nest in which to breed their young, and asks Mime where his wife might be. Though H114 and H115 evidently aren't directly related to any other motifs, H115 is a continuation of H114. Siegfried asks how Mime made Siegfried without a mother, and Mime offers the lame argument that Mime is Siegfried's father and mother. Siegfried also notes that in the natural world the young resemble their parents, and Siegfried looks as much like Mime as a glittering fish looks like a toad (we're reminded of Alberich's clumsily futile efforts to win the Rhinedaughters' love in R.1). Strikingly, Siegfried describes how he learned this by looking at the reflections in a brook, noting that Siegfried's image (represented by his motif H92) stared back at him so he could compare it with Mime's face (as we hear H70 recalling the tragic heroism of Siegmund's true father Siegmund), and we return in memory to Sieglinde's remark to Siegmund in V.1.3 that his face resembled her face as it looked back at her in the reflection of a brook. It suddenly dawns on Siegfried that he's always returned to Mime because it's only from him that he can discover his true heritage. Mime has co-opted Siegfried's heritage and kept it secret from him, fearing that this discovery would prompt him to yearn for independence from Mime:

> [pp. 203–4] **Siegfried:** (... H113 vari:) ... it now occurs to me ... : when I run off into the forest to leave you, how is it I still come home (:H113 vari)? (...) First I must learn from you who are my father and mother! [**Mime:** (...)] (H109 >>>:) So I must seize you to find out anything ... ! [Siegfried grabs Mime by the neck] (H32B vari? >>:) Thus have I had to force all things out of you: even speech I'd scarcely have mastered, had I not wrung it out of the rogue! (...) Who are my father and mother (:H109; :H32B vari? >>)? (...)
>
> **Mime:** You'll be the death of me yet! (...) (H110:) I'm neither your father nor any kinsman (:H110)—and yet you owe me everything! ... out of pity alone I sheltered you here ... . What a fool I was to hope for thanks!

I've proposed that Mime represents the common man whose sole concern is his immediate physical needs, safety, security, and life's little pleasures. In Wagner's view such men never grasp the special needs of the truly gifted, the genius, and instinctively feel threatened by more mentally and spiritually developed types. Such men tend to squelch all manifestations of authentic genius in their midst, to arrest human growth, to ensure that everyone remains on their level, figuratively dwarf-like. Of this stultifying dependence on the habitual at the heart of established society, Wagner says: "... Established Society has a terrible power over us, for it has deliberately arrested the growth of our strength. The strength for this holy war can come to us from nothing save perception of the worthlessness of our Society [Siegfried finds evil in all that Mime does]. When we have clearly recognized how our existing Society ... craftily ... withholds us from our mission, our right [Mime has deprived Siegfried of the knowledge of his heroic Wälsung heritage] ... , we shall have won the force ... to conquer it." [397W-{2/49} 'Man and Established Society,' PW Vol. VIII, pp. 230–231] Mime has striven to thwart what would otherwise have become Siegfried's true mission in life, to exploit him for the sole purpose of winning, through Siegfried's efforts, the Nibelung Ring and Hoard. But Wotan's confession to Brünnhilde of Siegfried's mission, unknown to Siegfried, also requires that he gain control of Alberich's Ring, Tarnhelm, and Hoard so Alberich can't regain them to overthrow the Valhallan gods. Wagner accused the German Jews of appropriating only the outer form of Germany's intellectual heritage (imitating authentic literature, music, science, language, etc.) but throwing away as profitless its vital spirit, just as Mime has appropriated the knowledge of Siegfried's true heritage, and (as we'll see) the pieces of Siegfried's father's broken sword Nothung (physical testimony to that heritage), which Mime is unable to re-forge, in the meantime offering Siegfried poor imitations. In light of this, it's noteworthy that Siegfried says he'd not even have learned to speak had he not forced Mime to teach him. As Wagner put it: "Taken strictly, ... our world was new to the Jews [after their political emancipation]; and all they undertook, to set them straight therein, consisted in the appropriation of our ancient heritage. This applies before all to our language—

for it would be rude to refer to our money." [904W-{2/78} 'Modern,' PW Vol. VI, p. 44]

We find in Mime's dubious efforts to profit from Siegfried's innocence and heroic nature, his inability to forge swords that only a true hero can wield, or to re-forge a true hero's sword, Nothung, and his co-optation of Siegfried's heritage, parallels to Wagner's remarks concerning Jewish nature, which are actually descriptive of the relationship of men and women of genius to the general mass of average human beings, who in Wagner's view don't understand the genius and see him or her only in light of their own practical concerns. In Wagner's following observations concerning what he regards as a specifically Jewish nature, by which he means philistinism in general, typified by artists whose work is the product of ulterior and therefore inartistic motives, he explores what it is he wishes to purge from his own artistic endeavors, just as Wotan wished for a hero in whom Wotan wouldn't find those qualities which Wotan loathes in himself: "... beautiful is that foible of the German's which forbade his coining into personal profit the inwardness and purity of his feelings and beholdings ... , (...) 'Tis as though the Jew had been astounded to find such a store of ... genius yielding no returns but poverty and unsuccess. (...) The Jew set right this bungling of the German's, by taking German intellectual labour [Siegmund's sword Nothung] into his own hands, and thus we see an odious travesty of the German spirit [Mime's useless swords] upheld to-day before the German Folk, as its imputed likeness." [721W-{9–12/65} 'What is German?,' PW Vol. IV, pp. 158–159]

On the subject of Judaism as an influence which, according to Wagner, has stunted the growth and development of an authentic German culture, Cosima recorded his following viewpoint: "... when he ["Friend Levi"] tells us that his father is a rabbi, our conversation comes back to the Israelites—the feeling that they intervened too early in our cultural condition, that the human qualities the German character might have developed from within itself and then passed on to the Jewish character have been stunted by their premature interference in our affairs, before we have become fully aware of ourselves." [956W-{1/13/79}CD Vol. II, p. 254] It's interesting that Wagner says the Jews intervened before the Germans had become fully aware of themselves (perhaps before national unification, which Wagner hoped would inspire the Germans to assert themselves culturally in a way true to their essential character), since Siegfried in S.2.2 will tell Fafner: "I still don't know who I am."

Mime's character as a self-serving, profit-driven egoist expresses itself in his harping here, again, on the fact that he's gained no profit from having reared Siegfried, and no thanks. Mime didn't rear Siegfried for Siegfried's sake, but only so Siegfried would win the Ring and Hoard for him. Wotan exploits Siegfried and his Wälsung parents seemingly for more exalted reasons, but in the final analysis his motives are just as craven as those inspiring Mime, as Mime's brother Alberich suggested in his indictment of Wotan's hypocrisy in R.4.

Mime now describes Siegfried's mother Sieglinde's tragic last moments. Brünnhilde had encouraged Sieglinde by telling her to take heart in spite of the great suffering (Noth) she'd have to endure to bring the greatest of heroes

Siegfried to birth. We hear H65 repeatedly as Mime speaks of her anguish: H65 expresses the Noth that the Wälsungs suffer as the heroic race to whom Wotan looks to pay the price of Alberich's Ring Curse, in order to redeem the gods from having to pay it:

> **[pp. 204–5] Mime:** Out there in the wildwood a woman once lay whimpering: (H65) I helped her into the cave (H62) … . (H63>:) She bore a child within her womb: in sadness she gave it birth here; … I helped as best I could: (H39:) great was her travail ["Noth"] (:H39); (H65) she died—(H93a) but Siegfried, he survived.
>
> **Siegfried:** So my mother died through me? (H65)
>
> **Mime:** She handed you over into my care: (H65: Siegfried stands deeply in thought.) … . What trouble Mime took! What pains ["Noth"] the good man went to! (H112/H110:) 'From a suckling babe I brought you up … (:H112/H110)'
>
> **Siegfried:** (…) (H65) Now say why (H93a) my name is Siegfried!
>
> **Mime:** (H93a:) Your mother said I might name you so … (:H93a)—(H112/H110:) 'I warmed the little mite with clothes … (:H112/H110)'
>
> **Siegfried:** (H65:) Now tell me, what was my mother called (:H65)? [**Mime:** (…); **Siegfried:** (…)]
>
> **Mime:** It's slipped my mind … no, wait! She who gave you to me in her grief may well have been called Sieglinde—(H112/H110:) I tended you as my second self ["eig'ne Haut"] …'
>
> **Siegfried:** (… H65 vari:) Now I ask what my father was called. [**Mime:** (…)] … didn't my mother speak his name?
>
> **Mime:** That he'd been slain was all she said (:H65 vari); …—(H110:; H112 frags:) 'And when you grew bigger, I waited upon you … (:H110 & H112 frags).'
>
> **Siegfried:** Stop that eternal squawking ("Staarenlied," i.e., "starling song")!

Siegfried has learned from Mime that his mother Sieglinde died giving Siegfried birth. While Sieglinde is Siegfried's birth-mother, Brünnhilde is his metaphysical mother by virtue of Wotan having inseminated her (his wish-womb) with the seed of his unspoken secret. Brünnhilde has figuratively given birth to Siegfried, who is Wotan reborn, minus consciousness of his corrupt history, craven identity, and guilt. But Siegfried's ultimate mother is Brünnhilde's mother Erda, Mother Nature. The fact that not only Siegfried, but Tristan and Parsifal, are guilty in some sense of causing their mother's death (Tristan's mother, like Siegfried's, having died giving him birth, and Parsifal's mother having died of a broken heart due to Parsifal's neglect), is a metaphor for the fact that Wagner's artist-heroes have inherited religious man's (Wotan's) sin against the truth (Erda's knowledge of all that was, is, and will be), and are figurative murderers of their mother, since their art is ultimately motivated by religious man's longing to transcend the world.

It's for these reasons that Siegfried meditates in anguish on how his mother died giving him birth, but will also confuse Brünnhilde with the mother who died giving him birth during their first meeting in S.3.3.

At Siegfried's insistence, Mime produces objective evidence (not for the ears, but for the eye) of Siegfried's heritage, the two pieces of the sword his father wielded when he was killed in battle, which Sieglinde evidently passed on to Mime. As always, Mime complains he wasn't paid, and therefore didn't profit, by offering Sieglinde his aid:

[pp. 205-7] **Siegfried:** I won't believe you with my ears but only with my eyes: what evidence bears you witness?

Mime: (H106: Reflecting for a minute, then fetching the two pieces of a broken sword: H56ab/H38:) Your mother gave me this (:H56/H38): (H38 frag:) for trouble, board and care she left it as paltry payment. See here, a shattered sword! Your father, she said, had borne it (:H38 frag) when he fell in his final fight.

Siegfried: (enthusiastically: [[H116 orch:]] [= H56/H108]; H108 end frags >>>:) And these fragments you shall forge for me: then I'll wield my rightful sword (:H116, :H108 end frags)! (H109 >>:) Come on now, Mime, bestir yourself and be quick about it; if there's aught you're good at, then show me your art ["Kunst"]! ... (:H109): (H56 vari over H109>>:) in those shards alone do I place any trust (:H56 vari over H109). (H56 frags?:). (...)

Mime: ... What would you do with the sword today?

Siegfried: ([[H117 voc:]]/H109 frag orch:) Go forth from the forest into the world: I'll nevermore return. How glad I am to have gained my freedom, nothing binds or constrains me! (H109 orch >>:) You're not my father, my home's far away ... . Fleet as the fish in the floodtide, free as the finch as it soars aloft (:H117 voc:; H109 orch), [[H118 voc:]] [= H112 vari] I fly from here and float away (:H118 voc), ... nevermore ... (H93c?:) to see you again (:H93c?)! (...)

Mime: ... Stop! Stop! Where are you going? (...) (H117 varis:; H118 varis and frag: he gazes in astonishment as Siegfried rushes away.)

Siegfried, thunderstruck at Mime's revelation of his true parentage, and that's he's fallen heir to his martyred father's sword, introduces the new Motif H116 as he peremptorily demands that Mime re-forge it for him. Dunning suggests that H116 is a synthesis of H56ab (Sword—Wotan's Grand Idea For Redemption) and H108 (Siegfried's Youthful Horncall). This implicates Siegfried in Wotan's futile scheme to restore the innocence lost through Alberich's forging his Ring of consciousness. Siegfried obnoxiously insists that Mime re-forge Siegfried's father's sword for him (H109, Siegfried's Contempt for Mime sounding), knowing full well that Mime is inherently unable! Siegfried's deliberate humiliation of Mime references the fact that though Wotan originally made that sword to serve as the instrument of redemption, leaving his son Siegmund heir to it, Siegfried will soon proclaim his autonomy from Wotan by re-forging the sword himself. However, it remains Wotan's sword, re-forged or not, because its motif remains identical to the one to which Wotan originally proclaimed his grand idea for redemption. Siegfried has demanded swords from Mime solely to prove their worthlessness, because Mime represents all that Wotan loathes in himself, and it was Wotan's futile longing for redemption (which he now loathes) which brought the sword into being. By proving Mime's incapacity to provide Siegfried with his rightful sword, Siegfried has unwittingly condemned Wotan's provision of this sword to Siegmund. This is tragically ironic since Siegfried is unwittingly the final refuge of Wotan's quest for redemption.

Siegfried introduces motifs H117 and H118 when—on being asked by Mime what he'll do with the re-forged sword—he declares he'll take it out into the world and leave Mime forever. H117 expresses Siegfried's newfound, joyous sense of freedom from the constraint under which Mime previously held Siegfried by keeping his true heritage and patrimony secret, and H118 ("Siegfried's Mission") likewise expresses Siegfried's ecstasy in emancipating himself from what he regards as Mime's false claims on him. But H118 is a curious candidate for a motif carrying this meaning. It's derived from H112 (Mime's Starling Song) in which Mime described how much Siegfried owes Mime for educating him on the world's ways. How interesting then that Siegfried musically expresses his emancipation from Mime, and absolves himself of all debt to him, accompanied by the motif Mime sang as he reminded Siegfried of all he owes Mime! H118 tells us Siegfried can't disown his true origin any more than a stone thrown into the air can defy gravity, but must fall back to earth. Significantly, Wagner's complaint to Franz Liszt that he could only mature as an artist if he could disavow his alleged dependence on, and imitation of, the Jewish opera composer Meyerbeer, tapped this vein: "Meyerbeer is a special case ... : ... I find him infinitely repugnant. This perpetually kind and obliging man reminds me of ... the most wicked ... period of my life, when he ... made a show of protecting me; ... when we were treated like fools by patrons whom we inwardly deeply despised. (...) But it was time for me to break away completely from so dishonest a relationship: ... even the discovery that he was playing me false could not surprise me ... since it was basically I who had to reproach myself for having wilfully allowed myself to be deceived concerning him. No, it was for more deep-seated reasons ... : I cannot exist as an artist in my own eyes ... without sensing in Meyerbeer my total antithesis, a contrast I am driven loudly to proclaim by the ... despair ... I feel whenever I encounter ... , the mistaken view that I have something in common with Meyerbeer. This is a necessary act if my mature self is to be fully born ... ." [See 556W-{4/18/51}Letter to Franz Liszt, SLRW, p. 222]

All that Siegfried is—his innocence, spontaneity, verve, passion, longing for freedom, hunger for love and belonging, etc.—stems from Alberich's emancipation from animal instinct (the Rhinedaughters) to forge his Ring of consciousness. Yet Wotan's primary impulse, inherited by Siegfried, is to disavow this true Nibelung origin, identity, and heritage, and emancipate himself from its claims. Wotan's quest is futile because, as Wagner said, we didn't long for redemption through the restoration of innocence until we'd lost it, and we lost it through the evolution of conscious human thought to become who we are. The meaning of the gods,' Brünnhilde's, and the Wälsungs' lives, is founded on the Fall Alberich brought to pass. All efforts to escape paying the price of Alberich's Ring Curse fulfill it, as in Greek tragedy. But Siegfried—freed, he feels, from Mime's repugnant claims on him—has run off into the forest, expecting to return for one last time to retrieve the sword which he's demanded Mime re-forge for him, to Mime's utter consternation:

> [p. 207] **Mime:** (H106:) to my age-old plight ["Noth"] (H17ab:) I can now add a new one (:H106; :H17ab); I'm well and truly trapped! (...) (H38) (H47:) How lead the hothead (H38:) to Fafner's lair (:H47; :H38)? (H38/H8 >>>:) How join the shards (H38) of insidious steel? (H38) ... (... H107 vari:) ... the Nibelung's envy ["Neid"], need ["Noth"] and sweat cannot join together (:H107 vari) (sobbing) [[H119 orch:]] nor weld the sword and make it whole!

Mime can't begin to fathom how—now that Siegfried has rediscovered his heritage and can free himself from Mime's influence—he can persuade Siegfried to serve Mime's purpose by killing Fafner and obtaining the Ring and Hoard for him. By the same token, how, Mime asks, can he re-forge Nothung, the only sword that would serve his purpose. But this, after all, is Wotan's problem. How, Wotan asked, could he make a hero, a friendly foe, who would do instinctively, from his own Noth, without Wotan's influence, that thing which Wotan needs, but can't do himself. Mime doesn't yet see Wotan, but as S.1.1 segues into S.1.2 we're introduced to the first of two motifs which identify Wotan as "The Wanderer," the slowly descending H119, as Wotan is about to enter Mime's forge, disguised. Dunning notes, echoing Cooke, that H119 is likely derived from Loge's Motif H32B. Loge, Wotan said, could draw advantage from the enemy's envy through his cunning.

When Wagner had almost completed *Siegfried* Scene One, he wrote: "During the next few days I shall finish the first scene. It is strange, but only in the course of composing the music does the essential meaning of my poem dawn upon me; secrets are continually being revealed ... which had previously been hidden from me." [646W-{12/6/56} Letter to Franz Liszt, SLRW, p. 361] It's worth recalling Wagner's oft-repeated assertion that his artworks weren't only the creation of his conscious mind, but also of unconscious inspiration, which made them strange and mysterious to him. The *Ring*'s music doesn't merely enhance the libretto's meaning through music's native expressive power, but also, as motifs, by playing the role of subliminal messenger of Wagner's hidden aim as a poet, an aim hidden even from himself.

SIEGFRIED ꞉ ACT ONE, SCENE TWO

(MIME'S FORGE)
MIME AND THE WANDERER—WOTAN IN DISGUISE

Wotan, disguised as the Wanderer, with a broad hat covering his missing eye, and using his Spear as his walking staff, enters Mime's cave. Mime is instinctively hostile, unwilling to welcome a stranger as guest, particularly one as thoughtful as the Wanderer. Wotan will propose a contest of knowledge whose sole purpose is to expose Mime—Wotan's prosaic self—as inherently unable to grasp what he needs to know in order to obtain redemption:

> [pp. 207–9] ([[H119 orch:]] The wanderer (Wotan) enters ... ... he carries a spear as a staff. On his head he wears a hat with a broad, round brim, which hangs down over his face.)
>
> **Wanderer:** Hail to you, wise smith! [[H120 orch:]] [Possible influence of H18b vari] To a way-weary guest you'll not begrudge your house's hearth (:H120 orch)! (H120 frag orch) [**Mime:** (...)] [[H119 voc:]] As Wanderer I am known to the world (:H119 voc): ... I've wandered widely [[H120 orch>>:]] ... over the earth's ["Erde"—Erda's] broad back ... .
>
> **Mime:** Then wend your way further (:H120) (H38) and don't rest here (H119 stopped chords:) ... .
>
> **Wanderer:** (H120 vari: [with a musical development of extraordinary nobility]) With good men I've rested as their guest ... : ... he who's ungracious fears misfortune (:H120 vari).
>
> **Mime:** Misfortune ever dwelt with me ... .
>
> **Wanderer:** (... H119>:) ... matters of moment I've made known to many and many I've saved from whatever irked them, (H35 hint voc?:) cares ["Noth"] that gnawed at their hearts ["nagende Herzens-Noth"] (:H120; :H35 hint voc?).
>
> **Mime:** (...) (H119:) Alone and apart I wish to be (:H119) ... .
>
> **Wanderer:** (... H119 vari:) Many's the man who thought himself wise but what he needed ["Noth"] (:H119 vari) he did not know; (H120:) ... my words he found worthwhile (:H120).
>
> **Mime:** (H119: ...) (...) (... H38/H8>>:) my wits suffice, I want no more: I'll show you on your way, you sage (:H38/H8)!

As the Wanderer (Wotan) introduces himself we hear his other Wanderer Motif H120, which according to Dunning may derive from H18b (Valhalla). Wotan told Fricka that in spite of securing the refuge Valhalla he wished to conquer the outside world. Wotan's status as Wanderer over the face of the earth (Erda) is Wagner's metaphor for historical, collective man's accumulation over time of a hoard of knowledge based on this experience of the world which grants man ever more power over his life and his environment. Wotan can know Erda either objectively, as Alberich does, or subjectively, through aesthetic intuition, as he does through Erda's daughter Brünnhilde, who sees what his objective eye, oriented to the outer world, can't see. The identification of the hoard of knowledge Wotan gains by wandering the earth (Erda) with the knowledge he obtained from Erda by going down to her to learn the full truth about why he must live in fear, and to learn from her also how to end his fear (which gave birth to Brünnhilde), and the identification of Wotan's (Light-Alberich's) endeavors with Alberich's accumulation of his hoard of treasure in the bowels of the earth (Erda), is a key to understanding the *Ring* allegory.

Not only does Brünnhilde in T.P.B describe the knowledge the gods (she means Wotan) imparted to her (presumably in his confession), which she gave in turn to Siegfried, as "a bountiful hoard ("Hort") of hallowed runes," but she describes Siegfried—who, by winning Brünnhilde, the repository of Wotan's confession, has inherited Wotan's hoard of runes—in S.3.3 as the "Hoard of the world," and as the "foolish Hoard of loftiest deeds." It's confusing that some English translations render "Hort" in these contexts as "treasure," since this ignores the link between Wotan's hoard of knowledge and Alberich's hoard of treasure, i.e., the identification of both Alberich's Hoard and Wotan's Hoard as a metaphor for knowledge and the power it brings. Though Fafner (religious faith's fear of truth) guards Alberich's Hoard to keep man from accessing it, i.e., to thwart intellectual inquiry, nonetheless, over time, Wotan (man) continues to accumulate that hoard of earthly knowledge. Feuerbach argued that over time, man teaches himself that what he'd formerly called God is actually Nature, and man understood as a part of Nature. [See 177F-PPF, p. 17; 77F-EOC, p. 83; 105F-EOC, pp. 152–153; and 234F-LER, p. 134] Alberich's and Wotan's accumulation of their Hoard of knowledge will inevitably overthrow the Valhallan gods.

Wagner's thinking, set forth in previously cited extracts, emulated Feuerbach's ruminations on man's historical acquisition of a hoard of collective knowledge. Wagner described how Mother Nature figuratively becomes conscious of herself in man through our scientific inquiry and accumulation of knowledge over time, which eventually overthrows our religious error in positing transcendent beings called gods. Wagner not only described objective knowledge of the kind which Alberich and Wotan gather, but another kind of knowledge, aesthetic intuition, a sympathetic, subjective way of knowing Erda (Mother Nature) through feeling (love), in which we feel one with ourselves and with her. [See 414W-{9–12/49} 'The Artwork of the Future,' PW Vol. I, p. 70; 417W-{9–12/49} 'The Artwork of the Future,' PW Vol. I, p. 72; 426W-{9–12/49} 'The Artwork of the Future,' PW Vol. I, p. 80; and 494W-{50–1/51} *Opera and Drama*, PW Vol. II, p. 164] It's this aesthetic intuition which Wotan alone acquires from Erda (through Brünnhilde) to redeem himself from objective knowledge. This is the redemptive knowledge Wotan speaks of as he tells Mime he's obtained knowledge of how to save men from the "Noth" that gnaws at their hearts. It's this knowledge of man's means to redemption which least interests Mime.

Because Wotan's longing for transcendent human meaning makes him dissatisfied with the real world, he's figuratively a Wandering Jew, or Flying Dutchman, who can't find his home, his redemption, in this world [See 957W-{1/23/79} CD Vol. II, p 258; and 562W-{6–8/51} 'A Communication To My Friends,' PW Vol. I, pp. 307–308]. It's ironic therefore that Light-Alberich (Wotan) continues to accumulate Alberich's hoard of knowledge after having dispossessed Alberich of his Ring, Tarnhelm, and Hoard of Treasure, since on this view Wotan both seeks redemption and undermines his chance of obtaining it in the course of his world-wanderings. We're reminded of the Flying Dutchman sailing the world's seas endlessly seeking but never finding redemption, collecting instead an ever larger hoard of treasure which impedes his quest for redemption.

Wotan informs Mime that in his travels he has, through knowledge he's acquired, helped many solve their problems, specifically the Noth that gnawed at men's hearts. He's speaking of those psychological problems which religious belief and art address, such as the disconnect between our religious and ethical and artistic values and practical reality. But Mime, further establishing himself as Wagner's archetype for the rude masses of men, the "rabble," who trouble themselves only about their immediate needs and advantages, and have no concern with truth or goodness or beauty for their own sake [See 442W-{9–12/49} 'The Artwork of the Future,' PW Vol. I, pp. 208–209], tells Wotan that he's solitary and wishes to remain alone, and has just as much knowledge as he needs to get by. Naturally, we hear H38 (the Nibelung Labor Motif) as Mime gives vent to his utilitarian world-view. Mime doesn't wish to be troubled by Wotan's longing for redemption, which is precisely the kind of alternative knowledge Wotan is speaking about. So Wotan tells Mime that though some have thought themselves wise (i.e., those who're conscious of their motives), what they needed they didn't know (just as Wotan doesn't know how to produce a free hero capable of redeeming the gods). Wotan is saying that Mime doesn't realize that what he needs is redemption from his conscious, ulterior thought. This is entirely foreign to Mime's prosaic, pedestrian mind, as an archetypal Philistine. The fact that Wotan is confronting his real—rather than ideal—self, the self he abhors, in Mime, lends a peculiar ironic resonance to the contest of knowledge which Wotan now proposes. When Wotan says he's staking his head in this wager of wits, he's staking Mime's life, because Mime represents Wotan's conscious, voluntary will (his head rather than his heart), his ulterior intent, from which Wotan seeks redemption:

> [pp. 209–10] **Wanderer:** (… H19:) I sit by the hearth here and (H119:) stake my head as pledge in a wager of wits (:H19; :H119): (H19) **[[H121ab voc:]]** my head is yours to treat as you choose, if you fail to ask what you need to know and I don't redeem it with my lore (:H121ab voc). (…)
>
> **Mime:** (…) … (H19:) As pledge for my hearth, I accept your head (:H19): (…) (H121a:) Three are the questions I freely ask (:H121a). (…) (H106:; H38: …) (H120:) You've traveled much on the earth's broad back and wandered far through the world (:H120):—(H38/H15 frag?:, H106:) now tell me … what is the race that trades in the depths of the earth ["Erde"—Erda] (:H38/H15 frag?, :H106)?
>
> **Wanderer:** (H38:) The Nibelungs trade in the depths of the earth: Nibelheim is their land. Black elves they are; Black-Alberich once watched over them as their lord (:H38). (H17/H38>>:) A magic ring's compelling power tamed his toiling people (:H17/H38); (H38:; H8/H45>>:) a glittering hoard of rich-gemmed jewels for him they heaped on high (:H38; :H8/H45): (H46 frag

orch >>:) it was meant to win him the world (:H46 frag orch). (H19/H38) (...)

Mime: (H38:; H106: ...) (H120 vari:) Much, Wanderer, I see you know of the earth's umbilical nest ["Erde Nabelnest"—Erda's "navel-nest"] ... (:H120 vari).

Wotan introduces a new motif H121ab while staking his head in this Contest of Knowledge, telling Mime that Wotan's head is Mime's if Mime fails to ask what he needs to know, and if Wotan doesn't redeem his head with his lore. Mime will indeed fail to ask what he needs (i.e., what Wotan needs) to know about how man might achieve redemption, and will lose his head (Mime is Wotan's head) to Wotan's proxy Siegfried (Wotan's heart). We can construe H121ab as the embodiment of the fact that while Mime's mind grasps practical knowledge of the real world, it fails to grasp the need for, and means to achieve, redemption. Mime is too wise, too conscious, for that.

Mime's first question is, who are the beings who "trade" in the bowels of the earth, i.e., Erda. The notion that the Nibelungs "trade" seems to be a holdover from a concept of the Nibelungs as businessmen or traders which, along with Wotan's remark in R.3 that Alberich's hoard seems useless since nothing can be "bought" with it in Nibelheim, Wagner hasn't carried over into his final conception of the Nibelungs. There are several other instances in which Wagner seems to have overlooked some passages when updating the whole of his *Ring* to make each detail consistent with his final concept of the characters and plot. Wotan summarizes the Nibelungs' history, particularly Alberich's enslavement of his fellow dwarfs. We learn from Wotan that the Nibelungs are black elves, and their lord Alberich is Black-Alberich, in direct contrast with Wotan's subsequent description of the gods of Valhalla as elves of light, and of Wotan as "Light-Alberich." Mime's unusual description of Nibelheim, where Alberich rules, as the earth's "umbilical-nest" (Erda's Navel-nest), is particularly striking. This further confirms that Alberich affirms Mother Nature's knowledge of all that was, is, and will be, the objective world.

Mime now asks Wotan to describe the race that inhabits the earth's broad back, and for his final question asks Wotan to tell who dwells on the cloud-covered heights:

[pp. 210–11] **Mime:** (H106:) ... what's the race that rests on the earth's ["Erde"—Erda] ... back (:H106)?

[The Wanderer tells Mime the Giants inhabit the earth's surface, that, envying Alberich's power, (H106:) they won his hoard and ring, and that Fafner having murdered his brother Fasolt, Fafner now guards the hoard as Dragon: (...)]

Mime: (...) ... (H38/H15 frag:; H106:) which is the race that dwells on cloud-covered heights (:H38/H15 frag; :H106)?

Wanderer: On cloud-covered heights there dwell the gods: (H18a >>:) Valhalla is their hall (:H18a). (H18b:) Light-elves they are; Light-Alberich,

Wotan, rules their host (:H18b). [[**H122 orch:**]] [= H2/H52 vari] From the World-Ash's holiest bough he made himself a shaft (H19 orch): though the trunk may wither (:H122 orch), the spear shall never fail (H19 orch); [[**H123 orch:**]] [Possibly a H19 vari] with the point of the weapon (H19 orch:) Wotan governs the world (:H123 orch; :H19 orch). [[**H124 orch:**]] [= H26 vari] Hallowed treaties' binding runes he whittled into its shaft (:H124 orch): [[**H123 orch:**]] he who wields the spear (H19) that Wotan's fist still spans (H43 orch:) holds within his hand control over all the world (:H123 orch; :H43 orch). (H17:) Before him bowed the Nibelungs' host (:H17); (H43:) the brood of giants was tamed by his counsel (:H43). ([[**H123 orch:**]]; H119:) Forever they all obey the mighty lord of the spear (:H123 orch; :H119). (H19: ... he strikes the ground with his spear; a distant roll of thunder can be heard, causing Mime to jump ... .)

Mime's question regarding the Giants Wotan answers in a straightforward manner, except that he seems to suggest the Giants alone secured Alberich's Hoard and Ring by omitting Wotan's and Loge's role in dispossessing Alberich of them and giving them to the Giants in exchange for Freia. However, since the Giants symbolize man's instincts of self-preservation and desire, in that sense the Giants did indeed secure the Ring and Hoard. Wagner's employment of H106, one of the motifs, derived from Loge's H24, which expresses cunning, as Wotan tells Mime " ... the mighty hoard they [the Giants] won for themselves ... ," informs us subliminally of the role Loge and Wotan played.

In Wotan's answer to Mime's question about the gods, Wotan describes himself, somewhat surprisingly, as "Light-Alberich." But Wotan doesn't call himself "Light-Alberich" merely because he calls Alberich "Black-Alberich," as a way of contrasting the lord of the dark elves with the lord of the light elves. The problem with this thesis is that Black-Alberich, throughout the *Ring*, is almost always called only "Alberich." If we construe the name "Alberich" as meaning "Elf-Lord," on the assumption that the German word Alb or Alp stands for elf, and erich references the word "reich," for kingdom, rendering "Alberich" in translation as something like "Lord of the elves' kingdom," then on this interpretation Alberich is the lord of all elves, both dark and light. For only Alberich is granted the generic title "Elf-lord" under this interpretation. Dark-Alberich and Light-Alberich are two halves of the same coin. This identity of Wotan (Light-Alberich) and Alberich can also be heard in Wagner's employment of H43 (Alberich's "Power of the Ring") as Wotan describes the power he wields as lord of the Spear.

Wotan the Wanderer recounts for Mime the history of his Spear of divine authority, describing how he cut it from the holiest branch of the World-Ash Tree, whose new motif H122 Dunning describes as the compound H2/H52, and Cooke describes as a rhythmic variant, in ¾ time, of H52. However, H122 is only the first of two wholly distinct motifs associated with the World-Ash. The second, H157, is introduced in T.P.A as the Norns narrate their version of world-history, repeating some of the things Wotan is now telling Mime. The orchestra also introduces here the definitive version of Motif H123 (Power of the Gods) as

Wotan proclaims that the wielder of the Spear, Wotan, rules the world, but it will re-occur in a variant form in *Twilight of the Gods*, ironically in association with the twilight of the gods. The World-Ash, whose most sacred branch Wotan broke off to make his Spear of Divine Authority, does double duty as a metaphor both for the Biblical Tree of Life, and also (in its embodiment as Wotan's Spear) the Tree of Knowledge, the cause of the Fall. Wagner may have been influenced by Feuerbach's metaphor in which the Tree of Life can be construed as the network of all living things, the Tree of Life's highest branch ultimately reaching the bitter fruit of human consciousness through evolution. [See 23F-TDI, p. 152] It's in this sense that the wound Wotan inflicted on the World-Ash Tree by breaking off its holiest branch to make his Spear kills it. This is an image of Wotan's sin of matricide, religious man's figurative killing of Mother Nature, Erda, through his ethic of world-denial. Cooke, in a somewhat tortuous argument, derived H123 (Power of the Gods) from H19, Wotan's Spear. But H123 seems almost to be a variant of H1, the Primal Nature Motif. It's perhaps significant that we hear the first World-Ash Motif H122, compounded of H2 and H52, each derived directly from H1, as Wotan describes how he broke a branch from the holiest bough of the World-Ash to make his Spear.

New Motif H124 is introduced as Wotan describes how he whittled "hallowed treaties' binding runes" into the shaft of his new-made Spear, with which he ruled the world. But H124's genealogy says otherwise: it's a member of the family of motifs which includes H24, H26, H42, and H106, a set whose conceptual associations include Wotan's intent to employ Loge's cunning to break the treaties he's made (H26, and H24), and Mime's cunning machinations (H42, and H106).

As the Wanderer declares the universal authority Wotan won through his Spear, and that his rule embraces both the Nibelungs and the Giants, we hear the Ring Motif H17, which is the basis for the Valhalla Motif H18, and H43 (Power of the Ring), further establishing the ultimate identity of Alberich and Wotan. The Wanderer's (Wotan's) assertion of power in Wotan's name is over-optimistic: he's rapidly losing his former power to both Alberich (and eventually, his proxy Hagen) and Wotan's heir Siegfried. Judging from Mime's subsequent remarks, after Wotan produces a thunder-clap with his spear, Mime presumably has guessed the true identity of his disguised guest.

Wotan has successfully answered Mime's three questions, which concerned only practical matters on which Mime was already fully informed. Mime tries to dismiss him, but Wotan insists on parity and requires of Mime that he now answer three questions correctly, or his head will be forfeit:

[p. 212] Wanderer: (H120:) You ought to have asked what you needed to know (:H120); (H119:) my head stood bail for knowledge (:H119): (H19) since you still do not know what you need to know, I'll now take yours in pledge. (H19) (H120 vari:) Your greeting, I thought, was unfit for a guest ... (:H120 vari). By the rules of the wager I'll take you as pawn if you cannot easily answer three questions: (H19) ... !

> **Mime:** (... (H38:; [[H125 orch:]]) It's long since I quit my native land, long since I left my mother's womb (:H38; :H125 orch); (H18ab:) Wotan's eye has lighted upon me. ... Into my cave he peered (:H18ab): my mother's wit grows weak before it. [[H125 orch >>:]] But since I now need to be wise, Wanderer, ask away (:H125 orch)! (H38)

Mime is precisely wrong: he doesn't need to be wise, but rather, he needs to have a heart, in order to answer the questions Wotan now asks him, the questions Mime would have asked Wotan had Mime acknowledged his need for redemption. This is what Wotan means when he tells Mime that he failed to ask what he needed to know. Mime needed to ask how Nothung could be re-forged, innocence restored, and who could do it. For Nothung, whose motif's second segment H56b is the Primal Nature Motif H1, is the means to restore lost innocence. Mime is fallen beyond hope of redemption: he lives too much in his head, which is why he'll soon lose it (figuratively). Mime, with unwitting irony insisting that he must now be wise, when he can only save his head by renouncing its wisdom, expresses his hope that he'll answer Wotan's questions and thereby save his head, as we hear Mime's new motif H125, which has the air of something furtive and privately conspiratorial about it. But Mime's effort to redeem his head will fail in the face of Siegfried's innocence. Mime says something else rather interesting: it's long since he left his native land, long since he left his mother's womb. Wotan's eye, he says, has peered on him, and his mother-wit grows weak before it. He seems to be acknowledging that his unwanted guest is the one-eyed Wotan, but perhaps he's saying something else as well. In S.3.2, when Wotan the Wanderer confronts Siegfried before Siegfried plunges into Loge's ring of fire to wake Brünnhilde, Wotan will describe Siegfried as the eye Wotan is missing, so Mime may be obliquely referring to Siegfried as well. Mime's appeal to his native land, his mother's womb, and his mother-wit, all seem to invoke Erda, Mother Nature, as she's known objectively to Alberich, a source of worldly power. It's Mother Nature—as known by the head—which grows weak before Wotan's missing eye Siegfried, Wotan's heart, who'll re-forge Nothung and eliminate Wotan's head Mime with it.

The three questions the Wanderer chooses to ask Mime concern the Wälsung hero-race, its greatest representative, Siegfried, the sword Nothung (i.e., the various means Wotan employs to redeem the gods from Alberich's Ring Curse), and Mime's formerly secret plan to exploit Siegfried in order to win Ring, Hoard, and power from both the gods and Alberich:

> **[pp. 212–14] Wanderer:** ... (H70:) what is the race which Wotan acted badly towards (:H70) ... : H104:) and yet which is dearest of all to him (:H104)?
>
> **Mime:** (...) (H125) (H70 vari:; H25a?:) The Wälsungs are the favoured race which Wotan fathered and fondly cherished (:H70 vari; :H25a?), while showing them disfavour. (H70 vari:; H25a?:) Siegmund and Sieglinde were sired by Wälse ... (:H70 vari; :H25a?): (H93a:) Siegfried they begat themselves (:H93a), the strongest scion of the Wälsungs. (H38) (...)

Wanderer: (...) (H67 voc?:) You've acquitted yourself of my opening question (:H67 voc?); ... (H106/H38>>:) A wily Nibelung cares for Siegfried (:H38; :H106): (H47 orch:) Fafner he's to kill for him, so that he may gain the ring and so be master of the hoard (:H47 orch). Which is the sword that Siegfried must wield if Fafner's death is to follow?

Mime: (... H125>>:) Nothung's the name of a fearsome sword (H56); (H19?:) Wotan drove it into an ash-tree's trunk (:H19?): it was meant for the man who could draw it forth ... . (H38:; H125:) ... Siegmund the valiant (H56ab) alone could do so; (H19 frag?) fighting, he bore it in battle until it was splintered by Wotan's spear. (H38>>:; H125:) A wily dwarf now keeps the fragments; he knows that only with Wotan's sword (H93a/H125:) can that foolish and foolhardy child, Siegfried, harm the dragon (:H38; :H93a/H125). (...)

Wanderer: (... (H125:) You're the wittiest of the wise: who could match you in cunning? (...) (:H125) (...) (H38>>:) Tell me, you wily weapon-smith, (H38) who do you think will forge (H93a) Nothung, the sword, out of these mighty fragments? (...)

Mime: (in a screeching tone of voice: H109>>>>:) The fragments! The sword! Alas! (...) (H108 vari or frag:) Accursed steel, alas that I ever stole you! (H8/H109>>:) It has trapped me in torment and need ["Noth"]; it remains unyielding, I cannot hammer it ... (:H108 vari or frag; :H8/H109 >>)! (... H110:) The wisest of smiths is now at a loss: (H107 vari:) who'll forge the sword if I cannot do so? How should I know of this wonder (:H110; :H107 vari)?

When Wotan asks Mime which was the race which he both favored and disfavored, and the name of the sword Siegfried must yield if he's to fulfill Mime's desire that he kill Fafner and win the Ring and Hoard for Mime, Mime answers readily. Mime's knowledge of the details of events which he presumably didn't witness is amazing. He not only knows the whole history of the Wälsungs (he could have learned much of this from Sieglinde), but he knows they were sired by Wotan, and that Wotan drove Nothung into Hunding's House-Ash for Siegmund to find. One explanation is that Wagner, the *Ring*'s author, knows all these things, and may not have worked out in detail the full range of knowledge that each of his fictional characters ought logically to possess. But another explanation is that Mime represents the practical, utilitarian, pedestrian aspect of Wotan's own persona. And of course Mime's knowledge could be part of the legendary history which is passed down through the generations from a distant past, as a common inheritance. However, when Wotan asks his third and final question, who'll re-forge Nothung's fragments into a new sword, Mime is thrown into an apoplexy of confusion and fear, and we recall how Wotan in his confession to Brünnhilde was thrown into an apoplexy by his inability to create a free hero. Mime wonders who could forge Nothung if he, the wisest of smiths, can't. We hear H93 (the fearless hero Siegfried's motif) as Wotan poses this question, since Siegfried alone can re-forge his father's sword Nothung. Mime can't answer Wotan's third question because Mime is too wise, too conscious, isn't gifted with the unconscious artistic inspiration which alone can grant wholeness to the sword with which Siegfried will eliminate Fafner (existential fear) and Mime (egoistic thought, Wotan's head), and win the muse of unconscious artistic inspiration, Brünnhilde.

Wotan chastises Mime for having asked of things wholly irrelevant to Mime's immediate concerns, while ignoring what most concerned Mime. Wotan now tells Mime what he needed to know:

> [p. 215] **Wanderer:** ... (H45?:) you asked after futile, far-off ["Fernen"] things (:H45?), (H35 vari or H107 vari?:) but what concerned you most closely and what you most need to know, you omitted to ask (:H35 vari or H107 vari?). (H56ab) (H19/H38:) ... I've won your wily head. ...(H47) listen, you ill-fated dwarf: [[**H126 voc:**]] only he who never knew fear (H56ab) will forge the sword anew (:H126 voc). (...) (H34:) Henceforth ward your wise head well: (H93a:) Forfeit I leave it to him (:H93a) (H93c vari voc:) who knows not the meaning of fear (:H93c vari voc). (H34: He ... disappears ... into the forest. ...)

If we examine Wotan's initial remark closely, and note that a H35 (Loveless) variant is heard as he points out that what Mime most needed to know he failed to inquire after, the implication is that Mime asked only about matters embraced by our general hoard of knowledge, which concern the ways of the world and its history, but neglected to ask about those things which could offer man redemption from the Fall, from lovelessness. It's Mime's objective knowledge—of what Wotan calls futile, far-off ("Fernen") things, accompanied by what sounds like the Hoard Motif H45 or a variant of it—which Brünnhilde redeems from its horror by distilling its essence as musical motifs. This term "far-off" ("Fernen") is Wagner's code-word for our objective knowledge, which Wotan had to cast away by storing it in Brünnhilde through his confession, so he could be reborn, minus the baggage of this worldly knowledge (which Mime wanted to teach Siegfried), as the innocent Siegfried, as per Wagner's following observation: "In the free self-determining of the Individuality there ... lies the basis of the social Religion of the Future ... ./(...) ... we may guess the measureless wealth of living individual relationships, if we take them as purely-human, ever ... present; i.e., if we think every extrahuman or non-present thing that in the State, as Property and historic Right, has placed ... between them, has torn asunder their ties of Love, ... if we think this all sent far away ["Fernen"?]." [514W-{50–1/51} *Opera and Drama*, PW Vol. II, pp. 202–203] This hoard of things that Wagner says we need to purge, to send far away, in order to leave the purely-human in its pristine innocence, includes all that's guarded by Fafner, namely, the Ring (the power of conscious, objective human thought), the Tarnhelm (imagination as employed by Alberich to acquire objective knowledge, rather than as employed by Loge for the sake of self-deception), and the Hoard of knowledge. What ought to have concerned Mime was how to re-forge Nothung (H107, heard here, symbolizes

Mime's inability to re-forge Nothung), i.e., how to restore lost innocence and obtain redemption from loveless, prosaic reality.

Wotan's head (Mime) was to all intents and purposes severed when Wotan confessed his unspoken secret to Brünnhilde, thereby repressing conscious thought of all that he loathed about himself into his unconscious mind. Siegfried's birth is tantamount to the substitution of Wotan's heart for his head, and therefore tantamount to Mime's (i.e., Wotan's) figurative decapitation by Siegfried. When Siegfried kills Mime with Nothung we're merely witnessing Wagner's dramatization of what's already effectively occurred, in much the same way that the events of R.2–4 are already implicit in the transformation of Alberich's Ring Motif H17ab into the first two segments of the Valhalla Motif H18ab. The same can be said of Siegfried's killing of Fafner in S.2.2. Siegfried's fearlessness and innocence, his birthright by virtue of being born metaphysically of Brünnhilde, is the death of Mime, who represents Wotan's prosaic aspect which Wotan (Siegfried) loathes and wishes to eliminate, and also the death of Fafner. As Mime said to Siegfried, "you'll be the death of me yet."

Mime isn't only incapable of being redeemed, but incapable of grasping his need for redemption. Mime is content with the real world as he finds it, in the sense that the means he seeks to satisfy his needs and desires and allay his fears are all found in the prosaic world. He doesn't reach out to art or metaphysics for consolation. He represents Wotan's reality principle. Wagner, of course, said this about the Jews, imputing to them an inherent egoism, and a lack of capacity for redemption, which he, however, suspected was the essential characteristic of all men, as dramatized in Wotan's paralyzing self-analysis. Wagner's observation that the Jews can't be redeemed because their nature condemns them to the real world is the thought behind Wotan's self-doubt and self-loathing, for Wotan is Wagner's portrait of man in all his facets. [See 1071W-{2/10/81} CD Vol. II, p. 618]

SIEGFRIED ≠ ACT ONE, SCENE THREE

(MIME'S FORGE)
MIME AND SIEGFRIED

Mime is about to expose himself as the very embodiment of the "… fear of harm that always accompanies man," the egoism at the root of Wotan's "religious imagination" which Siegfried, "the free imagination of the artist," will eliminate. [269F-LER, p. 196] Feuerbach authored another evocative description of the nature of this existential fear, "the *infinite* fear of the human soul," which he describes as a natural consequence of the abstract, generalizing nature of the human mind (the Ring's power), which transcends particular fears and seems to capture what Mime so vividly and comically illustrates. [319F-LER, p. 287] Wagner dramatized Feuerbachian existential fear, which besets man everywhere because it's his essence, in Mime's following bizarre attack of nerves. This prompts Mime's imagination to visualize a variety of inchoate, indefinable horrors (set to orchestral music evoking both Loge's protective ring of fire around

Brünnhilde and the Serpent Motif H47, which represents existential fear), culminating in his horrific vision of an attack by Fafner:

> [pp. 215–6] **Mime:** (H33:; H32B:) Accursed light! Is the air there on fire? (H105:) What's flashing and gleaming, (H34>>/H47:) what's glinting and whirling ... ? (...) (H34>>>:) It booms and crashes and crackles this way! (...) The dragon is trying to catch me! Fafner! Fafner (:H33/H32B; :H47)! (Siegfried bursts through the undergrowth. ... H56ab; H117; H118)
>
> **Siegfried:** (...) Quick! How's the sword coming on? (H109/H34, H38: ... .)

The most fascinating aspect of Mime's spell of delusional hysteria is that the music Wagner chose to depict it evokes Loge's ring of fire (intended to scare away all suitors of the sleeping Brünnhilde except the fearless Siegfried), for we hear Loge's Motifs H32B, H34, H33, and even H105 (Magic Fire). But we also hear the Serpent Motif H47, and recall that both Alberich and Fafner used the Tarnhelm (imagination) to transform themselves into Serpents of fear to warn away potential rivals for possession of the Ring's power. But Fafner sleeps while prohibiting man's access to Alberich's Ring, Tarnhelm, and Hoard, whereas Alberich hopes to impose their power on humanity. H47 represents not only the primal fear of pain and death, but fear of the truth, which unconsciously inspires religio-artistic heroes—modeled on their archetype Loge—to throw a veil of Maya (illusion), like Loge's protective and threatening Ring of fire, around that which instills existential fear in man, the truth. Brünnhilde, repository of Wotan's hoard of knowledge, the secret Wotan so feared that he daren't speak it aloud in words (consciously), holds that knowledge of the gods' fated doom which is the source of Wotan's (historical man's) collective fear. This is the fear which stems from our subliminal knowledge that in religious belief and our propagation of transcendent values we're deceiving ourselves, i.e., depending on Loge. Religious man's dependence on faith as a pretext to avoid having to reflect on the origin and true nature of his beliefs, is a key expression of this existential fear. Fafner, guarding the keys to Alberich's objective power to drive away anyone who might try to access them, is an image of the stranglehold which faith places on freedom of inquiry. Fafner/fear has imprisoned the human mind ever since Wotan and Loge launched human history by dispossessing Alberich of his Ring power and handing it over to the Giants.

Now Mime confirms what we've suspected, that he's too "wise," i.e., too motivated by conscious intention, and thus too fearful for his well-being, to be gifted with that unconscious inspiration necessary to instinctively re-forge Nothung. Having piqued fearless Siegfried's curiosity, Mime offers him the opportunity to learn what fear (the Fall) is:

> [pp. 216–8] **Siegfried:** (H109:) Were you honing my sword for me (:H109)?
>
> **Mime:** (...) (H47:) (...) (... H126:) 'Only he who never (:H47) (H56ab) knew fear can forge the sword anew (:H126).' (H34 orch:; H35 voc:) I've grown too wise for work like that (:H34 orch: :H35 voc)! [**Siegfried:** (...)] I've wagered away my wily head: (... H93a:) forfeit, I've lost it to him 'who

never learned the meaning of fear (:H93a).' [**Siegfried:** (...)] (H34:) Well might I flee from the man who knows fear (:H34):—(H110) but that I have failed to teach the child! Like a fool, I forgot what's uniquely good: (H114:) he was meant to learn to love me;—alas, that went amiss (:H114)! (H126 voc:) How shall I teach him what fear is (:H126 voc)?

Siegfried: (seizing him: H109:) (...) What have you furbished today (:H109)?

Mime: (H34:) Concerned but for you, I was sunk in thought of how to teach you something weighty (:H34). (H34) [**Siegfried:** (...)] (... H34:; H126 voc?:) For you, I have learned the meaning of fear, so I might teach it to you, you fool (:H34; :H126 voc?).

Siegfried: (... H109:) What's this about fear (:H109)?

Mime: You've never felt it and yet you want to leave the woods and go out into the world? (H56ab) What use is the stoutest of swords if fear is still a stranger to you? [**Siegfried:** (...)] (H65:; H110 orch:) (...) Your mother's counsel (:H65; :H110 orch) speaks through me: what I promised her (H65:; H110 orch:) I must now discharge and not let you leave for (:H65; :H110 orch) the cunning world until you've learned the meaning of fear. (H38; H109/H34)

Mime has suddenly realized that, having failed to teach Siegfried fear, Siegfried may be the fearless hero to whom Mime's head is forfeit. He urgently needs to teach Siegfried fear so he won't become Siegfried's victim. So Mime tells Siegfried he's learned the meaning of fear for him so Mime can teach it to him. Mime's sole purpose in bringing Siegfried up was that he'd be fearless enough to kill Fafner and win the sources of Alberich's power for Mime, so Mime would be invulnerable to Alberich's threat. Mime must solve this conundrum or risk either his head, or his bid for power, or both. Mime's plight suggests another parallel with Wotan. Wotan has, in a sense, learned fear for Siegfried, through his historical experience which Wotan confessed to Brünnhilde, so Siegfried, thanks to Brünnhilde keeping Wotan's unspoken secret for him and protecting him from its paralyzing influence, will have the courage to do that deed which Wotan's fear precludes him from performing. Through Siegfried's muse Brünnhilde Wotan can teach Siegfried fear safely, inspiring him to do what must be done to redeem the gods.

Since Mime represents Wotan's prosaic, practical motives behind his longing for redemption, the fact that Mime failed to teach Siegfried fear stems from the same motive as Wotan's longing for a hero who'd be freed from it. For Siegfried to fulfill Wotan's desire that he win control over Alberich's Ring, without being consciously influenced by Wotan, Siegfried the artist-hero must be subliminally inspired by Wotan's fear of the gods' doom to do that deed which the god can't do, take possession of Alberich's Ring from Fafner aesthetically. Mime asks himself how he can teach Siegfried fear, but Wotan already solved that problem by leaving Siegfried heir to Brünnhilde who, possessing Wotan's knowledge of all that he fears, will teach Siegfried fear, but unlike Fafner (from whom Mime will suggest Siegfried learn fear) teach Siegfried also how he can forget his fear, through art's Wonder. This is why Wagner musically anticipated Siegfried's loving union with Brünnhilde when he called up the motifs which evoke Loge's ring of fire to rise out of the orchestra alongside the Serpent Motif H47 (Fafner as Fear). This also explains the otherwise mysterious recurrence of H47 at the height of Siegfried's and Brünnhilde's love duet in S.3.3. Siegfried the artist-hero's unconscious mind Brünnhilde (repository of Wotan's hoard of fearful knowledge) gives birth to the redemptive musical motifs which are the secular world's substitute for dying religious faith, that faith predicated on, and protected by, fear of the truth (Fafner). To emancipate himself from the gods' protection and influence, i.e., from religious faith's fear of truth, Siegfried must seek inspiration solely in the muse of art Brünnhilde's love, in which religious man's longing for transcendent value (formerly the province of religious faith, Fafner) lives on subliminally, as music. Therefore H47 is transferred from Fafner, who can't teach Siegfried fear, to Brünnhilde, who'll teach Siegfried both fear and how to redeem himself from it.

In order to persuade Siegfried of the necessity of learning fear, Mime suggests Siegfried still lacks the one thing he most needs to make his way in the cunning world, fear. To overcome Siegfried's skepticism, Mime appeals to Siegfried's mother Sieglinde, intimating that Mime is acting on her desire that Siegfried not go out into the world without first learning fear. We hear H65, which calls to mind the tragic fate which the Wälsungs suffer as unwitting proxies in Wotan's futile quest for redemption, and Sieglinde's sympathy for their Noth. Presumably Mime invokes Siegfried's mother merely to exploit his sore point, since it seems unlikely that Sieglinde would've requested that Mime teach Siegfried fear. But since Brünnhilde (and in a sense even her mother Erda) is Siegfried's metaphysical mother, this poses the question from another standpoint. Erda taught Wotan existential fear, and their daughter Brünnhilde will teach Siegfried fear subliminally once he penetrates her protective ring of fire and wakes her. Perhaps Mime is invoking Siegfried's metaphysical mother Erda in this sense, as the source of Mime's "mother-wit."

Mime now describes for Siegfried what it's like to experience fear physiologically, recalling his spell of hysteria. He's accompanied this time not only by Loge's motifs evoking his protective ring of fire, and H47 (Fear), but in addition by H102, which Brünnhilde introduced as she begged Wotan to protect her defenseless sleep with something fearful which will keep all but fearless heroes (the unconsciously inspired artist hero) at bay, and by H105 (Magic Fire):

[pp. 218–9] Siegfried: (… H109/H34:) (…) What is this fear (:H109/H34)?

Mime: (H34 orch/H47 frag voc:) Have you never felt in the gloomy forest as darkness spreads to some twilit spot and, from afar, a rustling, humming, roaring sound draws near, a furious booming crashes closer (:H34 orch/H47 frag voc), (H105:; H102:) a whirling flicker flits around you and, swelling and whirring, floats towards you (:H105; :H102),—(trembling) (H34>>:)

have you not felt the terror then, that, creepingly, seizes hold of your limbs (:H34)? (...)—(H102>>:) If you've never felt all this, then fear remains unknown to you (:H102).

Siegfried: (... H102: [plus a beautiful orchestral rolling figure conveying a Nature-Mood]) Passing strange all this must be (:H102 [plus Nature-Mood rolling figure])! (H93a:) I feel that my heart beats firmly and strongly (:H93a). (H33: [in a transfigured variant of the "magic fire music" H105], H102>>:) The shuddering and shivering, searing and trembling, burning and fainting, hammering and quaking (:H33; :H102), how dearly I long to feel this dread (H102:) and yearningly crave (tenderly) such delights (:H102).

Siegfried isn't intimidated by Mime's description of fear, accompanied as it is by motival evocations of the sleeping Brünnhilde from whom—as Siegfried anticipates as he tells Mime he longs to experience this phenomenon—Siegfried eventually will learn the meaning of fear. When Siegfried poses the question, how could Mime, a coward, teach Siegfried fear, Mime offers the solution: Fafner, the Serpent, will teach Siegfried fear:

[p. 219] Siegfried: But, Mime, how can you teach me it? (H102/H34) How could a coward be my master? (H34)

Mime: (...) (H102) (H47>>:) I know of an evil dragon who's killed and devoured many: (H126:) Fafner will teach you fear (:H47) if you'll follow me to his lair (:H126). (H102) [**Siegfried:** (...)] Neidhöhle ["Envy-cave"] it is called: to the east, at the edge of the wood. (H102)

Siegfried: And so it's not far from the world? (H102)

Mime: It lies very close to the cave!

Mime's answer to Siegfried's question, where does Fafner live, is that Fafner's lair is Envy-Cave ("Neidhöhle"). Fafner's lair is the embodiment of all those aspects of society, the ways of the wider world, such as the desire for permanence, property, security, quiet, unquestioned faith, and unchanging tradition, which are enemies of the creative soul for whom change and variety are life-blood. Wagner clarifies this with a little piece of wit: to Siegfried's question whether Neidhöhle is far from the world, Mime answers that the world lies very close to the cave. Fafner's (self-preservation's) stranglehold over freedom of thought, in order to preserve the status quo, is the very essence of the human world into which Siegfried hopes to plunge once Nothung has been re-forged. Neidhöhle isn't far from the world: it is the world. And this world into which Siegfried told Mime he intends to go, wielding Nothung, is the world where Mime warns Siegfried cunning will trap him if he's not armed with the fear which everyone else in the world lives by. Siegfried will eventually succumb to the cunning ways of the world of men when in T.1.2 he arrives at the Hall of the Gibichungs, inhabited by Alberich's son Hagen (Mime's nephew), and Hagen's half siblings (children of Gibich and Hagen's mother Grimhilde) Gunther and Gutrune. But first, Siegfried needs to liberate knowledge (Alberich's Hoard), imagination (Alberich's Tarnhelm), and the gift of thought itself (Alberich's Ring) from the fear (Fafner) which religious faith engenders, to free art from its servitude to religion, so his new secular art (Wagner's art) can restore lost innocence.

Siegfried asks after his father's sword which he'd demanded Mime re-forge. Mime admits he hasn't the remotest idea how to re-forge it, so Siegfried tells him to get out of the way: Siegfried will take in hand the re-forging of his father's sword:

> [pp. 219–21] **Siegfried:** [[H127 orch:]] [= H108 frag vari] Thither you shall lead me (:H127 orch): when I've learned the meaning of fear, I'll away then into the world! (…) Make me the sword, in the world I mean to wield it.
>
> **Mime:** (H109:) The sword? O woe ["Noth"]! **[Siegfried:** (…)] (H110 orch >>:; H43 hint?:) Accursed steel! (…) No dwarf's resources can master the stubborn spell (:H110 orch; :H43 hint?). (H34:) He who's never known fear (H110 orch:) would sooner find the art ["Kunst"] (:H34; :H110 orch).
>
> **Siegfried:** (…) Away with the (H116) bungler! … For me my father's blade will doubtless fit together: (H116 hint?) I'll forge the sword myself! ([[H127 orch:]] Scattering mime's tools, he sets to work impetuously.)
>
> **Mime:** [[H127 orch:]] Had you attentively studied the art, (H38) it would surely have stood you in good stead; [[H127 orch >>:]] but you were always lax in your lessons: (H38:) how do you plan to prepare it now?
>
> **Siegfried:** [[H127 orch:]] Could the lad achieve what the master can't do, (H38:) even though he had always obeyed him (:H127 orch; :H38)? (…) [**Mime:** (…); **Siegfried:** (…)]
>
> **Mime:** [[H127 orch:]] You're filing the file away and rubbing the rasp to shreds: why pound the steel to pieces?
>
> **Siegfried:** Spun out into splinters I have to see it: what lies in two, I thus force together. (…)
>
> **Mime:** (aside) No sage can help here, (H108:) I see that clearly: here only folly can help the fool (:H108)! (H108) [[H127 orch:]] How he stirs and mightily strives: the steel's disappearing and yet he doesn't grow hot (:H127 orch)! (Siegfried has fanned the forge fire until it glows brighter than ever: H33/H32AB?/H105 vari over H108 frags [sounding like a laugh]; H34) I've grown as old as cave and wood but never saw the like! (H108/H108 frags)

Mime wonders how Siegfried, who never attentively followed Mime's lessons, could possibly re-forge the sword now on his own, but Siegfried retorts that since Mime's skill has always failed, Siegfried would have been wasting his time following his directions. When Mime complains that Siegfried has filed the sword's fragments into mere splinters, Siegfried insists that only by reducing this sword to its smallest constituent parts can he re-forge the whole in his own image, so to speak. Siegfried the artist-hero needs to be able to freely re-compose the elements of his religio-artistic heritage—i.e., man's historical quest to restore lost innocence in various religions, moral philosophies, and art-forms—to create something from it entirely new, coherent and whole. Mime notes that in this case only folly can help the fool to do something where no sage can help. Siegfried is accomplishing something—seemingly by spontaneous instinct—which transcends what an uninspired craftsman would require conscious intellectual labor to achieve. Mime, astonished at Siegfried's creative vitality, says to himself that he's grown old as cave and wood but never saw the like. We're reminded that Fricka's primary complaint to Wotan about the Wälsung twins' illicit activities was that they were unprecedented, and of Wotan's rebuke that she only understands what's habitual but can't recognize what's never before come to pass. Mime can only mime, repeat the past: Siegfried alone brings forth the new. Feuerbach captured this distinction between the uninspired laborer Mime, and the inspired genius Siegfried, neatly in his following observation: "Genius is immediate, sensuous knowledge. What talent [Mime] has only in the head genius [Siegfried] has in the flesh and blood ... ." [184F-PPF, p. 56]

In the meantime, Siegfried fans the flames of the fire in which he'll re-forge Nothung, accompanied by several of Loge's motifs. Nothung embodies Nature's creative principle, natural necessity, so Siegfried will wield his sword as a symbolic phallus which won't only penetrate Loge's veil of illusion to access the dangerous truth hidden within it (this is one of the things G. B. Shaw got right in his allegorical interpretation: he stated, accurately, that Loge's ring of fire is an illusion that hides the truth, which sleeps with Brünnhilde, that the church, religious faith, is founded on a lie—Shaw, pp. 32–33), but will penetrate the womb of Wotan's wishes, his unconscious mind Brünnhilde, to inseminate her with the poetic idea (Alberich's Ring Curse) which will bring the redemptive Wagnerian music-drama to birth.

Now Mime faces the same conundrum which besets Wotan. On the one hand, how can Mime obtain the Ring and Hoard, to keep Alberich from regaining their power and enslaving him, and instead subject Alberich and the gods to enslavement, if Siegfried learns fear from Fafner and is therefore too fearful to slay him? On the other hand, if Siegfried remains fearless, slays Fafner, and wins the Ring and Hoard, this is a moot point, since he's predestined to slay Mime:

[pp. 221–2] **Mime:** (H127 >>:) He'll succeed with the sword ... : fearless, he'll furbish it whole,—(H125/H32B:) the Wanderer knew he would (:H125/H32B)!—(H8/H34:) How can I save my timid head (:H8/H34)? (H93a voc:) It will fall to the valiant lad (:H93a voc) if Fafner doesn't teach him fear! (...) (H47 >>:) But alas, poor me! For how could he slay the dragon if he'd first learnt fear from the beast (:H47)? How could I win the ring for myself? (H125>>:) Accursed quandary! (...) (:H125; :H127).

The disqualifying disadvantage that Wotan's martyred heroes (assembling in Valhalla) labored under was that their heroic deeds perpetuated the gods' rule (religious faith) when Wotan knew their rule was founded on loathsome egoism and self-deception, sins which Alberich would inevitably expose. To obtain redemption from the Mime-like, prosaic aspects of religious faith which made it vulnerable to Alberich's threat to expose its hypocrisy, Wotan needs a hero who'll spontaneously breach faith without fear of suffering the consequences. Only the unconsciously inspired secular artist can fulfill his hidden purpose. Mime seeks to exploit the artist-hero Siegfried for egoistic ends, while Wotan, though covertly inspired by Mime's egoism, is prepared to sacrifice this prosaic aspect of his character so the artist Siegfried, purified of Wotan's egoism, can redeem the gods. Wotan will solve Mime's problem in the following way. Wotan needs to jettison all those aspects of religion which apparently stem from egoism, all religious beliefs and promises which stake a false claim on the truth by offering us the illusion that our fear of death and pain, and longing for bliss, will be assuaged infinitely in Valhalla. For this Wotan needs a hero who, of his own nature, will slay Fafner and Mime, i.e., slay the fear and practical egoism behind religious faith, to take aesthetic possession of our Hoard of knowledge, our imagination (the Tarnhelm), and our symbolic mind (the Ring), by covertly employing Alberich's mental gifts to produce redemptive art. Our religious longing for transcendent value can live on, reborn, seemingly purged of religion's practical egoism, in the secular art Brünnhilde will inspire Siegfried to create. Brünnhilde, not Fafner, will teach Siegfried fear indeed, but unconsciously and therefore safely. In figurative sexual union with his muse Siegfried will draw subliminal inspiration from Wotan's forbidden hoard of knowledge to sustain the protective veil of Wahn which masks the fatal truth under the consolation of illusion. So Wotan (religion) will lose his head (Mime), but not his heart, which will live on in Siegfried's love for Brünnhilde. By killing Fafner, religious faith's fear of freedom of inquiry, Siegfried will supplant practical faith with seemingly innocent, disinterested art-for-art's-sake.

After learning from Mime the name of his father Siegmund's sword, Nothung, Siegfried commences smelting it while singing a heroic song celebrating the sword's mysterious history, the process of its manufacture, and its personality. Wagner presents here and in Siegfried's forging song which follows a musico-dramatic celebration of the unfettered creative will claiming its freedom with vital heroic force. Mime, scrambling to sort out how he can exploit Siegfried to kill Fafner and win the Ring power for himself, without losing his head to Siegfried, hits on the idea of drugging Siegfried after Siegfried has won the Ring, so Mime can both win the Ring's power and free himself from the fearless hero predestined to take his head:

[pp. 222–3] (Siegfried has filed down the fragments and collected them in a crucible, which he ... places on the forge fire.)

Siegfried: Hey, Mime ... : what's the name of the sword that I've spun out into splinters? (H56ab)

Mime: ... [[H128 frag:]] Nothung's (:H128 frag) (H? voc [possibly motival]:) the name of the fearsome sword: your mother told me the tale (:H? voc—possibly motival).

(H127 >>: while singing the following Siegfried fans the flames with the bellows.)

Siegfried: (H127 vari:; [[**H128 voc:**]] [= H56a vari]) Nothung! Nothung! Fearsome sword (:H128)! Why did you have to shatter? [[**H129 voc:**]] [Possible H105 influence] I've turned your sharp-edged pride to chaff, in the melting-pot I smelt the splinters (:H129 voc). (H128 harmonic vari over H108 frags:) Hoho! Hoho! Hohei! Hohei! Hoho! [[**H130 voc:**]] Blow, you bellows, fan the flames (:H130 voc)! (H129 >>:) Wild in the woodland grew a tree: I felled it in the forest: the fallow ash I burned to charcoal, it now lies heaped on the hearth. (...)

Mime: ... He'll forge the sword and bring down Fafner: ... hoard and ring he'll wrest from the fray:—(H15 >>:) how can I gain what he's won (:H15)? (H38 >>:) With wit and cunning I'll win them both and keep my head unharmed (:H38). [**Siegfried:** (...)] (... H45 frag?:) When he's fought himself weary with the dragon, a drink may refresh him from his efforts (:H45 frag?). (H29b vari; H101 vari ["Brünnhilde's Magic Sleep" (based in turn on Fafner's motif Godhead Lost's second segment H29b), which sounds like the vari that accompanies Siegfried as he reaches the peak of the mountain where Wotan left Brünnhilde asleep, after breaking Wotan's Spear and penetrating Loge's ring of fire, in S.3.3]) From herbal juices I've gathered, I'll brew a drink for him; (H101: [strongly emphasized!!!]) he'll need to drink only very few drops (:H101 [strongly emphasized!!!]) before sinking, senseless, into sleep (:H29b vari; :H101 [music from S.3.3]): (H56ab vari:) with the selfsame weapon he won for himself ... I'll easily clear him out of the way and attain to both ring and hoard (:H56ab vari).

Siegfried's questioning Mime about the name of his father's sword, and Siegfried's smelting Nothung, has introduced three new motifs, H128, H129, and H130. H128's first segment, to which Siegfried sings "Nothung! Nothung!," is based on the octave drop introduced in Erda's proclamation that all things that are, end, the drop occurring on "Endet." This is the first segment of the sword motif H56a, which is followed by the Primal Nature Motif H1 in the second segment H56b. As a creative agent, an original artist who introduces the new, the revolutionary, into cultural evolution, Siegfried is an instrument of that natural necessity, including the necessity of death, which Erda acclaimed Nature's essence. This cosmic creativity embraces becoming and perishing. To embrace it, both Feuerbach and Wagner call on us to will the necessary. H129, "Siegfried's Smelting Motif," which follows the general contours of H118 (Siegfried's Mission), logically fits in with that musically related set of motifs which include H112, H118, and H135, the first being Mime's Starling Song concerning all that Siegfried owes to him, the second, H118, representing Siegfried's quest to emancipate himself from that debt, and H135 reminding us of Wotan's proclamation to Alberich in S.2.1 of Siegfried's ability to stand on his own feet. Siegfried's re-forging of the newly rediscovered sword Nothung, the link between his cultural ancestors and his destiny as a newly forged genius, the self-made hero Wotan longed for, is a key step in this process of emancipation. It dramatizes Wotan's remark during his confession to Brünnhilde that his imagined hero will have to make himself because Wotan can create only serfs. But the genealogy of this set of motifs also tells us that Siegfried can never escape his (Wotan's) debt to Alberich. H130, the last of these new motifs associated with Siegfried's smelting, is a frequently repeated descending refrain, heard as he sings "Blow, you bellows, fan the flame!"

Mime has devised a new scheme. By virtue of the vital force with which Siegfried is re-forging Nothung, Mime knows that Siegfried won't learn fear from Fafner, will kill Fafner, and will win the Ring and Hoard. So Mime hopes to cheat the fate the Wanderer laid out for him by mixing an herbal potion which will plunge Siegfried into sleep if he agrees to drink it as refreshment after his hard battle with Fafner. Mime then plans to dispatch Siegfried with Nothung and take possession of the Ring and Hoard he's won. But something wonderful and mysterious occurs in the play of motifs Wagner has chosen to convey Mime's machinations: we hear variants of H29b (Godhead Lost) and H101 (Brünnhilde's Magic Sleep) as he describes how he'll put Siegfried to sleep with this potion. These motival references aren't heard merely because Mime describes how he'll plunge Siegfried into sleep. H29b (Godhead Lost) is the basis for H101 (Brünnhilde's Magic Sleep). We also hear what seems a hint of H45 (Nibelung Hoard). H29b at its inception was associated with Fafner's intent to deprive the gods of Freia (goddess of love and immortality) so they'd die, i.e., lose their divine status, just as Wotan deprived Brünnhilde of her godhead while putting her to sleep. Wotan intends to let his free and fearless artist-hero Siegfried pay the price of Alberich's Noth so Siegfried can redeem the gods from Alberich's Ring Curse. Siegfried will not only ultimately be martyred by the Ring Curse, but must figuratively martyr himself by waking Brünnhilde to learn from her subliminally the meaning of Wotan's paralyzing fear, so he can draw the inspiration from Wotan's fearful hoard of repressed knowledge necessary to perpetuate man's religious longing for transcendence in the secular art Siegfried will create. Siegfried in a sense must die, while in union with Brünnhilde, to attain rebirth by producing a redemptive work of art, just as the allegedly immortal Wotan (religion) must pass away but is reborn in the immortal art that mortal Siegfried will create. In a manner of speaking, the fate Wotan's choice of Siegfried as his hero-redeemer condemns Siegfried to, inspired subliminally by Wotan's fear and self-interest, is akin to the fate which Mime plans to condemn Siegfried to suffer. We'll also learn later that Mime's potion, which Mime fails to persuade Siegfried to drink, will be recreated in Hagen's fateful potions that Gutrune and Mime's nephew Hagen will successfully persuade Siegfried to drink in T.1.2 and T.3.2.

As Siegfried continues singing his song extolling Nothung's virtues, he incorporates imagery strongly suggestive of a phallus penetrating a vagina (figuratively, a womb of conception), as he describes how the hot sword is stiffened when plunged into a vat of cool water, and hisses while it cools. This is a verbal foreshadowing of Siegfried's plea in S.3.3 that Brünnhilde cool and put out the flame of his ardor for her by letting him plunge into the depths of her flooding waters:

[pp. 224-5] **Siegfried:** (H128>>:) Nothung! Nothung! Fearsome steel (:H128)! Now your chaff-like steel's been melted down: you're swimming in your own sweat—(He pours the red-hot contents of the crucible into a mould, which he holds aloft: H116) (H116 voc:) Soon I'll wield you as my sword (H116 voc). (H116 or H56?: He plunges the mould into a bucket of water: steam and loud hissing follow as it cools.) (H130 chromatic vari:) A river of fire flowed into the water: in furious anger it fiercely hissed. Searingly as it flowed, it flows no more in the water's flood (:H130 chromatic vari); **[[H131A orch:]]** rigid and stiff it's become, lordly the tempered steel (H56 or H116?): soon it will flow (:H131A orch) with hot blood! (H129: He thrusts the blade into the forge fire and works the bellows vigorously. (H129 >>: Mime ... pours spices and herbs into a cooking-pot ... .) (...) (**[[H131B orch:]]** [Continuation of H131A: staccato horns again, transitioning into the oscillating figure which identifies "Mime's sleeping potion"]: While working, he [Siegfried] observes Mime, who carefully places his pot over the flames at the other side of the hearth.) (H131A:) What's that blockhead doing there with his pot (:H131A)? (H131B:) While I'm smelting steel, are you brewing slops (:H131B)?

Mime: (H131B end frag & vari >>:) ... his boy is teaching his teacher; the old man's lost his art ["Kunst"], he serves the child as cook. While he smelts the iron to pulp, (H119 hint?:) the old man cooks him broth from eggs (:H119 hint?). (...)

Siegfried: (H131B end frag:; H130 chromatic vari:) Mime the artist ["der Künstler"] (H38:) is learning to cook; he's lost his taste for forging (:H131B end frag; :H130 chromatic vari; :H38): (H108 inverted vari or H116 frag?:) I've shattered every one of his swords (:H108 inverted vari or H116 frag?); what he's cooking, I'll not savour.

Two motifs are introduced here, H131A and H131B. H131B seems to be merely a continuation of H131A. H131A, a staccato motif first heard on horns, is the motival accompaniment to Siegfried's statement that Nothung's tempered steel, now cold and stiff, is lordly, and will soon flow with hot blood, evoking sexual union in an image which also evokes death. We're reminded that as Siegmund prepared to withdraw Nothung from Hunding's House-Ash, he said that the highest need of love urged him on "to deed and death." H131A's continuation as H131B, which ends with an oscillating figure which seems to be the motival symbol for Mime's sleep (and death) potion, is the motival embodiment of a curious observation which both Siegfried and Mime make. It's first heard as Siegfried notes that while he's smelting the steel (of the sword Nothung), Mime is brewing slops (the sleep of death potion). This reminds us that shortly after Siegfried was introduced in S.1.1 he knocked a bowl of slops out of Mime's hand after Mime offered it to him, declaring he'd cook his own meals, just as Siegfried now informs Mime he'll not savor his cooking. Wotan is condemning Siegfried and Brünnhilde to martyrdom ensuring they'll inherit not only Wotan's futile quest to redeem the gods from Alberich's threat to overthrow them, but inherit Alberich's Ring Curse, which predestines its owners to destroy themselves.

Mime's sleep of death potion is a metaphor for the legacy Wotan left Siegfried in the sleeping Brünnhilde. The loving couple will confirm this parallel when, at the climax of their S.3.3 love duet, they cry out "Laughing Death!" Siegfried will succumb to Alberich's Ring Curse, just as Siegmund and Wotan did before him.

Siegfried now sings his "Forging Song" H132, adding more sexual imagery, but interspersed with passages in which Mime, ever more delirious with sinister joy, plans the coup through which he'll eliminate both Fafner and Siegfried and win the spoils of the fight for himself alone:

> [pp. 225–6] (... Siegfried removes the mould from the fire, breaks it and places the red-hot blade on the anvil: H130)
>
> **Siegfried:** (H129 vari:) He wants to lead me where I'll learn fear: a stranger will have to teach me (:H129 vari:) (H108 inverted vari:) what he can do best he can't impart (:H108 inverted vari) ... ! (while forging: **[[H132 orch:]]**) Hoho! Hoho! Hohei! Forge, my hammer, a hard-edged sword! Hoho! [etc.] (:H132)! **[[H132 orch >>>>:]]** Blood once dyed your faded blue; its bright red trickling made you blush: coldly then you laughed and licked the warm blood cool! Heiaho! Haha! Haheiaha! (...)
>
> **Mime:** (aside: H132 >> & varis:) He's making a sharp-edged sword for himself to bring down Fafner, the foe of all dwarfs: I've brewed a false drink to trap Siegfried once Fafner has fallen before him (:H132 & varis). My cunning is bound to succeed ... ! (...)
>
> **Siegfried:** (...) (H132 >>:) Through heat and hammer have I succeeded; with mighty blows I hammered you flat: now may your blushing shame disappear; be as cold and hard as you can! (He brandishes the blade and plunges it into the bucket of water: H131B) Heiaho! [etc.]! (H130 chromatic vari: ... While Siegfried attaches the newly forged blade to the hilt, Mime fusses about with his flask downstage. H38)

For the third time we've heard a comparison between Siegfried's smelting and forging, and Mime's brewing a potion to plunge Siegfried into a sleep from which he'll never wake. Siegfried and Brünnhilde were virtually condemned to martyrdom from the moment in the finale of R.4 when Wotan had his Grand Idea (H56ab—Sword Motif) of how he might redeem Valhalla from the dread and dismay caused by Alberich's Ring Curse. I've implied that Siegfried (by re-forging his father's sword Nothung) is actually brewing Mime's sleep-of-death potion by taking on the burden of his martyred father Siegmund's tragic destiny, to be an unwitting warrior in Wotan's futile endeavor to redeem the gods from the shameful end which Alberich's Ring Curse fates them to suffer. Wotan's futile endeavor is the Ring Curse itself in its most unendurable incarnation.

Mime, drunk with over-confidence, is already celebrating the world-power he'll enjoy, and the misery he'll impose on others, when he wins the Ring and Hoard from Fafner and Siegfried, even as Siegfried restores Nothung's glory and promises to strike down with it all who're false:

[pp. 226–8] Mime: (H125:) The glittering ring which my brother made (H32B >>:) ...—that ring have I won ... (:H125; :H32B)! (...) (H125 vari:) Alberich, ... who once enslaved me, (H32B >>:) I'll now reduce to dwarfish thrall: ... the whole of his host shall now obey me!—(H132/H131B/H38:; H125 >>:) The slighted dwarf, how he'll be honoured! (H131B, H132 >>) God and hero shall haste to the hoard: ... the world will bow before my nod, (H131B/H38:) it will tremble before my anger (:H125; :H131B/H38; :H132)! (...)

Siegfried: (H128:) Nothung! Nothung! Fearsome sword (:H128)! (H131B:) Now you are hafted once more in your hilt (:H131B). [**Mime:** (...)] (H132>>:) Though once in twain I forced you together, no blow shall ever break you again (:H132).

Mime: (H131B/H132/H38:) For him [Mime] shall others mine the eternal treasure (:H131B/H132/H38).

Siegfried: (H132 >:) The steel sprang apart in the hands of my dying father; his living son (H131B:) has made it anew: ... (:H132) for him its keen-edged blade cuts cleanly (:H131B).

Mime: (H38 shortened >>:) ... Mime is king, (H131B >:) prince of the elves, lord of the universe (:H38 shortened; :H131B)!

Siegfried: (... H128:) Nothung! Nothung (:H128:)! (...) (H56 or H116?) I've wakened you to life again, you lay there, dead, in ruins; [[**H133 voc:**]] [Possible H58d &/or H93c vari?—H133 is a *Siegfried Idyll* theme] now you glisten, defiant and glorious (:H133 voc). [[**H133 orch**]] (...) [[**H133**]] Slay him who is false (H129:) and fell the offender (:H129)!—(H127:) See, Mime, you smith: ... thus severs Siegfried's sword (:H127)! (H108/H116/H56 varis: He strikes the anvil, which splits from top to bottom and falls apart with a loud crash. (...)

In this frenetic passage which brings *Siegfried* Act One to a close, Wagner starkly contrasts the ultimate degradation of fallen, egoistic humanity, with the idealism through which we, at our best, seek to restore lost innocence and build a sublime future. Mime's self-delusion, his grandiose vision of holding absolute power over man and cosmos, unfettered by any longing for transcendent value, is Wagner's premonition of what the world would be like if the vulgar mass held all power through mob rule (or, more realistically, that a demagogue held all power by manipulating that mob's most dangerous impulses), or worse, if collective humanity, including all higher men, embraced Alberich's notion that all human feeling, thought, and action stem from egoism and self-aggrandizement. But the true pathos of this climactic moment is that Mime's claims (like Wotan's claims) on Siegfried are real. Siegfried's greatest achievement, the Wagnerian music-drama, the culmination of man's religio-artistic imagination, also expresses our primal will-to-power in Siegfried's bid to play god by recreating the whole world in his own image. We'll see in *Twilight of the Gods* that Wotan's ideal hero

Siegfried, Wotan's hoped-for agent of final redemption, is not so unlike Alberich as one might suppose.

The tools with which Siegfried creates himself by restoring to life his dead father Siegmund's broken sword Nothung are Nibelung tools, the hammer and anvil. But in Siegfried's first test of the now finished Nothung, he splits Mime's anvil, as if through his inspired labor he's transcended the very preconditions which made it possible for him to re-forge Nothung and forge his own independent identity. The almost frightening display of vital force (will-to-power) expressed by Siegfried in his re-forging of Nothung is a reflection of the distinction between himself and Mime: Siegfried is truly inspired, while Mime is only a journeyman who's learned his craft merely through hard labor and experience, but not by native genius. Mime expects thanks and concrete, material profit for exercise of his skills, whereas, according to Feuerbach and Wagner, the true genius is compelled by his very nature to create, oblivious to expectation of any reward. [See 169F-EOC, p. 321; and 399W-{4/49} 'The Revolution,' PW Vol. VIII, p. 236]). For Mime, labor, even in his own behalf, is a burden, as he proves when he anticipates with delight that once he wins the Ring's power others will do his work for him. [See 406W-{6–8/49} 'Art and Revolution,' PW Vol. I, pp. 48–49].

The sword Nothung which Siegfried has re-forged is a symbol for the legacy of works of genius that Siegfried has inherited from his spiritual ancestors, all prior inspired geniuses who left us a heritage in religious faith, moral heroism, and art. Wagner encapsulated this in the insightful passage previously cited, in which we may read the sword Nothung—which Siegfried, the individual genius of modern times, has re-discovered and re-forged—as the "long-since-hewn-causeway," the legacy all prior geniuses fashioned, so he can take up the task where they left off, and read the "Folk," the creative genius of primal, early man, which Siegfried inherits, as Wotan. [See 559W-{6–8/51} 'A Communication To My Friends,' PW Vol. I, pp. 288–289] Also, an unexpected, indirect source provides further evidence for our interpretation of Nothung as the legacy handed down by Siegfried's intellectual ancestors to him, an artist-hero. In the following passage Berthold Kellerman quotes Count Apponyi, who evidently during a celebration attended by Wagner at the time of his 1876 Ring premier spoke of Brünnhilde as a metaphor for Wagner's new national art, and described Siegfried's sword Nothung as the weapon which Wagner forged from the shards of his fathers' (the German masters') sword: "… Count Apponyi from Hungary spoke … . He spoke in the form of a parable … : 'Brünnhilde (the new national art) lay asleep upon a rock surrounded by a great fire. The god Wotan had lit this fire, and only the victorious … hero … who did not know fear, was to win her as his bride. (…) Along came a hero, … Richard Wagner, who forged a weapon from the shards of the sword of his fathers (the classical German masters), and with this he penetrated the fire and with his kiss awoke the sleeping Brünnhilde." [892W-{8/20/76} From a letter by Berthold Kellermann to his parents, reporting on the final performance of the *Ring* and the subsequent celebrations, WR, p. 250] I suspect that this reading of the *Ring* was common knowledge in Wagner's intimate circles at the time of the *Ring* rehearsals, and presumably its source was Wagner himself, though I possess no documentary evidence to prove this.

Wagner did, however, leave us an explicit clue to what Siegfried's sword Nothung might represent: "... the artist, without his knowing it, is always creating forms .... (...) ... has anybody ever seen a sabre borne without a hilt? Does not its swift and steady slash bear witness ... that it is mounted in a good strong hilt? No doubt, this hilt does not grow ... tangible for others, until the sword has been laid down; when the master is dead and his weapon has been hung up in the armoury, at last one perceives the handle ...—yet can't imagine that the next man who sallies forth to fight must necessarily bear his sword-blade also in a hilt." [649W-{2/57} 'On Liszt's Symphonic Poems,' PW Vol. III, pp. 242–243] The relevance of Wagner's curious remark to our discussion of Nothung is that its swift slash, which Siegfried proved by cutting the means of its creation—Mime's anvil—in half, might well represent the power of Siegfried's art (Wagner's art), which of itself proves it's grounded in potent, brilliant form, in other words, sits soundly in a hilt which the magic of his art hides from consciousness, perhaps, until after the artist's death. Wagner's art was accused of formlessness throughout his life, but, as he often said, the mere fact that we're emotionally and intellectually struck by its coherence, unity, and power, proves beyond doubt it's founded on the highest possible form, that which penetrates the soul of man. Wagner was beset all of his life by fools who, unable to respond to his revolutionary artworks with the naiveté and awe necessary for grasping their new forms, sought to critique his challenging art on the basis that it lacked traditional form. But, as he said, all new art of worth establishes its own new forms, and it's the responsibility of those who seek them to find them, as Hans Sachs put it when defending the novelty of Walther von Stolzing's audition song to the conservative masters (figurative Pharisees) in Act One of *Mastersingers*. This lends a special ironic punch to Mime's insistence that since Siegfried hadn't properly learned the techniques Mime taught him, Siegfried would be unable to grasp how to re-forge his father's sword: shades of Beckmesser!

SIEGFRIED ⋆ ACT TWO, SCENE ONE

(OUTSIDE FAFNER'S LAIR)
ALBERICH, THE WANDERER (WOTAN IN DISGUISE),
AND FAFNER TRANSFORMED INTO A SERPENT/DRAGON

This gloomiest prelude to any act in a Wagner opera or music-drama sets the stage for a confrontation between Alberich and his nemesis Wotan (Light-Alberich) in his role as the Wanderer, in the dark forest just outside Fafner's lair. We're introduced to the new motif H134ab, H134a being derived from the Giants' Motif H25a (which in this syncopated variant seems to invoke a heart-beat which misses a beat due to alarm or fear), and H134b stemming from a variant of the Serpent/Dragon Motif H47. H134ab is portentous with the fear at the heart of Fafner's transformation of himself into a Serpent/Dragon identical to the one into which Alberich transformed himself (in both cases through the Tarnhelm's

Wonder), the dread Fafner employs to prohibit man's access to Alberich's hoard of objective knowledge:

> [p. 228] Prelude: (...) It is a dark night ... . Alberich is stationed by the cliff-face ... : [[H134ab orch]] [= H25a/H47 vari]; H106 vari; H15 vari [a new vari expressing alarm], [[H134b orch]]; H106 vari; H15 vari; [[H134b orch]]; [[H134a orch]]; H50; [[H134ab orch]]; H50; H49; H15/H49; H51; H43/[[H134a orch]]; H15 vari; [[H134a orch]])
>
> Alberich: (H49:) In the forest at night I stand guard before Envy-Cave. My ear is cocked, my eye keeps effortful watch (:H49).

We hear a new variant of H15 (World-Mastery, embryo of the Ring Motif H17) which expresses alarm. As the prelude proceeds we hear the three primary motifs introduced when Alberich cursed his Ring in R.4, H49 (Envy), H50 (Ring Curse), and H51 (Death to the Ring's owner), as well as H43 (Power of the Ring) which forcefully underlined Alberich's demonstration of the power of his Ring over men in R.3. H106 recalls Mime's cunning intent to manipulate Siegfried into killing Fafner and winning the Ring for Mime. We find Alberich standing before Fafner's cave, as he must have from time immemorial, keeping watch for his chance to regain control over his Ring, his Tarnhelm, and Hoard, and to exact the Ring Curse's vengeance on those who've co-opted its power. Religious faith's stranglehold on freedom of inquiry (Fafner) has kept our potential for attaining Alberich's objective, scientific consciousness at bay for thousands of years.

As Wotan the Wanderer arrives on horseback, Alberich is startled by the storm-wind and strange bluish light Wotan's dramatic entrance produces. Alberich at first confuses this newcomer with the dragon-killer, by whom he means Siegfried:

> [pp. 228–9] (A stormwind blows up in the wood on the left; a bluish light also begins to glow there. H92/H82 vari >>:)
>
> Alberich: (...) (:H92/H82 vari) (H51 voc:) Is the dragon killer already coming? Is it he who'll lay Fafner low (:H51 voc)? (...)
>
> Wanderer: To Neidhöhle ["Envy-Cave"] have I come by night ... .
>
> (Moonlight streams in, as if through a sudden gap in the clouds, lighting up the Wanderer's form. H18ab: Alberich recognizes the Wanderer ... .)
>
> Alberich: You let yourself be seen here? (...) Get you hence, you shameless thief!
>
> Wanderer: (calmly:) Black-Alberich, are you roving here? Are you guarding Fafner's lair?
>
> Alberich: (H6 vari orch?:) (...) Enough deceit has steeped this spot in suffering ["Genug des Truges tränkte die Stätte mit <u>Noth</u>"] and so, brazen god ["du Frecher"—this mistranslation misrepresents Alberich's innocuous description of Wotan as something like an impudent or brazen scoundrel: he doesn't call him a god], let the place alone (:H6 vari orch?)!

Wanderer: (H119:) I came to watch (:H119) and not to act … .

Wotan's arrival is accompanied by H82 (Need of the Gods), the motif to which he confessed to Brünnhilde his need for a free hero who could, unlike Wotan, regain possession of Alberich's Ring from Fafner. Wotan hopes that his free hero Siegfried will preempt Alberich's long-awaited attempt to regain his rightful Ring power. It's his confidence stemming from his anticipation of this long-desired event which grants Wotan equanimity during his confrontation with Alberich. As the Wanderer is lit up by moonlight, and we hear the first two segments of the Valhalla Motif H18ab, Alberich instantly recognizes the Wanderer as Wotan. It's curious that Mime didn't at first recognize the Wanderer was Wotan. Alberich chastises Wotan for intruding at this spot which Alberich knows is Alberich's alone. Indeed, Brünnhilde noted in V.3.1 that Wotan shuns this spot. As Alberich demands that Wotan withdraw from this spot, since Wotan's deceit has steeped it in suffering (Noth), we're reminded of Alberich's diatribe against Wotan's hypocrisy in R.4, when he raged at the thought that the Noth he suffered to win the Ring's power would be exploited by Wotan to enjoy bliss at Alberich's expense, without paying his price. It was this offense, and Wotan's sin against Erda's (Nature's) objective reality, which Alberich designed his Ring Curse to punish. Alberich's accusation that Wotan's deceit has steeped this spot in suffering (Noth) expresses his critique of Wotan's dependence on religious faith's fear of the truth (Fafner), and religious self-deceit's substitution of a consoling illusion for the truth. It's in this sense that Wotan's self-deceit has steeped the world in Noth. It was through this cunning that Wotan and Loge co-opted Alberich's Ring-power. Significantly, this co-optation, inspired by Wotan's fear of the truth, occurred just after Alberich had transformed himself through the Tarnhelm's magic into a serpent. It can't be accidental that Siegfried will soon preempt Alberich's quest to regain his Ring from Fafner, who, like Alberich before him, has transformed himself into a serpent.

Wotan surprises Alberich by declaring he won't compete for the Ring's power (i.e., to determine what truth is) since he's merely come to Envy-Cave to observe, not to act. This recalls the analogous situation in Act Three of *Mastersingers* when Hans Sachs makes his dubious promise to Beckmesser that he has no intention of competing with him in the song-contest to seek Eva's hand in marriage, when in truth Sachs is preparing his proxy hero, the poet-composer Walther von Stolzing (analogous to Wotan's chosen hero Siegfried) to win the song contest and with it, Eva's (i.e. the muse Brünnhilde's) hand. Wotan is asserting that he's willing to pass the torch from religious belief (which promised man supernatural—i.e., imaginary—assuagement, supposed to be fulfilled in reality, and therefore staked an indefensible claim to actively intervene in the real world for man's sake) to secular art (in which man takes aesthetic possession of the terrible world without striving to alter it through miracles). In other words, in art, unlike religion, we observe, but don't act. Art's victory over the world is psychological, subjective, and emotional, not objective and actual, causing a change only in the individual's perception, not in the natural world which exists outside of pure subjectivity. Cosima recorded Wagner's following observation which tallies with our thesis: "Our morning conversation turns to perception and its freedom from sin; yesterday R. ... [said] that the best thing one could do was to occupy oneself with art, but not in the service of any great power; he ... says that art is the transfiguration of perception, just as religion is the transfiguration of the Will [Schopenhauerian "Will," man's inherent egoism]." [1060W-{1/30/81} CD Vol. II, p. 610] We observe a work of art, and contemplate it, but don't act. Christian faith, like many other religious traditions, but unlike secular art, promises that the real world's laws can be altered through miracles for man's sake, but art instead offers Wonder, which makes us feel "as if" we've transcended our natural limitations without affirming or accomplishing it in fact.

In admitting that he's resigned himself to pure subjectivism, and will no longer attempt to interfere with the objective world, Wotan is admitting that Alberich owns the real world, and that Wotan, man's religious impulse, has given up hope of fighting Alberich over his claim to reality. We're reminded that he informed Brünnhilde in his confession that he was leaving all that he despised, the real world and even the gods' legacy, now discredited, to Alberich's son Hagen. Wagner provided an approximate description of Wotan's position in his account of the moral effect the overall plot of the *Ring* had on him (previously cited), in which he stated that in the *Ring* he'd unconsciously admitted to himself [as Wotan had] the tragic truth that the world couldn't conform to his wish, and so turned inward to his art "... where alone can 'gladsomeness' abide." [694W-{64–2/65} 'On State and Religion,' PW Vol. IV, pp. 8–9] The place in which gladness alone abides is neither Alberich's scientific knowledge, nor illusory belief in a supernatural realm embodied in the gods' rule, whose false claim to truth's power can be discredited, but the subjective feeling which inspired art can impart in which alone gladness abides because, not staking a claim to the truth (the Ring), as both Alberich and Wotan have done, it's freed from the conflict between science and religion, yet satisfies man's longing for the feeling of transcendent value (figuratively restores Freia). [See 705W-{64–2/65} 'On State and Religion,' PW Vol. IV, pp. 29–30]. In Siegfried the secular artist-hero Wotan has found his preferred heir, so Wotan need no longer play the self-destructive nihilist, since through the observation of art, which doesn't strive to alter the world or escape fate, he can have peace. As Wagner put it: "... 'No dedicated artist or poet goes mad, and it is no credit to Kleist that he committed suicide, for it is precisely this which marks out the artist—that through all torments he retains the serene capacity to observe.'" [915W-{6/4/78}CD Vol. II, p. 84]

But Alberich suspects Wotan hasn't, in spite of his protestation to the contrary, taken a hands-off approach to who'll inherit Alberich's Ring. And Alberich warns him that he's gained greatly in experience and knowledge since Wotan deprived him of his Ring in primal times:

> [pp. 229–230] **Alberich:** Were I, as you wish, still as stupid as then, when you bound the foolish dwarf, how easy, indeed, it would prove ... to deprive me once more of the ring! (H80) Beware: I know your ways ["Kunst"] well

enough, (mockingly: (H80) but where you are weak has not escaped me either. ... my ring rewarded the toil of those giants (H18ab:) who built your stronghold for you (:H18ab); (H19:) what you once agreed with those insolent creatures (:H19) (H26 voc:) is still preserved today in runes on your spear's all-powerful shaft (:H26 voc). (H27:) What you paid the giants ... you cannot wrest from them again (:H27): (H19 vari:) you yourself would shatter the shaft of your spear (:H19 vari); in your hand the all-powerful staff ... (H33 vari or H46 vari?) would scatter like chaff.

Wotan: (H119:) By the faithful runes of contract it bound you not (:H119) (H19 vari:) to me ... : it bends you to my will by virtue of its might ... .

Alberich informs Wotan that he's much more knowledgeable about the world, and about Wotan's cunning, than he was in those primal times when Wotan, aided by Loge's artistic cunning (self-deceit), easily dispossessed Alberich of his Ring (reasoning power) and its derivative powers, the Tarnhelm (imagination) and the Hoard (of knowledge). In other words, man's gift of reason, which man initially involuntarily and unconsciously reified, imaginatively projecting the power of his mind's nature onto an idealized man-like form called God (Wotan), inevitably emancipates itself from its initial mistake which gave birth to those figments of the imagination, Valhalla's gods, and replaces them with Nature's (Erda's) implacable laws, the true source of power. As Feuerbach noted, human reason has acquired enough experience of itself and Nature that it will no longer posit itself as Godhead (and therefore Wotan must cease to play any active role in the world): "Religion is the childlike condition of humanity ... ... the historical progress of religion consists in this: ... what was formerly contemplated and worshipped as God is now perceived to be something human. (...) But the essence of religion, thus hidden from the religious [Wotan repressed his knowledge of this bitter truth into his unconscious mind, Brünnhilde], is evident to the thinker [Alberich/Hagen], by whom religion is viewed objectively ... ." [45F-EOC, p. 13; See also 215F-LER: p. 97, and 121F-EOC, p. 208]

Alberich won't be so easily cheated out of his Ring as he was in the past because he now knows where Wotan is weak, namely, in the fact that Wotan paid the Giants with Alberich's Hoard, Tarnhelm, and Ring for building Valhalla, and can't now take the Ring from Fafner lest Wotan break the contracts engraved on his spear through which the gods rule. But this is just what Wotan intends to do using his proxy Siegfried who'll, as Wotan desired, break Wotan's Spear in S.3.2, but hopefully preserve all that's worth preserving of Wotan's original Valhallan ideals in Siegfried's secular art. H80 (Wotan's Frustration), which expresses Wotan's reluctant acknowledgment that he can't create a free hero who can redeem the gods, is heard as Alberich notes that he now knows Wotan's ways, and sees where he's weak. But Alberich doesn't grasp that Wotan is reconciling himself to the gods' fated doom. Alberich's warning falls on deaf ears because Wotan hopes that his proxy Siegfried will preempt Alberich's quest to restore his lost power by forcibly breaking Wotan's contract in order to steal Alberich's Ring from Fafner, without Wotan directly intervening. Wotan, seemingly angered by

Alberich's ability to put his finger on the root of Wotan's problem, observes that though Alberich hasn't bound himself by contracts engraved on Wotan's Spear, nonetheless Wotan's Social Contract, as an externally coercive influence, can keep Alberich's threat at bay. While this may once have been true, during the lengthy period when the mytho-poetic world-view held universal sway, and political might at least nominally drew its sanction from this divine authority, it won't be true in the future. Wotan's authority (religious faith) has become a paper tiger in the modern, secular, scientific world, though it's still capable of rousing many people to passions and actions which stifle intellectual freedom, and may even yet bring about the demise of civilization as we know it.

Alberich, having astutely detected Wotan's hidden agenda, notes that Wotan's confidence arises from his hope to attain his desired end, theft of the Ring from Fafner to keep Alberich from regaining it, through proxy heroes:

> [pp. 230–1] **Alberich:** (H50:) Doomed to die through my curse is he who holds the hoard (:H50): ... . Will the coveted hoard once again belong to the Nibelung? (H49:) That fills you with endless care. For once I grasp it again in my fist (:H49), ... (H15 >>:) unlike foolish giants, I'll use the power of the ring (:H15): then tremble, (H51 vari:) eternal guardian of heroes (:H51 vari)! (H43:) Valhalla's heights I'll storm with Hella's host: then I shall rule the world (:H43)! (H46 orch)
>
> **Wanderer:** (... H15 frag voc?:) I know your mind full well; it gives me no cause for worry (:H15 frag voc?): (H121a vari:) he shall command the ring who wins it (:H121a vari).
>
> **Alberich:** (... H121a vari:) How darkly you speak of what I know clearly (:H121a vari)! (H56ab) (...) Haven't you nurtured a boy who would cleverly pluck the fruit ... which you yourself aren't allowed to pick? (H80)

Alberich reminds Wotan that if Alberich ever regains his Hoard, i.e., if the now matured scientific mind frees itself from society's dependence on religious illusions and independently disseminates an objective understanding of the world among men, Alberich will use the Ring's (conscious knowledge's) power, unlike the foolish Giants (the passion behind religious faith), to overthrow the gods' rule (faith's sway) over men, supplanting their power with his own. Fafner doesn't use the Ring's power or increase the Hoard, but just guards them to ensure their power can't be used. While one might read this as merely an indictment of the capitalist who acquires and hoards ever more wealth without using it, thereby depriving others, another plausible reading is that Fafner represents man's fear of any knowledge that might overthrow cherished traditions and beliefs, though these preclude our potential progress. So long as Alberich doesn't regain his Ring from Fafner (i.e., so long as scientific thought doesn't universally replace religious faith), Wotan and the gods are safe.

But just as Alberich said he's now learned enough about Wotan's weaknesses and cunning to defeat him, Wotan retorts that he knows Alberich's mind yet no longer fears him. Wotan mysteriously agrees with him that whoever wins the Ring will command its power, while H121 sounds. H121 was introduced when Wotan staked his head to compete with Mime in a contest of knowledge. The joke is that Mime is Wotan's head, and represents those aspects of the gods' rule (man's belief in them) which can readily be shown to have an egoistic origin, like fear of death and longing for eternal life which stems from it, the prosaic aspects of religion which Wotan loathes and wishes now to sacrifice to Alberich to free Siegfried from vulnerability to his threat. Siegfried will win the Ring, Tarnhelm, and Hoard, after killing Fafner (faith's fear of truth), but he'll take possession of them with his heart, aesthetically, rather than with his head. Siegfried won't use their potential power. Siegfried will also kill Mime, Wotan's ulterior thought, which is burdened by those things Wotan must jettison to free his hero Siegfried from them. Wotan is no longer fearful that Alberich will regain his lost power because religious faith, though falling before Alberich's onslaught, will live on subliminally in the art Siegfried and his muse Brünnhilde will produce, in feeling, music. Wagner expressed this in his following plea (previously cited): "Is it so utterly impossible to Theology, to take the great step that would grant to Science [Alberich and Hagen] its irrefutable truths through surrender of Jehova [i.e., the loathsome, egoistic aspects of the Old Testament God, Wotan, represented by Mime], and to the Christian world its pure God [Wotan minus consciousness of his true, egoistic motives] revealed in Jesus [the-artist hero Siegfried, religion's savior] ... ?" [928W-{3–7/78} 'Public and Popularity,' PW Vol. VI, p. 79] Jehovah can be read as Wotan, and Jesus as Siegfried. The part of Wotan that he loathes, his conscious, egoistic mind (Jehovah, or Mime), must go under, in order that Wotan's ideal, ageless part, his aesthetic feeling or music, can live on in the love shared by Siegfried and Brünnhilde, the secular art to which their loving union will give birth. However, as Alberich accuses Wotan of hypocritically seeking, through his proxy hero Siegfried, to do what Wotan can't do himself, we hear H80 again, recalling that Siegfried is as much a product of what Wotan loathes in himself as Siegmund was.

Now Wotan proffers a gambit even more daring than his false assertion to Fricka that he hadn't intervened to aid Siegmund. Wotan ingeniously and ingenuously argues that it's not he, but Alberich's brother Mime, who's been nurturing Siegfried to win the Ring for him and deprive Alberich of his property. But Wagner has revealed to us through a variety of musico-dramatic means that Mime represents the prosaic part of Wotan which Wotan loathes. Wotan has projected his own guilt on to Mime, who'll soon fall at Siegfried's hand. Since Wotan's ideal part has been reborn in Siegfried, Wotan disavows any link between Siegfried and his egoism (Mime), which originally inspired him to sire a heroic race who can redeem the gods from Alberich's Ring Curse:

[pp. 231–2] **Wanderer:** Haggle with Mime, not with me: ... he's leading a youngster here who's meant to kill Fafner for him. Of me he knows nothing; the Nibelung is using him for his own ends. (...) (H121 vari:) ... the boy doesn't know of the ring (:H121 vari) but Mime's found out about it.

Alberich: (... H19 vari:; H106 frag:) And would you withhold your hand from the hoard (:H19 vari; :H106 frag)? (H19 vari?)

Wanderer: Him whom I love I leave to his own devices; [[H135 orch:]] [= H118 vari] let him stand or fall, his own master is he: heroes alone can help me (:H135 orch).

Alberich: (H44?:) With Mime alone would I vie for the ring (:H44?)?

Wanderer: Save you alone, only he desires the gold.

This passage is psychologically intriguing. Wotan is projecting his worst motives on to Mime, so it's Mime, he says, who's prompting Siegfried to do what, after all, Wotan himself wanted Siegfried to do, kill Fafner and take possession of Alberich's Ring, Tarnhelm, and Hoard, so Alberich can't regain them (and bring about the gods' fated doom). Mime desires that Siegfried win the Ring for him for purely craven reasons. Wagner is suggesting that religious man's (Wotan's) impulse in seeking to control the world supernaturally is in the final analysis the same egoistic impulse which seeks practical control of the real world, minus practical effectiveness in achieving this. Wotan's motives, though seemingly more exalted than Nibelung motives, are at bottom our common concern for self-preservation and self-aggrandizement. This palpable hypocrisy Alberich brought to Wotan's attention in R.4. It's precisely because Wotan came to see himself as a moral dwarf (a Nibelung) that he confessed to Brünnhilde that he found, with loathing (Ekel), always only himself in all that he did to ensure the gods' redemption from Alberich's Ring Curse. The fact that Wotan will look to Siegfried's and Brünnhilde's loving union to redeem gods and world from Alberich's Ring Curse doesn't absolve Siegfried of guilt in unwittingly perpetuating Wotan's sin of religious world-denial. Siegfried's hidden motive for seeking Brünnhilde's love is Wotan's motive for seeking redemption from the bitter truth.

Hearing Wotan disavow personal interest in co-opting Alberich's means to power again, Alberich asks in disbelief if he really means to keep his hands off the hoard. We're reminded of Beckmesser's incredulity when Sachs asserts he has no intention of competing in the song contest to win Eva's hand in *Mastersingers*, and adds that Beckmesser is free to seek her hand in the song competition without Sachs's interference. Just as Sachs can safely disavow personal involvement in winning Eva's hand, yet take comfort in the knowledge that Sachs's proxy, the unconsciously inspired artist-hero Walther von Stolzing, will save his muse Eva from a tragic marriage to Beckmesser by winning her hand through victory in the song contest Sachs prepares Walther for, and redeem the Folk by performing the Mastersong she inspires, similarly, Wotan can safely disavow any intent to compete with Alberich directly for possession of his Ring, because Wotan expects his proxy Siegfried will win it and redeem the world from its curse through loving union with his muse Brünnhilde.

Wotan's retort to Alberich's query respecting Wotan's potential use of heroes, dearly descended from himself, to do what he can't do, is that he'll leave the hero he loves, Siegfried, to his own devices. Wotan sings the new motif H135 as he adds that he'll let Siegfried stand or fall himself, since he's his own master. H135 is musically related to H112, which conveys the notion of all that Mime claims Siegfried owes him, and to H118 (Siegfried's Mission), the motival embodiment of Siegfried's assertion of his emancipation from Mime. The first part of Wotan's retort is a paraphrase of Feuerbach about the quest of the individual man to assert his independence in the face of the overwhelming heritage of Nature and nurture (culture) which produced him: " ... I stand on the shoulders of my ancestors, but even on their shoulders I stand *on my own feet* ... . (...) ... no other being, not even a God, will help me unless I help myself; I stand and fall by my own resources." [216F-LER, p. 99; See also 251F] The point Feuerbach is making, and perhaps Wagner also, is that though each individual human is a product of Nature and nurture, and in that sense is unfree, nonetheless each individual brings into conjunction a specific set of factors unique to himself, and as he grows conscious of himself strives to assert that unique identity. Perhaps it's this unrepeatable uniqueness which is the closest we can come to any sort of transcendence. As Feuerbach put it: " ... individuality is the principle of generation and creation; only very individual conditions of the earth, geological upheavals such as have not taken place since, produced organic beings ... ." [256F-LER, p. 173] " ... *to love a man is to recognize his individuality. (...) But what is the principle or source of these infinite varieties and individualities that the senses disclose to us? It is nature ... .*" [344F-LER, p. 330] Wotan has acknowledged to Alberich that he loves Siegfried, and that he expresses this love by granting Siegfried his independence, that only in this way can Siegfried fulfill Wotan's wishes.

In *Opera and Drama* Wagner wrote a meditation on the proper relation of age to youth, in which he identifies the aged teacher with the poet-dramatist, and the youth with music. [See 518W-{50–1/51} *Opera and Drama*, PW Vol. II, p. 206]. Wotan we can identify with the experienced, aged one, who grasps the meaning of Siegfried's heroic life (having planned it in advance) in a way that the much less conscious Siegfried (who doesn't know who he is) can't. Wagner speaks of this aged teacher as "peaceful" not "passionate," as a "beholder," not a "doer." This recalls Wotan's description of himself to Alberich as one who has come to observe, not act. And Wotan will show Siegfried (the instinctive youth) Siegfried's inmost being, by leaving Siegfried heir to the ageless part of himself, in whom Siegfried will see himself reflected, Brünnhilde. Wagner adds that this teacher or "admonisher" (Wotan) is the conscious understanding (Wotan's hoard of knowledge, his treasury of worldly experience, as in poetic drama), while the "admonished" (Siegfried) is feeling (music).

But Alberich is still skeptical. How can it be that Wotan now fears Alberich so little he won't interfere to ensure Alberich doesn't win back the Ring's power? Wotan suggests he'll wake Fafner to inquire whether he'd agree to give Alberich his ring to thank Alberich for warning Fafner that he risks death in the coming fight with Siegfried, and for Alberich's offer to protect Fafner:

[pp. 232–3] **Alberich:** And yet I might not win it? (H106 frag?)

Wanderer: (...) A hero draws near to rescue the hoard; two Nibelungs covet the gold: ...—he who snatches it will have won it.—(H47:) (...) There lies the dragon (:H47): (... H134a:) if you warn him that death is at hand, then perhaps he'll be willing to give up his toy (:H134a).—(H134b:) I'll wake him up myself (:H134b). (...) [Wotan wakes Fafner. Alberich is incredulous: (...)] Someone has come to tell you of danger ["Noth"]: he'll reward you for it with your life if, in return, you repay that life with the treasure that you're guarding. [**Fafner:** (...)]

Alberich: (...) A doughty hero is drawing near who means to assail you, invulnerable beast. [**Fafner:** (...)] (H15:) The golden band alone he covets (:H15): give me the ring as reward and I'll change the course of the conflict; you'll keep the hoard for yourself and live a long life of peace!

Fafner: (H134a:) What I lie on I own: (yawning) leave me to sleep (:H134a)! (H134b inverted)

Alberich has joined Wotan to add that though a hero is coming to assault what he describes as the "invulnerable" beast Fafner, since Siegfried only wants the Ring, if Fafner will give it to Alberich he'll avert the fight so Fafner can enjoy the Hoard and live a long life of peace. But Fafner retorts that what he lies on, he owns, and asks them to let him sleep. Wotan has demonstrated that as long as religious faith and cherished tradition, characterized by the fear of anything new, any knowledge, which might overthrow faith and tradition, controls our conscious mind, Alberich will never be able to pry the Ring from Fafner. In other words, though religious faith has been weakening (which is why Fafner is now under threat at all), the values engendered or supported by religious belief live on still, and we humans won't easily give them up, even for the practical benefits of science and technology and political power. Alberich calls Fafner an "invulnerable" beast because Wagner himself (in a passage previously cited) described egoism as "invulnerable." [See 698W-{64–2/65} 'On State and Religion,' PW Vol. IV, pp. 14–15]. Fafner's remark that what he lies on, he owns, though, is usually taken to be an expression of the capitalist's nature, whose sole motive for striving to hoard more and more money and possessions and the power they bring, transforming these goods into luxuries beyond his capacity to use or enjoy, is a selfishness that deprives others of their most basic needs: "[Speaking of "the law of Property," Wagner said that:] ... in it ... the bent to satisfaction through the enjoyment of Nature and her products, became hardened into the unit's exclusive right over Nature beyond his capacity for enjoyment ... ." [390W-{1–2/49} *Jesus of Nazareth*, PW Vol. VIII. P. 302]

Though Fafner's role as guardian of Alberich's Hoard, Tarnhelm, and Ring probably owes something to this reading, a more enlightening perspective is offered by Feuerbach's critique of the inherent conservatism of religious man and traditional societies. [See 279F-LER, pp. 211–212; See also 141F-EOC, p. 274, and 283F-LER, pp. 216–217] Both the secular artist (Siegfried), and the cynical exponent of the objective scientific world-view which renounces our religious impulse (represented later by Alberich's son Hagen), having emancipated themselves from their former service to religious faith and its taboos on freedom of expression and intellectual inquiry, constitute a threat to Fafner's (fearful faith's) continued domination of human thought. If the popular view that Fafner represents the capitalist's lust for acquiring wealth was accurate, Fafner would be actively seeking to increase his hoard and exploiting the Ring's power. Instead, Alberich was correct when he declared Fafner doesn't use any of his potential power at all. Fafner merely keeps everyone, including himself, from exploiting it. His sleep is the sleep of faith and tradition, which, unless forced to by outside influences, won't change. Fafner guarding the Hoard is a symbol for possession in its most universal sense, man's desire to establish a secure foundation for the life of the individual within society, to preserve it or even to perpetuate it infinitely if possible, which is precisely what religious faith, custom, and tradition offer. Feuerbach argued that the elimination of the illusions which sustained human life for millennia, but have barred man (Hagen and Siegfried) from attaining his full potential, will bring about man's rebirth, a new, secular religion.

Wotan, in a final insult to Alberich in the guise of sympathy, acknowledges now not only that all things act in accordance with their innate character, their fate or natural necessity, but also accepts what follows from this, that in that case nothing can be altered. Wotan implies (but now with secret joy rather than in despair) there's no escaping the gods' fated twilight Erda foresaw:

[pp. 233-4] **Wotan:** This one thing—I advise you ... : H2 >>:) all things go their different ways; you can alter nothing (:H2).—I leave the field to you ... ! Try your luck with your brother, Mime; his kind you understand better. (... H19 vari) (H135 vari: [as a triumphant horn theme]) As for the rest, learn that, too (:H135 vari horns)! ((...) Alberich watches the Wanderer riding away. H56ab; H119; H92)

Alberich: (...) (H104/H92) (H119/H92:) ... laugh away, you light-hearted, high-living gang of gods (:H119/H92): (H50) I'll see you all perish yet! (H50) As long as the gold still glints in the light, (H50 voc:) then one who knows keeps watch (:H50 voc):—(H49:) his defiance will yet defeat you (:H49). (He slips into a cleft ... . (...) Dawn)

As Wotan acknowledges the truth Erda tried to teach him, that all things which occur in the real world must be, that everything that is, ends, and that he can alter nothing (there's no escape from fate), we hear H2, the first variant of the Primal Nature Motif H1 with which the *Ring* began, the basis for Erda's Motif H52 which expresses Nature's constant motion and change. I noted previously that the second segment of the Sword Motif (H56b), which represents Wotan's grand idea for ultimate redemption (Nothung), is the Primal Nature Motif H1. H1 reflects Feuerbach's concept of natural necessity. Siegfried's artistic creativity taps into this natural necessity, and it's from this that Wotan hopes for redemption from Alberich's Ring Curse of consciousness, which, ironically, is as much an expression of natural necessity (natural evolution from unconscious life to conscious humanity) as Siegfried's creative force and its impulse to restore lost innocence. By leaving the field (the world) to Alberich, Wotan has resigned himself to the fact that Erda's prophecy of Alberich's inevitable victory over the gods will come true. [See 627W-{10/7/54}Letter to Franz Liszt, SLRW, p. 319] Wotan has confessed that Alberich owns the truth.

When Wotan adds that Alberich should compete instead with Mime, whose kind Alberich understands better, Wotan is telling Alberich that Wotan willingly sacrifices to him only that part of Wotan which Wotan believes is reducible to Alberich's knowledge, namely, Mime, who represents Wotan's egoistic thought, but hopefully doesn't implicate his heartfelt feeling (Siegfried's and Brünnhilde's love) in its guilt. What Wotan doesn't tell Alberich directly but only intimates with the subtlest hint, is that Wotan has an alternative world to retreat to that doesn't claim to be supernatural, and doesn't stake a claim to truth's power (Alberich's Ring) which the truth could contradict, but in which nonetheless our longing for transcendent freedom from the bounds of the real world, which Alberich owns, can be satisfied. This alternative world is the secular art that Siegfried (the music-dramatist Wagner) will create under the muse Brünnhilde's inspiration. For this reason, when Wotan leaves Alberich with the unsettling remark: "as for the rest, learn that too," we hear H135, which stands for Wotan's intent to let Siegfried make his own way in the world, freed from Wotan's (direct, conscious) influence. One thinks of Sachs's cryptic, mysterious remark to Beckmesser, after leaving the field (wooing for Eva's hand in the mastersinging contest) open to him without Sachs's interference, that what else Sachs is thinking is of no concern to Beckmesser.

Wagner captured this complex array of ideas behind Wotan's covert intent to make Siegfried his heir in a passage previously cited, in which he says that the *Ring* shows us the necessity of acknowledging natural necessity, or change, and yielding to it, as Wotan does when he acknowledges the need to go under so he can give birth to his ideal self, Siegfried, who'll live on after him and be his heir. [See 615W-{1/25–26/54} Letter to August Röckel, SLRW, p. 307] When Wagner says that the ever-loving Siegfried is the final product of Wotan's self-destructive yet creative will, we recall that Brünnhilde described herself as Wotan's will, and that it was by virtue of planting Brünnhilde, Wotan's wish-womb, with the seed of his confession, that Brünnhilde was metaphysically able to give birth to the free hero Wotan had longed for, Siegfried. Religion as a set of beliefs, a faith, contradicted by knowledge, must die, so the savior, who'll preserve religious feeling in secular art, safe from refutation, can live.

Alberich is shocked by Wotan's newfound self-confidence in the face of certain destruction, but nonetheless asserts that so long as the gold glints in the light (so long as it's still possible to bring knowledge of the truth—his hoard—to the light of day) he, the one who knows, will defeat the arrogant gods (he'll overthrow the illusions which sustain the gods' rule over men). Though Alberich knows Wotan and the gods are predestined to destruction by the truth for which only Alberich possesses the courage, nonetheless Wotan's self-confidence has left Alberich uneasy. Perhaps Wotan's proxy Siegfried will succeed in pre-empting Alberich's quest to restore his rightful power where Wotan failed. If Wotan thinks he can find safe refuge for the mysteries of religion in his artist-hero Siegfried, then it's Alberich's or his son Hagen's task, the task of the modern scientific spirit, to expose the allegedly mysterious processes of unconscious artistic inspiration, and explain away the last stand of religious man's attempt to preserve the mystery of being. As Feuerbach said: "Here no barrier to human knowledge can excuse us. In the realm of nature ... there are still many things we do not understand; but the secrets of religion spring from man himself, and he is capable of knowing them down to their remotest depths. (...) The elimination of this lie is the condition for a new, energetic mankind." [284F-LER, p. 219]

SIEGFRIED ≠ ACT TWO, SCENE TWO

(OUTSIDE FAFNER'S LAIR)
MIME, SIEGFRIED, THE WOODBIRD,
AND FAFNER — TRANSFORMED INTO A SERPENT/DRAGON

As dawn is coming Mime arrives with Siegfried outside Fafner's lair, Envy-Cave ("Neidhöhle"). We hear H102 and H34 as they approach, reminding us that Loge's ring of fire protects the sleeping Brünnhilde from all except the fearless hero Siegfried, who'll not learn the meaning of fear from Fafner, but only from her. Siegfried, accordingly, expresses doubt he'll learn fear here, but Mime assures him that he can learn fear from Fafner, and won't likely learn it at any other time or place:

[pp. 234–5] (Prelude: H134b; H129; H109 vari; H129/H38 frag; H102: As day breaks, Siegfried and Mime enter. (...))

Mime: We've reached the place: wait here! (H102)

Siegfried: (...) (H102) (...) If I don't learn here what I'm meant to learn, I'll go on my way alone and be rid of you then at last! (H34)

Mime: Believe ... me, ... if you don't learn the meaning of fear here today, you're unlikely to find out what it is at any other place and any other time. (...)

[Mime graphically describes all that Fafner can do to harm Siegfried, and Siegfried confidently responds to each threatened harm with practical countermeasures. At one point we hear what seems to be (H6 or H86?): (...)]

When Mime describes in prosaic terms the specific ways in which Fafner can physically harm Siegfried, Siegfried self-confidently asserts, in response to each specific threat, that he'll prudently avoid them. But it's not so much Fafner, Wotan's guardian of the Ring, Tarnhelm, and Hoard (religious faith's fear of knowledge), which is the threat, but that knowledge itself. Because Siegfried is protected by his unconscious mind Brünnhilde from suffering consciousness of that threat which paralyzed Wotan, Siegfried doesn't foresee harm from Fafner (from what Fafner guards, forbidden knowledge). Siegfried the secular artist-hero can only free himself from religious faith's (Fafner's) control if he doesn't fear the truth. He has to kill Wotan's fear, incarnate in Fafner's prohibiting access to Alberich's power, to emancipate art from religious faith's control so Siegfried can win his muse of secular art, Brünnhilde, and take aesthetic possession of

Alberich's Ring, Tarnhelm, and Hoard. In this way Siegfried can transform religion's Wonder (belief in miracles), trapped in the past, into artistic Wonder, the artwork of the future. So we find Wotan's fear of anything which could threaten the gods' rule (Fafner) guarding access to the means Alberich would employ to overthrow the gods, knowledge and the means to attain it. Religious faith is the foundation of the state whose social contract Siegfried must break. [See 503W-{50–1/51} *Opera and Drama*, PW Vol. II, p. 184]

It's implicit that if Siegfried overcomes this existential fear which sustains religious belief and the state which depends on it, this will also grant Alberich or his proxy Hagen freedom of intellectual inquiry. Siegfried in this way unwittingly becomes potentially a fifth column for Alberich to exploit. For if Siegfried breaches faith (kills Fafner) to access Dark-Alberich's and Light-Alberich's forbidden hoard of knowledge and the Ring, so Siegfried can draw unconscious artistic inspiration from them, this greatly increases the risk that Alberich will regain control of them. Siegfried, by killing Fafner, also inherits from him the responsibility to keep this objective power inaccessible to other men (his audience), which Siegfried the artist-hero can best do by sublimating its horrors through aesthetic intuition into an unconsciously inspired artwork of tragic beauty, in which its horrors can be forgotten. So in Siegfried's case this hoard of forbidden knowledge will be placed off limits merely by the fact that in his inspired art thought has been sublimated into feeling, man's guilt-ridden but hidden history (Wotan's unspoken secret) sublimated into musical motifs.

Siegfried asks Mime an unusual question: does Fafner have a heart, and if so, does it lie where any man's or beast's does? H70 (the Wälsungs's tragic fate) sounds here to remind us of the most heartfelt experience the *Ring* has so far given us, Siegmund the Wälsung's tragic-heroic rescue of his sister Sieglinde from Hunding's clutches, punished by the miserable deaths to which this most sympathetic couple are condemned by their very nature. Mime certifies that Fafner's egoistic heart is, unlike that of the Wälsungs, "inhuman." Siegfried obviously asks this question because he wishes to learn how he can most efficiently kill Fafner. But Mime's answer suggests there's something more to Siegfried's question. Mime says that Fafner's heart lies just where it does in man or beast, and he, strangely, asks Siegfried if this fact has at last prompted him to feel fear:

[pp. 235–7] **Siegfried:** (H70) But tell me this: (H70) has the dragon a heart?

Mime: (H134a:) A fierce and inhuman heart (:H134a)!

Siegfried: But does it lie where it beats in everyone, be he man or beast?

Mime: Of course ... the dragon's heart lies there, too; are you starting to feel afraid now?

Siegfried: ... (H128 chord:) Nothung (:H128 chord) I'll thrust in the proud beast's heart. Is that what people call fear? (H109>>:) Hey, old man, if that's all that your cunning can teach me, ... I'll not learn what fear is here (:H109).

Mime: (H34 >>:) ... you have to see and hear him himself, then your senses will surely fail you! (H102 vari >>:) When your ... heart is quaking with fear in your breast (:H34; :H102 vari):—(H134a tympani: ...) you'll thank me ... .

Siegfried: (...) (H110 orch >>:) That loathsome nodding and blinking your eyes—when shall I finally see it no more? (...) (:H110 orch)

Mime: I'll leave you now (H10: [beautiful music foreshadowing the forest murmurs]) ... . when the sun's at its highest look out for the dragon (H47/H10:) ... (:H47/H10). [**Siegfried:** (...)] (H131A?/H10:) After the fearful struggle you surely won't stop me from bringing refreshment (:H131A?/H10)? (H109: Siegfried waves him away with some vehemence.) (...)

Mime's point seems to be that if Fafner's "inhuman" heart lies where every human's and animal's heart lies, then in a sense every human heart is egoistic like Fafner's, including the expansive hearts of Siegfried's Wälsung parents Siegmund and Sieglinde, whose tragic-heroic nature is invoked by H70. It's this possibility which is the ultimate ground of religious man's fear because, if all human motives and longings, even our longing for redemption, are egoistic, there's no possibility of supernatural transcendence or redemption from egoism.

Siegfried, having had enough of Mime's irritating and hypocritical protestations of his loving concern for Siegfried's welfare, now brusquely dismisses Mime with contempt, accompanied by H109. H10 begins to sound in the orchestra, foreshadowing the peaceful forest murmurs which will lull Siegfried into a virtually clairvoyant state after Mime has left him in peace. This has the effect of a brief pastoral interlude, a restoration of the natural world's innocence after civilized man's corrupting influence has been purged from it. Siegfried, now able to meditate in freedom, stretches out under the trees and listens to the forest murmurs and birdsongs which can gradually be heard in the peaceful forest. H2, the first variant of the original Nature Motif H1, now—Cooke notes—gives shape to the shimmering H10 as Siegfried reflects on the nobility and grace of his true parents, in contrast to the depravity of the repulsive foster father who poses as them:

[p. 238] Siegfried: (H10/H2 pattern:) That he is not my father—how happy I feel at that! Only now do the fresh woods delight me; only now does the day smile upon me in gladness now that the loathsome dwarf has left me and I'll nevermore see him again. (He falls into a silent reverie. (**[[H136 orch:]]** [Forest Murmurs: according to Cooke H10 now develops independently of the H2-based framework]) What must my father have looked like (:H136 orch—Forest Murmurs free-form)? Ha!—Of course, like me! If any son of Mime's existed, (H38:) must he not look just like Mime? (H6/H38:) Just as filthy, fearful and wan, short and misshapen, hunchbacked and halting, with drooping ears and rheumy eyes—away with the elf! I don't care to see him anymore (:H6/H38)! (He leans further back and looks up through the treetops. Deep silence. Forest murmurs. **[[H136 orch:]]** ["Definitive Forest

Murmurs"], H65 orch) (H65 voc:) But—what must my mother have looked like (:H65 orch/voc)? (...) (H65: [developing]) Like those of the roe-deer, her bright-shining eyes must surely have glistened (:H65)—only far fairer (:H136 "forest murmurs")! (H65 orch) (... H65 voc:) When, in her dismay, she gave me birth, why did she have to die then (:H65 voc)? Do all mortal mothers perish because of their sons? Sad that would be, in truth! (H113; H39) Ah, might I, her son, (H113:) see my mother (:H113)!—(H39) My mother—(H113:) a mortal woman (:H113)! (H36 >>:; H22/H10: [as heard during the musical interlude before Loge's narrative in R.2 about his inability to find anything which living beings would accept as a substitute for woman and love] (...) Deep silence. The forest murmurs increase. Siegfried's attention is finally caught by the song of forest birds. [[H137ab orch:]] He listens with growing interest to a woodbird in the branches above him. [[H138ab orch]] [= H4 varis])

The refreshment Siegfried draws from his aesthetic arrest in the midst of the now peaceful forest, purified of Mime's irritating, artificial presence, is an evocation of the important Wagnerian distinction between Nature (as experienced sympathetically) and the artificiality of Culture, which Wagner identifies with the "rabble," dissipated by civilization and its decadent discontents. Here, in Wagner's description of this rabble, who he suggests might have exemplified unspoiled, purely-human naiveté had they not been soiled by culture's artificiality, we find the basis for at least part of Wagner's characterization of Mime, the moral dwarf bound by the narrow spirit of utilitarianism and self-interest, and a basis also for Siegfried's instinctive abhorrence of Mime which, as one can see in this extract, isn't owing to Judaism, but rather to universal human egoism: "... this rabble is ... [not] the normal product of real human nature, but rather the artificial outcome of your de-naturalised culture; ... and ... these revolting features are ... [not] the real face of Nature, but rather the reflection of the hypocritical mask of our State-and-Criminal-Culture. (...)/(...) And—saddest tale of all!—when in this disproportionately burdened section of the Folk the sheerest utilitarianism has thus become the moving spirit of its energy, then must the revolting spectacle be exhibited of absolute Egoism enforcing its laws of life on every hand ... ." [442W-{9–12/49} 'The Artwork of the Future,' PW Vol. I, pp. 208–209] In the course of writing the *Ring* in reverse order, culminating in his attempt to create an allegory of the origins of human culture in *Rhinegold*, Wagner gradually gave up the optimistic idea that there was once, or ever could be, a purely-human nature which human culture (which, after all, was a product of that allegedly formerly innocent human nature) had corrupted. Mime's mythological account of such a time in R.3, his narrating the story of how Alberich's Ring power brought about the Fall of the Nibelungs from a once paradisal existence, was Wagner's attempt to posit such a purely-human nature. But as he wrote the *Ring* it dawned on him that human egoism is a legacy of natural necessity (evolution) and therefore inevitable. It's this artificiality, hypocrisy, and egoism, from which Siegfried now feels freed in the fresh, humming forest, in his reverie of innocence (allegedly) regained. But Nature isn't innocent.

Siegfried is experiencing the "Naïve," an instinctual relationship with Nature seemingly unmediated by conceptual interpretation. This calls up nostalgic longing for the true parents he never knew and overwhelming gratitude that discovering his true Wälsung heritage has liberated him from Mime's repugnant claims. The point of Siegfried's upbringing by Mime in the forest (note the contrast with Wotan's upbringing of Siegfried's father Siegmund in the forest) is that in Wagner's view the individual genius in the modern world suffers from alienation, for he finds himself almost universally among trivial, egoistic, small men, philistines, who're inherently incapable of grasping his naïve, straightforward, sympathetic relationship with Nature. In Wagner's view the overwhelming majority of men, whom Mime represents, are incapable of responding to the world in a purely aesthetic sense (or even in an objectively scientific sense, as Alberich does, who possesses a higher consciousness which discerns the laws and processes of Nature), because they construe all experience in terms of their desire to satisfy narrowly defined needs, while the artist-hero is presumably able to give himself to the world of experience without pre-judgment and without seeking the practical profit which might be obtained from the exploitation of things and experiences. Because true geniuses of this type are so rare, so widely dispersed in time and space as Wagner sometimes put it, most geniuses (of Wagner's type) are potentially very isolated and lonely, or at least were until the development of major urban centers to which creative minds could gravitate and increase their chance of having fellowship with similarly gifted associates. So when they do find the means to re-connect with their true heritage left them by prior geniuses of their stamp (represented by Nothung, and by Mime's likely distorted memories of the Wälsung twins), their sense of identity as a unique individual with special gifts, and sense of alienation from the majority of men such as Mime, is greatly increased. Such men and women of genius look for consolation, not to be found generally among fellow humans, in the mysterious haunts of Nature (in their aesthetic way of experiencing the world), where they can truly know themselves. Why else have shamans and mystics of all times and places (including Jesus) made pilgrimages into the wilderness so they can receive their revelations without distraction!

As Siegfried strives with difficulty to imagine what his mother looked like, the forest murmurs based on H10 and H2 increase, and ultimately we hear H36 and H22 over H10, which recalls that moment in R.2 when Loge was about to narrate how futile was his search for anything in the world which the living, and man in particular, could accept as substitute for love and woman's worth. Wagner is identifying the feminine, and love, with Mother Nature (Erda), and with the primal preconscious feelings embodied by the Rhinedaughters. We also hear H65, which in this instance specifically references Sieglinde. Siegfried's meditation on how his mother died giving him birth offers us what I think is the authentic cause for the recurrence of H65 here, for his mother Sieglinde's death in childbirth is a figure for the sin Wotan committed against Mother Nature's (Erda's) truth, in depriving Alberich the truth-teller of his Ring and its power. As Alberich said in R.4, Wotan would be sinning against all that was, is, and will be (Erda told Wotan in R.4 she knows all that was, is, and will be) if he stole the Ring from Alberich and co-opted its power for the gods' sake. Alberich's Ring Curse, which Brünnhilde and Wotan's Wälsungs suffer, is the price Alberich swore Wotan and his proxies would pay for trying to co-opt Alberich's Ring power without paying his price of Noth. Siegfried will unwittingly inherit Wotan's sin against Mother Nature, and H65 expresses the Noth the Wälsungs must suffer as heroes unwittingly and involuntarily dedicated to Wotan's futile quest to free the gods from Alberich's Ring Curse.

Within the forest murmurs Siegfried can now distinguish particular birdsongs played for us by specific wind instruments, and one bird in particular comes to his attention, singing snatches of the new motifs H137ab and H138ab, which are pentatonic tunes. H138ab is derived from the first segment of Woglinde's Lullaby H4, which gave birth to the *Ring*'s first words. This was the mother-melody out of which, according to Wagner, human language grew, by natural necessity. Woglinde's Lullaby H4 was a futile attempt to preempt the "Fall":

> [pp. 238–9] **Siegfried:** (H10 >>:) You lovely woodbird! I've never heard you before. (...) Could I only make sense of his sweet-sounding babble! He must be telling me something—perhaps about my dear mother?—(H137b) A querulous dwarf explained to me once that in time one could come to unriddle the babbling of little birds: but how could that be possible? Hey! I'll try and copy him: I'll sound like him on a reed! If I do without the words and attend to the tune, I'll sing his language in that way and no doubt grasp what he's saying. (H56ab vari:; H102:; H138b/H10: He runs over to the nearby spring, cuts a reed with his sword and rapidly whittles a pipe from it. (...)) (...) (He blows into the pipe. H138a frags offkey/H10:) (...) ... on the reed the delightful tune doesn't work. I think, little bird, I'll remain a fool. From you it's not easy to learn!

If Woglinde's Lullaby H4 is Wagner's motival metaphor for the mother-melody, or primal preconscious animal instinct, out of which language grew, H138ab, variants of H4, may well represent not only the European orchestral music tradition which according to Wagner restores this lost language of feeling, especially as it was developed by Wagner as an integral aspect of music-drama, but also Wagner's musical motifs. Wagner said that in our time, language (allegedly) having lost its instinctual roots, and the evolution of conscious thought having produced modern science which constitutes a wholesale renunciation of love or subjective feeling, humans seek redemption from this excessive consciousness by descending from their intellectual heights to the depths of love, to restore lost innocence. We strive to restore lost innocence by seeking a language, orchestral music, which retreats from prosaic conceptual thought to return to its instinctual roots in feeling. This links the Woodbird's song directly to the sleeping Brünnhilde, guarded by H102 (another of this set of pentatonic Nature melodies), which suggests that Siegfried's muse Brünnhilde has some mysterious influence on this Woodbird's as yet unspoken but purely melodic appeal to Siegfried.

Wagner authored a poetic image of his music-dramas' orchestral music's place in history with the following description, which links it to the forest murmurs and Siegfried's eventual ability to discriminate particular voices of nature, the birdsongs, in the forest's hum: "I have recourse to metaphor ... to give you ... a picture of the melody ... encompassing the whole dramatic tone piece .... First of all ... it should exert on him somewhat the effect produced by a noble forest, of a summer evening, on the lonely visitant who has just left the city's din behind; the peculiar stamp of this impression ... is that of a silence growing more and more alive. (...) But when, overwhelmed by this first general impression, ... the last burden of the city's hubbub cast aside, ... as if hearing with new senses, he listens more and more intently—he perceives with ever greater plainness the infinite diversity of voices waking in the wood. Ever and ever a new voice peers forth ... he thinks he has never heard as yet ... ." [690W-{9/60}'Music of the Future,' PW Vol. III, p. 339] How interesting it is, in light of this passage, that Siegfried tells the Woodbird he's never heard it before! Cosima's record of Wagner's description of Beethoven's music as a restoration of the bird language which man allegedly spoke before the birth of conscious conceptual thought ("ideas"), provides further confirmation of our thesis (I have Jean-Jacques Nattiez's *Wagner Androgyne* to thank for this particular insight [Nattiez, pp. 74–75]): "... he is still delighted with the picture of Beethoven: 'That is how he looked, this poor man who gave us back the language men spoke before they had ideas; it was to recover this language of the birds that Man created the divine art." [751W-{7/4/69}CD Vol. I, p. 119]

On a multitude of occasions Wagner cited Schopenhauer's notion that anyone who could translate inspired music into words would discover the key to the world's enigma. [See 1055W-{1/17/81}CD Vol. II, p. 600] This is especially intriguing in light of Siegfried's initially inept attempt to grasp the meaning of the Woodbird's song by imitating it musically. Since the Woodbird's music's hidden meaning, or programme, will be revealed to Siegfried after he tastes the dead Fafner's blood, and the Woodbird's last and most important message will be that Siegfried should fulfill his lifelong quest for a boon companion by seeking the sleeping Brünnhilde, Brünnhilde, recipient and safe repository of Wotan's confession of his unspoken secret of the key to world history (which must remain forever unspoken in words), holds the key to the enigma of the world in this sense. It's musical motifs which will give the music-dramatist Siegfried (and perhaps his audience) the key to his own unconscious mind, Brünnhilde, who holds for him the solution to the enigma of the world (or at least the enigma of man).

Siegfried instinctively seeks to grasp the meaning of the Woodbird's musical speech, intuiting that it may be trying to tell Siegfried something about his mother (who died giving him birth). This is true in three senses. (1) Wagner mentioned on several occasions that the presence of H65 here represents Siegfried's dead mother Sieglinde's effort to warn her son, through the Woodbird's tune (the Woodbird being Sieglinde's spirit reincarnated), about Mime's treacherous plan to murder him, and also to guide him to his predestined bride Brünnhilde. [See, for instance, 745W-{2/24/69}Letter to King Ludwig II of Bavaria, SLRW,

p. 740]. But H65 is also the motival symbol of the Wälsungs' Noth (tragic fate), the cost of Wotan's implication of them in his futile quest to restore lost innocence. (2) Brünnhilde, whom the Woodbird will soon call on Siegfried to wake, woo, and win, will be mistaken by Siegfried in S.3.3 for his mother Sieglinde. I've explained previously that she's his metaphysical mother, his surrogate for Mother Nature. (3) The Forest Murmurs invoke Mother Nature, Erda, who embodies the natural necessity Siegfried's inspired artistic nature has inherited. It's Erda whom Wotan figuratively killed by sinning against her knowledge of all that was, is, and will be. When we consider that the Woodbird tunes H138ab are variants of Woglinde's Lullaby H4, through which she sought to prevent our waking (the Fall), evidently Siegfried's primal, subliminal motive expressed by the Woodbird's song is to seek to restore our condition before the Fall, our lost innocence, by rendering Alberich's Ring Curse of consciousness dormant through aesthetic intuition. Siegfried intuits unconsciously that he's inherited Wotan's sin against Mother Nature, religious world-denial.

Siegfried also makes a curious observation of potential significance. He notes that "a querulous dwarf" (Mime) once told him that one could eventually unravel the meaning of birdsong. Were Siegfried to reveal the unconscious source of inspiration, or programme, behind the Woodbird's music (the significance of Wotan's having figuratively murdered his Mother, Nature, the substance of Wotan's confession of his unspoken secret to Brünnhilde), and thus bring to pass what the querulous dwarf Mime told him was possible, making feeling rise to consciousness as thought (as Alberich warned in R.3 his hoard will rise from the silent depths to the light of day and overthrow the gods), Siegfried would remember his true identity as Wotan. But the Woodbird will instead show Siegfried how he can remain safely unconscious of his true source of inspiration by joining his muse Brünnhilde in loving union. It's also noteworthy that Siegfried's remark that Mime told him that in time one could unravel the meaning of birdsong foreshadows Hagen's request in T.3.2 that Siegfried sing to his audience, the Gibichung hunting party, the tale of how he learned the meaning of birdsong. This song culminates in Hagen's persuading Siegfried to drink a potion (antidote to Hagen's potion of love-and-forgetting) which recalls to Siegfried's memory his muse of unconscious artistic inspiration Brünnhilde, whom he's forgotten thanks to Hagen's first potion.

Siegfried fails to properly imitate or mime the birdsong on a primitive flute he's made so he can understand the Woodbird's musical language the way the Woodbird does, through feeling. Though the natural course of evolution is from instinct (feeling) to conceptual thought, mother-melody to word, love to power, Wagner in the redemptive Music-Drama sought to reverse the natural necessity of evolution and restore to us a pre-scientific mythological consciousness, a subliminal musical intuition represented by the Woodbird's Songs. The Woodbird's song H138ab is Wagner's symbol for Western orchestral music in general and his musical motifs in particular, the art which, because it most retreats from consciousness to unconsciousness, Wagner looked to for redemption. But Wagner could only obtain proper inspiration for musical composition from a dramatic programme. Siegfried finally gives up his futile attempt to imitate this voice of Nature with a natural reed flute, and tries to meet the Woodbird's challenge instead with his horn. Though made for Siegfried by the conventional craftsman Mime, it's Siegfried's virtual embodiment on which he plays his own heroic motifs. As Wagner oft-explained, the inspired artist doesn't merely imitate Nature, but idealizes it. So, in a spirit of devil-may-care, having failed to communicate with the Woodbird on its own terms, Siegfried now says he'll play his own tune to the Woodbird on his horn with which he's sought to call up a loving companion in the past without result. What he calls up instead is Fafner, whom Siegfried wakes. Fafner (like Brünnhilde) keeps Wotan's unspoken secret (i.e., Dark-Alberich's and Light-Alberich's forbidden hoard of worldly knowledge):

> [pp. 239–41] (He hears the woodbird again and looks up at it. H10; H138a; H39; H10)
>
> **Siegfried:** ... so listen now to my horn; ... . (H18a hint?:) A woodland tune—the blithest I can—you shall lend an ear to now. With it I tried to lure boon companions (:H18a hint?): ... Now let me see whom it lures here now: (H93c voc?:) will it be some boon companion (:H93c voc?)? (He takes the silver hunting-horn and blows into it. H108; H108 >>; H93a; H93ab; H108 >>, H47 >>/H116: At each sustained note, Siegfried looks expectantly at the bird. (...) H134b: Fafner, in the shape of a huge, lizard-like dragon has risen from his lair in the cave ... . (...)) (...) You'd make me a fine companion! (...)
>
> **Fafner:** (H134a) What's that there?
>
> **Siegfried:** Hey, if you're a beast that's able to talk, there's someone here who doesn't know fear. Is he able to learn fear from you? [**Fafner:** (...); **Siegfried:** (...)]
>
> **Fafner:** (... H134a) I wanted a drink but food I find, too! (...)
>
> [They continue to spar, prompting Siegfried to set upon Fafner: (...)] (H116: He draws his sword, leaps towards Fafner and stands there, challenging him. [Fafner's attempted assaults illustrate each of the kinds of harm Mime had described in succession, all of which Siegfried parries. (...)] (... Siegfried ... notes the position of the heart and thrusts in his sword as far as the hilt. Fafner ... sinks down on the wound, as Siegfried releases the sword and leaps to one side. H134a, H116)
>
> **Siegfried:** Lie there, (H134a) you spiteful ["neidischer"] churl! Nothung is lodged in your heart. (H134a/H49; [[**H139 orch:**]] [a peculiar four note motif, a variant of H134b repeated, at each repeat preceded by the glissando from H25a])

Instead of performing poor imitations of the Woodbird's tunes H137ab and H138ab, Siegfried plays his personal melodies, his Youthful Horn Call H108, H92 (Siegfried), and H116, a synthesis of H56 (Sword) and H108 introduced when Siegfried learned from Mime about the legacy left to him by his mother, the pieces of his father's sword. The boon companion Siegfried has unwittingly been seeking throughout his life by playing his characteristic motifs on his wooing horn is the muse of art Brünnhilde, who'll fall heir to Fafner's role as guardian of Alberich's Ring. We've already been conditioned by Wagner's extensive employment of motifs which evoke sleeping Brünnhilde and her protective ring of fire, in conjunction with Fafner's Serpent/Dragon Motif H47 (the fear Siegfried doesn't learn from Fafner he'll learn from Brünnhilde), to see Brünnhilde as closely linked to Fafner. This is partly explained by the identity of Alberich's hoard of treasure, which Fafner (Wotan's fear) guards, with Wotan's hoard of dangerous, fearful knowledge, which he imparted to Brünnhilde in his confession, repressing what he couldn't bear to speak aloud in words. Near the end of Siegfried's and Brünnhilde's love-duet in the finale of S.3.3, H47 will be heard as Brünnhilde asks Siegfried whether he's blinded by her gaze, now that she's succumbed to his love, and a moment later she'll ask him whether he fears her. Brünnhilde, who represents the unconscious mind and its special language music, will be the secular artist Siegfried's substitute for lost religious faith (Fafner). The art she inspires will provide Siegfried a substitute for the fear of knowledge, the basis of faith, which prohibited the faithful from examining the religious mysteries which, as Feuerbach said, they'd involuntarily and unconsciously invented in the first place. Since the music-dramatist Siegfried is going to unwittingly deliver the death blow to religious faith (Fafner), in taking responsibility for guarding the Ring, Tarnhelm, and Hoard which Siegfried will soon win from Fafner, he must also take responsibility for keeping Wotan's unspoken secret, i.e. keeping anyone besides himself from accessing Wotan's hoard of knowledge which Wotan repressed into his unconscious mind Brünnhilde. Siegfried alone can safely woo Brünnhilde.

How curious it is that Siegfried describes Fafner as a beast who's able to talk, from whom Siegfried hopes to learn fear, since man is the one beast who's able to talk, and it's man alone among all the animals whose reflective consciousness (Alberich's Ring Curse) grants foresight of his inevitable death, the source of man's existential fear, Fafner! Siegfried's death-blow to Fafner is embodied in a new motif H139, which is a subtle variation of the second segment of Fafner's Serpent/Fear Motif H134b, a disturbing, ominous four-note motif which continuously punctuates Fafner's dying words to Siegfried. It's preceded by the glissando which always introduces H25a (the basis for H134a). I've granted it status as a numbered motif because it's associated exclusively with Siegfried's deathblow to Fafner and with Fafner's mysterious dying words to Siegfried, which suggest Siegfried is controlled by forces outside of his ken. H139 creates a uniquely unnerving mood which Wagner sustains and elaborates in Siegfried's falling into a mysteriously receptive state of clairvoyance prior to tasting Fafner's blood and finding himself suddenly able to grasp the meaning (subliminally) of the Woodbird's song H138ab.

Siegfried has now emancipated himself from religious faith's prohibition against examination of its taboo on dangerous self-knowledge. Wagner, in the spirit of Feuerbach's praise of freedom of intellectual inquiry, noted in the following extract the role the poet (say, Siegfried) plays in dramatizing the freeing of human thought from the insufferable bond of religious dogma and state support of religion: "It ... became the poet's task to display the battle in which the Individual sought to free himself from the political State or religious Dogma ... . (...)/The dangerous corner of the human brain, into which the entire individuality had fled for refuge, — the State endeavoured to sweep it out ... , by the aid of religious Dogma; but here the State was doomed to failure ... . (...) The first purely human stir of freedom manifested itself in warding off the bondage of religious dogma; and freedom of thought the State at last was forced to yield." [510W-{50–1/51} *Opera and Drama*, PW Vol. II, pp. 195–197] Fafner, mortally wounded by Siegfried, now delivers his parting words, asking who this young lad might be who's stabbed him to the heart, and who or what might have prompted Siegfried to do what clearly his young brain didn't hatch on his own:

> **[pp. 241–2] Fafner:** (... H49 >>:; H134a:; **[[H139 orch:]]**) Who are you, valiant lad, who has wounded me to the heart (:H49; :H134a;)? Who goaded the mettlesome child to commit this murderous deed (:H139 orch)? (H50:) Your brain did not brood upon what you have done (:H50).
>
> **Siegfried:** (H93a orch:; H93b voc:) There is much that I still don't know (:H93a orch; :H93b voc): I still don't know who I am: (H93a:) to join in murderous fight with you you goaded me on yourself (:H93a). **[[H139 orch]]**
>
> **Fafner:** (H49:; **[[H139 orch:]]**) You bright-eyed boy, unknown to yourself: I'll tell you whom you have murdered (:H49; :H139 orch). (H25a:) The giants' towering race, Fasolt and Fafner (:H25a), both brothers now have fallen. (H25a) (H15 frag/H25a:) For curse-ridden gold, bequeathed by gods (:H25a), (H134a) I dealt my brother his deathblow (:H15 frag): (H47:) he who, as dragon, watched over the hoard, Fafner, the last of the giants, (H116) (H93c voc or H133 voc?:) was felled by a rosy-cheeked hero (:H93c voc or H133 voc?). (H49/H134a >>:) ... he who goaded you on in your blindness is plotting the death of the radiant youth (:H49/H134a). (H50:) Mark how it ends:—(dying) Pay heed to me (:H50).
>
> **Siegfried:** Advise me yet on where I have come from; wise you seem, wild beast, in dying: (H93a:) divine it from my name (:H93a): (H93c voc:) Siegfried am I called (:H93c voc).
>
> **Fafner:** (sighing deeply: H134ab) Siegfried! (He rears up and dies.)

When Fafner asks Siegfried who goaded him to kill Fafner, the obvious answer is Mime, but it was Wotan who first contemplated the need for a hero—freed from the gods' divine law—who might, of his own volition, do what the gods are forbidden to do, slay Fafner and take possession of Alberich's Ring, Tarnhelm and Hoard so Alberich can't regain possession of them. And Wotan imparted this desire to Brünnhilde, who imparted it to Siegfried by metaphysically giving birth to him. But as Fafner asks who prompted Siegfried to deliver his death blow, H49 and H50 remind us that we can trace this back furthest to Alberich's Ring Curse, for anyone who possesses the Ring, Alberich said, would die, and Fafner is now dying at Siegfried's hands. Siegfried has fallen heir to Alberich's Ring Curse not only by taking the Ring from Fafner, but also by being heir to the curse's primary victim, Wotan, who brought it on himself. The artist-hero Siegfried's murder of Fafner to take aesthetic possession of Alberich's and Wotan's hoard of knowledge of our subjection to Nature (fate), is a perpetuation of Wotan's original sin against Mother Nature, so naturally Siegfried inherits the Ring Curse Alberich intended to punish Wotan's sin. Siegfried, waking Brünnhilde, will also fall heir to Wotan's repository of knowledge of the inevitability of Alberich's victory.

Siegfried's answer to Fafner is that he doesn't know a great deal, even who he is. The reason Siegfried doesn't know his identity or prehistory isn't only the obvious fact that he was orphaned and deliberately brought up by Mime ignorant of his identity and heritage, but that Brünnhilde, as the store-place for Wotan's unspoken secret, knows Siegfried's true identity as Wotan (reborn) for Siegfried, so Siegfried's conscious mind can be freed from suffering from Wotan's paralyzing conceptual contradictions and foresight of the gods' inevitable end. Simply put, Siegfried doesn't know who he is because Brünnhilde (as she'll tell him in S.3.3) knows this for him. And Brünnhilde knows his true identity for him because Wotan, who abhorred and loathed himself, couldn't bear to consciously contemplate his self-knowledge, so he repressed it into his unconscious mind by confessing it to Brünnhilde, expressing his desire for a new identity purged of Wotan's loathsome self-knowledge and fear of the end. It would be easy to aver that Brünnhilde knows all this about Siegfried for the mundane reason that Siegfried was brought up mostly ignorant of his past, and Brünnhilde, as witness to much of that past, knows it for him. But if that was all that Wagner meant to imply, it would make nonsense of dozens of both subtle and overt musico-dramatic intimations of Brünnhilde's status as both Wotan's and Siegfried's unconscious mind, numerous clues from Wagner's other operas and music-dramas, and a rather large proportion of Wagner's writings and recorded remarks which bear on the *Ring*'s plot.

Wagner surely meant to imply more by Brünnhilde's remark in S.3.3 that what Siegfried doesn't know she knows for him, than this, not only because we hear the Fate Motif H87 when Brünnhilde tells Siegfried this, but also because the heroines of Wagner's three other mature music-dramas also possess knowledge of their hero-lovers' identity and history which the heroes don't possess. Eva, Walther von Stolzing's muse of unconscious artistic inspiration in *Mastersingers*, not only inspires Walther to create his victorious mastersong unconsciously in a dream, but Sachs (in this resembling Wotan in his confession to Brünnhilde) in his cobbling song of Act II privately confesses to Eva her responsibility to inspire Walther's art through their figurative marriage, which will give birth to a legitimate child, the redemptive mastersong. The reason she has this responsibility is that, as a metaphor for Eve in paradise, who broke faith with god-the-father by giving the forbidden fruit of that Tree of Knowledge which brought original sin into the world, and caused our exile from paradise, to her brother and mate Adam, it's Eva's responsibility to inspire Walther's secular art as a substitute for religion's promise of a restoration of lost paradise, on earth. And Walther, like his model Siegfried, remains oblivious to the conceptual content of Sachs's confession to Eva, but Eva, like Brünnhilde, understands Sachs's "Noth." Sachs's confession, imparted to Walther subliminally by his muse Eva, is the unconscious source of inspiration for Walther's redemptive mastersong, just as Wotan's confession to Brünnhilde is Siegfried's unconscious source of inspiration by his muse. Similarly, Isolde possessed secret knowledge of Tristan's true identity and fate which, though he becomes fully conscious of it only in the third act of *Tristan* (as Siegfried will in his last moment before death in T.3.2), she hides in silence for Tristan's sake. And Parsifal, who doesn't remember who he is, learns his identity from Kundry, who knows for him what he doesn't know, in *Parsifal*.

The primary basis of this peculiarity in the relationship of the artist-hero with his muse of inspiration and lover, the heroine in Wagner's music-dramas, is the relationship of Elsa with Lohengrin. Lohengrin makes it a condition of his marriage with Elsa, and of his promise to redeem her from the charge of murdering her brother Gottfried, that she never inquire after his origin or identity. But *Lohengrin*'s plot centers on Elsa's insistence on asking the forbidden question. She asks in spite of Lohengrin's warning that if she breaches the unquestioning faith he demands, all their happiness will be ended, because she wishes to help him keep his secret to protect him from the harm ("Noth") she believes he'll suffer if his true identity and origin are exposed. As I stated in my essay *How Elsa Showed Wagner the Way to Siegfried* (published by Stewart Spencer in the May, 1995 issue of "Wagner," the scholarly journal of The Wagner Society, London, UK), the revolutionary step from Elsa to Brünnhilde was the following. Unlike Elsa, who only offered to protect Lohengrin from harm (Noth) by sharing with him the duty to protect the secret of his true identity and origin, by virtue of Wotan confessing his dangerous self-knowledge to Brünnhilde (that Wotan and the gods aren't divine, but mortal), and thus repressing his self-knowledge in his unconscious mind, Brünnhilde could know Wotan's secret for him so he needn't suffer from consciousness of it himself. In this way Wotan was reborn as Siegfried, the hero who, unlike Wotan, is fearless, because he doesn't know who he is. Siegfried is Wotan reborn minus consciousness of his true identity and origin, just as in Wagner's allegorical scheme man's religious longing for transcendent value is reborn in secular art, particularly the art of music, when it can no longer sustain itself as religious faith, as thought, in the face of the advancement of conscious knowledge in science. In other words, Elsa's offer to become Lohengrin's unconscious mind, his redeemer, is rejected by Lohengrin, but when Brünnhilde makes a similar offer to Wotan, he accepts it. This is the basis for Wagner's transition from the creator of traditional romantic operas into the creator of revolutionary music-dramas.

When we complete this picture by adding that the muse Venus knows things about the artist-hero Tannhäuser's true but disreputable and therefore hidden source of unconscious artistic inspiration, which he forgets on waking, and that the Dutchman doubts that Senta's love would be equal to knowing the full truth about the Dutchman's identity and fate, this leaves little doubt something profound is at stake in this striking trope, that the heroine knows something potentially damaging about the hero's identity, origin, and fate in all of Wagner's canonical operas and music-dramas.

Fafner has offered Siegfried a brief biography of who he's killed, noting Siegfried has now killed the last of the Giants. Wotan seems now to be freed from the debt and guilt inherent in his original contract with them. Siegfried has broken the original social contract founded on the basis of religious faith. Now both the cynical, scientific world-view (soon to be represented by Hagen), and secular art (represented by Siegfried's and Brünnhilde's love), fall heir to what had once been a unitary religious world-view, science taking on religion's former role as an explanation of the world, staking a claim to truth and the power it brings, including an intent to explain away the mysteries of being, and secular art expressing man's religiously inspired longing for transcendent value. Fafner with his last breath warns Siegfried that the one who prompted Siegfried to murder him contemplates Siegfried's death. Proximately he's Mime, but actually he's Wotan.

Siegfried now has a startling revelation thanks to inadvertently tasting the dead Fafner's blood: he's suddenly able to grasp the Woodbird's song's meaning:

[pp. 242–3] Siegfried: The dead can serve as no source of knowledge. (H116 voc?:) So let my living sword now lead me (:H116 voc?)! (… H116: Siegfried now draws his sword from his [Fafner's] breast; as he does so, his hand comes into contact with the dragon's blood … .) Its blood is burning like fire. (Involuntarily, he raises his fingers to his mouth in order to suck the blood from them. As he gazes thoughtfully in front of him, his attention is caught increasingly by the song of the forest birds. H10 >>; H137ab, H138ab) It's almost as though (H137b:) the woodbirds were speaking to me. Was this brought about by the taste of blood? (…) (:H137b)

The Voice of a Woodbird: (… H138a voc/H10 orch >>>>:) Hey! Siegfried now owns the Nibelung hoard: o might he now find the hoard in the cave (:H138a voc)! (H138b voc:) If he wanted to win the Tarnhelm, it would serve him for wondrous deeds: but could he acquire the ring, it would make him lord of the world (:H138b voc)! (…)

Siegfried: (…) My thanks for your good counsel, you dear little bird: I'll gladly follow your call. (He turns to the back of the stage and descends into the cave … .)

When Siegfried, preparing to withdraw his sword from Fafner's dead body, declares that the dead can provide no source of knowledge, so his living sword will lead him, this is Siegfried's farewell to the articles of faith, customs, social norms, traditions, rules, regulations, and other constraints engendered by a society whose social order rests on religious faith and fear of the new, which according to Wagner is death, not life. When he withdraws his sword his hand is burned by Fafner's blood and, sucking it, Siegfried experiences a revelation, not divine from on high, but a natural one from his own unconscious mind. Having gained access—by killing faith's taboo on dangerous self-knowledge—to the religious mysteries hidden in our collective unconscious, Siegfried can tap the unconscious processes behind not only the religious self-deception of divine revelation, but also behind unconsciously inspired artistic illusion.

The first thing the Woodbird tells him is that he must now take (aesthetic) possession of the Hoard, Tarnhelm, and Ring. The Woodbird proclaims that while the Tarnhelm would help Siegfried perform "wonders" (linking it with Wagner's notions of religious and artistic "Wonder"), the Ring will make Siegfried "lord of the world." But this gift granted to man by his Ring of consciousness, world-rule, only Alberich embraces. Siegfried will instead employ the Tarnhelm's Wonder (imagination) and the Ring's power subliminally, as the hidden source of inspiration for his art. We may surmise the Woodbird is telling Siegfried these things subliminally, not consciously. Dramatic proof will soon be presented, but Wagner's description of Siegfried under the Woodbird's sway as being under a "narcosis" (a spell of which he's unconscious), when he follows the Woodbird's prompting to take possession of the Hoard, Tarnhelm, and Ring, should suffice for now: "Siegfried has slain Fafner: the forest murmurs that had earlier captivated him so charmingly now exert their magic spell; he understands the woodbird, and—as though guided by some sweet narcosis and obeying, as it were, some instruction without knowing what he is doing—goes into the dragon's cave to remove the hoard … ." [744W-{2/24/69} Letter to King Ludwig II of Bavaria, SLRW, pp. 739–740] Through the Woodbird's music Siegfried enters an altered, dreamlike state which blinds him to the outer, objective world, but in which he can access his unconscious mind and therefore woo his muse of artistic inspiration, Brünnhilde: "So wakes the child from the night of the mother-womb, and answer it the mother's crooning kisses; so understands the yearning youth the woodbird's mate-call, … till over him there comes the dreamlike state in which the ear reveals to him the inmost essence of all his eye had held suspended in the cheat of scattered show … ./ The dreamlike nature of the state into which we … are plunged through sympathetic hearing—… that world from whence the musician speaks to us—we recognise at once … : … that our eyesight is paralyzed … by the effect of music upon us … ." [773W-{9–12/70} 'Beethoven,' PW Vol. V, p. 74]

Siegfried, at the behest of his own musical inspiration through the Woodbird's songs, is taking "aesthetic" possession of Alberich's/Wotan's hoard of knowledge of the terrible world, his Tarnhelm of imagination and his power of conscious thought (the Ring), to redeem man from the bitter truth through art's illusion. Wagner, by the way, wrote on several occasions that Siegfried effectively becomes a Nibelung himself by virtue of taking possession of these Nibelung treasures: [See 369W-{6–8/48} 'The Wibelungen'—Revised summer of 1849, PW Vol. VII, p. 276] Taking artistic possession of the world, re-interpreting it in one's own image through artistic idealization, expresses what Nietzsche called the will-to-power. But Siegfried won't use this newly won power in Alberich's practical sense. Rather, he'll see the outer world subjectively through music's inner eye. As Wotan will tell him in S.3.2, Siegfried is the eye Wotan sacrificed to win wisdom (consciousness) and the Spear of divine authority (the social contract), Wotan's Fall.

The capstone of our discussion of this scene is one of Wagner's most telling observations about the relationship of his inspired secular art to religion. He suggested that while religion should seek to influence ethics (as Wotan, by bringing Siegfried's father Siegmund up, instilled in him a conscience which Feuerbach said was religion's best legacy to secular man), art should represent faith, since it can transform illusion into truth: "In our times, R. continues, religion should seek to influence ethics, and allow faith to be represented by art, which can transform illusion into truth." [994W-{11/14/79}CD Vol. II, p. 395] Siegfried the artist-hero, having breached religious faith and broken Wotan's social contract, thus neutralizing the fear of truth on which they depended (Fafner), has fallen heir to the duty to guard man's unspoken secret in his own unique art of the future, the Wagnerian music drama. Brünnhilde keeps this secret not only "for" Siegfried but "from" him. So Siegfried will, waking her, risk confronting the fearful secret of his true identity she keeps.

SIEGFRIED ≠ ACT TWO, SCENE THREE
(OUTSIDE FAFNER'S LAIR)
ALBERICH, MIME, SIEGFRIED, AND THE WOODBIRD

Alberich and Mime stumble into each other while pursuing their mutually antagonistic schemes to gain control of the Ring, in a lurching, bubbling scene whose fantastic orchestration seems rather like music composed by a 20th century composer such as Stravinsky in, perhaps, his *Rites of Spring*. The main motif which expresses their confrontation is H5, which we're hearing for the first time since it was employed in R.1 to express the urgency and greed of Alberich in motion. This brief confrontation dramatizes Wotan's remark to Alberich in S.2.2 that, with respect to competition for the Ring, besides Alberich only Mime desires it, and that Alberich can best grasp motives of those who're his own kind:

> [pp. 243–5] **Alberich:** (H5 >>:) Are you lusting after my gold, you rogue? Are you after my wealth?
>
> **Mime:** (H5 >>:) Get away from this place! The field is mine: why are you rummaging here? [**Alberich:** (…); **Mime:** (…)]
>
> **Alberich:** Was it you who robbed the gold for the ring from the Rhine? (H49 frag:) Was it you who cast the tenacious spell on the ring (:H49 frag)? (H49 frag)
>
> **Mime:** (H40A:) Who made the Tarnhelm that changes men's shapes? (H49 frag:) Did he who needed it think it up (:H40A; :H49 frag)?
>
> **Alberich:** (H49 frag:) What have you ever known about beating metals, you bungler? (H106:) The magic ring first forced the dwarf to lend me his skill (:H49; :H106).
>
> **Mime:** (…) (H106:) What you yourself lost my cunning would gain for me (:H106).

Alberich: (...) (H49 frag) It doesn't belong to you at all: the bright-eyed boy himself is its lord!

Mime: I brought him up; he'll pay me now for rearing him: (H38 >>:) for my pains and all the burdens I've borne I've long lain in wait for my wages (:H38)!

Alberich and Mime debate who has foremost claim to the Ring, and when—to compete with Alberich's just claim that he made the Ring—Mime tries to take credit for manufacturing the Tarnhelm, Alberich reminds him it was only thanks to the Ring's power, which Alberich's labor produced, that Mime could achieve this. Mime's name implies he's an imitator, not a creative founder like Alberich. Mime represents the average man who, with respect to cultural achievement, receives rather than gives, though without his labor no one would be able to give. When Alberich points out Mime's claims are irrelevant because Siegfried now owns the Ring, Mime asserts Siegfried owes Mime the Ring as payment for rearing him. Mime reared Siegfried for the sole purpose of winning it from Fafner. After this verbally hostile, vulgar exchange, Mime tries a new tack, negotiation, but Alberich will have none of it since Mime can't be trusted:

[pp. 245–6] Mime: (... H38/H131B frag vari:) Well, keep it then and ward the bright ring well! (...) (H38/H131B frag vari) (H112 vari:) I'll give it to you in return for my Tarnhelm's delightful toy: it befits us both that we share the spoils in this way (:H38/H131B frag vari; :H112 vari). (...)

Alberich: (... H106 voc?:) I? Share with you? And the Tarnhelm too? (...) (:H106 voc?) I'd never sleep safe from your snares!

Mime: (...) I'm to go empty-handed, quite unrewarded? (screeching) Will you leave me nothing?

Alberich: (H43:) Nothing at all ... (:H43)!

Mime: (...) ... Siegfried and his warrior's sword I'll call on to help me against you ... !

While Mime pretends to negotiate with Alberich H131B and H112 tell us Mime's mind is focussed on his plan to have Siegfried secure Alberich's Ring from Fafner and to dispatch Siegfried in order to take the Ring and Tarnhelm from him. Accordingly, Alberich's intuitive suspicion of his brother's motives (which Alberich can be assured are like his own) is expressed in his assertion that if he gave Mime the Tarnhelm in exchange for the Ring Alberich would never sleep safe. We're reminded that in sleep the power of Alberich's waking consciousness is liable to be subverted by the involuntary unconscious, the dreaming through which our egoistic motives have been sublimated into religious belief and the beauty of art. Mime wants the Ring's benefits without cost, without possessing Alberich's genius or courage that would make him worthy of it. Mime—like Wotan with respect to his son Siegmund—expects Siegfried will pay for his rearing by winning for Mime what he can't win on his own merits, the Ring's power. This debate between the Nibelung brothers about the right of possession becomes a moot point as Siegfried emerges from Fafner's cave carrying the Ring and Tarnhelm (but leaving the Nibelung Hoard behind). As he emerges Siegfried meditates on his new-won treasures:

[pp. 246–7] **Mime:** (turning round: H15 modulations:) Children's toys he's doubtless chosen.—

Alberich: (H15:) He's holding the Tarnhelm!

Mime: (H15:) But also the ring! [**Alberich:** (...)] (... H15:) Get him to give you the ring! I still mean to win it myself (:H15). (With his final words, Mime slips back into the forest.)

Alberich: (H15:) And yet it shall still (:H15) belong to its lord alone! (He disappears into the cleft. ... Siegfried has emerged from the cave, slowly and pensively, with the Tarnhelm and ring: H58a: sunk in thought, he contemplates his booty ... .)

Siegfried: What use you are I do not know: (H9:) but I took you from the heaped-up gold of the hoard (:H58a; :H9) (H58b:) since goodly counsel counseled me to do so (:H58b). (H58c:) May your trinkets serve as witness to this day's events: may the bauble recall (H116:) how, fighting, I vanquished Fafner but still haven't learned the meaning of fear (:H116; :H58c)! (H10: He tucks the Tarnhelm under his belt and puts the ring on his finger. Silence.)

On the face of it, Siegfried took the easily transported treasures which the Woodbird told him of, but left the Nibelung Hoard (which the Woodbird also said he now owns) behind because, presumably, it's too cumbersome to carry. But in T.1.2 when Hagen asks Siegfried what he did with the Hoard, Siegfried will nonchalantly respond that he'd almost forgotten about it, and that he left it in the cave because he didn't treasure its "barren worth." This seems at first to solve the problem. But it's noteworthy that thanks to the Woodbird's prompting Siegfried has, after all, taken possession of the most important items in the Nibelung Hoard, Alberich's Ring of power, which Alberich forged only by renouncing love, and the wondrous Tarnhelm which Mime made following Alberich's instructions. As Alberich said in R.4, the Nibelung Hoard can be regenerated through the power and wonder of the Ring and Tarnhelm. The question is, why aren't these also of "barren worth" to Siegfried, especially in view of the Woodbird having spelled out their worldly value and having instructed him to take possession of them? He never consciously uses the Ring's power, certainly not to attain world-rule, and the only use he makes of the Tarnhelm is something he couldn't have foreseen, that in T.1.3.B, under the influence of Hagen's potion, he'll employ its wonder to disguise himself as Gunther, so he can abduct Brünnhilde on Gunther's behalf and delude her into thinking himself Gunther. Since Siegfried is the last of the Wälsung race, fathered by Wotan to pre-empt Alberich's plan to win back his Ring power from Fafner and overthrow the gods, Siegfried has been prompted subliminally by Wotan's intent. That Siegfried is being influenced by Wotan's unconscious mind Brünnhilde (perhaps through the Woodbird) follows from the fact she's his metaphysical mother and unconscious repository of Wotan's need for redemption.

Wotan's hoard of knowledge is now embodied in both Alberich's Ring and in the hoard of knowledge Wotan imparted to Brünnhilde in his confession. So by carrying off Alberich's Ring of power and Tarnhelm of imagination (which will allow Siegfried to transform truth into illusion through artistic Wonder), Siegfried virtually carries off Alberich's Hoard of treasure. But he's carrying it off not to keep it himself: in T.P.B he'll leave the Ring with Brünnhilde so she (his unconscious mind) can keep its power safe. Having taken this dangerous hoard of knowledge away from Fafner's protection, Siegfried is at risk it will become conscious for him, so, just as Wotan repressed his hoard of knowledge, when it was threatening to rise to consciousness, by storing it in his unconscious mind Brünnhilde through his confession, Siegfried will repress this hoard of knowledge by leaving Alberich's Ring with Brünnhilde to keep its curse of consciousness dormant. Siegfried will employ the Tarnhelm's Wonder (imagination, one of the Ring's powers) to create cunning deeds of art inspired by Siegfried's muse Brünnhilde which, so long as Siegfried loves her, will keep Wotan's unspoken secret.

But if Siegfried's leaving the Hoard behind—while keeping the Ring and Tarnhelm—seems inexplicable, it's even more mysterious that, having a moment ago learned from the Woodbird the "use" he could make of Tarnhelm and Ring (that through the Tarnhelm he can perform wonders, and through the Ring's power he can rule the world), Siegfried now says he has no idea what use the Tarnhelm or Ring have. It's not that he's now forgotten what the Woodbird told him: Wagner is telling us that thanks to the Woodbird's music Siegfried knows the Ring's and Tarnhelm's use unconsciously, musically. Brünnhilde, his unconscious mind, holds this knowledge for him. Similarly, when Siegfried and Brünnhilde have attained the height of rapture near the end of their love duet in S.3.3 (Wagner's metaphor for Siegfried's unconscious artistic inspiration by his muse Brünnhilde), and Wotan's dangerous hoard of knowledge has been sublimated into tragic ecstasy by Siegfried's wondrous art, Siegfried will triumphantly tell her that the fear she taught him he's now forgotten, as we hear the Woodbird's Songs H137 and H138. How interesting then that Siegfried says that though he doesn't know the Nibelung treasures' use, they'll serve as witnesses to the fact he killed Fafner but didn't learn the meaning of fear from him, since he'll learn the meaning of fear (Wotan's fear of the gods' doom) from his muse Brünnhilde, but only to forget it! Brünnhilde's identification with the Woodbird is also underlined by Hagen's remark to Siegfried in T.3.2, in answer to Siegfried's question "Is Brünnhilde making him [Gunther] brood?," "If only he understood her, as you do the singing of birds!"

Siegfried's new-found ability to grasp the essence of Alberich's Ring and Tarnhelm musically is reflected in Wagner's thesis about the special kind of knowing through feeling or clairvoyance that the audience for his music-dramas will experience, thanks to the fact that the essential motives of the drama, embodied by musical motifs, can now sound in the orchestra, telling us subliminally of these motives behind the action, without the drama's characters having to proclaim their motives in words. Wotan, for instance, has—in his confession—submerged his conscious understanding of his motives, which were too venal for him to acknowledge even to himself, in his daughter Brünnhilde, Wagner's symbol for the unconscious mind and its special language of feeling, music. Originally, Woglinde's Lullaby H4, Wagner's symbol for primal mother-melody, evolved into word-speech, but Wotan wished to retreat from word-consciousness (telling Brünnhilde that what he confessed to her would remain forever unspoken in words) back into the safety of feeling, or melody, by imparting knowledge too dangerous to admit to consciousness to his Will Brünnhilde, so that, reborn ignorant of his true identity and origin in the naive and ignorant Siegfried, Wotan could restore the pre-Fall naiveté and spontaneity of man's childhood. Brünnhilde represents the special musical language of continuous organically evolving music, and motifs, which redeem the dramatic action, the Poet's aim, which Wotan has confessed to her. Wagner said: "… that Melody to whose birth we now are listening [i.e., inspired modern orchestral music, especially Beethovenian, which Wagner employs in his music-dramas], forms a complete contrast to the primal Mother-melody; … we may … denote its course as an advance from Understanding to Feeling, from Word-speech to Melody: as against the advance from Feeling to Understanding, from the Mother-melody to Word-speech." [536W-{50–1/51} *Opera and Drama*, PW Vol. II, p. 284] The Woodbird's motifs H137ab and H138ab, H138ab specifically being a variant of Woglinde's Lullaby H4, presumably represent this melody which retreats from abstract language back to feeling and instinct.

Having repressed conscious knowledge of his loathsome motives, his true identity, and his corrupt history, by imparting it to his unconscious mind Brünnhilde, Wotan has been reborn as Siegfried who, purged of Wotan's conscious awareness of contradiction, can become a "knower through feeling" as Wagner described this phenomenon: "In presence of the Dramatic Artwork, nothing should remain for the combining Intellect to search for. Everything in it must come to an issue sufficient to set our Feeling at rest thereon … . In the Drama, we must become knowers through the Feeling." [520W-{50–1/51} *Opera and Drama*, PW Vol. II, pp. 208–209] It's in this sense that the Woodbird has informed Siegfried of the aesthetic use he can make of the Tarnhelm and Ring, allowing him to remain conceptually ignorant (unconscious) of their practical use. It's as if through Siegfried's inspired art he can transform the corrupting Ring, for which Alberich only sought its "use," back into the pristine, guileless gold which the Rhinedaughters celebrated in song, dance, and verse. The ultimate consequence of this is that thanks to Brünnhilde, Siegfried can live in the present, drawing subliminal inspiration from Wotan's fear of Alberich's Ring Curse without suffering from consciousness of it, while she holds for him, and protects him from, the disturbing knowledge of his venal origins, and fateful future. Wagner put it this way: "Siegfried lives entirely in the present, he is the hero, the finest gift of the will [i.e., the finest gift of Brünnhilde, who is Wotan's "Will."]" [820W-{3/12/72} CD Vol. I, p. 466] "Music cannot think: but she can materialise thoughts, i.e., she can give forth their emotional contents as no longer merely recollected, but made present. (...) ... and inasmuch as we thus make our Feeling [the *Ring*'s musical motifs] a living witness to the organic growth of one definite emotion from out another [motifs heard in association with the events and images, symbols and ideas of the evolving *Ring* drama], we give to it ... a faculty of higher rank than thinking, ... the instinctive knowledge of a thought made real in Emotion." [542W-{50–1/51} *Opera and Drama*, PW Vol. II, pp. 329–330] This aesthetic understanding through feeling, aesthetic intuition, which for Wagner is more powerful than objective truth itself (at least subjectively and psychologically), this "Wonder" which the Wagnerian music-drama's musical motifs offer, is Wagner's substitute for the old religious faith in the supernatural ("dogmatic Wonder") which, in fear of the objective truth (Fafner's guardianship over Alberich's Hoard, Tarnhelm, and Ring), had imprisoned the mind, as he said in his explanation of the artistic "Wonder" (previously cited). [522W-{50–1/51} *Opera and Drama*, PW Vol. II, pp. 213–214]

Thus, in killing Fafner (religious faith's fear of truth), Siegfried has seemingly freed our mind from the practical, egoistic drives which according to Feuerbach aren't only the basis of our political life, but also of faith in the divine, in order to enjoy playing with the world aesthetically, as an observer, not a doer, in art. Mime's suggestion to Alberich that Siegfried is likely to have taken from the Hoard merely children's toys is unwittingly ironic: Siegfried, by taking aesthetic possession of humanity's hoard of forbidden knowledge, in order to draw inspiration from its horrors to sublimate them into art, will indeed transform this horror and woe into play, for as Wagner said, art is a profound form of play. And to dramatize this with the most artful subtlety Wagner in this passage (as Siegfried emerges from Fafner's cave carrying Alberich's Ring and Tarnhelm whose "use" he's already forgotten) calls up several of the motifs which evolved out of, or were associated with, the Rhinedaughters' song and verse and dance and play in celebration of the pre-fallen Rhinegold in R.1, namely H9 (Rhinegold), H15 (World-Mastery), and H58abc, which was their lament for the stolen Rhinegold heard in the finale of R.4, which they wish will be restored to them so they can forever celebrate it in song, verse, dance, and play. These motival references to the Rhinedaughters and the pristine condition of the pre-Fall Rhinegold serve several dramatic purposes: they tell us the ultimate destiny of the Ring is that it will be restored to the Rhinedaughters, thereby ending Alberich's Ring Curse, but more immediately, they tell us that when Siegfried leaves the Ring in Brünnhilde's hands so she can keep safe its power, she'll figuratively become his surrogate Rhine. By leaving his newly won Ring with Brünnhilde, he'll be able to neutralize Alberich's Ring Curse of consciousness and heal man's un-healing wound temporarily, just as throwing it back into the Rhine where the Rhinedaughters can dissolve it will end Alberich's Ring Curse permanently (more or less!). Brünnhilde's inspiration of Siegfried's art will temporarily give religion a new, but covert, lease on life, as feeling, in inspired secular art, the new religion (New Valhalla).

Having seen Siegfried obey its instructions to take possession of the Hoard (left behind, but incarnate now in the Ring), Tarnhelm, and Ring, the Woodbird delivers the second of three messages: having tasted the dead Fafner's blood, Siegfried not only grasps the meaning of the Woodbird's music, but can divine the treachery behind Mime's hypocritical protestations of sympathy for him:

[pp. 247–51] **Voice of the Woodbird:** (H138a voc/H10 orch >>:) Hey! Siegfried now owns the helm and the ring! Oh let him not trust the treacherous Mime (:H138a voc)! (H138b voc:) Were Siegfried to listen keenly to the rogue's hypocritical words (:H138b voc), (H137b voc:) he'd be able to understand what Mime means in his heart (:H137b voc); (H138b voc:) thus the taste of blood was of use to him (:H138b voc). (H65: Siegfried's expression and gestures show that he has understood the meaning of the Woodbird's song. (…))

Mime: (H65 >>:; H10 >>:) He ponders and broods on the booty's worth:—has some wily Wanderer been … (H35?:; H113 hints?:) … beguiling the child with his counsel of cunning runes (:H35?; :H113 hints?)? … I'll set the most cunning snare now and fool the defiant child with falsely friendly words (:H65)! (**[[H140 orch:]]** He comes close to Siegfried and welcomes him with wheedling gestures.) **[[H140 voc/orch:]]** Welcome, (H138a) Siegfried! Tell me, brave boy, have you learned the meaning of fear? (H131A)

Siegfried: (H131A:) I've not yet found a teacher (:H131A).

Mime: (H140:) But you've slain (H138a) the snake-like dragon … (:H140).

Siegfried: (…) (H131B vari:) The man who bade me murder him I hate much more than the dragon (:H131B vari).

Mime: (very amiably: H140 >>:) (…) You'll not have to see me much longer: (mawkishly) I'll soon lock your eyes in everlasting sleep! You've done (as though praising him) what I needed you for; all that I still want to do is to win from you the booty (:H140):—I think that I ought to succeed in that; you're easy enough to fool after all!

Siegfried: (H65:) So you're planning to do me harm (:H65)?

Mime: (surprised: H138a or H138b?/H140 >>: [H140's development here is possibly an embryo for Gunther's Motif H163 and other Gibichung-related thematic material from *Twilight of the Gods*?]) What, did I say that? (continuing tenderly) (…) You and your kind I have always hated with all my heart; (tenderly) it was not out of love that I brought you up, … : my efforts were aimed … at the hoard in Fafner's safekeeping. (as though promising him pretty things) If you don't give it up to me willingly now, (as though he were ready to lay down his life for him) Siegfried, my son, you must see for yourself—(with amiable jocularity) you must yield up your very life to me!

Siegfried: (H140:) That you hate me (H138a) I'm glad to hear: (H65:) but must I also yield up my life (:H65)? (H87) [**Mime:** (…); **Siegfried:** (…)]

Mime: ... How you mistake my meaning! (...) (H106 vari:) I'm taking greatest pains after all to hide, by dissembling (:H106 vari), my secret thoughts and you, stupid boy, interpret everything wrongly! (...) (very amiable again, making a visible effort: H114:) Take this, and drink this refreshment! (...)

Siegfried: (H131A vari:) I'd be glad of something good to drink: how did you brew this one here?

Mime: (merrily joking, as though describing a pleasantly intoxicated state which the juice would induce: H131A vari:) Hey, just drink it: trust in my art ["Kunst"] (:H131A end frag [Mime's potion])! (H131A vari: [with the oscillating chords associated with Mime's potion suggested by pizzicato sounding like a clock's tick-tock or metronome]) In darkness ["Nacht"] and mist ["Nebel," as in Nibelheim]) your senses will soon be shrouded: unwaking, unwitting, you'll straightaway stretch out your limbs (:H131A vari). (H125:) And once you're lying there, (H32B or H46 hint?) then I could easily take the spoils and conceal them (:H125) .... (H125:) And so with the (H32B or H46 hint?) sword ... (:H131A) (in a gesture of unrestrained merriment: H131A vari [the tick-tock ascending and descending]) I'll ... hack off the child's head: then I'll have peace of mind and the ring as well! (sniggering) (...) (H140:) now, my Wälsung, son of Wolfe! Drink and choke yourself to death: you'll never taste another drop (:H140)! (sniggering)

Siegfried: (... H116 frag voc?:) Have a taste of my sword, you loathsome babbler (:H116 frag voc?)! (As though in a paroxysm of violent loathing, he deals Mime a sudden blow; the latter immediately falls to the ground, dead. H106 vari [expressing alarm]; H38; H106, H38: (...)) Nothung pays the wages of spite ["Neides-Zoll"]: for that I had to forge it. (H50)

This extensive passage draws a subtle comparison between Wotan's exploitation of his Wälsung race to suffer Alberich's Noth in the gods' behalf, represented motivally by H65, and Mime's exploitation of Siegfried. The fact that thanks to the Woodbird's music (the dead Fafner's blood) Siegfried has an insight into the egoistic motives behind Mime's two-faced protestations of interest in Siegfried's welfare, parallels the fact that, thanks to Wotan's unconscious mind Brünnhilde (which/whom Siegfried will soon wake), Siegfried will have access to Wotan's unconscious thoughts which Wotan can't afford to be conscious of. While Mime is fully conscious he's attempting to deceive Siegfried in order to exploit him, Wotan is unconscious of the fact he's lying, because he's—as he told Brünnhilde in his confession—deceiving himself. Wagner also provides an illustration here of how his musical motifs disclose the hidden motives of his protagonists.

While Mime expresses his suspicion that the Wanderer (Wotan) is responsible for tipping Siegfried off about the virtues of the Ring and Tarnhelm he's chosen from the Hoard (Mime being wholly unaware that the Woodbird imparted this to Siegfried), we hear H65. While H65 represents Wotan's implication of the Wälsung race in his tragic, futile quest for redemption from his fate, thus subjecting them to Alberich's Ring Curse, it also calls to mind Wagner's remark that the recurrence of H65 here represents the concern of the spirit of Siegfried's dead mother Sieglinde for her son, as if Sieglinde has become reincarnate in the Woodbird: "When the woodbird warns Siegfried afresh against Mime's approach, and as the latter now creeps up from afar, wondering who could have told the lad of the ring, we hear ... his mother Sieglinde's loving concern for her son sound forth with tuneful tenderness—the son to whom, dying, she had given birth." [745W-{2/24/69}Letter to King Ludwig II of Bavaria, SLRW, p. 740] This presents a problem. While it follows logically from Sieglinde's concern for her son's welfare that her spirit, taking the form of the Woodbird, would tip him off to Mime's treacherous intent (we must assume she intuited this during her all too brief sojourn, prior to death, with Mime), and we can rationalize the Woodbird's final request that Siegfried seek the sleeping Brünnhilde for his bride as a logical follow-up to Sieglinde's expression of hope to Brünnhilde that her woe (the yet unborn Siegfried in her womb) would smile on Brünnhilde someday, it's not so easy, on this hypothesis, to make sense of the Woodbird's notifying Siegfried that in killing Fafner he's inherited the Hoard, Tarnhelm, and Ring. At no point in the *Ring* is there even a hint that the Wälsung twins Sieglinde or Siegmund know anything about Alberich's property or the Ring Curse. Wotan's whole intent in bringing the Wälsungs into the world was that they should know nothing of his craven fears or desires, but should do what Wotan wants of their own free volition, uninfluenced by his concerns. The only characters in the *Ring* who express a longing for Siegfried to take possession of these Nibelung treasures are Wotan and Mime, and Mime represents the prosaic basis of Wotan's motives. If we read the presence of H65 here not merely as a reminder of Siegfried's mother Sieglinde and her sympathy for the Wälsungs' fated Noth, but understand it more broadly as representing the Noth which the Wälsungs must suffer as victims of Wotan's need for a hero who'll take on the burden of Alberich's Ring Curse to redeem the gods from it, it follows that all three of the Woodbird's messages to Siegfried convey Wotan's long-term plan for him, as confessed to Brünnhilde. Mime's suspicion that the Wanderer (Wotan) informed Siegfried about the value of the Hoard, Tarnhelm, and Ring might well be accurate.

Throughout the entirety of Mime's song-and-dance about the love he bears Siegfried—while simultaneously, involuntarily confessing his treacherous intent—we hear a new motif H140 which we can call "Mime's Wheedling Song of False Friendship." H140, expressing Mime's hypocritical protestations of false friendship to Siegfried, sounds in its second half very like an embryo for Gunther's Motif H163. Gunther in T.1.2 will also extend false friendship to Siegfried after having conspired with his half-brother Hagen (Mime's nephew) to drug Siegfried in order to exploit him, a crime akin to that which Mime has attempted to commit. I also detect hints of various related (according to Cooke) Gibichung motifs which are, like H163, introduced in T.1.1–2, including H167 ("False Friendship"), during Mime's futile attempts to persuade Siegfried of his benevolent intent, while unwittingly confessing his fell intent.

H114 and H115, motifs which previously evoked parental love, are heard—with great ironic effect—while Mime speaks of his potion, pretending he's offering as refreshment what's really his means to kill Siegfried. Siegfried inquires, rhetorically of course, how Mime brewed this drink. Mime responds: never mind, just trust in my art! If you drink this your senses will descend into night ("Nacht") and mist ("Nebel"), verbal references to Nibelheim. As Mime introduces this verbal image of Nibelheim we hear a new variant of H131A which ends with a sort of tick-tock resembling a metronome, and H131A carries this metronome effect until Mime's death at Siegfried's hands. One wonders what the symbolic significance might be: did Wagner once suffer from music lessons delivered by an obnoxious pedant time-beater and carry his resentment over into Siegfried's contempt for Mime? Or is this tick-tock just a rhythmic variant of the oscillations, standing for Mime's potion, which are appended to H131A and H131B? In any case, it's worth noting the resemblance between Mime's confusion as he unwittingly speaks truth when he meant to lie, and Beckmesser's (an uninspired pedant) confusion as he mangles Walther's mastersong which he sings, presenting it as if it's his own composition, in *Mastersingers*.

After Mime offers Siegfried his fatal potion, telling him with glee to choke on it, Siegfried has had enough and is so filled with an "access of loathing" for Mime that he stikes him dead with Nothung, declaring that Nothung has paid the wages of spite ("Neid"). In the wake of Mime's death we enter a mysterious realm of revelation. After dropping Mime's body into Fafner's cave so Mime can, in death, watch over the hoard he so lusted after in life, Siegfried laboriously drags the dead Fafner over to sit him on top of the cave so he can watch after the hoard—which Siegfried will leave in the cave unused—as well. Wagner places an extraordinary amount of emphasis on the strenuous labor Siegfried must expend to drag Fafner's dead body over to sit him atop the cave where the Hoard he once guarded lies, and we're reminded that the Giants are repeatedly described in the course of the drama as oppressively weighing down the world with their great bulk. This is testimony to what Wagner described as the invincible power of egoism as the prime mover for all human thought, feeling, and action. After his intense exertion Siegfried suffers what can only be described as something akin to heat-stroke, and lies down in the shade of a lime tree to await the next, and in the event final and most important, revelation of the Woodbird:

[pp. 251–3] (He snatches up Mime's body and carries it to the knoll outside the mouth of the cave, H108/H38 varis [here and in the following passage H108 seems to merge with H38] throwing the body down into the cave.)

Siegfried: (H38 & H108 varis:) In the cave here lie on the hoard! (H50:) With obstinate cunning you tried to win it: the wondrous hoard is now yours to command (:H38/H108 varis; :H50)! (…) ((H134a:) With a mighty effort, he rolls the dragon's body over to the mouth of the cave, so that it blocks off the entrance completely.) (H47:) So lie there, too, mysterious beast, (H15:) and guard the glistening hoard together with your booty grabbing foe (:H15) … (:H47)! (He gazes down into the cave for awhile, thinking, then returns slowly, as though exhausted, to the front of the stage. H134a/H38:; H108 frag:; H191 harmony hint? He wipes his hand across his forehead.) (H127 orch: [which expressed Siegfried's heroic "labor" in preparing to re-forge, and then re-forging, Nothung, and here expresses great exhaustion]) I'm feeling hot from my heavy burden! My raging blood's racing fiercely through my veins ... (:H127). The sun's already high in the heavens: its eye stares down on the crown of my head from the brilliant blue above. (H137a:) Gentle coolness I choose beneath the lime (:H137a)! (H137b) (...) (H113:) Once more, my dear little bird ... (:H113), (H113 >>:) I'd be glad to hear (H115:) your song: on the branch I can see you blissfully swaying, twittering, brothers and sisters surround you, fluttering gaily and lovingly round (:H113; :H115)! But I am so alone, have no brothers or sisters; my mother died, my father was slain. Their son never saw them! (H140/H38:) A loathsome dwarf was my only companion; ... (:H140/H38); he slyly set me cunning snares:—now I've had to slay him! ([[H141A orch:]] He raises his eyes again, in painful emotion, to the branches above him) [H141A orch:]] My friendly woodbird, ... (:H141A orch): (H115:) would you grant me a boon companion? (...) So often I've tried to attract one but never yet obtained one: you, my dear friend (:H115), (H137b voc:) would surely do better! (...) (:H137b).

Voice of the Woodbird: (H138a voc/H10:) Hey! Siegfried's now slain the evil dwarf! Now I know the most glorious wife for him. High on a fell she sleeps, fire burns round her hall (:H138a voc/H10): (H137b voc:) if he passed through the blaze and awakened the bride (:H137b), Brünnhilde then would be his! (...)

Siegfried: [[H141B orch:]] O welcome song! (...) How it thrills my heart with kindling desire (:H141B orch)!

When Siegfried says the sun stares down at the crown of his head, and its eye looks on him from the brilliant blue above, experts on the lore of the Norse gods will remind us that the sun is sometimes considered Wotan's (or Odin's) eye. Mime had already alluded to this when, in S.1.2, thanks to the clap of thunder the Wanderer called up by plunging his Spear toward the earth, he recognized Wotan under the Wanderer's disguise and told him Wotan's eye had lighted on him. Wotan in S.3.2 will tell Siegfried that Siegfried is the eye Wotan is missing. Wotan's intent was that Siegfried alone should wake, woo, and wed Brünnhilde, as Wotan promised her in the finale of *The Valkyrie*, so it's as if the Woodbird's final message was sent by Wotan. Siegfried complains to the Woodbird that he's lonely, never having known his mother or father, and never having had any siblings or loving companions, but only the vile Mime. So Siegfried lays down under a lime tree hoping the Woodbird can tell him of a boon companion who'd suit him. The Woodbird does, telling him that Brünnhilde lies asleep within a ring of fire, and will be his bride if he wakes her. The sudden violent onset of Siegfried's loneliness and the urgency of his long-thwarted longing for a loving companion culminates in the introduction of motif H141AB, H141A being the segment of this motif which expresses Siegfried's lonely longing for a companion, and H141B representing his excitement after learning of such a companion, Brünnhilde, from the Woodbird. One might have thought, given the profound significance of Siegfried's special relationship with his muse Brünnhilde, that this urgent motif of longing would belong to her alone, but surprisingly, when in T.1.2 Hagen's first potion makes Siegfried forget Brünnhilde and fall in love with Gutrune, H141 will express the urgency of his new-found desire for Gutrune, as if Siegfried's overwhelming longing for his true love Brünnhilde was transferred to the wholly unworthy Gutrune.

Siegfried asks the Woodbird to explain the cause of this feeling coursing through him, and the answer the Woodbird offers is the secret of unconscious artistic inspiration, the true basis of the love the poet-dramatist shares with his muse, the music produced by his unconscious mind:

> **[pp. 253–4] Siegfried:** (H141B orch:) What courses so swiftly through heart and senses? (…) (:H141B orch)! (…)
>
> **Voice of the Woodbird:** (H10/H137b voc:) Delighting in sorrow, I sing of love; blissful I weave my lay from woe (:H137b voc): (H138a frag voc:) lovers alone can know its meaning (:H138a frag voc; :H10).
>
> **Siegfried: [[H141B orch:]]** Exulting, it drives me away from here, out of the forest and on to the fell (:H141B orch)!—(H?—Possibly an orchestral figure from Wotan's reconciliation with Brünnhilde in V.3.3?) (H33:) But tell me again … : shall I break through the fire (:H33)? (H93a:) Can I awaken the bride (:H93a; :H141B orch)? (Siegfried listens again: H141B orch/H102)
>
> **Voice of the Woodbird:** (H137b voc:) He who wins the bride and awakens Brünnhilde (:H137b voc) shall never be a coward: (H138a frag voc?:) only he who knows not fear (:H138a frag voc?)!
>
> **Siegfried:** … The foolish boy who knows not fear, my woodbird, that is I! This very day I tried in vain to learn from Fafner what fear may be. Now I burn with longing to learn it from Brünnhilde: how shall I find my way to the fell? (The bird flutters up, circles over Siegfried and flies off, hesitantly, in front of him.) (H? voc: [Siegfried's vocal music gives the impression of his last moment of childhood, his last childish utterance]) Thus shall the way be shown to me: wherever you flutter, there shall I follow (:H? voc)! (…)

There are two distinct—though probably related—sources of the Woodbird's description of the special kind of love which has possessed Siegfried. In V.3.1, after Brünnhilde foretold Sieglinde would suffer great Noth to bring the world's greatest hero Siegfried to birth, Sieglinde ran off to take refuge near Fafner's lair, where Wotan never tread. But before departing, she spoke to Brünnhilde of her hope that her child Siegfried would smile on Brünnhilde someday, and with her parting words said: "Let Sieglinde's woe be your blessing." If it's true that Wagner intended the Woodbird to represent the departed spirit of Siegfried's mother Sieglinde, who died giving him birth, this would lend the Woodbird's poetic description of the love Siegfried and Brünnhilde will share special poignancy. There's also the possible influence of Siegmund's heroic and loving remark in V.2.4 that rather than enjoy the sorrow-less youth eternal in Valhalla which Brünnhilde offered him, he preferred a mortal life of weal and woe alongside his sister-wife Sieglinde. But there's more! Siegfried is Wotan: man's religious longing for transcendent value is reincarnate in the secular artist-hero. Brünnhilde is Wotan's collective unconscious, in union with whom Siegfried will now seek artistic inspiration. Thanks to Brünnhilde, who protects Siegfried from suffering from the un-healing wound caused by Alberich's Ring Curse of consciousness, Siegfried will be able to draw artistic inspiration from the source of man's woe (the Wälsungs' Noth embodied by H65), Wotan's unspoken secret, without having to pay the price of becoming conscious of it. As Wotan said of Loge, the archetype for the artist-hero Siegfried, Loge's cunning can draw advantage from the enemy's envy. Loge's cunning consists in his capacity to employ art to transform what inspires horror and fear in us when we're conscious of it into aesthetic bliss when the horrific source of inspiration remains repressed and therefore unconscious.

Siegfried has one more question for the Woodbird: will he be able to pass through the fire and waken Brünnhilde? The Woodbird answers that only he who doesn't know fear can achieve this, and Siegfried recognizes himself as the hero who hasn't learned fear from Fafner. Fearlessness was, according to Wotan, the primary qualification for re-forging Nothung, killing both Fafner and Mime, and penetrating Loge's ring of fire to win Brünnhilde. Siegfried says he's eager to learn fear from Brünnhilde, since he couldn't learn it from Fafner, as if he has a subliminal premonition that by winning Brünnhilde's love he'll be taking possession of Wotan's hoard of fearful knowledge and thereby falling heir to Alberich's Ring Curse. We can now understand why throughout the first two acts of *Siegfried* the music describing Brünnhilde's sleep, protected by Loge's ring of fire from all but a fearless hero, was continually heard in conjunction with H47, which symbolizes the serpent/dragon Fafner as metaphor for the fear which warns humans away from examining the true source of their faith, the fatal knowledge Wotan imparted to Brünnhilde in his confession. Brünnhilde holds this knowledge for Siegfried, and it's for this reason that she, not Fafner, will be able to teach him the meaning of fear, so he can safely draw inspiration from it to create redemptive works of art. With that, Siegfried proclaims that he'll follow the Woodbird (music) wherever it flies (back to its source, its unconscious programme). Thus Siegfried has left his childhood (his "initiation rite" into manhood) behind, and embarks on his journey to adulthood.

SIEGFRIED ≠ ACT THREE, SCENE ONE
(BELOW BRÜNNHILDE'S ROCKY PEAK)
THE WANDERER (WOTAN) AND ERDA

It's a remarkable factor in Wagner's composition of the *Ring*'s music that he stopped composing it for twelve years, from 1857 and 1869. In 1857 he completed the music for the second act of *Siegfried*, but he wouldn't return to composition, picking up where he left off at the third act of *Siegfried*, until five years after King

Ludwig II of Bavaria had undertaken to finance his work. During this twelve year period Wagner completed the libretto texts and music of two other revolutionary music-dramas, *Tristan and Isolde*, and *The Mastersingers of Nuremberg*, both of which are systematically conceptually linked with the plot of *The Ring of the Nibelung*. This will be examined in detail in two chapters covering these respective music-dramas in Volume Two of *The Wound That Will Never Heal*. Wagner's fluency in composing music for his music-dramas advanced dramatically while completing these two smaller (though nonetheless very large) music-dramas, so that when he returned to composing the *Ring* he undertook this task with even greater sophistication than he had before, but miraculously without missing a beat, since he was able to sustain the musical atmosphere of the *Ring* almost as if he'd never taken a break from composing it, as he and others have observed.

Wagner wrote an intriguing description of the import of S.3.1 which registers vividly just how important he regarded this scene to the development of his *Ring* allegory: "If I wanted to tell you more about Siegfried today, I should have to speak of a dark, sublime and awesome dread with which I enter the realm of my third act. We come here, like the Hellenes at the reeking crevice at Delphi, to the nub of the great world tragedy: the world is on the brink of destruction; the god [Wotan] seeks to ensure that the world is reborn ... . Everything here is instinct with sublime terror, and can be spoken of only in riddles." [747W-{2/24/69}Letter to King Ludwig II of Bavaria, SLRW, p. 740]

Some argue that his employment of musical motifs had by this time grown much more independent of the immediate passages of libretto text with which they're associated, and it's widely believed that in many cases his use of specific motifs and their variants is often inspired solely by musical rather than dramatic considerations. I'd argue that in many such alleged cases the commentators haven't sufficiently grasped the conceptual context in which certain motifs appear, nor the full range of conceptual association acquired by motifs by virtue of all their recurrences in the course of the drama (their dramatic profile), to make such a judgment. We'll examine several such instances in the course of our assessment of the last act of *Siegfried* and the entirety of *Twilight of the Gods*, whose music was composed after this long hiatus. Cooke's justifiably famous taped lecture on Wagner's development of the *Ring*'s motif families contains an impressive description of the prelude to S.3, for here, he says, Wagner arranges and combines no less than 9 distinct motifs within a short span of time, to capture the essence of Wotan's dramatic situation. Wotan, still disguised as the Wanderer, has ostensibly come to wake Erda to obtain primal knowledge of how he might alter the course of the fate she foretold, or, barring that, at least to learn from her how he, the god, can overcome the dread her prophecy of the gods' fated end instilled in him:

> [pp. 254–5] (**Prelude:** A wild place at the foot of a rocky mountain ... . Night. H52/(H92 beneath most motifs); H82; H19 [modulation]; H2 & H53/H119 & H92 [repeats twice with modulation]; H2/H1 [modulates];

H43/H92; H2 chromatic inversion modulates; H101; H87; H19; H87; H19 [modulates]: A raging storm. Lightning and violent thunder … . The Wanderer … enters. (…))

Wanderer: [[**H142 voc:**]] Waken, vala! Vala, awake (:H142 voc)! (…) [[**H142 voc:**]] From mist-clad ["nebliger"] vault (:H142 voc), from night-veiled depths arise! (H52>>:) Erda! Erda! Eternal woman! (H2:) From native depths rise up to the heights! (…) (H2:; H53:) All-knowing! Primevally wise! Erda! (…) [[**H142 voc:**]] (…) Waken, awaken (:H142 voc)! You vala, (H19:) awaken (:H19)! (H19)

(H87: H101: The vaulted cave begins to glow with a bluish light, in which Erda is seen rising very slowly from the depths. She appears to be covered in hoar-frost … .)

Erda: (H101:) … from knowing sleep am I roused (:H101): (H87:) who is it who drives away my slumber (:H87)? (H87)

Wanderer: (H82a—i.e. H52 orch:) Your awakener am I, and strains I sing (H82b—i.e., H53 orch:) that all may (H2:) wake whom heavy sleep enfolds (:H82ab orch; :H2 orch). (H119 vari:) I roamed the world … (H2:) to garner knowledge and gain primeval lore (:H2). (H36 vari orch >>:) None there is wiser than you: to you is revealed what the depths conceal, what fills every hill and dale and moves through air and water. Where men have life your spirit moves (:H36 vari orch); where brains are brooding your mind remains; (H87?:) all, it is said, is made known to you (:H87?). [[**H142 orch:**]] That I may now gain knowledge (:H142 orch), I wake you from your sleep. (H19 vari)

If Wagner's motival music could speak in words, the essential message of this famous prelude would be that Wotan is in desperate need of a hero (H82ab = [H52 & 53/H80]), freed from the gods' protection and influence (though Wotan ultimately comes to believe he can never find such a hero), who can redeem the gods from the fearful fate (H87) Erda predicted (H52; H53), the twilight of the gods, a fate to which they're inevitably condemned by the power of Alberich's Ring (H43). Since Wotan can't actually redeem the gods from the fate Erda foretold, Wotan has been wandering the world (H119) seeking knowledge from the sleeping Erda (H101), or perhaps from their sleeping daughter Brünnhilde (H101), of how the gods may forget their fear of the fate she foretold, and to this end Wotan must use his authority (H19) to wake Erda, the author of his fear, to compel her to grant him forgetting of fear and dread.

Wotan introduces a new motif, H142, as he cries out for Erda to wake. It's in the family of love motifs which includes H23, H37, H39, H63b, H79b, and H150. It was, after all, through his loving union with Erda that she gave birth to their daughter Brünnhilde, who lies asleep within Loge's protective ring of fire on the mountain crag above the spot where Wotan now wakes Erda. He's using love's spell (H142) to seek a special kind of knowledge from Erda, aesthetic intuition, as he did once before when their union produced Brünnhilde. Wotan (as he described in R.4) seeks not only the knowledge of what he feared from Erda, but also knowledge of how to end his fear. Wotan's two distinct desires of Erda have given birth to Brünnhilde, from whom Siegfried won't only be able to learn the meaning of fear, but also how to forget the fear she teaches him. Thanks to Brünnhilde's love Siegfried will be able to repress fearful knowledge into his unconscious and transfigure it, through artistic inspiration, into a sublime artwork which can keep its true source of inspiration an unspoken secret.

As Wotan tells Erda he wandered the world to gather knowledge and primeval lore, we hear the first variant (H2) of the Primal Nature Motif H1. This reminds us that Erda possesses the ur-knowledge of natural necessity, which is unconscious and only to be woken by conscious man, to whom she gave birth. Wagner concurred with Feuerbach that in man alone Nature becomes conscious of itself. As Wotan elaborates on the infinite depth and breadth of her knowledge we hear a H36 variant which takes us back to the moment in R.2 when H36 heralded Loge's paean to love, in which he told the gods how none among the living would ever renounce love or woman's worth (knowing full well that Alberich had already done so).

Erda asks who it is who's awoken her, and Wotan answers "Your awakener am I." Is it possible that she, Mother Nature, mother of all things animate and inanimate, and Wotan's former lover, doesn't recognize him at night under his disguise as the Wanderer, when Alberich recognized him under this disguise in moonlight at night? I've previously argued that Wotan and Alberich are virtual alter-egos, the light and dark sides of the same person as Donington put it. We'll revisit this question near the end of this scene, where it's raised again in a manner which should provide an answer. But there's a formal, ritualistic aspect to Wotan's conversation with Erda, at least initially, a distancing such as one finds in formal contexts in which the parties speak of themselves in the third person. In any case, Wotan tells Erda nothing in telling her he's her "awakener," as this is self-evident.

We've come now to the "nub" of the drama, for in the following dialogue Wotan will make the same two requests of Erda which he made in the finale of R.4. He'll ask how, or whether, he can alter fate (alter the truth), or, barring that, how he can end the fear which foreknowledge of his irrevocable fate engenders, i.e., how he can cease to be conscious of knowledge he's found intolerable. These are rhetorical questions, since Wotan already told Alberich in S.2.1 that he's resigned himself to the fact that nothing can be altered (as we heard, significantly, H2, heard here again as Wotan wakes Erda). He also found his answer to both questions in his daughter via Erda, Brünnhilde, who, in loving union with the artist-hero Siegfried, will inspire him to create artworks which render the terrible world and its horrors (including the gods'—religious belief's—fate) harmless by sublimating tragedy into beauty:

> [pp. 255–6] **Erda:** (H101:) My sleep is dreaming, my dreaming brooding, (H58a or H12 vari?:) my brooding the exercise of knowledge (:H58a or H12 vari?). (H2:) But when I sleep, then Norns keep watch: they weave the rope and bravely spin whatever I know—why don't you ask the Norns (:H2)?

Wanderer: (H52:) In thrall to the world (H17:) those wise women weave (:H52; :H17): (H35:) naught can they make or mend (:H35); (H17:) but I'd thank the store of your wisdom (:H17) (H142) to be told how to hold back (H142) a rolling wheel. (H142; H142)

Erda: (H17 varis:) Deeds of men becloud my mind: wise though I am (:H17 varis), (H35) a ruler once tamed me. (H18a:) A wish-maid I bore to Wotan (:H18a): (H18b >>:) for him he bade her choose slain heroes (:H18b). (H76) (H102:) She is brave and wise withal (:H102): (H87 voc:) why waken me (H102) and not (:H87 voc) seek knowledge from Erda's and Wotan's child? (H18ab)

Wanderer: Do you mean the Valkyrie, Brünnhilde, the maid? (H49) (H99A:) She defied the master of storms when, with utmost effort, (H19 frag voc?:) he mastered himself (:H99A; :H19 frag voc?): what the lord of the battle longed to do but what he forbade—in spite of himself—his dissident daughter, all too conversantly ["allzu vertraut wagte die trotzige"], (H76:) dared ... to do for herself (:H76). War-father punished the maid; (H97 voc:) he closed her eyes in sleep; on yonder fell she's sleeping soundly (:H97 voc): (H19:; H17 hint?:) the hallowed maid will awaken only (:H19; H17 hint?) (H35:) to love a man as his wife (:H35). (H99B orch) (H87 frag:) what use would it be to question her (:H87 frag)? (H104)

Erda notes that while she sleeps (her sleep being dreaming, her dreaming brooding) her daughters the Norns wake and spin her self-knowledge, world-knowledge (of time=space, matter=energy, and Nature's coherence—Fate). Erda is saying that Nature acts from unconscious natural necessity, but gradually wakens as life evolves to the point of human consciousness. She asks why Wotan troubles her about knowledge when he could obtain it from her daughters the Norns, in whom it wakes (for man) as natural law, object of scientific knowledge. But this objective knowledge of what he fears isn't what Wotan seeks. Shortly after Wotan declared in R.4 he'd descend to Erda's depths to learn the full meaning of the fear her prophecy instilled in him, to ascertain whether he could escape the gods' shameful fate she foretold, he amended this intention after witnessing the first fruits of Alberich's Ring Curse, Fafner's murder of his brother Fasolt. This shocked Wotan: the implication was that self-interest always trumps love and altruism. Wotan found this intolerable, especially its ultimate consequence, that the gods, who embody man's longing to transcend Nature's laws and our inherent egoism to attain a more exalted, spiritual existence, were doomed to destruction by truth. So he declared instead he'd seek Erda to learn how to overcome his care, since he couldn't overcome its cause, the truth.

Wotan tells Erda he refuses to seek knowledge from her daughters the Norns because they weave their rope of fate according to the world (which belongs to Alberich), and can't alter the fate they spin. What Wotan requires instead is knowledge of how to stop a rolling wheel (the wheel of fate, or natural law). Yet he'd just finished telling Alberich that one can alter nothing in Alberich's world, the substance of Erda's knowledge. Wotan's present requests of Erda are merely a rhetorical recitation of concerns which no longer belabor him because he hopes to sacrifice his insupportable claim to the power of truth (Alberich's Ring), and to the real world, to Alberich, yet live on, reborn, freed from Alberich's Ring Curse of consciousness, in the love Siegfried and Brünnhilde will share, the inspired secular art to which their love will give birth. Wotan seems to be seeking an artistic miracle, a "Wonder," in which he can at least feel as if he's broken natural law's bonds, as if he's conquered man's subjection to the self-preservation instinct (Fafner), fear. It's this second choice, in which feeling substitutes for thought, which will produce inspired art as the "new religion," secular man's substitute for lost faith in the gods. Secular art arises only because religious faith in miracles is being replaced by the scientific world-view, and because secular art stakes no claim to the truth (the Ring), doesn't, like religion, strive to alter the objective world's nature to make it correspond with what we feel it ought to be. Secular art alters the real world only symbolically, through perception, and thus acknowledges its practical powerlessness. Its power is subjective, psychological, emotional. [See 1021W-{6–8/80} 'Religion and Art,' PW Vol. VI, pp. 215–216]

H17 is heard prominently as Wotan and Erda speak of the Norns' spinning. The meaning is clear: the power Alberich obtains through his Ring (H17) is the power we gain through objective knowledge, Erda's knowledge of all that was, is, and will be, which the Norns spin. When Wotan complains that the Norns can't make or mend this fate we hear H35, which reminds us that such power can only be won by embracing lovelessness. The power man amasses through advancement of scientific knowledge is amoral, and undermines our belief that human value and love are transcendent, declaring rather that they're physical phenomena which can be altered by physical means. The world, understood objectively, in full waking consciousness, is loveless. It's this unbearable truth which the Norns can't mend, which Wotan once desperately longed to transcend supernaturally (by stopping the rolling wheel of natural necessity), but now, having learned this is impossible (having acknowledged to Brünnhilde and Alberich that it is), longs to forget in the dreamlike aesthetic oblivion of inspired art.

Since Wotan isn't content with Nature's objective truth—spun by the Norns—because he can't live happily with it, Erda seems to say to herself, 'well then, if you can't handle the truth, why don't you seek knowledge instead from our daughter Brünnhilde?' When Erda suggests Wotan seek knowledge from Brünnhilde if he can't live with the objective knowledge the Norns would teach him, Erda invokes a different kind of knowledge, aesthetic intuition, the antithesis of objective knowledge. Aesthetic intuition is knowledge of man's psychological, emotional needs. Wagner captured this distinction beautifully in his remark to August Röckel that he rejects scientific, objective knowledge of Nature only when it interferes with Wagner's personal, subjective idea of love, and of what life ought to be. [See 624W-{1/25–26/54} Letter to August Röckel, SLRW, p. 312] And Wagner added that he, like Brünnhilde, would sooner die than resign himself to a real world in which transcendent love is merely an illusion. Wagner renounced objective knowledge of Nature because in his view, the real world—invulnerable to the distortions of human imagination—is loveless, so the primary impulse prompting all the living must be fear of death, the self-preservation urge. [See 812W-{2/8/72} CD Vol. I, p. 456, and 658W-{9/30/58} Letter to Mathilde Wesendonck, RWLMW, p. 46] That Wagner was prepared to acknowledge manmade fiction as the source of all value, which trumps objective truth, we see in his observation on the teaching of history: "He ... talks ... about the study of history in childhood and where one should begin ... ... and this without questioning the legendary parts, for what human beings have themselves thought out and imagined is more important than what really happened." [995W-{11/17/79}CD Vol. II, pp. 397–398]

But Wotan hasn't even hinted in his recitation of his breach with Brünnhilde at his hope that through the love she shares with Siegfried the world will be redeemed. He hasn't yet informed Erda that he relented under the sway of Brünnhilde's plea that only Wotan's free hero Siegfried be permitted to wake her. Wotan's change of heart is reflected here only in motifs which recall Brünnhilde's successful plea to Wotan to sympathize with her rebellion for compassion's sake (H98AB), Wotan's agreement to protect her sleep from all except fearless heroes (H102), and Wotan's tender, parting words to her (H104), which contradict the bleak message Wotan is now conveying to Erda in words. For this reason Wotan's response to Erda's suggestion that he seek a different kind of knowledge from Brünnhilde is fascinating. He breezily dismisses this idea with the remark that since Brünnhilde did, "all too conversantly," what he desperately wished to do but couldn't because of the objective constraints on him, he punished her with sleep to wake only for a man who'll make her his wife. So he asks Erda what "use" it would be to ask Brünnhilde. Brünnhilde's "use" is that she'll wake only for Siegfried the artist-hero, who, alone among men, will have the gift of unconscious artistic inspiration which allows him to safely plunge into his own silent depths, his muse Brünnhilde, to confront Dark-Alberich's and Light-Alberich's (Wotan's) Hoard of knowledge (our repressed Serpent of Fear Fafner), to draw inspiration from it which gives birth to that redemptive art which reconciles us to the terrible world. During his confession to Brünnhilde in V.2.2 he asked what "use" his Will (Brünnhilde) could be to him, since he can't will a free hero into existence. But it was through his confession to her, the womb of his wishes, that god-the-father Wotan planted the seed (god's word, which became flesh) which gave metaphysical birth to the savior Siegfried, in whom Wotan's ideal self is reborn minus his prosaic, lower self Mime, i.e., minus consciousness of his true identity.

Having learned from her awakener of the fate Wotan condemned their daughter Brünnhilde to endure, Erda launches a diatribe against Wotan's hypocrisy and inconsistency. She asks why he punished Brünnhilde for doing what deep in his heart he wished her to do. She chastises him also for his inconsistency in making laws only to break them:

> [pp. 256–7] **Erda:** (H104:) I've grown confused since I was wakened: wild and awry the world revolves (:H104)! (H101:) The valkyrie, the vala's child, atones in trammels of sleep (:H101) while her (H87:) knowing mother slept

(:H87)? (H99A:) Does he who taught defiance (:H99A) (H87:) scourge defiance (:H87)? (...) (H99A) Does he who safeguards rights and helps (H87) uphold sworn oaths gainsay that (H87) right and rule through perjured oath?—(H87:) Let sleep descend once more (:H87): (H101:) let sleep enfold my knowledge (:H101)!

Making laws only to break them is something Mother Nature, in her self-consistency, would never do, since the universe's laws are coherent and unitary, just as Alberich's objective understanding of Nature is, whereas Wotan (religious man), who rebels against reality and his own human nature, is divided against himself. I previously cited Feuerbach's observation that gods can make their own laws or break them through miracles. [See 292F-LER, p. 241] This contrasts with Nature's laws which he said remain always the same, unbroken, unalterable: "A will that is not *manifested as a will*, but as an *unalterable law* is no will at all, it is only a clerical phrase and circumlocution for natural necessity .... A will that always does the same thing is not a will. If we deny that nature has free will it is only for one reason, because it always does the same thing." [293F-LER, pp. 241–242]

Erda's diatribe is the voice of Wotan's cosmic conscience, man's truth-instinct (in contrast to Fricka, Wotan's socio-religious conscience), the never-ending quest to know the reason for everything, a quest which insists on self-consistency and lawfulness, "fate" in its natural sense. So, as Erda castigates Wotan for his hypocrisy, H99, which expressed Brünnhilde's rebellion against Wotan's outward command in favor of his innermost desire (proof that Wotan is divided against himself yet refuses to acknowledge it because he punishes Brünnhilde for acting on it), is repeatedly contrasted with H87 (Fate). Wagner described Erda as Wotan's "conscience" and "superior." [See 877W-{6–8/76} WRR, p. 103] It's interesting that Wagner should say Erda is Wotan's conscience, since Wotan will at the end of S.3.1 consign her, his truth-conscience, to the oblivion of slumber and dreaming, damning her as "primeval mothers' fear, primeval care," since she's foretold Alberich's inevitable victory over the gods. This perhaps explains why Erda, Mother Nature, said she's grown confused since she became conscious of herself in the newly evolved human species. Since humans, in whom Nature first becomes self-conscious, are the first and only animals who've sought autonomy from their source by positing transcendent gods, who aren't only autonomous from Nature but in some cases are believed to have created Nature, we humans have figuratively murdered her. If Nature renounces herself in us, as she seems to do through our religious belief in a transcendent realm of being held to be free from her ur-law, then Mother Nature has indeed become confused since she wakened.

Having virtually repeated his initial request he made of Erda in R.4, that she tell him why he must live in fear, by asking her now to impart her objective knowledge of the gods' fate (and, implicitly, how he might overcome its cause, when he asks her how he might stop the rolling wheel of fate), Wotan now paraphrases his second request of Erda from R.4 by asking her how he, the god, can overcome his care. This is also a rhetorical question because Wotan not only knows he can't escape the fate Erda prophesied in R.4 (a fact he admitted to Alberich in S.2.1), but knows the objective knowledge which Erda and the Norns would teach doesn't embrace the redeeming love that their daughter Brünnhilde, his unconscious, alone can grant. Wotan seeks to remain unconscious of the fateful truth which can't be altered. He knew the answer to his questions before he asked them:

> [p. 257] **Wanderer:** (H142:) Mother, I'll not let you go while I yet have mastery over the spell (:H142). Primevally wise you thrust ere now the thorn of care into Wotan's venturous heart: (H2:) with fear of (:H2) (H53:) a shamefully adverse end your knowledge filled him till dread enmeshed his mind. (H81) (H119:) If you are the world's wisest woman, then tell me now (:H119): (H19:) how can the god overcome his care (:H19)?
>
> **Erda:** You are not what you say you are! (H17:) Stubborn and wild-spirited god ["god" isn't even hinted at in the German: "Was kam'st du störrischer Wilder, zu stören der Wala Schlaf?," so this mistranslation evidently destroys the meaning of this passage, in which Erda is telling Wotan that he isn't what he calls himself, a god!], why have you come (:H17) (H35:) to disturb the vala's sleep (:H35)? (H44 or H81 vari?)
>
> **Wanderer:** (H142:) You are not what you think you are (:H142)! The wisdom of primeval mothers draws towards its end: your knowledge ["Wissen"] wanes before my will. Do you know what Wotan wills? (long silence.)

Just after Wotan describes how Erda's prophecy in R.4 of the gods' shamefully adverse end thrust the thorn of care in his heart till dread enmeshed his mind, but before he asks her how the god can overcome his care, we hear H81 (Wotan's Revolt), introduced in V.2.2 just prior to Wotan's confession to Brünnhilde, through which he repressed his hoard of fateful knowledge of the gods' shameful end—imparted by Erda—into his unconscious mind. It was through his confession to Brünnhilde, symbolized by H81, that Wotan, reborn as the artist Siegfried, can overcome his care.

Erda's answer to Wotan's question, how can the God overcome his care, is that the Wanderer isn't "what" he says he is, not "who" he calls himself: "Du bist—nicht was du dich nenn'st." The Wanderer, in disguise, called himself Erda's "awakener," but whatever the Wanderer's true identity is, he's nonetheless also her awakener because he did wake her, so she can't be alluding to the name Wotan gave himself at the beginning of their S.3.1 dialogue when she says he's not what he calls himself. Erda must instead be denying that Wotan is what he (disguised as the Wanderer) just called himself, the "god." Also, is it likely Erda, Wotan's former lover and knower of all things (all things in the real world, if not the world of man's imagination, though that too, in the final analysis, has a natural origin, and must be embraced by her knowledge), wouldn't recognize the Wanderer as Wotan, when Alberich recognized him immediately? One reason for confusion here is that where Wagner's German has Erda say: "Was kam'st du störrischer Wilder zu stören du Wala Schlaf?," Spencer translated it as: "Stubborn, wild-spirited god, why have you come to disturb the vala's sleep?" There's not the least hint of the word "god" in the German, "störrischer Wilder," which might best be translated "disruptive madman," or "disturbing wild-man." Also, the fact that Erda doesn't assert that Wotan isn't "who" he says he is, but rather, tells him that he isn't "what" he says he is (and given the fact that he's clearly what he says he is, her awakener), implies that Erda is referring to Wotan's description of himself as the god. Erda's depreciation of Wotan's self-image as a god is merely another way of saying what she told him in R.4, that all things that are, including the gods, will end.

Wotan, enraged by Erda's (Mother Nature's) arrogance in the face of his self-proclaimed status as a transcendent God, now openly proclaims his intent to escape Alberich's Ring Curse (Fate) by suppressing consciousness of Erda's objective knowledge through the magic of his Will Brünnhilde, before whom, as he says, Erda's knowledge wanes. This tells us unequivocally that by virtue of having confessed the knowledge of world-history and the gods's fated doom (the destiny of religious belief), which Erda taught him, to their daughter Brünnhilde, his unconscious mind, Wotan has freed his reincarnate self Siegfried from Erda's fearful knowledge, and therefore freed him temporarily from Alberich's Ring Curse of consciousness. Erda's fearful foreknowledge thus wanes before Siegfried's muse Brünnhilde, Wotan's "Will."

Wotan parries Erda's thrust—her accusation that he's not what he calls himself, a god—brilliantly, by informing her he no longer fears the end of (belief in) the gods she once prophesied, because now he wills it. He wills it because, having once in despair left Alberich's son Hagen heir to the world, including all that Wotan despises about himself and the gods (the practical motives behind religious faith, represented by Fafner and Mime, now dead), which he willingly sacrifices to Alberich, he sees now that Valhalla's virtues, the promise of sorrow-less youth eternal, transcendent love, and freedom from fear of truth, will live on as pure feeling unadulterated by religious belief's refutable claims to the truth, in Wotan's chosen heir, the artist-hero Siegfried, to whom Wotan leaves his purified legacy:

> [pp. 257–8] **Wanderer:** (H52:) O unwise woman, I call on you now (:H52) (H53:) to sleep forever, free from care (:H53)! (H142 chord) Fear of the end of the gods no longer consumes me now that my wish so wills it! (H142) What I once resolved in despair, (H67 hint voc?:) in the searing smart of inner turmoil (:H67 hint voc?), (H142 vari:; H93c voc:) I now perform freely in gladness and joy (:H142 vari; :H93c voc): **[[H143 orch]]** though once, in furious loathing ["Ekel"], (H35 voc:) I bequeathed the world to the Nibelung's spite ["Neid"] (:H35 voc), (H93a) to the (H142) lordliest Wälsung (H142) I leave my heritage now. (H18ab vari) He whom I chose ... , though deprived of my counsel, has won for himself the Nibelung's ring: (H56ab) (H15 "Triumphant" varis:) rejoicing in love, while free from greed ["Neides"], (H23) Alberich's curse is powerless over the noble youth; (H93a) for fear remains unknown to him (:H15 "Triumphant" varis).

Wotan no longer fears the end Erda foresaw because he (religion) lives on in Siegfried (secular art). Wotan wills his own end because Alberich's threat to raise his Hoard of knowledge from the silent depths of Nature's sleep, and man's unconscious, to the light of day, will inevitably destroy belief in the gods in the course of history, so Wotan is merely willing the necessary. The "end" of the gods, which Wotan once resolved to bring about—in his confession to Brünnhilde—in despair at the inevitability that Alberich and his son Hagen would inherit the real world after destroying the gods, he now wills with the serenity which arises from his confidence that his legacy, Valhalla, will live on freed from Alberich's Ring Curse in Siegfried's and Brünnhilde's love, which will create a New Valhalla, a new religion of art. Siegfried won't fall heir to the real, loveless (H35) world which Wotan bequeathed to Alberich's spite ("Neid," embodied by Alberich's son Hagen), but to the purified essence of Wotan's legacy Valhalla, purged of man's compromising belief in the supernatural.

This is the Feuerbachian turning point when collective man, no longer requiring belief in gods to make life livable, acknowledges the gods were, all along, just man's projected ideals: "The necessary turning point of history is ... the open confession, that the consciousness of God is nothing else than the consciousness of the species; ... that there is no other essence which man can think, dream of, imagine, feel, believe in, wish for, love and adore as the *absolute*, than the essence of human nature itself." [139F-EOC, p. 270] "*Man is the God of Christianity, Anthropology the mystery of Christian theology.* The history of Christianity has had for its grand result the unveiling of this mystery ..... ." [175F-EOC, p. 336; [See also 377W-{6–8/48} 'The Nibelungen Myth,' PW Vol. VII, pp. 302–303] Wotan's bestowing his legacy on Siegfried has introduced one of the *Ring*'s most important motifs H143 ("World-Inheritance"), the only *Ring* motif which can truly be identified as "Redemption by Love," but only if love is grasped as a metaphor for redemption of dying religious faith by unconsciously inspired art. Feuerbach expressed it this way: "Love conquers god. It was love [the savior Jesus, a model for Siegfried, and the virgin Mary, a model for Brünnhilde as Siegfried's metaphysical mother] to which god [God-the-Father Wotan] sacrificed his divine majesty. (...) As god has renounced himself out of love, so we, out of love, should renounce god... ." [62F-EOC, p. 53; See also 517W]

As for who'll inherit this new world, on the one hand Alberich's son Hagen (the modern world's scientific, secular spirit) will inherit religion's former role of explaining the world and manipulating our knowledge of it for our benefit, because Wotan has acknowledged that he, the alleged God, can perform no miracles to alter Nature's laws. This is what Wotan meant when he told Alberich in S.2.1 that he leaves the field to him. What was once explained supernaturally and mythologically will now be explained from the perspective of Nature's laws. Siegfried the artist-hero, on the other hand, will fall heir to religious man's longing for transcendent value, the musical or aesthetic aspect of religious belief, by winning the love of his muse, Wotan's daughter Brünnhilde. According to Wagner, Feuerbach taught him what we've traditionally described as spirit (the gods), the object of religious faith, is actually man's aesthetic sense [Brünnhilde]: "The fact that he [Feuerbach] proclaimed what we call 'spirit' to lie in our aesthetic perceptions of the tangible world ... was what afforded me such useful support in my conception of a work of art which would be all-embracing while remaining comprehensible to the simplest, purely-human power of discernment [through the Wonder of Wagner's musical motifs], that is, of the drama made perfect ... in 'the artwork of the future' ... ." [387W {?/49} ML, p. 431]

As Feuerbach said (278F previously cited), both science (Hagen), and secular art (Siegfried's love for his muse Brünnhilde), originated in religion (Wotan), and fall heir to its two primary functions: "Everything which later became a field of independent human activity, of culture, was originally an aspect of religion: all the arts, all the sciences ... ." [278F-LER, pp. 209–210] "... the faith of this age [Wotan] is not an uncompromising, living faith, but a sceptical, eclectic, unbelieving faith, curtailed and maimed by the power of art [the music-dramatist Siegfried's loving relationship with his muse of inspiration, Brünnhilde] and science [Hagen]." [170F-EOC, p. 323] Wagner summed up Feuerbach's argument by ascribing the mind's highest "power" to science, and the mind's enjoyment (aesthetic pleasure) to art: "Science is the highest power of the human mind; but the enjoyment of this power is art." [470W-{49–51 (?)} Notes for 'Artisthood of the Future' (unfinished), Sketches and Fragments, PW Vol. VIII, p. 350]

So long as art is tied to religious belief and dogma it remains vulnerable to suffering religious faith's fate at the hands of modern scientific and secular thought. Religious belief in gods (Fafner, Wotan's faith's fear of truth, and Mime, the practical egoism behind religious belief) must go down to destruction as a concept for Siegfried to redeem the gods from destruction in feeling, or love. The escape hatch which Wotan's collective unconscious Brünnhilde offers as an alternative to his nihilistic impulse to self-destruction, which might otherwise wholly consume now disillusioned religious men (who'd previously staked life's meaning on redemption in heaven), is Wagner's redemptive secular art. This is the meaning of H143, the only *Ring* motif Wagner ever christened a "redemption motif," whose first occurrence here he described as sounding like the proclamation of a "new religion": "Wagner expressly demanded that the Redemption theme [H143], as it enters after Wotan's words, 'Was in des Zwiespalt's wildem Schmerze verzweifelnd eins ich beschloss, froh und freudig fuehre, frei ich nun aus' ["What I once resolved in despair, in the searing smart of inner turmoil, I now perform freely, in gladness and joy ... ." (H143)], ... should be ... 'very brought out ... . He once characterized the spiritual significance of this theme ... by the statement: 'It must sound like the proclamation of a new religion.'" [878W-{6–8/76} WRR, p. 103] In Feuerbach's description of his "new religion" of secularism we find a basis for Wagner's notion that his secular art is a new religion: "... our religious doctrines and usages ... stand in the most glaring contradiction to our present cultural and material situation; our task today is to do away with this loathsome and disastrous contradiction. Its elimination is the indispensable condition for the rebirth of mankind ... . (...) A new era ... requires ...—if we wish to retain the word—a *new religion*!" [283F-LER, pp. 216–217]

The only way out of Wotan's irresolvable existential dilemma—that he can no longer sustain religious man's consoling self-deception in the face of the inevitable rise to consciousness of Alberich's hoard of objective knowledge, yet can't psychologically bear to live within the prosaic world known to science in which egoism is universally accepted as our strongest or sole motive—is by retreating to feeling, man's innermost depth, in art. Only this way can Wotan salvage the best, ageless part of himself from the nihilistic self-destruction to which he originally consigned Valhalla (religious belief). In the following extract Wagner offers a striking description, surely a model for Wotan's relationship with Siegfried, of his historical position as an artist, whose creative gift allows him to rise above religious man's nihilistic longing to end it all in the face of the world's prosaic ugliness, and redeem himself from this insufferable existence in that "true-dream image" called art: "Who can look, his lifetime long, with open eyes and unpent heart upon this world of robbery and murder organized and legalised by lying, deceit and hypocrisy, without being forced to flee from it ... in shuddering disgust? Wither turns his gaze? Too often to the pit of death [Wotan informed Brünnhilde in V.2.2 that he now seeks "Das Ende!"]. But him whose calling and ... fate have fenced from that [the artist], to him the truest likeness of the world ... [the work of art] may well appear the herald of redemption sent us by its inmost soul. To be able to forget the actual world of fraud in this true-dream image, will seem to him the guerdon of the sorrowful sincerity with which he recognised its wretchedness. [Wotan's confession of his unbearable knowledge to Brünnhilde is the hidden source of Siegfried's unconscious artistic inspiration]" [1141W-{11/82} 'Parsifal at Bayreuth, 1882,' PW Vol. VI, p. 312; See also 580W; and 694W-{64–2/65} 'On State and Religion,' PW Vol. IV, pp. 8–9]

The notion that Wotan (religion) lives on reborn in Siegfried (inspired secular art) thanks to Brünnhilde, who holds for Siegfried—and thus protects him from the paralyzing effect of—Wotan's fatal self-knowledge, Wagner confirmed in the following extract: "It [S.3.1] is the most sublime of all scenes for the most tragic of my heroes, Wotan, ... ; greater now in renunciation than he ever was when he coveted power, he now feels all-mighty, as he calls out to the earth's primeval wisdom, to Erda, the mother of nature, who had once taught him to fear for his end, telling her that dismay can no longer hold him in thrall since he now wills his own end with that selfsame will with which he had once desired to live. His end? He knows what Erda's primeval wisdom does not know: that he lives on in Siegfried. Wotan lives on in Siegfried as the artist lives on in his work of art: the freer and the more autonomous the latter's spontaneous existence and the less trace it bears of the creative artist—so that through it (the work of art), the artist himself is forgotten, — the more perfectly satisfied does the artist himself feel: and so, ... his being forgotten, his disappearance, his death is—the life of the work of art." [693W-{11/6/64} Letter to King Ludwig II of Bavaria, SLRW, pp. 626–627]

But this idea also provided him with a conception of reincarnation which became a crucial aspect of his theory of the "Wonder" of his musical motifs, through which, as Wagner says in the following passage, the past life of a hero, now forgotten by him, can be made ever present to the audience by the sounding of motifs which link the hero's past and present lives, a concept to which Wagner later gave objective form in his final music-drama *Parsifal*, which some scholars have rightly described as, in effect, the fifth drama of the *Ring*: "Burnouff's Introduction a l'histoire du Bouddhisme was the book that stimulated me most; I ... distilled from it the material for a dramatic poem ... . I gave it the title Die Sieger [*The Victors*] ... . Apart from the beauty and the profound significance of the simple tale, I was influenced to choose it as much by its peculiar aptness for the musical procedures that I have since developed [motifs of foreboding and reminiscence]. To the mind of the Buddha [say Wagner, creator of Wotan and his reincarnate self Siegfried], the previous lives in former incarnations of every being appearing before him stand revealed as clearly as the present. The simple story owed its significance to the way that the past life of the suffering principal characters was entwined in the new phase of their lives as being still present time. I perceived at once how the musical remembrance of this dual life, keeping the past constantly present in the hearing, might be represented perfectly to the emotional receptivities ... ." [640W-{5/16/56?} ML, pp. 528–529]

This relationship between Wagner's theory of his musical motifs' "Wonder" and reincarnation attained its apotheosis in Wagner's remark recorded by Cosima, that reincarnation: "... is what I mean by God [Wotan], who runs parallel with nature [Erda] up to the point where the parallels meet." [1005W-{1/15/80} CD Vol. II, p. 246] Wagner's idiosyncratic theory of parallels suggests that where the parallel lines God and Nature meet space and time have been transcended, in much the same way that religious miracles are believed to do in actuality, but which Wagner's motifs' Wonder only makes us feel. That Brünnhilde is God's (Wotan's) and Nature's (Erda's) daughter, figuratively the place outside of space and time where the parallel lines meet, casts new light on my thesis that Brünnhilde redeems Wotan's confession of the guilt inhering in human nature and history by sublimating it into transfiguring musical motifs, Wagner's artistic "Wonder," which make all that's distant in time and space present, here and now, thus subjectively transcending space and time and offering us a secular substitute for dying religious faith's former dependence on belief in miracles. It's in this way that Wotan's Will Brünnhilde allows Siegfried to live in the present.

The notion that Siegfried is Wotan reborn minus remembrance of his true, original identity, and that this concept provides Wagner a basis for developing his art of associating musical motifs with characters, events, symbols, and ideas in his drama, is directly related to his idea that his musical motifs and revolutionary use of the romantic orchestra as both an extension of the drama and omniscient voice of the music-dramatist, offers a secular substitute for dying religious faith, through the motifs' (of reminiscence and foreboding) "Wonder," in which all that is distant in space and time can be made present, in a musical motif, but felt, not thought. This explains why Wotan's morale is lifted from the dregs of the despair he felt when he foresaw the gods' demise in shame, to an ecstatic embrace of his end, because it's solely through Wotan's willing the necessity of the gods' "going under" that Siegfried can be freed to redeem the gods' essence, love (feeling), as distilled in Wagner's musical motifs, from Alberich's Ring Curse. In this way Wotan can afford, sans fear, to sacrifice to Alberich the Valhallan gods and their illegitimate claim to power. [See 928W-{3–7/78} 'Public and Popularity,' PW Vol. VI, p. 79]

Since Brünnhilde, Siegfried's unconscious mind and muse, holds Wotan's paralyzing self-knowledge of his egoistic motives and fear of the end for Siegfried, protecting him from consciousness of the knowledge which demolished Wotan's agency, Siegfried is, as Wotan describes him, (seemingly) freed from envy and fear, and from Alberich's Ring Curse. Siegfried can act on his artistic inspiration unimpeded. He's therefore—unlike Wotan—not troubled by unbearable guilt in ruminating over a corrupt past nor paralyzed into immobility through crippling fear of the fateful future. Siegfried, thanks to Brünnhilde, seems childlike and guiltless and, in his apparent innocence, naive. It's through Wotan's imparting his disreputable motives to Brünnhilde that they can remain unconscious and hidden, yet secretly inspire Siegfried to act in Wotan's behalf unaware of the true source of his inspiration. In this way Wotan has fulfilled his desire, expressed in his confession to Brünnhilde, to find a hero who'd be free of Wotan's influence yet, of his own need, do what Wotan desires. Wotan has also told Erda that Alberich's Ring Curse is powerless over Siegfried because fear remains unknown to him. But this will be proven wrong not only because Siegfried will succumb to Alberich's Ring Curse in the end, but also because, though it's true Siegfried didn't learn the meaning of fear (Wotan's fear) from Fafner, Siegfried will learn the meaning of fear (Wotan's fear) from Brünnhilde. We noted previously Feuerbach's observation that the artist's imagination is free in a way religious belief isn't, because religion makes the practical though false promise that man in paradise will be immortal, whereas the artist makes no practical claims. [See 269F-LER, p. 196, and 202F-LER, p. 47] It's in this sense that Siegfried's fearlessness and freedom from greed makes him invulnerable to Alberich's Ring Curse of consciousness.

But this reprieve is only temporary. Just as Siegfried learned the use he could make of Alberich's Tarnhelm and Ring from the Woodbird and then immediately forgot their use, so Siegfried in S.3.3 will learn the meaning of fear from Brünnhilde, but in the ecstasy of their loving union will immediately forget that fear. Wotan's fearful hoard of knowledge, Wotan's unspoken secret kept for Siegfried by his muse Brünnhilde, will inspire Siegfried to create redemptive works of art, subliminally, and in these works of art man's existential fear can be forgotten. But this also means that Brünnhilde, Siegfried's unconscious mind, can redeem the artist-hero Siegfried (and presumably the audience for his art) from suffering Alberich's Ring Curse of consciousness only so long as she remains the inviolable repository for Wotan's hoard of forbidden knowledge, and keeps his unspoken secret.

Just before Wotan adds that he now performs this formerly bitter task—of willing the end of the gods—in gladness, and just before Wagner's introduction of his Redemption Motif H143 (World-Inheritance), we hear what sounds like the cadential figure which followed the introduction in Brünnhilde's vocal line of Siegfried's Motif H93ab in V.3.1, namely H93c (heard in V.3.1 only in the orchestra), in Wotan's vocal line as he sings "... I now perform freely in gladness and joy ...," i.e., performs the task of making Siegfried his heir. The importance of this cadential capstone of Siegfried's Motif, H93c, is that it also evidently is the vocal line for the final words Brünnhilde sings in T.3.3 just before she immolates herself and her horse Grane in Siegfried's funeral pyre, "... in bliss your wife bids you welcome!" It's through her self-immolation that Alberich's Ring is finally restored to the Rhinedaughters and dissolved in the Rhine, thus ending its curse.

It's noteworthy also that H94, to which Sieglinde sung her praise of Brünnhilde ("Sublimest Wonder") for intervening to save the life of the as-yet-unborn Siegfried in V.3.1, was introduced along with Siegfried's Motif H93 and its cadence H93c, at the same moment in V.3.1, since H94 is the primary motif which brings the finale of the *Ring* to a close in T.3.3, where it's juxtaposed with H93c again in Brünnhilde's last words. This musico-dramatic picture is completed by the surely not accidental fact that H93c seems to stem, in the first place, from H58d, the final cadential figure of the Rhinedaughters' first lament for the stolen Rhinegold in R.4, to which they sang "... o give us the guileless gold back again!" It's no accident because the consequence of Brünnhilde's self-immolation is the restoration of the Ring to the Rhinedaughters and its dissolution (along with its Curse) in the Rhine's waters. So H93c looks backward to the Rhinedaughters' lament for lost innocence and plea that it will be restored, and forward to the artist-hero Siegfried and his muse of unconscious artistic inspiration Brünnhilde who're to be the agents of its restoration. Though it might seem from H93c's occurrence both here and just prior to Brünnhilde's self-immolation, that Wotan is contemplating Siegfried's and/or Brünnhilde's eventual restoration of the Ring to the Rhinedaughters to end Alberich's Ring Curse, when he announces he now gladly wills the end of the gods Erda once taught him to fear, this isn't so, because during her visit to Brünnhilde in T.1.3.A, Waltraute will make it clear that Wotan's hope that Brünnhilde will restore the Ring to the Rhinedaughters is an afterthought, the result of his recognition that his hope to be redeemed by Siegfried's and Brünnhilde's loving union has been thwarted, since Siegfried has succumbed, after all, to Alberich's Ring Curse, and betrayed their love. Wagner confirmed this in his letter to August Röckel of 1/25–26/54. [See 616W-{1/25–26/54} Letter to August Röckel, SLRW, p. 307]

In the following passage H143 is heard again twice, once as Wotan informs Erda that her all-wise child Brünnhilde will—on waking (for Siegfried)—perform that deed which will redeem the world (from Alberich's Ring Curse), and is heard a second time as Wotan tells Brünnhilde that the god yields in gladness to the one who's eternally young. He then consigns Erda to eternal sleep:

[p. 258] **Wanderer:** (H39 >>:) Brünnhilde, (H63>>:) whom you bore to me, the hero will lovingly waken (:H39; :H63): **[[H143 orch:]]** waking, your all-wise child (:H143 orch) (H143 modulation!!!:) will work the deed that redeems the world (:H143 modulation). ... And so, sleep on; (H101:) close your eyes and, dreaming, behold my end (:H101)! Whatever they do— ["Was jene auch wirken": perhaps "whatever happens"?] **[[H143 orch:]]** to the one who's eternally young the god now yields in gladness (:H143). (H142:) Descend then, Erda! Primeval mothers' fear! (H87) Primeval care (:H142)! (H142:) Descend! Descend! (H101:) To ageless sleep (:H101)! (H87: Having already closed her eyes and begun to descend, Erda now disappears completely ... .)

This passage provides an astonishing example of the ambiguity Wagner often built into the *Ring*'s libretto and music, encouraging multiple interpretations which interact with each other, however, not as contradictory or inconsistent, but rather, as conceptually polyphonic strands which Wagner weaves together into an ultimately coherent whole. The most forthright and obvious meaning of Wotan's initial remark that on waking Brünnhilde will redeem the world, is that she'll ultimately restore the Ring to the Rhine, for we know that's her destiny. But that isn't what Wotan means. When Erda initially warned Wotan to flee the Curse on the Ring, by yielding it (implicitly, to the Giants), she could easily have told him, and the music could easily have told us, that he should restore it to the Rhinedaughters. But neither she nor the music spoke of this. Instead, Wotan paid off the Giants with it, rather than restoring it to the Rhinedaughters, as he admitted to Brünnhilde in his confession. No, Wotan doesn't contemplate restoring it to the Rhine yet, though Loge—the archetype for the Wälsung heroes to whom Wotan looks for redemption—reminded Wotan five times in R.2 and R.4 that he ought to do it. He doesn't because he believes that the love which Siegfried and Brünnhilde share (unconsciously inspired secular art, the Wagnerian music-drama, which as I've stated is a sort of surrogate Rhine) will redeem the world, and that Siegfried, being free from greed for the Ring's power, and from fear, is freed also from Alberich's Ring Curse. The temporary redemption from Alberich's Ring Curse provided by the art which Siegfried, under Brünnhilde's inspiration, will produce, is wholly distinct from the ultimate redemption from the Ring Curse which can only be won by returning the Ring to the Rhinedaughters and allowing them to dissolve it (i.e., dissolve human consciousness itself) in the Rhine.

The following extract from Wagner's letter to August Röckel of 1/25–26/54, aforementioned, proves that Wagner distinguished the redemption offered by the loving union of Siegfried with Brünnhilde, in which Valhalla's blissful dream can live anew, from the final redemption gained through returning the Ring to the Rhine, which, as we'll see, evidently can only be achieved through Siegfried's betrayal of his love for Brünnhilde, and Siegfried's and Brünnhilde's sacrificial deaths in atonement for Wotan's original sin against all that was, is, and will be, i.e., by fulfillment of Alberich's Ring Curse: " ... the pernicious power that poisons love is concentrated in the gold that is stolen from nature and put to ill use, the Nibelung's ring: the curse that clings to it is not lifted until it is restored to nature and until the gold has been returned to the Rhine. This, too, becomes clear to Wodan only at the very end, once he has reached the final goal of his tragic career; in his lust for power, he had utterly ignored what Loge had so frequently and so movingly warned him of at the beginning of the poem; initially—thanks to Fafner's deed—he learned to recognize the power of the curse; but not until the ring proves the ruin of Siegfried [when Hagen in T.1.2–3 influences Siegfried unwittingly to betray his love for Brünnhilde by abducting her for Gunther and forcibly taking Alberich's Ring, their wedding ring, back from her], too, does he see that only by restoring to the Rhine what had been stolen from its depths can evil be destroyed, and that is why he makes his own longed-for downfall a pre-condition of the extirpation of a most ancient wrong." [616W-{1/25-26/54} Letter to August Röckel, SLRW, p. 307] Wotan clearly hoped—as he expressed it to Erda, accompanied by H143 (Wagner's Redemption Motif)—that Brünnhilde's deed, on waking for Siegfried, in inspiring him to produce redemptive art, would redeem the world, without returning the Ring to the Rhine.

The fact that the love the hero and heroine share, though believed by Wotan to be the key to redemption, is distinct from the final redemption the Rhinedaughters will offer, is also implicit in the fact that both Brünnhilde and Siegfried in *Twilight of the Gods* will refuse pleas, from Waltraute and the Rhinedaughters respectively, to return the Ring to the Rhine by invoking love, that is to say, art, as an alternative to returning the Ring to the Rhinedaughters. The final redemption the Rhinedaughters offer will be, as Cooke put it, a metaphysical redemption. [Cooke: p. 247] There's motival evidence for this, but again, this is somewhat ambiguous. H143, the motif most associated with Wotan's hope that the love which his heirs Siegfried and Brünnhilde share—i.e., the creation of inspired art—will redeem the world, isn't heard in its definitive form in the finale (the moment of redemption) of *Twilight of the Gods*. Its final definitive, easily recognizable recurrence is heard a bit earlier in T.3.3 when Brünnhilde sets the record straight with Gutrune, who has accused Brünnhilde of bringing great harm ("Noth") to everyone because of her spite ("Neid"), by setting Hagen, Gunther, and the Gibichungs against Siegfried. H143 in its definitive form is last heard as Brünnhilde informs Gutrune that while Gutrune was merely Siegfried's "wanton," Brünnhilde was his lawful wife. Dunning, however, asserts that H143's modulation, as heard in the orchestra in S.3.1 when Wotan sings " ... (H143:) waking, your all-wise child (:H143) **(H143 modulation:) will work the deed that redeems the world (:H143 modulation),**" is heard again in the orchestra during the finale of the *Ring* just before Brünnhilde rides Grane into Siegfried's funeral pyre. However, it's not a self-evident motival reference. Instead, we hear in full flower, with no ambiguity, H94 as a capstone to the drama, the motif Sieglinde introduced in V.3.1 as she sang her praise of Brünnhilde as the savior of Sieglinde's unborn child Siegfried. H94 as the drama's capstone can be read perhaps more as an invocation of what might have been, an ideal never realized, than a redemption motif. Had Wagner wanted to employ the only motif he ever called a redemption motif, H143, in the finale, he surely would have in a manner that would have left no doubt of his intent. This is an important question and deserves a serious debate drawing on expert knowledge of those able to read a score.

Because the motif segment H93c to which Wotan sang "What I once resolved in despair, in the searing smart of inner turmoil, **(H93c voc:) I now perform freely in gladness and joy (:H93c voc)**," is also the motif to which Brünnhilde sings her last words, her final greeting to Siegfried, just before she immolates herself and her horse Grane in Siegfried's' funeral pyre, it seems Wagner allows us to have it both ways. In one respect Wotan's remarks about Brünnhilde's destiny as a redeemer look forward—in a way of which he hasn't yet become conscious—to Brünnhilde's final act, her immolation in Siegfried's funeral pyre and release of the Ring to the Rhinedaughters. However, insofar as Wotan's mind can contemplate the future, what he means is that Brünnhilde, on waking for Siegfried, will impart to him subliminally the fearful knowledge Wotan couldn't bear to contemplate and also the intuitive knowledge of the gods' need for redemption, so Siegfried can safely draw on the unconscious inspiration his muse Brünnhilde offers to create redemptive works of art, the New Valhalla, the new secular religion of which Feuerbach spoke.

It's thanks to the love of Siegfried and Brünnhilde—Wagner's metaphor for the artist-hero's unconscious artistic inspiration—that Wotan is now able to consign objective thought, science's understanding of man and Nature (Erda's wisdom, the source of her primal mothers' fear and care), to the oblivion of the unconscious mind, of dreaming. What would be horrific if experienced objectively in full, waking consciousness is transmuted into aesthetic bliss in the collective, shared dream, or artwork, that the artist-hero Siegfried will create, just as Light-Alberich's (Wotan's) horrific nightmare, Alberich's forging of his Ring of power and all that followed from it in Nibelheim, was sublimated into Wotan's waking dream Valhalla, an allegory whose true subject is Alberich's acquisition of the power of conscious thought. So Wotan has told Erda to behold his end (religion's death as thought and rebirth in art as feeling), dreaming. Erda's fateful knowledge won't wake again so long as Siegfried never betrays the unspoken secret which Wotan imparted to Brünnhilde, and which she, Siegfried's unconscious mind, keeps safe for Siegfried by keeping it secret even from him. Erda's fearful knowledge is consigned by Wotan to sleep and dreaming in redemptive art (music), which has taken aesthetic possession of it and made it sympathetic.

According to Wagner, where religion can't survive its conflict with science, art can live on eternally freed from that threat because it stakes no claim to truth, and therefore can never be guilty of falsehood: as feeling it's freed from the conflict between truth and falsehood which sustains the war between science and religion, Nibelheim and Valhalla. In this sense, by retreating to preconscious, pre-Fallen feeling (figuratively, to the Rhinedaughters), Wagner said, art can live on eternally where religion (illusion) and science (truth) cancel each other out. This explains why Wotan yields to the eternally young Siegfried, the artist-hero, and to Brünnhilde, who called herself the ageless part of Wotan. Immortal art, i.e., art made figuratively immortal by virtue of its profundity, universality, and longevity in cherished memory, which endears it to our hearts so long as there are humans capable of feeling as if they've resolved their most enduring contradictions in it, is Wagner's substitute for religion's bogus promise of immortal life to mortal man. Wagner attributed this insight to Feuerbach (in an extract previously cited), whose observation in our first extract below, that our only true immortality is a tribute to the everlasting youth of the collective human spirit, seems to have had a seminal influence on him: "That which is true in the universal belief in immortality ... consists only in the fact that it is a sensible representation of the nature of consciousness, ...—that is, the unity of past, present and future as one essential reality—is ... raised to the level of an object ... . Thus, your belief in immortality is a true belief only when it is a belief in the infinity of Spirit and in the everlasting youth of humanity, in the inexhaustible love and creative power of Spirit ... ." [21F-TDI, p. 137] In another previously cited remark Wagner gave testimony to Feuerbach's seminal influence on this subject, having declared he learned from Feuerbach that: "... the sole authentic immortality adheres only to sublime deeds and inspired works of art." [387W-{?/49} ML, pp. 430–431; See also 729W-{9–12/67} 'German Art and German Policy,' PW Vol. IV, pp. 79–80; 836W, and 900W]

Wagner summed this argument with his appeal to sacrifice the gods for the sake of love, his figure for authentically inspired secular art, through which man can emancipate himself from religion: "... we recognize the glorious necessity of love [Wagner's metaphor for his unconsciously inspired secular art, the music-drama] ... ; and so, in this way, we acquire a strength of which natural man had no inkling, and this strength—increased to embrace the whole of humanity—will one day lay the foundations for a state on earth where no one need yearn for the other world ... [i.e., a transcendent realm of the spirit, such as Valhalla, in which we can allegedly enjoy sorrow-less youth eternal thanks to Freia's golden apples] ... . For where is the man who yearns to escape from life when he is in love? (...) Now ... we must lose heart and go mad without any faith in the hereafter: I too believe in a here-after: ... though it lies beyond my life, it does not lie beyond the limits of all that I can feel, think, grasp and comprehend [i.e., it doesn't repudiate or transcend Erda's real world, all that was, is, or will be], for I believe in humanity and—have need of naught else!" [598W-{4/13/53} Letter to Franz Liszt, SLRW, p. 284] Clearly, Wagner based his notion that inspired secular art would become man's new religion, Wagner's art of the future, on Feuerbach's new secular religion founded on the hereafter of collective, historical man, the human race's future: "We must ... modify our goals and exchange divinity, in which only man's groundless and gratuitous desires are fulfilled, for the human race ... , religion for education, the hereafter in heaven for the hereafter on earth, ... the ... future of mankind." [316F-LER, p. 281]

SIEGFRIED ⚜ ACT THREE, SCENE TWO
(BELOW BRÜNNHILDE'S ROCKY PEAK)
THE WANDERER (WOTAN) AND SIEGFRIED

Siegfried now comes upon the scene of Wotan's confrontation with Erda, following his fluttering Woodbird up the slopes to reach the peak where Brünnhilde sleeps. It was Thomas Mann who said of this confrontation, between the old god and the new hero who supplants him, that it's of the highest poetry: "It has always seemed to me absurd to question Wagner's poetic gifts. What could be more poetically beautiful or profound than Wotan's relationship to Siegfried, the fatherly-mocking and condescending attachment of the god to the boy who will destroy him, the loving abdication of the old power in favour of the eternally youthful? The composer has the poet to thank for the marvellous sounds he finds here." [Mann, p. 190]

By this point in Wagner's application of his musical motifs to word and action, he'd attained such a degree of subtlety that each moment now seems so saturated with musico-dramatic meaningfulness, that it becomes increasingly difficult to account for the intensity and richness of the vivid yet idiosyncratic moods Wagner calls up through cross referencing between specific motifs and the drama. This isn't to say that in this advanced stage of his career Wagner's application of his musical motifs to the drama merely serves musical rather than poetic/dramatic purposes, and that his music is increasingly autonomous from the drama, as some aver, but rather, that his application of motifs to the drama is so natural and fluent, drawing now on so much ever accumulating material, that its capacity for cross-referencing the libretto text is increasingly nuanced and difficult to parse in detail. The associative power of his capacity for motival cross-referencing seems near infinite. Wagner can call up instantly subliminal reminiscences and premonitions not only of numerous events and characters in the *Ring*, sparked, sometimes mysteriously, by concerns of the present moment, but manipulate this ever more refined material in such a way that something new and profound is constantly being said about the past, present, and future, which is difficult to articulate. The *Ring* plot now lives a second, ghostly life in motival development alongside the events dramatized on stage, a parallel universe which distills what Wagner describes as the essence of what's presented on the stage, through a sort of musical x-ray revealing hidden motives.

Wotan the Wanderer, initially in a jocular mood, confronts Siegfried to interrogate him with the sole purpose, evidently, of insuring Siegfried can't trace his history and motives back to Wotan. Wotan also wishes to ensure Siegfried is the fearless, free hero he'd dreamed of. As Siegfried approaches we hear a H12 (the Rhinedaughters' cry: "Rhinegold! Rhinegold!") variant reminding us that Siegfried is protected from the Ring Curse of consciousness by the sleeping Brünnhilde, his surrogate Rhine, but also foreseeing its dissolution in the Rhine:

[pp. 259–60] **Wanderer:** (H12 vari:; H137b frag vari:) Siegfried I see approaching there (:H12 vari:; :H137b frag vari). (... H138b frag varis:;

H137b:; H?:—[chirping, fluttering woodbird frag from the finale of S.2.3.] Siegfried's woodbird flutters downstage. Suddenly the bird stops, flutters to and fro in alarm and disappears quickly towards the back of the stage ....)

Siegfried: [[H144 voc:]] My woodbird's flown away;—with fluttering flight and sweet-sounding song it blithely showed me my way (:H144 voc); now it has fled far away from me. (H56 varis:) It's best if I find the rock by myself: I'll follow the path that my guide pointed out (:H56 varis). (...) (H138b frag: He strides upstage.)

Wanderer: (...) Whither, my lad, does your journey lead you?

Siegfried: (...) There's someone speaking: (H138b vari frag:) perhaps he can tell me the way (:H138b vari frag). (H137b vari: (...) I'm seeking a (H12:) rock that's (H137b:) circled by fire (:H12; :H137b): there sleeps a woman (H138b:) I mean to wake (:H138b). (H137b vari)

Wanderer: Who told you to seek out the rock, who bade you desire the woman?

Siegfried: (H138b:; H10:) A forest songbird directed me (:H138b:; :H10) ....

Wanderer: [[H145 orch:]] A woodbird chatters of many things (:H145 orch); no human can understand it: how could you make any sense of its singing?

Siegfried: (H134a:) It was due to the blood of a fearsome dragon that fell before me at Neidhöhl' ["Envy-Cave"] (:H134a): its kindling blood had scarce wet my tongue (H10:) when I understood what the birds were saying (:H10).

Wanderer: [[H145 vari orch >>:]] If you slew the giant, who urged you on to defeat the mighty beast (:H145 vari orch)?

Siegfried: (H131B vari:) I was led by Mime, a false-hearted dwarf; he wanted to teach me fear (:H131B vari): (H116:) but the dragon itself provoked the blow (:H116) (H134 vari:) that proved to be his undoing ... (:H134 vari).

Wanderer: [[H145 vari orch:]] Who made the sword so sharp and hard that his fiercest enemy fell before him (:H145 vari orch)?

Siegfried: (H127 orch:) I forged it myself since the smith was unable (:H127 orch): (H38:) I'd otherwise still be swordless (:H38).

Wanderer: [[H145 vari horns:]] But who made the mighty fragments from which you forged the sword (:H145 vari horns)?

Siegfried: What do I know of that? (H132 varis:) I know only that the bits were no use unless I re-made the sword (:H132 varis).

Wanderer: ([[H145 orch:]] breaking into cheerfully good-natured laughter) That I can well believe! (H65: He observes Siegfried, well pleased.)

Something curious is at work here. The Woodbird, Wagner's metaphor for the new kind of music which will artificially restore lost innocence, leads Siegfried to Brünnhilde, to explore the depths of his unconscious mind, i.e., the secret of Wagner's artistic inspiration. Wagner had always said music was the link between the outer and the inner worlds, the ladder one could climb down into the silent depths of one's self (Wagner once called music "sounding silence."). Now, as Siegfried sings while introducing a new motif H144, the Woodbird has flown off after having shown him the way to Brünnhilde (alarmed by the sight of Wotan, or, as Wotan will tell Siegfried, scared off by Wotan's messengers, his two ravens). Siegfried will sing this motif only two more times, both in S.3.2: once while complaining that the Wanderer seems to be laughing at him and refusing to answer any more of the Wanderer's questions because all he's good for is to show Siegfried the way to Brünnhilde or shut up, and a last time when Siegfried's curiosity about the Wanderer prompts him to inquire what he looks like under that hat which hangs down over his head (hiding his missing eye, which the Wanderer will identify with Siegfried). In the latter two instances H144 is heard in conjunction with H65, the motif which references both Sieglinde's sympathy for the Wälsungs' Noth (and possibly her dead spirit's—in the guise of the Woodbird—attempt to guide Siegfried to Brünnhilde), and the cause of the Wälsungs' Noth, Wotan's implication of them in his futile quest to preempt the gods' doom foreseen by Erda. We can best describe the penumbra of meaning in Siegfried's three brief iterations of H144 as conveying the pathos of Wotan's relationship with Siegfried, of which Wotan knows the full import but of which Siegfried knows nothing. This is also conveyed by H65 when it sounds after Wotan has learned Siegfried can't trace his history back to Wotan.

Wotan the Wanderer asks Siegfried a series of questions intended to determine how far back Siegfried can trace his history, because Wotan wants to ensure Siegfried isn't conscious of Wotan's influence on him, since Siegfried is only of use to him if he does spontaneously, of his own Noth, what Wotan needs but can't do himself. Wotan first asks where Siegfried's heading. Siegfried's answer is that he's seeking to wake a sleeping woman encircled by fire. Wotan then asks who bid Siegfried to seek this woman. After Siegfried answers that it was a Woodbird, Wotan poses as skeptic and asks him how it's possible he could have understood the songs of birds, introducing by the way a new motif H145, which is repeated each time Wotan asks a question to ensure Siegfried can't trace his origins back to Wotan. It's curious, by the way, that Siegfried previously (in S.2.2), meditating on what the Woodbird might be trying to tell him, recounted how a querulous dwarf (Mime) had once told him that in time one could come to unravel the meaning of the Woodbird's song, since Wotan expresses his doubt about this, and Mime represents Wotan's prosaic self. One suspects Wotan's doubt is rhetorical, since I've argued that Wotan's hidden intent speaks to Siegfried through the Woodbird, the symbol of Wagner's musical motifs into which Wotan's original motives are distilled within the womb of his wishes Brünnhilde. Recalling Thomas Mann's comment that there's the highest poetry in Siegfried's confrontation with Wotan, this unusual staccato motif and its continual variation mysteriously conveys that feeling. Roger Scruton suggested H145 may be a satirical variant of H143, but I can't confirm this.

After Siegfried answers that he could grasp birdsong by tasting the blood of a dragon (Fafner) he'd slain, Wotan asks who urged Siegfried to kill it. Wotan's primary desire of his free hero was that he'd slay Fafner to take aesthetic possession of Alberich's Ring (Tarnhelm and Hoard) in order to keep Alberich from regaining his lost power and destroying the gods. Siegfried's answer is that the treacherous dwarf Mime led him into the forest to learn fear from it, but that the serpent's own arrogance incited Siegfried to kill him. To Wotan's question who made the sharp sword with which Siegfried killed Fafner, Siegfried's answer is that Siegfried forged it himself. And now Wotan poses his final question, who made the fragments of the sword which Siegfried forged. Siegfried answers with an incredulous: how should I know! Siegfried points out that the pieces would—in any case—have been useless without his personal labor to re-forge them. At that Wotan laughs contentedly and we hear H65, reminding us of the terrible fate to which Wotan has condemned the Wälsungs, of which Siegfried remains oblivious. Satisfied with his inquiry, Wotan has, he feels, successfully produced a hero who'll instinctively perform that deed of redemption which the gods need, and that's why he laughs with delight after Siegfried seems to have demonstrated his independence of (at least ignorance of) Wotan's influence. Siegfried has already slain Fafner, taken aesthetic possession of the Ring and Tarnhelm (and thereby also Alberich's Hoard), and slain Wotan's head, Mime. But to wholly fulfill Wotan's longing for redemption from Alberich's Ring Curse, Siegfried must still leave the Ring safely in Brünnhilde's protective hands (just as Wotan imparted his unspoken secret to her, his unconscious mind, leaving its secret safe in her hands), so Siegfried can draw artistic inspiration from her to recreate the world guided by her music. The fact that Siegfried doesn't know Wotan forged the original sword Wotan takes for the surest sign of Siegfried's independence.

Since there's a substantial analogy between Wotan and God-the-Father of the Old Testament, and between Siegfried and Jesus-the-Savior from the New Testament, Wotan's insistence that he find none of what he loathes in himself (what might be described in Wagner's terms as the "Judaism" of his true nature) in his ostensibly independent hero Siegfried, finds a parallel in Wagner's belief that though the Christian God is tainted by his derivation from the Jewish creator-god Jehovah, the creator of this terrible world (whom Wagner was glad to sacrifice to modern science if only he could keep his purified savior Jesus), Jesus, god's son, must be free from association with Jehovah: "That the God of our Saviour [the artist-hero Siegfried] should have been identified with the tribal god of Israel [Wotan, Light-Alberich, whose realm Valhalla (H18ab) is the product of Alberich's Ring power (H17ab)], is one of the most terrible confusions in all world-history; it ... avenges itself to-day by ... more and more outspoken atheism ... . (...) ... it almost seems right that Jehova ... should ... suppress the God so monstrously mistakenly derived from him [Wotan's debt to Alberich forces Wotan to abdicate his role as God-the-Father]. If Jesus is proclaimed Jehova's son [Siegfried is Wotan's grandson], then every Jewish rabbi can triumphantly confute all Christian theology ... ." [926W-{3–7/78} 'Public and Popularity,' PW Vol. VI, pp. 77–78] The futility of Wotan's quest to produce a hero truly free of all that Wotan loathes in himself, arising from the fact that Wotan's motive in seeking redemption through this hero is what Wotan loathes (his subjection to egoism and fear of the end), exposes the truth behind Wagner's absurd desire to purge Jesus of his Jewish roots, or for that matter purge Wagner's theoretical Germans or Aryans from taint by implication in the same evolution of species which produced all the so-called human races. Both cases represent Wagner's wish to imagine man freed from his natural egoism: the problem with this, as Feuerbach pointed out, is that everything both good and bad in human nature stems from egoism, even man's wish to transcend it. [See 208F-LER, p. 78, 250F-LER, p. 164, and 328F-LER, p. 304] This lends tragic pathos to Wotan's joy in finding what he takes to be his free hero in Siegfried.

Wotan and Siegfried now engage in a debate which again identifies Wotan with Mime in terms of their respective relationships with Siegfried. Siegfried has grown weary of Wotan's questioning and strongly suggests that if the "old man" can't show him the way to the sleeping woman (as Mime showed him the way to Fafner), then he should get out of the way. Siegfried's complaint—as he develops it—is accompanied by an increasingly intense variant of H65:

> [pp. 260-2] **Siegfried:** (surprised: H65:; [[H144 voc:]]) Are you laughing at me? No more of your questions, old man; don't keep me here talking any longer (:H65; :H144 voc). (H65: [definitive!]) If you can show me the way, then tell me: if you're unable, then hold your tongue (:H65)! (H65 [strongly pronounced!])
>
> **Wanderer:** (H145 vari orch:) (...) If you think that I'm old, you should show me respect (:H145 vari orch).
>
> **Siegfried:** A fine idea! (H114 >>:) As long as I've lived an old man has always stood in my way (:H114): (H138b frag voc:) now I have swept him aside. (:H138b frag voc) (H109 voc:) If you offer me more of your stiff opposition, take care ... (with an appropriate gesture) that you don't share (H109 orch: [more definitive]) Mime's fate (:H109 voc/orch)! (...) [[H144 voc:]] Let me see what you look like! Why are you wearing so huge a hat (:H144 voc)? (H65:) Why does it hang down over your face (:H65)?
>
> **Wanderer:** (... H119 vari >>:) That is the Wanderer's way when he walks against the wind (:H119 vari).
>
> **Siegfried:** (... H18ab:) But under it one of your eyes is missing (:H18ab)! (...) Be off with you now! Or else you could easily lose the other one, too.
>
> **Wanderer:** (very calmly: H18a:) I see (:H18a), (H18b >>:) my son (:H18b), that where you know nothing, you know how to get your own way. (H18ab:) With the eye which, as my second self ["das als and'res"], is missing, you yourself can glimpse (:H18ab) (H18c:) the one (:H18c) (H18d:) that's left for me to see with (:H18d).

Siegfried: (after listening thoughtfully now bursts out in a peal of spontaneous laughter (H17ab?) At least you're good for a laugh!

The most obvious reason why H65 so markedly punctuates Siegfried's complaint that if Wotan can't show him the way to Brünnhilde, he should just get out of the way, is the assumption, based partly on Wagner's testimony, that H65 represents the concern of the dead Sieglinde's spirit (who spoke to Siegfried in the form of the Woodbird) for her son Siegfried, and her longing to guide him to Brünnhilde. The meaning would be that the heartless Wotan is the antithesis of the loving and sympathetic Sieglinde, and therefore totally unqualified to lead Siegfried to Brünnhilde. But H65 also represents the Noth which the Wälsung race suffer as unwitting agents of Wotan's need for a free hero who'll involuntarily martyr himself to redeem the gods from Alberich's Ring Curse. The problem with the interpretation of H65's occurrence here as indicative of Sieglinde's spirit leading Siegfried to Brünnhilde, is that it's Wotan who stands to gain most from the redemptive love which Siegfried and Brünnhilde will bestow on the world, as Wotan confessed to Erda in S.3.1. Though Wotan would deny it, just as his prompting was behind everything Siegmund did to challenge the gods' rule, Wotan's motives subliminally drive Siegfried. Though Sieglinde could plausibly speak through the Woodbird to warn Siegfried about Mime, and guide him to Brünnhilde, it's not likely she'd have any motive to request he take possession of Alberich's Hoard, Tarnhelm, and Ring. Yet this was the Woodbird's first message to Siegfried. Only Wotan would have a reason to convey this message to him. The Woodbird is music (the "Wonder" of Wagner's musical motifs), the heart of man's religious longing for transcendent value.

Siegfried's complaint to Wotan that he's just like the old man who's always stood in Siegfried's way, and that if he doesn't clear out of the way he'll likely suffer the same fate as Mime, has explicitly identified Mime with Wotan, a fact highlighted by the sounding of several motifs linked with Mime such as H109 (Siegfried's contempt for Mime), H114 (the love parents owe their children, love Mime selfishly interpreted as the love which the child owes to its parent), and H131B (the simultaneity of Siegfried's re-forging of Nothung and Mime's brewing a sinister sleeping potion). The joke here is that Wotan's head, Mime, already suffered the fate Siegfried threatens Wotan with now. Siegfried's insult, telling Wotan an old man has always stood in his way, recalls the vivid remark Mime made in S.1.3 as he observed in astonishment Siegfried's ability to re-forge his father's sword Nothung instinctively rather than by instruction, that though he was old as cave and wood he'd never seen the like. Mime, like Fricka and Fafner, symbolizes the status quo, the bent of the majority of those in society. The Wälsung heroes are archetypal revolutionaries at odds with established society, seeking emancipation from traditional limits in the fresh and new.

Siegfried's curiosity is piqued by Wotan's unusual attire, so he asks Wotan (singing H144) why he wears his hat over his face, to which Wotan answers that that's the way the wanderer wears his hat when walking against the wind, i.e., against Nature. This feature of Wotan's personality, his world-renunciation, will be echoed by Siegfried in T.1.2 when Hagen, spotting Siegfried rowing his boat to Gibichung Hall upriver against the Rhine's natural current, says he recognizes Siegfried the dragon-killer from his strength alone. This identification of Wotan with Siegfried highlights their status as figurative killers of their mother, Nature. Siegfried then observes that under Wotan's hat Siegfried can see one of his eyes is missing, as we hear H18ab (Valhalla). We'll learn from the Norns in T.P.A that Wotan had to sacrifice one eye to obtain wisdom from the spring which flows from under the roots of the World-Ash, from which he broke off its most sacred branch to make his Spear of divine covenants. It was thanks to Wotan's contract engraved on his Spear that the Giants built Valhalla (H18ab). Siegfried insults Wotan gratuitously by suggesting that he might lose his remaining eye if he doesn't get out of Siegfried's way. But Wotan patiently responds with one of the most imposing passages of rhetoric in the *Ring*. He first notes, again accompanied by H18ab, that where Siegfried knows nothing, he knows how to get his own way. It's because Brünnhilde holds for Siegfried the knowledge of his true identity and history that he doesn't know who he is, and is spared that fear of the end which paralyzes Wotan, a privilege which frees Siegfried to act spontaneously. It's because Siegfried knows nothing that he can be heroic at all.

In the second part of this passage, accompanied by H18abcd, Wotan tells Siegfried something quite mysterious, that he's looking at Wotan with the eye which, as his other self, Wotan is missing. Wotan had to lose intuitive knowledge, or animal instinct (the Rhinedaughters' joy in the Rhinegold prior to Alberich's theft and forging of a Ring from it), to gain the power of symbolic thought, just as Alberich had to renounce love to forge his Ring of power. It's through the artist-hero Siegfried that Wotan hopes to restore, at least artificially, the aesthetic intuition (love) which was lost in the "Fall" through acquisition of reflective consciousness. This secular art which the artist-hero Siegfried and his muse of inspiration Brünnhilde will produce will become the New Valhalla (H18abcd). Donington was at least partly correct when he described Wotan's missing eye as his eye which looks inward into the unconscious mind [Donington: p. 69], which I've identified as Brünnhilde, into whose mysteries Siegfried will look when he wakes her and wins her love. Here's what Wagner had to say about man's inner eye, the eye of music (and the unconscious), long before his presumed first (direct) acquaintance with Schopenhauer's philosophy: "Man's nature is twofold, an outer and an inner. ... to the eye appeals the outer man, the inner to the ear./(...) ... the more distinctly can the outer man express the inner, the higher does he show his rank as an artistic being." [430W-{9–12/49} 'The Artwork of the Future,' PW Vol. I, p. 91] Siegfried, Wotan's missing eye, is the eye which looks inward to music and the unconscious (Brünnhilde). Furthermore, Brünnhilde in V.3.3 told Wotan that in time of war she guards his back, and therefore sees what he can't see. In this capacity for inner sight Siegfried and Brünnhilde are one, and distinct from Wotan.

Siegfried, accompanied by H145, tells Wotan that unless he can show Siegfried the way to Brünnhilde, he has no use for him. Siegfried has pricked Wotan's pride and, suddenly regretting his loss of divine power to him, Wotan strongly suggests, accompanied by H80, that if Siegfried knew him Siegfried wouldn't insult him. H80 calls to mind Wotan's capitulation to Fricka's argument that mortal men can't have a free will, since all merit comes from the gods, plunging Wotan into despair of ever finding a free hero. But Siegfried's defiance, which Wotan chastises because it's so arrogant in its ignorance, is after all the product of Wotan's desire for a hero who, in his defiance of the gods, would be their friend. Siegfried's arrogance, founded as it is on his ignorance of the Noth which besets Wotan, is ironic in the extreme:

> [pp. 262–3] **Siegfried:** (H145 vari orch:) But listen, I'll gossip no longer; quickly, show me the way (:H145 vari orch) and be on your way, too! For nothing else do I deem you of use! So speak or I'll send you packing! (H80)
>
> **Wanderer:** ... If you but knew me, brave-hearted youth, (H80) you'd spare me this affront! (H80 voc:) So dear to you, I'm sorely wounded by your threats (:H80). (...) (H80) (H21a vari voc?:) You to whom I'm well-disposed, too glorious by far (:H21a vari voc?) do not arouse my wrath ["Neid"] today—it could ruin both you and me!
>
> **Siegfried:** (H99A or H99B?/H80 vari:) (...) Get out of the way! For this slope, I know, must lead to the sleeping woman (:H99A or H99B?/H80 vari): (H12?) (H138b frag voc:) So I was shown by my woodbird that fled from here in flight just now (:H138b frag voc). (...)
>
> **Wanderer:** ... H41 vari >>: [the "Servitude Motif" in a vari which expresses alarm, also heard in V.3.3 when Wotan told Brünnhilde how he was going to punish her by putting her to sleep]) It fled from you to save its life; it guessed that (:H41 vari) (H97 vari:) the lord of the ravens was here (:H97 vari): (H41 vari) woe betide if they overtake it!—(H19) The way that it showed you shall not go!
>
> **Siegfried:** ... [[H146 orch >>:]] Hoho! You forbid me? Who are you then who would bar my way (:H146 orch)? [[H146 varis orch >>:]]
>
> **Wanderer:** Fear the guardian of the fell! Locked within my power the sleeping maid is held: (H? Voc:—[Back reference to Wotan's remark: "You to whom I'm well-disposed, too glorious by far ...," possibly a H21a vari?]) he who awakens her, he who wins her (:H? Voc—Back reference, possibly a H21a vari?) would make me powerless for aye ["ever"]!

Wotan accuses Siegfried of hubris which, if left unchecked, could result in catastrophe for both of them. Wotan isn't only accompanied by H80 in the orchestra, but sings what sounds like a variant of H21 as he tells Siegfried that though he's well disposed to him, Siegfried is excessively exalted. At the end of this passage Wotan again sings this vocal line (H21?) as he confesses the true motive behind his sudden revulsion toward Siegfried, for he notes that he who wakes and wins Brünnhilde would make Wotan powerless forever. This is ironic because Wotan told Alberich he was content to lose power to whoever wins the Ring, and told Erda he no longer feared the gods' doom she foretold because Siegfried and Brünnhilde would be his heirs and defeat Alberich's Ring Curse.

But Wotan has now exhibited an instinctive reaction against the inevitable, and a perverse jealousy toward Siegfried, in whom, after all, Wotan lives again. Wotan's vocal hints of H21 may well reflect Wagner's (if not Wotan's) recognition that Valhalla's domestic tranquility (H21's meaning when introduced by Fricka in R.2) is reborn in the love Siegfried will share with Brünnhilde, the New Valhalla of Art. This will be dramatized in S.3.3 in the most expansive version of H21 yet heard to express Siegfried's aesthetic arrest after he's penetrated Loge's protective ring of fire and finds himself above the clouds on the mountaintop where Brünnhilde sleeps. At this point a new motif H146 is introduced as Siegfried challenges Wotan to tell him who it is who dares to block Siegfried's way to Brünnhilde, and Wotan responds with threats embodied by H146, which illustrates the rolling fire with which Wotan will soon threaten Siegfried. In response to Siegfried's disrespect, Wotan's anger has gotten the better of him. He's asserted his old authority as Brünnhilde's punisher, suggesting it was Wotan's Ravens—associated here with H97, which at its inception expressed Wotan's intent to punish Brünnhilde with sleep and leave her powerless to prevent any man from waking and winning her as bride—who scared Siegfried's Woodbird away.

Wotan confesses that Brünnhilde lies under his power, and prepares to stop Siegfried from reaching her. We hear a variant of the Servitude Motif H41 (stemming from Alberich's "Wehe! Wehe!," H8a from R.1), introduced when Wotan and Loge in R.3 entered Nibelheim and found Mime moaning in pain from the beating Alberich had given him. We also heard this variant of H41 (again in association with H97) as Wotan told Brünnhilde of his plan to punish her in V.3.2. H41's presence here in a variant which conveys alarm expresses Wotan's demand that Siegfried submit to his authority. But Wotan, blocking Siegfried with Loge's ring of fire and with his Spear, is actually offering Siegfried the supreme test to certify him as the sole suitable suitor for Brünnhilde, since Wotan's last words in V.3.3, after he'd put her to sleep and commanded Loge to surround her with fire, was that he who fears Wotan's spear-point will never pass through the fire. Wotan hopes Siegfried will pass the test by breaking his spear and penetrating the fire.

We now hear the intimidating H146 again, as it embodies Loge's fire rolling down the slopes to frighten Siegfried away or consume him. It's only a descriptive motif which physically manifests Wotan's threat and doesn't carry any new conceptual weight. It's not heard again, but it's reminiscent of the powerfully rhythmic orchestral passage which expressed Siegmund's desperation to escape being captured and killed by Hunding's clan in V.1.1, based on H59 (Wotan's Storm), a variant of the embryonic version of the H19 (Spear). That prior episode, which musically illustrated Hunding's threat to punish Siegmund for breaking the gods' (Wotan's) laws, parallels Wotan's threat to punish Siegfried for seeking to win Brünnhilde, which Wotan describes as a mortal threat to his power (Spear of authority). Accompanied by H146, H34, H76, H33, H101, and H102, Wotan tests Siegfried to see if Loge's fire can frighten him away from the sleeping Brünnhilde:

[pp. 263-4] **Wanderer:** ([[H146 orch:]]; H34:) A sea of fire floods round the woman, a white-hot blaze licks round the rock: he who longs for the bride will find the fire raging towards him (:H146 orch; H34). (... H76 over H33 accompaniment:) Look up to the heights (:H76)! (...) The glow is growing, (H102:) the heat increasing ... . (H33:) A sea of light encircles your head (:H33): (...) (H101 vari voc:) Soon kindling flames will seize and consume you (:H101 voc vari):—get back, you foolhardy child!

Siegfried: (...) (H12) (H12/H138b:) There where the flames are burning, (H93a:) to Brünnhilde I must go (:H93a)! (...)

Wanderer: (H12:) If you're not afraid of the fire (:H12), (H93a) (H19:) my spear will bar your way for you (:H19)! (H146/H34:) ... the sword you wield was shivered ere now by this shaft (:H146): once more let it (H19) splinter upon my eternal spear (:H34)! (...)

Siegfried: ... (H65:) My father's foe! Do I find you here? What a glorious chance for vengeance is this (:H65)! Stretch forth your spear: (H56ab:) my sword shall strike it in splinters (:H56ab)! (With one blow, he strikes the Wanderer's spear in two. H19 broken up: ... The fragments of the spear fall at Wotan's feet. He calmly gathers them up.) (H52)

Wanderer: (H53:) Go on your way! I cannot stop you (:H53)! (H35: He suddenly disappears in total darkness.)

Siegfried: (H65:) Has the coward fled with vanquished weapon (:H65)? (H65) (...) (H93: H12>>/H137a vari:—[Possibly a H137a vari on flute which seems to reference the Motif of Siegfried's contempt for Mime H109. Is this an embryo for H155a, the first segment of the motif H155ab which brings *Siegfried* to a close?]) Ha, rapturous glow! (...) The pathway lies open, shining before me.—(H138b; H138b varis >>:) (...) To find the bride in the flames! Hoho! Hahei! Now I'll summon some boon companion! (Siegfried raises his horn to his lips and plunges into the billowing fire ... . H108/H33; H102; H102; H108; H102; H102 & H93a develop together; H12/H108; H102 repeated & developed; H93a?; H108: no longer visible, Siegfried seems to be moving away towards the summit. (...) ... the glow ... begins to fade, ... dissolving into ... clouds, which are lit as though by the red light of dawn: H93a?; H105; H101 >>; H102; H93a? repeated & developed over H12 & H102 & a H138b frag; H?—Harps; H87 interrupted by H108, and then interspersed with, & segues into, violins which ascend into H102; H?—Harps)

Siegfried hears Wotan's confession that Wotan was his father's enemy, for it was on Wotan's spear that Siegmund's sword Nothung once broke. Siegfried takes up the gauntlet of his betrayed father and breaks Wotan's Spear in revenge. Wagner had a tendency to compare some of his most striking characters, or himself, with the great protagonists of his models in literature, opera, and drama. On one occasion he identified himself with Shakespeare's Prospero from *The Tempest*, and in his following observation about Prospero's (and Shakespeare's) final act, his renunciation of his magic (and, Wagner adds, renunciation of knowledge and the modern world's achievements), and the breaking of his magical staff, in exchange for a world of music, we find Wagner taking Prospero as a model for Wotan. Like Prospero's magical staff, Wotan's spear is broken in favor of young lovers, but in Wotan's case by his heir, his ideal self Siegfried, who'll waken Brünnhilde, i.e., waken the legacy of music which Wotan left for Siegfried: "R. talks to me about 'The Tempest;' during the afternoon he had already expressed his astonishment and admiration for Prospero's words as he breaks his magic staff. 'He gives up everything, the miracle of knowledge—I have the feeling that I can understand that to mean the achievements of our modern world—for music!'" [1122W-{3/28/82} CD Vol. II, p. 832]

The occurrence here of H65—as Siegfried identifies the Wanderer, Wotan, as his father Siegmund's foe—proves that it represents the Noth which both Wälsungs, Siegmund and Sieglinde, suffered unwittingly for Wotan's sake, and not only Sieglinde. Siegfried is afraid neither of Loge's fire, nor of Wotan's Spear. But it's not Loge's fire itself which inspires fear: his outwardly threatening and inwardly protective ring of fire represents the veil of Maya, or Wahn, which first religious man, and then the artist-hero Wagner, employs to hide its true source of inspiration, Wotan's fearful Noth. Wotan's resignation in the face of the inevitability of the twilight of the gods has been conveyed by the recurrence of H52 and H53, recalling Erda's prophecy of the gods' end, as Wotan tells Siegfried to go on his way, since he can't stop him. Wotan has resigned himself to the fact that his free hero can only fulfill his mission to redeem the gods through loving union of the artist-hero with his muse of inspiration if the gods pass away, if religious faith declines and ceases. Accordingly, as Wotan departs we hear the Loveless Motif H35, symbol for the "Fall," suggesting that with Wotan's departure Siegfried will encounter no more stumbling blocks to thwart his unwitting mission, in Wotan's behalf, to restore lost innocence.

So far, Siegfried seems to have met all the conditions necessary to become Wotan's free hero and redeemer. With Wotan's departure, again accompanied by H65, Siegfried expresses his joy in his new-won freedom over the old, traditional, conservative powers which sought to block his progress towards his destiny as a revolutionary artist-hero. He blows his horn in the full certainty of winning the greatest of boon companions, his muse of inspiration Brünnhilde, and passes through the fire to win her. A variant of the Woodbird Motif H137a (which may not only originate, counter-intuitively, in H109, Siegfried's Loathing for Mime, but which may be a basis for the first segment of H155ab, with which S.3.3—Siegfried's with Brünnhilde's love-duet—comes to a triumphant end) seems to capture Siegfried's spirit of new-won freedom after having broken Wotan's Spear to clear a path to Brünnhilde. Siegfried's musico-dramatic ecstasy as he's emancipated himself from Wotan's burden of sin (from consciousness of sin) is overwhelming: rarely if ever has the sudden onset of the feeling of freedom, a falling away of ancient burdens and personal impediments, been so vividly captured in a work of art. This is because what we're about to experience in S.3.3, the *Ring*'s summit, is Wagner's allegorical representation of what it's like for him to be unconsciously inspired by his muse of art, his most inward experience, the most exalted feeling known to him.

SIEGFRIED ⚄ ACT THREE, SCENE THREE
(ON TOP OF BRÜNNHILDE'S PEAK)
SIEGFRIED AND BRÜNNHILDE

The thing which most strikes us in the wordless interlude during which Siegfried progresses up the mountain through the fire to reach Brünnhilde, is the sublimity of the music. It's as if we've entered an entirely new world, which though resembling the one we know, is transfigured to the point we feel we've attained the goal of earthly existence. This corresponds with Wagner's thesis about the redemptive power of his secular art which, though it doesn't truly transcend the world or stand outside it, makes us feel as if we've risen above it and its vulgar and stunted concerns. On reaching the peak of Brünnhilde's mountain Siegfried is overcome with aesthetic arrest as he surveys his new world, including Brünnhilde and her horse Grane asleep. Brünnhilde—her form hidden by her armor and helmet—Siegfried takes at first for a male warrior:

> [pp. 265–6] (H87: … a delicate veil of rose-coloured mist … now part[s] in such a way that the haze disperses towards the top of the stage, finally revealing only the cloudless blue sky … . (…) Brünnhilde lies asleep in full shining armour, her helmet on her head, her long shield covering her. H?— Harps [recalling the transition from R.1 to R.2, and our first view of Valhalla]; H?—A searching, alte-Weise-like string passage which may reference H22; H87; H102 [on high strings]; H?—Another searching, alte-Weise-like string passage which may reference H22: Siegfried reaches the rocky edge of the cliff from the back. (…))
>
> **Siegfried:** (quietly) Blissful wasteland on wondrous heights! (H12; H138b frag; H21: He … observes the scene in wonderment. (…)) (…) (… he stops in astonishment when, still some distance away, he notices Brünnhilde's form.) (H104 >>:) (…) What metalwork wrought in glittering steel? Is it the blaze that still blinds my eye? Shining weapons!—Shall I remove them (:H104)? (He raises the shield and sees Brünnhilde's form … .) (H104:) Ha! In weapons a man: how his likeness fills me with wonder! (…) (:H104) (H21:) Lighter it were if I loosened his headgear (:H21). (He carefully loosens the helmet and removes it from the sleeper; long curling hair breaks free. Siegfried starts.) … Ah!—How fair!—(He remains lost in the sight of it.) (H21 >>:) Shimmering clouds have fringed a celestial lake with their waves: the radiant sunlight's smiling likeness shines through a billowing bank of clouds! (…) His breast is heaving with swelling breath (:H21): shall I break the trammelling breast-plate open? (H76 frag) (…) Come, my sword, and cut through the iron! (H56ab: Siegfried draws his sword and, with tender care, cuts through the rings of mail on both sides of the armour. H65 on flute: He then lifts away the breastplate and greaves, so that Brünnhilde now lies before him in a woman's soft garment.)

One motif especially expresses Siegfried's aesthetic arrest, H21, which we hear as Siegfried enters the wondrous domain of the New Valhalla of art which will be inspired by his muse Brünnhilde, just as Fricka's introduction of H21 in R.2 (when she expressed her hope that Wotan would remain content within the safe haven, later christened by him Valhalla, and maintain his fidelity to her and her values), pointed to the Old Valhalla as the divine realm of the gods, religious faith. Siegfried has now taken notice of the sleeping warrior in armor, and initially has an impulse to ease his breathing by removing some of it. Siegfried removes Brünnhilde's helmet and, when her luxuriant, long hair falls out of it, is filled with amazement and awe, again expressed by H21. Siegfried resorts to Nothung to cut the armor away. Siegfried is metaphorically penetrating Brünnhilde's defenses, her Valkyrie chastity, with a phallus. Brünnhilde will later confirm this by complaining that Siegfried, by cutting lose her armor, has taken away her maidenly defenses, and will initially react with terror at the prospect of sexual union with him, recalling that as a goddess her virginity was always respected. Furthermore, in T.2.4 Brünnhilde will employ Nothung and its sheath as a metaphor for Siegfried's sexual union with her. When we recall also the graphic sexual imagery of Siegfried's smelting and forging songs in S.1.3, and Sieglinde's ecstatic response when Siegmund, her future lover, pulled Nothung out of Hunding's house-Ash in V.1.3, it's clear Wagner wanted his audience to regard Nothung as, among other things, a phallus, but not in the literal sense. Nothung represents the creative impulse in Nature itself, including sexual generation, which, according to Wagner, the artistic genius inherits. Wagner took his cue from Feuerbach, who equated natural necessity with sexual reproduction. [275F-LER, p. 174]

    H21 was introduced in R.2 as Erda expressed her hope that the domestic tranquility of Valhalla would content Wotan and keep him from wandering away in search of change and new sexual conquests. Wotan countered that he has an unconquerable impulse to wander and dominate the objective world. But he's now resigned to the powerlessness, the inwardness, of aesthetic contemplation, and also repudiated religious faith's quest to seek redemption in a supernatural realm, so H21's occurrence here seems to proclaim Wotan's (and therefore Siegfried's and Brünnhilde's) newfound peace and contentment. H21's next significant recurrence was later in R.2 when Loge told Fricka that with gold forged under the Ring's spell by Alberich's Nibelungs a wife might ensure her husband's fidelity. Loge's suggestion foreshadowed Siegfried's eventual oxymoronic use of Alberich's Ring as the wedding Ring he'll give to Brünnhilde in T.P.B to seal their love-bond. Wagner's employment of H21 to express the aesthetic arrest granted us by inspired secular art represents Wotan's hope that the love Siegfried and Brünnhilde share—the artist-hero's unconscious inspiration by his muse—will satisfy all we long for but can't find in the real world, minus the vulnerability of religious belief. In what may well be the most beautiful line of sheer poetry in the *Ring*, also highlighted by H21, Siegfried paints an image of Brünnhilde's beautiful face enveloped by her wavy hair in words which seems to capture H21's essence: "Shimmering clouds have fringed a celestial lake with their waves: the radiant sunlight's smiling likeness shines through a billowing bank of clouds," an image of the transcendent value we once hoped to find in paradise but can now find only in art. But can this newfound serenity be trusted? Won't Siegfried be prompted, as Wotan was before him, to venture outside the safe confines of his New Valhalla to conquer the outer world, and seek the suffering of change? Wotan's retort to Fricka underlined the instability and undependability of a paradise of faith which, after all, is just Wahn, self-deception. And yet, Siegfried's loving union with his muse of unconscious inspiration Brünnhilde will produce an art, the Wagnerian music-drama, in which man's age-old religious longing for transcendent value will attain its summit of expression, granting Wotan's hope a temporary lease on life.

On cutting loose Brünnhilde's armor Siegfried receives a profound shock: this warrior isn't a man. Never having seen a woman before, Siegfried doesn't know what to make of her, though desire draws him to her. This shock runs deep: Brünnhilde has taught him the meaning of fear:

> **[pp. 266–7] Siegfried:** (H141B: ...) No man is this!—(H21 vari: He stares at the sleeping woman in a state of utter turmoil.) (H141B >>:; H102 vari:) Burning enchantment charms my heart, fiery terror transfixes my eyes ... (:H141B; :H102)! (H65: He is filled with immense apprehension.) (H65 vari: [agitated]) To save me, whom shall I call on to help me? (H65 >> :) Mother! Mother! Remember me (:H65)! (...) How shall I waken the maid so that she opens her eyes for me? (H141B) (...) (H141B) (H102:) What though the sight might yet blind me! Might my bravery dare it? (...) (:H102) (H65>[[H147A orch:]] [= H80 vari] ... searing desire consumes my senses: on my quaking heart my hand is trembling! (H102) (...) Is this what it is to fear? O mother! Mother! ... (:H147A orch): ... a woman lies asleep: (H102) she has taught him the meaning of fear! (H22 vari plus music from the transition S.3.2–3) How can I overcome my fear? (...) (H44 or H81 vari orch?) That I myself may awaken, I must waken the maid! (As he approaches the sleeper anew, he is again held enthralled by the sight of her as a result of his more tender feelings. H56ab. He bends closer.) **[[H147A varis on strings:]]** Sweetly quivers her burgeoning mouth (:H147A varis on strings): (H21 vari:) gently trembling it lures me on, faint-hearted that I am!—(...) (:H21 vari) ... Awake! Awake! Thrice-hallowed woman! (H87: he gazes at her.) She cannot hear me. (H87:) ... So I suck life from the sweetest of lips (:H87)—... (H35 vari:) though I should perish and die (:H35 vari)!

Why is Siegfried afraid of Brünnhilde? There seems to be a near universal assumption that the fear Siegfried suffers during his first confrontation with her womanly form is a teenager's fear and awe at his first sexual experience. Generally, commentators add that since Siegfried has never seen a woman before, never experienced sexual desire, the experience overwhelms him. There are problems with this interpretation, not the least of which is that Wagner equates the fear Siegfried learns from the sleeping Brünnhilde with the existential fear which beset Mime, the fear Fafner failed to teach Siegfried. This fear was expressed with a conjunction of the Serpent/Dragon Motif H47 (which Alberich and Fafner share) with H32, H33, H34, and H105, which recalled Loge's ring of protective fire around Brünnhilde, which Brünnhilde and Wotan intended would frighten all cowards away from her, and with H102, the five-note motif to which Brünnhilde declared her desperate hope that Wotan wouldn't let cowards wake and win her but instead frighten them off. And most importantly, this fear stemmed from Wotan's fear of the gods' fated doom which Erda foretold, and which Wotan imparted to Brünnhilde in his confession. To grasp why Siegfried is afraid to wake Brünnhilde we need only recall that Wotan confessed to her an unspoken secret which was so traumatic that he told her he daren't speak it aloud in words. This troubling self-knowledge inspired so much consternation, terror, and revulsion in Wotan that he couldn't sustain conscious thought of it, and repressed it into his unconscious Brünnhilde during his confession. In Siegfried's fear of waking her he's having a premonition that he's about to risk becoming conscious of the forbidden hoard of knowledge which Wotan imparted to her. Siegfried was, until this moment, fearless, for—unlike Wotan—Siegfried doesn't know who he is. Wotan told Erda that Alberich's Ring Curse is powerless over Siegfried because fear remains unknown to him, yet Siegfried has now experienced fear in Brünnhilde's presence. Will this make him subject to Alberich's Ring Curse? Maybe not! At least not yet!

It's fascinating that Siegfried, afraid to waken Brünnhilde, calls on his mother for help. We hear H65, which links Siegfried to his blood mother Sieglinde, but Siegfried is also invoking Mother Nature, Erda (Brünnhilde's mother), who not only taught Wotan the price he must pay to possess Alberich's Ring, but also, Wotan hoped, might teach him how to end his fear. Furthermore, on waking Brünnhilde Siegfried will briefly confuse her with his mother Sieglinde, who died bringing him to birth. We recall that Wotan's sin, which Alberich cursed his Ring to punish, was his figurative murder of our Mother, Nature, through religious world-renunciation. Siegfried the artist-hero is falling heir to man's (Wotan's) collective unconscious Brünnhilde, who'll become his muse of inspiration. So Siegfried, by winning her, is also falling heir to Wotan's sin, his guilt, and Alberich's curse on it.

The relationship of Wotan's conscious mind to Erda (Mother Nature), and to that part of Erda in Wotan which links him to her more primevally, his unconscious mind Brünnhilde, is replicated in Siegfried. The key difference between Wotan and Siegfried in this respect is that where Wotan represents collective, historical humanity, the Folk in its widest sense (according to Wagner the involuntary creator of the elements of civilization, including language and the religious myths), Siegfried is a single individual, or at least an archetypal representative of a small group of individuals, the inspired modern, secular artist who's able to tap into man's collective unconscious Brünnhilde for inspiration. As Wagner might put it, the spirit of the primevally creative Folk (Wotan in collaboration with his trickster friend Loge) who invented the gods involuntarily during the collective dream-time when humans were rising, through evolution of species, to consciousness of themselves as distinctly human, has been reborn in the individual artist-hero Siegfried. Wagner described the key character from his only music-drama comedy, Hans Sachs of *Mastersingers*, as a last vestige of the art-creative spirit of the Folk: "I took Hans Sachs as the last manifestment of the art-productive spirit of the Folk (Volksgeist) ... ." [563W-{6–8/51} 'A Communication To My Friends,' PW Vol. I, p. 329] It goes without saying that if Hans Sachs is, like Wotan, a metaphor for the art-creative spirit of the Folk, then the poet-composer Walther von Stolzing parallels Siegfried as an unconsciously inspired artist-hero. In my chapter on that comedy in Volume Two I'll demonstrate that Hans Sachs is modeled on Wotan in numerous respects. One of the most startling is the fact that Sachs's confession to Eva—who'll become the muse of inspiration for the dream which gives birth to Walther's redemptive mastersong (secular art as a substitute for religious faith)—during his second act cobbling song, is modeled on Wotan's confession to Brünnhilde.

Wagner provided several explanations for Siegfried's fear of Brünnhilde, some of which might seem mutually exclusive. Some scholars have assumed, correctly, that since Siegfried must in some sense give up his distinct personal identity, or ego, to enjoy full loving union with Brünnhilde, that this is what frightens him. Wagner provided ample evidence for this reading. For instance, Cosima recorded his following remark: "... R. plays me his third act [*Siegfried*], great emotion. 'The kiss of love is the first intimation of death, the cessation of individuality, that is why a person is so terrified by it.'" [754W-{8/15/69} CD Vol. I, p. 137] But acknowledgment of the outer, objective world, at the expense of our subjective fears and desires, which diminishes our individual value and uniqueness but enhances Nature's prestige (a philosophy I've ascribed to Alberich, who sinned only against himself, but affirmed Erda's knowledge of all that was, is, and will be, by renouncing love for the Ring's power), threatens to diminish or eclipse our "self" in relation to the "all," also. Siegfried's fear of waking and having sexual union with her could stem as much from the objective hoard of knowledge she possesses (Erda's knowledge which Wotan imparted to Brünnhilde, i.e., Alberich's knowledge of men as things, as objects, rather than as persons, or subjects), as from a fear of the mystical loss of self through loving union with another "self." [See 146F-EOC, p. 285]

But Wagner also provided evidence that Siegfried's fear is the expression of his intuition that in waking Brünnhilde he's in danger of confronting Wotan's repressed thoughts. In the following remark which Cosima recorded, Wagner said Siegfried feels fear of guilt through love, as if Siegfried intuits he's taking on the burden of Wotan's confession of guilt to Brünnhilde by waking her and taking her as wife, and suggests also a link between Siegfried's fear of waking her and what Brünnhilde fears in her premonition of approaching doom: "A profound, indescribable impression; a wooing of the utmost beauty; Siegfried's fear, the fear of guilt through love, Brünnhilde's fear a premonition of the approaching doom ... ." [801W-{7/18/71} CD Vol. I, p. 391] In a remark recorded by Porges, Wagner said that in Brünnhilde's presence Siegfried is afraid of all that he's about to undergo, as if he has an intimation of the tragic fate to which he's condemned by unwittingly taking on the burden of Wotan's guilt: "Before singing the words, 'Wem ruf' ich zum Heil, dass er mir helfe?,' he [Siegfried] draws away somewhat from Brünnhilde. He should not look at her as he cries, 'Wie weck' ich die Maid, dass sie Auge mir öffne?' 'Siegfried is frightened by the thought of all he is about to undergo,'Wagner explained." [882W-{6–8/76} WRR, pp. 107–108] And in one of Wagner's more reflective moments he summed up the meaning of his art in the most startling way: " ... he says that he sometimes has the feeling that art is downright dangerous—it is as if in this great enjoyment of observing he is perhaps failing to recognize the presence of some hidden sorrow." [753W-{7/27/69} CD Vol. I, p. 130]

Wagner's point seems to be that the consolation of beauty which authentic art (his art) offers hides from us its true source of inspiration, a hidden sorrow. It's not merely that superficial art, fantasy as a refuge from harsh reality, distracts us from having a more profound and compassionate understanding of the earnest, terrible state of the world, but rather that Wagner's art (which no one, least of all Wagner, could justifiably call superficial, though he did later accuse himself of hiding from the bitter truth of the world through his dreamy art) hides within its magic circle (its veil of Maya, Loge's protective ring of fire) something very disturbing. Since Wotan's confession of his guilt and fear to Brünnhilde is Siegfried's true source of unconscious artistic inspiration, Wagner's insight into his own art seems a perfect explanation for Siegfried's fear of the sleeping Brünnhilde. In the chapters on *Rhinegold* I already cited a selection of Wagner's observations as evidence that Wagner identified Wotan's confession to Brünnhilde with the hoard of runes which Wagner stated on several occasions she imparts to Siegfried. In these extracts Wagner indicated that on Siegfried's death, this hoard of knowledge she imparted to him is revealed to be the Norns,' or Erda's, or the Ring's runes, i.e., the intolerably fearful knowledge which Erda taught Wotan during his sojourn with her in the bowels of the earth, that sojourn whose product was their daughter Brünnhilde. [See 380W-{6–8/48} 'The Nibelungen Myth,' PW Vol. VII, p. 310, and 382W-{10–11/48} *Siegfried's Death*, PW Vol. VIII, p. 16]

But we also have direct evidence from the *Ring* libretto that Brünnhilde taught Siegfried, subliminally, the contents of Wotan's confession, for in T.P.B she tells Siegfried: "What gods have taught me I gave to you: a bountiful store ["Hort"—"Hoard"] of hallowed runes ... ." And Siegfried's response strongly suggests that the knowledge she imparted to him is in some sense unconscious knowledge, because he tells her: "You gave me more, o wondrous woman, than I know how to cherish: chide me not if your teaching has left me untaught!" Her knowledge has left him untaught not merely because he decides not to use it, but because it never rises to consciousness for him. It was in this sense that he in S.2.3 emerged from Fafner's cave bearing Alberich's Ring and Tarnhelm, having already forgotten their use, which the Woodbird had taught him a moment before he entered Fafner's cave.

There's also an instance of indirect evidence which is quite dramatic. Wagner was greatly influenced in his development of the character Brünnhilde by the play attributed to Aeschylus, *Prometheus Bound*, presumed to be the first part of a Greek trilogy (the other two parts now presumably lost), like Wagner's model for the *Ring*, *The Oresteia*. It's part of the received wisdom of Wagner scholarship that Brünnhilde, like Prometheus, has been punished by the greatest of the gods (Wotan/Zeus) for striving to protect the Wälsungs/mortal man from the gods' punishment, and, in Prometheus's case at least, for granting mortal man what ought to be the gods' privilege alone. This privilege isn't only access to fire, as is often supposed (though, obviously, primeval man's first deliberate use of fire is a sure sign he's acquired reflective consciousness), but also the gift of foresight, foreknowledge. In Greek, Prometheus means "foreknowledge." Brünnhilde is Wotan's repository of foreknowledge of the twilight of the gods her mother Erda foretold. It's this fearful foreknowledge of their end (which, as we'll learn in *Twilight of the Gods*, also involves Siegfried's and Brünnhilde's love succumbing to Alberich's Ring Curse) which Wotan repressed into Brünnhilde, which is the hidden source of the fear which overcomes Siegfried just prior to waking her and falling heir to her hoard of knowledge. In *Prometheus Bound* Prometheus possesses secret foreknowledge of how the gods of Olympus will meet their doom, knowledge which Zeus tries and fails to obtain from Prometheus. Perhaps this explains why Wagner described *Prometheus Bound* as the most pregnant of tragedies: "To see the most pregnant of all tragedies, the 'Prometheus,' came they [the Greeks]; in this Titanic masterpiece to see the image of themselves, to read the riddle of their own actions ... ." [402W-{6–8/49} 'Art and Revolution,' PW Vol. I, p. 34]

But there's also decisive musico-dramatic evidence. During the initial onset of Siegfried's fear of Brünnhilde we hear H141B, which when introduced near the end of S.2.3 in its prior iteration as H141A expressed Siegfried's intense longing to win Brünnhilde's love. However, as Siegfried further analyzes his new feeling of fear we hear H65, and finally a new motif H147. I've noted that if one tallies all the contexts in which H65 recurs to obtain what I call its "dramatic profile," it seems to express the Noth (anguish) to which Wotan has condemned his Wälsung race by choosing them as martyrs to confront and overcome the full force of Alberich's Ring Curse, so the gods can be redeemed from it. But H65 also expresses their mutual sympathy as victims of this fate, as Cooke put it, and especially Sieglinde's sympathy for both Siegmund and Siegfried, a sympathy which includes her hope that Brünnhilde would meet her son Siegfried some day. The loving sympathy of the heroine for the hero's plight (Noth), central to his identity, is the core of all of Wagner's canonic stage works. But H65's newly acquired significance as a symbol for Siegfried's fear of the sleeping Brünnhilde is that Siegfried, preparing to wake her, has an intimation of the terrible fate to which Wotan condemns him by leaving him heir to the sleeping Brünnhilde and the horrific, unspoken secret she keeps.

Dunning describes H147, the primary motif which expresses Siegfried's fear of waking Brünnhilde, as an independent chromatic motif, while Cooke saw it as a twisted variant of H80 (in turn a gnarly variant of Wotan's Spear Motif H19). H80 was introduced in V.2.1 as a symbol for Wotan's reluctant acknowledgment that his quest for a hero freed from Wotan's egoism and fear was futile, and in V.3.3 H80 was heard in the context of Wotan's intent to let Brünnhilde suffer the punishment which she brought on herself by living for love in the face of Wotan's tragic awareness of its futility. It was this knowledge which Wotan repressed by confessing it to her, in whom he hoped his secret will remain forever unspoken. Later, H147 will evolve into H176, which expresses Brünnhilde's ultimate recognition that her blissful marriage to Siegfried was, ironically, the essence of Wotan's punishment. I favor Cooke's thesis that H147 is a baroque variant of H80. All in all, H65 and H147 bespeak the anguish of falling heir to Wotan's futile quest to redeem the gods from Alberich's Ring Curse. Siegfried and Brünnhilde, having unwittingly become implicated in the gods' self-deceit, will suffer the gods' fate: they'll betray the love which was Wotan's sole hope of redemption. These considerations justify Siegfried's fear of waking Brünnhilde.

Siegfried realizes that to end his fear he must wake the maid. As Siegfried loudly calls out for her to wake, we hear H87 (Fate) several times. It's Brünnhilde who holds for Siegfried the knowledge of his and the gods' fate (and thus his identity: for Feuerbach a man's identity is his fate) which her mother Erda imparted to Wotan. Then Siegfried introduces something quite novel: as we hear the Loveless Motif H35, he says he must suck life from Brünnhilde's lips, even should he die doing so. To draw unconscious artistic inspiration from Brünnhilde's terrible, forbidden knowledge that the world is loveless and irredeemable, Siegfried must confront the true source of our existential fear subliminally to create that redemptive art which will preserve the veil of Maya, Loge's ring of fire, which masks the terrible truth and sublimates it into tragic beauty. He must take aesthetic possession of Wotan's horror and draw advantage from it as Loge's cunning would. Symbolically, Siegfried must die during unconscious intercourse with the unspeakable truth to wake, figuratively reborn, with a new artwork in hand that allows us to forget the fear which inspired it and regain our lost innocence. Siegfried's model is singer-poet Tannhäuser's sojourn in the Venusberg, which he visits to obtain unconscious artistic inspiration from his muse Venus, a sojourn he normally forgets after waking, when he creates a new work of art and presents it to an audience. As with Tannhäuser, Siegfried's true but secret source of artistic inspiration would, if revealed to his audience (or even to himself), cause social mayhem and possibly destroy his artistic gift and even his life.

Now Siegfried summons his courage and kisses Brünnhilde awake. The best introduction to this key passage, which provides indirect evidence of how Wagner may have described the meaning of Siegfried's heroic act among his inner circle, is the remark by Berthold Kellermann (cited previously) regarding comments made by a Count Aponyi in 1876 during the rehearsals and premier of Wagner's *Ring*, in which Aponyi stated that sleeping Brünnhilde is the "new national art" which the hero Richard Wagner awoke after penetrating Loge's fire with a weapon forged "from the shards of the sword of his fathers (the classical German masters)." [See 892W-{8/20/76} From a letter by Berthold Kellermann to his parents, reporting on the final performance of the Ring and the subsequent celebrations, WR, p. 250] We'll find considerable evidence that Siegfried's and Brünnhilde's love-duet is Wagner's metaphor for the unconscious artistic inspiration which produced his unique, revolutionary art-form, the music-drama (the *Ring*), in what follows:

> **[pp. 267–8]** (H35: H?—Music from the orchestral transition S.3.2–3, including a H22 vari: He sinks, as though dying, on the sleeping woman, and, with his eyes closed, presses his lips to her mouth. H87; H?—Music from the orchestral transition S.3.2–3, including a H22 vari; H87; H?—Music from the orchestral transition S.3.2–3, including a H22 vari, developing to a loud climax; **[[H148 orch]]** [= H52 chord]; Harps; **[[H148 orch]]**; Harps: **[[H149 orch:]]** [= H22 vari] Brünnhilde opens her eyes. Siegfried starts up and remains standing in front of her. Brünnhilde slowly sits up. She raises her arms and, with solemn gestures, welcomes her return to an awareness of earth and sky.)
>
> **Brünnhilde: [[H148 orch:]]** Hail to you, sun! Hail to you, light (:H148 orch)! Hail to you, **[[H149 orch:]]** light-bringing day (:H149 orch)! (H87:) Long was my sleep! Awakened am I (:H87): who is the hero who woke me? (…)
>
> **Siegfried:** (H93a? >>> : … :H93a?): (H93a?:) Siegfried am I who woke you (:H93a?). (H93a [emphatic, powerful version])
>
> **Brünnhilde:** … **[[H148 orch/voc:]]** Hail to you, gods! Hail to you, world (:H148 orch/voc)! Hail to you, **[[H149 orch:]]** resplendent earth ["Erde"—Erda] (:H149 orch)! … awakened, I see it is Siegfried who woke me!
>
> **Siegfried:** (… **[[H150 voc:]]** [= H63b vari]) All hail to the mother who gave me birth; hail to the earth ["Erde"] that gave me nurture: **[[H149 orch:]]** that I saw the eye that smiles on me now in my bliss (:H150 voc; :H149 orch)!
>
> **Brünnhilde: [[H150 voc:]]** All hail to the mother who gave you birth; hail to the earth ["Erde"] that gave you nurture; your gaze alone was fated to see me, **[[H149 orch:]]** to you alone was I fated to wake (:H150 voc; :H149 orch)!
>
> (H65 frag/H93/**[[H151 orch:]]** Both remain lost in radiant delight as they gaze at one another.)

Cooke noted that from the finale of V.3.3 (when Wotan put Brünnhilde to sleep) till now, when Siegfried wakes her, the Fate Motif H87 hasn't modulated, but has remained in the same key, but now with her waking it begins to modulate again, as if fate is again at work now that Siegfried has woken her. If true, this would be most interesting, since it's often said that Brünnhilde in the end offers man redemption from fate. Wotan said Alberich's Ring Curse is powerless over Siegfried because Siegfried has never experienced fear. But we've just witnessed Siegfried experiencing fear in the presence of the sleeping Brünnhilde, fear he acknowledges he learned from her. It would be truer to say that Alberich's Ring Curse of consciousness is temporarily neutralized by Brünnhilde, Wotan's and Siegfried's unconscious mind, and that Alberich's Ring Curse won't be reactivated unless Siegfried betrays his love for her and thus betrays Wotan's unspoken secret, his hoard of forbidden knowledge (incarnate now in Alberich's

Ring), by bringing it up from the silent depths (where she'll keep its power safe) to the light of day.

This passage, in which Siegfried confronts his unconscious mind and muse Brünnhilde to seek inspiration for the first time, is one of the most sublime and ecstatic in Wagner's art, a dramatic representation of Wagner's paradise, his most exalted state of being, unconscious artistic inspiration. Wagner always said that for him, the greatest joy was in the original inspiration, not in the completion or the staging of his works. We've been introduced to four new motifs, H148, H149, H150, and H151. The awesome H148 is, according to Dunning, a chord evoking Siegfried's calling on Brünnhilde to wake based on H52, which at its inception in R.4 underlined Erda's two key proclamations of her knowledge, one, that she knows all that was, is, and will be, and two, that everything that is, ends. H52 evokes the passage of time, change, mortality, and natural necessity, Nature's laws of motion, its primal evolutionary creativity which lives on in the inspired artist Siegfried. The beautiful H149, a variant of H22 (Freia's Motif of Sensuous Love, which was heard frequently in the transition S.3.2–3), also evokes Siegfried's waking of Brünnhilde, who was destined to wake only for him. Only Siegfried can woo the muse Brünnhilde, for he alone is an authentically inspired artistic genius, who's able to access man's unconscious knowledge of the religious mysteries (their true source), knowledge too dangerous for the common man to handle.

On waking Brünnhilde hails the light, the day, the gods, the world, and earth (Erda), accompanied by H148 and H149. As she recalls how long was her sleep, we hear several repetitions of the Fate Motif H87. Brünnhilde possesses foreknowledge of the fated doom of the gods and their proxies, including herself and Siegfried. If—after experiencing fear and waking her—Siegfried fails to create that redemptive work of art in which the fear which inspired it can be forgotten, then the fate which Erda foretold, the gods' twilight, won't be long in coming. It's Siegfried's unwitting, involuntary duty now to share with Brünnhilde the task of keeping Wotan's secret, figuratively preserving Loge's ring of artistic illusion which protects the religious mysteries which Wotan imparted to her. If Siegfried can remain unconscious of the truth, thanks to Brünnhilde's protection, then as long as that's the case he has a temporary reprieve from suffering Alberich's Ring Curse of consciousness. Siegfried and Brünnhilde then exchange lines and duet for the first time to H150, which Cooke assigned to the family of love motifs which includes H23, H37, H39, H63b, H79b, and H142. This brief duet climaxes in an orgiastic, ecstatic orchestral explosion based partly on H65, but primarily on another new motif, H151, heard as Siegfried and Brünnhilde stare in wonderment and awe into each others' eyes. Neither Cooke nor Dunning have placed H151 in any of the motif families.

Thanks to the fact that Brünnhilde protects Siegfried from consciousness of the sin he inherited from Wotan, Siegfried's and Brünnhilde's love seems sinless, as if the preconscious innocence of man's animal ancestors (the Rhinedaughters' joy in the Rhinegold), experiencing the "present" in a pure way reflective humans can't—had been restored: "He [Wagner] then plays Siegfried's awakening of

Brünnhilde, is pleased with the character of this work, its trueness to Nature: 'Like two animals,' he says of Br. And Sieg. 'Here there is no doubt, no sin,' he continues ... ." [1134W-{9/5/82} CD Vol. II, p. 907] And thanks to Wagner's theoretical writings, particularly *Opera and Drama*, but especially to an observation by Cosima reproduced below (previously cited), we know that Wagner conceived of Siegfried as a metaphor for the poet-dramatist, and Brünnhilde as a metaphor for the music Siegfried embraces to produce that unique union of word, action, and music, the Wagnerian music-drama: "We speak also about my last conversation with Herr Levi. He does not seem to fully understand 'Parsifal,' and I tell him that R.'s [Wagner's] article theoretically bears almost the same relationship to the poem as his words on music (the loving woman) and on drama (the man) in 'Opera and Drama' bear to Brünnhilde and Siegfried." [933W-{8/2/78}CD Vol. II, p. 128]

The implications of this key metaphor for grasping Wagner's mature music-dramas and major theoretical writings were explored by Dr. Jean-Jacques Nattiez in his *Wagner Androgyne* (published in the original French in 1990, and in an English translation by Stewart Spencer for Cambridge University Press in 1993). I anticipated several important insights in this book—especially the notion that Siegfried is Wagner's metaphor for the music-dramatist Wagner himself, and Siegfried's loving union with his muse Brünnhilde the means by which he gives birth to the Wagnerian music-drama—in college papers written for anthropology classes in 1974 (Franklin and Marshall College, PA) and 1976 (Southern Illinois University at Carbondale), as well as essays copyrighted at the Library of Congress in 1981 ('In Dedication To Claude Lévi-Strauss') and 1983. The latter paper, entitled 'The Doctrine of the Ring' (which presented my thesis that Wagner's four music-dramas—the *Ring*, *Tristan*, *Mastersingers*, and *Parsifal*, can best be understood by treating the four as one single artwork), I hand-delivered to Nattiez at a symposium, "Wagner in Retrospect—A Centennial Reappraisal," held in 11/83 at the University of Illinois Chicago Circle campus. Nattiez independently applied a similar approach which he called the "paradigmatic" method to his treatment of Wagner's theoretical writings of the late 1840's and early 1850's as if they're a unitary argument [Nattiez, p. 13]. At this conference Nattiez presented his metaphorical reading of Siegfried and Brünnhilde (which he developed independently) in a paper entitled "The 'Ring' as a Metaphorical History of Music." I mention this because Nattiez's book, which I discovered long after having worked out most of my interpretation of the *Ring*, helped me to further solidify my interpretation of Brünnhilde as Siegfried's muse of unconscious artistic inspiration, by showing me just how far the concept that Brünnhilde is a metaphor for Wagner's special kind of dramatic music can be taken. Nattiez's independent findings have been a great aid to me in working out certain remaining conundrums in my own work (granting me insights which even he evidently didn't anticipate), and I believe my study enhances his book's value by grounding it in an even more comprehensive allegorical reading of the *Ring*, Wagner's other music-dramas and operas, his writings and recorded remarks, and Feuerbach's writings.

We've now come to one of several supremely important passages which, taken together, offer powerful evidence that Siegfried's loving union with Brünnhilde is Wagner's metaphor for the artist-hero's unconscious inspiration by Wotan's repressed hoard of knowledge he confessed to her. She tells Siegfried that long before he was born her loving protection nurtured him, a remark which taken by itself says only that through Brünnhilde's intervention—in defiance of Wotan's orders—to save the Wälsung twins' unborn child Siegfried, she was his guardian long before he was born. It's partly thanks to the ambiguity of her remark that Siegfried wonders whether in that case she might be the mother he'd assumed had died giving him birth, who it turns out may only have been sleeping all this time:

> [p. 268] **Brünnhilde:** (H150:) O Siegfried! Siegfried! ... (:H150)! (H151:) You waker of life, all-conquering light! (H151) If only you knew, you joy of the world, (H150:) how I have always loved you! (H150) (H150 >> :) You yourself were all I thought of, all I ever cared for (:H150)! (H150:) I nurtured you, you tender child, before you were begotten; even before you were born, my shield already sheltered you (:H150): (H143:) so long have I loved you, Siegfried (:H143).
>
> **Siegfried:** ... So my mother did not die? (H65:) Was the lovely woman merely asleep (:H65)? (Brünnhilde smiles and stretches out her hand to him in friendly fashion.)
>
> **Brünnhilde:** (H151 >> :) You blithesome child, your mother won't come back to you. (H151 orch:) Your own self am I, if you but love me in my bliss (:H151 orch); (H87:) what you don't know I know for you (:H87): (H143:) and yet I am knowing only because I love you (:H143)!

Siegfried's momentary confusion of Brünnhilde with his mother harks back further than Siegfried's being born through his mother Sieglinde's death. It looks back to Wotan's original sin against Mother Nature (Erda's knowledge of all that was, is, and shall be), as described by Alberich in R.4, a sin Siegfried has unwittingly inherited as Wotan's unconscious agent of redemption of the gods from Alberich's Ring Curse. Erda's daughter Brünnhilde, Siegfried's muse, is his surrogate mother, surrogate for Nature's truth. Brünnhilde is his music, and Mother Nature (Erda), according to Wagner, gave birth to music: " ... 'It took Nature a very long time to produce passion; this is what can lead one to the heights; music is its transfiguration, is, alone among all the arts, directly connected with it.'" [1143W-{1/5/83} CD Vol. II, p. 986]

Previously I presented evidence that Brünnhilde metaphysically gave birth to Siegfried after Wotan planted his confession in her (his wish-womb), the seed of his poetic intent that the artist-hero Siegfried should redeem the gods (religion) from Alberich's and Hagen's (science's) threat to overthrow them. Now, by virtue of Wotan's granting Siegfried access to Brünnhilde, Siegfried can draw artistic inspiration from Wotan's unspoken secret to redeem the world musically. This is represented by H143, which we hear as Brünnhilde concludes her description of how she cared for Siegfried even before he was born with the remark: "so long have I loved you, Siegfried." H143, introduced in S.3.1 as Wotan declared he no longer feared the gods' fated doom because his desire for redemption from Alberich's Ring Curse will be fulfilled by Siegfried's and Brünnhilde's love, represents the new religion, Wagner's revolutionary, redemptive music-drama.

Brünnhilde explains (as we hear H151) that though Siegfried's mother won't come back to him, Brünnhilde is Siegfried's self (Wotan's newly purified self) if he'll only love her in her bliss. And immediately afterward we hear H87 (Fate) as she makes the remarkable claim that what Siegfried doesn't know, she knows for him. We recall Siegfried's remark to dying Fafner: "I still don't know who I am." It's as if Brünnhilde is responding to Siegfried's remark to Fafner. She knows for Siegfried the fate (H87), the twilight of the gods, which her mother Erda foretold to Wotan, foreknowledge which paralyzed Wotan into inaction by benumbing him with existential fear. But she also knows for Siegfried the unwitting role Wotan assigned to his Wälsung heroes in Wotan's futile quest for redemption. H151 will be associated from now on with the concept that Brünnhilde knows Siegfried's true identity, history, and fate for him, as Wotan reincarnate, so she, Siegfried's unconscious mind, can protect him from suffering Wotan's un-healing wound of consciousness. There's no phrase more crucial than this, that Brünnhilde knows for Siegfried what he doesn't know, to understanding the *Ring*, and it's remarkable that evidently it hasn't previously disclosed its secret to an investigator, especially since it also offers a key to the innermost meaning of Wagner's other canonical operas and music-dramas, from *The Flying Dutchman* to *Parsifal*.

H143 is heard again giving expression to Brünnhilde's remark that she's knowing, in the special way she's described, only because she loves Siegfried. This new religion, the redemption of the terrible world through music (love), the language of the unconscious, gives birth to a new world created according to our human heart, an aesthetically conceived world of music-drama. This reverses the natural progress of evolution described by Feuerbach, in which the physical world, Mother Nature, gave birth to the human species which invented the illusory world of gods, but which ultimately resorted to music to express man's longing for transcendent value when belief in gods was no longer sustainable in the face of our advancement in objective knowledge. Wagner expressed it this way: "Everywhere we see the inner law, only conceivable as sprung from the spirit of Music, prescribe the outer law that regulates the world of sight ... . But that paradise was lost ... , (...) ... until the world-soul has been waked again [Wotan has woken Erda; Siegfried has woken Brünnhilde]. / (...) As for our present Civilisation, ... we certainly may assume that nothing but the spirit of our Music ... can dower it with a soul again. And the task of giving to the new, more soulful civilsation that haply may arise herefrom, the new Religion to inform it ... must obviously be reserved for the German Spirit alone ... [it must be reserved for Wagner's music-drama, the artwork of the future]." [791W-{9–12/70} 'Beethoven,' PW Vol. V, p. 121; p. 123] Siegfried's waking of Brünnhilde, Erda's (Mother Nature's) daughter, directly following Wotan's waking of Erda herself, can be construed as what Wagner described above as a paradise—once lost—which has now been regained, because Siegfried has wakened the world-soul (music) again. It's Siegfried's waking of Brünnhilde which Wagner has identified with Feuerbach's notion of a new, secular religion, which uplifts the human species and its mother, Nature, by consigning the gods, products of our fantasy, and an insult to Nature, to oblivion. This secular religion, which locates the source of all value in mortal man, will replace the old belief in supernatural gods. In this sense Siegfried's and Brünnhilde's redemptive love is a figurative twilight of the gods, as will be manifest in Brünnhilde's final invocation and dismissal of the gods to their destruction which brings *Siegfried* to its climactic close.

Feuerbach praised Eve's defiance of God's injunction against eating the fruit of the Tree of Knowledge [See 37F-TDI: p. 250] because he believed our gods are illusions, and therefore Eve's disobedience, her quest for knowledge which faith in god forbade, was according to Feuerbach a symbol for our first step toward freedom from dependency on the illusion of a divine creator or legislator. Because Siegfried's unconsciously inspired, redemptive art can only come to fruition with our emancipation from religious faith, Eve became Wagner's Feuerbachian symbol for the muse of secular art, particularly his revolutionary music-dramas. Wagner dramatized this explicitly in *Mastersingers'* heroine Eva, Walther's muse of unconscious artistic inspiration. Another way of putting this is that the death of God, Wotan's renunciation of active involvement in our human life, is the muse for Wagner's art. Religious belief was predestined to fail in the face of the human mind's inevitable disobedience to the divine injunction of faith, by breaking the prohibition on asking forbidden questions about our origin and true, natural identity, and about the origin of religious faith in particular. Feuerbach's heroine Eve is a natural metaphor for this because her disobedience to God's injunction not to eat the fruit of the Tree of Knowledge constitutes an archetypal instance of scientific skepticism toward opinion sanctified as divinely inspired tradition and therefore allegedly inherently unsusceptible to doubt. Religious belief must fail so that Wagner's secular music-drama can become religious faith's substitute or heir and compensate us poor mortals for the loss of faith's consolation. A close analysis of all of Wagner's heroines from his last romantic opera *Lohengrin* through his four mature music-dramas demonstrates that they—Elsa, Brünnhilde, Isolde, Eva (in whom Wagner's identification of the muse for art with Eve is self-evident), and Kundry—are all metaphors for Feuerbach's Eve. To an extent this can also be said of Tannhäuser's muse of unconscious artistic inspiration, Venus, a star identified with Eve.

Not only that, but Brünnhilde, a virgin—like Mother Mary—by virtue of her status as a celibate Valkyrie, as Siegfried's figurative mother, has given birth to the savior from Wotan's confession of his need for a free hero which Wotan planted in her. Wotan is the pagan equivalent of God-the-Father in the Old Testament. This gives a whole new meaning to the Biblical notion that Christ was born of God's word. In this way also, acting the part of Mother Mary through the virgin's metaphysically giving birth to god's son (in this case grandson), the savior Siegfried, Brünnhilde compensates for Eve's sin—which forged the Ring of human consciousness, and exiled us from the paradise of preconscious instinctual animality—by inspiring Siegfried to figuratively restore lost paradise through art, especially the art of music. [See 1103W-{10/23/81} BB, p. 202]

Now a strange and curious thing happens. Brünnhilde reveals to Siegfried that Wotan once confessed to her his thought, which she felt, and what she felt was her love for Siegfried, as we hear H143. But Siegfried remains oblivious to the conceptual content of Brünnhilde's confession:

> [p. 269] **Brünnhilde:** (H150 vari:) O Siegfried! Siegfried! (...) (:H150 vari) (H151 >> :) I loved you always (:H151): to me alone was Wotan's thought revealed. The thought which I could never name; (H82a:) the thought I did not think but only felt; the thought for which I fought, (H99 vari >> :) did battle and have striven (:H82a; :H99 vari); for which I flouted him who thought it; (H97 vari:) for which I atoned, incurring chastisement (:H97 vari), because, not thinking, (H99B >> :) I only felt it (:H98B)! Because that (H143:) thought ... was but my love for you (:H143). (H150 vari)

We hear H99 as Brünnhilde describes how she struggled and was chastised for fighting for Wotan's thought, which she only felt. His thought was his confession to her of the gods' need for a hero (represented here by the first segment of the Gods' Need Motif H82a, the portion which references Erda's Motif H52) emancipated from the gods' protection (faith), who could take on the burden of religious man's guilt, his sin against Mother Nature's truth, which Alberich's Ring Curse punishes, and redeem him from having to suffer from it. H99, ultimately derived from the embryo of H19 (Wotan's Spear), is a variant of H80, the motif which recalls Fricka's thwarting of Wotan's hope to obtain redemption through a free hero. We hear H143, a metaphor for the artist-hero Siegfried's unconscious artistic inspiration by his muse Brünnhilde, as she proclaims Wotan's thought (confession) to be her love for Siegfried. By confessing this thought to his wish-womb Brünnhilde, Wotan gave birth to his new, purified self, Siegfried. This was the thought she felt and fought for against Wotan's objections. What this tells us is that Wotan's confession to Brünnhilde of his unspoken secret, his hoard of fatal knowledge, is the secret source of Siegfried's unconscious artistic inspiration. What Wotan thought, she felt, and what she felt was her inspiration of Siegfried.

Brünnhilde has made a remarkable proposition. It's that a thought can have a corresponding feeling, linked with it irrevocably, which somehow carries the import of the thought without any conceptual element. This is what Wagner said his musical motifs do: they can't think but they can be messengers of thoughts with which they've been associated. [See 540W-{50–1/51} *Opera and Drama*, PW Vol. II, p. 324] Though the evidence for it in the *Ring* libretto is ambiguous, Brünnhilde is suggesting that the love she and Siegfried share is music, the "purely-human" which the soul of myth (Siegfried) and music (Brünnhilde) have in common.

In a passage previously cited Feuerbach argued that when religious faith, religion as conceptual thought, is dying out in the face of man's scientific advancement in knowledge, our religious longing for transcendence lives on, minus its conceptual component, in feeling, which Feuerbach described as "the last refuge of theology." [145F-EOC, p. 283] Feuerbach identified "feeling" as "the musical power in man." [65F-EOC, p. 63] In another passage previously cited, Wagner in his last years paraphrased Feuerbach with poetic flair on the subject of music as heir to dying religious faith, stating that when, thanks to scientific knowledge, God "had to vanish, he left us—in eternal memory of him—music." [See 999W-{12/25/79} 'Introduction to the Year 1880,' PW Vol. VI, p. 34] Elsewhere Wagner explained how music can save the essence of religious feeling, while religious thought fights on futilely against science in its quest to control thought. [1048W-{11/80} 'What Boots This Knowledge?'—First Supplement to 'Religion and Art,' PW Vol. VI, pp. 260–261] In another revelatory extract (previously cited) Wagner described music as the "living god within our bosom" and as our "last religion," which gives us the power of rebirth (just as Wotan, representative of religious belief, thanks to Brünnhilde is reborn in the artist-hero Siegfried) if we preserve her integrity. [1000W-{12/25/79} 'Introduction to theYear 1880,' PW Vol. VI, pp. 34–35] And, last, we found a basis for Wotan's (religious man's) insistence that he must wholly sever himself from Brünnhilde (music) and her concerns, and also for Brünnhilde's remark to Siegfried that what Wotan thought, she felt, in Wagner's (previously cited) comment that: "Only her final severance from the decaying Church [Siegfried's and Brünnhilde's independence of the Valhallan gods] could enable the art of Tone to save the noblest heritage of the Christian idea [Valhalla] ... ." [1026W-{6–8/80} 'Religion and Art,' PW Vol. VI, pp. 223–224; See also 539W-{50–1/51} *Opera and Drama*, PW Vol. II, pp. 316–317]

In other words, Brünnhilde will express Wotan's thought, his confession, only as feeling, in music, which is why Siegfried (as we'll see in the following passage) will remain oblivious to the conceptual message she's tried to convey about Wotan. Wagner described how the poet frees his subject matter of the burden of historico-social and state-religious relations and conditions through its ascension into music: " ... the Poetic Aim can only be realised through its complete transmission from the Understanding to the Feeling ... ." [532W-{50–1/51} *Opera and Drama*, PW Vol. II, p. 256; p. 263] This is precisely what Brünnhilde says Wotan has done by imparting his confession (of the burden of his corrupt history and egoistic nature) to her, so that what he thought, she feels. [See also 516W-{50–1/51} *Opera and Drama*, PW Vol. II, pp. 204–205, and 529W-{50–1/51} *Opera and Drama*, PW Vol. II, pp. 233–234] And finally, Wagner argued that music is most fitted to be the messenger of the purely-human because it's a language understood by all, through which the "inmost secret of the artist's thought" (Wotan's confession of his unspoken secret) can be transmuted into a universal message: "Though as regards Literature the diversity of European tongues presents an obstacle, yet in Music, that language understandable by all the world alike, there would be supplied the great conforming force, which, resolving the language of abstractions into that of feelings, would transmute the inmost secret of the artist's thought into a universal message ... ." [679W-{9/60}

'Music of the Future,' PW Vol. III, p. 302] These considerations should help us grasp the meaning of Siegfried's otherwise perhaps inexplicable remarks below:

> **[p. 269] Siegfried:** (H150 varis repeated:) Wondrous it sounds what you blissfully sing, yet its meaning seems obscure to me. ... the sound of your singing is sweet to hear: but what you say to me singing, stunned, (H87:) I cannot understand (:H87). (H147A:) With my senses I cannot grasp faraway things ["Nicht kann ich das Ferne sinnig erfassen"], (H150:) since all these senses can see and feel only you (:H147A [agitated but slow]; :H150). (H147A:) You bind me in fetters of anxious fear; you alone have taught me to dread it (:H147A). (H35 voc:) No longer hide that courage of mine (:H35 voc) which you bound with powerful bonds!

Siegfried describes Wagner's theory of artistic "Wonder" (the miraculous in art), which is attained by the music-dramatist when, by associating characters, events, symbols, images and concepts from the drama with specific musical motifs of remembrance and foreboding in evolutionary transformation, he's able to condense an immense array of experience, widely dispersed in time and space, into identifiable motifs, which capture particular feelings in tone and rhythm, resonant subliminally with all that with which they've been associated in the course of the drama. In this way, thanks to Brünnhilde, who felt what Wotan thought, Wotan's thought becomes Siegfried's feeling, which Siegfried can't understand conceptually, but can only intuit musically, or aesthetically. It's no accident that when Siegfried says he can't understand what Brünnhilde "sings" to him (Nattiez drew attention to the fact that she's described by Siegfried specifically as "singing" to him information he doesn't understand [Nattiez, p. 79]), we hear H87 (Fate), associated with all that Wotan learned from Erda about the gods' fated doom, which he confessed to Brünnhilde. Siegfried is seemingly freed from this fate (in truth, only freed from paralyzing consciousness of it) by his unconscious mind Brünnhilde, who holds knowledge of it for him. Thanks to Brünnhilde, the fearful, self-loathing, paralyzed Wotan is reborn, purged of all this malign baggage, as the fearless, proud, loving, and creative Siegfried, who lives in the present just as Wagner's musical motifs allow us to do through his "Wonder."

Pursuing his description of Wagner's "Wonder," Siegfried states, accompanied by H147A, that his senses can't grasp far away ("Ferne") things, since he can see and feel only Brünnhilde. H147A, originally associated with Siegfried's fear of what might be wrought by his waking Brünnhilde, is, like H99, based on H80 (Wotan's Frustration, recalling his acknowledgment that his allegedly free heroes are merely reflections of what he loathes in himself and can't transcend). However, H147 gradually begins to transform into this motif family's culminating variant H176, later to be identified with Brünnhilde's tragic recognition that the love she shares with Siegfried is, ironically, the fulfillment of the punishment Wotan said she brought on herself by living for love when Wotan had resigned himself to its futility. What's so "far away" that Siegfried can't grasp is Wotan's confession of the gods' and Wälsungs' tragic history to Brünnhilde, a hoard of knowledge of things widely dispersed in time and space, a sinister history recalled by the lengthy genealogy of transformations of the embryo of H19 (Wotan's spear), with which this drama began. This also explains why, as Siegfried complains to Brünnhilde that she's bound him in fetters of anxious fear, we again hear H147A. As he asks her no longer to hide his courage which she's bound with powerful bonds, he sings H35 (Loveless), a motival symbol for the Fall. These motifs evoke the objective knowledge of the world's lovelessness, and the inevitable destruction of the gods' ideal world by Alberich, which Erda taught Wotan, wisdom which he told Erda would wane before his Will (Brünnhilde). Siegfried's fear of Brünnhilde arose from his premonition that Wotan's hoard of forbidden knowledge, which she holds for Siegfried, might rise to consciousness in him if he wakes her. It's Brünnhilde's duty now, Siegfried seems to be saying, to help him forget the fear she's taught him. This becomes easier to understand when we recall that Wotan is reborn in Siegfried, and therefore Wotan's second desire of Erda, that she show him how to forget the care she taught, is reborn in Siegfried also.

Siegfried represents for Wagner, among other things, the Feuerbachian "free, self-determining individual" who, according to both Feuerbach and Wagner, is the foundation on which the future secular social religion will be built, which will replace our former belief in the gods and their supernatural "other world." Wagner asked (in a passage previously cited) what sort of paradisal, free human relationships we could create, "... if we take them as purely-human, ever fully and entirely present," if we send all that's "extra-human or non-present," which the State has placed between people, "far away (Fernen?)." [514W-{50–1/51} *Opera and Drama*, PW Vol. II, p. 203] We're reminded that when Mime, Wotan's prosaic self which he loathes and wishes to cast away, asked Wotan the Wanderer his questions about the depths and surface of the earth and about the gods above, Wotan castigated Mime for having only asked after remote, faraway ("Fernen") things, and not about what truly most concerned Mime (or ought to have concerned him). This is the basis for Siegfried's allusion to Wotan's confession of world history to Brünnhilde as something "far away" which he can't grasp with his senses, which can only grasp the here-and-now, i.e., the present as expressed by musical motifs, rather than the wide array of phenomena which are distilled in motifs through association. Brünnhilde, holding Wotan's hoard of knowledge for Siegfried, has sent it far away, and Siegfried only grasps it in the present, as music.

Siegfried's and Brünnhilde's description of the nature of their relationship, through which Siegfried can grasp Wotan's confession in feeling rather than thought, is Wagner's key metaphor in the *Ring* for his concept of the "Wonder," through which a musical motif can condense into a single, present moment of highly individualized feeling, intuited instantly, the entire history of its past and future associations with elements of the dramatic action and libretto, symbolized by Wotan's hoard of knowledge of human experience. [See 478W-{49–51 (?)} Notes for 'Artisthood of the Future' (unfinished), Sketches and Fragments, PW Vol. VIII, p. 371] This explains why Wagner's music-dramas always feel more substantial and meaningful at any given moment than the immediate musico-dramatic context might seem to warrant. One always feels as if each given moment is portentous with the tragic power of the whole. This also helps explain why directorial tampering with Wagner's stage imagery, which he deliberately left general and vague so as not to impose a particular or topical reading on his universal myth, can undermine the numinous, dreamlike effect, the universal, cosmic scope, which Wagner sought.

Now, thanks to this artistic Wonder (the whole web of motivic allusion in the *Ring*), the gift of the musical motifs she brings to birth, Brünnhilde is able to make Siegfried a knower through feeling, i.e., able to give him an aesthetic intuition of Wotan's thought, without the burden of fear this thought would engender if conceptually conscious. [See 542W-{50–1/51} *Opera and Drama*, PW Vol. II, pp. 329–330; See also 511W] As a knower (of Wotan's thought) through feeling, Siegfried is Wotan reborn minus conscious conceptual knowledge of his true identity and history. Guided by Wagner's suggestive remarks (previously cited) concerning the authentic artist's (Wagner's) ignorance concerning the true source of his own inspiration, we may regard Siegfried the artist-hero as unconscious of the true source of his inspiration, which remains a mystery even to him. [See 641W-{8/23/56}Letter to August Röckel, SLRW, p. 357] The key to the meaning of Siegfried's art (Wagner's music-dramas) lies in the musical motifs into which Wotan's confession of poetic intent, his guilt and longing to redeem himself from it, has been condensed through Brünnhilde's "Wonder," the "sublimest wonder" which Sieglinde celebrated with Brünnhilde in V.3.1 before running off to Fafner's tabooed realm in the East to painfully bring the greatest of heroes Siegfried to birth. The key, in other words, is music's relation to the drama.

Wotan seems to have attained his goal of creating the free hero who, uninfluenced consciously by Wotan's motives and autonomous from him, nonetheless has done, of his own volition, what Wotan needed for him to do, secure the Ring so Alberich can't regain its power. Though Wotan's confession to Brünnhilde of his unspoken secret is the true, hidden source of Siegfried's unconscious artistic inspiration, Siegfried is solely conscious of feeling, music, the sublimated form of this repressed knowledge, similar in this respect to Wotan's waking dream or allegory, Valhalla, whose true but forgotten source of inspiration was Alberich's forging of his Ring. Wotan desired of Valhalla a place of refuge from all debts, preconditions, and outward constraints. For this reason he imagined a hero freed from all that constrains the gods (free from religion's false claim to the power of truth). Musical feeling, as Wagner redefined it, seemed to offer Wotan the means to spontaneously produce the feeling of our transcendent value without having to acknowledge thinking's contradictions, which Wotan described to Brünnhilde in V.3.3 as his "Noth." What Wagner really meant when he began to proclaim after his introduction to Schopenhauer in 1854 that music produces the drama (contradicting his prior claim that drama inspired musical form), is that the artist's aesthetic intuition takes possession of our hoard of knowledge and Ring of consciousness, making us feel as if we've consigned their claim on us to oblivion. Wagner's concern to grant music pride of place over poetical drama as the ground of inspiration has its foundation in Wotan's need to create a hero freed from Wotan's (history's, or drama's) influence, who'll of his own volition redeem the gods.

It will be helpful for grasping Wagner's allegorical logic in S.3.3 to examine his thoughts on this subject of music's new status as the mysterious, unconscious foundation of the drama: "We ... should not go far astray, if we defined Music as man's qualification a priori for fashioning the Drama. Just as we construct for ourselves the world of semblances through application of the laws of Time and Space existing a priori in our brain [the Norns' rope of fate understood in light of Schopenhauer's Kantian concept of a priori knowledge], so this conscious representment of the world's idea in Drama would ... be foreordained by those inner laws of Music, operating in the dramatist equally unconsciously with the laws of Causality we bring into employment for apperception of the phenomenal world." [782W-{9–12/70} 'Beethoven,' PW Vol. V, pp. 106–107; See also 650W-{2/57} 'On Liszt's Symphonic Poems,' PW Vol. III, p. 247; and 781W-{9–12/70} 'Beethoven,' PW Vol. V, p. 104] Given Wagner's allegorical argument, it was inevitable he'd grant music, the new religion, an almost supernatural status as a religious mystery wholly inaccessible to conscious reason: "Here the might of the musician is conceivable as nothing but Magic. It certainly is an enchanted state into which we fall while listening to a true Beethovenian masterwork, when in every particle of the piece—which our sober senses would tell us was merely the technical means of exhibiting a given form—we discern a supernatural life ... , ... whilst it all appears to take its motion from the depths of our own inner being." [776W-{9–12/70} 'Beethoven,' PW Vol. V, pp. 86–87] This line of reasoning finally led Wagner to launch his grand Schopenhauerian attack on the main Feuerbachian thesis which had guided him in constructing the *Ring*'s plot. Wagner was prompted to launch his attack by Feuerbach's (for Wagner, cynical) assumption that religious mysteries and faith can be explained from mundane natural causes. But now, just as Wagner altered his original view that drama, real life, inspires music, to say instead that it's music which creates the drama, similarly, Wagner concluded that the religious mysteries couldn't be explained by natural causes, but rather, the ultimate source of all things (Schopenhauer's Will) is mysterious and in all probability supernatural. [See 896W]

This poses a question raised by Roger Scruton in his critique of my allegorical reading of Wagner's *Ring*, whether a counter-intuitive allegorical interpretation such as mine reflects only Wagner's most intimate and private (perhaps unconscious even for him) source of inspiration for his *Ring*, and therefore whether my allegorical reading can be said to constitute a part of what Wagner's audience experiences in the theater. It goes without saying that since much of my interpretation (with a few subtle exceptions) wasn't guessed at by prior commentators, if it authentically reflects what Wagner tried to convey in his *Ring*, it can only convey meaning to Wagner's audience, if at all, subliminally, in much the same way that Wagner's music conveys meaning subliminally, but not conceptually. In other words, perhaps my interpretation has explained the "mood" aroused in Wagner the musician by his unconscious poetic thought, by unearthing that thought for conscious contemplation. But does this explain the mood Wagner's *Ring* arouses in his audience? I would argue yes. My rebuttal of Roger Scruton's critique of my online Ring study can be found in the Epilogue to my published book posted at www.wagnerheim.com since 8/2021.

Having exhausted her initial exultation in the longed-for union with her artist-hero Siegfried, his muse Brünnhilde is now beset, as Siegfried was, by unnameable fear, expressed by a new motif H152, a compound of several older motifs preceded by two heavily accented notes in the bass which identify this motif as unique. It's a subliminal premonition that disaster will ensue if she consummates her love for Siegfried by joining him in sexual union, Wagner's metaphor for unconscious artistic inspiration:

[pp. 269–72] ([[**H152 orch**]] H35 frag:; H80 &/or H82 frag: [their initial grace-note twist]; H76 frag: He remains in a state of great agitation, gazing at her with an expression of yearning desire. Brünnhilde gently turns her head aside ... [[**H152 orch**]]; H80 &/or H82 frag [their initial grace-note twist]; H76 frag; H39 in a sad vari on oboe) [**Brünnhilde:** (...); **Siegfried:** (...)] (H147A:; [[**H152 orch**]]; H80 frags: Brünnhilde points with her hand to her weapons, which she now perceives. H76 frag; [[**H152 orch:**]]; H80 &/or H82 grace-note twist; H76 frag; H80 or H82 grace-note twist)

Brünnhilde: (H39:) There I see the shield that sheltered heroes (:H39); ([[**H152 orch**]]; H76 frag; H80 or H82 grace-note twist]) (H39:) there I see the helmet that hid my head (:H39): it shields and hides me no more!

Siegfried: (ardently: H81 vari:) A blissful maid has pierced my heart; a woman has wounded my head (:H81 vari) ... !

Brünnhilde: (... H80 frags & varis:) I see the brinie's resplendent steel (:H80 frags & varis): a keen-edged sword has cut it in two; it loosed my maidenly body's defences: (H80 &/or H82 grace-note twist) [[**H152 orch**]] (H39 voc?:) I'm stripped of shelter and shield, a weaponless, sorrowing woman (:H39 voc?)!

Siegfried: ... Through fierce burning fire I came to you; (H39 frag voc?:) no brinie or armour protected my body (:H39 frag voc?): ... (H147A frag/H34 vari:) my blood is pounding with rampant desire (:H147A frag/H34 vari); (H34 vari:) ... the flames that raged around Brünnhilde's fell are burning now in my breast (:H34 vari)! (H147A frag explosion on strings)— (H147B?:) O woman, quench the fire now! (...) (:H147B?) (He has embraced her violently: H147A-based string explosion: Brünnhilde ...repulses him with the strength born of fear ... .)

Brünnhilde: No god has ever dared draw near me: in awe the heroes bowed before the virgin maid: [I've altered the word order of Spencer's translation "she left Valhalla inviolate" below to reflect the original order of German words and motifs:] [[**H18e:**]] Inviolate ["Heilig"] [[:H18e]] (H18c:) she left Valhalla (:H18c)!—Woe! Woe! Alas for the shame, for my ignominious plight ["Noth"]! (H147A frag) He who woke me has wounded me, too! (H39 frag?; H34 vari) (H97 vari?:) He broke open my brinie and helmet (:H97 vari?): Brünnhilde am I no longer! (H147B vari?)

Siegfried: To me you are still the dream-struck maid .... (H81 or H44 vari?:) Awaken and be a woman for me (:H81 or H44 vari?)!

Brünnhilde: (... (H29b vari orch?:—[orchestration seems to reference R.2 when the gods grew old after the Giants took Freia, with her golden apples of sorrow-less youth eternal, hostage]) My senses grow clouded; my knowledge falls silent: is my wisdom to forsake me now (:H29b vari?—[possible orchestration reference from R.2])?

Siegfried: (H143 voc:) Did you not sing that your knowledge stemmed from the shining light of your love for me (:H143 voc)?

Brünnhilde: ... (H143 [fades away]; (H81:) Grieving darkness clouds my gaze (:H81); (H50:) my eye grows dim, its light dies out (:H50): (H81) (H50:) night enfolds me (:H50); from mist ["Nebel"] and dread ["Grau'n"] a (H81:) confusion of fear now writhes in its rage (:H81)! (H83/H78 >>:) Terror stalks and rears its head (:H83/H78)! (Brünnhilde impulsively covers her eyes with her hands.)

Siegfried: (gently removing her hands from her eyes.) Night encloses eyes that are bound; (H143 vari:) with your fetters your gloomy dread ["Grau'n"] will fade (:H143 vari): (H143:) rise from the darkness and see—bright as the sun shines the day (:H143)!

Brünnhilde: ... Bright as the sun shines the day of my shame! (H99B >>:) O Siegfried! Siegfried (:H99B)! Behold my fear ["Angst"]!

Erda (Mother Nature), Brünnhilde's mother, has in her sympathetic incarnation as Brünnhilde (now expressing her fear of consummating her love for Siegfried), become what Wagner called the artist's "bashful bride": "... Nature [Erda] has ... had her share in the birth of Art .... (...) From the over-tender mother [Erda, whose warning to Wotan in R.4 to yield the Ring to the Giants displayed her sympathy], she became to him ["Man, the creator of Art"] a bashful bride [Brünnhilde, fearful of sexual union with Siegfried], whom he [the artist] now must win by vigour and love-worthiness ... ." [448W-{2/50} 'Art and Climate,' PW Vol. I, p. 253] Why is Brünnhilde fearful of consummating sexual union (unconscious artistic inspiration) with Siegfried? The music tells all. During the onset of her doubt and fear, as she complains that Siegfried has cut away her maidenly defenses with Nothung, we hear that halting sequence of older motifs which express her rising doubt, preceded always by the new, heavily accented two-note motif in the bass, H152. The motif sequence which generally follows after it includes fragments of H76 (her former life as a chaste Valkyrie and inspirer of heroes to martyrdom for the gods' sake), the grace-note twist from H80 (recalling Wotan's rising consciousness of the futility of seeking to create a free hero), and H39 (a tragic variant of the basic love motif H23, love under the shadow of Alberich's curses on love and his Ring). Brünnhilde is facing for the first time the distasteful consequences which follow from Wotan depriving her of her divine status as a virgin Valkyrie by forcing her to become a mortal hero's wife, but of greater import is the fact that she's having a premonition of what Wotan warned her about during his confession in V.2.2 and his chastisement of her in V.3.3, that she'll bring down on herself the punishment Wotan meant to mete out to her, by living for love. The rarely heard H18e, by the way, sounds in one of its few occurrences in the *Ring* when Brünnhilde tells Siegfried: "... [[H18e:]] Inviolate (H18c:) she left Valhalla!"

The most dramatic motival confirmation that what Siegfried feared in the presence of the sleeping Brünnhilde was the prospect of waking remembrance of Wotan's repressed confession, is that as Brünnhilde's fear of Siegfried's embrace rises to the pitch of panic, we hear the same motif array last heard in V.2.2 when Wotan cried out in despair after Brünnhilde asked him what ailed him, when he invoked his divine Noth ("Götternoth"). The motif combination H81 (Wotan's Revolt), H50 (Ring Curse), and H78, but particularly H81, is the hallmark of his confession of his unspoken secret to Brünnhilde. This motif array reaches a pitch of intensity as Brünnhilde calls up images of Nibelheim: "from mist ["Nebel"] and dread ["Grau'n"] a confusion of fear now writhes in its rage!" H78 (Fricka's warning of the threat the Wälsungs represent to the gods), a variant of H57b, references the 'dread and dismay' Wotan invoked when, extolling the newly completed Valhalla, he sang: '(H57a:) Thus I salute the fortress, **(H57b:) safe from dread and dismay!**' Since this motif array heralded Wotan's confession to Brünnhilde of what ails him, his divine Noth, it calls to mind, subliminally, the entirety of Wotan's confession to Brünnhilde. Wotan, by virtue of making his confession to Brünnhilde, has given her the responsibility of keeping his unspoken secret. Siegfried's anticipated sexual union with her places Wotan's secret hoard of forbidden knowledge at potential risk of being brought up from the silent depths and exposed to the light of day by Siegfried. In a final motival coup, Wagner adds H83, associated with Wotan's anger at Brünnhilde for her disobedience, but which first sounded during Wotan's confession to her underlining his nihilistic remark that he finds with loathing always only himself in all that he undertakes, i.e., that he can't create a free hero because Wotan's ideal of a hero was inspired by his loathsome egoism and fear of the truth.

A subtlety in Brünnhilde's invocation of her fear to persuade Siegfried not to touch or violate her in his passion, is that she expresses her anxiety that her "wisdom" might forsake her, accompanied by what seems a hint of Fafner's Godhead Lost H29b and orchestration that echoes that heard in R.2 after the Giants temporarily abducted Freia and the virtue of her golden apples of sorrow-less youth eternal, music depicting the gods aging. What else is Brünnhilde's wisdom than Wotan's confession to her of what her mother Erda taught him! Siegfried is accompanied by H143 as he tries to reconcile her to their union by reminding her that she did, after all, tell him her knowledge (which she fears is forsaking her now) stemmed from the shining light of her love for him. What she fears is that if she has sexual congress with him (thereby inspiring his art unconsciously), she must impart to him (subliminally, of course) Wotan's heretofore unspoken secret. She instinctively fears that in granting Siegfried privileged access to Wotan's dangerous secret she places it at risk of being exposed to Siegfried (who depends on her protection from conscious knowledge of it) and by him to others. Powerful evidence for this reading can be found in T.2.5 when she'll complain to Hagen and Gunther that she gave all her wisdom to Siegfried, and that this left her vulnerable to betrayal by him. She's afraid that if she shares this secret with him he won't keep it, but may expose it to the light of day, just as Alberich threatened his hoard would rise from silent depths to daylight. Alberich had foreseen in R.3 that he'd someday turn Wotan's heroes against him, and that when Alberich's Hoard (embodied by Alberich's Ring and Wotan's confession to Brünnhilde) rises from the silent depths to the light of day, his host of night will storm Valhalla and end the gods' rule. Siegfried in T.1.3.B, under Hagen's influence, and therefore part of Alberich's host of night, will storm the New Valhalla, Brünnhilde, and forcibly take Alberich's Ring from her safekeeping, thus exposing the forbidden Hoard and betraying Wotan's secret. Brünnhilde's panic is her premonition of that tragic day of doom.

Siegfried again calls up H143 as he consolingly suggests to her that while night (fear that Alberich's Ring Curse will destroy Valhalla, both the old and the new) encloses eyes that are bound, with her fetters gone Brünnhilde's gloomy dread will fade. He asks her to rise from the darkness and see that bright as the sun shines the day. We're reminded of Tristan's and Isolde's fear of day (consciousness), which nonetheless gives way to their impulse to expose their secret and illicit love-bond to the light of day at the end of *Tristan* Act Two. Siegfried is unwittingly asking Brünnhilde to impart her knowledge to him so he can draw on it for unconscious inspiration to create his art which, though it originates in her silent depths, is to be presented by Siegfried to the public, an audience, in the light of day. Only by virtue of his muse Brünnhilde granting Siegfried unconscious artistic inspiration can Wotan's confession to her of the inevitability of Alberich's victory over the gods (the death of religious faith) safely rise to consciousness, sublimated into redemptive artistic form. Similarly, once Wotan and Loge had taken Alberich and his Ring [our human mind] captive in R.3, they thought they could safely take possession of his Hoard, Tarnhelm, and Ring in the open meadow below Valhalla in R.4, thereby voiding his threat that bringing his hoard up from the silent depths to day would end the gods' rule. But that turned out not to be altogether true. Brünnhilde's initial answer to Siegfried is that the sunlight will only expose her shame (as it will in *Twilight of the Gods*). Accompanied by H99B, which conveys the desperate passion through which she persuaded Wotan to grant her in marriage only to an an authentically inspired artist-hero, Brünnhilde asks Siegfried to behold her angst sympathetically.

With this we come to one of the most sublime and awe-inspiring yet unusual musico-dramatic moments in the *Ring*, for Brünnhilde's following appeal to Siegfried to respect her and not coerce her love with a force which will damage them both, is sung to two new motifs (H153 and H154) which initially seem independent of the genealogically inter-related motifs of the *Ring*, drawn as these motifs are from Wagner's chamber orchestra composition, the *Siegfried Idyll*.

However, H154, "Siegfried as Hoard of the World," Cooke stated is the basis for H161:

> [pp. 272-3] ([[H153 orch:]]/H102 accompaniment: Brünnhilde's mien reveals that a delightful image has passed before her mind's eye, at the thought of which she tenderly directs her gaze back to Siegfried.)
>
> **Brünnhilde:** ([[H153 orch:]]/H102 accompaniment:; [[H153 voc:]] [in minor]) Ever was I, ever am I, ever beset by sweet-yearning bliss—but ever working for your own weal (:H153 orch/voc/H102)! [[H154 voc:]] O Siegfried! Glorious hero! Hoard ["Hort"] of the world! Life of the earth ["Erde"—Erda]! Laughing hero (:H154 voc)! [[H154 orch:]] Leave, oh leave me! Leave me be! (...) Do not constrain me with chafing constraint (:H154 orch)! (...) (H153 vari voc:) Did you see your face in the limpid brook? Did it rejoice you, blithe hero (:H153 vari voc)? [[H147B varis orch:]] If you stirred the water into a wave, if the brook's clear surface dissolved, you'd see your own likeness no longer but only the billow's eddying surge (:H147B varis orch). (H154 frag; H?—[Orchestral figures representing water in motion may reference S.1.3 when Siegfried stuck his molten sword Nothung into a basin of water to cool and stiffen it?]) And so do not touch me, trouble me not: (H?—Horn fanfare) (H153 voc/H154/H102 develops >> :) ever bright in your bliss you will smile a smile that passes from me to you, a hero blithe and happy!—O Siegfried! Light-bringing youth (:H153 voc/H154/H102)! (H87:) Love but yourself and let me be (:H87): (H102:) do not destroy what is yours (:H102)!

While the first of the *Siegfried Idyll* motifs, H153, has been initially heard in conjunction with Brünnhilde's affirmation that she lives alone for Siegfried's well-being, H154 is linked at its inception with her description of Siegfried as the "Hoard of the World" and "Life of the Earth ['Erde']," i.e., the life of Erda, and with her appeal to him that he not rape her (as Alberich would have done), i.e., not force her to reveal her secrets. Brünnhilde is asking Siegfried not to destroy her function as his unconscious mind, not to trash the safe repository of his subliminal source of artistic inspiration, by forcing her to give up Wotan's unspoken secret, his hoard of knowledge, as Alberich would. This is as dramatic a piece of evidence for our reading as it's possible to imagine, for by calling Siegfried Hoard ["Hort"] of the world, life of the earth ["Erde"—Erda], Brünnhilde pronounces Siegfried heir to Wotan's Hoard of knowledge (and also to Alberich's Nibelung Hoard and the Ring which produced it), obtained from Erda, which Wotan confessed to Brünnhilde, and which she will now, during the height of ecstasy in their loving union, impart to Siegfried subliminally to inspire his art.

She invokes the image of his perfect reflection in a still brook (recalling Sieglinde's remark to her twin-brother Siegmund in V.1.3 that, just as she once saw her own reflection in a brook, she now sees it reflected back to her by Siegmund) in her effort to persuade Siegfried not to coerce her love, telling him that were he to stir this brook with his unbridled passion, its waves would distort its clear surface and Siegfried would lose the true reflection of his image, finding instead only the billow's eddying surge. Her description is accompanied by H147B, the new, second iteration of H147, the motif identified earlier with Siegfried's fear of waking Brünnhilde. H153 and H154 reach their climax of development in conjunction with H102, which conveys Brünnhilde's insistence that Wotan frighten away all suitors except an authentic hero, as she sums up her appeal by pleading with Siegfried not to sully the reflection of that smile which passes between them. Finally, as she warns him to love only himself, but let her be, we hear H87 (Fate). H87 calls to mind Erda's prophecy of the gods' inevitable fate, an end which Alberich's son and proxy Hagen is predestined to bring about with Siegfried's unwitting collaboration. Brünnhilde keeps the secret of Siegfried's fate and true identity. She's therefore calling on Siegfried to preserve her integrity as his unconscious muse of inspiration so she can keep Wotan's unspoken secret, and neutralize Alberich's Ring Curse of consciousness, just as his grandfather Wotan did by acquiescing in Brünnhilde's request to hear his confession of his divine "Noth."

A conceptual basis for Brünnhilde's comparison between herself and the reflection of Siegfried's face in a still brook can be found in Wagner's description of the union of poetical drama (Siegfried understood as the dramatist) with music (Brünnhilde as a metaphor for Siegfried's unconscious mind and its language, music), in which music takes on the specificity of language, while language enjoys the privilege of music's restoration of involuntary, instinctive feeling, the sense of infinitude and immediacy this brings, the oceanic feeling of absolute freedom which so many experience in Wagner's operas and music-dramas. As Wagner stated: "Melody is the redemption of the poet's endlessly conditioned thought into a deep-felt consciousness of emotion's highest freedom." Wagner added that in this way an endless reaching content (the *Ring* drama encapsulated in Wotan's confession to Brünnhilde) is condensed to a definite utterance of feeling, i.e., musical motifs. [534W-{50–1/51} *Opera and Drama*, PW Vol. II, pp. 280–281; See also 555W-{50–1/51} *Opera and Drama*, PW Vol. II, p. 376]

Siegfried, oblivious to Brünnhilde's cares, just as he was oblivious to her remarks about Wotan, now plunges headlong into passion accompanied by H141 and H147. He declares he's lost himself and can only find himself again in Brünnhilde, just as Brünnhilde told Siegfried she was no longer herself, having lost her godhead and the protective armor which preserves her chastity:

> [pp. 273–4] **Siegfried:** (H141 varis: [fast and furious figures]; H147A vari:) It is you that I love: if only you loved me (:H141 varis)! I no longer have myself: would that I might have you (:H147A vari)!—([[**H147B orch:**]] [an accompaniment from the *Siegfried Idyll*]) A glorious floodtide billows before me; with all my senses I see only it—the wondrously billowing wave: though it shatter my likeness, I'm burning myself now to cool raging passion within the flood; I shall leap, as I am, straight into the stream (:H147B orch): (H102/H153 vari:) o that its billows engulf me in bliss and my longing be stilled in the flood (:H102/H153 vari)! (H143:; H150 frag:) Awaken,

Brünnhilde! Waken, you maid (:H143; :H150 frag)! (H151 voc:) Laugh and live, sweetest delight (:H151 voc)! Be mine! Be mine! Be mine!

Brünnhilde: (very inwardly: H150 vari:) O Siegfried! Yours was I aye [ever] (:H150 vari)!

Siegfried: (... **[[H147B orch:]]** [an accompaniment from the *Siegfried Idyll*]) If you were once, then be so now (:H147B [*Siegfried Idyll* accompaniment])!

Brünnhilde: (H150:) Yours shall I be for ever!

Siegfried: (**[[H147B orch:]]** [*Siegfried Idyll* accompaniment]) What you will be, be today (:H147B—*Siegfried Idyll* accompaniment)! (H151 varis: [developing as in the lead-up to the finale a bit later]) ... as my heart beats wildly against your own; as our glances ignite and breath feeds on breath, (H150 vari:) eye to eye and mouth to mouth (:H151 varis; :H150 vari), (H143 voc:) then, to me (:H143 voc), (H151 voc:) you must be what, fearful, you were and will be (:H151 voc)! (H150 frags:; H151:) Then gone were the burning doubt that Brünnhilde might not now be mine (:H150 frags; :H151).

Contrary to Brünnhilde's resolve, Siegfried insists on plunging into the flood of that brook in which his image was clearly reflected back to him by her, to drown in his passion for her and obliterate his image, carrying her down into the flood of passion with him. He describes his passion as Loge's fire which longs to be cooled in Brünnhilde's flood, reminding us how Siegfried's molten sword and phallus Nothung cooled and stiffened in a vat of water. He climaxes with a shouted demand (H143 sounding in the orchestra): Brünnhilde must wake for him! Then Siegfried and Brünnhilde engage in a rather strange and off-putting argument: Brünnhilde says she was, and will be, Siegfried's own, while Siegfried insists she be so now. Siegfried sums up his demand, again with H143 in the background: "then, to me, you must be what, fearful, your were and will be!" This awkward grammatical construction makes sense only if we grasp it as Wagner's poetical paraphrase of his concept of the artistic "Wonder" of his musical motifs. Siegfried is saying that thanks to Brünnhilde's redemptive love, the entirety of Wotan's horrific, fearful confession of sinful world history and the gods' fate, all that's widely dispersed in time and space, has been condensed into redemptive moments of feeling in musical motifs, which make present both the past and future, because the sounding of a motif calls up memories of all the past with which it was associated, and foreshadows all those things with which it will be associated in the future. This is the true meaning of Wagner's concept of redemption by love, i.e., redemption of our religious impulse through Wagner's secular music-drama and its motival "Wonder." Siegfried correlates "fearing" with Brünnhilde's knowledge of past and future, the Norns' spinning of Erda's foreknowledge of the gods' fated doom and of all that was, is, and will be. It's implicit that by virtue of Brünnhilde's wondrous protection, only to be obtained through that loving union with his muse which allows Siegfried to live solely in the here and now, the present, without concern for all that is far away ("Fernen," distant in time or space), and that has been repressed into the unconscious through Wotan's confession to Brünnhilde, Siegfried can restore his courage and fearlessness.

Wagner had much to say which can enlighten us on Siegfried's experience of losing himself in a sea of musical harmony. This was Wagner's secular substitute for the religious man's mystical experience of oneness with the cosmos. He equated immersion in water or the sea with the oceanic feeling which music, especially harmony, engenders. This equation links Siegfried's oceanic experience of ecstasy in loss of self, with the experience of Tristan and Isolde, and even Senta and the Dutchman whose redemption and resurrection are preceded by immersion in the sea: [Speaking of musical harmony, Wagner said that:] Man dives into this sea … . His heart feels widened wondrously, when he peers down into this depth, pregnant with unimaginable possibilities … , whose seeming bottomlessness … fills him with the sense of marvel and the presage of Infinity. It is the depth and infinity of Nature [Erda] herself, who veils from the prying eye of Man the unfathomable womb of her eternal Seed-time, her Begetting, and her Yearning … . This Nature is … none other than … the human heart itself [Wotan's and Erda's daughter Brünnhilde, who feels what Wotan thinks]. [436W-{9–12/49} 'The Artwork of the Future,' PW Vol. I, pp. 112–113] Wagner added that through such immersion in music the poet-dramatist becomes the "lord of Nature": "Only the poet whose Aim we have here expounded [the inspired music-dramatist], will feel driven so irresistibly to a heart-alliance with the 'eternal womanly' of Tone-art, that in these nuptials he shall celebrate … his own redemption. / Through the redeeming love-kiss of that Melody the poet is … inducted into the deep, unending mysteries of Woman's nature … . To him the bottomless sea of Harmony … is no longer an object of dread, of fear, of terror [thanks to his loving union with his muse Brünnhilde, Siegfried the artist-hero will forget the fear she taught him] … . (…) [Wagner said of] … the Love in whose delight the poet is redeemed, … [that] through its might [he] becomes the lord of Nature." [537W-{50–1/51} *Opera and Drama*, PW Vol. II, pp. 285–286] The translator Ashton Ellis added a footnote in which he identified Siegfried's question prior to waking Brünnhilde, "How can I overcome my fear?," with this passage from *Opera and Drama*. What's particularly striking about this passage is that Wagner describes the poet (Siegfried) who joins in loving union with music (Brünnhilde) as becoming the "lord of Nature," which is to say that he takes aesthetic (musical) possession of the world otherwise known to us objectively.

According to Wagner's metaphor of the relationship of music (Brünnhilde) to drama (Siegfried), Siegfried likewise bestows redemption on Brünnhilde by condensing her infinitude, her limitless feeling, into the specificity of words and concrete events and images in the drama, which keep silent what her music speaks aloud: " … the poet's greatness is mostly to be measured by what he leaves unsaid, letting us breathe in silence to ourselves the thing unspeakable; the musician it is who brings this untold mystery to clarion tongue, and the impeccable form of his sounding silence is endless melody." [689W-{9/60} 'Music of the Future,' PW Vol. III, pp. 337–338; See also 437W] In other words, the unspoken secret of the *Ring*'s meaning can be found not only in its endless music's expression per se, but particularly in the infinite associative scope of its musical motifs which have an unlimited capacity for cross-referencing the dramatic action and protagonists' hidden motives and springs of action. The thing Siegfried's music-drama keeps silent, the thing unspeakable yet spoken by music, is Wotan's unspoken secret, his confession to Brünnhilde. As Wotan said to Brünnhilde just before he confessed his Noth to her: "What in words I reveal to no one, let it stay unspoken for ever: with myself I commune when I speak with you." So the *Ring*'s musical motifs must hold the key to unlock the secret of Wotan's confession.

As I stated previously, thanks to his muse Brünnhilde, Siegfried lives fearlessly in the present, unencumbered by Wotan's hoard of unspeakably horrific knowledge of all that was, is, and will be. There's no more cogent, striking evidence to support our allegorical reading of the *Ring* libretto and music than Wagner's remark recorded by Cosima, previously cited: "Siegfried lives entirely in the present, he is the hero, the finest gift of the will." [820W-{3/12/72}CD Vol. I, p. 466] Brünnhilde called herself Wotan's "Will." Siegfried is therefore Brünnhilde's finest gift, for he lives fearlessly in the present only because she (Wagner's musical motifs, product of Wotan's unconscious mind) knows for him the gods' (religion's) and man's history and fate, which Wotan imparted to her so Siegfried can be freed from Wotan's existential fear and paralysis. In this way Froh's hope that thanks to Alberich's sacrifice of love for the Ring's power, the gods could possess the Ring's power without suffering from its curse, without renouncing love, comes to fruition in Siegfried's love for his muse Brünnhilde.

In Wagner's descriptions of the means through which his music in general, and musical motifs in particular, carry the burden of knowledge of the protagonists' motives, so the characters are freed from having to reveal their motives in words, we find a basis both for Siegfried's innocence, ignorance and naiveté, and for Wotan's assumption that by imparting his confession to Brünnhilde it would remain forever unspoken: "An improviser such as an actor [the mime Siegfried, acting out the drama Wotan wrote for him] must belong entirely to the present moment, never think of what is to come, indeed not even know it ... . The peculiar thing about me as an artist ... is that I ... never say to myself, 'Since this or that will follow, you must do such and such ... .' I think, 'Something will turn up.' ... and yet I know I am unconsciously obeying a plan." [805W-{9/1/71} CD Vol. I, p. 407; See also 842W-{2/73} 'Prologue to a Reading of *Twilight of the Gods*,' PW Vol. V, pp. 305–306]]

In our final extracts which grant insight into this passage Wagner offered a description of the "Wonder" of his musical motifs which provides the best possible explanation of why Siegfried told Brünnhilde that while his senses only grasp and feel her, in the here and now, he can't grasp what's far away in time or space, and also why Siegfried calls on her to be for him, now, what, fearing, she was and will be: "... the most perfect Unity of artistic Form [is] ... that in which a widest conjuncture of the phenomena of Human Life—as Content [Wotan's confession]—can impart itself to the Feeling [to Brünnhilde] in so completely intelligible an Expression, that ... this Content shall completely stir ... and satisfy ... the Feeling. (...) ... only Thought can grasp the absent [Fernen?], but only the present can be grasped by Feeling. / In this unity of the Expression, ever making present, and ever embracing the full compass of the Content, there is ... solved ... the ... problem of the unity of Time and Space." [549W-{50–1/51} *Opera and Drama*, PW Vol. II, pp. 348–349] This could explain why Wagner identified Schopenhauer's Kantian notion of the ideality of time, space, and causation (Kant's thesis that a priori knowledge is a product of the mind and not an accurate understanding of the thing-in-itself) with objective, scientific knowledge, and the thing-in-itself ("Will") with Wagner's notion of the "Wonder" of his musical motifs, which make all time seem now, all space seem here, and gift us with the feeling of transcendence, the miraculous, as if we're freed from the material world and from fate itself. According to this reasoning what we call scientific knowledge of the objective world is illusory, and what we feel the world ought to be is authentic and true. And here Wagner explains why Siegfried urged Brünnhilde to be for him, now, what, fearing, she was and will be: "R.: 'The word 'eternal' is a very fine one, for it really means 'holy': a great feeling is eternal, for it is free from the laws of change to which everything is subject: it has nothing to do with yesterday, today, or tomorrow [Erda's objective knowledge of all that was, is, and will be, which Alberich affirms and Wotan denies]. Hell begins with arithmetic.'" [804W-{7/25/71} CD Vol. I, p. 396; See also 550W]

Brünnhilde, wholly enrapt in Siegfried's ecstatic self-abandon, now abandons her resistance and throws herself heedless of risk into his passionate embrace:

[pp. 274–5] **Brünnhilde:** (H87 voc:) That I'm not yours now (:H87 voc)? (H147B:; H?—Hint of orchestration from the moment in R.2 when the gods began to age due to being deprived of Freia and her golden apples of sorrowless youth eternal by the Giants, associated there with H29ab:) Godlike composure rages in billows; the chastest of light flares up with passion (:H147B; H?—orchestration suggestive of gods' aging); (H150 vari:) heavenly knowledge floods away, love's rejoicing drives it hence (:H150 vari)! (H150 vari) (H87 frag voc:) Am I now yours (:H87 frag voc)?—Siegfried! (...) (H150 vari) (...) (H150 vari) (H47:) As my gaze consumes you (:H47), are you not blinded? (H150 vari clarinet) (H47:) As my arm holds you tight (:H47), don't you burn for me? (H150 vari flute) As my blood streams in torrents towards you, (H76) do you not feel its furious fire? (H76/H77:) Do you fear, Siegfried, do you not fear the wildly raging woman (:H76/H77) (She embraces him passionately.)

Siegfried: (H93a: in joyful terror) Ha!—(H93a voc? >> :) As the blood in our veins ignites, as our flashing glances consume one another (:H93a voc?), (H74B hint:) as our arms clasp each other in ardour (:H74B hint)—(H93a?:) my courage returns (:H93a?) (H74B hint:) and the fear, ah! The fear that I never learned (:H74B hint)—the fear that you scarcely taught me: (H138b:) that fear—I think—fool that I am (:H138b), (H137b voc: [the frag which accompanied the woodbird's "blissful I weave my lay from woe"]) I have quite forgotten it now (:H137b voc)! (At these last words he has involuntarily released Brünnhilde.)

This is a totally overwhelming experience in the theater, drunk as we are with one of the most exalted, transporting scenes in Wagnerian music-drama (or any drama!), so it's necessary to sober up a bit to grasp the extraordinary musico-dramatic subtlety and nuance of Brünnhilde's dialogue with Siegfried. Accompanied by H147B (expressing Siegfried's initial fear of sexual union with Brünnhilde), and evidently by some other musical (and perhaps motival) content associated in R.2 with the gods' aging after the Giants temporarily deprived them of Freia and her golden apples of sorrow-less youth eternal, including perhaps H29ab, Brünnhilde makes the extraordinary remark: "Godlike composure rages in billows; the chastest of light flares up with passion." Then—accompanied by H150 (in the family of love motifs)—she declares: "Heavenly knowledge floods away, love's rejoicing drives it hence!" Siegfried has won her over to the conviction that it's only through their sexual union, her unconscious inspiration of Siegfried's redemptive music-drama, that she can still keep Wotan's unspoken secret. Love's rejoicing has driven heavenly knowledge (Wotan's confession and the fear it engendered) away, reminding us that Wotan told Erda that her knowledge waned before Wotan's Will, Brünnhilde. In the completed, inspired artwork the artist finds no trace of its original, subliminal source of inspiration, which is repressed below consciousness. It reaches consciousness only in sublimated or allegorical form, a waking dream of blissful feeling, wholly purged of all vestige of the existential angst which inspired it.

What does Brünnhilde mean when she says godlike composure rages in billows, and the chastest of light flares up with passion? This seemingly self-contradictory statement is the poetic equivalent of Wagner's critique of Schopenhauer's concept of redemption which, however, predated Wagner's first acquaintance with Schopenhauer in 1854. Schopenhauer believed, according to Wagner, that redemption was to be found solely in a stilling or quieting of the Will (man's primary instinctive impulses such as fear, self-aggrandizement, and sexual desire), and that this could be obtained through a mystical identification of one's ego with the "all," the entire cosmos and everything in it both animate and inanimate. Wagner's critique was that he found redemption not in stilling the Will, but in heightening it to the point of revelation through sexual love, in which one feels one's own limited, personal will expanded until it feels itself one with the universal will. But we can only make sense of Wagner's critique of Schopenhauer if we recognize that when he speaks of sexual love he's referring to his metaphor for unconscious inspiration of the artist by his muse.

A passage (previously cited) Wagner wrote three years (50–1/51) prior to his first known acquaintance with Schopenhauer's philosophy is the conceptual basis of what would later become his critique of Schopenhauer's concept of redemption. Wagner distinguished Nature as known to us objectively, "understanding's meditation" (Erda's knowledge of all that was, is, and will be), from Nature grasped organically by "feeling's highest agitation": "In Feeling's highest agitation, Man sees in Nature a sympathizing being ... ." [526W-{50–1/51} *Opera and Drama*, PW Vol. II, p. 218] "Feeling's highest agitation" is the oceanic feeling of infinitude and transcendence inspired music can give us, since according to Wagner such music expresses a hidden coherence underlying things the understanding divides and separates. Nature (Erda), when it's known to us as a sympathetic being, is Erda's daughter Brünnhilde, Wagner's metaphor for the unconscious, involuntary mind, and music. This I believe is the meaning underlying Brünnhilde's remark that "Godlike composure rages in billows; the chastest of light flares up with passion ... ," since it expresses a transition from Schopenhauer's religion-based notion of redemption as a quieting of the Will, to Wagner's concept of redemption as a passionate heightening of the Will to the point that it becomes conscious of itself as the cosmic Will in Nature. This is the distinction between religion and art.

And now we can understand what lies behind Wotan's leaving the virgin, formerly divine Valkyrie asleep on a mountaintop to be wooed, won and wed by the authentic artist-hero Siegfried, to whom her chastity and divinity must be sacrificed. It's only by renouncing the key religious notion of transcendence, whose symbols are divinity, immortality, and Valkyrie chastity, which deny man's physical nature, and reaffirming man's relationship with the real world in secular art, that the Wagnerian redemption by love, i.e. by art, can transpire. Chastity, a religion-inspired symbol of world-renunciation, is to be replaced by the secular artist's world-affirmation, sexual love. Wotan's religious impulse towards world-renunciation can find a new lease on life in secular art, without making the preposterous and falsifiable claim to spiritual transcendence.

There are two passages in which Wagner expounded his critique of Schopenhauer's concept of redemption. In the first he identified sexual love's ecstasy ("... the path to salvation ... which involves a total pacification of the will through ... sexual love ...") as a redemptive force of salvation which Schopenhauer didn't recognize, with genius, i.e., artistic inspiration: "... herein lies the only possible explanation for that marvellous and enthusiastic joy and ecstasy felt by any genius at the highest moments of perception, moments which seems scarcely to recognize, since he is able to find them only in a state of calm and in the silencing of the individual affects of the will." [664W-{12/1/58} Letter to Mathilde Wesendonck, SLRW, p. 432; See also [771W-{9–12/70} 'Beethoven,' PW Vol. V, p. 72, and 948W {11/3/72} CD Vol. II, p. 188] In one of his most intriguing commentaries on his artistic inspiration (previously cited), Wagner explained why he alone was privileged to grasp the true basis of redemption which Schopenhauer had missed. It was because he, as both composer and poet of his music-dramas, as master of both the unconscious and conscious minds, had an insight into inner processes unique to himself: [See 665W-{12/8/58} Letter to Mathilde Wesendonck, RWLMW, p. 78; See also 363W]

In the second half of our passage, just after Brünnhilde announces that heavenly knowledge (Wotan's hoard of knowledge) has flooded away, driven hence by love, she (accompanied by H47, Alberich's and Fafner's transformation into the Serpent/Dragon, a symbol for existential fear) asks Siegfried whether or not he's blinded by her gaze, and whether he burns for her. And finally, she inquires, in the context of H76 and H77: "Do you fear, Siegfried, do you not fear this wildly raging woman?" So Brünnhilde has now inherited Alberich's and

Fafner's H47 which represents the fear of truth which sustains religious faith. She's inherited H47 and teaches Siegfried fear where Fafner couldn't, because she, our collective unconscious, has inherited Fafner's status as the guardian of man's (Wotan's—the Folk's) religious mysteries, and as the muse for inspired secular art she's the guardian of the new faith, the involuntary and unconscious collective-dream realm of art in which all doubt and questioning is rendered moot by music's Wonder. In this context, it's no surprise that as Brünnhilde asks Siegfried, in ecstasy, "(H87 Frag:) Am I now yours?," we hear a fragment of H87, the Fate Motif, for he's taken (at least temporarily) aesthetic possession of Fate.

We can now grasp the meaning of Siegfried's exultant words: "(H74b hint) As our arms clasp each other in ardor (H93) my courage returns (H74b hint), ah! The fear that I never learned—the fear that you scarcely taught me: that fear—(H138b) I think—fool that I am, (H137b) I've quite forgotten it now!" Why do the Woodbird's songs H138b and H137b accompany Siegfried as he tells Brünnhilde that the fear he learned from her he's quite forgotten? Think back to Siegfried's peculiar case of amnesia as he emerged from Fafner's cave with Alberich's Ring on his finger and the Tarnhelm attached to his belt: "(H58a:) What use you are I do not know: (H9) but I took you from the heaped up gold of the hoard (:H58a) (H58b:) since goodly counsel counselled me to do so (:H58b). (H58c:) ... may the bauble recall how, (H116) ... I vanquished Fafner but still haven't learned the meaning of fear (:H58c)." The Woodbird had just moments before Siegfried entered Fafner's cave taught him the use of both Tarnhelm and Ring, that acquisition of the Tarnhelm would help him to work wonders, but winning the Ring would win him the world. Siegfried's amnesia was Wagner's metaphor for the fact that Siegfried only learned the use of the Tarnhelm and Ring from the Woodbird's singing subliminally, i.e., musically. What the Woodbird taught Siegfried has left him, insofar as his conscious mind is concerned, untaught. Similarly, Siegfried has now forgotten the fear Brünnhilde taught him. Now we can see the big picture. Siegfried's (the artist-hero's) relationship with Brünnhilde (his unconscious womb of inspiration) is modeled on Wotan's (religious man's) relationship with Brünnhilde's mother Erda, Mother Nature. Wotan, like Siegfried, learned the full meaning of all that Wotan had been taught to fear by Erda, by having figurative sexual union with her. But Wotan, as he suggested in R.4, also went down to Erda for another reason, to overcome his care and fear. Wotan satisfied these two wishes through Erda, and the product of their union was Brünnhilde, who, like Erda, teaches the artist-hero Siegfried subliminally the true meaning of his existential fear, and also how to end his fear, in this latter case through inspired art.

Now Siegfried and Brünnhilde attain the height of ecstasy in a final apostrophe to each other in which Brünnhilde remains the repository for Siegfried's unconscious knowledge of the wider world and history and his own true identity and origin, leaving Siegfried ignorant of everything but the bliss of union with her. Thanks to Brünnhilde, Siegfried the artistic genius remains childlike and foolish (in a higher sense), the unwitting guardian of Wotan's (man's) unspoken secret, Alberich's hoard of knowledge, which Siegfried has redeemed from Alberich's Ring Curse of consciousness temporarily through his art. Appropriately, Brünnhilde names Siegfried (the unwitting) heir to Alberich's/Fafner's Nibelung hoard, and Wotan's Hoard of worldly knowledge again, calling him the "foolish hoard ["Hort"] of loftiest deeds":

> [pp. 275–6] **Brünnhilde:** (laughing wildly and joyfully: H76/H77 >>:) O childish hero! O glorious boy! You foolish hoard of loftiest deeds ["Du hehrster Thaten thöriger Hort"]! (H151 >> :) Laughing I must love you; laughing I must grow blind: laughing let us perish … ! [[**H155ab orch:**]] [H155a possibly a H109 vari?; H155b possibly a H117 vari?] Be gone, Valhalla's light-bringing world! May your proud-standing stronghold moulder to dust! [[**H155ab orch:**]]; H150:) Fare well, resplendent pomp of the gods! End in rapture, you endless race! [[**H155ab orch:**]]; H150:) Rend, you Norns, the rope of runes! Dusk of the gods ["Götter-Dämm'rung"], let your darkness arise! Night of destruction, let your mists ["Neb'le"] roll in (:H150)! (H143:) Siegfried's star now shines upon me (:H143): [[**H155ab orch:**]] he's mine forever, always mine, my heritage and own, my one and all, (H151/H143 >> :) light-bringing love and laughing death (:H151/H143; :H155)!
>
> **Siegfried:** [[**H155 orch:**]] Laughing you wake in gladness to me: Brünnhilde lives! Brünnhilde laughs!—Hail to the day that sheds light all around us! Hail to the sun that shines upon us! Hail to the light that emerges from night! Hail to the world for which Brünnhilde lives! She wakes! She lives! She smiles upon me! Brünnhilde's star shines resplendent upon me! She's mine forever, always mine, my heritage and own, my one and all: light-bringing love and laughing death (:H155/H151; :H155)! (Brünnhilde throws herself into Siegfried's arms.)

We hear H151 as Brünnhilde exclaims that laughing, they must grow blind and perish. H151's first significant conceptual association was with Brünnhilde's statement to Siegfried that she'd be his self if he but loves her in her bliss, and that what he doesn't know she knows for him. H151 here expresses their loss of separate identity in each other's passion, and the fact that Siegfried remains unconscious of his true identity and origin because Brünnhilde knows this for him. Wagner said that music blinds us to the daylight, to the outer, objective world, so we can experience inner sight into the essence of things. [See 607W-{1/25–26/54} Letter to August Röckel, SLRW, pp. 302–303] Siegfried and Brünnhilde feel as if they've become one with the essence of all things, and we're reminded that at the height of their ecstatic sexual union in *Tristan* Act Two Tristan and Isolde, seemingly having lost their separate identities through their love, said to each other: "I've become the world."

As Brünnhilde celebrates their laughing doom the orchestra, and later the principals' voices, introduce the last motif of *Siegfried*, H155ab, a shatteringly manic motif which lifts us to the stratosphere. The libretto passage which H155 heightens is Brünnhilde's final renunciation of the gods, whom she asks to celebrate their own self-destruction in favor of the love Siegfried and Brünnhilde share, which will be Brünnhilde's sole concern from now on. Brünnhilde also rhetorically calls on her half-sisters the Norns (like the Valkyries, Erda's children) to rend their rope of runes, because, in the ecstasy of the moment, at the height of Siegfried's unconscious artistic inspiration by his muse, Siegfried and Brünnhilde feel "as if" the rope of fate, of natural law, has been rent by that "Wonder" of the music-drama which makes all the past and future, and all that's distant in space (all that is "Fernen"), seem present, here and now, which is to say they feel they've transcended the limits of time, space, and the lawful coherence of Nature. I strongly suspect Dunning was mistaken in declaring motif H155ab a member of the Love Motif Family. Its first, stepwise descending segment, H155a, seems rather to be a variant of H109, which conveyed Siegfried's loathing for Mime. This link of the romantically triumphant H155 to H109, a motif redolent of the most negative connotation possible, Siegfried's utter contempt for Mime, must seem counter-intuitive. However, if we consider Wagner's repeated adverse comparisons in *Siegfried* between Wotan and Mime, on the one hand, and Siegfried on the other, that Mime represents Wotan's prose and Siegfried Wotan's poetry, that Mime is a metaphor for all those things in Wotan he loathed in himself, and finally, if we consider that Brünnhilde has described Wotan and his divine realm Valhalla (which she conflates with Alberich's Nibelheim) as being consigned to oblivion as his heirs Brünnhilde and Siegfried unite in loving union while accompanied by H155, we can understand H155's sounding here in a triumphant variant as the motival symbol of the passing away of all that Wotan loathed in his own nature, and which Siegfried loathed in Mime, from which Siegfried is now freed thanks to her love. H155 also has a second, rising segment, H155b, which Dunning suggested might be a variant of H117, the first of two motifs (the second being H118, Siegfried's Mission) which together expressed Siegfried's joy in his emancipation from Mime, that with his sword Nothung re-forged Siegfried would strike out into the world and leave Mime behind. If H155b is indeed a variant of H117, then the motival symbolism in the derivation of H155ab from both H109 and H117 makes even more dramatic sense. Cooke, however, construed H155 as a variant of H75 (the Wälsung twins' remembrance of things past), which brought *Valkyrie* Act Three to its ecstatic close as Siegmund and Sieglinde, Siegfried's parents, embraced each other in loving union. This also makes musico-dramatic sense.

What Brünnhilde celebrates is Wotan's "going-under," the figurative twilight of the gods, in favor of religion's heir, inspired secular art, an end of the gods Wotan boasted to Erda he could now will with an open heart (accompanied by H143), since his heirs Siegfried and Brünnhilde can redeem the world from Alberich's Ring Curse of consciousness. Brünnhilde achieves this because, as Wotan told Erda, Erda's knowledge of world history (a world Wotan acknowledged belongs to Alberich)—and the inexorable laws of evolution it obeys—wanes before Wotan's "Will" Brünnhilde. That's why, as she sings of the wider historical and even cosmic context in which their love duet is taking place, Siegfried sings only of his love for her, wholly oblivious to this context, and ignorant of his own prehistory and identity. As a signal that Siegfried's love for

Brünnhilde, his unconscious artistic inspiration, has supplanted belief in gods as man's source of transcendent value, H143 sounds for the last time in *Siegfried* as both Siegfried and Brünnhilde bring the love-duet to a climax extolling the love they have for each other alone. The art their union will produce is the true Wagnerian redemption through love, the "new religion," the New Valhalla, the artwork of the future. With their final shout of "laughing death" the curtain comes down on one of the most electrifying climactic moments in all of world theater and opera (a climax hugely dramatically enhanced by contrast with the deep gloom with which *Siegfried* ominously began). But such manic joy can only spend itself in exhaustion, since one more great music-drama in the *Ring* tetralogy awaits us, in which we'll learn the true cost of this overweening joy, this cosmic hubris.

According to Wagner, it's the re-woken soul of music, the will to grasp the world aesthetically through feeling rather than thinking, that has temporarily restored lost innocence, and made humans feel as if they enjoy again paradise before the Fall. The new, aesthetic law of subjective feeling becomes our substitute for the natural laws of the objective world (the Norns' rope of fate): the new world is seen solely through the inward eye of music which blinds us to the outer world. As Feuerbach put it: "... the Christian made the requirements of human feeling the absolute powers and laws of the world." [90F-EOC, p. 120] We find an echo of Brünnhilde's hyperbolic—and purely figurative—rending of the Norns' rope of fate in Wagner's description of how music so transfigures all it touches that it sets us free from matter's realism: "... if every action, even humblest incident of life displays itself, when reproduced by mimicry, in the transfiguring light and with the objective effect of a mirror-image (as is shown not only by Shakespeare, but by every other sterling playwright), ... we shall have to avow that this mirror-image, again, displays itself in the transfiguration of purest ideality so soon as it is dipped in the magic spring of Music and held up to us as nothing but pure Form, so to say, set free from all the realism of Matter." [798W-{3–6/71} 'The Destiny of Opera,' PW Vol. V, pp. 146–147]

Thus, Wagner avers, through inspired music we feel as if we've regained lost innocence, and to this degree inspired secular art fulfills religious faith's promise that we can attain redemption from our earthly coils, and affirm and enjoy our transcendent value, but only subjectively, not in fact. Wagner described music as a means through which we can "play" with the grief of being (Noth), without suffering from it. Siegfried and Brünnhilde, accordingly, feel innocent, free from doubt, as if wholly unaware of their implication in Wotan's guilt: " ... all his [Beethoven's] seeing and his fashioning is steeped in that marvellous serenity ... which Music first acquired through him. Even the cry, so immanent in every sound of Nature, is lulled to smiling: the world regains its childhood's innocence. (...) / (...) The joy of wielding this new power turns next to humour: all grief of Being breaks before this vast enjoyment of the play therewith; the world-creator Brahma is laughing at himself ... as he sees how hugely he had duped himself ... . / (...) The effect upon the hearer is precisely the deliverance from all earthly guilt ... ." [777W-{9–12/70} 'Beethoven,' PW Vol. V, pp. 92–93] And Wagner thought of himself, the inspired artist, as a pre-Fallen being, not subject to the law (the original sin) which circumscribes the lives of uncreative men: " ... I [Cosima] maintain to R. [Wagner] that there are many things of which he understands nothing, since genius has no part in original sin. He: 'I live like a sort of animal.' I: 'Yes, in innocence.'" [977W-{9/21/79}CD Vol. II, p. 367]

Wotan, reborn ignorant of his past life (or lives) and true identity in Siegfried, therefore seems to have fulfilled the quest he once confessed to Brünnhilde was futile, the transcendence of his own self, the creation of a new identity unburdened by any debt to his past history and circumstances, freed from all pre-condition and causation (fate). Speaking of Tristan's and Isolde's union in death, Wagner said: "'Everything that is remains, what one already has persists, freed entirely from the conditions of its occurrence.'" [803W-{7/25/71} CD Vol. I, p. 396] It's worth recalling that in several comments previously cited Wagner critiqued the idea that religious man could renounce Nature yet go on living as self-deception, an idea which here he celebrates. Ironically, the Valhallan gods don't truly go to their doom with the rebirth of man's religious impulse in the music-drama, the loving union of Siegfried the artist-hero with his muse Brünnhilde, in spite of Brünnhilde's ecstatic invocation of the twilight of the gods. Valhalla (the Old Valhalla, abode of the gods) will only go to its doom when both Siegfried and Brünnhilde have betrayed their love in *Twilight of the Gods*, and solely as a consequence of the fact that they succumb, like Wotan, to Alberich's Ring Curse, in spite of Brünnhilde's celebration with Siegfried of their alleged cutting the Norns' rope of fate. The point is that our religious impulse lived on in Wagner's secular art (not to mention religious communities) until the moment when, according to Wagner's personal mythology, he betrayed the unspoken secret of his (man's) religious revelation and unconscious artistic inspiration to the light of day, in his *Ring*. Only then did our last remaining, vestigial religious impulse die out, according to him. And that is the subject of the final installment of the *Ring* tetralogy, *Twilight of the Gods*.

Twilight of the Gods

TWILIGHT OF THE GODS ≠ PROLOGUE, PART A

(BELOW BRÜNNHILDE'S ROCKY PEAK)
THE NORNS

As we embark on our analysis of the last of the *Ring* music-dramas, it should have become apparent that it's a hybrid masterwork which can't be grasped under one category, such as drama, poetry, music, or philosophy. It's, put simply, a dramatic, theatrical, poetic, musical, and philosophic meditation on the great questions which have confronted us humans since our emergence as conscious beings among the animals. The old, tired debate about whether Wagner's music-dramas are tone poems whose music is paramount and for which Wagner employed librettos as mere scaffolding or an organizing principle, which could be ignored once Wagner had completed the music for them, or rather, dramas set to music which must be taken seriously as artworks of philosophic import, can be laid to rest by acknowledging the necessity of experiencing Wagner's music-dramas, and the *Ring* in particular, as Wagner intended, with full attention to the dramatic action, the words, and the music. Some argue that only Wagner's music is important, and that the proof of this is that he'd still be remembered as one of the great composers if we eliminated his librettos for which the music was written and merely preserved the music, but that if we only had his librettos he'd be forgotten. This ignores the fact that his music-dramas' scores (with the exception of a few popular excerpts primarily of overtures, preludes, and orchestral intermezzos between scenes) require the drama to communicate their full meaning and emotional force. It's in this spirit that I commend my following critique of *Twilight of the Gods*, the last *Ring* drama.

The prelude to the Prologue to the final part of the four-part *Ring* drama, *Twilight of the Gods*, begins in darkness near the base of the mountain on whose summit Siegfried joined in loving union with Brünnhilde, protected by Loge's ring of fire. Erda's (Nature's) daughters, the three Norns, spokes-ladies for the past, present, and future (the world embraced by Erda's wisdom), meditate on the ways of the world as they spin their rope of fate:

[p. 280] (**Prelude:** H148; H3, H2; H148; H3; H2; H148 chord [transitions into H87; [[**H156 orch**]] [= diminished inversion of H3] (…) The scene is the same as at the end of the second day, on the Valkyrie's rock. Night. A fiery glow is visible … . The three norns, tall female figures in long, dark veil-like garments. The first (the oldest) is lying at the front of the stage on the left ... ; the second (the younger) is reclining on a stone terrace ... ; the third (the youngest) is sitting on a rocky outcrop of the mountain ridge ... .)

The Prelude begins, significantly, with H148, the chord—based on H52—to which Siegfried woke Brünnhilde in S.3.3. H52 represents Erda's knowledge of all that was, is, and will be, and that whatever "is" will end. H148 eventually transforms into H87, the fate the Norns spin. Their "Spinning Motif" H156, introduced in this prelude, is based, according to Dunning, on a diminished inversion of H3, the River Rhine's motion. *Twilight Of The Gods* opens with H148, in all probability, because it recounts the tragic consequences (or perhaps the redemptive consequences) which follow from Siegfried's waking our collective unconscious Brünnhilde, which will culminate in his inadvertent sharing of her secret (Wotan's unspoken secret) with the Folk, Wagner's audience, who were never meant to be privy to the religious mysteries. This is the secret of how we Folk involuntarily invented the gods, and how our higher, allegedly transcendent values were originally predicated on self-deception and fear. Brünnhilde has awoken for Siegfried, ultimately destined never to sleep again: our unconscious hoard of forbidden knowledge which she guards is about to rise, as Alberich threatened, from her silent depths to the light of day.

Wotan told Erda that when her daughter waked, she'd do that deed which will redeem the world. There are two distinct redemptive deeds which Brünnhilde performs. But there's also a third which Wagner saved for *Parsifal* Act Three: Parsifal's renunciation of Brünnhilde's reincarnate spirit, Parsifal's potential (but never realized) muse Kundry. The first is Brünnhilde's inspiring Siegfried to create redemptive deeds of art, which reconcile us to life in the real world by making us feel we've risen above its concerns. This secular art, in which our religious longing for transcendent value lives on as feeling, perpetuates Wotan's original sin against his mother, Nature (Brünnhilde's mother Erda), which Alberich's Ring Curse punishes. The second and final redemptive act in the *Ring* Brünnhilde performs (wholly distinct from the first) is undertaken in response to the fact that if we can't bear to live within the real world's (Alberich's world's) constraints, but can no longer call on religion, ethics, or art for consolation, there's the prospect of terminating consciousness altogether, either through personal suicide, or by ending that human consciousness per se which was the cause of our un-healing wound in the first place. This was "Das Ende" which Wotan—in his nihilistic despair, unable to accept the bitter truth, yet unable any longer to sustain the consoling illusions which he'd substituted for the truth—told Brünnhilde he fervently desired at the end of his confession in V.2.2. But Wagner explored a third option for redemption, our acknowledgment of our natural limitations and subjection to egoism, our ultimate reconciliation with our Mother Nature whom we sinned against in religious belief and unconsciously inspired art, in *Parsifal*.

Erda's daughters the Norns (Fates) are discussing the question whether the gleam they see is the dawn of day, or Loge's fire which still burns protectively round Brünnhilde's mountaintop home:

[pp. 280-1] **Second Norn:** (H52 vari:; H2:) Is day already dawning (:H2; :H52 vari)? (H33 vari)

Third Norn: (H33 vari:) Loge's host burns brightly round the fell (:H33 vari). [[**H156 orch:**]] Night still reigns (:H156 orch): why don't we spin and sing? (…)

First Norn: ([[**H156 orch**]]; H42/H106) (…)) [[**H156 orch:**]] For good or ill I wind the rope and sing (:H156 orch).—(H2:; [[**H157 voc:**]]) At the world-ash once I wove (H156 orch:) when, tall and strong, a forest of sacred branches (:H157 voc; :H156 orch) (H18d voc:) blossomed from its bole (:H18d voc); (H156 orch:) in its cooling shade there plashed a spring, whispering wisdom … (:H156 orch): (H18d voc:) I sang then of sacred things (:H18d voc). (H18d)—A dauntless god ["ein kühner Gott"] came to drink at the spring; (H18abc vari:) one of his eyes he paid as toll for all time: (H18d) from the world-ash Wotan broke off a branch; (H19) the shaft of a spear (H19 modified by H123 rhythm:) the mighty god cut from its trunk (:H19 modified by H123 rhythm).—(H101 vari:) In the span of many seasons the wound consumed the wood (:H101 vari); (H52 & H53 vari clarinet) fallow fell the leaves (:H52 & H53 vari clarinet), (H156 orch:) barren, the tree grew rotten (:H156 orch): (H52 vari:) sadly the well-spring's drink ran dry (:H52 vari); the sense of my singing grew troubled. [[**H157 orch**]] (H156 orch:) But if I no longer weave by the world-ash today, the fir must serve to fasten the rope (:H156 orch): ([[**H158 voc:**]]; H12 vari:) Sing, my sister,—I cast it to you (:H158 voc; :H12 vari)—(H88:) do you know what will become of it (:H88)?

The World-Ash having withered and died since Wotan broke off its most sacred branch to make his Spear from it, the Norns must attach their rope to any branch or rock which comes to hand. As they proclaim that they weave (spin) the rope (of Fate) for good or ill, we hear H42/H106 (Mime's Scheming), motifs in the family associated with man's cunning, our gift for distorting truth (man as trickster, or self-deceiver), which includes Loge's Motif H24 and H26. These Loge motifs convey Wotan's intent (inspired by Loge's cunning) to break the Social Contract he engraved on his Spear of divine authority. This cunning has tainted Nature's innocence with the self-deceit which was the cause of Wotan's sin against all that was, is, and will be, whose metaphor is the fatal wound Wotan made in the World-Ash (a figure for Mother Nature, Erda, and whose first motif H122 is a variant in 3/4 time of Erda's Motif H52, and H2.). As they sing of the sacred days when they wove their rope at the living World-Ash, the Second World-Ash Motif H157 is introduced vocally by the First Norn. H157 has no musical kinship with the first World-Ash Motif H122. As they sing of these primal, sacred times we also hear H18d, a segment of the Valhalla Motif which Cooke described as lending an air of nobility to anything seen or heard while it sounds in the orchestra. Its presence here, linked with that pre-Fallen time before Wotan broke off the World-Ash's most sacred branch to make his Spear, is somewhat mysterious, but I suspect it represents the underlying identity of the World Ash and its most sacred branch with Wotan's Spear, which he made from it. Also, it's noteworthy that unlike H18ab, this segment of the Valhalla Motif isn't derived from Alberich's Ring Motif H17ab.

We hear the first three of the Valhalla Motif's five segments, H18abc, as the Norns recall how Wotan sacrificed one eye (which he identified earlier with Siegfried, whose eye we assumed looks inward) to gain wisdom from the sacred spring which flows from the roots of the World-Ash. Is this sacred spring the Rhine's source? We may well ask, because the newly introduced Norns' Spinning/Weaving Motif H156 is a diminished inversion of H3, which represents the Rhine River flowing. Wotan had to sacrifice his instinctual knowledge, aesthetic intuition, his eye which looks inward (restored to him in Siegfried's love for Brünnhilde), to gain the power of reflective thought, just as Alberich had to renounce love to forge his Ring from the Rhinegold to obtain world-power (through acquisition of symbolic consciousness and language). Presumably Wotan's sacrifice of one eye to obtain the sacred spring's wisdom was also required to break off the World-Ash's most sacred branch to make his Spear of divine authority. This makes sense: Wotan's Spear is a symbol for the Fall (the Biblical Tree of Knowledge, figuratively derived from the Biblical Tree of Life, The World-Ash), and Siegfried's role is to redeem us from the Fall by restoring that inward sight (aesthetic intuition) lost due to our acquisition of the power of conscious thought.

Wotan's murder of the World-Ash is a metaphor for religious man's status as the killer of his mother, Nature. We hear H52 (the natural necessity of change, the end of all things) and H53 (twilight of the gods) as the Norns describe how the World-Ash died due to Wotan's abuse. Wotan's attempt to create cultural and social institutions of allegedly divine origin regarded as sacred and unalterable was a sin against the natural necessity for change, the everlasting creativity of the cosmos. Wagner had a fascinating insight into the idea underlying his World-Ash Tree. He told Cosima how modern, cultured man seems concerned solely with dead things (referencing Wotan's Spear), while in former, purer times we embraced living things, plants, animals, etc. (i.e., felt one with them): "… he [Wagner] says, 'It has occurred to me that we now seem to concern ourselves only with dead things; everything around us seems lifeless, whereas previously our existence was concerned with living things, with plants, animals; Wotan carved his spear from the growing ash tree.' When I say that … Siegfried and Brünnhilde give the appearance of sacred, living Nature, whereas the Gibichungs [Hagen, Gunther, and Gutrune, to whom we'll be introduced in T.1.1] are already among the dead, he agrees with me." [1114W-{1/8/82} CD Vol. II, p. 786] Though Wotan and the gods have figuratively murdered Mother Nature (Erda) by denying her truth and substituting a consoling illusion in her place, nonetheless, in the fulness of time, Erda's laws of change (embodied by H52 and H53) will wreak Nature's vengeance on those who've denied her. Feuerbach gave natural law (Erda's knowledge of all that was, is, and will be, which the Norns' spin into their rope of fate) pride of place when he said: "Space and time are not mere forms of appearance; they are conditions of being, forms of reason, and laws of existence

as well as of thought. (...) Limitation in space and time is the first virtue ... ."
[185F-PPF, pp. 60–61]

As the First Norn prepares to hand the rope of fate over to the Second Norn so she can spin and sing her knowledge, another new motif is introduced, H158, which is only heard in T.P.A during the Norns' colloquy when they call on each other to sing and spin. As the First Norn casts the rope to the Second, asking her what will come of the fact that the World-Ash has died through Wotan's sin, we hear H88, the motif generally associated with fated doom. I mention H88's occurrence here because it's often said that Wagner's application of musical motifs to the drama grew far more loosely linked to the immediate passages of libretto with which they're associated, and therefore more creative, heeding exclusively musical rather than dramatic considerations, during the final phase of his composition of the *Ring* music, starting with the last act of *Siegfried*. It's generally argued that Wagner's liberation of his motifs from subservience to the drama reflected Schopenhauer's influence, whose theory of music as a direct product of the Will inspired Wagner to give pride of place to music where music and drama interact. While it's true that his employment of his musical motifs for dramatic ends grew more complex, sophisticated, and nuanced as he neared completion of composition of the *Ring*'s music in 1874, I don't find that Wagner's employment of motifs has less dramatic relevance. Though Wagner's employment of motifs in this scene is often cited as a primary example of the motifs' gradual emancipation from the restrictions of Wagner's theory of music-drama, I find no dramatic examples of motifs employed purely for musical reasons which cut against the grain of the drama. Most if not all musico-dramatic interactions seem to me to remain fluent and comprehensible right up to the very finale of the *Ring*. But it's impossible to ascertain motifs' meanings definitively: each has a penumbra of meaning (based on their dramatic profile accrued throughout the drama) which sometimes overlaps that of other motifs. Take for instance the occurrence in this passage of a variant of H101 (Brünnhilde's Magic Sleep) heard as the First Norn says: "In the span of many seasons the wound [which Wotan inflicted on the World-Ash to make his Spear] consumed the wood." Wotan, on taking his final leave of Erda in S.3.1, having told her that her wisdom wanes before his will (i.e., before his unconscious mind Brünnhilde), consigned Erda to the oblivion of sleep and dreaming.

This isn't to say that from the drama's standpoint I can account for each occurrence of every *Ring* motif. To affirm with such certainty, where the best we can expect is well-informed speculation and guesswork, would be suspect in any case, because, with almost any *Ring* interpretation, one can find plausible reasons for the occurrence of almost any motif in almost any dramatic context. The only way to speculate intelligently about the presence in different dramatic contexts of various motifs is to remain cognizant of each motif's dramatic profile (the dramatic context of all occurrences in the *Ring*), and also of its family relationships, so we obtain a sense of the motif's thematic center of gravity, to maintain consistency in interpretation. If any motif can mean anything all hope is lost. It might be said (figuratively) that Wagner's motifs are a sort of musico-dramatic version of the concept of indeterminacy in quantum physics, an ambiguity (in our perception, or in Nature?) in which a wave of probability collapses into a particle of actuality on being observed.

The Second Norn now describes how Siegfried broke Wotan's Spear, and how Wotan then ordered his martyred Valhallan heroes to chop down the World-Ash, causing its sacred spring to dry up:

> **[pp. 281–2] Second Norn:** (H124:) The runes of trustily counseled treaties (:H124) (H123 Definitive:) Wotan carved on the shaft of the spear: (H19) he held it as his grip on the world (:H123). (H19 vari) A dauntless hero (H19 vari:) shattered the spear in combat (:H19 vari); (H124 voc:) the contracts' hallowed haft was smashed to whirling splinters (:H124 voc).—(H39?; H81 vari? >>:) Then Wotan bade Valhalla's heroes hew into pieces (H156:) the world-ash's (H53 >>:) withered boughs and bole (:H39?; :H81 vari?; :H156; :H53): the ash-tree fell; the spring ran dry for ever! (H157; H156) ... (H158 voc:; H12 vari orch:) sing, my sister,—I cast it to you (:H158 voc; :H12 vari orch)—(H88:) do you know what will become of it (:H88)?
>
> **Third Norn:** (H9?: catching the rope ...) Built by giants, the stronghold towers aloft; with the hallowed kin of gods and heroes (H53 vari) Wotan sits there within the hall. (H123) (H123 voc >>:) A rearing pile of rough-hewn logs towers on high around the hall (:H123 voc): (H157 voc:) this was once the world-ash tree (:H157 voc)!—(H105 accompaniment: [as heard in the finale of *Twilight of the Gods* as Valhalla burns—a new form of fire figuration?]) When the timber blazes brightly in sacred fire, when its embers singe the glittering hall with their searing heat (:H105 accompaniment), (H19:; H53:) the downfall ["Ende"] of the (:H19) immortal gods will dawn for all eternity (:H53). (H87)—If you know yet more, (H87) (H156:) then coil the rope anew ... (:H156): ... (H158 voc:; H12 vari:) spin, my sister, and sing (:H158voc; :H12 vari)!

Curiously, accompanied by H124 (linked at its inception with Wotan's intent—under Loge's sway—to break his contract with the Giants), the Second Norn speaks of the "runes of trustily counseled treaties" Wotan carved on his spear, which he holds as his grip on the world. H123 is also heard, recalling the power of the gods. It seems odd that the Norns would be so naïve that they could describe Wotan's runes as trustily counseled, or for that matter, that they would describe him as a god, since Wotan's sole purpose since making divine law has been to subvert it, and the Norns' mother Erda denied Wotan is what he calls himself, a God. Perhaps this is a rare instance in which Wagner forgot to revise a portion of his libretto to make it consistent with his final conception of the whole, before submitting it for publication and performance? In any case, the sounding of H124 here indicates these runes weren't trustily counseled.

The Third Norn recounts how Wotan now sits among the gods and heroes in Valhalla, which his heroes have surrounded with logs made from the wood of the dead World-Ash. He awaits that consuming fire which will bring about the twilight of the gods (H53). During her description of the events leading up to the gods' fated doom, H123, formerly associated with their power, heralds their downfall. H123's occurrence in this context highlights the irony of the gods' destiny. We're reminded that in the finale of R.4 Loge wryly observed that the gods, who think they'll last forever, are headed for destruction, and Loge imagined his fire would play a key role in their demise.

The first Norn now says her sight plays tricks on her, that she can't clearly recall the hallowed past when Loge flared up. Loge's motival references here, like so much of the motival content heard earlier in the *Ring* which is recapitulated here through Wagner's subtle variation of the motifs' harmony, melody-line, phrasing, modulation, instrumentation, etc., are now imbued with a nostalgic mood evoking time long past and dimly remembered. It's one of the most remarkable aesthetic effects in the *Ring*. Ernest Newman described this motival magic of *Twilight of the Gods* as granting the *Ring*'s motifs the patina of age:

> **[pp. 282–3] First Norn:** (... (H156:; H42/H106:; H32B vari:) Is daylight dawning? Or is it the light of the fire (:H156:; :H42/H106:; :H32B vari)? (H32B) Clouded, my sight plays tricks on me; (H33 vari:; H32B vari:) I cannot see clearly the hallowed past (:H33 vari), when Loge once flared up in white-hot flame (:H32B fades): (H88:) do you know what became of him (:H88)?
>
> **Second Norn:** (Once again winding the rope that has been thrown to her round the rock) (H19 vari >>:) By the spell of his spear Wotan tamed him (:H19 vari); (H32B) (H12 vari/H32B:) he whispered wisdom to the god (:12 vari/H32B): (H32B:) to work himself free (H34:) he gnawed and destroyed the runes on the shaft (:H32B; :H34). (H19 vari:) Then with the spear's all-powerful point (:H19 vari) (H12 vari/H32B:) Wotan cast a spell on him, bidding him blaze round Brünnhilde's rock (:H12 vari/H32B): (...) (H88:) do you know what will come of him (:H88)?
>
> **Third Norn:** (H123 definitive over H105 accompaniment:) The shattered spear's sharp-pointed splinters Wotan will one day bury deep in the fire-god's breast (:H123 definitive over H105 accompaniment): (H34:) a ravening fire will then flame forth, (H53 vari:) which the god will hurl (:H34) (H157 voc/H18a:) on the world-ash's (:H157 voc/H18a) (H18b voc:) heaped-up logs (:H18b voc). (...) (H101:) If you want to know when that will be, (H87) (H12 vari: [with trills]) sisters, wind the rope (:H12 vari [with trills.])! (H101)

The Second Norn recounts how, after Wotan tamed Loge to obey the authority conferred on Wotan by his Spear, Loge whispered wisdom to the god (the Second Norn may be alluding to Loge's five requests in R.2 and R.4 that Wotan restore the Ring to the Rhinedaughters, suggested here perhaps by the presence of H12 (the cry "Rhinegold! Rhinegold!"), and then gnawed at the runes on Wotan's spear to gain his freedom from servitude to the gods. Given Loge's status as the archetype for the revolutionary Wälsung heroes, particularly the artist-hero Siegfried, it makes sense that Loge would gnaw at Wotan's spear to gain freedom from the gods' rule, since the greatest Wälsung hero Siegfried gained this freedom by cutting Wotan's spear in half with the sword whose motif H56ab stands for Wotan's hope for redemption from the Fall through restoration of lost innocence. Wotan's Spear, the Social Contract, embodies the Fall. The Second Norn concludes her history with another curious detail of Wotan's involvement in his own demise: she foresees he'll light a fire (which will burn the logs of the dead World-Ash) with a torch made of his spear, splintered by Siegfried, which will burn Valhalla and consume its denizens, the gods and heroes. But in the event Brünnhilde will perform this last act. Metaphorically, Wotan and the gods (illusions of those humans who believed in gods) will go up in their own smoke and flames.

The First Norn notes that night is, after all, now waning, and that she can no longer see to find the strands of the rope of fate, as we hear H12 again, which seems in this context to represent Brünnhilde's protection of Siegfried from consciousness of Erda's (the Norns') fateful knowledge. H12 (the Rhinedaughters' "Rhinegold! Rhinegold!") tells us that Brünnhilde, who'll soon hold the Ring for Siegfried to keep its power safe (just as she's been holding for him the knowledge of his true identity, prehistory, and fate, to free him from Wotan's Noth), is Siegfried's surrogate Rhine, who temporarily neutralizes Alberich's Ring Curse through her wondrous protection:

> **[pp. 283–4] First Norn:** ... (H12 vari: [with trills]) Night is waning; I see no more: (H101:) the strands of the rope (H12 vari:) I can find no longer; the threads have become entangled (:H12 vari; :H101). (H17) (H17:) A desolate vision (:H17) (H35:) maddingly throws my mind into turmoil (:H35):— (H9ab:; H12:) Alberich once stole the Rhinegold (:H9ab; :H12):—do you know what became of him? (H17)
>
> **Second Norn:** ... (H17:) The stone's sharp edge is cutting the rope; ... the woven skein is raveled (:H17). (H17/H156:) From need ["Noth"] and spite ["Neid"] the Nibelung's ring stands proud (:H17/H156): (H43a orch:) an avenging curse (:H43a orch) (H43b voc:) gnaws at the tangle of threads (:H43b voc): ... (H56ab:) do you know what will come of that (:H56ab)?
>
> **Third Norn:** ... The rope's too slack! ... (H108 frag) if I'm to draw the end to the north, (H108 frag) tauter let it be stretched! (she pulls hard on the rope, which breaks.) It's snapped! (H56ab:)
>
> **Second Norn:** It's snapped! **First Norn:** It's snapped (:H56ab)! (...)
>
> **The Three Norns:** (H53:) An end to eternal wisdom (:H53)! (H50 voc:) Wise women no longer tell the world their tidings (:H50 voc).
>
> **Third Norn:** (H101:) Descend!   **Second Norn:** (H101:) To our mother! **First Norn:** Descend! (H87: They disappear.)

It's generally assumed that the fact that the First Norn recounts Wotan's history before she describes Alberich's history in brief, merely saying that he once stole the Rhinegold, implies Alberich's theft of the Rhinegold occurred after Wotan broke the most sacred branch off of the World-Ash Tree to make his Spear. But, just as in the account of world-history Wotan confessed to Brünnhilde, there's no way to ascertain the position of Alberich's theft of the Rhinegold within historical time from the First Norn's account because, in speaking of Alberich, she's speaking of a new topic, and so far as we can tell, going back in time to an indeterminate period. At no point has she definitively placed Alberich's theft of the Rhinegold in chronological context relative to Wotan's breaking the branch off the World-Ash. Similarly, the First Norn also noted she can no longer clearly see the hallowed past when Loge flared up in flame. This again provides us no concrete information about Loge's place in the chronological sequence of world history. The confusion is perhaps due to the fact that man's mytho-poetic, or religious phase, represented by the gods' reign in Valhalla, preceded in time the birth of modern science (whose origins lay in Classical Greece, approximately between 2,600 and 2,300 years ago, but which was not firmly established until the 17th Century in Europe), with which I identify Alberich's son Hagen. But Alberich's forging of his Ring and acquisition of his Hoard of knowledge isn't Wagner's metaphor for the birth of modern science (Hagen); rather, it's his metaphor for the birth of human consciousness per se which, though it began immediately to acquire useful knowledge, organized its knowledge originally within a religious framework. The gradual acquisition of objective knowledge which occurred throughout the mytho-poetic phase of human history didn't become a threat to religious faith until much later. Alberich's forging of the Ring of human consciousness is the logical—but not necessarily the temporal—precondition for the Folk's (Wotan's) unwitting and involuntary invention of the gods, and therefore for the development of the earliest human cultures.

The First Norn tells of a vision which throws her madding mind into turmoil, accompanied by H17 and H35, the motifs regularly associated with the Ring's power and with the lovelessness which Alberich affirms is man's essence in order to obtain that power he's imposed on his fellow humans. Noting that Alberich once stole the Rhinegold, she asks what became of him, while throwing the ever more invisible rope of fate to the Second Norn. At this point we hear H17 again plus H156 (the Norns spinning their rope of fate). Since Nature's rise to consciousness of herself in man, the Norns have been spinning the consequences of the Fall—man's burden of consciousness, Alberich's Ring and its Curse—into their rope of fate. But now the Second Norn, alarmed, observes that the stone's sharp edge is cutting the rope. From need ("Noth") and spite ("Neid"), she says, the Nibelung's Ring stands proud, and we hear H43ab (Power of the Ring) as she tells how Alberich's avenging curse gnaws at its threads, suggesting Alberich's Ring Curse is cutting the rope of fate. By cutting the Norns' rope of fate Alberich's Ring Curse would seem, ironically, to be fulfilling the task Wotan set for Siegfried, to free himself from all entanglement in the real world, its laws and egoistic impulses. It would be the height of irony if Alberich's Ring Curse was instrumental in cutting the rope of fate which includes the gods' doom the Norns' mother Erda foresaw, which is supposed to fulfill Alberich's Ring Curse. The only way we can make sense of this is to construe Siegfried's and Brünnhilde's love, their creation of unconsciously inspired art, as the fulfillment of Alberich's Ring Curse, the product of that key faculty of human consciousness which leaves man forever unable to find satisfaction in Nature as he finds it, but propels him to strive to transcend it, a futile quest which both religion and inspired secular art express. After all, Alberich had cursed his Ring to punish all who renounce Mother Nature's truth (his Hoard of earthly knowledge) for the sake of world-denial in religion and art. And Wotan warned Brünnhilde that in living for the redemption by love, an ideal he once championed but has now renounced as unrealizable, she'd be punishing herself. For the artist-hero and his loving muse perpetuate Wotan's sin against all that was, is, and will be, i.e., against the World Ash, in the inspired art they'll create together, and this fulfills Alberich's Ring Curse, since it will bring its own punishment.

That the Ring Curse's gnawing at the rope of fate is inwardly linked with Siegfried, who's the agent of Wotan's hope to transcend the limits of natural law and egoistic impulse by consigning to oblivion all that Wotan loathes in his own nature and origin, is proved by the sounding now of H56ab (Wotan's grand idea of redemption from Alberich's Ring Curse, incarnate in Nothung), while the Norns' rope of fate is being split. It's also proved by the sounding moments later of a H108 (Siegfried's Youthful Horncall) fragment. It's as if Siegfried, through his unconscious artistic inspiration by Brünnhilde (which is taking place in the cave on Brünnhilde's mountaintop while the Norns spin the rope of fate below it), is—at least figuratively—cutting the Norns' rope of fate with his sword Nothung, whose purpose was to restore the lost innocence of feeling and love, the time before the birth of human consciousness and its a priori knowledge of time, space, and causation. We hear the Ring Curse H50 precisely at the moment the rope of fate breaks. This isn't so much the neutralization of Alberich's Ring Curse as its fulfillment: his curse will have sated itself by *Ring*'s end, and Siegfried and Brünnhilde both will unwittingly play their part in this.

Wagner's dramatization of the breaking of the Norns' rope of fate isn't a foreshadowing of the moment, much later, when Alberich's Ring Curse will come to an end as the Rhinedaughters dissolve the Ring, restored to them by Brünnhilde, in the Rhine. In its current context it represents the figurative transcendence of the limits of time and space within the inspired artwork Siegfried creates, Wagner's "Wonder," the waning of Erda's knowledge before Wotan's Will, Siegfried's muse Brünnhilde. It's through her inspiration of Siegfried's art that he's freed from Wotan's fear of the fated end Erda foresaw (which the Norns have now foreseen), freed both of Erda's objective knowledge, and of religious belief's illusory claims to truth which were the cause of that fear. Alberich's Ring Curse doesn't end with the breaking of the Norns' rope of fate as described by them here, since Siegfried and Brünnhilde will succumb to it. The Norns don't foresee this because the knowledge they spin wanes before Wotan's Will Brünnhilde, who'll inspire Siegfried to go out into the wider world to undertake new adventures by performing heroic deeds of artistic creation. For this reason the Norns' scene T.P.A transpires between the two halves of Siegfried's love duet with Brünnhilde, S.3.3, and T.P.B (i.e., in the context of Siegfried's unconscious artistic inspiration). The rope of fate they spin breaks not literally, but figuratively, thanks to Siegfried's creation of a work of art inspired by his muse Brünnhilde, before whom Erda's knowledge of all that was, is, and will be—the real world's laws and egoistic impulses—fades. So after it snaps we hear H53 representing not a literal prophecy of the twilight of the gods which occurs in T.3.3, but the figurative twilight of the gods Brünnhilde spoke of in the ecstatic finale to S.3.3 when she described how the gods would go under in the face of the love she shares with Siegfried.

When, accompanied by H53 (twilight of the gods), the Norns proclaim "An end to eternal wisdom," their mother Erda's wisdom—which embraces the gods' fated doom—has temporarily been repressed into the unconscious where Brünnhilde hides it and keeps its secret safe. So long as Brünnhilde's unspoken secret sleeps in her and only emerges into consciousness sublimated as a waking dream or allegory (a work of inspired art) rather than as waking reality, the actual twilight of the gods won't occur. But the Norns' eternal wisdom lives on unchanged, in spite of any subjective psychological event which takes place in the artist-hero Siegfried and his audience. They descend now to sleep with their mother Erda, accompanied by Brünnhilde's Magic Sleep H101, and by H87 (Fate), the world-events whose historical necessity they spin. But their knowledge has only waned temporarily before Wotan's Will Brünnhilde. Should Siegfried or Brünnhilde betray their hoard of forbidden knowledge to day, the gods' fate will be sealed, not figuratively but in fact.

How has Siegfried's loving union with Brünnhilde made love, feeling, the heart's need, music, the aesthetic law of the world, and thus made the artist-hero Siegfried the figurative lord of Nature? It's through a trick our mind plays on us, as Wagner described below. Of all the arts music seems to aesthetic philosophers the least directly connected with our waking experience, since it contains no images or ideas from the real world, only abstract patterns of notes which somehow capture all the nuances of human passion and sentiment, as if music was their essence. But, as Wagner noted, these expansive moods which seem to us sui generis are the indirect product of events in our life which are transmuted over time by our unconscious mind into moods which presumably have lost all trace, for us, of the events which originally inspired them: "... grand, passionate, and lasting emotions, dominating all our feelings and ideas for months and often half a year, these drive the musician to those vaster, more intense conceptions to which we owe, among others, the origin of a Sinfonia Eroica. These greater moods, as deep suffering of soul or potent exaltation, may date from outer causes ... ; but when they force the musician to production, these greater moods have already turned to music in him, so that at the moment of creative inspiration it is no longer the outer event that governs the composer, but the musical sensation which it has begotten in him." [355W-{10/41} 'A Happy Evening,' PW Vol. VII, pp. 79–80] It's in this sense that Wotan's repressed hoard of knowledge (which he imparted to Brünnhilde) influences Siegfried seemingly spontaneously sans Wotan's influence. Through this means it seems as if music, heart-felt subjective feeling, is now the law of the world which trumps the objective laws represented by Erda's knowledge of time, space, and Nature's coherence. As Wagner put it: " ... whereas the world gets by and is held together solely by dint of experience

[Wotan's confession of his hoard of objective knowledge to Brünnhilde], the poet's intuition precedes all experience and ... comprehends what it is that gives all experience its significance and meaning. (...) / The common world, which is entirely subjected to the influence of experience forced upon it from without [the Norns' fateful knowledge of all that was, is, and shall be], ... can never understand the poet's attitude towards the world of his own experience [Neither Erda nor the Norns foresee what the artist-hero Siegfried and his muse of inspiration Brünnhilde will do]." [667W-{1/19/59} Letter to Mathilde Wesendonck, SLRW, pp. 441-442; See also 791W-{9-12/70} 'Beethoven,' PW Vol. V, p. 121, and 782W-{9-12/70} 'Beethoven,' PW Vol. V, pp. 106-107]

Feuerbach understood that when idealist philosophers like Kant and Schopenhauer spoke of a priori knowledge of time, space, and causality as if these are properties falsely imputed by the mind to the essentially unknowable thing-in-itself (what the world is in itself independent of man's artificial attempts to grasp and encompass it with ideas), implying that in some sense the objective world of our common experience is insubstantial and illusory, they were fooling themselves for the sake of a futile attempt to smuggle religious man's bid for transcendent meaning back into philosophy. It's through this mind-trick that such philosophers strove to restore to the allegedly mundane, desiccated existence left to us by science's demythologization of human life and the world, an element of mystery and transcendence, as if all man's effort to obtain knowledge of a reality outside our subjective impressions was destined to failure since our mind automatically imposes its ineradicable limits on its object of inquiry. But, he noted, time and space aren't the world's preconditions, they're qualities man abstracts from his experience of the world's phenomena: " ... from physical things man abstracts space and time as universal concepts or forms, common to them all ... . But although man has abstracted space and time from spatial and temporal things, he posits them as the first grounds and conditions of these same things. (...) ... man sets space and time before real things ... ." [227F-LER, p. 117] Similarly, the poet's aesthetic intuition isn't the essence of things-in-themselves, and it doesn't free him or his audience from life's natural constraints. It's merely our subjective, felt response to our experience. There's nothing transcendent about music or aesthetic intuition except that we feel as if it's transcendent, and it doesn't make the artist or his audience lord of the world, but merely lord of our aesthetic recreation of the world. Inspired art makes us feel as if we're transported outside the bounds of the real world and our own most mundane concerns. But we mustn't mistake the feeling for the fact.

TWILIGHT OF THE GODS = PROLOGUE, PART B

(ON TOP OF BRÜNNHILDE'S ROCKY PEAK)
BRÜNNHILDE AND SIEGFRIED

As the sun rises, Siegfried and Brünnhilde emerge from a cave on the peak of her mountain. The musical prelude to their final love duet, which invokes the dawn coming up over their last happy moment together, is one of the grandest orchestral passages in Wagner's oeuvre and justly famous as an independent piece in the concert hall (usually paired with 'Siegfried's Rhine Journey'). Having given Siegfried the unconscious inspiration he needs to create and perform heroic deeds of art in the wider world, she now prepares to send him off to undertake those new adventures ("adventures" a metaphor for Siegfried's artistic endeavors in the outside world). In the meantime, his vital Youthful Horncall H108 has, Cooke noted, evolved into a grand, harmonically rich theme H159, the Mature Siegfried's Horncall, played by multiple horns. When Siegfried emerges from Brünnhilde's cave, we know he's a mature man:

> [pp. 284–5] (**Prelude:** Dawn. (…) (H?—alte-Weise-like, searching passage for strings which seems to reference Siegfried's aesthetic arrest in S.3.3 as he reached the rocky peak where Brünnhilde lay asleep); [[**H159 frag orch**]]; (H?—alte-Weise-like searching passage for strings); [[**H159 horns**]] [= H108 vari]; [[**H160 clarinet**]]; [[**H159 horns**]]; H76; [[**H159 horns:**]]: Sunrise. Broad daylight. Siegfried and Brünnhilde emerge from the rocky chamber. He is fully armed; she leads her horse by the bridle)
>
> **Brünnhilde:** [[**H160 voc:**]] To new adventures ["Thaten"—deeds], beloved hero (:H160 voc), [[**H160 orch:**]] what would my love be worth if I did not let you go forth (:H160 orch)? [[**H160:**]] A single worry makes me falter (:H160)- [[**H161 voc:**]] [= H154 vari]; that my merit has brought you too little gain (:H161 voc)! [[**H161 orch**]] [[**H161 >>>:**]] What gods have taught me I gave to you: a bountiful store ["Hort"—Hoard!] of hallowed runes ["heiliger Runen reichen Hort"]; but the maidenly source of all my strength (:H161) (H150:) was taken away by the hero to whom I now bow my head (:H150). [[**H160 orch**]] [[**H160:**]] Bereft of wisdom [[**H160 orch**]] but filled with desire; [[**H160 orch**]] rich in love yet void of strength, I beg you not to despise the poor woman [[**H161:**]] who grudges you naught but can give you no more (:H161)! (H159 orch)
>
> **Siegfried:** You gave me more, o wondrous woman, [[**H161:**]] than I know how to cherish ["als ich zu wahren weiss," i.e., than I know how to keep, or guard] (:H161): [[**H161 orch**]] [[**H160:**]] Chide me not if your [[**H161 orch:**]] teaching has left me untaught (:H160; :H161)!

Another major new motif H160 has been introduced in the prelude. Cooke recognized this beautiful motif ("Brünnhilde as Siegfried's Mortal Wife") as part of a family of musically related motifs expressing the concept of man's inspiration by woman, which include H7, H21, and H94. I explained previously that "Woman's Inspiration" doesn't fully capture this family's essence, though H160 represents Brünnhilde's inspiration of Siegfried's heroic deeds (of art). H7 was introduced in R.1 as one of the motifs expressing the Rhinedaughters' cruel, mocking seduction of Alberich, and H21 at its inception in R.2 represented Fricka's futile effort to sustain Wotan's fidelity by offering him the domestic tranquility of their new home Valhalla, so he wouldn't seek romantic adventures outside the home. But Brünnhilde is inspiring Siegfried to leave their home to undertake adventures, and asks what value her love could have if it didn't serve this purpose. H94 invokes Sieglinde's apostrophe to Brünnhilde's loving intervention to save the as-yet-unborn Siegfried, "Sublimest Wonder" (so-called "Redemption by Love Motif"), introduced in V.3.1 and not heard again until the *Ring*'s finale in T.3.3. Cooke interpreted the "new adventures" which Brünnhilde inspires Siegfried to undertake as merely that, heroic adventures. But the only adventure we'll witness him undertake (besides, obviously, his journey to Gibichung Hall, where he'll meet the agents of his demise, the Gibichungs Hagen, Gunther, and Gutrune) is his unwitting abduction of his own true love and muse Brünnhilde to give her away as wife to his new blood-brother Gunther. Siegfried will commit this atrocity under the influence of a spell cast by Hagen's potion H165. The only candidate for an heroic adventure, inspired by Brünnhilde, which Siegfried undertakes in *Twilight of the Gods*, isn't strictly a heroic deed, but rather, the performance of a song narrating the story of his heroic life for his audience, the Gibichung hunting party, prompted by Hagen's question, how did Siegfried come to understand the songs of the Woodbirds. We can interpret Siegfried's narrative song as a heroic action since it's the tale of Siegfried's heroic adventures in the past, the meaning of his life. This, we'll learn, is truly the deed of art his muse Brünnhilde inspired him to undertake.

Brünnhilde has defined her love for Siegfried as having no other purpose than to inspire such adventures, for she's asked, accompanied by H160, what her love would be worth were it not to let him go forth to these new adventures. The purpose of her love for Siegfried is to inspire artworks which will redeem man's religious impulse from the threat posed by Alberich's Ring Curse of consciousness. Portentously, Brünnhilde expresses fear that her merit (as repository for Wotan's hoard of runes, and as Siegfried's muse of unconscious inspiration) has brought Siegfried too little gain, and her doubt is embodied in the next new motif H161. Cooke suggested H161 is a variant of H154 (Siegfried as Hoard of the World). Dunning disagrees, but I concur with Cooke. H161 represents the risk that Wotan's unspoken secret, his forbidden hoard of knowledge he imparted to Brünnhilde in his confession—which she imparts to Siegfried subliminally so he can draw unconscious inspiration from it—might be betrayed to the light of day. If this occurred Brünnhilde could no longer be Siegfried's muse of unconscious artistic inspiration. This is the explanation for her following comment, also accompanied by H161, that what the gods (Wotan's confession) taught her she gave to Siegfried, a bountiful hoard ("Hort") of hallowed runes. Brünnhilde adds, again with H161 sounding, that the maidenly source of all her strength was (now accompanied by H150) taken away by the hero to whom she now bows her head. Her strength's source is that she's the repository for Wotan's hoard of forbidden knowledge, and will become the safe haven for Alberich's Ring once Siegfried leaves its power in her safekeeping as the symbol of their loving troth, a wedding ring. Siegfried is now performing the role of co-keeper with Brünnhilde of Wotan's unspoken secret, though thanks to her he's wholly unconscious of his new status.

Wagner provided evidence for our reading in his prose draft of *Siegfried's Death*, his earliest version of the *Twilight of the Gods* (previously cited), in which Brünnhilde addresses Siegfried, now deceased, stating that "Of all my wisdom I must go lacking, for all my knowledge to thee had I lent ... ." [See 385W-{10-11/48} *Siegfried's Death*, PW Vol. VIII, p. 50; See also 381W] And in one instance Wagner said Brünnhilde sends Siegfried off to perform new deeds after teaching him secret lore which, interestingly, includes a warning about the deceit and treachery he'll meet in the outer world (recalling Mime's pretext for teaching Siegfried fear, that Siegfried's mother Sieglinde wished Mime to do so, and recalling also the Woodbird's warning against Mime's treachery): " ... he [Siegfried] marries her [Brünnhilde] with Alberich's ring, which he places on her finger. When the longing spurs him to new deeds, she gives him lessons in her secret lore, warns him of the dangers of deceit and treachery: they swear each other vows, and Siegfried speeds forth." [378W-{6–8/48} 'The Nibelungen Myth,' PW Vol. VII, p. 304]

But Siegfried is oblivious to any warnings Brünnhilde has taught him subliminally: he'll succumb to the world's cunning immediately after arriving at Gibichung Hall. However, we must consider the possibility that a long span of time has passed during the orchestral interlude (Siegfried's Rhine Journey) which follows, during which he's perhaps undertaken a series of adventures inspired by Brünnhilde prior to his final, fatal adventure at Gibich Hall, the main subject of *Twilight of the Gods*. If this is so, Siegfried may have had a series of successful adventures (have created and produced for a public a number of redemptive artworks inspired by his muse Brünnhilde) during this interregnum, which is suggested but not dramatized in the *Ring*. It's possible that Wagner dramatized this felicitous period in the inspired artist-hero Walther's life in *Mastersingers*. After all, in Wagner's essay "Epilogue to 'The Nibelung's Ring'" he described the plots of *Tristan* and *Twilight of the Gods* as virtually identical, describing them as essentially the same myth, while *Mastersingers* Wagner created as a virtual antithesis to *Tristan*, as Hans Sachs points out in *Mastersingers* when he tells Eva in Act Three that it's just as well he didn't woo Eva, as he might have suffered King Marke's fate from *Tristan*. In *Mastersingers*, unlike *Twilight of the Gods*, the artist-hero successfully creates and performs an unconsciously inspired artwork which offers his audience secular redemption.

Brünnhilde, noting (accompanied by H160) that she's bereft of wisdom and strength, yet rich in love and filled with desire, begs Siegfried not to despise her. But—accompanied now by both H161 and H160—Siegfried responds that the wondrous Brünnhilde has given him more than he knows how to cherish (keep, or guard), and he asks her not to chide him if her teaching (now accompanied by H161) has left him untaught. Siegfried hasn't only unwittingly described himself as beneficiary of the unconscious artistic inspiration granted him by his lover-muse, but has unwittingly foretold the plot of *Twilight of the Gods*. That Brünnhilde's teaching left him untaught follows from the fact that through her, his unconscious mind, Wotan's hoard of secret knowledge (identified moments ago with H161) influences Siegfried subliminally, i.e., she teaches him, but her teaching has left him untaught because he remains unconscious of it. Similarly, the Woodbird taught Siegfried the use he could make of the Tarnhelm and Ring, yet by the time he'd left Fafner's cave with these objects he'd forgotten their use. The Woodbird had taught Siegfried these things subliminally. And Siegfried in S.3.3 told Brünnhilde she'd taught him the meaning of fear, yet through her love he was able to forget it, as we heard the Woodbird tunes H137 and H138. As noted previously, we can trace this back to Wotan's relationship with Brünnhilde's mother Erda, from whom he learned the meaning of fear and also how to end it (their daughter Brünnhilde).

Siegfried unwittingly foretells the plot of *Twilight of the Gods* in his seemingly innocent remark that Brünnhilde gave him more (access to Wotan's unspoken secret) than he knows how to cherish (keep, or guard). Siegfried, the secular music-dramatist (Wagner), is now the sole authentic guardian of the religious mysteries (knowledge of the inner processes through which we humans involuntarily created our gods, to which Wagner claimed to have unique access). But, as Siegfried notes, since he remains unconscious of it, he doesn't know how to cherish, guard, or keep it. In other words, Siegfried unwittingly foresees he may one day innocently betray Wotan's unspoken secret, his hoard of knowledge, so that it rises as Alberich foresaw from the silent depths of our collective unconscious Brünnhilde, to the light of conscious day. This notion that Siegfried is destined to betray Wotan's unspoken secret to the light of day is embodied by H161. Wagner will dramatize this in T.2.5 when Brünnhilde, again accompanied by H161, expresses to Gunther and Hagen her anger at Siegfried for taking her knowledge away and betraying their love.

Now Brünnhilde asks Siegfried to honor their oath that they'll preserve the special love they share, i.e., that he'll preserve her function as his muse of unconscious artistic inspiration, so she can fulfill her sole purpose to inspire his heroic deeds of art. This is what she means when she tells him that if he'd bestow his love on her, he must be mindful only of himself and his exploits, i.e., his new adventures, a metaphor for the works of art she'll inspire him to create:

[pp. 285–6] **Siegfried:** ... (H160) one lesson I learned with ease: (H161 voc:) to be ever mindful of Brünnhilde (:H161 voc)! (H161 [as an orchestral explosion])

Brünnhilde: (H159 [H108] vari >>: [in a rhythmic, dance-like vari as heard in Siegfried's Rhine Journey]) If you'd bestow your love on me, be mindful only of yourself, be mindful of your exploits (:H159)! Recall the raging fire (H12/H108) through which you (H12/H108:) fearlessly passed—(H93a) ... (:H12/H108)—

Siegfried: (H161:) in order to win Brünnhilde (:H161)! (H108 vari) (...)

Brünnhilde: Recall the shield-clad woman (H76:) whom you found there deep in (:H76) (H87) sleep (H93a?:) and whose close-fitting helmet you loosed (:H93a?) –

Siegfried: (H161 >>> :) in order to waken Brünnhild' (:H161)!

Brünnhilde: (H160:) Recall the oaths that unite us; recall the trust that we place in each other (:H160); (H161) recall the (H160:) love for (H161:) which we (H160:; H?: [a painful, sustained note on "leben," i.e., "live," which follows]) live: (:H?) Brünnhilde then will burn for aye ["ever"] (H160 orch:; H93c voc?:) with holy fire in your breast (:H160 orch; H93c voc?)!—

(H143: She embraces Siegfried.)

As Brünnhilde asks Siegfried to recall the oaths which unite them, the trust they place in each other, and the love for which they live, we hear H161 and H160 alternating, reminding us that the unique love to which Brünnhilde alludes is the special Wagnerian redemptive love through which the artist-hero receives unconscious inspiration from his loving muse, through whom he can safely draw inspiration from Wotan's hoard of forbidden knowledge. But H161 also expresses the risk which underlies Brünnhilde's covert influence on Siegfried. The orchestra then highlights their embrace with H143, redemption of man's religious impulse (Wotan) by Wagner's unconsciously inspired secular art (the love which unites Wotan's heirs Siegfried and Brünnhilde).

Siegfried now gives Brünnhilde Alberich's Ring—oblivious to the fact (of which Siegfried is presumably ignorant) that it could only be forged by renouncing love—as her wedding ring, the symbol for their special Wagnerian love, in exchange for the subliminal runes she's taught him, and asks her to "… keep its power safe." How interesting it is that Siegfried should let slip that the Ring has "power" which needs to be kept safe! Siegfried forgot what the Woodbird told him of its power after retrieving it from Fafner's cave, because the Woodbird only imparted this knowledge of the Ring's "use" to him subliminally. Siegfried is repressing knowledge into his unconscious mind Brünnhilde, removing the risk it will rise to consciousness in him (just as Wotan did in making confession to Brünnhilde of his most bitter thoughts he daren't say aloud—i.e., consciously), in exchange for sublimation of this knowledge into inspired art:

> [p. 286] **Siegfried:** (H159 vari:) If, my dearest, I leave you here in the fire's hallowed guard, (H102 clarinet: He has removed Alberich's ring from his finger and now hands it to Brünnhilde.) in return for all your runes I hand this ring to you. (H17) (H93ab voc:) Whatever deeds I have done, their virtue it enfolds (:H93ab voc); (H47:; H159:) I slew a savage dragon that long had guarded it grimly (:H47; :H159). (H47) (H58a second frag voc?: [perhaps a hint of the Rhinedaughters' Lament for their stolen Rhinegold?]) Now keep its power safe (:H58a second frag voc?) in solemn token of my troth.
>
> **Brünnhilde:** (H17: rapturously putting on the ring) (H161/H76:) I covet it as my only wealth (:H17; :H161/H76). (H11:) For the ring now take my horse (:H11)! (H9) (H76:) As once, with me, he boldly clove the air in flight, with me he's lost that mighty power. (…) (H92 >> :) But wherever you lead him—be it through fire—(H159 vari/H92 [in the "Rhine-Journey" dance-like vari]) Grane will fearlessly follow … (:H159/H92)!

Siegfried proclaims that the Ring enfolds the virtue of all the heroic deeds he's performed, and he says more than he knows, because Alberich's Ring gave birth to Valhalla (H17ab>H18ab in R.1–2), and Alberich's threat to the gods inspired Wotan's longing for redemption from Alberich's Ring Curse, which is Siegfried's raison d'être. Siegfried knows nothing of this past history or of his true motive which is hidden even from him thanks to Brünnhilde, and the only instance of a heroic deed he's mentioned is his one great achievement in killing Fafner and taking his Ring, that heroic act which fulfilled the gods' need (Noth). By leaving the Ring's power safe under Brünnhilde's protection, it's as if Siegfried has symbolically restored the Ring to the Rhine where its waters will dissolve it and its curse, but only temporarily. A hint of the Rhinedaughters' lament for their stolen Rhinegold from R.4 (a fragment of H58a?) in Siegfried's vocal line heard at the moment Siegfried asks Brünnhilde to keep the Ring's power safe, seems to confirm this, but also looks forward to Brünnhilde's eventual restoration of the Ring to the Rhinedaughters. Brünnhilde, Siegfried's unconscious mind, is a surrogate Rhine because she neutralizes Alberich's Ring Curse of consciousness temporarily, which restoring the Ring to the Rhinedaughters will accomplish permanently (at least until the next *Ring* cycle begins). As Brünnhilde rapturously places Alberich's Ring on her finger she tells Siegfried, accompanied by both H161 and H76, that she covets it as her only wealth. This motivally identifies Alberich's Ring with the Hoard of knowledge Wotan acquired from Erda, which Siegfried is at risk of betraying to consciousness.

The notion that by leaving Alberich's Ring under Brünnhilde's protection Siegfried has found a surrogate Rhine to neutralize Alberich's Ring Curse is further confirmed by the sounding of H11 (the Rhinedaughters' joyful cry of "Heiajaheia! Heiajaheia!") and H9 ("Rhinegold Motif"), as Brünnhilde offers Siegfried her horse Grane in exchange for the Ring. However, the presence in this passage of a hint of H58a, as well as H11 and H9, and the transforming of other motifs into the dance-like form they'll take in Siegfried's upcoming Rhine Journey, may merely anticipate that journey. The flying Valkyrie horse Grane may be regarded as another metaphor for the feeling of transcendence which music gives us, which can be compared with the aesthetic joy the Rhinedaughters took in the pre-Fallen Rhinegold before Alberich stole and forged a Ring from it. It's noteworthy that Brünnhilde describes Grane as having lost his power to fly, because Wagner's theory of the music-drama requires that music in union with the drama sacrifice its freedom in order to attain the specificity of drama, of the word, in exchange for music lending drama and the word (Siegfried) ideal freedom. It's as if the Ring, in Brünnhilde's hands, has regained its pre-fallen innocence and been transformed back into the Rhinegold, so long as she keeps its power safe. The redemptive art Siegfried produces under Brünnhilde's spell will make his audience feel as if paradisal innocence has been restored.

Brünnhilde and Siegfried now sing their good-byes: Siegfried grants her credit for all the adventures he'll undertake inspired by her love, and they figuratively exchange identities, so that wherever one is, both are:

[pp. 286–7] Siegfried: (H76 vari:; H159:; H161:) Through your virtue alone shall I still undertake adventures (:H76 vari; :H159; :H161)? (H76) (H76:)

Is it you who'll choose my battles, you to whom all my victories redound? (H159 >>:) Upon your stallion's back, within the shelter of your shield (:H159) (H118 definitive:) no more do I think of myself as Siegfried, I am (H76:) Brünnhilde's arm alone (:H76; :H118)! (H161)

Brünnhilde: (H118:; H161:) If only Brünnhilde were your soul (:H118; :H161)!

Siegfried: (H161:) Through her my courage is kindled (:H161).

Brünnhilde: (H161:) So you yourself would be Siegfried and Brünnhilde (:H161:)?

Siegfried: Wherever I am, (H161 vari:) both will be safe (:H161 vari). (H118) [**Brünnhilde:** (...); **Siegfried:** (...)]

Brünnhilde: (... H118:) O holy gods, (H160:) hallowed kinsmen (:H118)! (H161:) Feast your eyes on this blessed pair (:H160; :H161)! (...) (H118:) Divided (:H118)—(H161:) they'll never part (:H161)! (H56 vari?) [Accompanied by a H118 vari and H161 vari, they hail each other goodbye: (...)]

Siegfried describes Brünnhilde as his unconscious mind, just as Wotan did when he acknowledged her as his Will, saying that with himself he communes when he communes with her, and that what he says to no one in words (because Brünnhilde is his Will), shall remain forever unspoken. For Siegfried says that through Brünnhilde's virtue alone he'll still undertake adventures, and that she'll chose his battles. This reminds us that Brünnhilde and her Valkyrie sisters once inspired Wotan's chosen heroes (H76) to martyrdom, so that after death the legacy they'd left could be enlisted in the ultimate fight to preserve Valhalla, man's religious impulse and ideals, from the reductive power of the scientific advancement of knowledge (Erda's objective knowledge, which Dark-Alberich and Light-Alberich, Wotan, accumulated through historical experience). Siegfried's unconscious mind Brünnhilde, rather than his conscious mind, chooses his battles and inspires him to adventures, because he's an unconsciously inspired artist-hero. And note, H161 (Wotan's secret hoard of knowledge, which Brünnhilde imparts subliminally to Siegfried but whose secret Siegfried is destined to betray) and H76, accompany Siegfried as he grants all credit for what he'll do in future to his muse Brünnhilde. Wagner meditated deeply on the nature of his unconscious artistic inspiration, and he felt that the more completely art is inspired involuntarily and unconsciously, like a dream, rather than through conscious calculation and taking audience's tastes, and one's personal finances, vanity, etc., into consideration, the greater, freer, more spontaneous and more sublime the art. But understanding, the kind of thinking Alberich does, and Wotan does too when he's objective, Wagner regarded as unfree: "... the artist confronting life: as long as he chooses, proceeds wilfully, he is unfree; only when he grasps the necessity of life, is he also able to portray it: then, however, he has no more choice, and consequently is free and true." [473W-{49–51 (?)} Notes for 'Artisthood of the Future' (unfinished), Sketches and Fragments, PW Vol. VIII, p. 352]

Wagner distinguished the art of music from the other arts on the probably spurious basis that he regarded music as uniquely unconsciously inspired. What he likely meant was that unlike the other arts which draw on concepts, dramatic situations, or images and activities taken from real life, music's true source of inspiration isn't so apparent, but remains hidden. Its link with the "mundane" and "everyday" isn't self-evident. His descriptions of the composer's procedure (as opposed to the allegedly more conscious creation by poet or painter), where the artist doesn't impose his aesthetic form but it's imposed on him by his inner vision, stemming from the mystic ground of the unconscious, make sense of Siegfried's declaration that Brünnhilde—taken as Wagner's metaphor for the language of the unconscious, music—chooses his battles (his artworks) for him. He said, for instance, that "... the great musician must always remain a complete enigma to us ..." because, while the great poets' creations are primarily a conscious act, "... where creation passes from a conscious to an unconscious act, i.e., where the poet no longer chooses the aesthetic Form, but it's imposed upon him by his inner vision ..." we find what characterizes the musician, whom Wagner added we can approach "... on the mystic ground of his unconsciousness." [763W-{9–12/70} 'Beethoven,' PW Vol. V, pp. 63–64; See also 418W-{9–12/49} 'The Artwork of the Future,' PW Vol. I, p. 73, 434W-{9–12/49} 'The Artwork of the Future,' PW Vol. I, pp. 110–111, 465W-{49–51 (?)} Notes for 'Artisthood of the Future' (unfinished), Sketches and Fragments, PW Vol. VIII, p. 345, and 466W-{49–51 (?)} Notes for 'Artisthood of the Future' (unfinished), Sketches and Fragments, PW Vol. VIII, p. 346]

When Siegfried adds that on her stallion's back, and protected by the shelter of her shield, he's ceased to be Siegfried but is Brünnhilde's arm alone, Wagner re-introduces H118 (Siegfried's Mission). H118 was introduced in S.1.1 in association with Siegfried's presumption that in restoring his lost link with his heroic Wälsung ancestors (or parents, to be literal), knowledge of which Siegfried's foster-father Mime had withheld from him, Siegfried was now free to cast aside Mime's claim of indebtedness, and emancipate himself from loathsome Mime to undertake heroic adventures in the wider world. There Siegfried would wield the newly re-forged Nothung, the sword which symbolizes the heritage of genius dedicated to restoration of lost innocence. Brünnhilde holds for Siegfried knowledge of his true identity as Wotan, which includes Wotan's lower, prosaic self, Mime, the very aspect of Wotan's character from which Brünnhilde frees Siegfried's conscious mind. Brünnhilde gave Wotan a new identity as Siegfried, so Siegfried isn't a complete "self" without his muse Brünnhilde, who knows for him his true identity as Wotan and, by extension, as a Nibelung. For H118 is based on H112, Mime's Starling Song, in which Mime reminded Siegfried of all he owes Mime. Similarly, H17ab (Alberich's Ring), the basis for H18ab (the first two segments of the Valhalla Motif), recalls all that the gods owe Alberich.

Considering Siegfried's and Brünnhilde's description of themselves as one self (Brünnhilde is after all his unconscious mind), Wagner, in a revelatory moment of self-awareness, described his unconscious artistic inspiration as a "marriage of myself to myself." I found the following passage cited by Donington in his book *The 'Ring' and its Symbols*, and it has always stimulated deep reflection on the metaphorical significance of the relationship of the heroes to the heroines in Wagner's three canonic romantic operas, and four music-dramas: "I had been distressingly but ... decidedly disengaging myself from the world; everything in me had turned to negation and rejection; even my artistic creativeness was distressing to me, for it was longing with an insatiable longing to replace that negation, that rejection, by something affirmative and positive, the marriage of myself to myself ('sich-mir-vermählende')." [657W-{9/18/58}Letter to Mathilde Wesendonck: Quoted by Robert Donington in his *Wagner's 'Ring' and its Symbols*; p. 152]

And so, riding on Grane's (music's) back, and protected by Brünnhilde's shield, Siegfried rides off on his famous journey down the Rhine, where he'll finally come to shore at the Gibichung Kingdom, Wagner's archetype for the modern State, essentially secular but still holding on to the old forms, the worship of the gods, to undertake his new adventures of art inspired by his muse Brünnhilde. Siegfried is inspired now by feeling alone, not thought. But his ultimate source of inspiration is Alberich's forging of his Ring of human consciousness from the Rhinegold, and Wotan's (man's) futile quest to preserve our religious longing for transcendent value in the face of Alberich's advancement of conscious knowledge (through Wotan's—Light-Alberich's—world-wandering in quest of knowledge, which ultimately produces Alberich's son and proxy Hagen). Siegfried the secular artist-hero is the unwitting pawn of historical man's desperate quest to restore an innocence forever lost. So he's journeying now out into the world to the tune of H118, which recalls both Siegfried's self-proclaimed emancipation from Mime in the finale of S.1.1, and Siegfried's debt to him. This echoes the symbolism of H155ab's (derived I believe from H109, the motif which expresses Siegfried's contempt for Mime, and from H117, another motif which like H118 expresses Siegfried's feeling of joyous emancipation from Mime) carrying the emotional weight of the ecstatic climax of Siegfried's and Brünnhilde's love-duet in S.3.3.

This redemption by love through unconscious artistic inspiration we've just witnessed is as close as Wagner comes to positing a miraculous event, the supernatural, in the *Ring*, aside from the instances of magic which, frankly, we can best construe as metaphors for more mundane, natural or social phenomena. In a sense their love, Siegfried's unconscious artistic inspiration by his muse, is on an even higher plane than conventional religious belief in supernatural gods. In sum, the artist-hero Siegfried and his muse of inspiration Brünnhilde, considered as one person, the genius, enjoying the ecstasy of unconscious artistic inspiration, feels "as if" he's transcended all the bounds of time and space and causality. Siegfried owes his inspiration to a forgotten past we can trace back to earliest man's involuntary and unconscious creation—in a collective dream—of an antidote for fear and meaninglessness, the gods.

Siegfried now leaves Brünnhilde behind protected by Loge's ring of fire, Alberich's Ring and its power kept safe from use, and its curse rendered dormant, through her Wonder, as he embarks down the Rhine on his quest for adventure.

But what is his quest? It's his subliminal impulse to offer modern man redemption from the angst caused by the failure of religious faith in the face of man's advancement of knowledge. What follows is Siegfried's famous Rhine Journey, aside from the 'Ride of the Valkyries' probably the most popular and oft performed musical excerpt from the *Ring*:

> **[p. 288] [Siegfried's Rhine Journey:]** (...) H161/H76/H159:; H118 vari: [in an even more emphatic vari] ... Siegfried disappears with his horse down behind the rocky promontory ... . H160 >>: (...) H160. Siegfried's horn is heard from below. H108: (...) H108. H160: (...) Her [Brünnhilde's] joyful smile indicates that she can see the hero as he merrily goes on his way: H39 vari: [expressing great tragedy]. H155ab:; H117 varis? [is this H155b?] :; H108 >> : At this point the curtain must be quickly lowered. H108 [in a playful, dance-like development]; H32B playful vari; H108/H32B mixed into H117? [perhaps H155ab] & H118: [a highly contrapuntal passage]; H2/H3; H53; H2/H3; H58a/H108/H14; H11 vari; H9 frag; H58b; H58c; H58d? [darkening and transforming into H15, then into H17, then into H35—played twice with trills]; H9 [complete but sad]; H9 [darkened and sadder]; H43ab)

There's something very playful, sportive, and dance-like in the opening minutes of Siegfried's Rhine Journey, in the unfettered exuberance with which Wagner juxtaposes motifs in counterpoint, which seems an expression of Siegfried's creative rapture as an artist, art being, according to Wagner, a profound form of play. It's as if this joyful conjuncture of motifs conveying Siegfried's intent to go out into the world and undertake great adventures (produce inspired works of art for an audience of his fellow men and women) expresses Wagner's notion that through music the composer becomes the Lord of Nature, because he can play with life itself, without suffering bad consequences. As Donington put it: "That is the advantage of an artistic experience; we pass through the gamut of human emotion, but not as literal participants. We learn from the experience without paying the heavy price which that lesson might cost us in a direct encounter." [Donington: p. 247] Or, as Wagner said (in a passage previously cited) when describing the creative joy of musical composition: "The joy of wielding this new power [music's power] turns ... to humour: all grief of Being breaks before this vast enjoyment of the play therewith ... ." [777W-{9–12/70} 'Beethoven,' PW Vol. V, p. 92] But Siegfried's Rhine Journey is an expression of his hubris, his wholesale ignorance of the tragic context within which he creates his art. Siegfried will not only suffer a tragic fate for his hubris, but will help bring it to pass.

H117 (or H155b?) and H118 recall Siegfried's feeling of freedom after learning Mime could stake no claim on him as he went out into the world on his own. H117 and H118 also remind us that Mime never succeeded in getting Fafner to teach Siegfried fear before he ran off to a life of adventure in the outer world (a lesson Mime described as essential if Siegfried was to survive in the cunning world). But Brünnhilde has taught him fear. H155ab recalls the ecstasy which brought Siegfried's loving union with Brünnhilde to its climax in S.3.3 We then hear a combination of H161, H76, and H159 in a festive mode. H160 stands for Brünnhilde's pride as Siegfried's muse in inspiring him to undertake these new adventures, the sole purpose for which she lives, and H161 reminds us that Brünnhilde holds for Siegfried his true source of inspiration, Wotan's hoard of knowledge, from whose ill effects she protects him, but whose secret Siegfried is doomed to betray. H39, in a very tragic, dark variant, informs us that love is again under threat, just as it did at its inception during the transition from R.1–2, when Wotan and Loge visited Alberich's realm of terror Nibelheim, the product of Alberich's renunciation of love for power's sake. A dance-like, celebratory counterpoint of motifs lightens this painful mood briefly, comprised of Siegfried's youthful horncall H108, and a Loge motif H32B, combined with H117 (or H155b?) and H118. Siegfried then casts a boat off the bank of the Rhine, taking Grane with him: this is announced by H2 and H3, the first and second variants of the Primal Nature Motif H1, the second (H3) invoking the Rhine's flowing. Then suddenly we hear H53 (Twilight of the Gods), and are brought back to reality: this is the whole point of this final *Ring* drama.

As Siegfried makes his way up the Rhine we hear a new combination of H58a, H108, and H14 (The Rhinedaughters' joyous swimming), which is somehow overwhelmingly moving. H58a calls to mind the Rhinedaughters' first lament for their lost Rhinegold. The poignancy of this moment in the Rhine Journey is that Siegfried will never return the Ring to them, not even when they plead with him in person. Then we hear Rhinedaughter music from scene one of *Rhinegold*, H11 (the Rhinedaughters' joyous cry of "Heiajaheia! Heiajaheia!"), and also H9 (the "Rhinegold Motif"), both expressing the Rhinedaughters' aesthetic delight in the gold. The orchestra then sounds the remainder of their lament from R.4, H58bc. However, as H58c ends it darkens and is transformed first into H15 (World-Mastery), then H17 (Ring), and finally into H35 (Loveless), recalling the sequence of events in R.1 when Alberich, thwarted in love, decided to call the Rhinedaughters' bluff, renounce love, steal the Rhinegold, and forge a Ring of power to rule over a loveless world. H9 (Rhinegold) then sounds several times, its harmony continually darkened and its mood growing sadder. Just before the introduction of new motifs from *Twilight of the Gods* which represent two members of the Gibichung Clan (Hagen and his half-brother Gunther), we hear a powerful version of H43ab (Power of the Ring), expressing the Ring's power to overthrow our hubris and puncture our illusions about ourselves.

What Siegfried's Rhine Journey tells us is that his ignorance of his situation and of his true identity is the reason he's a fearless hero, and that his ignorance is irrevocably leading him unwittingly to disaster, a fact expressed in the dark and tragic transformation of motifs heard in his Rhine Journey as we approach the opening of T.1.1 on the shores of the Rhine at Gibichung Hall. I take Siegfried's Rhine Journey to be Wagner's motival metaphor for the collective history of art which, since the Renaissance, had gradually been freeing itself from its religious affiliation and becoming more secular, branching out into the world of men without the protection or disadvantages of faith. This process culminated, according to Wagner's theory of history, in the Wagnerian music-drama, which will be figuratively represented in Siegfried's narrative of the story of his life, explaining how he came to understand the meaning of Woodbirdsong, in T.3.2.

TWILIGHT OF THE GODS ≠ ACT ONE, SCENE ONE

(GIBICHUNG HALL)
HAGEN, GUNTHER, AND GUTRUNE

As we're being introduced to the Gibichungs, we hear the first of the Gibichung Motifs H162ab belonging to Hagen, Gunther's and Gutrune's half-brother. All three siblings share a mother, Grimhilde, whom Alberich (as Wotan told Brünnhilde in his V.2.2 confession) previously wooed with gold, so he could sow the seed of his envy, spite, and resentment ("Neid") in her womb, and give birth to his agent of vengeance who'll fulfill his Ring Curse, his son Hagen. Cooke demonstrated that H162 is in the family of Gibichung Motifs which includes H167 (False Friendship), H168ab (Gutrune), and H181 (the Gibichung Horncall). Gunther's Motif H163 is heard next, and Dunning agrees with me that it seems to owe something to the Power of the Gods Motif H123. This would make sense because Gunther is, as a mortal ruler, a sort of earthly Wotan, his society exemplifying the gods' divine authority, but it's also through Hagen's influence on Gunther and Gutrune that the twilight of the gods will be brought about, and H123 will be associated more and more with the waning power of the gods and their ultimate doom. There also seems to be an echo of the second segment of Mime's Motif of False Friendship to Siegfried H140b in it as well. However, Cooke suggested that Gunther's Motif H163 arises out of the last three notes of H52 (Erda's knowledge), and therefore placed it in the family of heroic motifs associated with the Valkyries and Wälsungs. But this motif family ought not to include Gunther: he's no hero since he depends on Siegfried to do for him what he hasn't the courage or strength for, and his claim to heroism is mocked by Brünnhilde in T.2.5, accompanied by music which seems to hint at the heroic Wälsung heritage Gunther lacks.

The final measures of Siegfried's Rhine Journey transition into a new scene at Gibichung Hall on the Rhine, where the Gibichung king Gunther and his sister Gutrune hold court, and their half brother Hagen (common mother Grimhilde, Gunther's and Gutrune's father Gibich, Hagen's father Alberich) is an astute and respected advisor to the throne (like Friedrich in *Lohengrin*). Gunther's sole concern is his honor and glory: we recall Wotan's apostrophe to the gods' new abode in the opening moments of R.2: "... manhood's honour, boundless might redound to endless renown":

[pp. 288–9] ([[H162 orch:]]; [[H163 orch—in the bass:]] [Possibly a H123 vari?] The hall of the Gibichungs on the Rhine. (...) Gunther and Gutrune sit enthroned to one side ... . Hagen is seated in front of the table. [[H162 orch]])

Gunther: Now hearken, Hagen! [[**H163 end frag orch:**]] Tell me, hero (:H163 end frag orch)! [[**H163 orch>>:**]] Do I sit here in splendour by the Rhine, Gunther, worthy of Gibich's fame (:H163 orch)? (H163 frag orch)

Hagen: [[**H162 orch>>:**]] You who are said to be freeborn I deem to be worthy of envy ["Neiden"] (:H162 orch): [[**H163 orch:**]] she who bore us brothers both, the lady Grimhild, (H17:) gave me to know the reason why (:H163 orch; :H17).

Gunther: (H163 varis: [developing in an extraordinarily noble fashion]) I envy you: don't envy me! If I fell heir to the first-born's ways, (H163 end frag:) wisdom was yours alone (:H163 end): (H163 vari >>>:) ... I merely praise your sound advice (H162:) when I ask you about my fame (:H163; :H162). (H173b end frag)

Hagen: (H162 >>:) Then I blame my advice since your fame is still poor: (H22 vari, on clarinet) (H163 vari:) for worthy goods I know of that the Gibichung's not yet won (:H163 vari). [**Gunther:** (...)] (H163 vari:) In summer's ripe strength I see Gibich's line, you, Gunther, unwed, you, Gutrune, without a husband (:H163 vari). (...)

Gunther: (H163 vari >>:) Whom would you have me woo that it should serve our fame (:H163 vari)? (H163 frag)

Hagen: (H76 frag:) I know of a woman, (H76:) the noblest in the world (:H76):—(H33 vari—flutes:) high on a fell her home (:H33 vari on flutes); (H137b frag:) a fire burns round her hall (:H137b frag): only he who breaks through the fire (H138b) may sue for Brünnhilde's love. (H138b)

Gunther: (H76:) Is my courage equal to that (:H76)? (H163 end frag)

Hagen: (H162:; H123 vari descending?:) A man yet stronger is fated to win her (:H162; :H123 vari descending?). (...) Siegfried, the Wälsungs' offspring—he is the strongest of heroes. (H70 >>:) A twin-born pair, impelled by love (:H70), Siegmund and Sieglinde bore the truest of sons: (H116) (H116:) he who waxed mightily in the wildwood (:H116)—him would I have as Gutrune's husband.

Wagner described the Gibichungs as representing hypocritical society, the Establishment, much like that of which Hunding was the examplar, ordered by, and content with, strict laws and customs and traditional aspirations, and for that reason little inclined to self-reflection. Their kingdom is a sort of earthbound Valhalla, a society which pays tribute to the gods and obeys divine law: "We now enter a new world, pass from the boundless realms of nature into a settled, ordered society governed by strict laws of custom." [887W-{6–8/76} WRR, pp. 119–120] Metaphorically, the gods can be taken to mean man's religious heritage, and adherence to law and custom bespeaks a society ruled by the old norms of establishing quiet and order at the cost of human individuality and the free evolution of thought. But the mere existence in such a society of a Siegfried (an artist-hero who by definition is an extraordinarily individualistic and creatively gifted personality) and a Hagen (Wagner's metaphor for the cynical and skeptical, scientific and secular spirit of the modern age, destined eventually to overthrow adherence to religious faith and the values engendered by it) tells us that this is society transitioning to modernity. Gibichung society is typical of most societies up until, and including, modern times. As Wagner put it (in a passage previously cited), those sold on the value-system of such a society are already among the dead (never having truly lived), while vibrant life is the sole property of a few enlightened and/or gifted individuals capable of free self-expression and unafraid of the new. [1114W-{1/8/82} CD Vol. II, p. 786]

Gunther's preoccupation, like that of virtually all those who subscribe to the values of such a society, is to establish his power and honor and glory among his fellow men. His motive is egoistic self-aggrandizement. Hagen cunningly encourages this aspect of Gunther's character in his answer to Gunther's question whether Gunther is worthy of his father Gibich's fame on the Rhine. With subtle cruelty he notes Gunther, said to be freeborn, is worthy of envy, a fact the lady Grimhilde, their common mother, could well explain, as we hear H17 (Alberich's Ring Motif). We're reminded both by Hagen, and motivally, of what Wotan told Brünnhilde during his confession, that Alberich had won a woman's favors with gold who would give birth to the agent of Alberich's envy (his desire for revenge against the gods through his Ring Curse), Hagen. Gunther's mother Grimhilde, in other words, willingly prostituted love for power or money, and so Hagen has covertly mocked the heritage he shares with Gunther. This makes the extraordinarily noble variant of Gunther's motif H163 heard next, as Gunther lauds Hagen as having inherited what Gunther lacks, wisdom, feel all the more ironic as this dialogue proceeds. Wagner is granting us insight into the mundane, discreditable but hidden preconditions for the world's great show and ideals, and even our most sublime emotions.

Gunther as the first-born and true-born (Hagen is in effect a half-breed, son of a Nibelung father, Alberich) rules, but Gunther acknowledges his half-brother Hagen is the wiser of the two. Hagen is the intellect among the Gibichungs, just as his father Alberich was among the Nibelung dwarfs, an objective intellect unswayed by the consolation of illusions which motivate Gunther and his sister Gutrune (and Wotan). Hagen contradicts what he just told Gunther: there is something Gunther doesn't yet possess, lacking which his fame is still poor. Hagen notes Gunther and Gutrune remain unmarried, and suggests Gunther woo the noblest woman in the world. As he describes how Brünnhilde lives high on a mountaintop surrounded by a ring of fire, motifs such as H76 and H33 remind us of her Valkyrie status and of Loge's fire, but Hagen reproduces the description of Brünnhilde which the Woodbird gave to Siegfried word for word, repeating her formulaic expressions, and is even accompanied by the Woodbird's motifs H137b and H138b as he informs Gunther that only one who breaks through the ring of fire can sue for her love. Hagen is privy to knowledge hidden from others. Gunther doubts his own courage is equal to this, and Hagen responds that, indeed, only Siegfried the Wälsung (H70) is capable of performing this feat. Hagen also suggests Siegfried as a husband for Gutrune. Though what seems a conventional socio-politico-economic marriage alliance is afoot, we know Brünnhilde isn't merely the noblest or most beautiful of women, but that she's our collective unconscious, our muse of religious revelation and unconscious artistic inspiration. She possesses forbidden knowledge of the religious and artistic mysteries, and is the last refuge of dying religious faith. In Hagen's suggestion Gunther would attain the highest glory and fame by possessing her we might surmise that Hagen, the embodiment of Alberich's greed for loveless, worldly power which only objective knowledge in science and technology and politics can offer us, is effectively telling Gunther this power can best be obtained by knowing himself and his world fully, without reserving any privileged realm of the imagination and heart which is (or is at least considered to be) irreducible to reason. Alberich can only restore his lost Ring power if he (reincarnate as Hagen) discredits the beliefs, values, and refined feelings we humans have traditionally projected onto gods and heroes. But Gunther will initially see in this instead an opportunity to enhance his transcendent value.

The ultimate expression of the Rhinedaughters' promise to Alberich that if he renounced love and forged a Ring from the Rhinegold he could attain world-mastery, is the notion that we can only fully tap Nature's potential power, and only thoroughly exploit our fellow men for the sake of power, if we cast aside all moral reservations and all metaphysical illusions of our exalted human status. The most exalted religious faith and the most sublime art are presumably only of value if we don't examine them objectively too closely (this was the whole point of Lohengrin's prohibition on divulging the secret of his identity and origin to Elsa, or anyone else), since they satisfy our wish for the unattainable, rather than the requirements of reason and objective knowledge of the truth. The ultimate goal of science, technology, and real-politick is supreme power (over ourselves and our world), but man's emotional attachment to his religious, ethical, and artistic illusions remains a stumbling block to attaining it. Hagen isn't interested in furthering Gunther's fame, glory, or exalted view of his value, but interested solely in discrediting Siegfried's and Brünnhilde's love (religious sentiment's last refuge), and in re-possessing his father Alberich's Ring, so Hagen can supplant religion, morality, and art with the true source of power in this world, objective knowledge, and take possession of our collective mind for power's sake.

After learning from Hagen of Siegfried's heroic pedigree and achievements, both Gunther and Gutrune are doubtful anything can be done to prevail upon Siegfried either to win Brünnhilde for Gunther's sake, or to wed Gutrune. So Hagen offers a solution: he reminds Gutrune of a potion which will simultaneously make Siegfried forget any woman he's ever known, and love the first woman he sees, after drinking it:

[pp. 289–91] **Gutrune:** (H163 vari voc:) What was the feat that he performed so bravely that he is called the most glorious hero (:H163 vari voc)?

Hagen: (H47 vari:) Outside Envy-Cave ["Neidhöhl"] the Nibelung hoard (:H47 vari) (H17:) was guarded by a giant dragon (:H17); (H134 vari:)

Siegfried ... slew the beast with conquering sword (:H134 vari). From such a tremendous feat (H116:) the hero's fame has sprung (:H116).

Gunther: (... H15 vari:) I've heard of the Nibelung hoard: does it not hide ["birgt"] the most coveted treasure (:H15 vari)? (H17 vari)

Hagen: (H17: [darkened]) He who knew how to use it (:H17) (H35:) could bend the world ... to his will (:H35). (H9)

Gunther: And Siegfried (H9) won it in fair fight?

Hagen: (H43a:) The Nibelungs are now his slaves (:H43a). (H43b; H56ab vari)

Gunther: And he alone could win Brünnhilde?

Hagen: (H76:) Only to him would the fire yield (:H76).

Gunther: (H163 vari: ...) (...) Why make me long for what I can't gain by force? (H163 vari >>: ... H40A:; **[[H165 frag orch:]]** [= H40B vari] ... Hagen stops him with a mysterious gesture ... .)

Hagen: (H162:; H160?:; H163 vari:) If Siegfried brought the bride back home wouldn't Brünnhilde then be yours?

Gunther: ... (H163 vari >>:) What would force the carefree man to woo the bride for me (:H163 vari)?

Hagen: ... Your entreaty would ... force him (H161 voc:) if Gutrune bound him first (:H161 voc).

Gutrune: **[[H164 voc >>:]]** [Possibly a H22 vari?] You mock me, wicked Hagen! How should I ever bind Siegfried (:H164 voc)? If he's the world's most glorious hero, (H163 vari:; H22?:) the loveliest women on earth would have wooed him long ago (:H163 vari; :H22?).

Hagen: (H164 orch: ... **[[H164 voc:]]** Recall the potion in the chest; ... trust in me who obtained it (:H164 voc): **[[H164 orch:]]** it will bind to you in love (:H164 orch) (H35 voc:) the hero for whom you long (:H35 voc). (...) If Siegfried were to enter now (H56ab) **[[H164 vari voc:]]** and taste the herbal drink (:H164 vari voc), (H40A:) he'd be forced to forget (H22) that he'd seen a woman before you (:H40A), (H22) **[[H165 orch:]]** [= H40B vari] that a woman had ever come near him (:H165 orch).

Hagen informs Gunther and Gutrune that Siegfried's fame sprang from killing the Serpent/Dragon who guarded the Nibelung Hoard, and taking possession of that Hoard (Ring) which, if one knew how to use it, would bind the world to his will, as we hear both H17 (Ring) and H35 (Loveless). Hagen is saying in effect that Siegfried the artist-hero has taken aesthetic possession of that power of conscious thought, and knowledge, which in the hands of an objective thinker like Alberich or Hagen would grant the power to dominate the physical and human worlds lovelessly. Hagen, rightful heir to his father Alberich's Ring, has been dispossessed and disinherited by Wotan (man's religious impulse) and by Siegfried and Brünnhilde (man's religious impulse as expressed in secular art). If

Hagen regained his rightful legacy, the Ring, he'd employ its objective power to overthrow the usurpers who depend on self-deception for their happiness, and to establish a purely science-and-Nature-based worldview and world-order, which grants special power to those with knowledge of the truth and the ruthlessness to exploit it at all costs. Hagen is Wagner's metaphor for the modern, secular, scientific world-view which strives to solve all mysteries, leaving nothing in Nature or human nature free from human reason's power.

The answer to Gunther's question whether Siegfried won the Ring from Fafner in fair fight, is that Siegfried didn't. Siegfried, incarnation of Wotan's (collective man's) Loge-inspired need to deceive himself about the truth and replace it with a consoling illusion, has employed unwitting cunning to win the Ring from Alberich and keep it out of his hands by leaving it safely in Brünnhilde's hands. But this has provided Hagen with his opportunity: he can exploit Siegfried the music-dramatist's unique access to the inner processes of unconscious religious revelation and artistic inspiration (his muse Brünnhilde), so Siegfried will unwittingly betray the unspoken secret of which he's the unwitting guardian. What Hagen must do is find a weakness in the love which Siegfried and Brünnhilde share, an Achilles Heel in the inspired art to which their loving union gives birth. Hagen will accomplish this by manipulating Siegfried into giving his muse of unconscious artistic inspiration Brünnhilde and her secrets to Gunther, the artist-hero Siegfried's figurative audience, instead of a truly redemptive work of art which would keep Wotan's unspoken secret, and into wedding a false muse Gutrune who'll inspire Siegfried to make a public display of the profoundest secrets of the music-dramatist's aim, to betray the contents of his unconscious mind Brünnhilde to the light of day.

Hagen mysteriously addresses Gunther's doubt that he can win the hand of the noble woman to whom alone Siegfried's courage can gain access. He intimates (anticipated by the orchestra, which plays H40A (Tarnhelm), followed by a fragment of its variant, the new "Hagen's Potion Motif" H165, as Gunther paces in frustration) that if Siegfried brought Brünnhilde back to Gunther, Brünnhilde would belong to him. Gunther wonders how Hagen could persuade Siegfried to do this, and Gutrune, introducing another new motif H164 ("Seduction"), protests that such a hero as Siegfried has his pick of any woman he wants and would scarcely be interested in her. H164 is derived from the first of the two motifs associated with Freia as the goddess of love, H22. H22 is generally described as a symbol for the sensuous aspect of love, but it's also the basis of H149, the motif first heard as Siegfried was waking Brünnhilde in S.3.3.

Hagen provides the solution to this seemingly insurmountable problem. He notes, accompanied by H161 (the hoard of runes Wotan imparted to Brünnhilde, and she imparted subliminally to Siegfried, which Siegfried told her had left him untaught, and which he doesn't know how to guard), that Siegfried will abduct Brünnhilde for Gunther if Gutrune binds him first. Hagen reminds Gutrune that a potion he obtained will bind Siegfried to her in love if he drinks it, and make him forget any other woman. At this point we hear H35 (Loveless) and H22 (Freia's sensuous love) implying that Gutrune will bind Siegfried to her through sexual seduction, and therefore lovelessly rather than lovingly. While Hagen describes the potion's effects we again hear H40A (Tarnhelm) transform into H165, but now as the definitive Hagen's Potion Motif, which is a variant of H40A via H40B (Tarnhelm's Transformations). This motif family originated in Loge's H33 (Loge's Transformations), which is also the basis of H105 (Magic Fire Music—Loge's ring of fire, the veil of illusion which protects Brünnhilde from all men except Siegfried). Wagner has drawn our attention to H165's genealogy by having H40A segue into its variant H165. This motif family is an evolving symbol for Wagner's artistic "Wonder," his substitute in modern secular times for dying religious faith, and especially for the notion that what transmuted illusion into truth (the Tarnhelm of imagination) can also transform illusion back into the hidden truth from which it sprang. Just as Loge manipulated Alberich into using the Tarnhelm to involuntarily place it, the Ring, and his Nibelung Hoard in the gods' hands, so Hagen will now manipulate Siegfried to use the Tarnhelm to place these sources of power in Hagen's hands and thus into Alberich's hands.

Nattiez presented his hypothesis in his book *Wagner Androgyne* [Nattiez: pp. 84–86] that Gutrune is Wagner's metaphor for Italian opera and/or French Opéra Comique. Wagner called modern Italian opera a "wanton" who (like Gutrune) doesn't feel real love, and described French Opéra Comique as a "coquette" who enjoys men's adoration without feeling love. [See 488W-{50-1/51} *Opera and Drama*, PW Vol. II, pp. 112–113] Brünnhilde will accuse Gutrune of being Siegfried's "wanton" in T.3.3, and as Nattiez pointed out, there's evidence that some of the music Wagner wrote for Gutrune is modeled on music from French Opéra Comique (he traced some of the Rhinedaughters' singing to Parisian Grand Opera). Nattiez's thesis is the following: after noting clues in Gutrune's music that she's Wagner's metaphor for a lighter sort of operatic music, such as that of the Parisian Opéra Comique, he asks: "What role does Siegfried play here? He is the victim of Alberich's son Hagen, who is thus at least a half-Jew ... . It is a half-Jew, therefore, who lures Siegfried into the arms of French opera." [Nattiez: p. 87] Nattiez speculated that Siegfried's seduction by Gutrune (Opéra Comique), under the influence of the allegedly half-breed Jewish impresario Hagen, represents the music-dramatist Siegfried's betrayal of his true nature, symbolized by a properly loving relationship between poetic-drama (Siegfried) and music (Brünnhilde), essential for the creation of Wagner's mature music-dramas, for the sake of a lighter form of traditional opera represented by Gutrune, in which cheap effects, sensuous melody lacking a loving relationship with the drama, etc., would be the means to profit, fame, and fortune, rather than art for its own sake. Nattiez tells us that: "Siegfried ... perishes for having succumbed to the blandishments of a frivolous brand of opera." He adds that, Hagen having persuaded Siegfried to perform the role of an opera singer (in T.3.2) "... encouraged to perform his star turn ... ," (...) "... Siegfried is completely contaminated. He will be punished for having forgotten the woman with whom the poet could have achieved the perfect union of poetry and music," [Nattiez: p. 88] i.e., the music-drama. But Nattiez missed the main point: Siegfried doesn't betray his true identity as a music-dramatist by performing an Opéra Comique at

Hagen's behest, because Hagen in T.3.2 will prompt Siegfried to tell the Gibichung hunting party how he learned the meaning of birdsong, i.e., Hagen asks Wagner to explain how he became a music-dramatist, with his unique insight into the normally unconscious process of artistic inspiration. The narrative history of his past life which Siegfried will sing in T.3.2 at Hagen's behest is Wagner's metaphor for a performance of his redemptive artwork of the future, *The Ring of the Nibelung*, which recounts how he fell heir to dying religious faith's longing for redemption from truth and won his muse of inspiration.

There's one last difficulty not encompassed within Nattiez's thesis: he implies that Siegfried's seduction by Gutrune, under the influence of Hagen's potion, constitutes Siegfried's betrayal of authentic music-drama for the sake of trite satisfactions like cheaply won popularity with the audience and material profit, attainable through conventional operatic forms. But I believe Hagen's influence on Siegfried (Gutrune also being manipulated by Hagen, since he engineers all that she and Gunther do to trick Siegfried into serving their base needs) represents Siegfried's own (Wagner's own) impulse to present his innermost aesthetic intuition to an audience through his art, which ultimately was bound to betray the secret of unconscious artistic inspiration to his audience. Donington's Jungian interpretation of Hagen as Siegfried's shadow (as Dark-Alberich is Wotan's—i.e., Light-Alberich's—shadow), which represents a disreputable aspect of Siegfried's own character, has certainly influenced my reading, though Donington had no idea that Siegfried is Wagner's metaphor for Wagner in his role as a music-dramatist. It's not that Siegfried lowers his standard for operatic fare to produce a retro opera unworthy of an authentic music-dramatist, but rather, that he's too eager to share his innermost insights with his audience through a public performance of his authentically unconsciously inspired music-drama. But Nattiez was surely right to suggest that the sensuous music Wagner composed for Gutrune was inspired by the seductiveness of French opera. Wagner may have sought to make a similar musical impression in his Venusberg music he composed for his 1860 Paris version of *Tannhäuser*, and for Kundry and the flower-maidens in Klingsor's magic garden in *Parsifal*.

And then, (who would have thought!) Siegfried appears at Gibichung Hall on cue:

[pp. 291–2] **Gutrune:** (H164 orch: **||H168b voc?:||**) Might I only set eyes on Siegfried (:H164 orch; :H168b voc?)!

Gunther: How could we find where he is? (H50) (H162:; H108; H162; H163 frag: An off-stage horn is heard from the back on the right. Hagen listens. (…))

Hagen: (H108 >>:) When he rides out gaily in search of adventure, the world becomes a narrow pinewood. In restless chase he'll surely ride to Gibich's shores along the Rhine. [**Gunther:** (…)] (Horn closer, but still in the distance. H108. … (…) H162)

Gunther: (H163 vari:) The horn rings forth from the Rhine (:H163 vari). (H162; [[H181b orch]])

Hagen: (... H43a:) Hero and stallion on board a skiff (:H43a): (H93c voc?:) it is he who is blowing the horn so blithely (:H93c voc?). (H108: ... [[H166 orch:]] [= H39 vari/H58a/H108 combined with other motifs such as H11, H12, and H14, in an astonishingly moving passage]) (H58a voc/H108:) A leisurely stroke, as of idle hand, drives the boat headlong against the stream; (H11 vari/H56?/H108 >>>> :) only he who slew the dragon can boast such doughty strength in the sweep of the oar:—(H12/H108/H14) Siegfried it is: no other, surely (:H166 orch)! [**Gunther:** (...)] (H17 vari [as an orchestral explosion]) (...) ... Hoiho! Whither bound, you blithe-spirited hero?

Siegfried: ... To Gibich's stalwart son. (H163 vari)

Hagen: (H163 vari >>>> :) I bid you welcome to his hall (:H163 vari): (H163 vari: ...) (...) Put in to shore here!

That Siegfried would inevitably visit Gibichung Hall follows from the fact that the Gibichung society Siegfried visits in his search for adventure is an archetype for that society, still operating under the shadow of our religious heritage (man's futile and ill-fated quest for transcendent meaning), to which Siegfried presents the heroic deeds of art (adventures) which Brünnhilde has inspired him to undertake. Hagen's seemingly offhand remark that "when he rides out gaily in search of adventure, the world becomes a narrow pinewood," might well be a subtle evocation of Wagner's theory of the artistic "Wonder" through which his musical motifs distill a vast hoard of human experience, making what's widely dispersed in time and space present to us, here and now, through aesthetic intuition.

They listen more closely to Siegfried playing his horn in the distance and then spot a hero poling a skiff swiftly upstream toward Gibichung Hall. As Hagen describes how this hero easily poles his skiff upstream against the Rhine's natural current, we hear a remarkable, profoundly moving compound motif H166 comprised of H39/H58a/H108. Hagen concludes from the hero's strength he can only be the dragon slayer Siegfried, as H166 transitions to H11/H108, and then to H12/H108/H14, recalling the Rhinedaughters and Siegfried's tragic-heroic destiny as the hero to whom Wotan looks to redeem the gods from Alberich's Ring Curse, which will doom both Siegfried and Wotan. This profound motival meditation on Siegfried's tragic fate culminates in an orchestral explosion of a H17 (Ring) variant after Hagen recognizes this hero as Siegfried. This music is immensely moving and manically urgent in itself, but the motif combination evokes a tragic pathos stemming from the motifs' allusions to various aspects of the drama, which are quite extensive. H39 calls to mind the tragic destiny of love within Alberich's loveless world, and H58a, H11, and H12 recall both the Rhinedaughters' primal singing and dancing in celebration of the pre-Fallen Rhinegold, and their lament for its loss after Alberich renounced love to win the power inhering in a ring made from it, expressing their longing for it to be restored to them. H108, Siegfried's Youthful Horncall, which moves us by virtue of its vitality, optimism, and youthful naiveté, is driving Siegfried's skiff towards the unsafe harbor of his own unwitting and involuntary self-betrayal. And the H17 variant recalls Alberich's Ring, the prime mover of all the events in the *Ring*. This music's utmost pitch of intensity grants us a premonition of Siegfried's inevitable failure to restore the Rhinedaughters' lost Rhinegold, and his fated doom at the hands of the agent of Alberich's vengeance, the embodiment of his Ring Curse (H50), Hagen. Siegfried is about to lose his innocence, i.e., his protective veil of unconsciousness of his hidden guilt, permanently, irrevocably, irredeemably. And this is because the music-drama which Siegfried will create is the ultimate expression of Alberich's Ring Curse, *The Ring of the Nibelung*.

TWILIGHT OF THE GODS : ACT ONE, SCENE TWO

(GIBICHUNG HALL)
HAGEN, GUNTHER, GUTRUNE, AND SIEGFRIED

Now Siegfried steps ashore at Hagen's invitation, his future hosts in the greatest suspense about what will transpire. Hagen, portentously, calls Siegfried by his name as he hails him, the much-loved hero, accompanied by a powerful statement of the Ring Curse H50:

[pp. 292–3] **Hagen:** (H50 voc/orch: [as an orchestral explosion]) Hail! Siegfried, much loved hero (:H50 voc/orch)! (H164; H93ab: (…))

Siegfried: (… H93a voc?:) Which of you is Gibich's son (:H93a voc?)?

Gunther: Gunther, I, whom you seek. (H163)

Siegfried: (H93a?:) I heard you praised far along the Rhine (:H93a?): Now fight with me, or be my friend.

Gunther: Think not of fighting: be welcome here!

Siegfried: (H164 frags: … H92: Where shall I shelter my horse?

Hagen: I'll offer him rest. (H50)

Siegfried: (turning to Hagen: H50 voc:) You called me Siegfried (:H50 voc): have you seen me before?

Hagen: (H93a?:) I knew you only by your strength (:H93a?).

Siegfried: (H92: …) Take good care of Grane! (H160 >>:) You never held the bridle (H161/H92 >>:) of a horse of nobler breed (:H161/H92; :H160).

(H92 in the bass: [some orchestral music expresses Grane's instinctively negative reaction to Hagen, pulling against the reins] Hagen leads the horse away.)

Siegfried offers a traditional, tribal challenge to his potential host Gunther, who hails Siegfried not as foe, but friend. Then Siegfried asks, significantly, where he can shelter his horse. Hagen offers to take Grane and give him rest, followed by the Ring Curse H50. If Grane's ability to fly is a metaphor for Brünnhilde as the embodiment of music (Grane lost this gift to lend his wings of musical inspiration to Siegfried's dramatic poetry, so to speak), Hagen's offer is ominous indeed: he's effectively capturing Siegfried's musical inspiration as Hagen will literally do when he manipulates Siegfried to unwittingly abduct and give away his own true love and muse Brünnhilde as bride to Gunther. We hear H50 again as Siegfried asks Hagen how he knows Siegfried's name, and Hagen answers, plausibly enough, that he knew Siegfried by his strength (by his perpetuation of Wotan's religious sin against the real, natural world, for, just as Wotan wanders the world, as he told Siegfried, against the wind, Siegfried poled his boat up the Rhine, against its natural current). We're reminded of the Flying Dutchman's oath sworn to Satan to round the Cape of Good Hope against contrary winds, for which hubristic act (his sin against Mother Nature's truth) he was cursed by Satan, to endlessly sail the seas (like Wotan the Wanderer on land) seeking redemption but never finding it. Reassured, Siegfried hands Grane over to Hagen, and, accompanied by the two primary T.P.B love-duet motifs, H160 (Brünnhilde's unconscious inspiration of Siegfried's art and his spur to present it to audiences), and H161 (Siegfried's premonition he'll betray Wotan's unspoken secret Brünnhilde keeps), tells Hagen he never held the bridle of a nobler breed. As Hagen tethers the resistant Grane it's as if Alberich had captured the Rhinedaughters and forced his will on them. We hear an orchestral struggle evoking Grane's instinctive repulsion toward Hagen.

Siegfried has now entered society as man and artist, and as he begins to sober up from the ecstatic, mystical experience of his unconscious artistic inspiration, Siegfried will start to wake up, becoming too conscious of who he is, ultimately too conscious of the hidden processes underlying his inspiration to draw any longer on his muse Brünnhilde for inspiration. Hagen, the agent of Siegfried's waking, embodies the scientific, secular, skeptical and ultimately cynical spirit of the modern world, intolerant of man's consoling illusions in religion, self-sacrificial morality, and art. Gunther offers Siegfried an official welcome to Gibichung Hall, introducing a new motif H167 ("False Friendship"), which, Cooke says, is in the same family of motifs which identifies the manipulative, conspiratorial Gibichungs, H162ab (Hagen), H168ab (Gutrune), and H181 (The Gibichung Horncall, which later heralds the tragic double wedding of Gunther with Brünnhilde, and Siegfried with Gutrune). The loose variant of H167 which develops as Gunther offers himself and all he possesses to Siegfried is, ironically, of the most poignant nobility, considering this is a message of false friendship, Gunther, Gutrune, and Hagen having conspired to exploit Siegfried:

[pp. 293–5] ([[H167 orch:]] At Gunther's invitation, Siegfried advances into the hall.)

Gunther: [[H167 loose vari orch/voc:]] [music of the greatest nobility and poignancy, and therefore irony, given Gunther's craven character and bad faith] Greet gladly, o hero, my father's hall; wherever you tread, whatever you see, now treat it as your own: yours are my birthright, lands and men—

by my body I swear the oath (:H167 loose/vari orch/voc)! (H167 voc:) Myself I give you as liegeman (:H167 voc)! (H167 orch)

Siegfried: I can offer you neither lands nor men, (H163 vari) nor a father's house and court: (H70:) I inherited only this body of mine (:H70); (H151 voc:) living, I waste it away (:H151 voc). (H129 counter melody from S.1.3:; H116/H38:) I've only a sword, (H56ab) which I forged myself—(H167:) by that sword I swear this oath (:H167)!—With myself I present it as part of the bond.

Hagen: (... H162/H45/H38 >>: [H162 on horn's high notes]) But the tale names you lord of the Nibelung hoard (:H162/H45/H38).

Siegfried: (... H41:; H38:) I'd almost forgotten the treasure, so little I treasure its barren worth (:H41; :H38). (H47:) I left it lying inside a cave, where a dragon used to guard it (:H47).

Hagen: (H38:) And did you take (H39 vari:) nothing from it (:H38; :H39 vari)?

Siegfried: (H38:) This metalwork piece, (H39 vari:) not knowing its power. (:H38; :H39 vari)

Hagen: (H38 vari:) I recognize the Tarnhelm, (H40B frag vari?:) the Nibelungs' artful ["künstliches"] device (:H38 vari; :H40B frag vari?): (H40A:) when it covers your head, it serves to change you to any shape (:H40A); (H40B:) if you want to go to the farthest spot, it transports you there in a trice (:H40B).—(H38) You took nothing else from the hoard?

Siegfried: (H15ab [H17ab compressed into a lyrical vari]) A ring.

Hagen: (H161:) You're keeping it safe (:H161)?

Siegfried: ... (H161 voc:) A glorious woman is keeping it safe (:H161 voc).

Hagen: (aside: H38 vari:) Brünnhild' (:H38 vari)!

Gunther: (H167 vari >> :) I want nothing, Siegfried, by way of exchange; I would give mere dross for your jewels if you took all my wealth ["Gut"] in return! I serve you gladly without reward (:H167).

This entire passage may be modeled on Mime's greeting of false friendship to Siegfried in S.2.3, whose characteristic motif was H140 (Mime's Wheedling Song of False Friendship). Whether or not there's a musical foreshadowing of Gunther's welcome to Siegfried in that earlier passage from S.2.2 (I believe there is), during which Mime greeted Siegfried with false friendship after Siegfried killed Fafner and took possession of Alberich's Ring and Tarnhelm, there's certainly a dramatic parallel, since in both instances people with ulterior, sinister motives, kept hidden from the hero Siegfried, intend to exploit him for their own self-aggrandizement, and in both instances, they plan to fool Siegfried into drinking a fateful potion that will bring their goals within reach. The primary difference is that the Woodbird told Siegfried that thanks to tasting the dead Fafner's blood Siegfried would be able to hear, as Mime speaks, what Mime is thinking in his heart, forewarning Siegfried of Mime's treachery. We're reminded that Wagner described his musical motifs as conveying the motives of his drama's protagonists. Though Siegfried was previously the beneficiary of the Woodbird's subliminal advice, he's not now forewarned of danger even though Brünnhilde imparted to him subliminally foreknowledge of the doom her mother Erda imparted to Wotan. Thanks to his ignorance of the truth (Brünnhilde's gift to him) he's oblivious to the reality of his situation, of threats that lurk. But in T.P.B he had a premonition he wouldn't be a good guardian of Brünnhilde's teaching (Wotan's hoard of runes), which had left him untaught. We're reminded that Tristan and Isolde, in the throes of their loving union (also a metaphor for unconscious artistic inspiration), were oblivious to the threat that the secret their love keeps in silence (Tristan's identity) within the womb of night, was going to be exposed to the light of day. Thanks to unconsciously inspired secular art's freedom from religious faith's fear of truth (Fafner), it will be blindsided by the rise to consciousness of the bitter truth it had unwittingly consigned to oblivion.

Gunther has virtually granted Siegfried the keys to his kingdom, placing himself, his home, his property, his legacy, in Siegfried's hands. It's implicit that Gunther, representative of society still under the spell of the old religion and the old morality predicated on belief in a divine order, and sentimentally attached to what Siegfried has to offer, a noble, heroic art which has preserved the sublimest, most ageless part of the old religion as feeling, is more liable to make Siegfried his heir than make Hagen his heir, even though Gunther the hypocrite is motivated by an egoism identical to that which compels all of Hagen's actions. But, like Wotan, Gunther lacks the courage of his convictions, for he has a more exalted sense of his dignity than is warranted by his authentic impulses. Alberich and his son Hagen differ from him and from Wotan in that they're prepared to live in an openly egoistic world without the kind of divided loyalty known to Gunther and Wotan, for they strive to proclaim objective truth and despise consoling illusions which satisfy heartfelt feeling. Just as previously Wotan tested Fafner to ascertain if man was prepared to overthrow religious faith for the sake of the practical advantages of atheistic materialism, and Fafner (religious faith's fear of truth) said he'd remain as he was without change, letting the truth and its power sleep, so now Gunther, modern man, has granted his favor to the idealistic artist-hero Siegfried rather than the man of objective, practical wisdom, Hagen, whose intellect Gunther openly acknowledges to be greater than his own. Hagen's birthright is still being denied him, because collective man still wishes to smuggle religious sentiment into man's ever more secular life.

While Gunther offers Siegfried even his birthright, Siegfried, in a passage surely dear to Wagner's heart, tells Gunther that Siegfried has no birthright, no inheritance to offer in exchange (as we hear H70, invoking the Wälsungs' tragic-heroic destiny), merely his own body which wastes away (accompanied by H151, which recalls Brünnhilde's remark that she's Siegfried's self and knows for him what he doesn't know). Siegfried's only possession besides himself, he says, is his sword (which is Siegfried's self, the emblem of Wotan's desire to restore lost innocence), which he re-forged. In this passage Wagner has made a distinction crucial to his *Weltanschauung*, that the wealth we create of our own selves is our only true birthright, while inherited, unearned property, power, and status is a parasitical evil not fit to be compared with what one earns through one's own genius and labor, the foundation of that heroic self-worth of the type which is represented by Siegfried's Wälsung heritage, embodied by H70: [Speaking of "The plainnest type of heroism ... ," Wagner found this incarnate in the Greek Herakles and in the Siegfried of Teutonic myth, and characterized this archetypal hero in the following way:] "He knows no fear (Furcht), but respect (Ehrfurcht) ... ; whilst honour (Ehre) ... is the sum of all personal worth, and therefore can neither be given nor received, as is practiced to-day ... . From Pride and Honour sprang the rule that, not property ennobles man, but man this property ... ." [1088W-{6–8/81} 'Herodom and Christendom'—3rd Supplement to 'Religion and Art,' PW Vol. VI, pp. 277–288] Gunther's intent to win an honor (Brünnhilde) which only Siegfried's courage is equal to, and his dependence on inherited wealth, status, and power, marks him as the antithesis of the Wagnerian hero Siegfried, the self-created, original, revolutionary artist-hero, who brings the new to pass.

Though it was easy to grasp the rationale of H70's occurrence here, at first I couldn't grasp the link between H151 and Siegfried's remark that living, he wastes his body away. But I found a potential solution in Feuerbach's *Thoughts on Death and Immortality*. He speaks of the mortality of the human body as a loving sacrifice made by egoism, the particular and individual, to the wellbeing of the entire cosmos, that life is only possible with death, that the God to whom we sacrifice ourselves is actually the transitoriness of all things in Nature (Erda's "All things that are, end!"): "... love is not tranquil but is pure activity; love is consuming, sacrificing, burning; love is fire. It is wrath on that which exists singly and selfishly. The human, a particular being, is inflamed by consuming wrath on his natural selfishness and singleness. (...) / God is the ultimate ground of all transitoriness. (...) For death is produced by an inner longing of nature ... ." [TDI, pp. 20–21] It dawned on me that this is a key aspect of the symbolism of Siegfried's re-forged sword Nothung, which in part stands for Feuerbach's notion of natural necessity (willing one's own death as a sacrificial and necessary precondition for mortal life). The first segment of the Sword Motif H56, H56a, is based on the octave drop of Erda's vocal line as she sings "Endet," the last word of her proclamation (accompanied by H52) of the transience of all things, "All things that are, end." And H56b is based in the Primal Nature Motif H1, Wagner's motival symbol for natural necessity, which in turn produces Erda's H52 through a harmonic enrichment. Thanks to Feuerbach Wagner associated the artist-hero's creativity with Nature's necessity and evolutionary change, with acceptance of mortality and renunciation of spiritual transcendence. The only transcendence available in a secular world is the figurative immortality, the ageless youthfulness, of heroic deeds of moral rectitude, recorded in collective, historical memory (such as Siegmund's heroic self-sacrifice for love), and inspired art (the love Siegfried and Brünnhilde share), which never dies so long as collective, historical man honors it.

Hagen begs to differ with Siegfried, having learned that Siegfried isn't lacking in property or wealth, because it's said of him that he's lord of the Nibelung Hoard. Siegfried retorts with contempt (accompanied by the Nibelung Forging Motif H38 and the "Servitude" variant of H8ab, H41, associated initially with Mime) that he'd almost forgotten the hoard since he little values its barren worth. Siegfried describes how he left it unused in a cave where a dragon used to guard it. We recall Siegfried left the dead Mime alongside Fafner to guard the Hoard since Mime longed for it so much. But then Hagen asks whether Siegfried took nothing of the treasure, and Siegfried admits he took a helmet (Tarnhelm), not knowing its power. Siegfried doesn't know its power because, though the Woodbird taught him its power, it taught him subliminally, musically. The same is true of what the Woodbird told Siegfried of the Ring's use. Siegfried figuratively restored Alberich's Ring to the Rhinedaughters by having Brünnhilde, his muse of unconscious artistic inspiration, keep it safe. Since Woglinde's Lullaby H4 gave musical birth to the Woodbird's second song H138ab, we find Siegfried coming full circle here when Hagen reminds him of the Tarnhelm's use. But Hagen doesn't tell Siegfried of the Ring's power. Hagen informs Siegfried that the Tarnhelm serves to transform one to any shape one chooses (to change one's identity), and to go to the furthest ["fernsten"] spot instantly (not only in space, but also in time, as Wagner's evolving motifs of remembrance and foreboding do). This is a poetic description of the human imagination, and specifically of Wagner's artistic "Wonder," his substitution of the bliss of musical feeling (in his motifs) for religious faith in miracles and its existential fear of truth.

Hagen then asks if Siegfried took nothing else, and Siegfried acknowledges he took a Ring. To Hagen's question whether Siegfried is keeping the Ring safe, Siegfried says (accompanied by H161, Wotan's hoard of runes Brünnhilde imparted to him subliminally which Siegfried is fated to betray to consciousness) a glorious woman is keeping it safe. There's an awkwardness in the libretto here which can cause some confusion. Gunther must not have heard this part of Siegfried's dialogue with Hagen, because had he done so, he wouldn't display the confusion he does in T.2.4–5 about whether Siegfried, during his abduction of Brünnhilde, stole her Ring from her, since one would expect Gunther would logically draw the conclusion that the glorious woman who's keeping Siegfried's Ring safe, to whom Siegfried now alludes, is that Brünnhilde who, in T.2.3–4, will accuse Siegfried not only of stealing her Ring, but of coercing sexual favors from her. After all, Siegfried suddenly finds himself in T.2.4 in possession of his Ring (which he previously told Hagen he'd left for safekeeping with a glorious woman), which he asserts he took from a Serpent/Dragon he killed long ago, but which he hadn't been wearing until after he'd abducted Brünnhilde for Gunther and returned to Gibichung Hall. Gunther won't connect the dots at that time, and we can only conclude either that Wagner intended that Gunther should be presumed not to have overheard this part of Siegfried's conversation with Hagen, or that Wagner was clumsy in working out the dramatic mechanics of his greatest artwork on this point. The proof that the *Ring* libretto can't be grasped in everyday, common-sense terms, as for instance in a play by Ibsen, is that Siegfried might just as easily have identified this "glorious woman" as Brünnhilde when he answered Hagen's question. Had he done so, the plot of *Twilight of the Gods* would have fallen to pieces. The *Ring* is a dramatized myth, not a conventional, realistic drama.

There's another potential source of confusion here. I've identified Wotan's Hoard of knowledge with the Hoard of treasure Alberich and his Nibelungs mined in the bowels of the earth [Nibelheim is "Erde Nabelnest," Erda's umbilical nest] thanks to the Ring's power. Wotan obtained his hoard both through figurative sexual union with Erda (which Wotan in R.4 said was to gain knowledge from her), and by wandering over the earth (Erda) in quest of knowledge. I construed Alberich's Hoard and Wotan's Hoard as identical on the basis of Feuerbach's formulation that knowledge is power, that the first predicate of God is power, that God for Feuerbach is collective, historical man, and that the Ring grants its owner power over the world, both man and Nature. This is presumably the same Hoard of runes which, according to Brünnhilde, the gods (i.e. Wotan) imparted to her (during his confession), and which she in turn imparted to Siegfried subliminally during their loving union in both S.3.3 and T.P.B. Siegfried has told Hagen he left the Hoard unused in Fafner's cave, not valuing its barren worth, and we recall Siegfried told Brünnhilde she shouldn't be upset if her teaching left him untaught, and that he doesn't know how to guard the runes she gave him. The point is that Siegfried isn't "conscious" of the use he's making of the Nibelung Hoard, Wotan's Hoard of Runes, or Alberich's Ring itself, as the basis for his unconscious artistic inspiration, and this is as Wotan intended it, because he desired a hero free from consciousness of Wotan's influence, who'd nonetheless do, of his own need (Noth), as if spontaneously, what Wotan and the gods need for him to do to win them redemption from Alberich's Ring Curse. It wouldn't have been practical for Siegfried to take the Hoard with him on his journey to Brünnhilde's mountaintop, so he left it behind because, in any case, the Tarnhelm and Ring stand for the entire Hoard and can reproduce it. As further evidence for this we hear H161 as Siegfried tells Hagen that a glorious woman (Brünnhilde) is keeping the Ring safe: H161 embodies Wotan's Hoard of runes she imparted to Siegfried. Besides, if Siegfried had truly despised the Hoard's barren worth he wouldn't have taken even a portion of it with him, but instead, as Hagen's wry question whether Siegfried took nothing from the hoard draws attention to, Siegfried took the two key, generative items from the Hoard, the Tarnhelm and Ring, and what's more, it was the sympathetic Woodbird who prompted him to do this. This is of the utmost significance.

Gutrune has emerged from the Hall with Hagen's potion (Wagner's artistic Wonder) in hand, offering this drink to Siegfried in welcome as their guest:

[pp. 295–6] **Gutrune:** Welcome, guest, [[**H168a orch:**]] to Gibich's home (:H168a orch)! [[**H168b orch:**]] His daughter brings you this drink (:H168b orch). (…)

Siegfried: (quietly, but with extreme determination: H150 voc:) Were all forgotten that you gave me, one lesson alone I'll never neglect (:H150 voc):—(H143 voc:) this first drink (:H143 voc) (H149 voc:) to true remembrance ["Minne" according to Spencer can mean both love, and remembrance], Brünnhild,' I drink to you (:H149 voc) [Is the Remembrance Motif H192, introduced in T.3.2 when Hagen suggests that Siegfried tell the assembled Gibichung hunting party how he first came to understand birdsong, a reference to, or a variant of, this conjunction of H143 and H149? Dunning suggested previously that H192 may be a variant of H149 or an inversion of a segment of the Rhinedaughters' second lament for the lost Rhinegold, H174c]! (He raises the horn to his lips and takes a long draught. H165: He returns the horn to Gutrune who, ashamed and confused, stares at the ground. H168ab: Siegfried fixes his gaze on her with suddenly inflamed passion.) (H168b >> : [agitated vari]) (...) (... H141 varis:) Ha, fairest of women! Close your eyes! The heart in my breast is burned by their beam; in fiery streams I feel it consume and kindle my blood (:H141 varis)! (H173 end frag) ... Gunther, what is your sister's name? (H164)

Gunther: (H168a >: [definitive]) Gutrune (:H168a [definitive]).

Siegfried: (... H168b:) Are they goodly runes that I read in her eyes (:H168b)? (...) I offered myself as your brother's liegeman; the proud man turned me down:—(H167) would you treat me as brashly as he did if I offered myself as your husband? (H162:; H168ab:; H162; H168b: Gutrune involuntarily catches Hagen's eye; she ... leaves the hall with faltering steps. H22 vari: Watched closely by Hagen and Gunther, Siegfried gazes after Gutrune as though bewitched: H50)

As Gutrune offers Siegfried her drugged drink of alleged welcome we hear for the first time her definitive Gutrune Motif H168ab. Cooke states that H168a is in the same family of Gibichung motifs as H162 (Hagen), H167 (Gunther's false friendship for Siegfried), and H183 (the Gibichung Horncall). H168b seems to be in the family of motifs which includes H20 (associated in R.2 with Fricka's hope that in Valhalla she could entice Wotan to sustain his fidelity to her), H74, H104, and H113. H168's liquid, sensuous, poignant nature strongly suggests Gutrune possesses a sublime beauty and feminine mystique which would make it plausible that at least some married men would be capable of infidelity to their wives if she brought her seductive power to bear. But it could be argued that had she been such a great beauty she'd have married long ago. I think on balance Wagner intended her to be portrayed as a genuine seductress whose magic might prevail even without a love potion to aid her. Certainly Nattiez's reading of Gutrune as Wagner's metaphor for the Harlot, French Opéra Comique, in which the libretto (the dramatist) serves only as a pretext for pretty, seductive vocal music, would demand that Gutrune be presented as a beauty. It would enhance the realistic dramatic power of Siegfried's betrayal of Brünnhilde, the victory of the real over the ideal.

Siegfried holds the proffered drink aloft and softly (to himself) toasts Brünnhilde and all that she means to him. We must assume that though Siegfried has sung this toast for our benefit, it's not meant to be heard by the Gibichung siblings. If the Gibichungs heard his toast this would make the subsequent events nonsensical, because they proceed from the assumption that among the Gibichungs Hagen alone knows of Siegfried's true relationship with Brünnhilde. Gunther couldn't so easily have been persuaded to manipulate Siegfried into winning Brünnhilde for him as his bride had he known of Siegfried's prior relationship with her, since Gunther prides himself on at least preserving the veneer of honor. The verbal and subliminal (motival) content of Siegfried's toast to Brünnhilde is the following: "(H150) Were all forgotten that you gave me, one lesson alone I'll never neglect: (H143) The first (H149) drink to true remembrance/love, Brünnhilde, I drink to you!" H150 is the original love-greeting Siegfried and Brünnhilde sang to each other after he woke her in S.3.3, a member of the Love Motif Family. H143 was introduced in S.3.1 when Wotan told Erda the world will be redeemed through his heirs' Siegfried's and Brünnhilde's love. During their S.3.3 love duet H143 represented Siegfried's unconscious artistic inspiration by Brünnhilde, Wagner's secular substitute for dying religious faith. It's this that Wotan thought (confessed to Brünnhilde), which Brünnhilde felt (transmuted into redemptive musical motifs). H149 was identified in S.3.3 with Siegfried waking her, a prospect initially dreadful because Siegfried had a subliminal premonition of the danger in Brünnhilde's being the repository of Wotan's secret hoard of unbearable self-knowledge. Both H143 and H149 will be heard conjoined again in T.3.2 after Hagen has given Siegfried a drink containing the antidote to his original potion of love-and-forgetting, and Siegfried has remembered Brünnhilde as he sings "Oh! How clasped me in its ardor, the fair Brünnhilde's arm!"

As Siegfried drinks Hagen's potion we hear Hagen's Potion Motif H165 (from the motif family which represents Wagner's artistic Wonder). And now we understand: thanks to Hagen's influence (the Ring Curse of consciousness) Siegfried is unwittingly preparing to betray Wotan's unspoken secret—which Brünnhilde keeps for Siegfried to protect him from suffering its un-healing wound—from the silent depths of his unconscious to the light of day, by giving his muse Brünnhilde and her secrets away to Gunther (Siegfried the artist-hero's audience), and by marrying the false muse Gutrune (metaphor for the music-dramatist's need to present his sacred work to a profane audience in the modern world, in which the religio-artistic secrets which inspired artists formerly kept expose their mysteries and thereby desecrate and discredit them). Both Hagen's original potion of love-and-forgetting (H165), which makes Siegfried forget Brünnhilde, and Hagen's antidote to it (again represented by H165), which—at just the right moment for Hagen's machinations to bear fruit—allows Siegfried to remember her, are, taken together, the means through which Hagen manipulates Siegfried into revealing to his audience (Gunther and the Gibichungs) the unspoken secret of Siegfried's unconscious artistic inspiration. They both are one single potion designed by Hagen for a single purpose. Hagen hopes to explode the last of the religious mysteries by exposing the Feuerbachian historical mechanism whereby religion (the Valhallan gods) took refuge in musical feeling (the

Woodbird's song). To fully grasp the drastic import of this world-historical event, we must understand that Wagner in his *Ring* dramatized what he subliminally feared he himself was bringing to pass.

After drinking Hagen's potion Siegfried is overcome by a passion for Gutrune akin to the longing which he originally felt, in the finale of S.2.3, for the as yet unseen Brünnhilde, because it's expressed by the same motif H141 which in S.2.3 expressed Siegfried's passionate desire for the sleeping woman whom the Woodbird suggested he wake and win. Siegfried begs Gunther to tell him his sister's name, and as Gunther answers: "Gutrune," we hear an especially sinuous and provocative version of her motif H168ab. Siegfried then urgently offers her his hand in marriage, and we hear H50 (Ring Curse). Gutrune in her humility walks off into Gibichung Hall. Siegfried now asks Gunther whether he's already married because, evidently, it was an old Teutonic custom that a brother had to be married before any of his sisters could be. This provides Gunther the opportunity to repeat word for word what Hagen told him of the wondrous woman asleep on a mountaintop, surrounded by a ring of fire. Gunther explains to Siegfried that this is the ideal woman for whom Gunther longs, but whom he can't woo himself due to his fear of the ring of fire which protects her. This incites Siegfried to offer Gunther his aid in wooing her, but not before Siegfried has had a startling though brief moment of on-the-verge-of-conscious remembrance, accompanied by the Woodbird tunes to which it sang its description of Brünnhilde to Siegfried. Ultimately Siegfried can't call his latent memory of Brünnhilde up to consciousness:

[pp. 296–7] **Siegfried:** ... Gunther, have you a wife? (H167 vari)

Gunther: (H167 vari >>>:) I've not yet wooed nor shall lightly have joy of a woman (:H167 vari)! On one have I set my mind (H173 end frag) whom no (H162:) shift can ever win me (:H162). (H162)

Siegfried: (... H163 vari:) What would be denied to you (H151 voc:) were I to stand beside you (:H151 voc)?

[Siegfried echoes each of Gunther's repetitions of Hagen's original description of Brünnhilde accompanied by H33, H105's accompaniment, H137b and H138b, until Siegfried has totally forgotten her. (...)]

(H165: Siegfried's gesture at the mention of Brünnhilde's name shows that all memory of her has faded completely).

Gunther: Now I may not climb that fell: (H165) the fire will never die down for me!

Siegfried: (H32B: [the vari associated with the Norns, as heard also in the *Twilight of the Gods* finale they foresaw] ... I'm not afraid of any fire: for you I'll woo the woman (:H32B—Norns' vari); (H32A:) for your liegeman am I and my courage is yours (:H32A), (H168a:) if I can win Gutrune as wife (:H168a).

Gunther: (H32B:; H168a:) I grant you Gutrune gladly (:H32B). (H32B/H76)

Siegfried: (H32B/H76:) I'll bring back Brünnhilde for you (:H168a; :H32B/H76).

Gunther: How do you plan to deceive her? (H32 rhythm)

Siegfried: (H32 rhythm:) Through the Tarnhelm's disguise I'll change my shape with yours (:H32 rhythm).

As Siegfried tells Gunther nothing would be denied him if Siegfried stands beside him to help him win Brünnhilde, we hear H151 (Brünnhilde as Siegfried's self, who knows for him what he doesn't, his true identity and fate). By giving his muse of unconscious artistic inspiration Brünnhilde to Gunther, Siegfried will not only be losing her wondrous protection from the wounds of consciousness, but will also be sharing with his audience (Gunther and the Gibichungs) the knowledge which was so fearful that Wotan couldn't bear to face it. This is the profoundest secret of the poetical music-dramatist's artistic intent, which Wagner said he shares with his audience subliminally through his musical motifs, though it remains a mystery to himself. There's one thing Siegfried remembers, however. When Gunther complains that the fire will never die down so he can win Brünnhilde, Siegfried observes that since he doesn't fear fire, he'll win Brünnhilde for Gunther, if Gunther will give Siegfried his sister Gutrune in marriage. Gunther concurs, and they prepare to set off immediately to capture Brünnhilde. When Gunther inquires how they ought to deceive Brünnhilde so she'll think it's Gunther, not Siegfried, who's won her, Siegfried recalls Hagen's remark that he could use the Tarnhelm to change his form, and suggests he transform himself to resemble Gunther. Wagner found the notion of borrowing from others honors they alone have earned morally repugnant (Wotan's co-opting Alberich's Ring-power, which Alberich alone had the courage to win for himself, being a foundational example), and here we have Gunther agreeing to let Siegfried's courage stand in to cover Gunther's lack of it, and what's worse, Siegfried aiding and abetting this plan, just as Loge enabled Wotan's self-deception. But at least Loge was ashamed to abet Wotan's devious plans. One thinks here also of Wotan's quest for a hero who can do for him what he can't do for himself.

There's another fascinating aspect of Siegfried's offer to pose as Gunther through the Tarnhelm's Wonder, whose motifs H40A and H40B (derived from Loge's motif H33) are the basis for Hagen's Potion Motif H165. By transforming himself into Gunther, the artist-hero Siegfried effectively transforms himself into his own audience, making himself indistinguishable from his audience. And by granting Gunther access to his muse Brünnhilde (i.e., to those unspoken secrets kept by man's collective unconscious, to which formerly only the alleged recipients of divine revelation and inspired artist-heroes were privy) Siegfried transforms his audience into himself, granting his audience access to the innermost secrets of his unconscious artistic inspiration. Wagner did, indeed, say that through his musical motifs he could make his audience fellow-knowers of the artist's most profound secret, a secret unknown even to himself. In this way he grants his audience a grasp of those inner processes of which he claimed to have unique access by virtue of being both the author and composer of his own artworks.

Prior to shoving off in Siegfried's boat to abduct Brünnhilde, Gunther suggests they swear an oath. Previously I noted Wagner's moral distaste for oaths, inspired by Feuerbach's ruminations on this subject. Wagner believed the mere fact of requiring an oath implies the parties to it don't trust each other, for trust either comes naturally from both parties so oaths are superfluous, or it's unnatural to them, must be coerced by oath, and is therefore valueless. This is another example of Gunther's hypocrisy and cravenness which Siegfried aids and abets. It's this corruptly cunning society of which Mime was the exemplar, and whose nature Mime tried to teach Siegfried, though Siegfried in his repulsion for such teaching refused Mime's lessons. Siegfried's and Gunther's oath of blood-brotherhood introduces four new motifs, H169, H170, H172, and H171:

[pp. 297–8] **Gunther:** Swear oaths, then, as a vow!

Siegfried: [[H169 voc:]] To blood-brotherhood let an oath be sworn (:H169 voc).

(H50; H19; H32 vari [Norns' vari]; H32 vari [Norns' vari]; H56ab; H163; H162; H19: Hagen fills a drinking-horn with new wine and offers it to Siegfried and Gunther, who scratch their arms with their swords and hold them for a moment over the top of the horn. (...))

Siegfried: [[H170 voc >>:]] [Possibly a H107 vari?] The freshening blood of flowering life I let trickle into the drink (:H170 voc). (H162/H32)

Gunther: [[H170 voc >>:]] Bravely blended in brotherly love, may our lifeblood bloom in the drink (:H170 voc)! (H162/H19)

Both: [[H171 voc:]] Faith I drink to my friend (:H171 voc): (H168b vari) (H118 vari voc: [previously Dunning called this H135?]) Happy ["froh"] and free ["frei"] may blood-brotherhood (:H118 voc) (H169 voc:) spring from our bond today (:H169 voc)! (H19/H162)

Gunther: [[H172 voc:]] [= H17a vari] If a brother breaks the bond—

Siegfried: [[H172 voc:]] If a friend betrays his faithful friend—

Both: [[H171 vari voc:]] What we drank today in drops of sweetness shall stream in rivers (:H171 vari voc), [[H172 voc:]] in righteous atonement of a friend (:H172 voc).

Gunther: (H50; H19: Drinking and then offering the horn to Siegfried) Thus do I swear the oath!

Siegfried: Thus (he drinks and hands the empty drinking-horn to Hagen.) do I pledge my faith to you!

(H162; H19: Hagen strikes the horn in two with his sword. H167: Gunther and Siegfried join hands.)

The first new motif is H169 (to which Siegfried sings "To bloodbrotherhood let an oath be sworn"), the "Blood-brotherhood Oath Motif." Dunning suggests it ought to be considered part of the family of motifs which stem from H19 (Wotan's Spear: the Social Contract) and its variants. Wotan's oaths and contracts are recorded in runes on his Spear, and the fact that Siegfried and Gunther are now swearing an oath is illustrated by the fact that H19 is repeated here throughout it. H19 reminds us that the coercion and unnaturalness engendered by oath-taking was also part of what motivated Wotan's self-criticism in his confession to Brünnhilde in V.2.2. Wotan said that the Spear's agreements through which he rules trap him, and it was to the Wälsung heroes Wotan looked to free him from this trap and thus redeem gods and world from it. It's as if, by swearing this oath to aid the corrupt Gunther in abducting Siegfried's own true love and muse to force her into a loveless marriage, Siegfried has become indistinguishable not only from Wotan at his worst, but also from Alberich (who'd compel the Rhinedaughters to satisfy his desire, without love), and most strikingly from those Neidings who forced Siegfried's mother Sieglinde into a loveless marriage with Hunding, who (with Wotan's intervention) killed his father Siegmund. The key point of H19's sounding during their oath is that in spite of having cut Wotan's Spear in half and broken his contract with the Giants, Siegfried the artist-hero has fallen heir to it, for he too must preserve man's consoling self-deception from the bitter truth, just as Wotan with Loge's (the archetypal artist's) aid once did.

Siegfried introduces another new motif H170ab while singing that the freshening blood of flowering life he lets trickle into the drink, and Gunther adds the hope that, bravely blended in brotherly love, their lifeblood may bloom in it! I noted previously that the first segment of H170, H170a, is virtually identical to H107, the motif associated in S.1.1 with Mime's complaint that his Nibelung skill can't re-forge Nothung. Gunther is as unworthy to woo the authentic muse Brünnhilde as Mime was unworthy—because he's inherently unable (due to his too conscious and ulterior mind)—to re-forge the sword Nothung, which represents Wotan's hope to restore lost innocence. Yet, by sharing their blood Siegfried is becoming indistinguishable from Gunther. A third new motif is introduced, H171, as Siegfried and Gunther sing: "Faith I drink to my friend ... ." But now an older motif has been re-introduced in the most suggestive way as the blood-brothers sing "(H118 or H135?:) Happy (froh) and free (frei), (H169) may blood-brotherhood spring from our bond today," invoking the gods Froh and Freia, as we hear H118 (the basis for H135, the motif to which Wotan sang to Alberich that Siegfried is entirely independent of him and stands on his own), to which Siegfried sang of his joy in his emancipation from Mime's claims on him and of his newly won freedom. But both H118 and H135 stem originally from H112, Mime's Starling Song, in which he sung of all that Siegfried owes to Mime. This passage is remarkably ironic, for Siegfried has proven that he's not independent after all but instead is acting as if he never cut Wotan's spear in half with his sword Nothung. And H50's (Ring Curse's) occurrence here tells us that Siegfried, whom Wotan bragged to Erda is freed from Alberich's Ring Curse, isn't only succumbing to it, but actively (if unwittingly) bringing it to fulfillment. Siegfried is Hagen's unconscious pawn. Hagen is the instrument of Alberich's intent to co-opt Wotan's heroes to serve his vengeance against the gods for co-opting his Ring power.

Then the last of our new motifs originating in the Blood-brotherhood oath is introduced, H172, the "Oath of Atonement," which Cooke said is a variant of H67 (Hunding's Rights). H67 is based on the Ring Motif (H17's) chord. H67 expressed the honor of Hunding's hearth, home, and clan, the social stability engendered by traditional rights, property, and tribal affiliation, the things threatened by Siegmund's revolutionary impulse and personal conscience. It's H67's derivative H172 to which Siegfried and Gunther sing that if a brother breaks the bond, if a friend betrays his loyal friend, the drink of blood they drink today will stream in rivers in righteous atonement of a friend. It's to this broken oath that Hagen will appeal in T.3.2 as pretext for killing Siegfried. In other words, Hagen will accuse Siegfried, perhaps correctly, of breaking man's Social Contract. There's an interesting nuance in what Siegfried owes Gunther, i.e., what Wagner the music-dramatist owes to his audience. Loge, Siegfried's archetype, served Wotan's need to deceive himself. Similarly, the artist-hero Siegfried, heir to man's religious impulse, must protect Gunther's "honor," his sense of his transcendent value, but that honor is based on self-deceit and thus is dishonorable towards the truth. It's in this sense that Hagen is jealous of the power his half-brother Gunther wields. It was granted to Gunther only because Wotan and Loge had, in the earliest, mytho-poetic phase of human history, co-opted Hagen's father Alberich's potential power, to sustain the gods' rule through self-deceit. Hagen wishes to discredit the artist-hero Siegfried as a value-giver, and turn Siegfried's audience—who up until now have obtained their sense of value and truth from the Siegfrieds of the world—away from the consolations of self-deception, and base life instead on the power of objective truth. In this Hagen remains honorable towards the truth.

Put another way, it's through Siegfried's unspoken secret, his unconscious artistic inspiration by his muse Brünnhilde, that he can provide Gunther and his society with those sublime artworks which grant man the feeling of having transcendent value. However, should this secret be revealed, Siegfried will no longer be able to help Gunther and his society sustain the self-deception which lends their life this exultation. So long as the true nature of Siegfried's relationship with his muse Brünnhilde (the covert process of unconscious artistic inspiration) remains a secret hidden from Gunther and his society (Wagner's audience), Siegfried can honor his oath to Gunther and aid him in preserving his false values. But if the true nature of Siegfried's relationship with his muse Brünnhilde is revealed, if the unconscious process whereby man has obtained divine revelation and artistic inspiration was to rise from silent depths to the light of day, Gunther and his society would be exposed as having only false honor, and therefore no honor at all. If Siegfried betrays his unspoken secret, it's as if Siegfried became

Alberich and forced Wotan to disgorge the hoard of knowledge he'd repressed into Brünnhilde in his confession, to confront consciously the truth Wotan couldn't bear to contemplate. This would bring irrevocable, irredeemable dishonor and shame to Wotan, the gods, and the Gibichung society which is sustained by the ideals incarnate in godhead, and bring about the twilight of the gods Erda foresaw. The primary purpose of Siegfried's oath is that he's sworn to honor Gunther by abducting Brünnhilde (unbeknownst to Siegfried, his muse) to give her away to Gunther in marriage. Formerly, the artist-hero sustained man's false honor by creating inspired works of art in which their true source of inspiration was hidden from both the artist himself (who's unconsciously inspired) and his audience. But in this case, instead of giving Gunther a redemptive work of art in which man's consoling illusion of transcendent value is sustained, Siegfried would be giving his audience, within the context of his inspired work of art, a revelation of its true source of inspiration, which would doom religion's last refuge.

Wotan's Spear Motif H19 is oft-repeated during their oath-taking (even though Siegfried had previously cut it in two and broken Wotan's authority and divine law by killing Fafner and taking his Ring) because Siegfried's inspired art in a sense restores the broken social contract at a higher level than religious faith. Siegfried the secular artistic value-giver replaced Wotan (religion) as value-giver, and took over Wotan's responsibilities. This concept is similar to that inhering in the relationship of Jesus the savior, hero of the New Testament, to the hero of the Old Testament, God-the-Father, who're ultimately identified as one in the mystery of the Trinity. Jesus breaks the Mosaic Law, the coercive law of fear (the Ten Commandments, the "thou shalt nots"), to reconstitute it on a higher plane as the law of love.

Siegfried notices that Hagen didn't participate with them in the blood-brotherhood oath, and charitably inquires why. Hagen answers that his blood is dispassionate, so he's reluctant to mix it with the blood of those swayed by passion:

[p. 298] Siegfried: (H168a vari:) Why did you take no part in the oath (:H168a vari)? (H172)

Hagen: (H172:) My blood would mar your drink (:H172)! (H30 voc/H38:) It doesn't flow truly and nobly like yours (:H30 voc/H38); (H38) (H17:) stubborn and cold (H173 end frag:) it curdles within me (:H17; :H173 end frag;), (H38) (H35:) refusing to redden my cheek (:H35). So I keep well away from your fiery bond. (H162)

Hagen's cold, passionless blood would mar their drink, he says, as we hear H172 (Oath of Atonement) to which Hagen will appeal when he invokes his right to murder Siegfried for allegedly breaking his oath to Gunther later (T.3.2–3). We hear H38 (Nibelung Labor) which represents Hagen's base egoism, and Froh's optimistic H30 (variant of Freia's Golden Apples of Sorrow-less Youth Eternal H28), as Hagen adds that his blood doesn't flow truly and nobly like theirs, H30 standing for the nobility to which he can never aspire. Instead, he says (accompanied by H17—Ring) his blood is stubborn and cold, and curdles within him. Finally, we hear H35 (Loveless) as Hagen says his blood refuses to redden his cheek, which is why he avoids their fiery bond. Hagen suffers the fate Nietzsche assigned to overmen with the courage to face the world's terrible truth, that no transcendent meaning inheres in world or men, but is merely imputed to world and men by our imagination as consolation for the terrible truth. The martyr to truth, Nietzsche asserted, walks alone in solitude, and can't call himself happy. Hagen is sad because he's by his objective nature incapable of finding consolation in illusion, unlike the majority of men who draw their sense of self-worth from religion and/or art and the morality derived from these impulses. Hagen will vent his despair in a moving complaint to his father Alberich in T.2.1.

Quickly forgetting this sobering testimony to Hagen's alienation, Siegfried, beset by tempestuous, manic passion to win Brünnhilde for Gunther, so he can win Gutrune for himself, tells Gunther, quick! They must be off!:

> [p. 299] **Siegfried:** (… H162 or H164 vari? >>: [is this an embryo for H178, the Honor Motif?]) Quick, let's be off (:H162 or H164 vari?)! (H33/H32B/H105 accompaniment >>: [we hear extremely "manic" music based on these Loge motifs until Siegfried's and Gunther's exit]) There lies my boat; to the fell it will bring us swiftly: … H40A/H32B >> :) one night on the shore you'll wait in the skiff: (H162 or H164 vari?) you'll then bring the woman home. (…) (H32B: [**Gunther:** (…); **Siegfried:** (…)]
>
> **Gunther:** You, Hagen! Guard the hall! (H162 or H164 vari?) (H33/H105/H76: [reaches a pitch of great intensity] (…) … Siegfried and Gunther hoist the sail and prepare to leave, during which time Hagen takes up his spear and shield. (…)) (…)

The extraordinarily potent, explosive music depicting Siegfried's and Gunther's preparations to abduct Brünnhilde so Siegfried can marry Gutrune, impresses itself on us as if Siegfried is being compelled by a new, irresistible impulse. Porges recorded the impression, surely Wagner's own, that Siegfried's sudden passion for Gutrune, under the influence of Hagen's Potion, is indeed a "force of destiny": "Special attention must be paid to the moment when we have the feeling that Siegfried's sudden passion for Gutrune is a force of destiny impelling him." [888W-{6–8/76} WRR, p. 123] The point of this, surely, is that Hagen's potion's influence on Siegfried doesn't represent an externally generated intrigue or conspiracy foreign to Siegfried's nature: its influence on him is a force stemming from his own nature as an inspired artist-hero. It's as if it were a natural necessity of the evolution of human consciousness that Siegfried, the ultimate incarnation of the artist-heroes of history (whose archetype is Loge), who invented the various world-religions and produced all the truly authentically inspired art, should unwittingly and involuntarily reveal, within the context of his own greatest work of art (the pinnacle of man's age-old longing for restoration of lost innocence), the original source of inspiration for all prior religious mythology and art, thus retrospectively re-interpreting the meaning of the entire legacy of which Siegfried's ultimate artwork is the final cause. The motifs which comprise this manically urgent music during Siegfried's and Gunther's preparations are H33, H32b, H105 (Loge's motifs which recall his protective ring of fire surrounding Brünnhilde's mountaintop home), H164 (Seduction—whose steep interval drop seems to be an embryo for the "Honor Motif" H178 which marks Siegfried's decision in T.2.3.B to separate himself from Brünnhilde with his sword/phallus Nothung, to preserve Gunther's honor), and H76 (Valkyries). In combination, these reach a pitch of overpowering urgency as Siegfried and Gunther push off in Siegfried's boat on Siegfried's penultimate, tragic adventure, his betrayal of his muse of inspiration.

Gunther instructs Hagen to guard Gibichung Hall in their absence. Gutrune comes out to see them off, and then returns to her chamber as Hagen sits down with his spear and shield to guard the Hall. The following interlude, launched by Hagen's soliloquy on his sinister plan to exploit Siegfried to win back from Brünnhilde his father Alberich's Ring, transitions naturally into a purely orchestral passage, the musical transition from T.1.2 to T.1.3, "Hagen's Watch." This for me is the most impressive of the so-called "bleeding chunks," purely orchestral passages from the *Ring*, among which are several far more famous such as the "Ride of the Valkyries," "Siegfried's Dawn and Rhine Journey," and "Siegfried's Funeral Procession," which are played independent of the *Ring* staging in the concert hall. I'm not aware of any instance in which this particular orchestral passage has been played independently in the concert hall, but it seems to me the most subtle and impressive of all. The delicate orchestral transition from one motif to another, in some cases through transformations from one motif into another, materializing and dematerializing like clouds, is as fine an example of what Wagner considered his greatest orchestral art, the art of "transition," as any in the *Ring*. Another would be the orchestral transition from R.1 to R.2, during which the Ring Motif H17ab transforms gradually into the first two segments of the Valhalla Motif H18ab. "Hagen's Watch," the portentous and darkly suspenseful music which conveys Hagen's meditation on his plan to overthrow the power of the Gibichungs and Siegfried, gradually transitions into the music of Brünnhilde's reflection on the joy of being Siegfried's wife and muse of inspiration:

[pp. 299–300] (H162b; H108; H162b; H108 [plus some slow orchestral pulsations reminiscent of the Norns' music]: Siegfried has seized the oar and with its strokes drives the boat downstream, so that it is soon lost completely from view.)

Hagen: ... I sit here on watch, guarding the garth, defending the hall from the foe: (**[[H173ab orch]]** [= H43ab vari]; [H?—A Norn-like stir]) (H39 vari:) the wind wafts Gibich's son away, awooing he is going (:H39 vari). (H162/H108; H162/H108) (H93a voc:) His helm is held by a doughty hero (:H93a voc), (H93b voc:) who'll face every danger for him (:H93b voc). **[[H173ab orch]]** (H165:) His very own bride he'll bring to the Rhine; to me, though (:H165), he'll bring the ring. (H162/H35; H162/H35; H9) **[[H174a voc:]]** You freeborn sons, carefree companions (:H174a voc), (H35)

[[H174b voc:]] merrily sail on your way (:H174b voc)! [[H174b orch]] Though you think him lowly, (H84/H9b:) you'll serve him yet, the Nibelung's son (:H84/H9b).

This interlude begins with the second segment of Hagen's Motif H162b. Then a fragment of Siegfried's Youthful Horncall H108a depicts his sailing down the Rhine. H162 (Hagen) is mixed with H108a, and we hear orchestral pulses which recall the Norns' scene T.P.A. Hagen, motionlessly speaking to himself, notes he's defending the Hall from the foe. Then we're introduced to a new motif H173ab (whose end fragment we've heard previously on several occasions) as Hagen says the wind wafts Gibich's son (Gunther) away, wooing. H173ab has been appropriately christened "Hagen's Watch Motif." Cooke noted that H173ab is based on H43ab (Power of the Ring) which expressed the coercive power Alberich wielded as forger and rightful owner of the Ring. H43ab, which contains H17's (Ring's) harmony, is based in turn on two motifs which originally conveyed the Rhinedaughters' celebration of aesthetic joy in the Rhinegold, H11 ("Heiajaheia! Heiajaheia!") and H12 ("Rhinegold! Rhinegold!"), which in turn are based on Alberich's H8ab ("Wehe! Ach, Wehe!"). H173ab, therefore, contains a motival genealogy which channels the whole *Ring*, resonating with both the Golden Age and the Fall.

Hagen notes—accompanied by Siegfried's motif H92ab—that Gunther's helm is held by a doughty hero who'll face every danger (Wotan's unspoken secret, his divine Noth) for him. Siegfried is protected from suffering this unhealing wound by his artistic nature, which grants him the privilege of temporarily healing his wound each time he produces a new deed of art, thereby healing others not gifted with this virtue. This is why Siegfried faces danger for Gunther, why Siegfried alone has the courage to retrieve his muse Brünnhilde for him. We're reminded of Wagner's observation that if the average man was granted insight into the tragic truth within whose shadow the artistic genius lives daily, he'd be driven to madness or self-destruction. Then, accompanied by H165 (Hagen's Potion) combined with H108 (Siegfried's Youthful Horncall), Hagen boasts that Siegfried's bride he'll bring to the Rhine, but to Hagen Siegfried will bring the Ring. We then hear H35 (Loveless). Another new motif H174ab is introduced at this point, as Hagen sings: "(H174a) You carefree sons, carefree companions (H35; H174b), merrily sail on your way." This mournful motif will feature prominently in Hagen's complaint to his father Alberich in T.2.1 that it's thanks to Alberich's loveless upbringing of Hagen, as the agent of Alberich's Ring Curse, that Hagen can't share others' happiness. The truth, however un-conducive to human happiness, is what Hagen is bound by nature to stand up for.

Hagen ends his nihilistic meditation with the following ominous threat: "(H174 End) Though you think him lowly, (H84/H9b:), you'll serve him yet, the Nibelung's son." This conjuncture of H84 (a variant of H18ab—Valhalla, in the Minor) with H9b (the Rhinegold) recalls its introduction in V.2.2 during Wotan's confession to Brünnhilde that Erda informed him that once Alberich brings his own child to birth, "… the end of the gods won't be long delayed," and heard also moments later when Wotan in self-disgust left Hagen heir to his entire legacy and consigned all his ideals and hopes to destruction: "So take my blessing, Nibelung Son." The point of Hagen's remark, that while Siegfried abducts his own bride he also brings Alberich's Ring to Hagen, is that, by virtue of giving his muse of inspiration away to his audience Gunther, instead of giving Gunther a redemptive work of art, Siegfried will reveal to his audience and to himself the hoard of forbidden knowledge which Brünnhilde had held for Siegfried, and from whose wounds her Wonder had protected him. This knowledge, embodied by Alberich's Ring, Wotan found so intolerable that he confessed it to Brünnhilde to repress it into his unconscious mind.

This brings to mind Alberich's prediction in R.3 that he'd one day force himself on the gods' women, without love, and convert Wotan's heroes to Alberich's own service: this prophecy is being fulfilled in Hagen's manipulation of Siegfried to abduct Brünnhilde so Siegfried can compel her to wed Gunther (Wagner's audience), and restore the Ring, currently in Brünnhilde's possession, to Alberich. According to Alberich's prophecy, God's (religious faith's) last refuge (secular art) will be lost forever when modern scientific man discredits the old illusory consolations of religion and art and permanently establishes among all men an objective awareness of Nature's truth, at perhaps great cost to human happiness and social order. Here's how Feuerbach, summing up the implications of this foregone conclusion to world-history, that man through scientific endeavor will supplant the mysteries of religion and love with the mundane facts of Nature and the egoism inherent to all life, captures what's at stake: " ... are we to suppose that the head as a physical organ, that is, the skull and the brain, originated in nature, but that the mind within the head, that is, the activity of the brain, owes its origin to a product of our thought and imagination, a God? What inconsistency, what wrongheadedness! The source of the skull and the brain is also the source of the mind ... ." [241F-LER, p. 154; See also 111F-EOC, p. 180 and 284F-LER, p. 219] And here we have Wagner's strong veto (cited previously): "As the progress of the Natural Sciences involves the exposure of every mystery of Being as mere imaginary secrets after all, the sole concern must henceforth be the act of knowing ... . (...) / ... I believe we are justified in concluding that the purely comprehending Subject ... is left with sole right to existence [say, Alberich and/or Hagen]. A worthy close to the world-tragedy!" [924W-{3-7/78} 'Public and Popularity,' PW Vol. VI, pp. 74–76] Wagner feared that with the exposure of religion, altruistic ethics, and art as evasions of truth based on man's denial of Mother Nature, which depend on self-deception to ensure our happiness, religion and art would die out as value-givers, and scientific men (Alberich and Hagen) would be the sole humans left standing, the heirs to this world, as Wotan put it with disgust in his confession to Brünnhilde in V.2.2. This is the destiny Hagen contemplates.

What follows is the purely orchestral interlude which is Wagner's contemplative transition between T.1.2 and T.1.3.A, in which we'll see Brünnhilde meditating happily on Siegfried and on their wedding Ring (the height of irony, since it's Alberich's Ring won through lovelessness), the embodiment and guarantor of their loving troth, whose power he left in her safekeeping:

> [p. 300] **Interlude:** (A curtain downstage of the hall is closed, cutting off the stage from the audience: H173ab; H162; H17; H108a [as in Siegfried's arrival by boat at Gibichung hall in T.1.2]; H162; H93a; H19; H162; H17; H108a; H162; H17; H92; H19; H173b; H174b; H173a; H174b; H173a; H174b; H173a)

It's particularly in this musical interlude following Hagen's Watch soliloquy that we experience Wagner's art of transition at its full mastery. The sequence of motifs in play is recorded in detail above, and also in my following chapter T.1.3.A, so I'll only discuss motival recurrences of special interest. H93, Siegfried's Motif, is again paired with Wotan's Spear H19 as in Siegfried's and Gunther's bloodbrotherhood oath. The transition from the motival material evoking Hagen's meditation to the motival material calling up the image of Brünnhilde contemplating her love for Siegfried—embodied by Alberich's Ring and its Curse—is heard with the sounding of H160 (Brünnhilde as Siegfried's muse of artistic inspiration), which is followed by a H150 variant on clarinet reminding us of the first greetings Siegfried and Brünnhilde gave each other after he'd woken her in S.3.3. But then, ominously, we hear Alberich Ring Curse H50. We'll pick up our discussion of this musical interlude where I leave off here, in T.1.3.A, which follows.

TWILIGHT OF THE GODS ≠ ACT ONE, SCENE THREE, PART A

(ON TOP OF BRÜNNHILDE'S ROCKY PEAK)
BRÜNNHILDE AND WALTRAUTE

In T.1.3.A Waltraute makes a wholly unexpected visit to Brünnhilde which might involve considerable risk because Wotan in V.3.2 banished Brünnhilde's Valkyrie sisters from her rocky peak by threatening to bring down on them the same punishment he was about to administer to her, leaving them prey to a man. However, as Waltraute will explain, Wotan no longer seems to care:

> [pp. 300-1] H168 vari?; H160; H160 out of which clarinet plays a H150 vari; H50; H160; H50; H160; H150; H149 flutes; H17 varis; H160; H35; H160; H149 [plus trills]; H165; H154 "Hoard of the World" (...) The rocky height, as in the prelude. Brünnhilde is seated at the entrance to the stone chamber in silent contemplation of Siegfried's ring. Overcome by joyful memories, she covers the ring with kisses. distant thunder is heard .... (...) H92; H165; H76; H154: A distant flash of lightning. H165; H92; H76: (...) H76/H92; H77/H76)

> **Brünnhilde:** (H77b/H76:) Old familiar sounds steal to my ear from afar (:H77b/H76):—(H77b/H92 >>>:) A winged horse is sweeping this way at full gallop ... (:H77b/H92)!—Who's sought me out in my solitude?

Waltraute's Voice: (in the distance H77a:) Brünnhilde! Sister (:H77a)! (H77b:) (...)

Brünnhilde: (... H92 >>:) Waltraute's call, so blissfully dear (:H92)!—(... H77a:) Are you coming, sister (:H77a), (H149 vari or H133 vari?: [a *Siegfried Idyll* theme]) and boldly flying hither to me (:H149 vari or H133 vari?)? (...) (H149 vari or H133 vari? [a *Siegfried Idyll* theme]) (...) (H82a—based on H52; H77a) (...)

Variants of the Ring Motif H17 are followed by the Hoard of the World H154, first heard in S.3.3 when Brünnhilde called Siegfried "Hoard of the world" (including that portion to which Brünnhilde warned Siegfried to "leave, oh leave me be"). This is a poignant reminder not only that Siegfried is heir to Wotan's hoard of forbidden knowledge, but that Siegfried, under the spell of Hagen's potion, won't leave his muse Brünnhilde be, but will betray their love and abduct her to force her into an unloving marriage with Gunther (metaphor for Siegfried the artist-hero's audience), and will thereby betray Wotan's unspoken secret. The curtain opens, and we see Brünnhilde seated in front of her cave rapturously contemplating the Ring Siegfried gave her. Thunder and lightning and Valkyrie music herald the imminent arrival of Brünnhilde's sister Waltraute. As she joyously welcomes Waltraute and asks if she's boldly flying hither to her, we hear H82a, invoking Wotan's need for a free hero who can redeem the gods from Alberich's Ring Curse, suggesting that Waltraute has sought out Brünnhilde in response to Wotan's fear of the end.

Brünnhilde expresses her delighted surprise that her sister Waltraute—who in V.3.1-2 emulated her other Valkyrie sisters in shunning Brünnhilde because of her defiance of Wotan—should have braved Wotan's anger to come see her banished sister:

[pp. 301-2] **Brünnhilde:** Can you offer your greeting to Brünnhilde without feeling dread? (H98 vari or H141B?)

Waltraute: (H98 vari:) For you alone I hurried here (:H98 vari). (H98 vari or H141B?)

Brünnhilde: [[H175 voc:]] So, for Brünnhilde's sake, you've dared to break war-father's ban (:H175 voc)? Or what else? (...) Might Wotan's heart have relented towards me? [[H175 voc:]] When I shielded Siegmund against the god, erring—I know—I fulfilled his wish none the less (:H175 voc): (H98 vari) that his anger has passed I also know; (H141B; H98 vari) (H97 voc:) for, although he locked me in sleep at once, fettered me to the fell (:H97 voc) and left me, as maid, to the man who chanced to find and awake me, [[H175 frag]] (H99B vari—clarinet:) he granted my timid entreaty (:H99B vari—clarinet): (H76:; H32B:) with ravening fire he girdled the fell to bar the faint-heart's way (:H76; :H32B). (H99B vari:) So his (H149 vari:) punishment made me thrice-blessed (:H98b vari; :H149 vari): (H150 vari) (H93a voc:) the most glorious of heroes won me as wife (:H93a voc); (H150 vari) (H149 vari:) in his love I exult and glory today (:H149 vari).—(H150:; H149 vari:;

H77a/H76: (...) **[[H175:]]** Were you lured here, sister, by my lot? Do you want to feast on my joy and share in the fate that befell me (:H175)?

Waltraute's answer to Brünnhilde, accompanied by H98, is that she's come solely for Brünnhilde's sake. H98 combines H92 (Siegfried) and H88 (Brünnhilde's annunciation of fated doom to Siegmund), which expressed Brünnhilde's Valkyrie-sisters' horror that Wotan condemned virgin Brünnhilde to be forced into marriage with a mortal man (in the event, Siegfried). As Brünnhilde, proud of her sister's courage, exclaims to Waltraute that for Brünnhilde's sake Waltraute dared break War-Father's ban, a new, peculiar contrapuntal motif, comprised of two distinct melody-lines, H175, is introduced, which expresses both Brünnhilde's hope of reconciliation with Wotan and the cause of her hope, that in spite of Wotan's punishing her by putting her to sleep vulnerable to be won by a man, Wotan's acquiescence in her desire that he only allow a fearless man to win her (Siegfried) has proved that Wotan's punishment was actually her blessing. Brünnhilde recounts the history of her compassionate intervention against Wotan's stern intent to punish the Wälsungs and her (for aiding them) which, though performed by her in accord with Wotan's innermost wish, he couldn't openly countenance. But Brünnhilde makes a tragic error. Though she believes Wotan's anger against her for disobedience has passed, Wotan warned her in V.3.3 that since she'd decided to live for love and ignore his divine Noth he confessed to her (his anguished recognition of the futility of seeking a free hero who would redeem the gods, and the futility of living for love), her punishment for disobedience would follow naturally as the consequence of her choice. But she's now concluded that Wotan's punishment is her glory because its end result was her blissful marriage to Siegfried. This is her fateful mistake! She's set herself up for irredeemable failure, for she'll ultimately understand that her blissful, loving union with Siegfried was the very essence of Alberich's Ring Curse, her punishment in living for love in the face of the unbearable truth.

The new motif H175, whose recurrences are limited to T.1.3.A, conveys the irony in her misinterpretation of the reason for Waltraute's intrepid visit, that Wotan has reconciled with her rebellion against him and perhaps now glories in the loving relationship with Siegfried she won thanks to his benevolent amendment of his original intent to punish her lovelessly. Once Waltraute explains the reason for her visit, Brünnhilde will understand that Waltraute sought her out not because Wotan can now openly acknowledge her love for Siegfried, but because that love, according to Wotan, is so wanting in redemptive capacity that he's now desperate for her to cast the Ring back into the Rhine River to dissolve its curse in its waters, lest some irrevocable, irredeemable tragedy ensue. Wotan evidently is aware that Siegfried and Brünnhilde are destined to betray their love, and betray Wotan's original hope that their love (creation of inspired artworks in which religious man's longing for transcendent value can live on as feeling free from fear of truth) could redeem the world and gods from Alberich's Ring Curse. H175 conveys the ironic gap between the positive spin Brünnhilde has put on Wotan's punishment, and the bitter truth which instead prompts

Waltraute to seek her out. Waltraute now strives to bring her to her senses with an account of the terrible events at Valhalla which led Waltraute to seek her help:

> [pp. 302–3] **Waltraute:** (… H175:) Share in the frenzy that's seized you, you fool (:H175)?—Something else drove me in dread ["Angst"] to break Wotan's behest. (H176 embryo?: [as an orchestral explosion] Only now, to her surprise, does Brünnhilde notice Waltraute's wild agitation.)
>
> **Brünnhilde:** (H175 >>:) Poor sister, you're fettered by dread and fear? So the hard-hearted god hasn't pardoned me yet (:H175)? You quail at my punisher's wrath?
>
> **Waltraute:** (H80:) If only I feared it, my dread would be over (:H80)! (H80)
>
> **Brünnhilde:** Stunned, I don't understand you! [**Waltraute:** (…)] (alarmed) What ails the immortal gods? (H80 frag)
>
> **Waltraute:** (…) (H80) Since he and you were parted, Wotan has sent us no more into battle; (H80:) Lost and helpless (:H80) we anxiously rode to the field (H80>**[[H176 orch:]]** [= H147A vari]) The lord of the slain avoided Valhalla's valiant heroes (:H80>H176 orch): (H82a:) alone on his horse, without rest or repose (:H82a), (H82b:) he rode the world as the wanderer (:H82b). (H18a vari frag—possibly a hint of H84?) He came home of late; (H18a vari frag with H40A harmony—possibly a hint of H84?) (H19:) in his hand he was holding his spear's (H18a vari frag—possibly a hint of H84?) splintered shards (:H19): they'd been (H18a with H40A harmony—possibly a hint of H84?) shattered by a hero (H87 tympani). With a silent sign he sent Valhalla's warriors into the forest (H157 voc frag:) to fell the world ash-tree (:H157 voc frag); (H18a frag vari with H40A harmony—possibly a hint of H84?) (H18e in trumpet triplets:; H123 voc:) he bade them pile up the logs from its trunk in a towering heap round the hall of the blessed immortals (:H18e in trumpet triplets; :H123 voc). (H18ab voc/H123 orch >>>>:) He convened the council of gods; his high seat he solemnly took and on either side bade the anxious gods be seated, inviting the heroes to fill the hall in their circles and rows (:H18ab voc/H123 orch). (H18c) So he sits, (H87 voc plus H87 tympani:) says not a word, silent and grave on his hallowed seat (:H87 voc plus tympani), with the splintered spear held tight in his hand; (H28 vari:) Holda's apples he does not touch (:H28 vari): (H18ab vari:) wonder and fear hold the gods in thrall (:H18ab vari). (drum roll; H18ab vari/H17/H40A—possibly a H84 hint?)

Waltraute accuses Brünnhilde of enjoying the consolations of delusion while Valhalla and its gods, heroes, and Valkyries have been beset by dread, reminding us that Wotan once accused Brünnhilde of enjoying the bliss of love while he had to suffer divine Noth, a complaint which originated in Alberich's accusation that the gods above enjoy an illusory bliss paid for by Alberich's personal sacrifice of love. We hear the embryo of a new motif H176 as Brünnhilde becomes aware that Waltraute hasn't sought her out to share her bliss, but to apprise her of tragedy to come. H176 is based directly on H147, which expressed Siegfried's fear of waking Brünnhilde, prompted by his subliminal premonition of making Wotan's guilt his own. According to Cooke, H147 in turn stems from H80. H80 represents Wotan's acknowledgment that all his efforts to win redemption from Alberich's Ring Curse are merely expressions of it, that Wotan can never find a heroic redeemer freed from Wotan's loathsome motives, can never restore the love that allegedly has been lost to the world (I say allegedly because the *Ring* proposes that love as humans ideally define it may have been illusory). This family of motifs originates, according to Cooke, in H19, Wotan's Spear, and therefore symbolizes the Social Contract's contradictions, the fact that, as Wotan said, the law through which he rules now traps him, founded as it is primevally on Alberich's (man's) egoism.

When Waltraute's dread and dismay has been perceived by Brünnhilde, Brünnhilde says she's stunned and doesn't understand her, recalling Siegfried, who told Brünnhilde (when she tried to explain how her love for him was the product of Wotan's thought) that he was stunned and didn't understand her. But Waltraute's alarm prompts Brünnhilde to ask what ails the immortal gods, just as she once asked Wotan what ailed him, persuading him to confess his divine Noth to her. Waltraute answers by narrating Wotan's horrific history since he parted from Brünnhilde in V.3.3. Waltraute explains (accompanied continually by H80, the motif resonating with Wotan's sense that his proxies are as compromised as he is) that since that time Wotan no longer sends the Valkyries into battle (to inspire heroes to martyrdom so they can, resurrected, protect the gods' rule in the final battle against Alberich's host of night), and that the Valkyries are now lost and leaderless. Accompanied by H82ab (Gods' Need), Waltraute says that since Wotan last saw Brünnhilde he's wandered the world, after disavowing interest in his martyred heroes. Accompanied by what seems to be a new compound motif, a mixture of H18a (Valhalla) with H40A's (Tarnhelm's) harmony, Waltraute notes that Wotan came home of late, holding the splinters of his spear which had been shattered by a hero (Siegfried). The combination of H18a (including perhaps H18b) with H40A's harmony sounds like a variant of H84, which accentuated Wotan's acknowledgment to Brünnhilde in V.2.2 that Alberich's as-yet-unborn son Hagen will inevitably inherit the world, including Wotan's divine realm Valhalla, and bring about the twilight of the gods. H84 conveys Wotan's self-destructive intent to topple the ideal spiritual world he'd built because he'd renounced hope of redemption from Alberich's plan to compel humanity to acknowledge worldly egoism as the sole motive underlying all human thought, feeling, and action. This motif compounded of H18a(b?) and H40A's harmony is repeated as Waltraute declares with finality that Wotan with a silent sign sent his heroes into the forest to fell the dead World-Ash.

Waltraute narrates Wotan's preparations for the twilight of the gods Erda foresaw. He's evidently now resigned to it, since even his hope that Siegfried's and Brünnhilde's love would redeem gods and world has been dashed by Siegfried's involuntary capitulation to Hagen's influence. We must assume Wotan learned that Hagen has compromised Siegfried, perhaps from Wotan's messengers the ravens. We hear H123 (Power and Decline of the Gods) in its grandest tragic-heroic form (recalling its introduction in T.P.A as the Norns recounted this same story), which tells us of the fated end of the gods' power, as she describes how Wotan had his heroes pile up the logs from the World-Ash in a towering heap round the hall of the blessed immortals, in preparation for the burning up of Valhalla foretold by the Norns and Loge. The symbolism is disturbing yet rich, since Valhalla, product of man's self-deception, will be burned up by the archetype of man's artistic cunning (Loge) through which he deceived himself, using the dead World-Ash as fuel, i.e., the symbol for religious man's world-renunciation and figurative murder of his mother Nature (Wotan's sin against all that was, is, and will be, which Alberich's Ring Curse punishes). H123 embodies the gods' hubris (man's hubris in inventing the gods). In conjunction with H123, H18ab, heard here in a new variant expressing a sense of crisis (again evidently hinting at H84), accompanies Waltraute as she describes how Wotan convened a council of the gods in Valhalla. Wotan, she says, sits high on his throne, having bid the anxious gods to sit on either side, and bid his heroes to fill the hall. The repetition of a powerful figure made up of four descending notes, followed by the alternating chords of H18c, provides an awesome, sublime capstone to this towering music, capturing the essence of the *Ring* as an epic of world history which we've just heard Waltraute recount.

In her final portentous image, Waltraute tells Brünnhilde, accompanied by H87 (Fate), that Wotan now sits on his high seat, saying not a word, silent and grave. With the splintered spear held tight in his hand, she says, he no longer touches Holda's (Freia's) golden apples (of sorrow-less youth eternal). Wotan no longer stakes a claim to what Feuerbach described as the gods' most definitive trait which distinguishes them as supernatural beings from mortal beings, their immortality. Wotan no longer makes a bid for transcendence, and has rejected Freia, who as the goddess of transcendent love and sorrow-less youth eternal represented the essence of religious belief and its promise of redemption. Wonder and fear, Waltraute declares, now hold the gods in thrall (just as the existential fear which infected Wotan from the time he was impelled to go down to Erda to learn more about the gods' fate paralyzed him into inaction). Wotan's and the gods' final tableau before their fiery end in Valhalla anticipates Amfortas's culminating moment of desperation as King of the Grail Realm, for, like Wotan, Amfortas abhors immortality, refrains from serving the holy Grail any longer, and lives only for his own death, so he can finally be relieved from suffering from his wound that will never heal, the equivalent in *Parsifal* of Alberich's Ring Curse. Amfortas, like Wotan, also no longer looks to his heroes to serve the Grail, leaving them leaderless, as Gurnemanz describes the Grail realm's decadence to Parsifal in Act Three.

Considering that it's ultimately derived from Wotan's Frustration Motif H80, H176—in conjunction with the irony of H175, which conveys the notion that the positive spin Brünnhilde placed on Waltraute's visit has tragic implications— seems to express Wotan's punishment of Brünnhilde in its ultimate meaning, since Brünnhilde chose not to acknowledge the futility of Wotan's hope for redemption and so must suffer the consequences which Wotan had foreseen and confessed to her. H176, developed out of H80 via H147 (Siegfried's fear of waking Brünnhilde, his intuition of the danger he'd confront on gaining access to Wotan's hoard of forbidden knowledge), is the symbol for Brünnhilde's reinterpretation of the bliss of love she shares with Siegfried, in its wider tragic context. This love is Wagner's metaphor for secular art as the last refuge of religion (Valhalla). She'll soon understand that allegedly "thrice-blessed" love to be the climactic expression of Wotan's punishment. What had seemed bliss she'll soon construe as her woe, for Siegfried will betray their special Wagnerian love, prompting her to transform her love into a burning longing for vengeance, and hate. Ultimately, H176 represents Wotan's recognition that Siegfried is no more a free hero than Siegmund was. Wotan has lost faith in redemption by love (art) and now resorts to his original, nihilistic and desperate desire to end it all, but with an important difference.

Waltraute believes Wotan holds onto one last hope: eavesdropping, she heard him, as if in a dream, express his longing that Brünnhilde could be prevailed upon to do what Wotan never did, restore the Ring to the Rhinedaughters, to let the Rhine's waters wash away the sin inhering in its curse, and, dissolving the Ring, restore its gold to the pristine purity of the pre-Fallen Rhinegold:

> [pp. 303–4] **Waltraute:** (H173a voc >> :) Both his ravens he sent on their travels (:H173a voc): if ever they come back again with good tidings, (H12 vari voc:) then once again—for one last time (:H12 vari voc) (H11 voc:)—the god would smile for ever (:H11 voc). (H11 [transforming into a H76 vari]) (H80:) Clasping his knees we Valkyries lie (:H80): he is blind to our pleading glances; we are all consumed by dismay and infinite dread ["Angst"]. (H80/H176:) To his breast I pressed myself, weeping (:H80/H176): ... his glance grew less harsh; (H104 voc:) he was thinking, Brünnhilde, of you! Sighing deeply, he closed his eye and (:H104), (H12:) as in a dream, whispered the words (:H12): (H17 >> :) 'If she gave back the (H35 voc:) ring to the deep Rhine's daughters (:H17; :H35 voc), (H50 voc:) from the weight of the curse (:H50 voc) **[[H177 orch:]]** [= H12/H18c—as Cooke noted H177 occurs most powerfully in Brünnhilde's final judgment of the gods when she addresses Wotan: "Rest! Rest! Thou god!," in the finale of *Twilight of the Gods*, though in that case H12 is heard in its variant form H58a, from the Rhinedaughters' first lament for their lost Rhinegold]) both (H18c:) god and world would be freed (:H177 orch [H12/H18c]).'

The first segment of Hagen's Watch H173a, whose genealogy extends back to the very beginning (the pre-fallen part) of the *Ring*, has now been linked with Wotan's ravens, as Waltraute tells Brünnhilde that Wotan sent his ravens to fly away from Valhalla, hoping that, if they ever came back with good tidings, Wotan could smile one last time forever. The good tidings Wotan awaits are the message that Brünnhilde has restored Alberich's Ring to the Rhinedaughters, who'll wash away its Curse in the Rhine. However, the events of T.3.3 will clarify that this happy end is only possible after both Siegfried and Brünnhilde have died, giving up the claim of their love on the Ring which, ironically, has kept its curse in play. So Wotan is waiting to hear of Siegfried's Death, i.e., of Siegfried's atonement for Wotan's sin against all that was, is, and will be. This explains why Wagner's stage directions indicate that Wotan's two ravens, his messengers, fly off in the direction of the Rhine after witnessing Hagen fatally stab Siegfried with Hagen's Spear. Brünnhilde will direct the ravens to return to Wotan with anxiously longed for tidings of Siegfried's death, prior to Brünnhilde's self-immolation in Siegfried's funeral pyre, through which she restores Alberich's Ring to the Rhinedaughters in her ashes.

Waltraute speaks—accompanied by H80—of the Valkyries' desperation, dismay and infinite dread, which inspired her to clasp Wotan's knees, hoping to obtain guidance from him. H80 transforms again into its ultimate variant H176. Waltraute pressed herself on Wotan's chest, weeping, and his glance grew less harsh. Now, in one of the most tender, moving, and poignant motival reminiscences in the *Ring*, we hear the nostalgic H104 again for the first time in a long while, reminding us of Wotan's overwhelming anguish, and desperate hope, as he bid farewell to Brünnhilde in V.3.3, the last time he'd ever see his favorite daughter. Waltraute notes he was thinking of Brünnhilde. He closed his eye and, as if in a dream (H12), whispered the words: "(H17) If she gave back the (H35) Ring to the deep Rhine's daughters, (H50) from the weight of the curse (H177: [= H12 merges with H18c]), both god and world would be (H12) freed." This is a musico-dramatic foreshadowing of that key moment during Brünnhilde's final judgment of the gods in the finale of *Twilight of the Gods*, when she tells Wotan he can now rest, and H18c merges with H12's variant H58a, after the final sounding of the Gods' Need Motif H82, which formerly expressed the insupportable burden of Wotan's endless wanderings in futile quest of redemption, wanderings which now have ended, sealed by H18d. Many years ago I asked Dr. Dunning if he could inspect Wagner's *Ring* score closely at that point in V.2.2 during which Brünnhilde persuades Wotan to share with her the unspoken secret of his divine Noth, which troubles him and which he says he daren't speak aloud lest he lose the grip sustaining his will, by telling him that she herself is his "Will." Dunning discovered similar chord changes there, so I suspect that crucial moment in V.2.2 contains the musical embryo for H177. Wagner did say, after all, that Wotan's confession to Brünnhilde, which immediately follows the chord changes described above, is the most important scene in the *Ring*.

What evidence do we find in Wagner's writings or recorded remarks that Wotan realized his hope of being redeemed through the love which Siegfried and Brünnhilde share (redemption of religious longing for transcendent value by secular art) was destined to failure, and therefore Wotan decided the only hope of redemption left to him was to, after all, return the Ring to the Rhinedaughters and let the Rhine's waters wash away its curse? We have it in a letter Wagner wrote to August Röckel (previously cited) in one of several attempts to clarify the plot of the *Ring*, in which Wagner stated that Wotan doesn't acknowledge the need to restore Alberich's Ring to the Rhine " ... until the ring proves the ruin of Siegfried ... ." [616W-{1/25–26/54} Letter to August Röckel, SLRW, p. 307] Wotan's hope to be redeemed from Alberich's Ring Curse through the love which Siegfried and Brünnhilde share, through secular art, is completely distinct from the ultimate redemption, the restoration of the Ring to the Rhinedaughters, to which Wotan has resorted in prompting Waltraute to persuade Brünnhilde to restore Alberich's Ring to them and thereby take the weight of the curse off of gods and world. The Rhinedaughters themselves, ultimate agents of redemption from Alberich's Ring Curse, will make this distinction in T.3.1.

Wotan's despairing acknowledgment that his desire that his hopes and ideals live on, redeemed, in Siegfried's and Brünnhilde's love, is futile, finds an echo in Wagner's critique of his art, which expresses a despair that began to trouble him in the early 1850's while he was engaged in completing the *Ring* libretto. The notion of art as a profound form of play, once enthusiastically endorsed by him, in his later life seemed to him glib and shallow, given the earnest, terrible nature of the world, and the seemingly invincible egoism of man's (Schopenhauerian) Will, which was the ultimate subject of art: "… I cannot help finding that, if we had life, we should have no need of art. Art begins at precisely the point where life breaks off: where nothing more is present, we call out in art, 'I wish.' (…) Is our 'art' therefore not simply a confession of our impotence? (…) / Ah, how ludicrous it would be if, with all our enthusiasm for art, what we were fighting over were simply thin air!" [583W-{1/12/52} Letter to Theodor Uhlig, SLRW, pp. 246–247] "In full avowal of the Will-to-live, the Greek mind did not … avoid the awful side of life, but turned this very knowledge to a matter of artistic contemplation [in Greek Tragedy]: it saw the terrible with wholest truth … . In the workings of the Grecian spirit we … are made spectators of a kind of pastime, a play in whose vicissitudes the joy of Shaping seeks to counteract the awe of Knowing. … rejoicing in the semblance, since it has banned therein its truthfulness of knowledge, it asks not after the goal of Being, and … leaves the fight of Good and Evil undecided … . / (…) But the trouble of the constitution of the World is this: all steps in evolution of the utterances of the Will, from the reaction of primary elements, through all the lower organisations, right up to the richest human intellect, stand side by side in space and time, and consequently the highest organism cannot but recognise itself and all its works as founded on the Will's most brutal of manifestations. [H17ab> H18ab] (…) But a heartless mummery must the concernment with Art ever be, and all enjoyment of the freedom thereby sought from the Will's distress, so long as nothing more was to be found in art … ." [1029W-{6–8/80} 'Religion and Art,' PW Vol. VI, pp. 229–230]

Waltraute now tells how, on hearing Wotan's desperate desire, she flew to Brünnhilde to beg that she grant Wotan's wish and restore the Ring (source of all the world's evil) to the Rhinedaughters, to end its curse:

> **[pp. 304–5] Waltraute:** … (H80 frag/H176:) from his side, through silent ranks, I stole away; … (:H80 frag/H176) (H92 >>>> :) and rode to you like the wind (:H92). (H35 Voc loose vari:) (…) End the immortals' torment (:H35 Voc loose vari)! (…) (H19 vari [from Wotan's warning in V.3.2 he'd punish Brünnhilde by leaving her to be won as wife by any man who chanced to find her?])

Brünnhilde: (...) What tales of fearful dreams are you telling me, sad sister? (H80 vari) Poor fool that I am, I have risen above the (H17 frag?:; H18a?:) mists of the gods' hallowed heaven ["Himmels-Nebel"] (:H17 frag?; :H18a?): I do not grasp what I hear. (H80 grace-note twist) (H176 >> :) Your meaning seems wild and confused ... (:H176): (H176 vari [very concentrated]) ... wan sister (:H176 vari), what would you have me do in your wildness? (H17)

Waltraute: ... Upon your hand, the ring ... ! (H8 loose varis:) For Wotan, cast it away from you (:H8 loose varis)! [**Brünnhilde:** (...)] (H17 vari:; H173 vari:) Give it back to the Rhinedaughters (:H17 vari; :H173 vari)!

Brünnhilde: (H173 vari:) To the Rhinedaughters—I—the ring (:H173 vari)? (H17 vari) (H17 vari:) Siegfried's pledge of love (:H17 vari)?—(H149 frag) Are you out of your mind?

Waltraute: (H173 vari:) ... hear of my fears (:H173 vari)! (H11 varis:) The world's ill-fate ["Unheil"] surely hangs upon it (:H11 varis): (H173 vari >>:) cast it away, into the waves (:H173 vari)! (H11 vari >>:) To end Valhalla's distress (:H11 vari), (H173 vari:) cast the accursed ring into the river (:H173 vari).

As Waltraute, having weighed Wotan's words, tells how she flew to Brünnhilde to entreat her to take the burden of Alberich's Ring Curse from Wotan and restore the Ring to the Rhinedaughters, we hear H80 transform into H176 again. This motival transformation emphasizes Wotan's recognition that Siegfried is no freer a hero than Siegmund was, and was therefore bound to succumb to Alberich's Ring Curse just as Siegmund did. For this reason Wotan desperately wishes for Brünnhilde to restore the Ring to the Rhinedaughters before it's too late, before Siegfried forces the Ring out of Brünnhilde's hands and makes its power available to Hagen and Alberich. But, just as her lover Siegfried was once (in S.3.3) oblivious to Brünnhilde's attempt to place her love for Siegfried in the context of Wotan's confession of his divine Noth, telling Brünnhilde that what she sings to him he doesn't understand, so Brünnhilde, now living for love alone, likewise tells Waltraute that, fool as Brünnhilde is, the gods' tragic end doesn't concern her, as if Wotan's fate is a dream, as if she and Siegfried aren't complicit in Wotan's sin, not subject to Alberich's Ring Curse. Brünnhilde describes herself, like Siegfried, as a fool, who has risen above the mists of the gods' hallowed heaven, as we hear H18a (first segment of the Valhalla Motif) transform back into its true source, a fragment of Alberich's Ring Motif H17, a point Wagner also underscores verbally with Brünnhilde's description of "the mists of the gods' hallowed heaven," the word mists ("Nebel") invoking Valhalla's origin in Alberich's Nibelheim ("Mist-home"). The musico-dramatic point is that Wotan, having recognized his motives are no higher than Alberich's, is tainted, but Brünnhilde, living for love alone and freed therefore from consciousness of the contradictions inhering in Wotan's thought (his Noth), feels herself freed from the gods' fate and debts altogether. Brünnhilde's response to Waltraute's attempt to link Brünnhilde's fate with that of the gods is a firm no, because Brünnhilde claims not to understand what she hears (accompanied by H176 again, that motif which symbolically stakes Wotan's claim on Siegfried and Brünnhilde, since it informs us that their blissful love is Wotan's punishment, the fulfillment of Alberich's Ring Curse). Brünnhilde seems to have forgotten how she (in S.3.3) confessed to Siegfried what he didn't understand, that what Wotan thought (as imparted to her in his confession), she felt, and that was her love for Siegfried (H143). Their fate is tied inexorably to Wotan's and the gods' doom.

Brünnhilde, confused by Waltraute's plea, asks her what she expects Brünnhilde to do. Waltraute cries out that for Wotan's sake she must give the Ring back to the Rhinedaughters. Brünnhilde is incredulous: does Waltraute really imagine that Brünnhilde would give away Siegfried's pledge of love? The world's ill fate, Waltraute says, surely hangs on the Ring, so she begs Brünnhilde to cast it into the Rhine to end Valhalla's distress. Brünnhilde now says no, she won't return the Ring to the Rhine to redeem the gods, because she and Siegfried are now freed from their troubles, and can live for love alone, a love whose bond is now embodied by Alberich's Ring (the ring which, ironically, could only be forged by renouncing love for power's sake). She's fatally, blindly committed to Wotan's own unconscious poetic intent, confessed to her in V.2.2, that Siegfried the artist-hero be wholly freed from the gods' influence, while ignoring Wotan's warning that this hope is futile:

> **[p. 305]** (H?51.5 = H17ab vari [This vari seems to reference the moment right before Erda appeared to Wotan in R.4, and just after he refused to yield Alberich's Ring to the giants to redeem Freia.])
>
> **Brünnhilde:** Ha! Do you know (H17ab vari) what it means to me? How can you grasp it, you unfeeling child (:H17ab vari)! (H15ab varis >>: [a new, agitated but optimistic and triumphant vari of the World-Mastery Motif]) More than Valhalla's bliss, more than the glory of the immortals the ring is to me: one glance at its bright-shining gold ... (:H15ab varis) is worth far more to me than all the gods' eternal joy! (H143 voc:) For Siegfried's love shines blissfully forth from it (:H143 voc)! Siegfried's love—(H160:; H149:) if only my rapture could speak to you (:H160; :H149)! (H150—clarinet:; H93c voc:) That love the ring embodies for me (:H150—clarinet; :H93c voc). (H176 >> :) Go hence to the gods' hallowed council (:H176); of my ring tell them only this: (H16 voc:) I shall never relinquish love (:H16 voc), (H16 vari: [optimistic]) they'll never take love from me (:H16 vari), though Valhalla's glittering pomp should moulder into dust.

Brünnhilde's refusal to acknowledge Waltraute's demand that she restore the Ring to the Rhinedaughters is heralded by an orchestral explosion of a H17ab variant (Ring), which seems to reference a similar orchestral explosion based on H17ab (perhaps a hybrid with H18ab) heard in R.4 just after Wotan refused to give the Giants their agreed-on substitute for Freia, Alberich's Ring, and just before Erda rose from the earth's depths, to persuade him to yield Alberich's Ring to the Giants. I've designated this motif H?51.5. Both Wotan and Brünnhilde are at these respective moments confronted with the existential decision whether to keep Alberich's Ring and pay its price, to acknowledge the truth, or to relinquish it and hopefully escape its curse by resorting to consoling self-deception. Wotan decided to relinquish it under threat, but Brünnhilde (and Siegfried, in T.3.1) decides to keep it, though in Brünnhilde's case she seems oblivious to the fact that she and Siegfried will have to pay the same price the gods do. When Brünnhilde asks Waltraute how she can grasp what Siegfried's Ring means to her, accusing Waltraute of being an unfeeling child, we hark back to Brünnhilde's insensitive proffer to Siegmund in V.2.4 that he forget his love for Sieglinde so he could enjoy eternal bliss in Valhalla, and Siegmund's cutting rejoinder that she's a cold, unfeeling maid.

We're then introduced to a new variant of H15 (World-Mastery), the embryonic form of the Ring Motif H17, as Brünnhilde tells Waltraute that, more than the glory of the immortals the Ring is to her. This is an agitated but, ironically, radiant and optimistic variant expressing Brünnhilde's passionate love for Siegfried, now embodied for her by Alberich's Ring. It expresses Siegfried's (temporary) victory as a secular artist over the dread, dismay, and trauma engendered by Alberich's hoard of knowledge. When Brünnhilde tells Waltraute proudly that one glance at the Ring's bright-shining gold is worth far more than all the gods' eternal joy, adding (while singing the Redemption Through Unconsciously Inspired Art Motif H143) that this is so because Siegfried's love shines blissfully from it, she proclaims art's independence from dying religious faith. H143 sounded in S.3.3 when she told Siegfried that what Wotan thought (his confession), she felt, her love for Siegfried. Alberich's Ring, and Wotan's confession, are the hidden mainspring of this art and their love. Their love (evoked here by H160 and H150), Brünnhilde says, the Ring embodies for her. So she tells Waltraute (H176 conveying Wotan's understanding that redemption through love/art has failed) to go hence to the gods' hallowed council to tell them: "(H16 Variant [so-called Renunciation of Love Motif]:) I shall never relinquish love, [H16's second segment sounding optimistic:] they shall never take love from me, (H17 Variant—Ring) though Valhalla's glittering pomp should moulder into dust." Brünnhilde in her foolishness (which she shares with Siegfried) doesn't yet grasp that the love they've shared is the product of Wotan's repression of his unbearable hoard of knowledge in her through his confession, and that if the gods fall to Alberich's Ring Curse, the couple's love will be doomed likewise. Yet Wotan supposed their love/art was immune from Alberich's Ring Curse.

There are those who believe that the sorrow-less youth eternal which Freia's golden apples provide the gods is just an expression of Freia's nature as the goddess of youthful love. But Brünnhilde's renunciation of the gods' eternal joy is a renunciation of all that Freia represents, including transcendent love, but especially religious faith's promise of immortality. The religious promise of Freia's golden apples of sorrow-less youth eternal is nothing more, Brünnhilde suggests, than the satisfaction of egoism and alleviation of existential fear, and has nothing to do with the love she shares with Siegfried. She's channelling Siegmund's similar renunciation of the gods' eternal bliss. There's rich irony in the fact that the gods' glory (H18ab) was the product of Alberich's egoistic quest for power over the world (H17ab), but now Siegfried and Brünnhilde have not only taken aesthetic possession of Alberich's Ring power, but their love is predicated on it. And there we have it: H143, heard moments ago when Brünnhilde triumphantly told Waltraute that Siegfried's love shines blissfully forth from the Ring, is the motival emblem of the new religion of art, which is the product of egoistic impulses Wotan found so loathsome he couldn't bear to speak them aloud. Wotan's proxies, the Wälsung heroes, Brünnhilde, and her Valkyrie sisters, are all products of Wotan's fear of the truth, and therefore of Alberich's Ring of power. This ensures that Siegfried's and Brünnhilde's love is predestined to destruction, since it's founded on its antithesis.

Brünnhilde having abandoned Waltraute, her other Valkyrie sisters, the gods, and the martyred heroes of Valhalla, to their fate, Waltraute berates Brünnhilde for her lack of loyalty, to which Brünnhilde responds forcefully that Waltraute should take herself hence and never return:

[pp. 305–6] **Waltraute:** (H81:) Is this your loyalty (:H81)? (H50:) So, in grief, would you lovelessly send your sister away (:H50)?

Brünnhilde: (H81:) Betake yourself hence (:H81); (H50:) fly off on your horse: you'll never take the ring from me (:H50)!

Waltraute: (H101?/H78:) Alas! ["Wehe!"]! Alas! Woe betide you, sister (:H101?/H78)! (H173ab?:) Woe betide Valhalla's gods (:H173ab?)! (H77b; H76/H77a >>>: She rushes away. (…))

The most striking aspect of Waltraute's parting indictment of Brünnhilde is that its motival accompaniment replicates the sequence of three motifs to which Wotan's original explosion of despair over his divine Noth was set in V.2.2, just prior to his confession to Brünnhilde, namely, H81, H50, and H78. As this is the motif array which heralded Wotan's confession to Brünnhilde of his unspoken secret, which he daren't say aloud (consciously) to himself in words, its recurrence here informs us that his unspoken secret is now at risk of being compromised by Siegfried's imminent assault on her. The last time these motifs were heard together (one of only a few times in the *Ring*) was in S.3.3 when Brünnhilde had a premonition of danger in granting Siegfried her sexual favors, i.e., a forewarning of the risk she'd be taking that Wotan's unspoken secret might be revealed, his tabooed hoard of forbidden runes dredged up from her silent depths to the light of day, by the hero with whom she must share those runes that he might draw unconscious artistic inspiration from them. We can't help recalling Tristan's abduction of his secret but true love and healer Isolde to give her in unloving marriage to Kind Marke, and Tristan's exposure of the secrets of their womb of night, his private and forbidden union with his muse and lover Isolde, to the light of day, and its tragic consequences, in Act Two of *Tristan and Isolde*.

This is the ultimate fulfillment of Alberich's Ring Curse H50, whose motive was to punish religio-artistic man for co-opting the Ring's (conscious thought's) power to sustain the illusion of transcendence and deny Mother Nature's truth. H78, the last of the array of three musical motifs which call up remembrance of

Wotan's confession to Brünnhilde, associated in V.2.1 with Fricka's incomprehension of the gods' (Wotan's) need for redemption from the truth, is based on H57b, a motif to which Wotan acclaimed the newly built fortress of the gods as a refuge from the existential dread and dismay inspired in him by Erda's prophecy that Alberich's Ring Curse would bring about the twilight of the gods. Siegfried is now on the verge of destroying the last refuge of religion, music (Brünnhilde), by making it think. Thus, as she flies off in horror at the disaster Brünnhilde's indifference to the gods' Noth has wrought, Waltraute cries out: "Alas! Woe betide you, sister! Woe betide Valhalla's gods!"

TWILIGHT OF THE GODS = ACT ONE, SCENE THREE, PART B
(ON TOP OF BRÜNNHILDE'S ROCKY PEAK)
BRÜNNHILDE AND SIEGFRIED—DISGUISED AS GUNTHER

Having rid herself of Waltraute, Brünnhilde notices Loge's ring of fire has begun to glow more brightly, and tongues of flame come up over the crest of the mountain cliff. She hears Siegfried playing his own motif H93 and his Youthful Horncall H108 on his horn, and ecstatically prepares to welcome her god home, when, to her shock and dismay, another man (Siegfried transformed by the Tarnhelm into the image of Gunther) stands before her:

[pp. 306–7] (It is evening. H33/H105 [sans piccolo]; H102: from below, the glow of the fire gradually increases in brightness.) (...)

Brünnhilde: (H32BA) (H34 vari:) The fiery tide is rolling towards the top of the fell (:H34 vari).—(On stage horn in the distance. H93a Brünnhilde starts up in delight.) (H33/H105:; H102:) Siegfried! (H108) Siegfried is back! (H108/H33:) Hither he sends up his call (:H108/H33)! (H108) Up! Up! (...) Into the arms of my god (:H33; ;H102)! (H108: She hurries to the edge of the cliff in the utmost joy. Flames shoot up from below: Siegfried leaps from them .... On his head Siegfried wears the tarnhelm, which covers half his face, leaving only his eyes free. He appears in Gunther's form.) (H17 chord:) Betrayal (:H17 chord)! (...) Who forced his way here? (H40A end frag) (...)

Siegfried: (with a disguised—rougher—voice: H40A end frag:) Brünnhilde (:H40A end frag)! (H40A:) A suitor has come, whom your fire did not frighten (:H40A). (H165:) I woo you as my wife (:H165); (H163 frag:) follow me of your own will (:H163 frag)!

Brünnhilde: ... Who is the man (H173a:) who has done what only the (:H173a) (H40A end frag:) strongest was fated to do (:H40A end frag)?

Siegfried: (... H165:) A hero who'll tame you (:H165), (H163:) if force alone can constrain you (:H163).

Brünnhilde: ... (H173a vari >> :) an eagle came flying to tear at my flesh (:H173a vari)! Who are you, dread creature? (... H40A:) Are you of human kind? Are you from Hella's night-dwelling host (:H40A)? (H165)

Siegfried: ... A Gibichung am I, (H106 frag) (H163:) and Gunther's the name of the hero whom, woman, you must follow (:H163).

Brünnhilde: (... H95 varis >>:) Wotan, grim-hearted, pitiless god (:H95 varis)! (H176 voc:) Now I see the sense of my sentence (:H176 voc): (H173a >>:) to scorn and sorrow (:H173a) you hound me hence!

Wagner has repeated H102 with great irony at several points while Brünnhilde remarked on the increasing intensity of Loge's protective ring of fire, because H102 calls to mind her original request of Wotan that he protect her defenseless sleep from any but a true hero, by warding away cowards with great horrors. So when what appears to be another man, not Siegfried, stands before her, this gives her a traumatic shock. And of course, unbeknownst to her, it's Siegfried, disguised as Gunther through the Tarnhelm's Wonder, who's come to her through the flames. We hear a H17-based chord (Ring) as she sees, with horror, that it's not Siegfried and screams "Betrayal!" Since Hagen's potion made Siegfried forget he'd ever known Brünnhilde, Siegfried would have no reason to alter the characteristic melodies he plays on his horn (in this case his own motif H92, and his Youthful Horncall H108) to keep Brünnhilde from recognizing him, though hearing these melodies we know Brünnhilde would conclude Siegfried has returned. But these two facts, that she's heard Siegfried's two characteristic horncalls, and that the intruder now facing her did, like Siegfried beforehand, penetrate Loge's protective ring of fire to reach her, must tell her subliminally that it is, after all, Siegfried who confronts her.

Brünnhilde expresses her shock and surprise that anyone but Siegfried could penetrate the fire when she asks, accompanied by H173 (Hagen's Watch Motif) and H40A's end fragment, who the man is who has done what only the strongest was fated to do. Siegfried's aggressive, brutal answer expresses a sadistic tendency, the enjoyment of coercion through force, which didn't seem to be one of his characteristics previously, for he answers Brünnhilde's question with the vicious threat: "(H165—Potion) A hero who will tame you (H163—Gunther) if force alone can constrain you." But Siegfried was predestined by Alberich's Ring Curse to become its agent. By storming the New Valhalla and forcing himself on his muse Brünnhilde, to rip Alberich's Ring (Wotan's unspoken secret) out of her protective hands, he's replicating Alberich's original rape of the Rhinegold, and dramatizing Feuerbach's belief, and Alberich's argument, that egoism is behind all human thought, feeling, and action. Siegfried's sadistic brutality towards his true love makes him seem indistinguishable from Alberich. Wagner himself made the comparison, pointing out that no matter how big the gap seems to be between a noble and an ignoble person, they're ultimately motivated by the same egoistic Will which lies behind all human thought and action: "R. says, 'When the ring was snatched from her [Brünnhilde] I thought of Alberich; the noblest character suffers the same as the ignoble, in every creature the will is identical." [759W-

{6/5/70} CD Vol. I, p. 228] Siegfried's forcefully aggressive arrogance expresses the loathsome egoism which motivated both Alberich and Wotan, an egoism Alberich owned without shame, but which Wotan, in his longing for nobility of spirit, was ashamed to acknowledge in himself, so much so that he repressed knowledge of it into his unconscious mind Brünnhilde. The seed of Wotan's discontent gave birth to the seemingly innocent hero Siegfried, in whom Wotan hoped to be purged of his loathsome nature. He wasn't!

Brünnhilde is seized with terror and cries out that a demon has leaped on yonder stone, that an eagle came flying to tear at her flesh. Her mention of an eagle tearing at her flesh references Zeus's punishment of Prometheus with a wound that will never heal for standing up for mortal humans against the gods, and giving them the gods' prerogative of foresight and fire. Zeus punished Prometheus, as Wotan punished Brünnhilde for standing up for the mortal Wälsungs' right to the gods' prerogatives, by binding him to a rocky height and letting vultures eat his liver perpetually. The Greek Prometheus Myth is surely the origin of Wagner's concept of the un-healing wound, the price we humans pay for consciousness, and particularly for our ability to foresee our inevitable end (which produces existential fear), a fraught gift which gives birth to both religious faith (our futile striving to transcend our natural, physical limitations) and philosophy. She then asks Siegfried who he is, wondering whether he's human, or perhaps from Hella's night-dwelling host. Hella's night-dwelling host is Alberich's Nibelung host of night, with whom Alberich said he'd storm Valhalla. Siegfried's new status as Hagen's unwitting pawn, an involuntary and unconscious agent of Alberich's intent to avenge himself on the gods through his Ring Curse, makes Siegfried a member of Alberich's night-dwelling host, fulfilling Alberich's prophecy in R.3 that Wotan's heroes would serve Alberich, and that he'd force himself on the gods' women without love. Siegfried has in truth stormed the gods' refuge from Alberich's host of night, Old Valhalla, by storming New Valhalla, the seat of the new religion of inspired secular art (H143), his muse Brünnhilde.

Siegfried's answer to Brünnhilde's request to identify himself is that he's Gunther, a Gibichung. This provokes Brünnhilde to scream in despair: "(H95 Variants) Wotan, grim-hearted, pitiless god! (H176) Now I see the sense of my sentence: (H173) To scorn and sorrow you hound me hence!" H95 was the hallmark of Wotan's threat to punish Brünnhilde for her disobedience. Brünnhilde has now had a revelation about the true breadth of Wotan's punishment. It turns out, to her shock and dismay, that Wotan's punishment—which once seemed a blessing in disguise because he granted her wish to be wed only to a fearless hero, Siegfried—has turned out to be more horrible than she imagined, if its end result was that she'd be forced, after all, into marriage with a man wholly unworthy of her, or who would betray her secret. Yet she's unaware of that most tragically ironic of horrors, that Siegfried is perpetrating her figurative rape and outright abduction, channeling the Neidings (The Envious Ones) who abducted Siegfried's mother Sieglinde and murdered his grandmother, afterward gifting Sieglinde in loveless marriage to Hunding. It's as if Siegfried has become Alberich. Now we grasp the ultimate meaning of H176 (and thus the meaning of the motif family which stems from Wotan's Spear H19, which also includes H80, H99AB, and H147), heard here as Brünnhilde says she now sees the sense of her sentence. This is the punishment Wotan had warned Brünnhilde of in V.3.3, which follows from her choice to live for love without bothering to face the objective truth which troubled Wotan, his divine Noth. H80 stands to Siegfried's father Siegmund as its ultimate variant H176 stands to Siegfried: both proclaim the allegedly free hero Wotan longed for isn't free but entirely in debt to Wotan's original ego-driven longing to escape his true yet loathsome identity, corrupt history, and fate.

Wagner said (in a passage previously cited) that in reconfiguring the *Ring* plot to make Wotan, instead of Siegfried alone, a main focus, he realized Wotan is a kind of Flying Dutchman. Both are Wandering Jews in the sense of wandering the world without hope of redemption until the judgment day, the Twilight of the Gods. The full measure of the punishment Senta (Brünnhilde) will endure by choosing to fight for the Dutchman's (Wotan's) redemption, and willingness to pay the price entailed if this fails, arises from the fact that all efforts to redeem man's emotional attachment to the illusion of transcendent value from the truth are futile, because this longing depends for its satisfaction on the maintenance of a consoling illusion, and repression of the bitter truth, which is predestined to rise to consciousness to the utter shame and humiliation of those who live by that illusion. As Wagner put it: "… his [the Dutchman's] love for Senta displays itself at once in terror of the danger she herself incurs by reaching out a rescuing hand to him. It comes over him as a hideous crime, and in his passionate remonstrance against her sharing in his fate he becomes a human being through and through … ." [596W-{1/53} 'Remarks on Performing *The Flying Dutchman*,' PW Vol. III, p. 215]

Siegfried, in the guise of Gunther, brusquely informs Brünnhilde she must spend the night wed to Gunther in her cave:

[pp. 307–8] **Siegfried:** (H162:; H87 "Crisis" vari on trombones: [substituting for the usual tympani accompaniment] … H162; H?—Hagen's Watch Norn pulsation accompaniment) (H40A end frag:) Night draws on (:H40A end frag): (H165 voc:) within your chamber you'll have to wed me (:H165 voc).

Brünnhilde: (threateningly stretching out the finger on which she wears Siegfried's ring: (…)) (H83?:; H17 vari >>:) You'll never force me into shame (:H83?; :H17 vari) (H43:; H40A end frag:) as long as this ring protects me (:H43; :H40A end frag). (H173b)

Siegfried: (H162b? and vari with Hagen's Watch accompaniment >>:) Let it give Gunther a husband's rights: be wedded to him with the ring (:H162b? & vari with Hagen's Watch accompaniment)!

Brünnhilde: (…) Impious thief! (H17 vari:) Make not so bold as to near me (:H17 vari)! (H11 vari:; H164 varis: [these motifs seem to reference the end of T.1.2 when Siegfried and Gunther were preparing to sail off to capture Brünnhilde]) The ring makes me stronger than steel: you'll never steal it from me (:H11 vari; :H164 varis [possible T.1.2 reference])!

Siegfried: (H50:) To wrest it from you you teach me now (:H50). [They struggle: (...) (H173a/H76; H173a/H76; H76; H161; H162; H50; H76/H173a; H85 vari?; H50.] (He seizes her by the hand and tears the ring from her finger. Brünnhilde screams violently. H154 frag. As she sinks down in his arms, as though broken, her gaze unconsciously meets Siegfried's. H160 (...)) (H40A end frag) Now you are mine (H165:) Brünnhilde, Gunther's bride (:H165), (H164 frag:) allow me to enter your chamber (:H164 frag)! (H49 >>: [develops])

Brünnhilde: (H160: ...) How could you stop him, woman most wretched!

Brünnhilde threatens Siegfried with her Ring, hoping to wield its power to defend herself from the vile, ruthless intruder. However, in this case, as in that of Fafner, and even of Alberich in R.3–4, the Ring doesn't protect its owner. The Ring's ineffectiveness as a weapon of defense, even though the Rhinedaughters proclaimed that forging a ring from the Rhinegold would grant one limitless power, demands an explanation. Possession of the Ring represents possession of the power of conscious, objective thought, the power to amass, through hard labor over time, a hoard of knowledge of man and the world to gain power over other men and one's natural environment. Unlike divine, supernatural power, the Ring doesn't grant its owner omnipotence, but merely the ability to grasp the only omnipotent thing in this transient world, the unalterable laws of Nature, as a concept or idea, and to exploit this knowledge to obtain ever increasing power. We can know the true source of worldly power, but we can't be it. However, our power to "know" (to represent to ourselves our experience of the world in symbols, abbreviations for reality which nonetheless can capture its essential forms and laws), the source of our power, unique among animals, to dominate our world, was the infinite reach of our human mind which fooled our ancestors into taking our symbol-using mind for godhead, for something transcendent and autonomous from the laws of this world. This is what's behind Alberich's Ring (H17ab) having given birth to the gods' abode Valhalla (H18ab).

Brünnhilde also can't use Alberich's Ring for defense against Siegfried because she's his unconscious mind, which he's unwittingly plundering to repossess the Ring. During their struggle we hear, among other motifs, H161. She screams violently as Siegfried forcefully wrenches the Ring off her finger, just as Alberich screamed in R.4 when her father Wotan forced it off his finger. Strikingly, just after Siegfried takes possession of it we hear a segment of H154 (Hoard of the World) which Cooke noted is a basis for H161. H161, introduced in T.P.B, recalls Siegfried's premonition that he wouldn't be a good guardian of Wotan's hoard of runes Brünnhilde taught him. Siegfried, having won Brünnhilde, fell heir to Wotan's hoard of knowledge which he repressed into his unconscious mind Brünnhilde during his confession to her. But Siegfried is unconscious of this knowledge and ignorant of the risk entailed in removing it from its safe repository Brünnhilde, and revealing its secrets to himself and his audience. Wagner said Alberich's Ring is the source of Brünnhilde's strength (just as she told Siegfried in T.P.B: "I gave to you a bountiful store of hallowed runes;

(H161) but the maidenly source of all (H161) my strength (H150) was taken away by the hero to whom I now bow my head."), which is why she's spiritually deflated when she can't keep its power safe, as Wagner explained: " ... if you shudder at the thought that this woman [Brünnhilde] should cling to this accursed ring as a symbol of love, you will feel exactly as I intended you to feel, and ... you will recognize the power of the Nibelung curse raised to its most terrible and ... tragic heights: only then will you recognize the need for the whole of the final drama, 'Siegfried's Death.' (...) Why does Brünnhilde yield so quickly to Siegfried when he comes to her in disguise? Precisely because the latter has torn the ring from her finger, since it was here alone that her whole strength lay." [622W-{1/25–26/54} Letter to August Röckel, SLRW, p. 310] Alberich's Ring is the source of her strength because her sole purpose as Siegfried's muse is to hold it for the hero (just as she said in S.3.3 that what he doesn't know [H87—Fate], she knows for him), both to protect him from the wounds consciousness can inflict, and also to employ it to inspire Siegfried's art subliminally. Her whole strength lies in the Ring because Alberich's Ring (H17ab) gave birth to Valhalla and its gods (H18ab): man's abhorrence of the truth gave birth to religion, and inspired secular art is a sublimation of man's religious impulse. Alberich's Ring and his hoard of knowledge are the true source of religious revelation and unconscious artistic inspiration, the reason for which Brünnhilde lives. Once she loses her Ring to Siegfried, disguised as Gunther (Siegfried sharing with his audience his innermost secrets, unknown even to him), she inwardly collapses, wholly deflated, into Siegfried's arms.

After Brünnhilde collapses in Siegfried's arms while looking deeply into his eyes, H160 (Brünnhilde as Siegfried's muse) suggests she's intuited his true identity. Who would've thought that in Siegfried's quest for new adventures inspired by Brünnhilde, his last and greatest adventure would be his abduction and figurative rape of his muse Brünnhilde, and betrayal of her love by giving her in forced marriage to another man (his audience)! We hear H40A's end fragment (Tarnhelm) followed by H165 (Hagen's Potion), as Siegfried triumphantly announces that she belongs to Gunther. Both motifs are emblems of Wagner's artistic Wonder. As she meditates on her bottomless shame H49 develops: it symbolizes the force of envy (Neid) which Erda said was the seed Alberich planted in a mortal woman (Grimhilde), giving birth to the agent of Alberich's revenge on the gods, the instrument of his Ring Curse Hagen, who's manipulated Siegfried into abducting his true love Brünnhilde for Gunther unwittingly. So she'll now also become an unwitting instrument of Alberich's Ring Curse by collaborating with Hagen, as Siegfried did. Siegfried drives her, broken, into the cave where Siegfried embraced her in loving union previously, accompanied by alternations of H49 with H176. Once Siegfried is left alone outside the cave, he calls on his sword Nothung to separate him from the captive woman so he can honor his oath to hand her over as wife, unsullied, to his bloodbrother Gunther, and we're treated to a new motif H178, the "Honor Motif," which speaks to us of Siegfried's supremely ironic use of Nothung to protect her chastity rather than as a metaphysical phallus, its natural purpose:

[p. 308] (H162b: Siegfried drives her away with a gesture of command. Trembling and with faltering steps, she returns to the chamber. H49; H176; H49; H176; Siegfried draws his sword. [[H178 orch]] [Possibly 2-octave drop based on Erda's "Endet" and/or H56a]; H19/H56ab)

Siegfried: (in his natural voice: H169:) Now, Nothung, (H167:) attest that I wooed her chastely (:H169; :H167): (H168a) (H171 voc:) keeping faith with my brother (:H171 voc), (H168a) (H56ab:) keep me apart (:H56ab) from his bride! [[H178 orch]] (He follows Brünnhilde. H40A end frag; H165; H160; [[H178 orch]]; H40A end frag: The curtain falls.)

H178, comprised of a drop of two octaves, is perhaps a distant member of the Gibichung Motif Family which includes H162 (Hagen), H167 (Gunther's falsely friendly welcome to Siegfried), H168 (Gutrune), and H181 (the Gibichung Horncall, heralding the tragic double wedding of Siegfried with Gutrune, and Brünnhilde with Gunther). Its embryo seems to have been the similarly incisive and forceful orchestral interval drops which heralded Siegfried's and Gunther's deciding to set off by boat to abduct Brünnhilde in T.1.2. One characteristic which according to Cooke the Gibichung Motif Family shares is an interval drop which may be based on Erda's octave drop when she told Wotan: "(H52) All things that are, (H?—Octave Drop:) end!" Erda's octave drop on "Endet" was heard again when Wotan, during his despairing confession to Brünnhilde in V.2.2, told her he now only desired "das (H?—Octave drop) Ende!"

Aside from the obvious interpretation that Siegfried is preserving Brünnhilde's chastity to honor his oath to Gunther, the allegorical meaning of Siegfried's refusal to seek sexual union with his former lover Brünnhilde is the following. Siegfried is becoming too conscious of the inner processes of his formerly unconscious artistic inspiration to effectively seek temporary redemption from our un-healing wound in the arms of his muse Brünnhilde, his unconscious mind, any longer. By refusing for the first time to draw unconscious artistic inspiration from her by penetrating her womb with his phallus Nothung, to plant a new seed of poetic intent which might bear fruit as an inspired music-drama, Siegfried will create a work of art in which what had formerly remained hidden, its true source of unconscious inspiration, is revealed to consciousness. Siegfried will share his formerly unconscious source of inspiration with his audience, making them fellow-knowers of the profoundest secret of his (Wotan's, and Wagner's) poetic intent. By honoring his oath to Gunther to provide him the world's most glorious woman, i.e., muse of the world's most glorious work of art, in which man's transcendent value is most sublimely affirmed (yet denied), Siegfried will unwittingly expose Gunther (Siegfried's audience) to unbearable dishonor, the revelation of the disreputable source of what Gunther had formerly called his honor, the meaning of his life.

In calling on Nothung (now an anti-phallus) to attest and act as witness to Siegfried's original oath to protect and preserve his blood-brother Gunther's honor in exchange for Gunther's promise to give his sister Gutrune to Siegfried in marriage (represented by motifs which recall that oath such as H169 and H171, and Gutrune's motif H168), Siegfried swears a new oath accompanied not only by H56ab (Nothung the sword, Wotan's grand idea to redeem Valhalla), but significantly by H19, Wotan's Spear as guarantor of sworn oaths. Now, with supreme irony, Siegfried's sword, with which he'd once cut Wotan's spear in half, emancipating himself from the gods' influence and protection (emancipating art from its former service to religious ideology), is now supporting the contracts engraved on Wotan's spear, by attesting Siegfried's oath. What Wagner is telling us is that in some deep sense his inner need to favor his audience with the product of his unconscious artistic inspiration, his sacred womb of night, would in our modern age desecrate its sanctity by exposing its formerly unspoken secret to the light of mundane day.

Some may have wondered why Siegfried doesn't recognize his own Ring he won from Fafner on Brünnhilde's finger, at least after he's ripped it away from her and put it on his own finger, or why, for that matter, she doesn't recognize Siegfried's sword. There's a persuasive reason for this, wholly consonant with our allegorical reading, which I'll propose later in our discussion of T.2.

There's one last point of interest before we leave T.1 and move on to T.2. Wagner once noted that the plot of *Tristan and Isolde* is identical to the plot of the last of the *Ring*'s four parts (but the first libretto to be written), *Twilight of the Gods*, otherwise known as *Siegfried's Death*. In both instances, he said, a hero, under the influence of a spell which deludes him, woos for another man his predestined bride, and thereby finds his doom: "With the sketch of 'Tristan und Isolde' I felt that I was really not quitting the mythic circle opened-out to me by my Nibelungen labours ... . For the grand concordance of all sterling Myths, as thrust upon me by my studies, had sharpened my eyesight for the wondrous variations standing out amid this harmony. ... two seemingly unlike relations had sprung from the one original mythic factor. Their intrinsic parity consists in this: both Tristan and Siegfried, in bondage to an illusion which makes this deed of theirs unfree, woo for another their own eternally-predestined bride, and in the false relation hence arising find their doom. (...) [This expresses] '... death through stress of love (Liebesnoth) ... .'" What in the one work could only come to rapid utterance at the climax [the *Ring*], in the other [*Tristan*] becomes an entire Content, of infinite variety; and this it was, that attracted me to treat the stuff at just that time, namely [*Tristan*] as a supplementary Act of the great Nibelungen-myth ... . [811W-{12/71} 'Epilogue to *The Nibelung's Ring*,' PW Vol. III, pp. 268–269] Tristan woos his own predestined love Isolde for his uncle King Marke, and in so doing brings doom to himself and his lover Isolde. The meaning is the same in both instances, *Tristan* and the *Ring*: the artist-hero has betrayed the secret hoard of knowledge once kept for him by his muse, his unconscious mind (womb of night), to the light of day, so both he and his audience can become conscious of them, and with the revelation of this forbidden knowledge (of his true identity) comes unbearable shame, a figurative twilight of the gods for the New Valhalla of secular art. In this the artist-hero finds his doom, because, having become conscious of what heretofore was his unconscious source of inspiration, he can no longer produce genuinely inspired art. His art has become too self-conscious to be redemptive.

This plot scenario is the seed of Wagner's revolutionary, mature music-dramas, inasmuch as the first two of his four essays in this unique art genre have identical plots. What's more, this plot is also the basis for *Tannhäuser*, one of his three canonical, romantic operas which preceded his development of the revolutionary music-drama. Like Siegfried and Tristan, the unconsciously inspired artist-hero Tannhäuser unwittingly, as if under a spell, reveals the true but formerly hidden source of his artistic inspiration, his sojourn with his muse of unconscious artistic inspiration Venus in the Venusberg, during the performance of his song about love which is intended to win the hand of his waking muse Elisabeth (by waking I mean she's his conscious motive for artistic creation, whereas Venus is his muse of unconscious artistic inspiration). Each time Tannhäuser has left Venus and her Venusberg to go out into the world and perform the songs her love inspired, he's forgotten both her and the Venusberg and attributes his inspiration to something else, perhaps God in heaven, or Elisabeth on earth. But he finds irredeemable shame and doom in revealing to the assembled guests (his audience) at the Wartburg song contest his true, venal source of inspiration, which isn't divine, but rather, from the standpoint of the conservative religious folk, satanic. However, since *Tannhäuser* is the product of an earlier, more naive phase of Wagner's artistic career, he hadn't fully developed the allegorical scheme which lies behind his mature music-dramas created after 1848. Elisabeth's Christ-like compassion for the artist-hero Tannhäuser and intercession for him in heaven with God redeems both Tannhäuser and herself. Wagner would never again offer the world such a naive and comparatively uncomplicated and serene vision of redemption.

TWILIGHT OF THE GODS = ACT TWO, SCENE ONE

(GIBICHUNG HALL)
HAGEN AND ALBERICH

Act Two opens in the dark night outside Gibichung Hall, with Hagen still seated guarding the hall, presumably asleep. He's approached by his father Alberich in an eerie scene during which we can never be sure if Hagen is dreaming this dialogue, or experiencing it in reality. But one has the impression, nonetheless, that Hagen never truly dreams, but remains forever wakeful, even in sleep. Alberich has come to ensure Hagen doesn't sleep (and therefore dream), but is fully wakeful and conscious of his duty to be the instrument of Alberich's revenge against the gods (religion) and Wälsung heroes (secular moral heroes and artists) for co-opting his Ring power to sustain those illusions which, so long as humans cherish them, preclude the restoration of his Ring power:

> [p. 309] (**Prelude:** H148 vari?; Norn pulses; H179 end frag?; H173a; [[**H179 orch**]]; H179 end frag?; H12 vari; [[**H179 orch** >>]] [develops]; H179 end

frag?; H12 vari; H173a; H12 vari [drops off]; H173a; **[[H179 vari on trumpet?]]**; H174b; H174b; H174b: (...) An open space on the shore in front of the Gibichung hall ... . An altar-stone can be seen ... dedicated to Fricka; a larger one for Wotan is visible ... , with a similar one dedicated to Donner ... . It is night. Hagen ... is sitting asleep ... . Alberich can be seen crouching in front of Hagen ... H17 vari)

Alberich: (... H49 vari >>:) Are you sleeping, Hagen, my son? (H49 >>:) You're asleep and do not hear me whom rest and sleep betrayed (:H49). (H179 end frag)

Hagen: (... he ... seems to be asleep, even though there is a glassy stare in his permanently open eyes) I hear you, evil elf: what do you have to tell my sleep? (H173a)

Alberich: (H11 vari:) Be mindful of the power that you'll command (:H11 vari) (H17 vari:) if you're as mettlesome (:H17 vari) (H35 voc:) as the mother who gave you birth (:H35 voc). (H179 end frag)

Hagen: (... **[[H179 voc:]]** [definitive version, plus Norn pulses]) Though my mother gave me mettle, I've no reason to be thankful (:H179 voc) (H35 voc:) that she yielded to your cunning (:H35 voc): (H49 vari as Norn pulses:; H179 end frag:) old too early, pale and wan (:H49 vari as Norn pulses; :H179 end frag), I hate the happy, (H35 voc:) am never glad ["hass' ich die Frohen, freue mich nie!"] (:H35 voc)!

The Prelude to T.2 introduces a new motif H179 which expresses Hagen's anguish at being who he is, a lonely heir to Alberich's loveless *Weltanschauung*, who must stand for the objective, bitter truth even if this forever precludes happiness and contentment. He's someone we might describe loosely as a Nietzschean Overman. Dunning detects an element of H35 (Loveless) in H179, and H35 is heard several times as Hagen graphically describes his inner misery to his father Alberich. H35 evokes our irrevocable Fall from grace as reflectively conscious beings. An H12 Variant is heard which reminds us that Brünnhilde's wondrous love, Siegfried's surrogate Rhine, protects him from Alberich's Ring Curse only for a time, which is now ending. We see altars to several Valhallan gods, indicating that the Gibichungs still honor the gods (much, perhaps, as modern secular society, and the State, accommodate a large percentage of the public who are religious). Alberich, appearing to Hagen as if in a dream, asks him—accompanied by H49— whether he's sleeping. Hagen remains asleep with his eyes open during his dialogue with his father: Hagen asks Alberich "What do you have to tell my sleep?" Alberich had in S.2.1 described himself as forever watchful and waking. Alberich is fearful that Hagen sleeps and doesn't hear him whom rest and sleep betrayed. Loge in R.3 warned Alberich that he might be dispossessed of the Ring when he slept, due to the envy of those unable to obtain its power as Alberich had (those not willing or able to make his sacrifice of love). This was Wagner's metaphor for Feuerbach's notion that early man collectively dreamed his myths of a supernatural origin and world-order into existence. This is why Alberich insists that Hagen be wakeful.

Accompanied by a H11 Variant (recalling the Rhinedaughters' aesthetic claim to their Rhinegold) and H17 Variant (their Rhinegold forged by Alberich into his Ring of power), followed by H35 (Loveless), Alberich reminds Hagen of the power he'll command if he's as mettlesome as the mother who gave him birth. Alberich refers directly to Hagen's blood-mother Grimhilde, whose sexual favors Alberich bought with gold, but indirectly to Mother Nature, Erda, whose objective knowledge of all that was, is, and will be, Alberich affirms. Alberich is saying that he'll surely win back his Ring power if Hagen is sufficiently loveless and ruthless. Hagen's bitter response to his father (which echoes the despair he revealed to Siegfried and Gunther when Siegfried asked him why he hadn't joined them in their passionate blood-brother oath) is something of a shock in view of who Hagen is, Alberich's son and instrument of his vengeance against the gods. For Hagen complains, accompanied by the new motif H179, that though his mother gave him mettle, he isn't glad she yielded (H35) to Alberich's cunning. H35 stamps this as a loveless marriage. And the gold with which Alberich won Mother Nature's favors is his Ring of consciousness, his means to access Nature's power through accumulation of a hoard of knowledge. Accompanied by H49 (the resentment Hagen embodies), Hagen tells his father this legacy he inherited from him has made Hagen prematurely old, pale and wan. He concludes, again accompanied by H35, that he hates the happy, and is never glad. Hagen is beset by the envy ("Neid") of the happy which obsesses his father. This "Neid" is Alberich's burning resentment that the gods and Wälsung heroes co-opted his Ring power to sustain their consoling illusions without paying his price. Unsurprisingly, Hagen's complaint to Alberich verbally references both the god Froh (Joy) and his sister the goddess Freia (Free) in the original German text ("hass' ich die Frohen, freue mich nie!"). Those Hagen envies are happy only because they're ignorant of the bitter truth he was born to contemplate in lonely solitude, as all thinkers dedicated uncompromisingly to truth must do. Self-deception, on the contrary (according to Feuerbach), tends to characterize those dedicated to life within society who depend on a network of others for their happiness and sense of meaning. [See 68F-EOC, pp. 66–67] It's this indifference to the moral and social consequences of the quest for knowledge and its power, according to Wagner, which makes modern scientific studies heartless, loveless. [See 1108W-{11/24/81}CD Vol. II, p. 753]

But this is how Alberich likes it: he tells Hagen to hate the happy, but to love Alberich as Hagen ought to, accompanied again by H35:

> **[pp. 309–10] Alberich:** ... Hagen, my son, hate the happy! (H?:—[Possible subtle musical/motival references to Alberich's complaints about Wotan's hypocrisy in R.4?]) But me, the mirthless, much-wronged dwarf, (H35 voc:) you love just as you ought (:H35; :H?—Possible references to Alberich's complaints to Wotan in R.4)! (H173a) If you're stalwart, (H173a) bold and clever, those whom we fight in nightly feud already suffer our spite ["schon giebt ihnen Noth unser Neid"]. (H17 vari:) He who wrenched the ring from me (:H17 vari), Wotan, ... was worsted by his own kind: (H56 vari?:) to the Wälsung he forfeited power ... (:H56 vari?): (H17ab/H18ab frag:) in

company with the whole kindred of gods (:H17ab/H18ab frag [dies out]) he awaits his end (H40A end frag:) in dread ["Angst"] (:H40A end frag). Him do I fear no more ... !

Alberich reassures Hagen by telling him those they fight in nightly feud already suffer from Alberich's and Hagen's spite. Wotan, he says, was overthrown by one of his own, and forfeited his power to the Wälsung (Siegfried). Alberich is alluding to the notion that when religion could no longer be sustained as a set of beliefs and articles of faith, it lives on in feeling, in the art of music. Accompanied by a H17ab/H18ab hybrid variant (bespeaking the underlying identity of Alberich and Wotan), Alberich declares Wotan and the gods now await their end in Valhalla in dread (as we hear H40A's—the Tarnhelm's—end fragment, which now has become a motival sign for the gods' end). Wotan (man's religious faith) has, Alberich says, now been neutralized, so Alberich no longer fears him. At this moment in world history the State no longer universally suppresses independence of thought to protect religious faith. The nightly feud Alberich mentions is the war over who controls the Ring, the power of conscious human thought. Will it be those who misuse the Ring's might to sustain subjective, consoling illusions, or those who use its might to full advantage, to exploit Nature's power and control men through objective knowledge?

But Wotan's defeat, though brought about by his own kind, isn't complete. Although Wotan (man's religious impulse) had to concede the truth to Alberich and go under, Wotan's subjective ideal of a world known aesthetically, through feeling rather than objective thought, lives on in Siegfried, the secular artist-hero whose inspired art holds its own in the modern, scientific world which ought to belong entirely to Hagen. Alberich's victory over the gods (over our dependence on self-delusion for happiness) will only be complete when Siegfried, the archetypal secular artist-hero of the modern era, also succumbs to the same Ring Curse of consciousness which forced Wotan to go under. Hagen must ascertain where the artist-hero Siegfried is vulnerable, since Siegfried, unlike religious man, doesn't stake a claim on the power of the truth (Ring) which scientific man could refute, and seems according to Alberich to be freed from his Ring Curse:

[pp. 310–11] Hagen: (... H179 end frag plus pulses:) The immortals' power—who would inherit it (:H179 end frag plus pulses)?

Alberich: [[H180 orch:]] [= H17ab vari] I—and you (:H180 orch): (H33 Norns' vari:) we'll inherit the world if I'm not deceived in my trust in you, if you share my grief and rage (:H33 Norns' vari). Wotan's spear (H56ab) was split by the Wälsung (H19) who felled the dragon, (H134a?) Fafner, in combat (H32A frag?/H17?:) and, child that he is, won the ring for himself (:H32a?/H17?): every power he has gained; (H15 vari:) Valhalla and Nibelheim bow down before him; ... even my curse grows feeble in face of the fearless hero (:H15 vari): for he does not know what the ring is worth, he makes no use of its coveted power; (H108) (H108 developed >> :) laughing, in loving desire, he burns his life away (:H108). (H162b:) To destroy him alone avails us now (:H162b). (H35) Are you sleeping, Hagen, my son?

Hagen: To his own destruction he serves me even now.

Hagen asks his father rhetorically (because Hagen's seemingly fool-proof plan to discredit Siegfried and inherit Alberich's Ring-power is already afoot) who'll inherit the immortals' (gods') power. Alberich's answer introduces a new motif H180, the "Murder Motif," a tightly wound variant of the Ring Motif H17, with a very dissonant harmony. Alberich says Hagen, and he, will inherit the world if he's not deceived in Hagen, if Hagen shares his grief and rage. This is the grief and rage of those free thinkers who were suppressed and persecuted and martyred for thousands of years by traditional societies under the spell of religious mythology. Alberich introduces the novel problem of what to do about Siegfried, who felled Fafner (emancipated the arts from the stranglehold of religious faith and its fear of the truth) in combat, and child that he is, won the Ring for himself, split Wotan's spear, and inherited Wotan's power. It's Siegfried's artificial, childlike innocence (produced by Brünnhilde knowing for him his true identity and historical context) that allowed him to co-opt Alberich's Ring power without paying for it in Noth (anguish).

Accompanied now by a new variant of H15, Alberich explains that Siegfried has gained every power, that both Valhalla and Nibelheim bow before him. The conflict between subjective feeling and objective thought, religious faith and science, has been resolved by returning to pre-fallen feeling, music. Alberich adds with dismay that even his Ring Curse grows feeble before the fearless hero, for Siegfried doesn't know the Ring's worth and doesn't use its power. Siegfried knows the Ring's worth, knows its use, but only unconsciously, for Brünnhilde knows this for him, and it's through her, his muse, that he can safely make "use" of Alberich's Ring, Wotan's repressed hoard of knowledge, by drawing unconscious inspiration from it to create his redemptive art. Alberich decides, now that Siegfried has inherited Wotan's power and even control over the Nibelungs (i.e., control over man's view of himself), the only thing that can help them now is to destroy Siegfried. Hagen responds that Siegfried, to his own destruction, serves Hagen, as we hear H180 (Murder) again.

Alberich's and Hagen's victory would engender acceptance of a loveless universe, in which no transcendent meaning inheres, an objective reality with bitter consequences for our human preference for romantic idealism and utopianism. The advantage champions of such a loveless world would gain would be freeing up some mens' potential for accruing power through objective knowledge of man and Nature, which otherwise would be rendered inaccessible due to the need to cater to subjective human sentiment. The disadvantage would be that there could be no pretext found in objective knowledge of Nature for setting limits to the power individual men could accrue, no rational or lawful limit set to the exploitation of men vulnerable to the predatory instincts of those more capable of wielding power over others. A society wholly dedicated to objective truth, to be self-consistent, would have to wean itself of all humane impulses, all concern for individual expression and rights, the dignity of man, all the things we feel "ought" to be true. Any such respect for the rights of men would only be preserved, if at all, for the sake of the prudence of egoism, but such practical prudence is incapable of inspiring our passionate loyalty, as Wagner often said. It's this fear science will annihilate everything of value man's imagination has produced, everything which lends grace, dignity, pride, and magic to human life, that led religious men in the Renaissance and Nineteenth Century to violently resist accepting Copernicus's solar-centric cosmos (where previously it was believed God made the solar system revolve around man and his earth), and resist Darwin's attempt to place man in his true position within the animal kingdom (the evolution of man in Darwin's view being just another step in the sequence of the evolution of life, with no higher intrinsic value than that of worms). The quest for objective knowledge implicitly denies man a divine origin or transcendent value. It's this demoralizing truth which gives pause even to moderate secularists and avowed atheists, who still wish (as Nietzsche complained) to smuggle man's alleged transcendent value into their worldview. In previously cited passages Feuerbach spelled out the advantages which man might gain through scientific thought's triumph. [See 127F-EOC, p. 217, 34F-TDI, p. 231, 253F-LER, p. 167, and 254F] But it was left to Wagner to expose the disadvantages.

Wagner grew skeptical of Feuerbach's optimism about the victory of science over religion even before he first became acquainted with Schopenhauer. While Wagner was writing the libretto of the *Ring* he remained, to an extent, a Feuerbachian, with reservations (the *Ring* was his attempt to dramatize his reservations while nonetheless registering his doubt of their cogency in the face of objective truth). But shortly after he began composing its music he underwent a nearly wholesale conversion to Schopenhauer's atheist yet mystical philosophy, a system of thought which—though (like Feuerbach's philosophy) based largely on science and an atheistic critique of the religious notions of Godhead, immortality, and free will—tried to smuggle back into this secular outlook an element of mystery inherently irreducible to reason and inaccessible to conceptual knowledge, which we might call aesthetic intuition. In the following Schopenhauer-infused passages Wagner rebutted Feuerbach's atheistic materialism: "... the theory of Constant Progress takes refuge in the 'infinitely broader horizon' of the modern world ... . (...) Our world ... is irreligious. How should a Highest dwell in us, when we no longer are capable of honouring, of even recognising the Great? And if perchance we recognise it, we are taught by our barbarous civilisation to hate and persecute it, for it stands in the way of general progress. (...) How can it be asked to venerate the sorrows of the Saviour? (...) ... what 'educated' person gladly goes to church?—Before all, 'Away with the Great!' " [963W-{4/79} 'Shall We Hope?,' PW Vol. VI, pp. 118–119] " ... the world soon managed to abolish Sin entirely, and believers now look for redemption from evil to Physics and Chemistry." [1045W-{11/80} 'What Boots This Knowledge?'—First Supplement to 'Religion and Art,' PW Vol. VI, p. 256]

Wagner was particularly upset at science's threat to the morality of compassion and self-sacrifice (and even to man's natural instinct for love) which was, even according to Feuerbach, our best and most lasting legacy from the Christian tradition, because, Feuerbach noted, it had always existed independently of religion, which co-opted it. Wagner observed that such an amoral approach to scientific inquiry would inevitably culminate in the degradation of man, the explaining away of all goodness and beauty as merely products of natural law and human egoism: "Unfortunately our review of human things has shown us Pity struck from off the laws of our Society, since even our medical institutes, pretending care for man, have become establishments for teaching ruthlessness, which naturally will be extended—for sake of 'science'—from animals to any human beings found defenseless against its experiments." [983W-{10/79} Letter to E. von Weber 'Against Vivisection,' PW Vol. VI, p. 201] " ... quite apart from their value in the eyes of the world, in his sufferings and death man is able to recognise a blessed expiation; whereas the beast, without one ulterior thought of moral advantage, sacrifices itself wholly and purely to love ...—though this also is explained by our physiologists as a simple chemical reaction of certain elementary substances." [988W-{10/79} Letter to E. von Weber 'Against Vivisection,' PW Vol. VI, p. 207] For Wagner, once society acquiesces in science's explanation of mysterious love and creative genius as, figuratively speaking, merely a chemical reaction, predictable and natural-law-bound phenomena which can be reduced to mundane physical causes, and therefore alterable and corruptible by physical means, all hope of finding transcendent meaning in life is lost forever. That's what's at stake if Alberich regains his lost Ring-power. But after all, who, once in possession of the bitter truth, would have so little pride they could wish to cease to be conscious of it for the sake of an ersatz consolation! This is the existential question which has tormented Wotan (Wagner) throughout the *Ring*.

But Alberich is troubled by what—given the premises of our allegorical interpretation—can only be regarded as a metaphysical threat. Suppose, he says, Brünnhilde were to urge Siegfried to restore the Ring to the Rhinedaughters. In this case, he fears, its power could never be restored to him:

[p. 311] **Alberich:** (H180 vari:) The golden ring, the circlet, must be gained (:H180 vari)! (H19 frag?:) A wise woman lives for the Wälsung alone (:H19 frag?): (H12 vari?:) were she ever to urge him (:H12 vari?) [the order of phrases in Spencer's English translation which follows differs from the German, so the sequence of motifs is different also] (H15?/H17?:) to give back the ring (:H15?/H17?), (I14 >> :) to the deep Rhine's daughters who once befooled me in watery depths (:H4), (H15?/H17?:) the gold would be lost to me then (:H15?/H17?), no cunning could ever reclaim it. (H180 vari:) So strive for the ring without delay (:H180 vari)!

This is one of the most mysterious passages in the *Ring*, unless we take for granted everything the *Ring* presents to us naively as a child would, without question, a standpoint dear to Wagner's heart (and also mine, as regards how we ought to experience the *Ring* in the theater!). It seems at first as if it falls outside the objective frame of reference of our allegory. However, there are too many cases where a consistent, coherent allegorical account such as I've proposed makes sense of passages—in their wider musico-dramatic context—which would otherwise be meaningless or incomprehensible, for us to disavow the effort to accommodate or explain the surprisingly few passages which seem to make an awkward fit with our allegorical reading. This is one of the few which compels us to seek a metaphysical (as Cooke put it) rather than an objective, reality-based explanation. If we take Alberich's statement at face value, that if Siegfried restores his Ring to the Rhinedaughters it will be lost to Alberich forever, then we accept that in the world Wagner imagined for the *Ring* Alberich could never regain his power if the Rhinedaughters dissolved his Ring and its Curse in the waters of the Rhine and, presumably, were now better prepared—forewarned— to keep the Rhinegold out of the hands of thieves than they were when they first let Alberich steal the Rhinegold (and even prompted him to do it). And we can't overlook the fact that in the finale of *Twilight of the Gods*, the last words spoken are those of Hagen, who cries out "Get back from the ring" when he sees the Rhinedaughters take possession of the Ring from the funeral pyre which burned both Brünnhilde and Siegfried, and plunges madly into the waves after them desperately trying to retrieve his father's Ring. Hagen's last words, and his desperation to retrieve the Ring from the Rhinedaughters, were obviously prompted by Alberich's warning to Hagen that, were the Ring ever restored to the Rhinedaughters, no cunning could ever gain it back.

We'll save fuller consideration of this profound question for our discussion of T.3.3, in which similar questions are raised, but we can address a particular issue now. There's one big problem with this interpretation, which is that, looking back at R.1, we find Flosshilde reminding her Rhinedaughter sisters, with respect to Alberich, that their father (Father Rhine?) warned them about such a foe. Given this fact, it seems likely that no matter how many times the Rhinedaughters were warned about the impropriety of tempting intruders to sacrifice love to forge a Ring from the Rhinegold for the sake of power, they might nonetheless be predestined to let it happen. In my prior assessment of R.1 I discussed the likelihood that Alberich's winning of the gold and forging a Ring from it is an expression of natural evolutionary necessity. So let's reassess Alberich's curious observation in light of our allegory.

Alberich says if Siegfried ever restored his Ring to the Rhine Alberich would never be able to regain its power. I've argued that Alberich's renunciation of love to forge his Ring of world power represents the birth of man's reflective, symbolic consciousness, which grants us humans limitless power to control our fellow men and our physical environment. If the Ring (with its Curse) was restored to the Rhine of pre-fallen preconsciousness, the stage of life in which plants and animals (but not humans) flourish, presumably the human species will have gone extinct. And we hear—for the first time in quite awhile—Woglinde's Lullaby H4 as Alberich warns Hagen that Brünnhilde might persuade Siegfried to return the Ring to the deep Rhine's daughters who once befooled him in watery depths, reminding us that H4 is the mother-melody which represents preconscious animal feeling and instinct, from which reflective consciousness (the Fall, Alberich's Ring) evolved. So Alberich seems to be saying that his chance to obtain world power will be lost if human consciousness itself is lost. But how could Siegfried the artist-hero ever find himself in a position to bring about the end of human consciousness itself? He could never do this in reality, but only symbolically, within art, as Wagner does in the *Ring*, which ends with the twilight of the gods and dramatization of some sort of earthly or even cosmic catastrophe. Wagner's *Ring* can, after all, be construed as an allegorical model for the actual world, a work of art which may anticipate things to come. It's possible collective, historical man, could bring about his own extinction, perhaps the destruction of his earth, or even the whole cosmos, through the scientific and technological exploration of the bonds and forces and laws of Nature. One recalls the fears of those who first experimented with nuclear fission, that there was no way to be absolutely sure that once they started a chain reaction of fission that it could be contained. It was theoretically possible that once the process got started it could never be stopped, and the bonds holding all the atoms in the universe together into larger forms would be broken. This is pure speculation but it's one of several alternative hypotheses (one which Wagner encouraged, as we'll see in our discussion of the finale of *Twilight of the Gods* in T.3.3) we must assess if we wish to grasp what Wagner intended to express in the culminating moments of his *Ring*. I'll return to this problem in our assessment of the final moments of the *Ring* in T.3.3.

Alberich seems to confirm that the only way he can ever regain his Ring and its power is through Siegfried's death. *Siegfried's Death* is the original title Wagner chose for what later became the final drama of the *Ring* tetralogy, *Twilight of the Gods*, but which was the seedbed from which the whole tetralogy grew in reverse order. So, in grasping the meaning of Siegfried's death, we might well grasp not only the *Ring* as a whole, but also the basis of Wagner's transition from a romantic opera composer, to the revolutionary creator of the mature music-dramas. The meaning, I believe, is the following: for the secular, scientific world-view (Alberich and Hagen) to wholly control the contents of the human mind (regain the Ring), our human propensity to stake the meaning of our life on the consoling self-deceptions of religion and art must first be discredited, so we can wean ourselves away from them. To fully accomplish this secular art must be exposed for what it is, covert religion, so it'll succumb to the same critique through which scientific inquiry previously undermined religious belief and its articles of faith (Wotan and the gods), exposing its claim to the truth (Alberich's Ring power) to be false. This explains the necessity of Siegfried's death. It was the purpose of Wagner's *Ring* to do this.

Alberich now offers Hagen a pep talk, reminding him that Alberich brought him up solely to destroy the gods and Wotan's heroes, and to restore to Alberich his Ring and its power:

[pp. 311–12] **Alberich:** (H38 frag?) Fearless Hagen, I fathered you to take a firm stand against heroes. (H134a:) Though not strong enough to defeat the dragon (:H134a) (H116?) which the Wälsung alone was fated to do— (H180) (H180:) I brought up Hagen to feel stubborn hatred (:H180): now he'll avenge me (H35 vari voc?:) and win the ring in contempt of the Wälsung and Wotan (:H35 vari voc?). (H18ab/H162/H40A vari—Possibly a hint of H84?):) Do you swear it, Hagen, my son (:H18ab/H162/H40A vari—Possibly a hint of H84?)? (...) [**Hagen:** (...); **Alberich:** (...)]

Hagen: (H179:) To myself I swear it (:H179): (H50:) silence your care (:H50)! (...)

Alberich: Be true, Hagen, (H50:) my son! (...) (H179 end frag; [[**H181a orch**]]; H179 end frag; H8; H179 end frag; [[**canon on H181a orch**]]; [[**H181b orch:**]] Alberich has ... disappeared completely. Hagen ... stares motionlessly ... at the Rhine, over which the light of dawn is already beginning to spread.)

When Alberich, accompanied by H180 (Murder), incites his son Hagen to win back Alberich's Ring from those who co-opted it, saying that though Hagen wasn't strong enough to do what only Siegfried could do (defeat the dragon Fafner to win back Alberich's Ring), he fathered Hagen to take a firm stand against [Wotan's] heroes, Alberich references Wotan's experiment in S.2.1, when he offered Alberich a chance to see if he could persuade Fafner to part with his Ring by agreeing to save Fafner's life by protecting him from Siegfried, so Fafner could live a long life in peace. Fafner (religious faith's fear of intellectual inquiry) rejected Alberich's offer, saying he preferred to have, to hold, and to sleep, in other words, to enjoy life consoled by the illusions of religious belief, which would be impossible if Fafner attained full, waking consciousness. Society wasn't yet ready to renounce its religious impulse and the traditions (the Social Contract) which grew up around it, in favor of the modern, secular, scientific world which Alberich and Hagen offer. It's in this sense that Hagen didn't have the strength which Siegfried alone had, to kill Fafner (to kill the grip which religious faith, and its offshoots in morality and art, still held on man's heart). Siegfried the artist-hero alone had this power because, as heir to dying religious faith, the ultimate insider, he could best deliver the coup de grace to Wotan's sin against all that was, is, and will be. Alberich says that, this being the case, Hagen will now avenge Alberich. At this point we hear what seems to be a new compound motif, H18a/H162/H40A Variant, but it seems to hint at H84 (based on a H18ab variant), which in V.2.2 expressed Wotan's morbid resignation to leave Hagen, annihilator of all Wotan's hopes and ideals, his heir. Wotan resigned himself to this when he complained to Brünnhilde that though he could never create a free hero (even though he wooed the Wälsung twins' mother with love), Alberich, who wooed Grimhilde lovelessly through bribery with gold, could create this free hero. Hagen is free from the self-deception which is the basis of Wotan's fated doom.

Now the sun begins to rise, and Alberich's image to fade, as he repeatedly asks Hagen to swear he'll wreak (the Ring Curse's—H50's) vengeance on gods and heroes. Hagen, accompanied by H179 (Hagen's Despair) and H50, answers that he swears this to himself. As Alberich slowly disappears from view along with the night, we hear a new motif, H181ab, which evokes, as Cooke put it, the dawn of that day on which Hagen will set in motion the concluding phase of his plan to discredit the Wälsung hero Siegfried and regain possession of the Ring power which Siegfried (unwittingly) co-opted. Cooke called this two segment motif "Hagen's Day," and described the transitional music which depicts the rising sun as beginning with a variant of H1, the Primal Nature Motif with which the *Ring* began (seedbed of the *Ring*'s music), which then becomes a canon, and shortly thereafter is transformed into brutal brassy music associated with Hagen's expectation of victory, H181a. H181 then develops into its definitive form H181ab, the segment H181b repeating a powerful three-note figure which will later be sung by the Gibichung chorus in T.2.3 in praise of Hagen's newly acquired status as wedding herald.

TWILIGHT OF THE GODS : ACT TWO, SCENE TWO
(GIBICHUNG HALL)
HAGEN, SIEGFRIED, AND GUTRUNE

Siegfried startles Hagen by appearing from out of nowhere, having been transported back from Brünnhilde's mountaintop to Gibichung Hall in a trice through the Tarnhelm's Wonder:

[pp. 312–13] (… the Rhine begins to glow with the deepening red of dawn. (…) H40A end frag; H181ab; H165: Siegfried suddenly appears from behind a bush close to the shore. H108) (…)

Hagen: (H181ab >> :) Hey! Siegfried! Fleet-footed hero? From where have you sped (:H181ab)?

Siegfried: (H32B:) From Brünnhilde's rock; it was there that I drew the breath with which I called your name (:H32B): (H108:) so quick was my journey here (:H108)! Two others (H40A/H11 vari >> :) follow more slowly (:H40A/H11 vari): they're coming here by boat.

Hagen: So you overpowered Brünnhilde?

Siegfried: Is Gutrun' awake? [**Hagen:** (…)] (H32B vari:) I'll tell you both how I bound Brünnhilde (:H32B vari). (H168ab?/H183?: Gutrune comes from the hall to meet him.) [[**H182 voc:**]] Bid me welcome, Gibich's child (:H182 voc)! A goodly herald I am for you. (H168/[[**H183 orch**]])

Gutrune: [[**H182 voc:**]] May Freia give you greeting in honour of all women (:H182 voc)!

Siegfried: (H168/H183:) Be open handed and well-disposed to me in my happy state ["**Frei** und **hold**, sie nun mir **frohem**"] (:H168/H183): (H117 vari?:) today I won you as my wife (:H117 vari?).

Siegfried, optimistic in his ignorance of his true situation, exuberantly announces his return. The stark contrast between the grim, knowing Hagen and joyously ignorant Siegfried is telling. Siegfried, exclaiming at the Wonder of the Tarnhelm which transported him there from Brünnhilde's mountain with the instantaneity of a wish fulfilled, is celebrating Wagnerian Wonder, the artistic imagination at the service of Wagner's music-drama, in which all time becomes now, all space becomes here, all wishes fulfilled.

When Hagen asks Siegfried whether he overpowered Brünnhilde, Siegfried, with cruel, ironic indifference, ignores him to ask whether Gutrune is awake. They both call out to wake Gutrune, and at her entrance two new motifs are introduced. H183 is the bright, brassy "Gibichung Horncall Motif" (not yet in definitive form) which will at the end of the hunt in T.3.2 be contrasted with H108, "Siegfried's Youthful Horncall." Cooke described H183 as the antithesis of H108. H183 is in the Gibichung Family of motifs which include H162 (Hagen), H167 (Gunther's False Friendship With Siegfried), H168 (Gutrune), and perhaps H178 (Honor). H183 will serve as herald of the double wedding of Siegfried with Gutrune, and Gunther with Brünnhilde, which Hagen has engineered. The other new motif H182 is a festive musical figure which conveys Siegfried's tragic, uncomprehending joy in wedding his new love Gutrune, wholly ignorant of what he's lost in forgetting Brünnhilde under the spell of Hagen's Potion. H182 seems to subtly echo Mime's Potion Motif H131B, associated simultaneously in S.2.3 with Mime's concocting a sleeping potion to render Siegfried helpless so Mime can murder him, and with Siegfried's re-forging of his father Siegmund's sword Nothung (which has phallic associations). H182 is introduced as Siegfried ecstatically cries out his welcome to Gutrune, and is the vocal line of Gutrune's joyous response to him: may the goddess Freia give Siegfried greeting in honor of all women. Siegfried subtly invokes the sibling gods Freia (alternative name Holda) and Froh as he tells Gutrune that she should be open handed and well disposed to him in his happy state ("**Frei** und **hold**, sie nun mir **froh**en"), since today he's won Gutrune as wife. The tragic irony and hubris is overwhelming as Siegfried and Gutrune call on the gods to celebrate an event which will signal the gods' and Wälsung heroes' downfall, and even the downfall of that social order (the Gibichung way of life) which up until now has been based on either openly expressed religious faith, or secular traditions and sentiments which have been propagated and sustained originally by religious faith.

Siegfried is about to be wholly embraced by Gibichung Society. But the cunning society which Mime warned him to prepare for by learning the meaning of fear from Fafner, the society which Wotan created and came to loathe, and of whose corrupt history his hoard of knowledge speaks, is embodied by the Gibichungs who've set out, like Wotan, to exploit Siegfried. Siegfried is serving this corrupt society to grant it an ersatz sense of meaning and value, just as Siegfried's archetype Loge formerly served the gods' need to sustain their self-deceit. Siegfried's wooing of Gutrune is the artist-hero's impulse to produce redemptive art for a society founded on hypocrisy, and consoled by self-deception, which now is rising to consciousness of its true, craven identity. Gutrune displays jealous skepticism of Siegfried's intentions in wooing Brünnhilde for Gunther. She finds it implausible he could have posed as Gunther overnight in Brünnhilde's cave without winning her sexual favors. She expresses her suspicion in a musically light-hearted duet Nattiez described as channeling Parisian Opéra Comique [Nattiez: pp. 84–86]:

[pp. 313–14] **Siegfried:** (H40A/H8 loosely based >>:) The woman was easily wooed (:H40A/H8 loosely based).

Gutrune: (H40A/H8 loosely based:) Didn't the fire singe him [Gunther] (:H40A/H8 loosely based)?

Siegfried: It wouldn't have harmed him either, but I myself passed through it for him, (H174a frag?) (H117 vari?:) because I wanted to win you (:H117 vari?). [**Gutrune:** (...); **Siegfried:** (...)]

Gutrune: (H40A/H32B: [Norns' vari?]) Did Brünnhilde take you for my brother?

Siegfried: (H40A/H32B [Norns' vari?] >>>:) I resembled him to a hair: the tarnhelm brought that about, as Hagen wisely said it would (:H40A/H32B [Norns' vari?]). [**Hagen:** (...)]

[Gutrune skeptically parries each of Siegfried's assurances that though he stood in for Gunther during the night he shared with Brünnhilde, he remained loyal to Gutrune. (...)]

Siegfried: (H178 voc:) Twixt east and west (:H178 voc)—(H56ab/H19) the north: (H167: pointing to his sword) so close was the distance (H32/H40A vari >>>>:) between them [Siegfried and Brünnhilde] (:H167; :H32/H40A vari). [**Gutrune:** (...)] Down through the fire's dying embers (H32B >>:) she followed me in the morning mist from the fell to the valley below; close to the shoreline Gunther and I (H40A/H32B? >>:) changed places in a trice (:H40A/H32B?): (H40A:) through the trinket's magic virtue I wished myself straight back here (:H40A). (H108)

In the face of Gutrune's doubts Siegfried insists that though he slept next to Brünnhilde in her cave he nonetheless didn't violate Brünnhilde or dishonor Gunther or Gutrune. To prove his point Siegfried swears a new oath, reintroducing H178 (to which he sang he'd separate himself from Gunther's bride with Nothung in T.1.3.B), and also H19 (Wotan's Spear as guardian of oaths), as he says: (H178) Twixt east and west—(H56/H19) the north: (pointing to his sword) so close was the distance between them. Having reassured Gutrune, Siegfried explains how he changed places with Gunther secretly, and Gunther is now sailing with Brünnhilde back to Gibichung Hall. Siegfried, Gutrune, and Hagen prepare to welcome Gunther and his new bride to Gibichung Hall, after spotting them coming upriver. Gutrune calls on Hagen, of all people, to serve as wedding herald:

[pp. 314–15] **Siegfried:** (H108/H181? >>:) A strong wind's now driving the lovers back up the Rhine (:H108/H181?): (H108; H168a) and so make ready their welcome! (H168a/H181) [**Gutrune:**(...); **Hagen:** (...); **Siegfried:** (...)]

Gutrune: (H182 voc:) Let's welcome her fondly that, care-free, she's glad to stay here (:H182 voc)! (H181:) You, Hagen, lovingly call the menfolk (:H181) (H182 voc:) to Gibich's garth for the wedding (:H182 voc)!

(H168b:) Happy women I'll call to the feast: they'll be glad to follow me in my joy (:H168b).

TWILIGHT OF THE GODS ≠ ACT TWO, SCENE THREE
(GIBICHUNG HALL)
HAGEN AND THE GIBICHUNG VASSALS

Hagen blows a cow-horn to call the Gibichungs to the double wedding, as if he's preparing them for war, introducing a new motif H184, a variant of H8 (Alberich's primal scream "Wehe! Wehe!" which expressed his inconsolable woe finding there's no love for him in the world). The Gibichung men answer Hagen's call to arms in a tense chorus of alarm which introduces a new motif H185. Hagen's call to the double wedding as if for war, with "Hoiho! Hoho!" set to H184 and its associated music, has a bald vulgarity and brutality which can't be described as beautiful music but whose musico-dramatic meaning, with its philosophical resonance, transcends the conventional beauty of music with something impressive in the deepest, most disturbing sense, the sublime. This is portentous because Hagen is calling the Gibichungs (modern man, Wagner's audience) to witness a world-historical tragedy, the exposure of the final religious mystery—Wotan's unspoken secret, which he confessed to Brünnhilde—to the public eye of objective consciousness, in Wagner's *The Ring of the Nibelung*. This scene is modeled on Friedrich's and Ortrud's challenge to Lohengrin's prohibition against sharing knowledge of his true identity and origin with Elsa, prior to their wedding in Act Two of *Lohengrin*:

> [pp. 315–16] (H181b?: Hagen ... raises his cowhorn to his lips and begins to blow.)
>
> **Hagen:** [[**H184 voc:**]] [= H8ab vari] Hoiho! Hoiho! Hoho! You men of Gibich, bestir yourselves (:H184 voc)! (H8 voc:; H181b:) Woe! Woe! To arms! (...) (:H8 voc; :H181b) (H181) To arms throughout the land! [[**H183 orch >>:**]] (...) (:H183 orch) (H163) (H53 vari orch/H8 voc:) Danger ["Noth"] is here! Danger ["Noth"]! Woe! Woe (:H53/H8 voc)! [[**H184 voc >>:**]] (...) (:H184 voc)
>
> ((...) Armed vassals enter hurriedly ... before assembling on the shore outside the hall. H181b)
>
> **The Vassals:** [[**H185 orch:**]] Why does the horn ring out? Why does it call us to battle? (...) (:H185 orch) (...) (H53 vari:) What danger ["Noth"] is here? What foe is near? (...) Is Gunther in danger ["Noth"] (:H53 vari)? (...)
>
> **Hagen:** (H181; H163: ...) Arm yourselves well and do not rest! (H181; H163) Gunther you must welcome: he's wooed a wife for himself.
>
> **The Vassals:** [[**H185 orch:**]] Does danger threaten him? Is the enemy at his heels (:H185 orch)?

Hagen: A fearsome woman he's bringing home. **[[H185 orch:]]** [The Vassals: (...)] (:H185 orch) (H35 frag:) He's coming alone (:H35 frag): no one's following.

The Vassals: (H185:) So he triumphed over the danger ["Noth"]? (...) (:H185) (H108 frag)

Hagen: The dragon-killer averted the danger ["Noth"]: (H108 frag) (H108 vari:) Siegfried the hero made sure he was safe ["Heil"] (:H108 vari).

As Hagen calls the Gibichungs as if to battle, though it's merely to celebrate a double wedding, the dramatic sounding of H53 (Twilight of the Gods) tells us the events Hagen has put into motion, particularly the double (and tragically infelicitous) wedding, are going to bring about the end of the gods, the end not only of religious belief but of the secular, altruistic morality and art which fell heir to our religious longing for transcendent value when religion could no longer be sustained as a belief system in the face of our advancement in knowledge. Siegfried the artist-hero, influenced by Hagen (our natural evolutionary impulse toward greater consciousness), is going to reveal to his audience what should have remained concealed from it, the secret of that unconscious inspiration which gave birth to both religious faith and authentically inspired secular art.

It's a convention of most fairy tales that after a series of hardships and tests, the hero wins his true love and the story ends with their blessed marriage. Wagner has turned this narrative tradition upside down by making the culminating marriage, which normally resolves the conflicts in the tale, the undoing of the hero and heroine. One is reminded of Michael Tanner's remark about *The Rhinegold*, that it ironically reverses the archetypal tale of paradise lost, because in *Rhinegold* what was lost wasn't really a paradise: "Wagner has depicted a primal world which is corrupt from the start, thus producing something at odds with the central myth of Western culture." [Tanner: p. 118] Siegfried's unwitting yet reprehensible involvement in brutally forcing his muse of inspiration Brünnhilde into an unloving marriage with the coward and hypocrite Gunther, is Wagner's metaphor for his own unwitting, involuntary betrayal of the secret of his unconscious artistic inspiration to his audience through his musical motifs (not to say that any particular admirer of Wagner's art is either a coward or hypocrite). Wagner's motifs link consciously experienced feeling with subliminal, unconscious knowledge (they are our portal to our unconscious), and hold the key to those formerly hidden, inner processes to which Wagner claimed to have unique access by virtue of being both author and composer of his music-dramas. Cosima recorded his remark that he feared that in the enjoyment of creating his art he'd failed to acknowledge some danger hidden within it. This danger wasn't simply that art's capacity to substitute aesthetic play for the world's earnestness was a cowardly evasion that distracts us from our need to attune ourselves to moral imperatives. We're now about to confront this dangerous Noth since Wagner from this point onward in his *Ring* no longer offers us a euphemistic allegory for our tabooed secrets which we keep even from ourselves: he compels us to face what we most fear and can least afford to acknowledge. And the artist-hero Siegfried is about to wed the false muse Gutrune, who's Wagner's metaphor for the artist's natural impulse to share the ecstasy of his sacred—and private—inspiration with his audience in a public production, which in this unique case—coming at the culmination of the last phase of cultural evolution—has tragic consequences, since Siegfried's art will reveal the bitter Noth behind the bliss into which it was formerly sublimated through faith and artistic Wonder.

What's ultimately at stake in this double marriage is revealed in Hagen's endlessly repeated mantra that "Danger ["Noth"] is here!" This danger Hagen warns of is accompanied by the Twilight of the Gods Motif H53, so the danger which Siegfried's betrayal of his muse Brünnhilde engenders is the potential loss of all the illusions of transcendent value on which we humans have staked life's meaning. This is Wotan's divine Noth which he confessed to Brünnhilde in V.2.2. The Noth Hagen deliberately brought to Gibichung Hall is the risk that the hoard of knowledge which Siegfried's muse of unconscious artistic inspiration Brünnhilde kept safe for him up until now, from whose wounds she protected him, he's involuntarily going to dredge up from the silent depths to the light of day, as Alberich once foresaw (R.3). H184, a variant of H8 (Alberich's "Wehe! Wehe!," to which he expressed that despair of finding love in the world which prompted him to renounce it for power), is the hallmark of Alberich's revenge on the world for not granting him love, i.e., for his inability to find transcendent meaning in the real world, embodied now by Hagen. His revenge lies in denying the consolation of the illusion of transcendent value to those who, unlike him, have staked their life on it. Alberich is unable to evade the truth and won't let anyone else evade it either.

Hagen pursues this theme—that in winning Brünnhilde for Gunther Siegfried has introduced "Noth," danger and anguish, into the Gibichung realm—obsessively. When the Gibichung vassals demand to know what "Noth" (danger) is here, and ask if Gunther is in "Noth" (danger), Hagen answers that Gunther is bringing a fearsome woman, his new wife, home, Brünnhilde embodying the danger Wagner said lurked in his art. When the vassals ask whether Gunther has triumphed over the "Noth" (danger), Hagen avers that the dragon-killer (Siegfried) has averted the "Noth" (danger). This "Noth" is the secret, forbidden source of that unconscious artistic inspiration, existential fear, by virtue of which the primal Folk gave unwitting and involuntary birth, in a collective dream, to the gods. This allegedly divine inspiration is identical to that unconscious inspiration through which the single artist of modern times produces authentic art. Siegfried, archetype for all secular, unconsciously inspired artists (epitomized by Wagner), had formerly protected his audience (represented now by Gunther, primevally by Wotan) from this "Noth," confronting it subliminally to safely draw inspiration from it, so he could heal himself temporarily from the un-healing wound this knowledge dealt him, and redeem his audience, man, from it. But Siegfried is about to share it—unwittingly—with his audience. The art whose primal purpose was to temporarily heal man's un-healing wound will now inflict that wound without hope of healing. We're reminded of Tristan in Act Three of *Tristan* and Amfortas in *Parsifal*.

During the course of this frenetic dialogue between Hagen and the Gibichungs the new motif H185 is introduced. Though in its original context it bespeaks the Gibichungs' alarm inspired by Hagen's call to arms, eventually, as the vassals realize Hagen is merely playing a morbid game with them, it will settle down as they break into a jaunty chorus to which the vassals praise Hagen as wedding herald. It can be regarded, like H182 and H183, as one of those motifs which expresses Siegfried's, Gunther's, and Gutrune's tragically ironic joy in the Gibichungs' celebration of this double wedding, which will end in irredeemable disaster. Believing now (how little they suspect!) that Hagen was putting them on about the danger, the Gibichungs relax and ask how they can best celebrate the wedding. Hagen suggests, with dark humor whose mocking import is hidden from the Gibichungs, that they make sacrifices to the Valhallan gods to seek their blessing for the wedding, and that they drink themselves into a stupor:

[pp. 317–18] **Hagen:** Stout-limbed steers you're to slaughter: on the altar-stone let their blood flow for Wotan. [**One Vassal:** (...)]

Eight Vassals: (H181ab vari/H185:) What would you have us do then (:H181ab vari/H185)?

Hagen: Bring down a boar for Froh; a sturdy goat (H185) slay for Donner (H185): (H181ab vari:) for Fricka, though, you must slaughter sheep, so that she gives a goodly marriage (:H181ab vari)!

The Vassals: (... H185:) When we've slaughtered the beasts, what then should we do (:H185)?

Hagen: (H181a canon vari >> :) Take up the drinking-horn blissfully filled by your sweethearts with mead and with wine (:H181a canon vari). (H185) [**The Vassals:** (...)] (H181b:) Quaff all you can till drunkenness tames you (:H181b)—(H181a:) and all to honour the gods (:H181a), (H181 vari:) that they give a goodly marriage (:H181 vari)!

The Vassals: (H181b vari: breaking into ringing laughter) (H181ab voc:; H162:) Fair fortune and good now smile on the Rhine, since Hagen the grim can make so merry! The hawthorn bush no longer pricks (:H181ab voc; :H162). (H183 >> :) He's been installed as bridal herald (:H183). [Continuation of preceding lines set to H181ab voc] (...)

Hagen: (approaching some of the vassals: H181 vari:) To your lady be loyal, serve her truly: if wrong should befall her, be (H162:) swift to vengeance (:H162; :H181 vari)! (H183: (...) (... the boat bearing Gunther and Brünnhilde appears on the Rhine.) (H183 transitions into a H185 frag vari; H162) [**The Vassals:** (...)] (...)

The Vassals: (H181ab:) Welcome! Welcome! (...) Welcome, Gunther! (H181b >>:) Hail! Hail!

In bitter irony Hagen calls on the Gibichungs to make special sacrifices, one after the other, to each of the Valhallan gods (except Freia, whom Gutrune has already invoked), and in a final irony calls on Fricka to bless this double wedding which

Hagen has engineered, recalling how Fricka blessed Hunding's loveless marriage with Siegfried's birth-mother Sieglinde. Hagen's sole purpose in arranging these two marriages is to expose Siegfried's true relationship with his muse of unconscious artistic inspiration, revealing the secret their art has previously concealed, so that, Siegfried being discredited, Hagen can offer man (Gunther) the practical consolation of a bid for power which, however, precludes love and humane values. By exposing Siegfried's enabling of Gunther's and Gutrune's self-deception, Hagen will retroactively destroy faith in the old gods and the values and traditions which once flowed from religious faith, and continued to flow from it even after its day was done in the morality of compassionate self-sacrifice and in secular art.

The Gibichung vassals, taken aback and pleasantly surprised by Hagen's uncharacteristic gaiety, sing a choral song in mocking praise of his transformation into a jolly wedding herald, set vocally to H181ab (Hagen's Day), and orchestrally to H162, H183, and H185. Hagen asks them to grow serious now that Gunther and Brünnhilde are coming ashore, and sternly warns them—a premonition of dark things to come, set to H181—to loyally serve their new lady, and be swift to vengeance if wrong befalls her. They now prepare to sing a grand welcome to Gunther as he steps ashore with captive, crushed Brünnhilde in hand.

TWILIGHT OF THE GODS = ACT TWO, SCENE FOUR

(GIBICHUNG HALL)
HAGEN, THE GIBICHUNG VASSALS AND WOMEN, GUNTHER, GUTRUNE, BRÜNNHILDE, AND SIEGFRIED

Welcoming Gunther and his new bride home, the Gibichungs sing one of the most compelling and noble choruses in all of Wagner's oeuvre, all the more impressive and tragically ironic because we've born witness to its shabby pretext, its shoddy foundation (we recall Loge's ironic, mocking testimony to the alleged sturdiness of the gods' refuge, Valhalla):

[pp. 318–19] (H162?: Gunther steps out of the boat with Brünnhilde. (...) Throughout the following, Gunther leads Brünnhilde solemnly by the hand.)

The Vassals: (H163 loose vari:) Hail to you, Gunther! Hail to you, and to your bride! Welcome (:H163 loose vari)! (They strike their weapons noisily together. [this stage direction has been ignored in every production I've experienced])

Gunther: (H80 twist? [possibly a subtle reference to Brünnhilde's initial fear of consummating sexual union with Siegfried from S.3.3]; H76 frag/H176 vari: presenting Brünnhilde, who follows him pale-faced and with downcast eyes, to the vassals) Brünnhilde, most hallowed of women, I bring to you here on the Rhine (H185/H163 frag vari >>:): a nobler wife was never won! The gods have favoured the Gibichung race; now let it rise to the highest renown (:H185/H163 frag vari)!

The Vassals: (ceremoniously clashing their weapons: H185/H163 frag vari:) Hail to you, happy Gibichung (:H185/H163 frag vari)! (Gunther leads Brünnhilde, who never once raises her eyes, to the hall, from which Siegfried and Gutrune emerge, attended by womenfolk. H76; H176)

Gunther: (...) (H183 tragic vari voc:) Be welcome, dear hero! Be welcome, fair sister (:H183 tragic vari voc)! (H167 voc:) I see you happy beside him who won you as his wife. Two blissful couples I see here resplendent (:H167 voc): (H183 tragic vari: He draws Brünnhilde closer towards them.) Brünnhilde—and Gunther (:H183 tragic vari), Gutrune—and (H116:) Siegfried (:H116). (H162?)

This scene delivers a shock, for we must imagine that, allegorically speaking, Gunther, Wagner's audience, has laid claim to that which only the unconsciously inspired artist Siegfried ought to have had access to, the muse of art and all her forbidden secrets, and presents her here as his hostage, a present to him from the inspired artist himself. Heretofore, inspired artists had presented redemptive artworks to their audience, waking dreams or allegories in which the true, original source of inspiration, existential fear, was forgotten. But now, instead of presenting his audience with a redemptive work of art, Siegfried has presented his audience with his muse of inspiration, the sacred womb which formerly gave birth to his wondrous art, and has therefore made his audience a present of his formerly unconscious source of inspiration, the terrible Noth or existential woe, which in times past the artist-hero had to transform and sublimate into aesthetic bliss, to make his inspiration palatable to, and redemptive for, his audience, to make them feel as if he'd healed man's un-healing wound. We hear H176, which expresses Brünnhilde's gradual awareness that the blissful love she's shared with Siegfried (unconscious inspiration of his new adventures in art) is actually the horrific climax of Wotan's punishment of her for living for love, the fulfillment of Alberich's Ring Curse. Yet Gunther presents Brünnhilde—who carries this unbearable woe within her—to his fellow men, seeking their approval of his great triumph, as if, in winning her, he'd reached the apogee of joy of which human life is capable, the greatest honor it's possible to receive, a gift from the gods, the summit of human ideals, the very essence of the divine nectar of our entire religio-artistic heritage. And this in fact is how one feels experiencing the *Ring*, the most profoundly stirring and ecstatic of artworks, which nonetheless, because it sublimates the most abominable and unmentionable of truths, possesses for us a disturbing, subversive residuum, its controversial subtext, hidden evidence of Wagner's doubt about his entire artistic enterprise and its capacity for redemption.

Gunther then presents the two couples to each other, Brünnhilde and Gunther, Gutrune and—Siegfried! Siegfried's name calls forth H116 from the orchestra (which at its inception was the hallmark of Siegfried's unexpected discovery of his previously unknown Wälsung heritage, when Mime informed him of his martyred father's broken sword, a restoration which Siegfried would complete by reforging it as Nothung), and of course knocks Brünnhilde back with the greatest blow she'll ever suffer. Wotan's final hope for redemption through Siegfried's and Brünnhilde's love (the inspired art to which they give birth) ends right here. Brünnhilde raises her eyes and can't hide her shock, horror and dismay, causing everyone around her to note her terrible discomfiture with curiosity and concern:

> [pp. 319–21] (H176: Brünnhilde raises her eyes in alarm and sees Siegfried; her gaze remains fixed on him in amazement. Gunther has released her violently trembling hand and, like the others, shows genuine perplexity at her behavior.). (H87 vari)
>
> **Some Vassals:** (H87 vari:) What ails her (:H87 vari)? (H40A:) Is she distraught (:H40A)?
>
> (H165: Brünnhilde begins to tremble.)
>
> **Siegfried:** ... H162 [Hagen]:) What troubles Brünnhilde's features (:H162)?
>
> **Brünnhilde:** (scarcely able to control herself H183:) Siegfried ... here! ... Gutrune ... (:H183)?
>
> **Siegfried:** (H168:) Gunther's gentle sister (:H168): (H183 vari:) wedded to me, as you are to Gunther (:H183 vari). (H81 six-note vari orch?)
>
> **Brünnhilde:** (with terrible vehemence) I. Gunther? ...? You lie!—(H88 vari: She sways and appears about to collapse; Siegfried supports her.) The light is fading from my eyes ... (:H88 vari). (... looking weakly up at him: H160:) Siegfried ... knows me not (:H160)!
>
> **Siegfried:** (H160:) Gunther, your wife's unwell (:H160)! (...) Wake up, woman! Here stands your husband!
>
> **Brünnhilde:** (Brünnhilde sees the ring on Siegfried's outstretched finger and starts up with terrible violence.) (H17 vari:) Ha! The ring ... upon his hand (:H17 vari)! (H50:) He ... Siegfried (:H50)? (H35 frag) [**Some Vassals:** (...)]
>
> **Hagen:** (H162b vari:) (...) Mark closely now what the woman discloses (:H162b vari)!
>
> **Brünnhilde:** (... H49:) A ring I saw upon your hand:—it belongs not to you but was wrested from me (pointing to Gunther)—by this man here! How could you have got the ring from him (:H49)?
>
> **Siegfried:** (examining the ring on his finger) I did not get the ring from him. (H9/H165)
>
> **Brünnhilde:** (to Gunther: H173ab/H43ab:) If you took from me the ring by which I was wed to you, then tell him of your right to it, demand the token back (:H173ab/H43ab)!
>
> **Gunther:** (in great confusion: (H165 >>:) The ring? I gave him none.—but are you sure that it's the same (:H165)?
>
> **Brünnhilde:** (...) (H176 inverted vari—[as an orchestral explosion]) Ha! He it was who wrested the ring away from me: (H15 vari:) Siegfried, the

treacherous thief (:H15 vari)! (H176 vari:; H17 vari: All look expectantly at Siegfried, who is completely lost in contemplation of the ring.)

Siegfried: (H17 vari:) It was not from a woman the ring came to me (:H17 vari), (H15:) nor was it a woman (H47?:) from whom I took it (:H15; :H47?): (H176 frag:; H12:) I recognize clearly (H134a:) the spoils from the fight which I once won at (:H134a; :H12) (H173 vari:) Neidhöhle ["Envy-Cave"] (:H173 vari) (H58bc frags:) when slaying the mighty dragon (:H134a; :H58bc frags). (H9/H17 vari)

Hagen: ... Brünnhild' ... ! Do you recognize the ring? (H9) If it's the one that you gave to Gunther then it is his alone (H162b/H50 broad?:) and Siegfried won it by fraud, for which the traitor must pay (:H162b/H50 broad?)! (H165 frag)

As several Gibichungs ask what ails Brünnhilde, we again hear H176, but also H87 (Fate) and H40A's (Tarnhelm's) end fragment, followed shortly by H165 (Hagen's Potion). H87 tells us that this tragic event is fate at work, Erda's prophecy of the twilight of the gods. And H40A alongside of H165 recalls that the imagination (the Wagnerian Wonder), which religious man formerly employed to co-opt the mind's power in service to self-deception, will betray that self-deception to the light, now that it's in service to objective knowledge. When Siegfried asks what troubles Brünnhilde, she stumbles over her words trying to make sense of what's happening, and when he acknowledges he's now being wed to Gutrune, and declares Brünnhilde is being wed to Gunther, Brünnhilde calls him a liar, and nearly faints as we hear an H88 variant, recalling Brünnhilde's prior status as muse to martyrs and her annunciation of fated death to Siegfried's father Siegmund. Looking into Siegfried's eyes she implores him to tell her if he knows her, as we hear H160 (which recalls her inspiration of Siegfried's new adventures in art), but Siegfried's only response is to call Gunther's attention to the fact that Gunther's wife Brünnhilde seems unwell.

Suddenly, Brünnhilde sees her Ring on Siegfried's finger, the very one which Siegfried, disguised as Gunther, had forcibly ripped off hers, and is overcome striving to grasp the terrible implications, as we hear the Curse Motif H50. Hagen takes advantage of the situation, asking the vassals to mark closely what Brünnhilde discloses. Brünnhilde, composing herself, and accompanied by Alberich's "Envy Motif" H49, tells everyone that the Ring on Siegfried's finger doesn't belong to Siegfried, but was forcibly stolen from Brünnhilde by Gunther. Brünnhilde asks how Siegfried could have gotten the Ring from him. Siegfried, contemplating his Ring almost as if noticing it on his finger for the first time (and not only having forgotten that he'd given it to Brünnhilde, but also not having recognized it was his own Ring which he forced off her finger), accompanied by H9(Rhinegold)/H165, says distractedly that he didn't get the Ring from Gunther.

Siegfried isn't consciously lying: he really doesn't recall how he forcibly took his own Ring back from Brünnhilde. Hagen's potion (H165) not only made Siegfried forget Brünnhilde and fall in love with the first woman he saw after drinking it (Gutrune), but it precludes the possibility that he can become conscious of anything which might remind him of his former relationship with Brünnhilde. We must grasp that each time Siegfried visits his muse of unconscious inspiration Brünnhilde, by passing back through Loge's protective Ring of fire, the veil of Maya, which keeps all others except the authentically inspired artist-hero from accessing the religious mysteries Brünnhilde guards, Siegfried is unconscious, dreaming. And this will be true even when, later (in T.3.2), he unwittingly and involuntarily betrays the secret of his unconscious artistic inspiration within his completed work of art, the narrative he sings to the Gibichungs about how he came to understand birdsong. Wagner presents us with two metaphors for Siegfried's unwitting betrayal of the secrets of his unconscious mind to the light of day. The first is that Siegfried, under Hagen's influence (the Tarnhelm H40AB transforms into Hagen's Potion H165), gives his muse of inspiration Brünnhilde away to his audience, Gunther and the Gibichungs, by giving Brünnhilde to Gunther in marriage. The second is the song narrating his heroic history, and how he came to grasp the meaning of birdsong (H137ab and H138ab), which he sings at Hagen's behest to the Gibichung hunting party in T.3.2, during which he'll reveal his true relationship with his muse Brünnhilde to his audience, wholly oblivious to the serious implications of what he's confessing.

Brünnhilde then demands that if Siegfried took from her, by fraud, the Ring by which she was wed to Gunther, and which Hagen claims she gave to Gunther, Gunther should assert his right to have Siegfried return it to him. Gunther's confusion and inability to explain anything is expressed by H165 (Hagen's Potion). Gunther asserts he didn't give Siegfried any Ring, and asks if the Ring to which Brünnhilde alludes is the one Siegfried's wearing now. Brünnhilde's despairing struggle to solve this conundrum is accompanied by H9/H165 and H40A's end fragment, suggesting she's intuited that some sort of cunning subterfuge, a conspiracy between Siegfried and Gunther, is behind this. Suddenly we hear an orchestral explosion as Brünnhilde screams at Siegfried: "(H176 Inversion:) Ha! He it was who wrested the Ring away from me. (H15 Variant) Siegfried, the treacherous thief." H176 conveys Brünnhilde's growing recognition that the blissful love she's known with Siegfried is actually the instrument of Wotan's punishment for her insistence on living for love. Brünnhilde concludes Siegfried has won her love with the sole purpose of handing her over captive to a loveless marriage with Gunther. This is the punishment she initially supposed Wotan intended for her in V.3.2–3, that she'd be left asleep to be forced into marriage, and shame, with any man who found her, no matter how unworthy. It would be as if Siegmund, Siegfried's father, had aided the Neidings in abducting Sieglinde to hand her over to Hunding, rather than saving Sieglinde from her loveless marriage to Hunding which they forced her into.

But Siegfried is strangely oblivious, calmly contemplating the Ring on his finger as if under a spell, and recalling how he originally won it from Fafner, not remembering he's recently forced it off of Brünnhilde's finger. It wasn't from a woman it came to me, he says, as we hear Fafner's Serpent/Dragon Motif H47. Instead—accompanied initially by H12 (the Rhinedaughters' cry "Rhinegold! Rhinegold!") and H134 (Fafner's Fear Motif), Siegfried says: "(H12; H134:) I recognize clearly the spoils from the fight which I once won at (H173 Variant) Envy-Cave (H58bc) when slaying the mighty dragon." The sounding here of H12 (Rhinegold! Rhinegold!) and H58bc is extraordinary. We revisit that moment in S.2.3 when Siegfried emerged from Fafner's cave with the Ring and Tarnhelm (which the Woodbird told him to retrieve, describing their use in detail), accompanied by H58abc, the Rhinedaughters' first lament for their stolen Rhinegold from R.4. When he emerged he asked himself what use they might be, having already forgotten what the Woodbird told him. He knows the Ring's and Tarnhelm's use only in the safe way granted him by aesthetic intuition. By the same token Brünnhilde's subliminal teaching, founded on Wotan's confession, his hoard of runes, has left Siegfried untaught, i.e., unconscious.

So he now remains wholly unconscious of having forcibly taken his Ring back from Brünnhilde. That Siegfried speaks in this way, saying of the Ring that he recognizes clearly that he won it by slaying a mighty dragon, suggests he's almost surprised to find it on his finger. He wasn't wearing it before he left with Gunther to abduct Brünnhilde because, as he confided to Hagen, he'd left it with a glorious woman. But the contents of his unconscious mind are gradually rising to consciousness to contradict what would normally be his rational understanding of time, place, and self, because Siegfried unwittingly ripped the Ring, the incarnation of Alberich's Ring Curse of consciousness, out of Brünnhilde's (i.e. unconsciousness's) protective hands, and has now brought it from the silent depths to the light of day. Ironically, it's Brünnhilde's gift of wondrous protection from the wounds of consciousness which makes Siegfried unable to recall anything that happened when he was with her which might remind him of their former relationship. In like manner, Tannhäuser forgets the true source of his unconscious artistic inspiration by his muse Venus, in the Venusberg, each time he wakes, figuratively reborn, to create a work of art, originally inspired by Venus, but on waking attributed to some other source of inspiration (such as divinity). Similarly, Walther doesn't grasp the meaning of Hans Sachs's Act Two confession to Eva, Walther's muse of unconscious artistic inspiration, in *Mastersingers*. So we may deduce that Hagen's potion of forgetfulness H165, symbol for Wagner's artistic "Wonder," is in some strange way a product of Siegfried's unconscious mind Brünnhilde, just as we can deduce that Hagen's nefarious influence on Siegfried isn't an external influence, but comes from within Siegfried's own nature as an inspired artist-hero. This lends our ever more ramified plot (which nonetheless Wagner's motifs allow us to untangle) a uniquely provocative piquancy and fascination.

We might have expected Gunther would begin to suspect Brünnhilde is the wondrous woman with whom Siegfried told Hagen that he left the Nibelung Ring which he won from Fafner, to keep it safe. Did Gunther hear what Siegfried said to Hagen? Evidently not. Hagen now steps forward to suggest that if Siegfried took the Ring which, Hagen says, Brünnhilde gave to Gunther, Siegfried must have won it by fraud (represented here ironically by Hagen's Potion H165) and must be punished. Hagen knows that Siegfried is the heir to Wotan and Loge, who won the Ring by fraud from his father Alberich, and it's for this ancient, primal crime that Siegfried, Wotan's heir, must pay. Brünnhilde suddenly has an appalling revelation of the full scope and meaning of Siegfried's betrayal of their love, and cries out in agony to the gods, and to Wotan in particular, who're ultimately the cause of her despair:

> [pp. 321–3] **Brünnhilde:** (... H178 vari/H173 chord:) Deceit! Deceit! :H178 vari/H173 chord)! (H17 vari:) Most shameful deceit (:H17 vari)! (H178 vari/H173 chord:) Betrayal! Betrayal (:H178 vari/H173 chord)! **[[H186 orch:]]** [= H184/H176] As never before avenged (:H186 orch)! [**Gutrune:**(...); **Women and Vassals:** (...)] Hallowed gods! (H50 frag voc?:) Heavenly rulers (:H50 frag voc?)! (H176 voc:) Was this what you whispered within your council (:H176 voc)? (H49) (...) (H49) (H176:) Have you caused me (H39:) shame more painful than any yet felt (:H176; :H39)? (H43a:) Now teach me (H17 vari:) revenge as never yet raged! (...) (:H43a; :H17 vari;)! (H58a varis:) Bid Brünnhilde break her heart in twain to destroy the man who betrayed her (:H58a varis)!
>
> **Gunther:** (H8/H185:) Brünnhilde, wife! Control yourself (:H8/H185)!
>
> **Brünnhilde:** (H176 vari:) Keep away, betrayer! Self-betrayed (:H176 vari)! ... (H106 unison orch:) not to him [Gunther] (:H106 unison orch), but to that man there [Siegfried] am I wed. [**Women:** (...); **Vassals:** (...)] (H35 vari voc:) He forced delight ["Lust"] from me, and love ["Liebe"] (:H35 vari voc). (H176 vari)
>
> **Siegfried:** (H160 frag voc?:) Are you so careless of your own honour (:H160 frag voc?)? (H12 vari:) The tongue that defames it (:H12 vari), (H176:) must I accuse of lying ["Luege"] (:H176)?—Listen whether I broke my faith! (H162) (H169:) Blood-brotherhood (:H169) have I sworn to Gunther. (H178) (H178:) Nothung (:H178), my worthy (H19/H56ab/H162b) sword, defended the oath of loyalty; (H56ab:) its sharp edge sundered me from this unhappy woman (:H56). (H176)
>
> **Brünnhilde:** (H176:) You cunning hero, look how you're lying ["Lueg'st"], just as you're wrong to appeal to your sword (:H176)! (H58a or H12 vari:) Well do I know (H56ab) its sharp-set edge (:H58a or H12 vari), (H161 vari voc:) but I also know the scabbard in which your true friend (:H161 vari voc), (H56 sinuous vari) Nothung, rested (H161 vari voc >>:) serenely against the wall while its master won him his sweetheart (:H161 vari voc).

H178, the Honor Motif which recalls Siegfried's ironic employment of his phallus Nothung to separate himself from this authentic muse Brünnhilde (to lose the protection of his unconscious mind), is strongly emphasized as she cries out in shock about the shameful deceit to which she's been subjected, and we hear the new compound motif H186 (= H184/H176) as she screams for vengeance for his betrayal of their love. H184ab is Hagen's call to arms (which called up H53, the Twilight of the Gods) based on his father Alberich's foundational cry of "Wehe! Wehe!" (H8ab) in the face of his inability to find love in the world. H176 stems originally from H80 (Wotan's confession he couldn't create a free hero, the basis for his punishment of Brünnhilde for keeping his futile hope alive). H176 is emblematic of her ultimate recognition that the bliss she thought she'd won through loving union with Siegfried was predestined to be betrayed by him, and that Wotan had set her up for failure by insuring only the artist-hero Siegfried could win her love. The fact that Siegfried preserved Brünnhilde's chastity for Gunther's sake shows he's no longer capable of achieving unconscious artistic inspiration, but is becoming too conscious of both the process of his inspiration, once hidden from him, and also too conscious of the unspoken secret his unconscious mind Brünnhilde kept for him, and from him.

The vassals cry out in fear and confusion, asking who has betrayed whom. But Brünnhilde ignores them and speaks aloud of things she alone can understand. Accompanied by H176, she asks the gods if this is what they whispered in their counsel. She alludes to Wotan's confession to her in V.2.2, which was his attempt to explain what lies behind H80 (H176's basis), which expressed Wotan's conclusion that his allegedly free heroes of redemption weren't free but only reflected what he loathed in himself. What Wotan whispered to her in his counsel was that her foolhardy insistence on living for love when Wotan had resigned himself to the fact there is none, is the cause of her present tragedy. Siegfried's and Brünnhilde's betrayal of the love they shared, the most exalted love imaginable, proves Wotan's cynicism to have been well founded. Since there can be no redemption from this tragedy, no escape from Alberich's Ring Curse, Brünnhilde wishes to demolish her ideal world by bringing about her own destruction and that of her former lover Siegfried, just as her father Wotan in his confession wished only for "das Ende!," the end of everything he ever valued, once he acknowledged the inevitability of Alberich's victory. Thus she exclaims, to a combination of H39 (Tragic Love) and H176 that, if the gods would teach her greater shame than anyone ever felt before, that they must also teach her (H17 Alberich's Ring Variant) vengeance as never yet raged. And now, most poignantly of all, accompanied by H58a variants (Rhinedaughters' First Lament) she cries out: "Bid Brünnhilde break her heart in twain to destroy the man who betrayed her!" The soul of Brünnhilde's love for Siegfried was that through her protective Wonder it was as if he'd temporarily thrown the Ring back into the Rhine and restored the stolen Rhinegold to the Rhinedaughters (H58a), where they can wash away Alberich's Ring Curse.

Gunther asks her to contain herself, but she lashes out at him, again accompanied by H176: "(H176) Keep away, betrayer! Self-betrayed! Know then, all of you, (H106 unison) not to him [Gunther], but to that man there [pointing to Siegfried] am I wed." The H106 unison is a reminiscence of the moment in T.1.3.B when Siegfried in disguise falsely named himself Gunther, but also of the craven Mime, surviving by cunning, subterfuge, and deceit, the very exemplar of the human type of which Gunther and Gutrune are particular instances, but who, like Wotan, falsely suppose themselves exalted. Brünnhilde insists she's not wed to such an unworthy man, but only to Siegfried, who forced (H35—lovelessly) delight from her, and love. Siegfried is now implicated in Mime's cunning, as he's the involuntary instrument of the Gibichungs' cunning exploitation of his obliviousness. Siegfried couldn't free himself from his debt to Mime, just as

Wotan could never free his ideal realm Valhalla (H18ab) from its origins in Alberich's forging of his Ring (H17ab).

Siegfried asks her if she can be so careless of her own honor, saying, accompanied significantly by a special H12 (Rhinegold! Rhinegold!) variant made up of orchestral pulses, that the tongue that defames it, (H176) he must accuse of lying. It's Siegfried who's been unwittingly careless in making this accusation, because the H12 variant which accompanies his remark is, like H12's variant H58a, a hallmark of the wondrous protection from the wounds of consciousness which Brünnhilde's love has bestowed on him. He could only enjoy this gift through loving union with his muse, so it's especially ironic when Siegfried invokes his phallic sword Nothung, and his blood-brotherhood oath to Gunther, as he swears he never broke faith with Gunther's honor and never violated Brünnhilde. But Siegfried gets into deeper water when he insists—accompanied by a new variant of H56 (the Sword Motif taking a sinuous form)—that Nothing's sharp blade sundered him from this unhappy woman. Brünnhilde seizes the opportunity for some sharp wit at Siegfried's expense, referencing his sword Nothung as a phallus. She says: "(H176) You cunning hero, look how you're lying. Just as you're wrong to appeal to your sword! (H58a Variant) Well I know (H56) its sharp-set edge, but I also know the scabbard in (H161 Variant) which your true friend Nothung rested serenely (H56 sinuous Variant) against the wall while its master won him his sweetheart." This brings to mind the sexual imagery of Siegfried's smelting and forging songs as he re-forged Nothung in S.1.3, and Sieglinde's ecstasy as Siegmund first pulled the sword Nothung out of Hunding's house-ash in V.1.3. But the most important point being made lies in the motifs. The sexual union of Siegfried with Brünnhilde being a metaphor for Siegfried's unconscious artistic inspiration by Wotan's forbidden hoard of knowledge, it's no accident that we hear H161, the motif which symbolizes Wotan's hoard of runes which Brünnhilde imparted to Siegfried subliminally (of which Siegfried feared he couldn't be a good guardian), as Brünnhilde describes herself as the scabbard (if you will, Brünnhilde's vagina or womb) into which Siegfried thrust Nothung. H58a again recalls Brünnhilde's status as Siegfried's surrogate Rhine, who protected him from Alberich's Ring Curse of consciousness until Siegfried betrayed their love.

The Gibichung Vassals and women, and Gunther and Gutrune, now demand Siegfried swear an oath to refute Brünnhilde's abhorrent charges against him, which dishonor them all:

[pp. 323–4] **The Vassals:** What? Has he broken faith? (H161 vari:) Has he tarnished Gunther's honour (:H161 vari)? [**The Women:** (…)]

Gunther: (to Siegfried: H184ab:) I'll be disgraced (H161:) and held in shame, if you don't refute the words she utters (:H184ab; :H161). (H8/H161)

Gutrune: (H161:; H184ab:) faithlessly, Siegfried, you plotted deception (:H161; :H184ab)? (H32A/H161:) Bear witness that she accuses you falsely (:H32A/H161)!

The Vassals: (H32A/H161:) ... silence the charge, swear an oath (:H32A/H161)!

Siegfried: (H184a/H161:) If I silence the charge and swear an oath (:H184a/H161): which of you'll venture his weapon upon it?

Hagen: (H184ab:) The point of my spear (H162) I'll venture upon it (:H184ab) ... .

(H81 vari?: The vassals form a circle round Siegfried and Hagen. H172; H81 vari?; H172: Hagen holds out his spear. (...)) (H187 frag; H176)

Siegfried: [[**H187 voc:**]] (...) Hallowed (H162 or H178 frag?) weapon! Assist my (H162 or H178 frag?) eternal oath!—(H176) [[**H187 voc:**]] By the point of this spear (H162 or H178 frag?) I swear the oath (H162 or H178 frag?) ... (:H187 voc)! (H176) ... (H180 voc:) where death may strike, be it you that strikes (:H180 voc) (H162 or H178 frag?) (H176 voc:) if that woman's charge is true, if I broke my vow to my brother (:H176 voc).

Brünnhilde: (striding furiously into the circle, tearing Siegfried's hand away from the spear and seizing the tip of it with her own hand: H76/H77; H161 vari [as an orchestral explosion]; [[**H187 voc:**]]) (...) Hallowed weapon! Assist my eternal oath (:H187 voc)! (H176) [[**H187 voc:**]] By the point of this spear I swear this oath: (H178:) ... (:H178) ... (:H187 voc)! (...) (H178) (H180 voc:) I bless your blade that it bleed him (:H180 voc): (H178:; H176:) for just as he broke every oath he swore, this man has now forsworn himself (:H178:; :H176)!

The Vassals: ... Help, Donner! Let your tempest roar (H161 vari:) to silence this raging disgrace (:H161 vari)! (H17ab vari &/or H18ab?)

H161 is heard repeatedly as everyone present insists Siegfried swear an oath to silence Brünnhilde's presumably false, shameful charges. H161, embodying the hoard of runes Wotan taught her in his confession, which she imparted to Siegfried so he might draw subliminal inspiration of his redemptive art from it, represents Wotan's repressed knowledge of the inevitability of the fulfillment of Alberich's Ring Curse. H161 also calls to mind Siegfried's premonition in T.P.B that because he remained untaught by (unconscious of) the hoard of runes the gods (Wotan) taught Brünnhilde, he might betray its secret. Now, H161 is linked with her figuratively true but literally false accusation that Siegfried raped her and stole her (Alberich's) ring. She'd promised to keep Wotan's unspoken secret, but now, as a natural consequence of Siegfried's unwitting and involuntary betrayal of the contents of his unconscious mind (Brünnhilde) to the light of day, Wotan's formerly unspoken (in words, but not in music) secret can no longer be kept, and she must play her part in exposing what Siegfried has forced her to expose by giving her and her secrets away to his audience, Gunther and the Gibichungs. She'll collaborate with Hagen in destroying her true love Siegfried by depriving him of her protection, just as Elsa collaborated with Friedrich and Ortrud to betray Lohengrin's secret.

In answer to Siegfried's request that someone venture his weapon to back up Siegfried's oath, Hagen offers his spear-point, so Hagen's spear becomes a proxy for Wotan's Spear, guarantor of oaths and the Social Contract. Just as Wotan's Spear rendered Siegmund vulnerable to Hunding's fatal spear wound, to punish Siegmund for breaking divine law, so Hagen's spear will deliver a fatal wound to Siegfried for breaking an oath sanctioned by Wotan's Spear. Hagen holds out his spear accompanied by H172 (Oath of Atonement), and we hear a new motif H187, to which Siegfried and Brünnhilde swear their contradictory oaths. We hear H180 (Murder) during their oaths: it expresses Alberich's and Hagen's intent to deliver the coup de grâce to the gods by murdering their only hope of salvation from Alberich's Ring Curse, Siegfried. H180 embodies Hagen's spear-point, the instrument of Siegfried's atonement of the gods' sin against all that was, is, and will be.

Brünnhilde's version of the oath is sung to, and accompanied by, largely the same musical and motival material as Siegfried's oath, except that it's preceded by an explosive variant of H161. Since H161 stands for Wotan's hoard of runes which Brünnhilde taught Siegfried, her charge that Siegfried has forsworn himself, that he forced himself on her sexually, is in truth her complaint that he betrayed Wotan's unspoken secret, which Brünnhilde kept for Siegfried, by giving her away to another man (his audience), rather than loyally keeping his subliminal oath (made to her during their loving union) of fidelity to the love he owes his muse. Brünnhilde's subsequent collaboration as a co-conspirator with Siegfried's enemies is a natural consequence of his involuntary betrayal of the unspoken secret she'd been keeping. One point of interest in her accusation is that she implies Siegfried forced her to grant him her sexual favors and love during his most recent visit when he, disguised as Gunther, abducted her for Gunther. But she's alluding to Siegfried's prior visit when he first legitimately woke her and won her love, a visit that, in view of his more recent betrayal of their love, she now views retrospectively as preparation for his conspiracy to abduct her. So we must grasp both of Siegfried's visits to Brünnhilde as instances of his recurring visits to his muse, his unconscious mind, to heal the wounds caused by rising consciousness of the truth, by seeking inspiration for new works of art. The fact that his first visit in S.3.3 represents full-fledged unconscious artistic inspiration, whereas on his second visit he didn't achieve unconscious artistic inspiration because he separated himself from her with his sword Nothung, indicates that he's gradually becoming too conscious of the formerly hidden process of unconscious inspiration to seek inspiration from his muse any longer. It's in this sense Siegfried has betrayed their love.

The Vassals, in utter turmoil, and accompanied by H161, call on Donner to silence this disgrace with one of his tempests, echoing Donner's attempt in the finale of R.4—as the gods were preparing to cross over into their newly built refuge Valhalla—to clear the air of the taint of corruption in Wotan's hypocritical machinations to secure Valhalla, by calling forth his storm to sweep the heavens clear. Wotan's disgrace wasn't only that he was entirely dependent on Alberich's quest for power, the egoism which forged his Ring of consciousness, to dream the gods and their abode Valhalla (and even their ideal Freia) into existence, but that Wotan couldn't afford to acknowledge this debt, which is why he set in motion all the self-deceptive machinations with which the *Ring* drama abounds. It's no wonder Brünnhilde expressed her fear in T.P.B (accompanied by H160 and H161) that her merit as Siegfried's unconscious mind, her wondrous protection of him from the wounds of consciousness of this disgrace, would be too little to sustain his love.

There's another supreme irony in the oath Siegfried swears: he didn't dishonor Gunther by having sexual relations with Gunther's wife-to-be Brünnhilde, and not only for the obvious reason that Siegfried's loving relationship with Brünnhilde preceded Gunther's exploitative plan, inspired by Hagen, that Siegfried win Brünnhilde for Gunther (Gunther being unaware of their prior relationship). It was only through finding inspiration in muse Brünnhilde's loving arms that Siegfried could create those works of redemptive art which helped sustain the Gibichungs' self-deceit, their bogus sense of honor and glory, in an increasingly post-religious age. Siegfried could only accomplish this so long as the true nature of his relationship with his muse Brünnhilde (the inner process through which repressed knowledge of the truth is sublimated into blissful illusion) remained hidden both from himself, and from his audience. But now Siegfried has unwittingly revealed both the process of his unconscious artistic inspiration, i.e., the true nature of his relationship with Brünnhilde, and also the hoard of knowledge which this wondrous union formerly concealed (Alberich's Ring, now a metaphor for Wotan's hoard of runes). So in a sense Siegfried had to secretly break his oath to Gunther, by having figurative sexual relations with Siegfried's muse, to sustain his oath to Gunther by providing him with the false honor and glory on which Gunther's happiness depends. Only when this becomes clear near the end of the tale (in T.3.2–3) will Gunther reconcile himself with Siegfried.

Siegfried now condescendingly begs Gunther to curb his wife Brünnhilde's unseemly temper, suggesting that in time it will cool and she'll be thankful Siegfried won her for Gunther:

[pp. 324–5] **Siegfried:** Gunther! (H161 vari >> :) Stop your wife from shamelessly bringing dishonour upon you! Grant the wild mountain woman a moment's respite and rest that her brazen rage may abate, which a demon's cunning craft has roused against us all! (...) (:H161 vari) (H24 vari voc:) Like cowards we gladly give ground when it comes to a battle of tongues (:H24 vari voc). (H32B: He goes right up to Gunther.) (H32A:; H40A >>:) Believe me, it angers me more than you that I took her in so badly (:H32A; :H40A): (H32B:) I almost think that the Tarnhelm must have only half concealed me (:H32B). (H17 frag: [lyrical vari]) But women's resentment (H35 frag:) quickly passes (:H17 frag vari; :H35 frag): (H58a >>:) that I won her for you (:H58a) (H161 >>:) the woman will surely be thankful yet (:H161).

With tragic naiveté Siegfried in his ignorance has asked Gunther to stop his wife Brünnhilde from shamelessly bringing dishonor on him, accompanied by H161, when in fact it's Siegfried who has innocently brought dishonor on himself and the Gibichungs by presenting Brünnhilde, Siegfried's true muse, to Gunther as his prize. As an artist-hero it was Siegfried's unwitting duty to protect his audience, man, from the bitter Noth, the dangerous secret we can't afford to admit to ourselves, which formerly was hidden within our collective unconscious, not to make a gift of it to man. After Siegfried suggests they grant the wild woman a moment's rest so her brazen rage may abate, that a demon's cunning craft has raised against them all, we hear H24, which at its inception embodied Wotan's description of Loge as someone through whose cunning advantage could be drawn from the enemy's envy, a model for Siegfried's unconscious artistic inspiration by his muse Brünnhilde. Loge could be described as the cunning demon who set these tragic events in motion by falsely promising Wotan he could enjoy the bliss of his illusory paradise Valhalla without cost, and Loge, symbol for man's artistic gift of self-deception, is Siegfried's archetype. It was Loge who on five occasions advised Wotan to restore Alberich's Ring to the Rhinedaughters, but Siegfried's loving union with Brünnhilde, the source of inspired secular art, has been Wotan's substitute for restoring Alberich's Ring to the Rhine. So it's Siegfried who, on this interpretation, is the demon whose cunning craft has raised Brünnhilde's brazen rage against them. Siegfried, the solitary artist-hero, is the modern incarnation of religious man's futile longing for transcendence, and dependence on self-deception to feel as if that longing has been fulfilled. It's the collective artist-heroes of primal times whom Wagner called the Folk, those who involuntarily and unconsciously invented the various religions, and those individual secular artists of modern times who inherited the Folk's creative spark, who've made men dependent on illusion for their concept of the meaning of life, their sense of happiness and contentment. As Loge warned Wotan and the gods in R.2, the gods staked everything, the meaning of life itself, the basis of their happiness, on Freia's golden apples of sorrow-less youth eternal, i.e., on belief in man's transcendent value.

Siegfried condescendingly dismisses Brünnhilde's charges as if they arose merely from what he'd describe as a feminine mood-swing, which will swing back to contentment and happiness in time. The dramatic contrast between Siegfried's glib obliviousness to his true situation, and the tragedy lurking in the shadow of his ignorance, is breathtaking. And now he attributes her anger to a supposition that perhaps the Tarnhelm only half hid his true identity, so he surmises Brünnhilde may have guessed that the man who abducted her was Siegfried disguised as Gunther. However, Siegfried optimistically concludes: "(H17 fragment [a lyrical variant]) But woman's resentment (H35 fragment) quickly passes: (H58a) that I won her for you (H161) the woman will surely be thankful yet." Here's a supreme instance in which Wagner's motifs entirely contradict the content of a protagonist's words. The linking of H17 (Ring) with H35 (Lovelessness) as Siegfried tells Gunther that woman's resentment (over betrayal of love) quickly passes, tells us instead that it will never end, because Siegfried, unwitting agent of Alberich's Ring Curse, has wholly and irrevocably forsaken the love he shared with Brünnhilde. And as Siegfried adds that Brünnhilde will ultimately be thankful Siegfried won her for Gunther, we hear H58a (The Rhinedaughters' lament) bespeaking Brünnhilde's lost status as Siegfried's surrogate Rhine, but also anticipating her restoration of Alberich's Ring to the Rhinedaughters, and H161, which together remind us that she could offer Siegfried protection from Alberich's Ring Curse only so long as she—his surrogate Rhine—kept the Ring's power (Wotan's hoard of runes) safe.

Now, in what is perhaps the single most dramatic example of tragic irony and hubris in the *Ring*, Siegfried with ebullient optimism asks everyone to forget their troubles and prepare to join Siegfried and Gutrune, Gunther and Brünnhilde, in their joyous wedding feast:

> **[p. 325] Siegfried:** (… H161:) Cheer up, you vassals (:H161)! Follow me to the feast!—(H183) (… H183 >>:) Be happy to help at the wedding, you women!—(H183:) May blissful delight now laugh out aloud (:H183)! (H183 tragic vari:) In garth and grove you shall see me gladdest of all today (:H183 tragic vari). (H35: [in an optimistic-sounding vari of the utmost possible irony]) He whom love delights (:H35 [optimistic vari]), [the order of the German verses is reversed in the following English phrase] (H183 vari voc:) let the lucky man share in my happy frame of mind ["… meinem frohen Muthe thu es der Glückliche gleich!"—Siegfried sings a high, Gibichung-style interval leap on "Muthe" and "Glückliche"] (:H183 vari voc)! (H183: Siegfried throws his arm around Gutrune in exuberant high spirits and draws her away with him into the hall. The vassals and womenfolk, carried away by his example, follow him. (…) Only Brünnhilde, Gunther, and Hagen remain … . H183 tragic vari; H168a. … Gunther has sat down to one side in deep shame and terrible dejection. Brünnhilde remains standing at the front of the stage, gazing in her anguish at the disappearing forms of Siegfried and Gutrune … . H50; H35; H12 vari; H161; H49 vari; H172; H49 vari; H172; H49; H173a/H49; H180)

Siegfried's hubristic self-confidence and celebratory exultation is a classic instance of a final moment in a hero's consummation of glory, his apotheosis before the fall. The tragic irony attains such an apogee of intensity here that even the Loveless Motif H35 acquires an optimistic sounding coloration and feel in the orchestra, as Siegfried exclaims: "He whom love delights, let the lucky man share in my happy frame of mind." The vassals and their ladies follow Siegfried's and Gutrune's happy example and proceed after them into the Hall. Brünnhilde, Hagen, and Gunther remain behind, Brünnhilde confronting the annihilatingly wholesale, irrevocable disillusionment of all her life's ideals, hopes and dreams, and Gunther humiliated into silence, beyond hope of repair. The accompanying music expresses Brünnhilde's bereft, despondent and hopeless mood, capturing her total isolation and alienation. We hear H50 (Ring Curse); H35 (Loveless); a H12 Variant—with perhaps a hint of H11 (pre-Fall Rhinedaughter music); H161 (Wotan's secret hoard of runes Siegfried has betrayed to the light of day); H49 (Alberich's Resentment, embodied by Hagen), and reminiscences of Hagen's

Watch H173ab. Brünnhilde has plummeted into the nadir of her life, and the only meaningful thing she can now think to do in a world rendered—or rather, exposed as—meaningless is to destroy both herself and her true love who betrayed her, just as Wotan had hopelessly consigned his beloved Wälsungs to destruction by "Neid" in his confession to Brünnhilde in V.2.2.

TWILIGHT OF THE GODS = ACT TWO, SCENE FIVE
(GIBICHUNG HALL)
BRÜNNHILDE, HAGEN, GUNTHER, SIEGFRIED, GUTRUNE, AND THE GIBICHUNG VASSALS AND WOMEN

Brünnhilde takes a cue from Siegfried, asking what demon's art lies hidden in her tragic fate:

> [pp. 325–6] **Brünnhilde:** (… H176 voc:) What demon's art lies (H87:) hidden here (:H176 voc; :H87)? (H180) (H176 voc:) What store of magic (H87:) stirred this up (:H176 voc; :H87)? (H87) Where now is my wisdom against this bewilderment? (H87) Where are my runes against this riddle? (H87) Ah, (H8 voc:) sorrow! Sorrow (:H8 voc)! (H8 voc:) Woe! Ah woe (:H8 voc)! (H143:) All my wisdom I gave to him: (:H143) (H161) (H161 varis:) in his power he holds the maid; in his bonds he holds the booty which, sorrowing for her shame, (H161) the rich man exultantly gave away (:H161 varis).

This passage contains one of the primary clues which offers us a key to the innermost layer of our allegorical reading of the *Ring*. As Brünnhilde asks what demon's art lies hidden in Siegfried's betrayal of their love, we hear both H176 (her tragic recognition that her love for Siegfried which won her infinite bliss was actually Wotan's punishment in disguise) and H87 (Fate), foreknowledge of the gods' fated doom which Brünnhilde's mother Erda imparted to Wotan, he imparted to Brünnhilde, and she imparted to Siegfried. Again accompanied by H87, Brünnhilde asks where her wisdom has flown, that might have aided her against this bewilderment, and asks where she might find her runes against this riddle. And now it dawns on her. Siegfried, in forcing the Ring out of her safekeeping, and giving her (his muse) away to his audience Gunther and the Gibichungs, has dredged Wotan's hoard of runes (embodied by Alberich's Ring) up from the silent depths of his unconscious to the light of day, exposing man's irredeemable shame (the knowledge so unbearable that man—Wotan—couldn't tolerate being conscious of it). Thus we hear H143, the motif of redemption through unconscious artistic inspiration (the true meaning of redemption by love), as Brünnhilde helplessly laments that all her wisdom she gave to Siegfried. And as H161 (Wotan's hoard of runes Brünnhilde taught Siegfried subliminally, which he feared he wouldn't properly guard) sounds, Brünnhilde cries out that in Siegfried's power he holds her, in his bonds he holds the booty (Wotan's Hoard of runes, Alberich's Hoard of Treasure) which, sorrowing for her shame, the rich man Siegfried exultantly gave away. The supreme irony is that Siegfried's art had to reach its most sublime height of inspiration (*The Ring of the Nibelung*) to be capable of exposing the formerly unconscious process of his inspiration to his audience. Siegfried was blissfully blind in committing this sin against her. But Brünnhilde doesn't yet realize that her misery was inevitable, fated: she blames Siegfried and meditates vengeance against him for his betrayal of their love.

The emphatic repetition of H87 (Fate) in this passage calls up remembrance of Brünnhilde's comment to Siegfried in S.3.3, accompanied by H87 (and preceded by H151), that what Siegfried doesn't know she knows for him. This was echoed in T.P.B when, accompanied by H161, Siegfried told Brünnhilde that she gave him more than he knows how to cherish (keep, or guard), and that she shouldn't blame him if her teaching left him untaught (left him unconscious of Wotan's runes, which she imparted to him subliminally). Siegfried, in this way, unwittingly foretold he'd some day betray this secret knowledge to consciousness. And H143 brings to mind Brünnhilde's remark to Siegfried in S.3.3, accompanied by H143, that Wotan's thought (his confession of his runes to her) was the redemptive love Siegfried and Brünnhilde share, Wagner's metaphor for unconscious artistic inspiration. This is the true "Redemption by Love—i.e., Redemption by Art—Motif," which Wagner described at its inception as sounding like the herald of a new religion, inspired secular art in which religious feeling lives on when religion as belief had to depart. Wotan's unspoken secret, his forbidden hoard of runes, which Siegfried the artist-hero has taken from his muse Brünnhilde and is unwittingly revealing to his audience, isn't only the key to Siegfried's unconscious artistic inspiration, but is the key to all religious revelation, religious mysteries, and unconscious artistic inspiration. Whatever value is lost from Siegfried's formerly unconsciously inspired art by virtue of exposing its secrets to the light of day, retrospectively devalues all prior religio-artistic imagination going back to the beginning of human history. It's this world-historical knowledge that Siegfried holds without knowing it, and which, as Brünnhilde complains, he's glibly giving away. Remarkably, this is Wagner's own—perhaps subliminal—confession of the ultimate consequence which follows from his creation and public performance of his *Ring*.

Brünnhilde now asks who could offer her that sword which would sever her bonds with the damnable traitor Siegfried, and Hagen naturally volunteers. He's already acted as witness to the oath of atonement between Siegfried and Gunther, and to enforce the oaths Siegfried and Brünnhilde swore against each other, oaths Hagen accuses Siegfried of having broken:

[pp. 326–7] (H180)

Brünnhilde: (H186 >>:) Who'll offer me now the sword with which to sever those bonds (:H186)?

Hagen: (... H187:) Have trust in me, deserted wife! Whoever betrayed you, I shall avenge it (:H187). [**Brünnhilde:** (...); **Hagen:** (...)]

Brünnhilde: (H187 frag:) On Siegfried? ... You? (:H187 frag)? (smiling bitterly) (H161 vari:) A single glance from his flashing eye (:H161 vari)—(H165:) which, even through his false disguise ["Luegengestalt"] (:H165), (H161:) brightly lighted upon me (:H161)—(H108:) would make your greatest courage quail (:H108)!

Hagen: (H187:) Would not his false oath mark him out for my spear (:H187)?

Brünnhilde: (H12 vari:) Oaths true or false—an idle concern (:12 vari)! (H93) (H12 vari >>:) Seek stronger means to arm your spear if you'd best the strongest of men (:H12 vari)! (H180)

Hagen: (H180:) How well do I know his conquering strength, how hard it would be to kill him in battle (:H180): (H32A >>:) so whisper me sound advice and say how the hero may yield to my might (:H32A).

Brünnhilde: O rank ingratitude! Shameful reward! [[H188 orch:]] [= H161 vari/H12 vari or H58a vari, spectacularly expressive music!!!]) Not a single art ["Kunst"] was known to me that did not help to keep his body safe (:H188 orch)! (H151 vari>>:) Unknown to him, he was tamed by my magic spells (:H151 vari) (H?!!!: [foreshadowing of a motif from *Parsifal*]) which ward him now against wounds (:H?!!!—foreshadowing of a motif from *Parsifal*).

Hagen: (H187 vari:) And so no weapon can harm him (:H187 vari)? (H180)

Brünnhilde: In battle, no! (H49 >>:) But—if you struck him in the back (:H49). [[H188 orch:]] [the spectacularly expressive music from Brünnhilde's remark above: "Not a single art was known to me ... "]) Never, I knew (:H188 orch), (H93:) would he yield to a foe, (H12 vari:) never, fleeing, present his back (:H93; :H12 vari); (H56ab) ([[H188 orch:]] [from Brünnhilde's remark: "Not a single art was known to me ... ."]) so I spared it the spell's protection (:H188 orch). (H151 frag; H161 vari)

Hagen: And there my spear shall strike him!

The sword which will sever (indeed, has already severed) Siegfried's muse Brünnhilde—his source of unconscious artistic inspiration—from Siegfried the artist-hero, is Alberich's Ring Curse of consciousness, the inevitability that all who once were unconscious will rise to consciousness. Siegfried already employed Nothung (the phallus which once planted the seed of the artist-hero's hidden poetic intent in his womb of inspiration, the sword which formerly embodied art as a restoration of lost innocence) to sever himself from his muse Brünnhilde. The fact that he turned Nothung into an anti-phallus by using it to ensure he could no longer inseminate his muse with his poetic intent, meant that what once was only felt (music) will rise to consciousness as thought, what once was experienced as love will retroactively be reinterpreted as merely incipient will-to-power, a product of Alberich's Ring.

Brünnhilde's contempt for Hagen's offer to wreak vengeance on Siegfried for betraying her stems from Wagner's notion (cited previously) that the higher man (the artistic genius) lives daily in a world which, if imparted to the average, practical man, would drive him to despair and suicide. [See 707W-{64–2/65} 'On State and Religion,' PW Vol. IV, p. 32] However, she doesn't know her man Hagen, who's perfectly equal to this. She's mistaken him for such an average man, not realizing that the objective man of science is even more fearless than Siegfried, because he confronts the bitter truth head-on without consolation or self-delusion, no matter how much it degrades his self-esteem. This is why Hagen is permanently wakeful and melancholy, and Siegfried manically exuberant yet dreamy. Siegfried's ignorance produces his optimism, his seeming innocence merely the product of unconsciousness of his true, underlying motives. But given her mis-identification of Hagen as an average man, she says, unsurprisingly accompanied by a H161 variant, that a single glance of Siegfried's flashing eye would make Hagen's greatest courage quail. H161 evokes the forbidden hoard of dangerous runes which Wotan taught her in his confession. In S.3.3 she had a premonition of disaster, that in sharing with Siegfried Wotan's unspoken secret Siegfried might betray it to the light of day. In Siegfried's fear of waking Brünnhilde he also had a subliminal premonition stemming from the same cause, and at its inception in T.P.B H161 was linked with Siegfried's fear he wouldn't be a good guardian of the hoard of divine runes she taught him. It's because Siegfried guards a hoard of knowledge so unbearable that Wotan couldn't speak it aloud lest he lose his mind, that she says Hagen's greatest courage would quail before Siegfried.

But Hagen won't be put off. Accompanied by H187 (Siegfried's and Brünnhilde's counter-oaths), he asks whether or not Siegfried's false oath would mark him out for Hagen's spear. Brünnhilde responds, accompanied by H12 ("Rhinegold! Rhinegold!," and what sounds like a hint of other Rhinedaughter music, perhaps H11), that oaths, true or false, are an idle concern, and that Hagen must seek stronger means to arm his spear if he'd best the strongest of men. The wondrous protection she bestows on Siegfried from Alberich's Ring Curse makes her Siegfried's surrogate Rhine, an artificial and temporary substitute for restoring the Ring to the Rhinedaughters. This is why we hear H12 and possibly a hint of H11 as Brünnhilde declares that Siegfried is immune to concerns about oaths true or false. Debates concerning truth vs. illusion have no bearing on the protection she provides him because he only feels what Wotan thought, and therefore has no concern either with science's objective truth, or with the gods' (religious faith's) dependence on illusions which falsely stake a claim to the truth. As Wagner put it (in a passage previously cited), in the modern, materialistic, atheistic, science-based secular world, religion can't sustain itself, but lives on in "... the deepest, holiest inner chamber of the Individual: whither never yet has surged a conflict of the rationalist [Alberich and Hagen] and supranaturalist [Wotan—religious faith] ... ." [See 705W-{64–2/65} 'On State and Religion,' PW Vol. IV, pp. 29–30] That's what the Rhinedaughters meant when, in the final strains of their first lament for the stolen Rhinegold H58 in R.4, they sang that truth lives only in the depths.

Hagen acknowledges he knows Siegfried's conquering strength which would make him hard to kill in battle. Siegfried's strength is his ignorance, granted him by his unconscious mind Brünnhilde, and by Loge's ring of fire, which incarnates the entire legacy of religious belief and art which has hidden the fatal truth from man behind a veil of illusion for thousands of years. So Hagen asks her to advise how the seemingly invulnerable hero Siegfried might yield to Hagen's might. Her response to his request she expose the secret of Siegfried's Achilles' Heel, is one of the most important and meaningful passages in the *Ring*. She cries out in ironic, enraged frustration, introducing a new compound motif H188 (comprised of H161 Variant/H12 Variant): "O rank ingratitude! Shameful reward! (H188) Not a single art was known to me that did not help to keep his body safe. (H151 Variant) Unknown to him, he was tamed by my magic spells which ward him now against wounds." She feels revulsion at the irony that her love's magic, which unbeknownst to Siegfried protected him from wounds when his love was still true, still protects him now that he's betrayed her. It's no accident that H188 underlines her comment that not a single art was known to her that didn't keep his body safe. This is some of the most intensely expressive music in the *Ring* because it captures the soul of Brünnhilde's wondrous protection. H188's component H12 tells us she's Siegfried's surrogate Rhine, his temporary redemption from Alberich's Ring Curse, and H188's other component H161, representing Wotan's hoard of runes which left Siegfried untaught, and which Siegfried feared he didn't know how to cherish or guard, is the fearful foreknowledge of the gods' and their proxies' fated doom which Brünnhilde holds for Siegfried, protecting him from the wound of existential fear which paralyzed Wotan, i.e., protecting him from foreknowledge.

When (accompanied by H151) she says that unknown to Siegfried he was tamed by her magic spells which protect him from wounds, she describes herself as his unconscious mind. Siegfried is unconscious of the gift of protection her love grants, unconscious of the true source of his unconscious artistic inspiration, Wotan's hoard of runes. H151's first significant conceptual association was Brünnhilde's remark in S.3.3 that she's Siegfried's own self (keeper of the secret of his identity, a secret she doesn't reveal even to him) if he loves her in his bliss, and that what he doesn't know (H87—Fate, Siegfried's identity sounding) she knows for him. H151's occurrence in our current passage tells us Siegfried's unconscious mind Brünnhilde knows for him his true identity as Wotan and protects him from Wotan's fearful foreknowledge of the fate Erda foretold to him, the inevitable destruction of man's religio-ethical-artistic legacy. The portentous musico-dramatic resonance of this singular moment in the *Ring* stems from its condensation into the briefest time and singlest space of the most universal, cosmic ramifications of the *Ring*, thanks to artistic "Wonder," the capacity of Wagner's motifs to absorb like a sponge, as an intuition or felt memory, every idea, symbol, object, incident, and character with which they've been associated during the whole course of the drama.

Hagen remains unconvinced, and asks: "And so no weapon can harm him?" We now hear H180, the Murder Motif. Brünnhilde answers that in battle, no, nothing can harm him. However, accompanied again by H188, the terribly expressive music which underlay her remark: "Not a single art was known to me ... ," she says, "In battle, no! (H49) But—if you struck him in the back (H188) Never, I knew (H93) would he yield to a foe, (H93; H12 Variant), never, fleeing, present his back; (H56ab) (H188) so I spared it the spell's protection." Hagen, confident of the success of his sinister plan at last, responds abruptly: "And there my spear shall strike him!" Several important aspects of Brünnhilde's magical protection are outlined here. First, the fact that Siegfried is fearless means that, since he'd never turn his back to the foe and run away, Brünnhilde need only protect him at his front. This is subtle: it's because she protects him figuratively at his front from that fearful foresight of the gods's shameful end which Erda imparted to Wotan, paralyzing him into inaction through existential fear, that Siegfried is fearless and needs no protection at his back. Wagner has contrasted her magical protection of fearless Siegfried at his front with what Brünnhilde told Wotan (who's paralyzed with fear) in V.3.3, that in time of war she protects his back. Wotan, unlike Siegfried, runs from what he fears, hoping to put it behind him, out of sight and mind. Siegfried can be killed if the knowledge which Wotan in his fear repressed, and from which she protects Siegfried, rises to consciousness as a remembrance of things past, long forgotten and behind him, to stab him figuratively in the back.

Having settled how to dispatch Siegfried, Hagen turns to Gunther with surprisingly wry humor, asking him rhetorically, with subtle mockery, that since Brünnhilde stands before Gunther as his stalwart wife, why should he be hanging his head in grief. Gunther, accompanied by H172 (Vow of Atonement) and H35 (Loveless), cries out in despair which recalls Wotan's explosion of hopeless anguish just before he confessed its cause, his irredeemable disgrace, to Brünnhilde in V.2.2:

[pp. 327–9] **Gunther:** (... H172 vari:) O shame! O disgrace (:H172 vari)! (H172) Woe is me, (H35 voc:) most sorrowful of men (:H35 voc)!

Hagen: (H176:) You're beset by disgrace, can I deny it (:H176)?

Brünnhilde: (to Gunther: H176 >> :) O craven man! False companion (:H176)! (H? voc: [This musical passage seems to subtly reference Siegmund's heroism, hinting at some as yet undetermined music from *The Valkyrie* Act One and/or Act Two, as if in contrast to the craven, unheroic Gunther]) Behind the hero you hid yourself, that the harvest of fame he might reap for you (:H? voc)! (H180) (H176 voc:) The much-loved race has sunk far indeed (:H176 voc) that fathers such faint-hearts as you!

Gunther: (... H176 >> :) Deceiver I—and deceived! Betrayer I—and betrayed (:H176)! (H172 vari:) Crush my bones, break my breast (:H172)! (H43ab?:) Help, Hagen! Help my honour! (:H43ab?)! (H35:) Help your mother (:H35), who bore me too in truth!

Hagen: (H180 voc:) ... only Siegfried's death can help you (:H180 voc)! (H186)

Gunther: (seized with horror) Siegfried's death! (H186)

Hagen: (H186:) That alone can purge your shame (:H186).

Gunther: (… H170:) Blood-brotherhood we swore to one another!

Hagen: May blood now atone (:H170) for the broken bond!

Gunther: (H172:) Did he break the bond?

Hagen: When he betrayed you (:H172)!

Gunther: Did he betray me?

Figuratively speaking, Gunther has been made conscious of Wotan's unbearable knowledge by virtue of the fact that both the inner process of unconscious artistic inspiration (whose metaphor is Siegfried's formerly secret relationship with his muse Brünnhilde), and Wotan's unspoken secret Brünnhilde had kept (represented by Alberich's Ring), have been exposed to the light of day by Siegfried. So Gunther, modern man (Wagner's audience), has been made aware of the tragic meaning of life itself, that no transcendent value inheres, that all that Gunther had admired (or at least thought he valued), all that he believed gave him honor, dignity, and transcendent value, was only self-deception and the product of unwitting cowardice. For Gunther, like Wotan, had let Siegfried (representative of all culture-heroes of the past, in religion, social revolution, and art, who'd lent human life its majesty, through illusion) face the bitter truth for him, so he could enjoy the fruits of Siegfried's inspiration and live in blissful ignorance of this terrible truth. Wagner claimed that in Wotan's irresolvable existential dilemma he'd revealed something so profoundly disturbing that no audience for the arts had experienced it before, and he supposed such an audience would be completely overwhelmed by it: "Wotan's experiences …—his feelings toward Siegfried and Siegmund—people do not feel those inside themselves, the man of genius lays them bare, people look and are overwhelmed." [966W-{5/20/79}CD Vol. II, p. 311]

Gunther, like Wotan, is the not-so-innocent victim of all prior culture heroes, all Loges, who tempted man (Wotan) into believing the impossible, that human life is privileged, indeed divine, deserving everlasting glory (recall Wotan's apostrophe to the newly built Valhalla in R.2). Siegfried is just the latest and perhaps last Loge, whom Gunther and all such men before him favored with renown and power, because the illusions they created flattered prosaic, Nibelung-like men, redeeming them from having to contemplate their stunted Nibelung status by making them seem to themselves gods, or at least worthy to live among the gods, redeemed from their mortal finitude. Thus H35 (Loveless), hallmark of our Fall, the fact that transcendent value doesn't inhere in the real world, stamps itself on Gunther's self-lacerating explosion of guilt, as he calls himself the most sorrowful of men, echoing that explosion of self-doubt in V.2.2 which preceded Wotan's confession to Brünnhilde, when he told himself "(H35) The saddest am I of all living things!" Hagen is happy, in his Schadenfreude, to throw salt on Gunther's wounds, adding—accompanied by H176 (The motif which more than all others evokes the entire sad history of Wotan's increasing self-doubt)—that Gunther is indeed beset by disgrace, and Hagen can't deny it. The disgrace stems from having banked all he values on false change, a fact Hagen, who knows the pure coin of our earthly realm, will soon cash in.

Now Brünnhilde unloads her contempt on Gunther, a contempt she could as easily apply to Wotan, who was just as content to exploit Siegfried's naiveté to confront Alberich's Ring Curse for him, as Gunther was to let Siegfried do his wooing for him. Again accompanied by H176, she charges Gunther with being a craven man and false companion, who hid behind the hero, that the harvest of fame the hero might reap for him. [See 1088W-{6-8/81} 'Herodom and Christendom'—3rd Supplement to 'Religion and Art,' PW Vol. VI, pp. 277-278] But she gives her knife a final twist. She says that the much-loved race has sunk so far indeed that fathers such faint hearts as Gunther. She's saying Gunther can't compare himself with true heroes like Siegmund, who was willing to sacrifice paradise for the sake of his earthly love for Sieglinde. The music underlying her accusation seems to subtly reference Siegmund's heroism. Overwhelmed with self-loathing and self-doubt, Gunther gives vent to his feeling of irredeemable impotence, just as Wotan did in the final moments of his confession to Brünnhilde when he told her he found, with loathing, always only himself in all he undertook. Like Wotan, who admitted to her that in deceiving himself he'd deceived the martyred heroes he conscripted to defend Valhalla from Alberich's threat, Gunther describes himself as both betrayer, and betrayed. He's again accompanied by H176, the culminating form of the development of Wotan's Spear Motif H19, which references Wotan's troubled, self-deceitful contracts.

Having given up hope for transcendent meaning in this life, Gunther now turns for redemption from his misery to (of all people) Hagen. Again, we can't help thinking here of Wotan, who in his confession to Brünnhilde resigned himself to Alberich's victory over all Wotan stood for, preparing in his self-disgust to hand the world and Wotan's Valhallan legacy over to Alberich's as-yet-unborn son (Hagen). Accompanied by H43 (Power of the Ring), Gunther pleads with Hagen to help his honor. Unwittingly predicating life's value on self-deceit had been man's greatest dishonor, dishonor toward the truth, Mother Nature, Erda. And H35 (Loveless) underlies Gunther's request that Hagen also help Gunther's mother, who bore Hagen too. The mother to whom Gunther alludes is his blood-mother Grimhilde, but he's also speaking of the Mother of All, Erda, from whom we humans acquire that knowledge which gives us power over Nature and ourselves, if we consent to know her objectively, that is, lovelessly (H35).

Hagen says nothing can take away the stain of Gunther's dishonor except Siegfried's death, i.e., by demolishing man's heritage of religious faith and feeling, as expressed secularly in altruistic self-sacrifice and inspired art. Only if humans disavow this false source of value can they embrace the source of true, amoral power, Nature. But Gunther, having invested so much sentiment in his regard for the artist-hero Siegfried, is filled with horror at the thought of murdering him, especially in view of the fact that they swore an oath of blood-brotherhood, i.e., that Siegfried the artist-hero renewed Wotan's (religious belief's) social contract with man. Hagen insists that only Siegfried's death can purge Gunther's shame, and that Siegfried must in any case atone with his life for breaking his bond with Gunther. But Gunther intuits that Siegfried didn't wantonly break his bond with Gunther, for he asks Hagen whether Siegfried really broke his bond and betrayed his oath. Siegfried throughout *Twilight of the Gods* has consistently lived the life of the unconsciously inspired artist-hero on whom Gunther (modern man) could historically depend to invent and sustain those illusions on which most men depend for their happiness. Siegfried's unwitting, involuntary betrayal of the religious mysteries was an inevitable development of cultural evolution.

Brünnhilde interjects that if Siegfried betrayed them, they all betrayed her. She insists that though all the blood spilled in the world could never erase their guilt toward her, Siegfried's death will suffice to atone for their betrayal. She nominates him to be a Christ-like savior (or, as Roger Scruton put it, citing René Girard, a "scapegoat") who takes on himself the sins of the world and is sacrificed to expiate man's sin, i.e., Wotan's sin of matricide, collective, historical man's denial of Mother Nature's truth in religious belief, ethics, and art:

> [p. 329] **Brünnhilde:** (H172 frag vari) You he betrayed, (H172 frag vari) and me have you all betrayed! (H172 frag vari) If I had my due, (H172 frag vari) all the blood in the world (H172 frag vari) (H176 voc:) could never make good your guilt (:H176 voc)! But (H180 voc:) one man's death (:H180 voc) (H160:) will serve me for all (:H160): (H180 voc:) may Siegfried fall to atone (:H180 voc) for himself and you!
>
> **Hagen:** (turning to Gunther) May he fall—... for your good ["Heil"]! (H17 vari >>:) Tremendous power will then be yours if you win from him the ring (:H17 vari) (H35:) that death alone would wrest from him (:H35).
>
> **Gunther:** (... H161 vari:) Brünnhilde's ring (:H161 vari)?
>
> **Hagen:** The Nibelung's band. (H173b)
>
> **Gunther:** (sighing deeply H173b:) Must this be Siegfried's end (:H173b)?
>
> **Hagen:** (H186:) His death will serve us all (:H186).

What Brünnhilde wants Siegfried to atone for are two distinct sins which, in fact, are antithetical. Alberich's Ring Curse was meant to punish Wotan and his proxies for the sin of denying Mother Nature's truth, the hubristic sin of basing life's value on the illusion that man can transcend natural law and redeem himself from his subjection to egoistic animal impulse. Wotan's recognition that not only he, not only Siegmund and Sieglinde, but his proxies Siegfried and Brünnhilde must be punished to atone for Wotan's primal commission of this original sin, is embodied in Motif H176. But Brünnhilde's identity, her status as muse for the artist-hero Siegfried's redemptive artworks, is implicated in Wotan's sin. Siegfried and Brünnhilde have been committed by Wotan to the perpetuation of his original sin of world-renunciation, so Siegfried's unwitting revelation of the truth to his audience (Gunther) betrays Brünnhilde's function as his unconscious source of artistic inspiration and Wotan's hope for redemption. Brünnhilde is therefore asking Siegfried to atone, first, for the sin of betraying the secret she kept (for betraying her function as the muse who inspired Siegfried unwittingly to perpetuate Wotan's sin against all that was, is, and will be), and secondly, to atone for Wotan's sin in denying the truth in the first place. Siegfried the secular artist-hero, as heir to the founders of religions such as Moses, Jesus, Mohammed, and Buddha, must atone retroactively for man's sin of positing transcendence of Nature as the meaning of life.

With Siegfried's death, i.e., with both Wagner's (Siegfried's) and science's (Hagen's, or say, Feuerbach's and Nietzsche's) discrediting of the belief in our transcendent value, the last refuge of our religious illusion of transcendence will have fallen. Hagen can then offer us (Gunther) what seems the only alternative philosophy, of living for the power which objective knowledge of the truth, and the scientific mastery of man and Nature, grants those sufficiently ruthless to take advantage of it. Accordingly, Hagen suggests to Gunther he can draw great advantage from Siegfried's death, which would potentially place the full objective power of the Ring in Gunther's hands. Gunther, in spite of his sentimental attachment to the consolations of self-deception which Siegfried granted him, now seems reconciled, however reluctantly, to substituting for them the power which Hagen's Ring knowledge alone can provide. But Gunther, resigned to accepting life in Hagen's more bracing but emotionally desiccated world, fails to grasp that in a world whose highest value is the acquisition of power, neither he nor anyone else can guarantee their own well-being, since no individual human has any metaphysical status or dignity, but only a value equal to a mote of dust. Our only value in such a world would be our capacity to acquire and hold power. This surely is part of what Alberich meant when, as he was cursing his Ring in R.4, he said any who obtain its power will live in perpetual fear. But even if a person in such a loveless world could win for themselves perpetual security from threat, this couldn't compensate for the loss of that feeling of exaltation only to be obtained from satisfaction of our age-old longing for transcendent meaning.

Having already expressed his reluctance to relinquish all that Siegfried meant to him, Gunther speaks up for Gutrune's interest when he asks his co-conspirators to consider how they might rationalize Siegfried's death to her, so they won't incur blame for it. But this provokes a damning indictment of Gutrune by Brünnhilde:

[pp. 329–30] Brünnhilde: (H168b: ...) (H168a varis >>:) What did my wisdom tell me? (H168a:) What did my runes have to teach me? In my helpless distress it dawns on me now: (H168b:) Gutrune's the name of the (H173b Voc >> [sung very high on "spell," i.e. "Zauber"]) spell that spirited away my husband (:H168b; :H173b Voc)! May she be struck by dread!

Hagen: (to Gunther: H164 vari:) Since his death is bound to afflict her, then let the deed be hid from her (:H164 vari). (H108:; H164 vari:) Tomorrow let's merrily go a-hunting: (H108 >>:) the noble hero will rush on ahead— (H176:; H108 frag or vari:) a boar (H186 >>:) might bring him down (:H176; :H108 frag or vari; :H186).

Brünnhilde is enraged that Gunther should be so concerned with his sister Gutrune's feelings when Brünnhilde, Siegfried's true wife, has suffered the greatest anguish in being betrayed by him for Gutrune's sake. She asks herself what her wisdom (Wotan's confession) told her, what her runes taught: that Gutrune is the name of the spell which spirited Brünnhilde's husband Siegfried away, and Brünnhilde curses her. Wotan's confession taught her the price to be paid in living for the illusion of transcendent love, that it was destined to failure in the face of prosaic reality. Brünnhilde told Siegfried in T.P.B that the sole purpose of her love was to inspire him to undertake new adventures, i.e., to present to the public works of art she's inspired him to create. But the more man advances in knowledge and conscious self-awareness, the greater the risk that her artist-hero would betray the secret of his inspiration to the harsh glare of day. This is what Gutrune's seduction of Siegfried means to Brünnhilde. But Brünnhilde isn't yet conscious enough to grasp what Wotan told her in V.3.3, that she'd chosen her own punishment and is responsible for it. Hagen suggests they disguise Siegfried's death as a hunting accident. They'll tell Gutrune Siegfried died at the hands of a wild boar. Hagen, agent of Alberich's Ring Curse, is the boar who'll end Siegfried's life. One thinks here of Melot's fateful suggestion to Tristan that Melot plan a hunt for Marke's royal court so Tristan's and Isolde's love-tryst can escape notice, treacherously planning instead to make the secrets of their love-night the prospective prey of that hunt. The superficial difference between these cases is that, rather than surprising the lovers together to expose their illicit love, Hagen will give Siegfried the antidote to his love-and-forgetting potion so Siegfried will recall what will seem to Gunther to be Siegfried's illicit sexual relations with Brünnhilde, and confess them.

Now the three co-conspirators proceed to the infamous revenge trio, which tends to make some admirers of Wagner's mature music-dramas cringe because it seems such a throwback to the kind of operatic convention Wagner's revolutionary music-dramas had supposedly laid to rest. The libretto of *Twilight of the Gods*, though last in the chronological context of the *Ring* drama, was the first to be written, and therefore the part of the *Ring* libretto completed nearest in time to Wagner's earlier romantic opera period which culminated in *Lohengrin*, completed just a few years before (1848). Granted, Wagner could have brought the whole libretto of *Twilight of the Gods* up to date if he'd wished, but perhaps he had allegorical and/or purely aesthetic reasons for leaving such retro features intact. In any case, for this reason its libretto is the most backward looking of the *Ring* dramas stylistically, whereas its music is by far the most advanced in the *Ring*, having been composed last. This produces the most startling effect, allowing Wagner to update *Twilight* subliminally through his musical motifs, which place all its characters, events, and ideas in a world-historical, even cosmic context):

[pp. 330–1] **Gunther and Brünnhilde:** (H186:) So shall it be! May Siegfried fall (:H186): (H172:) let him purge the shame that he caused me! The oath of loyalty he has betrayed (:H172): (H11 vari:) with his blood let him cleanse his guilt (:H11 vari)! (H17ab or H18ab?:) All-wise, avenging god! Oath-knowing (:H17ab or H18ab?) guardian of vows! (H187 vari >>:)

Wotan! (...) Bid your awesomely (:H187) hallowed host (H162b:) come hither to hear this oath of vengeance (:H162b)! (H183)

Hagen: (H172:) So let him die, the radiant hero! Mine is the hoard, it must be mine (:H172): (H11 vari:) so let the ring be wrested from him (:H11 vari)! (H17ab or H18ab?:) Elfen father, fallen prince! Guardian of night (:H17ab or H18ab?)! (H187 vari >>:) Nibelung lord! Alberich! Heed me! Bid the Nibelung (:H187 vari) (H183) (H162b:) host obey you anew, the lord of the ring (:H162b)!

(H32AB vari: As Gunther turns ... to the hall with Brünnhilde, they are met by the bridal procession on its way out. H183/H32B; H183 >>; H168b. (...) Siegfried and the menfolk sound the wedding call on their horns. (...) H186 >>; H183 >>>>; H184a: (...) Brünnhilde is on the point of withdrawing impetuously, when Hagen ... pushes her towards Gunther, who seizes her hand ... and leads her over to the women. (...) H176. After this brief interruption, the procession quickly resumes its progress ... .)

The essence of this revenge trio is that, where Brünnhilde and Gunther call on Wotan (Light-Alberich), guardian of oaths, to wreak vengeance on Siegfried for breaking Siegfried's dissimilar oaths to Brünnhilde and Gunther, thereby dishonoring them, and in this way to cleanse Siegfried's guilt, Hagen calls on his father Alberich (Dark-Alberich) to prepare to reclaim his Ring's power, once Hagen's machinations have fulfilled the conditions of Alberich's Ring Curse. This oath of vengeance highlights the essential identity of Wotan and Alberich. This is expressed in the similarity of H17ab (Alberich's Ring) and H18ab (Wotan's Valhalla). T.2.5 ends with some stage business in which Brünnhilde expresses her disdain for her rival Gutrune and rage at her betrayer Siegfried, with final emphasis on H176, the motif which recalls Wotan's final acknowledgment that his quest for redemption from Alberich's Ring Curse was futile, and that his proxies in his bid for redemption are destined to succumb like him to Alberich's Ring Curse. This is the bleak message we're left to contemplate in this finale to the *Ring*'s penultimate act.

TWILIGHT OF THE GODS = ACT THREE, SCENE ONE

(A BANK ALONGSIDE THE RHINE)
THE RHINEDAUGTHERS AND SIEGFRIED

We come now to the final act in the great *Ring* cycle. The first notes of its musical prelude convey a sublime awe unmatched since the drama began with the prelude to R.1, because now, unexpectedly, after repeats of Siegfried's Youthful Horncall H108, of H180a (Hagen's call to arms, his version of his father Alberich's despairing admission he could never find love H8, "Wehe! Ach, Wehe!") and H181 (Gibichung Horncall), the orchestra, for the first time since the *Ring*'s prelude in R.1, reproduces H1's (Primal Nature Motif's) canon, with which the *Ring* began. H1 carries us back to our preconscious animal innocence before the Fall, which it was the underlying purpose of the Wälsung heroes—wielding their sword Nothung (whose motif H56ab's second segment is the Primal Nature Motif H1)—to restore. But Siegfried has succumbed to the inexorable evolution of consciousness, and is going to his predestined doom at the hands of Alberich's Ring Curse. H1 therefore sounds like an invocation of our primal, forgotten past, a distant call from man's origin in preconscious Nature for Siegfried (man) to return to his roots, the source of his art. As Hagen suggested in T.2.5, Gunther, Hagen, and the Gibichungs have taken Siegfried with them on a hunt whose ultimate prey is Siegfried himself. Siegfried loses track of his fellow hunters and stumbles on the three Rhinedaughters bewailing the loss of their Rhinegold by singing a new lament H189abc. H189 is one of the *Ring*'s most poignant motifs, miraculously making us feel the time that's passed since the beginning, and the degree of corruption the world has endured since the Fall. There's a sort of sickly beauty in it, the glamorous decay, over time, of a once pristine, noble world, now in ruins. Dunning suggests a segment of H189, H189c, is a loose inversion of H4, Woglinde's Lullaby (a lullaby intended to keep the world from waking, to forestall the inevitable rise to consciousness of man, who'd bring about the Fall). If this is so, H189c is related to the second Woodbird Song H138ab, because H138ab is a variant of Woglinde's Lullaby H4. H189 seems to sound a plaintive call to man to come home, to retreat permanently to his pre-conscious animal condition:

[pp. 331–2] (**Prelude:** H108; H108; H184a; H183; H184a; H183; H108; H1 canon; H58ab/H3 vari; H183; H108; H9; H189b frag varis: [[**H189abc orch:**]] [H189c possibly an inversion of H4] The curtain rises. A wild, wooded and rocky valley along the Rhine, …. . The three Rhinedaughters … swim to the surface and swim round in a circle, as though performing a dance.)

The Three Rhinedaughters: (pausing briefly in their swimming: H190 frag >>:); [[**H189b voc:**]] The sun-goddess sends her bright-shining beams (:H189b voc); [[**H190 orch**]] [= H14 vari] night lies in the depths. (H9 frag) [[**H189c voc:**]] Once it was light when, safe and hallowed, our father's gold (H9:) still gleamed there (:H189c voc; :H9). [[**H189a voc:**]] Rhinegold, radiant gold (:H189a voc)! [[**H189c voc:**]] How brightly you used to shine, you hallowed star of the deep (:H189c voc). ([[**H189a orch:**]] They resume their aquatic dance: [[**H189b voc:**]]) Weilala [[**H189c voc:**]] leia, [[**H190 orch**]] wallala leialala (:H189c voc)! (distant horn call. H108 frag: They listen, then beat the water in jubilation. [[**H190 orch**]]) [[**H190 orch >>:**]] O sun-goddess, send us the hero (:H190 orch) who may give us back the gold! (H9) [[**H189b voc:**]] If he left it with us, your bright-gleaming eye we'd then need envy (H9:) no longer (:H189b voc; :H9)! Rhinegold, radiant gold! [[**H189c voc:**]] How happily then you would shine, (H190 orch) you free-spirited star of the deep (:H189c voc)! (H190: [figurations representing water and fire seem to become indistinguishable during this scene]; H108: Siegfried's horn call is heard, closer than before.) ([[**H191 orch**]]; H108 frag)

Woglinde: I can hear his horn. (**[[H191 orch]]**; H108 frag)

Wellgunde: The hero's approaching. **[Flosshilde:** (...)**]** (**[[H191 frags orch:]]**; H190 orch: All three plunge beneath the waves. H189b frags: Siegfried appears on the cliff, fully armed. **[[H191 orch]]**)

Siegfried: [[H191 orch:]] An elf ["Albe"] has led me astray, so that I lost the trail (:H191 orch):—(**[[H191 orch >>**:/H108 frag:) (...) In which hill have you hidden the game so swiftly (:H191 orch/:H108 frag)?

The Three Rhinedaughters: (resurfacing and resuming their dance: H189b >>:) Siegfried! [The Rhinedaughters mock Siegfried's complaint about the elf who distracted him: (...)]

Siegfried: (... **[[H191 orch:]]**) Did you spirit away the shaggy haired fellow who disappeared from my sight (:H191 orch)? **[[H191 frag orch]]** If he's your lover, I gladly leave him to you, you light-hearted women. (The Rhinedaughters laugh. H190 [This music seems to reference the Woodbird's flight music with trills, in which H191 and H190 seem to mix])

Another new motif H190, heard as the Rhinedaughters joyously swim in the Rhine, is a variant of H14 which illustrated the Rhinedaughters' swimming in R1. We hear H190 as they swim a round dance and then in the orchestra while singing their new lament, describing how the deeps, which once were brightened by the Rhinegold, are now dark. Presciently, they ask the sun-goddess to send them the hero who'll give them back the gold, and we're reminded that it was the sun-goddess who brightened the gold one last time before Alberich stole it in R.1, commencing the Fall. Now we hear Siegfried's Youthful Horncall H108 again, as he's drawing closer. As Woglinde says she can hear the hero's horn, a new, mysterious, yet quirky motif is introduced, H191. Dunning detected a harmonic embryo of H191 in S.2.3 after Siegfried carried the dead Mime to Fafner's cave so Mime could figuratively guard the hoard which was his only goal in life, but just before the Woodbird's final revelation, that if Siegfried walks through a ring of fire and wakes Brünnhilde, he'll win her, his boon companion. Its overwhelming power arises perhaps from this, that it seems to be a link with the Woodbird's revelation to Siegfried that the sleeping Brünnhilde awaits him, i.e., an invitation to seek unconscious artistic inspiration. When Siegfried said in S.2.3 he'd follow the path laid out for him by the Woodbird's singing (H137ab and H138ab), this was Siegfried's premonition of his future as the music-dramatist Wagner, who'd strive to offer man one last chance of redemption in the face of the inevitable victory of science over man's metaphysical impulse to posit our transcendent value. The poignancy of H191 (which evidently owes something to the Woodbird's fluttering flight and chirping) seems to stem from our sense that this last hope is about to be lost forever. Siegfried has forever lost his way, having unwittingly repudiated his true relationship with Brünnhilde and exposed her secrets to the light of day.

As Siegfried walks down to the Rhine's bank the Rhinedaughters plunge deep underwater. He complains, accompanied by H191, that an elf ("Albe") has led him astray, so that he lost the trail (of his game). Siegfried has gone astray from his life's purpose, and the elf who lured him astray is perhaps Alberich (his Ring Curse of consciousness). Siegfried wouldn't recognize Alberich if he saw him. Perhaps the game he seeks, without knowing it (which he complains the elf has hidden from him), is his muse Brünnhilde, Siegfried's self, his other half. Thanks to the elf Alberich and his son Hagen, Siegfried has grown too conscious to seek unconscious artistic inspiration from her. Brünnhilde's raison d'être had been to protect the artist-hero and his audience from suffering wounds inflicted by Alberich's Ring Curse. The Rhinedaughters surface and jovially mock Siegfried's complaint about the elf who led him astray and futile search for the game he's lost. Siegfried asks them, again accompanied by H191, whether they spirited away the shaggy haired fellow who disappeared from his sight. He tells them that if this shaggy-haired fellow is their lover, he gladly leaves him to them. Siegfried's remarks are full of meaning for us, but not for him; it seems the elf who led him astray, whom he mockingly describes as their lover, might be Alberich, because Alberich once futilely sought their love after Woglinde introduced the seminal motif H4 (basis for the Woodbird's Motif H138ab) which is, according to Dunning, the inversion of the last segment of their new lament for the lost Rhinegold, H184c.

Like the Woodbird before, the Rhinedaughters will warn Siegfried of danger that awaits him. Accompanied again by H191, they offer to grant him the game he's seeking (presumably his muse of unconscious artistic inspiration Brünnhilde) if he gives them something, his Ring (which he gave to Brünnhilde to keep its power safe). The Woodbird, Wagner's metaphor for his special music, once granted Siegfried access to his unconscious mind Brünnhilde. The Rhinedaughters are in a sense making the same offer now, that Siegfried should retreat to the preconscious in the face of an imminent crisis, that he's about to become so conscious of who he is and of his past history, that he'll lose Brünnhilde's wondrous protection, her unconscious inspiration, forever:

[pp. 332–4] **Woglinde:** (H191 >>:) Siegfried, what will you give us, if we grant you your game (:H191)?

Siegfried: I'm still without a catch, so ask what you desire. (H12/H9)

Wellgunde: (H15/H17 vari:) A golden ring glints upon your finger (:H15/H17 vari)—

All Three: Give that to us! (H35)

Siegfried: (H47 >>) A giant dragon I slew for the sake of this ring (:H47); should I offer it now in exchange for a mangy bear-skin? (H190) (…)

Flosshilde: (H189a:) You ought to be openhanded with women (:H189a).

Siegfried: (H189c:) If I wasted my wealth on you, my wife would surely chide me (:H189c). [**Flosshilde:** (…); **Wellgunde:** (…)]

Woglinde: The hero's already feeling her hand! (H191: They laugh immoderately: H190)

Siegfried: (...) (H190 >>:) I'll still leave you to your sorrow: for though you desire the ring, I'll never give it to you, you teasers (:H190). (The Rhinedaughters have resumed their dance)

Flosshilde: (H189a/H3:) So handsome (:H189a/H3)! [**Wellgunde:** (...); **Woglinde:** (...)]

All Three: (H189b:) What a pity he's stingy (:H189b)!

The Rhinedaughters tell him what they want in exchange if they grant him the game he seeks, the Ring on his finger. Siegfried complains that this would hardly be fair, giving them the Ring he won heroically by slaying a dragon for the sake of a mangy bear-skin, and that in any case his wife would chide him, which further spurs their mockery. Siegfried petulantly retorts that he'll never give them the Ring, as they plunge again into the depths. But Siegfried, accompanied again by H191, and pleasantly persuaded by the Rhinedaughters' playful spirit, calls them back again to grant them the Ring after all. Unexpectedly, the Rhinedaughters, growing solemn, decide, seemingly unwisely, to let Siegfried know in detail the danger he'll escape by granting them his Ring, which suffers from a curse. Why don't they just play it safe and accept the Ring from him without further ado once he's offered it? Something else, something fateful, is at work here:

[pp. 334–5] **Siegfried:** (H191:) If they came back to the water's edge, the ring would be theirs for the asking (:H191). (...) You merry water-maids! Come quickly! I'll give you the ring (:H189b)! (H189a: He has removed the ring from his finger and holds it up. (...))

Flosshilde: Hold on to it, hero, (H9) and ward it well, until you (H17 vari:) divine the evil ["Unheil"] ...

Woglinde and Wellgunde: that you harbour within the ring.

All Three: You'll then feel glad (:H17 vari) (H35 voc:) that we freed you from its curse (:H35 voc).

Siegfried: ... (H191 inversion) (H17 vari:) Then sing of what you know (:H17 vari)! (H17 vari; H35)

The Rhinedaughters: (H173 chord:) Siegfried! Siegfried! Siegfried (:H173 chord)! Evil we know lies in store for you.

Wellgunde: (H17 vari >> :) To your own undoing ["Unheil"] you keep the ring (:H17 vari)!

[The Rhinedaughters describe how he who wrought this ring from the Rhinegold and lost it cursed it (...)]

All Three: [He] ... laid a curse upon it, (H50 voc:) until the end of time ["in fernster Zeit;" another translation is "till the furthest time"]) to bring about the death of him who wears it (:H50 voc:).

Flosshilde: (H17 vari:) Just as you felled the dragon (:H17 vari),

Wellgunde and Flosshilde: so you too shall fall

All Three: (H50 end frag:) this very day (:H50)—(H184ab>>:) this fate we foretell (:H184ab)—(H58a/H38:) if you don't hand over the ring to us (:H58a/H38)

Wellgunde and Flosshilde: (H58a >>>:) to be hidden away in the deep-flowing Rhine (:H58a).

All Three: (H58c/H2:) Its floodtide alone (H53:) can atone for the curse (:H58c/H2; :H53).

The Rhinedaughters' strategy with Siegfried—to instill in this proud, fearless man's heart fear of Alberich's Ring Curse, so he'll be prompted by gratitude to grant them his Ring to escape its threat—is bound to backfire, just as their original strategy in R.1 to discourage Alberich from stealing the gold and forging a ring from it, by telling him that to forge it he'll have to renounce his bid for the love they'd just finished rejecting, inevitably backfired, because they left Alberich with nothing to lose. Alberich's renunciation of love, under the circumstances dramatized in R.1, was just as inevitable as Siegfried's refusal to respond to the Rhinedaughters' appeal to his self-preservation instinct to prompt him to give them the Ring. Both are instances of natural necessity (Fate). The Rhinedaughters' futile efforts are therefore rhetorical. Alberich's Ring Curse of consciousness can only end, i.e., the Rhinedaughters can only dissolve it in the Rhine's redemptive waters, by virtue of Siegfried's death, his atonement of Wotan's sin against all that was, is, and will be, which Alberich cursed his Ring to punish. This curse, this punishment, can only end when man no longer posits his transcendent value. All must go down to destruction before we can release ourselves from the insufferable burden of predicating life on a lie.

In response Siegfried puts the Ring back on his finger and asks them what they know. They tell him of Alberich's Curse which he laid on his Ring till the furthest time ("in fernster Zeit"), and that Siegfried will die if he keeps it (just as he felled the serpent Fafner) this very day. Portions of their original song of lament H58abc and H53 (Twilight of the Gods) are heard as they describe how the Rhine's flood alone can atone for the Ring Curse, i.e., that only through life's return to animal preconsciousness can the curse of human reflective consciousness end. As Erda proclaimed in R.4, ending the Ring Curse won't spare the gods the shameful end she taught Wotan to fear; rather, the twilight of the gods (including their proxies Siegfried and Brünnhilde) is a precondition for the return of the Ring to the Rhine and the dissolution of Alberich's Ring Curse. Wotan's futile quest to escape the Ring Curse has actually fulfilled it. Siegfried, affronted by their appeal, now declares his immunity both to their initial flattery, and their current threats, as we hear H53 again:

[pp. 335–6] **Siegfried:** (H189c >>:) You crafty women, (H53:) have done! Since I scarcely believed your flattering tongues, your threats can alarm me still less (:H189c; :H53).

The Rhine-daughters: (H173:) Siegfried! Siegfried (:H173)! ... avoid, (H53 vari >:) avoid the curse (:H53 vari)! (H17 vari >>:; H156:) Night-spinning Norns have woven it into the rope of primal law (:H17 vari; :H156). (H43 frag; H19 vari)

Siegfried: My sword once splintered a spear: (H17 vari/H156) primeval law's eternal rope—though they wove wild curses into its strands (:H17 vari/H156)—(H93?) Nothung will hew from the hands of the Norns! (H116) (H47 vari:) A dragon once warned me against the curse (:H47 vari) (H35 voc:) but it did not teach me fear (:H35 voc);—(H58a: He looks at the ring.) (H84 frag voc: [an H18ab vari]) Though the ring were to win me the world's inheritance (:H84 frag voc: [an H18ab vari]), (H189a:) for the sake of love's favours I'd gladly forego it (:H189a); (H189c:) I'll give it to you if you grant me your favours (:H189c). But since you threaten both life and limb— (H51>>:) though it were not worth a whit (:H51)—the ring you'll never wrest from me! (H43:) For life and limb (:H43)—(H?51.5 = H17ab vari: [this vari may reference the H17ab/H18ab hybrid or H17ab vari heard in an orchestral explosion just before Erda's first appearance in R.4, after Wotan had decided to keep Alberich's Ring and not yield it to the giants in agreed payment for building Valhalla?]) lo: thus (He picks up a clod of earth ... and ... throws it behind him.) do I fling it far away from me (:H17ab vari [possible R.4 reference])! (H190)

Just as Brünnhilde, celebrating her banishment from the gods and their concerns, proclaimed her immunity to Waltraute's (Wotan's) appeal to restore the Ring to the Rhinedaughters to redeem gods and world from Alberich's Ring Curse, because the love she shares with Siegfried is her all in all, so Siegfried refuses the Rhinedaughters' request he grant them the Ring to end its curse and save himself (a request which included their promise to grant him his game in exchange for giving them his Ring), because he, the fearless hero, can never be prompted by fear (self-interest, ulterior motives) to do anything, but can only be inspired by love. Neither Siegfried nor Brünnhilde are aware that Wotan's ulterior intent, founded on his futile hope to redeem himself from truth through an illusory ideal, lives on in their love, so they're unaware their love will share the gods' fate. For this reason, only with the mutual betrayal by Siegfried and Brünnhilde of their love (their secular art exposed as covert religion) will Valhalla and its illusions finally burn up in Loge's fire of self-deceit.

The Rhinedaughters tell Siegfried the Norns have woven the Ring Curse into their rope of primal law (Fate) as we hear both H43 (Power of the Gods) and H19 (Wotan's Spear). Alberich's Ring Curse is an expression of natural necessity. Siegfried proudly retorts that since his sword once split a spear (Wotan's Spear), Nothung will also cut their rope of fate. This already happened figuratively in T.P.A, situated between the two halves of Siegfried's and Brünnhilde's love duet (S.3.3 and T.P.B), when the Norns' rope was split by the sounding of Motif H56 (the Sword Motif—Wotan's Grand Plan for redemption from Erda's truth) and Siegfried's Youthful Horncall H108, and also by Alberich's Ring Curse. Siegfried's unconscious artistic inspiration by his muse Brünnhilde had made him feel "as if" he'd transcended the world, but didn't achieve this in fact. Siegfried adds that a dragon (the Serpent Fafner) once warned him of this curse, but didn't teach him fear, as we hear H35 (Loveless). He then declares, accompanied by H84 (Wotan's First Bequest of the World and Valhalla to Alberich's as-yet-unborn son Hagen), that though the Ring were to win him the world's inheritance, for the sake of love's favors (accompanied now by H189a and H189c, segments of the Rhinedaughters' new lament for the lost gold) he'd gladly forego it. H84 recalls the motival genealogy H17ab>H18ab, the derivation of the gods' heavenly Valhalla from Alberich's earthly Ring power. Siegfried seems to be disavowing the corruption of soul inhering in this genealogy, since Wagner's motival "Wonder" makes us feel freed from the debate over truth and falsehood waged between objective science and subjective religious faith, between Alberich and Wotan. Siegfried is oblivious to the fact that the religious half of this debate lives on in the refuge of feeling, the love he shares with his muse (his music) Brünnhilde.

Now Siegfried sets forth his heroic credo: since the Rhinedaughters threaten him, though (accompanied now by H51—the portion of Alberich's Ring Curse which proclaimed death to any one who co-opts Alberich's Ring-power) the Ring were not worth a whit, the Ring they'll never wrest from him, adding (while we hear a special H17 variant) that, thus, (as he throws a clod of earth over his shoulder) he throws his life away. This H17 variant, H?51.5, seems to reference the hybrid H17ab/H18ab or H17 variant heard just after Wotan refused to hand Alberich's Ring over to the Giants as part of the negotiated substitute payment for building Valhalla which would redeem Freia, but just before Erda appeared to warn of the inevitable twilight of the gods. This motif hybrid or variant was also heard in T.1.3.A when Brünnhilde refused Waltraute's plea that she throw the Ring in the Rhine for the gods' sake. Like Brünnhilde, Siegfried's willing to die for love, or to be more accurate, he'd rather be dead than be forced to acknowledge that the fundamental motive of his life is self-preservation (fear) rather than love. This hybrid of H17ab/H18ab (or special variant of H17), H?51.5, calls dramatic attention to three key moments of decision by Wotan, Brünnhilde, and Siegfried, on whether to keep Alberich's Ring (and therefore pay its price), which both Brünnhilde and Siegfried do, or to relinquish it in the futile hope of escaping its curse, as Wotan did.

Wagner had very strong feelings on this subject, suggesting on several occasions suicide would be preferable to acknowledging that man's primary (or sole) motive is self-preservation (fear), as opposed to self-sacrificial love and compassion, which for Wagner was the sole worthy source of inspiration for human action (including the creation of art): "... my hero should not leave behind the impression of a totally unconscious individual: on the contrary, in Siegfried I have tried to depict what I understand to be the most perfect human being, whose highest consciousness expresses itself in the fact that ... [it] manifests itself solely in the most immediate vitality and action: the enormous significance I attach to this consciousness—which can almost never be stated in words [think here of Wotan's remark to Brünnhilde during his V.2.2 confession: "What in words I reveal to no one, let it stay unspoken forever: with myself I commune when I speak with you."]—will become clear ... from Siegfried's scene with the Rhinedaughters; here we learn that Siegfried is infinitely wise, for he knows the highest truth, that death is better than a life of fear: he, too, knows all about the ring, but pays no heed to its power … ; he keeps it simply as a token of the fact that he has not learned the meaning of fear. You will admit that all the splendour of the gods must inevitably grow pale in the presence of this man." [620W-{1/25–26/54} Letter to August Röckel, SLRW, pp. 308–309; See also 624W-{1/25–26/54} Letter to August Röckel, SLRW, p. 312] "… R. suddenly quoted Egmont's words, 'I set you an example,' and said … this was the German conception of freedom—not to want to go on living when all one could look forward to was fear and the need for circumspection. R. spoke these words with greatest vehemence, as if he were telling me the basic conviction of his life." [996W-{11/25/79} CD Vol. II, p. 401; See also 723W-{9–12/65} 'What is German?,' PW Vol. IV, pp. 161–162]

This was the great question of all questions in Wagner's life, and the primary theme underlying all of his significant repertory operas and music-dramas from *The Flying Dutchman* through *Parsifal*: do human beings have transcendent value, or not? Are we wholly subject to egoistic impulses, or is there something in us autonomous and free in relation to the primary animal impulses of self-preservation and sexual reproduction? Do we partake of, participate in, originate in, or have a stake in, a supernatural or metaphysical realm of being? Is our human consciousness, in its highest development, the self-consciousness of the all, the cosmos, Mother Nature, and if so, in what sense do we transcend our very being, and why would we wish to do so? If, on the one hand, we're purely a product of natural impulses and forces, why have we, in our various religions, based so much of our life's value on renunciation of our natural limits, and defiance of our natural egoistic impulses? And if, on the other hand, we do indeed have an irreducible, supernatural, divine spark in some sense, which is presumably the fount of our occasional manifestation of altruistic impulse, why are we so troubled when this possibility is brought into question and subjected to doubt?

Wagner seems to have believed that if men (at least certain women and men) are capable of conquering their egoistic instincts, then there's something more in the cosmos than natural law, something supernatural which can guide human action. But Wagner's intellectual conscience—informed first by the atheist Feuerbach, and later by the atheist Schopenhauer (who, however, tried to smuggle metaphysics back into Nature)—wouldn't allow him the cheap consolation of belief in a supernatural creator god, redemption in heaven, immortality, or free will. For Wagner, this potentially supernatural element in us remained a mystery he couldn't grasp, but posited theoretically on the basis of our inherent metaphysical impulse to defy our egoistic instincts and the trap of natural law. But if Feuerbach is correct, that all human action, even that dedicated to self-sacrifice for the sake of others and to redemption from our natural limitations, is ultimately motivated by self-interest (which Feuerbach doesn't quite say, but which is implicit in his philosophy), and that if we humans are put to a sufficiently rigorous test this sobering, depressing fact will prove true, then all the great ideals of heroism and love and compassion which human beings have held to be the best are illusions, predestined to be exposed by us in our historical search for the truth.

That's what's at stake as Siegfried declares his freedom of spirit to the Rhinedaughters, who've matured from preconscious animal innocence to expressing a melancholy, worldly wisdom worthy of Erda.

The fact that both Brünnhilde and Siegfried resist restoring the Ring to the Rhinedaughters, for the sake of love, strongly suggests that the redemption by love which Wotan proclaimed to Erda in S.3.1—which didn't involve restoration of the Ring to the Rhinedaughters, but was based on Wotan's hope that Siegfried's loving union with Brünnhilde would, of itself, redeem gods and world from Alberich's Ring Curse—is wholly distinct from the redemption from Alberich's Ring Curse which can only be attained through the Ring's restoration to the Rhinedaughters, a restoration which seems to depend on the destruction of Siegfried and Brünnhilde along with Valhalla and its gods and heroes. It's undeniable that Siegfried's and Brünnhilde's love succumbs to Alberich's Ring Curse, in spite of Wotan's hopes. Since the redemption through love which Wotan believed would be brought about through Siegfried's and Brünnhilde's loving union is Wagner's metaphor for the redemption of man's dying religious faith (the gods) in inspired secular art, particularly his special art, the music-drama, evidently he believed his personal attempt to redeem man from the ravages of reductive science was destined to failure in the face of truth, and that the only escape would be a return to animal preconsciousness. An alternative viewpoint would be that Siegfried and Brünnhilde prove themselves worthy to redeem the world from Alberich's Ring Curse by refusing to relinquish the Ring if prompted by fear, and holding on to it for the sake of love, an act of heroic martyrdom which on this view presumably neutralizes the curse's power. A key problem with this thesis, however, is that they've betrayed their love and will succumb to Alberich's Ring Curse, thereby fulfilling it.

Resigned to Siegfried's refusal, the Rhinedaughters castigate him for his unwitting ignorance of all he'll lose by not granting their request for the Ring, and of all he lost prior to his refusal, specifically the "hallowed gift," the wondrous protection from Alberich's Ring Curse which Brünnhilde's love formerly bestowed on him, and they consign him with cosmic equanimity and joy to the doom he's chosen. Cosima recorded Wagner's take on this: "... we talk about the Rhinemaidens' scene: he [Wagner] shows me how the maidens come very close to Siegfried, then dive down again, consigning him amid laughter and rejoicing to his downfall, with all the childlike cruelty of Nature, which ... indifferently sacrifices the individual—thus ... demonstrating a supreme wisdom which is only transcended by the wisdom of the saint [Siegfried reborn as Parsifal? One can't help noticing a resemblance between Siegfried's confrontation with the seductive Rhinedaughters and Parsifal's analogous confrontation with the amorous Flowermaidens in Klingsor's Magic Garden]." [816W-{2/23/72} CD Vol. I, p. 460]:

> [pp. 336-7] **The Rhinedaughters:** (H190 orch:) Come, sisters! Flee from the fool! (H191 voc:) Wise and strong as he weens himself, the hero is hoppled and blind (:H191 voc). (In wild agitation they swim close to the shore in widening circles.) (H189a vari:) Oaths he swore (H189b) (H189a

vari:) and doesn't heed them (:H189a vari); ... (H189a:) runes he knows (H189b) (H189a:) and cannot read them (:H189a).

Flosshilde, then Woglinde: (H160 voc/H189a>>:) A most hallowed gift was granted to him (:H160 voc/H189a)—

All Three: (H191 voc [a back reference to the Rhinedaughters' remark above: "Wise and strong as he weens himself, the hero is hoppled and blind"] that he has cast it away he doesn't know (:H191 voc).

Flosshilde: (H191 vari voc:) The ring alone

Wellgunde: which will deal him death—

All Three: ... he wishes to keep (:H190; :H191 vari voc)! (H17 vari) (H17 vari/H190 >>>> :) Fare well, Siegfried! A proud-hearted woman will be your heir today, you wretch: she'll give us a fairer hearing (:H17/H190). (H189a:; H190:) To her! To her! To her (:H189a; :H190)! (H189a: They quickly resume their dance and swim away ...)

The Rhinedaughters: H189abc:) Weialala leia, wallala leialala. [The Rhinedaughters' singing accompanies Siegfried's following remarks]

Siegfried: In water as on land I've learned the ways of women now: the man who's not taken in by their wheedling (:H189abc), (H190) (H189c/H190:) they frighten with their threats .... (H190)—And yet, ... were I not (H189c:) true to Gutrune (:H189c), (H189a:) one of these winsome women (:H189a) (H189b:) I'd have wasted no time in taming (:H189b). (...) (Hunting horns can be heard approaching over the heights at the back of the stage. H189c; H190; H18b vari?; H190; H189c; H190; H50; H183; H162)

Hagen's voice: (... H184a:) Hoiho (:H184a)!

(Siegfried starts up from his dreamy reverie and answers the call with his horn. H108. H183; H108)

The Rhinedaughters' critique of Siegfried is a critique of his status as the fool, the unconsciously inspired artist-hero who knows neither who he is, his history, nor the true source of the inspiration whereby he gives birth to redemptive art. Siegfried's foolishness, bestowed on him by Wotan's repression of his self-knowledge into his unconscious mind Brünnhilde, was the explanation behind Siegfried's fearless heroism, and also the reason why, for a time, he was immune from Alberich's Ring Curse of consciousness. But now, by virtue of this foolishness that once protected him, he's lost this protection forever, since his foolishness left him ignorant of—and thus not fore-warned of—dangers to come. As Siegfried said to Brünnhilde in T.P.B, he didn't know how to cherish the runes she'd given him, and she shouldn't chide him that her teaching of Wotan's runes left him untaught. The essence of the Rhinedaughters' critique is that Siegfried's heroism, strength, and indomitable will, have all been the product of his blindness, but his blindness, which allowed him to live solely in the present (freed from Erda's fearful knowledge of all that was, is, or will be, freed evidently from fate), was Brünnhilde's gift to him, which he's now lost forever.

Pursuing their critique, they add that though he swore oaths, he doesn't heed them. In Siegfried's earnest effort to keep his oath to protect Gunther's honor and grant him the privilege of marriage with the world's most wondrous woman Brünnhilde (redemption from conscious thought's contradictions through music), Siegfried unwittingly betrayed his oath to Gunther (Siegfried's audience), and simultaneously betrayed the oath he swore to Brünnhilde to honor her status as his muse of inspiration and not abuse it. Siegfried, the Rhinedaughters say, also possesses runes he hasn't heeded, echoing Siegfried's remark to Brünnhilde that her teaching left him untaught. But this was Siegfried's virtue, that he could draw subliminal inspiration from the most horrible thoughts man (Wotan in his confession) has ever entertained, and transmute or sublimate them into the most profound, transporting art. Woglinde adds, significantly—accompanied appropriately by H160, invoking Brünnhilde's inspiration of Siegfried's new adventures in art, and by H191, the quirky motif which represents Siegfried's going astray from the Woodbird's path of music, which once led him to his authentic muse Brünnhilde—that a most hallowed gift was granted him, yet he doesn't know he's cast it away. This was the gift of Brünnhilde's wondrous protection at the front from the wounds of foresight, and her unconscious inspiration of his redemptive art, a gift he took with him out into the world of men. The other Rhinedaughters add, accompanied again by H191, that the Ring alone, which will doom him, he wishes to keep. Having consigned Siegfried to the fate he's chosen (to which he's predestined), the Rhinedaughters now turn to Brünnhilde who, though she once refused to return the Ring to the Rhine for the gods' sake, at Waltraute's behest, they now assume will heed their message (once Siegfried, Brünnhilde's raison d'être, is dead).

And now, with ominous horns signaling the arrival of Hagen, Gunther, and the Gibichung hunting party whose prey is Siegfried, Siegfried calls his assassins to him with the horn with which he once sought his boon companion (calling up first Fafner in S.2.2, and then Brünnhilde in S.3.2–3), and Siegfried's final moment has come.

TWILIGHT OF THE GODS = ACT THREE, SCENE TWO

(A BANK ALONGSIDE THE RHINE)
SIEGFRIED, HAGEN, GUNTHER, AND THE GIBICHUNG VASSALS

As the Gibichung hunting party appears on a rise above the bank of the Rhine where Siegfried awaits them, his last horncall H108 recalls the moment in S.2.2 when Siegfried woke Fafner with his horn. Having finally found Siegfried, long missing from their hunt, on the bank of the Rhine, Hagen asks, rhetorically, if at last they've found where Siegfried's fled, to what sounds like H127 (a three-note segment of Siegfried's Youthful Horncall Motif H108) which accompanied his re-forging of Nothung, and represented his creative, vital force as an authentic artist-hero, as Hagen, Gunther, and the Gibichungs join Siegfried:

[pp. 338–9] **Hagen:** (catching sight of Siegfried) At last we found where you fled? (H108 frags—H127?)

Siegfried: Come below! (H189a:) It's cool and refreshing here (:H189a)!

(The vassals all arrive on the clifftop and, together with Hagen and Gunther, descend into the valley: H108; H183; H108; H189a/H108; H108)

Hagen: (H108:) Let's rest here and prepare the meal. (...) (H108: [developed] Wineskins and drinking horns are produced. All settle down. H134a [repeated, and strongly marked!!!]) (H162?:; H163 vari:) He who scared away our game, you'll now hear wondrous things of all that Siegfried hunted down (:H162?; :H163 vari). [**Siegfried:** (...); **Hagen:** (...)]

Siegfried: (H108 vari:) I set out in search of wood-game (:H108 vari) (H189a/H108>>:) but only waterfowl showed itself (:H189a; :H108): (H189b/H108 frag:; H190:) had I been better equipped, I might have caught for you three wild waterbirds (:H189b/H108 frag), (H189c:) who sang to me there on the Rhine (:H190; :H189c) (H186:) that I would be slain today (:H186). (Gunther starts up and looks darkly at Hagen. Siegfried settles down between Gunther and Hagen.)

Hagen: (H184ab: Giving instructions to one of the vassals to fill a drinking-horn for Siegfried, which he then offers to the latter H163 vari >>:) It would be an ill-fated hunt if the luckless hunter himself were brought down by a lurking head of game (:H184ab; :H163 vari;)!

As so often in Wagner's *Ring* libretto, which consistently conveys a fairy-tale-like naïveté in spite of being dense with allegorical/philosophical meaning, we find in Hagen's seemingly innocent remark that the hunting party has now found where Siegfried fled, a double meaning. Siegfried is the last in the long line of culture heroes of religious faith, altruistic morality, and artistic creativity who've temporarily redeemed man's religious longing for transcendent value from the Ring Curse of consciousness of the bitter truth. All have, figuratively speaking, fled to the preconscious Rhine with their Ring of consciousness (or, what's the same thing, fled to their unconscious mind, represented in the *Ring* by Brünnhilde) to escape the truth and substitute for it a consoling illusion or, where this wasn't possible, the feeling of transcendence (as found in music). So Hagen is announcing that in man's historical accumulation of his hoard of knowledge, scientific inquiry has finally hunted down and is about to solve the religio-artistic mystery itself, making conscious what for all past time was unconscious. Siegfried, the last of the heroes who sought refuge in the Rhine of human feeling, has unwittingly played his part in betraying Wotan's unspoken secret to the light of day, revealing it within the very work of art whose original purpose was to conceal it. And how much portentous musico-dramatic import there is in Siegfried's request that they "come below" to where it's cool and refreshing, as we hear part of the Rhinedaughters' new lament for the lost Rhinegold, H189a, i.e., that they come down into the depths of the self, the Rhine, with Siegfried!

Siegfried the music-dramatist is inviting his audience to descend into the depths of his own unconscious artistic creativity, depths unknown even to him.

After Siegfried asks the Gibichung hunting party to come down to where it's fresh and cool to join him, the music describing their fateful gathering around Siegfried, on the banks of the Rhine where the *Ring* cycle began, has the air of tragic destiny and finality, making us feel as though a great epic has reached its dramatic climax: something momentous and irreversible is about to happen! This feeling is dramatically enhanced by the presence of H134a, very strongly marked. H134a is the first segment of the motif identified with the serpent/dragon Fafner as teacher of fear, based originally on the Giants' Motif H25. It's as if the Giants have come back to stake their egoistic claim on Freia again, only this time to make their claim good by taking her away forever, thus bringing about the twilight of the gods Erda predicted. And indeed, we've already learned from Waltraute in T.1.3A that Wotan no longer eats Freia's golden apples of sorrow-less youth eternal, having renounced his age-old bid for transcendent value.

As the assembled hunters settle down around Siegfried and open their wineskins for refreshment, Hagen provocatively announces that, having scared away their game, Siegfried will tell the wondrous things he's hunted down. The wondrous things he's hunted down in his life include his father's broken sword Nothung, Fafner, The Nibelung Hoard, the Tarnhelm, Alberich's Ring, Mime, and Brünnhilde. Ultimately, what Siegfried will tell, with the aid of Hagen's antidote to the love-and-forgetting potion Hagen had Gutrune give Siegfried earlier, is how Siegfried woke—and won the hand of—the wondrous Brünnhilde (Wagner's artistic "Wonder"), thereby revealing what formerly had been hidden. Siegfried has lost the Woodbird's (music's) path to his unconscious mind and muse Brünnhilde, but now, thanks to Hagen's antidote (the historically inevitable rise to consciousness of what heretofore was unconscious) he'll find his path to her again, only this time by exposing to the light of day what formerly remained safe in the silent depths, protected by Brünnhilde's Wonder. We recall Tristan who, in giving his muse of unconscious artistic inspiration Isolde to King Marke in marriage (the artist-hero Tristan's audience, just as Gunther represents Siegfried's audience), similarly cast the searing sun of consciousness's light into the formerly sacrosanct womb of night, during a hunt whose ultimate objective, like this, was the exposure of the secret of Tristan's relationship with Isolde, who kept the secret of Tristan's true identity.

Siegfried complains he's empty handed. However, he notes that if he'd been better equipped, he might have caught three waterbirds who sang to him on the Rhine that he'd be slain today, accompanied by H186 (Hagen as Brünnhilde's instrument of vengeance). How interesting that he equates the Rhinedaughters, who warned him about Alberich's Ring's Curse, with the Woodbird who warned him of Mime's treachery! Gunther is startled and looks with alarm at Hagen, but Siegfried lays down between them, suspecting nothing. Hagen can't resist observing that it would be an ill-fated hunt if the hunter himself were brought down by a lurking head of game. But Siegfried has hunted himself down: it was inevitable that the hoard of knowledge he has unwittingly guarded would rise from the silent depths of the unconscious to consciousness within him. What's surprising is that he's played a key role in bringing this fated doom to fruition. Siegfried will expose the secret which religious faith, ethics, and art have long obscured. To this end, he suddenly tells the assembled hunters he's thirsty (accompanied by H165, Hagen's Potion), and it dawns on us he thirsts for self-knowledge, for Hagen's antidote to the love-and-forgetting potion which made Siegfried forget his authentic muse Brünnhilde and woo a false muse, Gutrune:

[pp. 339–40] Siegfried: (H165:) I'm thirsty (:H165)!

[[H192 orch:]] [Is H192, "The Remembrance Motif," derived from the transition from H143 to H149 heard as Siegfried quietly toasts his love and remembrance of Brünnhilde in T.1.2, just before he drinks Hagen's potion of love-and-forgetting? Dunning suggested that H192 might be either a H149 vari or an inversion of H189c]

Hagen: Siegfried, I've heard it said you can understand (:H192 orch) (H137b:) the language of birdsong: can it be true (:H137b)? (H137b frag)

Siegfried: It's long since I've heeded their warbling. (H189a vari; H183 vari: He seizes the drinking-horn and turns to Gunther with it. He drinks and offers the horn to Gunther.) (H183 vari:) Drink, Gunther, drink! To you your brother brings it (:H183 vari). (H172/H161?: Gunther looks into the horn with horror.)

Gunther: (dully: H172:) You've mixed it insipid and pale (:H172): (H172/H161?) ... : H186:) your blood alone is in it (:H186)! (H189a vari)

Siegfried: (laughing: H171 vari:) So mix it with your own (:H171 vari)! (H183: He pours wine from Gunther's horn into his own so that it overflows.) (H118 vari: [variant of "Siegfried's Mission" heard during the bloodbrotherhood oath when Siegfried and Gunther sang "... happy and free ... ," i.e. "froh und frei," evoking the god Froh and his sister Freia]) Mixed, it's overflowed (:H118 vari): to mother earth ["Mutter Erde"—Erda] (H168a/H32B:) let it bring refreshment :H168a/H32B)! (H33 vari/H32B) [Loge's motif H33 is the embryo for H40AB (Tarnhelm) and H165 (Hagen's potions of love-and-forgetting and remembrance), as well as H105, Loge's protective ring of magic fire around Brünnhilde. H32B is also a Loge motif]

Gunther: (... H33 vari/H32B:) You overjoyous hero (:H33 vari/H32B)! (H40A vari/H32B)

Siegfried: (quietly to Hagen: H40A vari/H32B:) Is Brünnhilde making him brood (:H40A vari/H32B)? (H40A vari/H32B)

Hagen: (quietly to Siegfried: H40A:) If only he understood her (:H40A) **[[H192 orch:]]** as you do the singing of birds (:H192 orch)!

Siegfried: (H189a vari:) Since I've heard women (H138b:) singing, I've quite forgotten those songsters (:H189a vari; :H138b).

Hagen: Yet once, you knew what they said? **[[H192 orch]]**

Siegfried: ... Hey! Gunther, woebegone man! (H163 vari) (H38 vari:) If you'll thank me for it, I'll sing you tales about my boyhood days ["jungen Tagen" (:H38 vari). (H38 vari)

Gunther: (H38 vari:) I'd like to hear them (:H38 vari).

Since Wagner compared Siegfried the redeemer with Christ the savior, as per an extract previously cited [See 372W-{6–8/48} 'The Wibelungen'—Revised summer of 1849, PW Vol. VII, p. 289], Siegfried's remark to the Gibichung hunting party that he's thirsty (just prior to his martyrdom) brings to mind Christ's identical remark on the cross during his martyrdom at Calvary, that he thirsts. As Brünnhilde said, Siegfried is to be martyred to pay man's debt for the sins of the world. But in this case of the secular artist-hero who inherited Christ's role in offering us redemption in an age dominated by science, in which religious faith is dying, Siegfried won't be atoning for man's original sin of disobeying God's ordinance not to break the taboo on partaking of divine knowledge of good and evil. Instead, his death will atone two antithetical sins: (1) Wotan's (religious man's) original sin of pessimistic world-renunciation (Wotan's sin against all that was, is, and will be, which inspired artist-heroes like Siegfried have, perhaps unwittingly, perpetuated), and (2) Siegfried's own personal sin, his betrayal of the religious mysteries, Wotan's hoard of runes, the unspoken secret kept by Siegfried's muse of inspiration and unconscious mind Brünnhilde. But the only way to atone for the first, greatest sin, Wotan's sin, is to commit the second sin against Brünnhilde, for only by disavowing all further perpetuation of our religio-artistic sin of world-denial, our sin against our mother Nature (Erda), by renouncing our impulse to seek redemption from Alberich's Ring Curse of consciousness, can the artist-hero (and we who've depended on, and aided and abetted him, in committing this sin of self-deception) hope to atone for this greatest of sins, against the truth. This means the artist-hero must never again seek to heal our un-healing wound through loving union with his muse of unconscious artistic inspiration, which would only rip that wound wider open. This is a primary theme of Wagner's final music-drama *Parsifal*.

We know Siegfried is hungry for self-knowledge when he says he's thirsty because H165 (Hagen's Potion-of-love-and-forgetting) sounds simultaneously in the orchestra, reminding us it was through Hagen's potion that Siegfried forgot (that is, betrayed) Brünnhilde, exposing the contents of his unconscious mind to consciousness. It's a natural consequence of Siegfried's thirst for self-knowledge that he'll soon remember Brünnhilde, Siegfried's "self" who knows for him what he doesn't know. We hear a new motif H192, the "Motif of Remembrance" (Dunning described it both as a H149 variant and a H184c inversion), just before Hagen, in answer to Siegfried's portentous remark that he's thirsty, asks him if it can be true what he's heard, that Siegfried can grasp the meaning of birdsong. H192 is perhaps a variant of a fragment from the transition from H143 to H149 as heard in T.1.2 during Siegfried's private toast to his love for, and remembrance of, Brünnhilde, just before he drank Hagen's potion, forgetting her and falling in love with Gutrune. H143 conveys Wotan's hope that his heir Siegfried's unconscious artistic inspiration by his muse Brünnhilde will redeem religious feeling from Alberich's Ring Curse of consciousness, when religious faith could no longer be sustained in the modern world. H149 at its inception captured Brünnhilde's waking for Siegfried. Dunning's alternate interpretation of H192 is that it's a H189c inversion, which he described as perhaps an inversion of Woglinde's Lullaby H4. H189c is the third segment of the Rhinedaughters' second lament for their lost Rhinegold, which expresses their longing for that decisive act Brünnhilde will later perform.

Hagen—advocate for objective consciousness—is trying to persuade Siegfried to transform his feeling back into thinking, to make music disclose its original source of inspiration in experience, to trace the *Ring*'s musical motifs' origin back to Wotan's confession of his hoard of knowledge to Brünnhilde. By asking Siegfried to recount how he came to grasp the meaning of birdsong, Hagen is virtually asking Wagner to explain how he, as composer and author of his music-dramas, came to grasp the inner process of unconscious artistic creation which formerly was hidden from his conscious mind and from scientific inquiry. Hagen is asking Wagner to tell us how he came to write and compose his *Ring*. And in this way Hagen is asking Siegfried/Wagner to present a performance of his *Ring* for us, since the *Ring* is Wagner's account of how he came to author and compose it as the heir to dying religious faith and the hoard of repressed knowledge it had concealed.

Siegfried in his naïve, heedless exuberance calls on his blood-brother Gunther to drink the drink Siegfried offers him. Gunther, horrified, looks into the drinking horn and, accompanied now by H172 (Oath of Atonement) and possibly H161, responds that Siegfried has mixed it insipid and pale. H161 is Siegfried's premonition he wouldn't be a good guardian of Wotan's hoard of runes Brünnhilde taught Siegfried. Then, under his breath, accompanied by H186 (Hagen as Brünnhilde's instrument of vengeance against Siegfried), Gunther murmurs that Siegfried's blood alone is in this drink. Siegfried asks Gunther to remedy the situation by mixing Siegfried's drink with his own, pouring wine from Gunther's drinking-horn into Siegfried's so that it overflows, a profound symbolic invocation of the blood-brotherhood bond Gunther and Siegfried swore. Siegfried's response to Gunther is one of the most breathtaking dramatizations of Wagner's allegorical master-plan (but nonetheless evidently unconscious for him, as Wagner said on more than one occasion). Initially, we hear two motifs recalling Siegfried's and Gunther's blood-brotherhood oath from T.1.2, during which they drank from a single cup which contained their mixed blood as Siegfried sings: "(H171) So mix it with your own. (H118) Mixed, it's overflowed: to Mother Earth [Erda] (H168a/H32B) let it bring refreshment." The artist-hero Siegfried's death at Hagen's hands is the sacrifice to Mother Earth (Erda) required to atone Wotan's guilt in having committed religious man's sin of world-denial against Mother Nature. Siegfried the music-dramatist must die because man's original religious sin of world-denial reaches its apogee in Wagner's music-drama, the last vestige of man's waning religious faith, and Siegfried is Wagner's metaphor for himself, the 19th Century music-dramatist who wished to restore a sense of the sacred to the theater.

Gunther now introduces the subject of tragic hubris, from Greek drama, into Siegfried's fate, saying to him (and of him): "(H32B/H33 [Loge motifs]) You overjoyous hero," recalling Siegfried's penetration of Loge's protective Ring of fire to wake and win his muse Brünnhilde. To Siegfried's question (aside to Hagen, and accompanied now by H40A variant/H32B), is Brünnhilde making Gunther brood, Hagen responds: "(H40A variant) If only he [Gunther] understood her (H192—Remembrance) as you do the singing of birds!" Hagen's seemingly off-hand remark makes explicit what has only been implicit up until now, the deep underlying connection between the unconscious, involuntary mind (Brünnhilde), which produces dreaming, and music (the Woodbird's song, which Siegfried alone can translate into words, or drama). Brünnhilde, Wotan's wish-womb, not only transformed Wotan's confession of the drama of world-history into transfiguring musical motifs, but evidently also is the spirit behind the Woodbird and its messages to Siegfried. Accordingly, Hagen's identification of the Woodbird with Brünnhilde is underlined by the Motif of Remembrance H192. By virtue of Siegfried having given away the secrets kept by his unconscious mind (Brünnhilde) to his audience (Gunther and the Gibichungs), Siegfried and his audience will become consciously aware of Wagner's unique insights into the inner processes of artistic creation of which he once spoke to Mathilde Wesendonck [See 665W-{12/8/58}Letter to Mathilde Wesendonck, RWLMW, p. 78], secrets previously kept by Wagner's musical motifs, symbolized by the Woodbird's song Siegfried is about to interpret for his audience of Gibichungs.

And Siegfried will give away the secret of his formerly unconscious artistic inspiration, his true relationship with Brünnhilde, by performing a play within a play, a metaphor for the *Ring* itself, in the narrative he sings to the Gibichungs explaining how he learned the meaning of birdsong, i.e., the hidden source of inspiration for the music of his music-dramas. Siegfried's narrative of his youthful adventures is the story of how Wagner the music-dramatist fell heir both to scientific man's hoard of objective knowledge of man and his world, and religious man's longing for redemption from this knowledge and for transcendent value (both this hoard and this longing being the hidden programme of inspired music), and how, finally, through inspiration by his muse, Wagner was able to wondrously, aesthetically transform all that man most fears into sublime art, particularly the Wonder of his musical motifs, represented by the Woodbird's songs. This play within the play is modeled on Shakespeare's *Hamlet*, in which the play Hamlet has written for the court about his fratricidal uncle's and murderous mother's conspiracy against his father is identical to the plot of *Hamlet* itself. Siegfried finds his doom in this narrative song. Nattiez was incorrect when he surmised the narrative Hagen persuades Siegfried to sing is Wagner's metaphor for one of the corrupt genres of opera, for the sake of which Siegfried has allegedly betrayed his true muse of inspiration of the Wagnerian music-drama Brünnhilde, in favor of a false muse, the coquette and wanton Gutrune, who represents a corrupt opera genre such as Parisian Opéra Comique. [Nattiez: pp. 84–88] Since

Siegfried's sung narrative of the story of his heroic life is Wagner's dramatization of a performance of his revolutionary music-drama, the *Ring,* Siegfried betrays his authentic art, his greatest music-drama, as a natural consequence of the *Ring*'s allegorical logic.

Siegfried's figurative music-drama will betray its secret source of inspiration, its hidden programme, symbolically, through Siegfried's conceptual interpretation of the meaning of the Wagnerian musical motif, represented by the Woodbird's second song H138ab (a variant of Woglinde's Lullaby H4). Woglinde's Lullaby H4 was Wagner's Mother-Melody, and the Woodbird's song H138ab is Wagner's metaphor for his artificial restoration of Mother-Melody (feeling, or instinct) in his special development for the drama of modern orchestral music. The Woodbird's songs are Wagner's symbol for his musical motifs, that womb of music which contains the drama and gives birth to it, as Wagner put it. After all, the *Ring* drama, its words, grew primevally out of Woglinde's Lullaby H4, which produced its variant, the Woodbird's second song H138ab. The Woodbird's tunes are the portal between Siegfried's conscious and unconscious mind, his aesthetic intuition of those inner processes of unconscious inspiration represented by Brünnhilde. In previously cited extracts Wagner described how his music, and particularly his musical motifs, provide a sound window into an inner world formerly hidden, a key to access mysteries of the psyche which normally remain unspoken and unseen, but aren't necessarily inherently inaccessible to the waking mind. [See 774W-{9–12/70} 'Beethoven,' PW Vol. V, pp. 75–76, and 838W-{10/72} 'On the Name "Music Drama,"' PW Vol. V, p. 303] Wagner on several occasions described his musical motifs as allowing his audience to share the artist's profoundest secret: "These Melodic Moments ... will be made by the orchestra into a kind of guides-to-Feeling (...) through the whole labyrinthine (...) building of the drama. At their hand we become the constant fellow-knowers of the profoundest secret of the poet's Aim, the immediate partners in its realisement." [547W-{50–1/51} *Opera and Drama*: PW Vol. II, p. 346; See also 679W-{9/60} 'Music of the Future,' PW Vol. III, p. 302; and See 967W-{6/79} 'On Poetry and Composition,' PW Vol. VI, pp. 140–141] What Siegfried is doing in disclosing to his Gibichung audience how he came to grasp the meaning of Birdsong, i.e., how Wagner came to grasp the hidden programme, the historical preconditions, which inspire all authentically great music, is that, as Wagner said, he's providing his audience with a philosophy which will explain the enigma of the world, through his musical motifs. [See 765W-{9–12/70} 'Beethoven,' PW Vol. V, p. 65, and 1055W-{1/17/81}CD Vol. II, p. 600]

After another invocation of the Motif of Remembrance H192, Siegfried, describing Gunther as a "woebegone" man, offers to cheer him up by singing to him tales of Siegfried's boyhood days. Wagner created his redemptive art, and his *Ring* in particular, to cheer up woebegone, fallen, modern man, who'd given up his religious faith and its promise of transcendent value for the sake of the power objective knowledge can grant us, and needed consolation for his loss. Siegfried's singing to the Gibichungs of his boyhood days is Wagner singing of man's childhood, of the prehistory of how man came to the point at which we find him in T.3.2 as Siegfried the music-dramatist is singing the narrative of his life's course for his Gibichung audience. Siegfried initially sings his narrative accompanied not only by the Woodbird's Songs H137b and H138b, but also by a new, jaunty, heroic and optimistic variant of H38, the Nibelung Forging Motif. It was Nibelung labor which produced the Ring, Tarnhelm, and Hoard in the first place, setting all the events of the *Ring* on their course. The tail end of this H38 variant sounds somewhat like the second segment of the Hagen's Watch Motif H173b. This lends to this H38 variant a peculiar narrative force. Siegfried begins with his account of his early childhood, which he endured under the shadow of his greedy, craven foster-father Mime:

> **[pp. 340–1]** (All settle down close to Siegfried, who is the only one to sit upright, while the others lie outstretched further downstage. H137b; H138b)
>
> **Hagen:** Sing on then, hero!
>
> **Siegfried:** (H38 vari; H38 vari; H173b; H106?:) In thrall to greed ["Neides"] (H38 vari:) a surly dwarf by the name of Mime brought me up (:H38 vari), so that, when the child was bigger and bolder, he'd fell (H47?:) a dragon in the forest (:H47?) that long had guarded a hoard there. (H112 vari/H38 vari) (H112 vari/H38 >>> :) He taught me forging and smelting ores (:H112 vari/H38): (H115 voc:) but what the artist ["Künstler"] himself could not do, the prentice's courage was bound to achieve (:H115 voc)—(H127 >>> :) to weld together into a sword the fragments of a shattered blade (:H127). (H116) (H108 triplet vari:; H128 harmony:) My father's weapon I fit together; as hard as nails I fashioned Nothung (:H108 triplet vari; :H128 harmony); (H106 vari [expressing alarm, as in the prelude to S.2.1]) it seemed to the dwarf (:H106 vari) to be fit for the fight: (H47 & H134b:) so he led me into the wildwood and there I felled Fafner, the dragon (:H47; :H134b). But now listen closely to the tale: (H65:) wondrous things I must tell you. The dragon's blood burned my fingers; to cool them, I raised them (:H65) (H192 vari orch: [this variant, the last occurrence of the Remembrance Motif in the *Ring*, seems to foreshadow a theme from *Parsifal* Act Three]) up to my mouth: the gore had scarcely wet my tongue when all at once I understood what the little birds were singing (:H192 vari orch [possible anticipation of a theme from *Parsifal*?]). (H10 vari:) On the boughs one sat and sang (:H10 vari;): (H10 orch:; H138a voc:) 'Hey! Siegfried now owns the Nibelung hoard: o might he now find the hoard in the cave (:H138a voc)! H138b voc:) If he wanted to win the Tarnhelm, it would serve him for wondrous deeds! But could he acquire the ring, it would make him lord of the world (:H138b voc)!'
>
> **Hagen:** (H10:) Ring and Tarnhelm you bore away? [**A Vassal:** (…)]
>
> **Siegfried:** (H65 orch:) Ring and Tarnhelm I'd gathered up (:H10 orch; :H65 orch) … .

In the first part of his narrative Siegfried has related how he did what Mime couldn't do, re-forge Siegfried's father's sword, and how Siegfried killed Fafner with it. So far, all is straightforward. But now, Siegfried relates events he describes as "wondrous" as we hear, for the first time in awhile, H65, the motif recalling Sieglinde's sympathy for Siegmund's Noth, and the Wälsungs Noth in general which they inherited as unwitting agents of Wotan's futile quest to redeem man's religious impulse from Alberich's Ring Curse. Siegfried, accompanied by H65, recalls how—the dead Fafner's blood having burned them—he licked his fingers to cool them and could suddenly grasp the meaning of the Woodbird's Songs. But in the second half of Siegfried's remark something noteworthy occurs: he's accompanied by a special variant of the Motif of Remembrance which not only is the last occurrence of H192 in the *Ring*, but which also seems to foreshadow a theme from Wagner's final music-drama *Parsifal*. Siegfried now recalls in detail what he'd once forgotten as he emerged with Alberich's Ring and Tarnhelm from the dead Fafner's Envy-Cave, what the Woodbird told him just before he entered it, that Siegfried, now owning the Nibelung Hoard, should retrieve the Tarnhelm, which will serve him for wondrous deeds, and the Ring, which would make him lord of the world. Though Hagen in T.1.2 informed Siegfried of the wondrous deeds the Tarnhelm could perform, he didn't tell Siegfried that the Ring could make him lord of the world. This is something Siegfried's remembering unaided for the first time since the Woodbird told him of it in S.2.2.

Accompanied by H65 again, Siegfried confirms that he followed the Woodbird's advice and retrieved these two items. The fact that Siegfried has now remembered expressly what the Woodbird once told him of the Tarnhelm and Ring, and what he'd forgotten, shows that Siegfried of his own nature is now bringing his hoard of formerly unconscious knowledge from the silent depths (Brünnhilde's safekeeping) up to the light of day, even before Hagen has him drink the antidote to the potion of love-and-forgetting which Gutrune gave Siegfried to drink in T.1.2. This suggests Hagen's potion represents a transformation taking place naturally in Siegfried's own psyche. After all, Loge is Siegfried the artist-hero's archetype, and both the two Tarnhelm Motifs H40AB, and Hagen's Potion Motif H165, derive from Loge's Motif H33. For corroboration we need only consider Tristan's admission (figurative certainly, but also truthful) in Act Three of *Tristan* that he himself brewed the love (and death) potion which Brangäne selected, a potion Tristan both describes as his true identity, and curses, in the context of Wagner's remarkable statement in his "Epilogue to 'The Nibelung's Ring'" that the plots of *Tristan* and *Twilight* are virtually identical, the story of how a hero, under a spell, gives away his own true love to another man, and thereby meets his doom.

Siegfried now recalls the second of the Woodbird's three revelations, that Siegfried shouldn't trust Mime, who's been exploiting Siegfried to win for Mime the Nibelung Hoard, and is now secretly plotting Siegfried's death. The essential point is that for Wagner inspired music is a truth deeper and more substantial than words can convey, and Mime's confession of the truth behind his deception is a function of that property of Wagner's music: music is Siegfried's portal into Mime's hidden thoughts (and therefore into Wotan's collective unconscious):

[pp. 341-3] **Siegfried:** (H10:) ... then I listened again to the wonderful warbler; it sat in the treetop and sang:—(H138a voc >>>:) 'Hey!, Siegfried now owns the helm and the ring: o let him not trust the treacherous Mime (:H138a voc)! (H138b voc:) He only wants him to win him the hoard; now he's craftily lying in wait and seeking to take Siegfried's life ... (:H138b voc)!' (H65) [**Hagen:** (...); Four **Vassals:** (...)] (H131B vari:) With deadly drink he came over to me; timid and stuttering he confessed evil thoughts (:H131B vari): Nothung laid the rogue low. (H38 vari) [**Hagen:** (...)] (Hagen has the drinking-horn refilled and squeezes the juice of a herb into it.)

Two Vassals: (H65:) What else did the bird have to tell you (:H65)?

Hagen: (H164:) Drink first, hero, from my horn: I've seasoned a sweet-tasting drink to stir your memory afresh (:H164) (H40A end frag: He hands Siegfried the horn H165:) so that distant ["Fernes"] things don't escape you (:H165)! (H165)

Siegfried: (gazing thoughtfully into the horn and then drinking slowly from it. H161 vari; H65; H160) In sadness I raised an ear to the treetop: (H10 vari:) it sat there still and sang:—(H138a voc >>>:) 'Hey! Siegfried's now slain the evil dwarf! Now I know the most glorious wife for him (:H138a voc):—(H137b frag voc:) high on a fell she sleeps (:H137b frag voc), (H138b frag voc:) fire burns round her hall (:H138b frag voc); (H137b voc:) if he passed through (H12) the blaze and awakened (H12) the bride (:H137b voc), (H137b end frag voc:) Brünnhilde then would be his (:H137b end frag voc)!'

Hagen: And did you follow (H137b frag) the bird's advice?

Siegfried: (H137b frag:) Without delay I set out at once (Gunther listens with increasing astonishment. H33 vari >>:) till I came to the fiery fell; I passed through the flames and found as reward (:H33 vari) (H22: with mounting ecstasy—(H22: or H149 as heard just before Siegfried woke Brünnhilde in S.3.3, heard here on "schlafend"—"asleep"?]) a wondrous woman asleep (H102>>:) in a suit of shining armour (:H102). (H102) I loosed the glorious (H102) woman's helmet (H102); (H102) emboldened, my kiss awoke her:—[I've reversed the order of phrases in Spencer's English translation below to accurately reflect the German original] (H143:) Oh! how clasped me in its ardor (:H143) (H149:) the fair Brünnhilde's arm (:H149) [is a fragment or variant derived from this transition between H143 and H149 a basis for H192, the Remembrance Motif?]!

That Siegfried could see through Mime's sinister hypocrisy, i.e., that Siegfried grasped the egoism of Wotan's lower self Mime, hidden behind the idealism Wotan consciously desired to express, thanks to Siegfried's knowledge of the true source of inspiration for music (the Woodbird's Song), reflects the music-dramatist Wagner's unique insight into the inner processes of religious revelation and authentic artistic inspiration. Wagner claimed he was uniquely gifted in this way because he was author and composer of his music-dramas, so he could experience them both through waking consciousness (objective knowledge) and unconsciousness (aesthetic intuition).

At this point—knowing that Siegfried, under the spell of Hagen's potion, has forgotten how the Woodbird told him of the sleeping Brünnhilde and guided him to her—Hagen prepares to offer Siegfried the antidote, so Siegfried will recall his former relationship with Brünnhilde and in so doing expose to Gunther what will appear at first to be Siegfried's breaking of the implicit oath he made to Gunther to bring Brünnhilde to him a virgin, unsullied. Hagen is out to prove Siegfried had sexual relations with Brünnhilde on the night he spent with her disguised (through the Tarnhelm's Wonder) as Gunther, but obviously it wouldn't be in Hagen's interest for Siegfried to reveal he'd had romantic relations with Brünnhilde prior to meeting the Gibichungs (as seems to be self-evident from Siegfried's account) since, in that case, Hagen would be exposed as having conscripted his half-siblings Gunther and Gutrune under false pretenses to conspire with him to make Siegfried forget his true love Brünnhilde and marry Gutrune, under the potion's influence. In a realistic drama Hagen would've taken this possibility that he'd be exposed as the guilty party into account, so we must suppose either that Wagner's dramaturgy got clumsy at this point, or that there's something else at work in Hagen's machinations.

For this intrigue is, after all, just a cover for what Hagen really wants. The ultimate goal of Hagen's influence on Siegfried, both through his original potion-of-love-and-forgetting, and his antidote to it, the potion of remembrance, is to make Siegfried expose the secrets of his unconscious mind to his audience consciously. Both Hagen's original potion and its antidote (they share motif H165) must be understood as a single potion with one purpose. In other words, thanks to Hagen's influence Siegfried is involuntarily fulfilling Alberich's old threat to bring his hoard of knowledge from the silent depths to the daylight and storm Valhalla. The exposure of Siegfried's true romantic relationship with Brünnhilde to Gunther, making it appear Siegfried has dishonored him, when in fact Gunther dishonored Siegfried by exploiting him and fooling him into betraying his own true love, is merely a metaphor for the fact that the Wagnerian artist-hero, modeled on the trickster Loge, helps his audience (Wotan, or Gunther) deceive itself, and is likewise exploited by his audience to serve its needs. The artist-hero's audience would naturally hope to project its own shame and guilt, once exposed, on to its enabler, the artist-hero, just as Wotan and the other gods projected the shame and guilt implicit in the gods' dependence on the liar god Loge, on to Loge himself. This is Wagner's twist on the Christian idea that Christ takes on the sins of the world.

Now several of the Gibichung vassals, warming to the story, ask Siegfried what else the Woodbird told him. We find astounding confirmation of our allegorical reading in a passage here which surely would otherwise be entirely ignored. As Hagen mixes the antidote to his original potion of love-and-forgetting in a drink, preparing it for Siegfried, he says, accompanied by H164 (Seduction), H165 (Hagen's potion and its antidote), and the end fragment of H40A (Tarnhelm): "(H164) Drink first, hero, from my horn. (H164) I've seasoned a sweet-tasting drink (H164) to stir your memory afresh (H40A End Frag: he hands the horn to Siegfried) (H165) so that distant ("fernen") things don't escape you!" Hagen's remark about distant ("fernen") things, which Siegfried will now be able to remember thanks to Hagen's antidote, is an oblique reference to the hoard of knowledge Wotan confessed to Brünnhilde, and she imparted to Siegfried, leaving him, however, untaught (unconscious of it). In S.3.3, after she told Siegfried that what he doesn't know, she knows for him (accompanied by H87, Fate), she told him that what Wotan thought, she felt, and what she felt was her love for Siegfried (accompanied by H143, redemption through unconscious artistic inspiration). In response, Siegfried (referring to Wotan's thought) told her he couldn't grasp faraway ("fernen") things but only feel her and her singing. Hagen thus identifies Wotan's confession of his hoard of knowledge to Brünnhilde as the hidden source of her unconscious inspiration of Siegfried's art. Wotan's "thought" is his confession to Brünnhilde which she felt, his hoard of runes which she imparted to Siegfried subliminally, i.e., musically, thus leaving Siegfried untaught. What Wotan thought, without fully grasping it, was how religious man's longing for transcendent value could live on, freed from the contradictions of religious belief, in Wagnerian music-drama, safe in the refuge of musical feeling, Wagner's and Feuerbach's inner chamber of the heart.

Wotan's thought, his confession of a hoard of knowledge of things far distant in time and space, which he couldn't bear to say aloud (consciously contemplate), is known to Siegfried only through feeling, Wagner's musical motifs, to which Wotan's wish-womb Brünnhilde gave birth. These redemptive motifs, through Wagner's artistic "Wonder" (symbolized now by the Woodbird's songs H137ab and H138ab in conjunction with the Tarnhelm Motifs H40AB and Hagen's Potion Motif H165), impart all those things faraway in time and space, all those distant, forgotten, and therefore subliminal things with which the musical motifs have been associated in the course of the drama, to Siegfried. [See 478W-{49–51 (?)} Notes for 'Artisthood of the Future' (unfinished), Sketches and Fragments, PW Vol. VIII, p. 371] All that's past and future (Erda's knowledge of all that was, is, and shall be, or Fate, she imparted to Wotan) becomes present for Siegfried through the messengers of Wotan's thought, Wagner's Musical motifs of foreboding and reminiscence.

Siegfried having unsuspectingly drunk Hagen's antidote to the love-and-forgetting potion, we hear H160 (Brünnhilde as Siegfried's muse of unconscious artistic inspiration), H65 (the Noth the Wälsung heroes suffer as Wotan's unwitting agents of his futile quest for redemption from the truth), and H161 (Wotan's Hoard of runes Brünnhilde imparted subliminally to Siegfried, which Siegfried foresaw he'd betray to consciousness), as Siegfried resumes his tale. We hear the Woodbird's tunes H138ab and H137b, as well as H12 (the Rhinedaughters' joyous cry "Rhinegold! Rhinegold!"), as Siegfried mimics the Woodbird's final message to him, that now that Siegfried's slain the evil dwarf Mime, he can wake, woo, and win the most wondrous wife who lies asleep within a wall of fire, Brünnhilde. H12 recalls Brünnhilde's status, about to be lost forever, as Siegfried's surrogate Rhine. Hagen brusquely encourages Siegfried to tell them whether he followed the Woodbird's advice, while Gunther grows increasingly livid at what seems at first hearing like evidence of Siegfried's dishonesty and betrayal. Siegfried, wholly oblivious to the potentially fatal consequences of his confession, now ecstatically recounts his joy in finding the wondrous Brünnhilde asleep. One thinks of Tannhäuser's Act Two confession—as if under a magic spell which renders him wholly oblivious to the risk he takes in exposing his secret source of unconscious artistic inspiration to his audience, particularly Elisabeth—during his performance of his contest-song in the Wartburg Castle, of his sojourn in the Venusberg with his muse Venus, an admission so repugnant, a confession of sin deemed so irredeemable by his audience, that it makes him subject to execution, banishment and excommunication from the church.

We now hear H22 or H149 (Siegfried's awakening of Brünnhilde) and multiple repetitions of H102 (Brünnhilde's plea that Wotan protect her sleep with terrors so only a fearless, worthy hero could wake her) as Siegfried describes how he removed her armor and kissed her awake. Siegfried's tale climaxes in bliss. Exulting, he says: "(H143) Oh! How clasped me in its ardor [following here the word order of the German original, not Spencer's English translation] (H149) the fair Brünnhilde's arm!" H143 and H149 were the two primary motifs heard in T.1.2 as Siegfried made a private toast to love and remembrance of Brünnhilde prior to drinking Hagen's original potion of love-and-forgetting, just before the potion made him forget Brünnhilde and fall in love with his false muse Gutrune. A variant of a fragment of the transition from H143 to H149 may, I suspect, be the basis of the Remembrance Motif H192. Siegfried, having drunk Hagen's antidote to his original potion, now fully recalls not only his former lover and muse of inspiration Brünnhilde, but presumably every secret she kept for (and from) him, including his true identity as Wotan and the full implications of Wotan's unspoken secret. Wagner didn't need to spell this out here: it's implicit in the dramatic context and in the wealth of meaning (hoard of knowledge) which the musical motifs we're hearing have accrued in the course of their history of association with elements of the drama, and even by virtue of their motival genealogy. Had Wagner spelled this out, making it self-evident, my allegorical interpretation would long ago have been anticipated. But much of my allegorical reading probably remained largely unconscious for Wagner anyway since, as he said, an authentic artist's art may remain as much a mystery for its creator as for his audience.

A remarkable aspect of Hagen's two potions, taken as one, is that what Mime failed to do, persuade Siegfried to drink his fatal potion (thanks to Siegfried being warned by the Woodbird's song translated into speech, which allowed Siegfried to grasp Mime's hidden motives), Hagen succeeds in doing, though the Rhinedaughters warned Siegfried of his fate. Hagen gives Siegfried the potion of remembrance at precisely that point in his narrative after Siegfried recounts Mime's failure to ensnare Siegfried with his potion. But this time Siegfried pays no heed to the Rhinedaughters' warning of danger to come. Siegfried's suspicion hadn't been aroused either by Gutrune when she offered Siegfried Hagen's original potion. This is because it was inevitable in the course of history that the secret he and all other authentically inspired artists and religious visionaries have kept, would someday rise to consciousness, and that the last inspired artist-hero would collaborate unwittingly in his own demise, by exposing to view, within his art, that which art and religious faith had long kept hidden, the secret of its inspiration. Hagen is as much a part of Siegfried's persona as Alberich was of Wotan's. How else does Hagen know so much about Siegfried's and Brünnhilde's most intimate life! But we might also surmise that Siegfried has determined now no longer to retreat in fear to the inner Rhine of his heart, but rather to confront the terrible truth Wotan had feared and run from head on, under the influence of a new sense of honor towards the truth.

Now Gunther leaps up in horror at what seems to be Siegfried's confession that he betrayed Gunther's trust and their blood-brotherhood oath, while Hagen prepares to deliver Siegfried's death-stroke, allegedly to avenge this betrayal, as Wotan's ravens fly up to carry the news to Wotan of Siegfried's death:

> [p. 343] **Gunther:** (leaping up in utter horror) What's that I hear? (H32B: Two ravens fly up out of a bush, circle over Siegfried and then fly off in the direction of the Rhine.)
>
> **Hagen:** (H34?:) Can you also guess what those ravens whispered (:H34?)? (Siegfried starts up suddenly and, turning his back on Hagen, watches the ravens fly away. H50/H184a:) To me they counseled vengeance (:H50/H184a)! (Hagen thrusts his spear into Siegfried's back. Gunther and the vassals throw themselves at Hagen. (…) H93a; [[H193ab orch]])
>
> **Four Vassals:** (having tried in vain to stop Hagen) Hagen, what are you doing? [[H193ab orch]] [Two Others: (…)] (H87)
>
> **Gunther:** Hagen, (H172:)—what have you done?
>
> **Hagen:** A false oath I avenged (:H172)!
>
> ([[H193ab orch:]] Hagen turns away calmly and disappears over the cliff top … . Griefstricken, Gunther bends down beside Siegfried. In a gesture of sympathy, the vassals form a circle round the dying man. H87 plus H87 "Crisis" on drums)

When Hagen asks Siegfried if he knows what the Ravens who just flew away whispered, Hagen perhaps doesn't suspect the full truth of what he's said, because those Ravens were sent by Wotan to report back to him when Siegfried is dead, and Hagen is the unwitting instrument of Wotan's need to relinquish all hope of redemption through Siegfried's and Brünnhilde's loving union. Only with Siegfried's death can the Ring be returned to the Rhine and the weight of Alberich's Ring Curse be lifted from gods and world, since Siegfried is the final, unwitting exponent of Wotan's original sin against all that was, is, and will be, and with his death, presumably this ancient sin will be atoned and no longer be perpetuated. Hagen delivers that fateful, fatal death-stroke by stabbing Siegfried in his vulnerable back where Brünnhilde's Wonder hadn't protected him.

Siegfried is stabbed in the back by remembrance of who he is and of things past, terrible things which Wotan seemed—by virtue of his confession to Brünnhilde—to have put behind him, and could permanently forget. He has, as the Rhinedaughters put it, lost his greatest gift, by giving it—his unconscious, which protected him from the wounds of consciousness—away, and keeping the Ring of consciousness. As Hagen delivers the death-stroke of remembrance, we hear H50/H184, as he cries out: "To me they [Wotan's ravens] counseled vengeance." Hagen hasn't wreaked vengeance on Siegfried for betraying Gunther's (false) honor. Hagen has avenged Wotan's original perjury in his foundational contract with the Giants, engraved on his Spear, which Wotan never intended to honor in its original form. Hagen has fulfilled the conditions of Alberich's Ring Curse, whose sole purpose was to punish all those who co-opted the Ring's (our human mind's) power in order to create and sustain the illusion that man has transcendent value, a sin against Mother Nature (Erda) and her truth. In this way Hagen has avenged perjury and deceit, and honored the truth.

The vassals try to stop Hagen in vain, and, after we hear Siegfried's motif H93, the last of the *Ring*'s motifs is introduced, H193ab, its first segment H193a being a heavy syncopation of four notes in the bass which is the hallmark of Siegfried's death-stroke, its second segment H193b being an orchestral flourish which somewhat resembles—at least in its subjective effect—the motif associated in V.2.4 with Siegmund's rebellion against the fate Brünnhilde announced to him, H89. H193 will soon introduce one of the most famous orchestral interludes from the *Ring*, Siegfried's Funeral Procession, often performed independently in the concert hall. The vassals, and now even Gunther himself, shocked, ask Hagen what he's doing, what he's done. We hear H87 (Fate) and H172 (Oath of Atonement) as Hagen grimly responds: "A false oath I avenged!" With that Hagen disdainfully walks off. Gunther, though initially horrified at the apparent evidence of Siegfried's dishonesty and betrayal, instinctively knows Siegfried is innocent and bends over him in remorse at what's been done, partly at Gunther's behest. Gunther in T.2.5 had already expressed his discomfort at Hagen's suggestion that Siegfried betrayed his oath to him. The loss of Siegfried, and Gunther's involvement in the scheme to kill him, is irrevocable: Gunther's remorse arises from the fact that the entire meaning of his life, his sense of self-worth and honor, was the self-deception which Siegfried's art had enabled, just as Loge formerly enabled the gods' self-deception (worship of the gods still practiced, at least formally, by the Gibichungs). How can Gunther find fault with Siegfried, any more than the gods can blame Loge for lying when their self-deceit, enabled by Loge, was the basis for their status as alleged gods!

What is the meaning of Siegfried's death? It's, after all, the reason Wagner authored and composed the *Ring*. The whole purpose of the tetralogy was to explain why Siegfried had to die, why it was inevitable. To do that Wagner had to trace the multiple causes of his death back to their roots in Nature, in evolution itself, and the origins of human thought, which is the subject of *Rhinegold*. Siegfried had to die because it was inevitable in human cultural evolution that the religious beliefs which gave our life meaning in the early phases of our cultural history, would eventually give way to objective knowledge of man and Nature, knowledge we acquired in the course of our experiences throughout history. That the last representative of man's religious impulse, the music-dramatist Siegfried (Wagner), would take a hand—however unwittingly and involuntarily—in bringing about the demise of that very tradition of which he was the exemplar and apex, was the ultimate tragic irony.

Curiously, Wagner's erstwhile friend and advocate, and latterly most vehement nemesis, Nietzsche, in his life-long critique of Wagner, played a role in relation to Wagner very like that which Hagen plays in relation to Siegfried. After Nietzsche broke off his formerly friendly relations with Wagner Nietzsche dedicated his life, as an Atheist, to bringing about the twilight of the gods, that is, the death of religion, the death of God, and the death of all those values and ideals which are predicated on illusory belief in humanity's transcendent value. A key component of his campaign was his effort to expose and destroy Wagner's romantic nihilism and decadence, Wagner's dedication in his secular art to the redemption of religious feeling from scientific inquiry's assaults on religion as a set of beliefs in the supernatural. Nietzsche, like Hagen (and to a certain extent Feuerbach), was a champion of egoism (which, however, he only valued if it was the self-expression of the higher man of creative genius and independence of spirit) at the expense of the romanticism which sustained humanism, compassion, and the high value set on romantic love. Nietzsche was prepared to live in a loveless world, even if happiness was forever banned from it, so long as it was true. And to this end, according to Wagner, Nietzsche set out to discredit and eliminate both religion and (in a certain sense) art, as Hagen has done in stabbing Siegfried in the back. [See 921W-{6/27/78}CD Vol. II, p. 103]

We can't help recalling that Wotan, in his confession to Brünnhilde, told her in despair he'd no longer strive to redeem the gods from Alberich's Ring Curse, and resigned himself to the fact his Wälsungs would be destroyed by Alberich's envy ("Neid"), incarnate now in Hagen. In another (previously cited) passage Wagner described the loveless world which Nietzsche's victory over religion and art and humanist values would leave in its wake, which provides a concrete illustration of the world Hagen would leave in the wake of Siegfried's death, in which "… the progress of the Natural Sciences …" would bring to pass "… the exposure of every mystery of Being as mere imaginary secrets … ." [See 924W-{3–7/78} 'Public and Popularity,' PW Vol. VI, pp. 74–76] But, in an apotheosis of ironic self-analysis, Wagner claimed he gave Nietzsche the means Nietzsche would use to destroy him: "… R. comes to Nietzsche, of whom he says: 'That bad person has taken everything from me, even the weapons with which he now attacks me.'" [934W-{8/2/78} CD Vol. II, p. 128] The weapon Wagner gave Nietzsche, which Nietzsche used against him, was Feuerbach's influence on Wagner's *Ring* and all (or almost all, if we exclude *The Flying Dutchman*, which may or may not have been influenced by Feuerbach's writings) of his other important artworks. It was Wagner's Feuerbachian roots in atheism and materialism which Nietzsche claimed Wagner betrayed in favor of Schopenhauerian mysticism, romantic nihilism and pessimism, and Christian sentimentality (Nietzsche's rather shallow reading of Wagner's last artwork, *Parsifal*, in which Wagner's critique of religious faith culminates). In view of the at least partial similarity between Hagen's relationship with Siegfried and Nietzsche's relationship with Wagner, it's amazing that in this case life followed art, because Wagner had already written the *Ring* libretto when Nietzsche was very young and hadn't yet met Wagner.

Now, presumably fully conscious of who he is, and of his formerly secret history, Siegfried, dying, sings his final apostrophe to Brünnhilde, in a death-song painfully reminiscent, for some lovers of revolutionary music-drama (but not for me), of the operatic clichés Wagner claimed to have put behind him, but which works on us with incomparable force in its dramatic context:

> **[p. 344] Siegfried:** (... H148:; H?—[a cryptic version of the harp music, trills, and shimmers from Brünnhilde's awakening in S.3.3]) Brünnhilde:— Hallowed bride—awaken (:H148; :H?—[harp, plus orchestral trills and shimmers)! (H149:) Unclose your eyes (:H149)! (H87 vari:) Who locked you in sleep once again? (...) (:H87 vari) (H?—[Morse-code-like pulses from Brünnhilde's original awakening:) One came to wake you; (H93a?:) his kiss awakes you and once again he breaks the bride's bonds: and Brünnhilde's joy laughs upon him (:93a?; :H?—[Morse-code-like pulses from Brünnhilde's awakening in S.3.3]). (H93a?) (H150>>:) Ah! those eyes— now open for ever! Ah, this breath's enchanted sighing (:H150)! (H151) (H151:) Sweet extinction ["Süsses Vergehen"],—blissful terror ["seliges Grauen"] (:H151):—(H87:) Brünnhild' gives me her greeting (:H87)!

This passage recapitulates, in brief, much of the musical/motival material heard in S.3.3 during Siegfried's original waking of Brünnhilde. We hear H148 (its chord based on Erda's H52, i.e. her knowledge of all that was, is, and will be), along with the orchestral trills, shimmers, and harp music from S.3.3 which recall Siegfried's waking of Brünnhilde, as Siegfried calls out to his hallowed bride. We hear H149, heard during her awakening, but also just before Hagen's potion made Siegfried forget Brünnhilde, as Siegfried calls on her to unclose her eyes. H87 (Fate) sounds as Siegfried asks who closed her eyes, which are locked in sleep once again. Siegfried describes how he comes to Brünnhilde and kisses her awake once again, breaking the bride's bonds. We hear his own motif H93 (Siegfried, fearless because Brünnhilde protects him from wounds) as he sings that Brünnhilde's joy laughs on him. As we hear H150, the love motif to which they launched their love-duet in S.3.3, making us feel that we've returned to that moment in the drama, Siegfried describes Brünnhilde's eyes, which he says are now open forever! By virtue of having betrayed the secret of his unconscious artistic inspiration (his love for Brünnhilde), and revealed the secret it kept— Alberich's and Wotan's hoard of bitter knowledge identified now with Alberich's Ring—to his audience, Siegfried has indeed awakened man's collective unconscious permanently, so it can never return to sleep and dreaming, never again inspire religious revelation and art. We recall Hagen's eyes remained permanently open and watchful, like his father Alberich, even in sleep. The fact that Brünnhilde's eyes are now opened forever means she's become indistinguishable from her mother Erda (Mother Nature) as known objectively to anyone possessing the Ring of consciousness, so Brünnhilde can now give voice to Erda's knowledge, which wakes alone in man.

Now, accompanied by H151 and H87 from S.3.3, Siegfried cryptically sums the essence of his life. He sings: "(H151) Sweet-extinction ["Süsses Vergehen"], (H151) blissful terror ["seliges Grauen"];—Brünnhilde (H87) gives me greeting." The German word Vergehen conveys a notion of "violation," or moral transgression, for Siegfried, by unwittingly betraying his oath to Brünnhilde to preserve her sanctity as his unconscious mind (as repository and guardian of Wotan's unspoken secret), by giving her and her secrets away to his audience, Gunther and the Gibichungs, violated or—in a sense—raped her, his muse of inspiration, irredeemably. And yet it was only by doing this, by betraying the secret of religious faith and unconsciously inspired art, that Siegfried could attain the apotheosis of ecstasy of which only the highest art is capable, in Wagner's *The Ring of the Nibelung*. When H151 was introduced in S.3.3 its primary conceptual association was with Brünnhilde's remark that she is his own self, if he loves her in her bliss, and that what he doesn't know (H87—Fate, his true identity), she knows for him. H151 simultaneously conveyed two notions which ostensibly oppose each other, but in reality cohere. On the one hand H151 can be construed as a metaphor for the mystical idea that by deep meditation, some sort of spiritual enlightenment, or by virtue of the deepest love of one person for another, the single individual can lose himself in the totality of the world, by—in some sense—identifying himself with it, and thereby renouncing and losing his ego. On the other hand H151 could represent what I've been suggesting throughout this study, that Siegfried (i.e., Wotan, Siegfried's prior incarnation) loses his loathsome identity in Brünnhilde only because she, his unconscious mind, knows it (his fate H87) for him, so he needn't suffer from consciousness of it. It was in this way that Wotan, who'd become unbearably conscious of who he is (Dostoevsky called consciousness a disease!), repressed knowledge of his true identity and Erda's prophecy of the gods' fated doom in Brünnhilde, and was reborn as fearless Siegfried, who didn't know who he was because Brünnhilde knew this for him. As Wotan said of Brünnhilde when confronting her mother Erda in S.3.1, Erda's wisdom wanes before his will, and Brünnhilde called herself his "Will" just prior to his confession to her in V.2.2. Thus H151 underlines Siegfried's perhaps otherwise inexplicable remark: "Sweet extinction (violation)."

H151 also highlights Siegfried's cryptic phrase "Blissful terror," because it was through his unconscious artistic inspiration by his muse Brünnhilde that the artist-hero Siegfried was able to suppress Wotan's (man's) objective, fearful knowledge of the terrible world, and sublimate it into beauty, in inspired art. As the Woodbird said, the lover's secret is how one draws bliss from woe, or, as Wotan said of Loge's cunning, how one draws advantage from the enemy's envy. But, now that he's fully awake (his unconscious mind Brünnhilde waking forever), Siegfried intuits that his formerly unconscious woe and his consciously felt bliss are identical. Thanks to Siegfried having made his unconscious mind indistinguishable from his conscious mind, by transforming himself (using Alberich's Tarnhelm's Wonder) into his audience (Gunther), so his audience could share secrets of inspiration unknown even to Siegfried himself, the abhorrent knowledge Wotan once feared to speak aloud (consciously) to himself has been exposed as identical with the aesthetic bliss the artist-hero Siegfried distilled from it. Thus Siegfried invokes the seeming oxymoron: "blissful terror." Siegfried had to learn fear from Brünnhilde to learn from her also how to forget it, just as Wotan once sought both full knowledge of what he feared from Brünnhilde's mother Erda, and also knowledge of how he might end his fear from her. Siegfried, in a blinding flash of self-knowledge, has now recognized these seemingly antithetical states of mind as one. Siegfried hadn't feared loving union with Brünnhilde because he feared he'd lose himself in her, but rather, because he (Wotan's reincarnation) feared he'd find his true self in her. In Wagner's *Ring*, "Know Thyself" is the most appalling of destinies.

With Siegfried's death, Hagen has realized Feuerbach's dream, exposure of the religious mysteries as nothing more than man's consoling fantasy [See 284F—LER, p. 219], leaving the way open to a new philosophy of materialism which, however, most men can't abide, once they fully grasp its horrific, depressing implications, its insupportable cost. Wagner on one occasion addressed the question why Siegfried had to die. According to a visitor to Wagner's home Tribschen in 1869, Valentina Serova, Wagner said Siegfried had to die because evil, exemplified by Alberich, always wins in the real, objective world: [Speaking of someone present at Wagner's home Tribschen on 7/8/69, who was asking Wagner to explain seeming contradictions in the *Ring*'s plot, Valentina Serova recorded his following question, and Wagner's answer to it:] "'… why must Siegfried be killed?' the questioner went on. / [Wagner answered:] 'Because evil always prevails over good. Alberich's powers are invincible: he is the spirit of evil who pursues his dark ends with a grim, unflinching determination. And he passes on this resolve to his son Hagen." [752W-{7/8/69} Valentina Serova's reminiscence of a visit to Tribschen on 7/8/69, WR, p. 203]

The mourners, including Gunther, now pick the dead Siegfried up and carry him in moonlight back to Gibichung Hall, to the accompaniment of one of the most famous orchestral passages from the *Ring*, 'Siegfried's Funeral Procession (March),' often performed as an independent piece in the concert hall, a staple of the Western classical repertoire:

> **[p. 344]** (**Orchestral Interlude:** Siegfried sinks back and dies. (…) H87's drum accompaniment "Crisis;" H193b; H65; H87's drum accompaniment "Crisis;" H193b; H65. Night has fallen. At Gunther's silent command, the vassals lift up Siegfried's body and, during the following, carry it away slowly in solemn procession over the cliff top. [H?—Three long, ever louder, higher notes in the bass]; H193a on brass; H193b; H193a brass; H193b; H70; H193ab: H69; H62/H65. The moon breaks through the clouds and casts an increasingly bright light on the funeral procession which has now reached the top of the cliff. H39; H63; H193b: [rising] Mists have risen from the

Rhine and gradually fill the whole of the stage ... . H65/H193 frag; H56ab; H193a in major [and loud]; H93ab/H193b major; H193a; H93bc; H159; H193a [loud]; H159; H193ab: From this point onwards the mists begin to divide again, until the hall of the Gibichungs can be made out once more, as in the opening act. H160 [a sad vari with melancholy harp accompaniment]; H193ab; H160 [in a sad vari]; H184ab)

The motifs Wagner chose for Siegfried's funeral procession are those evoking the tragic history of the Wälsungs from Siegmund and Sieglinde to Siegfried. But the keynote, gravely punctuating the interlude multiple times, is the last *Ring* motif H193ab, followed quickly by H65, which expresses the Wälsung's Noth (anguish), the Wälsung heroes' fate as unwitting martyrs to Wotan's futile campaign to redeem the gods from Alberich's Ring Curse, the curse of truth which will overthrow man's illusions of transcendent value. Siegfried, the last of the Wälsungs, has now been martyred by Wotan's Noth. Wotan's Wälsung heroes had to pay Alberich's price to spare the gods (those men dependent on belief in gods for their happiness) from having to pay it. This Wälsung motival genealogy begins with the sounding of H70 and H69, motifs introduced in V.1.2 after Siegmund had described the Noth-filled life which forced him to name himself Woeful. His tragic fate, conveyed by H69 and H70, is the price paid by the Wälsung heroes for being heirs to Wotan's futile quest for redemption, a concept conveyed in a different way by H65. While H65 expressed both Siegmund's woe and Sieglinde's sympathy for it, H69 and H70 manifested Siegmund's feeling of tragic alienation and loneliness in the midst of a society which didn't understand and felt threatened by him, in which he fought for the right to keep his own counsel and conscience against powerful pressures to do otherwise.

Following immediately after H70 and H69 are H62/H65, Sieglinde's motif plus that conveying the Wälsungs' Noth and her compassion for it. The moon then breaks through the clouds, casting an increasingly bright light on the funeral procession. Once the procession reaches the top of the cliff we hear the primary love motif in two key variants, H39, which conveys the tragedy of man's fight for love in a loveless world, and H63, the definitive love motif which was introduced in V.1.1 to express the growing love between Sieglinde and Siegmund. H63 stems from the second of Freia's love motifs, H23. H193ab, Siegfried's death-stroke, continually punctuates all of this music. Mists rise from the Rhine and hide everything on stage. Now we hear H56ab, the Sword Motif which tells us of Wotan's grand (yet futile) idea for redemption from Alberich's Ring Curse, that a race of heroes to whom he gave birth would take on the burden of that curse to restore lost innocence. The music grows ever louder as we hear Siegfried's motif H93 (bespeaking his onetime status as the hero rendered fearless by Brünnhilde's loving protection), which then transitions into H93c, a cadential figure or end fragment of H93. H93c was introduced in V.3.1 in association with Brünnhilde handing the two pieces of Siegmund's broken sword Nothung to Sieglinde so Sieglinde could give it in turn to the as-yet-unborn hero, her son Siegfried, to re-forge it, and also with Brünnhilde's naming of Siegfried. H93c may be derived from the last cadential segment of the Rhinedaughters' first lament for the lost

Rhinegold from R.1, H58d, to which they sang: "... o give us the guileless gold back again!" It's to H93c that Brünnhilde will sing her last words before riding Grane into Siegfried's funeral pyre in T.3.3, "In bliss your wife bids you welcome!" Finally we hear the Horncall of Siegfried's Maturity H159 on brass, but then the music, having reached perhaps the greatest volume in the *Ring*, quiets down to a mournful variant of H160, the motif which evokes Brünnhilde's loving inspiration of Siegfried's new adventures (creation and performance of redemptive works of art for his audience, man), adventures which have ended in tragedy.

Several commentators (including Michael Tanner) have asked whether such a naive and childlike hero as Siegfried, who lacks nuance, maturity, or depth, deserves such an epic accolade as this heroic musical genealogy and testimonial. Siegfried deserves it if one understands that his death is the death of the sole foundation we humans have had for our cherished notions of our transcendent value, and life's meaning, since we first evolved from animal forebears, and civilization began. Siegfried's seeming vacuity, lack of self-reflection, naiveté and innocence stem from Wagner's deliberate intent to portray in him Wagner's idea (based on his intense study of his artistic progenitors, and remarkably astute insight into his own nature as a genius of art) of the authentically unconsciously inspired artistic genius, and that the true, unconscious source of inspiration for his art remains as much a mystery to him as to his audience. Siegfried's heroism sprang from the fact that he didn't know himself, that the capacity of his unconsciously inspired art to offer us redemption depended on Siegfried's remaining innocent with respect to his true mainsprings of inspiration. One must understand this to grasp what's been lost with his death, and to grasp also why his personality seems so lacking in substance. He's an allegorical being. One of the most pernicious misunderstandings in the history of Wagner scholarship has been the widely held assumption that he was Wagner's metaphor for a failed 19th Century social revolutionary. Wagner assigned that role to Siegfried's father Siegmund. We can't grasp Wagner's characterization of Siegfried without recognizing that Brünnhilde and he can only be understood as the unconscious and conscious halves of a single individual, the unconsciously inspired artistic genius, and that they're subsumed by Wotan, Wagner's Feuerbachian symbol for collective, historical man, who gave birth to the world's various religions in primal times, perpetuated them as long as their self-deception could be sustained, and finally outgrew them through man's acquisition of a hoard of objective knowledge of man and Nature.

With that proviso in mind, we move now to the climax of the *Ring*, in which Brünnhilde will sum its meaning, and enact the twilight of the gods and the dissolution of Alberich's Ring and its Curse.

TWILIGHT OF THE GODS ⁼ ACT THREE, SCENE THREE

(GIBICHUNG HALL)
GUTRUNE, HAGEN, GUNTHER,
SIEGFRIED DECEASED (YET BRIEFLY RESURRECTED),
BRÜNNHILDE, THE GIBICHUNG VASSALS AND WOMEN,
AND THE RHINEDAUGHTERS

What is arguably the grandest and most heroic orchestral passage in the *Ring*, Siegfried's Funeral Procession, has slowly quieted and wound down to a brief orchestral interlude of silent melancholy, which introduces the *Ring*'s last scene. We've returned now to Gibichung Hall. Gutrune's brief soliloquy which follows is as central to the dramatic structure of the *Ring* as any other, though Wieland Wagner (Wagner's grandson) evidently thought it so negligible that he sometimes cut it from *Ring* performances at Bayreuth. Gutrune's brief moment alone is one of the most touching yet unnerving in the *Ring*, because we feel here a desolation of the spirit which tells us just what's been lost to the world through Siegfried's death. It's a little masterpiece of existential meditation on what a world might be like in which all hope for a higher spiritual life, all ideals, all longing for humane values has been utterly, irrevocably squelched:

> **[pp. 344–5]** (It is night. Moonlight is mirrored on the surface of the Rhine.
> H173a/H193ab frag; H50/H11 vari minor [H173 continued]; H159 [in a sad vari]; H11 vari: … . H168a vari; H108/H173a)
>
> **Gutrune:** (H108/H173a:) Was that his horn? (…) (H173b end frag >>:) No! He's still not come home.—Troubled dreams (:H173b end frag) (H108 vari>>:) disturbed my sleep (:H108 vari)!—(H77b:) His horse was neighing wildly (:H77b):—(H76 vari) Brünnhilde's laughter woke me up.—Who was the woman (H173b end frag:) I saw going down to the shore (:H173b end frag)?—(H12 vari; H118 vari; H160) I'm afraid of Brünnhild'!—(H87:) Is she within (:H87)? Brünnhild'! Brünnhild'! Are you awake? (H160: She opens the door timidly and looks into the inner chamber.) The chamber's empty! [could this be Feuerbach's and Wagner's 'chamber of the heart'?]—(H12 vari) So it was she whom I saw going (H11 vari:) down to the Rhine? (H183) Was that his horn (:H11 vari)?—No! Everywhere desolate!—(H168a/H176) (…) H168a/H176:) Might I only see Siegfried soon (:H168a/H176)!

The unbearably doom-laden mood of melancholy is produced initially by the mournful variant of H160 (Brünnhilde's inspiration of Siegfried's art), followed by the sad motif of Hagen's Watch H173 and a H50(Ring Curse)/H11("Heiajaheia!") variant in the minor. A depressing, tentative variant of the Mature Siegfried's Horncall H159, usually so proud and grand, adds to the melancholy. Gutrune's repeated refrain "Was that his horn," as we hear spectral echoes of the now deceased Siegfried's Youthful Horncall H108, forces on our wakeful attention more than anything could that Siegfried and all that he represented is gone forever, or rather, never truly existed.

Gutrune, troubled by nightmares, has been woken by Brünnhilde's ironic laughter in the night, a laughter which her reincarnate self Kundry will inherit in Wagner's final music-drama (which some consider, as I do, and with good cause, the fifth music-drama of the *Ring*), *Parsifal*. Gutrune thought she saw a woman going down to the Rhine. We'll soon learn from Brünnhilde that during her visit to the banks of the Rhine the Rhinedaughters persuaded her to fulfill their prophecy that she'd lend a more willing ear to their plea to restore the Ring to them, than Siegfried did. At this point in Gutrune's soliloquy we hear a H12 Variant (the Rhinedaughters' joyous cry of "Rhinegold! Rhinegold!" from before the "Fall"), an H118 Variant, and H160. H118 and H160 are echoes of T.P.B, when Brünnhilde inspired Siegfried to undertake the new adventures of art (Siegfried's ultimate "mission") which culminated in his self-betrayal of her, his muse, and their art. Gutrune, expressing her fear of Brünnhilde as we hear the Fate Motif H87, checks Brünnhilde's room to see if she's in. Finding she's not, Gutrune says Brünnhilde's chamber is empty, and that therefore it must have been Brünnhilde she saw going down to the Rhine. We can't help wondering if the chamber that's empty is that chamber of the heart of which both Feuerbach and Wagner spoke, the musical feeling to which Wotan, the alleged god, retreated when he could no longer sustain himself in the world through humanity's belief in him. Gutrune, thinking she's heard Siegfried's horn one last time, realizes finally that it wasn't, and then captures the essence of our experience of the *Ring*'s culmination in Siegfried's death, by saying: "(H173 End Fragment) Everywhere desolate!" H173, Hagen's Watch, speaks of his sinister intent which has now been fulfilled. We recall the bleak orchestral prelude of *Tristan* Act Three, a sort of musical evocation of "the wasteland" from legends of the Holy Grail which Wagner also captured in the orchestral prelude to Act Three of *Parsifal*. Finally, we hear Gutrune's Motif H168a in combination with H176 (Brünnhilde's recognition that her love for Siegfried was Wotan's punishment at its apogee of anguish, the consummation of Alberich's Ring Curse). H176 recalls the price Brünnhilde pays living for love.

Brünnhilde's laughter, I surmise, arises from the full knowledge of the place she and Siegfried, and their love, hold in the cosmic scheme of things, for in her final judgment on Wotan, and apostrophe to Siegfried, with which she introduces the *Ring*'s finale, the twilight of the gods, she'll proclaim she now knows all things (her mother Erda's knowledge of all that was, is, and will be) with full consciousness, and evidently will be reconciled to all things. Perhaps she concurs with the Rhinedaughters that all was play, thereby giving the victory, in the end, to art, after all!

Hagen now approaches heralding (the fact of) Siegfried's death (as previously he heralded the fateful double wedding of Gunther with Brünnhilde, Siegfried with Gutrune), with the greatest possible insensitivity, sadism, and Schadenfreude, at first suggesting Gutrune should greet the living Siegfried who's just returned from the hunt, but then, in announcing his death, placing special emphasis on all the things Siegfried, now dead, will never again be able to do, including love (H35 "Loveless" sounding at this point). Hagen scarcely tries to hide his role in Siegfried's death (though he says initially, invoking his prior conspiracy with Gunther and Brünnhilde, that a boar gored Siegfried), enjoying so richly his triumph over the hero:

> [pp. 345–6] **Hagen's Voice:** (approaching from outside: H186:) Hoiho! Hoiho (:H186)! (…) (H176 >> :) Wake up! (…) Spoils of the chase we're bringing home (:H176). (H186:) Hoiho! Hoiho (:H186)! (…) (H183:) Up, Gutrun'! Welcome Siegfried (:H183)! The doughty hero (H108:) is coming home (:H108).
>
> **Gutrune:** (in great fear. H176:) What's happened? Hagen (:H176)! (H108 end frag:) I didn't hear his horn (:H108 end frag?)! (…)
>
> **Hagen:** (H172 vari >>:; H179 hint?:) The bloodless hero will blow it no more; no more will he storm to hunt or to battle (:H172 vari; :H179 hint?) (H35 vari:) nor sue for the hand of fair women (:H35 vari)!
>
> **Gutrune:** (with mounting terror: H108 vari:) What are they bringing (:H108 vari)? (…)
>
> **Hagen:** (H43ab?:) A wild boar's prey (:H43ab?): Siegfried, your dead husband! (H147A or H176 vari?: Gutrune cries out and throws herself on the body. (…)) [**Gunther:** (…)]
>
> **Gutrune:** … Siegfried! Siegfried slain! (H50 frag or H51 frag?: She pushes Gunther violently away.) (H147 or H176 vari or possibly H81 vari?:) Away, faithless brother, my husband's murderer! Oh help me! (…) Woe! (…) They've slaughtered Siegfried (:H147 or H176 vari or possibly H81 vari?)!

As Hagen concludes his deliberately insensitive, mocking, and provocative remarks with his blunt announcement of Siegfried's death, we hear H43 (Power of the Ring), this being the final, most potent instance in which the Ring's power is wielded over men. It expresses Hagen's sadistic joy in power's triumph over love itself. Gutrune falls on Siegfried's body in grief (proving she isn't simply the loveless wanton or coquette argued for in Nattiez's reading), and then castigates her brother Gunther (who tries in vain to console her), accusing him of being a co-conspirator in Siegfried's death. Gunther, now fully aware of what he's lost in collaborating with Hagen to destroy Siegfried (Gunther's last hope of finding meaning in life) for the sake of practical, earthly power, now blames Hagen alone for Siegfried's death, cursing him as Judas was cursed in the New Testament for plotting Jesus's death (though Judas's martyring of Jesus was crucial to the fulfillment of Jesus's role as the world's savior). Hagen defiantly confesses to the murder, claiming he was the righteous instrument of vengeance in making Siegfried pay for breaking his oaths to Gunther and Brünnhilde:

> [pp. 346–7] **Gunther:** (H176 vari:) Hold me not to blame! Blame Hagen there: he's the accursed boar that rent the noble hero's flesh (:H176 vari). (H147 or H176 vari or H81 vari? [associated above with Gutrune's horror at

Siegfried's death]) [**Hagen:** (...)] (H180:) [to Hagen] May fear and misfortune hound you for ever (:H180)!

Hagen: (stepping forward with terrible defiance: H187:) Yes, then! ... I—Hagen—I struck him dead (:H187)! (H172:) He was marked out by my spear by which he'd falsely sworn (:H172). I've now acquired the sacred right of conquest: (H45?:) and so I demand this ring (:H45?). (H17 vari)

Gunther: Get back! What has fallen to me you'll never receive as your own. (H17 vari) (...) (H106/H17 vari:) How dare you touch (:H106/H17 vari) (H168a:) Gutrune's inheritance (:H168a), shameless son of an elf!

Hagen: (drawing his sword: H50:) The elf's inheritance his son now demands (:50:)! (H17 vari: ... they fight. (...) H43ab?: Hagen strikes Gunther dead.) Give me the ring! (He reaches towards Siegfried's hand, H56ab which raises itself threateningly. (...) All remain transfixed with horror.)

Gunther accuses Hagen of being the true traitor, since Hagen exposed the truth about Siegfried, and Gunther would rather have remained ignorant of it. Gunther would rather have enjoyed the false consolations provided by the artist-hero Siegfried than the objective truth, and the power it can bring, which Hagen offered, but now it's too late. We recall Wotan who, when Erda told him the full price he'd have to pay if he didn't yield the Ring to the Giants, that he'd have to acknowledge that the gods and love are predestined to destruction, relinquished the Ring to them, so he could fall back on his consoling illusions. But Siegfried's true nature has been exposed, and Gunther only has the Ring's power to fall back on as a basis for life, the open admission that self-interest rules the world, so he challenges Hagen for the right to exercise its objective power. Hagen defends his right to wreak vengeance on Siegfried for breaking his oaths to Gunther (H172—Oath of Atonement) and Brünnhilde (H187). Of course, Siegfried, like Oedipus, was unconscious he was breaking any oath: he thought he was acting in good faith. Hagen declares he's acquired the sacred right of conquest, and demands the Ring on dead Siegfried's finger. Gunther challenges Hagen's right to it, since Gunther considers it the widow Gutrune's—his sister's—inheritance. In a fight which echoes the first fight over the Ring between the giant Fafner and his brother Fasolt in R.4, the claims of egoism similarly prompt Gunther and his half-brother Hagen to fight over it. Gunther stoops to calling his half-brother Hagen the "shameless son of an elf," gratuitously introducing an element of class and/or race into the dispute. To H50 (Alberich's Ring Curse, of which Hagen is the agent), Hagen claims the elf's (Alberich's) inheritance, and strikes Gunther dead, accompanied by a H17 variant and H43. Hagen then shouts "Give me the Ring!," and reaches towards Siegfried's hand to take it, but Siegfried's dead arm rises threateningly to the tune of H56ab, the Sword Motif (Wotan's Grand Idea of redemption through restoration of lost innocence), and Hagen withdraws in awe, struck dumb by this seemingly supernatural intervention. This I believe is the final occurrence of the Sword Motif H56ab in the *Ring*.

What's the meaning of this seemingly unnatural incident? The fact that Siegfried's dead arm rises to the sound of H56ab calls to mind the Sword Motif's second segment H56b, the Primal Nature Motif H1, which evokes the pre-Fallen, paradisal time before the Fall. Knowing as we do that Siegfried's and Brünnhilde's love has failed to restore lost innocence except temporarily, and that Wotan's desire that their love would redeem the gods from Alberich's Ring Curse has been thwarted, the only redemption left to Wotan is his original plan to end it all. And Wotan can only bring about this desired end by acquiescing in Alberich's Ring Curse's fulfillment, resigning himself to the twilight of the gods and the failure and death of his vaunted hero and heroine. H56ab, sounding with Siegfried's dead hand rising in warning, points to the *Ring*'s original source, pre-Fallen, guiltless, guileless existence, the submersion of the Ring of human consciousness and its return to primal Nature and preconsciousness. The heroes, villains, and all their concerns are to be re-absorbed into the ephemera of an unceasingly changing world without end. That Siegfried's hand rises up from the dead to warn Hagen, the objective "Knower," away from it, has elements both of the metaphysical and also of the fact that Nature itself, in the end, with its space=time, matter=energy, laws of motion and evolution, and coherence, remains mysterious and in some ultimate sense beyond the grasp of objective reason. The implication is that, just when scientific man feels he has all of Nature's secrets in his grasp, including the mysteries underlying human consciousness, because he's emancipated himself from the self-made delusions which had obscured her bleak grandeur, they ultimately elude him. Nature swallows man (as the Rhine will soon swallow Hagen, desperately grasping for his father Alberich's Ring) in whom Nature becomes, in the course of evolution, self-conscious, but man doesn't digest Nature, except in part. And there's more to come. With the final cosmic cataclysm of the *Ring* we'll pose the question whether man's Promethean quest to grasp the "all" leads inevitably to its destruction.

Brünnhilde, with new, cosmic insight, now at peace with all that's happened in the course of the *Ring* drama, including the tragic part both she and her lover Siegfried played in it (often unwittingly), steps forward to judge Wotan and laud her dead husband Siegfried. Here's how Porges, presumably recording Wagner's opinion, described the significance of this moment: "As Brünnhilde ceremonially strides forward, Hagen picks up his shield from the ground. The scene has the grandeur of antique tragedy; Brünnhilde resembles, as Wagner put it, 'an ancient German prophetess.' All human passions extinguished, she is now a pure eye of knowledge—and the spirit of love that has taken possession of her, a world-conquering, redeeming love, carries her beyond all fear of death." [891W-{6-8/76} WRR, p. 143] And here's what I suspect may be one of Wagner's primary sources of inspiration for the cosmic wisdom and love, above all passion, that Brünnhilde gives voice to in her final words, a remarkably apt comment by Feuerbach that man's knowledge of himself and the cosmos expresses the universe's love for itself: "... how would it be possible that reason should exhibit the pure nature of things, the original text of the universe, if it were not itself the purest, most original essence? But reason has no partiality for this or that species of things. It embraces with equal interest the whole universe; it interests itself in all things and beings without distinction, without exception;—it bestows the same attention on the worm which human egoism tramples under its feet, as on man ... . Reason is the all-embracing, all-compassionating being, the love of the universe to itself." [151F-EOC, pp. 286–287] In other words, her mother Erda's knowledge, now waking, speaks through Brünnhilde:

[pp. 347–8] (H53 >>: Brünnhilde steps forward from the back of the stage and, firmly and solemnly, moves downstage.)

Brünnhilde: (... H2:) Silence your grief's exultant ("jauchzenden," [exultant?]) clamour (:H2)! (H53) (H2:) His wife, whom you all betrayed (H53 vari >>:) comes in quest of (H87:) revenge (:H53 vari; :H87). (H87:) ... no sound I heard of a worthy lament (:H87) (H88:) befitting the greatest of heroes (:H88).

Gutrune: (... H147 &/or H176 vari?:) Brünnhilde! Grieved by your grudge ["Neid"] you brought this harm ["Noth"] upon us! You who goaded the men against him, alas, that you ever came near this house (:H147 &/or H176 vari?)!

Brünnhilde: (H168a vari >> :) Wretched woman, peace! You were never his lawful wife (:H168a vari): (H168a/H164:) as wanton alone you bound him (:H168a/:H164). (H143:) His rightful wife am I, to whom he swore eternal vows (:H143) (H176 vari: [cuts off H143 midstream!!!]) ere Siegfried ever saw you (:H176 vari).

Gutrune: (... H165 >>:) Accursed Hagen! That you counseled the poison that robbed her of her husband (:H165)! (H168b voc:) Ah, sorrow! ... Brünnhilde was his one true love, whom the philtre made him forget (:H168b voc). (H168b: Filled with shame, she turns away from Siegfried and, dying, bends over Gunther's body... . H87/H3 vari: Leaning defiantly on his spear, Hagen stands deep in sombre thought ... .)

Having conferred with the Rhinedaughters and having reflected on her lifetime of experience (the entire scope of collective, historical man's, Wotan's, experience), Brünnhilde now grasps how inextricably her fate, Siegfried's fate, and the gods' fate were linked. She's willing the necessity of Siegfried's death, her death, their betrayal of each other, their implication in Alberich's Ring Curse and the gods' fateful destiny, the twilight of the gods. Therefore we hear H53 (Twilight of the Gods) and H2 (the second variant of the Primal Nature Motif, which can stand in for its variant, H52. Erda's Motif) as Brünnhilde steps forward and calls on the Gibichungs to silence their trivial grief. She's been betrayed by all of them, and she comes for vengeance. But her vengeance, her punishment even of herself, will be the destruction of the entire world of illusion of which Brünnhilde and her lover Siegfried, Gibichung society, and Valhalla's gods were a part. We hear H87 (Fate), apprising us of the evolutionary inevitability that the truth would rise to consciousness, that Brünnhilde would wake forever and become indistinguishable from her mother Erda. It was Erda's daughters the Norns who spun the rope of

Fate which has finally entangled Wotan and all his allegedly independent proxies in its coils, in spite of Siegfried's and Brünnhilde's prior celebration of their figurative cutting of it.

Accompanied by H87 (Fate) and H88 (Brünnhilde's annunciation of fated doom to Siegmund), Brünnhilde castigates all present for not making an outcry of lament worthy of the greatest of heroes Siegfried. It's noteworthy that if Siegfried were the puerile caricature of a hero, in whom Wagner allegedly lost interest as his interest in Wotan and Brünnhilde grew, subscribed to by several published *Ring* interpreters of recent years, Brünnhilde would never have said this. I think here of Dr. Philip Kitcher and Dr. Richard Schacht in their book on *Wagner's Ring, Finding an Ending* (2004), and to a somewhat lesser extent of Roger Scruton's *The Ring of Truth—The Wisdom of Wagner's 'Ring of the Nibelung'* (2016). Had Wagner lost his original admiration for Siegfried, he could easily have had Brünnhilde, to whom Wagner gave the last important words of the *Ring*, voice his depreciation of him. Had Wagner lost interest in Siegfried while completing his *Ring*, he'd never have replicated the plot of *Twilight of the Gods* (the first of the *Ring* librettos he wrote, and the basis for the entire four-part *Ring*) in *Tristan and Isolde,* which he completed in the course of composing the music for the *Ring* and long after Wagner had come under the influence of Schopenhauer, whom many suppose turned Wagner away from his allegedly Feuerbachian social revolutionary hero Siegfried. No, it was Siegfried's father Siegmund who was Wagner's idea of the Feuerbachian social revolutionary, whose outward, objective attempt to redeem society Wotan rejected in favor of turning inward to his art, embodied in the *Ring* by Wotan's confession to his unconscious mind Brünnhilde (Wotan's inner music), and reincarnation as the artist-hero Siegfried. If Wagner had lost interest in Siegfried, he wouldn't have resurrected the pure fool, who, like Siegfried, doesn't know who he is, Parsifal, in his last music-drama *Parsifal*. Parsifal like Siegfried doesn't know who he is, because his muse Kundry (like Brünnhilde in her relation to Siegfried), knows for Parsifal what he doesn't know, his true identity. Wagner authored and composed *Parsifal* long after he'd authored and composed the *Ring*, even after his *Ring* was first performed in public.

Gutrune, expressing concerns predicated on her ignorance of the true situation, confronts Brünnhilde, saying that grieved by her grudge ("Neid") Brünnhilde brought this harm ("Noth"), i.e., Siegfried's and Gunther's deaths, upon them. She blames Brünnhilde as the author of Hagen's and Gunther's conspiracy to kill Siegfried. But Brünnhilde shuts Gutrune down with the truth: it was Gutrune the wanton (accompanied here by the Seduction Motif H164) who was never Siegfried's lawful wife, who bound him. Highlighted now by the definitive version of H143, sounding here for the last time, Brünnhilde proclaims she alone was Siegfried's rightful wife, to whom he swore eternal vows ere Gutrune ever saw Siegfried (H176 cutting off H143 midstream as Brünnhilde is still speaking). H143 is Wagner's motival metaphor for redemption through love, i.e., redemption of the artist-hero and his audience through his unconscious artistic inspiration by his muse. H143 was for Wagner the *Ring*'s sole redemption motif, standing for the new religion of secular art (the New Valhalla), the Wagnerian music-drama, which was to compensate man for his loss of religious faith. The false muse Gutrune's—and her brother Gunther's—hold over Siegfried speaks of Wagner's need to present the sacred and formerly secret mysteries of his own unconscious inspiration, his muse, on the stage, where his audience could share them. But this was his downfall because he was the unconscious repository for the mysteries of religio-artistic revelation and inspiration, which he should have concealed, rather than revealed, to his fellow men.

Brünnhilde's judgment against the Gibichungs for betraying her is her indictment of man for succumbing to the natural necessity that all things that are unconscious must attain consciousness. She judges, and yet the crime was inevitable, its inevitability well known to Erda, Brünnhilde's mother. This crime was no less inevitable than the original Fall, which the Rhinedaughter Woglinde attempted to forestall by singing her lullaby H4, which birthed human speech, and finally produced Alberich's renunciation of love and forging of his Ring of power out of the pre-fallen Rhinegold. The Woodbird's Song H138ab, a variant of Woglinde's ur-melody H4, was Wagner's metaphor for the orchestral music, his artificial substitute for pre-fallen mother-melody, which Wagner employed in his ultimately futile attempt to forestall the final Fall, but which Siegfried similarly transformed from music into words in his narrative of his heroic life which culminated in his death. Brünnhilde, as a true daughter of Erda, is now reconciled to this supposed crime, and acknowledges the role Brünnhilde herself played, however unwittingly, in perpetrating it. We have Valentina Serova's testimony that Wagner more or less conceded this point with respect to Brünnhilde. She records that Wagner said the following: "'... evil always prevails over good. Alberich's powers are invincible ... . (...) One woman alone, Brünnhilde, is able to redeem the evil through her heroic action and to reconcile us at last to the crimes and intrigues of humanity. Those elements which lend dignity to our faults are concentrated in the arms of this loving woman.'" [752W-{7/8/69} Valentina Serova's reminiscence of a visit to Tribschen on 7/8/69, WR, p. 203]

Gutrune holds herself in contempt for having unwittingly let Hagen persuade her and her brother Gunther to engineer Siegfried's betrayal of his true love Brünnhilde, a betrayal in which all are complicit. Though he betrayed his muse of unconscious artistic inspiration Brünnhilde under Hagen's influence (under the influence of Wagner's artistic Wonder: Hagen's Potion H165 and the Woodbird's songs H137ab and H138ab), it was Siegfried who revealed the meaning hidden within the Woodbird's Songs, i.e., the meaning of Wagner's musical motifs, within the context of his own authentically inspired artwork, the epic tale of how Wagner came to be Wagner. Hagen, somber, sullen, and temporarily impotent (he'll raise himself to action one last time before the end), leans defiantly on his spear as we hear the portentous H87 (Fate) again.

Brünnhilde now sings her apostrophe to Siegfried and passes judgment on Wotan's and the gods' crime, her indictment of Wotan's exploitation of the unwitting hero Siegfried by making him the instrument of Wotan's futile quest for transcendent value, which predestined Siegfried (the allegedly free artist-hero) to succumb, like Wotan (religion), to Alberich's Ring Curse:

> **[pp. 348–9]** (H87; H87: ... after remaining lost for some time in contemplation of Siegfried, she [Brünnhilde] ... turns to the men and women in a mood of solemn exaltation. H123 "Definitive")
>
> **Brünnhilde:** (to the vassals: H123 voc >>:) heavy logs heap up for me here in a pile at the edge of the Rhine. ... (:H123 voc) let the (H33:) flames flare up and consume the noble limbs (:H33) (H93b voc/H33:; H53:) of the most exalted hero (:H93b voc/H33; :H53)!—(H123:; H76>>>>:) Lead his stallion hither: let it follow the warrior with me (:H123; :H76): (H93a voc/H33:; H76>>:) for my own body yearns (:H93a voc) (H93b voc/H33:) to share in the hero's holiest honor (:H93b voc/H33). (...) (H123: [gradually fades out] ... the young men raise a huge funeral pyre outside the hall .... H150>>: ... Brünnhilde becomes lost in contemplation of Siegfried's face. Her features grow increasingly transfigured.) (H150>>:) Purer than sunlight streams the light from his eyes (:H150): (H150: [a vari which seems to express a feeling of doubt]) the purest of men it was who betrayed me (:H150 vari)! (H39: [in a halting vari]) False to his wife (:H39 vari)—(H74B?:) true to his friend (:H74B?)—(H39 vari:) from her who was faithful (:H39 vari)—(H150:) she alone who was loyal (:H150)—(H56ab:) he sundered himself with his sword (:H56ab).—Never were oaths more nobly sworn; (H39 vari) never were treaties kept more truly (H39 vari); (H150 vari voc >>:) never did any man love more loyally (:H150 vari voc): (H8:; H39:) and yet (:H8) every oath (:H39), (H8:) every treaty (:H8), (H39 vari:) the truest love (:H39 vari)— (H178:) no one betrayed as he did (:H178)! (H88 frag:; H87:) Do you know why that was so (:H88 frag; :H87)? (... H18ab vari:) Oh you, eternal guardians of oaths (:H18ab vari)! (...) (H88 frag:) Behold your (:H88 frag) (H87:) eternal guilt (:H87)! (H99A:) Hear my lament (:H99A) (H87:) most mighty of gods (:H87)! (H99A:) By the (:H99A) (H87:) bravest of deeds (:H87), (H99A/H87:) which you dearly desired, you doomed him who wrought it to suffer the curse to which you in turn succumbed (:H98A/H87):—it was I whom the purest man (H87 voc:) had to betray, that a woman might grow wise (:H87 voc).

Brünnhilde calls for the Gibichungs to assemble logs to make Siegfried's funeral pyre on the bank of the Rhine, accompanied now by H123 (Power of the Gods), which has taken on a powerfully ironic character by becoming a symbol for the gods' inevitable destruction. She calls for the Gibichungs to light the funeral pyre so its flames will consume the most exalted hero Siegfried, as we hear H53 (Twilight of the Gods). This tells us Valhalla's fate and Siegfried's fate are one, though Wotan had desperately wished that his hero Siegfried and heroine Brünnhilde would be autonomous from the gods. Brünnhilde says she yearns to share the hero's fate, his holiest honor, invoking the Indian practice of Suttee. As she turns back to contemplate Siegfried's face, we hear H150 in a developed form, and she describes him as the purest of men who betrayed her. We hear H39 (Tragic love), as she makes her complaint to the dead Siegfried that he betrayed his faithful wife (his muse of unconscious artistic inspiration) while remaining loyal to his friend (loyal to his audience Gunther), by sundering her from himself with Nothung. To further variants of H39, Brünnhilde tells how she's been troubled by the conundrum that though nobody ever swore oaths more nobly, kept contracts more truly, or loved more loyally, Siegfried broke his oaths and contracts, and betrayed his truest love, like none before him. This is because Siegfried was the unwitting heir to Wotan, whose Social Contract was founded on self-deception. This inability to acknowledge the truth made Siegfried, even in his seeming purity, inherently self-contradictory, and the natural necessity of evolution made it inevitable that the irresolvable contradiction underlying Siegfried's apparent freedom and spontaneous love would rise to consciousness and storm, with shattering effect, the New Valhalla, the art-fortress of refuge from Alberich's unbearable truth which Siegfried's and Brünnhilde's love built. Brünnhilde's judgment of Wotan (and all humanity) for having implicated Siegfried in the guilt, hypocrisy, and self-deception which foredoomed the gods, echoes Erda's condemnation of Wotan in S.3.1, heightened immeasurably by the fact that Brünnhilde's judgment of Wotan is expressed by the same motifs, H87, H88, and H99A, heard as Erda condemned Wotan for hypocrisy and duplicity in S.3.1.

Brünnhilde looks upward towards Wotan and asks him (accompanied by H87 and H88, introduced in V.2.4 with her announcement to Siegfried's father Siegmund of the fated doom Wotan willed for him, when Wotan acknowledged Siegmund wasn't the free hero he'd hoped for) why Siegfried betrayed those who trusted him. Brünnhilde has acknowledged that Siegfried, like his father Siegmund before him, wasn't his own man either, that Siegfried's fate, his destruction by Alberich's Ring Curse, was similarly foredoomed by Siegfried being the unwitting agent of Wotan's self-deceit. To a variant of H18ab (Valhalla), she calls on Wotan, the eternal guardian of oaths, to hear her lament and behold his eternal guilt. H99A (Brünnhilde's appeal to Wotan for sympathy for her rebellion against him in favor of Siegmund) and H87 (Fate) are heard throughout her lament, which is the following: "(H99A) By the (H87) bravest of deeds [Siegfried's killing of Fafner and taking possession of Alberich's Hoard, Tarnhelm, and Ring, so Alberich couldn't regain their power], (H99A) which you dearly desired, (H99A/H87) you doomed him who wrought it to suffer (H99A) the curse to which you in turn succumbed." Wotan, like Mime (and even Gunther), intended not only to manipulate and exploit Siegfried to do what Wotan couldn't do, but also intended to martyr Siegfried, and all this—in Wotan's case—for the sake of a futile quest for redemption. Because Wotan's quest for redemption from Alberich's Ring Curse was futile, Siegfried was inevitably doomed to the same shameful end to which the gods would ultimately succumb. And Brünnhilde unwittingly played her own role in this tragic fate, by staging a rebellion (H99A) against Wotan's law in favor of his Wälsung heroes (whom he'd given up for lost) which, in the end, perpetuated Wotan's futile quest to renounce the real world and deny his true identity. Brünnhilde's rebellion made her an unwitting pawn in Wotan's master plan for redemption, which was sure to fail. It was inevitable

Siegfried and Brünnhilde would betray their love, since it was founded on Wotan's inability to confront the truth.

Brünnhilde concludes her indictment: "(H87—Fate) It was I whom the purest man had to betray that a woman might grow wise." Since she's Siegfried's and Wotan's unconscious mind, and the word "wise" is code in the *Ring* for self-conscious, she's echoing what Siegfried meant when he said her eyes are now open forever. Brünnhilde, humanity's collective unconscious, has now woken and can never return to unconsciousness. She's become the spokesperson for Nature's bitter truth. This is what Wagner added to Feuerbach's critique of religion, that the secular art, particularly music, in which Feuerbach admitted that God, man's religious feeling, had found refuge in the age of science, would someday succumb, of necessity, to the same spirit of scientific inquiry which had inevitably disillusioned man about religious faith. Our metaphysical impulse to seek to satisfy impossible demands, our futile quest to posit our transcendent human value, was destined to failure. The essence of Alberich's Ring Curse was that the quest to posit a consoling falsehood would, in the end, be more painful (engender more Noth) than acknowledging, and acting on the basis of, the sobering truth. This will be born out in Wotan's reincarnation as Amfortas: consciousness's wound that will never heal, Alberich's Ring Curse, man's inherent need to posit the impossible, will reach its climactic apocalypse of horror and misery in Amfortas's enslavement to the service of the Holy Grail (in *Parsifal*). It will also culminate in the loving muse of unconscious artistic inspiration Kundry, who formerly could provide suffering, fallen man, temporary balm, offering salves which instead only increase Amfortas's (man's) unbearable consciousness of his un-healing wound.

Having become wholly self-conscious, wholly awake, and embracing her mother Erda's objective knowledge (which now includes the previously unspoken secret imparted by Erda to Wotan and by Wotan to Brünnhilde), Brünnhilde says she now knows all things:

> **[p. 349] Brünnhilde:** (H87: [& "Crisis" on drums]) Do I now know what you need (:H87 [& "Crisis"])?—(H87:) All things! All things! All things (:H87) I know, all is clear to me now! (H173 chords/H97 vari voc?: [H?—Raven Motif?]) I hear the rustle of your raven's wings (:H173 chords/H97 vari voc? [H?—Raven Motif?]): with anxiously longed for tidings I send the two of them home. (H50) (H177: [H58a chord/H18c]) Rest now, (H82 vari: [H52 & H53 minus H80 frag]) rest now (:H177; :H82 vari [minus H80 frag]), you god! (H18d)

We hear H87 (Fate) as Brünnhilde describes herself as, effectively, her mother Erda, and we recall hearing it also in S.3.3 when Brünnhilde told Siegfried that what he doesn't know, she knows for him. Wotan in S.3.1 had told Erda that her wisdom waned before his Will (his unconscious mind Brünnhilde), and had consigned Erda to sleep forever, so she, dreaming, could behold the twilight of the gods, but now Erda's cosmic knowledge wakes in Brünnhilde, never to be put back to sleep again. The news Wotan has waited for his ravens (invoked now by

Brünnhilde) to bring home is Siegfried's death (which automatically includes his muse Brünnhilde's death, since they're two halves of a single person), the necessary precondition for the Rhinedaughters to retrieve Alberich's Ring from Brünnhilde's ashes and dissolve it and its curse in the Rhine. We therefore hear H50 (Ring Curse) as Brünnhilde sends Wotan's ravens home to him with these tidings. Wotan's only salvation was to cease longing for salvation.

In a final invocation of Wotan Brünnhilde grants him rest from his restless world-wandering, i.e., from his futile quest to redeem Valhalla's gods from Alberich's Ring Curse, in a musico-dramatic passage of stunning brevity to which Cooke devoted considerable attention, compressing as it does the entirety of the *Ring* drama into a few motifs with great subtlety. "Brünnhilde: (H177: [H58a chords plus H18c]) Rest now, (H82 minus H80 frag:) rest now (:H177; :H82 minus H80 frag), you god! (H18d)" The motifs in play are the following. H58a is from Rhinedaughters' original lament for the lost Rhinegold. H18c is the third segment of the five-segment Valhalla Motif H18abcde, which in its complete, definitive form is a symbol for Wotan's futile hope to secure in illusory Valhalla a refuge from Alberich's truth. H18c Wagner specifically employed in the finale of *The Valkyrie* as a symbol for Wotan's legacy, which slept with Brünnhilde, and to which Siegfried would fall heir. H82 (Need of the Gods) is a compound motif which in its definitive form is comprised of H52, Erda's Motif associated with her knowledge of all that was, is, and will be, her ur-law that all is ephemeral; H53 (Erda's prophecy of the Twilight of the Gods); and H80 (Wotan's Frustration), symbol for Wotan's unthinkable acknowledgment that his quest for a free hero who could redeem the gods from Alberich's Ring Curse was futile. But in the variant of H82 heard here H80 is missing, which tells us Wotan can now rest because he's reconciled himself to willing the necessity of the twilight of the gods and even of his proxies. The last motif is the fourth segment of the Valhalla Motif H18d which was associated in the Norns' scene (T.P.A) with their celebration of the sacred time before Wotan broke off the most sacred branch of the World-Ash to make his Spear of divine law and authority, i.e, before the Fall. It's significant that Wagner chose two segments of the five segment Valhalla Motif which aren't derived from Alberich's Ring Motif H17ab, namely, H18cd, to express the fact that by virtue of accepting the doom of all that he's stood for in life he also brings about the Rhinedaughters' dissolution of Alberich's Ring (which gave birth to Valhalla in the first place) and its curse.

Wotan's unspoken secret, that his quest for redemption was futile, which he repressed in his unconscious mind Brünnhilde, and which she sublimated into musical motifs, has now been spoken aloud as words. We've reached the climax of the *Ring*, whose plot's underlying import was summarized for Brünnhilde by Wotan in his confession, and now the true source of Wagner's inspiration in creating it is manifest.

After Wagner had written the entire *Ring* libretto (1853), with the exception of a few changes made afterward, he discovered Schopenhauer's philosophy in 1854, and subsequently renounced Feuerbach's materialist, optimistic (world-affirming) philosophy for the sake of Schopenhauer's pessimistic philosophy (of world-denial). Evidently during the writing of the libretto for the *Ring*, in which he traced the necessity for Siegfried's death back to the birth of human consciousness in evolution, and before becoming familiar with Schopenhauer, Wagner acknowledged something about human nature which disillusioned him about the possibility of predicating a humane and livable civilization on objective knowledge of man and Nature, that the atheist Feuerbach was promoting. He made a few changes in the *Ring* libretto but left most of its Feuerbachian content and structure intact, though Wagner, as we've seen, had already incorporated his personal critique of Feuerbach in the *Ring* libretto before having read Schopenhauer. It's generally argued that Schopenhauer's influence can be found not so much in the libretto as in Wagner's changing attitude to the music, most of which wasn't yet composed in 1854 when he first read Schopenhauer's works. It's argued that because Schopenhauer insisted that music is the Will, the thing-in-itself, Wagner concluded that the drama and poetry of the *Ring* is secondary to its music, a pale reflection of it, and that therefore he felt freer to manipulate the music and employ motifs for purely musical rather than dramatic reasons as his composition progressed. But Wagner in the course of writing the *Ring* libretto had already had, long before he read Schopenhauer in 1854, a revelation of man's irredeemably egoistic nature, especially of the egoism underlying our quest for redemption from our egoism. There was little Wagner found in Schopenhauer that wasn't already implicit in the *Ring* drama, Schopenhauer providing merely philosophic support for Wagner's turnabout in attitude toward his material prior to becoming familiar with Schopenhauer. Wotan's confession to Brünnhilde of the futility of seeking redemption from Alberich's Ring Curse through a hero freed from the gods' rule, Siegfried's betrayal of love, and Siegfried's tragic death, were already written into the *Ring* prior to Wagner's discovery of Schopenhauer.

Wagner described this change of attitude in a famous and oft-quoted passage from a letter he wrote on 8/23/56 to August Röckel, with whom he shared detailed insights into his creation of the *Ring*, in which he confessed that though his conscious conception of what his artworks meant was (Feuerbachian) optimism, his artistic intuition had long been following a different path predicated on "the high tragedy of renunciation" and "denial of the will." Schopenhauer, he said, merely made conscious for him what had instinctively motivated his art since he created what he regarded as his first truly inspired artwork, *The Flying Dutchman*. He then explained how he'd initially conceived Siegfried according to conscious world-affirmation, but eventually came to recognize the world's nothingness: "... my Nibelung poem ... had taken shape at a time when, relying upon my conceptions, I had constructed a Hellenistically optimistic [Feuerbachian] world for myself which I held to be entirely realizable if only people wished it to exist, while at the same time seeking somewhat ingeniously to get round the problem why they did not in fact wish it to exist. I recall ... having singled out the character of my Siegfried with this particular aim in mind, intending to put forward ... the idea of a life free from pain; ... I believed I could express this idea even more clearly by presenting the whole of the Nibelung myth, and by showing how a whole world of injustice arises from the first injustice, a world which is destroyed in order—to teach us to recognize injustice, root it out and establish a just world in its place. ... I scarcely noticed how, in working out this plan ... I was unconsciously following a quite different, and much more profound, intuition, and that, instead of a single phase in the world's evolution, what I had glimpsed was the essence of the world itself in all its conceivable phases, and that I had thereby recognized its nothingness ... . what emerged was something totally different from what I had originally intended." [642W-{8/23/56} Letter to August Röckel, SLRW, pp. 357–358]

This famous letter is a key basis for the popular assumption that Wagner initially conceived Siegfried as a Feuerbachian world-affirmer, a revolutionary in whom Wagner allegedly lost interest as he embraced Schopenhauer's pessimism and focused more on Wotan and Brünnhilde. But Wagner eventually relegated that role to Siegmund, reserving for Siegfried special status as the Wagnerian artist-hero. As we've seen, Wagner's deepest intuition was even deeper than what he allegedly learned about himself from Schopenhauer's pessimism. Wagner's pre-Schopenhauer pessimism which nihilistically seeks to nullify the world because it gives us no pretext to sustain our consoling religious illusions and longing for transcendent value, is presumably Wotan's frame of mind as the *Ring* reaches its climax. Recognizing the nothingness of the world includes Wotan's recognition that his lifelong quest to redeem himself from what he (religious, moral, and artistic man) considered to be the meaninglessness of the objective world known to Alberich, was an illusion. If man was to live in the only world he has he had to reconcile himself with the world's inherent and irredeemable anguish and with his own natural limitations. This difficult project of reconciliation with the bitter truth became the subject of Wagner's final essay in music-drama, his *Parsifal*.

Brünnhilde now withdraws Alberich's Ring from dead Siegfried's finger, only to give it away to the Rhinedaughters (who'd conferred with her along the shore of the Rhine). It's her wish that they take it from her ashes after she's joined Siegfried in death, consumed by his funeral pyre:

[pp. 349–50] (H123; H53; H2: She signals to the vassals to bear Siegfried's body to the funeral pyre; at the same time she draws the ring from his finger and gazes at it thoughtfully.)

Brünnhilde: My inheritance now I take as my own.—(H17 vari) Accursed band! (H17 vari) Fear-ridden ring! (H8/H12 vari>>:) I grasp your gold and give it away (:H8/H12 vari). (H58c/H189a>>:) Wise sisters (H4:) of the watery deep (:H58c/H189a) ... (:H4), (H58c/H189a:) I thank you for your sound advice (:H58c/H189a)! (H13·) I give you what you covet (:H13): (H9) from my ashes take it as your own! (H9 frag) Let the fire that consumes me (H9 frag) cleanse the ring of its curse: (H189c:) in the floodwaters let it dissolve, and safely guard (:H189c) the shining gold (H17 vari:) that was (H35:) stolen to your undoing (:H17 vari; :H35).

We hear a combination of H123 (Power and Decline of the Gods), H53 (Twilight of the Gods), and H2 (The Rhine's Motion), as Brünnhilde draws the Ring off Siegfried's finger and contemplates it as her inheritance. Describing it as the fear-ridden ring, she's accompanied by H8/H12 (Alberich's woe and the Rhinedaughters' joyous "Rhinegold! Rhinegold!" which was derived from H8) as she says that she grasps it and gives it away (to the Rhinedaughters). Accompanied by H58c and H189a (from the Rhinedaughters' original, and newer, laments for the lost Rhinegold, respectively), H9 (the guileless Rhinegold), H4 (Woglinde's Lullaby), and even H13, their song, dance, and verse in celebration of the Rhinegold, she calls on the sisters of the watery deep, thanking them for their sound advice. From her ashes they'll take back what they covet as their own. To a H9 fragment Brünnhilde proclaims that the fire which consumes Siegfried and herself will cleanse the Curse from the Ring. She calls on them to dissolve the Ring in the Rhine, and to safely guard the shining gold "… that was (H35) stolen to your undoing." Alberich's Ring of human consciousness is to return to its former, pristine state as guileless, preconscious Rhinegold.

In the first scene of the *Ring*, R.1, Flosshilde reminded the Rhinedaughters that their father (Father Rhine) had warned them about a foe like Alberich, and that they should take special care to protect the Rhinegold from such a foe, to no avail. So Brünnhilde's warning may be futile too: maybe all of this will happen again, and in much the same way. But what is Brünnhilde asking for? Is she not asking that the product of natural evolution, man's gift of consciousness (the Ring's power) be erased from the world, that a preconscious phase of life be restored, and therefore evolution—which one would have thought was irreversible—be reversed, a rolling wheel be stopped? Wasn't that Wagner's programme from the beginning? And won't the Ring Curse of consciousness evolve again out of this same natural world without beginning or end, of which Erda (Mother Nature) is the spokesperson (or becomes so once there exists a conscious being to wake her)? Is it possible to escape the eternal rebirth of reflective consciousness, since its occasional but rare occurrence in the vastness of all space and time seems to be an inevitable consequence of the laws of Nature, a sort of Wagnerian "Wonder" predicated on the supposition that, given enough space and time, i.e., enough matter and energy, it's not only possible, not only probable, but absolutely necessary, that reflective consciousness will occasionally evolve out of the stuff of Nature? Is it possible to accept the objective world known to Alberich and renounce our futile quest to posit our transcendent value, and therefore to repudiate the nihilistic impulse to crave an end to all things? Could we live a life of feeling without conceptually positing our transcendent value, without questioning our natural descent? Wagner addressed, and perhaps resolved, some of these ultimate questions in *Parsifal*.

Having removed Alberich's Ring from Siegfried's dead finger so she can wear it for her fiery apotheosis, thereby accepting martyrdom at the hands of Alberich's Ring Curse, Brünnhilde seizes a firebrand, and asks Wotan's ravens to tell Loge the time has come to set Valhalla and its gods and heroes and illusions aflame, as Brünnhilde prepares to light Siegfried's funeral pyre, and to be consumed by its fire with her lord in a world-historical self-immolation:

> **[pp. 350–1]** (H19:; H?—Loge's rising chromatic scales: She has placed the ring on her finger and now turns to the pile of logs on which Siegfried's body lies outstretched. She seizes a great firebrand … .)
>
> **Brünnhilde:** (H34:) Fly home, you ravens! (H33:) Whisper to your lord what you heard here by the Rhine (:H34; :H33)! (H32AB) (H33:; H32AB >>>>:) Make your way past Brünnhilde's rock: tell Loge, who burns there (:H32AB), to haste (H53 >>:; H35:) to Valhalla! For the end of the gods (H2) is dawning now (:H35): (H53 >>>:) thus do I hurl the torch (H43 chords) into Valhalla's proud-standing fortress. (H18ab [a mere hint, which breaks off]) (She hurls the firebrand on to the pile of wood, which quickly ignites. H34. Two ravens have flown up from the rock on the river-bank and disappear in the background. (…)) (H76/H34 >> :) Grane, my horse, take this my greeting (:H76/H34). (…) (H76:; H105 accompaniment:) Do you know, my friend, where I'm taking you now (:H76)? (H94 orch:) Lit by the fire (H93a?) your lord lies there, (H93a?) (H93a?:) Siegfried, my blessed hero (:H93a?). (H76; H77; H33; H105)—(H94 orch:) Feel how the flames burn in my breast, effulgent fires seize hold of my heart: to clasp him to me while held in my arms and in mightiest love to be wedded to him (:H94 orch)! (H77/H93a?:) Heiayoho! Grane (:H77/H93a?)! (H93a?) (H94 orch:) Greet your master (:H94 orch)! Siegfried! Siegfried! (H94 orch:) See! (She has leapt on to the horse and raises it to jump :H94 orch.) (H93c voc:; H143 vari or modulation orch?: [possibly referencing the moment in S.3.1 when Wotan told Erda that Brünnhilde, waking, "… will work the deed that redeems the world."?]) In bliss your wife bids you welcome (:H93c voc; :H143 vari or modulation orch? [possible S.3.1 reference?])! (With a single bound she urges the horse into the blazing fire. H77; H76)

Brandishing a torch, and accompanied by Wotan's Spear Motif H19 which has embodied her father Wotan's authority, Brünnhilde orders Wotan's ravens to fly home and whisper to their lord what they heard here on the Rhine, Brünnhilde's judgment of Wotan's guilt. Brünnhilde's final judgment includes her intent to restore the Ring—which Siegfried released in death—to the Rhinedaughters, fulfilling Wotan's last wish. She then calls on Wotan's ravens to tell Loge, still burning around Brünnhilde's mountain peak, to haste to Valhalla, since the end of the gods (H53) is dawning. Hurling her torch into Siegfried's funeral pyre, H43 (Power of the Ring) sounds as she proclaims she now hurls the torch into Valhalla's proud fortress. In so doing she draws attention to the identical destinies of Valhalla (religion) and the love she shares with Siegfried (inspired secular art), as well as Valhalla's origins in Alberich's Ring power.

As Wotan's ravens fly off to carry her messages both to Loge, and to Wotan in Valhalla, Brünnhilde leaps on to her horse Grane, and sings her final greeting to Siegfried. Addressing Grane, and accompanied now by H94 (Sieglinde's "Sublime Wonder!" from V.3.1—in its second and final manifestation), and also Siegfried's Motif H93a (introduced at the same moment as H94 in V.3.1),

Brünnhilde tells of her longing to join Siegfried in death, consumed by flames that have now entered her heart and breast (as Loge's flames once entered Siegfried's breast as he convinced fearful Brünnhilde to risk joining him in loving union, the unconscious inspiration of his art which was foredoomed). In an ecstasy of oblivion she sings: "(H94) ... to clasp him to me while held in my arms and in mightiest love to be wedded to him!" This lends a metaphysical air to Siegfried's and Brünnhilde's fate, since Brünnhilde is having an almost Isolde-esque vision of what could be described as an eternal (but also universalized, cosmic) love which can never die. But just as we find in Isolde's final apostrophe to Tristan, we can interpret Brünnhilde's hyperbolic words as the ecstasy of madness or Wahn, since their love, their inspired art, was the epitome of Wahn. Since the loving union of Siegfried with Brünnhilde is Wagner's metaphor for his unconscious artistic inspiration, which gave birth to the *Ring*, and the *Ring* triumphs as a work of art which will live on despite its revelation of tragic truths which are the underlying foundation of its inspiration, truths which call art itself into question—Brünnhilde's ecstatic proclamation can be construed as a victory for Wagner's art. As he said, the death of the hero is the life of the work of art of which he (or she) is the subject. Perhaps the death of man's age-old longing for transcendent value is the life of Wagner's *Ring*, art's greatest, climactic celebration of man's futile quest for meaning.

Grane rears up with Brünnhilde as she sings her last words: "(H93c voc:) In bliss your wife bids you welcome (:H93c voc)," and rides Grane into Siegfried's funeral pyre. The motifs Wagner has chosen for Brünnhilde's final moments, primarily H94, and the cadential figure which is the third but rarely heard segment of Siegfried's Motif H93abc, namely, H93c, recall that moment of highest drama in V.3.1 when Sieglinde—having been convinced by Brünnhilde to live for the sake of her unborn child Siegfried, who was destined to be the world's noblest hero (and whose motif H93abc Brünnhilde introduced at this crucial moment)—praised Brünnhilde's self-sacrificial love with the words "Sublimest Wonder!," sung to the new motif H94. H94 hasn't been heard again after its introduction in V.3.1 until it becomes here the basis for Brünnhilde's final apostrophe to the love she bears Siegfried. The presence in the *Ring*'s finale of these motifs H93abc and H94, which were introduced at that moment of decision in V.3.1, and which recall the hopes Sieglinde and Brünnhilde once placed in the as yet unborn Siegfried, doesn't provide justification for construing H94 as a symbol for redemption through love, since the hopes placed in Siegfried were dashed by Siegfried and Brünnhilde. It's difficult to see how his unwitting betrayal of his love for Brünnhilde, and her raging quest for vengeance for betrayed love, can produce redemption through love, except in the figurative sense that Siegfried's self-betrayal and death gave birth to Wagner's world-redeeming masterpiece, *The Ring of the Nibelung*.

The preponderance of evidence supports the proposition that they had to betray their love, to succumb to Alberich's Ring Curse, before Brünnhilde could end his Curse by restoring his Ring to the Rhinedaughters, since she only made the critical decision to do this once Siegfried and Brünnhilde had betrayed their love. The thesis that in refusing to relinquish Alberich's Ring if prompted by fear, but keeping it in the name of love, they thereby granted the world redemption by love, has several problems, not the least of which is that the Rhinedaughters, the agents of final redemption through the dissolution of the Ring in the Rhine's waters, blamed Siegfried for refusing to heed their warning, and persuaded Brünnhilde to change her mind and restore the Ring to them, but only after she'd initially refused to do this at Waltraute's request, standing up for her love for Siegfried against Wotan's counter-impulse to act on his fear of a shameful end. It's precisely this fact, that they were willing to martyr themselves for love's sake, that they were so committed, in their unconscious artistic inspiration (the basis of their love), to the illusion of man's transcendent value, that they couldn't bear to live in the real world, which is their tragic flaw, just as it was Wotan's tragic flaw. It's this very commitment to an illusion, held to be the truth, or at least held to be the only thing worth living for, which is the essence of Alberich's Ring Curse, the very thing his curse punished. The hope Wotan placed in the love Brünnhilde shared with Siegfried for redemption from the Ring Curse, was betrayed by the very agents Wotan looked to for redemption, which is why he finally concluded that the only way out was to restore the Ring to the Rhinedaughters, an entirely distinct means of redemption. It was (as Wagner wrote to Röckel) only after Wotan realized Siegfried would succumb to Alberich's Ring Curse, that he decided it would be best after all if Brünnhilde return the Ring to the Rhine. [See 616W-{1/25–26/54} Letter to August Röckel, SLRW, p. 307] H143, the incarnation of Wotan's hope for redemption through his heirs' love (unconscious artistic inspiration), could only identify their love with Brünnhilde's choice to restore the Ring to the Rhinedaughters through her self-immolation, if H143 is heard definitively in the *Ring* finale and emphasized in the manner H94 so obviously is.

But there's a problem. Dunning noted that just as Brünnhilde is singing her final words before riding into Siegfried's funeral pyre on Grane (intending that the Rhinedaughters retrieve Alberich's Ring from her ashes to dissolve it and its curse in the Rhine), out of the orchestra rises a modulation of H143. This is the only motif Wagner called a redemption motif. The relevant prior occurrence of H143 on which this modulation seems to be based was Wotan's proclaiming his prophecy to Erda in S.3.1 that their daughter, the all-wise Brünnhilde, would, on being woken by Siegfried, "... **work the deed that redeems the world.**" I've already described how Brünnhilde, muse of Siegfried's unconscious artistic inspiration, redeemed the terrible world temporarily through each artwork her love inspired Siegfried to create. This is what Wotan meant when he told Erda in S.3.1 that her daughter Brünnhilde, waking, would redeem the world, certainly not Brünnhilde's final decision to restore the Ring to the Rhinedaughters, since this was an afterthought which occurred to him only after he realized Siegfried's and Brünnhilde's love, betrayed, would fail to redeem the world from Alberich's Ring Curse. H143 represented for Wagner unconsciously inspired art (his music-dramas) as the new religion which would replace the old, and it has failed, just as religion did. It was for this reason Brünnhilde acknowledged to Wotan that

Siegfried succumbed to the same curse (Alberich's Ring Curse) which destroyed Wotan. So H143's occurrence here in a variant, and almost inaudible, form suggests the orchestra—at the moment of Wotan's proclamation that Brünnhilde, waking, would redeem the world—was presenting a subliminal premonition of Brünnhilde's final martyrdom and restoration of the Ring to the Rhinedaughters, which wasn't consciously willed or foreseen by Wotan. Otherwise, he wouldn't have been so joyous foretelling Brünnhilde's redemptive deed to Erda in S.3.1, but then become so morose and despairing, as described by Waltraute to Brünnhilde, when he spoke as if dreaming of his wish for Brünnhilde to restore Alberich's Ring to the Rhinedaughters, clearly an afterthought prompted by drastically altered circumstances. The deed that Brünnhilde performed on waking, which Wotan proclaimed would redeem the world, he surely understood (at that time) to be her inspiration of Siegfried's heroic deeds of redemptive art.

Furthermore, no motifs associated with the Rhine or Rhinedaughters were heard as Wotan proclaimed to Erda in S.3.1—accompanied by H143—that Brünnhilde, waking, would work the deed that would redeem the world, nor did Wotan allude to any hope she'd restore the Ring to the Rhinedaughters then. And at no time in the entire *Ring* has Erda, Wotan's lover and Brünnhilde's mother, ever hinted that Wotan should restore the Ring to the Rhine to end Alberich's curse on it. Wotan, after all, thought Siegfried was immune from suffering Alberich's Ring Curse because Siegfried seemed to be freed (through Brünnhilde's protection) from envy and fear. No, the motif Wagner chose as the capstone for his epic edifice, the *Ring*, is H94 which, though generally named "Redemption by Love," is best grasped as a nostalgic echo of the hopes once placed in Siegfried which have been dashed by experience. We can't construe redemption by love from mutual betrayal of love. Redemption here means something else.

We have contradictory evidence in the Wagner documents which allude to this finale and H94. On the one hand (in a previously cited passage), he called H94 merely his "hymn to heroes" (described by others, following Wagner's lead, as the "Glorification of Brünnhilde"): "'I am glad that I kept back Sieglinde's theme of praise for Brünnhilde, to become as it were a hymn to heroes.'" [832W-{7/23/72}CD Vol. I, p. 515] Porges on the other hand described H94 as representing the banishment of death's terror (fear), and as a song of redemption which overcomes Fate's power, something Porges says was well known, and presumably an interpretation advocated publicly by Wagner. [See 872W-{6–8/1876} WRR, p. 69] Assuming Porges based his interpretation of H94 on Wagner's own reading, Brünnhilde's self-sacrifice and reconciliation with Fate does indeed banish death's terror and redeems us from Fate's power in the sense that she doesn't resist her fate but wills it, an act which Wagner described as "willing the necessary." But we don't have any direct statement from Wagner himself to this effect. The only motif (for which we have documentary evidence) he ever described as a "redemption motif" was H143 [See 878W-{6–8/76} WRR, p. 103, where Porges tells us how Wagner described H143 as his "Redemption

Theme"], which most evidence suggests he identified with his art, the music-drama, as heir to dying religious faith.

It's hard to say how much stock we should place in Cosima's record of a remark Wagner made on 9/6/71, that Siegfried's and Brünnhilde's love produced no universal deed of redemption, no child, to which he added, significantly, that *Twilight of the Gods* is therefore the most tragic work of all: "We talk of the love between Siegfried and Brünnhilde, which achieves no universal deed of redemption, produces no Fidi [Wagner's and Cosima's son Siegfried]; *Götterdämmerung* is the most tragic work of all, but before that one sees the great happiness arising from the union of two complete beings." [807W-{9/6/71} CD Vol. I, p. 410] The difficulty here is that he may have been speaking merely sentimentally about the birth of his son Fidi (nickname for Siegfried). However, there's peculiar fascination in the fact that in *Mastersingers* Wagner employed the trope of Walther's and Eva's bringing their child to birth as a metaphor for the redemptive work of art which Eva, Walther's muse, inspires him to create during a dream, a metaphor enhanced by the fact their mentor Hans Sachs baptizes Walther's inspired mastersong as if this child in the form of an unconsciously inspired work of art is the product of their union, the union of the Poet-Dramatist with his muse of inspiration, music.

But there's further evidence to support our thesis in *Tristan* and *Parsifal* that the *Ring* finale can't be construed as dramatizing redemption by love. Wagner regarded the plots of *Twilight* and *Tristan* as identical. In both instances, he said, the hero (Siegfried, Tristan), while under a spell, gives his true love (Brünnhilde, Isolde) away to another man (Gunther, Marke), and thereby dooms himself to a tragic end. [See 811W-{12/71} 'Epilogue to *The Nibelung's Ring*,' PW Vol. III, pp. 268–269] Wagner saw Brünnhilde as allegorically identical to Isolde, so in a sense, whatever is true of Brünnhilde is also true of Isolde. This fact lends considerable significance to Wagner's illuminating comparison of Isolde with Kundry from *Parsifal*: "When there is mention on the train of the Wagnerites'" preference for 'T. und I.' even over '*Parsifal*,' R. says: "Oh, what do they know? One might say that Kundry already experienced Isolde's Liebestod a hundred times in her various reincarnations.'" [1135W-{9/14/82} CD Vol. II, p. 910] When we consider the question whether Siegfried's and Brünnhilde's love redeems the world, or whether Tristan's and Isolde's love lives on, transcendent, after their death, in light of Wagner's comment that Kundry, as the reincarnation of Isolde, experienced Isolde's Liebestod hundreds of times in her prior lives, and that Wagner regarded Isolde as allegorically identical to Brünnhilde, we realize that he's consigning Isolde and Brünnhilde to the status of failures. We can conclude this because their presumably most evolved reincarnation as Kundry fails in her bid to redeem Parsifal through loving union with him (love which he, similarly the most evolved reincarnation of Siegfried and Tristan, rejects), and it's precisely loving, immortal reunion with their lover which both Brünnhilde and Isolde long for in their final moments. Parsifal renounces Kundry's love (sexual love, yes, but the allegorical sexual love shared by hero and heroine is Wagner's metaphor for the poet-dramatist's unconscious artistic inspiration by his muse) altogether, and chooses celibacy rather than consort with her. Brünnhilde, Isolde, and Kundry are conceptually identical in being Wagner's metaphor for the artist-hero's unconscious mind, his muse of inspiration, and all three fail because, according to Wagner, art in the end fails to resolve man's existential dilemma. Eva alone among the heroines of Wagner's mature music-dramas, the artist-hero Walther's muse of unconscious artistic inspiration in *Mastersingers*, inspires her lover to create a redemptive work of art, because *Mastersingers* was Wagner's idealization of the golden age of secular art prior to the rise to consciousness of its true identity as covert religious faith and a cowardly evasion of bitter truth.

So we've arrived at the fateful conclusion of the *Ring* tetralogy, the twilight of the gods which Erda foretold in R.4. It's the ultimate fulfillment of Alberich's Ring Curse, his punishment of the gods (us) for favoring illusion over truth, for their (our) sin of matricide. With poetic justice, it's the fire god Loge (the liar) who burns the gods up, their illusions consuming them and dying with them:

> **[p. 351]** (The flames immediately flare up so that the fire fills the entire space in front of the hall and appears to seize on the building itself. H33/H105. H32B. Horrified, the men and women press to the very front of the stage. When the whole stage seems to be engulfed in flames H102 [repeats and develops]; H101; the glow suddenly subsides .... H58 chords/H3>>>>: At the same time the Rhine overflows its banks in a mighty flood, surging over the conflagration. The three Rhinedaughters are borne along on its waves and now appear over the scene of the fire. Hagen, who since the incident with the ring, has been watching Brünnhilde with increasing concern, is seized with extreme alarm at the sight of the Rhinedaughters. He ... plunges into the floodwaters like a man possessed, H12 vari: shouting the words 'Get back from the ring!' H50 [fragmented]. H190 end frag: Woglinde and Wellgunde twine their arms around his neck and, swimming away, draw him with them into the depths. Flosshilde leads the way as they swim towards the back of the stage, holding the regained ring aloft in a gesture of jubilation. H4/H3: A red glow breaks out with increasing brightness from the cloudbank that had settled on the horizon. By its light, the three Rhinedaughters can be seen swimming in circles and merrily playing with the ring on the calmer waters of the Rhine, which has little by little returned to its bed. H18ab; H4/H94/H3; H18ab [rising] From the ruins of the fallen hall, the men and women watch moved to the very depths of their being, as the glow from the fire grows in the sky. As it finally reaches its greatest intensity, the hall of Valhalla comes into view, with the gods and heroes assembled as in Waltraute's description in act one. H18ab [in a glorious vari]; H123 [as if on the verge of destruction, both repeated and developed]; H58abd?; H105; H93a Bright flames seem to flare up in the hall of the gods H53, finally hiding them from sight completely. The curtain falls. H94; H189a)

Siegfried's funeral pyre expands to embrace the earthly Valhalla, Gibichung Hall, as the Gibichungs witness the destruction of their world. We hear H101 (Brünnhilde's Magic Sleep) and H102 (Brünnhilde's plea that Wotan protect her sleep from all but worthy, fearless heroes) as the fire subsides. Accompanied by

H58 chords (the Rhinedaughters' original lament for their lost Rhinegold) and H3 (Rhine Motion), the Rhine overflows its banks, putting out the fire. Seeing the Rhinedaughters hovering over Brünnhilde's ashes, Hagen remembers his father Alberich's warning that if Brünnhilde ever persuaded Siegfried to return his Ring to them, no cunning would ever regain it, so he desperately jumps into the flood after them. The *Ring*'s last words are his frantic exclamation: "Get back from the Ring!" But the Rhinedaughters twine their arms around him and descend with him into the depths. This, presumably, is Wagner's metaphor for the ultimate incapacity of man's Promethean quest through scientific inquiry and technological advancement to master our precondition, Nature. Accordingly, the Rhinedaughters retrieve the Ring he desperately sought to reclaim, and carry him in triumph into the deeps, where they'll dissolve it and its curse, restoring it to pristine Rhinegold, as we hear a fragmented version of H50 (Alberich's Ring Curse).

We're left to wonder what became of Hagen's father Alberich, the author of this *Ring* drama. All we can say for certain is that in Wagner's prose sketch for *Siegfried's Death*, an earlier version of *Twilight of the Gods*, Alberich called on his son Hagen to rescue the Ring from Siegfried's funeral pyre, and Hagen jumped into the flames after it. When the Rhinedaughters retrieved the Tarnhelm and Ring from the dying embers of the fire, Hagen, as if demented, plunged after them, only to be dragged by them down into the deep. Wagner concludes this prose sketch with the cryptic remark: "Alberich sinks, with gestures of woe." [386W—{10–11/48} *Siegfried's Death*, PW Vol. VIII, pp. 51–52] Alberich, symbolic of reflectively conscious human life, a product of evolution, in whom Nature (Erda) first became self-conscious, will always be a potentiality within Nature, which, under the right circumstances, not only can, but must bring forth life, which then, from natural necessity, must evolve to produce conscious, reflective thought.

As a red glow appears in the clouds on the horizon, we hear H4 (Woglinde's Lullaby, to which the *Ring*'s first words were sung), and H3 (Rhine), as the Rhinedaughters perform their dance in celebration of the Ring's restoration and purification. This introduces the orchestral grand finale. We hear by far the most august variant of the Valhalla Motif's first two segments H18ab (that portion to which Alberich's Ring, H17ab, gave birth), intertwined with Woglinde's Lullaby H4, and H94. H94 is Wagner's hymn to heroes, his glorification of Brünnhilde, Sieglinde's praise of Brünnhilde's redemptive love for the Wälsungs. We hear these three motifs overlapping each other as the Gibichungs (whom we can now recognize as ourselves, Wagner's audience, as they become an audience for the twilight of the gods we're experiencing), who've witnessed Gibichung Hall burned to the ground, now stand within its ruins and, as Wagner says, watch—moved to the depths of their being—as the glow from the fire grows in the sky, and with its greatest intensity brings Valhalla into view with all its ersatz glory, the gods and heroes assembled as described by Waltraute to Brünnhilde in T.1.3.A. This sublimely glorious variant of H18ab is now heard alongside an apocalyptic variant of H123 (Power and Decline of the Gods), giving one the impression the world is on the verge of annihilation. We hear echoes of H58abcd (the Rhinedaughters' original lament for the lost Rhinegold) again, and the metaphysical orchestral orgy, a musical celebration of the End of Times, is capped by a loud proclamation of Siegfried's Motif H92a, as bright flames seize on the Hall of the gods and devour them and their heroes. Now for the last time we hear H53 (Twilight of the Gods), sounding like it did when Hagen proclaimed to the Gibichungs that "Noth is here!," as he prepared them to welcome Gunther and Brünnhilde, guardian of Wotan's unspoken secret.

As the flames finally hide the gods from view, the curtain falls as the orchestra recedes into a quiet, peaceful version of H94 and H189a (the Rhinedaughters' new lament for the loss of the guileless Rhinegold, a lament brought to a serene end by its restoration to them). With the last notes of H105 (Magic Fire, based on Loge's H33 as it was heard in the finale of V.3.3 after Wotan put Brünnhilde to sleep and compelled Loge to surround her with his protective ring of fire, except that this time H87—Fate—is missing), the curtain closes on what we, without hyperbole, can describe as the most comprehensive (and the most profound, original, and challenging) vision of human life, man's origin, nature, history and destiny, ever presented on the stage, leaving us with an intuition of the pathos of all that's been lost and is irretrievable.

It's well known that Wagner tried out five distinct conclusions to the *Ring*, including what has been described as the Feuerbachian finale, the Schopenhauerian finale, the Buddhist finale, etc. When he approached the completion of his ultimate masterwork he had to ask himself what it all meant. It's also well known that in the end Wagner decided on the ambiguous finale we've just experienced, because he said that the music would tell us everything we needed to know, all that was inexpressible in words. Is there redemption in the end, or not? If the world is redeemed from Alberich's Ring Curse, who redeemed it, and by what action? And just what is redeemed? In what does redemption consist? What after all was Alberich's Ring Curse? Do Siegfried and Brünnhilde live on after death in blissful immortality, or was Brünnhilde merely speaking figuratively, overcome by emotion? I've endeavored to address these questions as they've arisen in the course of the music-drama, and to do so within a coherent, unified, global conceptual framework, which follows a single narrative thread, but which also discloses deep conceptual, allegorical bonds with Wagner's other canonic operas and music-dramas, from *The Flying Dutchman* to *Parsifal*. There are psychological, social, historical, scientific, artistic, and metaphysical dimensions to this grandiose and morbidly glamorous twilight of the gods, which compel us to ask ourselves the ultimate question, what does it all mean? Why is there something instead of nothing? What is the meaning of our existence? Who are we and why are we here? Why am I Paul Heise and not somebody else? Wagner's *Ring* is so all-embracing that it can easily accommodate several layers of interpretation without contradiction. I will close by speculatively enumerating some of the primary levels of meaning of its mysterious, ambiguous conclusion.

Given the astonishing richness of the content of the *Ring* libretto (which must never be interpreted without considering the music as an integral part of its expression and meaning), its remarkable compression of the mass of all human experience into one narrative thread of drama (which, even at between fifteen and sixteen hours in performance, is nonetheless succinct if one considers all that's embraced within it), one thing the *Ring* clearly isn't is a mere allegory of the dangers of becoming obsessed by greed for money, property, or even power (social and political), though Wagner was wont to say this on occasion [See 1074W-{2/15/81} CD Vol. II, p. 624] The *Ring* may have begun there, as Wagner first imagined it, but in the process of completing its libretto and score he left that plot scenario far behind, incorporating elements of it within a more universal framework. His pet thesis, that the *Ring* concerns the disasters brought about by man's greed for money, is just one of many interpretations he applied to it in his lifetime, but ultimately he concluded that the definitive version of the *Ring* he was prepared to present on stage remained as much a mystery to him as to his audience.

Is George Bernard Shaw's interpretation of the *Ring* as an allegory of a socialist or anarchist revolution against the old order of inherited political power, wealth, tradition, and religion, and the historical succession of capitalist plutocrats (Alberich) to the power formerly held by blood-aristocrats (the gods), adequate to capture the full meaning of the *Ring*? At best, Shaw's allegorical reading works for portions of a few scenes in the 36 scene music-drama. Clearly, social revolution played a role in Wagner's original (but ever expanding) conception, as we see in his commentary on a passage from Carlyle below, which provides us one possible interpretation of the meaning of the final holocaust in which Valhalla and its gods burn up, leaving human beings free and independent: "Thomas Carlyle, in his 'History of Frederick the Great,' characterises the outbreak of the French Revolution as the First Act of the 'Spontaneous Combustion' of a nation 'sunk into torpor, abeyance, and dry-rot,' and admonishes his readers in the following words: — / 'There is the next mile-stone for you, in the History of Mankind! That universal Burning-up, as in hell-fire, of Human Shams. The oath of twenty-five Million men, which has since become that of all men whatsoever, 'Rather than live longer under lies, we will die!'—that is the New Act in World-History. (…) This is the truly celestial-infernal Event: … . (…) For it is withal the breaking-out of universal mankind into Anarchy, into the faith and practice of No-Government … . … When the Spontaneous Combustion breaks out; and, many-coloured, with loud noises, envelopes the whole world in anarchic flame for long hundreds of years … [etc.].'" [817W-{1-3/72} 'Introduction to "Art and Revolution," "The Artwork of the Future," and "Opera and Drama,"' PW Vol. I, p. 23] We may construe Wagner's reminiscences of the Russian anarchist Bakunin's apocalyptic vision of old Europe and its culture in flames, set by the revolution, as found in Wagner's autobiography *Mein Leben*, in the light of Wagner's remarks about Carlyle's universal combustion, which would burn up all human shams.

But in the course of his artistic evolution Wagner gradually expanded what had originally been a purely socio-historical concept of revolution, in which an old and tired order would make way for a new one with greater justice, tolerance, freedom, and happiness, into a quasi-scientific understanding of the cyclic nature of evolution (of both species, and culture), a philosophic development which eventually incorporated the entire cosmos. In the following extract, for instance, Wagner suggested that modern cultural decadence will culminate, vaguely, in some disaster whose consequence will be a return to Nature, though he doesn't describe the historical mechanism through which this will occur: "... he [Wagner] discusses the similarity between the present world situation and the fall of the Roman Empire, when national virtues also ceased to flourish, Christianity having torn down the national barriers; now the Jews are completing this work. 'At best,' says R., 'I anticipate a return to a kind of state of Nature, for the Jews will also meet their doom.'" [949W-{11/5/78}CD Vol. II, p. 190] It's implicit in Wagner's thesis that civilization will return to a sort of state of Nature after some general conflagration and cultural catastrophe, that something like what I've described as the end of human consciousness, and a restoration of preconscious animal instinct (which I take to be a primary meaning of Brünnhilde's restoration of the Ring to the Rhinedaughters), will occur after civilization has reached its nadir of degradation and perhaps wrought its own destruction.

On one occasion Wagner synthesized his otherwise purely metaphysical concept of an eternal return of the *Ring* cycle with his earlier theory of social revolution. In this instance, history must repeat itself, ending each time in cultural collapse, until man learns to distribute wealth equally: "If people cannot understand how to guard against the old (barbaric) abuses—such as unequal possession etc., history will have to begin from the beginning again in order to teach us anew and still more forcibly." [1101W-{10/23/81} BB, p. 201] But ultimately he broadened his concept of an end of civilization to include the earth and even the entire cosmos, offering us a metaphysical solution (as Cooke put it), but also a controversial one, to the problem of how to interpret the Ring finale: "'Not until all churches have vanished will we find the Redeemer, from whom we are separated by Judaism. But his ideas are not easy to grasp; God as the ending of the universe—that does not allow for a cult, though perhaps monasteries, in which people of similar beliefs could find a refuge and from which they could influence the world, from the solitary state [one thinks here of *Parsifal*]—but within the world itself it is not possible.'" [950W-{11/27/78}CD Vol. II, pp. 211–212]

Wagner applied his concept of an eternal return of the *Ring* cycle to the cosmos itself. For this he had ample precedent not only in Feuerbach, as instanced in our extract below, but also in various prior models of the world, including those of the Hindus (an end of times called the Kali Yuga, through which the cosmos is destroyed, ending one cycle, but is later reborn), Manicheans, Stoics, etc. Here we have Feuerbach's description of a pagan version of an eternal return of the world, or cosmos, in which it's continuously destroyed, and restored, in a never-ending cycle of rebirths (perhaps providing an inspiration for Nietzsche's concept that the higher man—"Overman"—must prove himself worthy by embracing the eternal return of all things, which was Nietzsche's antidote to the nihilistic, pessimistic Buddhist longing for escape from rebirth, and an antidote as well to the Christian emphasis on world-renunciation—Wotan's sin against all that was, is, and will be): "The Christians expected the destruction of the world immediately, because the Christian religion has in it no cosmical principle of development ... . (...) The heathens, on the contrary, set no limits on the development of the cosmos; they supposed the world to be destroyed only to arise again renovated as a real world; they granted it eternal life. The Christian destruction of the world was a matter of feeling, an object of fear and longing; the heathen, a matter of reason, an inference from the contemplation of nature." [We can't help thinking of the ultimate influence of the Second Law of Thermodynamics on the entire cosmos, a sort of universal dissolution of everything that is] [163F-EOC, pp. 309–310] In the following passage, Wagner applies this Feuerbachian model for an eternal return of the *Ring* cycle to his comparison between Indian (Hindu and Buddhist) mythology, and Scandinavian mythology, both of which posit a twilight of the gods and rebirth of the world: "Once more talked with R. about the Indians. The idea in Scandinavian mythology of a new world to follow the downfall of the gods is maybe a stray offshoot of the Indian religion." [852W-{11/25/73}CD Vol. I, p. 702] And in his comparison of what he describes as the "Buddhist theory of the origin of the world" with *Tristan*, Wagner posits the inescapability of eternal rebirth, an eternal return: "Everything is alien to me, and I often gaze around me, yearning for a glimpse of the land of nirvana. But nirvana quickly turns back into Tristan; you know the Buddhist theory of the origin of the world. A breath clouds the clear expanse of heaven: [Wagner placed here musical notation for the opening notes of the *Tristan* Prelude, the famous Tristan Chord] It swells and grows denser, and finally the whole world stands before me again in all of its impenetrable solidity." [673W-{3/3/60} Letter to Mathilde Wesendonck, SLRW, p. 486]

Wagner was troubled by his inability to hit on a capstone for the *Ring* drama which would tie up all its loose ends. It's possible that he authored and composed his final music-drama *Parsifal* to resolve the *Ring*'s remaining unresolved problems, though he'd been considering Parsifal as the basis for a music-drama for decades. But *Parsifal* actually provides Wagner an alternative ending for the *Ring* cycle, in which the eternally repeating cycle of world destruction and the cosmos' rebirth can be broken (at least figuratively) through man's acceptance of his true nature and acknowledgment of his natural origins. In describing such an optimistic solution in the following extract Wagner concluded with an account of what he regards as its only alternative, a catastrophic end to our world (or perhaps even the cosmos) brought about by man's Promethean, hubristic quest to grasp the nature and laws of all things in order to release Nature's latent power, which according to him might inadvertently unleash the chaos at the root of energy and matter, and obliterate the surface of the earth if not the cosmos. On this view the *Ring*'s finale can be construed as a poetic metaphor for the chaos set in motion by man's unrestrained quest for knowledge of the basis of all things, something not depicted in the *Ring*, but rather, implied symbolically: "'Do you want to found a new religion?'—the author of the present essay [Wagner] might be asked. (...) ... I grew convinced that Art can only prosper on the basis of true Morals ... . (...) ... it dawned on me that another, better state of future man—conceived by others as a hideous chaos—might well arise in comely order, if Religion and Art ... for the first time gained their right acceptance. From this path all violence is quite shut out ... . [Surely Wagner is referencing *Parsifal* here!] / But things may turn out otherwise, should Wisdom more and more recede from rampant violence. (...) ... it can but rouse our apprehension, to see the progress of the art-of-war departing from the springs of moral force, and turning more and more to the mechanical: here the rawest forces of the lower Nature-powers are brought into an artificial play, in which, for all arithmetic and mathematics, the blind Will might one day break its leash and take an elemental share. (...) 'Twere thinkable that all of this, with art and science, valour, point-of-honour, life and chattels, should one day fly into the air through some incalculable accident. When every pledge of peace was thus exploded in the grandest style, it would only need the outbreak of a general famine ... : then should we stand once more where world-Historical development began, and it really might look 'as if God had made the world that the Devil might take it,' as our great philosopher [Schopenhauer] found stated in the Judaeo-Christian dogma." [1038W-{6–8/80} 'Religion and Art,' PW Vol. VI, pp. 250–252] According to this reading, with the scientific mind's final victory over the mytho-poetic worldview which had guided man throughout all previous human history, the way would be opened to search more deeply into the nature of things than ever before. The ultimate consequence of this freedom to explore and unlock the bonds which hold the cosmos together might be the dissolution, through some incalculable accident caused by scientific experimentation (perhaps in the service of the development of weapons of mass destruction), of our planet, our solar system, or even the entire cosmos.

Finally, Wagner offered the following observations two to three years after the *Ring*'s premiere at Bayreuth, which strongly suggest *Parsifal* can be understood as an alternative to the *Ring*'s apocalyptic ending, and that Parsifal is a reincarnation (second coming) of the artist-hero and savior Siegfried, whose previously unwitting quest for redemption will on this occasion actually bear fruit (because, as we'll see in Volume Two of *The Wound That Will Never Heal*, Parsifal will in the end reject his prior role, in his former incarnations, as the hero of religion and art, by embracing Mother Nature in her truth and no longer seeking redemption from her): "Over coffee he said to me that in fact Siegfried ought to have turned into Parsifal and redeemed Wotan, he should have come upon Wotan (instead of Amfortas) in the course of his wanderings, but there was no antecedent for it, and so it would have to remain as it was." [964W-{4/29/79}CD Vol. II, p. 299] "Can one imagine the state of barbarism at which we shall have arrived, if our social system continues for another six-hundred years or so in the footsteps of the declining Roman world-dominion? I believe that the Saviour's second advent, expected by the earliest Christians in their lifetime, and later cherished as a mystic dogma, might have a meaning for that future date, and perchance amid occurrences not totally unlike those sketched in the Apocalypse. For, in the conceivable event of a relapse of our whole Culture into barbarism, we may take one thing for granted: namely, that our Historical science, our criticism and chemistry of knowledge would also have come to an end [Hagen will be drowned in the Rhine]; whilst it may be hoped, on the contrary, that Theology would by then have come to a final agreement with the Gospels, and the free understanding of Revelation be opened to us without Jehovaistic subtleties—for which event the Saviour promised us his coming back. [there's considerable evidence in *Parsifal* not only that Siegfried has been reincarnated in him, but that Christ the savior has been as well] / (...) And this would inaugurate a genuine popularisation of the deepest Knowledge. In this or that way to prepare the ground for cure of ills inevitable in the evolution of the human race ... might fitly be the mission of a true Art appealing to the Folk itself ... ." [929W-{3–7/78} 'Public and Popularity,' PW Vol. VI, pp. 80–81]

With those observations by Richard Wagner our argument is complete! The remaining chapters in Volume Two of *The Wound That Will Never Heal*, separate essays on Wagner's three canonical romantic operas (*The Flying Dutchman*, *Tannhäuser*, and *Lohengrin*) and three other music-dramas (*Tristan and Isolde*, *The Mastersingers of Nuremberg*, and *Parsifal*), will demonstrate that they're all best understood in the light of their systematic conceptual relationships to Wagner's *The Ring of the Nibelung*, the master-myth which subsumes all other myths.

I'll leave the last words for Friedrich Nietzsche, Wagner's greatest advocate and most vehement antagonist, since Wagner unwittingly wrote his future friend Nietzsche into his *Ring* libretto when he gave life to Siegfried's and the gods' nemesis Hagen, the author of Siegfried's death and the twilight of the gods (Hagen bears a not superficial resemblance to the author of *The Wound That Will Never Heal* as well). These were the two things Wagner set out to explain by writing and composing his *Ring*. Nietzsche wrote what I feel is the most touching and insightful one-paragraph tribute to Wagner in the literature, and it will provide the capstone to our tribute to Wagner's *Ring*, since it captures its essence: "There is a musician who, more than any other musician, is a master at finding the tones in the realm of suffering, depressed, and tortured souls, at giving language even to mute misery. None can equal him in the colors of late fall, in the indescribably moving happiness of the last, truly last, truly shortest joy; he knows a sound for those quiet, disquieting midnights of the soul, where cause and effect seem to be out of joint and where at any moment something might originate 'out of nothing.' (...) ... indeed, as the Orpheus of all secret misery he is greater than any." [*Nietzsche Contra Wagner*: p. 663]

Allen Dunning's Numbered List of The *Ring's* Musical Motifs, with 23 Motifs added by Paul Heise

Musical notation by Allen Dunning and commentary by Paul Heise

The following guide to the *Ring*'s musical motifs, 193 in number, including musical notation, was based originally on the list of 177 motifs provided by Dr. Allen B. Dunning from his online book *A Thematic Guide to the Musical Themes of Richard Wagner's 'Der Ring des Nibelungen.'* Though Dunning removed his website some years ago, his list lives on in my new guide to the *Ring*'s musical motifs which follows. Dunning's list was, until the publication of Scruton's *The Ring of Truth* in 2016, the most comprehensive list available. Scruton's list improves in some respects on Dunning's list, which was in turn an improvement of Deryck Cooke's list, but also omits, just as Dunning did, some motifs I regard as crucial. Thanks to Scruton's expanded list and to my own discovery of some new motifs I've added several motifs which were omitted by Dunning and by Scruton. Because the online Wagnerian community has long familiarized itself with Dunning's online list, either on his own website (now defunct), or on my website www.wagnerheim.com, and now also has access to the expanded list (including musical notation) Scruton has provided, my guide to the *Ring* motifs below offers a key to translate from Dunning's original list to its equivalents in my list and Scruton's list. Dunning's equivalents can be found in small print on the upper left side of each example of a motif's musical notation, distinguished by a hashtag # followed by the motif's number. My motifs can be found in larger print on the left above each example of a motif's musical notation, distinguished by the capital letter "H" (for Heise) followed by its number. Scruton's equivalents can be found to the immediate right of my motifs in smaller print, distinguished by the Capital letter "S" for Scruton, followed by their number. Each case in which I've omitted a motif originally included by Dunning, or Scruton, is also indicated.

Dunning and I collaborated to embed the numbered motifs from his list in the libretto wherever we could identify and verify their occurrence at any corresponding point in the orchestral score. This aspect of this study is primarily the product of Dr. Dunning's efforts: my contribution was comparatively small, though I did revise his original Herculean effort to embed in the libretto all discernible occurrences of motifs from his list by an extremely careful and painstaking listening over several months, one passage at a time, and also by embedding all discernible occurrences of the motifs I've added which he and/or Scruton omitted. In order to do this Dr. Dunning and I had to devise a set of symbols (again, mostly his contribution) to represent not only the numbered motifs but various aspects of their representation, or the conditions under which they're heard in the score, within the context of the English translation of the libretto.

Immediately following the musical notation of each numbered motif will be found the name and/or description of each motif in dark print. If the numbered motif has a commonly used name, I've indicated this with italics. I generally use commonly used names for motifs under discussion so that, wherever possible, the reader needn't depend exclusively on memorization of a motif's number to follow my discussion, but also so that, with practice, the motifs' identifying numbers may be committed to memory. However, not only does my interpretation suggest that quite a number of traditional names are inadequate or incorrect, but furthermore, Dunning has identified a number of motifs which either have never been named, or have never had a commonly accepted one. I've added a few motifs of my own which evidently have either not previously been identified as motifs or were equated with previously identified motifs (due to being variations of them) without their status as distinct motifs being taken into account. I distinguish motifs by number if they're musically distinguishable (even if they're variants of previously identified motifs), and if they're associated in the course of the drama with libretto passages which have a conceptual or dramatic profile which distinguishes them from other motifs. One difficulty in identifying motifs is that in some cases a compound motif, which synthesizes elements from other distinct, numbered motifs, becomes a new motif in its own right, by virtue of its association in the course of the *Ring* with a distinctive set of dramatic situations. Therefore, since quite often traditional names are either too one dimensional, or even altogether inaccurate, in expressing the discernible "meaning" of motifs, I've also provided a brief verbal description of each motif in dark print which readers should consider either my supplement to a traditional name, or as its replacement. For this reason readers must ultimately depend on my new list of 193 motifs' numbers, and on my descriptions of them, to identify motifs. My allegorical reading in the long run requires learning a new lexicon or allegorical language in order to grasp the deeper layers of meaning in Wagner's *Ring* libretto and the significance of the *Ring*'s motifs. To enhance ease of identification, to the far right of each motif's number, and above its musical notation, I provide the location of each motif's first occurrence in the libretto through abbreviations of its location in the *Ring* (for example, V.2.3 representing *The Valkyrie*, Act Two, Scene Three) followed by the page number in my book at which its first occurrence in the libretto can be found. At some as-yet-undetermined time I'll replace my online *Ring* study at www.wagnerheim.com with a revised version (not identical with the version you're reading, since it will include some material omitted from the published hardcopy, but subsuming all of it) which will include my revised list of 193 musical motifs along with their notation and sound files so you can click on the motifs to hear them. Until that time the numeration of motifs in this guide (193) doesn't correspond with the numeration of motifs in the guide available at www.wagnerheim.com.

To ascertain the full meaning of any given motif, i.e., the conceptual significance it carries by virtue of its occurrences in the course of the entire drama in association with persons, actions, statements, symbols, objects, ideas, etc., one would have to know the dramatic and conceptual context of all of its occurrences, including those of its variants. Surveying all of a motif's dramatic contexts or associations in the course of the drama offers us what I call the "dramatic profile" of a motif. An excellent example of a motif's entire dramatic profile was provided by J. K. Holman in his *Wagner's Ring—A Listener's Companion and Concordance*, where he reproduced 43 instances in the course of the *Ring* drama in which we hear the "Woman's Worth Motif" H35 (which Dunning christened the "Loveless Motif"). [Holman: pp. 393–396] Though it would be impossible within the covers of a book to reproduce all 193 motifs' dramatic profiles (this can, perhaps, be done on one's computer by using the "search" function in an e-book version of my book), my detailed verbal description of each motif attempts to convey something of the richness of resonance any given motif has acquired during its entire history of occurrences within the drama. This capacity of Wagner's musical motifs of reminiscence and foreboding to accumulate meaning in the course of the drama Wagner called his artistic "Wonder." For him it was a secular substitute for lost religious faith in a transcendent realm of being, because, like a supernatural miracle, which transcends the limits of time and space (Mother Nature's laws), musical motifs which recall the past and foresee the future give us the impression of making all things that are distant in time and space (i.e., within the drama) present, here and now. What would otherwise be thought, Wagner's musical motifs allow us to feel, offering us an aesthetic intuition of the drama.

However, given the many dramatic contexts with which most motifs are associated in the *Ring*, and therefore the multiple and often ambiguous conceptual associations which a motif accrues in the course of its life within the drama, to elucidate a definitive "meaning" for each recurrence of a motif within the context of the libretto is in most cases impossible. This problem was also demonstrated by Holman with respect to the difficulty of determining what the "Woman's Worth Motif," H35, means, since it's hard to discern a single unifying idea which makes sense of all of the instances in which we hear H35 within the drama [Holman: pp. 393–396] Though there are quite numerous instances in which motifs make unremarkable recurrences, in which one isn't surprised to hear them in their current dramatic context (such as when we see—or hear a verbal reference to—an object or person with which a motif has been previously associated, and concurrently hear this motif), there are comparatively few instances in which motifs recur which are unambiguously logical, yet dramatically surprising and brilliant in their effect. A classic instance of such a well-motivated, yet dramatically moving and unexpected employment of a motif, is the well-known recurrence of the first two segments of Wotan's Valhalla Motif (H18ab) in *The Valkyrie*, Act One, Scene Two, as Siegmund recalls how he lost his father Wolfe (Wotan in disguise) in the forest, finding only his wolf-skin. Its poignancy arises partly from the audience's awareness of something of which Siegmund is wholly ignorant, that Siegmund's father Wolfe (or Wälse) is the god Wotan in disguise.

But there are a comparatively small yet highly significant number of instances in which a motif's recurrence in a specific dramatic context is mysterious or at best ambiguous and perplexing. We should be alert to such instances because we may discover that they can become a portal to a deeper and more all-embracing level of allegorical meaning, assuming they mean anything at all.

Most of my interpretations of the recurrence of specific motifs within specific dramatic contexts are therefore speculative, educated guesses. There are after all a number of well-known instances in which the dramatic or conceptual motivation behind Wagner's employment of a specific motif in a specific dramatic context remains a mystery subject to endless debate. A famous instance is Wagner's employment of Motif H16 (the so-called "Renunciation of Love Motif"), which is first heard in *The Rhinegold* Scene One as the Rhinedaughter Woglinde tells the Nibelung dwarf Alberich that only one who's prepared to renounce love can forge a ring from the Rhinegold which will grant him limitless power, but which recurs in a surprising dramatic context later. The confusion arises from the fact that in *The Valkyrie*, Act One, Scene Three, as Siegmund, preparing to pull the sword Nothung out of Hunding's house-ash-tree-pillar, heroically embraces the love of his sister (and soon to be bride) Sieglinde, and therefore accepts the obligations of love, even unto death, he sings H16. Therefore, the so-called "Renunciation of Love Motif" in V.1.3 is employed as a motif which represents Siegmund's need for love. I've provided what I believe are logically and allegorically coherent explanations for each such instance in the *Ring*. However, this limitation—that many occurrences of motifs within certain dramatic contexts are so resonant with a variety of possible meanings that definitive elucidation is impossible—must be taken into account by any serious reader of this study. Experiment will show that any complex interpretation of this daunting masterpiece can probably supply a plausible rationale for the recurrence of almost any motif in any possible dramatic context, so an interpreter must be very careful not to overreach in drawing conclusions from the recurrence of specific motifs in surprising dramatic contexts. Therefore, we can only approach motival interpretation humbly with the full battery of knowledge at our disposal, taking into account not only the complete dramatic profile of each motif, but also all the other clues which Wagner and his mentor Feuerbach have given us. In order to propose a plausible interpretation of motival conundrums we must at least discern a logical, dramatically persuasive conceptual theme underlying the multiple recurrences—the history of dramatic associations—of any given motif, i.e., we must seek the allegorical logic underlying its "dramatic profile."

It's well known that not only does Wagner's employment of a comparatively small number of easily remembered musical motifs lend a remarkable feeling of unity and dramatic coherence to the *Ring*, but also, ever since the demonstrations provided by Deryck Cooke in his famous guide to the musical motifs of the *Ring*, recorded as a lecture, became available in the late 1970's, it's been understood that a large number of the musical motifs belong to different families, whose motifs are kin by virtue of common musical features and/or by virtue of discernible transitions from one variant into another. Cooke demonstrated that in many instances motifs give birth to other motifs by virtue either of a gradual process of musical transformation from one form to another, or at any rate in being the musical basis for a motif, or motifs, which are heard later. Dunning has incorporated most of Cooke's insights into Dunning's guide to the *Ring*'s motifs, and has added other discoveries of his own, some of which offer improvements on Cooke's work. Following the guidance of both Cooke and Dunning, in the following list of motifs I've also attempted to delineate the musical genealogy of each motif, and/or outline its musical relationship with other kindred motifs. The genealogy for each motif, as ascertained by Cooke and/or Dunning, can be found after each motif's verbal description in this guide, in light print. Unless otherwise indicated, nearly all the information provided in this guide regarding motifs' transformations and genealogical relations is based on Cooke's study.

Dunning provided most of the remaining insights on this subject. Those who wish to hear examples from his numbered list of 177 musical motifs can consult the motif guide at www.wagnerheim.com where, by clicking on any numbered motif in the guide (or embedded in passages of the libretto I've quoted), one can hear an mp3 computer simulation and simultaneously read its musical notation. Eventually I'll replace this with my expanded list of 193 musical motifs, including new sound files for the new motifs I've added.

Here's my list of symbols employed within both the guide to the musical motifs which follows, and also within the body of the text of *The Wound that Will Never Heal* wherever libretto text is quoted, or where Wagner's musical motifs are under discussion:

Symbols Employed to Characterize Musical Motifs

H   stands for specific 'music' or a specific 'motif.' It's always followed by either a description of the music in question, and/or the number which identifies a motif.

H: indicates that the following passage in the poetic text is sung to, and/or accompanied in the orchestra by, the specified music or motif. An example:
"Woglinde: (H4:) Weia! Waga! Welter, you wave, swirl round the cradle (:H4)!"

:H   indicates that the specified music, or motif, to which the previous text was sung, or which accompanied it in the orchestra, has now ended. (see example above)

H?   stands for music whose motival identity, if any, hasn't yet been ascertained.

/   a slash, "/," between two or more motifs, for instance, H32B/H18b, indicates that Wagner has combined the motifs in some way. Such motif combinations or hybrids sometimes give birth to new, numbered motifs.

[[H]]	indicates the first definitive occurrence of a numbered motif in the context of the score and libretto
Voc	indicates the specified music, or motif, is sung. For instance: "Woglinde: (H4 Voc:) Weia! Waga! Welter, you wave, swirl round the cradle (:H4 Voc)!"
Orch	indicates the specified music, or motif, is played by the orchestra. For instance: "(H6 Orch: His progress repeatedly obstructed, Alberich clambers to the top of the ledge with goblin-like agility)." In some instances, the specific instrument or section of the orchestra which plays the identified passage is identified.
a, b, etc.	Dr. Dunning has subdivided some motifs according to identifiable, distinguishable segments, which are sometimes heard independently within the *Ring*. Such segments are identified by lowercase letters following the motif's identifying number. For example, the "Valhalla Motif" H18 has five distinguishable segments, H18abcde, which will often be heard separately. Dr. Dunning indicated distinguishable segments in the images of 22 motifs: 18abcdef, 25ab, 29ab, 31ab, 32AB, 40A, 40B, 57ab, 58abc, 90AB, 99AB, 121ab, 134ab, 137ab, 138ab, 141AB, 147ab, 168ab, 181ab, 184ab, 189abc. The Motif Guide introduces distinguishable segments for 20 motifs that are not indicated in Dunning's images: 8ab, 9ab, 15ab, 17ab, 43ab, 44ab, 48ab, 56ab, 58d, 74AB, 79ab, 82ab, 93abc, 128ab, 155ab, 162ab, 173ab, 174ab, 193ab.
A, B	Wherever a motif number is followed by an upper-case letter, this generally indicates a variant of the Definitive Motif which sounds sufficiently like the Definitive Motif to be listed under its number yet sounds sufficiently different from the Definitive Motif to warrant designation as a key variant. **A** in general is the Definitive Motif, **B** its variant. In some cases, such a variant acquires a conceptual resonance which is kin to, but distinct from, the original motif from which it was derived.

Allen Dunning's Numbered List of The *Ring*'s Musical Motifs, with 23 Motifs added by Paul Heise

Vari A "variant" of a motif is sufficiently similar to the original motif to be identified by its number, but sufficiently distinct from it to be classified as a variant of the original, or "Definitive" motif. In general, whenever the word "vari" appears after a motif identified by number, this variant is, unlike cases in which varis are identified by a capital letter, a one-off and doesn't recur often enough in the same form to warrant designation by a capital letter. In some instances, a motif is so thoroughly transformed or varied in the course of the music-drama, both musically and in terms of its dramatic context and/or meaning, that it has been given its own identifying number as an entirely independent motif. In such instances, however, its musical genealogy will be indicated. A classic example, described by Cooke, is the transformation of H17ab, Alberich's "Ring Motif," into H18ab, the initial segments of Wotan's "Valhalla Motif." And Wotan's Spear Motif H19, as demonstrated by Cooke, undergoes such an astonishing series of transformations that you couldn't guess that its first and last iterations were related at all. Such cases often have great significance in interpreting the drama.

Frag A fragment of a musical motif, not necessarily identifiable as a lettered segment

> A specific motif transforms into another motif which usually (but not always) has a musical kinship to the original yet is sufficiently distinct from its parent to warrant its own identifying number. An example:
H17ab>H18ab

>> A musical motif develops of itself, but without necessarily transforming into a distinct motif identifiable by a different number

Embryonic Some motifs initially occur in a rather cryptic, premonitory form which hasn't yet attained a well delineated, easily identifiable "Definitive" Form

Definitive The well delineated form, with a distinctive musical profile, which motifs take on once they've attained the more or less fixed form in which they'll be heard throughout the *Ring* after their initial occurrence

Guide to Motifs in Richard Wagner's
The Ring of The Nibelung

The Rhinegold

H1 = S1   [[H1]] R.1. 30

Primal Nature. **Natural Necessity**

H1 basis of H2, H3, H52, H56b, and perhaps H123?; via H52, is a basis for H70, H76, H88, H93, H98, and perhaps for H163?

H2 = S2B   [[H2]] R.1. 30

Rhine Motion

H2 is based on H1; basis of H3, H14, H36, H52 and, by extension, of H53, which is approximately H52's inversion.

H3 = S2A and S3   [[H3]] R.1. 30

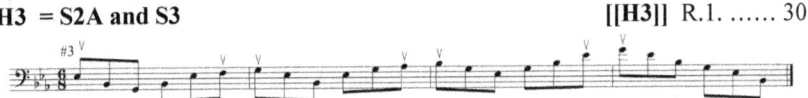

Rhine River **(Definitive Motif)**

H3 is based on H2; H3's diminished inversion is the basis for H156, the motif which represents the Norns' (who are Erda's daughters) spinning their rope of fate. See H2 above for H3's genealogy. H3 also a basis for H14 and H190

H4 = S4   [[H4]] R.1 31

Woglinde's Lullaby. **Ur-Melody**

H4 is basis of H138ab, while H189c is a loose inversion; related to H102 as a pentatonic Song of Nature.

S5 and S6 omitted

H5 S omits [[H5]] R.1 31

Alberich's lurching locomotion in his futile attempt to catch a Rhinedaughter
H5's motival links not ascertained.

H6 = S7 [[H6]] R.1 31

Alberich's Futile Wooing. [Reflective consciousness as a handicap]
H6 is basis of H86

H7 = S8 [[H7]] R.1 32

Wellgunde mockingly leads Alberich on. [Cruelty and exclusivity of sexual love]
H7 is in same family as H21, H94 and H160.

#9 omitted from Heise's and Scruton's Motif Lists

Alberich's desperation to win a Rhinedaughter
#9 is omitted because it isn't heard again or developed, and doesn't possess or accrue any conceptual meaning

#10 omitted from Heise's and Scruton's Motif Lists

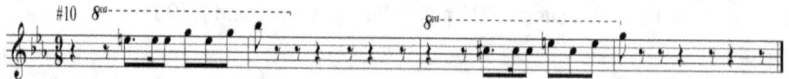

Possible embryo for the Nibelung Forging Motif (H38)
#10 is omitted because it isn't heard again or developed, and doesn't possess or accrue any conceptual meaning

H8ab = S9 [[H8ab]] R.1 33

Alberich's exclamation of woe upon rejection by the Rhinedaughters. [Love forever lost]
H8ab is basis of H11, H12, H38, H43ab and H173ab

S10, S11 omitted

H9ab = S13 [[H9ab]] R.1 34

***The Rhinegold.* From the time before the Fall of Man. [Before the birth of reflective consciousness]**
H9ab is based on a diatonic arpeggiated figure — same family as H1, H55 and H108

H10 = S12 [[H10]] R.1 34

Golden light shimmers underwater as the Rhinegold is brightened by the sun—one of Cooke's Motions of Nature
H10 belongs in the same family as H14, H36 and H190

H11 = S14B [[H11]] R.1 34

The Rhinedaughters' joyous cry: *"Heiajaheia! Heiajaheia!"* [Aesthetic delight in the gold]
H11 is based on H8ab; is basis of H38, H43b and H173b

H12 – S14A [[H12]] R.1 34

The Rhinedaughters' ecstatic cry: *"Rhinegold! Rhinegold!"* [Aesthetic delight in the gold]
H12 is based on H8a; is basis of H43a and H173a

H13 S omits   [[H13]] R.1 34

The Rhinedaughters' [muses'] song, dance and verse in praise of the Rhinegold
H13's motival links not ascertained.

H14 = S15   [[H14]] R.1 34

The Rhinedaughters' exuberant swimming in celebration of the Rhinegold— one of Cooke's Motions of Nature
H14 based on H2, basis of H36 and H190.

H15ab = S16A   [[H15ab]] R.1 35

World Mastery. **[Power of the Human Mind]**
H15ab grows naturally out of some of the Rhinedaughters' joyous singing in praise of the Rhinegold; is basis of H17ab and therefore also of H18ab; H17a is in turn basis of H45; H17ab is basis of H49, H50, H67 and H172

H16 = S17   [[H16]] R.1 36

Renunciation of Love. **[Need for Love]**
H16b is basis of H35; H35 seems to influence a large number of subsequent motifs

H17ab = S16B   [[H17ab]] R.1 38
                                                    [[H17ab→H18ab]] R.1>2 Trans 39

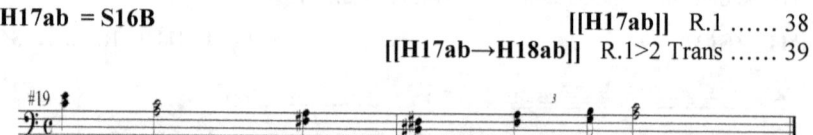

Alberich's Ring of World-Power. **[Limitless Power of the Human Mind]**
H17ab is based on H15ab, which in turn is based on Rhinedaughter vocal music which expresses their joy in the Rhinegold; is basis of H18ab; H17's chords are basis of H49, H17a is basis of H67 and H172; H17a's inversion is basis of H50; H17b is basis of H45; H17ab's harmony heavily influences many motifs, particularly under special dramatic circumstances

H18abcdef = S18ABCDEFG   [[H18ab]] R.1–2 39
                              [[H18abcd]] R.2 40
                              [[H18e]] S.3.3 337

***Valhalla*—The Gods' Heavenly Abode. [Symbol of man's earliest form of thought—Religious Belief]**
H18ab is based on H17ab, which in turn is produced by H15ab, derived in its turn from a transformation of music characteristic of the Rhinedaughters' song, dance and verse celebrating their delight in the Rhinegold. Dunning suggested H18b may be a basis for H120; related through its basis H17ab to all the H17ab-based motifs such as H45, H49, H50, H67 and H172. Since segments H18ef are always heard together, wherever one reads H18e it's understood that H18f follows. For this reason H18f is never mentioned in my book.

H19 = S19   [[H19]] (~ definitive) R.2 40
                [[H19]] (definitive) R.2 58

Wotan's *Spear* of Divine Authority and Law. [The Social Contract]
H19 is basis for H27, H31ab; H59, H61, H80, H99AB, H147AB, H176 and perhaps H123; H19's inversion is basis for H44 and H81; one of three motifs comprising H82ab

H20 = S20   [[H20]] R.2 49

***Love's Longing for Fidelity*. [Fricka's longing for Wotan to sustain faith in divine law]**
H20 is basis for H74, and perhaps H104, H113 and H168b?

H21 = S21   [[H21]] R.2 ...... 49, 50

Longing for the domestic bliss of Valhalla. [Fricka's longing for Wotan not to question divine faith—to accept it unconditionally]
Dunning suggests H21 is based on H7?; H21 is basis of, or related to, H94 and H160

H22 = S22A   [[H22]] R.2 51

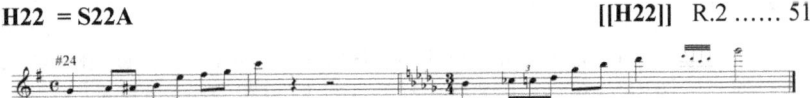

***Freia as goddess of sensuous love*. [Transcendent love has a physical basis]**
H22 is basis of H149; is possible basis of H164

H23 = S22B [[H23]] R.2 51

Freia as goddess of transcendent love—**(including romantic love)**
H23 is based on an embryo from the vocal line of Alberich's complaint at having his bid for love rejected by all three Rhinedaughters, who'd led him on:

> **Alberich:** "(H8a voc:) Woe! (H8b voc:) Ah, woe (:H8b voc)! (H23 and H37 embryo voc:) Has the third, so true, betrayed me, as well?"

is basis of H37, of definitive Love motif H39 and H63, of H79b, H142 and H150. Dunning suggests possible basis of H155a?

H24 = S33 [[H24]] R.2 51

Loge's Deceptions. **Loge the Fire God and Trickster. [Metaphor for artistic self-deception]**
H24 is basis of H26, H42, H106 and H124

H25ab = S23 [[H25ab]] R.2 52

Giants. **[Man's egoistic animal instincts of desire (Fasolt) and fear (Fafner - the self-preservation urge)]**
H25a is basis of H134a

H26 = S24A [[H26]] R.2 54

Irrevocable Law. **[The Social Contract must be dependable]**
H26 is based on H24; is a basis of H124; is related to H42 and H106

S24B omitted

H27 = S25 [[H27]] R.2 54

Treaty. **[The Social Contract must be dependable]**

H27 is based on H19; is in same family as H31b, H59, H61, H80, part of H82ab, H99AB, H147AB, H176, and possibly H123. Through H19's inversion it is related to H44 and H81

H28 = S26A [[H28]] R.2 56

***Freia's Golden Apples of sorrowless youth eternal.* [Immortality]**
H28 is basis of H30. Scruton suggests H28 is derived from H18ab. I'd go further and suggest that if this is so, H28 is derived from H17ab.

S26B omitted

H29ab = S27 [[H29ab]] R.2 56

***Godhead Lost.* Fafner threatens to deprive the gods of Freia's golden apples [their divinity]**
H29b is a basis of H101; H29b is possibly related to H32B. Scruton suggests that H29ab is a continuation of his S26B, which is Loge's ironical diminished version of the motif of Freia's golden apples H28.

H30 = S28 [[H30]] R.2 58

***Froh.* Freia's grateful, optimistic brother. [Religious faith stems from gratitude (Froh) and fear (Donner)]**
H30 is based on H28

H31ab = S29 [[H31ab]] R.2 58

***Donner.* Freia's threatening brother. Fearful God of Thunder. Enforcer of the Gods' Rule. [Faith]**
H31a is possibly a basis for H146; H31b is based on H19's embryo; H31b is related to H59 and H61; H31b is in same family as H27, H80, part of H82ab, H99AB, H147AB, H176, and possibly H123; inversion of H31b is related to H44 and H81

H32AB = S30 [[H32AB]] R.2 ...... 58, 59

***Loge.* [Man's gift of artistic self-deception]**
musically H32A forms a perfect pair with H32B, its inversion. H32B is possibly related to H29b and H101.

H33 = S32? [[H33]] R.2 58

Loge's Transformations. [Wagner's 'Artistic Wonder']. [Loge as metaphor for man's gift of artistic self-deception]
H33 is basis of H40AB, H105 and H165. Dunning suggests a possible relation to H47. Scruton calls S32 magic fire.

H34 = S31 [[H34]] R.2 58

Loge's Flickering Flames. Loge the Wily Fire God
H34 has no specific motival links, but is clearly in the family of Nature in Motion motifs such as H10, H36, etc.

H35 = S34 [[H35]] R.2 61

Loveless World. Woman's Worth. [Fall of Man]. [Conscious man's breach with Nature]
H35 is based on H16b; H35 influences many other motifs.

H36 = S35 [[H36]] R.2 61

Nature Weaving (Scruton). [The Cosmos's bonds of love]
H36 is one of Cooke's Motions of Nature; it is based on H2 and H14; it is related to H190

H37 = S36A [[H37]] R.2>3 Trans 69

Alberich's unbearable anguish: There's no love in the world
H37 is based on H23 but ultimately on the vocal line of Alberich's despair at being rejected by the Rhinedaughters: "(H37 embryo Voc:) The third, so true, betrayed me as well?;" Scruton describes it as the diminution of H23; it is basis of H39, H63b, H79b, H142, H150 and, according to Dunning, perhaps H155

H38 = S37 [[H38]] R.2>3 Trans 69

Nibelung Forging. Labor as drudgery rather than joy of creation
H38 is based on H8ab, and especially H11; it is related to H43b and H173b

H39 = S36B   [[H39]]   R.2>3 Trans 69

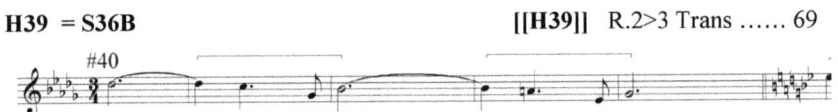

Tragic Love. **Love lost from the world**
H39 is based on H23 and H37; Scruton describes H39 as an augmentation of H23; it is basis of H63b, H79b, H142, H150 and, according to Dunning, perhaps H155

H40A = S38   [[H40A]]   R.3 70

Wondrous Tarnhelm. **[Man's Imagination]**
H40A is based on H33; it is basis of H40B and H165; it is related to H105 via H33. According to Dunning, it is possibly related to H47 and H48

H40B = S38   [[H40B]]   R.3 70

Tarnhelm's Transformations. **[Wagner's Wonder]**
H40B is based on H33 via H40A; it is basis of H165; it is related to H105. According to Dunning, it is possibly related to H47 and H48.

H41 = S37A minus S37A's 'Smithing' component   [[H41]]   R.3 72

Servitude. **[Dominance demands submission but engenders revenge]**
H41 is an H8a vari

H42 S omits, but ≈ S33   [[H42]]   R.3 72

Mime's Scheming **(First Motif)**
H42 is based on H24; it is basis of H106; it is related to H26 and H124

H43ab = S39   [[H43ab]]   R.3 75

Coercive *Power of Alberich's Ring*
H43ab is based on H8ab and H12 plus H11; it is basis of H173ab

H44ab S omits [[H44a]] R.3 77
[[H44b]] R.3 82

Alberich's Revolt. **[Alberich's intent to shatter the gods' illusions]**

H44a is an inversion of H19; it is basis of H81; via H19, it is related to H27, H31b, H59, H61, H80, part of H82ab, H147AB, H176, and perhaps H123. Dunning didn't provide musical notation for a second segment of H44 (H44b) which on three occasions follows H44a in R.3. H44b doesn't correspond to the second iteration of H44a to the right of the first iteration in the notation above, but is musically very distinct.

H45 = S40 [[H45]] R.3 79

Alberich's ever-growing *Nibelung Hoard of Treasure.* **[Man's Acquisition of Objective Knowledge]**

H45 is based on H17b; it is related to other H17-based motifs such as H18ab, H49, H50, H67 and H172

H46 = S103 [[H46]] R.3 86

Arrogance of Power. **Loge mocks Alberich's (and Wotan's) pretensions**

H46 is a compound motif comprised of H18b/H32B. See H18 and H32 for further motival links.

H47 = S41 [[H47]] R.3 87

Dragon/Serpent. **Alberich transformed through the Tarnhelm's magic. [Fafner as fear of death and religious faith's fear of objective knowledge]**

H47 is basis of H48; Dunning suggests a possible relation to H33, H40AB and H165

S42, S43 omitted

H48ab S omits [[H48ab]] R.3 87

Toad. **Alberich transformed through the Tarnhelm's magic into an amphibian [transition]**

H48a is based on H47; H48b's motival links not ascertained.

H49 = S44 [[H49]] R.4 95

Envy — **Alberich's Resentment against the gods' rule [religious man's rule]. Alberich's intent to avenge the gods' co-option of his Ring-Power**

H49 is a syncopation of H17's harmony; it is related through H17's harmony to H43, H45, H50, H67 and H172.

H50 = S45 [[H50]] R.4 95

Alberich's Curse on his Ring. **[The price man pays for being man, i.e., for being the symbol user with the gift of reflective consciousness]**

H50 is an inversion of H17a; it is related through H17 to H18ab, H43, H45, H49, H67 and H172

H51 = S46 [[H51]] R.4 96

Alberich's Death Curse. **[Consciousness as foreknowledge of the end]**

H51's motival links not ascertained.

H?51.5 [[H?51.5]] R.4 102

Wotan's, Brünnhilde's and Siegfried's moments of decision: do I keep the Ring?

Dunning doesn't distinguish H?51.5 as a unique motif, but described it as either an H17ab (Ring) variant or as an H17ab/H18ab (Valhalla) hybrid. H?51.5 is heard only three times in the *Ring* and, on each occasion, it expresses the moment of decision for Wotan (in R.4), Brünnhilde (in T.1.3.A) and Siegfried (in T.3.2): do they keep or relinquish Alberich's Ring? Dunning didn't provide musical notation.

H52 = S47 [[H52]] R.4 102

Erda as Mother Nature. **Erda's Ur-law. Knowledge of all that was, is, and will be. Erda: 'All things that are, end!'**

H52 is based on H2, and therefore on H1, and relates to H56b through H1. It is a basis for H82a and H122, and its modified inversion is basis for H53. Its concluding phrase generates H70, H76, H88, H93a, H98 and, according to Cooke, possibly H163.

H53 = S48   [[H53]]   R.4 104

Twilight of the Gods. **[The inevitability that man's advancement in objective knowledge will overthrow religious faith, ethics, and inspired art]**

H53 is approximately based on inversion of H52. It is related through H52 to H1 and H2, H56b, H70, H76, H88, H93a, H98, H122 and, according to Cooke, perhaps H163

H54 = S49   [[H54]]   R.4 112

Donner's thunderous cry: *"**Heda! Heda, Hedo!**.*" **Donner's futile attempt to purify Valhalla [from the taint of being founded on self-deception]**

H54 is basis of H60. It is possibly a basis for H83 and H85

H55 = S50   [[H55]]   R.4 112

Rainbow Bridge over the Rhine to Valhalla. **[Man's bridge from Nature to Culture]**

H55 belongs to the family of Nature motifs, variations on the Primal Nature motif H1 and Rhine motifs H2 and H3, which include H9ab.

H56ab = S51   [[H56ab]]   R.4 113

Wotan's Grand Idea **of Redemption of the Gods from Alberich's Ring Curse. [The *Sword* symbolizes man's longing to restore lost innocence]**

H56a is based on Erda's octave drop during her prophecy of the gods' doom (H52) "All things that are, end!" H56b is based on H1 (the time before the Fall). It is related through H1 to Nature arpeggiated figures like H9ab and H55, to H52, H53 and H122, and through H52's closing notes to heroic motifs such as H70, H76, H88, H93a and H98, and perhaps according to Cooke H163.

H57ab = S52   [[H57ab]]   R.4 113

Wotan's Salute to Valhalla—**Refuge of the Gods. [Religious man's illusory refuge from dread and dismay in the face of unpalatable secular truth]**

H57a's motival links not ascertained. H57b is basis of H78

H58abcd = S53ABC   [[H58abcd]]   R.4 117

Rhinedaughters' Lament for the Stolen Rhinegold (First Motif)
H58a is a variant of H12; H58bc's motival links not ascertained. Perhaps H58bc is a variant of H4 or H13 variant in the minor. Perhaps H58d is a basis for H93c, the close of Siegfried's motif in the following context:

> (R.4: "**Rhinedaughters**: (H58a voc: Rhinegold! Rhinegold! Guileless gold (:H58a voc)! How clear and bright you shone on us so sweetly! (H58b voc:) For you, bright toy, we now lament (:H58b voc)! (H58c voc:) Give us the gold (:H58c voc), **(H58d voc:) oh give us the guileless gold back again** (:H58d voc)!")

Dunning provided no musical notation for H58d.

The Valkyrie

H59 = S54   [[H59]]   V.1.1 121

***Wotan's Storm* of 'Noth' (Anguish). Wotan testing the independence of his son Siegmund**
H59 is based on H19's embryo and H31b; influenced perhaps by H14. It is basis of H61; related to H27 and H80, related by inversion to H44 and H81, related to H99AB, H147AB, H176 and, according to Cooke, possibly to H123.

H60 = S55   [[H60]]   V.1.1 121

***Donner's Lightning* (from Wotan's Storm of 'Noth')**
H60 is based on H54; may influence H78; possible influence on H83 and H85.

H61 = S56   [[H61]]   V.1.1 121

***Siegmund the Wälsung*—scion of Wotan (known only to Siegmund as Wälse or Wolfe)**
H61 is based on slowed tempo H59, itself based on H19's embryo. It is related through H19 to H27, H31b, H80 and part of H82ab. It is related to H99AB, H147AB, H176, and possibly to H123. Its inversion is related to H44 and H81.

S57 omitted

H62 = S58   [[H62]]   V.1.1 121

Sieglinde. **Siegmund's long-lost, but rediscovered, twin sister**
H62's motival links not ascertained, though Cooke described H62 as the musical complement of Siegmund's motif H61.

H63 = S59   [[H63]]   V.1.1 121

Romantic *love* of the siblings Siegmund and Sieglinde. (Definitive Love Motif)
H63a may be influenced by H20, but is more substantially a product of H23 via H37 and especially H39. It ultimately originates in Alberich's vocal line
    "The third, so true, betrayed me as well?"
as well as another embryo from R.1. It is basis of H79b, H142, H150 and, according to Dunning, possibly H155.

S60 omitted

H64 S omits   [[H64]]   V.1.1 123

Siegmund's ill-fortune. **Heirloom of Wotan's 'Noth'**
H64 motival links not ascertained.

H65 = S61   [[H65]]   V.1.1 123

The Wälsungs' Bond of Sympathy. **Siegmund's and Sieglinde's bond of sympathy for each other's sorrows as heirs to Wotan's 'Noth.' [Wotan's implication of the Wälsungs in his 'sin' of self-deception]**
H65's motival links not ascertained. H65 perhaps relates to H113.

S61A omitted

H66 = S62   [[H66]]   V.1.2 124

Hunding **('Hounding'). [Model representative of established (i.e., corrupt) society founded upon Wotan's divine authority (as interpreted by Fricka from fear of social change)]**
H66's motival links not ascertained; but there does seem to be some H25ab influence here

H67 = S63 [[H67]] V.1.2 124

Hunding's Honor, **Hearth and Home. Fricka's demand to maintain social order at all cost**
H67 is based on H17a; it is basis of H172; it is related through H17a to H15a, H18a, H45ab, H49, H50 and H180.

H68 = S65 [[H68]] V.1.2 126

The innocent, unloved bride's weeping. Siegmund's unsuccessful attempt to rescue Sieglinde from a forced, loveless marriage
H68 is basis of H79a.

H69 = S64 [[H69]] V.1.2 126

Infinite sorrow of the Wälsungs. **[The Wälsungs, as heirs to Wotan's divine 'Noth,' his fruitless, self-deceiving quest to restore lost innocence to the world through social revolution (Wotan as Wälse)]**
H69 is based on an embryo drawn from Siegmund's prior vocal line:
   Siegmund: (to Hunding and Sieglinde) "(H69 embryo:) A Wölfing [i.e., son of Wotan, who is disguised as Wolfe, and also disguised as Wälse] tells you this, whom as Wölfing many know well."
H69's motival links not ascertained.

H70 = S64A [[H70]] V.1.2 126

The tragic Wälsung Race. **[The Wälsung Race as heir to Wotan's divine 'Noth,' his futile, self-deceiving, quest to restore lost innocence through social revolution (Wotan as Wälse)]**
H70 is based on the last three notes of H52, and therefore ultimately on H1 and H2. It is related to H56b via H1. Cooke's family of heroic motifs based on the last 3 notes of H52 also includes H76, H88, H93a, H98 and, according to Cooke, possibly H163.

S66 ≈ H128 without Scruton's variant

H71 = S67 [[H71]] V.1.3 ...... 130, 130

Siegmund destined to win Wotan's sword 'Nothung' and rescue Sieglinde
H71 is a compound motif comprised of H18ab and H56b; see H18 and H56 for extensive series of motif links

554   The Wound That Will Never Heal:
An Allegorical Interpretation of Richard Wagner's *The Ring of the Nibelung*

H72 = S68   [[H72]] V.1.3 131

Siegmund's aria 'Winterstorms have waned': **'Spring' (Siegmund) is united with 'Love' (Sieglinde)**
H72's motival links not ascertained; Dunning suggests a distant relationship to H2.

S69 omitted

H73 S omits   [[H73]] V.1.3 131

Siegmund's and Sieglinde's delight in their loving union ("*United are love and spring!*")
H73's motival links not ascertained; this motif is employed in Wagner's independent chamber orchestra composition, the *Siegfried Idyll*.

H74AB = S70AB   [[H74AB]] V.1.3 131

Wälsung Twins' *Love-Longing*
H74 belongs in same family as H20, H104, and possibly H113

H75 = S71   [[H75]] V.1.3 132

The Wälsung twins' remembrance of things past—their common Wälsung heritage that stems from Wotan
H75's motival links are not ascertained. H75 is most prominent in the finale of V.1.3 as the Wälsung twins Siegmund and Sieglinde elope from Hunding's prison-like home. Cooke suggests that H75 is a basis for H155, the motif which brings the ecstatic love duet of Siegfried and Brünnhilde in S.3.3 to its climax. It is perhaps also a premonition of the Forest Murmurs H136.

H76 = S73A   [[H76]] V.2.1 136

The Valkyries. **Muses and angels-of-death to martyred heroes. Inspirers of heroes for the end-of-times battle against Alberich's Nibelung Horde of Night**
H76 belongs to a family of heroic motifs derived from the last three notes of H52, which includes H70, H88, H93a, H98, and perhaps H163. H76 relates through H52 to H1—and thus to H56b—and to H2 and H3.

H77 = S73C   [[H77]]   V.2.1 136

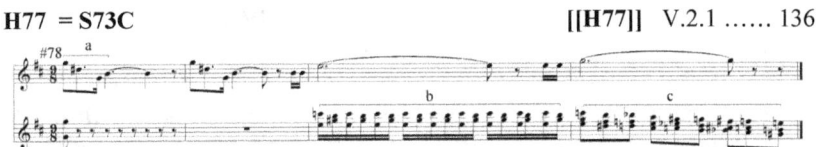

Brünnhilde's Valkyrie War-Cry
H77's motival links not ascertained.

H78 = S74   [[H78]]   V.2.1 ...... 136, 139

Fricka's indictment of the Wälsung twins for adultery and incest, as threatening the gods' eternal rule
H78 is based on H57b. Its initial rhythm influenced by H60.

H79ab = S75   [[H79ab]]   V.2.1 139

Fricka's indictment of Wotan for adultery, as threatening the gods' eternal rule
H79a is based on H68. H79b is based on H23; thus H79b belongs to the family of love motifs which includes H37, H39, H63b, H142, H150 and, according to Dunning, possibly H155.

H80 = S76   [[H80]]   V.2.1 141

Wotan's Frustration. **Wotan forced to acknowledge that allegedly free Siegmund is the unfree agent of Wotan's fear-inspired self-deception**
H80 is based on H19. It relates to H27, H31b, H59, H61, H99AB, H147AB, H176 and, according to Cooke, perhaps H123. It relates to H44 and H81 through inversion of H19. I designate the second half of H80 (above) as motif H95 [=S77].

H81 = S78   [[H81]]   V.2.2 145

Wotan's Revolt. Wotan's Despair. **[Hallmark of Wotan's confession to Brünnhilde. Wotan's repression into his unconscious mind of Alberich's inevitable victory over the gods, and of the futility of their seeking redemption through a hero freed from the gods' rule]**
H81 is an inversion of the definitive H19, based therefore also on H44; via H19 related to H27, H31b, H59, H61, H80, H99AB, H147AB, H176 and, according to Cooke, perhaps H123; Scruton notes that H81 ends on a chord which looks forward to *Twilight of the Gods* [not shown in the musical notation above]

556   The Wound That Will Never Heal:
An Allegorical Interpretation of Richard Wagner's *The Ring of the Nibelung*

H82ab = S79 [[H82ab]] V.2.2 156

Need of the Gods. **Need of the gods for a mortal hero who, freed from their rule [from religious faith], can redeem them from their fate—the twilight of the gods**
H82ab is a compound of H52 and its inversion—tantamount to Erda's prophecy of the twilight of the gods H53—overlain by H80, i.e., overlain by Wotan's awareness of the futility of hoping for a free hero who could redeem the gods from the fate Erda foresees; see H52, H53 and H80 for motival relationships

H83 = S81 [[H83]] V.2.2 159

Wotan's Anger **(First Motif).** ***Wotan's Self-loathing.*** **Wotan's anger at Brünnhilde for pursuing a cause he has renounced and which he forbad Brünnhilde from pursuing**
H83 is possibly based on H54.

H84 = S80 [[H84]] V.2.2 166

Wotan's First Bequest **(Scruton). Out of desperation, Wotan makes Hagen (Alberich's as-yet-unborn son) his heir because he reluctantly concedes the inevitability of Alberich's secular victory over the gods**
H84 takes a variety of forms, but its definitive form is a compound of a harmonic variant of the first two segments H18ab of the Valhalla motif and an H9b (Rhinegold) variant. H84 possibly reveals the gods as poor guardians of the Rhinegold's innocence, despite Loge's suggestion that the Rhinedaughters could once again find its stolen light in the splendor of the gods.

H85 = S82 [[H85]] V.2.2 174

Wotan's Anger **(Second Motif).   Wotan's anger at Brünnhilde for her disobedience in pursuing a forbidden cause**
H85 possibly is based on H54.

H86 = S83 [[H86]] V.2.3 176

Hunding's pursuit **of the Wälsung twins—to punish them for 'living for love'**
H86 is based on H6, Alberich's futile wooing [Scrambling] motif

H87 = S84   **[[H87]]   V.2.4 ...... 177**

Fate. [Erda's knowledge of the 'Coherence of Natural and Historical (Cultural) Law']
H87's motival links not ascertained. Cooke suggested a possible link with the family of so-called Magic motifs which includes H33, H40AB, possibly H47, and definitely H165.

H88 = S85   **[[H88]]   V.2.4 ...... 177**

Brünnhilde's Annunciation of Fated Doom to Siegmund. [Siegmund, martyred, will contribute his legacy to that of other culture heroes who met martyrdom in defense of Valhalla (= religious faith and transcendent value) through revolution]
H88 is based on the last three notes of H52, and thus relates to H1 and H2; related to H56b via H1. As one of the family of heroic motifs growing out of the last three notes of H52, it relates to H70, H76, H93a, H98 and, according to Cooke, perhaps H163.

H89 = S86   **[[H89]]   V.2.4 ...... 178**

Siegmund's resistance to his fated doom (of immortality in Valhalla)—Siegmund resists for the sake of his earthly love of his sister-bride Sieglinde
H89's motival links not ascertained; but H89 seems to be musically kin to H193b. Scruton suggests that H89 is related to Wotan's Frustration H80.

H90AB S omits   **[[H90A]] V.2.4 ...... 181**
                                                  [[H90B]] V.3.1 185

Brünnhilde's Compassion. Brünnhilde's heroic rebellion against Wotan in the service of the Wälsung race: Siegmund, Sieglinde and yet-to-be-born Siegfried
H90AB's motival links not ascertained.

H91 = S87   **[[H91]]   V.2.5 ...... 182**

Sieglinde's Nightmare. Sieglinde dreams of the most traumatic moment in the Wälsung twins' childhood, when the Neidings killed their mother, burned their home, abducted her and gifted her to Hunding
H91, the orchestral melody which heralds Sieglinde's nightmare is the 'Faust Theme' from the first movement (the 'Faust' movement) of Franz Liszt's *Faust*

558   The Wound That Will Never Heal:
An Allegorical Interpretation of Richard Wagner's *The Ring of the Nibelung*

Symphony. What private significance this orchestral theme may have had for Wagner is unclear, but it expresses the portentous mysteriousness of Sieglinde's dreamt recollection of her childhood's most traumatic moment. It apparently has no musical links to Wagner's other *Ring* motifs. It is only heard once.

S88 omitted

H92 = S72   **[[H92]]**   V.3.1.P. 185

A Ride of the Valkyries Motif. **The Valkyries riding their horses through the air, carrying martyred heroes to Valhalla**
H92's motival links not ascertained.

H93abc = S89 (Dunning and Scruton omit   **[[H93abc]]**   V.3.1 188
H93c)

Siegfried, the world's noblest hero. **[Siegfried is fearless because, unknown to him, he is Wotan reborn minus Wotan's fearful consciousness, his 'Noth.' What Siegfried doesn't know, Brünnhilde (his unconscious mind and guardian of Wotan's unspoken secret) knows for him]**
H93abc belongs to the family of heroic motifs stemming from the last three notes of H52. It therefore relates to H1, H2, H3 and, through H1, to H56b. This heroic family includes H70, H76, H88, H98 and, according to Cooke, perhaps H163. Dunning's musical notation above (as also Scruton's) includes H93ab, but not H93c, a cadential figure heard first in the orchestra. Brünnhilde's last words in the Ring, "In bliss your wife bids you welcome" are, I believe, sung to H93c, and H93c may in fact be a variant of H58d, the last portion of the Rhinedaughters' first lament for the Rhinegold which Dunning omitted.

H94 = S90   **[[H94]]**   V.3.1 188

Sieglinde's praise of Brünnhilde's heroic, self-sacrificial service to the Wälsung race, and her salvation of the as-yet-unborn Siegfried, the *"sublimest Wonder."* **Popularly, but incorrectly, called** *Redemption by Love*
H94 belongs to the family of motifs which includes H7, H21 and H160. Cooke regards the motifs of this family as unified under the theme of Woman's Inspiration, but that doesn't quite sum up their meaning, though it's a part of it.

H95 = S77   **[[H95]]**   V.3.2 191

Wotan's intent to punish Brünnhilde for disobedience
H95 is actually Dunning's motif #81B, which is the second half of his notation for H80 (=Dunning #81) above. I disagree with Dunning's assertion that H95 is a variant of H80, though both motifs share the initial gracenote twist of H80. H95's motival links not ascertained.

H96 = S91   [[H96]] V.3.2 191

Wotan's Reproach **(Scruton). Wotan's reproach to Brünnhilde for her disobedience. She fought for the Wälsung twins whom Fricka [moral law] had forced Wotan to abandon**
H96's motival links not ascertained.

S92 omitted

H97 S omits   [[H97]] V.3.2 193

Wotan's intent to punish Brünnhilde by putting her to sleep, defenseless, for any mortal man to wake and win as bride. [This punishment would not protect the hoard of forbidden knowledge (Wotan's unspoken secret) that he confessed to Brünnhilde, but would expose it to the light of day (consciousness)]
H97's motival links not ascertained.

H98 = S93   [[H98]] V.3.2 193

The Valkyries' protest against Wotan for his intent to leave Brünnhilde's divine Valkyrie chastity vulnerable for any passing mortal man to sully
H98 is a compound motif comprised of H88 and H93. It belongs to the family of heroic motifs stemming from the last three notes of H52, which includes H70, H76, H88, H93 and, according to Cooke, perhaps H163.

S94 omitted

H99AB = S95A and S95   [[H99A]] V.3.3 195
                              [[H99B]] V.3.3 197

Brünnhilde's appeal to Wotan not to debase her for attempting what he, in his innermost self, desired
H99AB belongs to the family of motifs derived either from H19's embryo, or the definitive motif H19, which includes H27, H31b, H59, H61, H80, part of H82, H147AB and H176. H99AB indirectly relates to H44 and H81 through inversion of H19.

H100 possible equivalent to S96, S97 and S97A [[H100]] V.3.3 197

Brünnhilde's appeal to Wotan to acknowledge what she saw: the conflict in Wotan's soul between his need to renounce Siegmund (H80) and Siegmund's refusal to accept his fate (H89) for the sake of a doomed love
H100 is a hybrid of H80/H89. Scruton describes S96 as derived from S76 [=H80], and S97 as a variation of S96 [possibly=H100], but he also describes S86 [=H89] as possibly derivative of S76 [=H80]

H101 = S98 [[H101]] V.3.3 203

Brünnhilde's Magic Sleep. **Wotan takes away Brünnhilde's divinity and leaves her Valkyrie chastity vulnerable to being sullied**
H101 is based, according to Dunning, on Godhead Lost H31b, with perhaps some influence, according to Cooke, of H32B. Cooke notes that H101 also contains some H17 harmony.

H102 = S99 [[H102]] V.3.3 203

Brünnhilde's plea to Wotan to protect her sleep with hideous terrors, so that only a fearless hero [the Wälsung artist-hero] Siegfried can wake and win her [his muse's] love
H102, being pentatonic, seems closely related to Cooke's Voices of Nature family, which includes H4, H138ab and #189abc.

H103 S omits [[H103]] V.3.3 206

Wotan's aria in praise of Brünnhilde's radiant pair of eyes
H103's motival links not ascertained. Though this motif is only heard twice, first as the theme of Wotan's song in praise of Brünnhilde's eyes, and second in the orchestral finale of *The Valkyrie*, I've designated it as a numbered motif because of its iconic stature, being one of the most recognizable themes from the *Ring*. It's part of Wotan's song of farewell to Brünnhilde.

H104 = S100 [[H104]] V.3.3 206

Wotan's Farewell to Brünnhilde. **Wotan will leave Brünnhilde [his unconscious mind and safe repository of his unspoken secret] to a man who is freer than the god [a man freed from religious faith—the secular artist-hero, Siegfried]**

H104's motival links not ascertained. Dunning believes H104 may be related to H113. Does any of the accompaniment for H104 generate H175?

H105 = S101   **[[H105]]** V.3.3 207

Loge's Protective Ring of *Magic Fire*. Wotan's protection of Brünnhilde from all wooers except the fearless Siegfried. [The veil of Maya (illusion) behind which religion and art hide their fearful truth]
H105 is a variant of H33; it's therefore a member of the family of H33-generated motifs which include H40AB and H165, and may be related, according to Dunning, to H47 and H48.

Siegfried

S102 omitted

H106 ≈ S33   **[[H106]]** S.1.1 209

Mime's Scheming **(Second Motif). [Mime represents what Wotan loathes in himself]**
H106 is based ultimately on H24 with H17's harmony. Through H42, it belongs to the family which includes H26 and H124.

H107 S omits   **[[H107]]** S.1.1 210

Mime's inherent inability to re-forge 'Nothung.' [Mime lacks authentically unconscious inspiration]
H107's motival links not ascertained. H107 may correspond to the first half of H170, the motif to which Gunther and Siegfried sing their oath of blood-brotherhood, though the motifs' harmonies differ. The implication would be that Gunther is unheroic, an unworthy blood-brother for Siegfried. Dunning detects the influence of H35.

H108 = S104   **[[H108]]** S.1.1 211

Siegfried's Youthful Horncall. **[Siegfried's vital creative force]**
H108 belongs to the family of diatonic Nature arpeggiated figures such as H1, H9ab and H55; it is the basis for Mature Siegfried's Horncall H159.

H109 = S105   [[H109]]   S.1.1 212
#104

Siegfried's [reborn Wotan's] contempt for Mime. [Expression of Wotan's self-loathing]

H109's motival links not ascertained. H109 is possibly a basis of H155, though Dunning regards a H155 as belonging to the Love motif Family based on H23. Cooke regards it as an elaboration of H75.

H110 = S106   [[H110]]   S.1.1 213

Mime's **mercenary** *Nibelung* **nature (Scruton)**

Dunning did not number this as a distinct motif, but identified it as an "H38 Duple Vari."

H111A S omits   [[H111A]]   S.1.1 213

Siegfried's debt to Erda (Mother Nature) (First Motif)

H111A's motival links not ascertained. Both motifs (H111A and H111B) philosophically foreshadow the Forest Murmurs and therefore also the Woodbird's songs, which Siegfried is ultimately able to translate into a language he not only feels but conceptually understands.

H111B S omits   [[H111B]]   S.1.1 217

Siegfried's debt to Erda (Mother Nature) (Second Motif)

H111B's motival links not ascertained. Both motifs (H111A and H111B) philosophically foreshadow the Forest Murmurs and therefore also the Woodbird's songs, which Siegfried is ultimately able to translate into a language he not only feels, but conceptually understands

H112 = S107   [[H112]]   S.1.1 213
#105

Mime's Starling Song. **The debt that Mime claims Siegfried owes him**

H112 is based on an embryo in Flosshilde's vocal line while leading Alberich on in R.1:

> "**Flosshilde:** (H112 embryo voc:) Your piercing eyes, your bristling beard, might I always see and hold them. (H112 embryo voc:) May your prickly hair's unruly locks flow round Flosshild' forever!"

It is basis of H118, possibly of H129, and definitely of H135.

H113 = S108 [[H113]] S.1.1 216

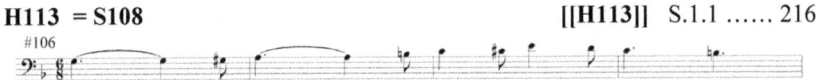

A child's longing for his or her authentic parents

H113 belongs to the same family as H20, H74 and H104. Scruton suggests S108 [=H113] is a reminiscence of S22B [=H23] and S100 [=H104]. Is H65 an influence?

S109 omitted

H114 S omits [[H114]] S.1.1 216

A child's longing for the sanctuary of his or her authentic parents' nest

H114's motival links not ascertained.

H115 S omits [[H115]] S.1.1 217

Siegfried asks Mime:
> "Since all animals and humans have loving fathers and mothers, where, Mime, is your loving wife, that I can call her mother?"

H115's motival links not ascertained.

H116 S omits [[H116]] S.1.1 221

Siegfried reconnects with his heroic Wälsung heritage through the pieces of his father Siegmund's broken sword 'Nothung.' [This represents Siegfried on the 'well-hewn causeway' laid down by all past heroes of religio-moral-artistic endeavor]

H116 is a compound motif comprised of H56 and H108, thus conceptually linking Siegfried—Siegfried's Youthful Horncall H108—with Wotan's Grand Idea for Redemption and Siegmund's sword 'Nothung,' both represented by H56ab; see H56 and H108 for motival links.

H117 = S110 [[H117]] S.1.1 221

Siegfried experiences the joy of emancipation from Mime. Freedom from Mime's repugnant, inauthentic, artificial claims upon him, and reconnection with his true Wälsung heritage

H117's motival links not ascertained. H117b may contain H19.

H118 = S111   [[H118]] S.1.1 221

Siegfried's Mission. Siegfried's declaration of independence from Mime. [Siegfried actually remains in debt to Mime, just as Wotan (Light-Alberich) remains indebted to Alberich's Ring-Power (H17ab→H18ab)]

H118 is based on Mime's Starling Song H112. It is possible basis of H129 and definite basis of H135.

H119 = S113A   [[H119]] S.1.1>2 Trans ......
                                                                          223, 224

The Wanderer (First Motif, descending). Wotan accumulates a hoard of knowledge while wandering into and over the earth (Erda). [Wotan's hoard of knowledge is identical to Alberich's hoard of treasure]

H119's motival links not ascertained. Dunning suggests a possible link with H33. Cooke suggests a link with Loge motifs such as H32AB. Loge restlessly wanders the heights and depths of the world, as does Wotan.

H120 = S113B   [[H120]] S.1.2 224

The Wanderer (Second Motif, ascending)

H120's motival links not ascertained. Dunning suggests a possible basis for H120 in H18b, the second segment of the Valhalla motif H18.

H121ab S omits   [[H121ab]] S.1.2 226

Wotan stakes his head [Mime] in a *Contest of Knowledge* with his heart [Siegfried]

H121ab's motival links not ascertained.

H122 = S112   [[H122]] S.1.2 228

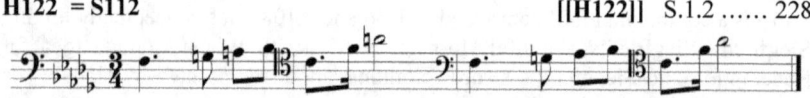

The World-Ash Tree (First Motif). [Tree of Life and Knowledge] Wotan killed the World-Ash Tree by making his Spear of Divine Authority out of its most sacred branch. [A metaphor for the 'sin' that Alberich accused Wotan of committing against Erda: religious world-renunciation]

H122 is a hybrid motif based on H2/H52, a Rhine motif, plus Erda's motif, in 3/4 time. This is musically distinct from the motif introduced in the Norns' recitation of world history in the Prelude to *Twilight of the Gods* that represents the World-Ash, H157.

H123   A = S114; B = S168 [[H123]] S.1.2 228

Former *Power of the Gods*, and Future Destruction of the Gods

H123's motival links uncertain. Cooke describes H123 as an H19 variant based on its inversion and transformation into a stepwise form. Similarities with H1 suggest that it might be an H52 variant? H123B is a variant of H123A not heard until Waltraute's narrative of how Wotan had his heroes chop down the World-Ash in order to make a bonfire to burn Valhalla. H123B is actually a compound motif H18e/H123A, H18e heard in triplets. Scruton numbers H123B as a distinct motif S168, and provides the musical notation, which Dunning omitted.

S115: omitted

H124 = S116 [[H124]] S.1.2 228

***Hallowed Contracts.* The allegedly binding runes, which Wotan whittled into the Spear that he made from the most sacred branch of the World-Ash Tree**

H124 is in the same family as H24, H26, H42 and H106: the original, archetypal contract Wotan engraved on his spear, he intended to break.

H125 = S117 [[H125]] S.1.2 230

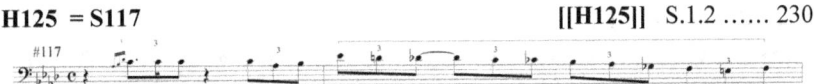

Mime's conspiracy-of-one. Mime is scheming to outwit the Wanderer, by answering his questions, saving his own head, and prompting Siegfried to kill Fafner to win Alberich's Ring for him

H125's motival links not ascertained. Scruton suggests S117 [=H125] is a prolongation of his Nibelung smithing motif S37 [=H38]

H126 S omits [[H126]] S.1.2 232

***Mime's [Wotan's] 'wise' head is forfeit to Wotan's heart [Siegfried]*. Siegfried is the fearless hero, who alone can re-forge 'Nothung' and redeem the world by restoring lost innocence**

H126's motival links not ascertained.

H127 = S118 [[H127]] S.1.3 238

***Siegfried's Labor* (Scruton). Expression of Siegfried's vital, creative, self-generating force**

H127 is a fragment of Siegfried's youthful horncall H108

H128ab = S119 [[H128ab]] S.1.3 241

Siegfried reclaims his father Siegmund's sword 'Nothung.' Siegfried restores the sword's name as he blows the bellows and smelts the sword's fragments

H128 is based on H56a, the octave drop on "Endet" in Erda's vocal line as she sings that "all things that are, end." Scruton adds that Siegmund sings this octave drop while crying out to his father "Wälse! Wälse!" (Wotan) to give him the sword he promised he'd provide in Siegmund's hour of need (Noth). It reflects the transitoriness of the world.

H129 = S120A [[H129]] S.1.3 241

Siegfried's Smelting Song

H129 is possibly based on H112, and thus possibly related to H118 and H135.

H130 = S120C [[H130]] S.1.3 241

Siegfried's invocation of the bellows (from his Smelting Song)

H130's motival links not ascertained.

S120BD omitted

H131A = S121 [[H131A]] S.1.3 243

[Siegfried's fiery phallus]. Siegfried cools and stiffens his fiery 'Nothung' in water. [A metaphor for cooling his ardor in Brünnhilde's flood]

H131A transforms into H131B. Their other motival links not ascertained.

H131B = S121A [[H131B]] S.1.3 243

Mime prepares his sleep-of-death potion for Siegfried as Siegfried re-forges 'Nothung.' [In truth, it is Wotan who is preparing to martyr Siegfried at the hands of Alberich's Ring Curse in order to redeem the rule of the gods]

H131B is a transformation or continuation of H131A. Their other motival links not ascertained.

H132 = S122 [[H132]] S.1.3 244

Siegfried's Forging Song (Accompaniment). **Siegfried imagines he is forging his own true identity [his independence from Wotan who is his own true identity]**

H132's motival links not ascertained.

H133 = S123 [[H133]] S.1.3 245

Siegfried's Triumph. The Re-forged 'Nothung.' [By splitting Mime's anvil Siegfried appears to have transcended the preconditions for forging 'Nothung']

H133's motival links not ascertained. Wagner employed H133 in his *Siegfried Idyll*.

H134ab = S124 and S125A [[H134ab]] S.2.1 248

Fafner as Dragon/Serpent of Fear. [Guardian of forbidden Secular Knowledge. Existential Fear–the basis of religious faith and social stability]

H134a is based on H25a. H134b is based on H47. See H25 and H47 for other motival links.

S125B omitted

H135 = S126 [[H135]] S.2.1 254

Wotan's futile hope that in Siegfried he has found his desired free hero. Wotan: "… let him stand or fall; his own master is he … ."

H135 is based on H112 and H118; possibly related to H129. Scruton says S126 [=H135] is based on S110 [=H117], but I consider S111 [=H118] is a better candidate for S126's [=H135's] basis.

H136 = S127 [[H136]] S.2.2 261

Siegfried's Forest Murmurs. Siegfried invokes his mothers: Sieglinde (who died giving him birth), Erda (the Mother of us all) and Brünnhilde (his metaphysical mother and muse)

H136 is a hybrid based on H2 and H10

H137ab   a = S128AB; b = S129   [[H137ab]] S.2.2 262

Woodbirdsong **(First Motif). [Music, as man's artificial bid to restore lost innocence]**

H137ab's motival links not ascertained.

H138ab = S130   [[H138ab]] S.2.2 262

Woodbirdsong **(Second Motif). [Wagner's musical motifs as man's artificial bid to restore lost innocence, as represented by the mother melody (Ur-melody H4) which attained consciousness in language as Woglinde's lullaby]**

H138ab is based on H4. H189c, according to Dunning, is a loose inversion of H4, and is therefore also related to H138ab. All of these pentatonic motifs are in the same family as H102.

#130 omitted

Selfishness and egoism of the Nibelung siblings Alberich and Mime

#130's motival links not ascertained. #130 is omitted because #130 is only heard a couple of times at one moment in association with Mime's anger at Alberich for not equably sharing the spoils of the Nibelung Hoard, Tarnhelm, and Ring. It lacks conceptual significance.

H139 S omits   [[H139]] S.2.2 ...... 267, 269

Dying Fafner speaks. [Siegfried has unwittingly committed Wotan's ultimate breach: the double breach of social contract and of religious faith]

H139 is a peculiar 4-note syncopated figure preceded by the glissando from the Giants' motif H25a, heard immediately after Siegfried has delivered his mortal blow to Fafner, but before Fafner expires from it. Dunning suggests it's a variant of the Dragon motif H47 linked to H26a through the common glissando, a hybrid of the two motifs similar in this respect to H134ab.

H140 = S131   **[[H140]]**   S.2.3 280

Mime's false [Gibichung-like] friendship
H140's motival links not ascertained. I speculate that some of the melody and rhythm of H140 and its associated music during this scene influences the dramatically similar scene in T.1.2 when the Gibichungs Hagen, Gunther, and Gutrune extend a falsely friendly welcome to Siegfried, while Gutrune, unlike Mime, successfully persuades Siegfried to drink a potion that Hagen has prepared, whose purpose is to exploit Siegfried to do what the Gibichungs Gunther and Gutrune cannot do, and whose consequence will be Siegfried's death.

H141AB = S132   **[[H141AB]]**   S.2.3 ...... 284, 285

Siegfried's loneliness and urgent need for a boon companion. Siegfried's joy at learning of Brünnhilde from the Woodbird
H141AB's motival links not ascertained.

H142 = S133   **[[H142]]**   S.3.1 288

Wotan's waking and wooing of Erda to obtain objective knowledge of what she taught him to fear, and aesthetic intuition (freedom from fear), is replicated in Siegfried's learning and forgetting fear through Brünnhilde's love.
H142 belongs to the family of love motifs stemming from an embryo in Alberich's vocal line:
    "(H37 embryo:) Has the third one, so true, betrayed me as well?"
which includes H23, H37, H39, H63b, H79b, H150, and perhaps H155.

H143 = S134   **[[H143]]**   S.3.1 ...... 295, 302

World Inheritance. **Wotan's Second Bequest (Scruton). [Wagner's proposed redemption of waning religious faith through unconsciously inspired Music-Drama (Siegfried's and Brünnhilde's love)—the new, secular Valhalla]**
H143's motival links not ascertained.

H144 S omits   (three occurrences) **[[H144]]**   S.3.2 ...... 307, 310

Pathos of Siegfried's ignorance of his true relationship to Wotan, as the Wanderer. Wotan is no longer able to guide his hero
H144's motival links not ascertained.

H145 = S135 [[H145]] S.3.2 307

Wotan's interrogation of Siegfried for reassurance that Siegfried is ignorant of his true identity

H145's motival links not ascertained. I suspect a harmonic link with the Valhalla motif H18ab, at least in several variants of H145. Scruton claims H145 is a satirical variant of H143, but I don't hear this, and can't conceive of a conceptual ground for it.

H146 = S omits (unique) [[H146]] S.3.2 ...... 313, 315

Wotan, 'guardian of the fell,' summons Loge's Ring of Fire to bar Siegfried's access to the sleeping Brünnhilde [Wotan's unspoken secret]

H146's motival links not ascertained. H146 can be considered one of the Motions of Nature. It recalls Wotan's storm H59 which chases Siegmund through the forest into the home of his nemesis Hunding and twin-sister Sieglinde.

H147AB A = S136; B = S136A [[H147A]] S.3.3 319
[[H147B]] S.3.3 ...... 341, 342

Siegfried learns fear from sleeping Brünnhilde. [Brünnhilde knows for Siegfried what he does not: his true identity and Wotan's repressed, fearful hoard of self-knowledge and the fate of the gods]

H147AB derives ultimately from H19, via H19's transformations into H27, H31b, H59, H61 and H80. Through H80 it is also related to a part of H82ab and H99AB. H147AB is the basis for H176. Scruton notes that the first bar of S136 [=H147A] and S136A [=H147B] is derived from S61 [=H65]. This is associated with the Wälsung's 'Noth' which they suffer unwittingly and involuntarily, and for which they offer each other sympathy and love, by virtue of being heirs to Wotan's divine "Noth," his futile desire for redemption.

S137, S137A omitted

H148 = S138? [[H148]] S.3.3 325

Kissed by Siegfried, Brünnhilde opens her eyes. [The artist-hero Siegfried can now access man's (Wotan's) collective unconscious to obtain inspiration from Alberich's Ring-Power/Curse without paying its price]

H148 is based on the H52 chord. Thus, H148 is related to H1, H2 and H56b, and also to the family of motifs stemming from the last three notes of H52, which include H70, H76, H88, H93, H98, and perhaps, according to Cooke, H163.

H149 = S139   [[H149]]   S.3.3 325

Brünnhilde, woken by Siegfried's kiss, surveys her newborn world. [Brünnhilde will inspire Siegfried's art by imparting Wotan's unspoken secret subliminally, through music]

H149 is based on H22. It is possibly related to H164. H149 may be a (or the) basis for H192, the motif of Remembrance, which Dunning also described as an inversion of a segment of H189, H189c.

H150 = S140   [[H150]]   S.3.3 325

Siegfried's and Brünnhilde's loving salute to each other

H150 belongs to the family of love motifs which includes H22, H37, H39, H63b, H79b, H142, and possibly, according to Dunning, H155.

H151 = S141   [[H151]]   S.3.3 325

What Siegfried doesn't know [his true identity as Wotan reborn], Brünnhilde [Siegfried's unconscious mind] knows for him.

H151's motival links not ascertained.

H152 S omits   [[H152]]   S.3.3 337

Brünnhilde's rising fear of sexual union with Siegfried. [Brünnhilde intuits that Siegfried, on taking possession from her safekeeping of Wotan's forbidden hoard of self-knowledge, may innocently divulge its secret]

H152 is a two-note motif, heavily accented in the bass, heard in conjunction with fragments of other motifs which follow, including H39, H80 and H76. H152's motival links not ascertained.

H153 = S142   [[H153]]   S.3.3 341

***Brünnhilde as Immortal Beloved.* Brünnhilde's demand for respect (Scruton). [Siegfried must now respect Brünnhilde's status as muse of his redemptive art and protector from the wounds that Alberich's Ring Curse of consciousness might inflict upon him]**

H153's motival links not ascertained. H153 is one of the primary themes Wagner incorporated into his *Siegfried Idyll*. Scruton, who calls S142 [=H153] Brünnhilde's sense of her unsullied nature, notes that it's an inversion of S99 [=H102], which is also heard in the bass.

H154 = S143   [[H154]] S.3.3 341

Brünnhilde calls Siegfried the "Hoard of the World." [Brünnhilde acknowledges that, by winning her love, Siegfried has fallen heir to Wotan's hoard of unbearable self-knowledge, his unspoken secret]

Cooke regarded H154 as a basis for H161, but Dunning disagrees. Both H154 and H161 are directly associated with the crucial concept that Brünnhilde is imparting Wotan's Hoard of Knowledge—his confession—to Siegfried subliminally. A musical kinship between H154 and H161 wouldn't be surprising.

#144 omitted

Siegfried, aflame with Loge's fire of artistic creation, longs to plunge into his surrogate Rhine, the floodtide of Brünnhilde's music

#144 is kin to the family of motifs Cooke called Motions of Nature, including #11 and #38. #144 was omitted because it's evidently only heard once, in S.3.3, and, though descriptive of Siegfried's passion for Brünnhilde, a passion she ultimately shares, it doesn't carry any conceptual weight.

H155ab = S144   [[H155ab]] S.3.3 350

Love's Resolution. Having learned the meaning of Wotan's fear but forgotten it through loving union with his muse Brünnhilde, Siegfried finally tastes freedom from Mime and Alberich [all that Wotan loathed in his own nature]

Dunning believes H155 belongs to the Love motif Family which includes H22, H37, H39, H63, H79b, H142 and H150. I suspect that H155a (the first 8 notes in a downward stepwise pattern) may be a variant of the motif of Siegfried's contempt for Mime, H109. If this is accurate, it would illustrate the concept which remains valid with or without motival support in this instance, that, thanks to Brünnhilde's loving protection, Siegfried (as the reincarnation of Wotan) has now entirely suppressed all those aspects of his own character which Wotan loathed in himself, namely those that are incarnate in Mime. If Dunning's speculation that H155b is a variant of H117 is correct, this would reinforce our suspicion that H155a is a variant of H109, since H117 was paired with H118—which itself stemmed from Mime's Starling Song, H112—in S.1.1 as an expression of Siegfried's emancipation from Mime.

Twilight of the Gods

H156 = S145 [[H156]] T.P.A 355, 357

The Norns spin their Rope of Fate. **Erda's knowledge of all that was, is, and will be. [Alberich affirms Erda's knowledge; Wotan 'sins' against (opposes) it]**
H156 is based on the diminished inversion of the Rhine Motion motif H3, and is often compounded with Alberich's Ring H17ab.

H157 = S146 [[H157]] T.P.A 357, 357

The World-Ash Tree (Second Motif). **Tree of Life and Knowledge. [Wotan's cutting down of the World-Ash Tree is his 'sin' against all that was, is, and shall be (Erda's Truth). It symbolizes delusional religious man's murder of objective Mother Nature]**
H157's motival links not ascertained. H157 is the second motif specifically associated with the World-Ash Tree, the first being H122, which is the hybrid H52/H2 in 3/4 time, according to Cooke. Scruton suggests that S146 (=H157) is a variant of S18 (=H18), the Valhalla motif

S147AB omitted

H158 = S148 [[H158]] T.P.A 357

The Norns Sing the Song of Fate. **Wotan admitted to Alberich that the Norns' objective message can't be altered [but our perception of it can be transformed through religio-artistic self-deception (imagination)]**
H158's motival links not ascertained. The actual motif which represents the Norns' spinning is a diminished inversion of H3, which is sometimes combined with the Ring motif H17ab.

H159 = S149 [[H159]] T.P.B 367

Mature Siegfried's Horn Call
H159 is a harmonically enriched variant of H108, which places H159 in the family of diatonic Nature arpeggiated figures which includes H1, H9ab, and H55.

H160 = S150   [[H160]]   T.P.B 367

Brünnhilde as Siegfried's mortal wife. **Siegfried's muse Brünnhilde inspires him [as artist-hero] to undertake new adventures. [To go forth into the world, create (Wagnerian) music-dramas and present them to the public (in Siegfried's case, to the Gibichungs as audience)]**
H160 is in the same family of motifs as H7, H21, and H94, which Cooke calls, only partially accurately, Woman's Inspiration. H160 sounds very close to H94, Sieglinde's Praise of Brünnhilde: "sublimest Wonder"

H161 = S151   [[H161]]   T.P.B 367

Siegfried as unwitting—and therefore poor—guardian of Wotan's Hoard of Runes. [He is involuntary keeper of Wotan's repressed, unspoken, secret confession to Brünnhilde]
Cooke suggests that H161 is related to H154, i.e. the Hoard of the World motif, but Dunning disagrees. However, both H154 and H161 are associated with the concept of Siegfried as heir to, and guardian of, Wotan's Hoard of knowledge.

H162ab = S153AB   [[H162ab]]   T.1.1 378

Hagen. **[Representative of our modern, secular, scientific age of skepticism and cynicism, which will deflate our age-old illusions—our consolatory religious faith, altruistic morality and inspired art]**
H162 is from the Family of Gibichung motifs, which according to Cooke incorporate a characteristic interval drop. This family includes H167, H168ab, H183, and perhaps distantly H178, but curiously, not Gunther's motif H163, which (uncharacteristically, because it makes little sense conceptually or dramatically) Cooke assigns to the family of heroic motifs associated with the Wälsungs

H163 = S152B? = S154?   [[H163]]   T.1.1 378

Gunther and the Gibichungs. **[The audience for Siegfried's (Wagner's) music-drama (the *Ring*)]**
Cooke describes H163 as one of the family of heroic motifs stemming from the last three notes of Erda's motif H52; if this is accurate, H163 would be related to H1, H2 and H56b, and would be included among the family generated from H52 which also includes H70, H76, H88, H93 and H98. However, conceptually it's hard to understand why Gunther, who is if anything the antithesis of a true hero, would deserve a motif linking him with Siegfried (H93) and his sword 'Nothung' (H56). Dunning agrees with me that H163 sounds closely related to H123A, generally known as the Power of the Gods, but which I note is also associated in its definitive form H123B with the fated destruction of the gods, in which all the Gibichungs play a role.

S154 omitted

H164 = S155 [[H164]] T.1.1 382

Seduction. The [music-dramatist] Siegfried, seduced by his false muse Gutrune [with the prospect of a public performance of his art. In our scientific age of skepticism and cynicism, Siegfried risks betraying his art's secret source, hitherto protected by his true muse Brünnhilde]
H164 is, according to Cooke, in the same family as H22 and H149, motifs sometimes thought of as a family representing sensuous love: this isn't always accurate!

H165 = S156 [[H165]] T.1.1 ...... 382, 382

Hagen's Potion. [The 'Artistic Wonder' of Wagner's Musical Motifs.] [The musical alchemy that brings forth in the present (here-and-now) that which was widely scattered over time and space]
H165 belongs to the family of motifs based on Loge's Transformation motif H33, including H40AB, possibly H47, and definitely H105

H166 ≈ S160 [[H166]] T.1.1–2 386

Siegfried's poignant leisurely rowing against the natural flow of the Rhine—to meet his fate [to rediscover his actual identity] at Gibichung Hall
H166 is a hybrid motif comprised of H39 vari/H58a/H108, which transforms as it gradually adds an H11 variant, H12, and H14, all together intended to musically evoke Siegfried leisurely rowing his boat against the natural current of the Rhine—by which feat of strength Hagen recognizes the rower as the dragon-killer whom he's promised to Gutrune in marriage, who'll abduct Brünnhilde for Gunther, to be Gunther's wife, and who'll restore Alberich's Ring to his son Hagen—towards the shore, and his fateful destiny, at Gibich Hall

H167 = S157 [[H167]] T.1.2 388

The Gibichungs' [Mime-like] proffer of *False Friendship* to Siegfried
H167 belongs to the family of Gibichung motifs based on a characteristic interval drop, which includes H167, H168ab, perhaps H178, and definitely H183

S158 omitted

H168ab a = S159; b = S159A?   [[H168ab]]   T.1.2 393

***Gutrune* as Siegfried's false muse and seductress**
Gutrune's motif H168a Dunning links to the family which includes H20, H74, H104 and H113; H168b is part of the family of Gibichung motifs which includes H162, H167, perhaps H178, and definitely H183

H169 = S161A   [[H169]]   T.1.2 398

Siegfried's and Gunther's *Blood-brotherhood Oath*. [Siegfried emulates his archetype Loge's relationship with the guardian-of-oaths, Wotan, by swearing to enable Gunther's willing self-deception that he possesses transcendent value and honor]
H169 possibly derived from H19, according to Dunning

H170 = S161B   [[H170]]   T.1.2 398

Siegfried and Gunther mix their life-bloods in the drinking bowl they share. [The artist-hero Siegfried blends with the audience of his art by sharing its secret (Brünnhilde) with his audience (Gunther)]
The first 7 notes or so of H170 correspond with H107, the motif which represents Mime's inherent inability to re-forge 'Nothung.' This suggests H170 grows out of H107, implying Gunther's craven nature is akin to Mime's: both Gunther and Mime seek to pull the wool over Siegfried's eyes to exploit him for their own unearned betterment, and both employ a potion to this end; though Gunther doesn't at first contemplate Siegfried's death, ultimately, he'll emulate Mime in wishing for it.

H171 = S161C   [[H171]]   T.1.2 398

Siegfried and Gunther pledge faith to blood-brotherhood by drinking each other's life-blood
H171's motival links not ascertained.

S162A omitted

H172 = S163   [[H172]]   T.1.2 398

Siegfried's and Gunther's *Oath of Atonement*. Each will pay dearly with his blood should he break the oath [which is predestined to be broken since it is based on self-deception]
H172 is based on H67, and both are based in turn on H17a; through H17a, H172 is kin to H15, H18a, H43, H49, H50 and H180; H172 is linked by association then also with H45, which is based on H17b.

H173ab = S164   [[H173ab]] T.1.2 403

Hagen's Watch. **Hagen knows that by abducting Siegfried's muse Brünnhilde [and her secret hoard of knowledge], and handing her over to Gunther and the Gibichungs [Siegfried's audience], Siegfried will reactivate the long dormant Ring Curse [of Consciousness]**
H173ab is based directly on H43ab, which is essentially a variation of H8ab with H17's harmony, via intermediate transformations of H8ab such as H12 and H11, and H38

H174ab = S165   [[H174ab]] T.1.2 403

Hagen's Envy. [Envy of those who enjoy the subjective, heartfelt, illusory consolations of religion, love, and art. Hagen's intent to take revenge on those who co-opted his father Alberich's Ring-Power without paying its price]
H174ab's motival links not ascertained; but Dunning detects H35's influence.

S166 omitted

H175 = S167   [[H175]] T.2.3A 407

Brünnhilde queries Waltraute about reconciliation with Wotan. Brünnhilde construes Wotan's punishment as a blessing since through it she won Siegfried's love
H175's motival links not ascertained; but I speculate it may owe something to music which accompanied H104 in V.3.3, when Brünnhilde had finally persuaded Wotan to protect her vulnerable sleep with a ring of protective fire so that she'd be woken by, and wed to, only a fearless hero (Siegfried). Wotan became, one last time, tender towards her as he reminisced about the past, and contemplated the anguish of never seeing her again, while leaving a freer man than himself heir to Brünnhilde.

H176 = S169 and S179A   [[H176]] T.2.3A 409

Brünnhilde's loving union with Siegfried reinterpreted as the culmination of Wotan's punishment
H176 is the last entry in a series of motif transformations, first described by Cooke, which started with the embryo for H19, followed by its definitive iteration. H19 transformed into H80, H80 into H99AB and also into H147AB [Siegfried's fear of waking Brünnhilde], and finally, H147AB into H176. Through its basis in H19, H176 is also distantly related to H27, H29b, H59, H61, and perhaps H123

H177 = S186   **[[H177]]   T.2.3.A 412**

Wotan's Ultimate Peace—no more world-wandering. Release from his futile quest for the redemption of the gods
We hear for the first of only a few times that hybrid motif H59a/H18c, which is heard for the last time in its most dramatic context in the finale of *Twilight of the Gods*, Act Three, Scene Three, when Brünnhilde tells Wotan—his futile wandering of the world seeking redemption, now over: "(H177 orch: [H58a/H18c]) Rest! Rest (:H58a/H18c)! (H82ab orch: You god (:H82ab orch)! (H18d)," except that here in T.2.3.A, H58a is replaced by its embryonic form H12. The ultimate embryo for this rarely heard motif hybrid seems to be in V.2.2, just prior to Wotan's confession to Brünnhilde, when she tells Wotan that she is his 'will,' and Wotan determines that because his daughter Brünnhilde is actually Wotan's true self, what he says to her will remain forever unspoken in words.

H178 = S162B   **[[H178]]   T.1.3.B 425**

Honor. **Siegfried employs 'Nothung' [as an anti-phallus] to protect Brünnhilde's chastity, before forcing her into loveless marriage with Gunther. [By failing to secure unconscious artistic inspiration from his muse, Siegfried will reveal what Brünnhilde would have him conceal, Wotan's unspoken secret]**
H178's motival links not ascertained; however, it has a two octave drop which may be a hyperbolic variant of Erda's "Ende!" This may link it to the set of Gibichung motifs based on the characteristic drop of an interval, namely, H162, H167, H168ab and H183

H179 = S170   **[[H179]]   T.2.1 ...... 427**

The anguish of being Hagen. [Hagen envies the cheap happiness of the self-deluded, but possesses the intellectual integrity not to share in it]
H179's motival links not ascertained; but Dunning detects H35's influence

H180 = S171   **[[H180]]   T.2.1 ...... 430**

Murder. **Alberich's Ring-Power can only be restored to Alberich through Siegfried's death [by discrediting the last refuge of dying religious faith in the modern world—the artist-hero Siegfried (Wagner)]**
H180 is a compressed H17ab variant

H181ab   a = S172(A?);   b = S172B   [[H181ab]]   T.2.1>2 Trans ......
                                                                  386, 436

Hagen's Dawn. **[Dawn of the day of his triumph over those dedicated to the consoling illusion of man's inherent transcendent value—an illusion that is embodied in religion, loving human relationships, and art]**
H181's motival links not ascertained; at its inception in an orchestral interlude it grows out of a canon based on H1, somewhat as heard during the Prelude to the entire *Ring* in R.1, but then the motif develops a brutal, brassy character associated with Hagen's evident day of triumph over Siegfried, Brünnhilde, and his Gibichung half siblings Gunther and Gutrune. For some reason I keep hearing distant echoes of H18b, the second segment of the Valhalla motif, in H181a.

H182   = S173   [[H182]]   T.2.2 437

Gutrune's festive welcome to her prospective husband Siegfried—in Freia's name and in honor of all women
H182's motival links not ascertained.

H183   = S174   [[H183]]   T.2.2 ...... 437, 440

The Gibichung Horncall. **Herald of the doom-laden weddings of Siegfried to his false muse Gutrune, and Gunther [Siegfried's audience] to his true muse Brünnhilde [safekeeper of the source of Siegfried's unconscious artistic inspiration]**
H183 is in the same family as other characteristic Gibichung motifs such as H162, H167, H168ab, and perhaps H178; Cooke described H183 as the musical antithesis of Siegfried's Youthful Horncall H108.

H184ab   = S175   [[H184ab]]   T.2.3 440

Hagen's rallying cry to the Gibichungs "Hoiho! Hoiho Hoho!," **"Danger, 'Noth' is here!" [Siegfried has disclosed the forbidden knowledge embodied in Alberich's Ring—The Twilight of the Gods, and of their proxies, is at hand!]**
H184ab is based on H8ab, Alberich's primal cry of woe at being rejected in love by all three Rhinedaughters, and thus linked with other motifs derived from H8ab such as H11 and H12, H38, H43ab and H173ab

H185 = S176　　　　　　　　　　　　　　　　　**[[H185]]　T.2.3 ...... 440**

Orchestral accompaniment to the Gibichung Vassals' chorus. The chorus is initially warlike but turns joyous on the impending arrival of Gunther with Brünnhilde.
H185's motival links not ascertained.

S177, S178 omitted

H186 = S179B?　　　　　　　　　　　　　　　　**[[H186]]　T.2.4 ...... 450**

Hagen as the instrument of Brünnhilde's vengeance against Siegfried for betraying their love [and revealing her unspoken secret]. [Hagen is the Judas-like proxy for god-the-father Wotan's Spear (with its sacred runes)—the punisher of oaths that are falsely sworn]
H186 is a compound motif comprised of H184/H176

H187 = S180　　　　　　　　　　　　　　　　　**[[H187]]　T.2.4 ...... 453**

Siegfried and Brünnhilde swear oaths against each other's testimony. The forgetful Siegfried denying, but the knowing Brünnhilde affirming, that they were lovers
H187's motival links not ascertained.

H188　S omits　　　　　　　　　　　　　　　　**[[H188]]　T.2.5 ...... 460**

Brünnhilde reveals the secret of her wondrous protection of Siegfried. She protects him from wounds at his front [foreknowledge of the gods' fated doom], but not at his back (remembrance), thus exposing Siegfried's fatal vulnerability to his nemesis Hagen
H188 is a compound motif comprised of H12 Variant/H161 Variant. See H12 and H161 for motival links. H12, originally the Rhinedaughters' cry of joy "Rhinegold! Rhinegold!" represents in this context Brünnhilde's status as Siegfried's artificial substitute for restoring the Ring to the Rhine to end its Curse. Brünnhilde is also the unconscious repository for Wotan's Hoard of Knowledge (Wotan's hoard of runes which he confessed to her, represented here by H161), through which Siegfried can access this knowledge subliminally, to obtain artistic inspiration, without suffering the wounds which consciousness would cause. Through this protection Brünnhilde grants Siegfried is, unlike Wotan, fearless.

H189abc   ab = S181AB;   c = S181C   [[H189abc]]   T.3.1 470

***Rhinedaughters' Lament for the stolen Rhinegold* (Second Motif)**
According to Dunning, H189c is a loose inversion of Woglinde's Lullaby H4, to which she introduced the first words of the *Ring*: H4 was Wagner's Ur-melody, or Mother-Melody; H4 is the basis for the Woodbirdsong H138ab; as a pentatonic primal melody H189 is related to H102

H190 = S181D?   [[H190]]   T.3.1 470

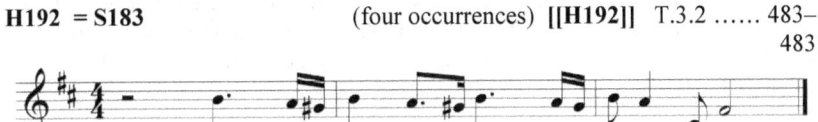

The Rhinedaughters swim jubilantly in expectation that Siegfried will restore Alberich's Ring to them—as once they swam in celebration of the Rhinegold from which Alberich's Ring was forged
H190 is a member of the motif family known as Motions of Nature, which includes H2, H3, H10, H14, H36, and H55

H191 = S182   [[H191]]   T.3.1 470

Siegfried Lost. **[Siegfried has lost his path back to his muse of inspiration and unconscious mind (Brünnhilde) owing to Alberich's Ring Curse of Consciousness]**
H191's motival links not ascertained; but H191 sounds as if it may contain scarcely recognizable fragments of one or two other motifs, including motival material relating to the Woodbird's motifs and/or fluttering of its wings, and/or Loge's fire, perhaps H105, the Magical Fire Music.

H192 = S183   (four occurrences) [[H192]]   T.3.2 483–483

Remembrance. **[Siegfried's play-within-the-play—the story he sings of his heroic life and of how he learned the meaning of bird song. Wagner presents a metaphor for the performance of his own *Ring of the Nibelung*: how Siegfried, as artist, fell heir to dying religious faith (Wotan) in the age of science (Hagen), and revealed to his audience (Gibichungs) what Wotan would have him conceal from them (and from himself)]**
H192, the motif of Remembrance, is, according to Dunning, either derived from H149, the music to which Siegfried woke Brünnhilde in S.3.3, or an inversion of the third segment of the Rhinedaughters' second lament for their lost Rhinegold, H189c (in which case it may evoke H4, Woglinde's Lullaby, since Dunning described H189c as a loose inversion of H4). I suspect H192 is a musical transformation of that moment in T.2.2 during which Siegfried privately toasted his love for, and remembrance of, his true love Brünnhilde, just prior to drinking the love-and-forgetting potion which Hagen had prepared but which Gutrune offered

Siegfried, unbeknownst to him, in his drink. At this very moment, before he drank and forgot Brünnhilde, falling in love instead with Gutrune, we heard the transition from H143, the so-called World-Inheritance motif which represents Brünnhilde's status as Siegfried's muse of unconscious artistic inspiration, to H149, the motif to which Siegfried woke Brünnhilde in S.3.3.

193ab = S184   [[H193ab]]   T.3.2 494

Siegfried's Death-Stroke. [**Wagner's thesis had long been that man, through his gradual acquisition of a hoard of objective knowledge (by Hagen, the embodiment of science), would inevitably undermine all those things which had affirmed his imagined transcendent value in religion, love and art. Wagner saw himself, like his Siegfried, as the last refuge of man's longing for transcendent value**]
H193ab's motival links not ascertained; however, H193b is superficially reminiscent of H89

S185 omitted

#178 omitted

Wagner's Hymn to Heroes. Sieglinde's Sublime Wonder. Hymn to the failed artist-hero Siegfried and his muse of formerly unconscious artistic inspiration, Brünnhilde, who—owing to Siegfried's betrayal of Wotan's unspoken secret, which she'd kept in silence, away from the light of day—now wakes forever, and becomes the voice of her mother Erda's (Nature's) objective knowledge of their fate. Sometimes called the Redemption Motif or the motif of Redemption by Love, but this is incorrect. See H94 for #178's motival links. I have omitted Dunning's motif #178 because it's redundant, having already been identified by Dunning as motif #93 [=H94].

References

Abbate, Carolyn — *Unsung Voices. Opera and Musical Narrative in the Nineteenth Century.* Princeton University Press. Princeton, NJ., 1991.

Aeschylus — *Prometheus Bound.* Translated by Paul Elmer More and Edited by Whitney J. Oates and Eugene O'Neill Jr., Random House. New York, 1938.

Berry, Mark — *Treacherous Bonds and Laughing Fire: Politics and Religion in Wagner's 'Ring.'* Ashgate, Burlington, VT, USA. 2006.

Borchmeyer, Dieter — *Richard Wagner. Theory and Theatre.* Clarendon Press. Oxford, 1991.

Cooke, Deryck — *I Saw the World End.* Oxford University Press. London. 1979.

Introduction to the Decca Recording of Richard Wagner's *The Ring of the Nibelung* (a spoken commentary on the musical motifs of Wagner's Ring, with musical examples) in three volumes, 1976.

Darcy, Warren — Wagner's *Das Rheingold.* Clarendon Press. Oxford University Press. Oxford, 1993.

Donington, Robert — *Wagner's 'Ring' and its Symbols. The Music and the Myth.* Faber and Faber. London, 1963.

Dunning, Dr. Allen B. — *A Thematic Guide to the Musical Themes of Richard Wagner's 'Der Ring des Nibelungen'* (an online publication)

Feuerbach, Ludwig — [EOC] *The Essence of Christianity.* Originally published in 1841. Translated by George Eliot [the novelist]. Harper Torchbooks. Harper and Row, Publishers. New York, Hagerstown, San Francisco, London, 1957.

[LER] *Lectures on the Essence of Religion.* Originally published in 1848. Based on book published in the early 1840s entitled *The Essence of Religion*, which was intended to fill in some gaps left by *The Essence of Christianity*. Translated by Ralph Manheim. Harper and Row, Publishers. New York, Evanston, and London, 1967.

[PPF] The *Principles of the Philosophy of the Future*. Originally published in 1843. Translated by Manfred Vogel. Hackett Publishing Company, 1986.

[TDI] *Thoughts on Death and Immortality*. Originally Published in 1830. Translated by James A. Massey. University of California Press, 1980.

Graves, Robert — *The Greek Myths*: In Two Volumes. Penguin Books Limited. Middlesex, England, 1960. Reprinted 1981.

Holman, J.K. — *Wagner's Ring A Listener's Companion and Concordance* Amadeus Press. Portland, Oregon, 1996.

Kitcher, Philip, and Schacht, Richard — *Finding an Ending—Reflections on Wagner's 'Ring'*: Oxford Univ. Press. New York, New York, 2004.

Kitcher, Philip — Private communication by email on July 27, 2016.

Lévi-Strauss, Claude — *The Raw and the Cooked—Introduction to a Science of Mythology*: Volume I. Translated from the French by John and Doreen Weightman. Harper Colophon Books, Harper and Row, Publishers. New York, 1975. Originally published in French by Librarie Plon, 1964.

The Naked Man—Introduction to a Science of Mythology: Volume IV. Translated from the French by Jonathan Cape. Harper and Row, Publishers. New York, 1981. Originally published in French by Librarie Plon, 1971.

Mann, Thomas — *The Sorrows and Grandeur of Richard Wagner*. From an anthology of Thomas Mann's writings on Richard Wagner entitled *Pro and Contra Wagner*. Translated from the German by Allan Blunden. The University of Chicago Press. Chicago and London, 1985. Originally Published in German in 1933.

Millington, Barry — Private communication by email on January 23, 2017.

Nattiez, Jean-Jacques — *Le Ring Comme Histoire Metaphorique de la Musique (The 'Ring' as a Metaphorical History of Music)*. A Contribution to *Wagner in Retrospect. A Centennial Reappraisal*. Edited and with an introduction by Leroy R. Shaw, Nancy R. Cirillo, and Marion S. Miller. Amsterdam, 1987. Nattiez presented this paper as a lecture at the 'Wagner in Retrospect: A Centennial Reappraisal' conference at the University of Illinois, Chicago Circle, in 11/83.

Wagner Androgyne. A Study in Interpretation. Translated from French by Stewart Spencer. Princeton, NJ. Princeton University Press. 1993. Original French Edition: *Wagner*

	Androgyne: Essai sur L'interpretation. Christian Bourgois Editeur. 1990.
Nietzsche, Friedrich	*Nietzsche Contra Wagner.* Translated by Walter Kauffmann. From 'The Portable Nietzsche.' The Viking Press. New York, 1954.
	The Case of Wagner. Translated by Walter Kauffmann. Vintage Books, A Division of Random House. New York, 1967. First published in 1888.
	Will To Power. Translated by Walter Kauffmann and R.J. Hollingdale. Vintage Books, A Division of Random House. New York, 1967. This work is a selection made by others from Nietzsche's notebooks dating from 1883–1888.
Porges, Heinrich	**[WWR]** *Wagner Rehearsing the 'Ring.'* Trans. by Robert L. Jacobs; Cambridge 1983. Cambridge Univ. Press. Written June through August 1876. Wagner commissioned Porges to record what Wagner said and did during the rehearsals for the *Ring*'s premier, as a permanent record of his intentions.
Rose, Paul Lawrence	*Wagner. Race and Revolution.* Yale University Press. New Haven and London. 1992.
Schopenhauer, Arthur	*The World as Will and Representation.* Vol. II. Translated from German by E.F.J. Payne. Dover Inc. New York, NY. 1966. Originally published in German in 1844. The First Volume of *The World as Will and Representation* was published in 1819.
Scruton, Roger	Introduction to www.wagnerheim.com, posted online in Spring of 2011
	The Ring of Truth—The Wisdom of Wagner's 'Ring of the Nibelung': Allen Lane, an imprint of Penguin Books. UK, 2016.
	'The Ring of Truth,' Published in the May, 2011 issue of 'The American Spectator'
Shaw, George Bernard	*The Perfect Wagnerite: A Commentary on the Niblung's Ring.* Originally published in London in 1898. Published by Time–Life Records. 1972, USA.
Spencer, Stewart	**[WR]** *Wagner Remembered.* Edited and annotated by Stewart Spencer. London and New York. Faber and Faber, 2000. An anthology of reminiscences of Wagner ranging from his early childhood until his death in 1883, including many conversations.
Tanner, Michael	*Wagner.* Princeton University Press. Princeton, NJ. 1996.

Wagner, Cosima — [CD] *Cosima Wagner's Diaries*. In two volumes. Ed. Martin Gregor-Dellin and Dietrich Mack. Trans. By Geoffrey Skelton. New York and London. A Helen and Kurt Wolff Book. Harcourt Brace Jovanovitch, 1978. Written by Cosima Wagner from 1869 through 1883.

Wagner, Richard — [BB] '*The Diary of Richard Wagner* 1865–1882—*The Brown Book*. Ed. by Joachim Bergfeld. Trans. by George Bird. Victor Gollanc Ltd., London, 1980.

[CWL] *Correspondence of Wagner and Liszt*. Trans. by Francis Hueffer. New York: Greenwood Press, 1969. Originally published by Charles Scribner's Sons, 1897.

[ML] *My Life*. Trans. Andrew Gray. Ed. Mary Whittall. Cambridge, New York, Melbourne: Cambridge University Press, 1983. Wagner's autobiography covers the years 1813–1864.

[PW] *Richard Wagner's Prose Works*. Eight volumes. Second Edition. Translated by William Ashton Ellis. Reprinted in St. Claire Shores, Michigan, by the Scholarly Press in 1972. Translation originally published in London by Kegan, Paul, Trench, Truebner and Co. Ltd., in 1895.

[RWMW] *Richard Wagner to Mathilde Wesendonck*. Translated by William Ashton Ellis. New York: Vienna House, 1972. Originally published in New York by Charles Scribner and Sons in 1905.

[SLRW] *Selected Letters of Richard Wagner*. Translated and edited by Stewart Spencer and Barry Millington. New York and London. W.W. Norton and Company, 1987.

Lohengrin. English translation by Dr. Karl Schumann, 1964, for E.M.I Records Ltd., plus translations of selected passages made especially for Paul Heise's article "How Elsa Showed Wagner the Way to Siegfried" [published by Stewart Spencer in the May 1995 issue (Volume 16, Number 2) of 'Wagner,' the scholarly journal of The Wagner Society (London, UK)] by Andrew Gray.

The Ring of the Nibelung. Complete Libretto text in an English translation by Stewart Spencer. 'From *Wagner's Ring of the Nibelung: A Companion*, ©1993 Stewart Spencer, Barry Millington, Roger Hollinrake, Elizabeth Magee and Warren Darcy. Published by Thames and Hudson Ltd., London and Thames and Hudson Inc., NewYork. Reprinted by kind permission of Thames and Hudson Ltd., London.'

The Flying Dutchman

Tannhäuser
Tristan and Isolde
The Mastersingers of Nuremberg
Parsifal

Index

A

Aeschylus 133, 195, 322
Libation Bearers, The 133
Oresteia 133, 195, 323
Prometheus Bound 162, 194, 195, 322, 583
Apponyi, Count Albert 246

B

Beethoven, Ludwig van 70, 265, 278, 352
Berry, Mark 22, 23

C

Carlyle, Thomas 525
Chaka, Zulu King 76
Cicora, Mary 22
Cooke, Deryck 7, 18, 24, 531, 534, 542, 546, 549, 550, 551, 553, 555, 557, 558, 559, 560, 562, 564, 565, 573, 574, 575, 577, 579
Corse, Sandra 22
Curie, Marie and Pierre 6

D

Darcy, Warren 7, 27, 43, 586
Deathridge, John 202
Donington, Robert 7, 16, 375
Dunning, Allen 18, 19, 24, 531, 543, 546, 547, 548, 549, 551, 554, 559, 560, 561, 562, 564, 565, 568, 571, 572, 574, 577, 578, 581, 582

E

Ellis, William Ashton 344
Everett, Derrick xii, 24

F

Feuerbach, Ludwig x, 1, 12, 14, 17, 20, 22, 23, 24, 25, 26, 29, 30, 32, 36, 37, 40, 41, 42, 43, 44, 45, 46, 47, 50, 51, 52, 53, 54, 55, 57, 58, 60, 62, 63, 65, 66, 67, 68, 70, 71, 73, 74, 75, 76, 77, 79, 80, 81, 82, 83, 84, 85, 88, 91, 93, 94, 95, 96, 97, 98, 99, 100, 102, 103-104, 106, 109, 111, 113, 128, 129, 134, 135, 138, 140, 141, 142, 144, 146, 147, 148, 149, 152, 155, 158, 160, 161, 163, 166, 167, 168, 169, 170, 174, 178, 180, 182, 187, 210, 212, 214, 225, 229, 233, 239, 241, 246, 251, 255, 256, 257, 259, 268, 274, 279, 289, 293, 296-297, 300, 304, 305, 310, 318, 324, 327, 329-330, 331-332, 334, 336, 352, 358, 366, 391, 393, 395-396, 398, 405, 411, 420, 428, 429, 432, 467, 477, 492, 496, 499, 501, 502, 503, 506, 508, 512, 513-514, 515, 524, 526, 527, 534
philosophical works of:
Essence of Christianity, The (EOC) 30, 36, 37, 44, 45, 47, 50-51, 63, 65-66, 66-67, 73, 75, 76, 77, 79, 80, 88, 91, 93, 95, 102, 128-129, 138, 142, 144, 148, 155-156, 167-168, 180, 226, 225, 246, 251, 256, 296, 297, 321, 331-332, 352, 405, 429, 432, 506-507, 526-527
Lectures on the Essence of Religion (LER) 29, 30, 32, 40-41,

43, 44, 47-48, 51-52, 53, 54-55, 57, 58, 60, 63, 65, 66, 67, 68, 71-72, 74, 80-81, 82-83, 84, 88, 91-92, 93, 94, 98, 99, 100, 102, 103, 104-105, 106-107, 111-112, 113, 122, 140, 141-142, 146, 152, 153, 155-156, 158, 168-169, 225, 233, 251, 255, 256, 259, 293, 297-298, 300, 305, 310, 318, 366, 432, 499
Principles of the Philosophy of the Future (PPF) 41, 80, 103, 225, 239, 358-359
Thoughts on Death and Immortality (TDI) 36-37, 54, 94, 103-104, 135, 160, 161, 163, 180, 207, 229, 305, 330, 391, 432
Freud, Sigmund 7
Furtwängler, Wilhelm 10

G

Goethe, Johann Wolfgang von 6
Faust 6, 182, 183, 557

H

Homer 183
Iliad, The 183

K

Kant, Immanuel 336, 346, 366
Keller, Hans 7
Kellermann, Berthold 246, 324
Kneif, Tibor 35
Kitcher, Philip 22-23, 508
Wagner's Ring: Finding an Ending 508

L

Lévi-Strauss, Claude 17-18, 327
Naked Man, The 18
Raw and the Cooked, The 18
Liszt, Franz 32, 45, 55, 57, 81, 115, 134, 144, 163, 168, 183, 204, 222, 223, 258, 305, 557-558
Faust Symphony 182, 183, 557-558

Ludwig II, King of Bavaria 5, 169, 265, 273, 282, 286-287, 298

M

Mann, Thomas 306, 308
Marx, Karl 1, 83
Kapital, Das 83
Meyerbeer, Giacomo 222
Millington, Barry x, 8, 26, 27

N

Nattiez, Jean-Jacques 8, 20, 21, 35, 265, 327, 333, 384, 385, 394, 438-439, 486, 504
Wagner Androgyne 20, 35, 265, 327, 384
Newman, Ernest 361
Nietzsche, Friedrich 14, 15, 24, 92, 166, 167, 273, 402, 428, 432, 467, 496, 526, 529
Case of Wagner, The 15
Will to Power, The 166

P

Porges, Heinrich 30, 33, 60, 111, 189, 190, 321-322, 402, 506, 520

R

Röckel, August 8, 45, 99, 104, 105, 120, 149, 172, 258, 291, 301, 302, 303, 335, 350, 413, 424, 477, 514, 515, 519

S

Schacht, Richard 22-23, 508
Wagner's Ring: Finding an Ending 508
Schopenhauer, Arthur 24, 25, 26, 37, 70, 108, 146, 147, 153, 163, 169, 174, 215, 265, 312, 335, 336, 346, 347, 348, 359, 366, 432, 477, 496-497, 508, 513, 514, 515, 524, 528
World as Will and Representation, The 163, 585

Scruton, Roger x, 1, 23, 24, 27, 190, 192, 308-309, 336-337, 466, 508, 531, 540, 545, 546, 547, 553, 555, 556, 557, 558, 559, 560, 562, 563, 565, 566, 567, 568, 569, 570, 571, 573
Ring of Truth—The Wisdom of Wagner's 'Ring of the Nibelung,' The 23, 24, 508
Serova, Valentina 186, 499, 509
Shakespeare, William 157, 315, 352, 486
Hamlet 6, 157, 486
Tempest, The 315
Shapiro, Alexander H. 23
Shaw, George Bernard x, 1, 7, 8, 15-16, 73, 81, 239, 525
Sophocles 183
Oedipus the King 183
Spencer, Stewart 24, 27, 271, 327

T

Tanner, Michael 7, 8, 10, 441, 501

W

Wagner, Cosima (wife of Richard) 8, 21, 81, 120, 162, 193, 219, 250, 265, 299, 321, 327, 345, 353, 358, 441, 478, 521
Wagner, Richard, 1, 3, 6, 9, 23, 25, 27, 246, 324, 529, 531, 539, 583, 584, 586
musical works of:
Flying Dutchman, The 6, 13, 110, 147, 171, 329, 422, 477, 496, 514, 524, 529
Jesus of Nazareth (planned) 53, 58, 69, 115, 134, 138, 142, 256
Lohengrin, 5, 9, 13, 25, 44, 113, 148, 149, 161, 162, 184, 201, 202, 271, 330, 378, 381, 440, 453, 468, 529
Mastersingers of Nuremberg, The 9, 13, 110, 120, 287, 529
Parsifal 6, 13, 21, 25, 44, 95, 104, 110, 120, 220, 271, 298, 299, 327, 329, 356, 385, 411, 442, 460, 477, 478, 484, 488, 489, 497, 503, 508, 512, 515, 516, 521, 524, 526, 527, 528, 529,
Rhinegold, The (*Das Rheingold*) 5, 15, 16, 29-120, 158-159, 322, 392
Ring of the Nibelung, The 1, 6, 9, 30, 105, 287, 385, 387, 440, 459, 498, 518, 529, 583, 586
Siegfried 5, 13, 14, 120, 159, 209-353, 359, 390, 399, 567
Siegfried Idyll 245, 340, 341, 342, 343, 407, 554, 567, 571
Tannhäuser 13, 25, 175, 271, 324, 330, 385, 427, 449, 493, 529
Tristan and Isolde 5, 9, 13, 15, 95, 120, 287, 344, 350, 390, 418, 426, 508, 529
Twilight of the Gods (*Götterdämmerung*) 23, 189, 521
Valkyrie, The 5, 14, 18, 19, 20, 58, 98, 112, 114,120, 121, 154, 158, 183, 195, 206, 284, 463, 513, 532, 533, 534, 551, 555, 560, 564
Victors, The (*Sieger, Die*, planned) 299
philosophical and literary works of:
"Art and Climate" 30, 37, 81, 180, 338
"Art and Religion" 33-34, 55
"Art and Revolution," 73, 76, 94, 211, 246, 323, 525
"Artwork of the Future, The" 29, 35, 42, 66, 85, 93, 102, 119, 173, 225, 226, 262, 312, 344, 374, 525
"Communication To My Friends, A" 5
"Destiny of Opera, The" 173, 352
"Epilogue to the Nibelung's Ring" 15, 426, 521

"German Art and German Policy"
36, 202, 215, 305
"Judaism in Music" 111, 164
Mein Leben (*My Life*) 525
"Music of the Future" 119, 265,
333, 344, 487
"Nibelungen Myth, The" 91, 111,
158, 296, 322, 369
"On Liszt's Symphonic Poems,"
247, 336
"On State and Religion" 41, 49,
55, 67, 93, 98, 109, 144, 147,
170, 184, 208, 250, 256, 298, 461
Opera and Drama 21, 31, 37, 41,
47, 55, 89, 125, 128, 135, 139,
142, 150, 151, 153, 157, 167,
181, 183, 200, 225, 232, 255,
260, 269, 278, 327, 331, 332,
334, 335, 342, 344, 346, 347,
384, 487, 525
"Public and Popularity" 171, 253,
300, 310, 405, 496, 529
"Religion and Art" 34, 46, 58, 65,
81, 86, 98, 153, 163, 168, 170,
202, 291, 332, 391, 414, 432,
465, 527
"Revolution, The" 73, 246
"Wibelungen, The" 43, 44, 98,
159, 273, 484
Wagner, Siegfried (son of Richard)
521
Wagner, Wieland (grandson of
Richard) 502
Weber, Carl Maria von 117
Freischütz, Der 117
Weber, E. von 66, 433
Wesendonck, Mathilde 7, 93, 119,
165, 292, 348, 366, 375, 486, 527